The Insider's Guide to the Colleges

2002

The Insider's Guide to the Colleges

2002

Compiled and Edited by the Staff of the Yale Daily News

St. Martin's Griffin
New York

Readers with comments or questions should address them to Editors, *The Insider's Guide to the Colleges*, c/o *The Yale Daily News*, 202 York Street, New Haven, CT 06511-4804.

Visit *The Insider's Guide to the Colleges* Web site at http://www.yale.edu/ydn.

The editors have sought to ensure that the information in this book is accurate at press time. Because policies, costs, and statistics do change from time to time, readers should verify important information with the colleges.

www.stmartins.com

ISBN 0-312-20415-9

n: August 2001

7 6 5 4 3 2 1

Contents

Preface

Congratulations! Although your head may be spinning and the college admissions process may seem daunting, you have begun your search on the right foot by picking up a copy of this book. Our staff has worked very hard on this new edition of *The Insider's Guide to the Colleges* to provide you with the tools necessary to give you an advantage in this hectic process.

We have one central objective, and that is to give you the *real* picture of what it's like to be a college student and not bore you with glossy brochure talk. After all, we have been through the process ourselves, and we owe it to you to tell you the truth. We tell you what we would love to have known when we were in your shoes. Through writing the book, we have discovered that there is more to college life than what is offered by any single institution. College is the godlike professor who stays after class to help you with a difficult concept in economics, and the dorm room friends whose late-night study breaks keep you from going insane. It is the dining hall where the lines are long and the food is bad, and the roommate who skips class and lets you cry on her shoulder after you get a D on your first English paper. College is gallons of coffee, alcohol, laughter, and stress.

All of this is well and good, but you are probably still thinking that it does not help you much. After all, you have to get there first. You can apply to no more than a handful of colleges from among thousands. Maybe you have a hazy idea of what you are looking for, but how do you even begin to narrow your choices?

That is where *The Insider's Guide* fits in. In this 28th edition, we provide a snapshot of life at 311 (7 additions in this edition!) colleges and universities in the United States and Canada. *The Insider's Guide* has changed a lot in twenty-seven years. In 1973, *The Insider's Guide* was little more than a handful of sarcastic, condescending articles by "Yale Men" about the "lesser Ivy League schools." Today, we strive for accurate and witty reports that capture the spirit and essence of a college. Most importantly, we give you the inside scoop on these places, directly from the students who attend these institutions.

We research each school in *The Insider's Guide* by interviewing friends (and friends of friends) at each of the 311 colleges covered. This allows us not only to keep in touch with high school buddies, but also gives *The Insider's Guide* a unique perspective from students whose opinions we trust. It also means that we are only as accurate as our sources. Though we have worked hard to ensure that each article is factually correct and current, you should still do additional research. As a good rule of thumb, never rely solely on any one source to decide something as important as choosing the right college. It is critical that you make every effort to learn as much about the school (or schools) of your choice before making a commitment.

In addition to the reports on each college, *The Insider's Guide* includes a number of special features to help you in your search. "The College Finder" gives you a rundown on some schools according to selected attributes. "Getting In" takes you step-by-step through all the intricacies of the admission process. In "The College Spectrum," we discuss some of the most important factors to consider when differentiating among schools, as well as give you a look at some of the current trends in college life. "Introduction for International Students" provides some tips on applying to American schools if you live outside the United States. "Disabled Student Services" introduces students with learning or physical disabilities to some of the issues they should be aware of when applying to college. Finally, we have included "Terms You Should Know," a humorous look at some of the often confusing jargon used in the world of college life.

We are confident that this edition of *The Insider's Guide* is even more lively and informative than its predecessors. We wish you all the best in finding the best match

' for your interests and talents and hope that you will think of us when you finally buy your first college sweatshirt. —*Seung C. Lee and Alexandra M. Rethore*

Editors-in-Chief
Seung C. Lee
Alexandra M. Rethore

Executive Editors
Brian Abaluck
Melissa K. Chan
William Chen
Jeffrey Kaplow
Marti Page
Alison Pulaski

Associate Editors
Jane H. Hong
Ellen L. Moskowitz
Shu-Ping Shen
Engin Yenidunya

Statistics Editor
Julita Ramirez

Senior Editor
Lisa E. Smith

Senior Writers
Robert G. Berschinski
Stephanie Manson
Johnny Swagerty
Jennifer B. Wang

Staff Writers
Amanda A. Ambroza
Kyla M. Dahlin
Alyssa Blair Greenwald
Nicole Jabaily
Conor Knighton
Sean McBride
Jessica Morgan
Edward Mundy
Yakut Seyhanli

Contributing Writers
Chiraag Bains
Jessica Bondell
Jason Friedrichs
Lauren Gold
Florence Han
Ludwig Johnson
Robert Lee
Melissa J. Merritt
Ann Sun
Kenneth Tseng
Robert Wong

Acknowledgments

Special thanks to Carrie McGinnis, our editor at St. Martin's Press, who has been instrumental in getting this book out on time and in excellent shape. We would also like to thank all the interviewees who were kind enough to let us get a personal peek into their lives and their colleges: Without you, this book would not have been possible.

Jamie Aaronson
Kristin Abbate
Kevin Adams
Jon Adler
Mathieu Ahlstrom
Ammar Ahmed
Gus Alberelli
Sylvia Alonso
Jozef Amado
Jessica Anderson
Jeff Atkins
Camille Atkinson
Lynne Bachand
Philip Bailey
Can Bakir
Stefanie Bala
Sarah Barkley
S.E. Barr
Ryan P. Barrows
Suzy Bass
Elizabeth Bates
Tatiana Becker
Kristine Behm
Kayce Bell
Chip Bennett
Robin Benson
Miles Berger
Denise Bilbao
Raffi Bilek
Pavel S. Blagov
Mary Bolt
Sonia M. Borrell
Alex Bragg
Virginia R. Brandt
Christin Brown
Jarrett Byrnes
Alberto Caban Jr.
Maria Caltabiano
Ashley Campbell
Greg Canfield
Abraham Caplan

Ursula Carliss
Leslie Carr
Matt Carter
Kristen Cartus
Maja Catipovic
Andrew Cencini
Taia Cesana
Janney Chang
Elaine Chao
Pei-Sze Cheng
Kate Childers
John Choi
Eugene Chung
Andrew Clark
Sarah Clarke
Enijin Cole
Vince Conte
Gracile Cook
Rob Curtis
Julie Cyphers
Mark Davis
Martha Davis
Dedric Day
Shirah Dedman
Michael DeLorenzo
Jaime Devereaux
Michael R. Dietrich
Gizem Dorter
Cameron Douglass
Joseph J. Doyle
Kelli Doyle
Anthony "Drazzy Draz" Draucikas
Sara Edelman
Joseph Esposito
Valerie Esser
Sarah Evans
Eileen Everett
Mark Farber
Dana Feinstein
Amanda Ferguson-Cradler
Rachel Fink
Noah Fisch
Erica Fisher
Kathleen M. Fregeau
Alison Mara Friedman
Marcus Friesen
Kelly Frisby
David Fuller
Lucy Garcia
Katharine Gatz
Selim Gokay

Melanie Goode
Ian Gopez
Paulina Grossman
Yola Habif
Laura J. Harris
Ethney Harrison
Karen Henderson
Kaysie Hermes
Thomas Hernandez
Kim Higbie
Anna L. Hillbrand
Joe Hoffman
Mary Holt
Anna Hong
Sibel Horada
Colleen Hsia
Carolyn Hunter
Hee-Jung Hwang
Ross Irwin
Lisa Jabaily
Nalo Jackson
Jane Jih
Carol Johnson
Kaleisha Johnson
Peter Johnson
Sarah Johnson
Victor Johnson
Lindsay Johnston
Meredith Jones
Olivia Jones
Tiffany Jones
Michael Joven
Deborah Kaufman
Bob Keary
Jocelyn Kenyon
Rashel Kesilman
Julie Kidd
Henry Kim
Tess Kim
David Knouf
Darrel Ko
Wendy Kobayashi
Galya Kohen
Ari Krepostman
Lynn Kuo
Sam Kusnetz
Kristin Kwasniewski
Elaine Lai
Wayne Lai
Stephanie Lambert
Kimberly Lau
Jung Min Lee
Dani Leiman
Steven Leong
Josh Levine
Nicole Levy
Tammy Li
Chris Liao
Angela Little
Jaemi Loeb
John Lofranco
Sue Lovoy
Cuitlahuac Lujan
Amber Luong
Staci Lyvers
John Mangin
Seth Manrow
Jeffrey Mansell
Eric Martens
Marissa Martinez
Michael Mayer
Lidia Meana
Maria Medlen
Keesha Melendez
Jay Le Melledo
Scott Merrill
Simon Messing
Teresa Metcalf-Johnson
Trisha Milazzo
Nicholas Miller
Vanessa Milsom
Jessica Minyard
Michelle Mitchell
Anne Moriarty
Isil Muderrisoglu
Tim Munn
Scotty Naigles
Kyle Najarian
Catherine Neuschler
Brianna Neville
Sarah Nuss-Waren
David Oehl
Meghan O'Mara
Stephen Osserman
Tanla Ozuzun
Andrea Partemore
Mukti Patel
Prapiksha Patel
Matt Pelowski
Ronald Petty
Natalie Pheasant
Andrew Philpott
Alissa Poisson
Jordan Posamentier
Harsha Ramachandra
Anne Reedstrom
Yonju Rhee
Jonathan Ritter
Sabin Rividi
Erin Rodgers
Trevor Rutledge-Leverenz
Ozer Sancak

Nalia Sanchez
Miguel Santos-Neves
Ipek Sarac
Shadron Sellman
Serra Semi
Steve Sendecki
Heather Shapiro
Shane Shariffskul
Jae Sung Shim
Yoko Shimizu
Laura Sideman
Matt Siedsma
Amanda Smith
Amy Smith
Andrea Smith
Andy Smith
Brad Smith
Courtney E. Smith
Jennifer Smith
Jaime Snape
Jay Snyder
Micah Spooner-Wyman
Jill Sprague
Stacy Steinhoff
Edward Stern
Volkan Stodolsky
Doug Strain

Keren Surowitz
Sarah Taylor
Irina Telyukova
William Terrin
Adam Thomas
Teneshia Thurman
Linda Tieu
Derrick Tung
Jodi Turrell
Joe Ursic
Toni Ann Vicari
Veena Villivalam
Sean Voscamp
David de Voursney
Marissa Wagner
Rita Wang
Rachel Wasser
Johanna Weinstock
Robert Whipple
Emily Woods
Forrest Woolery
Bean Worley
Jason Wirth
Ian Yohai
Juliette Yu
Selin Zalma

How to Use This Book

How We Select the Colleges

One of the most difficult problems we wrestle with is which schools should be included in *The Insider's Guide*. Out of the more than 2,000 four-year degree-granting institutions in the nation, we cover 311. The most important factor in our decision is the academic quality of the schools we select. Approximately 200 of the schools in the book qualified based on the excellence and breadth of their offerings alone. With that criterion established, making the other selections became more difficult. One key factor we carefully consider is the size of the colleges and universities in question. We make a particular effort to include a broad selection of larger universities, most of which are state affiliated. Further, we have included at least one such school from each of the fifty states. Although the overall quality of larger universities is often comparable to schools we chose not to include, these larger universities frequently have better facilities and offer more varied opportunities than do smaller institutions. Many have one or two outstanding programs that make them noteworthy. Finally, because large universities enroll thousands of students every year, more readers are likely to consider them on a list of prospective colleges.

We have also made every effort to include a broad cross section of smaller colleges. The smaller the school, the more we tended to view the quality of the student body—which we measured by admissions selectivity, average high-school class rank, SAT profiles, etc.—as the key criterion. Choosing among small liberal arts colleges is especially difficult because there are so many that are "selective" or "competitive" in admissions. However, like most admissions offices, we consider geographical distribution a virtue, so when faced with difficult choices, we favored colleges in less heavily represented regions of the country.

The Insider's Guide also includes a selection of two types of specialized schools—technical institutes and schools strong in the creative and performing arts. *The Insider's Guide*'s modest sampler of some of the better institutions across the nation is designed primarily to whet your appetites and to encourage you to continue your own independent research.

In sum, this book includes colleges we believe to be among the best and most noteworthy in North America. This does not imply in any way that you cannot get a good education at colleges that are not included in this year's *The Insider's Guide*. Nor, of course, does it mean that you are guaranteed a happy and prosperous four years if you attend any one of them. Rather, we believe that every school in *The Insider's Guide* offers students the raw materials for constructing an excellent education.

It's All Up to You

After your initial browse through *The Insider's Guide*, we suggest that you read the front section carefully and then go back and take a more careful look at the articles on the colleges that caught your eye. The opening features of the book are designed to help you zero in on what is unique and important about the schools you might be considering. The things we discuss in general terms in the introductory parts should give you a new perspective on the colleges as well as suggest options you had not considered before.

As you read through the *Guide*, you will notice that we have avoided the temptation to pigeonhole the colleges with some kind of catchall rating system, or worse, numerically rank these schools. Our reason is that the "best" college for one individual may come near the bottom of the list for another. Each person has his or her own particular set of wants and needs, so it would be pointless for us to try to objectively rank the schools.

Even so, people inevitably ask, "Can't you rate the colleges just on the basis of academic quality?" We think not. There are too many variables—from the many factors that contribute to the quality of a department and school as a whole to the articulateness and accessibility of the professor who happens to be your academic advisor. Furthermore, it is useless to try to compare a college of 2,000 with a university of 10,000 (or a university of 10,000 with one of 40,000) on any other basis than individual preference.

Despite all the reasons not to, report-edly reliable sources such as national magazines often insist on publishing numerical rankings of colleges. It is our hope that you can ignore such rankings when you find them elsewhere, or at the very least, take them with a healthy grain of salt.

We are dedicated to the notion that the quality of a college is largely in the eye of the beholder. What we want to do is help you to train your eye so that you can pick the college that is best for you. *The Insider's Guide* describes, explains, and interprets, but the choice is always yours.

Getting In

The task of applying to college can seem as intimidating as the thickness of this book. In the spring of your sophomore year in high school your Aunt Betsy, whom you have not seen in three years, pinches your cheek and asks you where you are going to college. *How the heck should I know?* you think to yourself. That fall, your mother tells you that the boy down the street with the 4.0 grade point average is taking the SAT prep course for the fifth time to see if he can get a perfect score and win thousands in scholarship money. You reply that you are late for school. We know you keep ducking the subject, but the hints keep coming with increasing regularity. You start dreading dinner time, which has suddenly become a time for "serious" conversations about schools with your parents. You find yourself choking on your broccoli. Pretty soon a few of your friends are visiting the guidance office periodically to talk to counselors or leaf through college catalogs. Finally, you decide to make an appointment yourself.

When you first talk to your counselor, preferably as soon as possible in your junior year, you may have only just begun to feel comfortable in high school, let alone prepared to think about college. The entire prospect still seems far away, but picking and getting into a good school takes a lot of work and organization. The earlier you begin the search, the better. A visit to your counselor is a good way to start. Most are very helpful, but a few should make you wary—such as those who do not want to disappoint anyone, and those who want to keep their track records unblemished. The first group will assure you that you do not have a thing to worry about about getting into the college of your choice. Although these counselors may be paying you a hard-earned compliment, it still pays to read everything you can about the schools that interest you and to follow application procedures carefully. The second group will tell you not to apply to any school whose admissions they consider "too competitive," and will try to limit your alternatives. Listen to reason, but trust your instincts. Getting a sense of how helpful your counselor will be is important. The good ones can be enormously valuable as advisors and confidants throughout the admissions process.

The next step is to read articles that interest you, ask questions, and begin to think about what factors about a school make a difference for you. What do you want in a college? A strong science department? A friendly atmosphere? A great social life? While your academic needs should be your primary concern at the outset, be wary of concentrating on only one or two academic departments and making them the sole basis of your judgments. In college, most people change their mind two or three times before finally settling on a major. If you do change your major midway through your sophomore year, you do not want it to affect the overall quality of your coursework or force you to transfer because your college does not offer a good program in your new area of interest.

We realize that you cannot possibly think of all the angles. No one can say for sure what your interests will be three or four years from now, or what things will ultimately prove most important to you at the college you attend. By taking a hard look at yourself now, and proceeding carefully as you begin looking at the colleges, you can be reasonably sure that you are investigating the right colleges for the right reasons.

In the early winter of your junior year, you will receive your PSAT scores (discussed later, in "The Tests"). Unless you request otherwise, you will also be deluged with mail from colleges throughout the nation. The College Search Service of the College Board provides these colleges with the names and addresses of students who scored in various percentiles, and the schools crank out thousands of form letters to those whose scores show promise.

At first, making sense of your flood of mail may seem impossible. Glossy brochures tend to portray a diverse group of students frolicking happily and thinking deep thoughts on every page. "They're all the same," recalled one college freshman, happy to be finished with the process. Each brochure speaks of "rich diversity" and "academic rigor" and dozens of other high-minded ideals that are often nothing more than hollow catchphrases. Likewise, any campus can look beautiful through the lens of an admissions-office photographer. Just remember that the building that looks so picturesque in the fading twilight could be part of the law school, miles from where the undergraduates study and live.

You should also consider that the schools who select you for their mailings might not be the ones you would choose. Schools can recruit you for any number of reasons: You could be from a part of the country that the school feels is underrepresented in its student body, or your test scores could be higher than their average, and they would like you to bring them up! Chances are you will have to take the initiative to get the mailing information on some of the schools that truly interest you.

Brochures and viewbooks can be useful if they are read critically. What themes does the college stress most? What is not mentioned? What does the SAT or ACT profile look like? Look for hard facts to back up the flowery prose. If nothing else, viewbooks reveal something about how the college perceives itself, as well as what it aspires to be. It is not much to go on, but then again you also do not have time to do a thorough analysis of all 2,000 four-year colleges in the nation.

There is one source of information that is often overlooked just because it is close at hand, namely your parents. They, and other adults who know you well, probably have some good ideas about which schools you ought to consider. Take their advice seriously and investigate the alternatives they suggest. Adults frequently have a better perspective on you as an individual than would most people in your age group. Do not, however, let anyone dictate which colleges you "must" consider. It is important to come to an understanding with your parents early on that the college choice is ultimately yours alone. You are the one who has to live with that choice for four years, not them. If money is a potential problem, reach an agreement on that as well. How much can your family afford to pay? Some colleges might offer substantial financial aid. How much will you be expected to contribute? It is much better to deal with these questions in the opening months of the process than to wait until later when emotions are running high.

There are two important things to bear in mind as you consult the opinions of others. First, every piece of advice you will get will be a reflection of a particular person's own life experiences and is likely to be highly subjective. Second, opinions are frequently based on stereotypes that are often false, outdated, or misleading. Still, these are the shortcuts most applicants use to begin narrowing their choices, an unfortunate but necessary phase. The more people you talk to, the better perspective you gain on the colleges you are considering. The primary purpose of this book is to give you an inside look at the colleges. If you like what you have heard about a particular school, follow up with some careful research and find out if it lives up to its name.

As the field narrows, you should begin to dig deeper. See what the guides have to say about schools that interest you. Do you know anyone in college? Do you know anyone who knows anyone in college? Talk to them. You do not have to interview everyone you know, but you may find that real students are your best resource. Do not be afraid to ask "real" questions (for example, "Is State U really the party school it is made out to be?"). Get the "facts" from your college guides, and opinions and insights from the people who really know the school—the students. College nights and visits from admissions officers can also be useful because you get to see and talk to a representative of the college in the flesh. As with the viewbooks, read between the lines. College reps are there to sell the school and will be reluctant to confess any serious problems with it. It is up to you to be critical in evaluating what they say.

At this point, all the things we have been mentioning are just bits and pieces, but if you start adding them up, you will begin to get an idea of what the college experience is like on each campus. We realize that college may still seem miles away.

Being editor of the school paper or winning the league championship often seems a thousand times more important than reading through stacks of college literature that all looks much the same anyway. You will be tempted to put off thinking about college until later. Resist the temptation. Getting off on the right foot is important, and it will take some serious effort. We hesitate to say "the earlier the better," for the fear of striking panic in the hearts of every parent, but the summer after sophomore year is not too bad a time to slowly start looking around.

The Visit

The summer vacation between junior and senior years is the best time to get serious about college visits. Your list of potential colleges should be narrowed to about 15 schools by this point.

The purpose of a college visit is not to get the basic information you already have. You can find out all about the academic particulars from the glossy promotional literature that each school is sure to send you. The goal, instead, is to figure out how each campus feels and how much you like it. You will want to see how the students act toward each other to know if you would be comfortable there. Said one student about visiting an Ivy League school, "I just wanted to see if they looked normal, or if they all wore preppy sweaters and drove BMWs. I wanted to be able to picture myself there."

The best time to visit schools is during the academic year. It is the best time to see prospective colleges in action; this is how they will look if you decide to attend. You want to see daily life. It is best to avoid the exam periods and breaks when students usually are not around. Also, you will want to schedule interviews with admissions officers as far in advance as possible. However, we warn you, from speaking with friends who work for Yale's admissions office, the on-campus interview is much more grueling and critical. Unless the school's admissions office hints that it is preferable to do an on-campus interview, opt for the alumnus interview instead. Largely, the idea that on-campus interviews are more important than alumni interviews is a myth.

Before you go, take some time for a little preparation. You will need to develop a system for evaluating the strengths and weaknesses of each college you see. Make up a short list of characteristics to have in mind when you visit: What is the atmosphere of the campus—is it fun and games or conducive to studying? How crowded are the freshman dorms? Try to think of a uniform way to record your findings, especially if you are visiting several colleges on one trip. By focusing on carefully selected criteria, it will be much easier to compare schools later in the process. Take a look at "The College Spectrum" section of this book for some ideas.

Staying on campus overnight with undergraduates is a good idea. Contact them through friends or ask the admissions office to help you find a host (most will be glad to do so). The prospect of staying with students might sound intimidating, but most hosts are genuinely interested in helping you. After a night or two, you will hopefully be sorry to leave. The real differences among most colleges are in daily life, so pay careful attention. "I found that it didn't matter much if I stayed over or not, as long as I got to talk to students," one recent applicant said. "But if you do stay over, Friday night is the best time." That's when you get to see what the students' social life is really like. And if you are staying with socially withdrawn hosts, just strike out on your own if you are feeling brave; just don't do anything you'll regret later.

"The best advice I got," another prospective student said, "was to talk to students. It's tough . . . I'm kind of shy. But it's worth it to ask." Indeed, the best source of information is the living, breathing student body. You will be surprised by how willing most students are to divulge the dark secrets of their daily lives. After all, most campuses have a healthy dose of school spirit. Who would miss a chance to promote their favorite place?

You can also learn a lot from the nonverbal clues students emit. Size up the typical student. Are his eyes glazed? Is her vocabulary limited to the words "intense" and "dude"? Is he tripping over his own feet, weighed down by a calculator, two slide rules, and physics and chemistry textbooks? These are caricatures, of course, but if you can identify some common thread running through most of the students on campus, you should be well on your way to an intelligent evaluation of the college.

Keep in mind that college life does not consist entirely of classes. Sample the food, which is, after all, a necessity of life. Check out the dorms. Take the campus tour. Though you are sure to be inundated with obscure facts about the college that do not interest you, it can be useful to see the buildings themselves and the campus as a whole. Look closely at the facilities. If you have questions, do not hesitate to ask. The tour guide is usually a student, so do not let the opportunity pass if there is something you really want to know.

Most important, though, is to get a sense of the campus atmosphere. How does it feel to walk across the main quad? Does the mood seem intellectual or laid-back? Do T-shirts read "Earth Day Every Day" or "Coed Naked Beer Games"? Look for postings of events; some campuses are alive and vibrant, others will seem pretty dead. Focus on these characteristics while you are on campus; you can read about the distribution requirements at home.

Should you bring your parents along when you visit? Maybe. If you feel comfortable going alone, leave them home. Although they mean no harm, parents can sometimes get in the way. If Mom or Dad takes a wrong turn and starts driving the car around on the main quad (it has happened before), your embarrassment may cloud your impression of a school you might otherwise have loved.

If your parents do go along, make sure you take some time to roam around on your own. Take the tours together, but send Mom and Dad to a hotel while you sleep in the dorm. In all fairness, having your parents along can be a good thing as long as they know when to step back and let you go your own way. They know you as well as anyone, and they might see things you miss. The drive home is often an excellent time to discuss with them the pros and cons of the school that you just visited.

The Interview

Just about every college applicant dreads the interview. It can be the most nerve-wracking part of the college application process. But relax—despite the horror stories you might have heard, the interview will rarely make or break your application. If you are a strong candidate, don't be too cocky (many have fallen this way); if your application makes you look like a hermit, be lively and personable. Usually the interview can only help you, and at some schools it is nothing more than an information session. "I was constantly surprised at how many questions they let me ask," one applicant reported.

It is best to look at the interview as your chance to highlight the best parts of your application and possibly to explain the weakest parts without being whiny or making excuses. Are your SAT scores on the low side? Did your extracurricular section seem a little thin? An interview gives you the opportunity to call attention to your successes in classes despite your scores, or explain that of the three clubs you listed, you founded two and were president of the third.

There are a few keys to a successful interview. The first is to stand out from the crowd. Keep in mind that the interviewer probably sees half a dozen or more people every day, month after month. If you can make your interviewer laugh, interest him or her in something unusual you have done, or somehow spice up the same old questions and answers, you have had a great interview. Don't just say that you were the president of something; you *must* be able to back up your titles with interesting and genuine stories. Second, do not try to be something you are not. Tell the truth. By doing so, you will be more relaxed and confident. Even if you feel that the "real you" isn't that interesting or amazing, think hard about your years of high school; you'll surprise yourself with the stories that will surface in your mind.

A few days before the actual interview, think about some of the questions you might be asked. Some admissions officers begin every interview by asking, "Why do you want to go to this school, and why should we let you?" You should not have memorized speeches for every answer, but try not to get caught off guard. Make sure you really know why you want to attend this college. Even if you are not sure, think of a plausible reason and be prepared to give it. Students often make the mistake of giving a canned answer, which is okay given most answers are similar, but admissions officers look to admit students who want to take advantage of all that is available at their school. Your answer must include the three essential elements of a good reply: your interests, whether academic or extracurricular; what you believe the school will provide; and how and why you are excited about the opportunity to take advantage of them. Other common questions include those about your most important activities, what you did with your summers, and what vision you may have for your future.

A note of caution: If your interview takes place after you have submitted your application, the interviewer might ask you questions about some of the things you included. One student wrote on his application that he read *Newsweek* religiously. During his interview, the admissions officer asked the student about a story in a recent issue of the magazine. The student had no idea what the interviewer was talking about. He was not accepted. Back up your claims or don't talk the talk.

It is always an excellent idea to indicate that you have a special interest in something, but make sure the interest is genuine—you may wind up with an hour-long conversation on the topic. Do not start talking about how you love learning about philosophy if you have only dabbled in it once. Do not try to use big words simply to sound impressive during what should be just a friendly chat. An open, thoughtful manner can do as much as anything else to impress your interviewer.

Having a successful interview usually amounts to being spontaneous in a contrived situation. If you are nervous, that is okay. Said one applicant, "I felt sick and I didn't eat for a day before the interview." The most common misconception is that admissions officers are looking for totally confident individuals who know every-

thing and have their entire future planned out. Almost the opposite is true. An admissions officer at a selective private college said, "We do not expect imitation adults to walk through the door. We expect to see people in their last year or two of high school with the customary apprehensions, habits, and characteristics of that time of life." Admissions officers know that students get nervous. They understand.

If everything in your life is not perfect, do not be afraid to say so when appropriate. For example, if the conversation comes around to your high school, there is no need to cover up if problems do exist. It is okay to say you did not think your chemistry lab was well equipped. An honest, realistic critique of your school or just about anything else will make a better impression than false praise ever could. Even more, someone with initiative who overcomes adversity is often more appealing to an interviewer than a person who goes to the "right" high school and coasts along.

If something you say does not come out quite right, try to react as you would with a friend. If the interviewer asks about your career plans, it is all right to say you are undecided. As a high school student, no one expects you to have all the answers—that is why you are going to college. Above all, remember that the admissions officer is a person, interested in getting to know you as an individual. As one interviewer explained, "I'm not there to judge the applicants as scholars. I'm just there to get a sense of them as people."

Do not get so worried about saying all the right things that you forget to listen carefully to the interviewer. The purpose of the interview is not to grill you, but to match you and the school in the best interest of both. Sometimes the interviewer will tell you, either during the interview or in a follow-up letter, that you have little chance of getting in. If she says so or implies it, know that such remarks are not made lightly. On the other hand, if she is sincerely encouraging, listen to that, too. If an interviewer suggests other schools for you to look into, remember that she is a professional and take note. Besides, many interviewers appreciate a student's ability to listen as well as to talk.

Your interviewer might ask you whether you have a first choice, particularly if her college is often seen as a backup. If the school is really not your first choice, fudge a little. Mention several colleges, including the one you are visiting, and say you have not made up your mind yet. Your first choice is your business, not hers. If the school really is your first choice, though, feel free to say so, and to give a good reason why. A genuine interest can be a real plug on your behalf.

Also know that you can direct the conversation. Do not worry about occasional lapses as some interviewers wait to see how you will react to a potentially awkward situation. Calmly ask a question, or mention something that really interests you. It is your job to present the parts of you and your background that you want noted.

Selective colleges need reasons to accept you. Being qualified on paper is not always enough. Think of the interviewer's position: "Why should we accept you instead of thousands of other qualified applicants?" The answer to that question should be evident in every response you give. Use the interview to play up and accentuate your most memorable qualities. Show flashes of the playful sense of humor that your English teacher cites in his or her recommendation; impress the interviewer with the astute eye for politics about which your math teacher raves.

Too many applicants are afraid to talk confidently about their accomplishments. If the interviewer is impressed by something, do not insist that it was not much, or he might believe you. If he is not impressed by something you think is important, tactfully let him know that he should be. But do not, under any circumstances, be "too cool" for the college. One well-qualified applicant to a leading college was turned down when the interviewer wrote, "It obviously isn't going to be the end of his world if he doesn't get in. And it won't be the end of our world, either." If there is any quality you want to convey, it is a sincere interest in the school. Always come to the interview armed with a good question or two and not one whose answer is easily found in the college's viewbook. Do not ask if they have an economics department, for example—ask

the average class size in introductory economics courses.

You will probably wonder what to wear. This is no life or death decision, but remember that your appearance is one of the first things the interviewer will notice about you. Wear something you will be comfortable in—a jacket and a tie or a nice dress are fine. Do not, however, be too casual. Faded jeans and a T-shirt will give the impression that you are taking the interview too lightly.

One crucial point: Keep your parents a thousand feet and preferably a thousand miles away from the interview session. When parents sit in, interviews tend to be short, boring, and useless. If the interviewer feels you cannot handle an hour without your parents, she might be concerned about your ability to survive the pressures of college life. Take the risk of hurting your parents' feelings and ask them to wait outside.

Once the interview is over, it is perfectly all right for your parents to ask any questions they may have if the interviewer walks with you back to the waiting room. Even if this makes you uncomfortable, do not let it show. Admissions officers can learn as much about you by the way you treat your parents as they do in the interview. The interviewer is not judging your parents. As long as you conduct yourself calmly and maturely, you have got nothing to worry about.

All of this advice applies for interviews given by alumni as well as those conducted by admissions staff. Alumni interviewers usually carry slightly less weight with the admissions office, but they are valuable contacts with the schools and should not be taken lightly.

What if you do not have an interview at all? Perhaps you live too far away, and you cannot get to the school itself. Or, perhaps you feel that your lack of poise is so serious that it would work against you in any interview you had. Talk it over with your guidance counselor. In general, geographic isolation is a valid excuse for not having an interview, and most colleges will not hold it against you. Yet, if the college is fairly close and makes it clear that applicants should have an on-campus interview if at all possible, make the effort to go. Otherwise, the college will assume that for some reason you were afraid to interview, or worse, that you simply did not care enough to have one. If the prospect is genuinely terrifying, schedule your first interview for a safety school, or ask your guidance counselor to grant you a practice interview. You might discover that the process is not as horrible as you originally thought.

The Tests

Standardized tests are known (not necessarily correctly) as the great equalizers. Whether you are an Olympic hopeful, a musical prodigy, or a third-generation legacy, you cannot avoid taking them. Whether you attend prep, private, public, or parochial school, your scores are meant to indicate the quantity and quality of education you have had in the past as well as your potential to excel in the future. Certainly, tests do not tell the whole story; grades, recommendations, extracurricular activities, application essays, and personal interviews round out the picture. Scores are often the only uniform admissions criteria available, and regardless of your opinion of them, they are necessary.

The Scholastic Assessment Test (SAT), by far the best known of admissions tests, is required by virtually all of the nation's highly selective colleges. The SAT is designed to measure verbal and mathematical abilities—as opposed to achievement—so theoretically you cannot study for it. After being administered in the same format for decades, the test changed slightly in March 1994. In the verbal section, antonym questions were replaced by a section on vocabulary in context, and more questions on reading comprehension and comparisons were added. For the first time, students were allowed to use a calculator for the math sections, which each included ten new "student-produced response" (fill-in-the-blank) questions along with 50 multiple-choice questions.

According to the Educational Testing Service (ETS), which administers the test, the format changes were minor, and they did not affect the way colleges used the test in their admissions decisions. Of course, it is difficult to speculate whether some colleges may lean more or less heavily on the new test in making their decisions. However, because ETS made the changes to improve the test's accuracy in determining students' scholastic ability, colleges are likely to find it a better indicator than before.

Beginning April 1, 1995, ETS also began reporting SAT scores on a "recentered" scale. The SAT was originally calibrated so that the average scores for the math and verbal sections would be 500 each, giving an average SAT score of 1000. These scores had slowly slipped over several decades to an average of 900—some say as a result of a declining American educational system, although others argue that the perceived "decrease" is not surprising considering that today's 1.8 million SAT-takers are much more representative of American education as a whole than the 10,000 primarily affluent prep-school students who took the SAT when it was implemented in 1941. The recentering returns the average SAT score to 1000 and thus gives the average test-taker a 100-point boost over the old system, which sounds encouraging only until you realize that almost everybody else gets a similar boost, and that as a result, your percentile "rank" will not change. Ultimately, the recentering, like the changes in the actual test, redistribute scores more evenly along the 200–800 score scale and therefore makes it easier for a school to differentiate between applicants. A few prestigious colleges and universities with many high-scoring applicants have complained that the recentering blurs the distinctions between top students' scores (yes, it is easier to get a 1600 now), although ETS and the College Board would argue that this is precisely why they changed the scoring; admissions committees should not be using minute differences in test scores to split hairs between applicants.

When you take the test, be sure to take advantage of two services offered by ETS upon registration. The first concerns the disclosure of your scores to recruiters. If you mark "yes" in the appropriate box, any colleges engaged in recruiting can find out the range in which your scores fall, and may send information about their programs directly to you. You might consider some of these pamphlets junk mail, but some of them might help you form the list of colleges to which you intend to apply. The SATs are also the qualifying round for the Presidential Scholar Award, a highly selective competition not as well known as the Merit Scholarship program (see "The Money").

The second service will mail your test scores to specified colleges. ETS will mail your scores directly to the admissions office of up to six colleges at no extra cost. If you have a "bad day," you have three days to cancel the mailing. If you take the test again, however, the form that reports the results of your second try will also contain the results of your previous attempt, so the colleges to which you apply will know about your bad day sooner or later.

Previously, the American College Test (ACT) was required mostly by colleges in the southern and western regions of the country, but now more colleges are accepting it as a substitute for the SAT I and SAT II tests. The ACT test consists of reading, math, science reasoning, and English grammar sections, each of which takes an hour. The ACT differs from the SAT in that it explicitly attempts to measure past achievement rather than aptitude. Many students feel that the ACT is easier, since wrong answers are not penalized.

Many of the more selective colleges also require up to three SAT II exams, formerly called Achievement Tests (also administered by ETS). Available subjects include English, a variety of foreign languages, math, history, and several of the sciences. Colleges may weigh these scores as heavily as the SAT I, so these tests should not be taken lightly. SAT II scores were also changed to reflect the re-centering. By now, you may have already taken the Preliminary Scholastic Assessment Test (PSAT). The PSAT is good practice for the SAT and high scores can qualify you for merit scholarships, although the scores themselves will mean very little after you have taken the SAT.

Advanced Placement (AP) exams are another animal altogether, since their purpose is not to get you into college, but instead to earn you credits once you get there. Administered in May, each test covers a specific subject area. Different schools require different scores for granting college credit. Some will offer credit but still require you to take classes in a subject that you aced on the AP exam. Since the tests require in-depth knowledge of specific subjects, do not put them off. If you plan on taking the American History AP test, take it right after you finish your American History course, be it sophomore or senior year. The fresher the material is in your mind, the better your score will be. In addition, the AP test scores can only help your college applications if you take them before your senior year and score high.

The most reliable way to keep up-to-date on test dates, sites, and registration deadlines is through your high school guidance office. After the PSAT, which most schools administer to sophomores or juniors every fall, you will be on your own about when and where you take the tests. Find out which ones are required by the colleges you are interested in way ahead of time; deadlines have a way of sneaking up on you. It is a good idea to begin taking the tests by the spring of your junior year. If you take the SAT in March or May of your junior year and do not do as well as you think you should, you will have a couple of other opportunities to improve your scores. The required SAT IIs should also be taken by June of the junior year so that if you decide to apply to an early-action or early-decision program, you will have completed the required testing.

Avoid postponing required testing until November, December, or January of your senior year. One new college student who put off the SAT until the last minute recalled his freshman faculty advisor saying to him, "I just don't understand it . . . you went to one of the best high schools in Chicago and did very well. How could your SAT scores have been so low?" He told her how lucky he felt just getting into college; he had contracted a nasty flu and thrown up before, during, and after the test! On the other hand, do not repeat the tests over and over. The ETS reports that students can gain an average of 25 points on both the verbal and math sections of the SAT if they take the test a second time. Two or three shots at the SATs are sufficient, and there is no need to sit for every SAT II imaginable.

If you have got the time and money, you might also consider taking a prep course given by a professional test-preparation service. Ideally, the object of the SAT is to measure raw ability, so studying should be forbidden. National test-prep companies like Kaplan and the Princeton Review, as well as dozens of local companies, remind us that our world is not an ideal one. There is a continuing debate among educators about whether these courses actually raise scores—but they certainly cannot hurt. The ETS maintains that there is "no surefire way to practice for standardized tests designed to predict aptitude." The testing agency adds that some students improve their scores after coaching, whereas others do better by preparing themselves. Coaching programs generally cost hundreds of dollars and seem to be most useful to students who are poor test-takers or who feel that they have a great deal of room for improvement. If you do take a prep class, take it seriously. You may have six or seven other high school classes to worry about and those might seem more important, but you cannot hope to get your money's worth if you do not attend all of the sessions and complete any homework. In general, the longer the program, the more likely it is to boost your scores.

If you choose not to take a practice course, at least read the instructions on the ETS practice exams carefully and thoroughly. You should not have to waste time during the exam rereading instructions. If you do choose to study by taking practice exams, treat them seriously. Simulating the test-taking environment (real questions, no interruptions, strict time limits) is a good exercise in familiarizing yourself with the situation so you will not freak out when it is for real. The official ETS book of practice tests, *10 SATs*, and commercially marketed practice books (the ones produced by the companies that also teach prep courses are the best) contain sample SATs.

In our opinion, one of the most effective ways to prepare for the SAT is to take as many practice tests as possible under simulated testing conditions. Actual SATs are much better than the practice tests in

SAT preparation books. True to its title, *10 SATs* has official SATs from two previous years. It is published annually and is available in most bookstores or can be ordered directly from ETS. Set aside three hours every Saturday for the ten Saturdays before the test; try to make it the same three hours when you will be taking the real exam. Instruct family, friends, and your dog to leave you alone for those hours. Such a regimen will give you a keener sense of the overall structure of the test and help you to work faster during the actual exam, and might help you relax a bit. Chances are that your actual score will hover somewhere close to your practice test scores.

A good student who is confident about test taking will probably do just as well studying on his or her own. One student endured a practice course only to score 100 points below what he received on a practice test he took before entering the course. He then prepared on his own with *10 SATs*, took the SAT a second time, and not only gained the 100 points but bettered his original practice score by 50 points. One thing to keep in mind: Although test preparation may or may not boost your SAT scores, it can make a huge difference on the SAT IIs, which measure your knowledge of a subject the way conventional tests do.

The night before the exam, get plenty of sleep. Do not cram the night before. Relax. "My teacher encouraged us to go out and have a good time the night before," recalled one first-year college student. "So I went to the movies as a distraction. I think it worked!" On the day of the test eat a full breakfast, dress comfortably, and do not forget to bring two pieces of ID, a couple of number-two pencils, and a pencil sharpener. Make sure you are up early and know where you will be taking the test as well as how to get there. The test center may be overcrowded, there may be no air-conditioning or heat, and a hundred construction workers may be drilling outside the nearest window—be prepared for anything!

The key to success on the SAT is to keep calm. During the exam, keep track of how many problems there are, and allot time accordingly. Read and attempt to answer every question since you do not get more credit for the hard ones than the easy ones. The SAT is one of the few standardized tests that penalizes the taker for wrong answers. The best overall rule is to eliminate one or more of the possible answers and try to select from the remaining choices. If you really have no idea about a question, it is best to leave it blank. Just remember to also leave a blank on your answer sheet!

A word of warning: Do not even think about cheating. It is not worth it, and your chances of getting caught and blackballed from college are high. To weed out cheaters, the ETS uses the mysterious K-index, a statistical tool that measures the chance of two students selecting the same answers. If your K-index is suspect, a form letter goes out to the colleges you are interested in, delaying your score until you retake the exam or prove your innocence. Know that looking at another person's test is not the only activity that the ETS considers cheating. Going back to finish work on a previous section is also against the rules. Do not tempt fate—a low score is better than no score at all.

At the beginning of this section, we stressed that standardized tests are important. How important? It varies. Generally speaking, the more selective the school, the less your scores will matter. At many state schools, admission depends almost entirely on test scores and grades. If you score above the cutoffs, you are in. At very competitive colleges, tests are just one of many factors. According to the dean of admissions at Harvard University, "If scores are in the high 500 to low 700 range, they probably have a fairly small impact on our decisions." Each of the schools in this book lists a mean SAT score. Remember that half of the students accepted to that college scored below the mean. Unless you score far below or far above the mean of your desired college, in most cases the SAT will not make or break your chances of getting in. If your scores are not quite up to snuff, but you have attended an inner-city school or a school in an area of the country where educational standards are below the norm, your apparent deficit might, in fact, indicate real strength—as long as you have passed certain minimum levels. Remember that a combined 700-point minimum is necessary to participate in NCAA athletic programs.

Many students mistakenly believe that the SAT is the only test that "really matters" in competitive college admissions. In fact, SAT II scores taken as a whole are usually of equal importance. Although most claim that SAT IIs are not taken into account for admissions, many colleges actually view these scores as a more accurate predictor of future performance than the SAT. In almost every case, your high school record is more important than your SAT scores. A strong performance in high school can sometimes compensate for weak scores, but standardized tests alone rarely make up for a poor showing in the classroom. If scores are exceptionally high or low, however, they do tend to take on more importance in the eyes of the admissions officer. The fact, for better or worse, is that currently test scores are an important factor in college admissions; try your best to make it an advantage point for you and don't panic if you don't get 1600.

The Application

By the time the leaves start to change in the fall of your senior year, you should decide on four to eight schools to apply to. If you are fairly certain about your first-choice school, you may apply to as few as two or three others, but if you are looking at highly selective schools, seven or eight is a more realistic number.

Ideally, the colleges you choose should range from highly selective to less so. A common tendency among applicants is to aim too low or too high. Do not let high median SAT scores and low acceptance rates at your two favorite schools intimidate you and keep you from applying. Even if the odds are against you, you will be happier attending your third choice knowing you at least tried for the other two. However, do not go to the opposite extreme of overconfidence and forget to choose a "safety school"—one where your chances of getting in are excellent and where you'll also be comfortable and happy. "At my school, we use the 2-2-2 plan," explained one senior. "Two 'safeties,' two 'middles,' and two 'reaches.'"

Once you have decided where you want to apply, start thinking about when. Make a list of when each application is due, and think about completing them in that order. You can put the schools most important to you closer to the front so you will not rush through them, or save them for last when you have had the most practice. If you truly want to go to a school, get the application in on time, preferably early. If a school needs to weed an applicant pool of thousands down to a few hundred, nothing is easier than immediately eliminating a late application.

Once you start considering due dates, you will want to decide whether to apply under any of the various "early" programs. These typically include early decision, early action, and rolling admissions. Early decision and early action are similar. Both require you to submit your application in the fall, usually mid-October to early November, and both will notify you by mid-to late December. The key difference is that early decision is binding, whereas early action is not. An early-decision candidate signs a contract stating that if he or she is accepted, he or she will enroll. Be sure to read carefully any early-decision agreement you sign. All applications to other schools usually must be withdrawn, and the student will most likely pay some sort of retainer fee immediately. Failure to comply with the agreement can lead to rather disagreeable consequences, typically blackballing from other schools. Needless to say, a student can apply to only one school as an early decision.

Early decision should only be used if you have a clear first choice in mind since it allows no room for flexibility. It does have advantages, however. Applying for early decision expresses a clear interest in the school and may give you an advantage over regular applicants. In addition, if you get accepted, you will be spared many of the hassles of the application process (and you can be wearing your college sweatshirt as early as Christmas vacation of senior year). If you feel your credentials will greatly improve during the first semester of your senior year, though, you might not want early deci-

sion. Rejections are final, regardless of when they arrive, and robbing yourself of an opportunity to put your best application forward for the sake of an earlier reply is not wise.

Early action is offered primarily by a few Ivy League schools, although other schools are beginning to offer similar programs. Because early action is not binding, it offers convenience without commitment, but for this reason it may not give as much of an advantage to the applicant. Typically only the top applicants are accepted, with borderline cases deferred for consideration with the main applicant pool.

Rolling admissions is another process offered by some schools, usually those that are larger and less selective. The process is a simple one. You send in the completed application, the staff considers it, and sends you a reply within a few weeks. Rolling admissions means you are judged on your own merits as opposed to being judged against the rest of a pool, but the relative difficulty of gaining acceptance increases as the spaces fill up, so apply as early as possible. Rolling admissions lets many students ensure acceptance to a "safety" school early in the process.

Once you know when to apply, you must begin the process of filling out the application, and there are some general rules to follow. Read the entire application carefully, cover to cover, before you begin. Always fill out or type the applications yourself. Never allow more than one person's handwriting to appear on anything you send to the admissions office. If you must write by hand, again, do so yourself and do it neatly. Keep ink color consistent throughout the entire application as well. If you use a word processor or computer for your essay, select a basic font, preferably the one that looks most like a typewriter, and use the best printer you can find.

You will find that each application has a certain "style." Some are very stiff and formal; others make an attempt to be casual. You can let the style of the application help you determine how to fill it in. Some schools insist that the application must be handwritten, for example, and others strongly encourage you to type. Some colleges do not make it easy to follow their own suggestions. "My Emory University application encouraged me to write, but there were no lines on the page!" complained one new freshman. Do the best you can.

Applications are usually divided into several sections. Treat every section as important, and use every page to your advantage. If a section gives you some degree of freedom to answer, do not repeat information you have listed elsewhere. The following explanations of the sections include some things you should remember when filling out your application.

- *Personal Information.* This usually is the first section, and is fairly straightforward. Certain questions of race or ethnic background may be optional, but it is not a bad idea to answer them, as they cannot hurt you and may help you. Again, do not try to be something you are not. Having a third cousin twice removed who has a Cherokee grandfather does not make you a Native American in the eyes of the admissions office. This part of the application may also ask for specifics about your parents—their careers, college degrees, and places of birth. You might want to write all this out on an index card to keep with your applications, so you only have to ask once.

- *Standardized Tests.* This section, also straightforward, tells you which tests are required, and gives you a place to list your scores and dates of past exams. You will most likely have to send an official copy of all your exam results to the school, through the Educational Testing Service. Make sure you request the copy of this report early enough for it to arrive before the deadline.

- *Extracurricular Activities.* Here is your first chance to be more than a statistic. Along with your essay, your activities define your personality in the eyes of the admissions office. Take the time to list them as the college requests. "Some schools want them chronologically, some want them in order of importance," said one recent applicant. If

it does not say, use the order of importance, and check this order against the rest of your application. If you intend to write your essay about your experiences as a hospital volunteer and you list it as your fifth most important activity, the committee will have doubts, either about the sincerity of your essay or the accuracy of your list. Make sure your information does not contradict itself.

As for which activities to list, remember that quality consistently takes precedence over quantity. Two or three activities to which you have committed yourself and that reflect your character in some manner will far outweigh membership in 20 clubs that you dropped after your first year. The general rule is that there are very few "superstars" of extracurriculars such as nationally ranked athletes or concert musicians in any applicant pool, and that activity lists are designed more to give some depth to your application than to tip the scales of an admissions committee in either direction.

- *Transcript.* Grades are a vital part of any application. There is little we can do at this point to help you improve them, but you can work on their presentation. Your percentile class rank counts for a lot, and those with the strongest applications will be in about the top ten percent. With any luck, you have taken the majority of your classes in the "meat and potatoes" disciplines: math, English, science, and so on. Colleges are not likely to be impressed with sociology, psychology, and other frill courses some high schools offer unless you have also mastered the basics. Senioritis makes offbeat electives tempting, but watch out. If the school of your choice sees that you have selected "Leadership Skills" instead of AP English, they will be somewhat less than impressed.

One more thing to remember: It is vitally important that any honors classes you have taken are marked as such on your transcript. (See your counselor to make sure.) If you are not taking honors classes, try to schedule some for your senior year. It can be damaging not to have taken the most rigorous courses offered at your school. Include any transcripts from summer programs at other schools or universities as well. Taking a college-level course shows initiative and is always a plus with the admissions office.

• *Recommendations*. Many colleges require one or more letters of recommendation. In cases where they are optional, the recommendation of a guidance counselor or teacher may not guarantee your acceptance, but it certainly will not hurt. Look for teachers who know you personally, perhaps as coaches or advisors. You should obviously choose teachers in subjects that are your strong points. Writing skills are highly valued by any college, so English teachers are a good choice, especially if your verbal test scores are strong. You should once again aim for a balance of subjects and viewpoints in selecting your teachers. Make sure they receive all of the necessary information in plenty of time to meet the deadline, and make sure to follow up. "I casually asked my bio teacher about my recommendation on the day before the deadline, and he hadn't even written it yet!" Most teachers are quite careful and considerate, but it never hurts to remind them when the deadline is near.

Most recommendation forms have a line at the bottom asking the student to waive his or her rights to see the completed recommendation. Unless you are extremely uncomfortable about allowing your recommendations to be submitted without your approval, sign the waiver. It shows that you have faith in those who have worked with you. Besides, many teachers will let you see what they have written anyway. "My teachers showed me the results voluntarily. I think they put a lot of time and effort into them, and they want us to know," said one applicant. A few schools demand confidentiality, including The College of William and Mary, which asks that the teacher seal the letter in an envelope and then sign over the flap.

• *The Essay*. Last but not least, you must write The Essay. Too many students needlessly stress out over the essay. If you think about it, the essay is, along with the interview, the only part of the application process that lets you determine the form and/or presentation. Even better, you get to go back and correct the parts of your essay that do not come out right the first time. There are some guidelines to follow, though.

Be concise. If the essay gives you a length limit, adhere to it. Pick a topic that not only will interest an admissions officer, but also truly interests you. Trying to write about something that you do not really care about just because you think it will make a good topic will only result in an essay no one else will care about either. Be yourself. If that means writing about a topic someone else might deem trivial, let an interesting, expressive essay be your answer to their criticism.

Begin thinking about your essay almost immediately, and do not be afraid to simply sit down and let some words pour out. Revision is the key to truly good writing, and under no circumstances should you send in a first draft. Procrastination, as tempting as it might be, can result in an inferior product. If you begin early enough, your writing will be relaxed and natural, and can be revised and tinkered with until it reaches the desired level of perfection. Writing your college essay the night before you mail it is a pressure-cooker situation that can only lead to disappointment. If you can, ask a teacher or counselor to work with you, not only to give grammatical and stylistic advice, but also to check for typos. Under no circumstances should you write on an application form until your essay is perfect.

Many schools ask what seem to be similar questions, but unless they are exactly alike, do not use the same essay more than once. Sometimes rewriting the introduction and conclusion can do the trick, but get a second opinion. Trying to make an essay written for one application "fit" a specific question from another college can be a fairly obvious ploy, and one that will only make you look bad. "I ended up writing about ten essays," explained one college freshman. "I wanted to be sure they were specific enough."

Essentially, your goal in writing an essay is to clearly and concisely discuss yourself by discussing something different. Your writing style should say as much about you as your words. To say people find you funny is one thing, but to make a reader laugh is quite another. You do not need an admissions officer to tell you which is more effective. Speak in your own voice and do so consistently throughout. Being humorous or unorthodox can make you memorable, but only if you are good at it and it is consistent with the tone of the rest of the application.

- *Miscellaneous.* If you feel that something about you speaks strongly in your favor, and it cannot be included in the application proper, think about sending it anyway. Many schools accept portfolios from aspiring artists and tapes from musicians. This does not, however, include such gimmicks as videotapes of your friends extolling your virtues, or sending your application inside a cake. Essentially, if your "creative writing sample" still needs to be written, do not bother. It probably is not worth the extra effort and certainly isn't the purpose of sending additional materials. Think "past accomplishments" when you are trying to decide if something should be sent.

Above all, be certain that your application is neat, honest, and all your own. Never put down anything fake, half-true, or almost true. Admissions officers have sensitive bullshit detectors, and if something in your work sets off their alarms, you've kissed your chances at that college goodbye.

Once all the stamps are licked and envelopes sealed, try to relax. This may be easier said than done, but if you are like most students, the months before your deadlines will have been frazzled ones. Go out, have fun, and enjoy the rest of your senior year. April is just around the corner. . . .

The Wait

We realize, of course, that no matter what we say, you will worry. From the day the final application goes in, students across the nation torture themselves with the ever-present "What if?" What if my first-term grade report got lost in the mail? What if my physics teacher forgot to send in my recommendation? What if ETS reports my SAT scores to the wrong schools? For some applicants, this period of suspense will be short-lived. Those who apply on a rolling admissions plan will have to wait only the few weeks it takes their application to be processed, while early-action and early-decision applicants should have their suspense ended (or prolonged) around December.

For those of you remaining, the pressure can be intense. "The whole school was waiting," recalled one college student. "We had all applied to the same schools, and we were all wondering who was going to get in!" The following information may help you understand what really happens while you are waiting.

Some colleges have relatively uncomplicated ways of evaluating applications. Many state universities use simple cutoffs for grades and SATs, accepting everyone who is qualified. At more selective colleges, however, the process is much more complex. After all the applications are in, every piece of information about each applicant, from the application to jotted notes from an interview, is assembled in a folder. Much of the applicant pool is academically qualified to attend; therefore, non-academic factors play a more important role. Each admissions office has its own criteria for organizing and reading the folders. Many do them by secondary school, others by state or region; sometimes all the "legacy" applicants (sons and daughters of alumni) are evaluated together. Each college starts with a rough idea of the optimal mix of "types" to enroll. Instead of being judged against absolute standards, applicants are evaluated relative to others who apply. Your fate will probably be determined by how well you rate within your subgroup.

Ethnic-minority status can be an important advantage in college admissions. Talented African-American students are much in demand. Being of Latino or Native-American descent also can be an asset. Recent years have seen a tremendous rise in the number of qualified Asian-Americans applying to prestigious colleges. Consequently, their acceptance rates have seen a steady decline at these schools—so much so that questions have been raised as to whether limits have been imposed on the number of Asian-Americans admitted each year.

Aside from ethnicity, chance diversity factors (as opposed to special talents or skills developed through a student's own initiative) are of limited importance. Relatives who attended the college or university may be an important asset at some schools and mean little at others. The same goes for geographic distribution. In general, the less successful a college is in attracting students from your school or region, the better your chances for admission. If you live very close to a selective college, you will sometimes get a break because the school wants to keep good relations with the community by admitting more local students. All these factors are far less important than the other parts of your application, but they can give you an advantage among applicants with similar qualifications, and sometimes that makes all the difference.

At most schools each folder is read and evaluated by one to three admissions officers. Many colleges have numerical ratings that are assigned to every application. Some rate the academic and non-academic sides of the folder; other systems are more complex. After a folder has been read, usually one of the staff will present it to the admissions committee as a whole for final action. Faculty members frequently are involved in the deliberations, either to contribute professional opinions on artwork, music, and so on or as full-fledged members of the committee. Coaches and alumni groups can also have their say about particular students they would like to see admitted.

Inevitably, the folders of marginal applicants get closer scrutiny than those of clear "admits" or "denies." Particularly close calls are saved until the end for final action by the committee. Sometimes, the director or dean of admissions retains a number of "wild card" acceptances for applicants denied admission by the full committee.

Although the process is subjective, it is by no means haphazard. Many admissions officers are recent graduates who vividly remember what it is like to be an applicant, and others on the committee bring many years of admissions experience to the evaluation process. In addition, each college has built-in safeguards to ensure that admissions officers with headaches or hemorrhoids do not bias the process.

Finally, after the admissions machine has ground to a halt, decision letters arrive in mailboxes across the nation. "My dad had about 1,000 copies of that acceptance letter made. And then he framed it!" reported one triumphant acceptee. "It's true what they say about a thick or thin envelope!" said one recent graduate. "But not for early action—the acceptances arrive in a thin envelope for those."

Making the waiting list, once a booby prize or a sop to the child of a potentially disgruntled alumnus, has come to have value in this age of overlapping acceptances. If schools underestimate the number of accepted candidates who will reject them, there will be holes in the incoming freshman class, which will be filled from the waiting list. Even so, the waiting list is usually a long shot. Final notification may not come until well into the summer, so for safety's sake it is best to accept an offer of admission from another school, even if it means sending in a non-refundable room deposit.

If you happen to be denied admission to a college you especially wanted to attend, never call the admissions office to vent your anger or ask why. If you are not satisfied, have your counselor make a discreet inquiry sometime later. As one admissions officer told us, "If somebody is contemplating transferring a year later, a bitter encounter with the admissions office can seal that person's doom forever."

When it comes to the final decision, go with your instincts. In the end, the best choice is probably the place where you will feel most comfortable.

Getting into the college of your choice is not the end of your worries, as four very expensive years lie ahead. Presently, the annual costs at the most expensive colleges are past the $25,000 mark, with some already costing more than $115,000 for a four-year education. Few families can afford this expensive price tag, especially if there is more than one member of the family going to college, but there are millions of dollars out there in the form of scholarship money each year. You should not hesitate to apply to a college because of its cost of attendance, so you should always look into the possibility of financial aid.

The most important step of the financial-aid process is to get organized (as with any step in the college application process). The money is not going to come to you, so you have to look for it. A good place to start is with your high-school guidance office. Often guidance counselors receive information about various types of scholarships (more on that later) and will usually post them somewhere in the school. Take note of these announcements and fill out the applications and you're on your way. The applications can be time consuming, but if you are well organized, there should be no problem. The following Web sites also provide information and services for students seeking financial aid: *www.finaid.org* and *www. fastweb.com*. The more persistent you are in your search, the better your chances are of finding all the funds you need.

By far the best sources of aid are the colleges themselves. Most colleges earmark large sums of money for financial aid and also distribute much of the money available from federal and state governments. Depending on the school, some may award only on the basis of need while others award on the basis of need and/or merit or achievement. The policies at various schools differ widely.

Carefully read the bulletins provided by the colleges you are considering. If you have any questions, write to the admissions or financial-aid office right away. Find out what their admissions policy is regarding financial-aid applicants. Some of the nation's wealthier schools have "need-blind admissions," which means that your application for admission is considered with no regard to your ability to pay. However, at some schools, financial need may affect the admissions decisions, especially in borderline cases where preference may be given to those with the ability to pay. Even if you do not think you can afford it, apply to the school and for financial aid. Then, just wait and see. Sometimes it is cheaper to attend a more expensive college because they sometimes provide superior aid packages. Of course this is not always the case, but it does prove that you should never decide against a school because of money until you have a financial-aid offer (or rejection) in your hand.

As a financial-aid applicant, you will soon notice all the paperwork involved. Most colleges require you to file a standardized needs-analysis form to determine an expected family contribution (EFC). Depending on the school, the form will either be the College Board's Financial Aid Form (FAF), the Free Application for Federal Student Aid (FAFSA), or occasionally the ACT Program's Family Financial Statement (FFS). The school will also have its own financial form for you to fill out, which you have to send along with the family's income tax forms for verification. The school will determine a reasonable family contribution for one year. (The student is also usually expected to contribute around $1,000 from summer earnings.) To come up with an estimate, a formula established by Congress is used. The formula takes into account family income, expenses, assets, liabilities, savings accounts, and other data. The cost of attendance minus this expected family contribution yields an approximate financial need. The school then designs a financial-aid package that may consist of a low-interest, federally guaranteed loan, a work-study job, and a combination of different types of grants. This would lead one to believe that all packages would be similar, yet this is not at all true. Even though all schools receive the recommended family contribution, they do not all use the same formula. The family contribution will thus vary slightly, but there will not be a big difference. The differences in aid packages comes mainly from the way the school issues money. Some schools may require you to get more loans, or they might give you more money.

Some schools will always make better offers than others. Wealthier schools guarantee to meet the full "demonstrated" need of every applicant they accept. At other colleges, however, the financial-aid package may leave an "unmet" need that you will have to cover on your own. In unfortunate cases like these, students can bear the extra financial burden or choose a college that gives them a better offer.

There are a few things you can do to improve your chances of receiving an adequate financial-aid package from a school. First of all, be efficient in getting all the forms in as early as possible. Some schools have a limited supply of funds available for financial aid, and the earlier they look at your application, the better your chance of receiving a larger share. Getting your forms in early shows a good-faith effort on your part, and schools are more likely to be cooperative with you if they feel you are being cooperative with them. Another thing you can do is write a letter to the financial-aid office explaining any special family circumstances that are not reflected on the financial-aid forms. If you do not let the school know about such situations, there is no way they can take them into account.

If a school offers you a financial-aid package that you consider inadequate despite your best efforts to let them know about your family situation, all is still not lost. After you have been accepted at the school, make a polite call to the school's financial-aid office. If you noted any special circumstances either on the financial-aid form or in a separate letter, ask if they took them into account when determining the award. Sometimes letters or comments get overlooked in the haste to get the aid awards out on time. If they say they took the circumstances into account, or if you did not mention any, tell them that you would really like to attend the school but do not think you can without more aid. If another school has offered you more aid, mention that, especially if the school is a competitor of the one

you're talking to. Calling may not help, but they are not going to withdraw your acceptance once you are in.

If you are eligible for money on the basis of need, then the school may list some federal government assistance. The first of the types of federal government assistance are grants. Grants do not have to be paid back, unlike loans, but they are also harder to obtain. The federal government offers two grants: the Federal Pell Grant and the Federal Supplemental Education Opportunity Grants. You have to demonstrate "exceptional" financial need for either, but the latter is harder to obtain since the government does not guarantee as much. A Pell Grant is as high as $2,340, and the FSEOG is as high as $4,000 annually.

The federal government also offers lower-interest loans. If you demonstrate "exceptional" financial need, you may be eligible for a Perkins Loan, which can be loaned at 5 percent interest up to a maximum of $3,000. There are two types of Stafford Loans, one subsidized and the other unsubsidized. The subsidized Stafford Loan is only for people who demonstrate financial need, and it has a cap of 8.25 percent interest. The government pays for the interest while you are in school and during the grace period after you graduate. The unsubsidized loan is for those who do not demonstrate financial need, and they have to pay interest the whole time. There is also a new loan called the Federal Direct Student Loan, which is just like the Stafford except that the lender is the federal government and not a bank.

There is also a federal government-sponsored loan for parents called the PLUS loan. It is particularly valuable for those who qualify for little or no financial aid. Each year, parents are allowed to borrow the full amount of tuition less any financial aid the student receives. The loan requires good credit, repayment while the child is still in school, and interest rates that are not far from market rates. Still, it can help to ease the burden on middle-class families.

You will also probably be required to take a job through the federal work-study program. Many applicants worry that working part-time will detract from study or, equally important, playtime. Yet, if you work on campus, you certainly will not be the only one: Most colleges report that about half of their students hold term-time jobs. It is possible to take a full load of courses, participate in extracurricular activities, and work 10 or 15 hours per week, all while maintaining a good grade point average. Although freshmen tend to get the least exciting jobs on campus, in later years you may well find yourself working on interesting research, in a lab, or in a library job.

Many private colleges also provide scholarships based on academic, athletic, or artistic ability. As competition among colleges for the best students intensifies, more and more colleges are offering lucrative merit awards to well-qualified students. There are many excellent schools, including many state universities, that offer merit scholarships in ever-increasing numbers. The best source of information is your high-school counselor and state Department of Education.

Be sure not to overlook the millions of dollars of aid available from private sources. Organizations ranging from General Motors to the Knights of Columbus offer money for college, often as prizes to assist students from your community. Sometimes large companies offer scholarships to children of their employees, so have your parents find out if their employers have such programs. There are also several scholarships out there related to specific majors, religions, or even ethnic heritage. Or if you scored very high on the PSAT, you could be in the running for a National Merit Scholarship. There is often a catch to merit-based awards, however: If you qualify for awards from private sources, your school will often deduct some or all of the amount from any need-based aid you receive.

The only other significant federal aid available that is not based on need is ROTC (Reserve Officers Training Corps) scholarships. Thousands of dollars are available annually for students willing to put in several years in a branch of the armed forces. Sometimes they will even repay a portion of the federal government loans. More and more, federal aid is being reserved exclusively for the very needy. Many families with incomes over $35,000 who qualify for PLUS loans must now pass a needs test to get Stafford Loans. Yet, if you play your cards right, your family should not have to undergo severe financial hardship to put you through school.

Advice for Transfers

If you are already in college and are thinking about transferring to another school, the preceding comments are mostly old hat. Theoretically, you know what to do now, but there are a number of new considerations that all potential transfers should keep in mind. The most important is the actual decision to transfer. If you are unhappy, it is easy to blame your school first. However, the cause of your troubles might not be your school in particular, but college itself, so do not assume that you will automatically be happy at another university. One dejected Ivy League student formed a transfer club during his freshman year and recruited friends to join him. Now, he is a happy senior at his original school, thankful that he and his friends ultimately decided not to transfer. Another student left Stanford in search of what she thought were "greener pastures," but found New England "cold, gray, and without pastures at all." According to one transfer student, "It's a big risk. You have to really want to leave where you were or really want to go where you will be."

Most schools accept transfer students who have up to two years of credit at another university. It is safer, however, to transfer after your first year, because your old university will be more likely to take you back if you change your mind. One student advised that it is better to take a leave of absence from your original school than to withdraw completely. This way, if you do not like the new school, you will have an "escape hatch" and little trouble returning. If you received financial aid from your former institution, make sure the schools you are applying to can offer an adequate aid package.

Another new consideration is the application itself. Be aware that colleges tend to consider a transfer student in a different light from a high school senior. Few students tend to leave top private universities, so the acceptance rate for transfers tends to be much lower than that for first-time applicants. The situation can be different for state schools. One student at UC/Berkeley reported that many of her classmates spent two years at Bay Area community colleges, then transferred to Berkeley to complete their degrees and benefit from the prestigious name. Each school looks for different students, but grades, recommendations, and the essay that explains why you want to transfer are usually the three most important parts of the application. Standardized tests and extracurricular activities are not as important. College grades will carry far more weight than your high-school grades. Although you rarely will be able to transfer out of a college at which you are getting low grades, admissions committees understand that many a high-school or freshman-year dilettante suddenly gets serious. It may not be too late. If your grade point average just shot up from 2.0 to 3.7, a tougher school than your current one may well accept you. As much as you might want to leave your school, do not ease up on classes.

Recommendations from college professors will be important. An English professor at Louisiana State University who is writing your recommendation, for example, might personally know an English professor at Tulane. In such a case your recommendation will naturally go much further than one from an unknown high-school teacher.

Because colleges will expect you to prove that you have developed and matured in your first year or two of college and to show why you absolutely cannot stay at your old school, your essay (and interview, if you can arrange one) is critical. Be definite about why you want to transfer and what you expect to find. Academic reasons are best; personal ones (such as a heartfelt need to live in a more rural setting after suddenly developing acrophobia in your skyscraper dormitory) are only as persuasive as you can make them. Never mention a long-distance love unless the two of you are married. It helps if the department in which you want to major is under-subscribed at the new school.

If you do transfer, consider your housing options carefully. College housing is often best because experienced students will be all around to answer your questions. Whether or not your dormmates are friendly is "the luck of the draw, but you can expect them to at least be responsive and civil," said one transfer student. Another successful transfer felt that sharing a room with a fellow transfer student in a regular dorm was ideal because "when you have two people in the same situation, you help each other, and when you have regular students close by, it's easy to make new friends." Once acclimated, transfers tend to be extremely adept at getting involved in campus life at their new schools. One Stanford admissions dean noted that "it's not unusual for transfers to take a lot of leadership positions."

The College Spectrum

Current Trends and How They Affect You

At first glance, the sheer number of colleges included in this book might seem a bit overwhelming—clearly you would never consider applying to 300 schools. Since colleges and their student bodies vary in so many ways, it can be difficult to identify schools at which you would feel comfortable. One way to get some perspective on different colleges is to identify where they stand in terms of various criteria—to figure out where they fall on a continuum we call the College Spectrum. Another is to be aware of the general social, political, and academic trends that schools are experiencing at the turn of the century.

We are not attempting to judge which types of schools are best, but instead to present a variety of perspectives and observations that can help students with the decision-making process. Our hope is that you consider all of these factors and sharpen your sense of the differences among schools, so that you can find the one that is best for you.

Size

The total enrollments of the schools in this book range from about 250 at Vermont's Marlboro College to nearly 50,000 at the University of Texas at Austin. Considering the size of the campus you want to attend is helpful in the initial narrowing-down process; the feel of a school can be very dependent on how small or large its student body is.

Academically, two important areas of comparison between large and small schools are class size and the accessibility of senior faculty. In this case, smaller colleges decidedly have the advantage simply because a smaller population usually translates into smaller classes. Students at small schools have greater opportunities for one-on-one student-faculty inter-

action. At large schools, students are more likely to complain of impersonal instruction and "being treated as a Social Security number."

To make up for this apparent disadvantage, many larger schools offer special programs intended to create the sense of community among professors and students that small colleges enjoy. Different universities have different approaches. Some offer honors programs for a limited number of students; others divide the whole undergraduate student body into separate living units. Some schools house all the students who are in special programs together, occasionally with faculty living in the same residence halls. Generally, students in such programs all take the same or similar courses, most of which are divided into small, discussion-oriented groups. Bear in mind that many honors and special programs are highly selective; do your best to make a realistic assessment of your chances to be included.

Another important factor to remember is that no matter how large a school is, not all of the classes it offers will be huge and overcrowded, and some of the huge classes will break into smaller discussion groups. Thus, although courses are generally larger, you can find small ones of interest. If you are considering a large university, take a close look at the quality of its special programs. Very often, there is a gap between the description of the program in the pages of a glossy admissions brochure and the reality.

Also, pay attention to who teaches the classes. At most liberal arts colleges, only professors do. Many large universities pad their student-faculty ratios by including graduate students, or they advertise discussion classes that turn out to be taught by people who are still working toward a Ph.D. By reading guides such as this one and by talking to students, you can find out roughly how many graduate students teach and whether or not senior professors teach undergraduates; this also gives you a good idea of how much the administration cares about the typical undergraduate student. Many times, courses taught by graduate students allow for a rapport between teachers and students that does not happen with some of the stodgier old professors. However, if graduate students appear to dominate the teaching, even if only for the freshman year, you should definitely consider this as you make your decision.

For highly specialized fields that require extensive facilities, the resources at small schools are generally limited. If you want to major in mineral engineering, for instance, neither the facilities nor the course offerings at most small colleges will suffice. For facilities not associated with technical research, such as the gym or the library, size and showiness are not nearly as important as accessibility. You will not care how many racketball courts the gym has as long as one is available when you want to play. Instead of asking how many volumes there are in the library, find out whether everyone has full access to all its resources. The same goes for labs: A large school may have state-of-the-art equipment, but it will not do you much good if only graduate students and professors get to work with it. While the facilities at smaller schools may be less impressive than those at big universities, they are often more accessible to undergraduates.

You should also carefully examine the scope and breadth of the curriculum offered. A course catalog may be packed with myriad offerings, but remember that in four years you will only be able to take a fraction of those, and that a larger student population means more competition to get into the classes you want to take. Some small colleges supplement and expand their own course selection by offering cross-registration with nearby large schools or a consortium of local colleges. Thus, if you are looking for a small college, but are concerned about the depth of the course offerings, you might want to consider one that has a close relationship with neighboring schools.

Social life, too, is affected by the size of a school. Consider carefully what kind of social life you plan to have and which type of school would be more conducive to your particular interests. The people you

associate with will likely be determined by your extracurricular interests—a sports team, the school newspaper, or student government. This is especially true for universities that do not provide more than one year of campus housing. The key is finding your own comfortable niche within any school. While there are usually more niches in large colleges, finding yours may require some initiative. The larger the school, the more subgroups there are likely to be within the student body. Fraternities and sororities are also more abundant and popular on bigger campuses. (Be careful, however, of large or small schools that tend to put too much pressure on being part of Greek life or on any other kind of affiliation.) An advantage to being a member of a very large community is that the supply of new faces never runs out. If you get tired of one circle of friends, you can always find another. But when you are on your own in the midst of all those people it is also possible to feel very lonely.

Typically, small colleges offer a stronger sense of community than larger ones. You probably will have an easier time fitting in and getting involved with activities. Such intimacy also has its drawbacks. On particularly small campuses, students can develop the feeling that "everybody knows everybody else's business," as one student put it. Another all too common problem at smaller schools are cliques. The social liabilities at a small college often do not become apparent until after you have been enrolled for a year or two. By the middle of your sophomore year you might feel as if you have met everyone. ("I was on a first-name basis with my entire class within a month," said one student at a small college in Ohio. "Sometimes I just want to meet new people.") Social stagnation can set in, and it might be difficult to break stereotypes or images that others have of you. To remedy this, many smaller schools offer popular junior-term exchanges or junior-year abroad programs that allow students to experience a change of environment. If you are considering a small school, particularly an isolated one, find out if it offers such programs.

One common misconception about smaller schools is that they are inevitably more homogeneous and have less school pride or spirit. On the contrary, many of them, especially the more selective ones, have just as many different types of people as do most large universities, only in smaller numbers. Although larger schools, especially those with a big emphasis on athletics, may have tremendous school spirit, smaller ones foster their own brand of pride, usually stemming from rich tradition and a strong sense of community.

Location

Students often have misconceptions about the differences between urban and rural schools because they know only their hometown atmospheres. Many college applicants are oblivious to the opportunities (and challenges) of going out of their own state, or even out of their own region, for college.

Going away to college can be an intimidating experience. However, it can also be invigorating and rewarding. If you are from a rural area and are considering the big move to the city, expect a lot of adjustment (to noise, traffic, people, crime, the hectic pace), but try not to make or accept any assumptions about "the horrors of city life."

The most important reason for rural and small-town people to consider attending a college in or near a city is that it is a good way to find out how the other half lives. Four more years of living in the country may sound appealing, but sooner or later you will probably want to try living in a big city. Although the transition to both college life and city life will make things more difficult at first, you may actually enjoy yourself sooner than you think. Do not let your wish to live in a particular city, however, outweigh other factors when you are looking at schools.

On the same note, applicants from cities tend to believe that they will "need" the cultural resources of a city during their college years. If you fall into that category, do not underestimate the ability of the college and its surrounding community to keep you busy. After academic work, extracurricular activities, dorm parties, visiting speakers, football games,

and the multitude of other school-sponsored events, few students have time to go to the theater or the opera every other night.

The most important thing to remember about rural campuses in general is that they tend to be more self-contained, both physically and socially, than most urban campuses. Many people head off to rural colleges expecting four carefree years studying by the shores of Walden Pond. In fact, these schools are sometimes academic pressure cookers. At a rural school, it is harder to get away, especially on the spur of the moment, when the academic grind gets oppressive. Then again, for some students a naturally beautiful and isolated environment may be the most conducive for a productive and successful academic life.

The biggest drawback of a rural school is the ease with which it is possible to fall out of touch with the "real world." In academic circles, this is called the "ivory tower" effect. It dulls the social consciousness and warps perceptions of how the world works. College, after all, is supposed to prepare you for adult life, which often includes facing the realities of poverty and crime.

Another point to consider is how far from home you want to be. Are you comfortable leaving the Golden Gate Bridge for the Brooklyn Bridge, or does being three hours away from your family make your knees start to quake? Distance is a very personal decision.

Your life will change in college, whether you travel far away or not. As tempting as it seems, it is generally not a good idea to sacrifice your choice of schools just to remain near high-school friends. Staying close to home does not keep your old relationships from changing, although it might make you feel secure to know that you can go home for the weekend if that is what you need or want. Make sure you are honest with yourself about your reasons for choosing a school either far away or nearby. Further, consider how the location will affect your life: Take the weather, the people, homesickness, phone bills, travel expenses, and your personal appetite for adventure into account.

Public or Private?

Choosing between a public or private school is a lot like buying a car. Some people think it is best to buy an inexpensive, fuel-efficient model that simply gets you where you want to go. Others head straight for a luxury-car dealership for a model that is more prestigious, has a better trade-in value a few years down the road, and may have several perks.

As with cars, the most obvious difference between public and private schools is their cost. As tuition at private institutions has skyrocketed in recent years, public universities have become an increasingly attractive option. Although less prestigious and usually less selective for in-state students than their private counterparts, many public universities offer solid departments in a wide range of fields, as well as top-notch honors programs for the most ambitious. Facilities at many state universities frequently equal and sometimes surpass those at the best private ones. While some of the wealthier private schools can offer extensive financial-aid packages, the fact remains that there is a large and ever-widening gap in the relative costs of attending public and private schools.

Academic offerings at both types of schools often do not differ to any great extent. Outside the classroom, however, differences become apparent. Highly selective private colleges have an intellectual atmosphere rarely matched at state universities. At any good college, public or private, much of the valuable learning takes place through interaction with students of backgrounds different from your own. Rarely do state universities approach the type of geographic diversity found at private ones, since by law they must reserve most of their places for state residents.

While some applicants consider attending a state university second-best compared to an elite private school, others make a public institution their first choice. Why might someone pass up the opportunity to attend a big-name school in favor of a state university? Some people find the atmosphere at many of the prestigious private colleges just a bit too self-centered. At a good state university, you might not find the geographic and cultural diversity of a private college, but you might just find a different type of diversity among the students. Some people may prefer the natural diversity of a public school to the carefully selected diversity of an elite private college.

It is important not to let your assumptions or prejudices about either type of school sway your decision. Not all private school students "prepped together" at the same boarding school and have names like Kip or Muffy, and not all state schools are centered on Greek life and football.

Coed or Single-Sex?

Since coeducation became the norm at American universities in the 1960s, the number of single-sex schools in the nation has dropped steadily. There are only four men's colleges remaining in this book: Deep Springs College, Hampden-Sydney College, Morehouse College, and Wabash College. The numerical decline does not at all reflect a decline in the quality of these schools or a desire among their students to admit women. Students at all-male schools state with some consistency that the absence of the opposite sex allows unsurpassed dedication to academics and a friendlier, more fraternal atmosphere. Weekends are far from single-sex: Road-tripping to nearby women's colleges and frat parties with women are still the pillars of social life. Not surprisingly, the few colleges that remain all-male tend to be traditional, conservative places.

Women's colleges are more abundant than men's colleges. Many women feel that women's colleges have more to offer them than coeducational institutions. While opponents of single-sex education might say that "sheltering" women does not prepare them for the "real world," advocates insist that four years at a women's college provides an invaluable opportunity to develop one's identity as a woman in a culture that historically has been defined in very masculine terms. In defending her institution, one professor remarked, "Yes, it's segregation, but so is taking a young plant and keeping it in its own pot with enriched soil, until it grows strong enough to withstand the rigors of the garden." At most women's colleges, women's experience is a clear and constant focus. While all-male schools tend to be conservative, all-female schools tend to espouse liberal views on topics such as abortion, AIDS, sexuality, and environmental protection. Sometimes sparks fly among those with different points of view, but the atmosphere tends to be thought-provoking, especially for those who have not confronted such issues before.

The female environment generally offers more support and leadership opportunities, and many graduates of women's colleges consider their institutions as important forces driving their success. One graduate of a women's college said she now feels "more confident when in a room full of males or in competition with males." Women's colleges are also an escape from sexual discrimination; because there are no men, there is no possibility of higher grades going to those who have not necessarily done better work. For many, these are considerations that make keeping women's colleges alive a valuable cause: In 1990, students at Mills College fought successfully to keep their school from going coed. Several women's colleges are part of coed consortia, such as Mount Holyoke and Smith, whose students can take classes at nearby coed Amherst and Hampshire Colleges and the University of Massachusetts. Others are paired with all-male or coed colleges, as Barnard is with Columbia.

The majority of college-bound seniors will be enrolling in a coeducational school, and for most of these students, entering such a college environment requires little, if any, adjustment. At some larger universities you may have to get used to coed dormitories and/or bathrooms. These setups are not nearly as uncomfortable (or as advantageous) as you might think. Most university dormitories are coed by floor, although some are coed by hallway. At some universities it is even possible for men to live next door to women. On the other side of the spectrum, single-sex dormitories still exist.

Make sure to check the housing information to see if the offerings match your preferences.

Advising

Not everybody is expected to ace college classes from day one, and even fewer people enter college knowing what they want to study for the next four years. Most colleges offer some sort of help for those who are struggling with a class or deciding which classes to take.

There is no way to predict whether you will need tutoring at your future college, but it can be reassuring to know beforehand that your school of choice has a safety net of academic help waiting for you if you stumble. Because many schools require knowledge of a foreign language and a smattering of math and the sciences for graduation, it is likely that these schools will provide tutoring for those who need it, free of charge. If a designated tutor is not available, it is the duty of the professors and teaching assistants (TAs), who are better prepared to answer questions about the homework than a generic dorm monitor, to fill the void. Professors and their TAs, who are usually grad students in the department offering the class, must hold office hours. (Whether the professors or TAs are easy to understand once you speak with them is a different matter.) Study groups with classmates are a useful last resort, but it is usually up to you to organize them. Many colleges provide their students with a writing tutor, which can be a tremendous resource for those willing to admit that their papers, though well-reasoned, could be better written.

Academic advising is often not as accessible as academic tutoring. Although some colleges pair their students with a faculty advisor starting freshman year, faculty advisors often are not a useful source of information on classes outside of their specific department. If you are concerned about the administration leaving you in the cold when it comes time to enroll in your classes, talk with freshmen to see how helpful their advisors are. Most of the students *The Insider's Guide* questioned about academic advising agreed that upperclassmen who had just passed through the stress of choosing a major were the best people to consult. Upperclassmen are also a prime resource for advice on choosing classes outside of your major, because they most often share your viewpoint as a student and have tried a wide variety of classes during their college years.

A Minority Perspective on the College Spectrum

As a minority student or a person of color, there might well be some additional factors to consider in your decision. You may, for example, be searching for a school with a high population of minority students or for a school that is predominantly African-American. A school with a high minority population may prove to be more supportive and even more comfortable. Regardless of size, though, a strong minority community can be helpful during the next four years and can even help reduce the racism and ignorance on some campuses.

Another factor to consider is the general attitude of both the administration and the student body. Unfortunately, racism still exists at many colleges, but do not assume a defensive attitude while visiting schools. Instead, be aware of possible situations and attitudes that may make you feel excluded and uncomfortable. What might have seemed like a diverse college in the brochures may not seem so open-minded after all. Take note of how integrated the minority community is, and what the school does to recognize and support other cultures. Some schools may foster a pressure to conform; if the school has a large population of a certain race, there may be a distinct sense of separatism. For some this may provide a stronger sense of belonging, while for others it will only increase the stress of college life.

To determine the true attitude of the administration, look at how it attempts to support the minority communities. Some schools assign ethnic counselors to help minority students adjust to college life. Some students appreciate this; others resent it. One student reported that her school was doing so much to accommodate her minority status she felt separated, rather than integrated. Many students, however, get used to the idea of special resources and ultimately find them supportive.

Another thing to look at is the extracurricular life. What kinds of organizations are there for specific minority groups, or minority students in general? The school may have cultural centers and politically oriented associations that focus on the traditional arts and dances of their culture. With any luck, the school's primary form of minority student recognition will not be an ethnic theme dinner once a semester.

For African-American students, an important decision may be whether to attend a predominantly black college over another school. Despite the improving financial situations of most private black colleges, you are likely to find better facilities and larger academic departments at predominantly white schools. Unfortunately, the continuing decline of federal funding is likely to exacerbate this situation, since black colleges rely heavily on such resources. Nevertheless, many students choose to attend a predominantly black college for many of the same reasons other students choose to attend a single-sex school. Some black students find them a more congenial and accepting community that is more conducive to personal growth. Likewise, students have a better chance to attain key leadership positions at a college where they do not have minority status. At a predominantly black school, the African-American experience is one of the central issues on campus. What does it mean to be a black person in America at the turn of the century? Of what importance is African-American heritage? At predominantly black schools, these questions are addressed in a manner and with a fervor unrivaled by other institutions.

In this book, we include reports on five of the best-known predominantly black schools in the United States: Howard University in Washington, D.C.; Spelman and Morehouse Colleges in Georgia; Florida

A&M University; and Tuskegee University in Alabama. For a more complete listing, we suggest you consult *The Black Student's Guide to Colleges* by Barry Beckham and published by Beckham House.

Ultimately, you have to decide where you will feel most comfortable. Whatever your choice, it is important to remember that your ethnicity is an integral part of yourself and is not something you should have to compromise in choosing a school.

Sexual Minorities

So far, we have spoken primarily of ethnic minorities. Gay men, lesbians, and bisexuals are also minorities, but unlike ethnic minorities, no college we know of has a recruitment program to attract them. The task of finding a school that will allow you to make your collegiate years the best they can be is largely up to you. One of the most important things to consider when choosing a school is whether you will be comfortable with the people around you, and whether other people (students, professors, administrators, even "townies") will be comfortable with you. Look for a place where your sexuality is respected and where there are others of the same sexuality with whom you can share your experiences. "One of the reasons why I chose [a liberal women's college] was because I knew it would have a very welcoming and accepting environment," said one student. "I think you'll find more lesbians here than at a traditional, conservative, coeducational school because it has a very safe atmosphere. It is not only easier to come out of the closet to your friends, but also to yourself," said one student.

So how can a gay or lesbian applicant assess the atmosphere at a particular college? The best way is to visit the campus, but there are also a number of other ways to evaluate schools. By looking through the official literature that a school mails to its prospective students, you can evaluate the attitudes of the administration. Check to see if there is a gay and lesbian student center. If there is not one, and this is most often the case, look for gay groups on the official list of clubs and organizations. If there are none, this could mean one of

three things: the administration refuses to officially recognize the gay and lesbian population; the homosexual population is "underground," or reluctant to attract publicity, perhaps due to potentially negative reactions on campus; or an openly homosexual population does not exist on campus. It is also helpful to browse the course catalog. Homosexual topics in history, modern culture, and the arts are subjects of legitimate academic inquiry; the absence of such course offerings might reflect the administration's ambivalence toward alternative sexual orientations.

Consider closely the vital statistics of a school. Urban schools tend to be more open-minded than small rural schools (see "Location"). Students at schools with a politically liberal climate tend to be more accepting of differences in lifestyles and backgrounds than do those at conservative schools. Schools with a large Greek scene tend to be more conservative as well (see "Greek Life and Other Social Options"). Greek systems can be oppressive toward homosexuality; many fraternity traditions reject alternative lifestyles. According to one gay student, on campuses where there are lots of fraternities, "it's cool to be macho, and they don't think homosexuality is macho at all."

These are all good indicators, but a campus visit is the best way to find out how other students view the gay community. Look for posters announcing lectures concerning homosexuality, rallies for homosexual causes, or simply meetings of gay, bisexual, or lesbian groups. Read the campus newspapers to see if they cover any prominent gay/lesbian issues. If so, what slant does the writer take on the issue? Are there publications dedicated solely to gay issues? Observe how people dress, and how the rest of the students react to alternative dress styles. If a number of people express themselves in an eccentric manner and onlookers treat them no differently than regularly dressed students, those are good indications that the school accepts individuality and self-expression.

Although the aim of this book is to help you choose a college, not to help you adjust once you get there, here are some suggestions to help homosexuals avoid potentially uncomfortable situations. If there are gay and lesbian student groups, seek them out. "Seeing that there are other people just like you will give you confidence in your sexuality, and for somebody who hasn't met many homosexuals before, they are a gigantic leap socially," one undergraduate suggested. Obviously, some people are more comfortable about their sexuality than others. If you are not yet comfortable, "remember that homosexuality is nothing to be ashamed of," one student said, "and that being homosexual does not have to dominate your life." Realize that coming out to roommates does not need to be as earth-shattering as the beginning of World War III. Bring it up in the proper context (for example, if a roommate is trying to set you up for a blind date) and do not be afraid to discuss the issue further as your roommates might be more uncomfortable than you.

Politics

How politically active a campus is may affect how comfortable you are there. A generation ago, political activism was as common as bell bottoms and tie-dye. Today, however, many students treat it as an extracurricular activity. "There is a hard core of committed activists on the left and right who believe that the struggle is everything, but most people don't seem to have a whole lot of time for that," said one student at Princeton University. In fact, one student remarked that a majority of her fellow students stay away from politics for social reasons: Many people at her college look down on those with strong convictions because they assume them to be close-minded.

Some schools, most often small liberal arts colleges, are highly politicized. "At my school, you don't just put your name on name tags, you put your cause, your oppressor, your god, and your sexual orientation," one student remarked. At less politically active schools, apathetic students might be in the majority. This does not mean, however, that those who espouse strong opinions and wish to discuss them have been silenced. Before you select a school, check to see if it has a politi-

cal forum that sponsors speakers and discussions. Most schools have politically oriented journals, both conservative and liberal, that provide outlets for issue-oriented thinking. Many schools also have party-affiliated organizations like the College Democrats and the College Republicans. Such partisan organizations tend to be most active in the year of a presidential election. Instead of joining political organizations, many students channel their activism into volunteer programs to confront such problems as urban blight or environmental destruction head-on.

If you have gotten the impression that campus activism has been institutionalized and domesticated in recent years, you are not too far off base. The average campus in the last decade was not the hotbed of radical reform that it may have been in the past. Nevertheless, certain incidents and issues garner community-wide attention. On Columbus Day at one school, for example, indignant students covered the sidewalks with brightly colored chalk-marked polemics against racism and genocide. The gay- and lesbian-rights activists at a different school sponsored a kiss-in where same-sex couples clustered around the campus's central promenade and necked.

Gay rights, AIDS awareness, and race-related issues are commonly on the collegiate slate of activist causes. Today, political correctness (PC), manifested by a tolerance for others' ideas and political orientations and an attempt to be inoffensive to any and all groups in speech as well as in print, is something of a secondary issue. Although PC was a hot topic on campus in the early 1990s, the debates on the spelling of the word "woman" and whether your floormate is disabled or "differently abled" seem to have faded. According to one student, "Political correctness is only an issue among the watchdog groups of the right and left."

The PC contingent has won some battles. Many schools now require students to take courses that focus on non-Western cultures, or courses aimed at raising sensitivity to minority issues and concerns. One student reported that the administration at his college goes so far as to hassle non-PC groups; although a gay rights coalition was not reprimanded for announcing events with explicitly sexual posters, a reactionary group on the same campus faced executive investigation for the minor infringement of staying in a classroom too late at night.

As a general rule, the more liberal the campus, the more concerned students are about political issues. If you enjoy informal political debates or thrive on dinner conversations about the Middle East or Proposition 187, you might want to consider a more liberal school, even if you are a Bush Republican.

By visiting a college you can learn just how important politics are to the student body. Read posters and student newspapers to gauge whether the political climate on campus is right for you. The best schools might be those that can absorb all viewpoints, so that no matter what you think, there will be others who will embrace your thoughts, challenge them, or respect your decision not to vocalize them.

Preprofessionalism vs. Liberal Arts

Preprofessionalism is a term you will see again and again throughout this book. All college curriculums are not created equal. Depending on what track or what major you choose, you will be receiving either a preprofessional or a liberal arts education.

Majors that do not lead directly to a specific career fall into the liberal arts category. Even if a student plans to be an accountant, for example, he or she might get a liberal arts degree in philosophy or math, and then go on to study accounting at the appropriate professional school. The goal of a liberal arts education is to teach students how to think creatively and analytically, thus preparing them to pursue any career.

The get-ahead attitude of the 1980s generated strong interest in both preprofessional and liberal arts programs, and these interests have continued into the 1990s. There are pros and cons to each track. Some argue that a liberal arts program is the key to a solid education, while

others believe that a liberal arts degree can be a waste of four years and thousands of dollars for students who already have their career plans mapped out. Many preprofessional programs require that a student take general education courses in liberal arts departments. In fact, almost all colleges insist that you take some courses outside your chosen field.

If you do not yet know your interests well enough to decide up front which option is for you, it may help you to know that the largest colleges and universities have both liberal arts and preprofessional students. The University of Michigan, for example, has a strong undergraduate school of business; many students in Michigan's liberal arts school also plan to go into business eventually but are pursuing a B.A. in a more general field first.

If you know exactly what you want from a school in terms of career preparation, then you probably will feel right at home at a preprofessional institution. However, be aware that getting a liberal arts education and getting a good job are not mutually exclusive. Furthermore, many students report that preprofessional schools tend to have a more competitive atmosphere that is unpleasant to those students who enjoy the intellectual exchange more common in purely liberal arts environments.

The 1980s also saw renewed interest in the various ROTC (Reserve Officers Training Corps) programs. These scholarships from the four branches of the armed forces help pay for tuition, books, and room and board during college. When you graduate, you are committed to four, five, or possibly eight years of reserve or active duty, depending on the program. As the supply of financial aid declines and the cost of a college education increases, many more students are viewing ROTC scholarships as a viable alternative.

Be very thorough when investigating ROTC programs. The system works differently at different schools. You will also want to explore the way that ROTC is received at your school. Some colleges tend to be very anti-military, and you may find yourself part of a controversial program on or off campus. Also keep in mind that your participation in the program does mean that you could be called to service, as a few graduates realized in a hurry during the Gulf War. Yet, the benefits of an ROTC program can be substantial for a student who joins after careful research and consideration.

Greek Life and Other Social Options

Social life at a given college is largely determined by the type of student body it attracts and by its location. At Arizona State, the fraternity scene is particularly dominant. At Loyola University, downtown Chicago clubs rule the party scene. At Harvard, intimate parties in the residences are typical Friday night fare. Your own social taste can be an important factor in choosing the type of school you want to attend.

Many students believe that fraternities and sororities are an American college staple—and the raising of the national drinking age to 21 during the 1980s has assured the Greeks an important role in campus social activity. The reason is, as one student put it, that at most schools "frats don't card." Membership in Greek organizations has increased dramatically in the past several years. Many once-defunct chapters have been revived and many new ones established.

Frats of the last decade generally had a cleaner image than their ancestral counterparts. At most schools, the notorious hazing rituals once associated with pledge initiation have been de-emphasized or abolished altogether. In addition, many Greek organizations have strengthened ties with charitable organizations and have become increasingly active in community service. On some campuses, the fraternities and sororities are the most active social-service organizations. Many new and revived Greek organizations, especially the sororities, are focusing on volunteerism. You may find that being in a sorority means more than socializing; it might also involve working on Saturdays in a soup kitchen with a group of socially conscious women.

Yet despite their best efforts, the Greeks still come under fire. Some of the old problems remain. In recent years, several pledges have been killed or seriously injured in connection with Greek-sponsored events. Hazing accidents and alcohol-related mishaps have carried the *Animal House* image into the present, and at schools where frats are one of the few places students can party, the image is likely to stick.

Whether Greek life appeals to you or not, make sure you understand how important the Greeks are at the school you choose. Going against the grain could make your social life different from most. Then again, that might be fine with you. You will also find that at many schools, it is perfectly normal to rush and also perfectly normal not to rush. While the Greeks are a presence on most campuses, at only a few do students report genuine social pressure to be part of the group.

While some other force besides Greek life may rule the scene at a given school, the odds are that alcohol has something to do with it. The sixties are long gone, and at most schools the use of hard drugs is no longer common. Among college students, alcohol is the current drug of choice.

Alcohol policies differ greatly from school to school. At some, there is a tacit understanding that students may drink in their rooms as long as they are not conspicuous about it. Other colleges are cracking down on underage drinking, eager to put an end to "party school" reputations. Many students escape the restrictions by moving off campus, which at some colleges leads to a fragmented social scene. Alcohol on campus continues to be an issue of debate among college administrations, and it is possible that the struggle will move to the federal level; in coming years, colleges might have to prove they actively oppose illegal drinking before they can receive federal money.

Visiting a school is the best way to be sure you will be comfortable with the social scene. Some would argue that the largest schools have a great number of cliques. However, it is also true that the largest schools have the most diverse social groups, due to the sheer numbers of personalities on campus.

Most college applicants worry about meeting people they will like, then find when they get to college that making friends was easier than they expected. Your interests will largely determine whom you meet. Therefore, you should be sure you find a school that has groups to represent your interests. Do you like journalism? Make sure that your school has an active newspaper. Pay attention to the social options you see. Fraternities, sororities, athletic groups, cultural groups, musical groups, and other activities can all be a part of your social experiences at college. Find what you think may be the right combination, and you will meet the right people.

Security

Security as an issue on college campuses is not simply a response to a few well-publicized campus murders. Although the tragedies at other colleges are by no means insignificant, crime in general is increasing on campuses across the country. In response to this trend, recent federal legislation has made it mandatory for all colleges receiving federal aid (which is almost every one) to publish crime statistics in several categories. At your request, the appropriate office (usually the public relations or admissions offices) at any college or university should release to you the crime count for the last calendar year.

Many colleges have also taken measures to beef up security. If you visit a campus and notice very stringent security measures (at the University of Pennsylvania, for example, you have to show your ID just to get into the quadrangle), remember that this means two things: there is a need for security measures, and the administration is responding to this need.

There are a number of features that any safety-conscious campus should have. Doors to individual dorm rooms and to the building entrances should be equipped with locks. All walkways should have bright lights, not only so that you can see, but so friends and classmates would be able to see you from a distance in case of danger. Another important security measure is a safety phone system with one-touch access to an emergency line. Each safety phone should have a distinct light to make it easily recognizable at night.

Ideally, there should be enough units so that you are never more than a half block from a phone. For getting around campus late at night, colleges should provide bus service or student safety escorts, free of charge. At least one of these services should be available 24 hours a day and should travel to every possible destination on campus. Every school should employ some type of security guard, whether unarmed monitors in or near the dorms or full-time police officers responsive solely to students and the affairs of the college.

Security problems are not limited to urban campuses. Some rural schools have crime rates as high as the urban ones. The sad truth is that many crimes are committed by other students, not outsiders. Why is campus crime such an issue now? College students are ideal targets—they keep expensive stereo and computer equipment in badly guarded areas, and they often walk alone across dark, seemingly safe campuses.

Therefore, it is important to understand that you cannot judge the safety of a campus simply by eyeing it from the safe confines of the viewbook's glossy photographs. Yet, by using a little common sense and preventive measures, the security problems of a given school should not prevent you from attending that school. By making yourself aware of potential problems and following the school's security guidelines, you can improve your chances of enjoying a safe four years. Security may be a fundamental problem with college life, but you can certainly do something about it.

Computers

Like it or not, computers are taking over. You cannot turn on the TV anymore without hearing a news report about "cyber" something-or-other or the "information superhighway"—of course, that is if you are old-fashioned enough to get your news from a boring old television set instead of downloading it off the Internet. Whether you are a literature major, art major, or major procrastinator, you are going to be using a computer of some sort, either your own or the university's. With that in mind, here is a list of things to look for when evaluating a college's computing facilities.

- *Twenty-four-hour computer rooms.* At some point you are going to have to type a paper at 3 A.M. and your machine will be broken. Make sure there is at least one room on campus that is available 24 hours a day. Ideally, the computers are recent models; a room with five Mac Pluses does not cut it these days.

- *Internet access from your dorm room.* Most colleges provide e-mail accounts and access to the huge international network called the Internet. The lame way to do this is to give you modem access, which usually means a slower connection and busy phone lines every time you check your e-mail. The cool way is to wire all the dorm buildings so that you have direct access, often through Ethernet, without using a phone line at all.

- *Public printing.* If the school offers free laser printing, you are in luck. If you have to pay for it, you are also lucky, but not nearly as much.

- *Support staff.* Are there students (or paid staff) available to rescue your term paper when it mysteriously vanishes from your floppy disk the day before it is due? Are there enough of them to deal with the entire campus? One computing assistant for every 75 people is a pretty good ratio.

- *Macs and PCs.* Unless the college requires you to use a specific type of machine, make sure it provides adequate support for both types. If the college requires you to buy a Mac (or a PC), that is actually a pretty good thing, because it means that the cost of purchasing a computer is factored into financial aid.

- *The administration's position on computing.* Does the college want to stay cutting-edge, or does it want to squeeze the last breath of life out of every obsolete machine it owns? Is the computer situation big on the administration's list of priorities? Does the administration favor free speech or censorship over

the network? Does the president of the college have an e-mail account?

- *Access to professors.* Look for professors who are accessible over the network. Many of them will answer questions via e-mail. More and more professors now allow students to turn in assignments over the network, which can save you a trek across campus on a cold winter day.

Few colleges will score high in every category, but as long as the school you are looking at is adequate in all areas, it will suitable for your needs.

A Final Note About Quality of Life

A final but crucial criterion for your decision is the overall quality of life you can expect to have at college. A school might have the best archaeology program in the nation, but if you are not happy at the school, there is no point in going.

While it is true that academics are the most important reason to go to college, they are not the only reason. Do not lose sight of the fact that we are talking about four or more years of your life. You should set your priorities not just in terms of academics, but also in terms of social life, extracurricular activities, housing, and even the weather. Do not go to the University of Miami if you cannot stand the sun! Will your freshman room be smaller than your closet at home? Will you have to share it with three other people? Is the food identifiable? Are you comfortable with the people you see walking down the street? Does the administration listen to the students? Is there a movie theater nearby? All of these factors make a difference in the way you will feel about a school. The best way to analyze them is to visit the school and to get your hands on a student newspaper. Do you like what you see?

You may also want to check that what you like about a school will still be there when you enroll. In recessionary times, more and more schools, both public and private, face a shortage of funds and are finding themselves forced to make budget cuts. This can take many forms: reducing the number of tenured professors, cutting entire departments or programs within departments, delaying campus renovations and additions, cutting sports teams and extracurricular activities, or a combination of the above. If you were your school's star varsity soccer player and want to continue playing soccer in college, check that the team is not rumored to be the next victim of the budget ax. If you are set on majoring in linguistics, find out how big that department is; frequently the smaller and less popular departments are the first to go. Talk to students and faculty to see how potential cuts could affect your interests. As recent newspaper and magazine headlines will tell you, even the best-known and supposedly best-endowed schools are tightening their purse strings.

We hope we have been able to give you a stronger idea about some of the decisions you will be making as you continue this process. Just remember that only you can make the final decision. —*Diana Sherman*

Introduction for International Students

International students, including Americans living abroad as well as citizens of foreign countries, might face special problems in submitting applications that conform to the standards and conventions American colleges expect from their applicants. Some of these deserve special consideration. They include the "strange" American insistence on external tests such as the SAT or the ACT, getting recommendations from teachers rarely confronted with American recommendation forms, the problem of writing the kind of essay that will best combine your cultural background with the style expected by American admissions officers, and assembling a list of extracurricular activities even if your school does all it can to de-emphasize them.

Unlike schools in many other countries, virtually all American colleges insist that applicants take standardized tests such as the Scholastic Assessment Test and the SAT IIs. These tests may be hard to come by, depending on the country, but the more selective schools tend not to accept otherwise qualified applicants without standardized test scores. In most countries, American consulates or high schools offer the SAT and ACT tests, as do many international schools. In Europe, several of the American cultural centers offer additional testing sites in metropolitan areas. The best way of finding out where the nearest testing center is located is to write to the Educational Testing Service (Rosedale Road, Princeton, New Jersey 08541) well in advance. A low score on the SATs can be compensated by many other factors in an application.

A word to the wise about the TOEFL (Test of English as a Foreign Language). Many colleges say that if English is your first language or language of instruction you do not have to take this test. If your verbal SAT scores are exceptionally high and you are confident about your language skills, you should not bother to take it. However, if you are in doubt about whether your SAT verbal scores are high enough, or you think you can do exceptionally well on the TOEFL, take it. Even if you are an American citizen or have grown up speaking English all your life, a near perfect TOEFL score can never hurt. Since many colleges substitute it for the verbal part of the SAT, a low verbal SAT score can be compensated to an extent by a high TOEFL result. Those who speak English only as a second language, of course, ought to take the TOEFL, since it is considerably easier than memorizing the rarely used vocabulary required in the verbal SAT.

At many schools, international students are eligible for acceleration credits. These credits, assigned by the individual colleges, permit students who hold foreign secondary-school degrees considered superior to the American high school degree to accelerate and graduate in less than four years' time—sometimes even one or two full years earlier, depending on the college. At most colleges, international students must apply for acceleration credits during their first year, so you must take action yourself if you want the opportunity to graduate early. Some of the more selective schools can be picky about awarding these credits; applicants should make sure to ask what their prospective colleges' guidelines are. Similarly, a college's language requirement for undergraduates can usually be met with a foreign high school diploma, but some schools require students to take placement exams when they enroll. Taking the College Board Advanced Placement (AP) exams before college is an effective way to avoid the hassle. A good score on any of these exams can translate directly into college credit.

Foreign students should be aware of two basic facts about the AP exams. First, they tend to be difficult to arrange. Although many people outside the United States take the SAT or the ACT, international students usually have to look harder for AP testing and must often arrange it themselves. If there is an American high school in your country, approach the guidance counselors directly and ask to be allowed to take the APs with their students. (In this, as in most other instances involving college applications, good relations with an American civilian or military high school are useful, especially since guidance counselors frequently are accessible and are excellent sources for all kinds of information about the application process.) Second, if you are in the early years of secondary school and know that you may want to apply to colleges in the United States, it makes sense to take AP exams as you complete certain courses of study. Doing well on a biology AP exam is next to impossible if you have not studied that subject for several years, even though your general level of knowledge may be superior to that acquired by students in the American high school system. Taking the tests not only helps to prove to college admissions officers that you have real proficiency in a subject, it can also entitle you to immediate "advanced placement" in college courses—a serious advantage for many international students. Unlike the SATs, for which all the scores you have received are reported when you request an official transcript to be sent to a college admissions office, individual AP scores are not reported directly to the colleges. So, if you do poorly on one of the tests, you can simply forget about it or retake the test without making a bad impression on the admissions board.

The most important issue, however, is the application itself. In getting teachers to write recommendations for you, be sure to approach those who not only know you, but are also apt to write enthusiastically about you. Many teachers, especially those in English-oriented school systems, tend to be more reluctant to award superlatives than their American counterparts. An otherwise perfectly qualified candidate's application could be marred by an amusingly cynical teacher's wry comment, "An excellent student, but I hardly know him outside the classroom. Appears to have a somewhat sound character." Obviously, recommendations should not go overboard, but if the recommendation form includes boxes for the teacher to check, his or her opinions of your academic and personal achievement ought to be in the highest category. In the essay sections, again, personality counts: The more personal insight the teacher can provide the better, and a rounded description can be more convincing than a one-sided laudation.

The lack of a "guidance counselor" at your school in no way means that your headmaster has to fill out the counselor recommendation form. Instead, have a teacher whom you know well, perhaps outside the classroom, fill it out. Especially in large schools, getting an administrative official who has never seen or heard from you to comment on aspects of your personal character is a formal statement without much meaning, and can have disastrous effects on your application.

A few words on translations: Even though many colleges will accept teacher recommendations in foreign languages and have them translated at their facilities, it is often a good idea to have them translated in your own country. A translation obviously makes the recommendation easier for the admissions officers to read. Also, since schools rarely require official translations, they offer the possibility of working with your teachers to do your own translations, especially if your own proficiency in English exceeds theirs. Generally, the more the recommendation is a communal effort, the better it will be.

The same applies to the parts of the application you have to fill out yourself. Most of the important general hints have been discussed in the preceding sections of this book, but international students unprepared for American college application essays can often be baffled by the empty page that says, in effect, "Write whatever you want, but remember that anything you say can be held against you." Some schools prepare special application forms for international students that require only a curriculum vitae (similar to a resume) and a book discussion instead of the "creative" essays the American applicants must complete. Do not feel you need to comply with this format; if you feel comfortable writing about yourself creatively, do not hesitate to submit the regular "American" application form. Do remember that many of the other international applicants to colleges will be as qualified as you are, so your essay and the personal impression you make are crucial, especially at the more selective colleges. It is important not only to write about concrete achievements, but also to be creative and to present an idea of what kind of person you are, even if this seems insubstantial compared to the more stringent essays required for university administration in other countries. Your cultural or family background can often be of more interest to admissions officers than the fact that you won a national academic award.

Many foreign schools do not place a great deal of emphasis on extracurricular activities, but as can be judged from the space they are allotted in the application forms you receive, they are of utmost importance to American schools. Contrary to many other university systems, American colleges frequently prefer a "well-rounded" applicant to someone who has received the highest marks in all his classes but has done little else. This means that you have to look actively for extracurriculars to include in your resume in order to make yourself competitive with other applicants. Activities you choose are obviously dependent on your own interests, but it is important to find your slot, even if this means founding your own newspaper or working for charitable organizations. Even though extracurriculars may be frowned upon in your educational system, they count in the U.S. An insincere pursuit of various activities is pointless, but demonstrated commitment to one or two activities that reflect aspects of your character are vital to a strong application. College admissions officers, of course, are aware of the differences among individual countries and have different expectations of American high school students than of international applicants. All this means, however, is that extracurricular involvement in a school system that de-emphasizes such activities shows all the more personality and strength of character.

It is important to note that many American colleges group all students applying from abroad into one category, with a limited number of admissions officers evaluating the applications. Frequently, all applicants from abroad—full American citizens, students with one American parent, and foreign nationals—are grouped according to the country they applied from. Some schools, especially the more selective ones, are rumored to have quotas on the number of international students they admit, in order to achieve a particular geographical and cultural mix. This can mean two things: If you are one of several dozen applicants from a Western European country, the competition for the few spaces available may be extremely stiff. On the other hand, if you are from a country that has few other applicants, you might stand a better chance of being admitted.

A consequence of this selection process poses a difficult question to American citizens who apply from abroad. You should consider whether or not you want to submit yourself to the "international student quota"—which may prefer "real" international students to Americans who went to high school in foreign countries—and take the chance of being one of only two or three students admitted from that country. In some countries, the actual percentage of acceptance to some of the more selective schools is lower than the American average acceptance rate. Depending on the individual case, it may be advisable to apply as a regular American student with an international background rather than compete with native residents for a limited number of acceptance slots.

Financial aid to international students can range from limited to nonexistent. Many colleges will send international applicants brochures that include all kinds of information on financial aid for Americans; only upon direct inquiry do they respond that they simply do not give financial aid to international students. This situation, unfair as it seems, is not likely to change in the near future. Some of the very large and wealthy colleges can afford to be virtually need-blind in their international admissions, but make sure you know the policy at every college you intend to apply to. There is no point in going through the entire application process only to find out that once admitted, you won't receive the aid you need to attend the school.

Federal regulations for visas vary from country to country. Generally, once you are accepted to an American university, you can obtain a student visa without much difficulty. However, do not expect to be able to work in the United States outside the university. Financial-aid recipients can usually work within their colleges, but finding an outside job is next to impossible unless you have a green card (a government document proving that you're a permanent U.S. resident) or outright American citizenship.

Despite these complications, do not despair. As an applicant from a foreign country, you have a distinct advantage over many American applicants. Getting into an American college might appear difficult, but at most of them, your cultural and educational background make you an attractive addition to their student roster. —*Amy Kappelman*

Disabled Student Services

This section is included in *The Insider's Guide* to give students with physical and learning disabilities an idea of additional considerations they might have in applying to or choosing a college.

Learning disabilities are defined as a collection of biological conditions that impede a person's ability to process and disseminate information. They are more common than any other disability. It has been estimated that as many as 5 percent of American schoolchildren are so affected. Leonardo da Vinci, Sir Winston Churchill, and President Woodrow Wilson were all learning-disabled. Physical disabilities are most often categorized as impairments of speech, vision, hearing, or mobility, but often include "hidden" disabilities like heart conditions or diabetes.

Students with disabilities are a rapidly growing element of the expanding collegiate student base. Many attend special schools that cater specifically to the disabled, but others are taking advantage of recent federal and state legislation demanding that non-specialty schools become accessible to the disabled. The accompanying rise in the disabled student body has prompted many institutions to accommodate students voluntarily (instead of after a legal battle), making many of the schools in this book within reach of the disabled student. Kay Runyan-Brown, the former coordinator of learning-disabled services for the Disabled Students' Program at the University of California/Berkeley, strongly encourages applicants to visit prospective campuses during the application process. "Visiting can allow for personal interviews, which deal with services available, the pace of campus life, and the expectations the LD Office has of prospective candidates," she said.

Advances in technology have given rise to many helpful services for disabled students. Many word-processing programs and pocket computers are equipped with spelling and grammar checkers. Students with reading disabilities should make sure voice synthesizers are available at their school of choice, while those with dexter-

ity impairments should be on the lookout for computers with the voice recognition feature. Those for whom a traditional collegiate program of lectures, reading assignments, and timed essay tests is a problem should ask about visual learning equipment. Multimedia encyclopedias on CD-ROM, which provide photos, movie clips, animation, and sound effects, are excellent learning tools that exploit the potential of visual learning. Because such technology is often brand new or even experimental, try to consider schools that are on the cutting edge of the information age.

Runyan-Brown suggests that students with learning disabilities identify themselves early on in the admissions process. Self-identification remains a personal choice, yet it is often crucial in order for your application to be placed in the proper context with the rest of the applicant pool or for you to be placed on a housing preference list.

Runyan-Brown also recommends that parents help guide LD candidates in finding out which colleges have strong support services, and then help the students examine their own needs to see what kinds of services they could not do without. "A lot of learning-disabled students do not go about the application process in an organized fashion; they simply don't know how to do it. And I think that is where the parents come in, in helping them organize themselves," she said. In the application process, a good way to encourage proper understanding of special needs is to have someone who knows you and your efforts to overcome disability write a letter of support that can be included in your college applications. A school principal or guidance counselor is a good choice. Have the letter describe your specific situation and encourage the admissions and student-affairs committees to take it into account.

Be on the lookout for universities that have a disabled student services office with counselors who can steer you clear of tough obstacles and unnecessary frustrations. Federal law requires that schools provide assistance for LD students, such as alternative testing. Unfortunately, professors may not assume responsibility for making suitable arrangements. A good counselor can notify professors with learning-disabled students and help the professor make accommodations.

Not all colleges operate a disabled-student services office. Many schools provide accommodations informally, as needed, through the Dean of Student Affairs. In these cases, Runyan-Brown recommends that the LD student learn the federal statutes applying to disabled-students' rights (Public Law PL 94-142 and Section 504 of the Rehabilitation Act of 1973 [Public Law PL 93-112]). "When you are at a school that doesn't have a formal program, being able to verbalize and understand your learning disability so that you can help someone else understand it is the way to be your own best advocate," she said. You might prefer a school without a formal program. According to Bill Scales, Director of Disabled Student Services at the University of Maryland, an "overly comfortable environment is an unrealistic preparation for real life."

Physically disabled students also have special needs. In July 1992, the Americans with Disabilities Act went into effect, ensuring that campuses be legally responsible for providing reasonable accommodation and access for disabled students. Subpart C of Section 504 of PL 93-112, on the books since 1973, mandates that campus facilities be made readily accessible for disabled students' use. A prevailing interpretation of this legislation, however, is that a school need not create a totally barrier-free environment, just one that does not significantly hinder the participation of students with disabilities. The case of Chris Powell, a University of Maryland undergraduate with limited motor control due to cerebral palsy, as reported by the *Washington Post*, reveals that hindrances still exist. The university is 95 percent accessible, but for Chris, getting up the ramp to his classroom building was always a struggle, the electric handicap doorway did not always function, he was not always able to push the small buttons for the elevators, the chairs in the classrooms were not designed for disabled students, and he had to rely on others' class notes because taped lecture notes were not available.

Bill Blanchard, at UC/Berkeley's Disabled Students Program, stresses the importance of the campus visit for physically disabled applicants. In addition to the regular campus tour, they should acquire a map and case the entire layout. Blanchard advises paying particular attention to the accessibility of key structures, such as libraries and the department building of the student's intended major. It is illegal for a college to be inaccessible, but some are more accessible than others. It is also important to contact the campus disabled student services office and to meet and chat with enrolled students who have similar disabilities.

Lastly, it is important to remember that students with either physical or learning disabilities should be free to approach the college selection process in the same way as other students. He or she should understand throughout the admissions process that college opportunities do exist and that acceptance to (and rewarding attendance at) competitive schools is a realistic possibility for the motivated disabled student. —*Marc Schwarz*

Terms You Should Know

Advanced Placement (AP)—College credit earned by students while still in high school. Many high schools offer specially designed AP courses that prepare students for the College Board's AP Exams. Administered in May, they can qualify students who score well for advanced standing when they enroll in college.

American College Test (ACT)—Test administered to high school juniors and seniors by the American College Testing Program. Traditionally it has been used as an admissions criterion primarily by Midwestern schools. Some Southern and Western schools use it as well.

American College Testing Program (ACTP)—The organization that produces the American College Test (ACT) and the Family Financial Statement (FFS). Many Midwestern universities use the ACT and the FFS in admissions instead of the SAT and the Financial-Aid Form (FAF). (See also "Family Financial Statement" and "Financial-Aid Form.")

arts and sciences (also called liberal arts)—A broad term that encompasses most traditional courses of study, including the humanities, social sciences, natural sciences, mathematics, and foreign languages. A liberal arts college is also a college of arts and sciences. (See also "humanities" and "social sciences.")

bagging—You're in bed. It's 9:30 A.M. You've got a class at 9:30. You are about to "bag" this class.

beer goggles—People start to look interesting when you've had too much to drink. If you hook up as a result of this phenomenon, you've been looking through "beer goggles."

candidate's reply date—The May 1 deadline, observed by most selective colleges, by which the applicant must respond to an offer of admission, usually with a nonrefundable deposit of several

hundred dollars. Colleges that require students to respond by May 1 in almost all cases notify them of their acceptance on or before April 15.

College Board—The organization that sponsors the SAT, the SAT IIs, the Advanced Placement tests, and the Financial-Aid Form (FAF). College Board admissions tests are developed and administered by the Educational Testing Service (ETS). (See also "Advanced Placement" and "Financial-Aid Form.")

Common Application—A form produced by a consortium of about 100 colleges (mainly selective liberal arts schools) that may be filled out and sent to member colleges in lieu of each school's individual application.

comprehensive exams (comps)—Tests, administered by some colleges (usually during the senior year), designed to measure knowledge gained over a student's entire college career. Schools that give comps usually require students to pass the test in their major field in order to graduate.

computing assistant (CA)—A university employee, often an undergraduate, who helps students with all varieties of computing problems, from how to use a word processor to how to download games from the network.

consortium—A group of colleges affiliated in some way. The extent of the association can vary widely. Some consortiums—usually among colleges in close proximity—offer a range of joint programs that may include cross-registration, interlibrary loans, residential exchanges, and coordinated social, cultural, and athletic events.

co-op job—A paid internship, arranged for a student by his or her college, that provides on-the-job training, usually in an occupation closely related to the student's major.

core curriculum—A group of courses all students in a college must take in order to graduate. Core curricula are becoming widespread.

couch duty—There are two people in your bedroom that you share with your roommate, and you are not one of them. Guess where you get to sleep? Also known as "sexile."

cramming—The process by which students attempt to learn a semester's worth of course material in a short period, often 24 to 48 hours. Cola, coffee, and/or caffeine pills are the staples of most all-night cramming sessions.

crew (rowing)—A sport, more familiar to those who live on or near either coast than to those from the South and Midwest, in which teams of two, four, or eight oarsmen or oarswomen race in long, narrow boats, usually on inland waterways. Crew is very "Ivy," very popular at many schools, and usually requires no high school experience.

deferral—A college's postponement of the decision to accept or reject an early-action applicant. The applicant's file is entered in with those of regular-action candidates and is reviewed once again, this time for a final decision.

distribution requirements—Requirements stipulating that students take courses in a variety of broad subject areas in order to graduate. The number and definition of subject areas and the number of courses required in each varies from school to school. Typical categories include the humanities, social sciences, fine arts, natural sciences, foreign languages, and mathematics. Unlike a core curriculum, distribution requirements do not usually mandate specific courses that students must take. (See also "humanities," "social sciences," and "core curriculum.")

dry—as in "dry campus." A school that does not allow alcohol for any students in its dorms or other campus facilities.

early action—A program that gives students early notification of a college's admissions decision. Like early decision, a student can apply early action only to one school, but unlike early decision, it does not require a prior commitment to enroll if accepted. Early action—far less common than early decision—is primarily associated with the Ivy League school that offers it: Brown. Deadlines for early-action applications are usually in late fall, with notification in December, January, or February. An applicant accepted under early action usually has until May 1, the candidate's reply date, to respond to the offer of admission. (See also "early decision" and "candidate's reply date.")

early decision—A program under which a student receives early notification of a college's admissions decision if the student agrees in advance to enroll if accepted. Students may apply early decision to only one college; it should be a clear first choice. Application deadlines for early decision are usually in November, with decision letters mailed by mid-December.

Ethernet—A direct, high-speed means of access to the World Wide Web and the Internet, as well as a way to keep in touch with friends via e-mail. Most campuses are either "wired" with Ethernet, or will be in the near future.

family contribution—The amount of money that a family can "reasonably" be expected to pay toward a student's education, as determined by one of the two standardized needs-analysis forms. (See also "Financial-Aid Form" and "Family Financial Statement.")

Family Financial Statement (FFS)—The financial-needs analysis form submitted to the American College Testing Program (ACTP), which, like the FAF, determines the expected family contribution. Colleges that use the American College Test (ACT) for admissions purposes usually require a copy of the FFS report from students applying for financial aid. (See also "American College Testing

Program," "family contribution," and "Financial-Aid Form.")

fee waiver—Permission, often granted upon request, for needy students to apply for college admission without having to pay the application fee.

Financial-Aid Form (FAF)—The financial-needs analysis form submitted to the College Board by students applying for financial aid. Like the Family Financial Statement (FFS), it yields the expected family contribution. Colleges that require the Scholastic Assessment Test (SAT) for admission typically use the FAF as the basis for financial-aid awards. (See also "Family Financial Statement," "family contribution," and "College Board.")

financial-aid package—The combination of loans, grants, and a work-study job that a school puts together for a student receiving financial aid.

five-year plan—The practice of stretching a four-year degree program over a five-year period.

four-one-four—An academic calendar consisting of two regular four-month semesters with a short "winter" or "January" term in between. Variations include four-four-one and three-three-two. In most cases, these numbers refer to the number of courses a student is expected to complete in each segment of the year, although at some schools they refer to the number of months in each segment.

freshman 15—A reference to the number of pounds students often gain during the freshman year. Usually caused by a combination of too little exercise, unlimited helpings in the dining hall, too many late-night runs for pizza, and overconsumption of alcoholic beverages.

government aid—Money that federal or state governments make available to students, most of which is administered through the colleges on the basis of need. Government aid can come in the form of grants, loans, and work-study jobs. Stafford Loans (formerly Guaranteed Student Loans) and PLUS parent loans of up to $2,625 and $4,000 per year, respectively, are made available through commercial lending institutions. For further information on government aid programs, contact the state and federal Departments of Education.

grade inflation—A situation in which average work is consistently awarded a higher letter grade than it would normally earn. At most schools, the grade for average work is about a B-/C+. But in classes or entire colleges with grade inflation, it can be as high as a B or even B+.

Greek system—The fraternities and sororities on a particular campus. They are called "Greek" because most take their names from combinations of letters in the Greek alphabet.

gut—A course widely known to be very easy, often with enrollments well into the hundreds. Guts are traditionally favorites among second-semester seniors.

hook up—To enjoy a person's nonplatonic company, often used in reference to a one-night deal. A very vague term that can range from an innocent kiss to sex, depending on usage.

humanities—Subjects in which the primary focus is on human culture. Examples include philosophy, language, and literature. (See also "social sciences.")

independent study—A course, usually in a student's major field, in which he or she studies independently and meets one-on-one with a professor on a topic of the student's choosing. Some colleges require an independent study essay or research paper for graduation.

interdisciplinary major—A major that combines two complementary subjects from different fields, such as biology and psychology. Students completing these majors take courses in each area as well as courses that explicitly join the two.

International Baccalaureate (IB)—A high school program found across the world which, like AP courses, can earn a student advanced standing upon college enrollment.

intramurals—Athletic leagues informally organized within a college. Students are free from the burden of tryouts and play with and against fellow classmates.

language requirement—A rule at many colleges that requires students to study a foreign language before graduation. Two years on the college level are usually required, although credit from Advanced Placement or SAT IIs often allows students to bypass the requirement.

legacy—An applicant whose mother or father is a graduate of a particular school. Students with legacy status are often given preferential treatment in admissions.

merit scholarship—A financial grant for some part of college costs, usually awarded for academic achievement or special skill in an extracurricular activity and not based on need. Private corporations and many colleges offer merit scholarships.

need-based aid—Money awarded solely on the basis of need, usually administered through the colleges. Some schools agree to pay the difference between their total fees and the expected family contribution; others pay only part of it, leaving some "unmet" need. Most financial-aid packages consist of some combination of three components: grants, loans, and work-study jobs. Some of the money comes from the college's own resources, although part is financed by federal and state governments. (See also "government aid.")

need-blind admissions—A policy in which the applicant's ability to pay does not affect the college's consideration of his or her application. Some schools with need-blind admissions also guarantee to meet the full demonstrated financial need of all accepted applicants as determined by one of the two standardized needs-analysis forms; others do not. (See

also "family contribution," "Financial-Aid Form," and "Family Financial Statement.")

office hours—A period during which a professor agrees to be available in his or her office for the purpose of talking with students about their coursework. Professors are not always required by their colleges to have office hours, but most do anyway.

open admissions—A policy under which any applicant with a high school diploma is accepted. State universities that have this policy usually limit open admission to state residents.

parietals—Regulations that govern the times when students of one sex may visit dorms or floors housing the opposite sex. Usually found only at the most conservative schools nowadays.

pass/fail or CR/F or CR/D/F—An option offered by some schools in some classes. A student may enroll in a class and simply receive credit or failure (or a D in "CR/D/F") for it on his or her transcript instead of a specific grade: God's gift to college students everywhere.

PLUS parent loans—A component of the Stafford Loan, for parents. (See also "government aid.")

problem set—An annoying weekly assignment you're inevitably faced with in any given science or quantitative class. This thankless task will keep you up till 2 A.M. Sunday nights but can count for anywhere from 1/50th of your grade to 1/2. Previously known as homework.

quad—An abbreviation for "quadrangle"; many dorm complexes are built in squares (quadrangles) with a courtyard in the middle. Quad can also refer to a suite of dormitory rooms in which four students live together.

quarter system—An academic calendar under which the school year is divided into four quarters, three of which constitute a full academic year. Less common than the semester system, it is most often used by large universities with extensive programs in agricultural and technical fields.

resident advisor/assistant (RA)—A student, usually an upperclassman, who lives in a dorm and helps to maintain regulations and enforce school policy, as well as offer advice and support to dorm residents. RAs receive compensation from the school for their services, usually in the form of free room and board.

rolling admissions—A policy under which a college considers applications almost immediately after receiving them. Decision letters are mailed within a month after the application is filed. Colleges with rolling admissions continue to accept applications only until the class is filled, so it is best to apply early.

Scholastic Assessment Test (SAT)—Test administered to high school juniors and seniors by the College Board of the Educational Testing Service, with math, verbal, and written language sections. Used as an admissions criterion at most colleges nationwide.

senior project—Many majors at many colleges require seniors to complete a special project during their senior year. Depending upon your major and institution, this could involve a thesis (anywhere from 15 to 100 pages), a research project, some sort of internship, or all of the above. Some colleges offer seniors a choice between taking comps or doing a project.

social sciences—Subjects that deal systematically with the institutions of human society, most notably economics and political science. The behavioral sciences, which include psychology, sociology, and anthropology, are often included in this group as well.

study break—An institutionalized form of procrastination involving food and talk. Often informally arranged—"I'm sick of calculus, let's take a study break at (insert name of local hangout)"—but can be sponsored by RAs, cultural groups, or even school administrators. Some nights, study breaks can take more of your time than the actual studying.

teaching assistant (TA)—A graduate student who assists a professor in the presentation of a course. Usually the professor gives two to four lectures a week for all the students in the class; the TAs hold smaller weekly discussion sections.

three-two program (3-2)—A program in which students can study three years at one school, followed by two at another, more specialized school. Upon completion, many of these programs award both the bachelor's and the master's degrees.

town-gown relations—The contact between a college (students, employees, buildings) and its host town (citizens, businesses, local government) and the set of issues around which this contact revolves. Such issues include taxes, traffic, local employment practices, and government services like road maintenance, sewage, and trash collection. Because a town and its university can be dependent on each other, good town-gown relations are important to both sides.

townie—A resident of a college town or city who is not enrolled in the college, but who might sit beside you at the local pub. Usually involves a "them vs. us" mentality.

trimesters—An academic calendar that divides the school year into three terms of approximately equal length. Schools on the trimester system generally have one term before the winter break and two after.

tutorial major (also called self-designed or special major)—A program offered by many schools in which a student can plan his or her own major, combining the offerings of two or more traditional majors, usually in consultation with a faculty member. An example is Medieval studies, in which the student might study the history, literature, philosophy, and art of the period, taking courses from a number of departments.

waiting list—A list of students who are not initially accepted to a certain school, but who may be admitted later, depending on the number of accepted students who enroll. Most colleges ultimately accept only a small fraction of the students on the waiting list, who are notified during the summer.

work-study—Campus jobs, for financial-aid recipients, that are subsidized by the federal government. Work-study jobs are a component of most need-based financial-aid packages. Students typically work 10 to 20 hours a week to help finance their education.

The College Finder

With so many colleges from which to choose, how can you zero in on one that is right for you? The lists that follow are designed to help you match your interests with a selected group of colleges. Our hope is that The Finder will introduce you to a number of colleges you might not otherwise have considered.

Regions

New England: Connecticut, Maine, Massachusetts, New Hampshire, Rhode Island, Vermont. Also includes Eastern Canada.

Mid-Atlantic: Delaware, District of Columbia, Maryland, New Jersey, New York, Pennsylvania, West Virginia.

Midwest: Illinois, Indiana, Iowa, Kansas, Kentucky, Michigan, Minnesota, Missouri, Nebraska, North Dakota, Ohio, South Dakota, Wisconsin.

Southeast: Alabama, Arkansas, Florida, Georgia, Louisiana, Mississippi, North Carolina, South Carolina, Tennessee, Virginia.

West: Alaska, Arizona, California, Colorado, Hawaii, Idaho, Montana, New Mexico, Nevada, Oklahoma, Oregon, Texas, Utah, Washington, Wyoming. Also includes Western Canada.

Schools with 1,500 Undergraduates or Fewer

New England
Bennington College
Hampshire College
Marlboro College
Simmons College
United States Coast Guard Academy
Wheaton College

Mid-Atlantic
Bard College
Bryn Mawr College
Cooper Union for the Advancement of Science and Art
Drew University
Eastman School of Music
Goucher College
Haverford College
Juilliard School, The
Manhattanville College
Sarah Lawrence College
St. John's College
Stevens Institute of Technology
Swarthmore College
Trinity College
Wells College

Midwest
Albion College
Alma College
Antioch College
Beloit College
Centre College
Cornell College
Earlham College
Grinnell College
Kalamazoo College
Knox College
Lake Forest College
Lawrence University
Wabash College

Southeast
Agnes Scott College
Birmingham-Southern College
Hampden-Sydney College
Hendrix College
Hollins College
Millsaps College
New College of the University of South Florida
North Carolina School of the Arts
Randolph-Macon Woman's College
Rhodes College
Sweet Briar College
University of the South (Sewanee)
Wofford College

West
California Institute of Technology
California Institute of the Arts
Claremont McKenna College
Deep Springs College
Harvey Mudd College

Mills College
Occidental College
Pitzer College
Pomona College
Reed College
Scripps College
St. John's College (NM)
University of Dallas
University of Redlands
Whitman College

Schools with 1,501 to 3,000 Undergraduates

New England
Amherst College
Babson College
Bates College
Bowdoin College
Clark University
Colby College
Connecticut College
Holy Cross, College of the
Middlebury College
Mount Holyoke College
Rhode Island School of Design
Smith College
Trinity College
Wellesley College
Wesleyan University
Williams College
Worcester Polytechnic Institute

Mid-Atlantic
Adelphi University
Alfred University
Allegheny College
Barnard College
Catholic University of America
Clarkson University
Colgate University
Dickinson College
Franklin & Marshall College
Gettysburg College
Hamilton College
Hobart and William Smith College
Lafayette College
Muhlenberg College
Parsons School of Design
Skidmore College
St. Bonaventure University
St. Lawrence University
Susquehanna University

Union College
Vassar College
Yeshiva University

Midwest
Carleton College
Denison University
DePauw University
Gustavus Adolphus College
Kenyon College
Macalester College
Oberlin College
Ohio Wesleyan University
Rose-Hulman Institute of Technology
St. Olaf College
Valparaiso University
Wittenburg University
Wooster, The College of

Southeast
Davidson College
Florida Institute of Technology
Furman University
Morehouse College
Spelman College
Stetson University
Tuskegee University
Washington and Lee University

West
Colorado College
Colorado School of Mines
Lewis and Clark College
Oral Roberts University
Pepperdine University
Puget Sound University
Rice University
Trinity University
University of Denver
University of Tulsa
Willamette University

Schools with Over 20,000 Students

New England
Boston University
Carleton University
McGill University
Northeastern University
University of Massachusetts/Amherst
University of Toronto
University of Western Ontario

Mid-Atlantic
New York University
Pennsylvania State University
Rutgers, The State University of New
    Jersey
SUNY/Buffalo
Temple University
University of Maryland/College Park
University of Pennsylvania
University of Pittsburgh
West Virginia University

Midwest
Indiana University
Iowa State University
Kansas State University
Kent State University
Michigan State University
Ohio State University
Purdue University
Southern Illinois University/Carbondale
University of Cincinnati
University of Illinois/Urbana-Champaign
University of Iowa
University of Kansas
University of Kentucky
University of Michigan
University of Minnesota
University of Missouri/Columbia
University of Nebraska/Lincoln
University of Wisconsin

Southeast
Auburn University
Florida State University
George Mason University
Louisiana State University & A&M
    College
North Carolina State University
University of Florida
University of Georgia
University of North Carolina/Chapel Hill
University of South Carolina
University of Tennessee/Knoxville
University of Virginia
Virginia Polytechnic Institute and State
    University

West
Arizona State University
Brigham Young University
California State University/San Diego
Colorado State University
Texas A&M University/College Station
Texas Tech University
University of Arizona

University of British Columbia
University of California/Berkeley
University of California/Davis
University of California/Los Angeles
University of Colorado/Boulder
University of Houston
University of New Mexico
University of Oklahoma
University of Southern California
University of Texas/Austin
University of Utah
University of Washington
Washington State University

Some Schools Over 200 Years Old

Bowdoin College
Brown University
College of William and Mary
Columbia College of Columbia University
Dartmouth College
Dickinson College
Franklin & Marshall College
Georgetown University
Hampden-Sydney College
Harvard and Radcliffe College
Princeton University
Rutgers, The State University of New
    Jersey
St. John's College
Union College
University of Delaware
University of Georgia
University of North Carolina/Chapel Hill
University of Pennsylvania
University of Pittsburgh
University of Tennessee/Knoxville
University of Vermont
Washington and Lee University
Williams College
Yale University

Some Schools Less Than 50 Years Old

California Institute of the Arts
Eugene Lang College of the New School
    for Social Research
Evergreen State College

Florida Institute of Technology
George Mason University
Hampshire College
Harvey Mudd College
New College of the University of South Florida
North Carolina School of the Arts
Oral Roberts University
Pitzer College
SUNY/Stony Brook
United States Air Force Academy
University of California/Irvine
University of California/Riverside
University of California/Santa Cruz
University of Dallas
University of Waterloo

Single-Sex Schools

Women
Agnes Scott College
Barnard College
Hollins College
Mills College
Mount Holyoke College
Randolph-Macon Woman's College
Scripps College
Simmons College
Smith College
Spelman College
Sweet Briar College
Trinity College (D.C.)
Wellesley College
Wells College

Men
Deep Springs College
Hampden-Sydney College
Morehouse College
Wabash College

Predominantly Male Schools (More Than Two-Thirds Male)

California Institute of Technology
Carnegie Mellon University
Clarkson University
Colorado School of Mines
Georgia Institute of Technology

Harvey Mudd College
Rensselaer Polytechnic Institute
Rose-Hulman Institute of Technology
Stevens Institute of Technology
United States Air Force Academy
United States Coast Guard Academy
United States Military Academy
United States Naval Academy
Worcester Polytechnic Institute

Predominantly Female Schools (More Than Two-Thirds Female)

Adelphi University
Bennington College
Bryn Mawr College
CUNY/Hunter College
Eugene Lang College of the New School for Social Research
Goucher College
Manhattanville College
Parsons School of Design
Sarah Lawrence College
Wheaton College

Some Schools with High Minority Enrollment (More Than 30%)

New England
Harvard and Radcliffe College
Massachusetts Institute of Technology
Wellesley College
Wesleyan University
Yale University

Mid-Atlantic
Barnard College
Columbia College of Columbia University
Cooper Union for the Advancement of Science and Art
CUNY/City College of New York
CUNY/Hunter College
CUNY/Queens College
Drexel University
Howard University
Johns Hopkins University
Juilliard School, The
New York University

Rutgers, The State University of New
  Jersey
Stevens Institute of Technology
SUNY/Stony Brook
Swarthmore College
Temple University
Trinity College (D.C.)
University of Pennsylvania

Midwest
DePaul University/Southeast
Florida A&M University
Morehouse College
Old Dominion University
Spelman College
Tuskegee University
University of Miami

West
California Institute of Technology
California Polytechnic State
  University/San Luis Obispo
California State University/Fresno
California State University/San Diego
Claremont McKenna College
New Mexico State University
Occidental College
Oral Roberts University
Pitzer College
Pomona College
Scripps College
Stanford University
University of Alaska/Fairbanks
University of California/Berkeley
University of California/Davis
University of California/Irvine
University of California/Los Angeles
University of California/Riverside
University of California/San Diego
University of California/Santa Barbara
University of California/Santa Cruz
University of Hawaii/Manoa
University of Houston
University of New Mexico
University of Southern California

Schools Accepting 30% or Less of Their Applicant Pool

Amherst College
Brown University
California Institute of Technology

Claremont McKenna College
Columbia College of Columbia
  University
Cooper Union for the Advancement of
  Science and Art
Dartmouth College
Deep Springs College
Georgetown University
Harvard and Radcliffe College
Juilliard School, The
Massachusetts Institute of Technology
North Carolina School of the Arts
Northwestern University
Princeton University
Rice University
Stanford University
Swarthmore College
United States Air Force Academy
United States Coast Guard Academy
United States Military Academy
United States Naval Academy
Williams College
Yale University

Schools Accepting 31% to 50% of Their Applicant Pool

Babson College
Barnard College
Bates College
Boston College
Bowdoin College
California Institute of the Arts
Carnegie Mellon University
Colby College
Colgate University
Connecticut College
Cornell University
Davidson College
Duke University
Eastman School of Music
Emory University
George Washington University
Hamilton College
Harvey Mudd College
Haverford College
Holy Cross, College of the
Howard University
Johns Hopkins University
Middlebury College
New York University
Pomona College

Queen's University
Rhode Island School of Design
Sarah Lawrence College
SUNY/Binghamton (Binghamton University)
Trinity College
Tufts University
University of British Columbia
University of California/Berkeley
University of California/Los Angeles
University of Notre Dame
University of North Carolina/Chapel Hill
University of Pennsylvania
University of Richmond
University of Southern California
University of Virginia
University of Waterloo
University of Western Ontario
Vassar College
Wake Forest University
Washington and Lee University
Washington University
Wellesley College
Wesleyan University
William and Mary, College of

Rose-Hulman Institute of Technology
Rutgers, The State University of New Jersey
Smith College
Spelman College
SUNY/Stony Brook
Syracuse University
Union College
University of California/San Diego
University of Chicago
University of Miami
University of Rochester
Vanderbilt University
Whitman College

Schools Accepting 51% to 60% of Their Applicant Pool

Bard College
Boston University
Brandeis University
Bryn Mawr College
Bucknell University
California Polytechnic State University/San Luis Obispo
Carleton College
Colorado College
Franklin & Marshall College
Georgia Institute of Technology
James Madison University
Lafayette College
Lehigh University
Macalester College
McGill University
Morehouse College
New Jersey, The College of
Parsons School of Design
Pennsylvania State University
Pepperdine University
Pitzer College

Private Schools

New England
Amherst College
Babson College
Bates College
Bennington College
Boston College
Boston University
Bowdoin College
Brandeis University
Brown University
Clark University
Colby College
Connecticut College
Dartmouth College
Fairfield University
Hampshire College
Harvard and Radcliffe College
Holy Cross, College of the
Marlboro College
Massachusetts Institute of Technology
McGill University
Middlebury College
Mount Holyoke College
Northeastern University
Rhode Island School of Design
Simmons College
Smith College
Trinity College
Tufts University
Wellesley College
Wesleyan University
Wheaton College
Williams College
Worcester Polytechnic Institute
Yale University

Mid-Atlantic
Adelphi University
Alfred University
Allegheny College
American University
Bard College
Barnard College
Bryn Mawr College
Bucknell University
Carnegie Mellon University
Catholic University of America
Clarkson University
Colgate University
Columbia College of Columbia
    University
Cooper Union for the Advancement of
    Science and Art
Cornell University
Dickinson College
Drew University
Drexel University
Eastman School of Music
Eugene Lang College of the New School
    for Social Research
Fordham University
Franklin & Marshall College
George Washington University
Georgetown University
Gettysburg College
Goucher College
Hamilton College
Haverford College
Hobart and William Smith College
Hofstra University
Howard University
Johns Hopkins University
Juilliard School, The
Lafayette College
Lehigh University
Manhattanville College
Muhlenberg College
New York University
Parsons School of Design
Princeton University
Rensselaer Polytechnic Institute
Rochester Institute of Technology
Sarah Lawrence College
Skidmore College
St. Bonaventure University
St. John's College
St. Lawrence University
Stevens Institute of Technology
Susquehanna University
Swarthmore College
Syracuse University

Trinity College
University of Pennsylvania
University of Rochester
Union College
Vassar College
Villanova University
Wells College
Yeshiva University

Midwest
Albion College
Alma College
Antioch College
Beloit College
Carleton College
Case Western Reserve University
Centre College
Cornell College
Creighton University
Denison University
DePaul University
DePauw University
Earlham College
Grinnell College
Gustavus Adolphus College
Kalamazoo College
Kenyon College
Knox College
Lake Forest College
Lawrence University
Loyola University of Chicago
Macalester College
Marquette University
Northwestern University
Oberlin College
Ohio Wesleyan University
Rose-Hulman Institute of
    Technology
St. John's University/College of St.
    Benedict
St. Olaf College
University of Chicago
University of Notre Dame
Valparaiso University
Wabash College
Washington University
Wittenburg University
Wooster, The College of

Southeast
Agnes Scott College
Birmingham-Southern College
Davidson College
Duke University
Emory University

Florida Institute of Technology
Furman University
Hampden-Sydney College
Hendrix College
Hollins College
Millsaps College
Morehouse College
Randolph-Macon Woman's College
Rhodes College
Spelman College
Stetson University
Sweet Briar College
Tulane University
Tuskegee University
University of Richmond
University of the South (Sewanee)
University of Miami
Vanderbilt University
Wake Forest University
Washington and Lee University
Wofford College

West
Baylor University
Brigham Young University
California Institute of Technology
California Institute of the Arts
Claremont McKenna College
Colorado College
Colorado School of Mines
Deep Springs College
Harvey Mudd College
Lewis and Clark College
Mills College
Occidental College
Oral Roberts University
Pepperdine University
Pitzer College
Pomona College
Puget Sound University
Reed College
Rice University
Scripps College
Southern Methodist University
St. John's College (NM)
Stanford University
Texas Christian University
Trinity University
University of Dallas
University of Denver
University of Redlands
University of Southern California
University of Tulsa
Whitman College
Willamette University

Some Schools with Religious Affiliation

Agnes Scott College
Albion College
Allegheny College
Alma College
American University
Baylor University
Birmingham-Southern College
Brigham Young University
Catholic University of America
Centre College
Creighton University
Davidson College
DePauw University
Duke University
Earlham College
Emory University
Fairfield University
Georgetown University
Gustavus Adolphus College
Hampden-Sydney College
Holy Cross, College of the
Kenyon College
Lafayette College
Lake Forest College
Loyola University of Chicago
Macalester College
Marquette University
Millsaps College
Muhlenberg College
Notre Dame
Ohio Wesleyan University
Pepperdine University
Randolph-Macon Woman's College
Rhodes College
Southern Methodist University
St. Bonaventure University
St. John's University/College of St. Benedict
St. Olaf College
Susquehanna University
Texas Christian University
Trinity College (D.C.)
Trinity University
University of Dallas
University of Denver
University of Notre Dame
University of the South (Sewanee)
University of Tulsa
Valparaiso University
Villanova University

Willamette University
Wittenburg University
Wofford College
Wooster, The College of

Small Liberal Arts Colleges (Under 3,000 Undergraduates)

New England
Amherst College
Babson College
Bates College
Bennington College
Bowdoin College
Brandeis University
Clark University
Colby College
Connecticut College
Fairfield University
Hampshire College
Holy Cross, College of the
Marlboro College
Middlebury College
Mount Holyoke College
Simmons College
Smith College
Trinity College
Wellesley College
Wesleyan University
Wheaton College
Williams College

Mid-Atlantic
Allegheny College
Bard College
Barnard College
Bryn Mawr College
Clarkson University
Colgate University
Dickinson College
Drew University
Franklin and Marshall College
Gettysburg College
Goucher College
Hamilton College
Haverford College
Hobart and William Smith Colleges
Manhattanville College
Muhlenberg College
Sarah Lawrence College
Skidmore College
St. John's College (MD)

St. Lawrence University
Swarthmore College
Trinity College (D.C.)
Union College
Vassar College
Wells College

Midwest
Albion College
Alma College
Antioch College
Beloit College
Carleton College
Centre College
Cornell College
Denison University
DePauw University
Earlham College
Grinnell College
Gustavus Adolphus College
Kalamazoo College
Kenyon College
Knox College
Lake Forest College
Lawrence University
Macalester College
Oberlin College
Ohio Wesleyan University
St. Olaf College
Wabash College
Wittenburg University
Wooster, The College of

South
Agnes Scott College
Birmingham-Southern College
Davidson College
Furman University
Hampden-Sydney College
Hendrix College
Hollins College
Millsaps College
Morehouse College
New College of the University of South
    Florida
Oral Roberts University
Randolph-Macon Woman's College
Rhodes College
Rice University
University of Dallas
University of Richmond
University of the South (Sewanee)
University of Tulsa
Spelman College
Stetson University
Sweet Briar College

Trinity University
Washington and Lee University
Wofford College

West
Claremont McKenna College
Colorado College
Deep Springs College
Lewis and Clark College
Mills College
Occidental College
Pitzer College
Pomona College
Puget Sound University
Reed College
Scripps College
St. John's College (NM)
University of Redlands
Whitman College
Willamette University

Rose-Hulman Institute of Technology
Stetson University
Stevens Institute of Technology
Susquehanna University
Texas Christian University
Trinity University
Union College
University of Mississippi
University of Pennsylvania
University of Richmond
University of the South (Sewanee)
Valparaiso University
Vanderbilt University
Villanova University
Wabash College
Wake Forest University
Washington and Lee University
Whitman College
Willamette University
William and Mary, College of
Wofford College
Worcester Polytechnic Institute

Large Fraternity/Sorority Systems (More Than 30%)

Albion College
Allegheny College
Birmingham-Southern College
Bucknell University
Centre College
Colgate University
Cornell College
Creighton University
Dartmouth College
Denison University
DePauw University
Dickinson College
Duke University
Emory University
Franklin & Marshall College
Furman University
Gettysburg College
Johns Hopkins University
Lafayette College
Lehigh University
Massachusetts Institute of Technology
Miami University
Millsaps College
Muhlenberg College
Northwestern University
Ohio Wesleyan University
Puget Sound University
Rensselaer Polytechnic Institute
Rhodes College

Schools with No Fraternities or Sororities

Agnes Scott College
Amherst College
Antioch College
Bard College
Barnard College
Bates College
Bennington College
Boston College
Brandeis University
Brigham Young University
Bryn Mawr College
California Institute of the Arts
California Institute of Technology
Carleton College
Carleton University
Claremont McKenna College
Clark University
Colby College
Connecticut College
CUNY/City College of New York
CUNY/Hunter College
CUNY/Queens College
Deep Springs College
Drew University
Earlham College
Eugene Lang College of the New School
    for Social Research

Evergreen State College
Fairfield University
Fordham University
Georgetown University
Goucher College
Grinnell College
Hampshire College
Harvard University
Harvey Mudd College
Haverford College
Hendrix College
Hollins College
Holy Cross, College of the
Juilliard School, The
Kalamazoo College
Lewis and Clark College
Macalester College
Manhattanville College
Marlboro College
McGill University
McMaster University
Middlebury College
Mills College
Mount Holyoke College
New College of the University of South
 Florida
North Carolina School of the Arts
Oberlin College
Oral Roberts University
Parsons School of Design
Pitzer College
Princeton University
Queen's University
Randolph-Macon Woman's College
Reed College
Rhode Island School of Design
Rice University
Sarah Lawrence College
Scripps College
Simmons College
Skidmore College
Smith College
St. Bonaventure University
St. John's College (MD and NM)
St. John's University/College of St.
 Benedict
St. Olaf College
Sweet Briar College
Trinity College (D.C.)
United States Air Force Academy
United States Coast Guard Academy
United States Military Academy
United States Naval Academy
University of California/Santa Cruz
University of Dallas
University of Notre Dame

University of Toronto
University of Washington
University of Waterloo
University of Western Ontario
Vassar College
Wellesley College
Wells College
Wheaton College
Williams College
Yeshiva University

Some Schools with Very High Graduation Rates

Amherst College
Bates College
Brown University
Bryn Mawr College
Bucknell College
California Institute of Technology
Carleton College
Claremont McKenna College
Colby College
Colgate University
Columbia College of Columbia University
Connecticut College
Cornell University
Dartmouth College
Davidson College
Dickinson College
Duke University
Emory University
Florida A&M University
Georgetown University
Hamilton College
Harvard and Radcliffe College
Haverford College
Holy Cross, College of the
Johns Hopkins University
Kenyon College
Middlebury College
Mount Holyoke College
Northwestern University
Rhode Island School of Design
University of Notre Dame
University of Richmond
University of the South (Sewanee)
Swarthmore College
Trinity College (CT)
Union College
United States Air Force Academy
Villanova University
Washington and Lee University

William and Mary, The College of
Yale University

Tuition, Room and Board

Note: Schools with asterisks (*) have tuition figures listed for the 2000–2001 academic year. When a school is followed by (I), that figure refers to in-state tuition only; out-of-state tuition is higher.

Under $6,000

NEW ENGLAND
United States Coast Guard Academy*

MID-ATLANTIC
CUNY/City College of New York (I)
CUNY/Hunter College (I)
CUNY/Queens College
United States Military Academy
United States Naval Academy

MIDWEST
Kansas State University (I)
University of Nebraska/Lincoln (I)
University of North Dakota (I)
University of South Dakota (I)
University of Wisconsin (I)

SOUTHEAST
Florida A&M University (I)
North Carolina School of the Arts (I)
North Carolina State University (I)
University of Mississippi (I)

WEST
Brigham Young University
Deep Springs College*
New Mexico State University (I)
United States Air Force Academy
University of Idaho (I)
University of Texas/Austin (I)

$6,000 to $11,999

NEW ENGLAND
Carleton University (I)
McGill University

McMaster University (I)
Queen's University (I)
University of Connecticut (I)
University of Maine/Orono (I)
University of Massachusetts/
  Amherst (I)*
University of New Hampshire (I)
University of Rhode Island (I)
University of Toronto (I)
University of Waterloo (I)
University of Western Ontario (I)

MID-ATLANTIC
CUNY/City College of New York
CUNY/Hunter College
New Jersey, The College of (I)
Pennsylvania State University (I)
Rutgers, The State University of New Jersey (I)
SUNY/Albany
SUNY/Binghamton (I)
SUNY/Buffalo (I)
SUNY/Stony Brook (I)
Temple University (I)
University of Delaware (I)
University of Maryland/College Park (I)
University of Pittsburgh (I)
West Virginia University (I)*

MIDWEST
Bowling Green State University (I)
Illinois State University (I)*
Indiana University (I)
Iowa State University
Kansas State University (I)
Kent State University (I)
Miami University (I)
Michigan State University (I)
Ohio State University (I)
Ohio University (I)
Purdue University (I)
Southern Illinois University/
  Carbondale (I)
University of Cincinnati (I)
University of Illinois/Urbana-Champaign (I)
University of Iowa (I)*
University of Kansas
University of Kentucky
University of Michigan (I)
University of Minnesota (I)
University of Missouri/Columbia (I)
University of Nebraska/Lincoln
University of North Dakota
University of South Dakota
University of Wisconsin

SOUTHEAST

Auburn University
Clemson University
Florida A&M University
Florida State University (I)
George Mason University (I)
Georgia Institute of Technology (I)
James Madison University (I)
Louisiana State University & A&M College
Mississippi State University
New College of the University of South Florida
North Carolina State University
Old Dominion University (I)
University of Alabama
University of Arkansas
University of Florida (I)
University of Georgia
University of Mississippi
University of North Carolina/Chapel Hill
University of South Carolina
University of Tennessee/Knoxville
University of Virginia (I)
Virginia Polytechnic Institute and State University (I)
William and Mary, College of (I)

WEST

Arizona State University
California Polytechnic State University/ San Luis Obispo
California State University/Chico
California State University/Fresno
California State University/San Diego
Colorado School of Mines (I)
Colorado State University (I)
Evergreen State College
New Mexico State University
Oklahoma State University
Oregon State University
Texas A&M University/College Station (I)
Texas Tech University
University of Alaska/Fairbanks
University of Arizona
University of British Columbia (I)
University of California/Berkeley (I)*
University of California/Davis (I)
University of California/Irvine (I)
University of California/Los Angeles (I)
University of California/Riverside (I)
University of California/San Diego (I)
University of California/Santa Barbara (I)
University of California/Santa Cruz (I)
University of Colorado/Boulder (I)
University of Hawaii/Manoa (I)

University of Houston
University of Idaho
University of Montana
University of Nevada/Reno
University of New Mexico
University of Oklahoma
University of Oregon (I)
University of Texas/Austin
University of Utah
University of Washington (I)
University of Wyoming
Washington State University (I)

$12,000 to $17,999

NEW ENGLAND

Carleton University
Queen's University
University of Maine/Orono
University of Massachusetts/Amherst*
University of Rhode Island
University of Toronto
University of Vermont (I)
University of Waterloo
University of Western Ontario

MID-ATLANTIC

Cooper Union for the Advancement of Science and Art
Howard University
New Jersey, The College of
Pennsylvania State University
Rutgers, The State University of New Jersey
SUNY/Binghamton
SUNY/Buffalo
SUNY/Stony Brook
Temple University
University of Delaware
University of Maryland/College Park
West Virginia University*
Yeshiva University

MIDWEST

Bowling Green State University
Creighton University
DePaul University
Illinois State University*
Indiana University
Kansas State University
Kent State University
Miami University
Michigan State University
Ohio State University

Ohio University
Purdue University
Southern Illinois University/Carbondale
University of Cincinnati
University of Illinois/Urbana-Champaign
University of Iowa*
University of Minnesota
University of Missouri/Columbia

SOUTHEAST
Florida State University
George Mason University
Georgia Institute of Technology
Hendrix College
James Madison University
Morehouse College
North Carolina School of the Arts
Old Dominion University
Spelman College
Tuskegee University
University of Florida
Virginia Polytechnic Institute and State
    University
Wake Forest University

WEST
Baylor University*
Colorado State University
Oral Roberts University
Rice University
Texas A&M University/College Station
Texas Christian University
University of British Columbia
University of California/Davis
University of California/Irvine
University of California/Santa Barbara
University of Colorado/Boulder
University of Dallas
University of Hawaii/Manoa
University of Oregon
University of Tulsa
University of Washington
Washington State University

$18,000 to $23,999

NEW ENGLAND
McMaster University
University of Connecticut
University of New Hampshire

MID-ATLANTIC
Adelphi University
Catholic University of America

Drew University
Drexel University
Fordham University
Hofstra University
Juilliard School, The
Muhlenberg College
Rochester Institute of Technology
St. Bonaventure University
Trinity College (D.C.)
University of Pittsburgh
Wells College

MIDWEST
Alma College
Case Western Reserve University*
Centre College*
DePauw University
Earlham College
Grinnell College
Gustavus Adolphus College*
Knox College
Loyola University of Chicago
Marquette University*
Rose-Hulman Institute of Technology*
St. John's University/College of St.
    Benedict
St. Olaf College
University of Michigan
Valparaiso University
Wabash College
Wittenburg University

SOUTHEAST
Agnes Scott College*
Birmingham-Southern College
Florida Institute of Technology
Furman University*
Hampden-Sydney College
Hollins College*
Millsaps College
Randolph-Macon Woman's College
Rhodes College
Stetson University
Sweet Briar College
University of Richmond*
University of the South (Sewanee)
University of Virginia
Washington and Lee University
William and Mary, College of
Wofford College

WEST
California Institute of Technology
California Institute of the Arts
Colorado School of Mines
Mills College

Puget Sound University
Southern Methodist University
Trinity University
University of California/Berkeley*
University of California/Los Angeles*
University of California/Riverside
University of California/San Diego
University of California/Santa Cruz
University of Denver
University of Redlands

Over $24,000

NEW ENGLAND
Amherst College
Babson College*
Bates College
Bennington College*
Boston College
Boston University*

Bowdoin College
Brandeis University
Brown University
Clark University
Colby College
Connecticut College
Dartmouth College
Fairfield University
Hampshire College
Harvard and Radcliffe College*
Holy Cross, College of the*
Marlboro College
Massachusetts Institute of Technology
Middlebury College
Mount Holyoke College*
Northeastern University
Rhode Island School of Design
Simmons College*
Smith College
Trinity College
Tufts University
University of Vermont

A Word About Statistics

Every college description in this book is preceded by a statistical profile. The figures are the most recent available. The data are supplied by the colleges themselves. When no figures were available, the symbol "NA" (not available) has been used. For the most up-to-date information, you should contact the colleges directly.

Please note that in general, except where doing so would be misleading, all percentages have been rounded off to the nearest whole-number percent. As an example, statistically speaking, there is no significant difference between an acceptance rate of 30 percent and 30.4 percent; in fact, even a difference of 3 to 5 percent would hardly be noticeable in everyday life situations.

As a rule, the statistics provided by a school are for the most recent year for which that school has information: in most cases, either the 1997–1998 or 1996–1997 academic year.

Below the name of each school is listed the **World Wide Web (WWW) site** and admissions office e-mail address for that school.

The **address** and **undergraduate admissions** phone numbers are the ones that a school's admissions office prefers applicants to use when corresponding.

Location describes the setting of a college: rural, suburban, small city, or urban. Of course, this can only give a general idea of a campus's surroundings.

Private/public refers to private schools versus "state" schools. **Founded** is the year that the school first accepted students. **Religious affiliation** indicates whether a school is affiliated with a particular religious establishment, either directly or indirectly.

Undergraduate enrollment is the number of full-time undergraduate students for the most recent year available at press time.

Total enrollment gives the total number of students, including not only full-time undergraduates, but also part-time students, graduate and professional students, and in some cases, evening and extension students.

Subtracting the number of undergraduates from the total enrollment will give an estimate of the number of graduate students; the ratio of undergraduates to graduate students will give you a rough indication of the relative emphasis a given university places on each.

Percent male/female (M/F) gives the percentage of undergraduates of each sex.

Percent minority is the percentage of enrolled students who indicated on their applications that they consider themselves members of a minority group. This figure is followed by percentages of students in three broad minority groups—African-American, Asian-American, and Hispanic—to give a measure of the ethnic diversity of the school. International students are not included in this figure.

Percent in-state/out-of-state is the percentage of enrolled undergraduates who are residents of the state in which the school is located. (For Canadian schools, the percentage given is the percentage of students from within Canada.) This figure gives a rough idea of the regional diversity of the school. Obviously, the in-state numbers will usually be much higher for public schools than for private schools, though in almost all cases, states provide incentives for private schools to take in-state students.

The figures for membership in **fraternities/sororities** are based on the approximate percentage of male students joining fraternities and female students joining sororities, as reported by the administration. Fraternity and sorority enrollment over 30 percent usually indicates a strong Greek system. Note that fraternity and sorority figures do not include non-Greek exclusive clubs or secret societies. Also, "NA" means that a school did not report a figure, while "0%" indicates that a school does not have fraternities or sororities.

Number of applicants is the number of completed first-year undergraduate applications received by the university.

Percent accepted is the number of applicants accepted for the most recent entering freshman class (in this case, usually the class of 2003) divided by the total number of applicants.

This is an imperfect measure of a college's selectivity, and does not necessarily reflect academic quality, since many factors can influence acceptance rates. Some schools with reputations for being easy after admission tend to attract larger numbers of applicants; public schools offer lower in-state tuition, often an attractive incentive for in-state applicants. Even winning sports teams can increase application numbers. And there are many other factors that can influence the quality and size of the applicant pool, from school to school and even year to year.

Despite these caveats, "percent accepted" can be a revealing statistic: Colleges that accept a relatively small percentage of their applicants are usually in the best position to maintain their academic quality. When the acceptance rate is less than one-third, you can be assured the school is one of the best around.

Percent accepted who enroll is the number of students who enroll divided by the number accepted. This figure, commonly called the "yield" by admissions offices, is another way to assess how well a school attracts qualified applicants. Since many applicants are accepted at multiple schools, the yield is a good indicator of which schools are first-choice schools, and which are "safety" schools: The latter usually have yields below 40 percent.

The main use of yields is to compare schools that have similar applicant pools; state universities tend to have high yields because some applicants are in-state students who don't apply anywhere else.

Number of transfers tells the number of students who were accepted for transfer to that institution each year. Keep in mind that "NA" here does not mean that there were no transfers, only that the schools did not report a number. A few schools, though, do not accept transfers.

This number gives an indication of the college's receptivity to transfer applicants. Colleges with many transfers are often fair to good academic institutions with one important feature (e.g., location, a particular program) that sets them apart

from other institution. Schools in or near Washington, D.C., are a good example because of their proximity to the seat of national government. Most schools with high transfer rates have as many students going as coming. Those who decide that whatever is there is not for them are continually replaced by fresh faces from other colleges. The transfer figure should not be considered an index of a school's popularity, since many limit transfers to a small number, and a few cases forbid them entirely. *The Insider's Guide* prints the number accepted rather than the number matriculated, because the former number better represents the opportunity to transfer than the latter. For example, if a school accepts 90 transfers, but only 4 matriculate, the "90" figure more accurately reflects the potential for a successful transfer acceptance.

Size of entering class is the number of first-years and transfers on campus at the beginning of the year.

The application deadline is the final deadline for completed applications (except for second-term grade reports and late admissions tests) for freshman students.

Many schools offer early-decision or early-action plans that allow students to submit applications for evaluation before the normal deadline. Early-decision usually requires a commitment to enroll if accepted (except in unusual circumstances), while early-action plans usually give you until April to decide. The main advantage of these plans is that you can have a definite answer by December or January. If you are interested in any of these plans, contact the schools for more information—the earlier the better.

A large number of schools have "rolling" admissions, where applications are reviewed in the order received. In most cases, however, these schools have priority deadlines after which applications are at a disadvantage.

A note to transfer students: As a general rule, transfer applications have a later deadline (often one to two months) than freshman applications. Nevertheless, the earlier you submit your application, the better.

Many colleges do not report **mean SAT scores** (SAT I), as they do not wish to discourage potential applicants by doing so; instead they either report a range of SAT scores, or none at all. If no figure is listed for the mean SAT, then the school is probably one of many that no longer report mean SAT scores. Keep in mind, though, a mean score implies there are approximately as many students with higher SAT scores as students with lower SAT scores. Some schools, notably in the South and Midwest, prefer the ACT (American College Test); for these schools, a single number (on a scale of 1 to 36) is reported. Where a school has reported both, only the SAT I score is provided; in most cases, though, schools will accept either test.

Middle 50% SAT range is the figure the College Board prefers schools to use in discussing actual SAT scores. The range represents where half of a particular school's new freshman students' scores fell. So, a mathematics range of 550 to 650 would mean that half of the incoming freshmen had SAT mathematics scores somewhere between 550 and 650. The middle 50 percent range are the numbers between the twenty-fifth and seventy-fifth percentile boundaries; someone whose SAT score falls on the seventy-fifth percentile scored higher than 75 percent of the people who took that particular test. The same applies for someone whose SAT score falls on the twenty-fifth percentile; the median is a score at the fiftieth percentile. So, if your SAT score falls within the middle 50 percent range, you are on par, SAT-wise, with previously successful applicants. But remember that this does not mean you have a 50-50 chance of getting in; instead, view this figure as an indication of your own competitiveness against the overall applicant pool that the school receives.

Most popular majors lists the three most popular majors among students in the most recent graduating class (usually class of 1999). Remember, though, that popularity is not necessarily a measure of quality; also, the exact number of students majoring in any given field can vary widely from year to year, though certain schools are particularly well-known for specific programs (e.g., criminology, biomedical engineering, government, journalism).

The **retention rate** is the percentage

of first-year students who remain enrolled at a given institution for their second (sophomore) year.

The **graduation rate** represents the percentage of students who successfully graduate within a specific amount of time: for example, "80% within 5 years." Most schools report a five-year graduation rate, as many now expect students to take five years to complete a degree program, while others report four- or six-year graduation rates.

Library figures list the physical number of volumes in the possession of the library. This includes book, audio and video recordings, but not micro-reproductions or volumes available through cooperative programs with other libraries.

Tuition and fees and **room and board** figures are given for the most recent year available. (The College Finder lists those schools that have provided tuition figures for the 2000–2001 academic year.) In cases where costs differ for in-state and out-of-state students, both figures are given. Also, many public schools charge tuition that vary with the course load taken.

Remember that these figures are meant as an estimate of the cost of a year at a given institution, and do not include such costs as travel, books, and personal expenses. Their main usefulness is as a relative measure of how expensive one college is to another.

On-campus housing, first-year gives the percentage of students living in school-controlled housing for their first year. This figure is given primarily for the benefit of students applying to state universities, many of which have reputations for literally leaving new students out in the cold. Be prepared to seek off-campus arrangements early if a school's housing percentage is less than 90 percent, or if no figure is listed.

Also, schools that reported that first-year students are guaranteed on-campus housing are listed with a (G) after the percentage. Schools that stated they require first-years to live on-campus are designated by an (R). Most schools, though, make exemptions for older students, married students, and/or students living nearby.

For **financial aid, first-year** figures, schools were asked to report the percentage of the entering class receiving need-based financial assistance from the institution out of those applying for aid (in some cases, though, schools responded with the total percentage of students on financial aid). This does not include students receiving only merit-based scholarships, federal loans not given out by the institution, and students who did not apply for aid. These figures are most relevant for comparing similar institutions. Questions about specific financial aid programs should be addressed to the schools.

A Note About Some Statistics We Do Not Include

We do not list student-faculty ratios in our statistics because we believe that such ratios form an inappropriate basis for judging student-faculty interaction. Large universities often pad their ratios by counting graduate students who teach undergraduate courses as faculty. Other schools distort their figures by including part-time professors, or full-time research and emeritus faculty who do not teach at all.

Many public universities maintain quotas for resident students who transfer from community colleges. These minimums usually are set by state laws enacted to encourage and provide motivated community-college students the opportunity to apply to major public universities within their respective home state. Often such transferees comprise a substantial proportion of a state university's incoming transfer students. If such minimums are on public record, this figure might be included in future editions of *The Insider's Guide* in order to serve this large body of students transferring from community college.

Previous editions of this guide included a percentage of international students. *The Insider's Guide* is aimed primarily at an American readership. Since the international student percentage was never greater than 9 percent in previous editions, the figure was dropped in favor of one that would better serve the needs of a predominantly American audience (percentage of students from in-state/out-of-state). International students should not feel slighted by this.

Alabama

Auburn University

Address: 202 Mary Martin Hall, Auburn University, AL 36849-5145
Phone: 334-844-4080
E-mail address: admissions@auburn.edu
Web site URL: www.auburn.edu
Founded: 1856
Private or Public: public
Religious affiliation: none
Location: suburban
Undergraduate enrollment: 18,616
Total enrollment: 21,525
Percent Male/Female: 52%/48%
Percent Minority: 9%
Percent African-American: 7%

Percent Asian: 1%
Percent Hispanic: 1%
Percent Native-American: 1%
Percent in-state/out-of-state: 69%/31%
Percent Pub HS: 83%
Number of Applicants: 10,542
Percent Accepted: 88%
Percent Accepted who enroll: 40%
Entering: 3,692
Transfers: 0
Application Deadline: 3 weeks prior to start of quarter
Mean SAT: 562 V, 580 M
Mean ACT: 23

Middle 50% SAT range: 480–590 V, 500–600 M
Middle 50% ACT range: 20–26
3 Most popular majors: business, engineering, education
Retention: 81%
Graduation rate: 29%
On-campus housing: 16%
Fraternities: 17%
Sororities: 30%
Library: 2,500,000 volumes
Tuition and Fees: $2,976 in; $8,766 out
Room and Board: $1,911
Financial aid, first-year: 11%

"Why do they have two mascots?" As you turn off the interstate on the way to Auburn University you'll drive over large tiger-paw prints showing you the way to the campus. Upon your arrival you'll meet Aubie the Tiger, who was 1997 NCAA mascot national champion. But at football games, you'll sing the War Eagle fight song and witness The Eagle in his cage outside Jordan-Hare Stadium. What does it all mean? At Auburn University, a school that prides itself on both its football and its friendliness, one emblem just isn't enough.

Two Heads Are Better Than One

Auburn University is divided into 12 different colleges. Students graduate with a major from one of these colleges, which include Agriculture; Architecture, Design, and Construction; Business; Education; Engineering; Forestry; Nursing; Human Sciences; Liberal Arts; Pharmacy; Science and Mathematics; and Veterinary Medicine. Once students declare their major at the end of their sophomore year, students are not ultimately bound to it and a change of major even between different colleges is easily accomplished. With some noted exceptions, Auburn students are pleased overall with their academic experiences. Grading is seen as fair, and homework is not too much of a burden, although as one student put it "your time here is all what you make of it. You can walk out without ever picking up a book, but you can also study your head off." While there are certainly exceptions, education is largely known as a "slack" major, while engineering and veterinary medicine are both considered "tough" and "prestigious." In addition to its tough subject matter, the math and science departments at Auburn also draw student criticism due to some of the faculty members. One student stated, "my teacher seemed to fall asleep during his own lecture, so I went in for a little personal help during office hours, and he fell asleep there too!" Other complaints stem from the fact that getting a professor or TA who speaks fluent English is often a rarity, although another student noted that the university is currently addressing this problem.

To Dorm or Not to Dorm

Freshmen aren't required to live on campus so many choose among other options available to them. For those who do decide to reside in university housing, there are two main areas of the campus to live in: the Quad and the Hill. Dorms in both of these areas are divided by sex but have regular visiting hours for students of the opposite sex. Dorms are also segregated according to student interests. For example, there is Sewell, the dorm for athletes, and Broun and Harper which house many honors-program students. Another point of interest surrounding dorm life is that the majority of the dorms are strictly female. For unknown reasons, many more Auburn women decide to spend their freshman year in the dorms than their male counterparts.

For the majority of students who live off-campus, housing options are plentiful. Many students decide to rent apartments or houses. Residential complexes often have reputations associated with them, like the College Park Apartments, which is known as "party central." Other options include the Commons, an interesting blend of apartment and dorm that is not run by the university but still supplies younger students with an RA system in order to help them with any problems they may have adjusting to college life.

Students rate the food at Auburn's two main dining halls, War Eagle Court and Terrell, "just average," but they consider their overall food choices plentiful. There are several fast-food chains around campus for students on the go, as well as other university-run options like the Dow Deli, where students can make their own pizza and sandwiches. There is no common meal plan at Auburn, but students can and often do make use of their "Tiger Club"

card to send the bill for any food purchases home to Mom and Dad. For more upscale dining, the town of Auburn hosts a large array of popular restaurants like Applebee's and Ruby Tuesday's, along with local favorites like Gutherie's, where students joke that one can choose from "chicken fingers, chicken fingers, or chicken fingers."

Y'all Come Back Now, Ya Hear?

Socially, Auburn considers itself one of the preeminent universities nationwide. Students pride themselves on their southern hospitality and amiability, although the university is somewhat homogeneous. "There is definitely a student stereotype here," said one upperclassman, "and those who don't fit in might feel a little out of it."

On weekends, Auburn students know how to have fun. "Friday night party, Saturday night party, and Sunday recuperate" is how one student described her weekend schedule. Most of these parties occur either in private apartments or at the many fraternities and sororities around campus. The Greek scene of Auburn is somewhat different from that at other large Southern universities. While the Greek presence is large, the frats and sororities don't have their own houses and students reside in the dorms. Thus, the first three floors of most dorms are populated with members of one particular fraternity or sorority.

> **"There is definitely a student stereotype here," said one upperclassman, "and those who don't fit in might feel a little out of it."**

This doesn't keep the Greeks from having a good time, however. Their large band parties and dressy formals keep members entertained and active. The band parties are attractive to Greek and non-Greek alike, and while police are required to be present at these gettogethers, students claim limitations on underage drinking are virtually never enforced. The cops do, however, enforce one popular safety rule known as "Sober Drivers" at major parties. Volunteers give their services to get partiers home safely at the end of the night, and are required to be on call at all times. Students say that non-Greeks don't feel particularly pinched by a lack of activity at Auburn.

Sports also play a large role in campus activities for all levels of commitment. Auburn football is followed with incredible zeal, especially when such noted rivals as the University of Georgia, Florida, and of course, Alabama come knocking. While no other varsity sport garners the attention given to football, Auburn plays host to a large group of well-supported intercollegiate teams. For those who take their sports a little less seriously, there are also many intramural and pickup games occurring on the campus at all times, as well as a bevy of local lakes and parks to which students frequently retreat.

Many students also engage themselves with a large array of social and community service organizations present around the campus. Popular groups include the University Program Council, commonly known as the UPC, which strives to bring famous entertainers and musicians to campus, and Campus Crusade for Christ, which regularly boasts over 800 members. Service groups also include Habitat for Humanity, which builds housing for the underprivileged in the area, Impact and Uplift, two groups that work with local families and children, and the Circle K, which works in conjunction with the local Kiwanas Club in community efforts.

A Walk in the Park

When asked to describe the campus, virtually every Auburn student replies "beautiful," "pretty," and "green." The campus is large enough that students don't feel cramped, yet not so big that getting from place to place is a problem. Grass and trees abound, and comparable redbrick buildings complete the campus.

When asked which of these buildings is the most noteworthy, most students reply with authority "the Haley Center." This behemoth of college life contains the university bookstore, cafeteria, and most of the large lecture halls on the campus. It is shaped into four quadrants that point (as rumor has it) towards four parts of Auburn life in decreasing importance, from Jordan-Hare Football Stadium to Draughton Library to Foy Student Union and finally to a 4-way intersection. Perhaps the importance of the intersection rests in Auburn's large automobile population. Cars have caused a slight dilemma on the campus due to a limited number of parking spaces. Most Auburn students do bring a vehicle to school, because as one student puts it, "a car is not a necessity for getting to classes, but socially it's a big plus." In fact, Auburn students seem to regard their entire collegiate experience as a big plus and with two mascots, how could you go wrong? —*Robbie Berschinski*

FYI
The three best things about Auburn are "the beautiful campus, the school spirit, and the academic diversity."
The three worst things about Auburn are "the size, the foreign-speaking TAs, and living in Alabama."
The three things every Auburn student should do before graduating are "go to a "Beat 'Bama" pep rally, relax during Splash into Spring week, and run in the 2.7 mile Cake Race across campus."
One thing I wish I'd known before coming to Auburn is "how humid it is."

Birmingham-Southern College

Address: 900 Arkadelphia Road, Box 549008 Birmingham, AL 35254
Phone: 205-226-4696
E-mail address: admission@bsc.edu
Web site URL: www.bsc.edu
Founded: 1856
Private or Public: private
Religious affiliation: United Methodist
Location: urban
Undergraduate enrollment: 1,434
Total enrollment: 1,531
Percent Male / Female: 40% / 60%
Percent Minority: 17%
Percent African-American: 12%

Percent Asian: 4%
Percent Hispanic: 0.5%
Percent Native-American: 0.5%
Percent in-state / out-of-state: 89% / 11%
Percent Pub HS: NA
Number of Applicants: 867
Percent Accepted: 95%
Percent Accepted who enroll: 41%
Entering: 337
Transfers: 0
Application Deadline: 15 Jan
Mean SAT: 598 V, 588 M
Mean ACT: 26

Middle 50% SAT range: 540–660 V, 530–640 M
Middle 50% ACT range: 23–29
3 Most popular majors: business administration, biology, English
Retention: 84%
Graduation rate: 48%
On-campus housing: 82%
Fraternities: 62%
Sororities: 65%
Library: 250,000 volumes
Tuition and Fees: $15,498 in; $15,498 out
Room and Board: $5,460
Financial aid, first-year: 47%

It's your senior year and you're sitting in your room stumped, with piles of applications lying around, without a clue about how to differentiate one college from another. Suddenly, out of the corner of your eye, you spot something. Is it the physics book you haven't opened since September? Is it a polished-off bottle of Dubra that you forget to shove under the bed? Is it your ex-girlfriend who, since her parents' divorce, has insisted on bumming around your house even though you broke up with her in seventh grade? No, it's a brand-spanking-new application from Birmingham-Southern College. Birmingham-Southern, ranked by *U.S. News & World Report* as one of the top liberal arts colleges in the country, should be on any applicant's short list. Founded in 1856, it is a college that's devoted to an undergraduate liberal arts education, hell-bent on shaping you into a viable member of society, and determined to help you experience all that Birmingham, Alabama, has to offer.

Polymaths!! So Many Polymaths!!

While decent academics can be found at many an institution and certainly are present at Birmingham-Southern, according to students, small class sizes, close student–teacher relationships, and highly accessible faculty are what make Birmingham-Southern unique. And while lecture classes abound, seminar formats are popular among the BSC faculty. First and foremost, BSC is a liberal arts university, and it requires of its students a working knowledge of numerous subjects. Students must accrue one unit credit in each of the following subjects: art, history, lab science, language, literature, math, philosophy/religion, social science, and writing. Following these initial core courses, students must take two additional arts and humanities courses and then an additional math or science, followed by two units outside of one's major or minor. Undaunted by the requirements, many students immerse themselves in pre-medical and pre-law tracks, which are both grueling career-oriented majors. Slacker majors, according to one student, are non-existent, "Everything is hard here, because it's a hard school."

But finding interesting and enjoyable classes is not difficult, so fulfilling the general education requirements is rarely looked upon as a burden. For 50 of the best and the brightest, BSC offers an honors college that has accelerated courses and even smaller class sizes, largely taught in seminar format. Other options include the Leadership Studies Program and the Service Learning Program. Students are assigned an advisor, often within the student's major, who assists with course selection, provides general guidance, and calms students during the trying academic times that they will likely encounter while enrolled at BSC. Good time-management skills are necessary to survive at BSC.

One aspect of their BSC education that students universally praise is the "Interim" session held every January. BSC still has the two-semester system, during which students generally take four classes. But the January interim session allows them to either take one class or travel abroad. Studying in such destinations as Greece, England, and France is always a popular option for the Alabama-weary student. Next year it is rumored that the study abroad options will include trips to Australia and New Zealand.

> **"Everything is hard here, because it's a hard school."**

The administration is reportedly very responsive to student complaints and concerns. The president routinely E-mails the students, informing them of the latest high-level decisions, and takes substantive complaints lodged against faculty very seriously.

Healthy, Wealthy, and Wise

Affluence is the hallmark of BSC students. Students report that most of their peers are upper-middle-class, white, and from some sort of prep or boarding school. While the environment may, from this brief description, sound relatively homogenous, the school has a minority enrollment of almost 20% and a substantial body of foreign students. But despite the apparent ethnic diversity, geographic diversity is lacking. Almost 90% of BSC students come from in-state, as BSC is a popular college option within the Alabama private school community.

Social life on campus centers around the Greek system at the school, with Naty Light being the preferred beer. Frat row is a frequent destination for weekend partiers, and the majority of students on campus are involved with either a sorority or a fraternity. Sigma Nu and SAE are known to throw particularly kickin' parties. Parties, save formal events, are generally open to all students regardless of Greek membership. Some, however, decry what they say is an overreliance among students on the Greek system. Traveling to the Southside of Birmingham is popular among fun-loving BSC students. There one can find myriad clubs and bars, generally for ages 18 and up. The drinking age is 21, of course, but no worries for the campus minors, as BSC is a "very wet" campus.

Major campus-wide events include the Entertainment Festivals in the fall and spring. Headliner bands in the past have included both Southern Comfort and Train. The college also sponsors free movie nights at the local cinema for interested students. The dating scene on campus is small, and most students search off campus for potential mates. At BSU, maintaining a relationship with a significant high school sweetheart or off-campus beau is usually not a problem. With most students coming from Alabama and the campus being a mere five-minute drive from downtown Birmingham, getting to campus for a little pillow talk is relatively easy. Of course, not everyone is involved in serious commitments, and random hookups are reportedly rampant.

Living Large

Living accommodations are regarded as adequate. The "Caf," BSC vernacular for the cafeteria, has numerous dining options designed to please the palate, including Pizza Hut, homestyle cookin', a grill, a deli, and a salad bar. The dorms themselves are all single-sex, with the most liberal option being 24-hour visitation. Hansen and Bruno are the most spacious and well outfitted of all the dorms. Living options range from singles to large suites with common rooms and bathroom.

Other suites have community bathrooms and kitchens. Each floor of the dorms has a residential advisor, who, depending on temperament, may or may not strictly enforce all university policies. Students report that RAs are readily available to lend help or a sympathetic ear to the concerned freshman.

The rest of the campus contains some fairly modern buildings, including the Norton Campus Center, which contains the food court, movies, computers, and games. The Cellar, a coffee shop on campus, is a popular option for students, having an open mike night on Thursdays and on other days providing a convenient place to study and chat with friends. The Learning Center is the place for hard-core studiers. The campus architecture runs the gamut from modern to neoclassical, with everything well contained and within easy walking distance.

Baseball and basketball are fairly big on campus. BSC just moved up into Division I play, something about which everyone on campus is excited. Besides sporting options, students wholly devote themselves to community service activities. BSC is, after all, a Methodist school with a tradition of lending a helping hand to the less fortunate. In addition, the student newspaper, the *Hilltop News*, attracts student writers, while the student government reins in the budding politicians on campus. BSC truly provides young scholars with the opportunity to live, learn, and grow while at the same time offering up a healthy dose of southern comfort, hospitality, and charm.—*Sean McBride*

FYI
The three best things about attending BSC are "the Southside, study abroad programs, and the students."
The three worst things about attending BSC are "the lack of diversity, frats everywhere, Abercrombie and Fitch all over the place."
The three things every student should do before graduating from BSC are "go to Frat Row, pull an all-nighter with friends, and get fined by your RA."
One thing I'd like to have known before coming here is "how everyone is Alabaman!"

T u s k e g e e   U n i v e r s i t y

Address: 102 Old Administration Building Tuskegee, AL 36088
Phone: 334-727-8500
E-mail address: admi@acd.tusk.edu
Web site URL: www.tusk.edu
Founded: 1881
Private or Public: private
Religious affiliation: none
Location: rural
Undergraduate enrollment: 2,859
Total enrollment: 3,023
Percent Male/Female: 45%/55%
Percent Minority: 96%

Percent African-American: 95%
Percent Asian: 0.5%
Percent Hispanic: NA
Percent Native-American: NA
Percent in-state/out-of-state: 29%/71%
Percent Pub HS: 80%
Number of Applicants: 2,834
Percent Accepted: 65%
Percent Accepted who enroll: 46%
Entering: 851
Transfers: 0
Application Deadline: 15 Apr
Mean SAT: 400 V, 500 M
Mean ACT: 20

Middle 50% SAT range: NA
Middle 50% ACT range: NA
3 Most popular majors: electrical engineering, biology, business administration
Retention: 77%
Graduation rate: 50%
On-campus housing: 0%
Fraternities: 6%
Sororities: 5%
Library: 310,000 volumes
Tuition and Fees: $9,500 in; $9,500 out
Room and Board: NA
Financial aid, first-year: 88%

Founded in 1881 by Booker T. Washington, Tuskegee University (formerly Tuskegee Institute) has drawn generations of African-American men and women searching for a strong, higher education and for cultural enrichment. Tuskegee's close-knit student community lives and studies in the shadow of one of America's most important African-American universities.

Changing Tradition

Tuskegee was founded upon the concept that African-Americans ought to train in specific, technical fields in order to gain a competitive stance in the job market. This approach has changed over the years, however, and today the school provides its undergraduates with a liberal arts education. Even with the change in curriculum, all freshmen are required to take an orientation course, which consists of history of the university—including the mandatory reading of Booker T. Washington's *Up from Slavery*—and advice for adapting to college life. Other requirements include two semesters each of English and math.

Most Tuskegee students are engineering or science majors. Pre-vet, pre-med, and nursing programs receive high student praise. Many introductory classes enroll between 40 and 50 students, but the average class size ranges from 20 to 30 students. The small class sizes and the fact that very few courses use TAs allow for interaction between students and faculty. Overall, students give Tuskegee's academics a high rating, calling the school "demanding." However, some students lament what they called "recent budget cuts" that have increased the faculty-student ratio and cut into instruction quality. The Guide could not independently confirm this allegation.

Tuskegee's history is clearly visible around its campus. Some of the brick buildings were built by students when the school was founded. Many of these buildings' interiors have been recently renovated. Although administrators claim that these renovations have produced air-conditioning, increased ethernet access, and an overall increase in comfort, students complain that the renovations were "incomplete because of funding problems."

Despite such recent work, however, students argue that the library still "needs work." It is small and limited in resources, and as a result students doing research projects often have to travel to nearby Auburn University to find information. In an effort to improve their library system, Tuskegee joined an interlibrary loan system and began a renovation project, to be completed shortly.

In Loco Parentis, or Just Loco

Dorms are the other main source of student complaints. Students must remain on campus for their freshman and sophomore years. One student called the dorms "ancient." A typical room is sparsely furnished. "You had better bring things that make you feel at home," said one undergrad, because "there's no real cozy feeling." Also, because the school's traditional atmosphere lends itself to conservative social rules, all dorms are single-sex, and members of the opposite sex are never permitted to visit each other's rooms. To help enforce these rules, male and female dorms are separated by a 10-minute walk. In addition, the university staff keeps a close eye on dorms; students are not allowed to be on the "wrong" side of campus after 11 P.M. and, if caught, may face punishment.

As a result of the strict rules and old facilities, many upperclassmen choose to move off campus. One student said of the coed policies, "I love my campus, but I had to leave it because of the rules." In an attempt to persuade more students to stay, however, the administration has announced plans for the construction of new on-campus apartments, but little has been said about the relaxation of rules.

Students tend to meet in the student union, which contains a movie theater, a grill, a game room, and offices for student organizations. The new cafeteria is another popular meeting place. Students report that the food quality is "ten times better" than it was several years ago. Tuskegee's many clubs and organizations also help to bring students together. Some of the biggest clubs are the state clubs, which unite students hailing from the same states to plan activities relating to their home turf. African-American groups such as the National Society of Black Engineers are also popular. Students are active in community service, and many students volunteer at the local hospital.

> **"The town of Tuskegee offers nothing except seclusion from the modern world, but you learn a lot trapped in the wilderness."**

Football and basketball games generate great excitement at Tuskegee. Students are sure to use their tickets for games against Morehouse College and Alabama State University. Homecoming is one of the biggest social events of the year. Aside from football, however, varsity sports tend not to be so popular.

Student Solidarity

Social life at Tuskegee changes with the season. In the fall, football brings the student body together. In the spring, Greek Weeks and Springfest attract large crowds. While the Greek system is a strong presence on campus, students report that they do not feel an urge to rush. There is little animosity between the fraternities, but they reportedly have a "friendly rivalry." Officially, alcohol is prohibited on campus and students who are caught with it face fines or other penalties. As a result, on-campus drinking is not a big activity; those wishing to drink can just search for off-campus parties.

Many students consider the town of Tuskegee "slow," but students agree that it contains the basics for college life. And, as one student put it, "Tuskegee has a lot of potential to grow," adding, "but you come for the school—not the town."

Tuskegee students say their campus is safe and claim that it is "getting better." Additional lights have been installed around campus in the past few years, and security patrols keep increasing. Security is "much, much better about patrolling both night and day," said one student. It has "really increased from years past," she added.

Tuskegee has a history of enriching young minds both culturally and academically. To this day, students take pride in the beliefs upon which their school was founded. The administration is more conservative and tradition-bound than the student body, but students are willing to accept this conservatism in return for the Tuskegee experience. As one student said, "There are a lot of good people here and you can meet a lot of great minds—not to mention we're friends for life. People might complain about things here, but in the end, you don't want to leave."
—*Melissa Chan and Staff*

FYI
The three best things about attending Tuskegee are "the teachers are very helpful, the people are friendly, and the parties are EXCELLENT."
The three worst things about attending Tuskegee are "the administration seems to have no respect or regard for the students, the registration process takes 3 days, and the dorms are really run-down."
The three things every student should do before graduating from Tuskegee are "try the food at the Chicken Coop, go to Homecoming, and visit the George Washington Carver Museum on campus."
One thing I'd like to have known before coming here is "that you need a car to survive here—the nearest mall is like 20 minutes away. The town of Tuskegee offers nothing except seclusion from the modern world, but you learn a lot trapped in the wilderness."

University of Alabama

Address: 1530 Third Avenue South Birmingham, AL 35294-1150
Phone: 205-348-5666
E-mail address: uaadmit@enroll.ua.edu
Web site URL: www.ua.edu
Founded: 1831
Private or Public: public
Religious affiliation: none
Location: suburban
Undergraduate enrollment: 14,357
Total enrollment: 18,744
Percent Male/Female: 48%/52%
Percent Minority: 16%
Percent African-American: 14%

Percent Asian: 0.5%
Percent Hispanic: 0.5%
Percent Native-American: 0.5%
Percent in-state/out-of-state: 75%/25%
Percent Pub HS: NA
Number of Applicants: 7,433
Percent Accepted: 89%
Percent Accepted who enroll: 41%
Entering: 2,720
Transfers: 1,231
Application Deadline: 8/15, 3/1
Mean SAT: 523 V, 532 M
Mean ACT: 22

Middle 50% SAT range: 480–620 V, 480–610 M
Middle 50% ACT range: 20–26
3 Most popular majors: business adminstration, communication, education
Retention: 80%
Graduation rate: 55%
On-campus housing: 70%
Fraternities: 15%
Sororities: 19%
Library: 2,187,000 volumes
Tuition and Fees: $2,872 in; $7,722 out
Room and Board: $4,154
Financial aid, first-year: NA

University of Alabama students have an enormous amount of pride in their school. It's not just the beautiful architecture ("This place must have more Greek columns than Athens!") that gets raves from undergrads. Rather, in the words of one senior, "The spirit I saw here is what attracted me in the first place. I've lived in college towns and have never seen anything like this place on a game day." In all likelihood, if you attend the University of Alabama a significant portion of your free time is going to be spent supporting tremendously successful athletic teams. In addition, Alabama students manage to fit academics and many extracurricular activities into their busy lives on the warm, southern campus.

The Necessities

Ferguson Center, the student union, houses the supply store, post office, dining hall, small movie theater, and food court with fast-food chain restaurants such as Burger King, Blimpie, Manchu Wok, and Chick-Fil-A. Taco Casa, students claim, "puts Taco Bell to shame!" On the meal plan, students buy 5, 10, or 15 meals a week plus $200 of credit per semester to use at the Ferguson Center and restaurants near campus. Students agree the food is acceptable for cafeteria cuisine. "It's nothing to write home about," one student said, and another added he "wouldn't call it home cooking." What does get raves, however, is the City Café's homemade biscuits with molasses on top.

For students who don't reside in Greek houses, dorm life is typical of campus living, getting "pretty loud" at times. "The dorms are not an ideal living situation, but you don't spend much time in them anyway." Freshmen are not required to live on campus, but for those who want to, suites with bathrooms and kitchens are available, as are coed and single-sex dorms. Friedman Hall is popular for its newer stoves and refrigerators. A junior advised that the smaller dorms tend to have bigger rooms.

Academics at Alabama

While many students study in their rooms, many study in Gorgas Library, which is the main library. Other options include the Science and Engineering Library, the

Business Library (where many go to socialize while studying), Mclure Library and the Arts and Sciences Library.

The options of what to study are diverse as well. In addition to the College of Arts and Sciences, Alabama houses a business school and colleges of engineering, nursing, and communication. Other schools include the College of Education, the College of Human Environmental Sciences and the College of Social Work. At the College of Arts and Sciences (which contains undergraduate liberal arts majors as well as many pre-professional programs) distributional requirements ensure that graduates of UA are well-rounded. These requirements include writing-intensive courses, computer or foreign-language literacy, humanities, literature, fine arts, history, social and behavioral sciences, natural sciences, and mathematics.

'Bama undergrads may take advantage of the prestigious honor program for incoming freshmen with high test scores and grades. This program allows for more student-faculty interaction, since participants work and research with professors. Also prestigious is the Computer-Based Honors Program. Along with the program's prestige comes a lot of hard work: one student recalled an assignment in which he was given a week to learn JAVA and write a complex program for presentation. The Women's Honors Program also allows students to capitalize on the intellectual resources of the University.

One of the biggest concerns for UA students is the lack of recognition given to its solid academics. Despite the school's vibrant and respected business and law schools, its noted communications program, and the successful accounting department, for the most part, UA's academics go unrecognized. Some students lament the lack of recognition; others consider UA "our little secret."

Crimson and White

As the team with the most national championships of any other college football team, the Crimson Tide garners the passion and spirit of many loyal Alabama fans. It would not be an overstatement to say that football is life for much of the student body. Much of the excitement cen-ters around an intense rivalry with Auburn University. Not to be outdone, the women's gymnastics team, the men's baseball team, and the girls' softball team sporting events are also very well attended. Intramural sports are also popular: students devote time to flag football, Ultimate Frisbee, soccer, and basketball. One popular place where students can be found playing casual sports is the Quad. One student remarked, "With its oaks and gentle breeze, this ten acre park in the middle of campus makes the school's character."

The Machine

Besides athletics, Greek life is one of the main binding factors among University of Alabama students. Esquire magazine once ran an article on the country's most powerful fraternity located at Alabama titled "The Machine." The article reported that this UA organization, a secret fraternity of fraternities, allegedly controlled student government.

> **The homecoming pep rally is an unforgettable event involving "fireworks, the Million Dollar Band, old alumni, a four-story bonfire, and 20,000 of your closest friends."**

According to students, the majority of voters in SGA elections still are Greek, and although Alabama students held a constitutional convention on the electoral system, a staff member of the Crimson White, the campus daily newspaper, said he believes the changes were purely cosmetic. "In a race in which a Greek was running a Greek won," he said of a recent SGA election. Despite the strong presence and influence of fraternities and sororities, students say there is no great pressure to rush and that it is possible to have a social life, if not political power, outside the Greek system. Students note that other popular activities are the Campus Crusade for Christ, the Crimson White newspaper, the national championship-winning debate team, the honorary organizations, and the community services groups. Active theatre, dance, and music programs also contribute to the diversity of cultural entertainment that UA has to offer.

The University of Alabama is known as a party school by outsiders and students don't go out of their way to discourage this view. Homecoming in late October is the biggest social event of the year. The homecoming pep rally is an unforgettable event involving "fireworks, the Million Dollar Band, old alumni, a four-story bonfire, and 20,000 of your closest friends." During homecoming, students can see the bond between the school and the community as "frat boys rally next to families."

In the spring, a big-name band performs on campus. Past performers have included Jimmy Buffett, Tom Petty, and James Taylor. On the weekends, students frequent the Strip, a street lined with restaurants, bars, and clubs. Many students have cars to get around in Tuscaloosa, which many call a typical college town. About five minutes away is the community of Northport while Birmingham is less than an hour's drive. Something that

every student should do, one senior claims, is to "drive somewhere insane on the weekend before exams and drive straight back that night." Popular road-tripping destinations have included Atlanta and the beach. On weekends without big basketball or football games, many students head home or to nearby Auburn.

The UA Student

"Most people think of UA as a typical white, southern, Greek school with a lot of alcohol. Few people actually fit the stereotype. There are students from many backgrounds here, though most are from Alabama and, reflecting the region, the majority are white." Students say they believe that all races and religions are welcome at UA, though they acknowledge that their school is relatively conservative. Efforts by the Student Government Association are aimed at improving diversity awareness and relations, to ensure a comfortable environment for all students on UA's campus. —*Marti Page*

FYI
The three best things about attending UA are "the Quad, football season, and flexibility of classes."
The three worst things about attending UA are "the lack of recognition for academics, the distance between classes, and the division between the Greek and independent students."
The three things that every student should do before graduating from UA are "eating breakfast at City Café at 5 in the morning after an all-nighter, attend the homecoming pep rally, and road trip to random locations."
One thing I'd like to have known before coming here is "that the University of Alabama is truly what you make of it."

University of South Alabama

Address: Administration Building Room 182 Mobile, AL 36688-0002
Phone: 334-460-6141
E-mail address: admiss@jaguan1.usouthal.edu
Web site URL: www.usouthal.edu
Founded: 1963
Private or Public: public
Religious affiliation: none
Location: urban
Undergraduate enrollment: 9,566
Total enrollment: NA
Percent Male/Female: 44%/56%
Percent Minority: 15%

Percent African-American: 13%
Percent Asian: 1%
Percent Hispanic: 1%
Percent Native-American: NA
Percent in-state/out-of-state: 77%/23%
Percent Pub HS: 92%
Number of Applicants: 2,739
Percent Accepted: 94%
Percent Accepted who enroll: 42%
Entering: 1,079
Transfers: 0
Application Deadline: 10 Sep
Mean SAT: NA

Mean ACT: 23
Middle 50% SAT range: NA
Middle 50% ACT range: 20–25
3 Most popular majors: nursing, health and physical education, adult degree program
Retention: 62%
Graduation rate: 25%
On-campus housing: 21%
Fraternities: 12%
Sororities: 9%
Library: NA
Tuition and Fees: $2,911 in; $5,581 out
Room and Board: $3,081
Financial aid, first-year: 84%

The University of South Alabama, "South" or "USA" to students, offers a bit of everything. It provides both a traditional Greek scene for the typical college age student, and unique dorm accommodations for non-traditional older students. The campus itself reflects a mixture of environments—the main campus sprawls across several grassy acres in the western outskirts of Mobile, but many classes, particularly in health-related fields, are located in the much more urban downtown area. Although relatively young, South is growing into a more traditional university as it ages.

Academic Options

South offers a variety of academic options to its students, including traditional degrees, an honors program, and several degrees geared towards older students returning to school. The university is divided into nine colleges: Arts and Sciences, Computer and Information, Business, Education, Medicine, Nursing, Engineering, Allied Health, and Continuing Education. The core requirements differ from college to college; however, all students must take two classes with a writing emphasis, although they do not have

to be English classes. Workloads vary according to majors as well. Health-related majors, such as nursing and physical therapy are considered strong departments, and students must have GPAs in the 3.8 range to be considered for admission to the BS/MS programs in these majors in their junior year. The Continuing Education program offers many night classes for students that work during the day and many students pursue this option. "Going to school here certainly is convenient for those of us who work all day," notes one night student.

Students generally praise their professors as "very helpful, not intimidating at all." Most classes are small enough to allow professor-student interaction, with average class size between 20 and 40 students. Professors teach nearly all the classes, which are primarily in lecture format. Students complain that due to poor English speaking skills, math professors are close to impossible to understand, but reading the textbook usually gave adequate instruction. Professors are happy to meet with students during office hours. "Go visit your professors," one student advised. "It's the best advice that I got freshman year—professors are helpful and inspiring as well as being nice people." The Honors Program offers opportunities for extended involvement with faculty. It pairs students with a faculty mentor with whom they do research and community service projects.

Registration for new students is conducted on campus during orientation. Everyone else registers over the phone, and priority is dictated by GPA. There are caps to classes, but students say they can often get around these by talking to professors and administrators. South recently changed its academic calendar from the quarter to the semester system. One student wonders if professors have completely adapted to the longer terms, commenting that the number of tests in some classes have not changed despite the lengthier time period.

Commuter Campus?

In years past, South has been primarily a commuter school, with many of its students living in Mobile or surrounding areas and driving to class every day. This is still true for many students, and, as a result, their interactions in the campus' social life are limited. Clubs meet in the afternoon, for instance, which is an inconvenient time for students who work fulltime. Many attribute the lack of school spirit to the fact that so many students do not live on campus or participate in campus events. "You have to jump into campus life here; nothing is going to pull you in like the school spirit that other schools have," says a frustrated student.

There are signs that this stereotype is beginning to fade, however. More efforts are being made to involve commuters, a newsletter, for example, tells commuter students about campus events. The recent completion of on-campus housing for Greek organizations is in part aimed at increasing student residence on campus. Another sign of growth is the Mitchell Center, the new home to the basketball team and site of concerts (Indigo Girls and Better Than Ezra played recently) as well as other campuswide events. The administration began fielding a football team, which many believe would bolster school spirit, especially in a region so focused on football. Alumni are very active in this effort as well and view a football team as necessary to put South on par with other state universities that have strong football programs, namely Alabama and Auburn.

> One student described her fellow classmates as "not extreme—you don't see a bunch of people with spikes or piercings running around here."

Few live on campus all four years, but those who do, dorm life is a great opportunity to meet other students. Epsilon dorms are newer, and their interior hallways are more conducive to getting to know others in the dorm. Other dorms include Beta and Gamma, which are set up like apartments, and Delta, which resembles hotel rooms. All freshmen who live on campus must have the university meal plan. But limited cafeteria hours on weekends reportedly create problems for meal plan holders. Resident assistants in each dorm occasionally sponsor activities to build community spirit. "Living in dorms is a terrific way to meet people—most of the people I hang out with now I met freshman year in dorms," raves one junior. South recently implemented the Essence Program designed to ease the transition to college life and encourage greater student involvement. It has several components, including living on campus, eating together with other students in the program, and an emphasis on mentoring and advising.

BYOB

The Greek system is responsible for most of the campus' social scene. The membership isn't huge, but they have a strong presence on campus since most of the students who join sororities or fraternities are also active in other activities at South. Non-Greeks are welcome at all social functions except date parties. The campus is officially dry, so frat parties do not usually supply alcohol (they can obtain licenses for special occasions). Party-goers are encouraged to bring their own drinks. Written warnings are given for alcohol violations and for storing alcohol in dorm rooms. Nevertheless, students emphasize that South is a dry campus "in name only."

A myriad of other activities cater to a range of interests. Outdoor movies, clubs relating to a particular major or to specific interests, like backpacking and rock climbing, and student government are some popular extracurricular activities. Religious alternatives are numerous, and include student fellowships, Bible studies, and mission trips. Students can also found a club if they so desire. Organizations often develop theme weeks to focus attention on a particular issue, like rape awareness, and speakers regularly visit campus in conjunction with these events. Sports are another option for students—the basketball team has made recent appearances in the NCAA Tournament and the baseball team regularly plays in the postseason. Intramurals cater to less serious athletes, and the on-campus gym is more than adequate for students looking for a good workout.

While the university's administration has made several changes to enrich the life of the school, characteristics of the student body remain the same. Nearly all students are from Alabama or surrounding states. Many are older students returning for a degree as they change careers or parents going back to school—as many as half the students are over twenty-one. Regardless of their age, students seem pretty uniform. One undergrad described her fellow classmates as "not extreme—you don't see a bunch of people with spikes or piercings running around here."

With the advent of new programs and buildings (the Mitchell Center and a new Fine Arts building are recent additions), South is going through growing pains as well. Poor investing, by the committee that controls the school's endowment, has led to the loss of a substantial amount of money. The administration is facing questions as it tries to institute a football team and as students protest the school's status as a dry campus. Nevertheless, the concerted effort to improve the quality of students' experiences have resulted in many changes that are fostering a great sense of community in this deep South school.
—*Alexa Frankenberg*

FYI

The three best things about attending South are "helpful, knowledgeable professors, strong programs in health-related fields, and a wide variety of activities."

The three worst things about attending South are "no school spirit, parking, and no football team."

The three things that every student should do before graduating from South are "play oozeball (volleyball in a knee-deep mud pit), go to an event in the Mitchell Center, and take advantage of the fine arts offerings."

One thing I'd like to have known before coming here is "that it's much different from other colleges in that it lacks of school spirit."

Alaska

University of Alaska/Fairbanks

Address: PO Box 757480
Fairbanks, AK 99775-
7480
Phone: 907-474-7500
E-mail address:
fyapply@uaf.edu
Web site URL: www.uaf.edu
Founded: 1917
Private or Public: public
Religious affiliation: none
Location: suburban
**Undergraduate
enrollment:** 3,991
Total enrollment: 9,012
Percent Male/Female:
44%/56%
Percent Minority: 26%
Percent African-American:
4%
Percent Asian: 3%

Percent Hispanic: 3%
Percent Native-American:
16%
**Percent in-state/out-of-
state:** 90%/10%
Percent Pub HS: NA
Number of Applicants:
1,301
Percent Accepted: 90%
**Percent Accepted who
enroll:** 68%
Entering: 790
Transfers: 0
Application Deadline:
1 Aug
Mean SAT: 462 V, 495 M
Mean ACT: NA
Middle 50% SAT range:
450–590 V,
560–580 M

Middle 50% ACT range:
18–25
3 Most popular majors:
education, biological
sciences, business
administration
Retention: 64%
Graduation rate: 26%
On-campus housing:
NA
Fraternities: 1%
Sororities: 1%
Library: 1,800,000
volumes
Tuition and Fees: $3,390
in; $8,310 out
Room and Board:
$4,150
Financial aid, first-year:
62%

At the University of Alaska at Fairbanks, Alaska's first state university, moose promenade through the streets and boiling water dumped outside freezes before reaching the ground. One student reported that even nose hairs become tiny icicles in the sub-zero Alaskan air. Yet, students who are hardy enough to brave the not-so-hospitable climate receive a unique and rewarding educational experience.

Unusual Academic Opportunities

All University of Alaska at Fairbanks (UAF) undergraduates must take a preliminary course in library skills as well as fulfill distributional requirements in communications, humanities, social sciences, mathematics, and the natural sciences. The university also offers an honors program that requires the completion of 27

credits as well as a senior thesis. Classes within this program range from "Aesthetic Appreciation" to "Differential Equations." UAF offers classes in environmental engineering, military science, and wildlife management. Additionally, there are two schools that provide students with excellent internship and research opportunities: the School of Fisheries and Ocean Sciences and the School of Mineral Engineering. For example, one special program enables students to spend a semester in the Arctic, offering an "amazing field-study experience."

Students are quick to point out that UAF is also the home of Denali, a supercomputer with one of the largest memories in the world. Although mostly graduate students and other researchers use it, Denali is accessible to undergrads as well. As one student notes, "Denali is just another example of the kind of unique, hands-on educational opportunities we are so lucky to have at our fingertips."

Another academic highlight is the renowned University of Alaska Museum, which attracts visitors every year, making the university a top tourist attraction in the state. Over a million objects, from fine arts to biological specimens, are housed in the museum's imposing, modern architectural framework.

Other prominent facilities enhance the UAF campus, too. Students at UAF hibernate in the all-hours room of the central Elmer E. Rasmuson Library for serious studying. The main social retreat is Wood Center, a two-level student center that includes a bowling alley, arcade, pub, and food court.

A Mixed Bag

Most UAF students live on campus for their first and second years. The eight dorms are divided into Upper and Lower Campus. Seven of the dorms are co-ed, while one is all-female. Students report that Lower Campus residence halls, especially McIntosh (the all-female dorm), are smaller and have a stronger community atmosphere. Alcohol-free housing is also available in Nerland Hall and suite-style living is available in the newly renovated Wickersham Hall.

Recently, dorm renovations for both the inside and the outside of existing buildings on Lower Campus have spruced up campus. In addition to renovations, the university also undertook the construction of a new multi-million-dollar residence hall specifically for Native Alaskan students. The dorm provides 25 to 30 students with an environment that will ease the transition from village to university life.

In addition to the eight dorms at UAF, there is the Student Apartment Complex, which offers students a chance to experience the feeling of living off campus without "actually having to deal with the nitty-gritty details of living off." Roughly half the student body lives off campus in Fairbanks, mostly in small cabins or special sections of local hotels reserved for students. Thus, undergraduate living at UAF is "a mixed bag and you can pretty much find a living arrangement that suits your needs."

The town of Fairbanks is a few minutes' drive or, alternatively, a short, $1.50 bus trip away from central campus. Fairbanks boasts a movie theater, several malls, restaurants, bars, and grocery stores. Though many students have cars, they report that "parking on campus is a hassle, although a shuttle bus does run from parking lots to the main campus."

UAF security "keeps an eye on those who live off- and on- campus." Security includes campus police patrols, nightly escort services, exterior lighting for pathways, and emergency phones strategically placed around campus. Guests also must leave a picture ID at the check-in desk upon entering any residence hall.

Eats and Social Treats

Students who live on campus must be on a meal plan, which one student thought "would explain the reason why half of the university lives off campus!" The food at the university's dining hall, called Commons, inspires descriptions that range from "bland" to "disgusting and fattening." Nevertheless, Commons is one of the more popular places for students to hang out and socialize. As one student joked, "Even if you don't know what to talk about, you can always chat about your eats—always a good topic of conversation." For alternative fare, students head over to the Wood Center, which offers hungry undergraduates pizza, hamburgers, and coffee. The Wood Center also becomes a place for entertainment as well. In the past, the Bust-a-Gut comedy series at the Wood Center Pub has featured big-name stand-up comedians, such as Chuck Milligan, Greg Fitsimmons, and Scott Falconbride. As one senior said, "these events are a big treat for us."

> **"Living and learning here is a remarkable experience."**

The majority of entertainment and social activity for UAF students, however, relies heavily on the weather. Popular outdoor activities include cross-country and downhill skiing and sledding. Students say that since the winters are so dark and cold, drinking is often prevalent "to warm us up." One student felt that the administration follows an "out of sight, out of mind" policy toward drinking on campus. In the fall, UAF students celebrate the coming of winter with Starvation Gulch, a carnival that includes a bonfire contest and "celebrity auction" for such treats as dinner with the university president. In April, UAF students commemorate the arrival of spring with events like Spring Meltdown, Spring Breakup, and All Case Day (an event where students try to "drink a case of beer before midnight"). Students also participate in mud volleyball games and, from several stories up, a watermelon toss and egg drop. No matter the season, UAF students enjoy school-sponsored dances and ice-skating in their own indoor rink.

The harsh winter weather limits UAF's intercollegiate outdoor sports program, but students and the surrounding community enthusiastically support the university's Nanooks Division I hockey team (whose name comes from the Eskimo word for polar bear). The cross-country ski team also performs well, and the rifle team, despite little fan support, ranks among the best in the NCAA. Other varsity sports include basketball and volleyball. Intramural sports (IMs) are popular on campus, especially volleyball, basketball, hockey, and broomball (hockey without the skates). At the Student Recreation Center, students take advantage of a climbing wall, indoor track, weight room, swimming pool, and ice arena either to hone their skills for IMs or simply to keep in shape.

A Little Spice in Life

While many UAF students are from Alaska (the school's Rural Student Services helps students from small villages adjust to college), a good number of international students enroll, mostly from Canada and Russia. Native Americans make up the largest and most closely-knit minority group.

Undergrads range from the "preppy" to "granola" outdoorsy types who live in cabins year-round. UAF also has a large nontraditional (older) student population. Although one student described the general political attitude as "apathetic and independent," many undergrads are politically active in matters that directly affect them, such as defending their departments from budget cuts. Many also aspire to return to their native villages after graduation to help their respective communities.

Extracurricular activities at UAF include a weekly newspaper titled the Sun Star, the Associated Students of UAF (student government), and the student-run radio station. Students are active in everything from College Republicans to specialized groups such as the Student Ceramics Art Guild. As one student said, "You have the freedom to do pretty much whatever you want." Greek life is also a new social option at UAF, though so far, there is only one sorority and one fraternity (the only one in Alaska). Both focus on community service and neither has attracted a large membership.

Students cite the quality of residential life, low tuition price, and academic offerings as UAF's strong points, but some warn that undergrads unaccustomed to Alaska's long, dark winters can easily become depressed. Alaska is not for everyone. For those hardy people who do decide on UAF, "living and learning here is a remarkable experience." —*Melissa Chan*

FYI

The three best things about attending UAF are "the hands-on educational opportunities, the abundance of outdoor fun, and the friendly student-body."

The three worst things about attending UAF are "the lack of parking, the terrible dining food, and the freezing COLD!"

The three things that every student should do before graduating from UAF are "visit the University of Alaska Museum (it really has lots of cool stuff), take a winter nightcap to warm up, and partake in 'Arrival of Spring' celebrations."

One thing I'd like to have known before coming here is "that it gets so cold here your nose hairs freeze!"

Arizona

Arizona State University

Address: Box 870112
Tempe, AZ 85287-0112
Phone: 480-965-0112
E-mail address:
ugradadm@asuvm.inre.as
u.edu
Web site URL:
www.asu.edu
Founded: 1885
Private or Public: public
Religious affiliation: none
Location: suburban
**Undergraduate
enrollment:** 33,948
Total enrollment: 47,000
Percent Male / Female:
48% / 52%
Percent Minority: 21%
Percent African-American:
3%

Percent Asian: 5%
Percent Hispanic: 11%
Percent Native-American:
2%
**Percent in-state / out-of-
state:** 74% / 26%
Percent Pub HS: NA
Number of Applicants:
17,082
Percent Accepted:
80%
**Percent Accepted who
enroll:** 43%
Entering: 5,868
Transfers: 0
Application Deadline:
rolling
Mean SAT: 543 V,
557 M
Mean ACT: 23

Middle 50% SAT range:
490–600 V,
490–620 M
Middle 50% ACT range:
21–26
3 Most popular majors:
psychology, education,
business
Retention: 73%
Graduation rate: 48%
On-campus housing: 17%
Fraternities: 8%
Sororities: 6%
Library: 3,000,000
volumes
Tuition and Fees: $2,261
in; $9,413 out
Room and Board: $5,010
Financial aid, first-year:
56%

In a climate where you can wear shorts 10 months out of the year, it is no wonder that most students at Arizona State care more about their tan lines than their grade-point average. Situated in Tempe, in the heart of what the locals call the Valley of the Sun, Arizona State is often a victim of its location. The sun provides the students with what is, in one undergrad's opinion, "a nine-month vacation." And as much as the university has tried, with numerous new programs over the past few years, ASU has not yet shed its reputation as one of the nation's top party schools.

Serious Sun Devils

The Sun Devils of Arizona State are a curious lot. Amid all of the distractions and beautiful weather, there are those who are serious about their studies. Arizona State's best programs are primarily pre-professional, and students rate the business, engineering, architecture, and broadcasting colleges as the university's best. The music school is also highly regarded. The main student complaint is the overall size of Arizona State, which has more than 32,000 undergrads and 47,000 students overall. "Seemingly simple things like registration for classes in my major can sometimes become a real hassle because of a required signature of a professor who has, on short notice, decided to take a vacation," one student said. To help ease this problem, Arizona State has implemented a phone registration process that has enabled students to check their grades, class schedules, and even their financial charges.

Introductory classes tend to be huge: classes such as Introduction to Sociology and Human Sexuality often enroll as many as 500 students. Undergrads report, however, that as they progress in their major, the class size radically decreases. Another student complaint centers on the English skills of some TAs. According to one undergrad, "Chemistry is hard enough as it is. It almost becomes impossible when the lab assistant can't speak English."

Students can sidestep some of these problems in ASU's nationally regarded Honors College. Housed in McClintock Hall at the center of the university, the program accepts top high school applicants as well as undergraduates who have performed well. The program includes such benefits as priority at registration and extended library checkout, as well as the opportunity to enroll in honors seminars taught by the university's best professors.

Living Off

With rare exceptions, only freshmen live in the campus dorms. The rest of the students can choose to live in nearby apartments, condominiums, or Greek houses. On campus, students have the choice of single-sex, coed, or theme dorms. Off-campus, students say having a car is a virtual necessity. Public transportation is poor in Tempe, and vast distances between many of the city's attractions cause even the most ambitious student to acquire a car. Arizona State does, however, provide ample parking on campus for a relatively small fee. Many students also purchase a bike to travel around the vast campus.

Between classes, students have a wide variety of activities to pass the time. Many choose just to lounge around the many lawns and quads, while others opt to study in the university library or hit the Memorial Union, the student center. Students generally rate the library system as "good" and "easy-to-use." Hayden, the main university library, is centrally located and provides students with ample study space and high-tech research equipment. Inside the enormous Memorial Union are various restaurants, a movie theater, a video arcade, lounges, and the popular basement bowling alley.

The Best Bodies on Campus

ASU's intercollegiate athletic program is perennially regarded as one of the best in the nation. The baseball and golf teams are among the nation's best annually. Every Saturday night, almost religiously, thousands of students head over to Sun Devil Stadium to watch the football team compete before they go, just as ritualistically, to the fraternity parties. The varsity athletes, however, are not the only ones working up a sweat. The enormous and well-equipped Student Recreation Complex is home to thousands of students who hope to add muscle to their already tanned and toned bodies. As one student said, "The lack of competition in the classroom is more than made up for by the extreme competitiveness for the best bodies on campus."

"You really have to be dedicated to be a good student here."

Many students also take advantage of Phoenix's professional sports scene. Football, basketball, baseball, and hockey games all take place during the academic year. The Arizona Cardinals play on campus in Sun Devil Stadium. For just a 20-minute drive west of campus, students can enjoy Arizona Diamondbacks and Phoenix Suns games in the Bank One Ballpark and American West Arena, respectively, in downtown Phoenix.

Party Central

At the same time, no one can completely forget the world-class social life at ASU that attracts so much media attention and annual rankings by college and national publications alike. The social life is heavily divided between those who are 21 (or, students say, those who have a fake ID) and those who are not. For the under-21 crowd, students say that dorm, apartment, and fraternity parties are the primary sites to socialize. Greek life at ASU is influential, with 36 chapters and over 3,000 pledges. Many students report feeling some pressure to rush, as "there is really no better way to meet other people."

For the over-21 crowd, Tempe offers students a large choice of bars, dance clubs, and pool halls that attract almost every eligible student. In fact, Mill Avenue, the city's most famous street for bars and entertainment, has become so crowded by partying university students that police have enacted measures to stop the frequent cruising by voyeuristic drivers. The more experienced barhoppers venture away from the trendy Mill Ave and praise such places as Maloney's, Famous Door, Cajun House, Martini Ranch, and Club Rio as the top bars. For truly adventurous and less thrifty-types, North Phoenix and Scottsdale offer the Valley's most upscale clubs and bars.

Those who are tired of the bar scene or just want to experience something different from the bustle of Phoenix can, in a few hours by car, travel to Tucson, Flagstaff, or the Grand Canyon. For spring break or long weekends, many ASU students pile into cars and head down south to Rocky Point, Mexico, for more temperate weather, a little beach-time, and unlimited alcohol. As much as it tries, Arizona State University cannot escape its party-school reputation. As one student said, "You really have to be dedicated to be a good student here."

Over the last few years this young university has made strong strides in developing programs to provide its student with a solid, well-rounded education. But for now, ASU's beautiful winter weather, attractive people, and world-class social life promise a social experience that is hard to beat. —*Alison Pulaski and Staff*

FYI

The three best things about attending Arizona State University are "the weather, the nice campus, and the friendly people."

The three worst things about attending Arizona State University are "the size, the lack of cultural events, and the bureaucracy of the university."

The three things every student should do before graduating from Arizona State University are "go bar hopping, go to the football games, and attempt to study."

One thing I'd like to have known before coming here is " how expensive dorms can be—they're hiking the dorm rates 12% next year!"

University of Arizona

Address: PO Box 210040
Tucson, AZ 85721-0040
Phone: 520-621-3237
E-mail address:
appinfo@arizona.edu
Web site URL:
www.arizona.edu
Founded: 1885
Private or Public: public
Religious affiliation: none
Location: urban
**Undergraduate
enrollment:** 25,356
Total enrollment: 26,157
Percent Male/Female:
47%/53%
Percent Minority: 26%
Percent African-American:
3%
Percent Asian: 6%

Percent Hispanic: 15%
Percent Native-American:
2%
**Percent in-state/out-of-
state:** 71%/29%
Percent Pub HS: 90%
Number of Applicants:
17,687
Percent Accepted: 84%
**Percent Accepted who
enroll:** 36%
Entering: 5,365
Transfers: 0
Application Deadline:
1 Oct
Mean SAT: 548 V, 558 M
Mean ACT: 23
Middle 50% SAT range:
580–600 V,
590–610 M

Middle 50% ACT range:
21–26
3 Most popular majors:
psychology, management
information systems,
finance
Retention: 77%
Graduation rate: 54%
On-campus housing:
20%
Fraternities: 5%
Sororities: 5%
Library: 3,900,000
volumes
Tuition and Fees: $2,264
in; $9,416 out
Room and Board:
$5,548
Financial aid, first-year:
34%

While much of the rest of the country braves the winter cold, students at the University of Arizona sunbathe on palm-lined lawns amid the desert landscape of Tucson. With such great weather, it can be difficult to concentrate on the university's varied academic offerings—a dilemma U of A students face daily. Indeed with spectacular winter weather and a relaxed environment, U of A students often treat academics as dessert to the main course of sun and fun.

TA Instruction

Regardless of student attitudes, U of A offers a serious academic program enhanced by distinguished faculty, adequate libraries, honors courses, and excellent research facilities, including astronomy observatories with telescopes that gaze into the bright Arizona sky. Undergrads report that the astronomy, earth science, and biology departments are standouts; the English, engineering, pre-medical, and social science programs also get excellent reviews. Business and communications are popular majors.

For the intensely academic student, U of A offers an honors program whose members enjoy smaller classes taught by professors, residence in an honors dorm, and professor-taught use of a personal computer lab, among many other privileges. Many students, however, believe the University of Arizona's large size has its academic disadvantages. According to one undergrad, "Nearly all of my first- and second-year courses were taught by TAs." TAs at U of A teach many of the introductory courses, especially in the more popular subjects such as psychology and English. Most intro-level courses are fairly large, enrolling 250 to 500 students. While some students sense a lack of personal attention from their professors, others find these courses "helpful in assisting students to decide on their majors." Many undergrads feel the advising/counseling system of U of A is weak because there are so many enrolled undergraduates that those in need of advice are lost in the shuffle.

The campus has several quiet study niches and libraries, and students like to work together in groups or study outside by the palm trees. The campus libraries are frequented by students during all hours of the night for studying and research. As one freshman said, "There is a place to study for everyone, no matter what your study habits are; studying can be intensely academic or social."

Students are excited by the possibility of a "new and improved" hang-out, when the Student Union and Bookstore renovations are completed in 2002. The new center promises to have sidewalk cafes, art galleries, fine restaurants with outdoor seating, retail operations, and the bookstore without eliminating old campus favorites, like The Cellar and Sam's Place.

Love It or Hate It

Students at U of A summarize their opinions of campus housing with one statement: you either love it or hate it. Campus housing is guaranteed only for first-semester freshmen, who are randomly assigned to dorms after filling out a brief questionnaire. Because housing assignments are "first come, first served," undergrads are advised to register early, especially for the small number of single-sex dorms. The four-person quads are a favorite among students because they easily break social tensions, but undergrads also live in doubles and singles as well. La Paz is apparently the "sweetest" dorm, although Coronado and Cochise, a guys-only dorm, are also reportedly two of the better dorms, with good lighting and facilities. Some residents complain that some dorms, namely Manzita-Mohave, are "prison-like" in appearance. Freshmen living will soon improve after the school completes the new Freshmen Center on the main mall of the campus. After freshman year, a large number of students move to off-campus apartments or houses, or live in one of the sorority or fraternity houses around campus to avoid "the overcrowding and frequent fire drills" that reportedly plague dormitory living.

Bring Your Shades and Spirit

Athletics are an important part of student life at U of A. The Rec Center, a large athletic and recreational complex, houses several tracks, an outdoor double Olympic-sized pool, and weight rooms. Club sports as well as varsity sports are based at the center. It is reportedly "always packed" because U of A students "don't mess around when it comes to working out." U of A's nationally ranked varsity basketball, baseball, football, golf, women's softball, swimming, and track-and-field teams draw substantial student support. The particularly popular U of A basketball team plays at McKale Center, and as one student said, "You simply cannot graduate from U of A without going to a b-ball game at McKale." Home basketball games feature "the Ooh-Aah Man," an unofficial mascot who strips down to his spandex pants to lead spectators in chants of "ooh-aah" in hopes of inspiring the team to victory. Football is also a great tradition at U of A, and each season climaxes with "the Game" against archrival Arizona State. Whatever the sport, wherever the event, U of A students are sure to be there in large numbers and in full support of their teams.

Sun, Sun, and More Sun

Undergrads like to say that "the sun always shines on the U of A," and this applies as much to the social scene as to any other part of campus life. Thursday-night fraternity and sorority parties mark the beginning of the weekend. The Greek system is alive and well at U of A, and joining it is reportedly the best way to meet people on campus, although students say there is never pressure to join or even to go to a frat party. One sophomore reported that "the U of A scene is a juxtaposition of Greeks, cool, artsy 1950s-ish beatniks, and fun, sun-loving, bright-eyed students."

> With such great weather, it can be difficult to concentrate on the university's varied academic offerings—a dilemma U of A students face daily.

The city of Tucson also has many hot spots for students (especially those over 21), including popular dance clubs and bars such as the Velvet Tea Garden, Bisonwithces, Gotham, the Rialto, and Club Congress. For weekend getaways, Mexico is only one hour away. The less adventurous crowd is content with theme parties (and the alcohol that often accompanies them) on campus.

Extracurricular activities at U of A reflect the diversity of the student population: ethnic organizations, political forums, literary publications, and environmental groups are especially popular. But what if there isn't a club to meet a student's interests? "Just start your own—it's that easy!" one undergrad said.

Many students call the U of A campus breathtaking. Students enjoy warm weather all year-round, and wake up each morning to mountains and palm trees outside their windows. U of A also houses a beautiful cactus garden that attracts many visitors.

Buildings on campus all have the same redbrick, Spanish architectural style. The campus is fairly self-contained, but at the same time, is well integrated into the city of Tucson, and many students get involved with the surrounding community through volunteer programs and environmental projects. The university reportedly has a good relationship with the Tucson community, and students claim that Tucson has all the benefits of a medium-sized city without the big-city problems.

Although a large percentage of U of A students are from Arizona, one senior said that there "really is no typical student here." One thing most students do seem to have in common is a strong sense of school spirit.

At the University of Arizona, students choose the combination of academics, sports, and socializing that suits them best. The relaxed environment and warm weather only add to the pleasure of university life. As one student said, "I don't think I could ever leave here—it would be like ending my dream vacation." —*Joel Karansky and Staff*

FYI
The three best things about attending U of A are "the excellent school spirit, the fabulous social scene (there is always something going on), and the sun, the sun, the sun!"
The three worst things about attending U of A are "the dorms (some are overcrowded and yucky), intro classes (they are too big and are often taught by TAs), and a weak advising/counseling system."
The three things that every student should do before graduating from U of A are "live off campus for at least a year, go to a Wildcats' basketball game, and take a weekend trip to Mexico."
One thing I'd like to have known before coming here is "bring the car, forget the warm-weather clothes."

Arkansas

Address: 1600 Washington Avenue; Conway, AR 72032
Phone: 501-450-1362
E-mail address: adm@hendrix.edu
Web site URL: www.hendrix.edu
Founded: 1876
Private or Public: private
Religious affiliation: United Methodist
Location: suburban
Undergraduate enrollment: 1,142
Total enrollment: 1,147
Percent Male/Female: 46%/54%
Percent Minority: 12%

Percent African-American: 5%
Percent Asian: 4%
Percent Hispanic: 2%
Percent Native-American: 0.5%
Percent in-state/out-of-state: 68%/32%
Percent Pub HS: NA
Number of Applicants: 962
Percent Accepted: 88%
Percent Accepted who enroll: 39%
Entering: 331
Transfers: 32
Application Deadline: 15 Jan
Mean SAT: 632 V, 603 M
Mean ACT: 28

Middle 50% SAT range: 590–690 V, 560–670 M
Middle 50% ACT range: 25–31
3 Most popular majors: psychology, history, biology
Retention: 86%
Graduation rate: 62%
On-campus housing: 99%
Fraternities: NA
Sororities: NA
Library: 197,995 volumes
Tuition and Fees: $12,638 in; $12,638 out
Room and Board: $4,625
Financial aid, first-year: 60%

Imagine canoeing down a turbulent river with nine friendly strangers. As you and your companions try to remain on course, a bond forms. Or, imagine participating in a charity house-painting project in which you and your fellow workers feel the satisfaction of lending a helping hand. These activities are a sampling of the many programs designed to welcome first-year students to Hendrix. In a week-long freshman orientation, students can choose one of 15 different trips that range from camping, rock climbing, and spelunking to visiting Memphis. These excursions allow students to get acquainted with both faculty and upperclassmen. One freshman explained, "I immediately felt like I belonged to the school after the program."

"The Best College in the State"

Students at Hendrix, a small liberal arts college in the small town of Conway, Arkansas, quickly identify their school as the "best college in the state," an assertion supported by its strong academic programs. Hendrix has a core curriculum that includes a foreign-language requirement, three courses in the sciences, and courses in English composition and literature. Along with these requirements, first-year students must enroll in Western Intellectual Traditions (WIT), a course that lasts two-thirds of the academic year and covers all elements of Western thought and history with lectures by professors from various departments, including history and physics. Students consider WIT a tough, but definitely worthwhile experience. One student said, "At the beginning, I thought WIT would be quite a hassle, and it was a lot of work, but I definitely feel that it was an interesting and vital experience that gave me a wider perspective on my studies."

Hendrix runs on a trimester system with three terms, averaging 10 weeks each. Students take three classes every trimester with each class meeting daily. Hendrix students feel that the science departments are the strongest, especially for pre-med students majoring in biology and chemistry. One student said, "Hendrix is very strong in the sciences; it has an exceptional record of getting students into prestigious medical schools." Some students feel that the school places too much emphasis on the sciences at the expense of the fine arts and theater departments.

One of the best things about Hendrix is its student-faculty relations. The largest lecture classes are usually no larger than 50 students, and most upper-level classes enroll no more than 10 to 15. All faculty members at Hendrix teach undergrads—there are no research fellows. As a result of small class sizes, student-faculty interaction is universally described as "amazing," and professors are reported to be very accessible.

In previous editions of the *Guide*, we reported that "registration is not a hassle at Hendrix." However, when we shared the good news with current students they laughed at us. The new consensus? "It is a huge hassle, complicated by rude and inefficient office workers, long lines, and general poor organization. It's universally dreaded."

Academics are reportedly rigorous, with studying taking up a large portion of students' time during the week. According to one student, "The amount of reading expected for many of the courses is unreal."

Natural Surroundings

One student described the self-contained Hendrix campus as "aesthetically pleasing with red brick as its recurring theme." A particularly beautiful section of campus is said to be its "pecan shell" courtyard, lined with trees, large rocks, and benches, with a fountain and goldfish pond, which students say make it "a relaxing study spot." Students give the suburb of Conway low marks; one student said it is "not exactly the quintessential college town" and another reported that it "offers very little for college kids," although the suburban nature of the surrounding community

poses few security problems on campus. To find activity, most students make the 25-minute trek to Little Rock on weekends, where the night life is a little more exciting.

The facilities at Hendrix are considered "very well maintained," and several new buildings are in the works or have recently been completed. Students consistently praise Hendrix's newly constructed Bailey Library, which is much larger than the old, underground library. However, the construction of the Jack Frost Campus Center, once slated for completion in late 1997, has been postponed for lack of funding. Students have placed lawn chairs and tables outside of the construction site, where they sit on sunny days. The new "center" is at the "campus crossroads, so you can usually see everybody if you sit there long enough . . . Few campuses are this groovy."

> **"Hendrix's diversity isn't ethnic; rather, it's in the varied interests and idiosyncrasies of its students."**

Most Hendrix students live on campus. There are three male dorms, three female dorms, and one coed dorm. Most students live in doubles, although there are some singles. All campus residents are required to buy a full meal plan, a policy some students despise for its expense and inflexibility. There is one cafeteria, and students are ambivalent about the food. One student said, "The food is decent, as cafeteria food goes, but the menu is very monotonous and repetitive."

Extracurricular Activities

One of the most popular extracurricular activities is the radio station, KHDX, which was recently rated one of the top college radio stations in the nation. Students are also active in the Student Senate and in the production of a biweekly newspaper, the *Profile*, and the *Aonian*, a literary magazine.

Varsity sports do not have a huge presence at Hendrix. With its recent change from NAIA to NCAA Division II status, the college no longer offers athletic scholarships. There is no football team, but the basketball, soccer, and swimming teams are all well supported and fairly successful. Students are active in intramurals. The Mabee Center athletic facility contains modern exercise amenities, such as aerobics rooms, a weight area, and exercise machines.

Dorm-based Social Scene

Hendrix has no Greek system, and since the town of Conway provides little in the way of entertainment, social life centers on the dorms. Many students describe their dorm as "a close-knit community." Each dorm holds dances and parties throughout the year. The Student Social Committee also organizes special events and often brings guest entertainers to campus. Some annual events sponsored by the social committee and the dorms include the Miss Hendrix Pageant, where men dress up as women, and Kampus Kitty Week, a carnival that raises money for charity. Some of the biggest social events of the year are the on-campus "Warehouse" Dances sponsored by the Student Social Committee. Some students say the alcohol policy is not heavily enforced on campus, and for many, alcohol plays a central role in the social life on weekends. On the issue of sex, the small community of Hendrix has no secrets: "If someone has sex here, at least 50 people will know about it within a week."

Students at Hendrix are primarily from Arkansas, although the school is drawing more and more students from other states in the South as its reputation grows. Even so, students say that "the vast majority of Hendrix students are upper-middle-class . . . white kids." Some argue "Hendrix's diversity isn't ethnic; rather, it's in the varied interests and idiosyncrasies of its students." However varied students' interests might be, Hendrix's social scene is known as "cliquish," and non-conformist students we talked to were quite bitter. The *Guide* once remarked in the past that "you will always fit in at campus." That may be true. But, it is equally true that you are more likely to fit in if you are an upper-class-white moderate conservative. Hendrix's bohemian reputation might be a product of affluence and convenience.

Hendrix, then, is a small college with all the advantages and disadvantages of its breed. It has a strong regional academic presence, and its science programs are strong for a liberal arts college. Its students are tightly knit, and many enjoy their Hendrix experience. Students who do not fit in to the Hendrix mesh are less sanguine. —*Melissa Chan and Staff*

FYI

The three best things about attending Hendrix are "that everyone is so different here, the campus is truly beautiful, and our core curriculum."

The three worst things about attending Hendrix are "its homogeneity, there are no Greeks, and people can be cliquish."

The three things that every student should do before graduating from Hendrix are "to get a place to stay off campus, buy some food—the dining hall sucks, put down the marijuana and start planning your future."

One thing I'd like to have known before coming here is "what Alabama Slammers are."

University of Arkansas

Address: 208
  Administration South,
  2801 University Avenue
  Little Rock, AR 72204
Phone: 501-569-3127
E-mail address:
  adminfo@uair.edu
Web site URL: www.uark.edu
Founded: 1871
Private or Public: public
Religious affiliation: none
Location: urban
**Undergraduate
  enrollment:** 8,706
Total enrollment: 11,679
Percent Male / Female: NA
Percent Minority: 29%
Percent African-American:
  24%

Percent Asian: 4%
Percent Hispanic: 1%
Percent Native-American:
  NA
**Percent in-state / out-of-
  state:** 93% / 7%
Percent Pub HS: NA
Number of Applicants:
  1,996
Percent Accepted: 67%
**Percent Accepted who
  enroll:** 79%
Entering: 1,061
Transfers: 0
Application Deadline:
  3 weeks prior to term
Mean SAT: NA
Mean ACT: 19
Middle 50% SAT range: NA

Middle 50% ACT range:
  NA
3 Most popular majors:
  psychology, biology, liberal
  arts
Retention: 59%
Graduation rate: 15%
On-campus housing:
  100%
Fraternities: 5%
Sororities: 5%
Library: 1,500,000
  volumes
Tuition and Fees:
  $2,724 in; $6,540 out
Room and Board:
  $6,170
Financial aid, first-year:
  70%

I magine this thrilling experience: You are attending a sold-out football game and the roar of the crowd surrounds you. Thousands of people dressed in red and white are cheering for the home team at the top of their lungs. School spirit fills the stadium, and you can feel the excitement in your body as you root for the Razorbacks. If this situation appeals to you, then you would probably love attending the University of Arkansas.

Pick a College
Similar to the policy at many other universities, undergrads at the University of Arkansas are required to take a core curriculum consisting of 44 hours of core courses. Students can take examinations to place out of certain core classes they feel they are already proficient in. There is also a language requirement for the core, which can be satisfied by successfully completing a competency exam or taking foreign language classes. Although some students may feel that the core limits them from taking all of the classes they are most interested in, there seems to be a general feeling that completing the core "prepares students well for more ad-

vanced courses and introduces them to new and different ways of thinking."

Undergraduates at Arkansas can enroll in one of several colleges: the College of Education and Health Professions, the College of Engineering, Dale Bumpers College of Agricultural, Food and Life Sciences, J. William Fulbright College of Arts and Sciences, Sam M. Walton College of Business Administration, and the School of Architecture. Each of these colleges has slightly different graduation requirements and programs, but students are not left alone in the dark. The university provides an Office of Academic Advising to keep students on the right track and make sure they take the courses they need.

One aspect of academics that Arkansas students appreciate is the accessibility of the faculty. Professors hold regular office hours and even go to meals with students. Some students, however, regret that not all classes are taught by professors. Teaching assistants supervise labs, and they occasionally teach introductory freshman classes. "Many TAs know the material well and are helpful, but they just don't have the same teaching experience yet as regular professors," commented one student. Due to the large student population at Arkansas, intro and core courses can top 400 students, and even some of the upper-level courses can be large.

Students generally consider accounting and engineering to be among the more difficult majors at the University of Arkansas. However, students shouldn't be too worried. One undergrad wisely commented, "If you are interested in the subjects, then the workload isn't too bad." Although some students may be busier than others, depending on what they choose to study, everyone's schedule is "challenging, but definitely manageable." Undergrads make the workload easier by studying with fellow students, and "the professors and TAs are always there to help you if you have trouble understanding the material."

Life in Fayetteville

According to students, Fayetteville is "definitely a great college town." This midsize town has "the benefits of a city but the intimacy of a small town." Students enjoy a feeling of safety at school and often step off campus to discover what the city has to offer. Favorite spots include a number of nearby restaurants and several popular bars, such as George's and River City. Dickson Street, which runs through the middle of the campus, is "a fun and convenient place to find something cool to do," commented one sophomore.

Aside from going out, there are plenty of activities that students can occupy themselves with on campus. The Arkansas Union, which contains a movie theater, a post office, a travel agency, and a large ballroom, as well as other resources, always attracts a large number of students. The school also holds larger special occasions, such as the annual non-alcoholic Red-Eye party featuring bands, dancing, and other entertainment. For a slightly more personal evening, many students also choose to spend time talking or watching videos in their dorms with friends.

Although there is definitely a Greek presence on campus, students are not pressured in any way to get involved if they are not interested. Only a small fraction of the student body actually pledge the fraternities and sororities, but anyone looking for a weekend party can usually find one at the houses, which are located near the middle of campus. The administration at Arkansas is becoming more strict about their alcohol policies, but as one student commented, "You won't get into trouble unless you are drinking in the street or doing something that makes it obvious you are drunk."

When they are not studying or out partying, Arkansas students also enjoy just relaxing in their dorms. People have mixed opinions of the housing, depending on whether they were fortunate enough to get one of the better dorms. The Gregson and Gibson houses, which are in a convenient location on campus and were recently renovated, are among the preferred dorms. In the words of one junior who lived in Gibson, "I feel sorry for the people who are stuck in Pomfret and Humphreys . . . those are definitely the worst."

> "I can feel the adrenaline pumping through my body every time I go to a game."

Another popular option is off-campus housing. Several residences such as College Park Apartments are inexpensive and convenient places to live for Arkansas students. Anyone living off campus can either drive to school or take a bus provided by the university's shuttle service. "The shuttles are useful because it's hard to find parking and the police are not afraid to give out tickets if you leave your car anywhere convenient," explained one senior.

Let's Go, Hogs!

Anyone who follows college athletics will be familiar with the Razorbacks, a perennial powerhouse in a wide range of sports. The most popular squads are the basketball team, led by coach Nolan Richardson, and the football team. Both are consistently ranked among the top in the nation. The school's track team has also enjoyed success over the years, including capturing

17 of the last 18 indoor national titles. High turnout at games is the norm, thanks to a combination of tremendous school pride and support from members of the Fayetteville community. As one enthusiastic student explained, "The Hogs represent all that we stand for! I can feel the adrenaline pumping through my body every time I go to a game." Yet another student declared that "every student should experience a basketball game! The new Bud Walton Arena can get so loud and fun." The rivalries between Tennesse, Ole Miss, Alabama, and LSU are pretty intense. New to this list of rivals is Texas, thanks to Arkansas' victory in the 2000 Cotton Bowl. Arkansas hopes to extend its impressive legacy of "over 30 national championships in the last 15 years!"

Perhaps motivated by the varsity Razorback teams, many students participate in intramural sports and work out at the House of Physical Education and Recreation (HPER). The "Hyper" building provides tracks, pools, racquetball courts, weight rooms, dance floors, basketball courts, and multipurpose rooms for students to use.

Getting Involved

In addition to the intramurals and academics, students can participate in various on-campus organizations and activities. Most agree that the extracurricular activities they choose play a big role in their college experience. Students can immerse themselves in KUAF radio or UATV, the campus television station. Those interested in campus publications can contribute to the *Arkansas Traveler*, the campus newspaper that comes out three times each week, the *Harbinger* magazine, or the yearbook. "You can find people interested in almost anything here. You just have to be willing to go out and look for them," stated one junior.

Sports fans or anyone else who wants an enjoyable college experience shouldn't overlook the University of Arkansas. Students describe themselves as "friendly and bursting with pride." One tradition at the university is the Senior Walk, which began in 1905 and has the names of over 100,000 graduates etched into it. The path, which already stretches over five miles, will surely continue to grow as future students experience the thrill of being a Razorback. —*Robert Wong*

FYI
The three best things about attending Arkansas are "the friendly people, the athletic teams, and the location."
The three worst things about attending Arkansas are "the lack of parking, dorm food, and the wind."
The three things that every student should do before graduating from Arkansas are "watch a football game, get involved in extracurriculars, and go to a frat party."
One thing I'd like to have known before coming here is "how much school spirit the students have."

California

California Institute of Technology

Address: Mail Code 5-63;
Pasadena, CA 91125
Phone: 626-395-6341
E-mail address:
ugadmissions
@caltech.edu
Web site URL:
admissions.caltech.edu
Founded: 1891
Private or Public:
private
Religious affiliation:
none
Location: suburban
**Undergraduate
enrollment:** 907
Total enrollment: 1,973
Percent Male/Female:
70%/30%
Percent Minority: 30%

Percent African-American:
1%
Percent Asian: 24%
Percent Hispanic: 5%
Percent Native-American:
NA
**Percent in-state/out-of-
state:** NA
Percent Pub HS: 79%
Number of Applicants:
2,894
Percent Accepted: 18%
**Percent Accepted who
enroll:** 45%
Entering: 234
Transfers: NA
Application Deadline:
1 Jan
Mean SAT: 715 V, 768 M
Mean ACT: NA

Middle 50% SAT range:
700–780 V,
750–800 M
Middle 50% ACT range: NA
3 Most popular majors:
engineering/applied
science, biology, electrical
engineering
Retention: 91%
Graduation rate: 86%
On-campus housing:
100%
Fraternities: NA
Sororities: NA
Library: 530,000 volumes
Tuition and Fees: $19,959
in; $19,959 out
Room and Board: $6,180
Financial aid, first-year:
58%

"Anyone with the slightest chance of maybe sort of thinking a little bit about not majoring in science/math should stay very far away from this campus. Do not pass Go; do not waste your money on the application fee." This is how one student at the California Institute of Technology, better known as Caltech, described the atmosphere of this science-heavy university. However, for those willing to make a commitment to science and engineering and looking for top-notch programs, Caltech is the place to be.

"Like Drinking from a Fire Hose" . . . a Caltech Education

The academic year of Caltech students, or "Techers," is split into three terms. Dividing the required 486 credit units over four years yields an average of 40.5 units per term. Each unit is designed to equal one hour students are expected to spend on work in or out of class; however, because of required classes, students usually take between 45 and 48 units, and course loads of over 50 units are not unheard of. Although some admit that the actual hours spent on the work are often less than the number of units, students are quick to point out the notorious difficulty of the problem sets that make up a significant part of their grades. Students generally spend anywhere from 2 to 10 hours on problem sets, and some report spending more that 15 hours on particularly difficult ones. According to one student, "It's possible that some work just as much, but I cannot believe that people at other schools work more than we do."

Freshman year and most of sophomore year, the source of these problem sets is Caltech's demanding core program, which includes five terms of math and physics, two of chemistry, one of biology, and two lab courses. Although they aren't Caltech's focus, 12 terms of humanities and social sciences are also required. Students add that many of the humanities faculty are better teachers than the rest of the professors—they just don't get as much respect.

Caltech professors include some of the most highly respected researchers in their respective fields, but students overwhelmingly remark that amazing researchers do not necessarily make for great teachers. "Professors here are almost always available, and are, as a rule, willing to give you a second chance, but they're not generally good lecturers," remarked one student. "But if you want to do research, this is a great place. If you like to attend classes, this might not be the best place."

Teaching assistants at Caltech receive high ratings from students, although English-speaking ability is sometimes a problem. TAs are ready and willing to help with course work, and because it's easy to change sections, leaving a TA with poor English skills doesn't seem to be a major issue.

Although it's clear that there's no easy way through Caltech, students report quite a variation in the difficulty of the major programs. One student commented, "You can't spell 'easy' without E&AS (engineering and applied science)." Others claim that literature and economics are relatively easy, but it's important to note that students rarely get these degrees solo; usually students majoring in a humanities subject will combine it with one of the easier science programs. On the other hand, physics is notorious for being the hardest major, while electrical engineering is rumored to be the most time-consuming.

Caltech students constantly speak about the sheer amount of knowledge they are expected to acquire in their four years. A popular school slogan is that "getting an education at Caltech is like drinking from a fire hose." In fact, prefrosh orientation t-shirts depict the school mascot, a beaver, trying to drink from a hose of rushing water.

Due to the huge workload, Techers are more often seen working than anything else. Even though the first two terms of their core classes are graded pass/fail, freshmen usually have to adjust to the overwhelming amount of work. Typical students work and attend class for about 10 to 14 hours a day, leaving little time for other activities. Not surprisingly, sleep is usually the first thing to go. "It's not unusual to see students up until four A.M., even frosh taking pass/fails—sleep is a very precious commodity," said one student.

Even though most core freshman work is pass/fail, grading for other classes seems to be quite fair overall. One student remarked, "Professors are not afraid to give you an honest grade. If you did C work, you get a C. And they're not afraid to fail you, either. If you get good grades here, you're either very smart, or you have no social life, or both." Because of the academic pressures, group work is encouraged and students find that not only does working together make the work go a lot easier, but commiserating builds friendships. Another example of freedom within this workload is the Honor Code, which students really seem to like and respect. The Honor Code System is based on the idea that "no member of the Caltech community shall take unfair advantage of any other member of the community." Because of the Code, students have access to most campus facilities at all times of day and night and are often given take-home tests and exams. One student explained, "The Honor Code is so respected that we get take-home exams; the professors trust us not to cheat, and the students, with few exceptions, honor that trust. That's why the students have so much freedom to explore the campus, underground and indoors, after-hours, whatever. The Honor Code is one of the things that make Caltech bearable."

Rotate, Please

At the beginning of frosh year, all students spend a week called "Rotation" touring the seven undergraduate houses, which can best be characterized as pseudo-frats. Each house has its own character and traditions, and since everyone is a member of one of them no one is left out and social skills are honed. As one upperclassman recalls, "Rotation lasts through the first week of classes, and is designed to help frosh choose houses and houses choose frosh. Frosh have dinner at each house, one per night, and then there's a whole lot of secret meetings where the houses talk about the frosh, and then the house presidents get together for a grueling twelve or fourteen hours and hash it all out." After being assigned to a house, frosh may choose their roommates and suitemates and are given a considerable amount of freedom in the house. After being placed in the houses, students select their own residential advisors who act as their counselors and sometimes supervisors. RAs are usually graduate students or younger Caltech employees, and overall students find them to be cool and laid-back, more like mentors or older siblings than disciplinarians.

Diversity?

One thing that strikes almost all students is a perceived lack of ethnic diversity. There is a decent amount of economic diversity, and most students come from public schools; however, students lament the overwhelming number of white and Asian males. Females comprise slightly over a quarter of the student body, about the same as Asian students, but African-American and Latino students make up only a combined 7% of students. Time and time again, students report sensing a lack of African-American students, as they make up only 2% of the student population.

As for dating, many Techers describe strange phenomena that occur on campus such as the "instant couple," whereby two individuals suddenly decide to go out, with little warning or dating. Such relationships often end as quickly as they begin, only to be repeated with different people. Like everything else at Caltech, dating is intense. Because of the disproportionately large male population, many men on campus complain about the lack of quality females. According to some, makeup is rarely seen, and many students pay little attention to appearance beyond basic grooming. Others praised this natural look, feeling it minimizes sexual tensions. Homosexual couples on campus seem to be completely accepted, and students report a very tolerant and accepting atmosphere on campus toward sexual diversity.

Everybody Likes a Prankster

Despite their heavy course load, most Techers have pretty active social lives. Although there are occasionally parties in off-campus housing, Caltech social life centers around the houses. Each weekend a party can usually be found at one of the houses, but students are quick to note that Caltech house parties differ considerably from parties at other schools. At the beginning of every academic year the Caltech administration advises the students on the university drinking policy, but in reality it doesn't seem to be strictly enforced. One student recalls, "The administration has some sort of policy about underage drinking. I'm pretty sure they're opposed to it, at least in principle. They send out an annual flier stating that drinking under the age of twenty-one is illegal in the state of California, and there's something about student bartenders and a spreadsheet full of things like 'thirty percent of undergraduates are of legal drinking age, so for a party of two hundred people, you should buy one bottle of rum.'" Apparently, the students don't take the administration's policy very seriously, but they add that drinking and partying are done with restraint, due to the small and largely respectful student body. Basically, as long as the police don't become involved, students are given plenty of liberty. Drug use on campus isn't a major issue, and most students note that it involves only a very tiny portion of the student body.

Caltech students' affinity for pranks carries over to parties, too, and Techers boast of pulling off an amazing array of stunts. One upperclassman recalls "the time we flooded our courtyard to eighteen inches and built boats to take us across it, all for a one-night party." Another popular prank is "the annual Pumpkin Drop, when Darbs (students who live in Dabney Hall) freeze 30 pumpkins in liquid nitrogen and drop them off of Milikan Library, the tallest building on campus, in an amazing display of gravitation. It is rumored that there was once a 'blue flash' seen when a pumpkin struck the concrete. People have been looking out for the blue flash ever since . . ." Like most activities at Caltech, pranks generally involve math and science, such as reprogramming the scoreboard at a football game to show that Caltech was beating MIT.

"If you want to do research, this is a great place."

Stemming from the prank tradition is the Senior Ditch Day, in which seniors leave their rooms unoccupied for the day and the underclassmen must break through or solve a series of "stacks" in order to gain entrance to the rooms and "redecorate." The stacks may be simple physical challenges, or they may involve more sophisticated puzzles and challenges. Once the underclassmen gain entrance to the rooms, they usually find a food "bribe" left by the seniors in order to persuade the underclassmen from rearranging the rooms too ridiculously.

Another way to relieve the stress caused by the work is by participation in athletics, either varsity or intrahouse. Intrahouse athletics are more popular and are as much social events as athletic endeavors. These games add to the spirit of friendly competition between the houses, and foster bonding within the houses.

Varsity athletics follow the same principle, as membership is based on desire and commitment more than ability. Anyone can participate on any team, and indeed some Techers take up entirely new sports in college. Winning is hardly a concern, and laughing about how bad many of the teams are is a great bonding experience. Everyone who comes to practices and makes an effort gets to play, even women on some of the men's teams, due to the small number of females. Since Caltech doesn't recruit athletes, everyone is given a fair shot at athletic glory. Because of the no-recruitment policy, it's understood that all athletes have an obligation first to aca-

demics, and coaches are extremely understanding about missing games or practices due to academic commitments.

Pasadena and Beyond

According to some students, the campus is beautiful and scenic but rather uninspiring for the average underclassman. They admire its architectural dichotemy— the early-twentieth-century buildings contrast nicely with the newer labs and buildings. The campus is fairly safe, and there is an excellent escort service for students who are walking home late or need a ride home.

Any students venturing off the campus will find a wealth of activities in nearby Pasadena, which is only a short drive away. There students will find movie theaters, clubs, and tons of great restaurants. Caltech students' meal plan covers five dinners and five lunches each week—the dining hall is open all day to purchase snacks or breakfast, but once the food grows boring the nearby restaurants are popular with students. Even though it's quite close, students still need a car to get into town or will need to find a friend with one. During the day, hiking, skiing, and swimming are feasible in the nearby mountain range.

Indeed, enjoying the fresh air may be a great way to take a break from what students describe as "the hardest school I could ever imagine." The workload is said to be ridiculous at some times and overwhelming the rest of the time, but students at Caltech are willing to work through it. Even if Techers could never imagine doing any more work than they already do, they somehow fight off procrastination and get it done, emerging from four years of attempting to drink from a fire hose with an unparalleled education. —*Brendan Muha*

FYI
The three best things about attending Caltech are "the amazing students, the amazing professors, and knowing that your diploma virtually guarantees a great job."
The three worst things about attending Caltech are "the ludicrous workload, the small number of undergrads, and varsity sports, if winning is your thing."
The three things that every student should do before graduating from Caltech are "pull an all-nighter or four (or ten or thirty . . .), drive a Daihatsu (the electric carts on campus), and see the steam tunnels."
One thing I'd like to have known before coming here is "that I would work much harder than I ever thought I could."

California Institute of the Arts

Address: 24700 McBean
Parkway; Valencia, CA
91355
Phone: 661-255-1050
E-mail address:
admiss@calarts.edu
Web site URL:
www.calarts.edu
Founded: 1961
Private or Public: private
Religious affiliation: none
Location: suburban
**Undergraduate
enrollment:** 804
Total enrollment: 1,125
Percent Male / Female:
56% / 44%
Percent Minority: 25%

Percent African-American:
5%
Percent Asian: 9%
Percent Hispanic: 9%
Percent Native-American:
2%
**Percent in-state / out-of-
state:** 35% / 65%
Percent Pub HS: NA
Number of Applicants:
1,271
Percent Accepted: 40%
**Percent Accepted who
enroll:** 29%
Entering: 146
Transfers: NA
Application Deadline:
14 Jan

Mean SAT: NA
Mean ACT: NA
Middle 50% SAT range: NA
Middle 50% ACT range: NA
3 Most popular majors:
animation, graphic design,
film / video
Retention: 92%
Graduation rate: 38%
On-campus housing: NA
Fraternities: NA
Sororities: NA
Library: 80,000 volumes
Tuition and Fees: $19,950
in; $19,950 out
Room and Board: $5,150
Financial aid, first-year:
75%

There's rarely a dull moment at the California Institute of the Arts. On its small campus in Valencia, California, students are constantly creating new ways to portray life, whether it be through devising a new interpretation of Hamlet, preparing for an exhibit opening, making a song completely out of Chewbacca sounds, or celebrating at the "My Bloody Valentine" party. Although the students are from an array of different backgrounds, they are tied together by their love of and total immersion in the arts. The result is a true cornucopia of passionate artists and an extremely focused yet admittedly eccentric student body.

Arts Aplenty
There is never a lack of daily activities at CalArts. Between academic responsibilities and alluring extracurricular activities, some students are at school for as much as 14 hours each day—and loving every minute of it. One sophomore's biggest complaint was that "classes are too short." CalArts is divided up into five different schools: music, art, dance, film/ video, and theater. Within each school,

there is a rough progression of classes that everyone must take, though this schedule is more defined in the music, theater, and dance schools. While academic requirements are different in each school, a senior found that "school politics make it hard to get into classes that aren't required. You really have to work at getting in the good classes, and it doesn't always pan out." However, students are required to take some classes outside of their school, and introductory courses in other schools are relatively easy to get into.

The assignments at CalArts are not traditional essay papers. One art student recounted, "I had to make art out of garbage and then sell it to someone. Then, I had to use the money to buy candy and bring it to class!" Students are also encouraged to join forces in their extracurricular activities; for many productions, theater students will make movies with the help of film students while music students write the score and art students create the sets.

Students are required to take 48 credits in the Critical Studies department in order to gain a strong liberal arts foundation.

Some students feel restricted by these "annoying" requirements, but many find the Critical Studies department a wonderful opportunity to explore unusual fields. One theater student was taking Narcissism, Holography, and a Theater Management class to fulfill his requirement, and found Critical Studies to be "a little tedious, but you can find some gems in there." For the most part, students consider Critical Studies little more than an interesting obstacle in their pursuit of the arts.

Cutting-Edge Arts

CalArts professors receive rave reviews from all students. "The student-teacher ratio is seven to one, and they can really focus on me. That's why I'm here," remarked one student. The professors are not just instructors, but usually also active participants in their field. "The training here is absolutely phenomenal. My theater professor just took time off from Broadway to teach at CalArts, and she's going back to be in a production with Uma Thurman. We're being trained by the professionals for the professionals," reported a junior. Professors are very accessible and friendly, and the school also manages to attract an impressive crop of guest speakers. Noted alum Ed Harris frequently makes appearances, while jazz virtuosos Charlie Hayden and Tim Allen have each held workshops recently. "There is always someone cutting edge here."

Although the CalArts campus is minuscule by most standards, students can lay claim to some of the best art resources on the West Coast. There are studios and practice spaces galore, not to mention the acclaimed Walt Disney Modular Theater, constructed entirely out of 3' 3 3' blocks. Hydraulic pistons make it possible to raise and lower segments of the wall, floor, and ceiling, paving the way for some bizarre sets. It is rumored that scenes from *The Empire Strikes Back* were filmed there, and one junior recalled a terrific modernized version of *Edward II* reorganized under the auspices of "the Mod." The animation department has just received expanded studios, and CalArts also boasts one of the biggest photo enlargers in the country. However, some students claim that getting access to facilities, even in your own school, can be trying.

Everyday Life with Not Your Everyday People

Students can live off campus all four years, but those who remain on campus don't complain about much. "The rooms are huge, and I have my own sink in the bathroom." However, not all experiences are positive. One student complained that "Ants really ruined my freshman year." The halls are also well-decorated by the students. "There is some really fantastic artwork; they make all these illusions. One hallway looks like it goes on forever. It's amazing!" Resident Advisors preside over the dorms, but like most CalArts students, they are fairly laid-back. "They might come in to tell us to stop smoking weed if they can smell it, but usually they're pretty cool." Half the students are blessed with a view directly over the courtyard and site of the CalArts heated swimming pool, which has inspired some unusual behavior. "I never expected so much skinny-dipping when I decided to come here!" exclaimed a junior.

Many cook at home or eat out, but CalArts does have a pretty good cafeteria. "Even though it's got a pretty wide range of choices, after a while it gets monotonous. But overall, it's pretty decent." Meals can be cooked to order and the food is considered fresh by most, although some students have gripes with the "rip-off" meal plan. If the meal plan gets old, there is always the student-run Mom's Cafe or the Tatum Coffee Lounge on campus. For those up for a journey, the Claimjumper in Valencia was lauded, but students also have the entire city of Los Angeles to peruse for an incredible array of dining options.

Tiny Town, Tall Talent

Valencia itself is considered one of the main drawbacks to CalArts. Although it boasts plenty of movie theaters, bowling alleys, and restaurants, students complain that "Valencia is really a cookie-cutter, soccer mom kind of place. You can always pick out the students." There is a Six Flags Magic Mountain in town, but to many "there's only so many times you can twist around the looping loops or swish down a hundred feet without getting bored." Fortunately, Valencia is only 20 minutes from L.A. and a half hour from the country, so students have a smorgasbord of options. Many have cars, and for those not swamped with rehearsals, jaunts into L.A. transpire several times a week. Students swing at the Derby, go clubbing around Hollywood, or just go out for a bite to eat.

> **"Someone made up a T-shirt last year that said 'CalArts Varsity Football,' but that's as close as we get to having a sports team."**

Those who opt to stay on campus are not living in a ghost town. The Rendezvous is a popular drinking hole, and there are always performances or art openings sponsored by the school. "Most Saturday nights there are raving parties on campus too; I usually don't go anywhere," remarked a junior. CalArts is renowned for its wild Mardi Gras party and especially the annual Halloween party, which necessitates the LAPD for security. "The costumes are awesome. Last year there was some guy dressed up as Jesus, and he actually nailed a cross through the thin skin in his hands!" Creativity even pervades the graduation ceremonies. There are no cap and gowns; instead each year, commencement is based on a theme. Last year the theme was the circus, so "the dean dressed up as a magician, people wore outfits, they served peanuts and hot

dogs, and there was hay everywhere. It was wild!"

Yet, very little at CalArts is as wild as the students who go there. "People here are very eccentric and different. They are all really into their work and have green hair and a lot of piercings," remarked a junior. Another student admitted, "there are a lot of freaks. But, they're nice freaks." CalArts students find ways to express themselves in all aspects of life, from their work to their appearance.

This sense of individuality is heightened by CalArts' lack of organized sports teams. "Someone made up a T-shirt last year that said 'CalArts Varsity Football,' but that's as close as we get to having a sports team." While arts are the main focus, many students miss sports—there isn't even a school gym! "There's no school spirit. I kind of wish we all had something to rally around like a football team." Fortunately, for the casual athlete, Nerf football and ultimate Frisbee games have been know to pop up in students' spare time.

If you like doodling in the margins during boring classes, the California Institute of the Arts is probably not for you. These students are extremely dedicated to their artwork and goals, and the overflowing creativity pervades everything from their personal appearance to their environment and even to their parties. But don't be scared off if you're not a pro just yet. For the truly motivated, CalArts provides an unparalleled opportunity to develop and refine your understanding of art as well as your ability to create it. —*Matt Stewart and Staff*

FYI
The three best things about attending CalArts are "the super talented students, renowned faculty, and the California weather."
The three worst things about attending CalArts are "the strenuous workload, no school spirit, and it's easy to feel burned out once in a while."
The three things that every student should do before graduating from CalArts are "take a good dose of non-art classes, attend as many student shows and presentations as you can, and hit the L.A. club district."
One thing I'd like to have known before coming here is "how your interests can change dramatically."

California State University System

The California State University system has continually grown since the enactment of the Donahoe Higher Education Act of 1960, which brought together a collection of individual colleges to form the California State University. The expansive system now contains 22 colleges, including the first public university in California, San Jose State University, and the most recently established campus, CSU Monterey Bay. A 23rd campus is planned to open in Ventura County within the next few years and will be founded as CSU Channel Islands.

> Unlike the research-oriented UC system, CSU schools concentrate most of their resources on undergraduate teaching.

From the metropolitan Los Angeles campus to rural CSU Sonoma to the coastal San Diego State, the individual campuses that make up the system are distinctive and vary greatly. San Diego State University, known for its party atmosphere and close proximity to fine beaches, is the largest campus, with about 31,000 full-time students. Maritime Academy and CSU Monterey Bay are the smallest, with total enrollments of 450 and 1,960 respectively.

CSU or UC?
Although often overshadowed by the better-known University of California system, the CSU system offers many features that the UC system does not. With campuses located throughout the state, the CSU system allows many Californians the option of commuting to a college close to home. For students concerned with the high costs of financing higher education, the tuition of the California State Universities are half that of UC schools, while still providing larger and better resources than two-year junior colleges. Even for an out-of-state student seeking California weather, the CSU system is still an attractive deal.

Differences and Similarities
All CSU schools offer financial aid and over 60% of the students are currently receiving aid. The larger campuses offer Division I varsity sports, while the smaller schools are in Division II. All campuses have organized club and intramural sports. Each campus differs greatly and prospective students should research the academic focus, size, location, and student makeup of each campus before deciding. To help high school students decide which of the twenty-three campuses is right for them, Cal State has implemented a specialized website named CSUMentor System (www.csumentor.edu). This site is very helpful and anyone interested in CSU should check it out.

Education, Not Just Research
The most popular undergraduate majors in the system are business and management, social science, and interdisciplinary studies. At the graduate level, education, business, and management majors top the list. The CSU system gives out more degrees in business, computer science, and engineering than all other California schools combined, reflecting the career-oriented focus of the programs.

Unlike the research-oriented UC system, CSU schools concentrate most of their resources on undergraduate teaching. Although the professors are less prestigious, it is for this reason that they can spend less of their efforts maintaining their reputation and more time focused on teaching. As tuition skyrockets at private colleges, the CSU system's offer of a good education at a reasonable price looks better and better. —*Seung Lee and Staff*

California Polytechnic State University / San Luis Obispo

Address: San Luis Obispo, CA 93407
Phone: 805-756-2311
E-mail address: admprosp@calpoly.edu
Web site URL: www.calpoly.edu
Founded: 1901
Private or Public: public
Religious affiliation: none
Location: suburban
Undergraduate enrollment: 15,406
Total enrollment: 17,000
Percent Male/Female: 56%/44%
Percent Minority: 24%
Percent African-American: 1%

Percent Asian: 11%
Percent Hispanic: 11%
Percent Native-American: 1%
Percent in-state/out-of-state: 98%/2%
Percent Pub HS: 80%
Number of Applicants: 15,407
Percent Accepted: 42%
Percent Accepted who enroll: 42%
Entering: 2,716
Transfers: NA
Application Deadline: 30 Nov
Mean SAT: 532 V, 569 M
Mean ACT: NA

Middle 50% SAT range: 463–665 V, 482–698 M
Middle 50% ACT range: 19–29
3 Most popular majors: business, agribusiness, mechanical engineering
Retention: 87%
Graduation rate: 57%
On-campus housing: 17%
Fraternities: 13%
Sororities: 10%
Library: 740,000 volumes
Tuition and Fees: $2,126 in; $9,506 out
Room and Board: $5,554
Financial aid, first-year: 51%

Well-respected as one of the top tech schools in the nation, Cal Poly places heavy emphasis on academics, offering students small classes and many required labs in a "learn-by-doing" atmosphere. But, despite the rigorous academic standards, students still describe Cal Poly as a "laid-back surfer-dude" type of school. Situated in a small coastal town only 15 minutes from the beach, Cal Poly offers a unique college experience through its mix of academic challenge and laid-back atmosphere.

Hands-On Learning

Cal Poly's "learn-by-doing" philosophy distinguishes it from most other schools. Beginning freshman year, students are required to take numerous labs, which one student described as "challenging and pretty tough, but you really do learn a lot from them." The general-ed (GE) requirements demonstrate this modern approach to learning: 15 credits each are required in science and technology distributions (labs included), as well as in Social, Political, and Economic Institutions and Life Understanding (psychology). Combined

with more traditional requirements of communication, arts, and humanities, the GEs are described as "fair," and contribute to the progressive learning philosophy of Cal Poly.

Another aspect of the "learn-by-doing" philosophy is the commitment to small classes. Even freshman year and at the introductory level, "large" classes usually only hold 40 to 50 students, and the 24 person upper-level classes and labs are the norm. A sixth-year super-senior reported that he'd only been in a class with 100 students twice. These small class sizes facilitate active discussions with professors, who are largely well-liked and easily accessible. Students comment that professors believe "they're really here to lecture and teach, not just to do research." This undoubtedly contributes to the learning environment. Of course, small classes have their disadvantages too: reportedly getting into desired classes is very difficult, even for required ones. This causes students to complain that "athletes have priority in the registration process" and "the faculty is under-staffed." However, there are ways around this problem, which mostly entail "crashing classes," or sitting in on a desired, but full course during the first week and requesting the professor to sign a form, giving a student permission to enroll.

Despite its California, laid-back atmosphere and close proximity to the beach, Cal Poly is no party school. Classes are "tough, usually not a joke," and the short quarter system creates an almost rushed environment. One student commented, "I feel like I have a test every other week." Certain areas, like the Business School, are considered "fluffy," but most students feel challenged by the rigorous academic schedule. Undergraduates recommend taking light course loads in order to do well in classes, which, combined with the difficulty of getting into desired courses, adds to the almost six-year average stay at Cal Poly before graduation.

> **Despite the rigorous academic standards, students still describe Cal Poly as a laid-back "surfer dude" type of school.**

Not surprisingly for a tech school, most students are engineering, technology, or science-related majors. And although the courses are challenging, students did not complain much about academics in general. Students have come to work hard in a progressive learning environment. This has led to Cal Poly's excellent reputation, especially in California's industry sector. Cal Poly graduates are highly sought after, both in California and out-of-state.

Life in SLO

The town of San Luis Obispo, or "SLO" in campus slang, is a small, comfortable town on the California coastline, halfway between Los Angeles and San Francisco. Cal Poly plays an important role in the economy of the city, and one student commented, "If the school weren't here, SLO wouldn't be here." Like their counterparts at other colleges in small cities, students at Cal Poly complained that there isn't much to do in the town. Although stu-

dents frequent a select number of town bars, they most often look toward the campus to entertain themselves. "Life in SLO is pretty slow."

Although the campus itself is technically dry, parties abound in the off-campus housing that surrounds campus. Most students will go to house parties on the weekends and the occasional fraternity fiesta. The Greek system is small and not strong at Cal Poly, leading students to comment that the frats "are only in the background, and not noticeable." On top of that, some say that frat parties are only "okay."

Partly because of the intense academic atmosphere and strict enforcement of the dry campus, the party scene is not raging; instead students describe it as "pretty kick-back." Drugs are reportedly commonplace in the community of SLO, but among the students, mostly upperclassmen experiment with "soft drugs."

The administration and student body all take advantage of Cal Poly's great weather. Every Thursday afternoon the school hosts "U-U Hour," (University Union Hour) where no classes are scheduled and different bands play outside in the university's main quad. Students attend this popular event and use the time to "sit with friends, chill out, and enjoy ourselves." On the weekends, students get away from campus and head to the outdoors. Pismo Beach, renowned for surfing, is only 15 minutes away, and students often go there to swim, sun, and surf. Students can also bike or hike in the range of grassy, rolling hills that lie just to the east of SLO.

Surfer Dudes and Brainiacs

Even with its rigorous academics, California's laid-back atmosphere and "surfer-dude" feeling prevail at Cal Poly, partly because of the short distance to the beach. Students describe the school as a "flip-flop kind of place" where shorts and T-shirts are the norm. The character of the student body also reflects the surfer mind-set. One female student said, "Freshman year in one of my labs there was this surfer guy in the class. He had a big blond afro, wore baggy shorts and tank tops, and seemed like a brain-dead kind of guy. I ended up being his lab partner, and I found out he was actually a computer engineering major. Now, I think he's one of the smartest guys I know." Because of its proximity to tubular surfing spots, many students will surf in the morning, go to class in the afternoon, and study at night. Another part of the California character, that of the "trendy, made-up sorority girl," also exists in full force at Cal Poly. However, Cal Poly's rigorous entrance standards ensure that all who come to the school are not merely "all tan and no brain."

In general, the student body at Cal Poly is dominated by white, upper-middle-class Californians. Shiny, new convertibles fill parking lots and undergraduates can be "very image-conscious, sometimes snobby," but most students agree that this facet of Cal Poly life is easily ignored. The school reportedly doesn't boast too much diversity, but this seems to be changing as more minority students—especially women and Asian-Americans—enroll.

Unfortunately, school spirit can be lacking at times. There seems to be a rift between athletes and engineers, and professors may have negative biases toward athletes in general. However, "when a team starts to win its games, the sport suddenly becomes really popular." The men's basketball team competes at the Division I-A level, and its home games are well attended by undergraduates. Many students participate in intramurals, so much that "it seems like there is always an IM game on the fields around campus."

Because of the academic atmosphere, extracurriculars are centered around academics as well. Most students participate in academic clubs, such as the Microbiology Society and the Society of Women Engineers. Between challenging classes, academic clubs, and enjoying California-opportunities, Cal Poly students keep plenty busy.

At few other schools can students obtain a hands-on technical education in small classes and labs, join academic clubs, take advantage of California's weather, beaches, and landscape, and all the while live in a "chill," laid-back atmosphere. With the myriad of unique attributes that attracts students to Cal Poly, it is no wonder students choose to stay so many years. —*Johnny Swagerty*

FYI
The three best things about attending Cal Poly are "small, intense, hands-on academic environment, the laid back atmosphere, and the close proximity to the beach."
The three worst things about attending Cal Poly are "difficulty of getting into courses, the boring town of SLO, and the average six-year stay."
The three things that every student should do before graduating from Cal Poly are "enjoying U-U hour, learning to surf at Pismo Beach, and purchasing a great pair of flip-flops."
One thing I'd like to have known before coming here is "that the stereotype of surfer-dude and sorority chick does prevail here, but the irony is that they are all smart!

California State University / Chico

Address: 400 West First St.; Chico, CA 95929-0722
Phone: 530-898-4428
E-mail address: info@csuchico.edu
Web site URL: www.csuchico.edu
Founded: 1891
Private or Public: public
Religious affiliation: none
Location: small city
Undergraduate enrollment: 13,397
Total enrollment: 13,919
Percent Male / Female: 46%/54%
Percent Minority: 18%
Percent African-American: 2%

Percent Asian: 4%
Percent Hispanic: 10%
Percent Native-American: 2%
Percent in-state / out-of-state: 99%/1%
Percent Pub HS: 84%
Number of Applicants: 6,827
Percent Accepted: 80%
Percent Accepted who enroll: 38%
Entering: 2,052
Transfers: NA
Application Deadline: 30 Nov
Mean SAT: 486 V, 487 M
Mean ACT: NA

Middle 50% SAT range: 440–560 V, 460–567 M
Middle 50% ACT range: 18–23
3 Most popular majors: liberal studies, business administration, psychology
Retention: 79%
Graduation rate: 50%
On-campus housing: 85%
Fraternities: 9%
Sororities: 9%
Library: 1,700,000 volumes
Tuition and Fees: $1,994 in; $9,374 out
Room and Board: $5,860
Financial aid, first-year: 17%

California State University/Chico is set among the foothills of the Sierra Nevada Mountains. The campus is replete with matching brick buildings, ". . . tons of trees and flowers," and the Big Chico Creek running through its center. Strolling around Chico, one often finds students and locals wandering through the twice-weekly farmers market that fills the streets of the small town; its homey feel welcomes students warmly.

A Varied Environment

Though some students feel isolated, others rave about the beauty of their surroundings, "Ten minutes from here there is snow, and five minutes the other direction is fishing, hiking, and the best mountain biking in the country." Students are quick to take advantage of their beautiful location. The salmon fishing is reported to be fantastic, and Chico also boasts Feather Falls, the sixth-largest waterfall in the country. A university-sponsored program, "Adventure Outings," takes groups of students on outdoor expeditions. They also offer day-long classes on

subjects such as wilderness survival. The group has sponsored whitewater rafting, long hiking trips, and even ventured outside of the country. Students looking for a less formal hike or mountain-biking trip walk downtown to Bidwell Park, a huge area with watering holes, places to relax, and a massive trail system.

Hitting the Books

Students don't flock to Chico for the environment alone; many believe that the small class size and the accessible professors are the school's best assets. The undergraduate program consists of six academic colleges as well as a School of Nursing and a College of Business. While core requirements are strenuous, students have few complaints. The average class size is 35 students. Students study diligently during the week, but admit that their books gather dust when the weekend hits.

TRAC, a telephone registration process, makes selecting classes easy, allowing students to plan their schedules up to two years ahead of time. Students report having very little trouble getting into the classes they want. An honors program is available to incoming freshmen with a high school GPA of 3.5 or higher. This program offers more one-on-one attention from professors, smaller classes with an average of 12 students, and an off-campus Honors House. Even if not enrolled in the honors program, students get to know their professors very well. "You see your professors out and about with the students." TAs are very rare, but when present, they get rave reviews as being very in touch with students' needs. Students claim that the friendly atmosphere and size of school leads to more networking with professors and other students, and therefore better jobs after graduation.

Dorm Living

Freshmen live in the dorms, which are co-ed by hall, and consist of small double rooms with "jail beds." The Resident Assistants program in the dorms is quite strict, as the campus is ". . . supposed to be . . . uhh, is, a dry campus." Any student caught with alcohol on campus must endure harsh penalties including community service and attendance at alcohol-related classes. Shafta is a dorm specifically for transfer students, while Whitney Hall is the largest dorm and the only one containing a dining hall. Sophomores traditionally move into Creekside Apartments and the upperclassmen to other off-campus complexes. The dorms tend to be noisy, and have recently become overcrowded.

Students linger over meals in the dining hall to chat about the weekend, but upperclassmen tend to avoid eating there altogether. Rather they choose to use their meal cards at the student union, the BMU, sometimes referred to as "the Moo." Here students gather at The Rainbow Cafe, a snack area where they can pay or use their meal cards. Students also frequent other area restaurants.

Wildcat Spirit

Cheering for the school colors—maroon and white—is also a popular activity. The football team was recently cut completely in order to fund golf and swimming teams, though few students seem upset by the loss. The gym itself is unpopular, with stu-

dents choosing instead to join independent local gyms. The basketball and baseball teams are particularly popular; the baseball team recently won a division II national title.

The Greeks

The Greek system at Chico is a prominent part of campus life. Approximately 40 percent of students join either a sorority or fraternity. The Greeks also sponsor intramural games for less serious athletes, and this often attracts students to the Greek system. Though a division exists between those within the system and those outside of it, students claim that the division is neither extreme nor hostile. The Greek organizations on campus host parties, which are well attended. Students do not date traditionally, but rather travel in large groups. The largest Greek-sponsored activity is Greek Week, a week filled with activities, including relay races to benefit various charities.

> **The students are "laid-back party animals."**

Halloween is the biggest social event of the year; people park all along the streets and get out their folding chairs to watch the costume parade—a town tradition. During this party, which lasts the whole week, the population of Chico nearly doubles. Parties abound, and students wander the streets attending haunted houses and admiring each others' costumes.

Local bands often frequent the Chico campus, and distinguished visitors are also common. The Cherry Poppin' Daddies and Red Hot Chili Peppers are bands who have recently played in front of the Rose Garden, a large grassy area backed by a large garden of roses. Prominent speakers such as the President of the Honda Corporation have also made appearances. A Free Speech area allows campus groups to voice their opinions and gain support for their causes.

Chico is home to the Sierra Nevada Brewery, and many students are proud to drink their locally brewed ales. Going to bars is a favorite weekend activity, with the Bear, a restaurant and bar, and the Crazy Horse, which has a mechanical bull, rating among the top hot spots off-campus. The beverage of choice remains beer, though martinis are a close second. Texas Tea, a stronger version of a Long Island Iced Tea, is thought to have developed in Chico. Students also say that marijuana is prevalent on campus.

Students laud the friendliness of Chico, and say that it is not unusual to smile and wave as they stroll across campus. The student body in general is quite liberal. In fact, the town of Chico holds the largest per capita lesbian population in California. Largely consisting of preppy, middle-class students, diversity at Chico is small, but improving. Described as "laid-back party animals," students are very happy with their experiences at Chico. "It is the typical college experience that you see in the movies," explained one student. Renowned for their partying, Chico students describe themselves as social: "We're like an island, secluded, but we still know how to have a good time."

—*Cynthia Matthews*

FYI

The three best things about attending Chico are "the beautiful campus, the opportunities for fantastic outdoors activities, and the small classes headed by visible, caring professors."

The three worst things about attending Chico are "strict drinking rules, overcrowded dorms, and lack of diversity."

The three things that every student should do before graduating from Chico are "see Feather Falls, participate in Adventure Outing, and share a glass of Sierra Nevada's best with a friend."

One thing I'd like to have known before coming here is "how big the Greek life is here."

California State University / Fresno

Address: 5150 North Maple; Fresno, CA 93740-8026
Phone: 559-278-2261
E-mail address: vivian_franco @csufresno.edu
Web site URL: www.csufresno.edu
Founded: 1961
Private or Public: public
Religious affiliation: none
Location: urban
Undergraduate enrollment: 14,765
Total enrollment: 18,113
Percent Male/Female: 46%/54%
Percent Minority: 44%

Percent African-American: 5%
Percent Asian: 11%
Percent Hispanic: 27%
Percent Native-American: 1%
Percent in-state/out-of-state: 99%/1%
Percent Pub HS: 99%
Number of Applicants: 5,886
Percent Accepted: 68%
Percent Accepted who enroll: 43%
Entering: 1,732
Transfers: NA
Application Deadline: 30 Jul
Mean SAT: 453 V, 473 M
Mean ACT: NA

Middle 50% SAT range: 390–520 V, 410–540 M
Middle 50% ACT range: 16–21
3 Most popular majors: business administration, liberal studies, agricultural sciences
Retention: 80%
Graduation rate: 37%
On-campus housing: 7%
Fraternities: 42%
Sororities: 58%
Library: 900,000 volumes
Tuition and Fees: $3,492 in; $10,880 out
Room and Board: $6,288
Financial aid, first-year: 67%

Looking for an urban agriculture school, or interested in education, engineering, or health sciences? In the center of the state of California, between San Francisco and Los Angeles, lie Fresno, and California State University, Fresno (a.k.a. Fresno State University). In the past decade, the city has developed into a metropolis, home to many software and Internet companies, and the university has matured into a diverse and well-respected state school.

Diversity is one of Fresno's strongest points. As one student put it, "There is awesome racial and ethnic diversity at this school, which I have not seen in many places; it truly makes it fantastic." In the heart of the San Joaquin Valley, Fresno has the resources and enthusiasm that make for an incredible agricultural department. However, it doesn't stop there. Students all have particular interests and ideas, preventing Fresno State from becoming an exclusively agriculture school. According to students, Fresno has highly respected education, engineering, health sciences, and criminology departments. "It can be hard to get into the more popular majors, but it's totally worth it," one student commented.

The Brain Part

Freshman and sophomore years at Fresno are mostly spent fulfilling General Education requirements, commonly known as the "breadth." These classes strive to "expose students to a variety of disciplines within a structured framework." Beginning in the 1999–2000 school year, a new format has been adopted, expanding the program and dividing it into four basic categories. Now students will be required to take their 21 class GE requirements from each of the four groups: "Foundation, Breadth, Integration, and Multicultural/ International Studies."

Along with this change in format, Fresno State has adopted an ambitious program to improve the school, both academically and socially. The staff and faculty's "Vision for the 21st Century" includes the development of an honors program, an intensification of research projects, and an increase in the overall diversity of the campus. The President of the university and his staff are "extremely committed to this school and its improvement," said one student.

The "breadth" allows students to explore many different areas before selecting a major, and is rarely an obstacle when it comes to taking classes in which one is interested. A second-year student confessed, "There are usually a few classes in the divisions that are required by your major anyway." Some of the required courses include a speech course and an English class. While many frosh are daunted by the prospect of giving speeches, this, according to one third-year, is the point, "Every student should take a good speech class their freshman year; it helps bring out some of those shy ones."

Getting into the classes you want is rarely a problem. Even students in popular majors, such as animal science, still found that they were almost never barred from a class and that most of the introductory courses remained relatively small. However, in some instances, when the phone registration system failed to cap the numbers registered, popular courses could end up with up to 300 people. On average, introductory science courses reportedly tend to enroll between 80 and 100 students, but most English and speech courses for freshman are capped at 30. While few students have had problems with TAs teaching courses, as one junior stated, she has "had a few problems with teachers not being able to speak English too well."

There aren't any notorious "slacker majors," or awful classes that everyone avoids. As one student pointed out, "Everyone has their own hopes and aspirations, which of course gives way for diversity"—one of Fresno's greatest qualities.

To escape the distractions of dorm or apartment life, many students choose to study in the Henry Madden Library, which is large enough and modern enough to accommodate a number of different study areas. Moreover, the digital "card catalog" is accessible from any computer.

The Life Part

Student life at Fresno centers around the University Student Union (USU). This building contains many student resources, including a food court, bank, post office, Tower Records, information center, lounge, balcony (for enjoying the beautiful California weather), administrative offices, graphic design center, and meeting rooms for student organizations. In the recreation center one can find billiards, bowling, chess, cards, pinball, video games, and even dominoes. "One could never leave the college and still have an awesome four years," noted one student.

However, most students do choose to leave campus occasionally. While Fresno is not a "commuter school," a fair number of students do live at home, and most after freshman year choose to live off campus. Generally people have cars and if they don't live in one of the "tons of apartments located very close to campus and at reasonable costs," then there are houses within a 5 to 10 minute drive.

Dorms are without question a "great way for frosh to meet people," and most of them are organized "like mini-apartments." The bathrooms are single sex and "the facilities are actually very nice." However, there are Resident Advisors (RAs) and certain "strictly enforced" regulations. Only eight people are allowed in a room at a time, and quiet hours are enforced from 11 PM to 7 AM on weekdays, and from 1 AM to 7 AM on weekends. In addition, there are no kegs allowed on campus.

When not in their rooms, students participate in a variety of activities, from varsity athletics to jobs to community service. On weekends, one sophomore found that "Fresno does not have that much to offer if you are under 21." However, there are movie theaters, restaurants, and clubs located near campus. People do date regularly, and it is not uncommon to see couples walking around the school. Great date spots are Romano's Macaroni Grill, the Bulldog Café, and later in the evening, Williker's or Baja's. Fresno is located almost exactly between San Francisco and Los Angeles, making both a 4-hour drive away, a distant, but not impossible, weekend excursion. Closer by are Shaver Lake and Yosemite, two "beautiful escapes from urban life."

The Outside World

Fresno State's 327-acre main campus and its 1,083-acre University Farm are located at the northeast edge of Fresno, California, at the foot of the Sierra Nevada

mountain range. The San Joaquin Valley, one of the richest agricultural areas in the world, surrounds the city. Fresno is the sixth largest metropolitan area in California and has all the amenities of a major urban area.

> **Said one undergrad, "If I had to go back and pick a school again, I would pick Fresno . . . the campus is beautiful and the diversity amongst students and faculty is incredible."**

The campus itself is spread out enough to seem full of lawn and trees, yet not so large that one can't walk to classes. Sitting in the middle of campus one would find "a large fountain with a row of roses up the center of campus . . . with trees and a grassy area." Directly across are the Student Union and the bookstore.

While crime is a problem off campus, within Fresno State are special designated paths that are very well lit at night, and there are emergency phones scattered throughout campus. In regards to on-campus crime, one student warned, "just like anywhere else, be wary, it's a cool place to meet people, but always keep your eyes open." A third-year added, "I feel safe on campus for the most part, but having a late class is not always a good thing." While for many students living in such an urban environment is quite a shock, the sizable number of students from surrounding areas creates an excellent town-gown relationship. Fresno State has grown up with the city, for the benefit of both, and that connection is not easily forgotten. Every year the Associated Student Body puts on Vintage Days, a celebration where people from all over the Central Valley come together for wine tastings, antique auto shows, sales, and other entertainment. Non-students also find interest in the University due to its dynamic sports teams, where the Red Wave (Fresno fans, wearing their color, "cardinal") have managed to break multiple records in numbers of spectators attending competitions.

The Cheering Part

Varsity sports are a huge part of Fresno State life, ranging from football to the equestrian team. Recently, Bulldog Stadium was expanded to add 11,000 seats to accommodate the increasing number of fans. The fans, called the Red Wave, financially support the entire Fresno athletic program. The athletic boosters club, Bulldog Foundation, has also had the number one fund drive since 1986. While football reigns as the most popular sport on campus, the men's basketball team is "a close second" and the men's basketball team's new coach Jerry Tarkanian has been making a splash and leading the team to numerous victories. Enthusiasm for athletics infects everyone at Fresno, as one student put it, "The sports here at Fresno are awesome. I really don't know too much about their programs, but the facilities and the games are always good."

And those facilities are about to get even better. Scheduled to open in the fall of 2001 is the Save Mart Center, a new arena for Bulldog basketball, volleyball, and wrestling. Sponsored primarily by Save Mart and Pepsi, this facility will not only serve for sporting events, but also concerts and cultural gatherings. It will include classrooms, banquet facilities, shops, and a gym. The enthusiasm of the student body and the surrounding population for sports is what allows this all to happen. The Red Wave is "deafening" at games, and literally looks like a "sea of red" in their Fresno school color.

Fresno State is a school with "an endless amount of opportunities, and a highly involved staff." It enjoys an urban setting in a rural area, meaning students have the best of both worlds. The school is diverse both in students and in faculty, allowing learning to span far beyond the classroom. —*Kyla Dahlin*

FYI
The three best things about attending Fresno State are "the people, the low cost of living, and the campus."
The three worst things about Fresno State are "the crime, the weather, and all the agriculture majors."
The three things everyone should do before graduation are "go to Shaver Lake, go to Vintage days, and participate in as many activities as possible."
One thing I'd like to have known before coming here is "that you MUST be a sports fan . . . or at least pretend to be one."

The Claremont Colleges Intro

The Claremont Colleges are a cluster of five small liberal arts colleges and two graduate schools, nestled in a suburban valley about 35 miles east of Los Angeles. The member colleges are Claremont McKenna, Harvey Mudd, Pitzer, Pomona, and Scripps, as well as Claremont Graduate University and Keck Graduate Institute, both of which are separate from the undergraduate colleges. Each college is independent, with its own faculty, campus, and academic focus. However, the schools' being adjacent to one another gives their respective students the best of both worlds: the feel of a small college with the resources of a large university.

Academic Integration

Cross-registration of classes between the colleges is easy and commonplace. The five campuses make up about 12 blocks total, so commuting is not a problem. Since each college has a particular academic focus and expertise, students can take advantage of specialized instructions in almost every subject. Claremont Mc-Kenna offers 26 majors with strengths in economics, government, and international relations. Harvey Mudd specializes in science and engineering with the option of a five-year master's program. Pitzer offers liberal arts majors with an emphasis on social and behavioral sciences. Pomona offers a variety of majors in arts, humanities, and social and natural sciences with a para-professional bent. Scripps is a liberal arts college for women. All the libraries are integrated as is the campus bookstore.

Campuswide Activities

The Claremont Colleges are also linked through athletic, social, and extracurricular activities. Pitzer and Pomona together comprise a NCAA Division III team, while Claremont McKenna, Harvey Mudd, and Scripps make up another. However, most athletic competition is usually among one another. Parties thrown in one college draw people from the other colleges. And there are several all-college parties thrown throughout the year. Many student organizations are comprised of undergrads from all the colleges, including the Claremont Collage, the student daily newspaper; the Claremont Colleges Model U.N., and the Claremont Shades, an a cappella group. The Claremont Center is the hub for social groups, organizations, and administrations on each campus, and orchestrates the activities of all five schools.

As integrated as the five colleges are, they still retain distinct characteristics, and prospective students should look to find the right fit. As one student summed it up, "It's really a matter of your academic interests as well as your personality. There is something for everyone at each of the colleges, but one college will definitely be the best fit."—*Seung Lee*

Claremont McKenna College

Address: 890 Columbia Avenue; Claremont, CA 91711-6425
Phone: 909-621-8088
E-mail address: admission@mckenna.edu
Web site URL: www.mckenna.edu
Founded: 1946
Private or Public: private
Religious affiliation: none
Location: suburban
Undergraduate enrollment: 1,022
Total enrollment: 1,022
Percent Male/Female: 56%/44%
Percent Minority: 35%
Percent African-American: 4%

Percent Asian: 17%
Percent Hispanic: 13%
Percent Native-American: 0.5%
Percent in-state/out-of-state: 63%/37%
Percent Pub HS: 72%
Number of Applicants: 2,827
Percent Accepted: 28%
Percent Accepted who enroll: 32%
Entering: 252
Transfers: 29
Application Deadline: 15 Jan
Mean SAT: 690 V, 690 M
Mean ACT: 29

Middle 50% SAT range: 620–720 V, 640–730 M
Middle 50% ACT range: 27–31
3 Most popular majors: economics, government, psychology
Retention: 94%
Graduation rate: 87%
On-campus housing: 100%
Fraternities: NA
Sororities: NA
Library: 2,011,000 volumes
Tuition and Fees: $20,795 in; $20,795 out
Room and Board: $7,420
Financial aid, first-year: 71%

Although the school enrolls fewer than a thousand undergrads, students at Claremont McKenna College do not feel isolated, claustrophobic, or bored. Instead, they are immersed in the social opportunities of the five-college system and the challenges of its rigorous academic standards. The "work hard/party hard" ethic is the rule here, but mixed with the laid-back atmosphere and

newness of southern California, Claremont McKenna creates a unique environment of its own.

Five-Colleges = Five-Star Social Life

A distinguishing feature of Claremont
McKenna is its membership in the five-
college Claremont Colleges System,
which also includes Pomona, Pitzer, Harvey Mudd, and Scripps. Students may
cross-register in classes, facilities are
open to all undergrads, and no social barriers prevent students from interacting
with those from the other colleges. Most
students agree that CMC is the kind of
place where everyone knows everyone,
including the professors, but the other
schools provide additional social options.
One junior commented, "It's small, but you
can make it as big as you want it to be."

Within the five-college system, students
pull resources together in order to party
hard. Almost every weekend there is a
five-college party, hosted in various conference rooms, dining halls, and other facilities in the schools. Professional dj's are
hired or student bands play, and attendance can reach over 200; not surprisingly, undergrads report that these parties
are usually pretty fun. College councils organize the especially popular theme nights,
such as Monte Carlo, a formal event with
jazz music and faux gambling, and the
Screw Your Roommate, a semiformal
dance where roommates set each other
up on blind dates. The vibrant five-college
scene keeps most social activity on campus, and students rarely venture into the
town of Claremont on the weekends.

Claremont is regarded as a retirement
community and its lack of entertainment
options draw disgruntled comments from
students. Students at CMC report that it is
not a huge party school but "you can go
out around three nights a week, if you get
your work done."

The CMC administration seeks a happy
medium between tolerance of campus
parties and the enforcement of strict
rules. In recent years, the number of kegs
allowed per weekend in school-sponsored
functions has been reduced to six, but students attest that "you won't be thrown out
of school if you're caught with beers in
your backpack." Kids who don't drink re-

portedly do not feel out of the social circle: the college provides a variety of other
activities, many students don't binge
drink, and there is a popular substance-
free dorm if students so choose. Drug use
at CMC usually doesn't extend beyond alcohol, as only a few students report smoking pot. There is also no Greek system
within the five colleges.

Besides parties, a variety of events are
organized on campus by individual
dorms, the CMC College Council, or the
Five College Council, with activities ranging from small get-togethers to movies to
semi-formal dances. Both Dave Matthews
Band and Third Eye Blind have played at
the college, much to the understandable
delight of students. Also, the college sponsors a weekly series of dinner lectures
known as Athenaeum, which has brought
speakers such as James Earl Jones and
the California schools superintendent to
speak.

Small Classes, Big Selection

As one would expect from a school with
an enrollment of a thousand, class sizes
are small at CMC. A typical class consists
of about 25 students, and a 75-person
class is considered big. Thanks to the five-
college system, students can choose from
a wide variety of classes from all five
schools and use common facilities, such
as the newly built Joint Science Center.

Students voice overwhelmingly high
opinions for the academics at CMC. They
never find it difficult to get into desired
courses or the required general education
(GE) classes. The GE classes are described as challenging and fair. Professors
welcome interaction with students both
in and out of class. One student attested,
"We eat lunch and dinner with our professors all the time. They even come to our
parties." Also, it is common for undergraduates to be an integral part of professors' research projects. One senior
reported, "Here professors will actually
ask students to work on their projects,
and they expect them to do real research."

CMC boasts a high academic standard,
so classes are not a breeze. Reportedly it
is very difficult to get an A or A- in a
course, and students definitely believe
that they have a lot of work. These aspects of CMC life may not be as popular as

the student/professor interaction, but it guarantees the respected academic reputation of the school.

Equal but Separate

Although the five-college system is extremely integrated, the student body at Claremont McKenna never loses its unity or identity. There are many opportunities for CMC students to meet and hang out with the other 3000 undergrads at the neighboring schools, but social circles rarely extend beyond CMC. One student claimed, "People interact but identify with their own school." Another student added, "I know people in the other schools, but most of my friends are from Claremont. But it's a good thing—the system is unifying rather than restrictive."

Diversity has increased at CMC in recent years, but students still say that it has room to increase further. The majority of the kids are from white, upper-middle-class backgrounds in California, but one student reported that people here aren't "snobby or spoiled." However, the student body is changing: more and more states and foreign countries are represented, enrollment of women and minorities is rising, and the political balance is shifting toward moderate after years of conservative domination.

> **"It's small, but you can make it as big as you want it to be."**

Besides studying hard, most CMC students fill their time with a wide variety of campus clubs and organizations, and like many other aspects of CMC, these clubs often involve all five colleges. Because of the popularity of the economics and business-related majors, academic organizations such as the Accounting and Student Investment Clubs are quite popular. A few atypical clubs exist at Claremont, such as the James Madison Society and the Winston Churchill Society, which convene to smoke cigars and drink fine wine, respectively.

Intra-Claremont Rivalry

By far the most popular undergraduate organization is sports. Students estimate that between 40 and 60 percent of students participate in at least one varsity sport in their four-year career, and almost everyone plays intramurals. The campus is filled with fields and grassy areas, and combined with California's sunny weather, CMC creates a great atmosphere for athletic competition. A student commented, "There is always a pick-up game of soccer or ultimate Frisbee going on, or maybe just a couple people throwing a baseball." On the varsity level, the Claremont College System's five colleges are divided into two teams, one team consisting of Claremont McKenna, Harvey Mudd, and Scripps Colleges and the other made up by Pitzer and Pomona. Basketball draws the largest student crowds, and the big game between the two Claremont teams can get wild: people dress up and supporters of each team try to steal the opponent's mascot.

CMC boasts many other traditions enjoyed by undergrads. Apart from the usually chaotic basketball festivities, on students' birthdays it is customary to "pond" them, or throw them numerous times into one of several campus fountains.

Dorm life is something else that distinguishes CMC from colleges across the nation. Almost 100 percent of students live on-campus all four years, choosing between the dorms or, as upperclassmen, on-campus apartments. Dorms are not segregated by year; students meet a variety of people from all class levels, interests, and ages with whom they share floors and buildings. Also, the RA system is very friendly. One student commented, "My RAs were not alcohol police, but focused on becoming friends with residents and being involved in dorm life."

Claremont McKenna does not fit the typical idea of a liberal arts college. By combining the benefits of a small school, such as interaction with professors, small classes, and a lively on-campus social life, with the resources, facilities, and class selection of a mid-size university, CMC provides students with the best of both worlds. —*Johnny Swagerty*

FYI
The three best things about attending CMC are "five college system, small classes, and great student-professor relations."
The three worst things about attending CMC are "the town of Claremont, the need for diversity, and LA smog."
The three things that every student should do before graduating from CMC are "go to a five-college party, attend an Anthanaeum lecture, and participate in intermurals."
One thing I'd like to have known before coming here is "how much I would love the CMC experience—the tough academics, the students, and a sense of community that includes your professors."

Harvey Mudd College

Address: 301 East 12th St.; Claremont, CA 91711-5990
Phone: 909-621-8011
E-mail address: admission@hmc.edu
Web site URL: www.hmc.edu
Founded: 1955
Private or Public: private
Religious affiliation: none
Location: suburban
Undergraduate enrollment: 693
Total enrollment: 699
Percent Male / Female: 74% / 26%
Percent Minority: 22%
Percent African-American: 0.5%

Percent Asian: 17%
Percent Hispanic: 4%
Percent Native-American: 0.5%
Percent in-state / out-of-state: 40% / 60%
Percent Pub HS: NA
Number of Applicants: 1,642
Percent Accepted: 33%
Percent Accepted who enroll: 32%
Entering: 170
Transfers: 9
Application Deadline: 15 Jan
Mean SAT: 700 V, 760 M
Mean ACT: NA

Middle 50% SAT range: 660–770 V, 730–800 M
Middle 50% ACT range: NA
3 Most popular majors: engineering, computer science, physics
Retention: 96%
Graduation rate: 79%
On-campus housing: 100%
Fraternities: NA
Sororities: NA
Library: 2,000,000 volumes
Tuition and Fees: $22,069 in; $22,069 out
Room and Board: $7,946
Financial aid, first-year: 72%

If you like math and science, that is, if you really like math and science, then Harvey Mudd College might be right up your alley. Located in suburban Claremont, California, Harvey Mudd offers students a rigorous and self-motivated education with top-quality academics and outstanding professors in a slightly unusual environment. Mudd students pride themselves on their strong work ethic, as well as the seemingly endless hours spent completing physics problem sets and math projects. They're also quick to point out the lighter side of life at Mudd—they live in a "crazy, weird, eccentric place," and they know how to break free from stress. "We may study a lot, but we're not nearly as uptight as Caltech," one junior pointed out. Mudd, like any other college, has its share of parties, student activities, and unique traditions.

Science Anyone?
Mudders are the first to point out the intensity of their curriculum. According to one junior, "The whole school is basically an honors program." Most of Mudd students' first two years are filled with core requirements, which amount to a total of 12 science and math courses, and additional humanities courses. Gut courses are unheard of, unless you consider Introductory Bio a walk in the park. Students estimate spending four to six hours a night on homework, and they insist this does not include time spent procrastinating.

Harvey Mudd College offers students only six majors: physics, chemistry, biology, math, computer science, and engineering. However, the opportunities to diversify one's education are growing. Students are offered the option of a double major, or more recently, the option to "off-campus major." The off-campus-major program allows students to complete requirements for a major at one of the other Claremont colleges, while still graduating with a degree from Harvey Mudd. With the academically diverse mix of the Claremont system, students can major in subjects ranging from music to Chinese, while still benefiting from their own math/science-rich environment. However, the off-campus major is a relatively new policy, and has not yet become popular among the science-hungry Mudders.

Most students praise the individual classes and professors at Mudd, noting that most classes have only 25 enrolled students. Some introductory lecture courses enroll up to 175 students, but these classes also have smaller tutorials led by professors. One student noted, "It's not particularly difficult to get into the classes you want to take—you might not get a time slot or a professor you want, but you aren't really restricted in your choice of actual courses." All courses at Mudd are taught by professors, and students appreciate the individual attention they receive. "The professors are easily accessible, and most are very good. They're excited to talk to students one on one, and being a small school, they usually recognize you and remember your name outside of class," noted one student.

Mudders raved about the "Clinic Program." It is very popular among engineering majors, but students in other majors can also participate. A large company, such as Kodak, develops a yearlong program in cooperation with Harvey Mudd, and students work together on a particular problem or project for the company. They design a system, solve the problem, and give the company a working prototype at the end of the year: one that actually gets used by the company. Students were quite pleased with the clinic program, and boasted of the superiority of Mudd's program to other schools' similar programs.

Campus and Community

"[The founders] decided that they really liked cinder block when they built Mudd," explained one junior. The modern cinder-block style is predominant on the small campus, which is about the size of a city block. Many buildings are accentuated with "warts," small square protrusions from the sides of buildings, which serve no functional purpose other than helping to differentiate Mudd from most other schools. Mudd is within walking distance from the other Claremont Colleges, thus helping to provide a change of scenery for most students. Another much appreciated aspect of the college's location is the relative closeness to Los Angeles, which allows students with cars to escape from the high-stress academic atmosphere and let loose in the city.

Only freshmen are required to live on campus, but most other Mudders choose to do so anyway. Students generally have positive responses toward their living quarters. There are seven dorms on campus, which consist of doubles and singles, some of which are grouped as suites into quads, sextets, or octets. South dorm, for example, is nearly all singles, while Linde has suites of six, and Atwood has suites of eight. Each dorm has its own distinct personality, or "dormunity," as Mudd students like to call it. "West dorm is really loud; the jugglers and martial artists live in East—they also have an old fire pit they use for a hot tub on weekends; North dormers stay to themselves more," noted one student who happened to live in the unicycler dorm. All dorms are co-ed; one female student lived in a suite with three males, and was quick to point out the logical nature of her living situation. As only a Mudder would phrase it, "There's a pi:1 ratio of guys to girls here, so it makes sense." One can only guess where the extra $0.14159\ldots$ came from. Students report that the dorm rooms are moderately sized and well furnished, with ethernet connections in all the rooms. Mudd dorms each have a few proctors (similar to RAs), but "they're not very strict—it's a pretty relaxed atmosphere in the dorms."

All Mudd students living on campus

must have a meal plan, which most students consider pretty flexible. Harvey Mudd has one main dining hall, but hungry Mudders can look to any of the five dining halls of the Claremont colleges for their meals. In addition, there are restaurants in the area to provide a bit of variety to one's diet. However, don't look too hard for a McDonald's—the town of Claremont does not allow chain restaurants or stores within the city limits. The Mudd Hole, a student hangout, also provides snacks to students looking to relax among the pool tables and video games.

Mudd shares its library cnd athletic facilities with the other four Claremont colleges. A new recreation center just opened on campus, and is growing in popularity among Mudders. "It takes a while to rip us away from our computers," noted one student.

Attractions and Distractions

Yes, despite what some may believe, there is life outside of academia at Harvey Mudd, and students take advantage of their convenient location and unique student body to get the most out of their free time. As one student points out, "Most Mudders have average IQs higher than the rest of the world, so it's a very interesting atmosphere."

Watching television is a big part of any college campus social life, and Mudd students have their own favorites in the X-Files (do you like science much?) and The Simpsons. Many students also often pile into cars and hit the L.A. club scene. "It's so cool to be able to leave campus and go dancing in Hollywood," noted one junior. Like most other colleges, Mudd is also no stranger to the alcohol/party scene. "Dorms throw parties every couple of weekends because there are no frats, but on any given weekend, there are always some random, small things going on," noted one student. "There's not much pressure to drink for those who choose not to, but if you do, there's pressure to drink more. The social life doesn't revolve around liquor, but it's always available."

> "There is a pi:1 ratio of guys to girls here."

Dating is a tricky issue at Mudd, because of the lopsided ratio of guys to girls. A male student pointed out, "We spend a lot of time at Scripps [a women's college within the Claremont system]." Mudd is not completely lacking in romantic relationships, though, and students point out that a lot of people are involved in relationships, or at least random hookups.

Students can also participate in a slew of student activities, such as the Gonzo Unicycling Club, Shades singing group, swing dancing, intramurals, club, and varsity sports (varsity teams are formed together with Scripps and Claremont Colleges). Inter-collegiate sports competition consists of competing against the combined teams from Pitzer and Pomona Colleges. While athletic activities are available to students, they are not a big priority for most people. Said one student, "Most Mudders don't care too much about attending sporting events; our school spirit comes from being nerdy together."

Other types of stress relief for Mudders include getting drunk and running around all five of the Claremont colleges campuses and jumping in every body of water in sight. Even the annual food fight in North Dorm, and the Mudders' common hatred of their academic rival, Caltech, brings the students closer together. One large-scale prank involved stealing a giant cannon from Caltech, who had previously stolen it from the National Guard. Added one Mudder, "Large trucks and heavy manpower were used."

Harvey Mudd students consider themselves to be extremely close-knit and community-oriented. "The way it's designed, if you weren't a part of the community and wanted to exclude yourself, you wouldn't survive. It's a team effort because we all work so hard and are usually in high-speed mode," said one sophomore.

Harvey Mudd College is no scene out of Animal House. Its intense academic programs require a great deal of effort from students, and in turn, the school offers students one of the most respected science and math curricula in the country. Students are always quick to mention their concentrated workload. However, Mudd is more than just math and science classes, and most people truly enjoy the stimulating and often silly environment in which they find themselves. Members of the diverse student body always seem to be able to find ways to amuse themselves and have fun when they are not working, whenever those precious times come.

Students get a kick out of their own craziness, but it's justified by the intensity of their academic programs. As one Mudder explained, "We really do work that hard."
—Melissa Andersen

FYI
The three best things about attending Mudd are "the intensity, the ability to intensely concentrate on one subject, and the personal attention from the professors."
The three worst things about attending Mudd are "the intensity, the lack of females, and the cinder-block campus!"
The three things that every student should do before graduating from Mudd are "academically diversifying by taking a non-science course at a Claremont college, participate in the Clinic Program, and revel in the eccentric student body."
One thing I'd like to have known before coming here is "what a crazy, intense, and amusing environment Mudd really is."

Pitzer College

Address: 1050 North Mills Avenue; Claremont, CA 91711
Phone: 909-621-8219
E-mail address: admission@pitzer.edu
Web site URL: www.pitzer.edu
Founded: 1963
Private or Public: private
Religious affiliation: none
Location: suburban
Undergraduate enrollment: 930
Total enrollment: 930
Percent Male / Female: 36% / 64%
Percent Minority: 31%
Percent African-American: 5%

Percent Asian: 11%
Percent Hispanic: 14%
Percent Native-American: 0.5%
Percent in-state / out-of-state: 59% / 41%
Percent Pub HS: 50%
Number of Applicants: 1,716
Percent Accepted: 72%
Percent Accepted who enroll: 20%
Entering: 246
Transfers: NA
Application Deadline: 1 Feb
Mean SAT: 601 V, 584 M
Mean ACT: NA

Middle 50% SAT range: 540–650 V, 520–640 M
Middle 50% ACT range: 21–27
3 Most popular majors: psychology, sociology, art
Retention: NA
Graduation rate: 58%
On-campus housing: 75%
Fraternities: NA
Sororities: NA
Library: 2,000,000 volumes
Tuition and Fees: $24,096 in; $24,096 out
Room and Board: $6,240
Financial aid, first-year: 50%

Considered to be the most care-free school of the Claremont Colleges, this small college has made a unique name for itself. As one of the five schools that make up the Claremont system, Pitzer's academic flexibility, numerous opportunities to get involved in extracurricular activities, and great location combine to make it "an extremely fun and diverse environment to be in." True, Pitzer's activities provide "a lot of distractions to take you off track," but students

promise that "there's a very supportive community here that will help you along the way."

Pitzer is located about 40 minutes outside Los Angeles. Its location attracts a very diverse student body: people of different ethnicities, opinions, fashions, interests and backgrounds hail from California to Illinois to the Middle East. Students do report, however, that there is a "liberal leaning" among those who attend.

Pitzer students appreciate the safety

and cleanliness of the city of Claremont. Although it has "lots of pretty houses and trees," students complain that "it's not a college town." Still, they enjoy the restaurants and shops in the area which provide them with the opportunity to relax and get away from campus for a while. Students have the freedom to roam about Claremont, thanks to the fact that the area is basically "free from crime." The overall consensus is that the city is a "peaceful place to be."

No Shortage of Academic Options

Because of its relatively small student body of less than a thousand undergraduates, the faculty to student ratio at Pitzer is low, allowing students a good deal of interaction with their professors. "It's awesome—you get so much help," says one student. "Even if a class is hard, it's so easy to do well because professors are always ready and willing to help you." Class sizes in general range anywhere from 7 to 20 students, and even introductory courses are small. Says one student, "I don't think I had a class that enrolled more than 40 students." Close contact with professors is enhanced by a college-sponsored program in which students invite faculty members to their dining halls to discuss courses or just to get to know each other better. The contact with professors is so close that some instructors occasionally have classes right in their own homes.

There are few complaints about the limited number of required courses. According to one student, "The requirements are really easy to fulfill and they don't hinder your ability to take the classes you really want to take."

Among the most popular and strongest of Pitzer's departments, according to students, are sociology and psychology. Because of the popularity of some departments, classes fill up quickly, and students can get shut out. Students aren't limited to Pitzer's courses, however, for everyone has the option of taking class at any of the Claremont colleges. These Joint Courses provide the wealth of academic options that makes Pitzer "everything you can ask for in a college academically."

Where Should I Live?

Like many other private schools, Pitzer requires all freshman to live on campus. Sophomores and juniors can live off campus, but they must apply for permission to do so. Most students, however, opt for on-campus housing, which consists of three dorms: Holden, Mead, and Sanbourn Halls. All freshman and almost all sophomores live in Holden, nicknamed the "suburbs," and Sanbourn, also called the "ghetto." Upperclassmen live in Mead, which is referred to as the "projects." Despite the name, however, Mead is characterized by large apartment-style suites and huge rooms and is also known as the "party Hall." Within these dorms, there are numerous "theme halls," on which students can choose to live. Students who want a noise-free environment live in "Hush Hall" in Holden, which is known for its quiet and serene atmosphere. "Involvement Tower" in Mead Hall is designed for students who want a support network of other students for their academic, as well as their non-academic, concerns. And "Wellness Quarter" in Sanbourn is occupied by students who neither smoke nor drink.

There is one dining hall on campus, McConnell, which serves the entire Pitzer student body, and many students complain about the quality of food it serves. "Sometimes the food is good; sometimes it's not," explained one undergrad. "Students frequently dash off to Collins [at Pomona] to satisfy their hunger," says another student. All students who live on campus are required to purchase a meal plan, but they have the freedom to eat at any of the other dining halls in the Claremont Colleges. In addition, they can use their meal plan to eat at either the Gold Mine or the Groove House, two on-campus eateries, up to twice each week. Other options include going to the numerous off-campus restaurants and cafes.

What's On Campus?

Newly built facilities include the Gold Mine, the Groove House, and the Gold Center, where students can get their minds off school work. The Gold Mine is a student-run eatery where students can grab a quick bite to eat or substitute their regular dining hall meals. The Groove

House is a coffeehouse frequented by students who want to relax, talk to friends, or just simply catch up on some reading. The student union building, the Gold Center, allows students to "kick back and unwind after a long, hard day of studying." It contains an arcade room, a swimming pool, a TV room complete with pool and ping-pong tables, and a weight room. It also includes meeting rooms that are used by various campus organizations.

Varsity sport teams are shared by the colleges, something unique to the Claremont system. Pitzer and Pomona team up to form the Sage Hens and Harvey Mudd, Scripps, and Claremont McKenna come together to form a rival team. There is a strong rivalry between these two teams, and though students concede that athletics are not a big deal, sporting events between these two teams are sure to draw crowds.

> **"The requirements are really easy to fulfill and they don't hinder your ability to take the classes you really want to take."**

Since Pitzer doesn't have its own library, many students go to Honnold at Pomona, which is the most popular of all the campus libraries. Those looking for books of mathematics and the hard sciences usually go to Sprague library at Harvey Mudd. Dennison, the Scripps library, specializes in books on the fine arts and humanities. Students enjoy this variety; according to one, "It gives me the opportunity to go to any library I'm in the mood for."

What To Do?

Pitzer offers many extracurricular activities that keep students active and involved. Students can write for the daily newspaper, *The College,* offered to all five colleges, or they can host a radio program on the student-run radio station, also managed by all five colleges. Community service is one of the more popular ways in which students get involved. Other activities range from student government,

which is considered to be very influential, to intramural sports. These activities equip Pitzer with "every opportunity to get involved with something." You can tutor at high schools, volunteer at community centers, or participate in campus activities. Basically, "all you have to do is just figure out what you want to do and then do it."

On the weekends, many students hit the party scene. Most activities are held in Mead Hall. Events sponsored by a student organization which spans all five colleges take place in McKenna Auditorium. Students' choices of parties are diverse, ranging from dance parties that play hip-hop, dance, or house music, to wild concerts with live bands, to parties that serve "lots and lots" of alcohol. Drugs and alcohol are part of the party scene and it's not too hard to fund them if that's what you're looking for. According to one student, students drink freely because "Pitzer is not really strict about cracking down on them." Instead, claims one, the administration "[tells] you that whatever you do is your business."

Besides the typical weekend parties, Pitzer throws a couple well-known parties every year. OSCAR, a student activity group, organizes a party called "The Super Tri Fly," featuring hip-hop and house music. The once-a-semester party called "Screw Your Homey" involves setting people up on a blind date. However, the social event considered by students to be the best of the year is the weekend-long party called Kahoutek. Celebrating the coming of the spring, it attracts some big-name bands and arts and crafts from all over southern California.

Beyond the confines of the Claremont campus, students needing an escape can flock to the many attractions of Los Angeles and the surrounding area. Nearby, students can shop and hang out at the Montclair Mall or catch a movie at the local cinema, Edward's. For students with cars, Los Angeles is a popular destination. The beaches, Hollywood, sports events, and Disneyland are just some of the many places students go on the weekends.

Pitzer is a diverse and vibrant community that thrives on the opportunities offered by the larger Claremont Colleges community. Students enjoy these opportunities, claiming that "you have a great time at Pitzer; overall, it's a really great and exciting place to be." —*Edward Mundy*

FYI

The three best things about attending Pitzer are "accessibility to professors, great opportunities to study abroad, and its diversity."

The three worst things about attending Pitzer are "prevalent drug use, you have to go to the Pomona library to get some quiet study time, and you get absolutely no privacy."

The three things that every student should do before graduating from Pitzer are "travel abroad (it's so easy to do), get really drunk the day before finals, and pull at least one all-nighter each semester."

One thing I'd like to have known before coming here is "that there was so much drug use here."

Pomona College

Address: 333 North College Way; Claremont, CA 91711
Phone: 909-621-8134
E-mail address: admissions@pomona.edu
Web site URL: www.pomona.edu
Founded: 1887
Private or Public: private
Religious affiliation: none
Location: suburban
Undergraduate enrollment: 1,530
Total enrollment: 1,530
Percent Male/Female: 53%/47%
Percent Minority: 33%
Percent African-American: 4%

Percent Asian: 18%
Percent Hispanic: 10%
Percent Native-American: 1%
Percent in-state/out-of-state: 39%/61%
Percent Pub HS: 70%
Number of Applicants: 3,612
Percent Accepted: 32%
Percent Accepted who enroll: 34%
Entering: 390
Transfers: 16
Application Deadline: 1 Jan
Mean SAT: 720 V, 710 M
Mean ACT: 32

Middle 50% SAT range: 670–760 V, 670–750 M
Middle 50% ACT range: 29–32
3 Most popular majors: biology, psychology, history
Retention: 99%
Graduation rate: 94%
On-campus housing: 100%
Fraternities: 9%
Sororities: NA
Library: 2,000,000 volumes
Tuition and Fees: $24,170 in; $24,170 out
Room and Board: $8,170
Financial aid, first-year: 51%

Even in the great multitudes of California's outstanding educational institutions, Pomona College stands tall among the masses. Pomona is a relatively small school, but the quality of its academic program has propelled it to high standing. In recent years, *U.S. News & World Report* has ranked Pomona among the top national liberal arts colleges in the nation. In addition to its intimate feel, Pomona enjoys the resources of a larger university through its affiliation with the Claremont Colleges system. To its credit, Pomona has risen to the top ranks through an unusual blend of traditional and innovative methods.

Unique Academics

Besides attracting some of the nation's best students, Pomona's liberal arts approach ensures that every student is provided with a broad education. Besides the usual courses that reportedly produce sleep-deprived students, Pomona has its own unique selection of courses. All first-year students have to take an ID1 course, which is a writing/thinking-intensive class. Although it may sound like a typical class,

Mind, Culture, and Sport allows students to chat, think, and play sports on the same day the paper is due. Furthermore, Pomona requires its freshmen to take a P.E. class for the first semester. The courses range from aikido to Brazilian jujitsu techniques—talk about a liberal education! However, Pomona still keeps its share of the classics. Even at a school with such academic diversity, the most popular majors include psychology, economics, English, political science, and chemistry.

Although Pomona has an abundance of social opportunities, any prospective sage hen should understand one important aspect about Pomona's social scene. One student describes it as "a socially awkward place where there doesn't seem to be a set group of friends that you hang around with." Many students claim that the school is so small that "even if there were cliques on campus, you would know at least two or three people in that group." Pomona's small size makes social life quite different. For the most part, Pomona is one of those "you know everybody" schools. As one student put it, "The whole school is almost one big group of friends."

Drinking is a common part of most colleges and Pomona is no exception. Pomona's social scene generally centers on parties, so alcohol often finds its way into the mix. Says one student, "The rules for alcohol at Pomona are very, very liberal." Another quips, "The rules are almost amusing because nobody cares if you are of age or not." Take heart, though, if you are not into drinking. "There are many non-drinkers on campus, so it's not a big thing if you don't drink."

Living at Pomona

Even if you're not into the activities on campus, there is much to do in and around the community. Pomona College is close to Ontario Mills Mall and about an hour away from Los Angeles. Of course, many students claim that a car is a must. Echoes of "I really need a car" can be heard all over campus. But students say the great likelihood is that you will have a friend who drives, so if you are vehicularly challenged, you won't be left stranded and bored.

> **For the most part, Pomona is one of those "you know everybody" schools.**

Some think that size is all that matters. In the case of Pomona College, small size definitely does matter. Pomona has among the lowest student-to-faculty ratio (9 to 1) of any college and 79 percent of classes have fewer than 20 students. "Most classes are taught by professors and there is a very free and open climate when it comes to class discussions." Students report great individual attention from the professors.

If all that isn't enough for you, one of the greatest advantages of going to Pomona College is its affiliation with the other Claremont colleges. Based on the Oxford University system, the Claremont Colleges are a group of five colleges that include Pomona, Claremont McKenna, Pitzer, Scripps, and Harvey Mudd. As a Pomona student, you have the opportunity to enroll in each college's courses. If you opt to take courses from the college that specializes in a particular field, you are essentially getting the best of five worlds.

Social Pecking Order

Pomona's social life is lively and enriching. Pomona's mascot is the Sagehen. If you're one of those people who are just into hanging around, then Pomona has a huge student center called the Coup. "The Coup is a great place to meet fellow Sagehens, eat, study, and of course . . . sleep," says a current student. However, if you require more than hanging around, Pomona can deliver. You can try a whole host of activities that range from the Filipino Club to the Hawaii Club. Sports definitely abound. Pomona is a Division III school and you can try your hand at varsity sports or intramural—whatever strikes your fancy.

Students say the food at Pomona inspires many different eating habits. One student claims that "no one even touches the beef and everyone is slowly becoming a vegetarian." Apparently, the food at

Pomona not only inspires vegetarian conversions, but a general migration to Claremont McKenna College. If you're dying for some decent food, "you will have to hike over to Claremont McKenna for the best grub."

Most freshmen live on South Campus, which is a group of dorms made up of long, big hallways. Rooms vary in size from small to large. Pomona's dorms are generally described "as happy living quarters, filled with camaraderie and bonding. They are definitely livable places."

Pomona is an extremely open and tolerant community. There are lots of interracial couples and ample opportunities for relationships abound. One student noted that, "Although there are not very many homosexual people at Pomona, many people here respect others' beliefs and behaviors." It is apparently very common to see posters on people's doors that sport such phrases as-"I respect 'Queer' [name of homosexual support group] rights". Overall, many see Pomona as a community that is very accepting of diversity.

So what makes Pomona rise above the rest? Pomona is like the David of colleges surrounded by many Goliaths. It may be small, but there are so many advantages and beneficial aspects of a Pomona education that it definitely warrants consideration from anyone looking for a small-college environment with all the advantages of a university education.

—*Aaron Johanson and Staff*

FYI

The three best things about attending Pomona are, "the students are amazing, the professors really care, and the weather is spectacular."

The three worst things about attending Pomona are, "a poor relationship with the surrounding community, the lack of school spirit, and the lack of diversity."

The three things that every student should do before graduating from Pomona are, "go to a professor's house for dinner, go skiing and to the beach all in one day, and be part of a live television audience in Hollywood."

One thing I'd like to have known before coming here is "no need for winter clothing!"

Scripps College

Address: 1030 Columbia Avenue; Claremont, CA 91711
Phone: 909-621-8149
E-mail address: admofc@d.scrippscol.edu
Web site URL: www.scrippscol.edu
Founded: 1926
Private or Public: private
Religious affiliation: none
Location: suburban
Undergraduate enrollment: 769
Total enrollment: 769
Percent Male/Female: 0%/100%
Percent Minority: 25%
Percent African-American: 3%

Percent Asian: 15%
Percent Hispanic: 6%
Percent Native-American: 0.5%
Percent in-state/out-of-state: 53%/47%
Percent Pub HS: 53%
Number of Applicants: 1,063
Percent Accepted: 70%
Percent Accepted who enroll: 28%
Entering: 212
Transfers: 11
Application Deadline: 1 Feb
Mean SAT: 640 V, 620 M
Mean ACT: 27
Middle 50% SAT range: 600–690 V, 560–670 M

Middle 50% ACT range: 25–30
3 Most popular majors: psychology, politics and international relations, biology
Retention: 88%
Graduation rate: 69%
On-campus housing: 100%
Fraternities: NA
Sororities: NA
Library: 2,000,000 volumes
Tuition and Fees: $21,130 in; $21,130 out
Room and Board: $7,870
Financial aid, first-year: 51%

If life among independent, motivated women strolling between Spanish Mediterranean architecture, sprawling lawns, and rose gardens sounds appealing, check out Scripps College! This small, all female institution boasts the intimacy and community of a single-sex school, and the resources and entertainment of the surrounding four colleges and nearby Los Angeles.

Students are quick to point out that they are not members of a stereotypical women's college. "It's not about feminism and activism, but about equality and community spirit." The advantages of a single-sex environment range from the supportive environment and relaxed atmosphere, to the attention given to women's educational issues. Most students did not choose Scripps because of its all-female status, but rather fell in love with the school itself.

All in the Family

Scripps is part of a consortium with Claremont McKenna, Pomona, Pitzer, and Harvey Mudd. Students cross-register frequently, and claim that doing so is easy, and often rewarding. "Going to one of the other schools is just like walking to another part of campus." Claremont McKenna, Pitzer, and Scripps have a Joint Science Center, where resources, and often classes, are shared between the schools. This state-of-the-art facility (completed in 1992) allows Scripps to benefit from resources that it would not be able to afford alone.

Students rate academics highly, praising their professors, as well as their small classes. The campus is evenly divided between humanities and science majors. With an average of 10 to 15 students in a Scripps class, and up to 150 in a joint science lecture, personal attention is one of Scripps' greatest attributes. There are no teaching assistants, and the professors are helpful and always willing to talk.

A core curriculum is required of all Scripps students. Students must also fulfill general requirements, which include three semesters of foreign language, one of laboratory science, two of social sciences, and one inter-cultural class. Students note that these requirements are not difficult to meet.

Scripps registers students by randomly choosing a letter, and proceeding alphabetically from that point, circling back around to cover the letters passed initially. This provides a fair way to register students, though some students are occasionally denied their first-choice classes.

The Scripps campus is located in the rather upscale town of Claremont, dubbed "the village" by students, and student interaction with the townspeople is very congenial. The campus is built in a loose square, with lawns and walled gardens filling the middle. A set of steps forming a semi-circle in the middle of campus is laughingly called "the Miss America Steps." Add Spanish Mediterranean architecture and rose gardens to these lawns, and it is easy to understand why the Scripps campus is a National Historic Landmark. Students feel extremely safe on the Scripps campus. It is a quiet and closed community in which students "never feel endangered." The dorms have an escort policy stating that a Scripps student must always accompany visitors to the dorms.

Home Sweet Home

Dorms at Scripps vary widely but all have resident assistants. Scripps has a few newer dorms, which are largely suite-style, with air-conditioning, and several older dorms, which students often prefer. "The older dorms have more character, with larger rooms, vaulted ceilings, and just more charm," one student explained. Designed to foster a close community, the older dorms each have a living room with a piano, and a fireplace, as well as a "browsing room" in which students may make use of uninterrupted quiet, reference books, and couches. One particularly unique dormitory, Toll Hall, has a star-shaped fountain in its courtyard with balconies running around it. Students call residing in this part "living on star court."

Students live in double rooms their first year, and singles thereafter. Housing was once tight, but a new dorm has helped alleviate the space crunch. Further campus additions include a new Commons, built to replace three smaller dining halls and to make dining at Scripps more accessible to students at other Claremont schools. Commons also houses administrative offices, student organizations, and mailboxes.

A new food service was introduced recently, and students were not happy with the results. Students unhappy with the menu can use their meal plans at grills and pizza places off-campus, as well as at the Motley Coffee House, which shows movies every Friday night and hosts bands every Sunday night.

Athletics, Activities, and Dateless Dances?

Sports are played in conjunction with the other four colleges, with Pitzer and Pomona forming one league, and Claremont McKenna, Scripps, and Harvey Mudd forming another. There is intense rivalry between the two leagues. Within the Scripps league students can participate in intramural sports. Though many Scripps students are involved in sports, the Scripps campus houses few athletic facilities. One of these facilities is a small gym, with plans for a new, expanded gym facility under way.

> **"Going to one of the other schools is just like walking to another part of campus."**

Other extracurricular activities abound, from student government to NOW, the National Organization for Women, or the literary magazine. One sorority recently opened a local chapter on campus, though it received a lot of student resistance. This chapter associates largely with the three fraternities at Pomona, and is not a large part of campus life.

Weekend activities often involve cultural events such as concerts, guest speakers, or art openings. Some of Scripps' most memorable speakers include the Supreme Court Justice, Sandra Day O'Connor, author, Jane Smiley, and former President of NATO Parliament, Karsten Voigt. Students also travel to the other colleges for Five College parties. Until this year, a Five College Organization worked to organize a large party at one campus each weekend. This organization has broken up for administrative reasons, and is currently being reconstructed. The Dean of Students organizes several Saturday afternoon trips into Los Angeles. Students might also spend several weekends a semester visiting LA, or going to Disneyland.

Scripps students attend several formal occasions a year, one where Scripps women get dressed up and go to a dance on their campus without dates. A more conventional Spring Formal is also held on the Scripps campus.

Other Scripps traditions include students signing their names in a book of Scripps students as freshmen, and as seniors having a special champagne brunch, after which some streak the campus. The Dean of Students serves students cookies and tea during the traditional Scripps Tea.

Students at Scripps form a tight community based on mutual support. "Scripps is a small college with personal attention, yet you don't know every person that you see, every day." For many, Scripps presents the best of both worlds, one where diverse students can bond and "not be on guard all the time," experience small class sizes, and yet reap the benefits of an active college town. —*Cynthia Matthews*

FYI
The three best things about attending Scripps are, "that professors are truly interested in helping their students; the dynamics of a women's college: mutual respect and support, an openness to new ideas, and a lack of cut-throat competitiveness; and the combination of a small college with a high teacher/student ratio and the five college consortium."
The three worst things about attending Scripps are, "the smog, the location, and the housing crunch (which will soon be alleviated with the new dorm)."
The three things that every student should do before graduating from Scripps are, "go to one of Professor Hao Huang's concerts, take a professor to the Motely for coffee and talk about anything but class work, and find an excuse to spend time in the Rare Books room in Denison Library."
One thing I'd like to have known before coming here is "it all goes by too quickly!"

Deep Springs College

Address: Application Committee, Box 45001 Dyer, CA 89010
Phone: 760-872-8088
E-mail address: apcom@deepspring.edu
Web site URL: www.deepsprings.edu
Founded: 1917
Private or Public: private
Religious affiliation: none
Location: rural
Undergraduate enrollment: 26
Total enrollment: 26
Percent Male / Female: 100% / 0%
Percent Minority: 0%

Percent African-American: NA
Percent Asian: NA
Percent Hispanic: NA
Percent Native-American: NA
Percent in-state / out-of-state: 99% / 1%
Percent Pub HS: NA
Number of Applicants: 120
Percent Accepted: 11%
Percent Accepted who enroll: 100%
Entering: 13
Transfers: NA
Application Deadline: 1 Nov
Mean SAT: NA

Mean ACT: NA
Middle 50% SAT range: 700–800 V, 700–800 M
Middle 50% ACT range: NA
3 Most popular majors: NA
Retention: 96%
Graduation rate: 92%
On-campus housing: 100%
Fraternities: NA
Sororities: NA
Library: 26,000 volumes
Tuition and Fees: NA in; NA out
Room and Board: NA
Financial aid, first-year: 100%

At Deep Springs College, located in a large desert valley set deep in the mountains, isolation is the name of the game. Even the *New York Times* arrives a couple of days late. "The joke is it's the best place to be if the world ends because we'll have a couple of days," smirks one student. Of course, that is the least of what this unique school has to offer.

Just the 26 of Us
The feature that most sets Deep Springs apart is its tiny student body—26 students, all male. Each year, out of around 200 applicants, a committee composed of students and a few faculty members chooses between 10 and 13 new students for admission to the two-year associate degree program. Ethnically and racially, there is not much diversity, though a committee devoted to diversity has been formed to address the issue. In other regards, though, "there is a good variety of people," says one student. "We have some international students, a fair spread in economic background, and we have a wide range of views on different issues. We didn't *all* vote for Nader." An admis-

sions committee member agrees that Deep Springs looks for no one type of student. "Some are just straight amazingly intelligent people who were incredible in high school," he explains, "while others just seem like they're really interested in service and have a lot of potential even if they didn't necessarily live up to it in their high school years."

Serving the Time
The idea of service is central to Deep Springs' philosophy. The education students receive is tuition-free, but by enrolling, students agree to devote their lives to serving others. "A dedication to service and desire to serve mankind—that's something we look for in our applicants," says another admissions committee member. "I don't think there's a particular type we accept. Some people would say weirdos, but I would like to contest that."

It's certainly true that Deep Springs is not for everyone. After all, living in seclusion in the California desert with only 25 guys is not exactly everyone's cup of tea. A good thing about it, though, is that the guys form incredibly tight relationships, compared by many to a brotherhood. "They are really incredible people to be around, and very, very smart," says a second-year student. "They can also be gigantic assholes. I mean, living with the same twenty-five people, we get on each other's nerves sometimes."

The lack of girls also takes some getting used to. "It's really hard on some people," says one student. "We don't meet or interact with any girls, and it's a death trap for long-distance relationships." Still, the student adds, "I like to think it's worth it." Another student said the upside is that "you can concentrate better, and honestly, I do find that I can concentrate better here than anywhere else." Other students agree that the situation precludes distractions from studies and labor.

By *labor*, they mean *farm* labor, because Deep Springs is an almost entirely self-sufficient farm. Students work on the farm about 20 to 30 hours per week, rotating duties ranging from harvesting and planting, to shoveling horse dung, to milking cows. The fresh milk at every meal is a definite bonus, but for every glass some poor student has to get up at six in the morning to milk ol' Bossie (even on Saturdays!).

I Want to Be a Fireman When I Grow Up

In addition to staying up to task on farm duties, the guys also have to stay on top of a large workload for classes in a curriculum chosen by a student committee. Each of the three long-term and two short-term faculty members has a list of classes they can teach, voted on by the committee each semester. Recently offerings have included classes on the civil rights movement, the history of higher education, German philosopher Heidegger, painting, and the literature of love. There are no majors and only two requirements—Composition and Public Speaking. Students can do independent studies, too. Not surprisingly, students' roles in choosing the curriculum have caused some tension between students and faculty. "We granted leave to one student so he could take an emergency medical technician course because he wants to become a firefighter," says a member of the curriculum committee, "and it really ticked off a bunch of the faculty members."

"We didn't *all* vote for Nader."

Students are mostly very satisfied with their professors. One student says the only class he hasn't liked was one on conservation biology, and not because of the subject matter. Actually, "I was the only student in the class, so there wasn't much in the way of class discussion, which would have been interesting." Classes usually have about six or seven students, providing an intensely personalized educational experience. After getting their two-year associate degree at Deep Springs, most students transfer to prestigious colleges throughout the nation to earn their bachelor's degree. In recent years, students transferred to Yale, the University of Chicago, Swarthmore, and Harvard.

Got Milk? Got Beef? Get Bossie.

Though Deep Springs is almost entirely student-governed, it has strict rules. There are two big ones. First is the isolation policy: visitors usually don't come into the valley, and students are not permitted to leave the valley. The second forbids the students from using drugs and alcohol. Still, the guys don't feel totally imprisoned. For one thing, the quality of life at Deep Springs, labor aside, is pretty excellent. The buildings in the beautiful valley were recently remodeled, and double and triple dorm rooms are "absolutely gigantic; it's almost ludicrous," says one student.

The farm-fresh food that sustains the hard workers is described as "amazing. We have a chef who used to work at a really good restaurant in the Bay Area," says a second-year Deep Springster. "Tonight we had herb-roasted chickens for each table, risotto and vegetables, homemade ice cream and cake, and salad from the greenhouses. We always have our own fresh milk and beef, too. We are definitely spoiled."

Nothin' like Sliding Your Bare Butt down a Giant Sand Dune

In their rare free time, the guys enjoy outdoor activities like rock climbing, hiking, camping, and horseback riding. When it's hot, they also like to go swimming to cool off. Guys also look forward to silly traditions like the yearly "naked lunch," followed by a game of naked Frisbee, and sand-dune sliding: "In the summer, when it's warm at night and there's a full moon, we go out to the really big sand dunes and slide down them. It's a lot of fun." Students also get together at some of the staff's satellite-equipped houses to watch the Superbowl. Sometimes they get bands together and periodically put on performances. "One kid is really into techno music, so he's put on a few dance parties," says a student. Also, almost all of the guys leave Deep Springs with an affinity for country music, "since the only radio station we get is a country music station. It's hard not to get a thing for it."

For most who attend, Deep Springs is a life-changing experience. "It's hard to say how it's changed you," says one second-year student. "We struggle with that all the time. I mean, I've learned so many things I never thought I would—how to horseback-ride, how to plant alfalfa. But it's changed me in so much more important ways that I can't even describe." Another second-year agrees that his time at the school has been an incredible journey: "I would come back to Deep Springs in a second. I really love it here, and I don't think I could have been as happy anywhere else. Now I'm really looking forward to going out in the world and doing something worthwhile." There couldn't be a better preparation for it than attending an inspiring institution like Deep Springs. —*Patricia Stringel*

FYI
The three best things about attending Deep Springs are "the amazing food, the close relationships with classmates, and the influence students have on every aspect of it."
The three worst things about attending Deep Springs are "life without girls, the isolation, and getting on each other's nerves because you spend every waking hour with the same 25 guys."
The three things that every student should do before graduating from Deep Springs are "hike to the Druid (a rock formation in the mountains), milk a cow, and slide naked down the sand dunes in the light of the full moon."
One thing I'd like to have known before coming here is "how hard it is to leave."

Mills College

Address: 5000 MacArthur
Boulevard; Oakland, CA
94605
Phone: 510-430-2135
E-mail address:
admission@mills.edu
Web site URL:
www.mills.edu
Founded: 1946
Private or Public: private
Religious affiliation:
none
Location: urban
**Undergraduate
enrollment:** 768
Total enrollment: 1,169
Percent Male / Female:
0% / 100%
Percent Minority: 20%

Percent African-American:
7%
Percent Asian: 6%
Percent Hispanic: 7%
Percent Native-American:
NA
**Percent in-state / out-of-
state:** 79% / 21%
Percent Pub HS: NA
Number of Applicants:
461
Percent Accepted: 78%
**Percent Accepted who
enroll:** 34%
Entering: 121
Transfers: 124
Application Deadline:
1 Feb
Mean SAT: NA

Mean ACT: NA
Middle 50% SAT range:
540–660 V,
490–590 M
Middle 50% ACT range: NA
3 Most popular majors:
English, psychology,
communication
Retention: NA
Graduation rate: 69%
On-campus housing: 100%
Fraternities: NA
Sororities: NA
Library: 220,000 volumes
Tuition and Fees: $18,262
in; $18,262 out
Room and Board: $7,296
Financial aid, first-year:
80%

M ills College is a small, private, all-
women's liberal arts college located in Oakland. Aside from the
obvious difference in that all students are
female, Mills offers something unique that
students would not be able to get just anywhere: focus on the individual female student. The diverse student body includes a
sizable group of "resumers" who are over
the age of 23 and either returning to
school or seeking a degree later in life. According to one senior, "Students come
here for many different reasons, but what
they find here is a supportive and friendly
atmosphere backed by a great education
from top-notch professors."

Political Activism Is Alive and Kicking

When Propositions 187 and 209 affecting
immigration and affirmative action respectively were heatedly debated back in
1997, students protested with as much fervor as students did in the '60s. In recent
years, students have boycotted classes to
protest the school's lack of faculty diversity and an ethnic-studies department.
Students report that the administration is
doing much better at addressing student

concerns. Currently, resumers are protest-
ing that their special child-care needs and
older-age concerns are not being met and
are working to bring about change. Students involved in Amnesty International
often hold protests and events to focus on
political prisoners. Current hot issues include the Free Tibet movement and
gay/lesbian rights.

Women's issues are also of great concern to students. The National Organization of Women (NOW) has a strong
presence as do other organizations for the
advancement of women's rights. Even
those who are not politically active view
the activism with high regard. Says one
Mills woman, "Students here are very passionate about their beliefs and are very involved in bringing about change."

Activists Have Classes Too

However, life isn't all protest and no work
for students. All Mills women must take
two classes from each of the four major
academic divisions: humanities, fine arts,
social sciences, and natural sciences. The
curriculum guidelines also require two semesters of English and one course on
multi-culturalism. One student voiced a

common complaint: "The multicultural-ism requirement is a good idea, but only requiring one course hardly seems diverse." Students favor the English and music majors, but some criticize the math and computer science departments for their dwindling faculty, though the administration has made an effort to reverse this trend. Although the computer science department has recently hired a new professor, the math department is still less than fantastic. Some students report that the absence of male students limits production options in the theater department. However, the science and art departments tend to have integrated upper-level classes with the coed grad students, and one woman noted, "It's a nice change of pace."

> **"Students here are very passionate about their beliefs ad are very involved in bringing about change."**

Students herald small class size and individual attention as the most positive aspect of Mills College. Introductory science courses rarely enroll more than 70 students, and the majority of classes have no more than 25. Some classes have capped enrollments, especially those in the art department, which give priority to art majors. "Classes in the art department are sometimes hard to get into, but other than that it's pretty easy to get the classes you want." Students report that "professors are willing to negotiate paper deadlines and are very understanding if students have problems, or unique situations." In addition to the offerings at Mills, students are allowed to cross-register one class per semester at UC Berkeley or other nearby colleges if Mills doesn't offer a class in their topic of interest.

An Oasis in an Urban Desert
Students describe the Mills campus as an oasis in the middle of an urban environment. Eucalyptus trees and a small stream add beauty to the picturesque Spanish-style buildings that dot the campus. Mills Hall, the main administration building, underwent extensive renovations after a

1989 earthquake caused severe structural damage. The main campus library, Olin Library, holds over 210,000 texts, a rare book room, and cushy study rooms, but many still travel to nearby UC Berkeley to do "serious research."

All residence halls include a kitchen, library, laundry, and computer room. The favored dorms include Orchard Meadow, with its homey atmosphere, and Ethel Moore, despite its rather secluded hillside location. While about half of the students choose to live off campus, those who live on campus live in dorms with spacious singles and shared common rooms.

While the dining halls provide salad and pasta bars in addition to the hot entrees, students still complain about the food, though they admit that it is "better than at most other places." One student also lauded "the taco stand on the corner of Fruitvale and High, which makes the best tacos I've ever had."

Social Options
While students feel defensive about their neighborhood of East Oakland, they describe Mills as being a pretty self-contained campus with only one entrance onto the campus. "The school is located next to a major freeway on-ramp . . . so when students leave campus, they go far away." Others believe that the line of restaurants and coffee shops along the border of the campus provides a great atmosphere. "There are some really nice movie theaters in close range, including one that has couches for seats and serves food to you while you watch the movie." For the club scene, students take the Mills van shuttle service to the city of Berkeley. Students sometimes complain that the last shuttle pickup is at 10:30, leaving tardy students stranded. Nearby San Francisco also provides great entertainment opportunities.

Students, typically outfitted in jeans, tank tops, and Birkenstocks or running shoes, often stop at the Tea Shop, an on-campus beverage and food shop, to socialize or take a break from studies. The Black-and-White Dance and the Boat Dance are two annual campus activities. For the Boat Dance students and their dates dance the night away on a chartered boat that cruises around the San Francisco Bay. One student explained "It's almost like prom."

Students either participate actively in extracurricular organizations or ignore them altogether. A small, dedicated group of women publishes the Mills Weekly, the college newspaper. The Walrus, a literary magazine, comes out every semester. The on-campus social scene is described as, "reserved." Students report that many off-campus students tend to be resumers and they often do not participate as much in the day-to-day campus activity and social scene. For obvious reasons, the typical college frat parties are absent from the social scene and most students really like not having ragers around. One junior offered this advice, "The social life at Mills is really what you make of it. A lot of people tend to travel to San Francisco and partake in the great cultural life there. Others like to hang around and relax. But everyone finds their niche."

Mills College is a Division III school and therefore does not offer athletic scholarships. Few students consider athletics a big deal on campus, though they still support their teams. The crew team competes against top California teams, and a win over UC Berkeley is always a sweet victory. Varsity athletes and weekend athletes all use the Haas Pavilion, whose facilities include basketball and volleyball courts, as well as aerobic and weight-lifting rooms.

While Mills women readily point out their perceived isolation, they are also quick to praise Mills strengths. Students of all ages can expect to find a supportive network of women who are as passionate about learning as they are. Mills students care about their school, know its history, and love it. Many children of alumnae, called "bent twigs," are currently enrolled, attesting to the ties that students have to their school. The women are strong, active, and as one busy student explained, all "have a million things going on; maybe too many things!" —*Seung Lee*

FYI

The three best things about attending Mills are "focus on the individual, female student, the political and social activism, and the shared passion for learning."

The three worst things about attending Mills are "the East Oakland neighborhood, the reserved social scene, and the weak computer science department and overly popular art department (it is difficult to get into its classes)."

The three things that every student should do before graduating from Mills are "attending the Boat Dance, enjoying the cultural/social opportunities in Berkeley and San Francisco, and taking the time to get to know women of all ages."

One thing I'd like to have known before coming here is "my fears about an all-women's college were wrong: Mills' women live in a supportive, wonderful environment."

Occidental College

Address: 1600 Campus Road; Los Angeles, CA 90041
Phone: 323-259-2700
E-mail address: admission@oxy.edu
Web site URL: www.oxy.edu
Founded: 1917
Private or Public: private
Religious affiliation: none
Location: suburban
Undergraduate enrollment: 1,552
Total enrollment: 1,552
Percent Male / Female: 44% / 56%
Percent Minority: 41%
Percent African-American: 6%

Percent Asian: 20%
Percent Hispanic: 14%
Percent Native-American: 1%
Percent in-state / out-of-state: 60% / 40%
Percent Pub HS: NA
Number of Applicants: 3,002
Percent Accepted: 60%
Percent Accepted who enroll: 23%
Entering: 411
Transfers: NA
Application Deadline: 15 Jan
Mean SAT: 600 V, 600 M
Mean ACT: NA

Middle 50% SAT range: 550–660 V, 550–660 M
Middle 50% ACT range: NA
3 Most popular majors: English, psychology, economics
Retention: 89%
Graduation rate: 77%
On-campus housing: 100%
Fraternities: 16%
Sororities: 13%
Library: 470,000 volumes
Tuition and Fees: $22,518 in; $22,518 out
Room and Board: $6,490
Financial aid, first-year: 60%

Just outside the bustling city limits of Los Angeles is the small campus of Occidental College, with its quiet lawns and balanced architecture. If you were to wander around the campus, you would probably find it uncannily familiar; Occidental was the site of the mythical "California University" that the kids of Beverly Hills 90210 attended. But while camera crews used to crowd onto the campus weekly, now the 90210 gang has moved on, and most Oxy students agree that this is a good thing. The homogeneity of the popular show could not be farther from the true makeup of the Occidental student body, which hails from a wide variety of cultural, economic, and geographic backgrounds.

Oxy Academics

Oxy has a large number of core requirements that students describe as "a lot of work," but well worth it. One student said the courses "prepared me to be a better student as a whole," and that they laid a good base for later classes. Requirements include courses in history, science, math, foreign language, fine arts, and writing, as well as a special Cultural Studies course required for freshmen. For this require-

ment, first-years choose from four classes, which are different every semester. These are considered some of the best classes at Occidental, because they focus on current issues and are taught by passionate professors. The sciences are reportedly strong; one student went so far as to say "most students do something with chemistry or biology." Other popular majors include psychology, history, English, and sociology.

Occidental undergrads say that student-teacher relationships are very strong. Professors are often young, with new teaching styles and fresh ideas, and they are "very accessible and more than willing to assist in the individual education of the students." Classes generally have one professor, as well as one or two TAs, but most large classes enroll no more than 40 or 50 students, and smaller ones usually enroll around 12 to 18. Students usually get into the classes they want during registration, even though sizes are so limited; "no one will be denied a class that he/she wants, it just takes some running around and signing forms," one student said. Registration is done at the end of the previous semester, and seniors have priority, but in the fall, freshmen register during orientation, and a certain number of spots in classes are reserved for them.

Studying at Occidental is intense, but balanced. Students say that the time just before exams can be very stressful, but most of the time they feel fairly relaxed. Students are also "good about studying together and sharing information," one student said, and the atmosphere is one of cooperation, not competition. The library, considered adequate both for research and for studying, has group study rooms as well as quiet rooms. If students can't find the books or periodicals they need at Occidental, they can order the books from other local college libraries of Pomona and UCLA.

Living on the Oxy Campus

Most Occidental students live on-campus in the dorms (freshmen are required to do so), and those who live off-campus generally live within a few blocks of the college, creating a tight-knit community. Students cite Norris Hall as one of the best dorms, with mostly quads composed of two double bedrooms, a bathroom, and a large common room. There are also a few singles in Norris, and other halls contain either all singles or a mix of doubles and singles. Students say the rooms are "not luxurious, but they are large," and students are generally pleased with their options.

> **"A lot of Oxy life is centered around campus activities."**

Some students report that there are only two sizes of rooms, "huge and tiny." But even the smaller rooms generally have enough space, and some have additional perks, like balconies. Off-campus housing may be cheaper, but students find that off-campus housing is often "ugly and out of the way." All dorms are co-ed, although some have single-sex wings, and bathrooms are all single-sex.

Many students who live off-campus choose fraternity or sorority houses. Occidental has three national fraternities and three local sororities, which organize a lot of events open to the entire campus. "A lot of Oxy life is centered around campus activities," one student said. The Associated Students of Occidental College (ASOC) plans campus social activities such as movie screenings every Friday, and parties such as the annual Sex at the Beach Party, which includes dancing and drinking in a mock-beach environment. Students also hang out at the on-campus Tiger Cooler or the Ozone, a campus coffee shop.

On and Off Campus Fun

Whether sports, community service, writing for a publication, or theater groups, "most students try and find the time to participate in extracurriculars." Some popular activities include the A-team (the admissions team); Tour Guides; La Encina (the yearbook); and the Tango/Swing Dance Club. Students also cheer on the O, X, and Y, three guys who go to all of the football and basketball teams and cheer like crazy.

Occidental also offers a variety of sports. Oxy competes in Division III, so sports are not a huge part of campus life, but students say that this means "the students who participate do it because they love the game." Large numbers of students turn out and cheer for both home and away games, particularly against their chief rival, Pomona College. Students say that the athletic facilities are "up to date and easily accessible," and completely open to non-athletes as well. For those who want to compete on a less intense level, Occidental organizes intramural football, basketball, volleyball, and softball. Teams are generally organized from within fraternities, dorms, or clubs, but anyone who wants to organize a team can do so.

Even with so much to do on campus, many students are drawn off campus to Los Angeles or other nearby areas for entertainment. The college runs a free shuttle service to Pasadena's Old Town, but students say that having a car is a big advantage. With a car, students have access to countless restaurants, clubs, stores, and other entertainment in Los Angeles, or recreation areas like beaches and parks outside the city. Closer to campus, students can walk to coffee shops and restaurants in the surrounding suburban area when they need a break from traditional Oxy food.

Occidental students are very proud of their school's commitment to diversity. Ranked number one in the country for diversity, with roughly half of the student body comprised of minorities, Oxy students find that they have avoided some of the problems that other colleges face. At some other schools, students of different backgrounds may tend to divide off into cliques, but Oxy students find their classmates not only extremely tolerant, but also integrated. The strong, tight community and well-integrated diversity are what makes Occidental College stand out from busy Los Angeles and trendy Pasadena; students say they are glad that they can visit the city, but still live in their community. —*Melissa Andersen and Staff*

FYI
The three best things about attending Occidental are "strong teacher-student relationships, the atmosphere of cooperation not competition, and the diversity of the student body."
The three worst things about attending Occidental are "the 90210 image (which is so far from the truth), the small library, and the poor off-campus living options."
The three things that every student should do before graduating from Occidental are "getting to know the incredible people, play intermurals, and enjoy the opportunities that LA offers, with out having to deal with the negatives of living in the city."
One thing I'd like to have known before coming here is "that a school in such an urban area could be so tight-knit—a car is necessary if you need a break."

Pepperdine University

Address: Seaver College; 24225 Pacific Coast Highway; Malibu, CA 90263-4392
Phone: 310-456-4392
E-mail address: NA
Web site URL: www.pepperdine.edu
Founded: 1955
Private or Public: private
Religious affiliation: Church of Christ
Location: suburban
Undergraduate enrollment: 3,063
Total enrollment: 7,802
Percent Male/Female: 41%/59%
Percent Minority: 22%

Percent African-American: 6%
Percent Asian: 6%
Percent Hispanic: 9%
Percent Native-American: 0.5%
Percent in-state/out-of-state: 51%/49%
Percent Pub HS: NA
Number of Applicants: 5,219
Percent Accepted: 35%
Percent Accepted who enroll: 30%
Entering: 552
Transfers: NA
Application Deadline: 15 Jan
Mean SAT: 590 V, 600 M
Mean ACT: NA

Middle 50% SAT range: 570–670 V, 580–680 M
Middle 50% ACT range: 25–29
3 Most popular majors: business administration, telecommunications, sports medicine
Retention: 85%
Graduation rate: 70%
On-campus housing: 65%
Fraternities: 25%
Sororities: 25%
Library: 480,000 volumes
Tuition and Fees: $23,070 in; $23,070 out
Room and Board: $7,010
Financial aid, first-year: NA

Overlooking the Pacific Ocean from the hills of Malibu stands the coastal castle that is Pepperdine University. Students rave, "This place is absolutely gorgeous." But there is more here than sunny beaches and stunning views. Pepperdine is a Christian, conservative, private institution that offers an intimate academic experience shared among classmates from all over the world.

Caring Professors and Small Classes
Many students claim that the regular small class size (usually under 20 students) was a major factor in choosing

Pepperdine. Especially compared to the larger public universities in California, students here can brag about having "great relationships with professors." Professors are reportedly very understanding of students' needs. "They'll work really hard for you. They always give the extra effort." Between holding regular office hours and even inviting students over for dinner, the typical Pepperdine professor is accessible, friendly, and truly cares about the students.

Students are also very satisfied with the classroom instruction, a feeling shared by majors in all departments. Before choosing a major, students fulfill their general education requirements (GEs) which include courses in English, math, religion, Western Heritage, and physical education. Of the majors to choose from, business tends to be the most popular. Many students also major in communications.

Diversity . . . Students from All Over California?

The student body is a fairly diverse bunch. Although more than half of the student body comes from California, there are also many international students who "fit in just fine," according to one student. Most seem satisfied with the diversity on campus. "There is no stereotypical Pepperdine student and you can always wear what you want," reported one junior, although another student commented, "There are definitely those who always dress up." An undergraduate organization called Campus Life holds two major events each year to celebrate the cultural diversity at Pepperdine. An example is Rainbow Fest, which is a weeklong festival full of multi-ethnic food tables and international dance presentations.

Sexy but Dateless Students

If you think the campus is pretty, just wait until you see the students. Complete with dark tans appropriate for sunny California, Pepperdine undergraduates are "a really good-looking bunch" and very health-conscious. However, there is one minor problem with these sunbathing studs and hot chicks: they don't date. "Nobody ever dates at Pepperdine; you just get engaged." There seems to be a general consensus on the two main romantic op-

tions: you are either in a serious relationship, or you are in no relationship at all. One student called this "the sore spot of Pepperdine." A female student agreed, lamenting, "the guys here are wimps." Yet many students say that the lack of dating is more than made up for by the intimate, long-lasting friendships that emerge on campus. "Some date, many don't, but everyone has great friends."

Social life is generally geared toward off-campus activities. Pepperdine is in such an exciting part of California it would be hard not to venture off campus during the weekends. Los Angeles, Santa Monica, and Hollywood are just a hop, skip, and a jump from Pepperdine. As one student happily reported, the surrounding cities offer "everything you'd ever want to do." Many students, especially freshmen, opt to go home for the weekends as well, since often home is not too far away, then return on Sunday for a hard day of studying.

> "Nobody ever dates at Pepperdine, you just get engaged."

This is not to say that on-campus life is dead. Greek life most definitely plays a role in Pepperdine's social scene; it engages over half of the student body and is growing more popular every year. Fraternities and sororities on campus have become part of their respective national charters since 1995, whereas before they were limited to being merely local organizations due to administrative restrictions. Students say one of the nice things about the societies is that it's not too difficult to get in if you're interested. One of the priorities of Campus Life is to make sure that all girls who want to get in to a sorority can do so. Because Pepperdine is a dry campus (a policy that is strictly enforced), almost all drinking takes place away from campus.

To Convo or Not to Convo— Got No Choice

Pepperdine University is affiliated with The Church of Christ, a relationship not taken lightly by the student body and the administration. A strong religious atmosphere is an integral part of the Pepperdine experience. For the most part, students love this religious element tied in with their years of higher education. Although many students attend church regularly and are actively involved with the Campus Ministry (an undergraduate organization that focuses on community service projects), not everyone is devout. One student who doesn't consider herself to be very religious commented that the "presence is not overbearing." There are no requirements to attend church or the Bible studies on campus, but all undergraduates must attend the weekly convocation. "Convo" is a meeting held every Wednesday morning during which a variety of issues are discussed. Often guest speakers are featured, ranging from popular celebrities to local ministers, and not all discussions focus around a religious theme. Topics range from "community service, school spirit to 'how to be a better lover,'" said one senior. For the most part, students feel that convo is an important and interesting part of campus life at Pepperdine. "It truly builds a community feeling." The diverse meetings are cited as building an "awareness on important issues" that students often encounter during the rest of the week. However, some say that the mandatory aspect of convo makes it feel "more like an obligation." One student reported that at times, "some feel uncomfortable" attending the convocation if they are "not that serious about religion."

Community Clusters

Incoming freshmen can look forward to a dormitory experience "geared toward a community feeling." Freshman dorms are single-sex buildings, which typically hold 40 students. Each building has five suites with eight people in each suite. The suites have two bathrooms, a community living area, and four doubles. Although they are not air-conditioned, the mild and "not too humid" weather allows students to live comfortably. Most important, the small buildings really foster a sense of community. However, as with all deals, some restrictions apply: members of the opposite sex are only permitted in the rooms from 11 A.M. to 11 P.M., although they can stay in

the dorm room lobby until 2 A.M. Also, you must leave your door open if someone of the opposite sex is in your room. Each dormitory has a Resident Advisor and a Student Advisor whom students can approach with questions and problems. Juniors and seniors sometimes petition to live in on-campus apartments. The apartments, while still single-sex, have later time restrictions (you don't have to kick your partner out of your room until 1 A.M.).

Given the small student population, there is only one large dining hall, located at the Tyler Campus Center. Students select from a wide variety of different food stations, such as the Grill. For the most part, the food at Pepperdine is described as really good. And why not, it's catered by Marriott Services. Although students complain that the cafeteria cuisine can sometimes get boring, they take comfort in the fact that there's "always pizza."

Competitive Sports and Fun Activities

Pepperdine is also widely known for its excellence in varsity sports, with many teams often competing for Division I national championships. In recent years, Pepperdine has gained recognition with the men's water polo team 1997 national title, a consistently successful men's volleyball team, which has placed as high as second in the nation, and a talented men's basketball team. But don't be afraid if you're not an incredible athlete. Club and intramural teams play on more relaxed turf, and it is easy to get involved. This "easy to get involved" mentality extends over most extracurricular activities at Pepperdine. Students generally feel they can find clubs that satisfy their interests and they are very easy to join. For singers, there is a Church of Christ a cappella group, which tours often. Pepperdine also has its own student-run radio and television stations.

A diverse student body, whose members share a common respect for Christian beliefs, characterizes Pepperdine University. These students enjoy the small, intimate, well-taught classes at Pepperdine. The campus on the coast of sunny California is beautiful. The weather is beautiful. Even the people are beautiful.

One word of advice, though—if you decide that Pepperdine is the place for you, don't be afraid to ask somebody out on a date. —*Carl Shephard and Staff*

FYI

The three best things about attending Pepperdine are, "its location, its small class size, and the abundance of personal attention given to student, and its standing as a reputable university."

The three worst things about attending Pepperdine are, "the lack of school spirit, a poor Greek system, and too much emphasis on religion."

The three things that every student should do before graduating from Pepperdine are, "get a professional internship through the school, take a day off to enjoy the incredible weather and scenery, and make sure you acquire a car."

One thing I'd like to have known before coming here is "how much emphasis would be put on religion. There is quite a diverse crowd at Pepperdine, and many students feel that they are being forced to participate in the religious aspects of the school."

St. Mary's College of California

Address: PO Box 4800 Moraga, CA 94575-4800	**Percent African-American:** 6%	**Mean ACT:** NA
Phone: 925-631-4224	**Percent Asian:** 13%	**Middle 50% SAT range:** 500–590 V,
E-mail address: smcadmit@stmarys-ca.edu	**Percent Hispanic:** 13%	510–590 M
	Percent Native-American: 1%	**Middle 50% ACT range:** NA
Web site URL: www.stmarys-ca.edu	**Percent in-state / out-of-state:** 87% / 13%	**3 Most popular majors:** business, communications, English
Founded: 1963	**Percent Pub HS:** NA	**Retention:** NA
Private or Public: private	**Number of Applicants:** 2,830	**Graduation rate:** NA
Religious affiliation: Catholic	**Percent Accepted:** 85%	**On-campus housing:** 100%
Location: suburban	**Percent Accepted who enroll:** 26%	**Fraternities:** NA
Undergraduate enrollment: 2,863	**Entering:** 620	**Sororities:** NA
Total enrollment: NA	**Transfers:** NA	**Library:** NA
Percent Male / Female: 39% / 61%	**Application Deadline:** 2/1, 11/30	**Tuition and Fees:** $18,320 in; $18,320 out
Percent Minority: 33%	**Mean SAT:** NA	**Room and Board:** $7,560
		Financial aid, first-year: NA

Looking for a small Christian liberal arts college near a major urban center? Nestled amongst the hills east of Oakland and Berkeley, across the bay from San Francisco, lies the city of Moraga and St. Mary's College. With its white walls and red tile roofs this school is as picturesque as any California mission, but filled with students living the modern college life. St. Mary's is one of 914 Christian Brother schools throughout the world, and one of seven in the United States. The philosophies of the Brothers, stemming from Saint John Baptist De La Salle, patron saint of teachers in the Roman Catholic Church, serve as a basis for traditions involving community support and service through education.

Life is a Journey of Learning

St. Mary's was founded on the basis of education of the person. As one professor put it, "The capacity to think critically and live life as a journey of learning are not, after all, skills to be listed on a resume. They are, rather, traits of the heart and the soul as much as of the mind." Students at St. Mary's choose to enroll in one of four schools, the School of Liberal Arts, the School of Science, the School of Economics and Business Administration, or the Intercollegiate Nursing Program. All of these schools (except the INP) have different majors, and within each major there are concentrations to choose from. It is also possible to combine majors or double major as you see fit. The most popular majors are Psychology and Business Administration, though students can major in anything from Computer Science to Physical Education and Recreation.

In order to graduate from St. Mary's, each student must participate in four seminar courses and two religion classes. Students feel that "the seminar program is a very important part of our education." It allows them to discuss topics more intimately, and examine ideas further than a normal class would allow. The seminars generally involve the reading of classic literature and topics range from "Greek Thought" to "19th–20th Century Thought." The religion courses "have also provided insight into unfamiliar faiths and a foundation for my own beliefs," according to one student. Another pointed out, "religion classes are not all based in Catholicism," which provides for more objective perspectives in this area.

The school is experiencing a surge in popularity, but students complain that "due to increasing size, it is becoming more difficult to get the classes we want." Classes are also not as small as most incoming students had expected. According to one upperclassman, "[Classes] are still on the small side. My smallest class this semester has 11 students, my largest has 30." So while class sizes increase, "they are still small compared to most universities." But not everyone experiences these problems. "Since my freshman year I think that I have always gotten my first choice of classes," notes one student. There are no TAs at St. Mary's, hence all classes are taught by professors and "all teachers speak fluent English."

"Students strive to do well, but it is not a competitive atmosphere to the extent that they do not help one another." As one student pointed out, "The courses are not graded on a curve. If you deserve an A you get an A. This makes it less competitive and encourages students to work together."

> **"This liberal arts college was founded on the basis of education of the person."**

The High Potential program is one that makes St. Mary's stand out from the crowd. This program is "for students who could not normally get into college on their grades." After an additional application process, students who, due to extenuating circumstances did not do as well as they could have in high school, may be admitted. As one student put it, "it is a program that allows those that normally would not get the opportunity to go to college, to go." This program, an interesting alternative to Affirmative Action, helps increase the school's diversity and helps deserving students.

Fun and Games

While St. Mary's is not a commuter school, weekends involve dashing home for some home cooked food and free laundry because so many students grew up in the area. As one student put it, freshmen either "drink in the dorms or go home" on the weekends. Most people on campus own cars, and "if you don't, you'll know someone who does" so quick trips to Berkeley or San Francisco for a night of clubbing or bar hopping is always an option. Also, there are "buses that run from campus to BART [Bay Area Rapid Transit] regularly."

Student life, while fun, is not centered on the college. There is no Greek system, and one mildly disgruntled student pointed out that, "student apathy is really bad here. There is no collective spirit or passion about anything on campus." But just because "everyone does their own thing" doesn't make it all bad. Students participate in many extracurriculars, like the Student Alumni Association and the service group run through Circle K (a national community service organization).

Many students have jobs either on campus or in nearby cities, and play intramural or club sports.

Students say that there are plenty of attractive people—however, dating is fairly uncommon. According to one student, "there is a lot of sex, for some." Cliques exist, but it is easy to meet people through any sort of activity or class. Students complained that "people think we're all rich," and that there are virtually no interracial or homosexual couples on campus. While almost the entire student body is either Catholic or Protestant, few of the activities are religious in nature and "we are not required to attend church services."

Every year there are several dress-up events, two boat dances on San Francisco Bay, junior formal, senior ball, and casino night. Also, "two of the most popular events of the year are the Luau and Jamaica-me Crazy" theme dances for the entire school.

Freshman Dorms Build Character

Freshmen and sophomores are guaranteed housing, though it's not always the best. As one upperclassman put it, dorms "are small and crowded, sometimes three to a room." Floors are divided by gender, and there are community bathrooms. Freshman dorms "build character."

All on-campus housing is overseen by RAs and Brother Counselors who live in the dorms. Though they are not police, the "level of discipline varies from person to person." The primary rules of the dorms are "no cohabitation past 2 am, no alcohol, and quiet times that vary." The dorms are clean and pest free, but students warn, "don't live in Assumption Hall." Students who live off campus find rent to be high and proximity to the school to vary. How-

ever, this choice is often "a nice alternative to dorm life."

Dining hall food is, for the most part, good. The vegetarian options are "getting better," and flex dollars on the meal plans allow students a bit more variety. In addition to the cafeteria there are "a Taco Bell, a grill, and a café" on campus.

Sporting Gaels

Both the men's and women's sports teams at St. Mary's are highly respected and receive a lot of attention from the student body. The most popular team to watch is Men's Basketball, and last year the Women's Basketball team was co-champion the West Coast Conference. Club sports and intramurals are also played by many at St. Mary's, and Gaels pride is a must.

St. Mary's is a small liberal arts college with all the benefits of a major metropolitan area. It has cross registration programs with the University of California at Berkeley, Cal State University, Hayward, Mills College, and Holy Names College. It is also connected to the Hearst Art Gallery. The Saint Albert Hall Library is extensive for such a small college, and through the Interborrowing Library Service, any book in the bay area is at your fingertips.

St. Mary's College is a typical college in many respects. However, it may serve prospective students to consider the administration's Catholic influence, albeit it small, in the academic and social life and how they feel about that. Most students report being very happy at St. Mary's and profess to choose it again if given the opportunity. Given the mild Bay Area weather and vibrant on-campus life who can blame them?—*Kyla Dahlin*

FYI
The three best things about attending St. Mary's are "having professors who know your name and getting to know them on a personal basis, walking through campus and knowing most of the people you see, and the collegiate seminars."
The three worst things about attending St. Mary's are "cafeteria food, getting housing, and the fact that rumors spread so quickly."
The three things that every student should do before graduating from St. Mary's are "to paint 'SMC' on the hill, attend the Luau and Jamaica-me Crazy dances, and go to 'the Grove.'"
One thing I'd like to have known before coming here is that "class sizes aren't as small as they are advertised."

Stanford University

Address: Old Student Union; Stanford, CA 94305
Phone: 650-723-2091
E-mail address: undergrad.admissions@forsythe.stanford.edu
Web site URL: www.stanford.edu
Founded: 1867
Private or Public: private
Religious affiliation: none
Location: suburban
Undergraduate enrollment: 6,404
Total enrollment: 14,219
Percent Male / Female: 51% / 49%
Percent Minority: 45%

Percent African-American: 9%
Percent Asian: 24%
Percent Hispanic: 11%
Percent Native-American: 1%
Percent in-state / out-of-state: 46% / 54%
Percent Pub HS: 65%
Number of Applicants: 17,919
Percent Accepted: 15%
Percent Accepted who enroll: 65%
Entering: 1,749
Transfers: 20
Application Deadline: 15 Dec
Mean SAT: NA
Mean ACT: NA

Middle 50% SAT range: 670–770 V, 690–780 M
Middle 50% ACT range: 28–33
3 Most popular majors: biology, economics, English
Retention: 99%
Graduation rate: 90%
On-campus housing: 100%
Fraternities: 21%
Sororities: 10%
Library: 7,000,000 volumes
Tuition and Fees: $24,991 in; $24,716 out
Room and Board: $8,030
Financial aid, first-year: 39%

Stanford students can be found wearing T-shirts that read, "Harvard: the Stanford of the East." As the T-shirt attests, Stanford has long been recognized as one of the top universities in the nation, competing with Ivy League schools such as Harvard, Yale, and Princeton for top students. However, Stanford boasts California weather, a slew of nationally ranked sports teams, and a relatively low-stress environment—things no East Coast school could dream of mentioning in its glossy brochures. Students feel that because Stanford does not stand out in merely one area, it stands out even more as a whole.

Cornucopia of Academic Offerings

The Stanford academic year is divided into three 10- to 11-week quarters, followed by a summer session. A total of 180 credits are required for graduation. Most courses are worth 4 to 5 units, and students generally take 14 to 18 units (4 classes) per quarter. Stanford also has general education requirements (GERs), which students must complete. A freshman core program—either Cultures, Ideas, and Values (CIV), or Introduction to the Humanities (I-Hum)—is required, along with courses in each of the following groups: Science, Technology, and Math; Humanities and Social Sciences; and World Culture, American Culture, and Gender Studies. In addition to the GERs, students must meet writing and foreign language requirements. Course requirements generally are not a significant problem. As according to one student, "Often many of them fit into your major or interests."

Stanford students have a reputation for being laid-back and easygoing compared to their peers at other prestigious institutions. Although students report having on average 5 to 6 hours of work every day, "whether or not it gets done depends on the weather." Perhaps because of this reputation, a student reported, "It's a big thing here to not stress about work. . . . Everyone does their work; they just do it without complaining." "Generally there isn't any homework you have to turn in, so everybody does their estimate of what they can get away with. I think we're a little bit more relaxed," says another student, though there are always people who are "really intense."

While the daily workload is generally

not a problem, students claim that getting As is by no means easy, especially in science classes. "I guess the stereotypical thing to say about Stanford is that even if you don't know what's going on, you can get a B," said one student, "but to get an A you really need to work hard." As a result, there is competition—"You're always fighting against a pretty tough curve"—but students are quick to add that competition takes place "anonymously" rather than on a personal level and that "it's not a competitive place." Even though getting good grades may be difficult, "No one compares GPA or rankings."

Students note a heavy contrast between humanities ("fuzzy") and science ("techie") classes, in "everything from structure to time to units to grades." It is widely agreed that science and engineering courses are more time-consuming and tend to cover more material faster; another significant difference between the two groups is that science classes require more written homework, rather than just reading. "You spend more time on a 5-unit techie class than a 5-unit fuzzie class. . . . It's harder to not turn in a problem set than it is to not do your reading, so you have to keep up a lot more," said one student.

As at most major universities, students can expect some crowded introductory classes. Introductory economics courses, "far and away the biggest classes on campus," usually enroll over 700 students. Fortunately, class size "gets smaller pretty quickly" in higher-level courses, which generally enroll 60 to 70 students. Seminars and the highest-level courses, usually have 20 students or fewer.

Stanford's most popular majors include economics, computer science, and biology, so lectures in these subjects tend to be largest. Both professors and teaching assistants (TAs) are described by students as "very, very qualified." Opinions of the faculty are almost overwhelmingly favorable, ranging from "pretty good" to "fabulous." But some students report that the quality of teaching is "not nearly as good in the sciences as they are in the humanities." All lecturing is done by professors, and lectures are broken up into discussion sections (usually made up of about 15 students) led by TAs, who are, according to one student, "often as good as the professors."

Student-faculty relations are also reputedly good, especially for a major research university like Stanford. Professors tend to be pretty friendly and open, and "they're always there for office hours." Some students note that reaching science and engineering professors tends to require more effort, since humanities classes are often smaller. But all professors are accessible through office hours or by appointment. Dorms also periodically hold "faculty nights," when students get to invite faculty members to dinner.

Feeling Lucky for the Housing Draw?

Entering Stanford freshmen are asked to give a preference between co-ed and single-sex dorms, and between freshman, four-class housing, and the new freshman/sophomore housing. Now with the freshman/sophomore housing, freshman can bond with their classmates but get advice from upperclassmen at the same time.

In order to help get freshmen started on the right foot, each dorm has its own Residential Adviser (RA), who is typically "active with freshmen, and very depended upon." Residential Fellows (RFs), faculty members affiliated with the dorms ("the parents of the dorm"), are meant to "add a family feel." Some students and faculty also serve as Academic Advisors (AAs), and certain dorms have live-in tutors. "The feeling of being taken care of really helped me freshman year," said one student. Some dorms have more active staffs than others.

Students report that rooms are "decent size" but claim that housing at Stanford is better than what they hear from friends about other schools. However, the university's lottery system for placing students in housing is the subject of complaints from many seniors, who would obviously favor a room draw based on seniority rather than a mere lottery. Groups of up to 8 students each draw a number and are given priority in choosing rooms based on the results of the draw.

Dorms usually house several hundred students. Row houses, apartment-like complexes housing 50 students, are also available but very hard to get. One student complained, "It's almost impossible to get a single in a dorm, and lots of students live in one-room doubles." Whether students get the housing they want depends largely upon luck, and the students often find themselves feeling "screwed."

Dining In

Several different meal systems are available at Stanford. Students' choices depend on where they live: some dorms offer a set number of meals per week, others give students a certain number of meal "points" to be used by the end of the quarter. Some dorms allow students to choose between meal plans. Food in the dining halls is described as "generally not too bad, but some places are better than others." Students can eat at dining halls outside of their own dorms, but because the halls often use different meal plans and all have different management, "it's not always easy to eat wherever you want."

Beautiful Campus and Surroundings

Stanford's sprawling campus features many walkways and wide-open spaces among predominantly red-roofed buildings, which were supposedly built so that the university would be visible from the air. Trees and grass can also be found everywhere. The campus is so big that most students get around on bikes. With beautiful surroundings and near-constant California sunshine, the environment is described as "amazing." According to one enthusiastic student, "[The atmosphere] is one of the reasons I came here in the first place. I can't think of anything I'd change."

> "We have a lot of very committed athletes—and they're smart too."

Students report that there are "always quite a few things going on" on campus. Most activities are planned by student organizations, but the administration also arranges events. "We always have guest lecturers and people visiting, but a smaller group of people pay attention to those things." Common hangouts for students include the Coffee House ("CoHo") and Tressider Student Union, a student center featuring various eateries. Also popular are Sunday night movie showings, which are always preceded by a massive, auditorium-wide paper fight. "People bring their phone books. I feel bad for whoever has to clean up afterward," said one student. Every weekend, one can find lots of campus parties. Parties organized by fraternities can be found most weekends, and dorm-organized parties are also frequent. Alcohol is "definitely there, but I wouldn't say there's more than there is anywhere else," said one student. Any drinking that goes on is usually "not too crazy."

The nearby town of Palo Alto draws mixed reviews from students. The area is described as "cute," but it is agreed that Palo Alto is "not quite a college town," and that as a result, a sense of isolation is common among students. For many, there is just not enough to do. Students report taking trips to Safeway (grocery store) or the Palo Alto Shopping Center, but otherwise "there aren't that many hangouts," said one student. Despite Palo Alto's limitations, one student offered, "It's a nice town to look at. There are about a million really nice restaurants, but that's about it." In general, getting around off campus requires a car, or the services of a friend with a car (reportedly, not many students drive). Visits to San Francisco (a 45-minute drive) and other nearby cities are possibilities for a weekend trip, but "when things start to get hot and heavy academically, there's not a lot of that."

Finding a Niche

Students at Stanford agree that "people here do a lot." A wide variety of activities and student groups can be found on campus; "the campus is active enough so that if there's some niche that needs to be filled, someone will come along and fill it." Likewise, Stanford is large enough for anyone to find his or her own niche. The more popular activities include the marching band and a cappella singing groups. Many students also tutor at elementary schools in disadvantaged areas. Though fraternities organize many parties, students report that the Greek system "isn't very big here." Frats tend to be more popular than sororities, but neither have a large influence on social life.

Stanford sports, on the other hand, command the attention of not only students but also that of sports fans all over the country. Stanford's varsity sports teams, among the best in the nation, get a lot of support from the student body. This winter alone, many a Stanford student could be found rooting for the home team as Stanford played Wisconsin in the annual Rose Bowl, and the school's winning basketball team is a perennial heavyweight in the NCAA Tournament. "We have a lot of very committed athletes—and they're smart too," said one student, who also estimated that half of the *Stanford Daily* is taken up by the sports section. Intramural sports are also very popular, but the emphasis in IM sports is more on having fun than on winning. Even with the more popular sports, students say that Stanford is "still a very academic place."

Because Stanford is so good in every area, students have trouble deciding which aspect of Stanford is their favorite. "It's hard to say—it really is all things to all people." However, students are proud that "people definitely seem more laid-back here" than at other top universities. Although the school is without a doubt one of the best academic institutions anywhere, it is ultimately this sense of balance that makes Stanford "a good place to live, as well as a great place to learn."
—*Chiansan Ma*

FYI
The three best things about attending Stanford are "the weather, the beautiful campus, and the Rose Bowl."
The three worst things about attending Stanford are "the hard course loads, housing lottery draw, and Palo Alto is boring."
The three things every student should do before graduating from Stanford are "attend the Rose Bowl and cheer for Stanford, play frisbee golf, and listen to a band in the CoHo."
One thing I'd like to have known before coming here is "how much Palo Alto is not a college town."

University of California System Intro

The schools comprising the University of California System are renowned as some of the top research and academic institutions in the world. Since the founding of the first school in Berkeley in 1868, the UC schools have produced over 20 Nobel Prize winners. Currently, the system spans the entire state with universities in Berkeley, Davis, Irvine, Los Angeles, Riverside, San Diego, Santa Barbara, and Santa Cruz and one medical school in San Francisco. Each of the eight undergraduate institutions receives a large number of applications from all over the nation and competition to enroll is high.

Distinctive Campuses
The foremost determining factor for many applicants is the location and climate of the schools. UCLA and Berkeley are in urban settings, and offer the exciting bustle and sophistication of cities. San Diego, Irvine, Santa Barbara, and Santa Cruz are near beaches, settings that tend to lull their respective students to take a day off to surf or sunbathe. Davis and Riverside are in more secluded rural areas, surrounded by the tranquil outdoors. Perhaps because their urban atmospheres appeal to more people, LA and Berkeley tend to have the most applicants and most competitive admissions process. Academically, all eight schools are top-notch and were recently recognized by U.S. News & World Report as some of the best schools in both the national public universities category as well as the national universities category.

Fall of Affirmative Action

With the recent fall of affirmative action in California, a casualty of Proposition 209, the demographic shift in the student body of the UC schools was dramatic. At UCLA and Berkeley, the Asian-American population has skyrocketed to the mid-40 percent range, while African-American and Hispanic acceptance rates have suffered. In addition to the lower acceptance rates, many African-Americans and Hispanics who were accepted have declined admission in favor of more "minority-friendly" campuses with higher African-American and Hispanic enrollment. Many students have noticed that with this change has come greater self-enforced segregation among the student body. The future ramifications of this decision are still hard to foresee, but as of now, California has become the testing ground for a non-affirmative action educational policy.

Why Attend a UC School?

Despite the recent admissions changes and financial hardships, the hard fact is that the UC System provides a great education at a comparably cheap price. The tuition for an in-state resident is six times less than tuition at an Ivy League college, and out-of-state students still pay half what they would at a similar private college. With the warm and temperate California weather, it is no wonder that students from all over the U.S. and the world choose one of the UC System universities to spend four blissful years.
—*Seung Lee*

University of California at Berkeley

Address: 110 Sproul Hall Berkeley, CA 94720
Phone: 510-642-3175
E-mail address: ouars@uclink.berkeley.edu
Web site URL: www.berkeley.edu
Founded: 1926
Private or Public: public
Religious affiliation: none
Location: urban
Undergraduate enrollment: 22,705
Total enrollment: 30,290
Percent Male/Female: 49%/51%
Percent Minority: 56%
Percent African-American: 5%

Percent Asian: 39%
Percent Hispanic: 11%
Percent Native-American: 0.5%
Percent in-state/out-of-state: 89%/11%
Percent Pub HS: 84%
Number of Applicants: 31,108
Percent Accepted: 27%
Percent Accepted who enroll: 43%
Entering: 3,618
Transfers: NA
Application Deadline: 30 Nov
Mean SAT: 655 V, 685 M
Mean ACT: NA

Middle 50% SAT range: 580–700 V, 620–730 M
Middle 50% ACT range: NA
3 Most popular majors: molecular/cell biology, English, psychology
Retention: 93%
Graduation rate: 77%
On-campus housing: NA
Fraternities: 11%
Sororities: 9%
Library: 8,500,000 volumes
Tuition and Fees: $4,046 in; $13,850 out
Room and Board: $8,266
Financial aid, first-year: 73%

Without a doubt the most rigorous and reputable of the University of California schools and the flagship of the California system, Berkeley is considered by some to be the flagship institution of the U.S. public university system. With a faculty replete with Nobel Prize winners and a phenomenally diverse student body, Berkeley is a gem of a college for intellectually enthusiastic and highly motivated undergraduates.

Harboring top-notch research facilities and kick-butt sports teams to boot, Berkeley rivals any of its eastern Ivy League counterparts and has managed to keep pace with local Bay Area rival Stanford. One would be remiss in passing up an opportunity to attend "Cal."

Uncovering the Periodic Table

With over 20,000 undergraduates, one would think it difficult to be anything but a "number" at Berkeley. However, specialization begins upon application as potential students compete for spots in one of Berkeley's several colleges, which include the College of Letters and Science, the College of Chemistry, and the College of Natural Resources.

Requirements for graduation certainly depend upon the college in which you enroll, but one breadth requirement needed for all students, regardless of college, is American Cultures. This core credit can be fulfilled through numerous courses offered by the top-notch Cal faculty. Some might look down on core courses, but Berkeley students universally praise the American Cultures requirement.

In addition to American Cultures, students say that those enrolled at the College of Natural Resources must complete "weeder" courses such as Math 1a and 1b, as well as Intro Chem, and the ever-feared Organic Chemistry. Weeder classes, according to one student, are designed to "give bad grades to students who can't do well, to deter them from majoring in the subject."

Some of the more reputable departments at Berkeley include chemistry, chemical engineering, computer science, and English—certainly an eclectic mix. The chemistry department, considered by most to be the best in the world, is responsible for the discovery of over 16 elements, the most of any institution in the U.S. Nobel Laureates routinely teach introductory level courses. In addition, Berkeley has one of the best English departments in the country, surpassing, in some respects, such old stalwarts as Harvard and Yale.

Classes run the gamut in terms of size. Intro Chem and Orgo courses can have as many as 650 students in lecture, while requiring discussion sections of around 25 people. Other intro courses can enroll upward of 1,000 students. But almost all professors have office hours, making it relatively easy for the confused or curious student to seek help or ask questions. Teaching assistants for most courses speak English with ease. One complaint, however, is the mathematics TAs' tenuous grasp of the language. But even without a firm command of English, all TAs are said to possess an "intelligence bordering on brilliance."

Science courses are regarded as some of the toughest courses on campus, but even so, the curve is somewhat generous. Usually about 10% of students receive As, another 25% receive Bs, and 50% receive Cs. Rarely are Ds and Fs given out. The university allows the unlucky students who happen to receive such grades to take the course over. If one is looking for a slacker major, students say political science fits the bill.

When registering for classes, students generally need to be aggressive in going after the courses that they want to take. Registration is done by phone, and students routinely complain that classes fill up too quickly. However, Berkeley gives priority in class registration to its freshmen, something that most universities fail to do. Enrolling in advanced courses generally requires taking a placement exam or having the prerequisites that mainly juniors and seniors possess. Overall, students are "thoroughly impressed" with the academics but remark that "Berkeley is hard as hell. You must work really hard freshman year!"

"Stop! Hey, What's That Sound?"

Everybody's definitely looking at what's going down at Berkeley. Despite having over 89% of its students from in-state, Berkeley has an incredibly diverse student body, encompassing various interests and attitudes. And even with the majority of students residing in California, the 11% of students from out-of-state come from places as far away as New York or New Jersey. But don't go in thinking that the Berkeley of the new millennium in any way resembles the Berkeley of the '60s. Certainly student activism still abounds, but as one student put it, "It's not the '60s anymore. We have our preps, our punks, and our hippies."

The activist movement centers mainly on the University of California's elimination of affirmative action. When asked if the elimination of affirmative action has had a noticeable effect on the diversity of the student body, students generally say no. But statistically there has been a drop in the number of African-American admittees. Berkeley students are actively lobbying in the hope of getting affirmative action back.

> **"It's not the '60s anymore."**

At Berkeley, the typical weekend revolves around the Greek system. For those students unafraid of the Friday morning hangover, partying begins on Thursday evening with a frat, sorority, or COOP bash. (COOPs are an alternative form of living for people with similar interests.) Partying continues through Friday and Saturday nights. Some students who possess cars head into San Francisco (SF) for a night of clubbing and general merriment. Upperclassmen, along with those who have fake IDs, tend to hit the bar scene in Berkeley or SF. Despite administrative admonishments, being underage is generally not a problem when attempting to acquire alcohol. Underage students can easily get willing upperclassmen to purchase a case or handle of beer or vodka. Marijuana smokers are certainly a presence on campus, but it is easy for non-smokers and non-drinkers alike to have a great time.

Frats and sororities have invitationals and formals, routinely rated by *Playboy* magazine as some of the best collegiate bashes in the U.S. Two of the most happening fraternities and sororities on campus are Kappa Delta Roe and Delta Gamma, respectively. Generally, one student reported, the first floor of an all-night frat bash has the dancing, the second floor alcohol, and the third floor pot—a perfect little hierarchy.

What about sex on campus? While casual sex appears to be infrequent, Berkeley, unlike many colleges, has a fairly active casual dating scene. Random hookups are also somewhat infrequent, but the aggressive boy or girl has about 10,000 potential hotties to choose from.

Living on Berkeley Campus

The only group guaranteed housing on campus is the freshmen. Dorm options include the ever-popular all-girl and all-boy dorms, Stern and Bowles, respectively, which both, incidentally, team up to throw a giant party during the year. Unit housing tends to be more social, and Clarke Kerr is home to the male and female athletes. Dorm rooms vary greatly in size. Generally speaking, however, the standard fare abounds—one bedroom with two beds and two desks. The exceptions are Clarke Kerr, Bowles, Stern, and Foothill Dorms, where students generally live in suites of up to 20. Dorm floors provide a convenient place to just chill with friends. RAs (residential advisors), who are usually juniors, are reportedly cool about things like drinking as long as students don't flaunt the rule-breaking.

With no guaranteed housing for upperclassmen, students tend to be very aggressive in seeking off-campus apartments. Most students begin the search the winter before the fall move-in. Other housing options include COOPs, sororities and frats, and cultural houses. Some complain that these "groupings" tend to contribute to the formation of cliques, but most see them as a positive.

Campus safety is somewhat of a concern to students. Past muggings have forced Berkeley to install blue phones throughout the campus, enabling students to easily contact campus security. The university is also fighting crime with its SWAT Team, and students are encouraged to take advantage of this safe walk program.

What about eating on campus? Students get to choose anywhere from 10 to 19 meals per week. Cafeteria food can, after a while, get "bland." Luckily, there are several eateries around campus to satisfy the hungry Berkeley man or woman—including the aptly named "Gourmet Ghetto."

Learning to Love Berkeley and Hate Stanford

Hating Stanford is a popular pastime on the Berkeley campus. Certainly the most talked about and anticipated football game of the year is the annual Berkeley-Stanford football game. Since red is Stanford's color, students are encouraged to take off red shirts. Other oft-watched sports are men's crew and basketball. Women's volleyball and soccer are also worth waking up for.

Extracurriculars abound on campus. It is difficult to find an uninvolved student.

The *Daily Cal*, the campus daily, as well as the *Heuristic Squelch*, the campus humor magazine, are frequent havens for budding writers.

Overall, Cal/Berkeley, according to one enthusiastic freshman, is the "most diverse place I've ever been in my entire life. There's definitely something happening in here . . . and it's definitely groovy."—*Sean McBride*

FYI

The three best things about attending Berkeley are "the quality of the faculty, San Francisco, and not having to attend Stanford."

The three worst things about attending Berkeley are "the huge introductory classes, the end of affirmative action, and 'Berkeley vision.'"

The three things every student should do before graduating from Berkeley are "go to the Blacklight Party, take advantage of San Francisco, go to the top of the Campanile."

One thing I'd like to have known before coming here is "that you need to take a very active role in your education. No one is holding your hand anymore."

University of California/Davis

Address: 175 Mrak Hall, One Shields Avenue Davis, CA 95616
Phone: 530-752-2971
E-mail address: thinkucd@ucdavis.edu
Web site URL: www.ucdavis.edu
Founded: 1863
Private or Public: public
Religious affiliation: none
Location: suburban
Undergraduate enrollment: 19,393
Total enrollment: 23,092
Percent Male/Female: 44%/56%
Percent Minority: 49%
Percent African-American: 3%

Percent Asian: 35%
Percent Hispanic: 10%
Percent Native-American: 0.5%
Percent in-state/out-of-state: 97%/3%
Percent Pub HS: 85%
Number of Applicants: 22,766
Percent Accepted: 63%
Percent Accepted who enroll: 27%
Entering: 3,819
Transfers: NA
Application Deadline: 30 Nov
Mean SAT: 556 V, 593 M
Mean ACT: NA

Middle 50% SAT range: 510–630 V, 550–650 M
Middle 50% ACT range: 21–27
3 Most popular majors: biological sciences, psychology, engineering
Retention: NA
Graduation rate: 77%
On-campus housing: 65%
Fraternities: 6%
Sororities: 7%
Library: NA
Tuition and Fees: $4,214 in; $18,145 out
Room and Board: $7,163
Financial aid, first-year: NA

Located in the heart of the Central Valley, University of California/Davis is the largest of the nine UC campuses, with 5,200 plush acres. Although Davis started out as the "University Farm," you'd be wrong if you called it that today! The academics at this top public university are among the best in the nation. Its sports put other schools to shame thanks to a number of NCAA titles. And the students who walk on its campus are friendly and diverse in their interests. Davis students still get a hint of the farm that the campus once was with the cows and large open spaces, but "this school is just like any other college. Parties, dating, you name it. We've got it."

Do U.C. Intensity Here?

Although Davis was once an institution for only those interested in agriculture, today it offers its students an opportunity to pursue a broad range of disciplines. The school has a general education requirement, which has three components: topical breadth, social-cultural diversity, and writing experience. To fulfill this requirement, six courses must be taken from the two topical breadth subjects that don't include your major, one course must be taken from the social-cultural diversity component, and three courses are required from the writing experience component. One student comments that "the GE system really helps us get a better background in subjects outside of our concentration. I like it a lot." UC/Davis also has University Requirements and separate requirements for whichever college the student decides to enter (College of Agricultural and Environmental Sciences, College of Engineering, and College of Letters and Science). Although it seems as though the school has way too many requirements, one student says, "It's not too rigid and strict, nor loose and easy. I just take what I want to."

But it's not always easy to get the courses you want at Davis. "A lot of people don't get into the classes they want because the school is so big," says one student. With such a large student body, people complain that the courses have too many enrollees, making interaction with professors almost impossible. Another complaint students have is that some of the professors and "way too many TAs are foreign," making it hard for them to understand lectures and the weekly discussion sessions. On the one hand, some students say that they are "happy with a lot of the professors and TAs. They're usually willing to help you out if you ask." On the other hand, one sophomore says, "I think our professors aren't qualified, to tell you the truth, and the TAs are pretty weak all around so far."

Davis offers a couple of different honors programs, including the Davis Honors Challenge Program and the Integrated Studies Program. Davis Honors Challenge involves an application process, while Integrated Studies is an invitational first-year residential honors program limited to the top 3% of the entering class. Both programs require members to be highly motivated and grant students the opportunity to enhance their educational experience at Davis. When asked about the Davis Honors Challenge, one student in the program commented that "the seminars we're required to take are a joke!"

Students claim that biological sciences, psychology, and computer science are among the more popular majors at Davis. "Computer science is hard as heck and so competitive!" Some students comment that managerial economics and design are probably the easiest majors at their school. As far as classes go, "everyone seems to want to do design and nutrition . . . probably since they are so easy." The overall workload at Davis is "easier than high school" for some students and quite the opposite for others. "The work they give here is by no means unbearable," says one student. "As long as you keep up with the reading and seek help when you need it, you'll be on top of things." Indeed, students must keep up with their studies, because it's fast-paced at Davis. Their 10-week quarter system requires students to "take in a lot of information in a very short time period." Some students complain that they don't get as much out of their classes because of this, while others think that it's a great system that allows them to take more classes. One thing that Davis students *do* agree on is the necessity of the weekends to recuperate and relax.

Where Do You Want to Go Today? Off Campus!

The social life at Davis is pretty limited. Some students party at the frat houses, some catch movies on campus, and others just chill with their friends. If they have access to a car, Davis students will probably leave campus for their fun. With Sacramento to the east and the San Francisco Bay Area to the west, students can find a plethora of places to eat, shop, and go clubbing. The campus tries to engage its students with speakers, performances, and dances. Turbulence is a dance that freshmen go to every year to meet new people. "I think it's easy to meet new people here. It's just a matter of whether or not you're willing to go out and actually meet them," says one junior.

Even though there is a Greek system at Davis, it only consists of about 20% of the student body. So non-Greeks definitely don't feel left out. Alcohol is pretty big among the frats and smoking is prevalent all over campus, but if you don't do either, you won't feel out of place. The student body is ethnically pretty diverse, although predominantly Caucasian and Asian. Most of the students are California residents, from a wide range of economic backgrounds. The typical look varies widely as well, with some students looking "like they just rolled out of bed" and others dressing up in nice clothes. But on the average, students at Davis are very fit and athletic. "Everyone wants that Cali bod," laughed one student.

> "You can't beat a place that has smiling faces and Cali's sunny weather to complement it!"

As far as extracurriculars go, with such a large student body and over 300 different organizations, there's sure to be something that interests each individual. "Everybody tries to do something to get involved on campus." Intramural sports are pretty big, as are the religious groups at UC/Davis. Students say that "it's a good way to make friends and find out more about yourself."

Davis Got Game
Even though Davis doesn't offer athletic scholarships, its sports teams consistently rank among the top in Division II of the NCAA. Men's basketball won the national championship in 1998 and the football team has also been doing extremely well. In addition, Davis has won the Sears Directors' Cup for overall excellence in both men's and women's athletic programs for NCAA Division II schools and was recently named the top Division II school for female athletes by *Sports Illustrated*. The annual Causeway Classic football game against Sacramento State

University usually attracts a lot of Davis students cheering for their school. With the "Aggie Pack," Davis' cheer organization (acclaimed as the largest in the nation), students get pretty hyped for their teams as shirts, food, and other items are thrown into the crowd: "The Aggie Pack really gets us going! It's amazing how the school spirit just rises to a different plane when they come out!" The facilities for non-athletes at Davis are "wonderful, but there could always be more of everything since there are always so many guys working out and playing basketball all the time." The campus offers a swimming pool, tennis courts, and even a roller hockey rink!

Green Acres Is the Place to Be
The open areas of green and abundant trees on campus make it a "peaceful and enjoyable place to be, whether you are by yourself or with other people." Most of Davis is flat, spread out, and very nature-oriented: "I don't think I could survive without my bike here. The campus is way too big to walk." Some students complain about the odor from the cows near Tercero dorm, but most say that it's bearable after a while. "The arboretum is a great place to go. It's so relaxing to be surrounded by the ducks and the serenity there," says one student when asked about his favorite hiding place on campus. The surrounding town of Davis is "small, quiet, and suburbanlike . . . it's nothing different from any small college town."

Students say they feel safe on campus despite some small crime incidents here and there. Recent disturbances on campus include some racially motivated hate crimes. Violent confrontations between an Asian-American frat and a Caucasian frat have resulted in an increased awareness of racial tensions within the student body. Still, Davis students say that for the most part they still feel safe, just more wary of their surroundings.

Most freshmen live in campus dorms overseen by residential advisors, but the bulk of upperclassmen live in off-campus apartments. Most dorms are comprised of coed floors with single-sex bathrooms, and many are air-conditioned. Some dorms have different programs and all vary in size. "I met most of my closest friends in my dorm. Everyone should live in a dorm their freshman year because you get to meet and live with so many interesting people!" After freshman year, most people are booted off campus to apartments. The rent is "good compared to other schools nearby like Stanford and Berkeley," but the degree of expense really varies depending on whether you get a shack or a model home. One accommodation Davis makes for its students living off campus is the UNITRANS bus system that connects the surrounding area with the main campus.

The meal plan is pretty flexible. Students choose how many meals they want and pay accordingly. One student complained, "It's a rip-off for the quality of food we get," while another said that "it's fine." With plenty of restaurants surrounding the campus, however, students don't starve to death. There are the usual fast-food restaurants like Jack in the Box, McDonald's, KFC, and Wendy's. Some of students' favorite restaurants are Woodstock's Pizza, Pluto's, and Fuji's all-you-can-eat sushi bar. And one can't forget about the late-night Chinese food deliveries!

Nothing's Better than Some California Sunshine

The small-town, country atmosphere of UC/Davis is what attracts most students to the school. Although the fast-paced schoolwork and abundant extracurriculars provide challenging opportunities, they don't keep the students from maintaining a friendly, laid-back attitude. "The one thing that separates us from other schools is our friendly and open student body. You can't beat a place that has smiling faces and Cali's sunny weather to complement it!" —*Jane Pak*

FYI
The three best things about attending UC/Davis are "the relaxed atmosphere, the freedom to do whatever you want, and its closeness to Tahoe, San Francisco, and Sacramento."
The three worst things about attending UC/Davis are "you feel like you're a number rather than a person, the cliques, and Davis (the city)."
The three things every student should do before graduating from UC/Davis are "make a trip to Sacramento, get lost in the boonies at night with some friends, and live in the dorms."
One thing I'd like to have known before coming here is "the variety of things Davis has to offer in terms of the social life, clubs, and academic programs."

University of California / Irvine

Address: 204
Administration Building;
Irvine, CA 92697-1075
Phone: 949-824-6703
E-mail address:
oars@uci.edu
Web site URL:
www.ucap.edu / pathways
Founded: 1885
Private or Public: public
Religious affiliation:
none
Location: suburban
**Undergraduate
enrollment:** 15,235
Total enrollment: 16,129
Percent Male / Female:
47% / 53%
Percent Minority: 70%

Percent African-American:
2%
Percent Asian: 56%
Percent Hispanic: 11%
Percent Native-American:
0.5%
**Percent in-state / out-of-
state:** 96% / 4%
Percent Pub HS: 88%
Number of Applicants:
22,118
Percent Accepted: 73%
**Percent Accepted who
enroll:** 23%
Entering: 3,674
Transfers: NA
Application Deadline:
30 Nov
Mean SAT: NA

Mean ACT: NA
Middle 50% SAT range:
495–600 V,
540–655 M
Middle 50% ACT range: NA
3 Most popular majors:
biological sciences,
economics, psychology
Retention: NA
Graduation rate: 36%
On-campus housing: 50%
Fraternities: 7%
Sororities: 7%
Library: 1,500,000 volumes
Tuition and Fees: $3,871
in; $14,193 out
Room and Board: $6,407
Financial aid, first-year:
61%

One of the first things that students at UC/Irvine comment on when asked about their school is how much they love their campus. The beautiful modern 1,500-acre campus is located in Orange County, only minutes from the Pacific Ocean. In addition to being close to the water, UCI is also close to home for much of the student body. And although it is one of the younger campuses in the UC system, UCI is "one of the fastest-growing in stature and size" and is the first public university to have faculty members awarded two Nobel Prizes in two separate fields the same year.

A Wide Variety of Classes

To accommodate its large student population, UCI boasts a renowned faculty and a broad range of course offerings. Academics are considered intense, and students are happy with the diverse course offerings at UC/Irvine. UCI offers majors in seven schools: Engineering, Social Ecology, Art, Humanities, Physical Sciences, Biological Sciences, and Social Sciences. The biology department is particularly strong and boasts the most majors. UC/Irvine is on the 10-week quarter system, and the first thing students mention when you ask them about their courses is the heavy workload. General education requirements (or "breadth requirements," as students call them) are extensive and varied and include competence in a foreign language, three natural science courses, and three writing courses. While some complained about the hassle of the requirements, they were quick to mention "cool and interesting" classes such as Greek Literature and The History of Jazz.

Students need 180 credits to graduate, which means most undergrads take three or four classes a quarter. Some mentioned difficulties enrolling in classes at times and anticipated taking five years to graduate. UCI is a large public university with an undergraduate enrollment of over 12,000 students, and class size can often reach "intimidating proportions." Introductory courses often enroll about 400 students, though discussion sections with only about 15 to 20 students provide a more interactive atmosphere.

A Growing Campus

When UCI was founded in the 1960s, the campus consisted of 1,500 acres of treeless terrain. Less than 40 years later, it has been filled with facilities that make life easier for its thousands of students. Among the newest buildings on campus is the Anteater Recreation Center (known among students as the ARC), where students participate in sports and other planned activities, such as dance lessons, karate classes, and rock climbing. The Bren Center, UCI's student activity center, hosts banquets, exhibitions, concerts, and other events. Some of the center's more popular recent events have been the World Championship Wrestling tournaments and MTV's Campus Invasion Tour. The center can also be rented out to the general public for activities, such as dance competitions and sporting events. As one student says, "Residents from all over Orange County and other areas of California often visit the Bren Center for its most popular events."

> **"As long as you make an effort, it is not hard to meet a lot of great people here."**

The Irvine Barclay Theatre hosts orchestras, cabaret, concerts, and other performances several times a week. The theater sponsors an arts education program called ArtsReach that is designed to provide students with knowledge and appreciation of the performing arts. Crawford Hall is where men's and women's volleyball games are held. Students who are fond of water sports should be sure to visit the Aquatic Complex, where they can watch the Anteaters compete against other colleges. The Anteater Pool, which holds nearly 1 million gallons of water, is one of the largest competitive pools in the United States.

Go, Anteaters!

Although UCI does not have a football team, sports still play a major role in the lives of students. As one student commented, "All we are missing is a football team." Despite this shortcoming, students at UCI still have plenty of enthusiasm for their school's athletics. Perhaps the most popular team on campus is men's basketball, which consistently does well and was recently seeded third in the Western Division of the Big West Tournament. A lot of students enjoy participating in intramural sports, where different organizations and fraternities engage in friendly competition for an invigorating break from their studies.

Life on and off Campus

While the percentage of students involved in the Greek system is relatively small, fraternity and sorority mixers are cited as the places to go for parties. Thursday and Friday nights are party nights, and fraternities and sororities provide the alcohol. But there is very little pressure to participate in the Greek system, and ethnic fraternities and sororities are also options. Fraternities and sororities are prevalent at UCI, where "students can often be found hanging out with their brothers or sisters at the food court." Every Thursday night, people at UCI look forward to attending frat parties, since Irvine can reportedly be boring at times. The surrounding cities also offer much to do for students. As one student noted, "Ring Road is like the promenade of UCI. There is always something going on, whether it be a fair, clubs offering food, games to attract people, or speakers." Popular options include Newport Beach, Costa Mesa, and Los Angeles, as well as clubbing and going to raves, where students "dress to impress."

Flashy cars are common sights in the parking lots at UCI, and many of them are "fixed up and lowered to the ground with great sound systems." However, many students don't feel a pressure to conform to this "fashion show," because they can easily blend into the large student body. A portion of the student body at UCI takes fashion very seriously. As one student said, "Many people are indifferent about what they wear, while for others their clothing is a top priority."

Freshmen are guaranteed housing and in their subsequent years usually seek off-campus housing in apartments and homes in town, which are plentiful. Two housing complexes named Mesa Court and Middle Earth are freshman residences, each accommodating about 1,200 students. A fairly large portion of the student body commutes, and as a result "parking can be a hassle at times."

In addition to the regular weekly options for hanging out, there are numerous special events held at UCI each year. Celebrate UCI is the annual open house held each April. This event gives the community, alumni, and prospective students and their families the opportunity to tour the campus and observe performances throughout the day. The semiannual formal dance also allows students a chance to get dressed up and have fun with their classmates and meet some new people. As one student put it, "As long as you make an effort, it is not hard to meet a lot of great people here."

Students who live on or off campus enjoy the all-you-can-eat dining facilities on campus, which also provide the option of packing a bag lunch if you have classes during regular meal times. There are two main dining halls, which students feel are not bad at all, although one cautioned, "Keep away from the pasta sauces."

Although academics at UCI are a top priority for students, it is often difficult to resist the temptation of extracurricular opportunities. Whether it be intramural sports, research, studying abroad, clubs, or organizations, students have an array of opportunities to take advantage of at the University of California at Irvine.
—*Robert Wong*

FYI
The three best things about attending UCI are "the campus, the beach, and the parties."
The three worst things about attending UCI are "the large number of students, the heavy workload, and large class sizes."
The three things that every student should do before graduating from UCI are "go to a concert at the Bren Center, hang out at the beach, and get to know people."
One thing I'd like to have known before coming here is "how flashy many of the students are."

University of California / Los Angeles

Address: 1147 Murphy Hall; Los Angeles, CA 90095-1436
Phone: 310-825-3101
E-mail address: ugadm@saonet.ucla.edu
Web site URL: www.ucla.edu
Founded: 1919
Private or Public: public
Religious affiliation: none
Location: urban
Undergraduate enrollment: 24,668
Total enrollment: 36,351
Percent Male/Female: 45%/55%
Percent Minority: 58%
Percent African-American: 5%

Percent Asian: 37%
Percent Hispanic: 15%
Percent Native-American: 0.5%
Percent in-state/out-of-state: 97%/3%
Percent Pub HS: 79%
Number of Applicants: 35,681
Percent Accepted: 29%
Percent Accepted who enroll: 40%
Entering: 4,131
Transfers: 2,249
Application Deadline: 30 Nov
Mean SAT: 620 V, 655 M
Mean ACT: 26

Middle 50% SAT range: 570–680 V, 600–720 M
Middle 50% ACT range: 23–30
3 Most popular majors: psychology, economics, political science
Retention: 97%
Graduation rate: 79%
On-campus housing: 85%
Fraternities: 11%
Sororities: 9%
Library: 7,401,780 volumes
Tuition and Fees: $3,698 in; $13,872 out
Room and Board: $7,692
Financial aid, first-year: NA

Surrounded by the Santa Monica
mountains and exclusive neighborhoods of Beverly Hills and Bel Air,
it's easy to see why UCLA is one of the
most popular UC schools. But don't let the
ideal location fool you. UCLA is one of
the most academically elite universities in
America, its location being only one of its
many enviable qualities.

Solid Academics
Although a relatively young university,
UCLA has established a strong academic
reputation firmly rooted in a commitment
to undergraduates. "Even though some of
my classes were quite large, the professors always advertised office hours where
I routinely went to ask questions and
really got to know the professor," one student said. Professors teach all of the lecture classes at UCLA, with TAs leading
many of the discussion sessions. "The TAs
were an invaluable source of information
for me. Without their help, I quite honestly
don't know how I would have survived!"
another student said.

Many introductory math and science
classes enroll up to 300 students. However, upper-level courses are much
smaller. Students in introductory humanities courses report classes of as few as 20
students. Like many other schools in California, UCLA is on a modified-quarter system with three 10-week periods. This
system accelerates the pace of learning:
during a typical year, students take three
sets of courses instead of the usual two.
Students complain that one disadvantage
of the quarter system is having to take
midterms every few weeks. However,
most students find the system manageable, even if they are not overly enthusiastic about it.

UCLA has a general education (GE)
requirement that includes classes in a
variety of departments. The College of
Arts and Sciences requires undergrads to
choose from an extensive list of classes in
the humanities, social sciences, life sciences, physical sciences, and foreign languages, while the School of Engineering
requires only seven humanities courses.
Some GE requirements can be met with
advanced placement credits earned in
high school.

"Everyone is a bio major."

Choosing a major at UCLA can be a relatively complex procedure. Students must
apply to a major upon completion of their
pre-requisites and admission to many programs such as business-economics or
engineering is highly competitive. Undergraduates report that biology, engineering, economics, business-economics, and
chemistry are among the most popular
majors and best departments. One student complained, "Everyone is a bio major," and many among them hope to enter
the esteemed UCLA medical school.

Students rate the library system at
UCLA very highly. Powell Library is the
main campus library, and serves mainly
as a study center. Undergraduates report
that they also study outside in the sun,
in dorm study rooms, and in campus
restaurants. Research is primarily done
in the University Research Library and
various graduate school libraries around
campus.

Off Campus or On?
UCLA has many different housing options. Four high-rise dorms offer a social
atmosphere to their primarily underclassmen tenants. Upperclassmen tend to
choose to live in apartment-like, university-owned buildings. Students report that
these accommodations, such as Sunset
Village, provide more luxury in a "hotel-
like" atmosphere that includes picnic and
volleyball areas. Students report that
while these apartments are quite social
and friendly, they are nothing compared
to the "roar and mania" of the freshman
high-rises. Many students also choose to
live off-campus, though students often
travel to the neighboring towns of Santa
Monica, Culver City, and Westwood to
find affordable apartments. Many students do have cars despite the university-
wide shortage of parking spaces.

Students rate the food at UCLA with
great enthusiasm. Ackerman Union, the
main student building, serves regular
cafeteria-style meals, and is also home to
Taco Bell and many similar restaurants
that are part of the meal plan. Students

can choose between plans of 11, 15, or 19 meals a week.

Far and Away

The campus is divided into North Campus, where the majority of humanities classes are held, and South Campus, where the math and science courses take place. Though UCLA tries hard to keep its buildings on campus, its huge size often defeats this goal. Students say that aside from the occasional rickety classroom, the university is doing a good job maintaining and upgrading the campus facilities.

Security is a main priority of the university, and the campus is "unquestionably safe even in the wee hours of the morning." Blue-light emergency phones and security escorts are easily available.

Students report great ethnic diversity at UCLA, although some claim that the diversity is misleading. Students from similar ethnic backgrounds tend to self-segregate, creating an uneasy tension between groups. Students are quick to point out, somewhat defensively, that this is true everywhere, and that race issues at UCLA are probably better than at most universities.

Divided Social Life

The social life at UCLA is often divided between those who live on campus and those who live off. Fraternity parties are the main attraction on campus, with frequent dorm and campus-wide parties drawing students as well. Students with cars often leave campus for the weekend to go home or visit friends; they also take advantage of nearby Los Angeles. Located just minutes away from the clubs of Sunset Boulevard and the beaches of Santa Monica, students rarely have trouble finding weekend entertainment.

Recently, Sports Illustrated rated UCLA the number one "jock school" in the nation. This distinction is well deserved. The enormous John Wooden Recreation Center provides all students the opportunity to sweat off those hours spent in the library. Intramural sports are also incredibly popular, and team spirit is high. In recent years, the varsity basketball, gymnastics, volleyball, and tennis teams have had huge national success. The football team is also highly supported and the rivalry between UCLA and the University of Southern California peaks each year when the football teams battle it out on the gridiron, often with both conference title and bowl game hopes at stake.

UCLA has much to offer its students. Along with its vast resources as a major university and its relatively low costs, UCLA provides an exceptional education, with a spirited student body. With its enviable weather and superior education, students say it is no wonder that UCLA has few competitors. —*Sathya Oum and Staff*

FYI

The three best things about attending UCLA are "sunny weather, Los Angeles, and the diversity of the student body."

The three worst things about attending UCLA are "Los Angeles, huge lecture classes, and bureaucracy."

The three things every student should do before graduating from UCLA are "go to a Bruins game, hang out on the beach, and party at Mardi Gras."

One thing I'd like to have known before coming here is "how difficult science classes would be."

University of California / Riverside

Address: 1120 Hinderaker Hall; Riverside, CA 92521
Phone: 909-787-4531
E-mail address: discover@pop.ucr.edu
Web site URL: www.ucr.edu
Founded: 1905
Private or Public: public
Religious affiliation: none
Location: suburban
Undergraduate enrollment: 10,120
Total enrollment: 10,888
Percent Male/Female: 46%/54%
Percent Minority: 68%
Percent African-American: 5%
Percent Asian: 41%
Percent Hispanic: 21%

Percent Native-American: 0.5%
Percent in-state/out-of-state: 99%/1%
Percent Pub HS: 86%
Number of Applicants: 16,316
Percent Accepted: 84%
Percent Accepted who enroll: 19%
Entering: 2,610
Transfers: NA
Application Deadline: 30 Nov
Mean SAT: 512 V, 554 M
Mean ACT: NA
Middle 50% SAT range: 440–570 V, 480–620 M

Middle 50% ACT range: 18–24
3 Most popular majors: biology, psychology, business administration
Retention: 86%
Graduation rate: 43%
On-campus housing: 60%
Fraternities: 13%
Sororities: 12%
Library: 1,800,000 volumes
Tuition and Fees: $3,757 in; $13,561 out
Room and Board: $6,579
Financial aid, first-year: NA

UC/Riverside has an unfortunate reputation as a safety school for the more popular UCLA and Berkeley. However, its newness and smaller size offers its own charms to its students. The quiet town of Riverside affords the students a tranquil academic atmosphere, and as the school is a major research center, Riverside's undergraduate population is given great opportunities to participate in research activities.

"Boonie-hill"

Students characterize the town of Riverside, located east of downtown L.A., as "Boonie-hill." Even with grass and mountains in the background, the town inherits the smoggy air characteristic of L.A., but not the bustling urbanity. As one student reported, "It wouldn't be considered desolate, but it's definitely a lot quieter than parts of L.A. just thirty minutes away."

To date, UCR remains one of the smallest UCs; a five- to ten-minute walk is all it takes to walk from one edge of campus to the other. The architectural design of the campus is distinguished by its lack of uniformity. According to several students, there seems to be no underlying theme that connects the modern buildings. UCR is continually upgrading its campus, renovating its current buildings as well as constructing new ones. One of the three dorm buildings was recently refurbished, and others are continually being renovated. The improvements to the dorms have been met with great enthusiasm among the students. As one student said, "There's new carpeting, and the AC and heating can now be adjusted within each room. There's more than enough space—as long as your roommate isn't too messy." The majority of the dorms are doubles, but some residents have singles or triples. There are no suite arrangements. While the majority of freshmen live in the dorms, on-campus housing is not required, even for freshmen. Some students choose to live in apartments on- or off-campus, or in one of the many fraternity houses.

Studying Made Possible

With reportedly few attractions in the immediate area, "Riverside is a school where you can study because, well, there's not much else to do." One heralded aspect of UCR is the Biomed Program, a joint association with UCLA Medical School. Twenty-five spots are made available in UCLA Med each year for graduates of the program. Competition for these spots is fierce, and students often gripe about the curve being set by "those overachievers in the Biomed program." The most popular majors at UCR are business, engineering, and the natural sciences. As one senior noted, "I haven't met that many people in the humanities, but I am sure there are some out there." UCR expanded its science programs by recently building a new Science Library.

> With a social scene that sometimes lags on campus, some students argue, "Come on. It's L.A. There's always something to do; you just have to look around and deal."

With many classes being held in large lecture halls, a common complaint is the size of classes, particularly in the large introductory courses required for specific majors. Capping enrollment frustrates those who cannot get in, and prevents the professor from "giving us some individual attention." These classes, even when broken into discussion sections, often have 15 to 40 people. One student stated, "I wish that they would open up more sections of major impact classes. Course selection is done on the phone by appointment, and it sucks to be late."

It Can Get Pretty Gross

Food receives mixed reviews from students. Some indicate that food on-campus is "actually not that bad," while others state that "the slop we're served in the dorm dining halls is awful." Another student noted that "food here can get pretty gross." Not only does UCR offer dining hall facilities, but it also makes food stands available around campus that offer hamburgers, beef bowls, and other fast-food items. Those who choose to eat off campus find that the main road through Riverside also offers eateries including Baker's, Church's Chicken, and the Spaghetti Factory.

Night Life

While frats are popular, the Greek scene does not dominate campus activities. Rather, many students indicate that student organizations thrive alongside them. "There are a good deal of frats around, but there are also a lot of clubs where we hang out on weekends." Though frat parties are often exclusive, there are many dances open to the entire student body. There is also a UCR movie night once a week that is popular with students. Beyond that, however, students complain that they are left to find their own entertainment. Downtown Riverside is 5 to 10 minutes away, but few undergrads have cars, and those who do often "don't want to risk losing their parking spaces. So we're left to find another way to get off campus." With a social scene that sometimes lags on campus, some students argue, "Come on. It's L.A. There's always something to do; you just have to look around and deal."

Sagging Spirit

Sports do not muster much school spirit at UCR, a Division II school. On the whole, students are reportedly "apathetic and saggy" about their teams. As one student stated, "Really, are we known for any sports at all? No, we're just known for the Biomed Program." While students do not appear to rally behind their teams, involvement in sports certainly exists. Intramural sports are particularly popular as friends sign up to form teams, and play "for the sheer fun of it—you can't study all the time because it wears you down after a while."

Though the university is somewhat isolated from the heart of Los Angeles, many students praise UCR for enabling them to work in a much more "tranquil environment." Students often forget that UCR wasn't their first choice because of all that UCR has to offer. Its proximity to L.A. and its quiet setting allow students to concentrate on studying during the week and have fun over the weekend. If a good education is more important to you than bragging rights, UCR isn't a bad choice at all. —*Seung Lee and Staff*

FYI
The three best things about attending UCR are "the great faculty, its great location, and a very flexible program."
The three worst things about attending UCR are "the isolated campus, lack of sports, and self-segregated student body."
The three things that every student should do before graduating from UCR are "make use of resources at UCLA, go celebrity sighting, and go to nearby national parks."
One thing I'd like to have known before coming here is "how homogeneous the student body is because most come from California."

University of California / San Diego

Address: 9500 Gilman Drive, 0337; La Jolla, CA 92093-0337
Phone: 858-534-4831
E-mail address: admissionsinfo@ucsd.edu
Web site URL: www.ucsd.edu
Founded: 1965
Private or Public: public
Religious affiliation: none
Location: urban
Undergraduate enrollment: 16,230
Total enrollment: 18,324
Percent Male/Female: 48%/52%
Percent Minority: 40%

Percent African-American: 2%
Percent Asian: 35%
Percent Hispanic: 2%
Percent Native-American: 1%
Percent in-state/out-of-state: 98%/2%
Percent Pub HS: NA
Number of Applicants: 32,539
Percent Accepted: 41%
Percent Accepted who enroll: 25%
Entering: 3,286
Transfers: NA
Application Deadline: 30 Nov
Mean SAT: 601 V, 640 M

Mean ACT: NA
Middle 50% SAT range: NA
Middle 50% ACT range: NA
3 Most popular majors: biochemistry, biology, psychology
Retention: NA
Graduation rate: 74%
On-campus housing: 86%
Fraternities: 10%
Sororities: 10%
Library: 2,300,000 volumes
Tuition and Fees: $3,847 in; $14,021 out
Room and Board: $7,134
Financial aid, first-year: 50%

Soaked in sun and minutes from beautiful California beaches, the University of California/San Diego offers its students a world of opportunities in the idyllic setting of the San Diego suburb of La Jolla. How, you may ask, does anyone ever work with great waves and warm beaches closer to your dorms than your classes are? However, in spite of the weather, UCSD students do find time to get their academics in and live up to the school's reputation as one of the top academic institutions in the country.

Beach Reading
Like many California schools, UCSD is on the quarter system. Most students attend three quarters a year and do not take classes during the fourth quarter, which is during the summer. Because of the quarter system, each student gets to take a wide variety of classes. However, many students complain that because of the short duration of quarters, they are not able to study material in-depth. One student observed, "The quarter schedule is pretty hectic—you're either in the middle of midterms or getting ready for finals!"

Apart from the quarter system, students are generally pleased with their academic experience. One of UCSD's most unique aspects of academics is the college system. There are five colleges, each with different core requirements and mission statements. Marshall College emphasizes diversity and public policy. Undergrads at Muir College study the humanities, and Warren College promotes a liberal arts education. Roosevelt College is focused on international policy, and Revelle College is geared toward students interested in math and the hard sciences. Because of UCSD's core requirements, introductory classes are often large in size and can enroll as many as 400 students.

The complaint at many universities is that teaching assistants do not speak English. However, at UCSD the problem is not the TAs (often undergraduates themselves) but the professors. In fact, students report a recent decrease in English proficiency among the faculty. At the upper level, class size decreases dramatically and professors are generally better. However, as one student reports, "Classes are becoming hard to get because of overcrowding." How do students get into classes? As is done throughout the UC system, students register by phone or on the Internet. Priority is given to more advanced students—freshmen with AP credits are able to register before those without. However, students who are not able to get into a class they want through traditional means are often able to squeeze in by talking with the professor once the semester starts.

Students must work for their grades once they have gotten into their classes. The biggest complaint about UCSD is that students are constantly studying. Because undergrads must apply to some of the majors, there is reportedly a high level of competition among students. As one reports, "It is not totally uncommon for pre-meds and engineering students to be victims of sabotage or commit academic dishonesty in the form of cheating." However, there were no reports of such competition among students in less quantitative subjects. And if you want to take it easy with academics, the majors to think about are communications and economics.

Creative Campus

With all this studying, one might wonder where students go to do work and research papers. The center of academia on the UCSD campus is Geisel Library. Besides housing the bulk of texts on the UCSD campus, the Geisel Library is one of the most architecturally unique structures on campus: a massive structure that widens until the sixth floor, after which its width then decreases to the top. And if the library is not unique enough, the route to the library is by the "snake path." "Everyone likes to walk on the snake path on their way to the library; it's a path with colorful tiles in the shape of a snake."

California Casa

Besides the library, the UCSD campus is sprawling, and many students need cars to get from where they live to their classes. For freshmen, however, this is not the case. Housing is guaranteed for freshmen and sophomores, and most students live in doubles along hallways. Dorm life is far and away the most complained-about part of life as a UCSD student. According to one student, "Dorms and dorm living are difficult for most people because the residents and RAs (residential advisors) tend to be uptight about everything. Also, dorms are usually about a fifteen-minute walk from most classes." According to another student, "From the first week of school freshman year, I quickly discovered that partying was a big no-no."

The best part of dorm living is the food. Each of the five colleges (Marshall, Warren, Revelle, Roosevelt, and Muir) has its own "restaurant," which means you can always find people you know at dinner. Also, the food is apparently well liked by most students.

Because of such a limiting dorm life, students tend to move off campus as soon as they are able to find housing. However, this is easier said than done. Not only is La Jolla the most expensive area of San Diego, but also all housing is a good drive away from campus, "and if you're a freshman, don't bother bringing a car," because parking is largely unavailable. And even if you are able to park, it is still a good walk to class. However, the upside to this ritzy area of California is that the town of La Jolla is safe for students. Also, there is a campus police agency that will walk students who find themselves alone at night.

What Football Team?

Because studying takes so much time, "people at UCSD aren't really into organized extracurriculars." Many students can be found studying or relaxing at the heart of campus at the Price Center, which has a bunch of restaurants, a theater, a travel agency, a smoothie joint, a coffee shop, and the bookstore, as well as a pool hall. Most people hang out there between classes. In spite of the apparent apathy of many students toward extracurriculars, UCSD does offer a wide range of student organizations that allow for everyone to get involved if they so desire. One example is the *UCSD Guardian*, a student newspaper listing all the campus happenings.

> **"Nine out of ten girls in San Diego are pretty and the tenth one goes to UCSD."**

For the athletes, UCSD is a Division III school with sports available on the varsity level. However, one apparent gap is the lack of a football team, a factor that many students say contributes to the lack of school spirit. However, the absence of a football team does not discourage participation in all athletics. UCSD has a good water polo team, and with students rallying behind water polo "school spirit has increased in the past few years."

"Take Genesee to Governor . . ."

As for evening activities, student opinions vary widely. It depends on who your friends are and what kinds of things you like to do. The on-campus party scene is fairly subdued, and most parties are broken up by 10:00 P.M. due to the strict policies of the campus police and RAs. Off-campus parties tend to be the most talked about. According to one student, "I think everyone who has ever gone to UCSD knows the intersection of Genesee and Governor. About seventy-five percent of the off-campus parties start

with the directions 'Take Genesee to Governor . . .'" Also, the fraternity scene is not as omnipresent as it is on many state school campuses due to the fact that the frats do not have their own on-campus houses. Thus frat parties are held at members' apartments and houses and it can sometimes be a drive to get there. Furthermore, recent laws passed in La Jolla to limit the noise level can result in eviction if offenses are committed multiple times.

With strict laws on parties, most under-21 undergraduates find themselves hanging out with friends or going to the movies. For those over 21, there are a few local bars that students frequent. Also, brand-new this year is the first on-campus club in the UC system: Club Ritmo's hopes to cater to the students' desire to party and features DJs from UCSD's DJ club, the Vinylphiles.

Besides the weekly party scene, the most anticipated event of the year is the campus-wide Sun God Festival. Not only is it near the end of the academic year, but it is one of the only times in the year that the whole campus comes out to celebrate and take some time off. Huge obstacle courses are set up on the athletic field and top name bands such as Cypress Hill, Reel Big Fish, and others play for students under the rays of San Diego sun.

As for the students themselves, the running joke is that "nine out of ten girls in San Diego are pretty and the tenth one goes to UCSD." Whether this is true or not is a matter of opinion. With the sun always shining, the campus is conducive to athletic participation, and many people play intramural sports and jog on a regular basis. There is also a state-of-the-art gym facility on campus known to students as RIMAC (Recreation and Intramural Athletic Complex). Also, there is always the possibility of going to the beach nearby if you want a healthy tan.

The warm climate and beautiful beaches, along with top-ranked academics, make UCSD one of the most highly sought after schools in California. After all, who could turn down a school that has a campus-wide festival dedicated to a celebration of the Sun God? —*Sophie Jones*

FYI

The three best things about attending UCSD are "living in San Diego, the excellent quality of the academics, and the annual Sun God Festival."

The three worst things about attending UCSD are "the lack and cost of housing, the lack and cost of parking, and the absence of a social scene on campus."

The three things that every student should do before graduating from UCSD are "go to Black's Beach (a local nude beach) for a night bonfire, go to BJ's Pizza, and go to Ralph's in La Jolla."

One thing I'd like to have known before coming here is that "having a car is absolutely necessary!"

University of California / Santa Barbara

Address: 1210 Cheadle Hall, Santa Barbara, CA 93106
Phone: 805-893-2881
E-mail address: appinfo@sa.ucsb.edu
Web site URL: www.admit.ucsb.edu
Founded: 1909
Private or Public: public
Religious affiliation: none
Location: suburban
Undergraduate enrollment: 17,685
Total enrollment: 20,056
Percent Male / Female: 46% / 54%
Percent Minority: 32%
Percent African-American: 2%

Percent Asian: 15%
Percent Hispanic: 14%
Percent Native-American: 1%
Percent in-state / out-of-state: 96% / 4%
Percent Pub HS: 82%
Number of Applicants: 26,964
Percent Accepted: 53%
Percent Accepted who enroll: 26%
Entering: 3,781
Transfers: NA
Application Deadline: 30 Nov
Mean SAT: 578 V, 601 M
Mean ACT: 24

Middle 50% SAT range: 530–630 V, NA M
Middle 50% ACT range: NA
3 Most popular majors: business economics, sociology, communications
Retention: 89%
Graduation rate: 61%
On-campus housing: 46%
Fraternities: 10%
Sororities: 10%
Library: 2,571,000 volumes
Tuition and Fees: $3,844 in; $14,018 out
Room and Board: $7,156
Financial aid, first-year: 58%

Picture yourself strolling down the beach on a sunny afternoon. The waves lap at your feet and the soft sand squishes between your toes. What a nice break from the stress of college life! But wait, this *is* college! At least for those who attend University of California campus at Santa Barbara (UCSB). Though technically located in Galeta, ten miles outside of Santa Barbara, UCSB is bordered on three sides by the Pacific Ocean. Most students are California natives, and admit it is easy to be distracted from academia when the surf is calling.

A Top 5 School

Perennially regarded as one of the greatest party schools in the nation, UCSB does not disappoint. With a ban on kegs in all university housing, only about 2,500 undergrads choose to live on the campus itself. But with Galeta and Isla Vista right next door, there are about "20,000 college students living together," particularly in Isla Vista, one resident said. Affectionately called I.V., Isla Vista is the center of UCSB party life. In addition to its shops, cafes, and parks, "beer is available seven days a week" in I.V., either at apartment parties or at the "raging [frat house] parties."

Social activity peaks every October as students from UCSB and other local colleges celebrate Halloween. On other weekends, however, there is still a plethora of stuff to do, including dance recitals, movies, intramural sports, and enjoying the outdoors. "With Mother Nature looking so beautiful," many hike, mountain bike, or surf when not cheering for the popular UCSB Gauchos' varsity basketball and volleyball teams.

Seriously, We've Got Academia

Seeking to shed its timeworn image as a party school, however, UCSB has followed the lead of other UC schools and has been placing more emphasis on academics for the past decade. There was a recent increase in minimum admission requirements, and students remarked that "UCSB is not as big a party school as I thought it'd be. Sure, there's still parties up the gazoo, but you actually have to put in some effort to maintain good academic standing." Commonly regarded as some of the school's better departments, biology, environmental studies, engineering, economics, and psychology attract a good number of the undergraduate population. Marine biology is also popular, as is the perennial favorite Shakespeare course by Professor Frank McConnell.

> **"Beer is available seven days a week" in I.V., either at apartment parties or at the "raging [frat house] parties."**

Distinguished speakers have also grazed the campus, many through the efforts of the Interdisciplinary Humanities Center. Recently, the Dalai Lama visited and spoke to UCSB students.

Classes tend to be large, like those at most state schools, particularly at the introductory level. Some lectures enroll as many as 800 students, though most are closer to 150. Additional instruction is usually provided in these large lecture courses through TA-led discussion sessions. As one heads toward upper-level courses, however, classes are as small as 30 students. There is "not much one-on-one with professors, but if you find them in their offices, they're usually really easy to talk to," one student reported. "The [professors] are pretty chill. There isn't too much of a rift between students and professors, and you can usually see a couple of them getting a beer at the same bars we're at," added one undergrad.

UCSB also offers undergrads opportunities to explore various career fields while still in college. The UCSB Washington Center Program, for instance, assists students pursuing internships, research, or creative activities in the nation's capital. In addition, the Education Abroad Program provides students with an overseas program connected to nearly 100 colleges and universities in 32 countries throughout the world.

There *is* a Campus to Be On

For the few living on campus, rooms tend to be small despite the continual renovations. "They're always fixing or building something, but the dorms just don't seem to get any bigger." Several dorms have themes, including the Scholars Hall, the Multicultural Experience Hall, and the Performing and Creative Arts Hall. Inhabited mostly by freshmen, campus dorms are often geared toward freshmen interests to help them adjust to college life. Likewise, one dorm is reserved for transfer students. Most upperclassmen, however, prefer to seek off-campus apartments in I.V. or Galeta. "Sure, it might actually be a little more expensive to live in a nice off-campus apartment, but it's well worth it," said one such upperclassman. "Living off-campus is more like real life," explained one undergrad. "You take care of your own mess, but you get to do whatever you want."

Stores for all sorts of daily supplies are nearby, making life in an apartment a "very manageable chore." Cars aren't totally essential around campus, but "they really make travel a lot more manageable, especially when lugging home the groceries. But practically everyone has a car, so you can always bum a ride."

Some students living off-campus have also found life away from the college scene. A number have been elected to positions on the local and county boards, working to represent both the college and community interests. On campus, meanwhile, the student newspaper, *Daily Nexus* is popular and well-regarded. In each of the last four years, it has been rated either first or second in the statewide Newspaper Publishers Association's college newspaper competition.

Ongoing renovations around campus have resulted in "shutting down all the roads at times, but I think it's worth it," one student asserts. The fruits of this labor have been seen in a new recreation building and aquatic center, fondly known as the "Rec-Cen." It adds two swimming pools and room to work out to the old Robertson Gym and Event Center. Also on campus is the Davidson Library, home to over 2 million volumes. There is a new humanities and social science building, as well as a student service center.

Well-Rounded

Combining one of the academically better state school systems with all walks of social life, students argue that UCSB is a "total thing to do," a "complete package." It provides academic challenge, a friendly atmosphere, and a fabulous setting. With warm weather year-round, the ocean-side location, and nearby mountains ideal for biking and hiking, it is difficult to think of more ideal surroundings. Pull out the shades, get some sunscreen, add a desire for knowledge without the intensity found at some more cutthroat schools, and you're all set. —*William Chen*

FYI

The three best things about attending UCSB are "the beach, the weather, and the women/men."

The three worst things about attending UCSB are "the beach, the weather, and the women/men. With all these distractions, I'm amazed we actually get work done."

The three things that every student should do before graduating from UCSB are "live in Galeta, surf in the Pacific, and party on a random mid-week school night."

One thing I'd like to have known before coming here is: "that this is actually a school—people learn."

University of California / Santa Cruz

Address: 1156 High Street; Santa Cruz, CA 95064	**Percent Asian:** 11%	**Middle 50% SAT range:** 510–640 V, 510–620 M
Phone: 831-459-4008	**Percent Hispanic:** 13%	**Middle 50% ACT range:** 20–26
E-mail address: admissions @cats.ucsc.edu	**Percent Native-American:** NA	**3 Most popular majors:** biology, psychology,
Web site URL: admissions.ucsc.edu	**Percent in-state / out-of-state:** 94%/6%	literature
Founded: 1904	**Percent Pub HS:** NA	**Retention:** NA
Private or Public: public	**Number of Applicants:** 14,485	**Graduation rate:** 37%
Religious affiliation: none	**Percent Accepted:** 77%	**On-campus housing:** 50%
Location: suburban		**Fraternities:** NA
Undergraduate enrollment: 10,242	**Percent Accepted who enroll:** 19%	**Sororities:** NA
Total enrollment: 11,308	**Entering:** 2,108	**Library:** 1,200,000 volumes
Percent Male/Female: 43%/57%	**Transfers:** NA	**Tuition and Fees:** $4,235 in; $14,409 out
Percent Minority: 26%	**Application Deadline:** 30 Nov	**Room and Board:** $7,337
Percent African-American: 2%	**Mean SAT:** 510 V, 510 M	**Financial aid, first-year:** 50%
	Mean ACT: NA	

What exactly can one guess about a university whose mascot is the banana slug? As the slug suggests, UC/Santa Cruz is arguably the most liberal and laid-back of the University of California schools, and it is sometimes still associated with the hippie movement of the '60s. However, despite their relatively casual attitude, students find that the low-stress environment, along with a pleasant city and a beautiful campus that is literally built into the surrounding redwood forest, provides a great atmosphere for learning.

Grades Optional

The academic year at Santa Cruz is divided into four quarters, but because most students leave during the summer usually only three are taken in any given year. A typical course load is 15 units, consisting of three courses, each worth 5 credits. Everyone must have 180 credits, or roughly 36 classes, to graduate.

Students speak very highly of the faculty, who are generally described as "really excellent." Registration for classes is done by phone or over the Internet and is "pretty cut-and-dry." Internet registration is considered "really easy" and "useful." Students who have completed more credits get registration priority. The most popular majors at UC/Santa Cruz include psychology and biology—students of marine biology utilize nearby Monterey Bay and its abundant valuable marine life resources. As at many universities, intro-level classes are the biggest and hardest to get into, especially classes in popular majors such as biology and photography.

The most distinctive aspect of the UCSC academic system is the grading policy; you can pass without ... well ... grades. Students are allowed to take as many courses pass/fail as they wish. Instead of a letter grade, students who choose the pass/fail option receive a written narrative evaluation from their professor or teaching assistant, assessing their performance in the course. This way, the emphasis is less on the grading curve and more on learning the material. However, in very large classes, the sheer number of students can mean that "you'll get an evaluation that's two lines long, which kinda kills the intent," but such cases are the ex-

ception rather than the rule, and students agree that "it's a really good system." Students also have the option of receiving a letter grade along with their evaluation. The majority of students in the more competitive majors (think Premed) tend to opt for the grade to validate their efforts.

Not surprisingly, the pass/fail option means, that for most classes, the level of competition is close to nil. "There's no need to do better than everyone else," said one student. "There's not a lot of pressure from your peers," agreed another. "It's you versus the course load." But students are quick to point out that, "you've still gotta pass the class—if you pass by the skin of your teeth you're still going to get the rundown of how you did in the evaluation." It is also observed that "you could get away with doing very little, and a lot of people do, but they don't do well. Don't come here if you're not self-motivated. There are too many opportunities to slack off." Although there are slackers on campus, other students are more focused on academics: "Once you get into what you like, you'll have a lot of work."

Meat Dish

Students are assigned to one of eight residential colleges, each with requirements that students take a special core course. Particular colleges also have reputations for drawing certain types of students. Crown College is said to attract more science majors, while Porter College is supposedly favored by performing arts majors. Students can also choose to live in substance-free, same-sex, or ethnic theme dorms.

Freshmen generally live in a residential college dorm, and usually move into an on-campus apartment ("a big room with a kitchen") for sophomore year, though staying in the dorms is also possible since "there's no trouble finding friends," especially within one's college. The majority of students move off campus after sophomore year to one of several nearby houses.

Life in the dorms is "social and loud at times," but parties are "easy to get away from since there's always somewhere quiet to go." Drugs and alcohol are present, although "not obvious." "You don't have to look that hard," claimed another student. "You will find people smashed on

Saturday morning." The administration has reportedly been "trying to buckle down [on drug use and drinking], but it's always there."

> **"I could totally live here. Maybe when I'm really rich, I'll have a house here."**

Dorm food is described as "not bad" and "bearable." Yet students warn of hearing past comments such as, "they try to make real meal-type foods and fail miserably," and "I once saw something that was labeled simply 'Meat Dish.'" Fortunately, students can choose to eat at any dining hall, and since the food quality varies from college to college, students who explore all of their options will have a better chance of avoiding the dining services' apparent fixation with things containing pasta and/or tofu.

School Upon a Hill
To those looking for outside entertainment, Santa Cruz offers "lots of options," including various restaurants, stores, and movie theaters. The university sits on a hill overlooking downtown Santa Cruz, which is only a short ride away on "the Magical #1 Bus," and is free for students making frequent trips between the campus and the city. The city is a very popular student hangout and easily accessible via car, bike, bus, or even on foot. With the amount of leisure time students have, going off campus is "a big thing . . . almost a necessity," said one student. Many students also get around on bikes; some have cars, but "it's not necessary to have a car. You can get around without one." Students report that parking is "terrible."

Excursions to the city often involve going bowling or watching an independent film, but "sometimes it just involves going to Taco Bell." The downtown area is considered safe at night by some students, perhaps due to a recent increase in the police presence, but "it's not advisable to go out alone." Hiking, camping, and going to the beach are also popular, especially on weekends. For students with cars, San Jose is only 30 miles away, and a drive to San Francisco takes an hour and a half.

Higher praise is given to the campus itself, which was founded in 1965 and built with the surrounding redwood forest (home to the banana slug) in mind. While constructing the university, "they attempted to harm as little of the forest as possible," and as a result, many buildings are nestled among the trees. "Nature lovers out there, have we got a place for you!" Students use words such as "beautiful" and "amazing" to describe their campus, and many comment on the frequent encounters with wildlife on campus, especially deer. Signs warning passersby to watch out for mountain lions are also a common sight. "The deer come on campus and eat the flowers," said one student, "the mountain lions come on campus and eat the deer." UCSC's location also offers views of the surrounding forest and of the ocean; the two can sometimes be seen through the same window. The "cool environment" on campus and in the city is cited as the greatest thing about UC/Santa Cruz by many students: "I could totally live here. Maybe when I'm really rich, I'll have a house here."

No Vibrant Campus Scene
Extracurricular activities are not a big part of life on campus, and there is "very little in the way of sports," at least at the varsity level. The swimming, water polo, and ultimate Frisbee teams do get attention, but one student reports, "I've never seen anything posted for any sporting events." However, participating in intramural and club sports is very easy: "If you can get five people together and field a team, then you can play."

There are fraternities and sororities, but they are not overly influential. One student said, "There are some frosh who are surprised to know that we even have fraternities." The student body is described as "a lot of everything and everyone can find their niche." With such a loose, open environment on campus, "everyone's friendly," and "you can always find someone playing a guitar." As for activities during their spare time, students often take classes like self-defense and belly dancing, and "there's a lot of the environmental thing up here; CALPIRG (California Public Interest Research Group, a consumer/environmental watchdog agency) gets a lot of support." Overall, though, "students are more inclined toward their studies."

But students also note that recent university projects, including a new science library and the establishment of a school of engineering, reflect a shift toward the hard sciences and away from the liberal arts. The university, which is in the process of hiring new faculty in order to expand its engineering departments, "might get a little bigger" as a result of this shift. The growth of Santa Cruz itself may parallel that of the university, according to one student: "It's an expanding city desperately trying to stay small." Another student expressed worries that the development of the university may result in "more red tape," and that "UCSC might become more of a normal university, which is scary. There needs to be more places like this."—*Chiansan Ma*

FYI

The three best things about attending UCSC are "narrative evaluations and the awesome pass/no record system, the gorgeous campus nestled in a redwood forest, and the free public transportation system that takes you almost anywhere."

The three worst things about attending UCSC are "that it's becoming more like every other UC and they're slowly dismantling the narrative evaluation system, people pretend to be progressive but really aren't, and the way the UC system takes every opportunity to take money from you."

The three things that every student should do before graduating from UCSC are "walk the length of the campus (via trails, not roads!), celebrate Halloween or New Year's Eve on Pacific Ave, and make use of the UC transfer system and take classes in other UC Schools."

One thing I'd like to have known before coming here is "how bad the financial aid system is."

University of Redlands

Address: 1200 East Colton Avenue; PO Box 3080; Redlands, CA 92373-0999	**Percent Asian:** 7%	**Middle 50% ACT range:** 21–26
Phone: 800-455-5064	**Percent Hispanic:** 12%	**3 Most popular majors:**
E-mail address: admissions@uor.edu	**Percent Native-American:** 1%	social sciences, business administration and management, liberal arts and sciences
Web site URL: www.redlands.edu	**Percent in-state / out-of-state:** 69%/31%	**Retention:** NA
Founded: 1959	**Percent Pub HS:** 87%	**Graduation rate:** 56%
Private or Public: private	**Number of Applicants:** 1,975	**On-campus housing:** NA
Religious affiliation: none	**Percent Accepted:** 80%	**Fraternities:** 18%
Location: suburban	**Percent Accepted who enroll:** 30%	**Sororities:** 20%
Undergraduate enrollment: 1,669	**Entering:** 474	**Library:** 230,000 volumes
Total enrollment: 1,697	**Transfers:** 309	**Tuition and Fees:** $20,581 in; $20,581 out
Percent Male / Female: 47%/53%	**Application Deadline:** rolling	**Room and Board:** $7,590
Percent Minority: 23%	**Mean SAT:** 560 V, 552 M	**Financial aid, first-year:** 75%
Percent African-American: 3%	**Mean ACT:** NA	
	Middle 50% SAT range: 510–610 V, 520–610 M	

Majestic mountains rise out of the Californian desert landscape. Nestled at the foot of the mountains on a patch of green is University of Redlands, a small liberal arts college of about 2,000 undergraduate students. One week during Christmas season, students trail on the green to attend the Festival of Lights, a three-hour performance by the orchestra and choir in their chapel. "It's beautiful, and it's a big deal at the school," says one student. The Festival of Lights displays the essence of University of Redlands—its quaint and serene existence among the mountains.

Academics Without Distractions

While the remoteness of Redlands can keep students from getting distracted, its small size can also be a blow. On the positive side, it means professors pay a lot of attention to each student, with class size averaging seven people. "All my professors know me by name and greet me when I see them outside class," says one student fondly. But having a small school may also mean that course selection may be limited. The problem is especially true for the Liberal Arts Foundation, LAF, in which certain core requirements must be taken before graduating. "There are a lot of requirements for students not in a specialized program," says one student. If students are averse to taking a distribution of classes, they can use Advanced Placement exam credits to avoid the requirements. Every student must, however, complete a community service requirement before graduating.

Redlands excels in the humanities; the music, art, and creative writing departments are particularly good. But some other facilities may fall short of student expectations. "It's inconvenient that the computer cluster is only open until midnight," noted one student. Such inconveniences are one of the problems of being at a small school.

There are many options for getting away, however, such as the winter term and study abroad programs. *Winter term* refers to one month of intensive study in January, usually undertaken abroad. The school has an impressive gamut of study abroad programs, in locations that include Japan and a number of African countries, which any student can pursue for winter term or for a junior term/year abroad. The biggest study abroad program is in Germany, especially popular among music students.

Overall, students seem satisfied with the academics at their school. "Redlands is not really easy, but it's not really difficult, either," comments one student. "If you want to work, you can, but here you are not stressed out as you might be in some other schools."

Activities—from Sports to Music Theater

As Redlands is such a humanities-oriented school, students admit readily that the athletics are not the strongest part of their school. "I've never gone to a sports game, or heard of anyone going to one," says one student, and wonders who Redlands' rival school is. Another student explains that there is some school spirit: "The sports teams are not that good, so we get excited when we win." Outside organized sports, however, there are plenty of opportunities for the athletically minded. The location of Redlands makes it ideal for those who love skiing or swimming. Hiking in the nearby mountains is another popular activity. One student describes one of her favorite activities as "hiking into the mountains and looking at the stars."

> "The small community feel is nice because you get to know people really well, but you probably want to go out sometimes."

Redlands also boasts a variety of clubs and organizations, including choir, mock trial team, and Christian organizations, and the school hosts lecture series and other academic events. Students note the visibility of Christian organizations and events on campus, although their popularity does not compare to that of musical theater, which involves an excellent orchestra and a trained choir. Traditionally, an opera is staged one semester and a musical the other semester. The theater productions, as well as the Festival of Lights, are school-wide celebrations showcasing students' musical talents.

Town of Redlands and Beyond

Redlands is a small Southern Californian town that students describe as relatively safe. The trade-off, however, is that it doesn't offer much by way of fun. "The only thing we can do is watch movies, and that's what we do for dates," says one student, referring to the nearby Krikorian Theater. About 30 minutes away from campus in downtown, there are quaint Italian and Mediterranean restaurants, as well as coffee shops. "We don't hang out in the town, though," claims one student. "You would get bored of it if you stayed here for four years."

That is why Redlands students recommend having a car, which allows them to shop at outlet malls, take a trip to Wal-Mart, and get some food after the student eatery closes at midnight. Students can also venture into L.A., which is only about one hour away. San Diego is also within driving distance, and Las Vegas is a 4.5-hour trip. San Francisco, about 9 hours away, is close enough for weekend getaways.

Social Life on Campus and the Myths of Johnson

"Parties at Redlands suck," exclaimed one student. The party scene at Redlands revolves around the Greek system, which provides students who want it an ample supply of alcohol and pot. Less prevalent are hookups, which people feel happen less frequently than dating because of the size of the school. All in all, students feel that the administration knows of the party activities, but that it generally adheres to a "hear no evil, see no evil" approach to maintaining order.

Students would say the Johnson Center is the exception. The Johnson Center is a competitive program that lets students design their own majors. The students in the program live in one dorm and are seen by outsiders as being "really smart, but really weird." Johnson Center adds spice to campus life; its parties are notoriously crazy, lewd, and fun. Theme parties such as kissing parties are open to all students, but rumor has it that plenty of mysterious activities go on behind closed doors.

Food and Living

The living situation for Redlands students depends on the dorm that they are placed in. Single-sex dormitories have the largest rooms, while Cortner is popular because of its central location and Melrose for its hotel-like quality. All dorms have a kitchen and washing machines, although some students might complain there aren't enough. The popular dorms are harder for freshmen to get into, so while the university does not separate freshmen housing, firstyears typically end up getting the less desirable dorms. Students must live on campus the first year and can decide to live off campus after if they so desire.

Students feel that the food at Redlands is not bad compared to other colleges. They do complain, however, about the inflexibility of the meal schedules and plans. Students who live on campus must select from one of a number of meal plans, which don't reimburse students for missed meals. The Plaza, the student center, is only open until 12, and, according to students, the menu hasn't changed in the past few years. The Plaza café is the only eatery open on campus late at night, and if you miss those hours, there is nowhere within walking distance to buy food.

"The small community feel is nice because you get to know people really well, but you probably want to go out sometimes," says a student, summarizing the majority of opinions about her school. Redlands seems to be about surprises, however, whether in the form of its large international population, the Johnson Center, or the Festival of Lights. It is through uncovering these hidden treasures that the students of the University of Redlands make the most of their four years out in the California desert.

—*Mariko Hirose*

FYI

The three best things about attending Redlands are "the small size of the school, the good weather, and the small but beautiful campus."

The three worst things about attending Redlands are "the lack of entertainment, the limited class choices, and the lack of economic diversity among the students."

The three things every student should do before graduating from Redlands are "hiking in the mountains, visiting market night in town, and attending the Festival of Lights."

One thing I'd like to have known before coming here is "that there are weird and interesting people here, especially in Johnson Center."

University of Southern California

Address: 700 Childs Way, University Park; Los Angeles, CA 90089
Phone: 213-740-1111
E-mail address: NA
Web site URL: www.usc.edu
Founded: 1880
Private or Public: private
Religious affiliation: none
Location: urban
Undergraduate enrollment: 15,594
Total enrollment: 28,342
Percent Male/Female: 50%/50%
Percent Minority: 44%
Percent African-American: 6%

Percent Asian: 23%
Percent Hispanic: 14%
Percent Native-American: 0.5%
Percent in-state/out-of-state: 67%/33%
Percent Pub HS: NA
Number of Applicants: 24,650
Percent Accepted: 37%
Percent Accepted who enroll: 31%
Entering: 2,828
Transfers: NA
Application Deadline: 10 Jan
Mean SAT: NA
Mean ACT: NA

Middle 50% SAT range: 570–670 V, 690–700 M
Middle 50% ACT range: NA
3 Most popular majors: business, engineering, social sciences
Retention: 92%
Graduation rate: 69%
On-campus housing: 65%
Fraternities: 15%
Sororities: 15%
Library: 3,300,000 volumes
Tuition and Fees: $22,636 in; $22,636 out
Room and Board: $7,282
Financial aid, first-year: 61%

Upon her admission to the University of Southern California, one undergrad remembers being told: "When you come to USC, you will become a part of the Trojan family." As cheesy as that may sound, it may not be too far from the truth. When they arrive in sunny South-Central Los Angeles, students find themselves steeped in the Trojan spirit in classrooms, at football games, and at Greek parties. The ties forged during the undergraduate years continue after graduation, assuring USC students that "there will be a Trojan always, wherever you go."

Studying in the City of Angels

One sentence sums up the academic strengths of USC: this is L.A. The popular undergraduate programs reflect the city's status as the world headquarters of cinema and communications. "The music program, communication, and the film programs are really wonderful," raves one student majoring in cinema and minoring in music industry. "These popular programs have a lot of funding and top-line equipment." Also popular is the business school, which students agree is not too intense. The five-year architecture program, on the other hand, is nicknamed architorture; no explanation necessary there. For most of the programs, however, "your workload depends on how well you want to do." One student in the arts and sciences explains, "If you want an A in the class, you have to put in an A effort."

USC programs tend to emphasize preprofessional focus. A slew of internships available in the areas of communications, film, music, and business support such a focus. "We're in L.A., so we get a lot of cool internships," boasts one student. Being situated in Los Angeles is also an advantage when looking for speakers to educate the students outside the classrooms. USC invites an impressive list of speakers each year; in the recent past, they have had Jason Alexander from *Seinfeld*, Rev. Jesse Jackson, and former president George Bush.

Sometimes the big names that stand at the podium at USC are not guests but professors. One cinema undergrad, for example, was excited to take a class with a cool, Oscar-winning professor. World-renowned or not, however, students agree that their professors are "well educated and experienced" in their fields and easy to approach. "Every year I have at least one class where the professor is excellent," comments a student in the arts and sciences.

Despite all the focus on pre-professional programs, USC has not abandoned its liberal arts education. Students in all programs are encouraged to take classes outside of their schools to fulfill the general education requirements and to pursue a minor in another field of study. General education requires credits from various categories of study, plus a writing requirement. "It is not that bad, and I understand why they have it," says one student, "but it's not very interesting, either." For students in the small programs like architecture or cinema, the big GE classes are social occasions where they can easily meet people outside their major. If students ever get tired of LA, studying abroad is a popular option for junior year. The school itself has a selection of programs, and students can also petition to go on a separate program.

The Other Face of L.A.

For all the glitz and glamour associated with L.A., prospective students might be disappointed if they expect Hollywood and Beverly Hills to be at the doorstep of USC. "South-Central L.A. (where USC is located) is a pretty bad area," warns one student. "There is not much around it." The campus of USC is like a little island— beautiful, traditional Ivy League–style brick buildings surrounded by an area undergoing development. Students hanging around campus restrict themselves to visiting friends off campus, grocery-shopping at University Village, or UV, or visiting one of the "hole-in-the-wall" bars. New clubs targeted toward USC students such as Club Envy have also emerged in the recent past.

Despite the relative wealth of the population that attends USC, students agree that Trojans still interact with the less privileged surrounding community. "College kids go out and tutor inner-city kids and do other community service activities," says one student. Outside the USC neighborhood, L.A. is the Trojans' playground; there are clubs along the Sunset Strip, beaches for the warm days, and lots of shopping. Many students leave the

campus on weekends to frolic in the glamorous parts of the city. However, one student warns, "Having a car is the only way to get around. Absolutely."

Partying with Beautiful People

Staying on campus can't be that bad, though, when yours is one of the 10 most beautiful schools in the United States. "Everyone at this school is like a model," says one sophomore girl. If you are looking for a long-term prince-in-shining-armor, however, you may not find him here. One sophomore testifies, "I don't think many people long-term date here." "I hear a lot more about random hookups than about people going out for a long time," confirms one guy. "People are busy doing a lot of other things, and they just want to have fun."

> **"Everyone at this school is like a model."**

After all, having fun is what USC is about. Students think that it is fairly easy to meet people and just as easy to find alcohol, even if you are underage. The Greek system is big, and the Row (frat row) is open to non-Greeks on Thursdays for parties. One student commented that the center of social life is focused on the Greek system, although less now that the university is cracking down a little bit. Overall, however, the consensus remains that the school is a paradise for party lovers.

Fighting, the Trojan Way

There is no better way to cultivate the Trojan fraternity (outside of the Greek system) than at football games. The King of all games is the one against USC's major rival: UCLA. "The rivalry is so intense that they tape up the mascot on our campus a couple of weeks before the game to protect it," says one student. Tradition on the day of the big game dictates that the whole school walk together to the Coliseum, kicking the flagpole on the way to bring luck to the Trojans.

Besides football, basketball and swimming are popular, as well as Cal Week and games against Stanford or UC/Berkeley. Because of the focus on athletics, the school has good fitness facilities, which one student calls "intimidating, but nice." On the negative side, one student complains, "the school is too athletic and obsessed with the sports people."

Living and Dining

Students at USC have no complaints about any of the facilities on campus, including their living situations. Most agree that the dorm is where people meet one another freshman year. "I think it's virtually impossible to live in a dorm freshman year and not to make friends," says one sophomore. The rooms in the dormitories are allegedly big, although it depends on the dorm. Upperclassman may live in apartments or off campus.

Trojans generally like the food at their school. Students agree that the cafeteria does a good job, considering the number of students in the school. "The quality of the food depends," clarifies one student, "but there is always diversity." The ice cream, Betty Crocker, and sushi that embellish their main dining hall confirm such diversity. Such good food lures students to hang out in the Commons, a central area where the food court and a bookstore are located.

Diversity

Diversity seems to be the theme of this urban campus. "I'm very surprised at the diversity, especially racially," says one student from the East Coast who had grown up in less diverse areas. "Contrary to the stereotype that USC is a rich people's school, there is a large financial aid pool," says one Trojan proudly.

Campus activities reflect the diverse interests of the student body. Intramural sports, the Student Senate, and Christian campus organizations are popular. Special interest clubs, like a sky-diving club, entice the adventurous. Whatever students choose to do, there is a place for them in the Trojan family. It is obvious that there is no stereotypical USC student.

Diversity for the loyal Trojans is about maintaining a mixture of experiences and activities. "I feel like there is enough academics and academic reputation at this school, so I am getting a good education without frying out," says one student. USC nurtures strong and healthy Trojans by allowing them to enjoy a balance of sports, academics, the arts, real-life preparation, and, most of all, fun.

—*Mariko Hirose*

FYI

The three best things about attending USC are "the wide variety of majors, the tight alumni community, and being in LA."

The three worst things about attending USC are "the obsession with sports and athletes, the bad neighborhood, and having too big of a Greek system."

The three things every student should do before graduating from USC are "go to a frat party, go to a football game, and go to the beach."

One thing I'd like to have known before coming here is "the administration never really knows what they are doing, and it is impossible to get straight answers from people."

Colorado

At Colorado College, it's easy to understand why the snowcapped mountains of Colorado, visible from any window, might tempt students from their studies and up to the slopes for extended ski trips. Fortunately for CC students, their school's unorthodox academic schedule, the block plan, leaves plenty of four-and-a-half-day breaks during the school year that are perfect for skiing, community service, and any other adventure CC students can think up.

Focusing and Concentrating

Students agree that the block plan, for better and for worse, is a unique aspect of their college and the main reason they chose to come to CC. The academic calendar is divided into eight three-and-a-half-week blocks, with four-and-a-half-day breaks in between each block. During a block, students immerse themselves in a single subject. "I get to concentrate on one thing; I learn more about what I'm taking, and I don't have to worry about a test in another class," one student said of the plan. The schedule, which students say is good for those with a "one-track mind," spares the residents of this small school the stress of juggling four or five different classes. Professors know they have their students' undivided attention, and it's not uncommon for them to take classes on overnight field trips or out for a midnight viewing of the stars. Classes like geology and astronomy especially benefit from this freedom.

Although the block system can be intense and stressful, students said they don't feel an overwhelming sense of competition at CC. "It's what you put into it," said one student. Another agreed, "You can get away with slacking." With all classes held for two or three hour sessions in the morning, some students say they feel spoiled by having so much free time on their hands.

According to students, though, the plan is not without its drawbacks, and can be quite rigorous. Classes are "intense" and if you miss more than one class or fall behind, especially in a language class, it can be very difficult to catch up before the next exam, since the learning for each class goes on during such a short, concentrated period of time. One student also commented that, due to the small class size, you can't just expect to skip unnoticed, and professors know if a student is not there. Academic life at CC is definitely not for everyone.

"Buying" Classes

The block plan isn't the only thing that's different about Colorado College—registration at CC is as unorthodox as the academic calendar. Students receive 80 "points" at the end of each spring for the next year. To register, they assign these points to courses they want to take, putting more points on preferred classes. Those who assign the most points to a particular class get priority.

Introductory classes and film courses are in high demand and sometimes hard to get. Human Sexual Behavior is reportedly among the most popular courses. Students who manage to "buy" their way into their class of choice reap the benefits of smaller class sizes. For the most part, classes taught by one professor have no more than 25 students, and classes taught by two professors have no more than 32. TAs, called "paraprofessionals," help with labs and tutoring, but don't teach classes.

Requirements at CC are described by students as "loose." During their four-year career in Colorado Springs, students must take two blocks each of lab and natural sciences, and by the end of sophomore year, four blocks of "Alternative Perspectives," two in Western culture classes and two in non-Western. The required courses are not seen as a heavy burden. "They're great, because otherwise I wouldn't have taken [these classes]," one student insisted. Although undergrads report that there are no gut courses at Colorado College, they admit that some classes are eas-

ier than others. Some less-challenging courses cited by students were Jazz and Exercise Physiology. An end may be near to even these less stressful block choices. "They are making them harder," lamented one student. Geology, biology, economics, psychology, and English are all popular majors, and many students choose to double major.

Natural Beauty and Artificial Modernity

Located at the foot of Pike's Peak and the majestic Rocky Mountains, CC attracts many students for the scenery and the entertainment it provides. Skiing and other outdoor pursuits are definitely high priorities in the lives of most CC students. Despite the natural beauty and the fact that the campus is within walking distance of the city's downtown, students are "not too impressed with Colorado Springs." The dominant style of buildings at the school has been described as "modern ugly," but the campus is framed by breathtaking mountains, so students say they love the setting and spend a lot of time within the confines of CC's campus.

Because of the block plan schedule, students have concentrated amounts of work to do in the afternoons, and Tutt Library is the place of choice for doing it. Dorms have study lounges as well, but in nice weather, many students opt to bask in the warm Colorado sun in Armstrong Quad, reading and dodging Frisbees. Some students complain that the library is not adequate for in-depth research, and often travel to the library at nearby University of Colorado in Colorado Springs for a better stock of books.

> "With the block plan, I get to concentrate on one thing; I learn more about what I'm taking, and I don't have to worry about a test in another class."

All dorms at CC have been renovated recently, or will be in the near future. There are three large dorms: Loomis, which houses most freshmen, is "definitely the loudest"; Mathias is a "very sterile" dorm with the reputation of being "full of jocks"; and Slocum is the "quiet dorm" with "substance-free wings." The dorms are coed, with mostly doubles and singles, but bathrooms are single-sex. Other on-campus housing options include five language houses, three fraternity houses (there are also three non-residential sororities), and a couple of theme houses. Themes change every year; last year CC was the proud home to an "eclectic arts" house and a "multicultural" house. First-years and sophomores must live on campus, but some juniors and several seniors live in nearby off-campus housing.

Veggies for Granolas

Deciding how to eat can be as difficult for students at CC as choosing what class to take next block, though the options are fairly straightforward and flexible once you get used to them. First-year students may choose between five different meal plans, which offer combinations of meals in one of CC's dining halls, and a "flex-point" system that can be used at Benjamin's snack bar, housed in the Worner Student Center, and a campus convenience store. Rastall, the main cafeteria, serves standard college fare, described by some as "better than average." It serves a variety of entrées at each meal, in addition to a salad bar, grilled items, and pasta almost every day. Students advise avoiding the pasta, and added that the daily entrée is usually a student's best bet for an edible meal. The smaller Bemis, with less variety and shorter hours, is preferred by some because "the food's healthier and it has a really nice environment." Both dining halls serve vegetarian food.

When dorm food becomes too much for students to take, CC dining hall patrons head out for Mexican fare at La Casita or pizza and beer at Old Chicago's. One "really cool place" near campus is Poor Richard's, a coffee shop/bookstore/movie theater/pizza joint.

Like many Coloradans, students at CC take physical fitness seriously. Varsity and intramural sports are probably the most popular extracurricular activities at CC. The Division 1 Tigers men's hockey team

draws the largest crowds on campus, especially when the school is playing its big rival, the University of Denver. The school's football and women's soccer teams also have large followings.

For the less serious sports enthusiast, CC's active intramural sports program provides an antidote to the freshman 15. Especially popular are hockey, flag football, broomball (played with a ball in tennis shoes on an ice rink), and ultimate Frisbee. Outdoor activities, like mountain climbing, camping, hiking, biking, and (especially) skiing in the nearby mountains meet the needs of the more solitary CC student. Some students warn that frequent ski trips can burn a hole in your budget, however, and popular outdoor recreation spots are usually accessible only by car.

The less sports-minded can join student government, write for the college's weekly newspaper, the *Catalyst*, play in student bands, or perform with Room 46, CC's prominent a cappella group.

In addition to being outdoor fanatics, students at CC are generally Birkenstock-clad liberals. Some students describe their classmates as "crunchy granola" and "suffocatingly liberal," and grumble that their peers conform to nonconformity. Ethnic diversity is not CC's strong point either. For the most part, campus politics (which some students complained lack enthusiasm) stand in stark contrast to those of politically conservative Colorado Springs, the birthplace of Colorado's anti-gay amendment a few years ago. One student described CC as an "oasis in conservative Colorado Springs." Still, according to one student, "If you read between the lines, there's more diversity; people aren't just how they look."

Students report that alcohol and pot are the drugs of choice at CC, and because of the unorthodox class schedule at CC, which leaves some students with lots of extra time on their hands (so they claim), there are usually parties every night of the week. Frat parties, often themed, are common on campus. The most popular are the Harley-Davidson party, beach parties, and DU Sucks, an anti-University of Denver party. Still, with only four fraternities and an equal number of nonresidential sororities, there is no pressure to rush. As one student described it, the frat presence on campus is "low-key."

Room parties in the dorms are not unheard of, but "you have to be kind of discreet." Many students have turned to off-campus locations for their more drunken nighttime escapades. Still, most drinking takes place on or around campus, as Colorado Springs has a limited bar scene.

There are people on campus who do not drink, and students say even at a school the size of CC, it's possible to find a niche of people with similar social preferences. Movies, plays, and concerts—both on campus and in the city—provide alter-

natives to alcohol-centered social events. A few nondrinkers on campus have become militant recently, and are trying to lobby the administration to make the campus dry, or at least drier than it is. The social life is also greatly affected by the fact that there is a mass exodus off campus every four weeks on block breaks, somewhat breaking the continuity of socialization.

Many Colorado College students choose the school for its outdoorsy atmosphere and unconventional academics. A prevailing attitude is "do what you want, not what people tell you to do," and Colorado students do just that. —*Brian Abaluck and Staff*

FYI

The three best things about attending Colorado College are "the block plan when you are taking a class you love, the beautiful setting and all of the opportunities for activities that it affords, and block breaks every four weeks."
The three worst things about attending Colorado College are "the block plan when you are taking a class you hate, the ugly buildings, and the limited bar scene in Colorado Springs."
The three things every student should do before graduating are "play broomball, go on a cool road trip on block break, and take Human Sexual Behavior."
One thing I'd like to have known before coming here is "how liberal everyone is."

Colorado School of Mines

Address: 1811 Elm Street; Golden, CO 80401-1842
Phone: 303-273-3220
E-mail address: admit@mines.edu
Web site URL: www.mines.edu
Founded: 1874
Private or Public: public
Religious affiliation: none
Location: small city
Undergraduate enrollment: 2,463
Total enrollment: 3,193
Percent Male/Female: 76%/24%
Percent Minority: 14%
Percent African-American: 1%

Percent Asian: 5%
Percent Hispanic: 7%
Percent Native-American: 0.5%
Percent in-state/out-of-state: 75%/25%
Percent Pub HS: 90%
Number of Applicants: 1,984
Percent Accepted: 76%
Percent Accepted who enroll: 38%
Entering: 566
Transfers: 80
Application Deadline: 1 Aug
Mean SAT: 590 V, 650 M
Mean ACT: 28

Middle 50% SAT range: 530–650 V, 600–700 M
Middle 50% ACT range: 25–30
3 Most popular majors: chemical, mechanical, and electrical engineering
Retention: 84%
Graduation rate: 64%
On-campus housing: 86%
Fraternities: 16%
Sororities: 16%
Library: 320,000 volumes
Tuition and Fees: $5,370 in; $15,780 out
Room and Board: $4,920
Financial aid, first-year: 80%

Located at the base of the Rocky Mountains, the Colorado School of Mines campus as well as the Coors Brewery are the main hot spots of Golden, Colorado, a town of 15,000 people (of which about 3,000 attend the college). The university offers 14 bachelor of science degrees, 10 of which include the word "engineering," along with degrees in chemistry, economics, mathematics, and computer sciences. The bevy of engineering majors at Mines, says one student, makes for a very "homogeneous student body and a rather dull college experience."

Highly Academic Minded

Almost everyone would agree that students consider academics a top priority at the Colorado School of Mines. All students are required to take a number of courses including those in calculus, chemistry, economics, physics, physical education, and a course called Nature and Human Values (described as "a lousy excuse for a liberal arts class"). Freshmen are also required to take EPICS (Engineering Practices Introductory Course Sequence), in which groups are given a real-life project to solve each semester. Projects range from re-mediating mine tailing waste to making solar cookers. Basically, freshmen are "all in the same classes for the first year and a half." The larger classes, physics and chemistry, range from 100 to 200 students while most others enroll about 40 to 50. The larger classes are broken up into weekly recitations so students know that "you can get help if you need it." However, one senior described some of the required courses as "of no interest and kind of a waste of time, even though they give us a broad (academic) basis." These classes are tough and most students believe that the requirements are imposed "to weed out" those who cannot stay afloat, which accounts for the high class dropout rate. Indeed, students say that the first few months are "very overwhelming at first," though many tend to "get used to the pace and rigor as the semester rolls along." Nevertheless, one Mines student described the workload as "challenging, engaging, and gratifying." Students here are devoted to their studies and proud of the work that they do.

The school's heavy emphasis on engineering sets Mines apart from other schools. One student said that he came because "I always loved science and math classes and hated English and history classes in high school. Here, I'm not required to take any of those classes." However, the Guy T. McBride Honors Program offers students a liberal arts dimension to their education. In this program, students are required to read one book a week and write an essay on it. Most students love that the Mines is generally focused on the areas that they enjoy the most, yet some students were bothered by the small number of liberal arts opportunities. This heavy emphasis on the sciences and engineering creates an environment often described as "intense," though not overly competitive.

Your Place or Mine?

The social life at Mines can be summed up by the fact that most students complain that it is "pretty lousy." The school enforces its no-tolerance policy for drugs. Although drinking goes on, especially at frat parties, security is required at all parties that serve alcohol. Guards work doors, check IDs, and give out wristbands in an effort to curb underage drinking.

Students report that Mines is not much of a party school. On weekends, many Mines students migrate toward UC/Boulder or Colorado State University to find both the "girls and the parties." One student said that the party scene is "the worst in the country. I am from Anchorage, Alaska, and my high school parties were better than this." However, Golden does offer a few bars for the upper-age crowd as well as a movie theater, though many students indicated that neither option is a major source of distraction from the academic rigors of the school week. Other students turn to their computers, video games, or homework on the weekends.

Colorado also provides many modes of escape for students. Outdoor activities such as rock climbing, hiking, and camping are popular among students here. Students are frequently found skiing on the weekends, as Golden is not more than half an hour away from many top ski locales including Vail, Copper Mountain, and Winter Park. One student commented that the opportunities to interact with nature and the outdoors offered at Mines "are unlike anything else that any other school could offer."

The dating scene, however, suffers from the fact that 77 percent of the student body is male. One male student commented that "the girls who have a social life turn into sluts and the girls that were decent-looking in high school become goddesses." For women, the debilitated dating scene is also complicated because "all the guys are geeky losers." The best advice for those seeking love and romance is that "while most people here are very nice, most students would be best looking off-campus for love."

Mind and (Student) Body

Adjectives students use to describe their classmates are "unathletic," "quiet," "smart," and "conservative." One student characterized the variety of students here as "about as diverse as the Ku Klux Klan." Nonetheless, most students are not greatly bothered by the lack of minorities. As for homosexuals, one student said that "this is not the campus to be openly gay on because it's way conservative."

Many students do raise complaints about other personal characteristics of the student population. One said that "many students don't interact much with the outside world. They just kinda sit in front of the computer all day—there are a number of people here who wake up at 6 A.M. to play on their computers." Multiplayer games such as Quake and Starcraft are very popular as most floors are known to have big games every day. Another student commented that "most people are nerds; they don't have any social life and live in the dorms all four years. They don't do anything but homework." One student concluded that the large portion of introverts "goes along with the type of people that major in engineering. They are not very social for the most part so the school is pretty much dead, and those people who want to party end up doing a lot of stuff off-campus."

The Colorado School of Mines is not the best place to be for those who are likely to be found picketing outside of state buildings or lobbying for better U.S.–Arab relations. As far as an activist scene, one student commented that "nobody seems to care because they are either just not interested or too busy doing a problem set." When asked about student involvement in campus life, one student responded with a "resounding no." The Greek system accounts for most of the philanthropic activity while most students get involved with the engineering department either through working with their professors or joining academic organizations.

This Life of Mine

Freshmen comprise a great majority of the students in Mines's five residence halls. The four halls that offer "traditional" housing are comprised mostly of doubles and singles. Though housing is "comfortable," these are the older buildings that tend to be "old and dirty." Bathrooms are shared, closet space is limited, and most do not have carpeting. Apart from the traditional dorms are the more luxurious and more expensive Weaver Towers. Students in the Towers live in suites of six to eight people in "newer and nicer" facilities, particularly noted for their air-conditioning. Students receive postcards on which to rank their housing preferences, and dorm assignments are on a strictly first come, first served basis. However, most students move to nearby off-campus apartments after their first year because of a strict resident advising system and expensive on-campus meal plans. Although the food was described as "satisfying" and "good for a university," there were some complaints about meal variety and options.

> "I always loved science and math classes and hated English and history classes in high school. Here I'm not required to take any of those classes."

The Mines campus is very small, but "beautifully green." The main campus covers about one square mile and students report that they can walk from one end to another in just a few minutes. There are large common areas, such as Kassador Commons, where students can play Frisbee or set up tents for campus events. One student praised the wildlife around campus, remembering one day when he saw 30 wild deer passing in front of his dorm. This intimate size of the Mines community receives mixed reviews from the student body. One student stated, "I feel like I know the whole campus, and can talk to most of the students or faculty, but it is limiting because sometimes there is nothing I want to do here." Another student noted that the campus lacks a collegiate atmosphere when he stated, "I drive through campuses of other universities and can almost always see students walking around or studying on the grass. Here, you hardly ever see that."

Golden is a generally safe town located only about 20 minutes from downtown Denver. Students have no problem commuting for the occasional sporting event or concert. The Coors Brewery is also nearby and offers students a couple of free beers at the end of every tour. Many students comment that they can smell the malt from the brewery from the dorm rooms. Golden also offers many popular off-campus opportunities to grab some food with friends, including McDonald's, Wendy's, Pizza Hut, and Subway. Other popular off-campus hangouts include the Ace Bar and the Buffalo Rose Saloon.

Taking to the (Mine) Field

Mines offers 16 varsity sports, the most by any state school in Colorado. About 20 percent of the student body is involved at the varsity level. Also, more than 35 percent of students actively participate in the intramural sports program at Mines. Soccer, ultimate Frisbee, flag football, and basketball are the most popular. School spirit, though, is generally considered "dead as a ghost." One student said that "sometimes the cheerleaders will yell; that's the closest thing to team sprit I can think of."

The Colorado School of Mines is a great place for those who can find their niche in a very rigorous and academically focused program. One insightful senior noted that the college is "so geared toward engineering that you want to go here and be an engineer or go to a different school—most people realize they don't want to be engineers and transfer." The Mines is a great place to be for those who enjoy a small campus life and a strong emphasis on the applied sciences. —*Kurtland Ma and Staff*

FYI

The three best things about attending Mines are "gratification of hard work, focus on math and science, and great location (close to Denver, close to nature)."

The three worst things about attending Mines are "homogeneous student body, weeding out process (high student drop out rate), and the poor social life."

The three things that every student should do before graduating Mines are "take a nonscience class, participate in outdoors activities for an escape, and look for love and a life with the outside world off campus!"

One thing I'd like to have known before coming here is "how terrible the love life is for both men and women."

Colorado State University

Address: Fort Collins, CO
80523-0015
Phone: 970-491-6909
E-mail address:
admissions@vines
.colostate.edu
Web site URL:
www.colostate.edu
Founded: 1870
Private or Public: public
Religious affiliation: none
Location: suburban
**Undergraduate
enrollment:** 18,800
Total enrollment: 22,344
Percent Male / Female:
49%/51%
Percent Minority: 10%
Percent African-American:
2%

Percent Asian: 1%
Percent Hispanic: 6%
Percent Native-American:
1%
**Percent in-state / out-of-
state:** 80%/20%
Percent Pub HS: NA
Number of Applicants:
10,465
Percent Accepted: 77%
**Percent Accepted who
enroll:** 39%
Entering: 3,137
Transfers: 0
Application Deadline: 1 Jul
Mean SAT: 551 V, 561 M
Mean ACT: 24
Middle 50% SAT range:
510–610 V,
520–620 M

Middle 50% ACT range:
22–26
3 Most popular majors:
general business, liberal
arts, biological science
Retention: 81%
Graduation rate:
26%
On-campus housing:
95%
Fraternities: 11%
Sororities: 12%
Library: 1,800,000
volumes
Tuition and Fees:
$3,062 in; $10,748 out
Room and Board:
$5,142
Financial aid, first-year:
38%

I t's been called by *Your Future* one of the four "Best Places to be Young." *Money Magazine* ranked it among the twenty safest cities in the U.S. *Reader's Digest* noted that it was the third best city in the country to live based on the absence of crime, low rate of drug and alcohol abuse, clean environment, and affordable cost of living. Where can you find such a city? Find where the Great Plains meet the Rocky Mountains, and you'll see the vibrant city called Fort Collins; and nestled in the heart of Fort Collins are 642 green acres, home to Colorado State University.

Students hail from Colorado and beyond to enjoy the beauty of Fort Collins, experience the "exceptional academics" without exceptional costs, and join in the multitude of activities that CSU has to offer. And few are disappointed. Students report that they love CSU and its "exciting and relaxed" environment.

Hidden Resources
Students claim that the solid academics at CSU are consistently underrated. The university boasts eight academic colleges with concentrations in agricultural sci-

ence, applied human science, business, engineering, literary arts, forestry and natural resources, veterinary medicine, and biomedical sciences. Students who haven't decided on a major can postpone enrollment in a specific college and register with the more generic "open option." Although liberal arts are offered at the school, its strengths lie in the natural sciences. The well-respected veterinary school is ranked among the top in the nation; the business school is "top notch;" the forestry and natural resource management school is well-respected; and the engineering program is earning increased attention and respect, due in part to extensive facility renovations, an easily accessible internship program in Fort Collins, and great research opportunities.

With this respect, however, comes a "kind of challenging" workload. CSU requires its students to take classes from each of five general categories, including Communications and Reasoning, Natural Sciences, Arts and Humanities, Behavioral and Social Sciences, and Physical Education and Wellness. Although most students claim these requirements are relatively simple to fulfill, some students have complained that these requirements ensure that "there will always be that one semester when you cannot avoid an 8:00 A.M. class." Students also get frustrated with class sizes in some of the introductory courses, some of which enroll 200–300 students. Whether the class has 10 or 300 students, however, students claim that "professors genuinely care for their students on an individual level and make themselves accessible."

The workload varies by class. Many perceive studio art to be easy but time consuming, and some students report that psychology is relatively easy. Science courses, particularly engineering, tend to be more challenging. One student joked that "if you're a genius, even the sciences will be easy, and if you're not, you'll have to work fairly hard."

So where do people do this hard work? Some students study in their rooms, but usually that's a luxury of people who have singles. Popular places to study include the Sunken Lounge at Lory Student Center, the newly renovated Morgan Library, or outside on the grass. Despite the work load that CSU students expect, students guarantee that "there's always time to have fun!"

Fort Fun

The new Lory Student Center provides not only the Sunken Lounge for study, but also a popular place to take a break from the books. After the old facility flooded, the school decided to renovate its main gathering place. After the student center underwent complete renovation, the *New York Times* ranked Lory as one of the country's ten best student centers. With video arcades, pool tables, a ballroom, a theater, a computer store, a bookstore, restaurants, bowling alleys, comfortable places to sit and sleep, TVs, and more, this ranking was no shock to CSU students.

Other recent renovations on campus have included the engineering building, the environmental sciences building, and the student recreation center/gym. Students report that the engineering building is "very attractive," but the real enthusiasm is for the environmental sciences building, with its copper fountain cascading from three stories. Students consider

the new gym to be a "great facility," but sorry professors, you're not allowed.

> **Despite the work load that CSU students expect, students guarantee that "there's always time to have fun!"**

Students are required to live on campus for their freshman year. Those who live on campus prefer Corbett, the party dorm, and Braiden, the closest dorm to central campus. Dorm rooms tend to be small, but students enjoy the "great big windows" from which you can enjoy Colorado's 300 days of sunshine. After freshman year, many students move off campus. Fort Collins offers many apartment complexes like Rams Village for its college students.

Many students opt to live off campus because the on-campus alcohol policy strictly enforces that no alcohol be consumed in the dorms. Fraternities and sororities, while they do constitute about 10 percent of the student body, aren't a huge presence. Students have a wide selection of bars and clubs in Fort Collins from which they can choose. Some of the more popular clubs include Ramskellar (on campus, actually), Linden's and Felipe's (in Old Town Fort Collins), Suite 152, the Matrix, the Martini Bar, and Washington's. Students who want to get a bite to eat off campus enjoy Coopersmith's, a brewery with reportedly good food, El Burrito and Rio Grande, Bisetti's, Canino's, the Charcoal Broiler, CB & Potts, Young's Vietnamese Cuisine, and the Red Dragon. Students have a similarly broad selection of coffee places: Starry Night, Starbucks, Déjà vu Coffeehouse, and the Coffee Connection, to name a few.

300 Days of Sunshine

Colorado boasts of nice weather, but Fort Collins has the added benefit of avoiding "those huge storms that Denver gets." Students capitalize on this weather by hanging outside, hiking, biking, roller blading, running, skiing (2 hours away), snowshoeing, and rock climbing. River rafting is popular, as are the water sports on nearby Horsetooth Reservoir. With the exception of surfing, Fort Collins offers almost everything for the outdoors enthusiast.

This enthusiasm for outdoor activity extends into sports: CSU students enjoy participating in and/or watching the many sports that CSU has to offer. The women's basketball team has had strong performances in the past, making bids for the NCAA tournament. The football team has also had strong showings, recently winning the Liberty Bowl. Both the community and students come out to support the games.

Intramurals are a popular activity on campus. Team lists, sometimes arranged by dorm floor or apartment complex, fill up quickly. Students are especially eager to play softball, basketball, innertube waterpolo, soccer, flag football, volleyball, tennis, racquetball, and inline hockey (a new offering). Part of the popularity of intramurals stems from the fact that students recognize them as a fun way to get to know people and to get some exercise.

Student enthusiasm isn't limited to sports and outdoor activity; students have a wide selection of extracurricular activities from which to choose. Those interested in writing can work for the *Rocky Mountain Collegian*, and those interested in television can participate in Campus Television, which one student claimed "has won more Emmy's than the cast of Seinfeld." His claim might be slightly exaggerated, but students agree that the television and the radio station, KCSU, are great. The arts are also popular at CSU. The dance school hosts recitals; there are open auditions for plays and musicals, and there are frequent poetry and fiction readings. Community service is also a popular activity. CSU students can volunteer to tutor in the Fort Collins community, give time to the Northern Colorado AIDS Project, run and bike in marathons to help raise support for various causes, and conduct food drives for the homeless and needy.

Students at CSU, therefore, benefit not only from a strong academic program, but also from gorgeous surroundings and countless opportunities to get involved in social and community life. —*Marti Page*

FYI

The three best things about attending CSU are "being in Colorado, the opportunities on and off campus to learn, volunteer, and have fun, and the caring and devoted faculty."

The three worst things about attending CSU are "parking, limited library hours, and large student body."

The three things that every student should do before graduating from CSU are "go to a lady Rams basketball game, hike to the Aggies sign above Fort Collins, and go into Old Town on Friday night."

One thing I'd like to have known before coming here is "how spread out the campus is."

United States Air Force Academy

Address: HQ USAFA / RRS, 2304 Cadet Drive; Suite 200; USAF Academy, CO 80840-5025
Phone: 719-333-2520
E-mail address: rrmail.rr@usafa.af.mil
Web site URL: www.usafa.edu
Founded: 1954
Private or Public: public
Religious affiliation: none
Location: suburban
Undergraduate enrollment: 4,075
Total enrollment: 4,075
Percent Male / Female: 84% / 16%
Percent Minority: 16%
Percent African-American: 5%

Percent Asian: 4%
Percent Hispanic: 7%
Percent Native-American: NA
Percent in-state / out-of-state: 5% / 95%
Percent Pub HS: NA
Number of Applicants: 8,828
Percent Accepted: 20%
Percent Accepted who enroll: 75%
Entering: 1,330
Transfers: 0
Application Deadline: 31 Jan
Mean SAT: 626 V, 649 M
Mean ACT: NA
Middle 50% SAT range: 590–660 V, 610–690 M

Middle 50% ACT range: NA
3 Most popular majors: management / engineering management, biology, political science
Retention: 92%
Graduation rate: 80%
On-campus housing: 100%
Fraternities: NA
Sororities: NA
Library: 700,000 volumes
Tuition and Fees: paid for by US Government in; paid for by US Government out
Room and Board: paid for by US Government
Financial aid, first-year: 0%

F reshmen at the United States Air Force Academy undergo a rigorous academic and military regimen that occupies almost every waking minute, and cadets do not spend much time asleep. Arriving in late June, freshmen spend six weeks at "Basic," a boot camp that prepares them for academy life. They then begin the Academy's most difficult year. Those who choose to remain at the Academy report that their hard work definitely pays off. Looking back on his experience, one senior said, "Freshman year is really tough. It's not fun here, but it's rewarding. Now that I'm a senior, I love it."

A Cadet's Life

Cadets, nicknamed "zoomies," praise the Academy for providing leadership opportunities that will help them in later life, regardless of whether they continue to pursue a military career. The entire student body, called the Cadet Wing, is divided into 40 squadrons of approximately 100 cadets each. Cadets in the same squadron live together, eat together, and train together. Seniors, called "first classmen," hold major leadership positions

in the squadron. One first classman is squadron commander each semester; his or her duties include assigning rooms, marching the squadron to breakfast and lunch, and knowing the schedule of every cadet in the squadron. Other cadets in the squadron make up the commander's staff.

Each squadron lives in either Vanderberg or Sijan halls, two large dorms with mostly two-person rooms. Many freshmen have triples, but almost all upperclassmen have doubles. Cadets with rooms in the same hallways share communal bathrooms, which are all single-sex. Female cadets live on the same floors as males, but because of the high male-to-female ratio, women often live far away from one another. "In the dorm, there's me and my roommate. The closest room with girls is quite a bit away," one cadet said. She added that women receive the same treatment as men and enjoy the same leadership opportunities.

The freshmen's day starts early in the morning, usually between 5:30 A.M. and 6 A.M., when they wake up and attend to their squadron duties. Squadron duties include delivering newspapers to upperclassmen's rooms and cleaning the squadron's offices and common areas. At 6:40, cadets line up for morning formation and march to Mitchell Hall ("Mitch's") for breakfast. Freshmen eat all their meals at attention, making as little noise as possible. The entire cadet wing takes its meals during the same 20-minute period, so cadets eat quickly. The food receives mixed reviews, though the cadets' main complaint was the lack of choices. Classes start at 7:30 and last until 11:30, when cadets line up again for another formation. They march into Mitch's for lunch and hurry to afternoon classes, which run from 12:30 to 3:30.

After class, a variety of activities occupy the cadets' time. Athletes head to practice, and some students attend club meetings. Popular extracurricular activities include the jump team, whose members parachute out of airplanes; KAFA, a campus radio station; the Drum and Bugle Corps; the Warrior Update, a student newspaper; and community service opportunities. Students report that service projects such as tutoring and working at soup kitchens "give you a chance to get off base, especially for us freshmen." Students without time commitments to varsity teams or certain clubs must play one intramural sport each semester; intramurals meet every other day.

> "Many people complain, but with the challenges come definite rewards. I fly upside down every other day, and I haven't paid a dime."

Dinner is the Academy's only optional meal, so students can stay in if they need to study or rest. The cadets' evenings are unstructured. Freshmen, however, must be in their rooms studying after 8 P. M. Most cadets report going to sleep around midnight so that they are be ready for the next morning's early wake-up.

Academics

Academy cadets face the same academic challenges as students at any competitive college or university. Cadets often take twenty-one credit hours (or seven classes)

in a semester, and some majors, such as aeronautical engineering, require even more course work. One student was surprised by "the other cadets' dedication to academics here." He added, "There's no letdown at all. You're taking so many classes." Students divide majors into technical and non-science "fuzzy" majors, where the non-science majors are considered slightly easier. Many aspiring pilots flock to the political science and management majors, which prompt some nonpilots to chant, "Wanna fly? Poli-sci." Cadets agree that even the somewhat less rigorous majors demand a great deal of work since "none of the majors are easy."

Many students have reported that they have "no problem getting into classes we want," but they also said the core curriculum often dictates most of their course selections. After satisfying the requirements for the core and her major, one senior said, "I haven't really had that much opportunity to choose my courses." Each year, the Academy assigns each freshman to an academic advisor and also to a sophomore who looks out for the cadets and ensures that they follow regulations. Students who studied a subject at an advanced level in high school or at another college before entering the Academy (transfer students enter as freshmen), may be able to place out of some core classes. Otherwise, students should count on taking classes in chemistry, calculus, one year of a foreign language, computer science, and writing mechanics among other fields during their first year. In the last year or two, more elective choices become available, such as music appreciation, American philosophy, medical ethics, and "499 courses," which are independent research programs guided by the professors in various departments.

Weekend Leave

Weekends often provide a much needed break from academy life. Each cadet is assigned a host family in the Colorado Springs area, often a retired military serviceman, which provides a home for the cadets on weekends. After freshman year, cadets can leave campus on almost any weekend, and many students go to Denver, Fort Collins, or Boulder, the homes of

Colorado State University and the University of Colorado, respectively. Cadets say that you can spot an academy student on leave in Colorado Springs by his demeanor. Cadets are generally "very conservative," "polite," and "are very much in line."

For those who do not leave the base, the Academy plans social activities for freshmen in Hap Arnold Hall ("Arnie's"), which serves as a campus social center. Seniors are allowed to leave the base on weekdays after completing their military duties, so they often leave around 5 P.M. and return by 11 P.M. One thing that might prevent students from leaving base on a weekend is the "triple threat" which include Saturday morning inspections ("Sami's"), a home football game (which all cadets must attend), and a parade put on by cadets for spectators. Weekends also allow students some free time to enjoy their surroundings. "It's just beautiful up here," one cadet said. "We're right in the mountains."

Most cadets seem truly grateful for the opportunity to attend a top-notch school at absolutely no cost. One cadet said, "Many people complain, but with the challenges come definite rewards. I fly upside down every other day, and I haven't paid a dime." In return for a free education, cadets pledge to serve for at least five years in the Air Force after graduation; pilots accept an extra service requirement (so they cannot immediately use their expensive government-funded training to get jobs at commercial airlines). The Air Force pays for some graduates from the Academy to attend medical school, law school, and other postgraduate schools; however, years spent in professional school do not count toward a graduate's service requirement.

Cadets warn prospective students not to come to the Academy without learning a lot about it. As one cadet advised, "If you are a recruited athlete [who sometimes know less about academy life], make sure you find out more about this place because it can be really brutal if you don't know what you are getting into." Cadets consistently stress the importance of time management at the Academy and of having a real understanding of the place's military rigor. Overall, however, cadets consider the intense effort that the Academy demands more than worthwhile. Many genuinely respect the Air Force and what it stands for, and they look forward to putting their education and training to work both in and out of the military.

—*Ben Trachtenberg and Staff*

FYI

The three best things about attending the USAFA are "the free top-notch education, the beautiful campus, and the camaraderie with fellow students."

The three worst things about attending the USAFA are "the entire freshman year, a lack of vacation time, and the bureaucracy."

The three things that every student should do before graduating from the USAFA are "the Jump (parachuting) program, take advantage of the skiing, and break the rules at least once."

One thing I'd like to have known before coming here is "you have to know how to study and write because you won't make it otherwise."

University of Colorado/ Boulder

Address: Campus Box 30; Boulder, CO 80309-0030
Phone: 303-492-6301
E-mail address: apply@colorado.edu
Web site URL: www.colorado.edu
Founded: 1876
Private or Public: public
Religious affiliation: none
Location: small city
Undergraduate enrollment: 21,781
Total enrollment: 28,373
Percent Male / Female: 52% / 48%
Percent Minority: 14%
Percent African-American: 2%

Percent Asian: 6%
Percent Hispanic: 5%
Percent Native-American: 0.5%
Percent in-state / out-of-state: 66% / 34%
Percent Pub HS: NA
Number of Applicants: 14,647
Percent Accepted: 85%
Percent Accepted who enroll: 37%
Entering: 4,595
Transfers: 1,375
Application Deadline: 15 Feb
Mean SAT: 573 V, 587 M
Mean ACT: 25

Middle 50% SAT range: 520–620 V, 540–640 M
Middle 50% ACT range: 22–27
3 Most popular majors: psychology, biology, English
Retention: 84%
Graduation rate: 64%
On-campus housing: 95%
Fraternities: 10%
Sororities: 13%
Library: 2,000,000 volumes
Tuition and Fees: $3,118 in; $15,898 out
Room and Board: $5,202
Financial aid, first-year: 54%

In a valley at the foot of the Rocky Mountains, where the Great Plains abruptly meet the front range, sits the University of Colorado at Boulder. Known locally as CU, the beautiful campus is located just 25 minutes from Denver and 45 minutes from Eldora, the closest ski resort. Students can take advantage of the great outdoors, which is virtually in their backyards, without giving up city life. Boulder is a small city that is growing at a tremendous rate, but is still small enough to lack urban problems like high crime rates. The campus has a relaxed feeling about it, and some students say anyone who is easygoing would love CU's environment because "here, students do their own thing."

Academics—What You Make Them

At CU, academics are as easy or as tough as you make them. Students say that you can earn a degree from CU having worked hard or having hardly worked at all. Graduation requirements include a distribution core that requires students to be reasonably proficient in a foreign language, writing, critical thinking, and have basic mathematical skills. Among the best departments, according to undergrads, are engineering, the natural sciences, sociology, and business. Anthropology is an especially popular department. Professors are reportedly very approachable, and one student said he especially liked how most professors interact with students and love what they are doing. However, one student warned that some calculus professors are "brainy Nobel prize–winners that really don't know how to teach," and who sometimes like to fail students. Another student said some profs are "egomaniacs." Overall, though, CU students are satisfied with their professors. Difficult classes include calculus, those in the natural sciences, and engineering classes, especially physical chemistry. Slackers reportedly major in open-option arts and sciences—otherwise known as the "arts and parties."

Freshmen tend to get stuck with leftover classes in the fall term because they register at orientation over the summer, and all other students register the previous April. Class size averages 200 to 500 for introductory and popular courses, but after freshman year the classes get progressively smaller, with an average class size of about 50. By senior year, classes usually range from 10 to 30 students. Large classes break into smaller sections taught by teaching assistants (TAs). Students report that TAs are usually good, despite the occasional problems with those TAs whose English is not strong. CU also has an honors program with smaller classes, averaging 9 to 10 students per class discussion in classes with 40 students or fewer. CU students also get their share of outside education when famous guest speakers come to campus. In recent years, guest speakers have included the CEO of the company that produces Tootsie Rolls (who came to a business class to lecture in addition to giving out product samples), Secretary of the Interior Bruce Babitt, and Olympic diver Greg Louganis.

Much More Than Academics

At CU, life is much more than just academics. CU students have diverse interests, and can likewise choose from a large number of social options. Greeks are a definite presence in Boulder social life, but they don't offer the only option for fun on the weekends. The most popular Panhellenic groups are Alpha Chi Omega, Kappa Kappa Gamma, Kappa Alpha Theta, and Delta Gamma. The most active fraternities are Alpha Tau Omega, FIJI, Pi Kappa Phi, Pi Kappa Alpha, and Sigma Alpha Epsilon. Sororities are usually harder to rush than fraternities, since they are more formal and have more rules and regulations than frats. Frat parties are said to be "a blast," but they are officially dry. Many Greek bashes are inter-house, date, or theme parties. The Sink is a favorite watering hole for fraternity boys. However, if you are not into the frat scene, one student warns that it is hard to mix in with the crowd. Fraternities occasionally rent out dance clubs, which are especially well-attended affairs. But, it is a definite "scene." One student felt that, "Greek life is lots of skinny girls in trendy dresses and piles of wasted frat boys."

If you're not into the Greek scene, Nick's Sports restaurant is a popular hangout. On the weekend, students frequent the bars of Boulder, such as the Foundry, the Wallace, and the Walnut Brewery, which all offer "good music, good drinks, and lots of fun." There are also large school parties around campus. Every year people attend the party "Xmas" dressed as Santas and elves (this party can draw a crowd in excess of 2,000 people). Many people go out on dates and one student said that "Fridays are pretty laid-back; they are the date night." However, students report that there are just as many random hookups. Although there are a lot of gay and lesbian couples, students say they are not as visible on campus as at some other schools. CU has a reputation as a party school, and many students agree with the stereotype to a degree, saying that "there are more people that party [than don't]" but that not everyone parties in the same way.

Chemical Fun

CU has had some alcohol-related problems in recent years, which students say have changed the relationship between police and undergrads from one of mutual tolerance to one of mutual disrespect. Recently, the police have been cracking down harder and harder on underage alcohol consumption, and students agree that being underage is much more of a problem if you want to drink than it used to be. Some students gripe that Boulder police are "horrible" because they never "let students be without giving them a hard time." Therefore, students basically "despise" them and there are several major "incidents" between students and police each year. The administration is as unpopular as the police among students for its regulations against kegs on campus ("but people get them anyway"), and the beer ban at sports events. Even with the crackdown, students say alcohol is still widely consumed both on and off campus, and there are more students that drink than that don't. However, being a nondrinker reportedly will not hinder your social life. Those who don't drink say they are not pressured to do so.

Drugs do not present as much of a problem on the CU campus as alcohol. Although CU is known to many as a "druggie school," a large number of students don't do drugs. Students agree that there are at least as many people who don't use drugs on a regular basis as those that do. The most common drug is marijuana, which almost everyone encounters at some point whether he or she is involved with drugs or not. According to one student, "Drugs are there for those that want them."

Kicking Back

Dorm life at CU is not for everyone. Freshmen are required to live on campus, but after freshman year more and more people move off campus. By senior year, a large percentage of students are living off campus. Dorms are said to be good, but some residents dislike the "childish rules that are not well-enforced"— like no alcohol. Dorms vote on quiet hours, and RAs are usually easy on the students they supervise. The best dorms are said to be Kittridge, because of its scenic location, as well as Baker, Reed, and Crosman. Libby Hall, Cheyenne/Arapaho, and Hallet, are popular for social students because they party so much in them that the dorms have received national recognition for it. However, some residents complain that these dorms are too loud, too crowded, have bad facilities/small rooms, are ugly, or all of the above.

CU students are a very diverse group, and resist categorization. However, some say there is a "common CU student" if not a typical one: wealthy caucasian. Some undergrads would like just a bit more diversity among the student body. Stereotypes of CU students include "hippies" and "granolas," as many come from suburban or urban environments and are trying to "get back to nature." Students at CU are very easygoing and friendly, and although there are cliques, you can choose to hang out with just about anyone. At CU, "you always feel welcome," one student said. Many people are the "outdoorsy" type, and love to camp, hike, bike, and join environmental clubs. Engineers, pre-meds, and math and science majors are all identified separately from other majors, largely because these majors require less partying and more work. The administration discourages cars because of the traffic problems and limited parking space in

Boulder, though many students ride bikes. Despite this, one student said cars are popular because so many people like to travel to the mountains or to Denver.

Rocky Mountain High

Students agree that both the environment and location of CU make it one of the most beautiful campuses in the nation. The buildings are uniform in architectural style, and are quite attractive on the outside, but sometimes "junky on the inside." In recent years, additions to the Music School, the engineering building, and the Integrated Teaching and Learning Labs have provided for new, attractive sights on campus. The engineering addition is the only regular classroom building on campus that students need an ID to get into. The CU gym is very large and modern. Norlin Library offers students a quiet environment and all the resources they need for research. Folsom Stadium, where the varsity football team plays, has a gorgeous view of the front range of the Rockies. Since the CU campus is in a suburban area, students mostly feel safe there. However, in Boulder there "are a lot of weirdos running around that aren't dangerous, just really weird," and students recommend using caution.

The Buffs

Sports at CU are a major attraction. The football team has been in the top 25 in the nation for the past 10 years, and the basketball team "is on the way up" with a new coach. The CU Buffaloes, known locally as "the Buffs," have excellent sports teams and a popular mascot, Ralphie the buffalo. Popular sports include varsity football and basketball (mostly spectator sports, unless you are good enough to get on the teams), and skiing and snowboarding. Students pursue every other sport imaginable, including rock climbing on the Flatirons (huge stone slabs that jut out of the faces of mountains) and in nearby Eldorado Canyon. Intramurals are also popular. Saturday football is a tradition with many students, and the games against Nebraska and Oklahoma, CU's Big Eight archrivals, always fill the stadium. Of course, students have local professional teams to support as well, including the

Broncos, the Avalanche, the Nuggets, and the Colorado Rockies.

The Stuff on the Table

One aspect of CU that students do not praise is the food. The dinning halls at CU serve food that draws such comments as "interesting," "barely tolerable," and "gets old fast after freshman year." Perhaps because of the food, students rarely hang out in the dining halls but instead "eat and leave." The campus meal plans give students the option to use their "dining dollars" at vending machines. The city of Boulder has many excellent restaurants, especially on the Pearl Street Mall (an out-door mall popular with students). Students also go to Pearl Street for its "good" bars. Students often go to restaurants right off campus on the Hill. Pizza delivery and takeout is also a favorite option among undergrads.

The beautiful outdoors, the gorgeous campus, and the easygoing atmosphere all make CU a unique university. People in Boulder and on campus are generally accepting, tolerant, and liberal. The laid-back mood is so pervasive that students warn it can completely win you over. Students say they love their campus and their school and "would choose CU again in a minute." —*Alison Pulaski and Staff*

FYI

The three best things about attending CU are, "outdoor activities, casual atmosphere, and geographic location "

The three worst things about attending CU are, "parking sucks, ethnic diversity is limited and the groups are sometimes hostile toward each other, and police are lame . . . they are either over-reactive or under-reactive, and they are prejudiced toward college students."

The three things that every student should do before graduating CU are, "hike to the Flatirons, do the Pearl Street Mall pub crawl, and see a concert at Fox Theater."

One thing I'd like to have known before coming here is "that you should have a good academic plan because advisors are clueless."

University of Denver

Address: 2199 South University Boulevard; Denver, CO 80208

Phone: 303-871-2036

E-mail address: admission@du.edu

Web site URL: www.du.edu

Founded: 1864

Private or Public: private

Religious affiliation: none

Location: suburban

Undergraduate enrollment: 3,715

Total enrollment: 9,188

Percent Male / Female: 42%/58%

Percent Minority: 16%

Percent African-American: 4%

Percent Asian: 5%

Percent Hispanic: 6%

Percent Native-American: 1%

Percent in-state / out-of-state: NA

Percent Pub HS: NA

Number of Applicants: 3,303

Percent Accepted: 84%

Percent Accepted who enroll: 30%

Entering: 834

Transfers: NA

Application Deadline: rolling

Mean SAT: 557 V, 560 M

Mean ACT: 24

Middle 50% SAT range: 510–610 V, 500–610 M

Middle 50% ACT range: 21–27

3 Most popular majors: biology, communication, psychology

Retention: 84%

Graduation rate: 54%

On-campus housing: 41%

Fraternities: 29%

Sororities: 22%

Library: 1,155,981 volumes

Tuition and Fees: $19,440 in; $19,440 out

Room and Board: $6,165

Financial aid, first-year: 52%

At an elevation of 5,280 feet with 300 days of sunshine every year, the University of Denver is a paradise for the student who loves the outdoors. With the snowcapped Rocky Mountains nearby, access to the ski slopes is a hop, skip, and a jump away, while the city itself teems with enough life to satisfy any student. Of course, the academic reputation of the University of Denver is fairly strong as well. Thus, students who decide to obtain a degree from DU will reap the benefits of a study hard, play hard environment.

What TAs?

By far the distinguishing factor of DU academics is the predominantly small class size. Class enrollment ranges from as few as 6 students to approximately 60 students. The relationships between professors and students flourish in this more personalized setting, and the faculty for the most part "are approachable, knowledgeable, and grade fairly." The "one-on-one relationship we have with professors," says one student "opens great opportunities for research." There are also very few TAs teaching except in science laboratories.

DU does have a core curriculum. All entering freshmen must take first-year English; one course in oral communications, math, computer science; and demonstrate proficiency in a foreign language. The DU Campus Connection ensures that freshmen adjust to the rigors of college life by assigning each one a faculty member who serves both as an academic advisor and a mentor for the entire first year. Special programs include the unique and highly selective Pioneer Leadership Program, which allows students to receive a minor in Leadership Studies that may be applied to any major. Students who apply to the Pioneer Leadership Program must be able to demonstrate leadership and devotion to community service. The Honors Program offers a variety of opportunities: seminars with lectures by guest scholars, a student-run Honors Association, special checkout privileges at Penrose Library, and special "honors floors" in each of the residence halls. Students in the Honors Program must take special honors courses while maintaining a GPA of 3.4 or higher.

The most difficult classes on campus are the courses on genetics and Organic Chemistry. As one student noted, "Since we are on a quarter system, if you miss a week of class, you can lose up to 10 percent of your grade in the course!" But, as another student said, "If you keep up and study hard, classes are not too strenuous." In addition, the university also hopes to "maximize the educational benefits that are associated with having a computer" by requiring all first-year students to purchase a laptop, beginning in fall of 1999.

> **"It is extremely easy to become involved in this school."**

One extremely popular DU offering is the Interterm classes. Because DU operates on a quarter system, the period of time between quarters, known as the Interterm, provides priceless opportunities for DU students. Each Interterm (in fall, winter, and spring), DU offers one-to-two-week classes that take students out of the classroom. Some popular classes include a painting class in Santa Fe, New Mexico; a business class that includes a trip to Wall Street in New York City; and a photojournalism class in Brazil.

The New and the Old

DU has a mix of old, almost Gothic-style buildings juxtaposed with brand-new structures. Evans Chapel near the student center has beautiful stained-glass windows, while not too far away, Penrose Library maintains a sleek, rectilinear style. The new science building, F. W. Olin Hall, is topped with a gleaming copper dome. DU will continue to make major capital improvements on buildings in coming years. A new business building, tennis pavilion, and the Wellness Center are slated for construction. The architecture is not the only aesthetically pleasing characteristic of DU. There's a breathtaking view of the mountains, and also lots of "unique specimens of flowers and trees" scattered throughout campus.

Besides the main University Park Campus, DU also has a "satellite" campus an inconvenient 10 miles away known as the Park Hill Campus. Students at Park Hill often complain about feeling disconnected from the rest of campus and the big hassle of having classes on both campuses.

DU also requires that students living outside a 90-mile radius of the school live on campus for the first two-years. There are only two residence halls on campus: Centennial Halls and Johnson-McFarlane. Centennial Halls is comprised of twin high-rises 10 stories tall. Special features include a convenience store located in the residence hall as well as air-conditioned suites with furnished kitchens. Centennial Halls is where the Living-Learning Centers and Special Interest Floors are located. Living-Learning Centers are designed to bring American and international students together to "explore far-ranging global concerns." Each quarter, students take a one-credit course focusing on critical global issues. Special Interest Floors are available in the form of business floors, math and science floors, substance-free floors, and single-gender floors. Centennial Halls is also the home for students involved in the Honors Program. Johnson-McFarlane, commonly known as J-Mac, is a three-story building containing facilities similar to those at Centennial Halls. Students involved in the Pioneer Leadership Program live here, and J-Mac is considered the "tamer" of the two residence halls because Centennial Halls is "a-LOT wilder than J-Mac." Dorm food in these residence halls is regarded as "regular, nasty college food." As one senior stated, "Prepare to lose weight when you get here due to the terrible food."

Drink and Ski

"The city of Denver considers us at times a rich kid's school where all we do is drink and ski," commented one student. Admittedly, many students agree that there is some truth to the stereotype. Numerous students come from wealthy families, and a common joke among all undergrads is that they "drive Range Rovers that their Republican fathers bought for them." The preppy type of student definitely seems to be the majority on campus, but the "friendly, intelligent, mature, and generous" attitude of all DU students makes being a minority on campus comfortable.

Students say that alcohol is prevalent throughout campus. There are a few Greek houses going dry, though most are establishing a "bring your own beer" policy. At parties, students report plenty of random hookups, but a lot of serious dating also exists on campus as well. The Greek system at DU reportedly drives the social scene on campus. Little hostility exists between Greeks and non-Greeks, but one sophomore who decided not to rush said, "The Greek system runs the school. When I went through rush, people told me that if I wanted to be something on campus, I had to join a house." The frats and sororities open their parties to all students and hold big theme parties ranging from the "Beachcombers" (featuring sand and beach attire) to the very formal "Casino Royale" (where students gamble with fake money). There are parties and events not associated with the Greeks running throughout the year, which include fall homecoming, Winter Carnival, and May Daze in the spring. The DU Programming Board also sponsors weekly movies and guest speakers.

So Many Things to Do

"It is extremely easy to become involved at this school. All activities are open to everyone," exclaims one junior. The most popular organizations include the campus newspaper (*The Clarion*), the Alpine Club, and the DU Programming Board. Ethnic and cultural organizations and professional honors associations are also popular. Other, more specialized, organizations include the Forensics Club, the Kayak Club, and the Rescue Team. DU offers enough variety to satisfy almost any student. Many students participate in DU's club sports program, which allows students to join any team they like. No one is cut from a team, and "everyone has the chance to play in competition." Sports groups range from cycling to ultimate Frisbee to skiing (of course!). The most popular spectator sport is hockey. The Pioneers garner strong student support with DU "bleacher creatures," who often sit together in a designated section of the stadium to cheer loudly and stamp their feet incessantly during games.

Student enthusiasm and support for the Division I hockey team is a reflection of the general love the students have for their school. "People are very laid-back and casual here," says one student. DU undergrads at once enjoy the benefits of a city and the seclusion of suburban surroundings. Students agree that DU provides a solid undergraduate education while still allowing for an active social life and, more importantly, frequent ski trips to the Rockies. —*Melissa Chan and Staff*

FYI

The three best things about attending DU are "the proximity to the Rockies, the small class size and one-on-one relationships with professors, and Interterm classes."

The three worst things about attending DU are "the pressure of a quarter system, the terrible food, and the plethora of rich, preppy kids who have gone Greek."

The three things that every student should do before graduating DU are "take advantage of the Rockies, join the bleacher creatures at a hockey game, and enjoy the incredible social scene."

One thing I'd like to have known before coming here is "how much life at DU is a balance of work, partying, and skiing."

Connecticut

Connecticut College

Address: 270 Mohegan Avenue; New London, CT 06320
Phone: 860-439-2200
E-mail address: admit@conncoll.edu
Web site URL: camel.conncoll.edu
Founded: 1911
Private or Public: private
Religious affiliation: none
Location: suburban
Undergraduate enrollment: 1,645
Total enrollment: 1,857
Percent Male/Female: 43%/57%
Percent Minority: 10%
Percent African-American: 4%

Percent Asian: 2%
Percent Hispanic: 3%
Percent Native-American: 0.5%
Percent in-state/out-of-state: 81%/19%
Percent Pub HS: 58%
Number of Applicants: 3,700
Percent Accepted: 39%
Percent Accepted who enroll: 33%
Entering: 477
Transfers: 30
Application Deadline: 15 Jan
Mean SAT: 636 V, 621 M
Mean ACT: 25

Middle 50% SAT range: 582–685 V, 580–677 M
Middle 50% ACT range: NA
3 Most popular majors: psychology, government, economics
Retention: 90%
Graduation rate: 76%
On-campus housing: 100%
Fraternities: NA
Sororities: NA
Library: 480,000 volumes
Tuition and Fees: 31,985 total expenses
Room and Board: NA
Financial aid, first-year: 0%

"Looking for a typical, small, New England liberal arts school? Well, in that case, Connecticut College is a great place to come," reported one sophomore. His description of his school as "typical," however, does not capture its honor code, close-knit community, great location, and solid academic programs that are hallmarks of the college.

The Best Programs

The best and most popular departments at Conn include government, psychology, economics, history, English, art, and dance. Although the humanities reign supreme in terms of popularity, by no means does this indicate that the science departments are weak. Thanks to great facilities like the Connecticut College Arboretum and the new Olin Science Center, sciences are stronger than ever at Conn. Perhaps the main reason for the low levels of par-

ticipation in the sciences is that many students dread the formidable pre-med track that requires introductory chemistry, regarded as the most difficult course at Conn.

In the true spirit of the liberal arts, students at Conn are required to take one course from each of seven different areas, including Physical and Biological Sciences, Mathematics and Logic, Social Science, Critical Studies in Literature and Arts, Creative Arts, Philosophy and Religious Studies, and Historical Studies. Students view the requirements as positive, not as some burden. "It's good because you go through the whole potpourri," said one student. This potpourri also contributes to the great flexibility offered to Conn students. One particularly impressed student noted that, "It's easy to design your own major, double major or minor, area of concentration, certificate program, or any other course of study you may desire, along with the dozens of already established programs." One complaint that students did voice was the requirement that students go to tutorials with their pre-major advisors during the first and second semesters. Students are also asked to attend at least six General Education events designed around an annual theme.

The international program is extremely popular at Conn. Students applaud the administration's belief in the importance of studying abroad. The college has recently become involved in CISLA, an intensive program that offers funding for students who want to pursue their self-designed projects. One of the students commented that CISLA "is a way to explore your dreams and learn about another culture."

Class sizes at Conn are usually small, but do include large lectures. Typically, upper-level seminars enroll only a few students, and the introductory courses are large. The classes are reportedly "challenging, but not overwhelming." Perhaps this relatively relaxed atmosphere can be attributed to the professors, who are "very approachable and personable." All classes at Conn are taught by professors, although TAs are there for tutoring. Office-hours meetings or e-mail are the most popular means for getting help from instructors.

Social Life—Unity on Campus
While the students do spend much time studying in Shain Library or their rooms, Conn students find room in their schedules to hang out with friends. "Students here get along and work well with others, probably because we're all stuck here together." Although New London "leaves much to be desired," the president is launching a campaign to integrate the school with the city development. Still, campus life is "active, busy, and fun." The Student Activities Council (SAC) provides events every Thursday, Friday, and Saturday night. Some of these activities include movies shown by the film society, performances by the a cappella singing groups or drama groups, and concerts. Although drinking does play a role in campus social activities, students agree that "you don't need to be drunk to have fun on this campus." Many students are attracted to Conn

simply because there is no Greek life on campus. Not having a Greek system "doesn't impede the social life at all . . . it actually contributes to a certain unity on campus."

Extracurriculars
Students can enjoy a variety of activities at Connecticut College. Those interested in journalism can write for the *College Voice* or the *College Journal*. Those who have musical talent can join one of Conn's multiple singing groups or orchestra. Those particularly interested in broadcasting can participate in the operation of the school radio station, WCNI. Involvement in student government is also popular.

> "It's easy to design your own major, double major or minor, area of concentration, certificate program, or any other course of study you may desire."

Sports also are a big part of student life at Conn. This Division III school receives much community support at games, especially in soccer and hockey. New on campus is the women's ice hockey team. Those students who do not wish to participate in a varsity sport can take advantage of the newly renovated Athletic Center. Conn also has a popular intramural sports program. Making intramurals especially entertaining is the friendly competition fostered by Dorm Olympics. This series of games also increases dorm loyalties.

Location and Rooming
Students comment favorably on the school's location. The campus is very safe according to one student who said, "I have never felt unsafe walking alone late at night because the campus is well lit and there are phones scattered throughout for emergency use." Although New London does not receive rave reviews as a college town in terms of fun, students enjoy the 721-acre campus that overlooks the Thames and the Long Island Sound. The on-campus Connecticut College Arboretum provides students with a great place

to study and conduct research, but is also an ideal place to visit for an outdoor experience.

The rooming situation at Conn is reportedly very good. Most freshmen live in doubles or triples, but all upperclassmen get singles. Dorms are co-ed and run by a house fellow. One alternate housing situation is the Unity House, a dorm staffed by a full-time director who works "to bring all sorts of people together, from race to ethnicity to culture to lifestyle." Other housing options include the Earth House for environmentally concerned students, Quiet Housing, Substance-Free Housing, and Thematic Housing. Three of the four previously "ugly" Plex dorms have undergone renovations, so they are modernized, air conditioned, and have brand new furniture. Also, all the dorms now have cable television.

The dining halls are said to be "great" due to the reconstruction of Harris Dining Hall. Renovations have helped eliminate long lines and broaden dining options for students. Dining halls serve vegetarian as well as standard fare. Students can choose among several dining halls on campus, Harris being the largest. But each dining hall has its own special attributes. For example, Freeman is known as the "stir-fry dorm" and Harkness is the "deli dorm." Those looking for something different can go to the newly renovated Crozier-Williams Student Center (the "Cro"), where they can get pizza, mail a letter, or have a beer at the "Cro" bar.

Students and their Honor Code

One student admitted that "Conn leaves something to be desired in terms of diversity." Students described the typical Conn student this way: "Rich, white, athletic, shops at Abercrombie and Fitch and North Face, drives a SAAB, and lives in a suburb of Boston."

One defining trait of Connecticut College is its honor code. Upon matriculation, every student must sign an agreement that he or she will abide by the honor code. In the academic vein, students agree that they will not cheat or plagiarize, rules that enable students to enjoy "completely self-scheduled, unproctored exams." Students regard this as a "great perk because students can study as long as they need to, and take exams when they're ready." Socially, students agree to respect others and their lifestyles and space, and those who infringe on the honor code rules deal with the Judiciary Board, a board of students who "take their jobs seriously."

Connecticut College is a place where students can learn in an academically supportive atmosphere with small classes and accessible professors. Conn students also learn the value of responsibility and integrity through the honor code. Conn students are proud of their school and see it as a constantly improving institution where they can make great friends. As one student said, "Conn is a fun and interesting place to go to school. I am excited about what my future here will bring."

—Marti Page and Staff

FYI

The three best things about attending Connecticut College are "the small size allows for wide access to professors and their work, a cappella groups, and the flexibility in major design."

The three worst things about attending Connecticut College are that "students tend to be apathetic toward the outside world, the honor code is taken too lightly, and that politics get in the way of administration."

The three things every student should do before graduating are to "do an internship, go to Harkness beach, and sing in an a cappella group."

One thing I'd like to have known before coming here is that "students here don't always take their time as seriously as I'd expected."

Fairfield University

Address: 1073 North Benson Road; Fairfield, CT 06430-5195
Phone: 203-254-4100
E-mail address: NA
Web site URL: www.fairfield.edu
Founded: 1942
Private or Public: private
Religious affiliation: Jesuit
Location: suburban
Undergraduate enrollment: 4,064
Total enrollment: 5,127
Percent Male / Female: 47% / 53%
Percent Minority: 11%
Percent African-American: 3%

Percent Asian: 3%
Percent Hispanic: 4%
Percent Native-American: 0.5%
Percent in-state / out-of-state: 22% / 78%
Percent Pub HS: 50%
Number of Applicants: 6,457
Percent Accepted: 61%
Percent Accepted who enroll: 21%
Entering: 837
Transfers: 31
Application Deadline: 1 Feb
Mean SAT: 575 V, 584 M
Mean ACT: 25

Middle 50% SAT range: 530–620 V, 540–620 M
Middle 50% ACT range: NA
3 Most popular majors: English, biology, psychology
Retention: 89%
Graduation rate: 81%
On-campus housing: 100%
Fraternities: NA
Sororities: NA
Library: 206,849 volumes
Tuition and Fees: $19,935 in; $19,935 out
Room and Board: $7,380
Financial aid, first-year: 65%

With pristine green lawns, golden-red trees, and beautiful buildings, the Fairfield campus of 2001 may not look, at first glance, like the typical New England college. But that is because one's eye lingers over the evidence of renovation. Fairfield will soon be finished with its now three-year-old project of improving each of its seven dorms, with the installation of air-conditioning in the common spaces (a big plus!). More good news for freshmen: the frosh dorms are in the Quad, which is the central campus area, making it easier for new students to feel like part of the college immediately. Another bonus at Fairfield is that housing is guaranteed for all four years. Upperclassmen enter a lottery to get into beach houses or condominiumlike town houses. The upcoming Fairfield classes will be able to enjoy a new campus center, a totally renovated library, and new on-campus apartments. Students say that the worst dorm is Campian, but it is being renovated during the 2002–2003 year.

A Unique Academic Experience

Fairfield's Jesuit tradition is still visible in the academic arena. Rising sophomores are offered the opportunity to apply to the college's Honors Program, based on first-year GPA, which exempts its students from some of the distributional requirements in favor of an interdisciplinary program that is writing-intensive. Students say that the foreign languages are the weaker programs academically and the arts program is small. The college is divided into four schools: the School of Arts and Sciences, the Business School, the School of Nursing, and the Graduate School. The core curriculum consists of three semesters of English and two semesters each of math, science, language, history, social science, and fine arts. Besides these, Fairfield Stags are required to take two semesters of religious studies and philosophy, with one additional semester in either religion, philosophy, or ethics. Such a complicated core is not for students who dislike the liberal arts, but for those who do, Fairfield's program is intellectually rewarding and, most important, improves writing skills. Besides the core curriculum, another respected Fairfield institution is its pre-med program. About academics in general, students say that "with a little time and effort you will be fine" because professors "are more than willing to help you out."

Fairfield's small size makes it easy to

get individual attention, and classes are small enough to foster stimulating discussions with the professors. Introductory lecture classes rarely enroll more than 40 people, and seminars often have around 12 or less. Because of the class sizes and the helpful attitude of most professors, Fairfield students have plenty of time to develop extracurricular interests.

What's a Naked Mormon?

Extracurriculars at Fairfield are as diverse as those of any other school of its size and quality. Prospective freshmen can look forward to participating in activities ranging from the community service–oriented Campus Ministry, to campus radio, to the popular Glee Club, and FUSA, the extremely enthusiastic Fairfield student government. One extracurricular that Fairfield does not offer is a Greek system, but the school still maintains an active party scene. Students here love their "Beach," a four-square-mile strip of school-owned houses, most of which are "right along the Long Island Sound." These houses host the best parties, and often have fun, wacky names like the "Naked Mormon," the "Dugout," and the "Red Barn." Next door to the Beach is the Sea Grape, or just the Grape, which is the campus bar. When students are not at the Beach or the Grape, they head to New Haven for its nightclubs. The most popular for Fairfield students is the Van Dome, but a new club called Risk just opened with college Thursdays. One student says that the social life at Fairfield revolves "totally and utterly" around alcohol. The Fairfield way of life: work hard, party harder! When asked about the presence of drugs on campus, one student says that while marijuana has always been around, recently 'shrooms and ecstasy have become more visible.

Incoming Frosh Without ID— Fear Not!

The college itself has begun to devote more attention to enhancing the weekend activities available to its undergrads. Free bowling, discounted movie tickets, and trips to see Broadway shows are all being sponsored with greater frequency. Sometimes bands play at the Levee. There are

two major semi-formals during basketball season: the Harvest and the Dogwood-Midnight Madness, but the best-loved college-sponsored event at Fairfield is its spring weekend. On Saturday is "Spam Jam" and on Sunday is "Clam Jam." In the words of one student, "There are bands, games, contests, and lots of activities, and of course tons of drinking." Another student claims, "We look forward to luau and Alumni weekend, but especially Clam Jam—it's insanity!"

> **"[Students look like] they just stepped out of a J.Crew or Abercrombie catalog."**

When it comes to sports, Fairfield holds its own in men's and women's soccer and women's volleyball. All three have made it to the NCAA tournament in the past few years. Men's club volleyball is a relatively new activity here as well. Students consistently rate school spirit as very poor. Intramurals at Fairfield are a good way to combat stress, with floor hockey, flag football, soccer, and basketball being most popular. Men's basketball games get the greatest turnout when it comes to fans. Fairfield also began its own football tradition in 1996, allowing more opportunities for Fairfield's bright school colors—red and white—and the University Pep and Dance team to enliven the social scene. Despite this recent addition, the student body just is not as sports-oriented as most Division I schools are.

Chemistry at Fairfield Is Not Just a Science

The student body is a homogenous group, and many complain about a lack of diversity. When asked what the typical Fairfield student is like, students responded that most look like "they just stepped out of a J.Crew or Abercrombie catalog." The majority are Christian, hail from New England, and are middle- to upper-class economically. Students warn that some of their fellow classmates are very snobby. The advantage of having an attractive student body is obvious: "there is a lot of chemistry between students here," and "meeting people is not a problem." However, as at many colleges, the dating scene is nearly non-existent. With some exceptions, casual hookups are predominant.

Fairfield, Connecticut

The college is located in southwestern Connecticut, and the campus is characterized by the Egan Chapel of St. Ignatius, a reminder that Fairfield is a school founded upon the Jesuit ideals of education and community service. The town of Fairfield, Connecticut is the typical New England college town, but it is on the quiet side. Stoplights turn off after 9:00 P.M. The closest mall is in Trumbull, and for undergrads with transportation, Fairfield is about a half hour from New Haven, seven minutes from Bridgeport, and an hour from New York City. New York is a popular trip, especially for upperclassmen, but Fairfield is by no means a "suitcase school." There are a number of boutiques in Fairfield but few restaurants. Students generally enjoy going to Joe's, which is close to the campus and has good food.

Dining Options: For Better or for Worse

The dining experience at Fairfield University, according to the upperclassmen, is no different from those of other colleges. There are many choices, but for those nights when nothing looks appetizing there are the old standbys: peanut butter and jelly, cereal, and grilled cheese. The campus has two dining halls, one for freshmen and one for upperclassmen, but the school has been experimenting to see which dining hall is best for the freshmen. Campus residents are on either a 19- or 14-meal-a-week plan, and off-campus residents have the option of a 7-, 10-, or 12-meal plan. There are Stagbucks that can be purchased in order to obtain snacks during the day. Those tired of cafeteria food can go to Joe's, Spazzi's, or Sidetracks.

Student body diversity is one issue Fairfield has recently taken steps to improve. The creation of the Multicultural Task Force is an important addition, as it emphasizes awareness and tolerance by sponsoring guest lecturers to give talks and by sponsoring ethnic and cultural awareness days. Also, the administration added a class in diversity to its distributional requirements, and the students were very pleased by this step. It requires students to take at least one course with a focus on another culture, religion, or ethnic group during their four years.

The Fairfield Experience

Between extensive renovation projects, the creation of a football team, and the recent addition of a diversity requirement and the Multicultural Task Force, Fairfield University is a school steeped in both the tradition of reputable academics and an enthusiasm for continued improvement of both the structural body of the school and students themselves.
—*Christina Merola*

FYI
The three best things about attending Fairfied are "the proximity to New York City, the beach, and the hotties."
The three worst things about attending Fairfield are "the homogeneity, the lack of dating, and the core requirements."
The three things every student should do before graduating from Fairfield are "go to New York City for the night, go to Clam and Spam Jam, spend a night at the Beach."
One thing I'd like to have known before coming here is "what the hell a Stag is."

Trinity College

Address: 300 Summit Street; Hartford, CT 06106
Phone: 860-297-2180
E-mail address: admissions.office@trincoll.edu
Web site URL: www.trincoll.edu
Founded: 1823
Private or Public: private
Religious affiliation: none
Location: urban
Undergraduate enrollment: 2,146
Total enrollment: 2,371
Percent Male / Female: 45% / 55%
Percent Minority: 17%
Percent African-American: 6%

Percent Asian: 5%
Percent Hispanic: 5%
Percent Native-American: 0.5%
Percent in-state / out-of-state: 24% / 76%
Percent Pub HS: 45%
Number of Applicants: 4,648
Percent Accepted: 40%
Percent Accepted who enroll: 30%
Entering: 560
Transfers: 23
Application Deadline: 15 Jan
Mean SAT: 630 V, 630 M
Mean ACT: 27.3

Middle 50% SAT range: 590–680 V, 590–680 M
Middle 50% ACT range: 26–29
3 Most popular majors: economics, English, political science
Retention: 92%
Graduation rate: 85%
On-campus housing: 100%
Fraternities: NA
Sororities: NA
Library: 1,000,000 volumes
Tuition and Fees: $25,440 in; $25,440 out
Room and Board: $7,160
Financial aid, first-year: 47%

Although it is a small school with only 1,900 students, Trinity is an academically rigorous liberal arts college located in Connecticut's capital city, Hartford. The main part of the campus, Long Walk, is graced with rows of Gothic buildings jarringly offset by the ultramodern Life Sciences Center, nicknamed "Castle Grayskull" by students. The campus, as a whole, is lovely. As one enthusiastic freshman stated, "This place is paradise in so many ways, it really is."

Hitting the Books at Trinity

Trinity's small size promotes an intimate academic environment; students find professors friendly and accessible. One upperclassman philosophy major said, "Professors in the philosophy department are thrilled whenever students come up to them outside of class to talk about their work." Many students, however, often do not take advantage of professors' accessibility. "If you're not too shy to open your mouth, you'll get all the attention you can stand," commented a junior English major. TAs at Trinity are undergraduates who have taken a course and done well in it, and are used at Trinity

only as lab assistants and leaders of review and extra help sections, although they do grade homework assignments in many science courses. Class sizes are generally small (15–20), though there are some large introductory courses, such as freshman biology and freshman English, which may contain close to 100 students.

Trinity's academic requirements are fairly easy to fulfill. "There are few distribution requirements because the school really wants people to focus on their majors," said one student. To fulfill the distribution requirements, students must take one course in each of five general areas: Humanities, Numerical and Symbolic Logic, Arts, Social Sciences, and Life Sciences. Each freshman is also expected to take a non-traditional first-year seminar on an interdisciplinary topic like Images of Light or Representations of Gender. There is no foreign-language requirement. Many students complained about the mandatory math proficiency test, which is administered the first Sunday of school. "It's the first weekend of college," complained a sophomore, "everyone is hungover." To make matters worse, Trinity does not allow those with high SAT I or

SAT II math scores to waive the exam. Students who do poorly are placed into Math 101, a course generally regarded as a waste of time. Trinity's strongest departments were cited as English and the sciences, in which there are lots of research opportunities, even for freshman science majors. Facilities are notably "excellent," though music and theater arts are relatively small departments "without many course offerings," one junior said.

For particularly motivated students, Trinity offers an intensive two-year program in Western philosophy, history, and literature called Guided Studies. Guided Studies consists of three reading- and writing-intensive courses each semester for two years and is open to first-year students by invitation only. The program is rewarding, but also very limiting and restricted to non-Classics or English majors, according to a freshman in the program. "I want to be a theater arts major, and being in Guided Studies makes it pretty hard for me to fulfill all my requirements," she said.

There are no easy-A courses at Trinity. Although one student recommended the History of Flight as an easy way to fulfill the Life Sciences requirement, another warned, "Even courses that sound like guts are not blow-off courses." Music Appreciation and Philosophy of Sports were two prominent examples of unexpectedly difficult courses.

Grading at Trinity was described as fair, neither too severe nor too lenient. Since As are not easy to come by, many students report that Bs are considered average. Very few people graduate with honors. "In my major [English], the profs really peer to see if you're straining before they'll give you a decent mark," said one junior. Political science was cited as one of the easier majors.

Socializing, Camp Trin-Trin Style

"It's like summer camp here," explained a sophomore. "Most people know how to have a good time." They do indeed—Trinity students work hard and party hard. Greeks are very active on the campus, but, since frat parties are generally open to all students, few people feel the need to become members. Frats do arrange and host popular campus theme parties, like "Gender Bender," "Tropical," and the extremely popular "Disco Inferno." "I never thought you could have so much fun in polyester," raved one junior. Another student said "Tropical" was the single worst thing about life at Trinity, a night "of too many drunk people with no control." Lately, student organizations have been hosting more parties.

As on many college campuses, drinking and smoking are widespread at Trinity; in fact, several upperclassmen suggested that a beer keg would be the most appropriate mascot for the school. However, students who do not drink are by no means social outcasts. "I know a lot of people who don't drink. They still go out on weekends, even to bars, and still have a good time," one sophomore commented. One student expressed pleasant surprise about the attitudes of his peers. "I am straight-edge, and it's not that hard to not drink here," he explained. "People are actually understanding and sometimes even impressed by your strength." Nevertheless, "students who don't drink are in the minority," a sophomore added. Pot is smoked by a large percentage of the campus population, at least according to the estimates of several upperclassmen. "I'm a freshman Residential Advisor," one sophomore explained, "and I'm trained to be alert for the smell of pot in any of the dorm rooms. But it's pretty easy for students to get away with it." Cigarettes are not prohibited on campus or even in dorms. In fact, students may smoke anywhere except in common rooms, lounges, and a few other areas that are designated smoke-free. One of the campus dorms offers two floors of smoke-free housing, which is available upon request.

The administration has made a concerted effort to crack down on underage drinking and drug use on campus, and students still find carding strict at the Tap, an on-campus bar. Among other measures, the administration in the fall of 1997 introduced a new class of enforcement officers called Junior Fellows. In 1993, kegs were banned in residence halls, although frats and other groups can make arrangements to use party halls, where kegs are allowed.

Junior Fellows have the right to academically expel anyone they catch drinking illegally, but one student noted that Junior Fellows handle "a variety of issues" and most of their attention is focused on the freshman dorms.

> **"It's like summer camp here. Most people know how to have a good time."**

Although there is a school-sponsored shuttle system providing transportation into Hartford, students rarely go into the city. The school administration encourages weekend parties and other social events that keep students on campus at night. Trinity is located in Frog Hollow, a run-down area of Hartford that one junior characterized as a "ghetto." Broad Street, which borders the campus on one side, is not a good place to go walking at night. The campus itself, though, is fairly safe, at least in the opinion of many students. "There was one person accosted on the campus with a gun last year and made to hand over all his money, but that was just one incident," said a sophomore. "It's a very well lit, protected campus and I feel safe here."

Social life consists of party-hopping or hanging out with small groups of friends. Very little dating goes on at Trinity, according to students. "There is not much of a thing called love at Trinity," said one upperclassman, yet "there are a lot of random hookups." The Trinity student body is more sexually active than most, according to one frustrated junior who said, "Being a person involved in a long-term relationship, I can, as a partial observer, say the sexual activity at Trinity is among the highest in the known universe." Sexual assault and sexual harassment are very prominent campus issues, although there have not been many reported instances of them in the past few years. "It's definitely a concern, because so much of the hooking-up that goes on here is alcohol-induced," said a sophomore Resident Assistant.

A Sell Point

Although the area may be somewhat dangerous, Trinity can still boast about its location in Hartford, which is the home of the Bushnell Theater and the Wadsworth Atheneum, the nation's oldest public art gallery. "The city is a selling point for the school," one sophomore said. "Some other liberal arts colleges are isolated from the real world." Another student added, "Hartford's not like New York or Boston, but it is a city and it does offer certain things." Music fans can always find an abundance of concerts in the city. Also, Hartford is a great source of internships for Trinity students. Until the late 1980s, Hartford was known as "the insurance company capital of the world." Although the city's economy has declined slightly in recent years, there are still many large business firms in Hartford willing to employ Trinity students. The administration is very encouraging and supportive of students who pursue internships, study-abroad opportunities, or other special programs. Trinity has a Rome campus of its own, but also allows people to participate in programs offered by foreign universities for credit. "Nearly everyone here goes abroad," said one sophomore. According to one junior who is currently studying in London, "All I had to do was fill out a simple form. Really, it couldn't have been much easier."

The campus, like a summer camp, is alive with spirit. "We are aggressive athletes, students, partygoers, and for the most part, we are ambitious beyond that," said a junior. Unlike summer camp cabins, however, Trinity dorms are comfortably furnished (although some gripe that the college-issued desks are far too small). Also, as is not the case at most summer camps, many students even like the food, which is provided by Marriott Catering. There are three on-campus dining halls: the standard cafeteria; the Cave, a grill and social center; and the Bistro, a dinner and lunch restaurant that serves smaller portions of better-quality food. All three are covered by the campus meal plan. There are not many restaurants nearby, and students rarely eat off campus.

Trinity's Extracurriculars

The Trinity student body is very athletic. The vast majority of people participate in varsity or intramural sports, with football and rugby being two popular choices. Even students who do not play a sport work out frequently. Outside of sports, the most popular extracurricular activities include a cappella singing groups and the student newspaper, the *Tripod*. Student government at Trinity is more active than on most campuses. "It has a strong voice in decisions made by the faculty," said a sophomore. Not surprisingly, the campus is not a hotbed of social activism, although "we do try to be very politically correct," one junior said.

Students rarely interact with the Hartford community, although the administration strongly encourages community service and is currently involved in massive neighborhood revitalization plans. There is a community service dorm at Trinity devoted to social activism, and there are several small, but devoted groups, such as Habitat for Humanity and tutoring groups. Fewer than 400 out of the 1,900 students at Trinity participate in community outreach programs. Trinity life is centered on campus activity. Ninety-two percent of Trinity students spend their four years on campus.

Currently, 16 percent of the student body consists of minorities. Starting with the class of 2001, the administration is making more of a commitment to increase the socio-economic diversity of the student body. "I'm impressed. There's a tremendous difference in diversity between the senior class and the incoming freshman class," said a sophomore. One junior noticed a surprising number of Slavic and Eastern European international students. "I don't know how they heard of Trinity," he commented in amazement.

The student body is predominantly preppy and consists mostly of students from wealthy, white families who have attended boarding schools. "J.Crew and North Face outfit our entire campus," one junior said. A frustrated student said the campus consists entirely of "rich, white conservative Republicans." One junior railed against Trinity social life, saying "Meeting new friends is completely dependent on your age and economic status, the sports you play, the music you listen to, and, rarely, your actual worth as a human being." Other students, however, had no problems meeting new people and found the campus comfortable socially.

Very few people are openly homosexual, although Trinity is by no means a homophobic school. Encouraging Respect of Sexualities (EROS) is one of the most socially active groups on campus. However, one student did say that "there are more homosexual and interracial couples on campus than you'd expect given our preppy reputation."

By and large, though, Camp Trin-Trin is still a place where people buy their clothes from J.Crew, travel to Europe in the summer, and watch *Party of Five*, *Dawson's Creek*, and reruns of *Melrose Place*. One undergrad noted, however, that "the current freshman class is comprised of individuals who come from different backgrounds and styles," and they stand to break that Camp Trin-Trin image of Trinity. Overall, it is a place trying to redefine itself, a unique school that offers its students both an excellent liberal arts education and, in the apt words of a Trinity sophomore, "a good time." —*Erik Johnson and Staff*

FYI

The three best things about attending Trinity are "the small size, the parties, and the Freshman Seminar program."

The three worst things about attending Trinity are "the location, the math proficiency exam, and the homogeneity."

The three things that every student should do before graduating from Trinity are "to dress all out for the Disco Inferno, to go to the Wadsworth Atheneum, and to play an intramural sport."

One thing I'd like to have known before coming here is "that I'd have to revamp my wardrobe to be completely J.Crew and Abercrombie, or risk social exile."

United States Coast Guard Academy

Address: 31 Mohegan Avenue; New London, CT 06320-4195
Phone: 860-444-8501
E-mail address: uscgatr@dseg.uscga.edu
Web site URL: www.cga.edu
Founded: 1876
Private or Public: public
Religious affiliation: none
Location: suburban
Undergraduate enrollment: 830
Total enrollment: 830
Percent Male/Female: 72%/28%
Percent Minority: 8%
Percent African-American: 3%
Percent Asian: 1%

Percent Hispanic: 3%
Percent Native-American: 0.5%
Percent in-state/out-of-state: 6%/94%
Percent Pub HS: NA
Number of Applicants: 5,458
Percent Accepted: 10%
Percent Accepted who enroll: 62%
Entering: 326
Transfers: 0
Application Deadline: 15 Dec
Mean SAT: 614 V, 643 M
Mean ACT: 26
Middle 50% SAT range: 570–660 V, 600–670 M

Middle 50% ACT range: 25–29
3 Most popular majors: government, civil engineering, marine science
Retention: 89%
Graduation rate: 75%
On-campus housing: 100%
Fraternities: NA
Sororities: NA
Library: 180,000 volumes
Tuition and Fees: paid for by US Government in; paid for by US Government out
Room and Board: paid for by US Government
Financial aid, first-year: 0%

The United States Coast Guard Academy is not your average college. Life at the academy emphasizes military life, not social life. Although it's not for everyone, it offers the attractive combination of strong academics and an eventual career as a United States Coast Guard officer.

The academy offers eight major courses of study, including civil engineering, electrical engineering, mechanical engineering, naval architecture and marine engineering, marine and environmental sciences, operations research, and government and management (the only two non-engineering majors). Government is said to be the easiest major, but "that's just because it's tough to fail someone when they're writing papers interpreting things," one cadet said. However, cadets say all of the majors are challenging, mainly because cadets must balance military obligations, academics, and sports.

Coast Guard Courses

All cadets must take a set of core courses. The freshman curriculum includes Calculus I and II, Chemistry I and II, Organiza-

tional Behavior and Leadership, Nautical Science, Introduction to Engineering and Design, English Composition and Speech, among others. Essentially, cadets spend their freshman and sophomore years fulfilling the necessary requirements. Cadets must maintain a 2.0 cumulative GPA to remain at the academy, but it's also possible to make up failed core courses. Classes are small and range from 25 to 40 students. All are taught by professors. Courses also can be taken at Connecticut College, across the street from the academy. Most internships and training take place during the summers at Coast Guard stations or aboard ships.

The academy is a functioning Coast Guard base and is small compared to most college campuses. Built mainly in the 1930s, the buildings are brick and the landscape is meticulously kept. The hilly grounds fit "just beautifully against the background of the Thames River," according to one cadet. Regardless of rank, all cadets must live on academy grounds, in Chase Hall, the barracks/dorm. Rooms and roommates are reassigned every semester. Most cadets live in doubles; the few available singles go to lucky upper-classmen. Keeping the modestly furnished rooms spotless is a never-ending task, and aside from monthly formal inspection, cadets can receive demerits from wandering upperclassmen who spot a messy room. The emphasis on cleanliness and organization is reportedly designed to help future Coast Guard officers adapt to the close quarters that are the norm on a ship.

Before beginning your academic career at the academy, you must first survive the grueling six weeks of summer training known as "Swab Summer," which is organized and run by the junior class. During this time, the "swabs," or pre-freshmen, perform rifle drills, march, run obstacle courses, and learn military courtesy and customs. One cadet described the process as an "intense indoctrination into the military," an experience that is challenging mentally, physically, and emotionally. After the successful completion of swab summer, the pre-freshmen become fourth-class cadets and begin the rigorous academic schedule.

> **Cadets must balance military obligations, academics, and sports.**

A typical day at the USCGA begins with morning formations at 6:20 A.M. Breakfast is at 6:40, and by 7:40 the cadets await personal inspection, when the shine on their shoes and the creases in their uniforms are checked carefully. The academic day continues from 8 A.M. to 3:40 P.M. and is followed by two hours of mandatory athletic activity. Dinner is served from 5 to 7 P.M. and is followed by a mandatory study period from 8 to 10 P.M., during which students either study in their own rooms, the library, or classroom buildings. At 10 P.M., when "Taps" is played, all cadets must be back in their rooms.

All cadets eat in the wardroom (the cafeteria) and are required to attend breakfast and lunch. These meals are eaten "family-style" in tables of ten with a mixture of all classes, freshmen through seniors. Dinner attendance is optional, except for freshmen: upper-class cadets can eat in the wardroom or take out using plastic containers. On the whole, cadets offer no complaints about the cuisine, although fourth-class cadets say meals are difficult because they must eat "braced up," without looking at their food. All meals are paid for by the academy, but cadets can eat off campus or order food from local fast-food restaurants. Plenty of fast-food joints and restaurants are located close by, and according to one cadet, "Campus Pizza is the big cadet hangout."

Academy Activities

The academy offers a variety of clubs, and most cadets participate in at least one or two. These include several campus bands, singing groups, a debate team, student government, and a political affairs association. Cadets interested in journalism publish a monthly magazine, the *Howling Gale*, and a yearbook, Tide Rips. However, the focus remains on academics, military life, and sports. The Coast Guard Bears compete in NCAA Division III. The Merchant Marine Academy is the big rival, and the two football teams compete every year for the Secretary's Cup. "Since everyone here is pretty athletic, we usually have good records," one student said. Cadets have a strong school spirit, and leading the way is the academy's mascot, the bear, which is affectionately referred to as "Obje" (the name is derived from "objectionable," the label the Humane Society gave to the academy's former practice of keeping a live bear mascot in a pen). Every cadet at the academy must participate in intercollegiate or intramural sports each year.

Life of Discipline

The social sphere is where the academy differs the greatest from most other colleges. Although cadets must remain on campus for most of the week, "liberty," or free time, allows them to venture off-campus occasionally for a break from the military regime. Underclassmen (juniors and below) cannot have cars and cannot leave campus until Friday night. Seniors get one night off a week, but can earn more. On the weekend, cadets only have time off until midnight on Fridays, 1 A.M. on Saturdays, and 8 P.M. on Sundays. Cadets say drugs and alcohol do not exist on campus. "We do have plenty of mixers and formal dances, though," reported one cadet. The towns of New London and Groton provide adequate distractions for cadets, and New York City, Boston, and Newport are also close enough (each less than two hours away) for road trips.

Upon graduation from the academy, the new officers of the Coast Guard patrol the seas while participating in such activities as drug enforcement, rescues, and protection of the American people in peacetime. Cadets are required to serve five years after graduation, and many stay on past their period of mandatory service. Cadets strongly suggest that prospective students visit the academy before making a commitment, because it's not for everyone. They point out that although the life they live at the U.S. Coast Guard Academy is a disciplined one, rewards and opportunities are many. —*Melissa Droller and Staff*

FYI

The three best things about attending the Academy are "the academics here are very strong, the sports is great, and you gain a strong sense of discipline and achievement at the Academy."

The three worst things about attending the Academy are "6:30 A.M. roll call, the mandatory meetings we have, and trying to keep your uniform clean during meals."

The three things that every student should do before graduating from the Academy are "to join an extracurricular club (on top of everything else we already have), to head out to New York City or Boston one weekend, and hang out at Campus Pizza for hours."

One thing I'd like to have known before coming here is "there is no alcohol, only water."

University of Connecticut

Address: 2131 Hillside Road, U-88; Storrs, CT 06268-3088
Phone: 860-486-3137
E-mail address: beahusky@uconn.edu
Web site URL: www.uconn.edu
Founded: 1881
Private or Public: public
Religious affiliation: none
Location: rural
Undergraduate enrollment: 11,987
Total enrollment: 15,936
Percent Male/Female: 47%/53%
Percent Minority: 16%
Percent African-American: 5%

Percent Asian: 6%
Percent Hispanic: 4%
Percent Native-American: 0.5%
Percent in-state/out-of-state: 83%/17%
Percent Pub HS: NA
Number of Applicants: 11,781
Percent Accepted: 70%
Percent Accepted who enroll: 36%
Entering: 2,956
Transfers: 443
Application Deadline: 1 Mar
Mean SAT: 562 V, 573 M
Mean ACT: NA

Middle 50% SAT range: 510–610 V, 520–620 M
Middle 50% ACT range: NA
3 Most popular majors: psychology, English, human development and family relations
Retention: 86%
Graduation rate: 68%
On-campus housing: 96%
Fraternities: 11%
Sororities: 5%
Library: 2,475,851 volumes
Tuition and Fees: $5,404 in; $13,922 out
Room and Board: $5,694
Financial aid, first-year: 74%

Could you cheer, "GO, HUSKIES!" for one of the nation's finest basketball teams? Perhaps you are also interested in a solid liberal arts education at an affordable price? If so, the growing athletic and educational programs at the University of Connecticut might have just what you are looking for.

A Broad Education

Undergraduates at the University of Connecticut are offered a comprehensive education and the freedom to choose classes that best suit their interests. All students must fulfill requirements for the core curriculum by taking credits in a variety of disciplines, including art, science, philosophy, and computer science. Most meet these requirements by sophomore year and feel that the core classes help rather than hinder the education process: "It's great being able to take classes in so many interesting subject areas that we want to learn about and have them count towards graduation." The level of technological advancement at UConn is also highly beneficial to its students. Most classrooms are equipped with Internet access, and many classes are run primarily through the Internet; students are even able to observe on-screen research occurring in a separate facility on campus.

By their junior year, students must apply to one of nine schools of specialized study. Undergraduates finish their years at UConn with the majority of their remaining classes taken within the focus of their school. The schools of pharmacy, engineering, and physical therapy are three of the most popular of the specialized schools. The business school is not only very popular, but also very widely recognized on campus, because "the econ department at UConn is really awesome." When it comes to class size, there are a fair number of large introductory lectures, but the average class size ranges from 18 to 25 students. For those seeking smaller classes and more difficult work, a challenging honors program is available. Overall, as one sophomore put it, "I feel the university has some very good teachers here, but at such a big school, it's always up to the student to make the most of it all."

Where to Live, What to Eat?

Dormitories are both single-sex and coed, consisting of high-rises as well as smaller buildings. The majority of the rooms are doubles, with some singles and triples. Upper- and lowerclassmen are mixed in the dorms, allowing for integration and bonding among the classes. Floor regulations are relatively lax. As long as alcoholic beverages are not carried in their original containers, residential advisors usually do not bother students. Many students do complain, however, that dorms are barely in satisfactory condition due to a lack of upkeep and renovation. "Our living conditions aren't the best; you're lucky if you can get to live in the recently built dorms on South Campus," commented one undergrad. Buckley and Shippe (an all-female dorm) are considered two of the better dorms available. As freshmen, many students choose to live and party together in "the jungle"—a dorm on North Campus rumored to throw wild parties. A good number of upperclassmen live in apartments and houses off campus. The apartments are not very close to class buildings and can be expensive. Off-campus houses include Blue, White, Yellow, Brick, Stone, and Fire Houses.

> "I thought there'd be much less of a social life here because of the location, but that's not the case at all."

In regard to food, "the meal plan itself is fine; it's the food that sucks." Another student stated just as plainly, "The dining halls serve food that you really just shouldn't eat." Although the food may be horrible, students enjoy the luxury of having an on-campus creamery that offers delicious fresh-made ice cream and milk. Located in rural Storrs, UConn is a virtually self-sufficient campus: on-campus stores and facilities meet most students' needs. "We're in the middle of cow country, but that's not really a problem," remarked one undergrad.

Partying, for Sure—but That's Not All

Well-known as a party school, UConn does not disappoint. Fraternities, sororities, and the Rugby House are all notorious for their huge parties. Students also head to Carriage House and Celeron apartments to let loose. Popular hangouts on campus are Ted's, a restaurant; Civic Pub, a pool hall/bar; and Huskies, a bar/dance club. Although alcohol is the central focus of the party scene, non-drinkers do not feel left out, as UConn's social activities include much more than just alcohol and parties. The campus is a popular stop on the tours of many famous entertainers, such as Jewel, Reel Big Fish, Harry Belafonte, and David Spade. The Student Union sponsors weekly dances and movie nights, while the Student Union Board of Governors (SUBG) plans such large events as homecoming weekend, a winter party, and spring fling weekend. "I thought there'd be much less of a social life here because of the location, but that's not the case at all," insisted one sophomore.

Extracurricular activities and service-oriented clubs also play a major part in the non-academic pursuits of undergraduates at the University of Connecticut. Varied opportunities exist to accommodate the full range of interests. Students can play in bands and sing in groups, join political unions, or write for the *Daily Campus* newspaper. Many undergrads join the Student Union Board of Governors to voice their opinion in the student government, while other students choose to pledge fraternities and sororities in order to be part of a more tight-knit community. The Public Interest Research Group (PIRG) is a protest group focused on improving government environmental issues. Other outlets of service allow students to volunteer with children, the elderly, and the state government in nearby Hartford, Connecticut's capital.

Not Just Basketball

Ranking among the top teams in the nation, UConn's men's and women's basketball teams have recently been major contenders for both the NCAA Division I Big East Conference and national championships. The two teams command the spirit of the students who fill the stands of Gampel Pavilion to cheer for UConn's primary sports teams. In recent years, men's and women's soccer have also become increasingly popular, as has football. In an effort to upgrade the football team to Division I-A status, UConn and the state of Connecticut finalized budget approvals to construct a state-of-the-art football facility. For those students not involved in a varsity sport, intramurals are a great way to be involved in sports.

The University of Connecticut is an excellent example of a school that offers top-notch athletic and educational programs as well as a great social atmosphere—all at a very affordable price.
—*Victoria Yen*

FYI

The three best things about attending UConn are "the local bars, the great people, and, of course, the basketball games."

The three worst things about attending UConn are "the hills on campus, the long distance to good shopping, and walking past the cow pasture."

The three things that every student should do before graduating from UConn are "go to a basketball game, of course; go to the big party at X-lot on spring weekend; and take the train to New York City."

One thing I'd like to have known before coming here is "that you can party every day of the week if you want."

Wesleyan University

Address: 70 Wyllys Avenue; Middletown, CT 06459-0265
Phone: 860-685-3000
E-mail address: admissions@wesleyan.edu
Web site URL: www.wesleyan.edu
Founded: 1831
Private or Public: private
Religious affiliation: none
Location: suburban
Undergraduate enrollment: 2,734
Total enrollment: 2,900
Percent Male/Female: 48%/52%
Percent Minority: 23%
Percent African-American: 9%

Percent Asian: 7%
Percent Hispanic: 6%
Percent Native-American: 0.5%
Percent in-state/out-of-state: 9%/91%
Percent Pub HS: 58%
Number of Applicants: 6,402
Percent Accepted: 29%
Percent Accepted who enroll: 39%
Entering: 732
Transfers: 70
Application Deadline: 1 Jan
Mean SAT: 666 V, 658 M
Mean ACT: 28

Middle 50% SAT range: 640–730 V, 640–720 M
Middle 50% ACT range: NA
3 Most popular majors: English, government, economics
Retention: 96%
Graduation rate: 78%
On-campus housing: 100%
Fraternities: 4%
Sororities: 3%
Library: 1,200,000 volumes
Tuition and Fees: $25,120 in; $25,120 out
Room and Board: $6,510
Financial aid, first-year: 50%

You are watching *PCU*, the movie. The camera pans over a beautiful college campus of dignified ivy-covered buildings and a chapel. You wonder, Is there really a college campus that looks like that? Indeed there is. Go to Wesleyan University and you will recognize that the scene was a scroll across Wesleyan's college row. The ivy-covered buildings include the psychology department building, the 92 Theatre, and the administration buildings (North and South College).

A Comfortable Learning Environment

Freshman year begins with a special orientation program in which students have the option of community service or a two-day camping adventure. A great way to meet others, the program is also intended to give students the feeling that they can accomplish anything: "It definitely put me in the right frame of mind going into first semester freshman year." Meeting the general educational requirements is probably less challenging. In order to graduate, undergraduates at Wesleyan must take two classes in natural sciences, two in behavioral and social sciences, and two in arts and humanities. For students, these requirements are considered "very few, almost non-existent." As one sophomore describes it, "The dearth of requirements really allows the student to pursue any academic venture unimpeded . . . one of the beauties of attending this small, liberal college."

For students who want to be challenged, there are two interdisciplinary programs to which they may apply during their sophomore year. The College of Letters combines work in English, writing, and languages, while the College of Social Studies, which has earned the nickname "College of Suicidal Sophomores," focuses on history, philosophy, political science, and sociology. There is also the Science and Society program, which enables participants to double-major in one natural and one social science simultaneously or to concentrate solely on science and medicine and their implications in society. Even though students feel their workload can be overwhelming at times, Wesleyan does not have a very competitive environment. Students feel that they are there to genuinely help one another and that they "have the privilege of going to school with extremely intelligent people but are not hampered by the competitiveness that is often detrimental to students at other schools." Getting into classes is not really a problem: "If you want a class badly enough, odds are you will be able to get in." The "drop and add period" also helps students take the classes they may originally have been denied. For freshmen, the First-Year Initiative Program affords the opportunity to take small seminar classes in several departments, enabling them to get to know professors early on in their college years. This program is just an example of how intimate the academic environment is at Wesleyan: "Undergrads really do get a lot of individualized attention here; it's a common reason why many students choose Wesleyan over Ivy League schools."

A Good Time for All

Weekends offer almost every type of student the opportunity to get out, meet people, and have a good time. And since the surrounding area of Middletown has little to offer students and is not considered by many to be the safest of places, most students stick around on weekends, making campus life busy and exciting.

The partying and drinking scenes are based in the fraternity and residential houses. Each weekend, several fraternities and residential houses throw parties that are open to all students. Fraternities are "ridiculously easy" to rush because not many people really want to rush. "I rushed for a few days and instead of being hazed, it seemed more of a courtship; they need you to keep the frat going," quipped one student. "We only use them for the dancing, drinking, and grinding," said another. According to students, being underage is "HA-HA, not a problem at all." "Freshmen are welcome anywhere," said one such freshman, "whether it be a frat house or a house party—or if that is not your cup of tea, you can take in a show, go to a concert." The general rule of the administration about alcohol seems to be "if they don't see it, they don't care." Besides the weekly parties, big events such as the Fall Ball, Spring Fling, Homecoming, Halloween Dance, Screw-Your-Roommate Dances, and the '80s theme dance also draw big crowds throughout the year.

All kinds of couples find acceptance at Wesleyan. There are many homosexual and interracial couples and, according to students, they are accepted on campus. When it comes to dating, however, well . . . there is none. One student woefully reported, "I am an ex–Homecoming King, and I haven't been on a date in a year." Meaningful relationships tend to become marriagelike, while "random hookups are what make the party world go round."

Great Housing, Not-So-Bad Meal Plans

Freshman dorms are scattered throughout the campus, but most freshmen reside in Clark and Butterfield Halls. They can also live in Wesco, where the residents do not have to wear clothes (some call it "the naked dorm") or on "well-being" floors, which specifically forbid any use of drugs and alcohol. The rooms range from nice-sized singles to quads, and some rooms even have balconies. One residential advisor lives on each floor of each dorm. For the most part, students report that the RAs allow you to do whatever you want: "They aim to be a friend and usually end up to be. They are really no different from any of the other residents." Floors and bathrooms are coed, but students can vote for the latter not to be.

> "If there weren't decent vegetarian options here, the student body would mobilize and protest; that is what we do at Wesleyan."

After freshman year, students enter a lottery for housing, either with the group of people they want to live with or alone if they want a single. In this lottery, drawn in order of seniority, each student or group gets to list housing preferences. Upperclassmen also have the option of living in residential houses, some of which cater to particular interests. For example, students can live in the Malcolm X House, La Casa, the Gay and Lesbian House, or one of a few literary societies.

Most students feel that "the food's not too too bad, especially since there are many options." As freshmen, students choose between plans consisting of either 19 meals per week or 13 meals per week and flex points. The meals can be eaten in a few places, the most popular of which is Mocon, the McConaugh cafeteria, which always offers a salad bar, a deli car, and a buffet of hot foods. Flex points can be used at various on-campus eateries and mini–grocery stores. The points can also be used at the supermarket for students who want to make the food themselves. As upperclassmen, students have even more meal plan opportunities, including a completely point-based plan. Diners nearby are also very popular among students at Wesleyan. Athenian is one such diner that is open late and "perfect for an omelet when you are not all there . . . if you know what I mean." There is also the renowned Oroukes Diner, which makes "a mean breakfast."

A Passion and Energy— Outside of Class

When not in class, Wesleyan students put their passion and energy to work: "People tend to do things that make them stand out and show that they aren't just another smart kid." Wesleyan boasts more than 180 undergraduate organizations, many of which perform community service in Middletown. A cappella groups, theater troupes, and the student newspaper, *Argus*, are among the most popular student activities. "Activities here are awesome because they give you something to do and people to know without forcing you to identify yourself as one type of person," remarked one student. In short, nearly anyone could find his or her niche in the extracurricular world of Wesleyan.

Athletes at Wesleyan are recruited but maintain a low profile. Wesleyan sports fans, however, take their sports very seriously, and several teams have recently met with great success. Football, crew, and Ultimate Frisbee are particularly hard-core competitive teams. The teams also foster different traditions as well as close friendships. One soccer player recounts: "We soccer folk, the night before the first game [of the year], strip down to our nakedness, run laps, and take penalty kicks. It is a real bonding experience." Those interested in participating in athletics on a less competitive level can choose from a large and active array of non-competitive club and intramural sports at the Freeman Athletic Center, which was built a few years ago and has "an amazing pool and field house."

The Wesleyan campus is very diverse and open to virtually any sort of personality or activity: "Kids are really laid-back; no one cares what you look like. It's a comfortable, accepting, awesome environment." Many students even claim that the idea of being politically correct began at Wesleyan and that *PCU* was written with Wesleyan in mind. As one student asserted, "If there weren't decent vegetarian options here, the student body would mobilize and protest; that is what we do at Wesleyan." —*Victoria Yen*

FYI
The three best things about attending Wesleyan are "the low-key environment, the easy access to both New York and Boston, and the great academic atmosphere."
The three worst things about attending Wesleyan are "Middletown, Middletown, and a tie between Middletown and the dining hall food."
The three things that every student should do before graduating from Wesleyan are "study abroad, take advantage of all the programs, both academic and extracurricular, and spend time on Foss Hill in the spring (it's easy to get wrapped up in schoolwork, but one afternoon on Foss Hill will remind you what college is really about)."
One thing I'd like to have known before coming here is "how accepting the student body really is."

Yale University

Address: PO Box 208234;
New Haven, CT 06520-
8234
Phone: 203-432-9300
E-mail address:
undergraduate.admissions
@yale.edu
Web site URL:
www.yale.edu
Founded: 1701
Private or Public: private
Religious affiliation: none
Location: urban
**Undergraduate
enrollment:** 5,413
Total enrollment: 11,059
Percent Male/Female:
51%/49%
Percent Minority: 29%

Percent African-American:
7%
Percent Asian: 15%
Percent Hispanic: 6%
Percent Native-American:
0.5%
**Percent in-state/out-of-
state:** 10%/90%
Percent Pub HS: 54%
Number of Applicants:
13,270
Percent Accepted: 16%
**Percent Accepted who
enroll:** 64%
Entering: 1,371
Transfers: 30
Application Deadline:
31 Dec
Mean SAT: 720 V, 730 M

Mean ACT: NA
Middle 50% SAT range: NA
Middle 50% ACT range: NA
3 Most popular majors:
biology, history, economics
Retention: 98%
Graduation rate: 85%
On-campus housing:
100%
Fraternities: NA
Sororities: NA
Library: 10,800,000
volumes
Tuition and Fees:
$25,220 in; $25,220 out
Room and Board:
$7,660
Financial aid, first-year:
66%

T hanksgiving Weekend heightens
Yalies' school spirit like nothing
else. Generations of alumni and
students gather together to cheer their
football team to victory against their Cambridge archrival in one of the most anticipated events of the year, the Yale–Harvard
football game, commonly referred to as
simply "the Game." Shirts, hats, and ban-
ners emblazoned with the blue "Y" dot the
landscape. The festivities in the stands and
at the tailgates outside the stadium are a
strong display of the solidarity, spirit, and
dynamism that pervade the campus of one
of the nation's premier institutions, long
after the Game weekend is over.

Located in the Elm City neighborhood
of New Haven, Connecticut, the Yale campus offers undergraduates a glimpse of
city living without sacrificing the intimacy
of a suburban campus. "That is, if you
would go so far as to call this a city,
though it's certainly not one of your nicer
ones," said one student. Modeled after England's Oxford and Cambridge Universities, Yale's large Gothic buildings loom
beside both Georgian and modern architectural styles. Many students are quick to
call Yale "your quintessentially charming
traditional New England campus." But
this prominent liberal arts university pro-

vides more than just a beautiful campus
for the enthusiastic undergraduates who
matriculate each year.

A Rigorous Academic Pace

The incoming freshman class learns very
quickly about the pace and rigor of academic life at Yale. Yale requires 36 course
credits for graduation, compared to the
standard 32 at other Ivy League schools.
Still, many Yalies end up exceeding the 36-
course requirement by graduation, finding
themselves overwhelmed by the sheer
volume of classes available in the "Blue
Book" (the Yale College Programs of
Study). As one junior stated, "Poring over
the Blue Book and making decisions
about my courses gets harder each term. I
just need a few more semesters to take all
the classes I like!" A two-week-long period at the beginning of each semester
helps student make the right choices. During that time, students can "shop" as many
different classes as they want without
making an official commitment. While
some students use shopping period as an
extension of their vacation, many consider it a "great way to try to see as much
of what Yale academics have to offer to
make sure you don't get stuck taking
something you will regret later."

And the choices do not end there. Each semester, the university offers a full spread of residential college seminars, small classes taught by visiting professors, grad students, or individuals in the community. Recent topics have included the physics of baseball, writing portraits, and capital punishment and criminal justice in the United States. Pre-frosh also have the option of applying to one of two special programs for first-year students. The Perspectives on Science program is a lecture and discussion course designed for freshmen who are strong in math and science, and the Directed Studies program is a writing-intensive yearlong interdisciplinary program in the humanities. The latter program, often labeled "Directed Suicide," requires a particularly high reading load and weekly papers that keep many "DS-ers" chained to their desks on Thursday nights.

Students definitely love the academic freedom Yale's curriculum offers. There are no core curriculum requirements. Instead, students must take three classes in four major subject groups, roughly divided into language and literature, history, social science, and natural science, and complete two years of study in a foreign language. Students can waive the language requirement by demonstrating proficiency on a Yale-administered test or on the AP exam. The Yale proficiency exams are reportedly very difficult, though. "I took six years of Spanish before coming to Yale, and I left the proficiency test wondering whether I had learned Portuguese by mistake," one sophomore said.

Aside from these basic requirements, Yale students are encouraged to experiment and take classes in as many different departments as they wish before officially choosing their major at the beginning of junior year. Popular majors include history, English, molecular biophysics and biochemistry (MB&B, the "pre-med major"), political science, economics, and psychology. Yale is particularly strong in history and English but "pathetically lacking" in ethnic studies and women's and gender studies course offerings. One student lamented: "You'd think that with as much money as it has, Yale could afford to get with it—I mean it's the twenty-first century." Slowly but surely, the administration is attempting to do just that. Thanks to a recent donation, Yale has commenced construction of a $500 million Science Park. This project will provide new science facilities and update many existing labs. The initiative will also result in the hiring of more faculty and researchers to utilize the technologically advanced facilities. This move, and others like it, shows Yale's support for the sciences.

Yale also has its share of "guts." As one senior noted, "If there is one thing I have learned, it's that you have to strike a happy medium with your courses. Unless you want to pitch a tent in the library all term, then you need at least one class you can let slide." Electrical Engineering 101, The History of Jazz, and Astronomy 110 are among the more popular "fluff" courses. The Credit/D/Fail option is also a popular way to lighten the pressure of rigorous academics and encourage experimentation in new areas without the fear of a "crummy grade."

According to many Yalies, one of the highlights of the academics is the chance to learn from some of the most important scholars in academia. Students often look to such star professors as history's John Gaddis ("Mr. Cold War"), history of art's Vincent Scully ("his fervor for art is infectious"), history's Jonathan Spence ("think brilliant Chinese history scholar who looks like Sean Connery"), and the English department's Harold Bloom ("the man has written literary criticism of every great piece of literature you can think of"). Undergrads particularly comment on the strong degree of student–faculty interaction, citing regular office hours as "one of the best ways to get to know profs more personally."

There is no shortage of places on campus where students can study. Many find themselves working amid the intricate woodwork, arches, and cathedral ceilings of Sterling Memorial Library, the recently renovated "researcher's dream." The Yale library collection is the second–largest in the nation, and its 10 million volumes are housed in almost 40 libraries spread across campus. For those undergraduates who prefer to study closer to home, the residential colleges each have their own libraries, which are open 24 hours a day.

Each library is lined with shelves of books donated by each college's respective alumni. They cover a wide range of topics and time periods. Many of them even date back to the 1800s. One student recalls having picked up a random book off the shelf and seeing that it was more than 150 years old: "I remember I couldn't believe they had just left it lying around like that."

Residential College Life

Just about every aspect of life at Yale is influenced by the residential college system. Before arriving at Yale, freshmen are randomly assigned to one of the 12 residential colleges, where they will live beginning sophomore year. Each college has a distinctive architectural style and tradition. For example, Pierson is Georgian, while Branford and Jonathan Edwards, among others, are Gothic. Each residential college is overseen by a master and academic dean, both of whom live and work within the college. While the deans oversee student academics, masters often work closely with the college councils and student activities committees to improve student life.

> "Unless you want to pitch a tent in the library all term, then you need at least one class you can let slide."

Residential colleges are equipped with their own dining halls, music rooms, snack bars, computing facilities, laundry rooms, TV rooms, exercise facilities, and college kitchens. Some colleges have special features such as Davenport's darkroom, Silliman's movie theater ("Silliflicks"), Branford's printing press, Jonathan Edwards' racquetball court, Berkeley's woodshop, and Calhoun's sauna. Facilities range from "ghetto" to "brand-spanking-new." Dorming conditions also vary markedly across colleges, though generally students live in quads their sophomore year and doubles and singles their junior and senior years. Most rooms follow the same basic layout—single and double bedrooms set off a common room marked by poor overhead lighting and "ratty old" radiators.

But that is set to change soon. Nineteen-ninety-eight marked the beginning of a 12-year, $1 billion project to renovate the residential colleges, starting with Berkeley College and moving on to the rest of the colleges one at a time. While Saybrook is being renovated during the 2000–2001 school year, Saybrugians live in a newly constructed dorm, informally called "Swing Space," complete with small kitchenettes, great overhead lighting, and private bathrooms with bathtubs. Many students would say it "looks just like a hotel." When the Saybrugians move back into their college next year, the structural integrity of their college will have remained the same, but the interior and underground basement areas will have been completely renovated, with reconfigured rooms, generous lighting, and air-conditioned common areas. Students in Berkeley, the first college to be renovated, rave about the improvements. One sophomore was so enthusiastic about the changes that she exclaimed, "I don't want to graduate; I'll just enjoy my spacious room-with-a-view for the rest of my life."

Students have a love-hate relationship with the college system. Some love it, calling it a great "support system for students" giving individuals a small-college feel within the larger university community. Others complain that it "makes maintaining friendships with people in other colleges more work" and is annoying because students can only room with other people in their respective colleges, which, in one student's words, "can really suck." Every year, a handful of students do transfer colleges, but for the most part, students stay where they are assigned, if only because transferring can be a hassle. Each college has its own reputation—Calhoun is known as the "rich college," Davenport the "legacy college," and Pierson the "jock college." The colleges carry on a friendly intercollegiate rivalry, a reality that becomes readily apparent at intramurals sports (IMs) and varsity football games (where members of each college invariably sit together, wave their college flags, and shout insults at the other colleges).

Yalies generally associate strongly with their colleges, and social interaction is often centered on the residential college system. Annual parties such as the Silliman Safety Dance (an immensely popular all-'80s revival), the Pierson Inferno (a Halloween costume ball), Exotic Erotic (Timothy Dwight's "the less you wear, the less you pay"), and the Morse and Stiles Casino Night (a formal '20s event) are all sponsored by the residential colleges. The Holiday Balls are also a favorite student event, as each college hires either a band or a disc jockey and students dress up and "ball-hop" from college to college over the course of a single night.

Yalies, All Dork Losers?

The social scene at Yale also revolves in large part around non–college-sponsored events. As one junior stated, "One of the biggest misconceptions about Yale is that we are all dork losers who hate a good time and are too busy saving the world or padding our resumés. It's just not true. There is a definitely hard-core party network of people who love to let loose," though it's a common complaint the same people go to all the parties. Events such as Alpha Epsilon Pi's Jell-O Night, Swing Dance parties, Naples nights, and Co-op Dances (sponsored by the Lesbian, Gay, Bisexual and Transgendered Cooperative at Yale) draw a large crowd of Yalies on Friday and Saturday nights. Students also show their support for student drama productions, dance performances, a cappella concerts, and musical performances. The more popular productions include the Yale Symphony Orchestra's Halloween Extravaganza, the Anti-Gravity Society's Fire Show, Rhythmic Blue's contemporary dance show, and anything with Shades, without a doubt the "coolest singing group at Yale." Other cultural venues in the area are the Yale Repertory Theater, which offers special student discounts, as well as the Yale University Art Gallery (complete with a van Gogh, Degas, and lots of Edward Hopper), British Art Center (the largest collection of British art outside of Great Britain), and Peabody Museum (featuring one of the world's few *T-rex* dinosaur skeletons). Students can also catch a movie at nearby York Square Cinema, which primarily shows "artsy" films, with only a smattering of first-run movies. The Yale Film Society regularly offers better movies for a few bucks, so many students will opt to take advantage of those screenings instead. Still, for many students, York Square is a "favorite date spot for those of us who actually do the dating thing."

Several Yalies point to a prominent casual hookup scene as the only alternative to a "meager" dating environment. "You either have zip in the relationship department or something really long and intense. There isn't much in between," one student remarked. Many Yalies are so committed to their academics and extracurricular activities that "essentially dating gets lost in the shuffle."

A typical weekend for Yalies involves a visit to one of the area's great restaurants as an alternative to dining hall food. As one junior noted, "One of the best things about living here is being able to break out of the dining hall doldrums and enjoy either Thai, Mexican, Japanese, Chinese, Italian, French, Cajun, American, or Middle Eastern fare." Some of the most popular dinner destinations in New Haven include Scoozi's, Thai Taste, Rainbow Gardens, Consiglio's, and Union League. Some places can get pretty pricey, though, so to appease late-night cravings on a budget, students frequent Au Bon Pain, Copper Kitchen, Durfee's, Yorkside Pizza, Krauszer's, and Gourmet Heaven (the last two both open 24 hours). Students will also frequent nightspots such as Viva's, Kavanaugh's, Gecko's, Richter's, BAR, and Toad's Place, a nightclub located right on campus and once honored by *Rolling Stone* magazine as one of the best clubs in America.

Neighborhood shopping is limited. According to one student, "You got Gap and Ann Taylor—and not much else." That is soon to change, however. A Yale branch of the popular clothiers Urban Outfitters is slated to open next academic year. Developers have long toyed with the idea of building an upscale shopping mall near campus, but such plans have been shot down for the moment. Still, fairly decent nearby mall shopping can be found by those students with cars.

Passion, Action, and Drive

But partying and studying aren't the only things Yalies take seriously. Extracurricular commitments have a high priority for many students who want to "take a breather from work and give something back to Yale." Organizations abound on campus. Freshmen often find themselves inundated by the possibilities, particularly during the Freshman Bazaar in late August, when campus groups set up booths in Beinecke Plaza and vie for the first-years walking by. Student interests are varied, resulting in a mind-boggling number of extracurricular campus groups. Publications include the *Yale Daily News*, the nation's oldest college daily, and *Rumpus*, a humor paper/tabloid best-known for its "Yale's 50 Most Beautiful People" issue each fall. According to one student, roughly 18 a cappella singing groups exist at Yale, of which the Whiffenpoofs and the SOBs (Society of Orpheus and Bacchus) are the oldest in the nation. Debate and political organizations, including the Yale College Student Union, the Yale Debate Association, and the Yale College Mock Trial Association, are notoriously time-consuming. The campus religious presence is strong: groups like Yale Students for Christ (YSC), the Muslim Students Association (MSA), and Yale Christian Fellowship (YCF) are both visible and active. Community service organizations like TIES (Tutoring In Elementary Schools), Project SAT, and YHHAP (the Yale Hunger and Homelessness Action Project) also enjoy wide student participation.

Sports have a significant presence on campus, though some would say their popularity is limited to specific pockets of the Yale community. There are approximately 30 varsity teams, including traditional favorites such as football and ice hockey but also extremely successful fencing, crew, and squash teams for both men and women. Some varsity teams, such as lacrosse, tennis, soccer, and volleyball, were so popular that JV teams were recently established. There are also a wide variety of other club sports teams, including serious rugby and Ultimate Frisbee teams for both men and women, and informal badminton and croquet teams. In addition, there is a popular intramural sports program, in which students on residential college teams compete in fall, winter, and spring seasons for the prestigious "Tyng Cup."

A Yale Type?

Is there such a thing as a typical Yalie? According to one senior, "It's no big secret that Yale strives for diversity in its student body." Yalies come from all over the world, though the highest concentrations seem to come from the Northeast and California. One student complained, "I swear every other person here is from New York, New Jersey, or California." Though some students lament that "everyone seems to come from the same socioeconomic group," looking closer at the Yale body, one can find great variety ethnically, religiously, and geographically, as well as socially. Though it's taken Yale a long time, ethnic students would agree Yale is becoming a more diverse and minority-friendly place. The ethnic organizations on campus are still horrendously underfunded, but representatives report that the situation is gradually getting better. Cultural centers such as the Asian American Cultural Center, Casa Cultural Julia de Burgos, and the Af-Am House serve as gathering places for those respective communities.

Yalies love their school. One student gushed, "Every day I am struck by the awesome privilege I enjoy of being here in such a great community full of amazing people. There's nowhere else like it." Other students would agree that there is no place they'd rather spend "those bright college years," as the alma mater goes. Yale, they say, is the best of all possible worlds, characterized by unparalleled diversity, intellectual challenge, and passionate people who make life on this campus "the perfect conglomeration of the absolute best college has to offer."
—*Jane H. Hong and Staff*

FYI
The three best things about going to Yale are "you go to Yale! (need I say more?); the campus' proximity to New York; people are passionate about what they're doing. "
The three worst things about going to Yale are "New Haven, the incompetence of the registrar's office, the gross weather."
The three things that every student should do before graduating from Yale are "toast at Mory's, go to the Game, go to a Master's Tea or campus speaker series."
One thing I wish I'd known before coming to Yale is "that residential college life is so big."

Delaware

Address: Newark, DE
19716-6210
Phone: 302-831-8123
E-mail address:
admissions@udel.edu
Web site URL:
www.udel.edu
Founded: 1743
Private or Public:
Independent
Religious affiliation: none
Location: suburban
**Undergraduate
enrollment:** 15,463
Total enrollment: 18,230
Percent Male/Female:
41%/59%
Percent Minority: 12%
Percent African-American:
6%

Percent Asian: 3%
Percent Hispanic: 2%
Percent Native-American:
0.5%
**Percent in-state/out-of-
state:** 42%/58%
Percent Pub HS: 75%
Number of Applicants:
14,107
Percent Accepted:
63%
**Percent Accepted who
enroll:** 40%
Entering: 3,534
Transfers: NA
Application Deadline:
15 Feb
Mean SAT: 560 V,
575 M
Mean ACT: NA

Middle 50% SAT range:
520–610 V,
520–630 M
Middle 50% ACT range:
22–26
3 Most popular majors:
business management,
education, engineering
Retention: 87%
Graduation rate: 54%
On-campus housing: 0%
Fraternities: 15%
Sororities: 15%
Library: 2,300,000
volumes
Tuition and Fees:
$4,858 in; $13,228 out
Room and Board: $5,132
Financial aid, first-year:
44%

The University of Delaware is a large state college nestled in the rolling hills of picturesque Newark, Delaware. It is a place where intellectuals and frat boys co-exist in eternal bliss. As one Delaware freshman states, "we talk about everything from Heideggar to Heineken."

Rollin' with the Scholars— Academics

The University of Delaware offers the full range of the usual college majors. Particularly intense majors, according to some students, are Engineering, Visual Communication, Chemistry, and Physics. Chemical Engineering is of especial interest to many students since the DuPont Company endowed the university with millions of dollars resulting in a Chemical Engineering program that rivals the best technical schools in the United States. On the other end of the spectrum, for those not interested in masochism, the Psychol- ogy major is apparently a popular option for the slacker student population. But one student emphatically asserts that Delaware has "no joke majors."

In order to attract top-notch students the university has also implemented numerous programs. In particular, the Honors Program provides students with challenging classes in small settings. Honors students praise the close contact between students and professors that they enjoy.

The Jefferson Scholars program offers would-be doctors guidance and aid in applying to medical school and gives them a slight competitive edge. For minority students interested in engineering there is the RISE (Resources to Insure Successful Engineers) program, which offers them tutelage and career counseling. In addition to these programs Delaware also offers the Dean's Scholar Program whereby students can devise their own major.

When it comes to academic distributions Delaware students are fairly lucky. They are required only to fulfill basic core courses that include such courses as E110-otherwise known as Freshman English. Full time students are required to take 12 credits per semester but most studious Blue Hens opt for 15.

Although there are some large introductory courses, many students enjoy schedules where none of their classes have more than 30 or 35 students. Despite the perks of small classes and "incredible professors," one student complains that she has a mere 3.5 hours of sleep a night and has absolutely a "TON" of work.

To help students diminish the intensity of the workload the university offers a much taken-advantaged of "winter term" during which students remain in school to take classes during their incredibly long winter break. The university, however, does not require anyone to partake in this pseudo-semester.

Many would-be college students are greatly concerned about having TAs as teachers. At Delaware, many large lecture courses are actually taught by the professors but have TA s leading sections. But take heart, pre-frosh, there are some excellent professors at the University of Delaware including big names such as Robert Straight and Katherine Varnes who one student calls "absolutely incredible!"

Students love to relax at some of the university's most popular study locations. Morris Library is called "indispensable" by one student and the Chemistry, Physics, or Honors Centers are notoriously quiet locales ideal for the angst-ridden student. Overall, "The University of Delaware has a strong academic program. What you get out of it depends on how you treat the courses."

For those looking to kick back, there are also some nice off-campus hangouts that include the famous Klondike Kates and the ever hip Iron Hill Brewery. According to several sources the Hartsoe House, located in Nonantum Hills, is *the* location for popular parties and cool sounding music. Local musical talent includes Phil Lamplugh and his band *The Grieder's*. All three locations offer food and some places accept UD flex dollars whereby students "pay" for off-campus food with specially distributed UD cards. Many students complain about the meal plan and the varying quality of the food, as one student does by calling Delaware's meal plan an absolute "rip-off." Unfortunately, many students list dining hall food as one of the worst aspects of university life.

Getting Jiggy Wit It—The Social Scene

Social life at UD centers heavily on the drinking scene. According to some upperclassmen the freshman have been spotted in huge groups desperately trying to locate parties they hear about through the grapevine. The upperclassmen, on the other hand, are the ones who throw these much sought after parties. On a more serious note, drug use exists on campus, but it is not widespread and mainly consists of marijuana usage.

> "We talk about everything from Heidegger to Heineken."

There is a definite frat scene on campus and as much as 15% of UD students belong to either a frat or a sorority. For those interested in rushing frats or sororities, the process of joining one isn't difficult. According to students, the most popular frats and sororities are Sigma Chi and Alpha Zeta Delta. Though Greek life is a presence on campus, it is not an integral part of the social scene at UD.

For the serious daters on campus, dating is rare but according to one student, there is "a load of random hookups." Sex is apparently commonplace on campus and "attractive individuals," according to one sophomore girl, "abound." For students lucky enough to find a date, Klondike Kate's followed by a movie is always a popular option for burgeoning couples.

Students wary of the drinking scene have available to them a large number of on-campus non-alcoholic activities. There are frequent movie screenings, as well as "art under the stars."

It is very easy to meet new people on campus and most people form friendships with individuals from classes and activities. When asked about stereotypes of UD students, some boldly stated that none existed while others characterized their fellow classmates as "upper-middle class white kid beer guzzlers." Many students feel there is a definite categorization of the student body along the lines of athletes, Greeks, nerds, etc. A common complaint from the students centers on the lack of diversity at the school. Many students come from Delaware and the surrounding Mid-Atlantic States, so geographical diversity is not commonplace. As for racial diversity there is very little interracial mixing on campus but race relations are still described as "good."

Leaving Campus—Extracurriculars

Extracurricular life at Delaware is booming. When asked about the workload at Delaware one student replied that he was "swamped" with mainly extracurricular activities. Like any major state school Delaware has the ROTC, theater groups, and some singing groups. There is a very active Black Student Union, as well. The inter-varsity Christian Fellowship and the Greek groups are active in community service in and around Newark. Many students at Delaware enjoy actual paying jobs on and off the campus. Popular places of employment are clothing stores, restaurants, and on-campus jobs.

Of all extracurricular activities, the largest and most popular one at Delaware is athletics. Delaware has a superb men's basketball team that has reached the NCAA Tournament and helps drum up school support for the Fighting Blue Hens. The football team is also a popular source of school spirit. The opening game versus archrival West Chester University is always a fun-filled and exciting event for all involved.

Living it in UD

Housing problems, with the recent increase in the number of students, is one of the greatest problems on campus today. Last year, some students were forced to live in common rooms until suitable accommodations could be found. Freshmen describe the dorms as comfortable but certainly not "palaces." One dorm to particularly avoid is the Dickinson dormitory. The RAs at Delaware are notoriously strict and hand out offenses for underage drinking and other frowned upon dormitory activities. One RA claimed that Delaware RAs are as "strict as they have to be" in order to enforce the alcohol policy on campus despite the fact that many students maintain that alcohol still flows freely at Delaware.

Most upperclassmen move off campus and housing is apparently readily available to students in the Newark area. Some others choose, however, to live in the house of their respective fraternity or sorority. Theme houses, such as the French house, also exist on campus.

Ultimately, most students are content with their decision to attend the University of Delaware. With wonderful professors and interesting visiting speakers (from Chris Rock to Maya Angelou), the experiences students enjoy while at the University are extraordinary and "eye opening." Overall Delaware students are healthy, somewhat sober, and very, very wise. —*Sean McBride*

FYI

The three best things about attending The University of Delaware are "the Ethernet connection, the traffic stops for students, and every time you do work friends try to get you to go to a party."

The three worst things about attending The University of Delaware are "the parking, the meal plan, and the inadequate showers."

The three things every student should do before graduating from The University of Delaware are "learn how to take an ice block shot, walk around campus at night and appreciate the architecture and lighting, and visit Nonantum Mills."

One thing I wish I knew before coming here is "how many students there are from Jersey."

District of Columbia

American University

Address: 4400 Massachusetts Avenue NW; Washington, DC 20016-8001
Phone: 202-885-6000
E-mail address: afa@american.edu
Web site URL: www.american.edu
Founded: 1893
Private or Public: private
Religious affiliation: Methodist
Location: urban
Undergraduate enrollment: 5,161
Total enrollment: 10,894
Percent Male/Female: 39%/61%

Percent Minority: 16%
Percent African-American: 7%
Percent Asian: 3%
Percent Hispanic: 5%
Percent Native-American: 0.5%
Percent in-state/out-of-state: 5%/95%
Percent Pub HS: NA
Number of Applicants: 7,554
Percent Accepted: 74%
Percent Accepted who enroll: 21%
Entering: 1,203
Transfers: NA
Application Deadline: 1 Feb

Mean SAT: 604 V, 582 M
Mean ACT: 26
Middle 50% SAT range: NA
Middle 50% ACT range: NA
3 Most popular majors: international studies, political science, international business
Retention: 85%
Graduation rate: 65%
On-campus housing: 60%
Fraternities: NA
Sororities: NA
Library: 870,000 volumes
Tuition and Fees: $21,399 in; $21,399 out
Room and Board: $8,372
Financial aid, first-year: 47%

I f you are looking for an internationally diverse campus, then consider American University. The undergrad student body, made up of over 5,000 people, draws from over 150 countries. Located in the heart of urban Washington, D.C., American offers an international experience right in our nation's capital.

Small Classes, Great Variety

American University, or "AU" as it is called by students, places a strong emphasis on its core curriculum general education program. This program requires students to choose 10 specific courses in different disciplines. Out of the 120 credit hours necessary to graduate, this requirement doesn't seem too taxing. But although this program may sound fabulous on paper, many students complain that

there are too many required courses. If you have tons of AP credits, however, don't worry—the hours you spent slaving over European history and calc in high school pay off, and exemplary scores on AP tests place you out of many general education classes. As one student said, "I got lucky! I came to American with the equivalent of twenty-four credits from AP courses, which got me out of most of the GenEd requirements."

Students speak highly of the classes at AU. Most courses follow a Monday/Thursday or Tuesday/Friday schedule, with very few classes meeting on Wednesday. Because of the small class size, usually 20 to 25 in a course, students enjoy personalized attention from full professors. There are many different courses offered each year, but there are some perennial favorites. Although it is difficult to get into some of these classes, like Kevin Spacey's film course, most students are able to enroll in most of their first choices for other courses.

AU is divided into separate undergraduate schools. While some people think that international relations, at the School of International Service, is the most popular major, others believe that the government major, in the College of Arts and Sciences, is number one. One thing is certain—whether you are enrolled in those two schools or in the School of Public Affairs, the School of Communication, or the Kogod School of Business, the education is top-notch.

For those who want a challenging course of study, AU provides an honors program in addition to the regular course offerings. Acceptance to this program usually depends on SAT scores and high school GPA. But it is also possible to move into the honors program following the first semester of freshman year. One student said, "If you want to get As, you need to work a couple of hours each night. Then, you can get into the honors program." AU also provides an extensive program for study abroad. The World Capitals Program, which includes an intensive language study, core seminar, and predetermined internship, allows AU students to study in 17 cities around the world.

And needless to say, AU maximizes the value of its location—Washington, D.C. About half of the student population are involved in unpaid internship programs either on Capitol Hill or in local businesses. Many students cite these internships as the highlights of their weeks at AU. An enthusiastic student exclaimed, "I have an internship two days a week, and those two days are actually the highlight of my week!" These partnerships give students the ability to gain valuable exposure and experience in addition to receiving a great education.

Location, Location, Location

When asked to name the best thing about AU, most people give the same answer—"WASHINGTON, D.C.!" Whether they are shopping at Dupont Circle, grabbing a bite to eat in one of Georgetown's many restaurants, or strolling on the Mall, AU students always take advantage of their location in the nation's capital.

> **"If you want to get As, you need to work a couple of hours each night."**

Most of the organized parties actually take place off campus right in the city, so students will quickly familiarize themselves with the Metro, the D.C. train system, an easy and safe mode of transportation. This is also great for the many students who live off campus. Two of the most common places to live, the Berkshires and Tunlaw Apartments, are within close proximity to the university. While it is common for students to live off campus, many remain on campus as well. With the exception of Centennial Hall, freshmen may live in any of five residence houses on campus. Although the dorms are coed, there is at least one all-female floor in each building. In addition, some houses boast non-smoking floors, wellness floors, and international floors. Students are happy with their accommodations and enjoy such luxuries as air-conditioning, carpeting, and even small kitchenettes. But the presence of strict residential advisors, who have duty rounds each night, often pushes students to live off campus.

The dining services on campus are well regarded by most students. A combination of points and meals, dining plans come in all varieties. The main dining hall, the Terrace Dining Room (TDR), is buffet-style and catered by Marriott. Using points, students also grab food à la carte at the Tavern and the Marketplace, which offer sandwiches, salads, sushi, and wraps. Off campus, students love to hang out at Guapos Tex-Mex Restaurant. Despite the dining options on campus, some students decide not to buy a meal plan. But whatever you choose, you won't go hungry at AU.

Time for Fun

If you love to party, you'll love AU. Over 30% of students are involved in a strong Greek system. Although they cannot have houses on campus, the 11 fraternities and 11 sororities make their presence known.

Because very few students have classes on Wednesdays, Tuesdays are popular nights for Greek-sponsored events at local clubs. Greeks also have formals, crush parties, and mixers, which provide students with opportunities to dance up a storm. Hookups are common at these events, but don't hope to land a significant other: relationships at AU are the exception rather than the norm.

The AU administration has a very strict policy concerning drugs and alcohol. One student revealed, "If you get caught, it sucks, because the administration is VERY strict." While parents of first-time offenders won't be notified, second- and third-time offenders run the risk of losing their scholarships. Despite these policies, however, students have ample access to substances should they want them.

Even if you aren't interested in the Greek scene, there is plenty to do for fun. One student said, "Even if there isn't an official event, people still go out almost out of tradition!" Last semester, Moby gave a concert in a club downtown. There are tons of movie theaters that offer block-buster hits and artistic films. Many people also choose to chill in bookstores and coffee shops listening to local musicians and jazz music. Last, AU students benefit from the Kennedy Center, which is always hosting musical ensembles, ballets, and other artistic performances.

Washington, D.C., Here I Come

Because of the urban atmosphere, most students feel a stronger connection to Washington than to AU itself. Without a football team or a strong athletics department, AU does not top the charts for school spirit.

On campus, you'll see students from many different backgrounds and ethnicities. There is definitely a large number of people toting Louis Vuitton bags or sporting Chanel sunglasses and Gucci loafers. But many others lean toward the business-casual end of fashion. However you choose to dress, you'll find an extremely diverse population ready to welcome you to Washington, D.C. —*Shira Tydings*

FYI
The three best things about attending American are "D.C., the totally unique class schedule, and the clubs."
The three worst things about attending American are "the lack of school spirit, the campus, and no football team!"
The three things every student should do before graduating from American are "go abroad, go clubbing for 48 straight hours, ride the Metro at 1:00 A.M."
One thing I'd like to have known before coming here is "that it lacks community."

The Catholic University of America

Address: 102 McMahon Hall; Washington, DC 20064
Phone: 202-319-5305
E-mail address: cua-admissions@cua.edu
Web site URL: www.cua.edu
Founded: 1887
Private or Public: private
Religious affiliation: Catholic
Location: urban
Undergraduate enrollment: 2,494
Total enrollment: 5,616
Percent Male/Female: 46%/54%
Percent Minority: 19%

Percent African-American: 8%
Percent Asian: 5%
Percent Hispanic: 5%
Percent Native-American: 0.5%
Percent in-state/out-of-state: 8%/92%
Percent Pub HS: 39%
Number of Applicants: 2,604
Percent Accepted: 88%
Percent Accepted who enroll: 35%
Entering: 797
Transfers: NA
Application Deadline: 15 Feb
Mean SAT: NA
Mean ACT: NA

Middle 50% SAT range: 530–640 V, 520–630 M
Middle 50% ACT range: 22–28
3 Most popular majors: architecture, engineering, politics
Retention: 82%
Graduation rate: 70%
On-campus housing: 100%
Fraternities: 1%
Sororities: 1%
Library: 1,500,000 volumes
Tuition and Fees: $19,930 in; $19,930 out
Room and Board: $8,073
Financial aid, first-year: 79%

For some reason the idea of a "religious" school always seems to strike fear into the hearts of prospective students. Fear not, my friends! Despite its ominous name, CUA is not Vatican City. In fact, it might be more aptly characterized as the prototypical American institution of higher learning.

Although Roman Catholics are the majority at CUA, all faiths are not only tolerated but also openly studied. The administration encourages students to study and explore the numerous faiths of the world. According to one student, "There isn't the least bit of pressure to convert to anything!" Although Intro to Religion is a thorn in the sides of most freshmen, non-Catholic freshmen report feeling very little discomfort attending class.

God Loves Smart People

CUA does have numerous core requirements for many of its majors. Some students enjoy the regimentation while others find it particularly annoying. According to one student, "sometimes the core courses don't make sense in light of your major." Despite having an exceptional architecture program, students who intend to major in this field must fulfill requirements in such oddly incongruous courses such as Religion and Philosophy. Many students regard the large introductory classes in math and English as rudimentary to the point of ridiculousness.

The core requirements, for most majors, include courses in English, the humanities, philosophy, social science, foreign language, science, and math. One of the more popular majors, and considered by some to be a slacker major, is political science. CUA is, after all, centered in Washington, D.C., the heart of what we fondly call the "political process." As a consequence, many of the incoming freshmen at Catholic are interested in political science, political philosophy, and history. There are myriad internships available for these future practitioners of democracy. Special programs in Europe are available for the particularly scholar of history, as well. Professors are readily available to help out the student-in-need. As one student creatively put it, "My English professor is the best thing since Shakespeare and mangos!"

In terms of the actual facilities on campus, students give them mixed reviews. The main library, Mullin, is good, in part because of the quiet rooms for studying. However, the actual card catalog is somewhat confusing and on occasion the book the student so desperately needs cannot be found. Membership in the D.C. College Consortium, consisting of CUA, Howard, George Washington, and American, helps many hapless students find much-needed research material. The Library of Congress, the largest library in the United States, is also a few metro stops away.

Perhaps the best features of academics at CUA are the superb graduate schools. The Nursing School is consistently ranked in the Top 10 and offers motivated future RNs an absolutely superb education. The Law School also carries a positive reputation. Perhaps one of the more popular graduate schools is the School of Drama, which has graduated such blockbuster stars as Jon Voight of *Deliverance* and the versatile Susan Sarandon. The strong graduate schools attract top-notch professors and great graduate students so that the TAs are "excellent and very helpful," according to one student.

And on the Fifth Day He Created Dorms . . .

Are you tired of the same old cookie cutter dorm room with your hand-held-fan being the only source of relief from the sometimes-stifling humidity of the Mid-Atlantic? Do you like *Dawson's Creek* as much as the next college freshman? Go no further! CUA has two of the greatest luxuries afforded to the college freshman—air-conditioning and cable. And for you "playas" out there, CUA offers coed floors and wings, with the only all-female dorm being Conaty. The prize of these palatial housing options is Centennial Village. CUA has an odd policy regarding dorm visitation. All visitors must be signed in by 8 P.M. and must leave the dorm by 2 A.M. As a result, many students complain of a "booty gap" that exists at Catholic. Centennial Village is popular for several reasons, foremost of which are its lack-

adaisical guards who, according to one senior, are "easily bypassed." Those who cannot find housing in Centennial usually move off campus, a once popular option that has fallen by the wayside in recent years. The two apartment complexes near campus, Heights and the Cloisters, provide many upperclassmen with adequate housing. But why, you ask, has this option declined in popularity? According to one student, there is a growing racial tension in the neighborhood in and around Catholic. "The neighborhood seems to be getting worse, not better." Fewer and fewer upperclassmen opt to live off campus because of the safety issue that now exists. The administration discourages students from walking alone anywhere in the area. "The campus itself is incredibly safe with the guards and all . . . but just watch out when you step outside the gates. Use common sense and you'll be fine." The university provides escorts to concerned students.

But, living on campus is not all bad. The campus itself is "gorgeous" and overflowing with green things (a.k.a trees and shrubs). Students have nicknamed the campus "The Mall II" after a more famous mall in Washington, D.C. On sunny days, students can be seen reading and doing other collegiate activities on the Mall. Students have also been able to enjoy a relatively new athletic center. Also nearby is the third largest Catholic Church in the whole world, The National Shrine.

Finding food on campus is a different story. Catholic is notorious for "shitty" meals. A popular option among students is to eat in D.C., which has "some really fine restaurants." However, there are some decent meals on campus and the campus Taco Bell is a popular destination. The neighborhood around Catholic is also replete with fast food joints and surly counter people.

God Hates Keggers

Don't go to CUA expecting to find kegs all over campus—the administration forbids underage drinking on campus. But for all you hedonists out there, there are a plethora of off-campus bars and pubs that'll liquor you up to your heart's content. But be forewarned that late night drinking in D.C. also means a late night walk through the hospitable streets of D.C. By hospitable, I mean there are a lot of muggings. Thankfully, for the inebriated CUA student, blue phones are in abundance on campus. Blue phones allow students to contact the police in the event of an emergency.

> **"You just step outside and you're in the nation's capital. It's kind of awe inspiring."**

Although there is no Greek System, fun does exist on campus. The Program Board dominates campus social activities. The board brings in cool bands and popular guests to talk to students. They also sponsor such infamous dances as the "Screw Your Roommate Dance," where you have to have sex with your roommate. I'm just kidding. "The Screw" involves roommates setting each other up on blind dates. Other popular on-campus events are the Mistletoe Formal, and Movies on the Mall nights.

Although Catholic is a Division III school, sports are still popular on campus. The football team and basketball teams are perennial favorites. The team mascot is the Cardinal. Although most teams at Catholic are Division III, the rugby team is at the Division I level and routinely performs well. Games against cross-town Jesuit rival Georgetown are heavily attended.

CUA, on the whole, is a place where students can allow their own individual talents to flourish. The social life in a major city, especially one chock-full of college students, cannot be beat. "You just step outside and you're in the nation's capital. It's kind of awe-inspiring." Although the school has its Catholic traditions, which many students praise, DMX can also be routinely heard in the hallways. And as DMX would say, "Stop, Drop . . . and come to The Catholic University of America." —*Sean McBride*

FYI
The three best things about attending Catholic University are "the love, the independent-minded student body, and the cool bands that visit."
The three worst things about attending Catholic University are "the neighborhood, Intro to Religion, and the food sucks!"
The three things that every student should do before graduating from Catholic University are "go clubbing in D.C., visit the Shrine, and kick Georgetown's ass."
One thing I'd like to have known before coming here is "the condition of the surrounding area."

George Washington University

Address: 2121 Eye Street NW, Suite 201; Washington, DC 20052
Phone: 202-994-6040
E-mail address: gwadm @gwis2.circ.gwu.edu
Web site URL: www.gwu.edu
Founded: 1821
Private or Public: private
Religious affiliation: none
Location: urban
Undergraduate enrollment: 8,168
Total enrollment: 19,356
Percent Male/Female: 44%/56%
Percent Minority: 23%

Percent African-American: 7%
Percent Asian: 10%
Percent Hispanic: 5%
Percent Native-American: 0.5%
Percent in-state/out-of-state: 7%/93%
Percent Pub HS: 70%
Number of Applicants: 14,326
Percent Accepted: 49%
Percent Accepted who enroll: 30%
Entering: 2,120
Transfers: NA
Application Deadline: 1 Feb
Mean SAT: NA
Mean ACT: NA

Middle 50% SAT range: 570–670 V, 570–660 M
Middle 50% ACT range: 24–28
3 Most popular majors: international affairs, psychology, biology
Retention: 89%
Graduation rate: 68%
On-campus housing: 94%
Fraternities: 16%
Sororities: 14%
Library: 1,900,000 volumes
Tuition and Fees: $24,430 in; $24,430 out
Room and Board: $8,538
Financial aid, first-year: 34%

I s it getting late? Are you looking for an exciting place to hang out? Why not head over to the Lincoln Memorial or the Washington Monument to spend some time or cruise over to Capitol Hill to watch the U.S. government firsthand? If this sounds enticing, then George Washington University may be just the place for you. With a campus located only three blocks away from the White House, George Washington students rarely miss an opportunity to take advantage of the fact that they go to school in the center of the nation's capital. Whether you are interning in government offices or spending the afternoon at the Smithsonian, Washington, D.C., provides a seemingly limitless source of potential activities. Influenced by the overwhelming political atmosphere, George Washington University thrusts its students into not only the academic world but the political world as well.

A Future Monica Lewinsky?

The city of Washington is often integrated into the academic curriculum at GW. Therefore, it comes as no surprise that George Washington has particularly strong international programs, since Washington, D.C.,

is, as one student stated, "the international center of the world." Similarly, students at the university are provided with endless opportunities if they are interested in government. In particular, government internships are very popular and are very easily accessed through the university. However, the university also makes many other types of internships available to its students, and one freshman was quick to observe that "if you want to get involved in something and really have a strong feeling toward it, then the university has you covered. That is one of our biggest assets."

Political influence from the city also pervades extracurricular life on campus. Students feel that "political activism is everywhere," and one student said that "there's no other school that I'd rather be at for the presidential elections than George Washington."

Internship opportunities aren't the only way GW taps into the city's resources. Many classes at George Washington waste no time in taking their students to the capital. One freshman claims that his English class alone visited four museums before the first half of his first term ended. Furthermore, classes often invite speakers from the community to pay a visit. One member of the business school was particularly thrilled with his freshman finance class because prominent people of the business world frequented his class discussions.

George Washington is divided up into several schools, each of which has its own set of requirements. The Colombian School is the school of liberal arts. For students interested in a more specialized education, there is also a business school, engineering school, and school of international affairs. But despite the focused nature of these schools, students are permitted to take classes outside of their specific school and must fulfill liberal arts requirements. George Washington also offers many special programs for students to take advantage of. About 100 students in each class are members of the honors program, and there are also accelerated MBA and medical school programs. George Washington students are particularly pleased with the relative ease with which one can double-major. One student double-majoring in finance and international relations and minoring in Spanish felt that the "great accessibility of professors" helped him quickly and efficiently manage his concerns regarding his majors.

Class size at George Washington ranges from lectures of about 150 to discussion-oriented courses of about 15. Impressions of the workload also seem to vary. While one honors student claimed that his entry-level classes were "easy," there are other students who feel that they "need to be in the library every single minute of every single night." The easiest major on campus seems to be business, while the more difficult majors are engineering and pre-med. George Washington students tend to be "definitely pleased overall" with their academics, especially because their "studying can always be related with what's going on in the city."

Good Luck Drinking

When the weekend rolls around (or, more precisely, when Thursday rolls around), students generally head off campus to the city, where, as one student remarked, "everywhere you turn there's a club." However, the novelty of the clubbing atmosphere does eventually dwindle as

students come to realize cover charges can be expensive. Room parties are a common alternative, but students warn that "the school can be pretty harsh with underage drinking." Community facilitators, known commonly as CFs, are upperclassmen quick to write up any freshman caught with alcohol. Accumulate three write-ups, and the school requires that you live off campus. Similarly, GW requires its students to move off campus immediately if caught with drugs. However, as one freshman pointed out, "The strict policy does not really stop the use of drugs and alcohol; it just makes it more of a hassle." While freshmen typically hit clubs or stay on campus, "upperclassmen go to bars more." In particular, they can often be seen in Adams Morgan, a neighborhood known for its bars and pubs.

One favorite activity for both upper- and underclassmen is visiting the monuments—especially during times of less-than-soberness. As one freshman exclaimed, the monuments are "great when you're retarded." Another exclaimed, "They're just powerful at three in the morning when you and your friends are the only people there."

> **"There's no other school that I'd rather be at for the presidential elections than George Washington."**

Students say the social opportunities at George Washington seem almost endless. They have the option of joining a sorority or fraternity, but since the school is only 18% Greek, the Greek scene tends not to be very prominent. And because Greek life is so time-consuming, the university itself discourages students from joining. As one non-Geek student related, "You don't want to confine yourself in a city with so much to do." Furthermore, the school provides a plethora of activities and events on campus. However, some say that for the amount of effort the university invests in these events, student turnout is relatively poor, as an event is generally considered "kind of geeky if it is campus-involved." During the day on weekends, students often try to get to one of the magnificent museums in the city. One college Democrat said, "I try to get to a museum once a week because it's just nice and relaxing."

We've Got Lookers

The students at George Washington tend to be typically "white, rich, Jewish, and from the Northeast." However, at the same time, some students feel that it has a particularly diverse student body. One freshman expressed: "What I love is that there is every type of person here that I can imagine." Aesthetically, the students also seem to be quite pleasing, and in particular, the girls "are really attractive." Furthermore, these good looks do not go unnoticed, as many students claim the campus is very "sexually active." Whether they are hooking up randomly or actually dating, students at George Washington do not seem to be sexually frustrated, and there is also a noticeable homosexual presence on campus. Interestingly, though, while students do tend to be physically fit and take advantage of the school's excellent student gym, George Washington is "much more of an artsy school than a jock school." GW officially recognizes no contact sports. However, students do come out in numbers to cheer on their Division I basketball team. Even with the loss of popular coach Mike Jarvis, George Washington basketball is without a doubt the best-attended sport in the school and graduates professional prospects each year.

A Nice City Campus

The George Washington University campus consists of four-by-four square city blocks. Students feel that it is "very compact," and one honors program student said, "The longest walk from one side of the campus to the other is only fifteen minutes." Students appreciate this compact campus, but one did say he wished "there were more green space to throw a Frisbee." Despite the fact that the campus is in a city, students feel relatively safe. One freshman said, "I'd walk anywhere on campus alone during any time of the day." However, the same freshman did express reluctance to wander off campus alone.

Starting in 2001, all freshmen and sophomores at George Washington will be required to live on campus. Upperclassmen, however, are not guaranteed housing and therefore often live in city apartments. New housing for upperclassmen has recently been built, and while these rooms provide great living conditions, they are hard to get.

The hub of the George Washington campus is the student union, known as the Marvin Center. Inside is "pretty much anything that you can ever need." Aside from student organization offices and headquarters, there are a ton of restaurants inside the Marvin Center, which all belong to the George Washington meal plan. Restaurants such as Subway, Little Caesars, Starbucks, and Taco Bell are where students typically eat their meals. The student union also has a grocery store and even a travel agency. George Washington students can also take advantage of the study lounges in the Marvin Center, but the lounges in the library are more popular for studying.

If the center of the political universe is your dream campus location, then George Washington University is probably your dream school. Integrating its students' learning with one of the most exciting cities in the world, GW offers an undergraduate experience few others can match.
—*Jonathan Levy*

Georgetown University

Address: 37th and O Streets, NW; Washington, DC 20057	**Percent Asian:** 9%	**Middle 50% SAT range:** 620–730 V, 630–720 M
Phone: 202-687-3600	**Percent Hispanic:** 6%	
E-mail address: NA	**Percent Native-American:** 0.5%	**Middle 50% ACT range:** 27–31
Web site URL: www.georgetown.edu	**Percent in-state / out-of-state:** 2%/98%	**3 Most popular majors:** international affairs, government, English
Founded: 1789	**Percent Pub HS:** 42%	
Private or Public: private	**Number of Applicants:** 13,244	**Retention:** 98%
Religious affiliation: Roman Catholic	**Percent Accepted:** 23%	**Graduation rate:** 83%
Location: urban		**On-campus housing:** 100%
Undergraduate enrollment: 6,089	**Percent Accepted who enroll:** 50%	**Fraternities:** NA
Total enrollment: 12,629	**Entering:** 1,498	**Sororities:** NA
Percent Male/Female: 46%/54%	**Transfers:** NA	**Library:** 2,000,000 volumes
Percent Minority: 22%	**Application Deadline:** 10 Jan	**Tuition and Fees:** $23,295 in; $23,295 out
Percent African-American: 6%	**Mean SAT:** NA	**Room and Board:** $8,693
	Mean ACT: NA	**Financial aid, first-year:** 53%

Interested in politics, government, or international relations? Students at Georgetown University have the nation's capital as their classroom. Located in one of the most affluent areas of Washington, D.C., Georgetown undergrads have at their disposal the resources of one of the country's finest universities and the opportunity to experience life in a hub of national and international activity.

A World of Learning

In addition to the law, medical, and graduate schools, Georgetown offers undergraduates four different schools to which one applies specifically: the School of Business, School of Nursing, College of Arts and Sciences, and School of Foreign Service (SFS), which many cite as Georgetown's strongest program. Each of the colleges has slightly different academic guidelines. The College of Arts and Sciences requires two courses each in philosophy, English, theology, and natural sciences or math. Students must take one course each semester toward their major, which they declare during their sophomore year. Many students praise the history program and the humanities in general, but some find Georgetown's science department relatively weak. Well-known easy courses include Fun with Numbers and some sociology classes.

Business school undergrads take two classes of history or government, philosophy, theology, and English, as well as a semester each of psychology and sociology. SFS (School of Foreign Service) has perhaps the strictest set of core requirements, especially for freshman year when students must take political theory, economics, theology, English, history, and a foreign language (proficiency is required for graduation). While the relatively small nursing school is considered one of the easier programs, SFS (also known by students as Safe from Science) is among the most rigorous courses of study available.

One of the biggest complaints among freshmen is Georgetown's large class size, especially in SFS. All classes are taught by professors, but many lectures break down into weekly small-group recitations led by TAs. Many students say their professors are what they like best about Georgetown. "They know what they're talking about and they really try to make it interesting," said one undergrad. "All my professors are characters with great personalities." Famous Georgetown profs include Ben Bradlee, Madeleine Albright, and Dean Galluchi.

That students are required to study theology is one of the more obvious results of Georgetown's Jesuit origins. Other manifestations of its Catholic roots include nuns on the faculty, crucifixes in the classrooms, representations of saints adorning the walls, and the administrative decision against condom distribution. "Sometimes you can really tell Georgetown is a Catholic school and other times it's not very pervasive," explained one student.

Georgetown draws students from a variety of geographic areas, including many international locations. Many students say, however, "the diversity is not as great" as they had expected. Self-segregation is a problem many undergrads identify. "Being a minority here tends to translate into a minority status." Students say there doesn't seem to be much of a gay community on campus, "at least not one that is clearly visible. There are definitely religious undertones which guide certain standards of behavior."

Students identify the stereotypical Georgetown students as Jane/Joe Hoya (after the school mascot—the Georgetown Hoyas), who is best described as "white cap, plaid shirt, khakis . . . clean-cut preppy East Coast kid." Many expressed their initial surprise at how dressed up students tend to get for classes and especially for evenings out. "The student image here is blond hair, blue eyes—a perfect Ken and Barbie . . . Sometimes people put too much pain into their fashion," said one student.

A More Social Side

"During the week, tension levels are so high that everyone goes crazy on the weekends, and it's one non-stop party," said one student. Clubbing seems to be a popular nighttime activity for weekend partying which starts on Thursday night. Friday night tends to be slightly more low key, as many students decide to stay on-campus and hang out or party quietly in dorms.

All the freshmen dorms are dry dorms, and students who are caught with alcohol in the dorms are assigned community service and are fined $25 for the first offense, with increased punishments for subsequent offenses. As a result, many students go off-campus to party. Popular destina-

tions include bars like the Tombs, Chadwicks, or Champs, or keg parties at off-campus upperclassmen apartments.

Drug use on campus is not very visible, according to several students. "If you use drugs, you're considered an outcast," said one student. "Pot is totally taboo." And although much of the social scene seems to be related to alcohol consumption, students claim non-drinkers do not feel left out and are under no pressure to drink. There are no official fraternities or sororities on campus. "There's a lot of other stuff to do—plays and movies every weekend—and there's all of D.C. for you to hang out in." Recent speakers include the U.S. national security advisor, the former king of Rwanda, and Jerry Springer.

Classic Hoyas

Tradition abounds at Georgetown. A favorite of the students is the Healy Howl, which began after parts of *The Exorcist* were filmed on campus. On Halloween everyone gathers on the quad, watches the movie, and howls at the nearby graveyard. Another superstition that new students at Georgetown learn early on is that if they want to graduate in four years, they should never step on the giant seal in the doorway of Healy Hall.

The campus itself is a mixture of seventeenth-century brick buildings with heavy Gothic influences and some modern buildings, all clustered together. "When you walk on campus, it looks so majestic," said one student. "And there's a lot of grass—it's very aesthetically pleasing." One complaint is that everything on campus is uphill—the entrance to one building will be on the first floor, but when you walk into the building next door, you're already on the fourth floor. "I'll be in such good shape by the time I graduate," joked one student.

Outside Academics

Freshmen live in one of four dorms on campus: Harbin and New South are older dorms built in typical dormitory style while Village C East and Village C West are newer dorms with smaller rooms and private bathrooms, considered by those who live there to be a "huge plus." Dorm halls are coed with common areas and kitchens on every floor, and students enjoy air-conditioning in their rooms. Undergrads from all five schools are mixed in the dorms, which "eliminates any feeling of segregation between colleges."

Georgetown has an RA (resident advisor) system that assigns an upperclassman to each freshman hall. Some RAs "hang out with us all the time and organize activities as a floor," while others are "really strict" in their role as policemen. RAs take turns patrolling the halls each night to keep the noise level down and watch for alcohol. Security is not an issue for Georgetown students, who feel quite safe with the security clerk on duty checking IDs until 3 A.M., when an electronic system goes into effect. "On our hall, we always keep our doors open—I feel perfectly secure," said one student.

> **"If you use drugs, you're considered an outcast," said one student. "Pot is totally taboo."**

Hallmates form the nucleus of a freshman's social circle, at least during the first several months. Huge groups are often seen heading off together for dinner in one of Georgetown's two dining halls. Students choose from a wide variety of meal plans (including "munch money," which can be used for some local takeout, groceries on campus, and snacks at Fast Break), although most do not consider the variety of dining hall food to be satisfactory. Standard fare includes such items as pasta, pizza, rice and vegetables, and a salad bar. Many students also enjoy weekend dinners out—Middle Eastern, Egyptian, Vietnamese, and Indian food can all be found nearby, in addition to more traditional cuisine.

The Washington, D.C. area offers many opportunities for participation in community service—DC Reads (elementary school tutoring), Increase the Peace (workshop seminars with troubled teens) and jail/inmate programs are just a few ways Georgetown students find their way out into the greater community. Many students also take advantage of D.C.'s political life and find internships with congressmen, at international firms, or at the Smithsonian Institute. Some feel frustrated that they do not take more advantage of their surroundings, especially since the Kennedy Center for Performing Arts and a multitude of museums, fairs, historical monuments, and off-campus lectures are all accessible by the Metro subway system.

Popular activities on campus include the International Relations Club and various special-interest groups for students from different areas of the country. Although many people come to Georgetown with backgrounds in student government, "it's kind of looked down upon here . . . student government has no power."

Lots of Georgetown students get involved in sports, whether on the varsity, intramural, or spectator level. The men's soccer team is one of the more popular teams to watch—fans bang pots and pans together to show their support at soccer games. Undergrads don't consider football to be a very big draw, but school spirit is definitely high during basketball season, as students flock to cheer on one of the top-ranked teams in the country.

The life of a Georgetown student is not easy. Like other colleges, the challenge of balancing rigorous academics, engaging activities, and an active social life can be quite trying at times. "Although the campus itself is serene and calm," said one student, "you never see people who aren't rushing somewhere with an agenda." Students say that after four years at Georgetown, they have gained more than just an academic education. Said one undergrad, "There's a great mix of studying and learning a lot with real-life experiences."—*Marti Page and Staff*

FYI

The three best things about attending Georgetown are "the small, pretty campus; the tight-knit student body, and the location in Washington, D.C."

The three worst things about attending Georgetown are "the lack of racial diversity, the religious presence of nuns teaching classes, and class size."

The three things that every student should do before graduating from Georgetown are "walk through the cherry blossoms, eat a chicken madness at Weismiller's, and howl on Halloween."

One thing I'd like to have known before coming here is "that SFS was going to be so much work."

Howard University

Address: 2400 6th Street NW; Washington, DC 20059	**Percent Asian:** 0.5%	**Middle 50% SAT range:** 430–640 V, 410–680 M
Phone: 202-806-2752	**Percent Hispanic:** 0.5%	
E-mail address: admission@howard.edu	**Percent Native-American:** 0.5%	**Middle 50% ACT range:** 16–27
Web site URL: www.howard.edu	**Percent in-state/out-of-state:** 91%/9%	**3 Most popular majors:** biology, psychology, radio/TV, film
Founded: 1867	**Percent Pub HS:** 80%	**Retention:** NA
Private or Public: private	**Number of Applicants:** 5,964	**Graduation rate:** NA
Religious affiliation: none	**Percent Accepted:** 53%	**On-campus housing:** 100%
Location: urban	**Percent Accepted who enroll:** 42%	**Fraternities:** 4%
Undergraduate enrollment: 6,540	**Entering:** 1,325	**Sororities:** 4%
Total enrollment: 11,839	**Transfers:** NA	**Library:** 1,800,000 volumes
Percent Male/Female: 37%/63%	**Application Deadline:** 1 Feb	**Tuition and Fees:** $9,330 in; $9,330 out
Percent Minority: 89%	**Mean SAT:** 526 V, 493 M	**Room and Board:** $5,714
Percent African-American: 87%	**Mean ACT:** NA	**Financial aid, first-year:** 60%

One of the nation's premier historically black universities, Howard has produced more African-Americans with advanced degrees than any other institution in the world. It is no surprise that Howard counts such distinguished people as Nobel Prize–winning author Toni Morrison and world-renowned singer Roberta Flack among its alumni.

Best Is Best

According to students, Howard's strongest areas are communications, business, and engineering. Undergrads attribute much of Howard's academic success to warm student-professor relationships. It is not unusual, students say, for professors to make themselves very available to their students, even giving out their home phone numbers. "The professors here have a particularly important philosophy in their teaching," one student said. "They truly want you to be the best you can be for yourself and for your community." Another student commented, "They want you to succeed and then give back to the community. They feel that we have the power to strengthen the African-American community." Undergrads report that the work is very challenging, but they are rewarded by the knowledge they gain. They feel that, at Howard, excellence is not a goal—it is a requirement.

Those who desire further challenge can participate in the school's honors program, which students may qualify for after freshman year and which involves a heavier course load than the average five classes per semester. All students are required to take courses in physical education, African-American history, English, speech, and math. Students highly recommend the courses in African-American history and communications as among Howard's best. Others recommend the class on sexuality as an "easy A."

Undergrads at Howard say they mostly study in the Founder's Library, the undergraduate library, or in their rooms. The undergraduate library is popular among those who like to study in groups, while Founder's is the favorite for intense independent study.

Something for Everyone

With over 150 student organizations, students say it is extremely easy for everyone to get involved with campus life, meet friends, and have fun. Student government, intramural and varsity sports, and community service are among Howard's most popular activities. Undergrads have taken the university's highly renowned media groups far beyond campus boundaries. The student newspaper, *The Hilltop*, is internationally circulated. Students also produce an Emmy-nominated program called *Spotlight*, which is aired on one of the nation's few black-owned and operated television stations. WHUR, the campus radio station, has a large following in the Washington, D.C., metropolitan area.

> A unique feature of Greek life at Howard and other black colleges is "stepping," an inter-fraternity and -sorority competition that mixes choreographed dance routines with stomping and taunting chants to a beat.

Students describe Howard's social scene as "adequate" in terms of excitement. Many students congregate outdoors on "the Yard," located at the heart of the campus; the Blackburn student center is also popular. Students say on-campus parties occur fairly frequently, but many also appreciate D.C.'s intense and varied club scene, including 18-and-over "college nights" at the Ritz, Mirage, and other hip spots. Howard's social scene tends to revolve around football games. Although many students say they are dedicated fans, others say they go to the games just to hear the marching band, nicknamed the Thundermachine, whose powerful drum section can make even the least rhythmic person get up and dance. School spirit is always high at games, but students say that it turns into a frenzy during homecoming, when the Howard Bisons battle their bitter rival, Morehouse. Homecoming also features such activities as the Miss Howard Beauty Contest and a fashion show.

Most freshmen and sophomores live on campus; the majority of freshmen live in single-sex dorms. Cook Hall, which mainly houses sophomores, is considered Howard's best dorm for its walk-in closets, air-conditioning, and student lounge equipped with a large-screen TV and weight room. Most upperclassmen that elect to live off campus prefer the 10-story Howard Plaza Towers for its prime location.

Growing Diversity

Undergrads say Howard's population is becoming more diverse, with an increasing number of non-blacks matriculating each year. Many of these students cite Howard's strong academic reputation and D.C.-area campus as their reasons for attending the school: "I came here for the challenge," reported one, "and I stay here for the friends I've made."

Although part of Howard's agenda is to foster unity among its students, the campus environment welcomes a variety of ideas. According to one student, "It's very intellectually stimulating to be around people with such different opinions about everything from politics to sports." Some students feel that there are "a lot of snotty, rich" people on campus and that "going to class is like going to a fashion show." One student reported his first memorable experience upon arriving at Howard for the first time. "I was lucky—in the first couple of days a girl took me aside and told me exactly what clothes I needed to buy to fit in." Others, however, argue that such stereotyping is unfair. "You'll find all kinds of people here, all with different styles, and everyone is accepted."

A Greek History

There is a strong Greek presence on campus; in fact, many of the national black fraternities were founded at Howard. Students report that the Greeks at Howard are interested in more than just throwing wild parties: they also emphasize racial unity and community service as focusing on ways of uplifting all African-Americans. A unique feature of Greek life at Howard and other black colleges is "stepping," an inter-fraternity and -sorority competition that mixes choreographed dance routines with stomping and taunting chants to a beat. Yet, one student expressed some misgivings about the strong Greek presence on campus, saying some people have the impression that "if you are not Greek there must be something seriously wrong with you."

Most students declare that the best thing about Howard is the opportunity a Howard degree provides. One student declared, "When current community leaders want to reach out to the community leaders of tomorrow, to give them guidance and inspiration, they come to Howard because they know Howard teaches us more than math or engineering. It teaches us to lead." —*Dylan Howard*

FYI
The three best things about attending Howard are "the cultural solidarity, living in D.C., and the alumni network."
The three worst things about attending Howard are "social life is just okay, the utter lack of diversity, and PE requirements."
The three things that every student should do before graduating from Howard are "go clubbing, learn to 'step,' and go to a bunch of football games."
One thing I'd like to have known before coming here is "how strong our spirit is."

Trinity College

Address: 125 Michigan Avenue, NE; Washington, DC 20017
Phone: 202-884-9400
E-mail address: admissions@trinitydc.edu
Web site URL: www.trinitydc.edu
Founded: 1897
Private or Public: private
Religious affiliation: Catholic
Location: urban
Undergraduate enrollment: 1,018
Total enrollment: 1,489
Percent Male/Female: 0%/100%
Percent Minority: 73%

Percent African-American: 60%
Percent Asian: 3%
Percent Hispanic: 10%
Percent Native-American: NA
Percent in-state/out-of-state: 68%/32%
Percent Pub HS: 60%
Number of Applicants: 277
Percent Accepted: 95%
Percent Accepted who enroll: 69%
Entering: 183
Transfers: NA
Application Deadline: rolling
Mean SAT: 490 V, 460 M
Mean ACT: 21

Middle 50% SAT range: 450–560 V, 410–590 M
Middle 50% ACT range: NA
3 Most popular majors: business administration, political science, English
Retention: 76%
Graduation rate: 56%
On-campus housing: NA
Fraternities: NA
Sororities: NA
Library: 170,000 volumes
Tuition and Fees: $14,440 in; $14,440 out
Room and Board: $6,700
Financial aid, first-year: 85%

In the heart of the nation's capital is a place where women's issues always receive a fair hearing—Trinity College. This small college has been educating women in the liberal arts, while maintaining its Catholic roots, for a century. According to students, Trinity is a melting pot of political activity, tradition, new ideas, and learning.

New Ideas in Academics
Upon acceptance, undergraduate students enter the School of Arts and Sciences. Political science is said to be the most popular major and a strong department, likely influenced by the school's proximity to Washington, D.C. In order to graduate from Trinity, students must complete the Foundation for Leadership curriculum, which includes courses from six areas. Communication Skills enables students to develop critical reasoning and to speak or write a second language. Cultural Diversity explores the traditions and civilizations of different groups worldwide, and Knowledge and Beliefs involves

the study of religious and intellectual perspectives. Traditions and Legacies looks at Western civilization, Scientific and Mathematical Inquiries requires study in those two areas, and Individual and Society investigates how individual and group behaviors affect societal institutions.

Within these areas, classes are designated as either Group One or Group Two, and students must take some of each group. For Group One, they must take a set number of hours. Then, students choose at least three out of the six areas available and take a Group Two course out of each of these. Most undergrads find these core requirements a bit on the extensive side, although they can usually complete them by the end of their sophomore year. One recent grad said, "You definitely have to keep it in mind, but it's really not a headache to fulfill." Recently, students have been given more choice within the core requirements. Instead of a list of specific courses, students now have more course options in the required areas of study, which makes the requirements less of a hassle.

Small classes are the norm at Trinity. Classes range in size from 4 or 5 students to 20 at the most, and the majority have between 10 and 15 students. Students value the approachability of their professors. "The professors are involved in and become a part of your life," one sophomore stated. Unproctored tests are also routine for Trinity women, who are serious about upholding their honor code. The code also includes restrictions on underage drinking and men in the dorms after hours, but rumor has it that reports of these social violations are less common. Trinity also offers a highly popular Weekend College Program for working women through which adult students may take classes on the weekends to earn their undergraduate degrees.

Social Life and Migration Patterns

The social scene at Trinity always involves both its own campus and the lively areas surrounding it. Transportation on the Metro, D.C.'s subway system, provides easy access to the movies, shopping (at Union Station, Pentagon City, and Dupont Circle), dance clubs, and bars. Other college hangouts in the neighborhood also enhance the social scene; undergrads frequently migrate to nearby Georgetown, Howard, and Catholic Universities for mixers or just to hang out in a coed environment. While the surrounding area has its attractions, the campus has its fair share of hangouts as well. Most popular is the Pub, which offers fast food, video games, billiards, occasional dances, and karaoke nights.

> **"The neighborhood isn't very good. When you walk onto campus, it's like stepping into a different world."**

Certain campus social events and traditions are an integral part of the Trinity experience. Twice a year, each class convenes on one of the four floors of the Main dorm to sing canons. The college sponsors a Christmas party called the Holly Hop, and a Beaux-Arts weekend during the spring semester. Toward the end of the year, rising juniors don their graduation caps and gowns for the first time at a special mass. Class dinners and class color days take place as well, but according to one student, these are "nothing special."

Politicking and Other Activities

Because Trinity is in Washington, D.C., political involvement is naturally the most popular extracurricular activity for the Trinity undergrad. A good number of students work on Capitol Hill and are active on campus in various leadership roles. The student government plays an important role at Trinity and has a strong rapport with the administration. Interning is a common activity for students, sometimes to receive course credit and in other cases for enjoyment and experience. Some students travel to other states in order to work on political campaigns. In general, students interested in politics find that at Trinity their extracurricular activities and academic endeavors complement, if not overlap, each other.

It's Like Stepping into a Different World

Although very many Trinity students find politics near or at the top of their priority list, other activities also find their place. The monthly paper, the *Trinity Times*, and the literary magazine, the *Record*, attract aspiring writers. The school has a strong a cappella group, the Bells, and the Pan American Symphony Orchestra is in residence at Trinity and some students play for the orchestra. Some students also take piano or voice lessons for credit. Trinity has six varsity sports teams—lacrosse, soccer, tennis, field hockey, crew, and track and field—all of which are quite popular. Because of the small student body, the teams will accept anyone who wants to play. Trinity became a member of NCAA Division III in September 1995, and as a result both the number of participants and spectators have surged.

Living Standards

Overall, Trinity students are satisfied with the quality of the housing on campus. Although single rooms are not available to first-year students, the doubles are reportedly roomy. Some undergrads prefer Main for its convenient location, and Cuvilly Hall remains a favorite because of its spaciousness and easy staggering distance from the Pub. Seniors and some fortunate juniors live in Alumni Hall, which is popular for its two-bedroom suites with private bathrooms, underground tunnel leading to Main, and proximity to the cafeteria. Students are required to purchase a 19-meal plan the first semester of their first year, but after that they may choose either 19, 14, or 10 meals a week. Some students are also pushing for a pay-as-you-eat plan, citing the inflexibility and inefficiency of the set meal plans. Approximately 25 percent of all students, including commuters, live off campus.

Relations between the school and the largely residential area that surrounds it are reportedly good, although the area surrounding the campus is not flourishing quite as well as the university. According to one senior, "The neighborhood isn't very good. When you walk onto campus, it's like stepping into a different world." Security, however, is not a problem. Campus buses leave for the Metro stations every twenty minutes, and escort services are always available. Trinity and its neighbors are working together on plans for a new campus center. The center has not begun yet, but plans are definite, and the college is set to break the ground at any time.

Trinity students say that over the years they have earned a reputation for being "white, Catholic, feminist snobs," but many report that this stereotype is outdated and incorrect. Trinity's Catholic population is down to approximately 50 percent, minority enrollment is increasing, and need-based student financial aid is prevalent. According to one first-year student, "There are some snobs—but the stereotype is really misleading."

At Trinity, women find a small, friendly environment, enlivened by the excitement of being in a major city. In the political center of the nation's capital, Trinity students thrive and learn, receiving hands-on experience to complement their work in the classroom. *—Lisa E. Smith and Staff*

FYI

The three best things about attending Trinity are "you're in the nation's capital, it is a small all women's community which has given a lot of students confidence in their academic life, and the people are always willing to help you here."

The three worst things about attending Trinity are "financial aid is weak, the dorm life is TERRIBLE—there is no air-conditioning in the first year dorms, and the school does not offer enough selection in terms of majors."

The three things that every student should do before graduating from Trinity are "to get a great internship, use this opportunity to network, and do something spectacular—there are a lot of opportunities here."

One thing I'd like to have known before coming here is "that Trinity is a hub of activity."

Florida

Florida A & M University

Address: Foote Hilyer Administration, G-9; Tallahassee, FL 32307-3200
Phone: 850-599-3796
E-mail address: bcox2@famu.edu
Web site URL: www.famu.edu
Founded: 1887
Private or Public: public
Religious affiliation: none
Location: urban
Undergraduate enrollment: 10,691
Total enrollment: 11,091
Percent Male/Female: 42%/58%
Percent Minority: 94%

Percent African-American: 92%
Percent Asian: 1%
Percent Hispanic: 1%
Percent Native-American: NA
Percent in-state/out-of-state: 76%/24%
Percent Pub HS: 85%
Number of Applicants: 5,663
Percent Accepted: 70%
Percent Accepted who enroll: 48%
Entering: 1,914
Transfers: 727
Application Deadline: 12 May
Mean SAT: NA

Mean ACT: 20
Middle 50% SAT range: NA
Middle 50% ACT range: 18–24
3 Most popular majors: business administration, health professions, liberal arts
Retention: 64%
Graduation rate: 27%
On-campus housing: 70%
Fraternities: 70%
Sororities: 70%
Library: 490,000 volumes
Tuition and Fees: $2,336 in; $9,324 out
Room and Board: $3,896
Financial aid, first-year: 75%

While most of the country braves the winter cold, Florida A&M students, with sunblock and books in hand, settle back on well-manicured, flower-filled lawns. Located in quiet and scenic Tallahassee, Florida A&M University (also known as FAMU) provides solid educational opportunities in a variety of disciplines.

Pre-professionals

Academics at FAMU are centered on specific pre-professional programs. Students report that the business, architecture, engineering, and pharmacy departments are among the strongest. While one senior particularly praised the administration for "teaching us practical information with tons of realistic applications instead of abstract ideas and principles that we will forget an hour after the final," another freshman complained that "my academic program is way too narrowly defined and there is little room for personal explo-

ration." All classes at FAMU, including some recitation sections, are taught by professors. Graduate TAs only help with labs and occasionally substitute for faculty. While each department has its own specific requirements for graduation, all students must complete at least one course each in history, English, math, humanities, and a physical or biological science. The academic program on the whole is considered both "very manageable" and "reasonable, with enough work to make you feel like you are learning without being ridiculously overwhelmed."

Most of the facilities at FAMU are reportedly satisfactory. Although Coleman Library "needs a bigger collection," according to one student, it is a great space to "spread out your stuff, get focused, and accomplish a lot." Empty classrooms are also popular places to get to work when classes are done for the day. Several students said that the sports facilities are "small and mediocre at best" due to a lack of modern gym equipment. Yet, students are also quick to compliment the administration for investing in building improvements and point to the recent additions of a new music building and general classroom building.

An Off-Campus Student Body

Most undergraduates at FAMU live off campus in either rented houses or apartments. The situation draws mixed reviews. While an off-campus student body can be "great because you are really living on your own without dealing with the bullshit regulations that often accompany on-campus housing arrangements at other schools," others are not as convinced. One undergrad said "off-campus living is limiting socially because you are confined to your own group of friends and lose the close proximity that on-campus dorms offer." Residents consider campus housing "fine—nothing great, nothing awful." All students who live on campus must be on a meal plan. The food ranges from "nasty" to "fair." Several students reported that the quality and variety of the meal plan has improved under a new policy that allows them to take their meals in delis and pizza places as well as in the school cafeterias. Off-campus, students enjoy eating at Jake's, "a greasy BBQ dive," and Shingle's, "a decent seafood restaurant."

> Students rally behind the school mascot, the Rattler, and FAMU students show their school spirit during game weeks when the "whole school is covered" with orange and green, FAMU's colors.

FAMU's campus is relatively self-contained and somewhat separated from the town of Tallahassee. Students say town-gown relations are "great." Undergrads enjoy shopping, hanging out at several local clubs, or just wandering around the city's two malls. As one junior reported, "Everything you need is right here." Tallahassee is also only an hour and 15 minutes away from the beach. Fraternity parties are another social venue for those who

have exhausted the Tallahassee club scene. Students agree that FAMU's top on-campus hangout is the "Set," a common area near the Student Union Building, which has a post office, TV room, bookstore, and market. As one sophomore said, "It is great to have the Set so that off-campus people like myself can still stay connected with the rest of the student body." One senior added, "It is awesome to be able to come to campus for something more than just going to class."

Getting Involved

Many undergrads are quick to praise the active student government at FAMU for helping to get students involved in campus life. One person noted that student government leaders "have a really tough task trying to keep an off-campus student body involved with the school, but they do a terrific job." The student government is responsible for planning many social events throughout the year including their biggest event of the year, "Be-out day," which occurs in the spring and features food, games, and contests on the athletic field. It also organizes the extensive Homecoming festivities, activities that "we all look forward to each year," one student said.

Most undergraduates join extracurricular activities connected to their future professions, such as the pre-medical society. Some students also participate in FAMU's theater group, which stages four performances every semester. The gospel choir, several bands, and the *Faumuan*, FAMU's weekly paper, are also popular among students. Community service activities are largely sponsored by fraternities and sororities. Varsity sports also draw student support, and intramural competition is reportedly "fierce and fun." Students rally behind the school mascot, the Rattler, and FAMU students show their school spirit during game weeks when the "whole school is covered" with orange and green, FAMU's colors.

Diversity at FAMU?

The students at FAMU are predominantly in state African-Americans. Some students have questioned the lack of diversity at FAMU. As one senior reported, "I love this community, but I also think there is much to be desired in terms of creating a more diverse student body—I look outside and everyone is so much like me." While not ethnically diverse, FAMU students say that they have very different interests and backgrounds. The small number of openly lesbian and gay students, however, are not organized, and according to one sophomore, not very welcome on campus. "Students are not very open-minded when it comes to that,"

said one student. FAMU undergrads also consider themselves more environmentally than politically aware.

FAMU offers an opportunity to take advantage of a strong pre-professional academic program in a warm, relaxed environment. In the words of one senior, "I am going out into the real world with not only solid academic training, but a host of life experiences that I won't soon forget."—*Jeff Kaplow and Staff*

FYI
The three best things about attending FAMU are "do theater, do sports, do something."
The three worst things about attending FAMU are "the largely in-state student body, orange and green school colors, and an off-campus culture."
The three things that every student should do before graduating from FAMU are "chill at the Set, volunteer in Tallahassee, and attend Homecoming."
One thing I'd like to have known before coming here is "how much energy these people have."

Florida Institute of Technology

Address: 150 West University Boulevard; Melbourne, FL 32901-6975	**Percent Asian:** 3%	**Middle 50% SAT range:** 530–630 V, 500–610 M
	Percent Hispanic: 5%	
	Percent Native-American: NA	
Phone: 321-674-8030	**Percent in-state / out-of-state:** 55%/45%	**Middle 50% ACT range:** 22–27
E-mail address: admissions@fit.edu		**3 Most popular majors:** marine biology, aviation management, mechanical engineering
	Percent Pub HS: NA	
Web site URL: www.fit.edu	**Number of Applicants:** 1,939	
Founded: NA		
Private or Public: private	**Percent Accepted:** 79%	**Retention:** 76%
Religious affiliation: none		**Graduation rate:** 55%
Location: NA	**Percent Accepted who enroll:** 26%	**On-campus housing:** 96%
Undergraduate enrollment: 1,933		**Fraternities:** 17%
	Entering: 397	**Sororities:** 13%
Total enrollment: NA	**Transfers:** 47	**Library:** 368,517 volumes
Percent Male / Female: 67%/33%	**Application Deadline:** rolling	**Tuition and Fees:** $18,450 in; $18,450 out
Percent Minority: 13%	**Mean SAT:** 550 V, 580 M	**Room and Board:** $5,290
Percent African-American: 5%	**Mean ACT:** 25	**Financial aid, first-year:** 86%

After a day of classes at the Florida Institute of Technology, some students head for nearby beaches along Florida's Space Coast while others study under the tall palm trees on campus.

The motivated pre-professional student who chooses FIT is rewarded not only with its picturesque, tropical setting but also with its intense, challenging curriculum.

Sun and Studies

Despite the temptations of the sun and beach, students at FIT take academics seriously. The core curriculum includes heavy doses of science and math (something most FIT students are happy about), along with courses in English composition and rhetoric. Many FIT students have a strong sense of what they want to do later in life and focus on their major early in their college career at one of the five undergraduate schools: the College of Engineering, the College of Science and Liberal Arts, the School of Aeronautics, the School of Business, or the School of Psychology.

Each major requires an intensive curriculum in addition to the core requirements, so freshmen and sophomores have little flexibility in their schedules. According to one student, FIT "gives you a schematic for your major—there aren't too many electives." One sophomore described the first-year program as "rather difficult. They test you to see whether or not you can handle it." The rigorous course load, however, does not translate into cutthroat competition: students report that they "don't go after each other." On the contrary, study groups are popular, and some professors encourage team problem solving. Easy courses are hard to come by in the science departments, but many students use their elective opportunities to take stress-free courses such as scuba diving or sailing.

The College of Engineering is especially popular at FIT. The School of Aeronautics and the departments of oceanography and marine science are also well respected. According to one oceanography major, FIT is one of the few places where students receive "in-the-field" training from almost the first day of class. FIT maintains an extensive co-op program with many of the major companies on the Space Coast, which enables undergrads to alternate semesters in the classroom with semesters on the job. Students can become involved as early as sophomore year, and one participant said of his job experience, "You're not a gopher. You are asked to do the work and get it done. It is a real job." Students work (earning course credits and money) at places such as NASA, Rockwell International, Martin Marietta, McDonnell Douglas, Harris, and Lockheed.

Living Arrangements

Dorm life at FIT is quiet, but as one RA confirmed, "there are parties." The six campus dorms surround a large quad. Evans and Brownly are considered upperclass dorms, although some upperclassmen live on halls with freshmen in the other four dorms, two of which are single-sex. Most rooms are designed for three people, although freshmen generally live in doubles. Residents consider the rooms "quite large." Brownly Hall is especially popular: although the rooms are smaller on average, each has its own bathroom. All rooms at FIT are air-conditioned, and many also have ceiling fans. While freshmen must live on campus, many upperclassmen move to the university-owned Southgate Apartments or to other off-campus housing. Southgate units typically have two or three bedrooms, a large living room, and a kitchen.

Students say they feel safe hanging out on campus. University security officers, most of whom are ex–law enforcement or ex-military officers, are on duty 24 hours a day. Call boxes are located around campus, and an escort service walks students from place to place at night.

> **"Who else takes their calculators to the beach?"**

Students call the food in FIT's Evans cafeteria "decent—it could be better, it could be worse." Freshmen are required to be on the meal plan. Students looking for tastier food head for the popular campus hangout called the Rat (short for Rathskeller), whose specialties include burgers, grilled chicken, and sub sandwiches. Pool tables, a large-screen TV, and small bar make the Rat a favorite place for eating, talking, and hanging out. Seven fraternities and two sororities dominate campus social life by hosting parties and events. According to one student, "The most fun you have in Melbourne is at the fraternities and sororities. You're not going to die if you're not involved in one, but they're pretty big." Drinking is a popular pastime despite the administration's efforts to curb it, but students say that those who don't want to drink are under no pressure to do so.

The surrounding city of Melbourne, home to a large retirement community, has little to offer students (who have nicknamed it "Melboring"). Many students drive or find rides to the bars, malls, and other entertainment venues outside the Melbourne area. Orlando is an hour away, and the beach is a mere ten minutes from campus. Hangouts just off campus include a pizza place called the Mighty Mushroom (locally known as "the 'Shroom"), the local bowling alley, and a miniature golf course. There is also a 7-Eleven store for late-night snack runs.

FIT's lopsided male-female ratio affects campus social life. Many male students lament that it is difficult to meet women, and one female student reported that the situation sometimes causes "a little tension" between the sexes. Another student pointed out that as more women enroll at FIT, the ratio and the tension are slowly improving.

The FIT student body hails from all parts of the globe, with especially large contingents from the Northeast, Florida, and the Caribbean. A burgeoning international community on campus has led to the formation of a number of ethnic clubs, including the Caribbean Students Association. FIT supports many extracurricular organizations, ranging from student government to the school newspaper, the *Crimson*, and from a biology fraternity to a theater group called the College Players.

The FIT Panthers compete in the NCAA Division II Sunshine State Athletic Conference. Popular varsity teams include women's volleyball, men's and women's basketball, crew, cross-country, softball, and baseball. The administration's efforts to start a football program have been unsuccessful so far; homecoming revolves around basketball instead. Many students are active in intramural flag football, innertube water polo, and cycling. For the size of the school, students consider the athletic facilities "pretty good."

In general, FIT students take a lot of pride in and are happy with their school. ("Who else takes their calculators to the beach?" one tanned undergrad questioned). As one student emphasized, "if you work hard, you will receive a good education here." And the weather and waves aren't bad, either. —*Ellen Lee Moskowitz and Staff*

FYI

The three best things about attending Florida Institute of Technology are "how Florida Tech gives scholarships to nearly everyone who applies, the proximity to the ocean where I can surf between classes or in the mornings, and the weather during the 'winter.'"

The three worst things about attending Florida Institute of Technology are "the campus apathy, the buildings are old and need improvements, and there's no flavor here because a lot of people here are engineering majors = boring."

The three things that every student should do before graduating from Florida Institute of Technology are "learn how to dive, go watch the shuttle lift off, and attend Daytona 500 at least once."

One thing I'd like to have known before coming here is "that the humidity is intense in the summer and fall."

Florida State University

Address: Tallahassee, FL
32306-2400
Phone: 8550-644-6200
E-mail address:
admissions@admin.fsu.
edu
Web site URL: www.fsu.edu
Founded: 1851
Private or Public: public
Religious affiliation: none
Location: suburban
**Undergraduate
enrollment:** 25,040
Total enrollment: 30,519
Percent Male / Female:
45% / 55%
Percent Minority: 24%
Percent African-American:
12%

Percent Asian: 3%
Percent Hispanic: 8%
Percent Native-American:
0.5%
**Percent in-state / out-of-
state:** 18% / 82%
Percent Pub HS: 89%
Number of Applicants:
21,159
Percent Accepted:
64%
**Percent Accepted who
enroll:** 38%
Entering: 5,183
Transfers: 3,458
Application Deadline:
3 Mar
Mean SAT: 576 V, 571 M
Mean ACT: 24

Middle 50% SAT range:
520–620 V,
530–630 M
Middle 50% ACT range:
22–27
3 Most popular majors:
biology, criminology,
psychology
Retention: 85%
Graduation rate: 38%
On-campus housing: 51%
Fraternities: 10%
Sororities: 10%
Library: 2,200,000 volumes
Tuition and Fees:
$1,697 in; $8,685 out
Room and Board: $4,951
Financial aid, first-year:
33%

A lmost every weekend during football season, the streets around Florida State University are blocked off and an organized chaos engulfs the campus. Such is the atmosphere during football season, when thousands of students and alumni pack in to watch their Seminoles destroy the competition. Waves of painted faces enthusiastically cheer their team to victory but also revel in their school's social atmosphere and dedication to academics.

Studying Seminole Style

Although their university is consistently ranked among the top party schools in the nation, FSU students are quick to point out that there is much more to the school than its reputation implies. "Despite what a lot of people think, we actually do have to work and have to study to do well in classes," said one sophomore. Most students enter the School of Arts and Sciences, but the university has a number of specialty schools. Some of the stronger ones include the School of Music, the College of Engineering, the College of Business, and the nationally renowned School of Motion Picture, Television, and Recording Arts. The degree requirements vary from school to school, but in general all students must receive course credit in English, mathematics, history, social sciences, humanities, and natural science. They were described as "nothing you can't finish easily, and they usually overlap with a major's requirements as well." In addition, all students must satisfy the statewide Gordon Rule, which requires students to write 24,000 words by graduation. FSU students must also take two "x-and-y" multicultural classes before graduation. "Some of the requirements are really annoying. They can be very large courses and in some of them I never really learned anything," said one sophomore.

Most people generally agree that one of the easiest and most popular majors is psychology. Communications was cited as an easier concentration, which was explained as "something you do when you don't know what else to do." Several introductory courses were described as easy or, in some cases, "easy As." Introductory sociology, religion, and theater were among the most popular. "The hard-core science classes are definitely the hardest, and they usually weed out a large portion of students who thought they were going to be pre-med," said one junior.

Many classes at FSU tend to be very large, especially introductory courses.

"Some of the lectures are so large, I feel like an anonymous number," said one freshman. While some classes can enroll upward of several hundred students, FSU tries to keep most classes at 20 students or under. "The more individualized attention in my music class is spectacular," exclaimed one sophomore. For those looking for more personalized attention, the honors program is ideal. Applicants who graduate from high school with a 3.8 GPA and 1300 SAT score are invited into the program, which includes special classes and colloquiums.

> **"Going to FSU football games is one of the most incredible experiences. Looking out and seeing thousands of people do 'the chop' just fills you with such a sense of school pride."**

One student described FSU's registration system as "absolutely horrible. It can be extremely hard to get into classes." Students can register either by phone or through the Internet. Undergrads commonly complain that classes fill up quickly and jammed phone lines prevent registration. In addition, three summer courses are required for graduation. AP credit earned in high school is often used to get out of these requirements, but one student warned, "They'll charge extra if you take too many classes." One happy undergrad said of his FSU education, "I feel that my major has really prepared to send me out into the world."

Sunning like a 'Nole

In the capital of Florida, a wide variety of social options await Seminoles. On campus, the fraternities reportedly "dominate a large portion of your social life," and alcohol can be a big part of that scene. Some students claim that it can be easy to feel left out if you don't drink. "Sometimes there can be a real limit on your social life if you don't drink. It seems that a lot of people plan their weekend schedules around getting drunk," claimed one freshman. Marijuana use is present on campus but not something that is overwhelming. Recently the university has been cracking

down on underage drinking on campus. "You can get arrested if you're not careful," said one freshman.

Although it may appear as if the Greek system dominates social life at FSU, a number of alternatives await students. Among one of the more popular options is going to a movie at Moore Auditorium. The screenings are sponsored by the Student Government Association and occur every few days. "They actually play really good movies and they're free," exclaimed one freshman of the movie screenings. The Oglesby Union also has many different things for students to do, offering such amenities as a bowling alley and art studio. The Leach Center, FSU's incredible gym and recreational building, offers a myriad of activities to keep students entertained. The fitness center offers state-of-the-art cardiovascular and strength-training machines. Multipurpose courts can be used to play anything from basketball to badminton, and an indoor running track and pool are available. Racquetball courts are also housed here, and students make good use of this popular fitness center. Intramurals ranging from basketball to tennis run year-round for students who are interested in becoming involved in organized sports but don't have the time to make a serious commitment. Students with other extracurricular interests can participate in a wide variety of clubs and activities, such as Habitat for Humanity or the Student Government Association.

Off campus, many students frequent clubs and bars in the city of Tallahassee. One student claimed that "clubbing" is one of the biggest social alternatives. Floyd's is a particularly popular destination. Students gave the city of Tallahassee varying reviews. "The city seems kind of dirty, and there are some parts I really wouldn't want to walk into," said one sophomore. The city has two shopping malls for the most essential shopping, and an IMAX theater under construction should add even more options for off-campus relaxation. Bike trails and a nearby lake invite swimmers and canoeists year-round, thanks to Florida's temperate climate.

Picturesque and Poor Parking

Dotted with old red-brick architecture and set amid a rolling countryside, FSU's campus has been described as "very pretty. There are lots of nice brick buildings and it's usually very well maintained." "I was kind of surprised when I got here. I thought all of Florida was supposed to be really flat, but around FSU it's really hilly," said one freshman. The campus is spread out over a large area, so many students take advantage of the campus-wide bus system. A large percentage of students, including freshmen, bring cars, and insufficient parking is, by far, the most widespread complaint of students. "The parking sucks here. It's hard as hell to even find a spot. I've gotten hit twice because of the way the lot is laid out, and I've only been up here a few months!" said one freshman.

Many students choose to bring a car, because off-campus housing is a very popular alternative for upperclassmen. The surrounding area of Tallahassee has a wide array of affordable housing. Many freshmen choose to live on campus, but dorm quality varies. "If you're not in a renovated dorm, watch out!" warned one sophomore. Reynolds, Bryan, Gilchrist, and Broward dormitories have all been recently redone and are considered to be very clean. Sally and Kellum are known as the party dorms, but they have not been renovated recently and, according to students, do not provide the most pleasant living accommodations. Dorms are coed by floor, except for the all-female Dorman and Jennie Murphree Halls. Rooms are assigned on a first-come, first-serve basis and also by class seniority. Thus the older students leave freshmen to fend for themselves, as the nicer dorms fill up quickly. Residential advisors are available on each floor for counsel and friendly advice. Off-campus private dormitories are ideal for those who want a college atmosphere without actually living on campus.

A surprising number of students do not use FSU's meal plan. Most go to the Food Court, which has a Burger King and Pizza Hut, among others. "I wasn't terribly impressed with the school's food. I think that's why a lot of people just cook for themselves," said one junior. The dining halls "don't seem to be very social places. Sometimes if you're not in a clique it can be hard to find people to sit with," said one sophomore. FSU is a school filled with southern charm and friendly students, but many find that tight social groups tend to form, making it difficult to meet new people.

Football at Its Finest

Not surprisingly, the most popular activity on campus is attending football games. FSU's football team consistently ranks among the best in the nation, and the entire student body supports them. Painted faces and bodies clad with Seminole merchandise fill the stadium during the season. "Going to FSU football games is one of the most incredible experiences. Looking out and seeing thousands of people do 'the chop' just fills you with such a sense of school pride," said one freshman. When students make the tomahawk motion and sing the sacred tune, they are carrying on a tradition that characterizes Florida State as much as football itself. Although football is the most popular and well known FSU sport, others, like baseball and crew, are gaining prominence.

FSU students exhibit an enormous amount of school spirit. They are proud of their school's success in the field and in the classroom. Being one of the top party schools in the nation has not permitted academics to fall through the cracks. The school may be extremely large, but southern hospitality allows most students to feel welcome. Says one student, "FSU is the best of both worlds. The party scene is incredible, but you can really come out after four years with a great education if you take advantage of the resources made available to you." —*Aaron Droller*

FYI

The three best things about attending FSU are "the football games are so much fun because FSU kicks ass, absolutely beautiful girls, a beautiful campus with a great location."

The three worst things about attending FSU are "finding a parking spot around here can become very frustrating, waiting in line to turn in financial aid every semester, some of the classes are really big, so you can't have a personal relationship with your professor."

The three things that every student should do before graduating from FSU are "live in a dorm as a freshman, get thrown in the fountain on your birthday, and go to class."

One thing I'd like to have known before coming here is that "the city is boring."

New College of the University of South Florida

Address: 700 North Tamiami Trail; Sarasota, FL 34243-2197
Phone: 941-359-4269
E-mail address: ncadmissions@sar.usf.edu
Web site URL: newcollege.usf.edu
Founded: 1960
Private or Public: public
Religious affiliation: none
Location: suburban
Undergraduate enrollment: 617
Total enrollment: 617
Percent Male/Female: 37%/63%
Percent Minority: 14%
Percent African-American: 2%

Percent Asian: 5%
Percent Hispanic: 7%
Percent Native-American: NA
Percent in-state/out-of-state: 62%/38%
Percent Pub HS: 81%
Number of Applicants: 298
Percent Accepted: 75%
Percent Accepted who enroll: 58%
Entering: 129
Transfers: 63
Application Deadline: 1 May
Mean SAT: 679 V, 622 M
Mean ACT: 27

Middle 50% SAT range: 630–730 V, 580–660 M
Middle 50% ACT range: 26–29
3 Most popular majors: psychology, literature, biology
Retention: 88%
Graduation rate: 67%
On-campus housing: 99%
Fraternities: NA
Sororities: NA
Library: 254,889 volumes
Tuition and Fees: $2,492 in; $10,878 out
Room and Board: $4,663
Financial aid, first-year: NA

With a name like "New College" there's no mistaking the small Sarasota, Florida school for a traditional undergraduate institution. With only six hundred students and no grades or core curriculum, New College attendees report that their four years of striving for success takes place "in an experimental milieu."

Independent Intellectuals

New College students make much of the fact that self-motivation is key for success at their school. There is no core curriculum. Rather, students design their course plan with the help of a faculty advisor. Students can easily design their own majors, though many choose from the variety of already-established ones. Traditional liberal arts majors like anthropology, literature, and biology are common. Students caution, though, that the "literature theory classes will completely exhaust your brain and overload your reading time." In addition, "Psychology is very popular . . . but the department walks you through the thesis, which is the most difficult aspect of New College." Some even get degrees in "general studies," which is "sort of a catch-all." As for those who plan to continue their education, faculty members can suggest programs of study appropriate for future graduate students.

Another hallmark of the New College education is the lack of grades. Said one sophomore, "There can't really be competition—there's nothing to compete about." Nevertheless, one student did note that "it can be a hard adjustment from high school. You have to train yourself to study for the right reasons." Students don't point to any particularly strong area of faculty expertise, but note, rather, that they are all "high-caliber." Like the college as a whole, class sizes are almost universally small. As a result, professor-student interaction is lauded at New College. "You'll definitely have professors who know you well—some'll probably cook your whole class dinner." There are TAs, but they only assist professors and students and do not teach classes.

Students say that partly as a result of the atmosphere of "intellectualism," most students spend more time on academics than any other aspect of college. The Jane

B. Cook Bancroft Library, the main library, is complimented for having "the best librarian I've ever met." Because New College is a state school, it is part of an inter-library book exchange program with other Florida colleges. Upperclassmen are also pleased that they get their own study carrels. Other places to study, which tend to be more social than Bancroft, are the student center and individual dorm rooms.

Time flies when you're saving the world

While studying occupies the biggest chunk of a New Collegian's life, many students are involved in extra-curricular activities. The *Catalyst* is the weekly paper written by students. Other popular activities include student government (through the New College Student Alliance) and Amnesty International. Politically, "the overwhelming majority is liberal." A senior cautioned, though, that "more than being of one view or another we are open-minded." Nevertheless, students noted that the campus isn't as good at activism as it is at "theorizing about activism." New College does not have a varsity sports program, but its athletic facilities include a gym, racquetball, tennis, and basketball courts, a soccer field, and a pool.

> "You'll definitely have professors who know you well—some'll probably cook your whole class dinner."

On the weekends, New College students party like their peers at other institutions—sort of. There are no fraternities or sororities, and students say that the social scene is "fairly laid-back." The majority of socializing takes place on campus. "Walls" are parties randomly thrown together whenever the urge hits. Cross-dressing is reportedly popular at these parties. A more organized dance is the Palm Court Party (PCP), where a laid-back atmosphere of tie-dyeing, listening to music, and dancing pervades. Students say that both drinking and drugs are prevalent at the school, though the latter is mostly confined to marijuana. "Cops look the other way most of the time," said one student.

Outside of campus Sarasota does not offer much for night-time activity, though its tourist-friendly beaches are appreciated by New College students. Said one student, "Sarasota is a small, artsy town with not a lot to do, but it's beautiful and has more cultural opportunities than any other city in Florida. Which I guess makes me a bit sad for the rest of Florida..." Tampa is less than an hour way and students in need of a break from the quiet suburban life occasionally make the trip.

Sleeping and Snacking in Sarasota

Most freshman and sophomores live on campus while upperclassmen generally move off campus. All B and Viking rooms are singles, while Pei residents share doubles. Viking is actually a converted motel, which some students say, has "charm." The newer Dort and Goldstein dorms are said to be much better than their counterparts. Dort features large suites with single bedrooms, complete with appliances. In all the dorms, though, residents often keep their doors open, which contributes to a more suite-like atmosphere. Security concerns are minimal among students; locking doors is the only precaution most students take. There are two RAs for each dorm. Students enjoy the "very Florida" campus, calling the architecture "'70s Spanish" style. The school is located on a bay, which, "during good weather, is awesome." In general, students appreciate going to school in sunny Florida. "I don't know why my friends put up with snow up north!" said one.

Campus residents eat in one central cafeteria and are required to be on the meal plan. The food is prepared by the Marriott food service, and students can use their meal cards at the local convenience stores as well. Many undergrads complain about the quality of the food. As one student explained, "There's a reason we were ranked as the worst college food in the South." Students also enjoy eating at the Granary, a health-food restaurant, and at Taco Bell.

Lack of Cultural Diversity

While students have diverse interests, they generally come from similar backgrounds: white, upper-middle-class, and suburban.

Said one student, "I wouldn't say New College is particularly diverse, unless you consider a school nearly 85 percent full of white, suburban, overly intelligent kids diverse. Of course, everyone welcomes diversity, but it's part of the 'program' here." The homosexual community is said to be "well-accepted." In general, said one student, "due to self-selection, we're a pretty alternative, easy-going bunch. Students are proud to be a part of their "thoughtful—in both senses of the word" community and don't mind missing the "traditional" college experience. "I belong here. I can't imagine most of us truly belonging anywhere else."

—*Ellen Moskowitz*

FYI

The three best things about attending New College are "freedom of education, meeting lots of strange and exciting people, and the intimate atmosphere of a small school."

The three worst things about attending New College are "freedom to accomplish nothing, living with lots of strange people, and the atmosphere of a small school—where everyone knows everything about everyone else."

The three things that every student should do before graduating from New College are "dance naked in Palm Court, listen to one of John More's storytimes, and win a game of one-on-one with John Newman."

One thing I'd like to have known before coming here is "there's a small social sphere."

Rollins College

Address: 1000 Holt Avenue; Winter Park, FL 32789-4499	**Percent Asian:** 3%	**Middle 50% SAT range:** 540–630 V, 540–630 M
Phone: 407-646-2161	**Percent Hispanic:** 8%	**Middle 50% ACT range:** 24–28
E-mail address: admission@rollins.edu	**Percent Native-American:** 0.5%	**3 Most popular majors:** psychology, economics / international business, English
Web site URL: www.rollins.edu	**Percent in-state / out-of-state:** 50% / 50%	
Founded: 1885	**Percent Pub HS:** 55%	
Private or Public: private	**Number of Applicants:** 1,748	**Retention:** 83%
Religious affiliation: none	**Percent Accepted:** 73%	**Graduation rate:** 68%
Location: suburban	**Percent Accepted who enroll:** 35%	**On-campus housing:** 95%
Undergraduate enrollment: 1,519	**Entering:** 448	**Fraternities:** 27%
Total enrollment: 3,483	**Transfers:** 68	**Sororities:** 27%
Percent Male / Female: 40% / 60%	**Application Deadline:** 15 Feb	**Library:** 277,671 volumes
Percent Minority: 14%	**Mean SAT:** 570 V, 580 M	**Tuition and Fees:** $22,868 in; $22,868 out
Percent African-American: 2%	**Mean ACT:** NA	**Room and Board:** $7,000
		Financial aid, first-year: 55%

"Don't forget to bring your suntan oil," joked a Rollins College student when describing the reputation Rollins has among its neighboring schools. With its Spanish Mediterranean architecture and majestic trees hung with Spanish moss, this college in the sunny climes of Winterpark, Florida, garners a certain amount of envy from other southern universities. Add to this the fact that U.S. News & World Report ranked Rollins number two behind the University of Richmond and above rival Stetson (number four) in its "2001 Top Southern Universities" rankings, and you have a group of satisfied, if slightly smug, students.

Tom and Tammy Tar

Take Tom and Tammy Tar (the school mascots), for instance. "Tom's basically this big, brawny sailor guy, and Tammy's his, ahem, mate," one student explained. These tan, lean mascots inspire generations of Tars to sports excellence in the traditional sports of golf, tennis, and crew. Rollins has several nationally ranked teams, including men's golf and men's and women's tennis. The Tom Tar men's and women's basketball team also do well in their tough Division II conference. In 1997, one senior male basketball player set an all-division NCAA record for 93 consecutive games with three-point baskets. "Hey, we got it great. Nice weather, great sports . . . uh, oh yeah, I guess we study a little bit, too," one student said.

Working Hard

Rollins students study more than a little bit. "My reasons for coming here were academics first, and that other stuff second," said one studious freshman. Another student emphasized that "active participation in classes is essential for good grades." Rollins's three-story Olin Library comfortably seats the hard-core studiers on the basement floor, while the first floor is home to the more social studier. Rollins has several programs catering to such students: the Winter Term (or J term, short for January term), the Honors Degree Program, and the Rollins Advantage Program (RAP) are the primary vehicles for particularly motivated students. The J term, which was once mandatory for students, now consists of a totally optional term after the winter holidays in which classes meet three times per week for three hours, and finish with an exam before the start of the spring semester. Although the J term is no longer required, most students still take the opportunity to partake in the more hands-on classes that the shorter term provides. Students who do not stick around for the J term often go abroad or take internships in nearby Orlando, which, as one of the fastest-growing cities in the nation, is home to myriad large corporations, as well as Universal Studios and Disney World.

Hmm . . . What To Study?

The business-oriented environment of Orlando makes the Rollins environment conducive to the study of economics, one of the most popular majors of the 28 that Rollins offers. Rollins's psychology, political science, English, and theater departments were also cited as popular, while some students report that the language departments are weaker. All students must satisfy course requirements before graduating, and while the requirements "help some people make up their minds about their possible major, I think they're a crock," said one undergraduate.

> **"Hey, we got it great. Nice weather, great sports . . . uh, oh yeah, I guess we study a little bit, too."**

Greeks play a large role in the Rollins social scene, with approximately 40 percent of students choosing to pledge. Some students say the Greek scene "really opens up a lot of social opportunities," while others feel that it makes the already close-knit community of Rollins "damn near suffocating." "I think that they're good for the campus as a whole, but some people just rush and then lose themselves in the organization, never really becoming an individual," one perceptive student said. But, according to one undergrad, "There is nothing on campus, so we either have to do the bar scene or hit an off-campus party." Since there are few school-wide dances (the annual President's Dance is an informal theme dance), Greek formals take prominence.

Dating and Relationships

On the topic of dating and coed relations, one student summed up with, "I'd say there's a lot of sex, I mean, hooking up here. Perhaps it's because we're so small that you hear about it all the time, but then again, maybe there's something in the water, because you hear about it all the time." Same-sex relationships are also treated with respect, and gay students can join R-FLAG, Rollins for Lesbians and Gays. International students make up only about 5 percent of the Rollins student population, but they do organize activities and contribute to campus life. Minority students are represented by LASA (Latin American Student Association), BSU (the Black Student Union), and the Muslim Student Association among others. Since Rollins is small, these groups tend to coordinate campus events together.

With a country club-like campus and over 70 student organizations to choose from, very few students opt to live off campus. Those who do "are the type that commute and just come to get their degrees. They're very rare," one junior said. The only incentive that students cited to move off campus is the quality of the dining hall food. "If you ask me, it pretty much bites," a disgruntled senior remarked, but several underclassmen said they were satisfied: "Even though the menu is ultra-predictable, they still do some novel stuff, like a teriyaki bar." Another student said, "You pay the same price everyone else does, then you're charged for each item of food you buy at the on-campus convenience store or at the dining hall. Problem is, everybody is always running out of money toward the end of the semester, so you've gotta call Mom and Dad and ask for more money."

The Rollins administration takes a hard stance on alcohol, but ignores what some students see as a pressing campus drug problem. According to one undergraduate, "There's a lot of money here. A lot of kids should be in AA." A recent change allows for "catered kegs" at fraternity parties, which means an outside company is hired to provide beer to students with proper ID. According to several undergrads, a "surprising number" of students smoke pot, and "some of the rich, snobby types are involved in cocaine and heroin— it's really pretty sad."

Despite these issues, Rollins students in general enjoy a laid-back life of sun, fun, and Orlando at a bargain that cannot be beat this side of the Mason-Dixon Line. Students interested in such a "work hard, play hard" atmosphere should consider applying to Rollins. —*Ellen Lee Moskowitz and Staff*

FYI
The three best things about attending Rollins are "the sun, the beautiful country club of a campus, and Florida."
The three worst things about attending Rollins are "the dining hall food, there are too many rich preppies, and a close-knit school can be stifling."
The three things every student should do before graduating are "to play golf, to play tennis, and to get a tan."
One thing I'd like to have known before coming here is "how big the Greek system is."

Stetson University

Address: 421 N. Woodland Blvd, Unit 8378; DeLand, FL 32720-7100
Phone: 904-822-7100
E-mail address: admissions@stetson.edu
Web site URL: www.stetson.edu
Founded: 1883
Private or Public: private
Religious affiliation: none
Location: small city
Undergraduate enrollment: 2,062
Total enrollment: 2,380
Percent Male/Female: 40%/60%
Percent Minority: 12%

Percent African-American: 4%
Percent Asian: 2%
Percent Hispanic: 5%
Percent Native-American: 0.5%
Percent in-state/out-of-state: 80%/20%
Percent Pub HS: 78%
Number of Applicants: 1,913
Percent Accepted: 80%
Percent Accepted who enroll: 37%
Entering: 563
Transfers: 120
Application Deadline: 15 Mar
Mean SAT: 561 V, 557 M

Mean ACT: NA
Middle 50% SAT range: 510–620 V, 500–610 M
Middle 50% ACT range: NA
3 Most popular majors: general business, biology, psychology
Retention: 81%
Graduation rate: 60%
On-campus housing: 90%
Fraternities: 33%
Sororities: 26%
Library: 344,452 volumes
Tuition and Fees: $18,385 in; $18,385 out
Room and Board: $6,070
Financial aid, first-year: 98%

In the 1860s, the Stetson hat was called the "Boss of the Plains." Indeed, the students who call themselves Hatters at Stetson University take charge of any obstacle that gets in their way. Through one-on-one academics and fervent school spirit, students who choose to call De-Land their home can be assured of obtaining a good education amid the intimate setting of a small school.

Hats Off to Academics

Educational opportunities abound at Stetson. The university is divided into the College of Arts and Sciences, School of Business, School of Music, and Law School, which is located in nearby St. Petersburg. Graduation requirements are extensive. Students must take courses in English, communications, math, social and natural sciences, and religion and demonstrate proficiency in a foreign language. Many requirements can be waived by presenting satisfactory AP scores. Also required is attendance at cultural events such as music recitals and lecture series. "All the requirements can be irritating, but at the same time they help broaden your horizons. If you're an English major, at least you have the experience of having taken some science," commented one ju-

nior. Some students choose to take advantage of the honors program, which mandates that they take a junior honors seminar. Students in the program have the luxury of being able to design their own major but need to have graduated from high school in the top 10% of their class with an SAT score of at least 1270 to enter the program.

> **"Having Daytona so close really gives you something great to do on weekends."**

Due to Stetson's small size, students are given many opportunities to learn one-on-one with professors. Classes are intimate and even introductory lectures will only have about 25 to 30 students. "People get to know their professors so well here. Some even invite students from their class over for dinner. I know all of my professors by first name," exclaimed one freshman. Registration is done through an advisor, and most students do not have a problem getting into desired courses. Students said that chemistry and biology are among the harder majors but also pointed out that the music major is extremely competitive.

"Watch out for the music theory class; it has the highest failure rate on campus!" warned one student. Easier majors were said to be education and communications.

Hatter Living

Although upperclassmen can request to live in suites, all freshmen live in doubles that are "definitely a little cramped" and share a hall bathroom. There are residential advisors on every floor to offer friendly advice. The two honors dorms, Carson and Hollis, are single-sex, dry, and have enforced quiet hours for study. All of the other dorms except one are coed and separated by floor. Nemick is reportedly the worst dorm, because it is the oldest. Emily has a reputation for having a party atmosphere, with more drinking than other dorms. Students said they felt very safe on campus. It is necessary to pass through two key locks for room access, and Public Safety, Stetson's security force, is constantly walking around campus. In addition, phones around campus allow those who do not want to walk home alone at night to call for escorts. Although off-campus housing is always an option, most people choose to live on campus all four years, because apartments in the small town of DeLand can be costly.

Many students have positive opinions of the culinary options at Stetson. The dining hall, Commons, is catered by Marriott, so "the food seems to be a level above what you would find at other colleges." There is a well-stocked salad bar and a vegetarian entrée at each meal for those who are inclined, and there are also omelets on Sunday. The meal plan ranges between 5 and 17 meals per week. Those who don't use all of their meals can convert them to points that can be used at the Hatrack, a fast-food restaurant that is open until late at night. In addition, points can be used to order in Domino's pizza if you who feel like leaving the dorm. The dining hall is a social place where "you can just pick up a conversation with anyone, really." In addition, minutes away by car are several restaurants, including the popular Boston Coffee Shop.

Brimming with Spirit

Stetson students say that there is a "club for almost everyone here." Many people are involved in some type of extracurricular activity. Religious organizations, such as the Wesley house, a Methodist student union, and the Baptist student union, seem to be popular on campus. Community service also draws a number of students at Stetson, and Circle K is a particularly large volunteer group. The Council for Student Activities organizes campus-wide events like concerts and has recently brought bands like Sister Hazel to campus. "Stetson is a very musical campus. Lots of people are in choirs or play an instrument, and the School of Music brings performers to campus throughout the year," said one freshman.

Athletics play a large role on campus. Many students get involved with intramural sports that range from basketball to flag football. A complaint among some students is the lack of a varsity football team, but the basketball and soccer teams always enjoy student support at games. "Humiliating yourself by doing the Stetson cheer in front of everyone is a time-honored tradition that everyone should do," said one junior. The Hollis Center, the recently renovated gymnasium, has many facilities to keep the athletically inclined student entertained. Its offerings include basketball courts, an Olympic-sized pool, a game room, an aerobics studio, and a fitness center offering state-of-the-art workout machines.

Night on the Town

The town of DeLand, although small, is located conveniently about an hour away from Orlando and is just a short ride from Daytona. In Orlando, students can go to theme parks such as Walt Disney World or Universal Studios on weekends. In Daytona, students find some of the best beaches in all of Florida and also one of the hottest spring break destinations for college students around the country. "Having Daytona so close really gives you something great to do on weekends," exclaimed one freshman. Accordingly, many students at Stetson choose to bring cars, although some warned that it can sometimes be difficult to find a parking spot on campus. The town of DeLand itself, although not large, holds a certain southern appeal for students. It is filled with lots of "mom and pop shops" that give it the feel of small-town America. "Since Orlando is close by, I never feel smothered by how small DeLand is," said one sophomore. One student said she liked the fact that the residents of DeLand get involved with what goes on around campus, such as attending sporting events to show their support for the home team.

The weekend starts for Stetson students on Thursday night, when the Greek influence on campus starts to become noticeable. Fraternities throw large parties that are inclusive of everyone, and generally free. Drinking does happen, but it's definitely not overwhelming. Drug use is said to exist but is not tremendously visible. "People who don't drink really do not feel pressure to do so," said one freshman. More than 30% of the students are involved in Greek life. Those who are not in frats said there is not a terrible amount of pressure to join. Since many of Stetson's students are from Florida, there is often a "mass exodus of students" who drive home on Friday and the campus is not as active for the rest of the weekend.

Students at Stetson recognize both the advantages and disadvantages of attending such a small school. The intimate setting of the school allows students to truly get to know their professors and receive real individualized attention. The small town of DeLand adds to the personal atmosphere, but with Daytona and Orlando so close by, students have no problem getting away if they need to. The small-school ambiance ultimately adds to a feeling of togetherness that makes the time spent at Stetson a worthwhile experience. —*Aaron Droller*

FYI

The three best things about attending Stetson are "the one-on-one attention from professors, extremely nice and well-rounded people, and the small classes—even at the introductory level."

The three worst things about attending Stetson are "the quiet weekends, the small town of DeLand, and the feeling of sometimes being left out if you're not in a fraternity or sorority."

The three things that every student should do before graduating from Stetson are "get thrown into the fountain, [do] the Stetson cheer, and ring the bell at the Hollis Center."

One thing I'd like to have known before coming here is "because DeLand and the school are so small, you sometimes feel claustrophobic."

University of Florida

Address: 201 Criser Hall, Box 114000, Gainesville, FL 32611-4000
Phone: 352-392-1365
E-mail address: freshman@ufl.edu, transfer@ufl.edu
Web site URL: www.ufl.edu
Founded: 1853
Private or Public: NA
Religious affiliation: none
Location: NA
Undergraduate enrollment: 30,883
Total enrollment: 43,382
Percent Male/Female: 48%/52%
Percent Minority: 24%
Percent African-American: 7%

Percent Asian: 6%
Percent Hispanic: 10%
Percent Native-American: 0.5%
Percent in-state/out-of-state: 94%/6%
Percent Pub HS: NA
Number of Applicants: 13,967
Percent Accepted: 60%
Percent Accepted who enroll: 44%
Entering: 3,717
Transfers: NA
Application Deadline: 29 Jan
Mean SAT: NA
Mean ACT: NA

Middle 50% SAT range: 570–670 V, 600–690 M
Middle 50% ACT range: 26–29
3 Most popular majors: business management, education, engineering
Retention: 91%
Graduation rate: 67%
On-campus housing: NA
Fraternities: 15%
Sororities: 15%
Library: 3,401,279 volumes
Tuition and Fees: NA in; NA out
Room and Board: NA
Financial aid, first-year: 27%

While UF students are proud that their school has been noted as one of the top universities in the country according to *U.S. News and World Report*, they'd toss that accolade aside for a #1 ranking where outside opinion really matters: football. The school has a winning tradition in the sport, and the game against Florida State makes for the biggest weekend of the year, as well as one of the biggest pep rallies in the country. GatorGrowl, as the pep rally is known, typifies both American college life and the UF experience—quality football, parties, and fun.

Pride's for more than Saturday

Students are proud of their fun-loving reputation but emphasize that their education is both high-quality and strenuous. As admission standards of recent years have risen markedly, the school's prestige has increased accordingly. The general education core curriculum requires students to complete classes in math, English, the biological sciences, the humanities, and social and behavioral sciences. Nearly all Gators note the reputation of UF's teachers and programs as having been a decisive factor in their college choice. In particular, architecture, journalism, and engineering are quality programs. Business-related majors are popular as well. Choice of major is a decision that should be made early at UF. Said one student, "If you are going to change your major, change it early. If not, expect to stay an extra year. An honors program is available, acceptance to which is based on SAT score and high school GPA. In addition, study abroad programs are gaining popularity. Gripes about the academic experience at UF include the lecture classes of as many as seven hundred students and the preponderance of graduate students in teaching positions. One junior noted, however that the "personal attention" from TAs is a valuable asset.

Prowling Grounds

The main library, used for both studying and research, is the Smathers Library, which houses 2.5 million volumes, in two main libraries and nine branches. Students report that they often study in other quiet places, such as the computer labs or the Plaza of Americas park, due to the limited hours of the libraries. Social studying is based in the dorm lobbies. Other facilities available for student use on campus include the Florida Museum of Natural History, the Center for the Performing Arts, Harn Museum of Art, and the University Art Gallery. Further contributing to the breadth of Gators' opportunities are the world's largest citrus research center, a world-renowned institute for the study of the brain, a public television and radio station, and one of the largest health centers in the Southeast, the Shands hospital. Students enjoy the Florida sunshine on a gorgeous campus characterized by a variety of brick and Gothic-style buildings. One section of campus is on the National Register of Historic Places.

Quarters and Cuisine

Dorm living does not get as much praise as the dorms themselves. While one upperclassmen said, "It's good to experience it," she acknowledged that, "people are always happy to move off campus after the first year." Living on campus is optional, and most take advantage of the option freshman year in order to get acquainted with their classmates. Only upper-class students have the opportunity of getting into an ARF (apartment residence facility) and even these are rare. The rest of the dorms are generally small but comfortable doubles. There are RAs on every floor, and floor residents vote on visiting hours for members of the opposite sex. The only particularly undesirable dorms are Murphree and Buckman, which have no air-conditioning.

Students say that their dining options have improved recently and that they appreciate not being forced into a meal plan. Many take advantage of the offer, though, and food ranges from cafeteria-style, to fast food at the Hub, to vegetarian at the Gator Dining Corner.

Living the Florida Life

The campus is mainly self-contained and Gators can easily keep themselves occupied on its grounds. Besides the opportunities to be a spectator at premier college sporting events, UF students can participate in popular intramural sports including football, soccer, and tennis. Extracurricular activities abound; students can't point to the most popular ones because "there's seemingly as many groups as there are students." The *Alligator*, a student-run daily newspaper, and Florida Blue Key, a campus activity involvement organization, are two of the most well-known. Popular community service activities include Habitat for Humanity and volunteering for the Shands hospital.

Greek life is influential at UF. The fraternities and sororities dominate social life but non-Greeks don't feel left out. "We can still go to the parties and there's plenty other ways to meet people. You probably have to make more of an effort, though, and that's why there's some pressure to rush." All year long, Gators expect opportunities for socializing and drinking. Drugs are "without question available, but completely avoidable."

> "We all bleed orange and blue down here! FSU fans are the only thing we're not open-minded about."

Students do report that Gainesville caters to the university and that movies, malls, and restaurants are easily accessible with a car. Local clubs such as Torches and Maui's are popular too. Tampa, Talla-hassee, Jacksonville, and Orlando are all located within a two-hour drive, and students often make weekend trips to other colleges. Fans of the outdoors can take advantage of great year-round weather in Gainesville—and at the hour-away beaches located on the Gulf of Mexico or the Atlantic Ocean.

A Gator?

A junior laughed in response to the question, "Is there a student stereotype?" "With 42,000+ students we've got 'em all," he said. Florida students come from all over the country and remarkably diverse cultural backgrounds. Cultural organizations like the Black Student Union are popular. The lesbian and gay communities are large and in general students point to a "live and let live" feeling on campus. "We all bleed orange and blue down here! FSU fans are the only thing we're not open-minded about."

The spirit UF students exhibit for more than football reflects confidence in their school. Said one junior, "If you are looking for a good academic school and you want to experience all that college has to offer then UF is your place." At first overwhelmed by the great size and many opportunities of the University of Florida, students ultimately find niches at UF and unite to scream, "'If You're Not a GATOR, You're GATORBAIT!'" —*Ellen Moskowitz*

FYI
The three best things about attending University of Florida are "football, either the weather or the highly-ranked programs, and football."
The three worst things about attending University of Florida are "huge classes, parking (or lack thereof), and the sometimes sweltering heat."
The three things that every student should do before graduating from University of Florida are "watch the bats leave the bat house at dusk, attend a UF football game, and hang out on Payne's Prairie and watch the stars on a clear night."
One thing I'd like to have known before coming here is "that every freshman should come to summer classes before they come in the fall—it's a great time to meet new people."

University of Miami

Address: PO Box 248025;
Coral Gables, FL 33124-
4614
Phone: 305-284-4323
E-mail address:
admission@miami.edu
Web site URL:
www.miami.edu
Founded: 1925
Private or Public: private
Religious affiliation: none
Location: suburban
**Undergraduate
enrollment:** 8,235
Total enrollment: 13,715
Percent Male / Female:
45% / 55%
Percent Minority: 45%
Percent African-American:
11%

Percent Asian: 5%
Percent Hispanic:
28%
Percent Native-American:
0.5%
**Percent in-state / out-of-
state:** 55% / 45%
Percent Pub HS: NA
Number of Applicants:
12,280
Percent Accepted:
55%
**Percent Accepted who
enroll:** 28%
Entering: 1,859
Transfers: 643
Application Deadline:
1 Mar
Mean SAT: NA
Mean ACT: NA

Middle 50% SAT range:
520–630 V,
530–640 M
Middle 50% ACT range:
22–27
3 Most popular majors:
biology, psychology,
nursing
Retention: 83%
Graduation rate: 61%
On-campus housing:
72%
Fraternities: 13%
Sororities: 13%
Library: NA
Tuition and Fees:
$21,354 in; $21,354 out
Room and Board: $7,782
Financial aid, first-year:
71%

Thousands of students nervously watch as the football sails up in the air in the closing seconds of the annual University of Miami–Florida State University matchup. The ball arches and it's . . . wide right. With a collective sigh of relief and excitement, a wave of orange-and-green-clad students rush the Orange Bowl to celebrate a hard-earned victory and show the pride they feel in being a Hurricane. The passion students exhibit at the University of Miami isn't just for athletics but is also for the strong academic departments that will shape the education they receive in tropical South Florida.

No Suntanning 101

The University of Miami is comprised of 14 schools, which include arts and sciences, architecture, business administration, communications, education, engineering, international studies, law, medicine, music, marine and atmospheric science, continuing studies, nursing, and graduate studies. Until they declare a major, usually during sophomore year, students enroll in the College of Arts and Sciences. Course requirements vary depending on the school, but everyone must take English, social sci-

ence, and natural science core courses. Many students get out of these requirements through AP credits, but most "don't mind the core at all, because major requirements often overlap with required courses."

Typically there are about 15 students in each course. Large introductory lectures, such as biology and chemistry, can enroll upward of 200 students. Most agree that getting into a class does not pose a problem, even for freshmen. Reportedly, the science courses are "the toughest around" and weed out many pre-med students. Exclusively open to Florida residents is the elite six-year medical school program, which grants automatic entrance into UM's medical school after two years. Competition to get into the program is tough, as only 25 students are granted admission per year. In addition to science, the architecture and music programs are also considered rigorous, as is the internationally renowned School of Marine Science. Business, education, and communications are reportedly easier majors.

Most students enjoy their classes because of the excellent faculty. Professors try to be accessible to students, even in the largest of lecture courses. "I know my professors on a first-name basis," said one junior. Classes are mostly taught by professors, even at the introductory level. Teaching assistants are also available to help students and often conduct review sessions before exams. Freshmen are assigned to faculty advisors to help devise a course of study that is both broad and focused on specific interests. After declaring a major, students are assigned to an advisor in their respective departments. Undergrads generally agree, "Advisors are great and supportive. They're there to help with all kinds of academic problems."

Applicants who score at least 1360 on the SAT and rank in the top 10% of their class are invited to join the honors program. Students enrolled in the program must maintain a GPA of 3.3 and take at least one honors class per semester. In addition to the six-year medical school program, Dual Admission Honors programs are available, which offer both a bachelors and masters degree in biomedical engineering, marine geology, or physical therapy. The university also offers an extensive study abroad program for those who are interested in a wide variety of majors, such as international studies and marine science.

Clubbing and Sunning (Social)

The weekend begins on Thursday at UM, when a wide array of social options await students, both on and off campus. Advance movie screenings at the university's theater or on the outdoor screen are popular for on-campus relaxation. Toga and patio-themed parties also provide entertainment for students. A significant portion of on-campus social events revolve around the Greek scene. Many frats advertise parties all around campus and tend not to charge admission. Some, however, are by invitation only. Although drinking is prevalent on campus, one student said, "Non-drinkers don't feel left out." "If you do, do; if you don't, don't," seems to be the general attitude toward drinking on campus. Alcohol is not allowed in any dorm with residents under 21, but it is still present in many on-campus apartments. For a campus with "lots of attractive people," random hookups do happen but not with oppressive frequency; as one junior put it, "UM is not a sex melting pot."

The University Center, with comfortable couches, TVs, an arcade, and Ping-Pong tables, offers a relaxing and social environment. The Rathskellar, referred to as "the Rat," frequently hosts bands and comedians and is another place where students go for a bite or a game of pool.

Clubbing and the Tropical Paradise

The university's close proximity to South Florida hangouts offers students a number of off-campus activities. Parking is a major problem, and many students opt out of bringing cars to campus. While some find not having a car to be constricting, they have no trouble getting around thanks to the aboveground railway, the Metrorail, which is close to campus. Just a short ride away on the Metrorail are Coconut Grove and South Beach, where students shop, go clubbing, or hang out on the beach. At South Beach, where beautiful people come from all around to sunbathe in the unique Miami atmosphere, students "get an eyeful every day." A law was recently passed increasing the minimum age for admittance to clubs to 21 for women, who were previously let in at 18. This has made clubbing a less viable social option than it once was, although "a lot of people try to get fake IDs." Students also frequent Sunset Place to catch a movie and Bayside, where they can shop at the boutiques that line the streets. Although there is a lot in Miami to tempt them away from schoolwork, students claim, "You can't slack off, or the work will catch up with you." The work-hard, play-hard attitude prevails across campus.

Back from South Beach

Students rave about the beauty of the campus. Lake Osceola sits at its center and is surrounded by palm trees and other tropical foliage. "It feels almost like a resort," said one junior. Many students enjoy the very "relaxed and laid-back atmosphere." The campus is kept clean, and students claim that one can rarely find graffiti. The warm tropical climate lends itself to t-shirts and shorts all year round. Students also praise the diversity of the campus. "No matter what ethnicity you come from, there is always someone [like you] here," said one freshman. Some, however, noticed that certain groups form cliques, which can make it difficult to meet people. Despite the wealthy Coral Gables neighborhood that surrounds campus, there are areas nearby that students try to stay away from.

The coed dorms include Eaton, Stanford, Walsh, Pentland, McDonald's, Pierson, Mahoney, and Hecht. All dorms are air-conditioned, but many students lament the fact that the windows cannot be opened. All freshmen who do not commute to school are required to live on campus in the same dorms as upperclassmen. Generally, freshmen will live in a unit consisting of two doubles and one shared bathroom. Pierson and Mahoney are regarded as the best dorms, although Eaton also received high marks. Security is "very tight." Students are required to swipe their "Cane Card" for dorm access and have to check in with residential advisors, who live on the same floors as freshmen, late at night and early in the morning. Students who need quiet study time head to study rooms in their dorms or to Richter Library, which is open 24 hours a day and has copy machines and computer labs.

> **"If you don't go to the game, you have no school spirit."**

Dining is viewed as "adequate, but it gets tiresome." A popular food court, called the Hurricane, offers food from chains such as Panda Express and Sbarros. The general complaint about the two main dining halls, Hecht-Stanford and Pierson-Mahoney, is that their hours aren't flexible enough for most students' schedules. On-campus students must purchase a meal plan that ranges from 8 to 21 meals per week. The Caf is a popular place not only to eat but also to socialize. Salad bars and meal options such as quiches provide vegetarians with adequate culinary alternatives.

Hurricane Force Wins

Athletics play a huge role at the University of Miami, and the school has a long winning tradition in a multitude of sports. The biggest event of the year is the annual football game against Florida State University at the historic Orange Bowl. "If you don't go to the game, you have no school spirit," claimed one sophomore. Football isn't the only sport that the Hurricanes excel at. Recently, the University of Miami basketball team made it to the Sweet Sixteen for the first time in team history, and the baseball team won the College World Championship in 1999. Tickets to sporting events are provided to all students free of charge, and, as a result, games are widely attended and the teams are enthusiastically supported.

The recently constructed Wellness Center received rave reviews from almost all students. The facility contains modern weight training equipment, racquetball and basketball courts, Olympic-sized swimming pools, an elevated jogging track, and even a health juice bar. At the Wellness Center, many students participate in a variety of intramurals, ranging from touch football to floor hockey. For those not looking for a huge commitment, the Wellness Center is a sure bet for a quick pickup game.

Students praise the university's strength and dedication to a wide variety of disciplines. For those who don't need cold New England winters to force them to study, UM offers a tropical climate all year round with a unique South Florida atmosphere. Students demonstrate a strong sense of pride in their school's academic and athletic accomplishments. "The focus isn't just on academics and it isn't just on partying. There's no better place to spend four years than sunny South Florida."
—*Aaron Droller*

FYI
The three best things about attending the University of Miami are "medium-sized school with big-school sports, proximity to the beach, and small classes."
The three worst things about attending the University of Miami are "sucky dorms, the parking situation, and people are kind of snobby."
The three things that every student should do before graduating from the University of Miami are "go to South Beach, visit the Everglades, and learn to speak Spanish!"
One thing I'd like to have known before coming here is that "everyone is huge, so I wish I started working out before."

Georgia

Address: 141 E. College Avenue; Atlanta / Decatur, GA 30030
Phone: 404-471-6285
E-mail address: admission-@agnesscott.edu
Web site URL: www.adgnesscott.edu
Founded: 1889
Private or Public: private
Religious affiliation: Presbyterian
Location: urban
Undergraduate enrollment: 834
Total enrollment: 887
Percent Male / Female: 0% / 100%
Percent Minority: 29%

Percent African-American: 20%
Percent Asian: 5%
Percent Hispanic: 3%
Percent Native-American: 0.5%
Percent in-state / out-of-state: 50% / 50%
Percent Pub HS: 80%
Number of Applicants: 688
Percent Accepted: 77%
Percent Accepted who enroll: 45%
Entering: 241
Transfers: 25
Application Deadline: 1 Mar
Mean SAT: NA
Mean ACT: NA

Middle 50% SAT range: 580–680 V, 530–640 M
Middle 50% ACT range: 24–29
3 Most popular majors: biology, English, psychology
Retention: 82%
Graduation rate: 66%
On-campus housing: 98%
Fraternities: NA
Sororities: NA
Library: 208,283 volumes
Tuition and Fees: $16,745 in; $16,745 out
Room and Board: $6,900
Financial aid, first-year: 72%

W hat is your favorite scary movie? *Scream 2*, perhaps? The beautiful college campus featured in the blockbuster movie is none other than all-female Agnes Scott College in Decatur, Georgia. Of course, Agnes Scott comes free of the gore and scary masks. The women who attend Agnes Scott swear that the luxurious buildings shown in the film are definitely for real and assert that the campus is one of the most appealing aspects of their school.

Beautiful Setting

Agnes Scott is a very small campus located six miles outside of Atlanta. According to one sophomore, "it only takes about 15 minutes to walk the entire campus." When asked what she most loved about her school, another student said, "I love the fact that it's a really nice-looking campus." The campus is built around the Quadrangle, simply called the "Quad," which one student described as "a nice, green area in the middle of the campus." From the Quadrangle, one can soak in the splendor of Gothic architecture, which is a characteristic of many of the dorms and buildings on campus. According to the students, Agnes Scott possesses many other scenic locations where students can go to relax. Some cited the most peaceful place on campus as the amphitheater, an outdoor area that now largely goes unused. "A lot of people don't go down there, so it's a good place to go when you need to be alone." Another sophomore mentioned the "Secret Garden." To get there, "you have to walk through the first floor of the library, then walk down some steps, when you come to this really cute walled-in courtyard. It's a fun place to be." The "Secret Garden," however, is currently not accessible to students due to a massive renovation project that Agnes Scott is now undergoing. Hoping to increase enrollment, the college has made renovations to a number of buildings, including Bradley Observatory and McCain Library, and built the new Alston Campus Center, which houses a bookstore, snack shop, meeting rooms for student groups, administrative offices, and a post office. Aside from the construction, the beauty and seclusion of the campus are still present and the students make sure to take advantage of it.

> **"We sometimes get flak for being a women's college, but they don't prepare us to be housewives. They're trying to empower us."**

Being on a small campus in a small city, however, does come with a number of drawbacks. Most students have cars, including freshmen, because certain student necessities are not readily available on campus. One student stated, "I wish we had a grocery store on campus. To get to the nearest grocery store or the drug store, you have to have a car." Another student complained that "Agnes Scott really needs more coffeehouse sorts of establishments. I get tired of having to walk to a coffeehouse all the time." Despite any complaints the campus might garner from students, most students say they do feel safe. One student contended that "the public safety officers are pretty on top of everything, so I'm not terribly worried."

It is also on campus that Agnes Scott students celebrate Black Cat, which one student summed up as "our equivalent of homecoming." During the week-long celebration, the four classes—frosh to seniors—engage in "Color Wars." Each class is assigned a color, which it uses to determine a mascot. Students play jokes on each other during the week and upperclassmen try to guess what the frosh have chosen as their mascot. The celebration includes singing of "sister songs" and a bonfire. The juniors put on the Junior Production, a two-hour extravaganza consisting of skits poking fun at first-years, professors, the administration, and Agnes Scott in general. The week culminates in a big formal on Saturday night, where one

of the classes is announced as the winner, based on various competitions, such as the one for best hall and door decorations.

Classes: Small but Challenging

Students of Agnes Scott say they study hard. As one student put it, the classes are "not-too-hard, but it's hard to get an A." The college sets specific and distribution standards for its students. The specific standards consist of two courses in English composition, intermediate competency in a foreign language, and two semester hours of physical education. The distribution standards require students to take courses in literature, history, philosophy, fine arts, and social sciences. In addition, one math course must be taken, as well as a natural science course including laboratory work. Regarding these requirements, one student said, "they're pretty lenient, really. Whatever you major in, you're going to go ahead and fulfill the standards somehow." Though the requirements are generally well accepted, one student did say that "parts of the requirements are sort of stupid."

Almost all students said that getting into classes was rarely a problem. Registration, as one student put it, "is very laid back. You fill out a registration card, go to the registration place at the assigned time, and they put it in the computer." Most students who do not get into their desired courses are freshman because they register a few days after the upperclasswomen, and, as a result, some of the bigger, introductory classes may already be filled. One student praised academics at Agnes Scott as giving "lots of opportunities. You get to take a lot of classes. Very few classes fill up, and even then, they open up a new section." Students insist that class size is small. "I've never had a class with more than 30 people, and as a freshman, I was in a class composed of only four people including myself," said one student. The small size, however, is also a cause of grievance among many of the students. One sophomore said that due to the small enrollment, professors "care too much about attendance. They always know who's absent." Another student cited the small size of the college as contributing to the fact that "sometimes, they don't have as many classes as you might want." If course selection is indeed a problem, however, Agnes Scott students are given the option of taking classes at any other Atlanta university. "It's great because you can take the course and the school pays for your cab fare," exclaimed one student.

Students unanimously declared the sciences as the harder classes, although English is also rumored to have some fairly difficult courses. Biology and English appear to be the strongest departments, as well as the most popular majors. The English department has drawn a number of prominent female writers to come and speak, including Alice Walker, Jamaica Kincaid, and Margaret Atwood. Professors are reportedly "very accessible. They have office hours and the faculty hall doors are always open." Only professors teach courses, with the exception of instructors who teach foreign languages or lab components to the science classes, although in the latter case, there is always a professor involved as well. Students have generally been very pleased with their professors and appreciate the interdisciplinary approaches sometimes used in class. Another aspect of academic life that Agnes Scott students are particularly happy with is the International Education Office, which provides high quality study abroad programs to upperclasswomen.

The Draw of Atlanta

Although Agnes Scott students do study hard and some freshman say they stay on campus all the time, most of the students enjoy leaving the Agnes Scott campus to do some partying. "We're really close to downtown Atlanta, so we just go to parties there, usually frat parties at Georgia Tech," said one student. For those interested in dancing, there are reportedly lots of clubs for the over-21 crowd. Students without cars can take the MARTA, the local public transport system and arrive in the city within 15 minutes. One freshman did say that, "There are some clubs where you only need to be 18, but some of the over-21 clubs have a college night anyway." While Atlanta may be popular, there are also things to do on the Agnes Scott campus. "They show movies on the Quad and sometimes we even have big-name

comedians come, such as Bobcat Goldthwaite and Tommy Davidson," stated one student. Official parties are also thrown on campus, but one student said that "it's hard to get guys to come here from their own campuses." Free beer is always served at these parties, but "it's really silly because only about 10 people on the campus are old enough to drink and the administration is very strict about underage drinking." Other popular weekend options include eating out at restaurants or coffeehouses in Decatur.

Bad Food, Great Rooms

Many Agnes Scott students enjoy eating off campus because the dining hall food does not receive terribly good reviews. One student did concede, however, "it's not bad for dining hall food. You can always find something edible." All Agnes Scott students are required to purchase a meal plan, which, in addition to a certain number of meals, in a week, includes a declining balance used when the dining hall is not open. Agnes Scott students have the option of going to Ebans dining hall or the snack bar, once termed Scotland Yard. One student griped about the dining hall hours, saying that, "the hours are pretty narrow and the system is sometimes slow." Vegetarian students are accommodated in the dining hall. "They have veggie burgers, yogurt, the salad bar, and there's always at least one vegetarian entrée." Due to the short hours, however, one student said, "I have to depend on the snack bar quite a bit." Students who go to the snack bar can choose from fast-food-style food, namely hamburgers. One upperclasswoman said, "Actually, I usually eat out unless I'm broke. There are good restaurants in the area, particularly in downtown Atlanta."

While the food is not stellar, Agnes Scott students certainly rave about the dorms. One student described the dorms as "huge." First-years live in two dorms, Winship and Walters. Most dorms have air-conditioning, and many frosh get singles. Due to the renovations, however, many students are now required to have roommates, which "isn't as luxurious, but it's still nice," said one student. All rooms have cable access and a phone line on each side, so it is possible for those students living in singles to use both a telephone and a modem at the same time, if necessary. After first year, room assignments are decided by lottery, with preference given to upperclasswomen. Agnes Scott students are required to live on campus, unless they are over 21 or are married. The college, however, recently purchased a nearby apartment building, which is also considered on-campus housing. In certain dorms, students have the option of living in language halls, where TAs of a particular language can be found and where foreign-language tables are held.

In Their Spare Time

Students like to joke that there are two stereotypical views of the Agnes Scott student: either she is a "preppy, southern, well-off girl" or else she is a lesbian. They are quick to point out, though, that at Agnes Scott, neither of these stereotypes constitutes the majority. When they aren't watching TV or going to work out at Woodruff, the gym, the women at Agnes Scott also engage in extracurricular activities. According to one student, however, "there doesn't seem to be much of a presence from what I've seen. Community service isn't all that popular." Nevertheless, there are clubs for those interested in joining. There are a number of ethnic clubs for students of color and service clubs such as Circle K and the Campus Civitan, which focuses on helping the disabled. There are also organizations for ecology buffs, as well as outdoor activities, such as hiking and rafting.

Aside from extracurricular activities, some students do participate in sports. As one student declared, "We have them, but they're not very visible. Only the people who play them are into them." There isn't a particularly high level of school spirit, but students do attend some of the games nonetheless. The most visible teams at Agnes Scott are the softball team and the rugby team. Students not interested in intercollegiate sports can participate in activities at Woodruff gym. One sports club, the Century Club, makes a goal of running 100 miles by the end of the semester.

Set in the heart of Georgia, Agnes Scott College provides a rigorous academic environment and the pleasures of both the suburbs and the big city. Agnes Scott students love their school and, for the most part, have never regretted their decision to go there. One sophomore said, "I definitely think this is a good school and that it's preparing me for my future." Regarding the fact that Agnes Scott is a women's school, another student commented, "We sometimes get flak for being a women's college, but they don't prepare us to be housewives. They're trying to empower us." —*Shu-Ping Shen and Staff*

FYI

The three best things about attending Agnes Scott are "there are no TAs—all classes are taught by professors, it's near Atlanta, a great city with many opportunities for internships and things for college kids to do, and classes are small, so there are lots of chances for class discussion."

The three worst things about attending Agnes Scott are "there is a great deal of bigotry and racism, not much variety in terms of things to do, and it is all girls, and some people here preach that virtually all men are evil and should not be trusted."

The three things every student should do before graduating from Agnes Scott are "study abroad—the school pays for it, get engaged—there's this great tradition that when you get engaged, you get thrown into this stinky pond behind the alumnae house, and mud wrestle on field day during Black Cat week."

One thing I'd like to have known before coming here is "that virtually every girl goes home for the weekend. The campus is very dead after about 7 P.M., and on the weekends there is no one around."

Emory University

Address: 200 B. Jones Center; Atlanta, GA 30322
Phone: 404-727-6036
E-mail address: admiss@emory.edu
Web site URL: www.emory.edu
Founded: 1836
Private or Public: private
Religious affiliation: none
Location: urban
Undergraduate enrollment: 6,190
Total enrollment: 11,000
Percent Male/Female: 45%/55%
Percent Minority: 29%
Percent African-American: 10%

Percent Asian: 15%
Percent Hispanic: 3%
Percent Native-American: 0.5%
Percent in-state/out-of-state: 13%/87%
Percent Pub HS: 70%
Number of Applicants: 9,866
Percent Accepted: 43%
Percent Accepted who enroll: 36%
Entering: 1,520
Transfers: 125
Application Deadline: 15 Jan
Mean SAT: NA
Mean ACT: NA

Middle 50% SAT range: 630–710 V, 650–720 M
Middle 50% ACT range: 27–31
3 Most popular majors: biology, political science, business
Retention: 92%
Graduation rate: 90%
On-campus housing: 100%
Fraternities: 43%
Sororities: 58%
Library: 2,700,000 volumes
Tuition and Fees: $23,130 in; $23,130 out
Room and Board: $7,650
Financial aid, first-year: 57%

Located just outside Atlanta, Emory University is a thriving institution committed to academic excellence, social discovery, and comfortable living. Emory has been described by some as a northeastern institution located in the heart of Dixie. However, as any visitor to this beautifully modern campus can tell you, Emory does have that distinctive southern charm. Within the last decade, Emory has enjoyed a meteoric rise in popularity and, consequently, applications have risen almost 100%. It appears students are flocking to Atlanta to take advantage of an educational cornucopia.

Academia Personified

Students rave about the academics at Emory University. Most departments at Emory maintain a world-class reputation while still managing to concern themselves with the undergraduate population. Notable professors include former United States president Jimmy Carter and Nobel Prize winner in literature Wole Soyinka. The most recent freshman class has a particularly pre-professional bent, with over one-third intending to enter medical school and a sizable minority interested in law school. As a result, introductory courses, commonly known as weed-out courses, are fairly difficult and, by all measures, serve their purpose.

Psychology, biology, and political science are the most popular majors. Business and English are also favorites and are rumored to be among the best undergraduate degree programs. Competition, although not cutthroat, can be intense. Most upperclassmen see the competitive atmosphere slowly diminish as time goes by, and it certainly is not something that defines Emory.

All Emory students are required to fulfill distributional requirements in the natural sciences, history, aesthetics and values, and writing and complete a Phys Ed credit. PE course offerings include "health" class, widely regarded as a "complete waste of time, energy, and overheads." Studying abroad is also a popular option for Emory students, and the university offers programs in Mexico, Kenya, France, India, Israel, Italy, Japan, and Russia. Students interested in biomedical sciences certainly have access to some enviable resources, since the CDC and American Cancer Society are located along the Clifton Corridor right near the university. The School of Medicine also sponsors outside research projects that are open to interested, qualified undergraduates.

Within the university system there is Oxford College, located in Oxford, Georgia. Oxford is a two-year institution, and upon completion of those two years students move to the main campus in Druid Hills. Emory also offers a full scholarship to students of exceptional academic merit. Known as the Emory Scholars, these students are paired up with professors who act as advisors and aid them in research and study.

Thank You, Coca-Cola

Renovations on campus are occurring at a feverish rate. Structurally, many of the buildings at Emory are brand-new, including recently opened Emerson Hall, which will house new offices and classroom space for chemistry, mathematics, and physics. The project is part of Science 2000, an initiative meant to provide more facilities to the burgeoning Emory science program. The funds for the recent rash of renovations come from the ever-increasing Emory endowment, now totaling more than $4.5 billion. Emory currently has 20 projects under construction with a budget of an estimated $190 million. There are 20 further projects in the pipeline, adding another $236 million in costs. On tap are new science buildings, residential halls, research centers, and renovations to existing structures. There is even talk of creating a residential college system that mimics Yale's and Stanford's.

The campus itself is replete with grassy courtyards and windy tree-lined roads. On balmy days, students can be seen sunning, reading, and tossing around Frisbees and footballs. The administration is currently planning to make Emory more pedestrian-friendly and hopes to remove cars from the main portion of the campus.

Ole' Times There Not Forgotten

Most students live on campus and first-years have a variety of housing options. Turman East is notoriously far away from central campus locales. Longstreet is located right next to the Dobbs University Center, which houses the main dining

hall, mailroom, and bookstore. Dining options include Chick-Fil-A and Burger King. A McDonald's recently opened on campus. Other freshman dorms include Harris, which is small and cramped. Dobbs is also on the small side, but fosters an incredible sense of community. The gem of Emory housing is undoubtedly the Complex, containing three residential halls, Thomas, Hopkins, and Smith. It is both spacious and conveniently located. Freshman rooms tend to be doubles, but upperclassmen have the option of living in on-campus apartments. After a year or two of dorm life, this can be a popular option. Freshman floors in the dorms have both a residential advisor and a student advisor. The RA is charged more with rule enforcement while the SA is the sagacious confidant who still remembers the trials and tribulations of freshman year.

Campus facilities include the Woodruff Gym, which houses an indoor track, swimming pools, weight rooms, a dance studio, and a rock-climbing wall. The Woodruff Library, the largest library on campus, is open 24 hours a day to accommodate the studious Emory student body.

> "The Greek system is ubiquitous and plays a major role in many campus events."

Partying on campus is mainly centered on the Row, a street lined with sorority and fraternity houses. One of the largest parties of the year, Bid Day, celebrating the taking on of new pledges, is widely regarded as a "complete and total saturnalia." Dooley's Ball is another "orgy of fun, alcohol, and mad hookups." The ball, located on McDonough Field, draws upward of 3,000 students. Maggie's, the big campus watering hole, is a popular weekend destination and is known for "sporadic carding." Freshman can also look forward to their semi-annual ball and songfest, a gala freshman musical extravaganza, is an oft-anticipated event. The popular Homecoming event allows students to get their groove on to some awesome bands. This year's headline act: Naughty By Nature.

Students report that alcohol is prevalent on campus, and drug use is also not uncommon. As one student put it in a newspaper editorial, "Drinking is fun and it's going to happen." As for significant others, it appears that the hookup has replaced the date on the Emory campus. Homosexuals, while tolerated, are not a very active part of the campus community.

Greek life is indeed dominant on campus: "The Greek system is ubiquitous and plays a major role in many campus events." Some lament that the Greeks play too big a role, but others welcome their participation and parties. The rush process is a big obstacle for most freshmen, with a sizable minority deciding to go for bids.

Atlanta provides a variety of options for those dissatisfied with on-campus fun. With the public transportation earning only mediocre reviews, the truly social student must have a car. Unfortunately, frosh aren't allowed to have cars. Atlanta has its famed underground mall, students can always catch championship baseball with the hometown Braves, and Fox Theatre earns rave reviews. Little Five Points is a place where the hippies can chill and is filled with coffee shops and retro stores. Upscale Buckhead has some kick-ass clubs, including the Chili Pepper and Cotton Club. One Emory student calls Atlanta "the best thing to happen to Emory since Coca-Cola stopped adding cocaine to their soft drinks" and says it allows a lot of students to "blow off steam."

Your Fellow Men and Women of Dixie

Emory has a student body that is extraordinarily diverse, both ethnically and geographically. The ethnic diversity has led to some self-segregation on campus, which students often complain about. The *Princeton Review* identified Emory as having significant problems with race relations. Emory has a relatively large Jewish community, leading some students to identify Emory as "Early Methodist and only recently Yiddish." Although conservatives do have their place, Emory is certainly a bastion of liberalism in the increasingly Republican South. However, despite some complaints, students uniformly praise Emory as, "a place that lets you mature, grow, and discover those things that will help define you for the rest of your life. There's a feeling I get that I can't quite describe upon arriving back on campus after a long summer, perhaps a mix of relief and excitement. I'm finally back home." —*Robert Wong*

FYI
The three best things about attending Emory are "internships, the diversity of students and opinions, and Atlanta."
The three worst things about attending Emory are "no cars for frosh, the public transportation, and the fact that I've gained 10 pounds eating Big Macs."
The three things every student should do before graduating from Emory are "attend Dooley's Ball, hear Jimmy Carter speak, and go to Buckhead . . . a lot."
One thing I'd like to have known before coming here is "how everyone is pre-med!"

Georgia Institute of Technology

Address: 225 North Avenue; Atlanta, GA 30332-0230
Phone: 404-894-4154
E-mail address: admissions @success.gatech.edu
Web site URL: www.gatech.edu
Founded: 1885
Private or Public: public
Religious affiliation: none
Location: urban
Undergraduate enrollment: 10,171
Total enrollment: 14,072
Percent Male/Female: 71%/29%
Percent Minority: 26%

Percent African-American: 9%
Percent Asian: 13%
Percent Hispanic: 3%
Percent Native-American: 0.5%
Percent in-state/out-of-state: 67%/33%
Percent Pub HS: 75%
Number of Applicants: 7,579
Percent Accepted: 69%
Percent Accepted who enroll: 45%
Entering: 2,320
Transfers: 455
Application Deadline: 15 Jan
Mean SAT: 630 V, 674 M
Mean ACT: NA

Middle 50% SAT range: 590–690 V, 630–725 M
Middle 50% ACT range: NA
3 Most popular majors: industrial, electrical, and mechanical engineering
Retention: 88%
Graduation rate: 70%
On-campus housing: 95%
Fraternities: 25%
Sororities: 25%
Library: 3,500,000 volumes
Tuition and Fees: $3,107 in; $10,349 out
Room and Board: $4,976
Financial aid, first-year: 43%

The Degree and the Ratio. Ask any student at the Georgia Institute of Technology about the best and worst aspects of life as a Yellow Jacket, and he or she is likely to mention one or both of these subjects. The Degree refers to the pride and prestige students feel having graduating from one of America's premier engineering schools. The Ratio, however, pertains to the nearly 3-to-1 proportion of male and female students on campus—which may be seen as either positive or negative, depending on one's gender of preference.

Survival of the Fittest

When asked about the rigors of the academic curriculum at Georgia Tech, or just "Tech," as it's more commonly known, one student replied that "around here, it's not graduation; it's survival." All Tech students are required to fulfill a core curriculum including classes in English, math, science, and the humanities. Most students complete this requirement by the end of their freshman year, and many regard the core classes as helpful in selecting a major of interest. Most students go on to major in some field of engineering—

indeed, each of the three most popular majors at GT end in the formidable "E-word." While "this is definitely a school for math and science people," Tech students majoring in English and other non-technical fields are happy with their education. Said one, "Yes, the school as a whole caters to engineering, but not at the expense of the classes that interest people like me." Computer science is commonly regarded as the single hardest course of study, with classes in programming and Java script known to aggravate even the toughest self-described "computer geeks." A special term known as "hopping on the M-train" has been created for those students who begin their time at Tech as engineering majors but become overwhelmed with the work. "M" is short for "management," and most GT students agree that this business degree is the easiest path toward a diploma on campus.

Many students wishing to gather real-world experience while still in school participate in GT's Cooperative Education Program, known around campus simply as "Co-op." In this largest program of its kind in the U.S., students usually complete their undergraduate degrees in five years on an alternating schedule of a semester in school and a semester at a job of their choice. Over 650 employers work with Georgia Tech under the program, and around one-third of the students Co-op at some point in their studies. While students are not obligated to work for the company they Co-op with once they graduate, many choose to do so, and recent employers have included such well-known companies as AT&T, Coca-Cola, and Sony Entertainment.

Tech prides itself on staying on the cutting edge of technology and requires every student to own a computer. Financial aid is available for those who cannot afford them, and expenses for necessary software are included in each semester's tuition. In addition, all course registration is accomplished via the Internet. Priority is given to upperclassmen and athletes, but few students report major difficulties getting into the classes they want. Many intro classes are large, especially in the more popular majors; however, as students begin more advanced courses, class sizes decrease. All classes are taught by professors, with graduate students often leading recitation sections. Students warn that grading can sometimes be harsh, especially on freshmen used to earning near-perfect grades with little effort in high school. Thus joining the "square-root club," in which a student's GPA is less than 1.0, is a common yet dreaded fate. Other students remark that while tough, grading is relatively fair across departments, but "if you're not ready to work, just getting out of here will be a challenge."

Atlanta and Beyond

While students stop short of saying that the social scene on the Tech campus is dominated by the Greek system, over a quarter of both men and women join a fraternity or sorority. Pi Kappa Alpha and Phi Gamma Delta are well known among the university's 31 fraternities, while Alpha Chi Omega and Alpha Delta Pi are two of Tech's eight sororities. Most of the year's large parties are hosted by various fraternities and have recently included themes such as Mardi Gras and Beach Party. Most Greek parties are open to the entire university; however, male non-Greeks generally do not attend. Given Tech's gender ratio, most women are usually welcome at parties. As stated by one fraternity member, "We never close our doors on a pretty face."

Although one non-Greek sophomore noted that it's hard for non-Greeks to fit into the GT party scene, other options abound. Tech's location in the middle of Atlanta is considered its greatest asset, socially speaking. One senior summed up this situation by saying, "I think we might miss out on some of the campus-related events held at other, less urban state schools, but then again, we have a thriving city right in our backyard." Atlanta does play a large role in the lives of many Tech students. Favorite eateries include the Varsity, notable for being the world's largest drive-in restaurant, and pizza hangouts such as Fellini's and Mellow Mushroom. Atlanta also boasts a flourishing music scene, allowing GT students to hear up-and-coming acoustic acts at Eddie's Attic, dance to the latest swing music at the Masquerade, or rock to nationally known bands at the Roxy or Cotton Club. Also popular for its vast array of bars and nightspots is the Buckhead district, although underage students are warned by upperclassmen that fake IDs are commonly spotted and confiscated.

For those who wish to stay on campus, intramural sports are a common pastime, as are SGA, the Student Government Association, and SWARM, an organization of over 500 members known for going crazy in support of their GT Yellow Jacket athletic teams. Community service is also popular, especially Atlanta-based Habitat for Humanity. In addition, each November students organize TEAM (Tech Enhancing Atlanta Metropolitan) Buzz, after the university's mascot, Buzz the Yellow Jacket. In 2000, TEAM Buzz placed 1,800 student, faculty, and alumni volunteers in over 60 separate community service projects.

The majority of Tech students are crazy about their varsity sports teams. The social scene during fall semester revolves around Yellow Jacket football, especially the big game with the University of Georgia. During the spring, the Jackets focus on perennially powerful basketball and baseball programs. School spirit always runs high, as evidenced by the ever-present yellow paraphernalia worn by students on their way to class.

Freshman Experience

Most Georgia Tech students begin their college careers living with other members of their class in a program called Freshman Experience. Although the program is not mandatory, a majority of freshmen participate. Those involved live together in a group of seven residence halls located around Brittain Dining Hall on East Campus or in a group of four residence halls near Woodruff Dining Hall on West Campus. Each Freshman Experience group is led by an upperclassman peer leader, or "PL." Tech freshmen note that PLs, similar to residential advisors, are present to offer help and guidance and rarely enforce dorm regulations. All Freshman Experience participants also take Psychology 1000, a class geared toward helping each new student adjust to the rigors of college life.

> "I think we might miss out on some of the campus-related events held at other, less urban state schools, but then again, we have a thriving city right in our backyard."

After freshman year, those who wish to remain on campus may choose between dorms on either East or West Campus, as well as apartment-style dorms left to the university after originally housing athletes during the 1996 Atlanta Olympic Games. Many upperclassmen also elect to find a private apartment in or around Atlanta. Only students in Freshman Experience are required to buy a meal plan, although most students who live in university-provided housing elect to purchase this option. While the East and West Campus dining halls offer "standard, not-so-great cafeteria fare," students find them attractive and always clean. For those craving fast food, the Student Center also offers Burger King, Chick-Fil-A, Pizza Hut, Häagen-Dazs, and Krispy Kreme, all of which accept the university "BuzzCard" and bill students directly, without the use of cash.

The BuzzCard also acts as a Tech student's access card to many buildings on campus, including the "gargantuan" Student Athletic Complex, or SAC. Home to weight rooms, racquetball, squash and tennis courts, a pool, a jogging track, and various other sports-related facilities, the SAC is a favorite destination for many Yellow Jackets. Also impressive is the Aquatics Center, another remnant of the 1996 Olympic Games. Even non-swimming students enjoy this beautifully engineered outdoor structure, home to one of the fastest pools in the world.

While some students complain that the Tech campus is lacking in greenery, others commend the university for its "grass-covered nooks and crannies." As one student explained, "I heard people in my high school call Tech the 'concrete campus,' but once I got here I realized that really isn't true." Being right in the middle of Atlanta, however, means the university is constantly in a state of near crisis over parking. Bikes are encouraged by the administration and students alike, as driving to class "is a big no-no." Despite this fact, many students own cars and use them for traveling around the city.

Though they may moan over tough courses and heavy workloads, Tech students enjoy the prestige of learning at one of America's top engineering schools. With the skyscrapers of Atlanta rising over their heads and a world of social and academic opportunities at their feet, this should come as no surprise. —*Robert Berschinski*

FYI

The three best things about attending Georgia Tech are "the absolutely amazing engineering departments, the strength of almost all the sports teams, and being right in downtown Atlanta."

The three worst things about attending Georgia Tech are "the ratio of men to women, the grading, which can often be terrifying, and freshman housing."

The three things that every student should do before graduating from Georgia Tech are "attempt to tear down the hedges at the University of Georgia, find a favorite restaurant in Atlanta, and learn how to use MARTA [the city's rail system]."

One thing I'd like to have known before coming here is "that the school isn't just for computer nerds—although there are lots of those, too."

Morehouse College

Address: 830 Westview Drive, SW; Atlanta, GA 30314
Phone: 404-681-2800
E-mail address: apattillo@morehouse.edu
Web site URL: www.morehouse.edu
Founded: 1867
Private or Public: private
Religious affiliation: none
Location: urban
Undergraduate enrollment: 3,012
Total enrollment: 3,012
Percent Male/Female: 100%/0%
Percent Minority: 100%
Percent African-American: 99%

Percent Asian: 0.5%
Percent Hispanic: 0.5%
Percent Native-American: NA
Percent in-state/out-of-state: 31%/69%
Percent Pub HS: 82%
Number of Applicants: 2,785
Percent Accepted: 66%
Percent Accepted who enroll: 41%
Entering: 748
Transfers: 85
Application Deadline: 15 Feb
Mean SAT: 526 V, 530 M
Mean ACT: 23

Middle 50% SAT range: 440–680 V, 470–680 M
Middle 50% ACT range: 19–32
3 Most popular majors: engineering, business administration, biology
Retention: 82%
Graduation rate: 31%
On-campus housing: 45%
Fraternities: 7%
Sororities: NA
Library: 550,000 volumes
Tuition and Fees: $11,738 in; $11,738 out
Room and Board: $6,970
Financial aid, first-year: 85%

U ndergrads may learn engineering or biology in their time at Morehouse, but most important, students say, they learn the true meaning and value of the word brotherhood. For many of Morehouse's illustrious alumni, such as Dr. Martin Luther King, Jr., brotherhood has been much more than just a buzzword. Morehouse, known affectionately by its graduates as the "House," changed their lives and, in turn, allowed them to change the world.

Men Only!

The only historically African-American all-male college in the United States, Morehouse prides itself on its traditions of brotherhood, which date back to the college's beginnings in 1867. Incoming students are taught the meaning of brotherhood early in their time at Morehouse with the tradition of Spirit Night. In this traditional ceremony, underclassmen link their arms and form a circle that upperclassmen try to break. Through this struggle, Morehouse men say they learn to hold on to their brotherhood above all else. As one freshman said, "Spirit Night made me realize how much I could trust my new friends. I'd only known them for a little while, but we all held on, supporting one another like we'd been together forever."

The tradition of brotherhood is supported by Morehouse's strong academic reputation, reflected today in the extensive General Studies requirements, which comprise 68 of the 124 credits needed to graduate. Each student must complete one-year courses in composition, literature, history of civilizations (which has a special focus on ancient African civilizations), social science, and physical education. Also required is one semester each of art, music, speech, religion, philosophy, physical science, and biological science, as well as two years of a foreign language. The completion of this rigorous academic program lends truth to the school's unofficial motto: "You can always tell a Morehouse man, but you can never tell him much." Academics are further supplemented with cultural instruction. Students are required to attend the Crown Forum, a weekly address by prominent African-American leaders that many students see as a vital part of the House's social mission. "The speakers at the Crown Forum are one of the most important parts of a Morehouse education. Knowledge is just knowledge without the ability to make a difference in the real world. The speakers teach us that," one student said.

One major benefit of Morehouse's urban Atlanta location is its membership in the Atlanta University Center (AUC), a consortium of five schools including Clark Atlanta, Morris Brown, the Interdenominational Theological Center, and Morehouse's sister school, all-female Spelman. Morehouse students can cross-register at any of the other four AUC schools, provided that the chair of the department at each school grants permission and that the course is not offered at Morehouse if it is within the student's major.

Pre-professionals Rule

The most popular majors at Morehouse, biology, business, and engineering, hint at the student body's strong preference toward pre-professional subjects. For students who desire further challenge and achievement, the college offers "3–2" programs in engineering and architecture. After three years at Morehouse, students can earn an advanced degree (in two years) at such schools as Georgia Tech or the University of Michigan. Morehouse also has an honors program, beginning in the freshman year, that offers dedicated students more advanced classes and a special diploma. Students report that a definite "easy A" is Intro to Visual Art, whose toughest requirement reportedly involves "just visiting a few museums in the area."

Morehouse is also notable for its professors. Spike Lee, one alumnus, returns to lecture fairly often. Students describe their relationships with professors as "extremely close." Many students say that it is common for undergrads and teachers to have lunch together, or go to museums or parks outside of class. One student claimed that he got invited to dinner at professors' homes on a regular basis.

Although some students said that the academics at Morehouse can be very competitive, many declared that the tradition of brotherhood on campus extends into the classroom. "At Morehouse all of your fellow students want you to do well. If you are having trouble, all you have to do is ask the person sitting next to you. People are always tutoring one another," said one student.

Where'd Everybody Go?

One statistic that attests to Morehouse's challenging academic regimen is its low student retention rate. One student declared "it's definitely a tough school to be successful in—people drop out of here like flies," while another added that his junior class of 600 began as a freshman class of 900. Other academic problems related by undergrads include difficulty with getting into required classes. Occasionally, seniors are forced to postpone their graduation because they were shut out of one or two classes, students said. Students cited financial-aid problems as a common reason for leaving Morehouse.

> "These programs enable us to teach our code of brotherhood to younger students in Atlanta who are particularly in need of love and respect," one student said.

Undergrads report that they spend much of their time studying at one of several libraries in the close vicinity of Morehouse. Woodruff Library, the central library for the five-member institutions of the Atlanta University Center, gets mixed reviews. While some students reported that it is especially good for "social" studying, others declared that the number and variety of students who share the library make resources hard to come by. Students who desire more quiet studying travel to the libraries at either Georgia State University or Emory. Hard-core studying takes place in the Frederick Douglass Commons, a student center at Morehouse where students have access to study rooms and materials. "What you learn here, they don't teach anywhere else."

Undergrads live in seven dorms on campus. Graves Hall, the oldest building on campus, is reportedly the best, as it has air-conditioning. Hubert is said to be the least appealing, with no air-conditioning and small rooms. Students can unwind at Kilgore, a dorm that houses pool and Ping-Pong tables, big screen TVs, and a snack shop that stays open until midnight. Dorms have friendly rivalries and are unofficially identified by Greek letters and hand signals. Dorm restrictions include no alcohol and specific visiting hours for women.

Some residents call restricted visitation "an initiation for freshmen," but admit that the rules are obeyed without much active enforcement. Undergrads seeking relaxed rules of conduct say the best bet is to move off campus. Most students say they prefer private apartments on Fair Street to those in the West End, where there is college-owned housing removed from the main dorm area. However, residents say that facilities in this area are "run-down."

Students who live on campus are required to be on a full meal plan that they describe as "below average," but "improving." Those desperate for improved fare eat out at places like Spegal's, a popular pub and restaurant, or fast-food restaurants at West End, a mall close to campus.

Athletics play an important role at Morehouse. The most popular teams, football and basketball, draw dedicated fan support, particularly when Morehouse plays its perennial rivals Howard and Tuskegee. Students say the tennis team is also extremely popular and successful. Archer Hall, the gym, underwent several renovations for the 1996 Summer Olympics.

Reaching Out

Students say they are particularly proud of the extracurricular activities at Morehouse, citing a strong devotion to community service programs, particularly several mentoring programs in which students act as big brothers or academic tutors to inner-city youth. "These programs enable us to teach our code of brotherhood to younger students in Atlanta who are particularly in need of love and respect," one student said. Students are also quick to point out that the popular Glee Club performed at President Clinton's first inauguration. Other organizations, such as the Pre-Law Society, the Health Care Society, and the Business Association, reflect the high aspirations of Morehouse students.

Although some students report that they were skeptical about attending an all-male college at first, many say that Morehouse provides them with the best of both worlds. They feel the all-male environment on campus allows them to cultivate a strong feeling of brotherhood. In fact, undergrads say, the high female-to-male ratio of the AUC provides students with more than adequate opportunities to meet and party with women.

Students say that the Morehouse social scene is "perfect for the challenging academic atmosphere." The campus is reportedly calm during the week, to allow for plenty of studying. Over the weekend, however, students can choose from innumerable parties, AUC unity rallies, picnics, concerts, or excursions to a local nightclub called Club Garage. Many students say that homecoming is one of the prime social events of the year and is traditionally a time for graduates and their families to return to the House to reminisce. The largest social event of the year, Freaknic, is one that is alternately loved or despised by the student body. While many students report the annual event, which consumes most of Atlanta, is the best party in the entire country, others complain that the large number of visiting students, reportedly 20,000 in recent years, absolutely prevents the students from being able to drive anywhere in downtown Atlanta.

Students consistently say that the one aspect that makes Morehouse unique is its deeply ingrained sense of tradition and brotherhood. As one student said, "What you learn here, they don't teach anywhere else. And I don't mean pre-law. I mean the overwhelming sense that you are truly a part of something great and that you can accomplish anything you want, simply because you are a Morehouse man. Even today, when students say they are only attending their college for a diploma and a few connections, being a Morehouse man still means something."—*Dylan Howard and Staff*

FYI

The three best things about attending Morehouse are "Spirit Night, solidarity, and being a Morehouse man."

The three worst things about attending Morehouse are "no women in classes, calm social scene during the week, and tough academics."

The three things that every student should do before graduating are "go to Freaknic, tutor inner-city youth, and go to Spegal's."

One thing I'd like to have known before coming here is "how many people drop out after the first year."

Spelman College

Address: Box 277, 350 Spelman Lane, SW; Atlanta, GA 30314
Phone: 800-982-2411
E-mail address: admiss@spelman.edu
Web site URL: www.spelman.edu
Founded: 1881
Private or Public: private
Religious affiliation: none
Location: urban
Undergraduate enrollment: 2,065
Total enrollment: 2,065
Percent Male/Female: 0%/100%
Percent Minority: 98%
Percent African-American: 96%

Percent Asian: NA
Percent Hispanic: NA
Percent Native-American: NA
Percent in-state/out-of-state: 42%/58%
Percent Pub HS: NA
Number of Applicants: 3,275
Percent Accepted: 53%
Percent Accepted who enroll: 33%
Entering: 576
Transfers: NA
Application Deadline: 1 Feb
Mean SAT: 549 V, 524 M
Mean ACT: 22

Middle 50% SAT range: 480–590 V, 460–570 M
Middle 50% ACT range: 21–25
3 Most popular majors: psychology, biology, English
Retention: 86%
Graduation rate: 77%
On-campus housing: 62%
Fraternities: NA
Sororities: NA
Library: 350,000 volumes
Tuition and Fees: $9,260 in; $9,260 out
Room and Board: $6,730
Financial aid, first-year: 80%

Spelman College strives to give each of its students more than just a diploma after four years of hard work; it also wants its graduates to walk away with a strong sense of cultural identity. As the first institute of higher learning specifically designed for African-American women, the college is in a unique position to do just that.

Challenging, Yet Worthwhile

Students describe Spelman academic life as "extremely rigorous." Every student is required to fulfill a core curriculum that consists of classes in the natural sciences, social sciences, fine arts, and humanities. In addition to these broad divisions, students are required to take several specific classes in black history such as African-American Women's Studies and the African Diaspora in the World. Although many students say the requirements are both necessary for a proper education and fulfilling in their own regard, most say the classes just add extra stress to students already worried about finishing the requirements for their major in four years. As one student put it, "I don't have as much time as I'd like to take classes in my major—I don't need this added stress."

Popular majors at Spelman include English, biology, chemistry, and psychology. Many students are pre-professional, preparing themselves for medical and law school. Undergrads stress that the most important aspect of Spelman academics is the faculty. One student said, "The professors here are incredibly nice and accessible. I haven't had a single class yet when I didn't feel completely comfortable with just walking up and talking to my teacher." Many students echoed this sentiment, declaring that the level of student-faculty interaction is unusually strong: "Teachers want to know you by your first name; they ask you to come by and talk all the time. It's important to them that they know you on a personal level," another student added. Many students said that this warmth is extremely valuable at Spelman, where "it makes the challenging classes seem possible and the extra work worthwhile."

To meet the academic challenge, students use the many study rooms located in each dorm. Spelman's Woodruff Library is shared by all of the other schools in the Atlanta University Center (AUC), including Morehouse, Clark Atlanta, and Morris Brown. Although the library is a long walk from the center of campus, students say it is particularly useful for research and serious studying, one of the perks of a university-like community.

No Alcohol

Woodruff does, however, provide common ground for Spelman students and those at their unofficial "brother" college, all-male Morehouse. Students say that much of their social life is centered off campus, at parties hosted by local clubs or on the Morehouse campus. Undergrads say the strict rules of conduct, the campus ban on alcohol, and limited visiting hours for males may seriously limit the potential for an on-campus social scene.

Campus residents describe their dorms as "adequate," although this judgment varies greatly depending on which dorm a student lives in. The Living and Learning Center II earns high marks for cleanliness and convenience. The Laura Spelman house is ancient in comparison, described by one student as "old, rickety, hot, and unstable." McVicar, located above the infirmary, is also unpopular. Many upperclassmen opt to live off campus in "nice residential neighborhoods" within 15 minutes of campus.

> "Spelman is the perfect place for young, determined women to find themselves and to learn how they can really make a difference in the world."

Another fact of campus life at Spelman is the required meal plan. Students say the cafeteria food is "pretty bad," although some feel that "in the not-so-grand scheme of college food, Spelman's is about average." As a result, many students opt to pay for food at the two campus eateries located in the Manley Student Center: the Grill (a burger joint), and Subway, the sandwich franchise. The most popular off-campus restaurant, Mick's, serves typical American fare.

Weekly Prayers

Many students attribute the strict code of conduct to Spelman's Christian philosophy. Students are required to attend weekly meetings that include a guest speaker and an opening prayer. Student opinions on the religious tradition vary widely. Some students say that religion is an extremely important part of their life and education. Others feel that it infringes upon their personal beliefs, and warn that the depth of religious sentiment can surprise new students. As one student said, "The religious nature of the school isn't made clear during the admissions process; it's a feeling you get once you're here."

Spelman students say that the historical philosophy of the school administration is not indicative of current student sentiment at all. Many describe the political climate of the student body as liberal and engaging. Informal debates and discussions "rage daily." One student said that one important distinction between Spelman and other colleges is that at Spelman, students act on their political convictions. "If a Spelman student feels that there is some problem that needs to be solved, social or political, you better watch out because something is going to be done about it."

Spelman students say that sororities are very important to campus life. Although they lack actual houses, each sorority fosters a communal spirit as sisters plan social events and spend time together. Many students also join the wide variety of academic clubs available. Aside from sororities, students say the most popular extracurricular activities include journalism, student government, and community service in the neighboring low-income areas.

What's a Sport?

According to students, one aspect typical of college life that is lacking at Spelman is sports. Although the basketball team is noted for its devoted following, sports are not at the forefront of students' thoughts. One senior reported that she had just recently discovered Spelman even had a mascot. This does not mean that Spelman students are not athletically inclined, however. Many students say they regularly use the campus gym to keep in shape. For those less energetic, the required physical education classes can be happily spent in the campus bowling alley.

Spelman primarily attracts African-

American women from the South, California, New York, and Washington, D.C., and is widely considered the most selective black women's college in the country. Some students believe this reputation leads to Spelman students being perceived as snobbish, which "may be true of some people here, but not generally."

Students assert that their time at Spelman has provided them with an experience unequaled at other colleges. One student said, "Spelman is the perfect place for young, determined women to find themselves and to learn how they can really make a difference in the world."
—*Melissa Droller and Staff*

FYI

The three best things about attending Spelman are "the supportive environment fostered by students and professors, the rigorous academics, and the opportunity to get an education at an all-women's school but still have access to a coed social life through exchange with Morehouse."

The three worst things about attending Spelman are "the importance placed on sororities, the overemphasis on religion, and the food."

The three things every student should do before graduating from Spelman are "have dinner at Mick's, participate in a community service group, and engage in a discussion with someone who challenges your personal beliefs."

One thing I'd like to have known before coming here is "how important religion is to the institution."

University of Georgia

Address: 212 Terrell Hall; Athens, GA 30602-1633
Phone: 706-542-2112
E-mail address: undergrad @admissions.uga.edu
Web site URL: www.uga.edu
Founded: 1785
Private or Public: public
Religious affiliation: none
Location: small city
Undergraduate enrollment: 24,040
Total enrollment: 31,000
Percent Male/Female: 46%/54%
Percent Minority: 11%
Percent African-American: 6%
Percent Asian: 3%

Percent Hispanic: 1%
Percent Native-American: 0.5%
Percent in-state/out-of-state: 91%/9%
Percent Pub HS: 15%
Number of Applicants: 13,402
Percent Accepted: 63%
Percent Accepted who enroll: 51%
Entering: 4,285
Transfers: 1,834
Application Deadline: 1 Feb
Mean SAT: 598 V, 597 M
Mean ACT: 27

Middle 50% SAT range: 550–650 V, 560–650 M
Middle 50% ACT range: NA
3 Most popular majors: business, education, biological sciences
Retention: 87%
Graduation rate: 65%
On-campus housing: 85%
Fraternities: 14%
Sororities: 18%
Library: 3,400,000 volumes
Tuition and Fees: $3,034 in; $10,276 out
Room and Board: $4,902
Financial aid, first-year: NA

To attend the University of Georgia every student must become familiar with one word and one place. "Dawg" is the word. It's short for "Bulldawg," and it's used to denote both the sports teams and each and every student on the UGA campus. Between the Hedges is the place known to outsiders as the field at Sanford Football Stadium but understood by students to be the epicenter of this football-proud school.

And in the words of one Dawg: "What a school it is!" UGA plays host to a total enrollment of approximately 30,000 students. The size of the school, located in the "classic city" of Athens, allows for an immense range of activities, sports, clubs, and social groups. This diversity coupled with the university's comprehensive list of degrees and programs, has made UGA one of the South's premier state universities.

Keeping the Hope Alive

At UGA, academics are spelled "HOPE." This is because a large percentage of student tuition is paid by Georgia's HOPE grant—a fund created through state lottery proceeds that allows any student who maintains a B average free tuition and $100 toward books each semester at any public school. The relatively cheap cost of attending UGA has made it very popular among Georgia's top students and is also reflected in the school's admissions numbers. Students must now have noticeably higher GPA and average SAT scores than their predecessors to be eligible to walk around the famous Georgia "arch." (But don't walk through it! It's campus lore that those who prematurely pass under the arch are doomed never to graduate.)

Once inside the hallowed halls, students have a large scope of classes from which to choose, ranging from pre-law and Greek lyrical poetry to calculus and chemistry. While opinions differ among students on whether the university caters more to the humanities- or science-focused student, both are thought to be very well represented on campus.

> **"Frats have a great time, but if you're not in one, then you hardly know they exist."**

For those who take a long time to commit to any path, the university allows students to wait until the end of their sophomore year to declare a major, prompting one student to notice that "slackers major in undecided." Those students who wish to really flex their mental might may choose to enroll in the university's honors program. While time-consuming (honors students must take at least nine honors classes throughout their career in order to graduate from the program), the honors program was cited in *U.S. News & World Report* as one of the nation's best. Other perks for honors students include smaller class size and closer contact with their professors.

In general, students at UGA are happy with their professors. Most lecture classes are admittedly large, but most meet in weekly discussion sections of only 20 or so. Teaching assistants are known to be good and grading to be fair, although some students have had occasional problems with the English-speaking abilities of their teachers.

Did Someone Say, "Party"?

The social scene at UGA is considered by students to be as much of an institution as the school itself. Dawgs love their football team, and throughout the fall much of campus life revolves around the weekly games between the hedges. Tailgates and post-game parties are a rite of passage in Athens, and season tickets sell out months before the first kickoff. Students and adult alumni also support their Dawgs on the road, and no classes are held on the Thursday and Friday prior to the all-important yearly contest with the University of Florida, allowing most of the classic city to head south for the rumble in Jacksonville with the Gators.

Parties can be found at UGA seven days a week, prompting many students to consider themselves at the center of the party universe. The Greek system at UGA is very popular among students and annually holds the country's second-largest rush period. The approximately 40 fraternities and sororities at Georgia are known to party hard, but non-Greeks are invited to many of the events and do not find themselves without social alternatives. One student sums up the atmosphere by stating that "frats have a great time, but if you're not in one, then you hardly know they exist." Greek or not, the one thing that unites nearly all parties at UGA is the large quantity of alcohol, leading one student to exclaim, "A Dawg's favorite food is usually beer."

And the Winner Is . . .

No doubt about it, *the* sport on the Georgia campus is football. With each home football game, Athens turns itself from a moderately busy college town into a sea of Dawg-crazed fans, as students past and present swamp Sanford Stadium to see the boys in red.

While football is certainly king of the sports scene at UGA, it is not the only game around. UGA fields many perennial powerhouses in a wide variety of intercollegiate athletics, including women's gymnastics and swimming. For those who take their sports a little less seriously, UGA also offers a wide variety of club and intramural teams to fit any level of participation. Students who just want to keep in shape can use the university's state-of-the-art Ramsey Student Physical Activity Center. The "Ramsey Center," as it's known, is a sprawling gym that contains, among other things, an indoor track, two pools complete with diving equipment, a rock-climbing wall, basketball and volleyball courts, and a large weight room.

Owing to the immensity of the student body at UGA, the options for extracurricular activities and social organizations are broad. Students with a journalistic bent can work for one of the many publications, including the *Pandora Yearbook* or the student newspaper, the *Red and Black*. There are also several active religious groups on campus, including the Baptist Student Union and Campus Crusade for Christ. Habitat for Humanity is a very popular organization on the UGA campus. Participants help build houses for financially challenged families in the community. A broad spectrum of organizations, including the fraternities and sororities, actively engage in community service as well.

A Dawg's Life

It is not mandatory that students live in dorms at UGA for any period, although most freshmen take advantage of on-campus housing. Two of the more popular dorms are Russell, which is known for its party atmosphere, and Oglethorpe. Many other students choose to live in Myers, but this un-air-conditioned dorm tends to elicit complaints until late fall rolls around. Female students who want a single-sex dorm can live in Brumby, known on campus as "the virgin vault." Rules on dorm visitation vary from dorm to dorm and even floor to floor. The severity of the restriction ranges from no admittance at any time to 24-hour-a-day visitation—but students are allowed to place themselves in housing situations according to their preferences. UGA has a comprehensive residential assistant program, and at least one RA lives on every floor in each dorm. Students remark that RAs do not act as police and are not overly strict. Students at Georgia are relatively happy with their dorm experiences, but few remain in the university-provided housing for more than a year. Apartments abound on and around the campus, and the majority of upperclassmen choose to move off campus after their freshman year. Students who live off campus find that having a car is a must, and even the majority of those who live on campus bring a car from home. One student summed up the situation at Georgia by saying, "The traffic problem is getting rather large, but I can't imagine what I'd do here without a car."

One aspect of dorm life consistently given high marks is the food. Students on the meal plan can eat their meals at any of the three dining halls: Bolton, Oglethorpe (commonly known as "O-House"), and Snelling. As with dorm living, the meal plan at UGA is totally optional, although most freshmen tend to take advantage of the university-supplied food. Some students who do not live in the dorms also purchase full or limited meal plans for weekday stops in the cafeterias. Food off campus is rated as very good as well, although it can sometimes get expensive to eat all meals out. Many students avoid this situation by buying groceries and cooking for themselves in the apartments.

A large state university in a picturesque college town, UGA has something to offer each and every one of its students. Whether a challenging course load or a never-ending series of parties, there is rarely a lack of things to keep someone busy at UGA. One simply has to find his or her own home among the "Dawgs." —*Robert Berschinski*

FYI

The three best things about attending UGA are "Bulldog football, the 'classic city' of Athens, and the party atmosphere."

The three worst things about attending UGA are "class registration is a pain, having to leave for class a half hour early to find a parking space, and being lost when you first get here."

The three things that every student should do before graduating from UGA are "go watch the Gym Dogs, catch a concert at the Georgia Theatre or 40 Watt Club, and tailgate with the old alumni at a football game."

One thing I'd like to have known before coming here is "classes are what you make them— you can make them hard if you want, or you can not think about them at all."

Hawaii

University of Hawaii / Manoa

Address: 2600 Campus Road, SSC Room 001; Honolulu, HI 96822
Phone: 808-956-8975
E-mail address: ar-info@hawaii.edu
Web site URL: uhm.hawaii.edu
Founded: 1907
Private or Public: public
Religious affiliation: none
Location: urban
Undergraduate enrollment: 11,458
Total enrollment: 17,344
Percent Male/Female: 45%/55%
Percent Minority: 78%
Percent African-American: 0.5%

Percent Asian: 76%
Percent Hispanic: 1%
Percent Native-American: 0.5%
Percent in-state/out-of-state: 95%/5%
Percent Pub HS: 69%
Number of Applicants: 4,466
Percent Accepted: 70%
Percent Accepted who enroll: 49%
Entering: 1,529
Transfers: NA
Application Deadline: 1 Jun
Mean SAT: 520 V, 565 M
Mean ACT: NA

Middle 50% SAT range: 470–570 V, 520–620 M
Middle 50% ACT range: NA
3 Most popular majors: biology, information and computer science, psychology
Retention: 82%
Graduation rate: 56%
On-campus housing: 21%
Fraternities: 2%
Sororities: 1%
Library: 3,000,000 volumes
Tuition and Fees: $3,142 in; $9,622 out
Room and Board: $4,435
Financial aid, first-year: 28%

Despite the exotic location, being a student at the University of Hawaii is not all about sitting on the beach, getting a tan, and surfing. The mission of the University of Hawaii is to provide quality education and training, to create knowledge, and to contribute to the cultural heritage of the community. At this major research institution, students not only enjoy their surroundings but also seek knowledge.

Academics

"There are too many core requirements here," one student said about the academic requirements at the University of Hawaii. Each student must take two years of a foreign language, in addition to numerous other arts and sciences courses. Many students take more than four years to graduate, due to the large number of core courses and the difficulty they have

getting into classes. Registration at the university is a rigorous procedure, unless you're in the honors program whose students receive priority. Despite the high demand for most classes, the student-to-teacher ratio is pretty low—most classes average 20 to 30 students. Introductory classes are reportedly much larger than the upper-level courses within a major. Attitudes about professors run the gamut. When asked about the quality of the teaching, many students replied "average." On the bright side, TAs are rare in upper-level courses, and one student described the grading as "generally easy." The University of Hawaii has been increasing its enrollment in recent years, and this has put more of a strain on resources. Undergrads report that geography, geology, science, and business courses are among the toughest at the University of Hawaii. One student said the university offers more to chemistry majors than other science majors because the chemistry department has more professors who are better teachers.

What's on for Tonight?

The social options at the University of Hawaii are ample. Many freshmen spend their weekends going to parties. Drinking and smoking are part of the social scene, but non-smokers and non-drinkers do not report feeling uncomfortable. Students say that not many of their classmates use illegal drugs. One undergrad described the typical freshman weekend as "Drink, party, smoke." There are few dress-up formal occasions on the weekends, and few students go on formal dates, but random hookups are a regular occurrence. "Yes, it's easy to meet new people," one student said. Students are reportedly open-minded about their social groups and can easily move in and out of different cliques on campus. Cliques do persist, however, even though fraternities and sororities are not major forces in the campus social scene.

> The University of Hawaii is not all about sitting on the beach, getting a tan, and surfing.

One undergrad described the student stereotype at the University of Hawaii as "female, short, and Asian." In general, students are laid-back and most often wear T-shirts, shorts, and sandals to class. Some students find the campus population "homogeneous—Asian."

Where We Live

Freshmen who live on campus live in co-ed dorms with students in all class years. This situation provides for a great introduction to college life, as students avoid the craziness of all-freshman dorms. Campus housing has become limited as more and more students enroll in the university. Hawaii residents receive first priority, and those who don't get campus housing usually commute from home if possible, since a lot of students live nearby. The campus apartments, which offer more privacy and space than the regular dorms, are considered the best on-campus housing, but still, many students choose to live off campus to avoid the hassle of competing for the vacancies.

The campus is "nice, lots of trees," as one student said. Another student described the buildings as "cramped and overcrowded." "One architecture professor characterized the buildings as the worst part of the campus," a student reported. The campus is near major bus routes, and students rave about the convenience of this transportation system, although there is some debate over the safety of the campus. Some students say they feel safe, others say they feel insecure at night on the campus. One student said, "in general, you shouldn't walk anywhere alone at night, no matter how safe the city, but [at UH] I would." Some students complain that the campus lacks a 24-hour eating establishment.

The dining hall food is "overpriced," according to many students. One said that the food is "pretty good for the first week, after that it's not so good." Another said the dining halls are "clean, big, and not bad." Although the campus social scene is open to movement between groups, the dining halls are characterized as more cliquey; students often eat with their friends from high school or even grade school. Extracurriculars do not dominate the lives of most university students, yet intramurals are popular. According to one student, "It's a commuter school," and most students work part-time.

Team spirit at the University of Hawaii abounds, though, and the school actively recruits athletes for its teams. Major sports teams participate in the Western Athletic Conference, and basketball and volleyball are two of the most popular sports. The football team has also made recent strides toward improvement. One student called the athletic facilities, particularly the new special events arena, "great, since the school spends the most funds on the sports program," but some students complain that the campus lacks a good track.

The three four-year campuses, seven community colleges, and five education centers that make up the University of Hawaii emphasize different levels of instruction, research, and service, but all focus on a Hawaiian and Pacific orientation and an international leadership role. Students agree that the University of Hawaii is a great place to spend four or more years, as long as you learn early on how to balance the beach with your studies. —*Rebecca Pace and Staff*

FYI

The three best things about attending the University of Hawaii are "the weather, meeting people from different ethnic backgrounds, and the live music every Friday night at Manoa Gardens (the bar on campus)."

The three worst things about attending the University of Hawaii are "the limited space to study in the library, the unkempt school grounds, and the continuing rise in tuition."

The three things every student should do before graduating from the University of Hawaii are "to check out the oriental garden by Kennedy Theatre, attend a volleyball game, and relax at Manoa Gardens."

One thing I wish I knew before coming here is "tuition increased eleven times in ten years here."

Idaho

Address: University of Idaho; Moscow, ID 83844-3133

Phone: 208-885-6326

E-mail address: admappl@uidaho.edu

Web site URL: www.uidaho.edu/index-ext.shtml

Founded: 1889

Private or Public: public

Religious affiliation: none

Location: small town

Undergraduate enrollment: 7,989

Total enrollment: 11,305

Percent Male / Female: 54% / 46%

Percent Minority: 6%

Percent African-American: 0.5%

Percent Asian: 2%

Percent Hispanic: 2%

Percent Native-American: 1%

Percent in-state / out-of-state: 80% / 20%

Percent Pub HS: 98%

Number of Applicants: 3,487

Percent Accepted: 85%

Percent Accepted who enroll: 49%

Entering: 1,453

Transfers: 846

Application Deadline: 1 Aug

Mean SAT: 550 V, 554 M

Mean ACT: 24

Middle 50% SAT range: 490–610 V, 490–620 M

Middle 50% ACT range: 21–26

3 Most popular majors: engineering, education, business

Retention: 80%

Graduation rate: 51%

On-campus housing: NA

Fraternities: 27%

Sororities: 18%

Library: 1,566,081 volumes

Tuition and Fees: $2,348 in; $8,348 out

Room and Board: $3,952

Financial aid, first-year: 60%

O ne junior captured the essence of his years at the University of Idaho as "cheap, fun, and a great education." Tucked between the potato fields and rolling hills of Moscow, Idaho, the University of Idaho is wrapped up in its own world—a world immersed in frat parties, intramurals, and academics.

Engineering Future Engineers

Engineering is widely recognized as the toughest major on campus. Even so, undergrads flock to the department. The University of Idaho engineering programs are regarded as some of the best in the country. The university attracts candidates early on through an engineering camp for juniors in high school. Future engineering majors earn credit at the university during the intense two-week program. All undergrads, regardless of major, are required to fulfill basic core require-ments. These include math, science, social science, and communications. The easiest classes are found in the PE department (one can get credit for playing football or bowling) and in general studies, but most students feel that "for the most part there are not too many easy classes."

Students were split in their feelings on class size and TAs. Some undergrads thought their TAs were generally very good while others thought they "suck royally." Feelings about class sizes ran along similar lines. Opinions on class size varied from "perfect" to "fine as long as the room is big enough" to "too big." Many introductory classes fall into the "too big" category, but are broken down into sections and labs taught by TAs.

Undergrads also have the option of enrolling in classes offered by Washington State University, located eight miles away in Pullman, Washington. Students are able to take classes at WSU that the U of I does not offer, though course selections are very limited.

It's All Greek to Me

With 18 fraternities and 8 sororities for the approximately 8,000 member campus, Greek life dominates every aspect of non-academic life at the U of I. About 27 percent of men and 19 percent of women go Greek. There is an unspoken but pronounced division between Greeks and independents. As one undergraduate put it, "There are two separate worlds. You're proud to be where you are."

> **"I have only been on one date and I went to the rodeo!"**

Freshmen are free to choose their living arrangements. Their options include living in a fraternity or sorority house, living in a residence hall, or living off campus. Just as each Greek house has its own personality, each dorm has its own character. Residents may choose their dorm, but dorms have unofficial designations such as "athletic" housing. Despite the variety of options, the administration has had to deal with a housing crunch in recent years, and dorms and Greek houses were renovated to provide extra space. There are also apartments available on campus. Many students opt for off-campus housing but find that a good location at a decent price is difficult to come by if they don't look early.

Greeks also dominate social and extracurricular life. There are fraternity and sorority parties nearly every weekend. There is no cover charge for the parties, but they are open only to those on the guest list (usually the membership list of other Greek houses). There have been no publicized problems with Greek life recently, though one fraternity chapter lost its charter a few years ago. However, underage drinking is "the epitome of the U of I. There are constant minor-in-possession citations." Greek life revolves around dances, cruises, socials, and philanthropic events. Strong friendships are a part of the package. A sorority member

claims, "The friends that I have made through the Greek system will be my friends for life."

Those not involved in Greek life take quite a different view, "[The Greek system] has TOTAL control of this place. We have the second-largest Greek system in the Northwest here (next to U. of Washington). It sucks because the Greeks here think they are God's gift to life and everything else." However, social life outside of the Greek scene is abundant. Many undergrads take advantage of the nearby mountains and rivers to camp and hike. Others head for neighboring Pullman, Washington, or for Spokane, Washington, which is about an hour's drive away.

Where's the Kremlin?

Moscow, Idaho, itself has very limited opportunities. Described as a "typical college town," this tiny town of about 18,000 boasts fast-food restaurants, movie theaters, a small mall, and an abundance of bars. Students complained that there is nothing social to do off campus. Many students own cars and escape from Moscow over the weekends. The U of I campus is fairly compact. It takes about 15 minutes to get from one end to the other. With both a small campus and a small town, students said they generally feel safe on campus and in town, although like anywhere there are "certain places [where] you don't walk after dark."

Dating at the U of I is very low-key. A typical date involves attending a Greek event or going to the movies. Those who are not in serious relationships generally just try to meet people at parties. With such limited options, dating often gets creative. "I have only been on one date and I went to the rodeo! Whoa, pardner, easy!"

"Vandal"izing Fun

School spirit runs high among the University of Idaho Vandals, and sporting events are heavily attended. U of I athletes, both men and women, compete in NCAA Division I as members of the Big West Athletic Conference. The men and women Vandals represent the university in 14 varsity sports, including the recently added women's soccer program. The rivalry with the Boise State University Broncos is especially intense. Outstanding recreational facilities, available to the campus and the community, include an excellent 18-hole golf course, swimming pool, indoor and outdoor tracks, indoor and outdoor tennis courts, and racquetball courts.

Extracurricular activities are unfortunately quite limited at the U of I. The engineering department offers several organizations and teams, but these usually appeal only to students in the major. Outside of academic organizations, there is a large Christian group on campus that has some presence. The campus also hosts various concerts, including the widely known Lionel Hampton Jazz Festival held every spring. The most popular activity, by far, is intramural sports, although they are often "Greek dominated."

Despite its isolated location and the deep division between Greek and non-Greek undergrads, students love the U of I. Whether they are looking for an awesome social life or a decent education at a decent price, U of I meets its students' needs, and creates many fond memories for them along the way. Students feel that they are getting the "college experience." As one enthusiastic Vandal put it, "I thought that high school was the best time of my life, until I got to college. This is where my best memories are!" —*Jennifer Rogien and Staff*

FYI

The three best things about attending the University of Idaho are "the incredible Greek life, the Vandals are crazy fans, and the alcohol flows over the weekends."

The three worst things about attending the University of Idaho are "that there aren't a lot of extracurriculars, dating doesn't happen often, and this place is out of the way."

The three things that every student should do before graduating from the University of Idaho are "make a road trip to one of the cities, attend a game against the Broncos, and participate in intramurals."

One thing I wish I knew before coming here is "how much Greek life dominates everything!"

Illinois

Address: 1 East Jackson Boulevard, Suite 9100; Chicago, IL 60604
Phone: 312-362-8300
E-mail address: admitdpu@wppost.depaul.edu
Web site URL: www.depaul.edu
Founded: 1898
Private or Public: private
Religious affiliation: Catholic
Location: urban
Undergraduate enrollment: 10,914
Total enrollment: 16,747
Percent Male/Female: 40%/60%
Percent Minority: 34%

Percent African-American: 12%
Percent Asian: 9%
Percent Hispanic: 12%
Percent Native-American: 0.5%
Percent in-state/out-of-state: 81%/19%
Percent Pub HS: 64%
Number of Applicants: 6,050
Percent Accepted: 78%
Percent Accepted who enroll: 37%
Entering: 1,749
Transfers: NA
Application Deadline: 1 Feb
Mean SAT: NA
Mean ACT: 24

Middle 50% SAT range: 510–620 V, 490–620 M
Middle 50% ACT range: NA
3 Most popular majors: accounting, finance, communication
Retention: 83%
Graduation rate: 52%
On-campus housing: 17%
Fraternities: 2%
Sororities: 2%
Library: 960,000 volumes
Tuition and Fees: $14,700 in; $14,700 out
Room and Board: $6,300
Financial aid, first-year: 68%

Chosen by *Time* magazine and the *Princeton Review* as having the happiest student body of any college in the country in 1999, DePaul University manages to maintain a small-school, student-oriented atmosphere. It probably helps that classes are small and almost all taught by professors, and that the main campus is in one of the best parts of Chicago, Lincoln Park. One political science major referred to the neighborhood's inhabitants as "rich, young yuppies."

Safety is rarely an issue, whether in Lincoln Park or on the downtown campus, which is located near the Art Institute of Chicago. No wonder the students of DePaul are so pleased: they can go to the nation's third-largest city for fun, get a great education, and still find time for top-notch extracurricular activities and sports.

Educational Priorities

"The school is very passionate about making education the first priority," said a pleased senior. While DePaul offers more than 100 academic programs and more than 1,000 different courses, every single class is taught by a professor as opposed to a teaching assistant, like at other large schools. More than 88 percent of the faculty have Ph.D.s, and average class sizes max out at 25 students and can be as small as 5 students. Notable professors include Wayne Steger, who teaches political science; Deena Weinstein, the authority on rock concerts and audiences (one student said that "she knows everybody in the music industry"); and Lorilee Sadler of computer science, telecommunications, and information systems. Professors and students maintain a comfortable atmosphere both in and out of class—the professors give out their home phone numbers on syllabi and are flexible with grading. As one freshman described, "You can call them up and be like, 'Hey, what happened with this grade?' A lot of times, they'll change it and be reasonable." Students are encouraged to participate in class, and one senior raved that the professors "encouraged individuality and helped guide me."

DePaul is known for being a humanities and business-oriented school, but one student pointed out that the "computer science program is gaining national attention" and that "the School of Computer Science is one of the largest in the country." Slackers can be found in any major, but, in particular, the exotic cat management major seems to attract a large share of the loafers for some reason.

DePaul is on a quarter system, and students must take at least three courses a quarter and maintain a 2.1 GPA. Those in the liberal arts program must take a core curriculum. First-year students have a special curriculum that they must follow, but they have "a lot of room for other classes," according to one freshman. Honors programs can be found in each college, and classes are even smaller in those; one honors student raved, "You end up taking the majority of your classes with the same group of people, and you get to know each other, which is nice when a school is large." However, a sophomore mentioned that while "my honors and political science classes are the most challenging, the rest seem like a joke at times." On the other hand, a freshman said that he felt like he had a ton of work, although he did say that it was manageable.

> One thrilled female student also mentioned that "I think there are some fine-looking men here!"

The professors are available to help those who need it. One invited students over to his house to help them with projects that he had assigned. Other positive aspects of classes at DePaul include, said a senior, "their locations. You can be in the Chicago Loop downtown in the center of business, then take a ten-minute train ride into Lincoln Park and be at a standard college campus that's surrounded with history and all kinds of things to do."

An Extracurricular Experience

Extracurricular activities are also a big part of student life. There are about 120 different student organizations: ethnic clubs, political groups, honor societies, a radio station, and many more. Students are often identified by the activity they are involved in. As one student put it, "Everyone knows who works on the *DePaulia* [the student paper], partly because our lives revolve around it. It's like that for anyone, if they are really into one thing, they will be associated with it." Many students are involved with community service, and student government is also well respected. Perhaps gaining the most attention are the sports teams, which compete in NCAA Division I. In particular, the men and women's basketball teams, which recruit heavily, are popular and bring in a lot of fans.

While DePaul is a commuter school, students did not mention that as having an adverse effect on their social lives. The most obvious reason for this is that the "city is our campus. Even if you don't drink, there's still a lot of stuff to do." Similarly, another student said that "DePaul utilizes Chicago to the extreme; it's awesome." Students can go to concerts, bars, clubs, and plays, although one upperclassman remarked that freshmen just "find the nearest party and travel there in large packs." Students agreed that it was easy to meet people, that "people are very friendly." Good parties include swing dances, Halloween parties, '70s parties, and toga parties hosted by the fraternities. There is a lot of drinking, and one sorority member pointed out that "the Greek life is really starting to grow."

Punks v. Dawson

Because, as one senior put it, "DePaul is a very liberal school," students mentioned that there is a large gay population. "We live near one of the largest gay communities in the country, North Halstead," explained a freshman. Many students tend to be trendy, and a common stereotype is "a bunch of rich, Chicago, suburban kids."

This stereotype might stem from the fact that, as one disgruntled junior pointed out, DePaul, as a rule, does not give scholarships to international students. Student dress tends to differ between the campuses. The Lincoln Park campus is really laid-back, while students at the downtown campus tend to be more dressed up. The student population is "pretty diverse," with a large number of Hispanic and African-American students, although there are not many Asian students. One thrilled female student also mentioned that "I think there are some fine-looking men here!" Music-wise, the punk scene is reputedly quite big, despite the somewhat antithetical popularity of *Dawson's Creek*.

Also big, although in a different sense, are the dorm (called "residence hall") rooms, for the few who opt to stay in them (students complain about the high prices of housing). All student rooms have private bathrooms, air-conditioning, and cable with movie channels; upperclassmen get to stay in "town houses and beautiful apartments with a killer view of the skyline." Freshmen must stay on campus, but even their dorms are complete with "tall ceilings," an attribute not found at too many other universities. Cafeteria food is good, but "gets boring," (DePaul has just one cafeteria) so students often go off campus to eat. Popular restaurants include Potbelly's, My Pie, Demon Dogs, and "Taco Burrito Place is where every DePaul student goes after hitting the bars." Campus buildings are indistinguishable from the rest of the city, and anywhere on the undergraduate campuses students can be awed by the sight of the magnificent Chicago skyscrapers.

Winner? Chicago

So there are great academics, extracurricular activities, and parties. But what epitomizes DePaul University? Students seem to love, above all, their school's deep bond with the city of Chicago. As one senior reflected, "I got to do things here that I could never do at a huge university, and I'm in the center of a huge city." Just like Chicago, the DePaul community is connected through close-knit classes and a dedication to community service. Even the sororities and fraternities are friendly with each other, said one member. What creates this great atmosphere? As one freshman put it, "The city. It's all about the city." —*Jennifer Wang and Staff*

FYI

The three best things about attending Depaul are "the great diversity among the students, the very knowledgeable and approachable faculty, and the exciting and diverse atmosphere of Chicago."

The three worst things about attending Depaul are "the quarter system, the expectation that every student is rich, and the special treatment of the basketball team over the other varsity sports teams."

The three things that every student should do before graduating from Depaul are "go to the Midnight Madness pep assembly in the fall, take a class on a campus other than Lincoln Park, and see different areas of Chicago other than the immediate Lincoln Park area."

One thing I'd like to have known before coming here is "that I wish that I could have been reminded to always keep an open mind!"

Illinois State University

Address: Campus Box 2200; Normal, IL 61790-2200
Phone: 309-438-2181
E-mail address: ugradadm@ilstu.edu
Web site URL: www.ilstu.edu
Founded: 1857
Private or Public: public
Religious affiliation: none
Location: small city
Undergraduate enrollment: 17,596
Total enrollment: 20,470
Percent Male/Female: 42%/58%
Percent Minority: 12%
Percent African-American: 7%

Percent Asian: 2%
Percent Hispanic: 2%
Percent Native-American: 0.5%
Percent in-state/out-of-state: 99%/1%
Percent Pub HS: 90%
Number of Applicants: 11,049
Percent Accepted: 75%
Percent Accepted who enroll: 37%
Entering: 3,080
Transfers: 1,824
Application Deadline: 1 Apr
Mean SAT: NA
Mean ACT: 23
Middle 50% SAT range: NA

Middle 50% ACT range: 20–25
3 Most popular majors: elementary education, business administration, applied computer science
Retention: 78%
Graduation rate: 53%
On-campus housing: NA
Fraternities: 13%
Sororities: 11%
Library: 1,398,742 volumes
Tuition and Fees: $4,340 in; $10,778 out
Room and Board: $4,238
Financial aid, first-year: 40%

Located in the small town of Normal, Illinois State University provides students with both the resources of a large university and the comforts of a small community. With its central quad containing all the academic buildings, and the residence halls surrounding the quad, the campus is very central and accessible to students. One student described the campus as "small enough that the environment is very comfortable and relaxed."

Intimate Academic Setting

The small feeling created by the comfort of the campus contrasts with the vast number of academic opportunities. The theater, political science, education, and accounting departments are all reportedly strong and competitive. Although one student described the academics as "not really hard, not really easy," another political science major described the classes as "challenging and interesting." Professors teach most classes, with some introductory classes taught by graduate assistants. Students rate the student-faculty interaction as "very good," and one student said that "compared to some uni-

versities we have a good, solid relationship between students and faculty." Students also report that interaction is encouraged through many available resources to students, and the professors are very accessible during office hours. They are always "willing to do what they can for students."

According to one student, registering for classes is "not a problem." Students can easily register by phone or computer. Getting shut out of classes is not the problem at ISU that it is at other large universities. If a class is a requirement of a major, the administration puts a block on a certain number of openings. In this way, students who need the class for their major can apply to the specific department for a position in the class. Undergrads must also fulfill general requirements within the University Studies areas. These groups include humanities, natural sciences, social sciences, arts, mathematics, communications, contemporary life studies, and non-Western cultures and traditions. While some students pronounce the requirements a "waste of time," many find them enriching. Freshmen are assigned a general advisor when they arrive, and after declaring a major receive an advisor in their specific department. Students find this system helpful.

Freshmen also have the opportunity to participate in a recently implemented program called Connections, which brings small groups of students with common interests together in "learning communities." These groups take three classes together during the year, study together, and often form close social groups. One participant praised the program as a "great transition tool from high school to college."

Where We Work?

One undergrad explained that "students who are here for the education study a lot." The recently built Milner Library is a six-floor building with up-to-date resources. It is reportedly a good environment for serious studying. The second floor has equipment and resources that are available 24 hours, which students find helpful. Many students also study in the Prairie Room in the Bone Student Center. It is reportedly a popular place to study at any hour with "couches, TVs, and a really cozy atmosphere."

Dorm Life

Undergrads also study in their dorms. Freshmen and sophomores are required to live on campus in one of the 14 residence halls. The dorms on East campus, Hewett, and Manchester, are considered to be social. West campus, with the Tri Towers (Wilkins, Haynie, and Wright), is also a popular place to live. Waterson, where the floors are divided by a staircase, is sometimes considered "anti-social." While one student complained that "the rooms are pretty small," the university is currently in the process of a campus enhancement project to renovate all dorms. Adding computer access to the dorm rooms was recently approved as well. After their first two years, many students choose to either live in Greek housing or in apartments in Normal.

Eats

Students who do live in the dorms are required to be on a meal plan. The university runs on a debit-card system, where students use their IDs at any of the five dining

halls on campus. There are two food courts, two all-you-can-eat cafeterias, and one coffeehouse/deli. One undergrad commented that "the food is average" while another student felt that it was "pretty gross." Most students do like the variety, however, and as part of the enhancement plan the dining halls are increasing their options and responding to student input. Now all the cafeterias always offer a vegetarian bar, a pizza bar, a sub bar, and many other choices.

> **Freshmen also have the opportunity to participate in a recently implemented program called Connections, which brings small groups of students with common interests together in "learning communities."**

There are also several places to eat off campus. As one student explained, "Normal grew when ISU grew, so there are a lot more places now to eat and socialize off campus." Popular options include Avanti's, an Italian restaurant close to campus, Micheleo's Pizza, and La Bamba, which serves "burritos as big as your head." The Pub, a bar and grill, is a popular place for older students to hang out.

Social Life

The town of Normal provides other social opportunities for students as well. Many students frequent the local bars, which admit 18-year-olds on certain nights. Popular bars include Rocky's, Spanky's, and the Pub. ISU has a very strong, established Greek system, with around 20 percent of students participating. For those who seek it out, it can be a major part of their lives, but one student reported that "it is not the major influence on campus." Frat parties are extremely popular on the weekends, but for those students not involved in Greek life, there are private parties and house parties. One student adds, though, "it is fine if you are not a partier. The town is pretty big and you can go to the movies or out to eat." There are also two malls in Normal, and the campus bus system provides students with transportation to off-campus locations, which makes it "okay not to have a car."

For extracurricular interests on campus, ISU has over 180 student organizations, ranging from political groups, to dancing troupes, to Habitat for Humanity. With so many interests represented, one student felt that "you have to make an effort to get very involved in a few things, because, with 20,000 students, it's easy to get lost here." ISU has a school newspaper, the *Daily Vidette*, which attracts a high amount of student involvement. The Student Government Association is also very strong. This year's student body president's main goal is to target different campus organizations to get more students involved in campus life.

An Athletic Lot

Many students are involved in athletics. As a Division I school, ISU has a very strong athletic reputation. Last year, the men's basketball team had a great year, earning a spot in the NCAA tournament. While the football team has not been great lately, the team is currently rebuilding under a new coach. The softball, baseball, and volleyball teams are reportedly strong as well. School spirit is "pretty good," reflected in the large number of students wearing various ISU apparel around campus.

People from Normal strongly support the university, attending athletic events and offering discounts in the local stores and restaurants. Along with varsity sports, intramurals are extremely popular and competitive, attracting Greeks, dorm residents, and any other students who want to participate.

Student Body

Along with a diversity in interests, the student population as a whole is diverse as well. Many different ideas and ethnicities are well represented. However, one student, disappointed by the lack of interaction between ethnic groups, described the population as "not exactly unified," and the social atmosphere as "self-segregated." Support services for minority students include a multicultural center and the Minority Student Development Service, and many active groups on campus such as the Black Student Union. ISU also has one of the oldest LGB (lesbian, gay, and bisexual) groups in the country.

Students at Illinois State University praise the small-school feeling they get from this large university, and the incredible opportunities they encounter. As one student concluded, "Whatever you're looking for, you can find it at ISU. You just have to be willing to go out and look for it."—*Melissa Kantor and Staff*

FYI
The three best things about attending ISU are "small-school feel, decent school spirit, and a student government that really represents."
The three worst things about attending ISU are "self-segregation, invitation-only parties, and there are too many ways to get involved."
The three things that every student should do before graduating from ISU are "head to La Bamba, root for men's basketball, and wear ISU shirts."
One thing I'd like to have known before coming here is "how such a big place can feel like home."

Knox College

Address: Box K-148;
Galesburg, IL 61401
Phone: 309-341-7100
E-mail address:
admission@knox.edu
Web site URL:
www.knox.edu
Founded: 1837
Private or Public: private
Religious affiliation: none
Location: small city
**Undergraduate
enrollment:** 1,220
Total enrollment: 1,220
Percent Male / Female:
40% / 60%
Percent Minority: 12%
Percent African-American:
3%

Percent Asian: 5%
Percent Hispanic: 3%
Percent Native-American:
1%
**Percent in-state / out-of-
state:** 50% / 50%
Percent Pub HS: 75%
Number of Applicants:
1,357
Percent Accepted:
75%
**Percent Accepted who
enroll:** 30%
Entering: 300
Transfers: 44
Application Deadline:
1 Feb
Mean SAT: NA
Mean ACT: NA

Middle 50% SAT range:
550–680 V,
550–650 M
Middle 50% ACT range:
24–29
3 Most popular majors:
biology, political science,
economics
Retention: 88%
Graduation rate: 74%
On-campus housing: 95%
Fraternities: 33%
Sororities: 12%
Library: 169,661 volumes
Tuition and Fees:
$21,174 in; $21,174 out
Room and Board: $5,436
Financial aid, first-year:
90%

I magine arriving for your first day of college and before the day is done meeting every single student at the school. Welcome to Knox College. Every year begins with a tradition called Pump Handle, a two-hour event where students line up and shake everyone's hand. This is just the first glimpse of the friendliness of a school "where everybody wants to know your name."

Reaching Your Potential

Academics at Knox push students to reach their academic potential. As one junior put it, "I don't know anyone who isn't working really hard." All Knox students must take two credits in each of the humanities, social studies, and math and science. Beyond this, first-years are required to enroll in a preceptorial, a discussion class about a variety of controversial topics. Preceps are taught by professors from all departments and are meant to foster personal growth. As a follow-up, seniors are given a choice between several advanced preceptorials. Although it has a strong liberal arts philosophy, Knox is particularly well known for its excellent science and math departments, though students said the computer science department leaves much to be desired.

The faculty has a lot to do with the excitement Knox students feel about learning. They are highly accessible and it is not uncommon to be invited to a prof's house for dinner. As one student explained, "They have a 'Yes you can!' philosophy. They make you want to learn."

"A different perspective is really important to the way we learn at Knox," stated one undergrad. As evidence of this philosophy, two of the unofficial rites of passage of a Knox student are study abroad and staying at Knox over the summer. In fact, there are even some majors that require time abroad. There is also a big emphasis on multiculturalism, with approximately 15 percent of students coming from outside the United States. A strong overseas recruiting program has drawn a large contingent of Indian students as well as students from East Asian nations. A very generous financial-aid program also promotes diversity on campus.

Social Life

One junior explained the social scene at Knox: "We live in a pretty small town, so it's not really going on." Another agreed, "You have to come up with your own fun." The biggest mainstay is the fraternity scene, which is always a popular option for first-year students. Being underage generally isn't a problem, and there is also a prevalent non-drinking scene. There are few formal events, but that doesn't mean that there is not dating. However, students complained that there is little casual dating and instead, most dating is serious.

> "A different perspective is really important to the way we learn at Knox."

The housing at Knox earns much praise, and one sophomore even said that it was the housing that drew him to Knox. The rooms are generally large and well maintained, but there is not much diversity in the type of rooms available within dorms. However, there can be a distinct difference between dorms. This is especially evident in dorms like Seymour, where first-year men are housed, which offers markedly inferior accommodations compared to the hotel-like Post dorm, where the first-year women are housed. There are also theme houses, which are an option after the first year, offering excellent living accommodations. The RA system has drawn praise as being "a little more intimate" than the typical college RA system. RAs tend to act a lot more like an older sibling and less like enforcers.

The food is generally described as run-of-the-mill college food, being neither spectacular nor inedible. One student described the food as "mundane," and a common student complaint is that they do not receive good value with their meal plan. There is an attempt to offer larger variety with facilities like the Oak Room, a special dining area where students can eat sit-down dinners.

Extracurriculars
According to one student, "The attitude surrounding extracurriculars at Knox is 'Join!'" People are very involved in many organizations and they are an important part of the Knox education. Music and drama are among the most popular activities, and multicultural groups also have a large presence on campus due to the high level of diversity at Knox. The student newspaper, the *Knox Student*, has also received many awards.

Sports at Knox tend to take a backseat to other interests. Recently, Knox's team name has changed from the Siwashers to the Prairie Fire because the former was considered a derogatory term for an alcoholic Native American. Although many students see Knox sports as a joke, the teams do work very hard. The cross-country team and the men's golf team have achieved recent success.

Knox students still find plenty of time to participate in intramurals, which in many ways have a larger presence on campus than varsity sports. There is fierce competition in men's volleyball and ultimate Frisbee in particular, and basketball and soccer are popular as well. To support the non-varsity athlete, sports facilities are constantly improving. The latest change has been the addition of a new pool. Athletic facilities also include an excellent field house with basketball, volleyball, tennis courts, and an eight-mile track.

Traditions
One of the harbingers of summer is a special festival called "Flunk Day." No one knows when this day is going to be held. When it is announced, it is the responsibility of several drunk seniors to run around campus at 5 A.M., banging on pots and pans and letting the entire campus know that Flunk Day has arrived. Classes are canceled for the day and the campus turns into a big carnival with an amusement park appearing on campus overnight. Students and professors alike spend the day outside, sunning themselves, relaxing with friends, and taking the time to sit back and enjoy life.

Knox is truly a place that comforts students with its homey atmosphere, yet will challenge them to expand their minds in ways that might not always seem comfortable. The Knox education extends far beyond academics to prepare students to be successful in the real world. *—William Chen and Staff*

FYI

The three best things about attending Knox College are "the small student population, the closeness of people, and the philosophy behind teaching."

The three worst things about attending Knox College are "the small student population— there's fewer people to date, there's not much to do in Galesburg, and small schools come with smaller resources."

The three things that every student should do before graduating from Knox College are "study abroad, stay at Knox over the summer, and be immersed in the traditions."

One thing I'd like to have known before coming here is "that despite the desolate area, there's a great wealth of things to do, you just have to figure out what you want to do."

Lake Forest College

Address: 555 North Sheridan Road; Lake Forest, IL 60045
Phone: 847-735-5000
E-mail address: admissions@ifc.edu
Web site URL: www.ifc.edu
Founded: 1857
Private or Public: private
Religious affiliation: Presbyterian
Location: suburban
Undergraduate enrollment: 1,275
Total enrollment: 1,275
Percent Male / Female: 46% / 54%
Percent Minority: 15%
Percent African-American: 6%

Percent Asian: 4%
Percent Hispanic: 4%
Percent Native-American: 0.5%
Percent in-state / out-of-state: 48% / 52%
Percent Pub HS: 67%
Number of Applicants: 1,246
Percent Accepted: 81%
Percent Accepted who enroll: 34%
Entering: 341
Transfers: 68
Application Deadline: 1 Mar
Mean SAT: 570 V, 560 M
Mean ACT: 25

Middle 50% SAT range: 520–630 V, 520–640 M
Middle 50% ACT range: 22–28
3 Most popular majors: business / economics, English, psychology
Retention: 79%
Graduation rate: 61%
On-campus housing: 83%
Fraternities: 20%
Sororities: 15%
Library: 280,000 volumes
Tuition and Fees: $21,190 in; $21,190 out
Room and Board: $5,000
Financial aid, first-year: 75%

Set in the wealthy suburb of Lake Forest, a five-minute walk from the beach of Lake Michigan, a fifty minute drive from Chicago, and filled with close, extremely social, and hardworking professors and students, Lake Forest College sounds a bit too good to be true. Sure, it has the makings of a great vacation getaway, but a real, four-year college? Get out of here. There must be a catch.

It's a Ton of Fun

One junior, when asked when the weekend started at Lake Forest College, was confused by the question. "The weekend doesn't quit," he said. Then he added, "But people have got their priorities, and not a lot of people say their priority is to party." However, one student double-majoring in

computer science and business said that parties are great: "They're so much fun. You go there, and it's 1,300 of your closest friends. If you bring a freshman to a party, it's like a dream for them. If an upperclassman brings a frosh, he'll introduce you to everyone, and everyone wants to know where you live, what do you do. It's so cool."

Lake Forest administration allows legal-age students to consume alcohol, as long as they're in their rooms behind closed doors. "They give us a little leeway; if we [mess] up there's consequences," explained one student. After being caught outside with alcohol three times, students are "kicked off housing."

When asked what differentiated Lake Forest from other schools, one student gushed, "The socialness. I can't even express it in words. It's unbelievable. When you go to class you say hi to everybody, if you go to a party, you know everybody. If you don't know somebody, it's like a long-lost brother. You're like, 'Where have you been? Why don't I know you?' Everyone hangs out; everyone knows everyone. It's literally like an oversized family at our school."

And when students are not at the parties, which usually take place on Fridays, they can easily hop on a train downtown for $1.75 (the station is about a mile away; students drive and park their cars there), or get a $5 unlimited weekend pass. As one English major put it, "We like to mix some culture in our social/party schedule." And of course, the city of Chicago speaks for itself.

Students who want to stay on campus and sober (some undergrads estimate that between 30 to 40 percent do not drink) have plenty of options too. Lots of movies, sporting events, community service, and dry social activities run by the Student Council can be found, although one sophomore mentioned that the turnout at the events is pretty small, since "it's a small school, and people are too busy getting trashed." But even so, it seems hard to knock a social scene where, as one athlete put it, "Everyone is welcome everywhere."

And the Academics Are Good

If the weekends "don't quit," then the classes could not be too challenging, right? No. Students all agreed that classes are difficult, entail a lot of work, and ultimately, are very rewarding. A junior said that after finishing a test one time, his professor gave him a high five, saying, "You studied so hard for this." Professors invite students to their houses for dinner, attend sporting events, and "want you to succeed and come back to visit and say 'Thanks for kicking my [butt] all through college—look where I am now,'" said a student. Students are close to their professors, who tend to be relatively young. Freshmen introductory courses are sometimes a source of complaint because they average 30 to 40 students, but upper-class courses max out at 25 and average between 6 and 10 students per class. Another junior said that "the professors are

very competent and willing to let students exercise intellectual freedom and reward them accordingly."

In fact, some illustrious profs can be found at Lake Forest: the inventor of holography is in the physics department. There is also a world-renowned art historian, a nationally recognized postmodern theorist, and the leading authority on the philosophy of erotics. The "all-around, most competent, rewarding prof?" asks one student. "Bob Greenfield in the English department. Ph.D. Columbia, amazing." Students also mentioned Dawn Meyer in the music department, Jason Cody in chemistry, and Ben Goluboff in English. Professor Matheson in business/economics starts off every class with a joke to "loosen everybody up." Professor Guglielmi in the psychology department is "awesome, gets so pumped up in class. He'll throw chalk and erasers at you." There are no TAs, class participation is encouraged and necessary, and as one chemistry major quipped, "I'm taking organic chemistry, which is taught by two professors. Both meet with me on a regular basis. The Dean of the College helps me out. My advisor calls me in my room, to see if I need something. Professors really care. If there's anything that stands out about this school, it's that they really care, won't let you fail. They really encourage interaction and challenge you. Students rise to the occasion and really get a decent education."

The Sports Teams Are Good Too!

The Lake Forest handball team is the best in the nation, literally, since there is only one division and Lake Forest is on top of it. Other sports are also top-notch. The men's swimming team has won three Midwest Conference titles recently, and the women's team has a tradition of first-place finishes. Men's tennis has also won titles the last couple of years. The men's soccer team is reputedly good, but the most popular varsity teams are men's hockey and women's basketball.

Juniors referred to a poll of students taken every year that revealed "astronomical statistics. Sixty-five percent of the freshmen class has played varsity athletics. Forty percent were captains of their teams. Thirty percent had a varsity letter in three or more sports." As one student put it, "Our school goes out and gets people that are leaders, that can express their feelings, who are able to perform well in the academic world. A 36 ACT is not what they're looking for. They want students that are well-rounded."

> **"The music is just as diverse as the people who go here. People listen to anything from swing to alternative to jazz to metal to rap to R&B."**

Student organizations mentioned included the campus radio station, Student Council, an environmental organization that is helping out with the reforestation of Lake Forest, and GLASS, the gay, lesbian, and straight society, one of whose events was to watch the Grammys together and cheer on Madonna. The student in charge of the radio station, when asked what type of music the undergrads listened to, answered, "The music is just as diverse as the people who go here. People listen to anything from swing to alternative to jazz to metal to rap to R&B."

"Our school thrives on diversity," emphasized a junior. She went on to explain how students were from all over the place, both from all over the States and other countries. There are also "all sorts of minority groups, an intercultural relations center, and all sorts of scholarships." However, students tend to be quite wealthy. A junior, when asked what students typically wore to class, said, "Polo, Prada, and Banana Republic." Somewhat antithetically, he went on to say, "There is certainly a spectrum of other people [not predominantly wealthy] here." There are also quite a few homosexual and interracial couples. And what brings the diversity of students together? As one student put it, "Everyone drinks. All races, they all get drunk and plastered together."

The Dorms Finally Get Renovated

Students report Lake Forest dorms were once in a "sad condition," but renovations begun in 1999 have significantly raised the caliber of on-campus living. Even without the renovations, students all agreed that the dorms are "livable," a good thing since not many can live off campus because of the costly surrounding neighborhood. Lake Forest is home to multimillion-dollar houses, and "one of the most expensive places to live in the entire nation." (The town is not exactly a college town, although students did mention the popularity of the Lantern, which has Wednesday-night drink specials, and Rainbows for Thursdays.)

The campus itself is "very, very beautiful. It's slightly hilly, but crisscrossed with ravines and an oak forest. It's just a mile or so from the lakefront." Buildings are red brick, and one building, Holt Chapel, is the center of an unusual tradition. Every year, "these super-religious people come out and all sit around it. They meditate and try to levitate the chapel. Just the concept of trying to levitate the 120-year-old building . . . it's pretty solid." There are three campuses: North, Middle, and South. Middle is where the classroom buildings are, and "it is a lug" from South Campus, where most of the students live (and where the parties are). Five dorms are on South Campus, and "all the jocks live down there because the sports center is down there. It's usually the crazy area," explained a Middle Campus resident. Along with the class buildings, there are two dorms on Middle Campus, including the Blackstone, which students need to apply to live in, since it is the "academic dorm." North Campus includes Cleveland Young, a residence hall for international students and those who have lived abroad. It was "just renovated. It's really, really nice," gushed one student.

Even the food is good, because Lake Forest switched to Aramark food service a few years ago, which does "a good job," say students. There's full salad and pasta bars daily, and "compared to other colleges, it's really good," said a junior. There are a couple of exceptions, however. "Some of the meats are bad, but it's tough to get good-quality meat," said one junior, while another mentioned, "They don't have enough seating, but it's getting fixed."

Ferris Bueller, Macaulay Culkin, Harrison Ford Are Right.

So, it seems the catches are small and getting fixed, and the great parts of Lake Forest College are going to last. Reputedly, Lake Forest has produced the most CEOs of any small college. And even Hollywood likes Lake Forest. Movies like *Ferris Bueller's Day Off*, *Home Alone*, and *The Fugitive* have all been shot here. Students cannot stop gushing, and as one said, "all sorts of races and ages come together, it's a super-friendly campus." It seems there is not much to lose and a whole lot of fun, learning, and friends to gain when it comes to Lake Forest College. —*Jennifer Wang and Staff*

FYI

The three best things about Lake Forest are "the beautiful campus, the friendly student body, and the caring *and* renowned faculty."

The three worst things about Lake Forest are "the freezing winters, a weak football team, and the eggs and hamburgers in the dining hall."

The three things that every Lake Forest student should do before graduating are "go to the Lantern and Rainbows, go to a Winter Ball, and spend the day touring Chicago."

One thing I wish I'd known before coming to Lake Forest is "how to juggle a moderate course load with all the activities on campus."

Loyola University

Address: 820 North Michigan Avenue; Chicago, IL 60611-9810
Phone: 312-915-6500
E-mail address: admission@luc.edu
Web site URL: www.luc.edu
Founded: 1870
Private or Public: private
Religious affiliation: Catholic
Location: urban
Undergraduate enrollment: 7,456
Total enrollment: 13,604
Percent Male/Female: 35%/65%
Percent Minority: 27%
Percent African-American: 7%

Percent Asian: 12%
Percent Hispanic: 8%
Percent Native-American: NA
Percent in-state/out-of-state: 80%/20%
Percent Pub HS: 60%
Number of Applicants: 3,670
Percent Accepted: 89%
Percent Accepted who enroll: 36%
Entering: 1,188
Transfers: 871
Application Deadline: 1 Apr
Mean SAT: 572 V, 570 M
Mean ACT: 24

Middle 50% SAT range: 520–630 V, 510–620 M
Middle 50% ACT range: 22–27
3 Most popular majors: psychology, business, biology
Retention: 83%
Graduation rate: 65%
On-campus housing: 31%
Fraternities: 7%
Sororities: 5%
Library: 1,700,000 volumes
Tuition and Fees: $18,190 in; $18,190 out
Room and Board: $7,200
Financial aid, first-year: 75%

In a city known for the Bulls, stuffed pizza, and the Sears Tower, Loyola University continually strives to make its mark with strong academics and a diverse student body.

Academic Flexibility

While seeking to be different, Loyola instills the traditional set of core requirements, hoping to ensure that students graduate with a well-rounded education. Among the requirements are three courses each in natural sciences and literature, two in history or social science, one in communicative and expressive arts, and one in the mathematical sciences. Unique to Loyola, however, are the requirements (three semesters each) in theology and philosophy. This is in keeping with the university's Jesuit affiliation. Despite the number of courses required in this core, few students are dissatisfied. They find that there is still enough academic flexibility: "It really provides you with alternatives," said one student. Class sizes are in general fairly small. While there are classes that exceed 150 students, like the popular Dr. Linda Heath psychology course, most classes enroll approximately 30, and some upper-level classes have as few as 4. Professors match the intimacy of their classes with personal accessibility. Reported one student, "most professors even give out their home numbers."

While there is a core requirement, students have reported that Loyola's strength lies in its division into five different campuses. Among the strongest is that which includes the nursing department. While business, communications, and biology are among the most popular, it is the 16-month intensive nursing program that draws the largest crowds and some of the fiercest competition; "there's a large pre-med/nursing crowd on campus," reported one sophomore, "and some of the requirements for that track are really hard." A selective program, nursing is open to application during undergrads' third year.

But Loyola is not just about nursing. There are a "lot of liberal arts people, as well." Since the recent merger with Mundelein College, Loyola's music department now offers instrumental as well as choral courses. To accommodate an expanded campus, there are shuttle buses that allow students to commute between the main Lake Shore main campus which houses most of the undergraduate facilities, classes, and dorms and the four satellite campuses.

Living in Chicago

Freshman dorm life is the norm, and Loyola does not encourage moving off campus until junior year, but many upperclassmen nonetheless eventually move out to nearby, furnished, campus apartments. All campus dorms are monitored by RAs, and are coed by floor. Opposite-sex visitors are not allowed on dorm floors after midnight during weekdays and 2 A.M. on weekends. "It is a Catholic school, you have to understand," ex-

plained one undergrad. In short, strict security dominates dorm life. But students do report the policy in campus apartments to be "a bit more open." While there is a sign-in at the door, ID cards need not be deposited for entry. And for those seeking even more freedom from regulations, Chicago provides all of life's essentials, from housing to eateries. Which is not to say that the food on campus is bad—most declared the food at Loyola's two cafeterias to be "tolerable." But nonetheless, "it is school food, and you just get sick of it after a while," one sophomore professed.

> Opposite-sex visitors are not allowed on dorm floors after midnight during weekdays and 2 A.M. on weekends.

While most students do in fact remain on campus, with local transportation so convenient a large portion of Loyola's student body is made up of commuters. As such, these students have a markedly different experience in Loyola's social scene than do those who live on campus. Although Loyola does offer many activities, ranging from Christian groups to ethnic clubs to the Lake Shore Student Government Association, there is a general consensus that these social offerings are somewhat lackluster. Proclaimed one student, "some organizations do stuff; a lot of people do their own thing." Added another, "Greeks are not big at all; we don't have enough people throwing parties." But the few frat houses present still garner enough support to sponsor the annual "Night on Ice" skating party held downtown.

While alcohol regulations are strictly enforced at dorm parties, students find alcohol readily available at off-campus parties or at city bars. Despite the apparently quiet campus, one commuter strongly recommended living on campus. "You really don't get to meet a lot of people if you always have to leave after class." The sports center at Loyola provides facilities for various levels of athletic involvement, from intramural to club sports. School spirit for team sports is not strong, however. Without a football team, Loyola students find themselves "supporting Chicago sports teams" more than they do their own.

But not all events are uninspired; Loyola students are reportedly among the most politically active in Chicago. Debates often rage over gay rights and abortion legislation, and some are vocal in their discontent with administrative policy—most noticeably against the student health center's policy of not distributing birth control.

Social life? It's in Chicago

If Loyola's social scene sounds fairly tame, the plethora of resources in Chicago make up for it. Many students prefer Chicago nightlife, just a short bus ride or train ride away. Along with excellent museums and other cultural attractions, the city has an abundance of dance clubs, comedy clubs, shops, and bars. Local coffeehouses like Coffee Chicago and Pannini Pannini are popular hangouts. Many also are fans of the vibrant local jazz and blues scene. Chicago even provides employment opportunities for students. Local companies recruit on campus, and undergrads generally find the career-placement center adept in counseling and assisting with job searches.

Impressively diverse for its size, Loyola offers, as one student said, "college life without a college town." With Chicago as an integral part of social and academic life, undergrads say they enjoy "more of the real world." If you're looking for a combination of strong pre-professional programs, solid liberal arts courses, and an exciting urban setting, Loyola offers this and more. —*William Chen and Staff*

FYI

The three best things about attending Loyola are "the location, the faculty, and the lake."

The three worst things about attending Loyola are "studying, the lack of a football team, and the weather."

The three things that every student should do before graduating from Loyola are "ride the ferris wheel at Navy Pier, enjoy local ethnic restaurants, and sit on the rocks up by the lake."

One thing I'd like to have known before coming here is "not to take 8:30 classes."

Northwestern University

Address: 1801 Hinman Avenue, Box 3060; Evanston, IL 60204-3060	**Percent African-American:** 6%	**Middle 50% SAT range:** 630–720 V, 650–740 M
Phone: 847-491-7271	**Percent Asian:** 17%	**Middle 50% ACT range:** 28–32
E-mail address: admission@northwestern.edu	**Percent Hispanic:** 3%	
	Percent Native-American: NA	**3 Most popular majors:** economics, political science, engineering
Web site URL: www.northwestern.edu	**Percent in-state / out-of-state:** 76% / 24%	**Retention:** 96%
Founded: 1851	**Percent Pub HS:** 66%	**Graduation rate:** 91%
Private or Public: private	**Number of Applicants:** 15,460	**On-campus housing:** 98%
Religious affiliation: none	**Percent Accepted:** 32%	**Fraternities:** 32%
Location: suburban	**Percent Accepted who enroll:** 39%	**Sororities:** 34%
Undergraduate enrollment: 7,842	**Entering:** 1,952	**Library:** 3,958,508 volumes
Total enrollment: 15,406	**Transfers:** 70	**Tuition and Fees:** $23,496 in; $23,496 out
Percent Male / Female: 48% / 52%	**Application Deadline:** 1 Jan	**Room and Board:** $6,847
Percent Minority: 26%	**Mean SAT:** NA **Mean ACT:** NA	**Financial aid, first-year:** 47%

At the heart of Northwestern University lies a solitary rock laden with uncountable layers of paint. Students will camp out overnight to stake their claim on this unofficial campus bulletin board in order to let their voices be heard. It displays everything from fraternity pride to campus events, such as AIDS Awareness Week and Gay/Lesbian Pride Week. The rock brings together and provokes dispute within a student body of boundless diversity, interest, talents, and opinions. The rock is a monument to how so many diverse ideas can come together and create a community with strength and spirit.

Work Hard . . .

Northwestern is definitely the place to go for serious academics. The school year runs on a quarter system, and courses are taught in a 10-week period. This fast pace leaves little room for slacking. As one sophomore said, "You can study your butt off, but it doesn't guarantee a good grade. It is very easy to feel mediocre in the midst of such intelligent classmates." The faculty is excellent, but many students feel that they spend too much time on research.

Students must enroll in one of the six undergraduate schools: the College of Arts and Sciences (CAS), the School of Music, the Medill School of Journalism, the School of Speech, the School of Education and Social Policy, or the McCormick School of Engineering and Applied Sciences. Several of these schools have received high acclaim, especially Medill School of Journalism and the School of Music. Northwestern has several departments that are highly acclaimed, including theater, economics, and bio-medical engineering.

All of the University's colleges offer several highly selective honors programs. The best known is the Honors Program in Medical Education (HPME) that guarantees entrance into Northwestern's medical school after three years. There are also several honors programs in engineering, the Integrated Science Program (ISP), the Mathematical Experience for Northwestern Undergraduates (MENU), and Mathematical Methods in the Social Sciences (MMSS), all of which provide an opportunity for accelerated study in the field of choice.

Distributional requirements vary from college to college, but, for the most part, they are quite similar. In the College of Arts and Sciences, which has the largest enrollment, students are required to take two quarter classes from each of the six distributional groups: formal studies (math); natural sciences; social and behavioral sciences (sociology, economics, political science); historical studies; values (civilizations, philosophy, religion); and literature and fine arts. Freshmen also take two seminars with an emphasis on writing and literature.

. . . Play Hard

Located right on the shore of Lake Michigan, Northwestern offers a picturesque college setting. The college is divided into the Chicago and Evanston campuses. Over a mile long, the Evanston campus is further divided into North and South campuses. South Campus is generally more quiet and houses most of the freshmen, while the fraternities and sororities are housed on North Campus, making it the place to party. With 40 percent of the students belonging to fraternities or sororities, the social scene focuses around Greek parties. However, recent administration crackdowns on underage drinking have pushed a significant amount of parties off campus. Despite the freshman freeze on Greek parties that is in effect for the first quarter, first-years still find it easy to get in to them. Northwestern's proximity to Chicago also spices up the social scene, and students find that their weekends often entail the half-hour trip to the Windy City.

> "We are intelligent, but we definitely know how to have a good time."

The social scene also includes many formal events. There are formal parties practically every weekend. At a recent Winter Ball, 4,000 students attended. As one freshman commented, "There is always an opportunity to get dressed up." But, not all special events require getting dressed up. Every May, the university sponsors Armadillo Day (Dillo Day) in celebration of the coming of summer. The celebration lasts the entire weekend, as students move out onto the lakefill, which is the peninsula that the university built to extend out into Lake Michigan. It gives overworked students an opportunity to forget about all their worries and listen to different bands in an atmosphere reminiscent of the 1960s. As an upperclassmen said, "It is a time when everyone sheds any reservations they might have."

There is a common view on campus that people are so caught up in studying that they do not have time to date. As a sophomore said, "There is not enough dating, not enough parties, and too much studying." In spite of Northwestern's intense academics, students who can find the time discover there is no lack of dating possibilities. As a freshman put it, "People are too busy doing their own thing."

And extracurricular opportunities abound at Northwestern. As one student lamented, "There's just too much stuff to choose from!" Artistic groups, especially theater and a cappella troupes, are prominent. The Associated Student Government is also popular, though the students admit that "this is a very apathetic campus." Despite the apathy, Northwestern sponsors Dance Marathon, the second largest college philanthropic event in the nation. The entire campus is drawn into participating in this 30-hour fund-raising dance.

The student union, Norris University Center, is a great place for students to chill and houses several franchises, in-cluding Pizza Hut and Higher Grounds, which is open 24 hours a day during reading week and is a popular destination for people who want to study and be social.

Let the Games Begin!

Sports have long been an important part of Northwestern. Being a Big Ten school, they find themselves with stiff competition, but they have been able to hold their own as they proved by their back-to-back football championships in 1996 and 1997. Their strong spirit is embodied in the clock tower that is purple when the football team wins and white when they lose. Unfortunately, in the 1998 season there was a lot more white than purple. Besides football, the men's basketball team enjoys particular success, and women's sports in general are very popular, often ranking higher than the men's sports. Intramurals are a popular alternative that draw a great number of participants.

The Sports Pavilion and Aquatic Center (SPAC) provides state-of-the-art facilities for athletes and non-athletes alike to work out. In fair weather, in-line skaters, joggers, and bicyclists are drawn to the path that runs along the lakefront offering a beautiful change in scenery.

It does not matter if Northwestern students are studying or being social, they do it in style. Although there are many complaints that the school is too focused on academics, a balance between work and play does exist as long as you are prepared to look for it. As an upperclassman said, "We are intelligent, but we definitely know how to have a good time." —*Seung C. Lee and Staff*

FYI

The three best things about attending Northwestern are "the people, being a Big Ten school, and Chicago."

The three worst things about attending Northwestern are "the cold, the serious effect of Greek life, and the tough academic curriculum."

The three things that every student should do before graduating from Northwestern are "hang out in Chicago, play intramurals, and take a gut class to alleviate some of the pressure."

One thing I'd like to have known before coming here is "how snowy Chicago gets."

Southern Illinois University / Carbondale

Address: Carbondale, IL
  62901-4701
Phone: 618-453-4381
E-mail address:
  admrec@siu.edu
Web site URL:
  www.siu.edu/oar
Founded: 1869
Private or Public: public
Religious affiliation: none
Location: suburban
**Undergraduate
  enrollment:** 17,735
Total enrollment: 21,908
Percent Male/Female:
  57%/43%
Percent Minority: 20%
Percent African-American:
  14%

Percent Asian: 2%
Percent Hispanic: 3%
Percent Native-American:
  0.5%
**Percent in-state/out-of-
  state:** 81%/19%
Percent Pub HS: NA
Number of Applicants:
  11,486
Percent Accepted: 71%
**Percent Accepted who
  enroll:** 31%
Entering: 2,493
Transfers: 4,108
Application Deadline:
  rolling
Mean SAT: NA
Mean ACT: 22
Middle 50% SAT range: NA

Middle 50% ACT range:
  20–24
3 Most popular majors:
  work force education,
  health care management,
  psychology
Retention: 66%
Graduation rate: 37%
On-campus housing:
  24%
Fraternities: 3%
Sororities: 3%
Library: 2,300,000
  volumes
Tuition and Fees:
  $4,113 in; $7,123 out
Room and Board: $4,104
Financial aid, first-year:
  57%

W hile Southern Illinois University has always been famous for its party-school image, the administration is making a conscious effort to direct attention back to academics. Numerous attempts at curbing undergraduate drinking and promoting alcohol-free fun have not earned a warm reception from students feeling the effects of the crackdown, however. Even though they are not thrilled with the new changes, many are still impressed with SIU's building up of academic programs.

Southern Education

SIU undergraduates are convinced that their school is the best in southern Illinois; they cite their communications, psychology, and political science majors as proof of that assertion. Students are especially proud of their unique aviation program, one of the few existing programs of its kind in the country, which attracts top students interested in flying. Other undergrads participate in the equally distinctive hotel and restaurant management program. During their freshman and sophomore years, all undergrads are required to take courses within the core curriculum

that range from English to the environment to music. While most introductory courses are large and many classes are taught by TAs, students are generally happy with the level of instruction. They rave about the professors, especially retired U.S. senator Paul Simon, who teaches a political science and a journalism course. Students claim that SIU is not strictly composed of humanities majors or science majors. In fact, many revel in the fact that their fellow students are involved in diverse fields. One student said that his three best friends were interested in forensic chemistry, art, and engineering.

The Social Scene

If you go to SIU and do not drink, you may feel left out. Practically all social functions revolve around drinking. Many underclassmen say they have no problem finding alcohol to fill their weekend, which usually begins around Wednesday and does not end until late Sunday. Upperclassmen spend most of their free time consuming alcohol at local Carbondale clubs and bars. Fraternities and sororities sponsor popular parties, although only about 15 percent of the student body goes Greek. One student chalks this up to the fact that "frats really don't recruit aggressively enough." Other undergrads feel that the number of students rushing will slowly decline in the next few years due to the unpopular Select 2000 program. Under this nationwide pilot study, SIU frats and sororities must all be dry by the turn of the millennium. Students say that some Greeks aren't really sure how to hold parties without alcohol.

> **Practically all social functions revolve around drinking.**

By necessity, the alternatives to drinking are becoming more and more popular. The Student Programming Council, one of the most well-respected organizations on campus, coordinates film screenings and concerts. Acts as diverse as Garth Brooks and 311 have recently played SIU. Undergrads report that random hookups also are a favorite pastime and that there is not much steady dating. Students claim to be liberal on the whole, but homosexual and interracial couples reportedly are still not fully accepted in the mainstream. Undergrads also perceive that a large number of their classmates smoke pot. As one upperclassman said, regarding the alternatives to alcohol consumption, "Options are there, but people think they have to drink to have fun."

Cornfields and College

SIU students rave about the beauty of their campus. Instead of being located in the stereotypical Midwestern flatlands and cornfields, SIU is situated among rolling hills, and a lake stands in the middle of campus. Minutes away, there are hundreds of acres of forest preserve. While town-gown relations are admittedly tense because many Carbondale residents dislike the seasonal influx of boisterous, reveling students, the town provides all of the amenities, including restaurants of practically every ethnicity.

That is not to say that the dining hall food is bad, though. The typically dining-hall-jaded college student is rare at SIU; those who eat at the dining halls are content. Many upperclassmen both eat and live off campus. Freshmen and sophomores are required to live on campus, and tend to be happy with their dorm rooms; most have doubles with air-conditioning, cable, and private bathrooms.

Extracurriculars

While fraternities and sororities are by far the most popular activities on campus, there are many different clubs to join. *The Daily Egyptian*, the campus newspaper, has won many awards and has one of the largest circulations in the country for a college newspaper. Minority groups, such as the Black Affairs Council and the Asian Student Council, also attract many members. In addition, community service is an extremely popular activity on campus. The Saluki Volunteer Corps, named after the SIU mascot, an Egyptian hunting dog, actively raises money for needy groups and organizes volunteers. Many students also have jobs, both on- and off-campus. One student estimated that as much as 90 percent of the part-time work force in Carbondale is composed of SIU students.

Saluki Athletics

Students describe the SIU recreational center as "awe-inspiring." It has six indoor basketball courts, twelve racquetball courts, and an Olympic-size pool. Some claim that this single building is responsible for most undergrads' above-average bodies. Popular intramurals are also a factor in keeping the student body in shape. Many sports classes for athletes and non-athletes alike are offered each semester, and students describe these sports as fun and well-attended.

As for varsity sports, the actively recruited basketball team has a huge following throughout SIU. Football, on the other hand, has been decidedly less successful and consistently fails to gain much support.

There is a lot of change happening at SIU. An advisory committee has been formed to find a new chancellor. This new appointment and the Select 2000 rule are the administration's attempts to focus on creating a new SIU geared toward academics and sobriety. —*William Chen and Staff*

FYI
The three best things about attending SIU are "its gorgeous campus, an internationally diverse student body, and WIDB radio."
The three worst things about attending SIU are "the administration's alcohol policy, a lack of school spirit, and the drinking-centered social life."
The three things every student should do before graduating from SIU are "go abroad, watch a varsity basketball game, and see a play at the Shryock Auditorium."
One thing I wish I'd known before coming to SIU is "how central drinking is to weekend activities."

University of Chicago

Address: 1116 East 59th Street HM 186, Chicago, IL 60637
Phone: 773-702-1234
E-mail address: college-admissions@uchicago.edu
Web site URL: www.uchicago.edu
Founded: 1891
Private or Public: private
Religious affiliation: none
Location: urban
Undergraduate enrollment: 3,561
Total enrollment: 12,117
Percent Male/Female: 54%/46%
Percent Minority: 36%
Percent African-American: 4%

Percent Asian: 27%
Percent Hispanic: 5%
Percent Native-American: NA
Percent in-state/out-of-state: 27%/73%
Percent Pub HS: 73%
Number of Applicants: 5,472
Percent Accepted: NA
Percent Accepted who enroll: NA
Entering: 980
Transfers: 120
Application Deadline: 1 Jan
Mean SAT: NA
Mean ACT: NA

Middle 50% SAT range: 640–740 V, 640–730 M
Middle 50% ACT range: NA
3 Most popular majors: economics, biology, psychology
Retention: 83%
Graduation rate: NA
On-campus housing: 95%
Fraternities: NA
Sororities: NA
Library: 6,000,000 volumes
Tuition and Fees: $21,485 in; $21,485 out
Room and Board: $7,275
Financial aid, first-year: 69%

Every year for three and a half days at the beginning of May, students at the University of Chicago get caught up in the frenzy of Scavenger Hunt, an event that provides a classic example of life in Hyde Park. To win, teams try to rack up as many points as possible by finding items from the master list. Last year, contestants road-tripped through the Midwest to pick up objects from Big Ten universities, chugged cans of creamed corn in the Scav Hunt Olympics, and seized control of university buildings. "One year, a homemade nuclear reactor was on the list and, as it's the U of C, two students actually made one in their dorm room. I'm less frightened that someone made a nuclear reactor than by the number of students I know who know how to make them," said one senior. An interesting blend of the quirky, the creative, and the intellectual, Scav Hunt exemplifies the "sheer madness" that is an undeniable part of one of the most highly regarded schools in the nation.

Work Hard . . .

As one independent studies major put it, "U of C students are masochistic in a way. We hate it, but we love it." The University of Chicago is known for its particularly demanding academics, and most students there agree that the work is intense. The sometimes-overwhelming atmosphere of Chicago is due at least in part to the university's trimester system. Classes run on a 10-week schedule, so that students take finals three times during the year; midterms can begin as early as four weeks into the term. Using the pre-med requirements as an example, one student said, "It takes a year and a half at most schools to finish organic chemistry and biochemistry . . . Here, you do it in one." As most would expect, these time constraints can translate into heavy assignments. One fourth-year student characterized the workload as "both excessive and necessary. I haven't had a class where I felt as if the problem sets or the reading assignments were not necessary. At the same time, I'm always behind in my work." Still, some people at U of C said that their work was "not too bad," emphasizing that the level of difficulty often depended on an individual's course load and study habits.

In addition to the trimester system, students must also deal with the requirements of the Common Core, a program meant to give undergrads a "true liberal arts" education. Although less stringent than in previous years, the Core requires students to take six classes in the humanities, six in mathematics and natural sciences (with at least two courses in the physical sciences and one in mathematics), and three in social sciences, in addition to fulfilling a language and physical education requirement. The Core takes up roughly a third of the credits required to graduate, with the remaining two-thirds split evenly between electives and classes necessary for a "concentration" (the U of C term for a major). Although they admitted that the Core requirements were a source of controversy, most students praised the Core as "a way to get a taste of every subject" before committing to a particular concentration. Students can use high AP and IB tests scores to minimize the Core requirements, but one senior felt that most people at Chicago would dabble in each of the academic areas, regardless of the graduation criteria: "Part of what makes U of C students different is our desire to know anything and everything inside out. The Core plays a big part in facilitating that sort of outlook."

Such an extensive list of requirements means that relatively few classes are freshman-only, as most people are still trying to fulfill the Core during their third and fourth years. The exceptions are Hum (the U of C name for the humanities requirement, pronounced "hume") and calculus classes; most freshmen take the

former to improve their writing (members of the Little Red Schoolhouse, Chicago's nationally renowned program for writing, help new students hone their skills) and the latter to complete the math requirement while it is still fresh in their minds from high school. Classes are split between lecture and discussion formats, with lecture classes ranging from 50 to 75 students and discussion sections generally maxing out at 30. Students pointed out that class size is not as important as the skill of the professor: "I was in a discussion class of about forty that . . . the professor made a great class because he really made discussion possible. I've also been in classes of twelve that were not handled nearly as well." Teaching assistants are prevalent in large classes, but in the opinion of one freshman, "Professors, unless it's a large science intro class, don't depend too heavily on the TAs for anything other than grading." In general, students consider their professors to be accessible. Still, the grading practices, considered "WAY too harsh" by some and "fair . . . but honest" by others, are universally acknowledged as tough.

Nerd Pride

Not surprisingly, Chicago's academic environment has in large part been formed by the students themselves. One senior fondly said, "Smart to the point of geeky is what I heard and what I expected and what I see. There *are* some stereotypically cool people on campus . . . however, I eventually see their nerdy sides, and then I know why they're here." There is "school spirit in terms of our nerd pride," and most students bond with one another, thanks to their mutual bookish sensibilities. While the vast majority of undergrads are white or Asian, students called the campus "very culturally diverse," pointing to the large number of ethnic student organizations. One freshman was particularly impressed by the visibility of these groups, since they seem to be "always organizing big events that the whole student body can take part in, like cultural shows, festivals, and formals." Although they are admittedly "dedicated to studying," U of C students are all quick to point out that a commitment to various extracurricular activities is the norm. Several students cited MUNUC

(Model United Nations of the University of Chicago) as one of the biggest groups on campus. This popular organization conducts a conference on international relations every year for roughly 2,000 high school students. Students are unashamed of their complete lack of interest in varsity sports. A fourth-year scoffed, "I've never been to a game, and most people don't even go to play-off games if they know about them in advance." This indifference about U of C teams is consistent with the attitude about sports in general. Club sports "have been having a hard time recently," although intramural sports are popular. Many students were underwhelmed by the quality of the athletic facilities on campus, but a new gym is under construction. One freshman summed up the concern for fitness on campus saying, "It's just not what dominates conversations."

. . . Play Moderately

In keeping with the academic atmosphere of the University of Chicago, "we aren't known for the wild parties and social extravaganzas of other universities," one first-year said. With only six fraternities and three sororities, the Greeks do not control the social scene with much force. An international studies major noted, "Rushing is not hard. They are almost always under quota, so they're always trying to recruit." Campus-wide participation is more likely to occur in events like lectures, theater productions, and classical music concerts. One party that *is* well attended by most of the student body is Summer Breeze, scheduled just before the last round of midterms begins. The student group COUP "turns the quads into a carnival complete with hypnotists, giant sumo wrestler suits, orbitrons . . . just generally fun stuff," sighed one senior. MAB, an organization in charge of recruiting big-name talent to play on campus, throws its biggest show of the year, featuring performers such as Moby, Sonic Youth, Busta Rhymes, and G-Love and Special Sauce. Orientation (also known as "O-week") is "like summer camp in late September" and offers similar events before school truly begins.

> **"Smart to the point of geeky is what I heard and what I expected and what I see."**

In general, the same principle that governs life at the U of C applies to free time. As summarized by one freshman, "Here a person's experience really depends on what he or she makes it out to be." After-hours activities during freshman year seem to happen mostly on campus, but upperclassmen typically venture outside of Hyde Park for fun. While most clubs are 21+, many are reportedly not very strict about enforcing this rule. As one upperclassman was quick to point out, "You can do so much without having to be twenty-one. There are so many large and small theaters, plenty of film festivals, cool restaurants, ethnic neighborhoods, protests, and rallies." When asked about the dating scene, one freshman replied, "One thing you should know about Chicago is that it is NOT known for social aptitude . . . we're nerds, most of us at least, and we're definitely not known for an attractive population." Relationships, if they do occur, are generally more serious, and "the random hookups of other schools" tend not to be as common here.

Where the Living Is Easy

"The social scene also depends greatly on where you live, as each dorm has its own social characteristics," one undergraduate observed. Currently, students are dispersed among the 11 dorms, regardless of year, although buildings with dining halls that are closer to campus (Woodward, Pierce, and Burston Johnson) generally have higher concentrations of freshmen. The style and layout of the rooms vary from dorm to dorm. One senior recommended, "If you want a single and want to be near the lake, you should live in Broadview . . . If you want a social dorm with older students and apartment-style rooms, try Shoreland. Every dorm has its benefits and drawbacks." Residents are fairly devoted to the place they live because of U of C's housing system. With the exception of the small dorms, each residence hall is divided into "houses." Each house has a residential advisor (houses with over 70 students have two), a third- or fourth-year undergraduate, and a residential head (RH), a member of the junior faculty or a grad student. Buildings that consist of more than one house also have a resident master drawn from the senior faculty. Masters plan large events involving the entire dorm (such as Shoreland's "infamous Karaoke Night"), while RAs and RHs organize various outings for their house each quarter, such as movie nights or trips to inexpensive plays. The dorm currently under construction will be exclusively for first- and second-years. Some students have criticized the new plan, saying that by limiting the mixing of the different classes it misses "the beauty of housing." At the same time, only about half of the upperclassmen at Chicago live on campus. While Hyde Park has the reputation of being unsafe, students said that basic "street smarts" are all the protection that is really necessary. Even the defenders of the area will admit that "the neighborhoods surrounding Hyde Park aren't very

nice" but add that these pockets are "rapidly being gentrified, which is another issue in and of itself." All students living on campus must be on the meal plan, but only freshmen are required to have the full meal plan (17 per week). With vegan and vegetarian options, students generally praised the offerings in the dining hall, going so far as to call the fare "great," the single critique being the early hours for dinner.

According to one freshman, students at the University of Chicago are critical of their school by nature. "We make fun of ourselves, put ourselves and the school down, make numerous derogatory comments, but that is the way we are, and we know it, and love it." Although there is no school spirit in a traditional sense—Chicago is not the "traditional" university of beer, frats, and football—with the amenities of Chicago, a star-studded faculty, and an intensely intellectual environment, the University of Chicago offers its students the resources to make their college experience their own. —*Lauren Johns*

FYI

The three best things about attending U of C are "that it's where being dorky is okay, the housing system, and breaks."

The three worst things about attending U of C are "the way that U of C students complain about their work all the time, the dining hall hours, and the lack of school spirit."

The three things that every student should do before graduating from U of C are "go to the Checkerboard, be on a Scav Hunt team, and step on the seal in front of Reynolds."

One thing I'd like to have known before coming here is "that it's the kind of school where you need to find your niche."

University of Illinois / Chicago

Address: Box 5220;
Chicago, IL 60680-5220
Phone: 312-996-4350
E-mail address:
uicadmit@uic.edu
Web site URL: www.uic.edu
Founded: 1965
Private or Public: public
Religious affiliation: none
Location: urban
**Undergraduate
enrollment:** 16,384
Total enrollment: NA
Percent Male/Female:
46%/54%
Percent Minority: 50%
Percent African-American:
10%

Percent Asian: 22%
Percent Hispanic: 17%
Percent Native-American:
0.5%
**Percent in-state/out-of-
state:** NA
Percent Pub HS: 81%
Number of Applicants:
9,304
Percent Accepted: 63%
**Percent Accepted who
enroll:** 48%
Entering: 2,807
Transfers: NA
Application Deadline:
1 Feb
Mean SAT: NA
Mean ACT: NA

Middle 50% SAT range: NA
Middle 50% ACT range:
19–25
3 Most popular majors:
business, health
professions, engineering
Retention: NA
Graduation rate: NA
On-campus housing:
NA
Fraternities: 1%
Sororities: 1%
Library: NA
Tuition and Fees:
$4,648 in; $10,924 out
Room and Board: $5,856
Financial aid, first-year:
NA

"UIC is a very worldly school. It gets you ready for the real world," described a third-year transfer student, summing up the difference between the University of Illinois at Chicago and her previous private college. UIC is not your typical life-in-a-fishbowl college, as concrete-clad UIC is right in the city with the looming Sears Tower and world-renowned theaters, restaurants, and stadiums at the students' disposal. Many students save money by commuting and have jobs to put themselves through UIC, which is known for its affordability. Students warn that the school is 92% commuter, leading to little participation in extracurricular activities and a less than happening social scene, as the campus is dead after 4 P.M. Said a sophomore—"*No one* is around at all!" However, that's not to say UIC ignores its population. Students can find plenty of faculty support if they have the desire to research or to start a club. Explained an enthusiastic first-year, "UIC is constantly looking to raise its profile in the educational system of Illinois."

Academics

Opinions differed as to whether UIC is more humanities or math and science-oriented, but one student said that the school is probably stronger in science because of the impressive research facilities and the medical school—UIC has the largest medical center campus in the nation. One second-year mentioned, however, that the music program is "underfunded and small, but excellent." The school is strengthened by the presence of its students in the math and science oriented Guaranteed Professional Program Admissions (GPPA—affectionately pronounced "guppa"), where select incoming freshmen (Illinois residents only) are automatically admitted into specific graduate programs at UIC. Especially well-known is the medical program, where students are guaranteed a medical school spot for three to five years without having to take the MCAT. Many GPPA students thus opt to finish their undergraduate career in three years. GPPA students still need to do pre-med requirements as specified by the medical school, including chemistry, biology, physics, and social science courses. These GPPA students up the curve in classes—cautioned one student, "stay away from the GPPA kids and the curve's a beautiful thing. With GPPA kids, the curve's definitely a lot higher."

While admission into the GPPA programs is quite competitive, regular admissions, according to a second-year student, are "too easy. Anyone can get into this school as long as you passed high school." Students cited requirements as 1000 on the SAT and approximately 22 on the ACT. "However," added the same student, "our standards are going up and within the next few years, academically, our standards will be as high as our brother school U of I at Champaign." Regular students need to maintain a 3.0 on a 5.0 scale to continue at UIC, while GPPA students must maintain a 4.5. Grading is pretty easy, although, one economics major said, "Sometimes there are teachers who, even though the whole class failed the test, choose not to curve the scores."

Classes range from "intimate," at around 20 students to "huge," with as many as 340 students in the large lecture courses. While one second-year student said that not many students participate in class—"it's a pretty apathetic campus," another pointed out that "students for the most part are very focused. The ones who don't pay attention don't show up."

Unfortunately, the lack of interest in many classes may stem from the plethora of TAs. "Discussion can be stupid and worthless especially if you can't understand what the TA is saying," complained one student. Chemistry TAs have an especially bad rep, although biology TAs are "pretty good." Yet, even professors do not fare so well in their students' eyes. "Lecture is sometimes useless because you can always get notes off the web or rely on others." Further, "labs are absolutely stupid in the general courses." Some professors who have good reputations on campus include: Stanley Fish, a well-known writer and the Dean of Liberal Arts and Sciences; Professor Young, who somehow gets "rave reviews every year" despite teaching organic chemistry; Ackles in psychology; and Fetzer in chemistry.

Students agreed that the slacker major is psychology, which one psych major gloated as requiring just 27 credits (roughly nine classes) out of the 120 credit hours required to graduate. Other popular majors are criminal justice and biology; biology being especially important to pre-med GPPA students since "it's only a few more classes than the requirements for the program." "There are a lot of requirements for the Liberal Arts and Science College, but it's easy to understand if you talk to upperclassmen about them," said one freshman. The toughest class at UIC, students say, is physical chemistry—"everything else pales in comparison unless you're taking grad classes," said one victim. Other tough classes include an embryology class and calculus-based physics.

UIC takes care of its honors students, giving them priority in class choices, but this does not mean that it forgets the rest of its population either. "The University has various counseling services that are available to aid with career placement, tutoring, advising, scheduling, and various other things that overwhelm the student body," described a third-year student. "There are even counseling services for those with math anxiety!"

Social Life—Well, Sort Of

Unfortunately, "unless you're part of the small Greek system, UIC isn't that much of a social school," reported one sorority member. Cool frats and sororities are Sigma Alpha Mu, the third largest national fraternity, and Alpha Sigma Tau. Anyone can rush, but pledging is selective. However, there is no hazing at UIC. Greek mixers or exchanges are closed to other students. Cool theme parties include Toga, Graffiti, Cowboys and Indians, Tropical, and Cops and Robbers. The administration does not allow alcohol for minors, and "athletes can not be associated with alcohol *period*," said one Greek.

Being underage poses problems at Chicago clubs and bars, as some card hard. "But there are always places that don't card. Most importantly, meet someone that's 21 and you'll be fine," assured one student. However, beware: while those of drinking age are allowed to drink in the dorms, "if they catch you drinking below age, you get one warning before getting kicked out," stated a freshman. Freshmen who do not go home tend "to go to the city, find one of maybe five parties, watch movies, or go clubbing." Upperclassmen do roughly the same, with the addition of visiting Hawkeyes, the closest campus bar. Students visit clubs at Rush and Division, as well. Especially popular are The Drink and The Crowbar, where Dennis Rodman has been known to hang out and party.

> **"This school isn't called University of Indians and Chinese for nothing. It's very, very diverse."**

Because of the lack of resident students, there are very few campus-organized activities aside from those in the beginning of the year for freshmen to meet each other and members of the administration. However, it is easy to meet people in classes. "Most people are pretty friendly," said a second-year student. "You could stand in the middle of Inner Circle (fast-food place) and meet someone new everyday," described a first-year student. Many students frequent the student center to hang out, exercise, and eat.

Student Body

At UIC, "there are racial cliques that just can't be beat. Indians and blacks and Asians all stick—it's just the way it is," one student said. But one freshman, after describing the cliques, said that ultimately, "it doesn't really matter because there are so many people that go to school here. You're bound to find a friend somewhere." As for significant others, upperclassmen tend to have long-term relationships while freshmen and sophomores "play the field and do more stupid stuff." Interestingly enough, despite the cliques which students say tend to form and remain cemented (especially among religious groups and athletes), one freshman declared that there are quite a few interracial couples. "This school isn't called University of Indians and Chinese for nothing. It's very, very diverse," said one second-year student. Many students mentioned the multitude of Indians, Koreans, and Chinese students. As for dress, "there are really a lot of people that look like they're about to go clubbing at any moment, but you have your relaxed outfits and pajamas and grungier styles like anywhere else. I think for the most part people dress pretty well," observed a biology major. In general, though, the student population is "pretty middle class," according to one student.

The Neighborhood

Most students said they feel safe on and around campus, as the campus police have a strong presence. However, one second-year student mentioned that she hears sirens pass by her room almost nightly. Like most places, it is not safe to walk around alone at night. "It's not a good-looking campus either," insisted one student. "But within the next ten years or so, the school is planning to tear down the projects separating the east and west campuses. The older architecture at UIC, explained one student, "is built mostly with concrete and other rather blah-looking materials, and the windows are puny. The newer buildings are pretty nice, and lately the school has been working on beautifying the campus so it's getting better—more grass and flowers, less concrete." UIC buildings are riot-proof since they were built during the civil rights movement. For example, rumor has it that University Hall, the tallest building on campus, was built with the bottom narrower than the top so that people couldn't climb it in the event of a riot. Also, UIC is adding a south campus in the next five years, having bought up all the land in the surrounding neighborhoods.

Most students live off campus, either at home or in apartments nearby, although the school guarantees housing for the next year after students live on campus. However, warned one student, "it's kind of a pain to live on the west side of campus and have classes on the east side." However, the west side "has more community" than the east. Students said that they were very happy with their freshman-year dorms. One second-year student said that her floor "happened to bond very well together and we're all pretty tight." Specific dorms mentioned were PSR, which is an older dorm that is being torn down in two years, and SSR, a dorm for people over 21. In SSR, two to four people share a kitchen and a common room and have their own bedrooms. Exterminators come every month to the dorms, "whether you need them to or not," and while there is an RA system, RAs are not strict.

Food and Sports Perks

There are plenty of great restaurants off campus. Giordano's, the famed Chicago pizzeria, is a five-minute walk from school, and Greektown, which is open 24/7, is just another five minutes down from Giordano's. Little Italy and Chinatown are within walking distance as well. There is "pretty good food" on campus, said a first-year, ticking off Wendy's, Sbarro's, Subway, Taco Bell, and KFC. "The cafeteria food isn't too bad either. It's actually pretty good on the west side because all the doctors eat there for lunch."

The school's most popular sports team is by far the men's basketball team, as UIC does not have a football team. "Our homecoming is in February with a basketball game. Weird, huh," said one student. Facilities for non-athletes are reportedly nice and well-populated by bench-pressing giants. The athletes have a new $10 million dollar Flames Athletic Center that regular students are not allowed to use. And while most students do not participate in extracurriculars, one student said that "the best thing about attending UIC is having one consistently nationally known dance team. We are ranked 5th in the nation."

UIC, with its location right in the hub of Chicago, has a lot to offer to the city-loving student: the advantages of its affordability and location also lead to its drawbacks of a mostly commuting student body. With its unique GPPA programs and top-notch research facilities, as one first-year student summed it up: "I believe UIC has a lot to offer to an ambitious student . . . you just have to look for opportunities." —*Jennifer Wang*

FYI

The three best things about attending UIC are "Chicago and all its splendiferous glory, 3:00 Pizza Puff runs at the still very much awesome Greektown, and you never run out of people to meet."

The three worst things about attending UIC are "the dangers of city living, the lack of a college campus atmosphere, and the fact that almost everyone's a commuter."

The three things that every student should do before graduating from UIC are "to explore the city, to get involved in a club or activity, and to share a 50-piece Chicken McNugget meal at the Rock 'n Roll McDonald's with someone."

One thing I wish I'd known before coming here is "that AP credit counts for massive amounts and if you want to register early, you need that credit."

University of Illinois / Urbana-Champaign

Address: 901 West Illinois; Urbana, IL 61801
Phone: 217-333-0302
E-mail address: admissions@oar.uiuc.edu
Web site URL: www.uiuc.edu
Founded: 1867
Private or Public: public
Religious affiliation: none
Location: small city
Undergraduate enrollment: 27,492
Total enrollment: 36,019
Percent Male/Female: 56%/44%
Percent Minority: 26%
Percent African-American: 7%

Percent Asian: 13%
Percent Hispanic: 5%
Percent Native-American: 0.5%
Percent in-state/out-of-state: 91%/9%
Percent Pub HS: NA
Number of Applicants: 17,867
Percent Accepted: 71%
Percent Accepted who enroll: 51%
Entering: 6,479
Transfers: 1,366
Application Deadline: 1 Jan
Mean SAT: 602 V, 638 M
Mean ACT: NA

Middle 50% SAT range: 550–650 V, 590–710 M
Middle 50% ACT range: 25–28
3 Most popular majors: biology, psychology, electrical engineering
Retention: 92%
Graduation rate: 78%
On-campus housing: 33%
Fraternities: 19%
Sororities: 22%
Library: 9,000,000 volumes
Tuition and Fees: $4,744 in; $12,192 out
Room and Board: $5,424
Financial aid, first-year: 83%

Host to the nation's first homecoming football game, first supercomputer, oldest marching band, and largest Greek system, the University of Illinois/Urbana-Champaign has grown from its youth in the 1860s as the chartered "land-grant" public college for the state of Illinois into one of the nation's foremost public research universities. U of I today includes eight undergraduate colleges and more than 26,000 undergrads, offering a plethora of academic, extracurricular, and social options.

Academic Powerhouse

The university's nine undergraduate divisions include the Colleges of Agriculture, Applied Life Studies, Business, Communications, Education, Engineering, Fine and Applied Arts, Liberal Arts and Sciences, and the Institution of Aviation. The university's reputation, especially in engineering, computer science, and business, is excellent, and the programs in these fields consistently rank among the best in the nation. Admission to most undergraduate schools is selective, with more than half of the student body coming from the top 10% of their high school class. The variety of academic options makes U of I a popular destination for undecided majors; one undergrad remarked, "If a person is unsure about what major he/she wants to pursue, UIUC is a great place to come." However, transferring into a different undergraduate college—particularly into the competitive College of Engineering—can be a difficult task for students who change their minds. "It's discouraging how much red tape one needs to go through in order to switch," stated an LAS-to-engineering transfer. "But it weeds out people who don't really know what they're doing."

Graduation requirements are generally considered demanding, and some students find it difficult to fulfill both the distributional requirements and their major curriculum in four years. "Many of my friends in engineering came here knowing they'd be likely to take four and a half years or more," said one freshman. Grading is also generally considered tough. "There's not a lot of grade inflation," stated a junior. "It's not like high school. You work very, very hard for your courses, and sometimes an A is just not worth the extra effort." One freshman characterized her schedule as "an endless stream of work . . . there's never enough time!" However, there are known ways of circumventing the academic rigors; the kinesiology and leisure studies departments in the College of Applied Life Studies, along with popular intro courses like Geology 100 ("Rocks for Jocks"), are notorious for serving as quick and easy ways to a degree.

"Like a Huge Farm"

The University of Illinois campus is described by various students as "gigantic," "majestic," and "unbelievably flat." More than one student drew an analogy between the setting of the campus and a large farm: "There's lots of open space, the campus is entirely flat, and there's even some experimental crops growing next door to the library!" In the heart of the campus, the Quad, the architecture is primarily Georgian revival, with large brick buildings and tall white pillars. The Illini Union, sitting at the north end of the Quad and serving as the center of much of campus life, houses small shops, banks, bowling alleys, cafeterias, hotel rooms, meeting rooms for student organizations, and a branch of the university's library system, which contains more volumes than any other public university in the country. The Undergraduate Library, situated at the south end of the Quad behind the prominent 1,750-seat Foellinger Auditorium, is a popular place to study and is almost entirely underground. It was built so as not to block the sun from shining on neighboring Morrow Plots, the country's oldest agricultural experiment field still in use and a National Historic Landmark since 1968.

Although the campus sprawls over nearly 1,500 acres, most buildings are grouped according to academic departments. North Campus primarily houses the sciences and the school of engineering, while the south is home to the business and agriculture schools and the athletic complex. "I really don't have a problem with the size of the campus," noted one student. "Once you're in your major and can choose where to live, it hardly feels big at all."

Beyond the large expanse of university-owned land are the cities of Urbana and Champaign, which form a combined metro area of nearly 100,000 people. Students affectionately refer to the area as "Chambana," although as several students confess, "outside of Campustown, there's really not all that much to do." Students with cars (and most U of I students have access to them) often take trips to grocery stores, movie theaters, or the mall in Champaign. Many students enjoy visiting Allerton Park, a university-owned recreation area and conference center 40 minutes away in the town of Monticello. Originally a privately owned estate, the grounds were donated to the university in 1946 by the Allerton family, and the park now includes formal gardens, sculptures, hiking trails, and lots of well-maintained green space. "It's a perfect place to study, relax, or have a picnic, if you're willing to make the drive," commented one sophomore.

Social Illini

The University of Illinois student population is one of the largest in the Midwest. Although the student body is represented by all 50 states and 100 foreign countries, students overwhelmingly come from in-state, especially from the Chicago area. "It seems like everyone I've met is from the suburbs," noted a freshman. And while large African-American, Latino, and Asian-American populations exist on campus, most students are dismayed by how much self-segregation exists among different ethnicities. "Cliques are definitely a problem, and many of them are drawn solely along racial or ethnic lines," remarked one student. Everyone primarily "eats, lives, and socializes" with members of their own group.

> **"It's not like high school. You work very, very hard for your courses."**

When the weekend rolls around, U of I students are no strangers to an active social life. Campustown, a large nearby business area with a multitude of bars, stores, and restaurants, is a popular destination. Once inside a bar, "it's very easy to score drinks, and many people go overboard with it," commented one sophomore. Because the bar entrance age is 19 in Champaign, many freshmen are initially excluded from the scene. However, fake IDs are said to be relatively easy to obtain, and many students are able to get in by knowing friends who work in the various drinking establishments.

The Greek scene maintains a huge influence on campus social life and provides the primary social outlet for a large portion of undergraduates. GDIs ("god-damned independents") are mixed about whether they felt left out socially, though many agreed "there is plenty to do on a Friday night besides get wasted." Still, the pressure to drink, especially for those interested in becoming members of frats or sororities, can be very heavy. "Practically everyone" seems to get drunk at least one night over the weekend, lamented one critic of the "hyperactive" drinking scene.

Outside of partying, there is a wide array of events and activities to keep students entertained. Recent guest speakers to campus include Rubin "the Hurricane" Carter, Roger Ebert (an alum), Dr. Drew Pinsky, and Jesse Jackson. U of I is known for drawing famous musical acts to campus as well; within the past few years, the Dixie Chicks, Foo Fighters, Matchbox 20, Red Hot Chili Peppers, Smashing Pumpkins, and Cher have all come to the campus to perform. The Krannert Center for the Performing Arts brings in notable artists in other musical genres, including renowned symphonies, opera companies, and jazz ensembles. Many students throw themselves wholeheartedly into the extracurricular scene, participating in noteworthy groups like Volunteer Illini, the student newspaper (the award-winning *Daily Illini*), and a vast array of political organizations, activist groups, performing arts ensembles, and social clubs. "U of I is a very active campus. You name it and we probably have it," commented a student. Quad Day, an event that takes place at the beginning of the year, draws hundreds of student organizations to set up booths on the Quad and recruit new members. "Quad Day is huge!" exclaimed one sophomore. "You can walk around for hours and still not find all the groups that interest you."

As a member of the Big Ten athletic

conference and a perennial powerhouse in many sports, the University of Illinois is also a very athletically oriented campus. Teams like men's football and men's basketball consistently sell out their venues. "Sports are very, very important here," noted a student. "Even non-athletes follow the teams, and the fitness and intramural facilities are wonderful . . . and free for students!" While one junior lamented a "slight increase in student apathy" for athletic teams over recent years, U of I is still home to some of the nation's most rabid fans.

Living in a Cage

Despite ongoing attempts by the administration to improve campus living spaces, housing still ranks among one of the largest grievances of the student population. "My freshman-year dorm room was very small . . . it felt like I was in a cage," complained one upperclassman. Dorm food also gets low marks. "The food here is awful, even by dining hall standards," commented a dorm resident. Still, many are satisfied with their arrangements; air-conditioning is available in a number of residences, and students "do a good job" of making their rooms feel like home. Most students eventually move off campus into nearby apartments or houses, some of which are maintained by the university. Fraternity and sorority houses also are popular places to live, as is the residential hall area nicknamed the "Six-pack" as much for its fervent party scene as for the six towers that constitute it.

"Jewel in the Cornfields"

While the size of the university deters many would-be Illini, most students easily acclimate to their surroundings and quickly fall in love with their school. In fact, many respondents cite the size of the University of Illinois as the best thing about it. "The huge size just means that there's a wealth of opportunities available here that you can't find . . . anywhere else. It's everything I'd want or need in a school," commented one enthusiastic student. Said another, "Everything about this place is engaging and exciting . . . it's truly a jewel in the cornfields." —*Jeff Sandberg*

FYI
The three best things about attending UIUC are "the stellar academics, the diverse party scene, and Big Ten athletics."
The three worst things about attending UIUC are "the cafeteria food, the dorm room sizes, especially freshman year, and the different ethnic groups tend to self-segregate."
The three things that every student should do before graduating from UIUC are "visit the echo spot in front of Foellinger Auditorium, sleep outside on the Quad with Habitat for Humanity's 'Shantytown,' and go to lots of football and basketball games!"
One thing I'd like to have known before coming here is "just how big the campus is!"

Wheaton College

Address: 501 College Avenue; Wheaton, IL 60187
Phone: 630-752-5005
E-mail address: admissions@wheaton.edu
Web site URL: www.wheaton.edu
Founded: 1860
Private or Public: private
Religious affiliation: none
Location: suburban
Undergraduate enrollment: 2,302
Total enrollment: NA
Percent Male/Female: 48%/52%
Percent Minority: 10%

Percent African-American: 2%
Percent Asian: 4%
Percent Hispanic: 3%
Percent Native-American: 0.5%
Percent in-state/out-of-state: 21%/79%
Percent Pub HS: NA
Number of Applicants: 1,964
Percent Accepted: 54%
Percent Accepted who enroll: 55%
Entering: 584
Transfers: NA
Application Deadline: 15 Jan
Mean SAT: NA
Mean ACT: NA

Middle 50% SAT range: 610–720 V, 600–700 M
Middle 50% ACT range: 27–31
3 Most popular majors: English, music, Biblical studies
Retention: NA
Graduation rate: NA
On-campus housing: 100%
Fraternities: NA
Sororities: NA
Library: NA
Tuition and Fees: $15,540 in; $15,540 out
Room and Board: $5,260
Financial aid, first-year: NA

When the Blanchard Hall bells ring, Wheaton students cannot help but smile. It is a school tradition that when a Wheaton couple becomes engaged, the two must climb the bell tower and ring the bell twenty-one times, in three sets of seven. Then they are to leave behind some sort of memorabilia or token in memory of their trip there. One of the school's most famous alumni, Christian evangelist Billy Graham, is reported to have visited the site himself more than 50 years ago with his then-fiancée, Ruth. Every week, three or four couples follow his same path up the bell tower stairs.

Founded in 1860, Wheaton College is known today as one of America's premier Christian colleges. As one student joked, "People call us the Harvard of Christian colleges." And indeed it is true that many Wheaton students reject offers from top secular universities to attend Wheaton. For them, it is often a matter of where they think they will grow the most, stemming from a desire to learn in a Christian-friendly environment absent at secular institutions. Christian faith is a requisite for entrance to Wheaton, which asks its applicants to submit a personal testimony as well as a recommendation from a church pastor. At Wheaton, biblical Christian values underlie every aspect of life as the school strives to realize its motto, "Christo Et Regno Ejus"—"For Christ and His Kingdom."

In the Christian Classroom

When asked to name her favorite place on campus, one student jokingly replied, "My bed because I don't get to see it very often." Students at Wheaton work hard. All majors must fulfill a general education requirement, which includes two social science courses, Philosophy 101, two science courses, and two Bible classes concentrating on the Old and New Testaments. "We're definitely a liberal arts school," said one student. "I don't think most people realize that before coming here."

As a Christian college, Wheaton offers a number of specifically Christianity-related majors in addition to more traditional ones. Among those distinctive to Wheaton are Biblical Studies, Christian Education, and various ministry-related Music majors. Students say Communications and Christian Education are the easiest fields of study, while Chemistry and the sciences can be "absolutely killer." In the words of one science student, though, "Wheaton is really good if you're gonna major in Bible, but not-so-great if you're doing science. It is a liberal arts school, after all." Music students were said to work especially hard. "You never even see music majors because they're always in the conservatory practicing," one student noted.

Like students, all professors at Wheaton are Christian. Many will open their lectures by reciting a short prayer or bible verse. Students agree that having Christian professors can be both good and bad. As one student said, "It's good because we have the opportunity to learn in an academic atmosphere that is not hostile to the Christian faith." But because professors and students share a core of Christian beliefs, the classroom can sometimes "lack challenge and diversity of opinion." According to one student, "The environment here is conducive to close-mindedness because everyone thinks the same way. One person will say something and everyone else will just nod in agreement. Where's the challenge in that?" Another student added, "Sometimes it's like you're cheating yourself out of figuring out things for yourself by having it spoon-fed to you."

The Wheaton Pledge

Every semester, Wheaton students sign an official statement of responsibility, promising to uphold certain Christian values. In taking this Wheaton pledge, they agree to refrain from smoking, drinking alcohol, social dancing, and premarital sex. Most students do adhere to these guidelines, but there are exceptions. One student remarked, "I kinda had the impression that everyone here is a perfect Christian and never breaks any of the rules. But I've realized that's not true. It's kinda disappointing. Then again, Christians are human too—we all make mistakes."

In addition, students must attend a morning chapel service three times a week—Monday, Wednesday, and Friday. They are allowed up to 9 skips a semester; those students who miss more than 9 may be placed on "chapel probation." Students on probation cannot participate in school activities and lose seniority in housing privileges. "It's not too big a deal, though," said one student.

"Bro-Sis" Housing

Almost all Wheaton students live in dorms or university-owned apartments. First-year students are required to live in dorms. Fischer was named the most social freshman dorm, while Saint and Elliot were cited as the worst places to live because of their distance from main campus. Frosh do have a curfew—midnight on weeknights and 2 A.M. on weekends—but according to one upperclassman, "it's not enforced too strictly. Coming in late is okay as long as you don't do it too much."

Males are generally not allowed in female dorm rooms and vice versa except during special hours called "open floors," which take place twice a week for about three hours. One stipulation is that dorm room doors must be kept open throughout visits, so that floor RAs (residential advisors) can oversee everything that goes on.

Dorms operate on a "Bro-Sis" system, in which each male floor has a corresponding "sister floor." "Brother" and "sister" floors will regularly do stuff together, including meet for weekly dinners at Saga, the campus dining hall, and have "raids," party-like get-togethers that happen a couple of times a semester. Wheaton has one dining hall to accommodate its 2300 undergrads. Officially known as Centennial Cafeteria, students informally refer to it as "Saga" after the food service Wheaton employed during the 80s. Food is cited as "pretty good—much better than what you'll find at some other schools." After hours, students can find munchies at the school eatery, called "The Stupe." Most students will only go there during certain times, though. "It's okay at night, but during the day, it's like a junior high hangout, so we all kinda avoid it then," said one sophomore.

On Campus

Primarily residential, the town of Wheaton has been nationally recognized as one of America's safest cities. "I feel really comfortable walking around even at night," said one student. But most students will agree, local life can get really boring. The handful of coffee shops and food places near campus "all close at like 8!" lamented one student.

Wheaton is a dry, Greek-free campus. But even in the absence of traditional frat party life, students find lots to do. A couple of times a month, Wheaton will host popular Christian bands, with students attending in hordes. Classical music is also a big draw. The school conducts an Artist Concert Series of six or seven concerts every year. Recent guests have included Dawn Upshaw and the Vienna Boys' Choir. Another popular event is a weekly Praise Night hosted by the campus World Christian Fellowship group every Sunday night. For a few hours, students will gather and sing Christian praise and worship songs. The school talent show and February formal are two other well-attended Wheaton events.

Wheaton does not permit its students to engage in social dancing. Square dancing performed to traditional American hoedown music is the only kind of dancing allowed, and it is only permissible at school-sponsored events. Square dances happen a few times a semester and remain popular despite the dance's "hickish" reputation. Most students will go as singles, but it is not uncommon for people to go with dates.

Going for an M.R.S. degree

According to one student, dating at Wheaton tends to get "very complicated." "Everyone's pretty much looking for marriage, so dating here involves a lot of pressure," noted one sophomore. Another male student explained dating at Wheaton, "The way it works, if you're seen walking around campus with a girl, people will jump to conclusions and automatically assume you're engaged. Needless to say, casual dating is lacking."

On the female side, a common joke circulating among Wheaton women is that "you've come to get your M.R.S. degree." One female student went so far as to call Wheaton a "meat-market." Every week the school newspaper runs a section called "Up the Tower," listing newly engaged couples; a minimum of two or three pairs of names appear each week with numbers soaring near the end of each semester.

Off Campus

Many students own cars, a luxury which makes finding fun off campus considerably easier. A big nearby movie-plex is a popular weekend destination. After shows, students often get coffee and talk at the local Borders or Barnes & Noble bookstore. The Front Street Cocina was cited as a fun place to satisfy cravings for salsa and other Mexican treats. Despite their popularity, cars are not a necessity. Said one student, "You can get by without a car, but it's nice to have one." With on-campus parking becoming scarcer many students are choosing to leave their cars at home.

> "I'm convinced that 99% of the people on this campus play the guitar."

Twenty-five miles from Wheaton campus is Chicago. Many Wheaton students take trains there to enjoy the bustle of metropolitan life. Train fare is inexpensive—$5 for a weekend pass—and the trip takes less than an hour, making for a mass student exodus to the city on weekends.

Extracurriculars

Most Wheaton students are involved in at least one extracurricular campus activity. In particular, Christian campus ministry groups abound at Wheaton, ranging from local community service to international evangelism groups. Some well-known student organizations include the College Union, the school's social planners, which are in charge of bringing groups and speakers to campus, and Student Government, comprising Wheaton's student body representatives.

Many Wheaton students are musical, so participation in campus singing and music performance groups is naturally very high. One student joked, "I'm convinced that 99% of the people on this campus play the guitar. Moving in, almost everyone is carrying one."

Wheaton tends to lack ethnic diversity, but for the less than 10% minority student population, the Office of Minority

Affairs organizes a number of ethnic organizations, such as Koinonia, the Asian-American group, and Unidad Cristiana, the Hispanic and Latino-American group.

Sports at both the intercollegiate and intramural levels are very popular among Wheaton students, with soccer being especially big. Wheaton students attend school games en masse, and the crowds tend to become "very enthusiastic," said one frequent attendee.

Always Changing

In 1980, world Christian evangelist Billy Graham led a crusade at Wheaton College, celebrating the completion of the Billy Graham Center, dedicated to advancing world evangelism. Almost two decades later, the Center houses its own museum, which chronicles world evangelism history using art. As the Center adapts to changing world needs and conditions, it serves as a paradigm of advancement and useful adaptation.

Wheaton, too, is a dynamic being. But the school never loses its foundation rooted in faith. Amidst a changing world, the school strives to remain a Christian bastion of higher learning. But, as the new millennium begins, recognizing the school's need to adapt and grow, the Wheaton administration has announced a school-wide "New Century Challenge," which includes plans to foster greater ethnic diversity as well as more practical plans for building construction and renovation. An improved Sports and Recreation Center was recently completed. And having successfully finished Anderson Commons, the administration has plans for a new student center underway.

In a further effort to keep up with the times, Wheaton changed its macot. Historically, the school mascot has been the Crusaders, a modern take on the medieval Christian soldiers who fought for their faith. But, some people feel the current "Crusaders" image inaccurately depicts Christians and may unnecessarily offend. The new mascot name is the Wheaton Thunder. A competition to design the new logo is currently being held.

A Personal Decision

Wheaton can be a great place for some to grow in their Christian faith. But, as one student warned, Wheaton life can quickly become a "super-saturation of the Christian experience." As always, the final decision is a personal one. But Christian students considering Wheaton are encouraged to really look at the school. As it has been for hundreds of Christian greats, it may be the stretch in the straight and narrow that leads them to places they never dreamed they would go. —*Jane H. Hong*

FYI
The three best things about attending Wheaton are "the integration of faith and learning, good professor-student interaction, and being in a Christian community that supports and encourages."
The three worst things about attending Wheaton are "the lack of ethnic diversity, its being kinda isolated from the rest of the world, and it's easy to over-commit yourself to too many things here."
The three things every student should do before graduating from Wheaton are "to go up the bell tower of Blanchard Hall—or in other words, get engaged, visit Chicago, and live in an apartment."
One thing I wish I had known before coming here is "how easy it is here to cut yourself off from the real world."

Indiana

DePauw University

Address: 101 East Seminary St; Greencastle, IN 46135
Phone: 765-658-4006
E-mail address: admission@depauw.edu
Web site URL: www.depauw.edu
Founded: 1837
Private or Public: private
Religious affiliation: United Methodist
Location: rural
Undergraduate enrollment: 2,173
Total enrollment: 2,173
Percent Male/Female: 44%/56%
Percent Minority: 12%

Percent African-American: 6%
Percent Asian: 2%
Percent Hispanic: 3%
Percent Native-American: 0.5%
Percent in-state/out-of-state: 47%/53%
Percent Pub HS: 89%
Number of Applicants: 2,687
Percent Accepted: 67%
Percent Accepted who enroll: 32%
Entering: 581
Transfers: 15
Application Deadline: 1 Feb
Mean SAT: NA

Mean ACT: NA
Middle 50% SAT range: NA
Middle 50% ACT range: 24–28
3 Most popular majors: communication, English, economics
Retention: 84%
Graduation rate: 79%
On-campus housing: 99%
Fraternities: 78%
Sororities: 73%
Library: 254,806 volumes
Tuition and Fees: $18,840 in; $18,840 out
Room and Board: $6,080
Financial aid, first-year: 99%

In the small Indiana town of Greencastle, Marvin's is the home of good, greasy eats like the garlic cheeseburger (GCB). Venture inside and you will discover more than a thousand pictures covering the walls, of people holding "Marvin's Delivers" signs at locations across the globe, from Antarctica to the bottom of the ocean. Famous for delivering its GCBs at almost any hour of the day or night, Marvin's is just one of many traditions at DePauw University, a private liberal arts college located in Greencastle.

This small college was founded in 1837 to provide students of all religious denominations with a sound liberal arts education. According to students, the current academic environment reflects those original intentions. A total of 31 course credits is required for a B.A. degree, along with distribution requirements in six categories: natural science and mathematics; social and behavioral sciences; literature and the arts; historical and philosophical understanding; foreign language; and self-expression, which includes classes in physical education, communications, and musical performance. DePauw students must also demonstrate proficiency in writing, quantitative reasoning (mathematical problem solving), and oral communication skills by taking classes in each of these three areas. In addition, students are required to attend a winter term held in January, an opportunity many DePauw students use to pursue internships and real-world experience in their field of study. Although the requirements are numerous, there are few complaints. Students describe the curriculum as "very challenging." One undergrad said, "Initially, most students here have to adjust to the difference in workload between college and high school."

DePauw has several honors programs for exceptionally talented and ambitious students. These include Management Fellows (a pre-business program), Media Fellows (focused on mass media—print and broadcast), and Science Research Fellows (focused on independent laboratory research). Students report that the humanities and social science departments at DePauw are exceptionally strong, while some find the sciences slightly weaker. Many say the real strength of a DePauw education is the intimate learning environment provided by small classes and professors; DePauw has neither TAs nor large introductory courses. According to one student, the largest class has only about 90 students, and most have enrollments of less than 30. "I love the small classes and the fact that teachers actually know your name!" said one student.

A Huge Petrified Turtle?

The small size of DePauw's campus also contributes to the intimacy of the school. The walk from one end of campus to the other "takes about 10 minutes," said one student. Undergrads universally praise the beauty of the DePauw campus, noted for its attractive brick buildings, especially the centrally located East College, one of the oldest buildings at DePauw. Also, on the East Campus lawn is the Boulder, donated to the university in 1892 by a farmer who reportedly thought it was a huge petrified turtle. Every year, a group of adventuresome students streak around the Boulder to celebrate the first snowfall.

Going Greek

The intimacy of the school, the small student body, and the lack of entertainment options in Greencastle result in a social scene dominated by the Greek system. According to one student, "Social life exists only because of the Greek system." The high percentage of Greeks has a significant impact on the independent (non-Greek) students at DePauw. Those outside of the Greek system are more likely to be dissatisfied with the school, and some feel left out of the social scene. "At DePauw it is very hard not to go Greek. It is harder to make friends, especially if you're a quiet person," reported one student. Another student said that if you are not planning on going Greek at DePauw, "there's a good chance you wouldn't stay here." For the majority who do make the plunge into Greek life, the

rush process is a painless, noncompetitive, and relatively enjoyable experience. "Rush was one of the most unique experiences I've had. If you go to DePauw, you should rush just to check it out," said one freshman. Several students who had not planned on going Greek before coming to DePauw commented on how rush changed their stereotypes of fraternities and sororities.

> **"Social life exists only because of the Greek system."**

However, members agree that one stereotype is true: fraternities and sororities provide a multitude of opportunities to drink and party, including theme parties and formals throughout the year. Delta Chi, for example, hosts a Hawaii Five-O party every year, complete with sand and 40-ounce drinks. Though kegs are officially banned on campus, some students say it is fairly easy to find alcohol, if you so desire, at Greek parties and local bars. Several restaurants also serve as popular hangouts, especially Marvin's, Hathaway's (slightly upscale), Jackson's (for breakfast), and the Phoenix Orient Chinese Restaurant.

These restaurants are a much-appreciated reprise from the standard fare served in the dining halls. The food was uniformly described as average to mediocre, primarily for the limited choices and "recycled menus." Vegan and vegetarian options are available, but that's where the variety ends. First-semester freshmen are required to purchase a full 21-meal plan—a requirement that annoys many at DePauw. Beginning sophomore year, Greeks can take their meals in their respective houses, which many feel is a much more economical and tasty alternative to dining hall food.

Beginning sophomore year, the majority of Greek students move into their fraternity or sorority houses. All first-year students are required to live in on-campus dorms. The average freshman room "isn't anything special" but is fairly large; students share common bathrooms with hallmates. All dorms are co-ed; most have mixed floors, but a few floors remain single-sex. Many freshmen consider their RAs more as friends than authority figures. For those who do not go Greek, the university guarantees single rooms in Huber and other upperclass dorms.

Who Goes to DePauw?

The general consensus is that people at DePauw do not fit a certain stereotype. The school may be 80 percent Greek, but students described the Greek scene as different from those of larger state universities. "It's not as exclusive and elitist," said one student. The general fashion style is an eclectic mix that ranges from preppy to alternative. Most of the students are upper-middle-class, white in-staters, with a good mix of political conservatives and liberals (leaning more to the conservative side). The school has a visible gay and lesbian group that is generally accepted. Many undergrads believe that black, Latino, and Native American students are underrepresented at the university and thus have been the focus of recruitment efforts. A large number of scholarships are available for traditionally underrepresented minorities.

The majority of DePauw students get involved with some sort of extracurricular activity. Intramurals and exercise are popular pastimes, although several students complain that the gym and athletic facilities could be better. DePauw is a Division III school and offers no athletic scholarships, so sports teams are "good but not great." Basketball and football games are the best-attended events.

The intense rivalry between DePauw and its long-standing local archrival Wabash comes to the forefront in the last football game of the season-the Monon Bell Game ("the Game"), when each school battles to proudly display the old railroad bell at its respective campus until the next Bell Game comes around. The nationally televised Monon Bell Game unifies all of DePauw, past and present, Greek and non-Greek, students and alumni, by demonstrating their spirit and pride. On game day, DePauw spirit peaks at a school deeply entrenched in both the academic liberal arts tradition and the Greek social system. —*Madhu Pocha and Staff*

FYI

The three best things about attending DePauw are "the low faculty-to-student ratio, the Greek system, and the friendly people."

The three worst things about attending DePauw are "the location, the weather sucks, and there's not a lot of entertainment options."

The three things every student should do before graduating from DePauw are "to attend a Monon Bell Game, do a roadtrip, and go abroad."

One thing I wish I knew before coming here is "what Green Castle has to offer."

E a r l h a m   C o l l e g e

Address: 801 National Road West; Richmond, IN 47374
Phone: 765-983-1600
E-mail address: admission@earlham.edu
Web site URL: www.earlham.edu
Founded: 1847
Private or Public: private
Religious affiliation: Quaker
Location: small city
Undergraduate enrollment: 1,123
Total enrollment: 1,191
Percent Male/Female: 43%/57%
Percent Minority: 13%

Percent African-American: 8%
Percent Asian: 2%
Percent Hispanic: 2%
Percent Native-American: 0.5%
Percent in-state/out-of-state: 23%/77%
Percent Pub HS: 75%
Number of Applicants: 1,038
Percent Accepted: 84%
Percent Accepted who enroll: 34%
Entering: 296
Transfers: 26
Application Deadline: 15 Feb
Mean SAT: 594 V, 565 M
Mean ACT: 25

Middle 50% SAT range: 520–660 V, 500–630 M
Middle 50% ACT range: 21–27
3 Most popular majors: biology, psychology, English
Retention: 87%
Graduation rate: 70%
On-campus housing: 96%
Fraternities: NA
Sororities: NA
Library: 477,161 volumes
Tuition and Fees: $21,070 in; $21,070 out
Room and Board: $4,936
Financial aid, first-year: 80%

Many things have changed at this small Quaker college. Jeans and t-shirts have replaced the traditional Quaker plain dress. Liberal thinking has seeped through the conservatism. A student body that more closely resembles a cross section of America's young adults has replaced the once all-Quaker student population. Yet, after more than a century of modernization, Earlham College still holds on to many of the ideals upon which it was founded. In the flat plains of the Midwest, these traditions help make Earlham stand out.

Small Classes, Big Ideas

A classroom with seven people is a fairly common sight at Earlham—and it's not because students don't like going to class. The school's small size makes for small, intimate classes, like *Literature of the Industrial Age* and *Humanism and Personology.* "Earlham provides opportunities to students that aren't available to my friends that go to larger universities. If there is something you wish to pursue in your studies, Earlham provides an informal, supportive, and comfortable setting in which to do it." As with all colleges, Earlham does have its share of large introductory lecture classes, but even these classes are reported to have only seventy or eighty people.

Professors teach every class at Earlham. As a result of small class sizes and Quaker tradition, students are on a first name basis with their teachers. Even the president of the school is greeted with a, "Hey Doug!" But informal doesn't mean pushover. In fact, getting to know the professors helps students get to know the subject matter. One student gushed, "The professors are *wonderful*—they are accessible, challenging but caring about their students, and very passionate about the subject matter." One student explained the dedication of the professors, "If you move to Richmond, Indiana to teach for the pay that they provide at Earlham, you have to be pretty invested in your work." Professors play a part outside of the classroom, too. In addition to the usual invitations to dinner, or parties on the front lawn, professors are known to participate in student activities. "The oldest member of the English department, his daughter (also a professor), and two other professors performed Bananarama's 'Venus' at our annual Air Guitar show."

Academics at Earlham can be challenging, but you have to make the effort. Even the general education requirements, which can be a hassle to fulfill, can be enriching experiences. Claimed one student, "The Freshman Humanities program, which is required, could have made Tolstoy a better writer." Students are also given opportunities to get into seminar-level classes as first year students, although first years ("we don't say freshmen") often aren't prepared for the level of difficulty in these seminar courses. Academic advisors are always willing to help students decide whether or not a class is right for them. Some classes that students recommend taking include German Film, Topics in the History of Ideas: Thucydides and Plato, and Theory and Practice of Nonviolence.

The Heart of It All

The center of the campus is a grassy circle known as The Heart. "You can see just about every major building from the middle of the heart." On a nice, spring afternoon, students are found playing Frisbee, barbequing, or just relaxing on The Heart. The rest of the campus is a blend of sixties architecture, newly constructed buildings and backcampus—an undeveloped area of campus great for quiet walks and peaceful thoughts. As a whole, the campus is beautiful and cozy; no streets run through campus. Students are excited about the new field house, recently completed and housing new weight machines and an indoor pool. A new social sciences building and a fine arts building are still planned.

> Outside of bowling, Wal-Mart, movies, Little Sheba's, and el Rodeo, students find that Richmond doesn't have much to entertain them.

The two opposite ends of the campus each have their own libraries: Lilly Library and the Science Library. Both libraries have computer labs where students can print out their reports and are considered good places to study. Lilly library—the larger of the two libraries—has Japanese mats to sit on. Another important piece of

the campus is the Runyan center which houses has several classrooms, a small coffee shop, the bookstore, a theatre for plays, and is attached to the dining hall. Most students find themselves at Runyan at least twice a day, if not more.

Living

The types of housing at Earlham vary, and most people are able to find an accommodation that works for them. The variety of housing options runs the gamut from Hoerner (the quiet dorm) to Barrett ("the loud dirty drugs dorm") to Warren and Wilson (the each-room-has-individual-adjustable-thermostats-and-air-conditioning dorm). All of the dorms have a kitchen on each floor and students often make their own meals for special occasions or just to get out of eating dining hall food. All of the dorms have RAs who help out for all four years that a student is on campus, and most of the RAs are reportedly "wonderful." Students also have the option of living in campus-owned housing. Some of these campus-owned houses are theme houses. Each theme house plans a theme week for the other students sometime during the year, For example, the residents of Peace House are responsible for planning Peace and Justice Week every year in the fall. Students think that the food in the dining halls has been steadily improving, especially with the most recent addition of pizza. A vegetarian contingent has also gotten the college to add more "edible" vegetarian options, in addition to the usual meaty fare. One vegan student recommended the vegan potpie, "It's delicious."

Trials and Tribulations of a Small Town

However, the small town of Richmond, Indiana, doesn't provide the entertainment that Earlham's college kids crave. Outside of bowling, Wal-Mart, movies, Little Sheba's, and el Rodeo, students find that Richmond doesn't have much to entertain them. Instead, weekend jaunts up to Oxford, Ohio (home of Miami University), Indy, and Dayton are common. Students do find that Richmond offers a lot in the way of volunteer activities, though, and most students take advantage of these opportunities to help out their community. A select group of students are offered the Bonner Scholarship, which helps students pay for school in exchange for ten hours of volunteer work a week. Students cite the extra bonus in that it also gives them a chance to meet the people of Richmond. But students recommend strongly, "Bring a car (or make friends with someone who has one) because it's hard to get around Richmond without one."

Living It Up

Earlham's extracurriculars are as numerous as the interests on campus. From Earlham Environmental Action Coalition to the radio station, from the Film Society to the Rainbow Tribe (Earlham has a history of supporting gay and bi students), most students find something that suits their interests. Within this bastion of liberalism ("a stifling political oneness"), one brave force battles to bring bipartisanship back to the campus: the Earlham Progressive Alliance—group activities include infiltrating the school newspaper staff.

Spectator sports are not popular at Earlham. Although not many people go to the football games or other athletic events, participation is popular. The less athletically inclined can form an intramural team—IM soccer team names include "Southern Comfort" and "the Green Nuggets"—play a club sport, or just join a pick-up game of football on the Heart. Playing a varsity sport requires more of a commitment—about three hours per day—but success doesn't come without hard work. The men's soccer team is one of the most successful teams in its division and other Earlham teams have seen considerable success.

Many Earlham students count going abroad as one of their best experiences in college. Earlham offers programs to such exotic locales as Japan, Kenya, Jerusalem, and others. And if a student wants to go someplace that isn't part of Earlham's off-campus program, the school gives them the opportunity to go abroad through other schools' programs; their financial aid goes with them, too.

Runnin' the Hash

Earlham is a dry campus so no alcohol is sold on campus, but that doesn't mean that nobody drinks. "The Hash" has been an Earlham tradition for about 10 years: students follow a set trail of flour for three miles through the woods to find a body of water and a keg of beer at the end. Then a wild party ensues. "[The beer] is usually Schaeffers, the nectar of the gods. As you drink, standing in the water, the rest of the crowd sings bawdy hash songs. There are a variety of rules and veteran Hashers have Hash names. The best part is that it's all underground—sort of. It's really hard to hide a flour trail."

The social atmosphere is very laid back, so those who don't feel like drinking find that "you can easily not drink and still have fun. There isn't pressure to drink." "It's not the basis of a social life." The film society usually shows a movie every weekend and the Student Activities Board brings in comedians every now and then. The college often sponsors concerts (like Louis Belson, the jazz performer). Annual events include the Sunsplash—a reggae concert, the International Festival, and a lip synching competition. Some people say that the best parties, though, are the small ones with their friends. "The best party I've been to was backcampus in the woods around a campfire. We had some musical instruments and played and sang into the night." For late night cravings, Sunshine is open 24/7 and Papa John's delivers until 1:30AM. And for those who can't live without a hot cup of joe, Java Jazz is a little college run coffee shop about a block off campus.

Quaker Friends

Earlham is not as racially diverse as most here would like. One athlete pointed out, "I'm concerned that the relatively few African Americans on campus are recruited by the sports teams. I think more should be recruited by the academic departments." Racial diversity aside, students are often very different and come from different parts of the country. However, students find themselves moving among the different groups on campus—the "gamers, jocks, activists, punks, hashers"; "there is a lot of permeability within these groups." Most people on campus are very friendly and will say "hi" to you if they see you. Chalk it up to Quaker tradition or Midwestern hospitality, Earlham is a great place to meet new people. A third year gives this piece of advice: "GET INVOLVED. LEAVE YOUR DORM ROOM."

You will meet great people, get job skills, and have an excuse for never handing in work on time—works with some profs but not others." —*Kenneth Tseng*

FYI

The three best things about attending Earlham are "accessible professors, the sense of community, and being able to take peace studies classes."

The three worst things about attending Earlham are "the food (I could just say that three times), the red tape associated with housing, and Richmond."

The three things that every student should do before graduating from Earlham are "take a walk on back-campus, do some volunteer work, go abroad for a year, and (four), gotta run the hash."

One thing I'd like to have known before coming here is "when they say that the Midwest is flat, they ain't kidding."

Indiana University / Bloomington

Address: 300 North Jordan Avenue; Bloomington, IN 47405-1106
Phone: 812-855-0661
E-mail address: iuadmit@indiana.edu
Web site URL: www.indiana.edu
Founded: 1820
Private or Public: public
Religious affiliation: none
Location: urban
Undergraduate enrollment: 27,461
Total enrollment: 34,937
Percent Male/Female: 46%/54%
Percent Minority: 10%
Percent African-American: 4%

Percent Asian: 3%
Percent Hispanic: 2%
Percent Native-American: 0.5%
Percent in-state/out-of-state: 77%/23%
Percent Pub HS: NA
Number of Applicants: 20,095
Percent Accepted: 81%
Percent Accepted who enroll: 41%
Entering: 6,583
Transfers: 1,227
Application Deadline: 1 Feb
Mean SAT: 466 V, 530 M
Mean ACT: 24

Middle 50% SAT range: 490–600 V, 490–610 M
Middle 50% ACT range: 22–27
3 Most popular majors: biology, psychology, journalism
Retention: 87%
Graduation rate: 70%
On-campus housing: 49%
Fraternities: 11%
Sororities: 9%
Library: 5,700,000 volumes
Tuition and Fees: $4,212 in; $12,920 out
Room and Board: $5,492
Financial aid, first-year: 38%

Ask 10 different students at Indiana University at Bloomington for the definition of a Hoosier, and expect to get 10 different answers. Located in the small city of Bloomington, IU can boast about its excellent academic reputation in addition to its nationally recognized basketball team. In fact, the only thing you may not learn at IU is the definition of a "Hoosier."

Tough Stuff

Academics at IU are reported to be tough, but not overwhelming. As one student noted, "It's only as bad as you make it." Music, journalism, and business are extremely popular majors at IU, and the business school is known to be especially demanding. While most students say that slackers are "weeded out" pretty quickly during the first year, others say the School of Public and Environmental Affairs has gained a reputation as "the school for business dropouts." Also, one student said that "the English department has a real attitude. It's impossible to get an A." The biggest academic complaints are about the strict language requirements (four semesters).

For those willing to work hard, the university offers several honors programs for both underclassmen and upperclassmen. On the other hand, when looking for those easy classes, students give warning about elective courses offered for credit through the HPER (Health, Physical Education, and Recreation) Departments like archery and tae kwon do. "The teachers all know that you're probably taking them for an easy A, so they make it tough on you."

Overall, students are happy with the classes and professors at IU, but some complain about large intro classes freshman year. Freshmen are last to register, and one student said that you can "sign up early and get a 30-person class, later and get a 300." However, even the smallest classes usually break up into smaller sections taught by TAs. In a sea of over 25,000 undergrads, students say that sometimes they feel like "just a number." "However," as one student countered, "something about big universities that people don't take into consideration is that once you're accepted into your chosen school . . . it feels like a family."

The Resources at IU

One of the advantages of a large university are the resources it can offer. Indiana is home to the nation's largest student center, a building that includes restaurants, eateries, a bookstore, a movie theater, a bowling alley, pool tables, and a four-star hotel. Also, the Recreational Sports Building, which students love to brag about was recently finished.

Though Hoosiers complain about the food in the dining halls, there are plenty of other places to eat around campus, and most dorms now include fast-food chains like McDonald's and Sbarro's Pizza.

Most freshmen and sophomores live in the dorms, since a large number of upperclassmen decide to live in fraternity and sorority houses or apartments off-campus. As one student described it, "people flock off-campus after freshman year." Students

who do live in the dorms say they are not too bad. Most housing is coed by floor with several RAs. Students claim each dorm has a definite personality and some say that "you can usually tell what someone is like by which dorm they live in." For example, Ashton is known for its academics, Eigenmann for its international student population, and Collins Living-Learning Center is the place for "free spirits" on campus.

> "The English department has a real attitude. It's impossible to get an A."

Though a majority of students are from in state, undergrads agree that there is no stereotypical Hoosier. Some people come in with a set group of friends from high school, but it is "very easy to meet people here." Many students mention the very liberal attitudes of students and their open-mindedness. Bloomington has a large gay and lesbian population, and the IU campus is "well known for its gay rights activism."

Greek Glory

A typical Hoosier is known as a big party fiend, and it is no coincidence that the fraternity and sorority presence on the IU campus is huge. One student reported that sometimes tension exists between Greeks and independents. While some said non-drinkers do not feel out of place (campus is "technically" dry), other students disagree, saying that "a large portion of the social life does revolve around alcohol." Drugs, mostly marijuana, are on campus, but they are "only around if you are into it." A typical weekend for under-classmen includes frat parties every night. Many of these parties are exclusive and tickets are checked at the door. However, many upperclassmen, even those who are frat members, tend to prefer the local bar scene. Other than bars, students talk about the lack of off-campus activities, saying "everything closes early here." Frequent road trips to Chicago, St. Louis, Indianapolis, or a weekend at home are also common.

One of the most anticipated events at IU is the annual "Little 500" bike race (the subject of the film Breaking Away, which was filmed in Bloomington). Students from all different organizations on campus participate, the days beforehand are filled with parties, and it is said to be "one of the wildest weeks ever."

100 Percent Basketball

"Basketball, basketball, basketball. That's what IU is!" Bobby Knight's team is legendary around the country, and IU school spirit reaches its peak during March Madness, the month of NCAA playoffs, known here as "Hoosier Hysteria." Students can easily get tickets, but school officials, anticipating a rush, often do not announce or downplay the opening of ticket sales.

Most IU students played a sport in high school, and many continue on at some level in college, either at the intramural or the varsity level. The campus has two main athletic facilities: "HPER is a big warehouse . . . that's where all the no-nonsense people work out. The SRSC is where all the sorority and frat people go to work out . . . so they look really good in their matching workout outfits."

Extracurriculars are also important to students. *The Indiana Students* is a full-size student-run paper that most students read. Also, community service organizations abound. The IU Student Organization is recognized by the administration as the most important on-campus organization, "But no one knows exactly what they have their hands into."

Whether they come for the noteworthy academics, the Big Ten experience, or the closeness to home, the Hoosiers are happy with their school. Freshmen should be warned that the sheer size of IU can be overwhelming, however, and the transition from high school to college can often be difficult. Everyone finds their niche though, and once settled in, students can expect four years of work, fun, and basketball galore. —*Sarah DeBergalis and Staff*

FYI

The three best things about attending IU are "the open-mindedness everywhere, the Greek system, and HPER classes."

The three worst things about attending IU are "the language requirement, the Greeks, and being in a small town."

The three things that every student should do before graduating from IU are "to bike in the 'Little 500,' to figure out what a Hoosier is, and to take an HPER class for credit."

One thing I'd like to have known before coming here is "all the rules of basketball . . . I had to learn fairly quickly."

Purdue University

Address: 1080 Schleman Hall; West Lafayette, IN 47907-1080
Phone: 765-494-1776
E-mail address: admissions@purdue.edu
Web site URL: www.purdue.edu
Founded: 1869
Private or Public: public
Religious affiliation: none
Location: suburban
Undergraduate enrollment: 30,300
Total enrollment: 35,715
Percent Male / Female: 57% / 43%
Percent Minority: 9%
Percent African-American: 3%

Percent Asian: 3%
Percent Hispanic: 2%
Percent Native-American: 0.5%
Percent in-state / out-of-state: 26% / 74%
Percent Pub HS: NA
Number of Applicants: 19,625
Percent Accepted: 84%
Percent Accepted who enroll: 42%
Entering: 6,860
Transfers: 1,966
Application Deadline: 10 Apr
Mean SAT: 540 V, 568 M
Mean ACT: 25

Middle 50% SAT range: 480–590 V, 500–630 M
Middle 50% ACT range: 22–27
3 Most popular majors: electrical and computer engineering, elementary education, comunication
Retention: 87%
Graduation rate: 64%
On-campus housing: 43%
Fraternities: 20%
Sororities: 18%
Library: 2,200,000 volumes
Tuition and Fees: $3,724 in; $12,348 out
Room and Board: $5,500
Financial aid, first-year: 41%

Purdue is more than just a great engineering school. While its reputation for academic excellence in engineering draws some of the most promising prospects from all over the world, Purdue also boasts a campus teeming with school spirit, a friendly, down-to-earth student body, and a vibrant social scene.

Speaking of Engineering . . .
Known as one of the top engineering schools in the nation, Purdue gives students a run for their money not only in engineering but also in physics and computer science, all considered the hardest and most competitive majors. Anything in liberal arts, interior design, and elementary education are considered somewhat easier. Even though they complain about the difficulty of many of their classes (Physics 152 is one of "the toughest physics course nationwide," one student claims), students realize the value of their labor when recruiters start their bidding for engineers at $50,000.

Six hundred or even more are enrolled in many introductory classes, but the size of the classes decreases as students advance. Students say they don't feel that having a class of 600 affects the quality of their learning experience since many of the lecture halls have big screens and other equipment that allow everyone to follow the lecture. However, problems may arise when the class meets in smaller groups with teaching assistants, many of whom do not speak English as a first language.

Greeks Get to You
The lively social life on campus surpasses many students' expectations. "Call-outs, especially those of dance clubs and sports and of many other events, are handed to you all the time," said one student, who reported feeling overwhelmed by the active social life. Greek organizations play a major role in the social scene, and lots of students attend their parties. Fraternity rushes have nightmare stories compared to more tame sorority rushes, students say. And although the school has a strict policy on drinking, the Greeks continue to party on. Police visits, however, have recently ended in court. Purdue's alcohol policy is more strongly felt in the dorms, where residential advisors are strict about the possession and consumption of alcohol and uphold the no guests after-2:00 A.M. rule.

For those who find the Greek scene a turnoff, Purdue boasts plenty of alternatives: Pete's Bar is popular on Wednesday nights, Neon Cactus dance bar packs them in on Thursdays, and Fridays find students at Harry's Chocolate Shop (a former chocolate shop, now a popular bar) and the Where Else and Boiler Room dance bars. Theme parties such as "$5 Prom," "White Trash," "Dress Your Buddy," and "Food Fight" also add color to the social life, as well as the funny organizations like the Vanilla Ice Club and the Unicycle Club. A great number of nearby restaurants, discount stores, malls, and many theaters are other alternatives to weekend partying and barhopping. Three campus movie theaters, each with nine screens, show first-run films.

> "As a freshman, you are the center of attention—they [campus groups] come and check you out. If they like you, you join the group; if not, you've got to find new people."

Cheers for the Boilermakers

The huge sports complex, CO-REC, offers students everything from volleyball to swimming and weight lifting, and there are a number of golf courses close to campus. Sports are a part of almost everyone's life at Purdue; intramurals bring many to the playing field, and football holds special meaning for each student at Purdue. Tailgating, before and during the games, means great barbecue on the weekends, and the marching band entertains and enlivens the devoted supporters of the Boilermakers. The world's largest drum also adds to the excitement of games at the Ross-Ade Stadium. Most students attend the annual battle against Indiana University, where the winner keeps the Oaken Bucket, a traveling trophy that signifies the schools' strong rivalry. The basketball team also benefits from the support of the entire student body. Tickets for games at Mackey Arena quickly sell out, since fans are eager to watch the Boilermakers compete against their Big Ten rivals and other Division I teams in the NCAA.

Life of a Boilermaker

Purdue's campus stretches over a wide, flat terrain, and some dormitories are far away from central campus. However, if you live on campus, a car is not a necessity, or more correctly, as one student explained, "It doesn't feel like a necessity until you have to walk from your room to classes for fifteen minutes during winter." Many upperclassmen and international students prefer to move off campus, while first-years and sophomores generally live in frat houses or in the dorms. Parking is a big problem on campus; freshmen aren't given parking permits in the areas that are around central campus, and the police are strict about enforcing the time limits. Therefore, bringing a car freshman year is not recommended.

Student groups are often formed along ethnic and national lines, with a great deal of interaction among all, and students say socioeconomic backgrounds don't matter at all. New students are especially welcomed by campus groups. Said one upperclassman, "As a freshman, you are the center of attention—they come and check you out. If they like you, you join the group; if not, you've got to find new people."

All Relaxed and Spread Out

Purdue continues to grow as plans for a new management building, engineering building, civil engineering testing lab, and fine arts center are under way. School spirit, the lively social scene, and the satisfaction that comes from participating in such strong academic programs make for an excellent experience for Boilermakers.
—*Yakut Seyhanli*

FYI

The three best things about attending Purdue are "good reputation (especially in engineering), layout of campus, diverse community including lots of international students."

The three worst things about attending Purdue are "Indiana winters ('It gets COOOLD around here'), large class sizes, 7:30 AM classes."

The three things that every student should do before graduating from Purdue are "ride the Boilermaker train, run through all of the water fountains, and eat at the Triple X at three in the morning."

One thing I'd like to have known before coming here is "how small and boring West Lafayette is."

Rose-Hulman Institute of Technology

Address: 00 Wabash Avenue-CM 1; Terre Haute, IN 47803-3999
Phone: 812-877-8213
E-mail address: Admis.Ofc@Rose-Hulman.edu
Web site URL: www.rose-hulman.edu
Founded: 1874
Private or Public: private
Religious affiliation: none
Location: suburban
Undergraduate enrollment: 1,545
Total enrollment: 1,678
Percent Male/Female: 83%/17%
Percent Minority: 5%

Percent African-American: 1%
Percent Asian: 3%
Percent Hispanic: 0.5%
Percent Native-American: 0.5%
Percent in-state/out-of-state: 45%/55%
Percent Pub HS: 85%
Number of Applicants: 3,295
Percent Accepted: 67%
Percent Accepted who enroll: 18%
Entering: 395
Transfers: 18
Application Deadline: 1 Mar
Mean SAT: 650 V, 700 M
Mean ACT: 30

Middle 50% SAT range: 580–700 V, 650–750 M
Middle 50% ACT range: 28–31
3 Most popular majors: mechanical engineering, electrical engineering, chemistry
Retention: 96%
Graduation rate: 67%
On-campus housing: 98%
Fraternities: 40%
Sororities: 30%
Library: 74,205 volumes
Tuition and Fees: $19,948 in; $19,948 out
Room and Board: $5,751
Financial aid, first-year: 90%

For intelligent students who care more about getting a quality education than attending a name-brand university, Rose-Hulman Institute of Technology is a jewel. The small technology specialty school lacks the name recognition of rivals MIT and Caltech but offers a relaxed environment where students are genuinely friendly and cutthroat competition is unheard of.

Scenic, Up-to-date, and Safe

Located amid trees and rolling hills on the outskirts of Terre Haute, Indiana, Rose-Hulman Institute of Technology is beautiful and improving every day. The campus sports two lakes, although one is "an unnatural turquoise color." While the grounds are attractive, huge amounts of money aren't shelled out for perfectly manicured lawns. "Our tuition goes to what it should—academics," one student said.

Rose has a small campus where everything is within walking distance. Students can wake up 10 minutes before class and still get there in time, as long as they're not picky about how they look. Students brag that the quaint setting fosters a close-knit environment. "There's a very personal atmosphere here," one student said.

One of Rose's biggest assets is its state-of-the-art facilities. The multimillion-dollar Sports and Recreation Center and the brand-new observatory, technology center, and residence hall are several buildings Rose prides itself on. A new chapel and fine arts building are currently under construction. One student joked that the only thing she wished Rose had that it doesn't was finished construction.

Rose is far enough away from the city of Terre Haute that safety isn't much of an issue. A couple of cars have been broken into around campus lately, but that's usually the extent of campus crime. One student claimed that she left her car doors unlocked all through freshman year and never had a problem. Dorm room doors are left wide open even when people are gone. The only threat is friends playing a prank. "I would let my girlfriend walk across campus at three A.M. on a Friday night without worrying . . . it's that safe," one junior remarked. To further deter crime, emergency phones are located all over campus.

Good Things Don't Come Easy

Most Rose-Hulman students got A's in high school with little difficulty. Things change. It's extremely hard to earn an A at Rose. One student said, "Getting a 4.0 is damn near impossible." However, Bs are feasible if a student is willing to work hard. It's rumored that no student who's attended every class has ever failed the course.

The first two years at Rose are difficult, and the sophomore curriculum in particular is known to be a killer. It consists of a set of classes that teach students the basics of all disciplines. For the first time students cannot get by with only knowing how things work. They also need to know why things work. This is the year when Rose starts teaching students to teach themselves.

To accommodate this difficult year most sophomores live in the newest dorm, built largely to help with studying. There are peer tutors on every floor and study rooms at the end of each hallway. Professors are also extremely helpful. They give out home phone numbers and are always available for questions. All classes at Rose are taught by professors, but teaching assistants also help students with questions.

There are no easy majors at Rose, but civil engineering is rumored to be more painless than the rest. "The real slackers' major in economics," one student commented. Chemical engineering is without a doubt the most difficult curriculum, but most say the hard work is worth the trouble. "The professors are the best in the world, and even though you will work hard and be challenged, you will be well respected for the rest of your life," one student said. Students praise Rose's 100% job placement rate.

Living in Luxury

Most freshmen live in the newly constructed and impressive Deming Residence Hall. Others live in BSB, which is also nice. The triplets (Mees, Blumber, and Scharpenburg) are "kind of scary." For the most part, students are happy with their dorms. One senior has lived on campus all four years and said he wouldn't change much of anything. The rooms are big, most are air-conditioned, they come with nice oak furniture, and

students can customize them as they wish (painting, building lofts, etc). Frosh floors are segregated by sex, but the halls are not. Upperclassmen live on coed floors. All dorms have residential advisors, and frosh dorms also have two sophomore advisors. "I was an SA and would have given any of my guys the shirt off my back if they needed it," one upperclassman said. The SAs are there to help with anything and everything freshmen could possibly need.

> **"Getting a 4.0 is damn near impossible."**

After their first year students are allowed to live off campus, but many remain in the residence halls. Those who don't stay on campus typically move into fraternity or sorority houses. Some also live in off-campus housing. Nearby Village Quarter reportedly has cheap rent.

Something Edible

With a salad bar, deli, wok, main course, grill, cereals, and veggie bar in the cafeteria and "the Worx" in the basement, Rose students can "usually find something digestible." They complain, however, about having the same choices over and over. They are also unhappy with the mandatory meal plan—18 meals per week. Since the cafeteria is closed for dinner on weekends and breakfast on Saturdays, students rarely eat that often.

Making Their Own Fun

Known for Indiana State University Sycamore Larry Bird and a funny stench from a nearby paper mill, Terre Haute is not exactly an entertainment mecca. "There's really nothing to do in town besides going to Super Wal-Mart and making fun of the local Hautians,'" one student said. Rose students must make their own fun. With eight fraternities and two sororities on campus, Greek life dominates the social scene.

Graffiti parties—where everyone wears a white shirt and draws on others with markers—are popular events. The annual Camp Out party finds a frat house transformed into the wilderness, completely filled with leaves and a 25-foot-tall tree. The popular Mafia party has hit men and fake money that can be used to give people "hits." While there's beer at all parties, students aren't pressured to drink. However, one student said, "It's pretty boring at Rose without drinking."

Life Beyond Engineering

With more than 60 clubs and student organizations, Rose-Hulman students have a plethora of activities to be involved in. And if students can't find clubs that interest them, Rose encourages them to create their own. One of the most popular organizations is the Solar Phantom team, which competes in a biannual cross-country solar car race called Sunrayce. Most students are involved in several activities, but academics are their first priority. "Devotion only lasts until we have to do homework," one student said.

Intramurals are very popular, as are varsity sports. Rose is a Division III school, which means it isn't allowed to offer athletic scholarships. Consequently, school comes before sports. So is Rose-Hulman bringing home any athletic glory? "Our teams are the fighting *ENGINEERS* . . . we obviously aren't very good," one student joked. But football and basketball games still manage to draw pretty big crowds. Every year during homecoming the fresh-man class constructs "an absolutely enormous, blazing hot, butt-kicking bonfire." It's built solely by manual labor. Upperclassmen try to knock it down, but the freshmen protect it.

A Less than Satisfactory Student Body

If you're looking for a school with culture and diversity, Rose-Hulman might not be the place for you. A typical Rose-Hulman student is a white upper-middle-class male from the Midwest. "We're talking about a whole school that hasn't heard of Costco," said one East Coast student. Another complained that she was the only non-white student on her freshman floor. But while there's not much diversity, there's certainly no discrimination.

With a 7-to-1 male to female ratio, there is not much dating at Rose. The school has only been coed since 1995. A girl can generally get a guy if she wants to, although she might have to settle a bit. One female joked that there are too many "Steve Erkels" running around campus. Guys are not happy with the selection of females, either. One male commented, "There aren't enough females, there are few girls, and absolutely no women." Many guys look for girls at nearby Indiana State University and St. Mary-of-the-Woods College. —*Alexis Wolff*

FYI
The three best things about attending Rose-Hulman are "the family atmosphere of the school, the experience you have in the freshman residence hall, and the relationships with professors."
The three worst things about attending Rose-Hulman are "the lack of a Big-Ten-like athletic atmosphere, we're about an hour from any major city, and the campus is not very diverse."
The three things that every student should do before graduating from Rose-Hulman are "see a movie in historic Indiana Theatre, draw on somebody at a Graffiti party, have one of those conversations that keep you up until the wee hours of the morning."
One thing I'd like to have known before coming here is "calculus."

St. Mary's College

Address: LeMans Hall;
Notre Dame, IN 46556
Phone: 800-551-7621
E-mail address: admissions
@saintmarys.edu
Web site URL:
www.saintmarys.edu
Founded: 1844
Private or Public:
private
Religious affiliation:
Roman Catholic
Location: suburban
**Undergraduate
enrollment:** 1,355
Total enrollment: 1,355
Percent Male/Female:
0%/100%
Percent Minority: 6%

Percent African-American:
1%
Percent Asian: 4%
Percent Hispanic: 1%
Percent Native-American:
NA
**Percent in-state/out-of-
state:** 24%/76%
Percent Pub HS: 54%
Number of Applicants:
920
Percent Accepted: 85%
**Percent Accepted who
enroll:** 52%
Entering: 406
Transfers: 75
Application Deadline:
1 Mar
Mean SAT: 560 V, 550 M

Mean ACT: 25
Middle 50% SAT range:
00–610 V,
500–600 M
Middle 50% ACT range: NA
3 Most popular majors:
business administration,
communication, nursing
Retention: 88%
Graduation rate: NA
On-campus housing: 82%
Fraternities: 0%
Sororities: 0%
Library: 198,729 volumes
Tuition and Fees:
$16,184 in; $16,184 out
Room and Board: $5,632
Financial aid, first-year:
77%

A student at this small Catholic women's college can be assured that she will not get lost in the crowd. At St. Mary's College in Notre Dame, Indiana, one can have the best of both worlds: the intimacy of a small single-sex campus, with the facilities of the large University of Notre Dame just across the street.

Liberal Arts Curriculum

Academically, St. Mary's "belles," as they're known, pursue one of five degrees: bachelor of arts, bachelor of business administration, bachelor of fine arts, bachelor of music, or bachelor of science. All students are required to declare a major at the beginning of their sophomore year. Through the core curriculum at St. Mary's, students are encouraged to pursue a broad-based liberal arts education. Most students fulfill all of the core requirements, along with the foreign-language requirement, by the end of their sophomore year, after which they take more specialized classes suited to their major. One first-year student who had not yet decided on her major said that "the core requirements are a relief. They give me some direction."

Students at St. Mary's can take classes at Notre Dame, and many do. Notre Dame students take St. Mary's courses as well. St. Mary's courses have a great advantage because of their small size: one frosh said each of her five classes had fewer than 20 students. The largest classes on campus are the introductory science classes, which are still remarkably small—around 50 students. In addition, at St. Mary's there are no teaching assistants, so students say a professor "with the highest degree in the field" will be teaching your courses. The student-teacher interactions are also excellent. In addition to having her professors' home phone numbers, one student even attended a Halloween party given by her philosophy professor.

Registration takes place over the summer. First-year students are sent a guidebook of courses, from which they select 10. A schedule is then sent home, usually including the student's top five classes. Upperclasswomen generally do not have difficulty enrolling in their first-choice courses.

Academics at St. Mary's are rigorous, but manageable. "The classes are small enough so all my questions are answered and I understand the material, which makes the classes seem easier," one student said. Undergrads claim that there are no true "gut" courses, although Beginning Acting is an easy class according to some.

An Integrated Campus

St. Mary's has its own library, named Cushwa-Leighton, which is separate from the Notre Dame facilities. To study quietly, many students go to Cushwa, which reportedly is so conducive to studying that Notre Dame students like it too. For social studying, and for simply socializing, most St. Mary's students go to the larger library at Notre Dame.

> "The classes are small enough so all my questions are answered and I understand the material, which makes the classes seem easier"

The majority of St. Mary's students live on campus in four residential halls. McCandless, the most modern of the four, provides each student with a small study carrel space across the hall from her bedroom. According to one student, "Each dorm has its own personal character." Each small study room is equipped with air-conditioning, which helps beat the hot Indiana weather at the beginning and end of the year. Students also live in Le Mans Hall, which is relatively old, but beautiful; Holy Cross Hall, which has larger rooms and big suites; and Regina Hall, which has only singles. All of the dorms (with the exception of McCandless) as well as the computer clusters and various other facilities across campus are connected via underground tunnels.

There are stringent rules, called parietals, dictating when members of the opposite sex are allowed in the dorms. Males have to be out of the dorms by midnight during the week, and by 2 A.M. on weekends. The same rules apply at Notre Dame.

There is one main cafeteria on campus, and the food there is reasonably tasty. Students can frequent the dining hall as many times a day as they like (it's open from 7 A.M. to 7 P.M.). Vegetarian options are always available, as are a salad bar and a grill. Most students eat on campus because there are few options in the local town of South Bend. When the women of St. Mary's do leave campus for a meal, their choices "tend to be limited to fast food."

Midwestern Belles

Because South Bend has little to offer a college crowd socially and culturally, much of what happens at St. Mary's centers on life at Notre Dame. Since neither has a Greek system, the schools are interrelated through clubs and extracurriculars. One student claimed that "going back and forth to Notre Dame is an extracurricular activity." However, "some people have a love-hate relationship with Notre Dame," another student added. St. Mary's undergrads participate in a wide range of activities from student government to intramural sports to writing for the *Observer*, the daily paper. The main connection between the two schools is athletics. St. Mary's has its own, recently built athletics center (the Angela Fitness Center) and Belles play competitively in basketball, volleyball, and tennis, yet their true allegiance is to Notre Dame. One frosh said, "People try to rile up some school spirit, but it's just not there. Mainly, it's for Notre Dame."

In addition to Notre Dame sports, St. Mary's students take part in Notre Dame social events. St. Mary's itself is a dry campus, but that does not stop undergrads from busing over to Notre Dame to drink (a shuttle runs between the two schools almost 24 hours a day). Popular events on campus also include "screw your roommate" dances. At these events, roommates fix each other up on blind dates, using the "Dog Book," a book with photos of all the freshmen. Although St. Mary's does offer some social venues, the majority of St. Mary's students spend their free time socializing at Notre Dame.

Students at St. Mary's date, but random hookups also occur, despite the strong Catholic overtones at the school. General, informed discussions on safe sex are rare, and the administration has something of a "don't ask, don't tell" policy, according to students.

The campus is politically conservative, and while the college is not as diverse as larger institutions, it makes a concerted effort to attract women from different backgrounds and geographic areas. Currently, the majority of the students at St. Mary's are from the Midwest.

St. Mary's is a small Catholic college with all the resources of a large university (as a result of its proximity to Notre Dame)—and St. Mary's students rely on their neighboring university for social, athletic, and academic enrichment.
—*Heather Topel*

FYI

The three best things about attending St. Mary's College are that you get the benefits of both single-sex education and co-educational, great professors, underground tunnels (who wants to walk in the rain?)

The three worst things about attending St. Mary's College are how everyone spends all of their time at Notre Dame, parietals, the lack of restaurants in town

The three things that every student should do before graduating from St. Mary's College are setting up your roommate for the "screw your roommate" dance, go to a sporting event, take a class that you had never considered taking before

One thing I'd like to have known before coming here is that the picture I sent them before freshman year was going to be put into something called the "Dog Book"—how insulting.

University of Notre Dame

Address: 220 Main Building; Notre Dame, IN 466
Phone: 219-631-7505
E-mail address: admissions.admissio.1@nd.edu
Web site URL: www.nd.edu
Founded: 1842
Private or Public: private
Religious affiliation: Catholic
Location: suburban
Undergraduate enrollment: 8,005
Total enrollment: 10,275
Percent Male/Female: 55%/45%
Percent Minority: 15%

Percent African-American: 3%
Percent Asian: 4%
Percent Hispanic: 7%
Percent Native-American: 0.5%
Percent in-state/out-of-state: 9%/91%
Percent Pub HS: 52%
Number of Applicants: 10,010
Percent Accepted: 35%
Percent Accepted who enroll: 56%
Entering: 1,971
Transfers: 131
Application Deadline: 7 Jan
Mean SAT: 650 V, 668 M
Mean ACT: 29

Middle 50% SAT range: 620–710 V, 640–720 M
Middle 50% ACT range: 29–32
3 Most popular majors: accounting, political science, finance
Retention: 97%
Graduation rate: 86%
On-campus housing: 79%
Fraternities: NA
Sororities: NA
Library: 2,600,000 volumes
Tuition and Fees: $23,357 in; $23,357 out
Room and Board: $5,920
Financial aid, first-year: 52%

Not far off the interstate in South Bend, Indiana, a statue of a bearded man in flowing robes stands atop the library of the University of Notre Dame. "Touchdown Jesus," as he is known to students, is representative of all that Notre Dame stands for—Catholic ethics, a rigorous education, and football.

Serious Academics

Notre Dame offers four different schools for undergraduates—Business Administration, Engineering, Science, and Arts & Letters—with differing requirements within the specific colleges. In the College of Arts & Letters, which includes the largest number of undergrads, students must take two each of philosophy, theology, math, and natural science, as well as one class each in the social sciences and in fine art/literature. There are approximately 50 majors to choose from. ND's academic offerings are described as a broad spectrum of everything, "except communications, which is a bit lacking." Otherwise, "they offer everything I might ever want to take," said one student. In the College of Arts & Letters students said that philosophy and English are both known as tough majors, and theology and government are both strong departments. Intro philosophy is a favorite class, but if you are looking for guts, students recommended intro sociology, intro government, some arts classes, and the math and science classes for non-majors. Intro to biology enrolls approximately 300 students, which is one of the largest classes undergrads ever encounter. Most average about 30, with some class sizes slightly higher.

The most popular majors are government and finance. Students say that engineering and science majors are set apart from others by the intense number of hours they find themselves consumed with work. Many come to Notre Dame already having decided on a major, but find they want to change their minds after the first year; most notably, many students who enter as business majors transfer into the College of Arts & Letters, a relatively easy process.

Students praised the school's emphasis on undergraduate education: "Grad students don't really have a presence, except for some TAs in big lab classes. The administration is actually trying to recruit more heavily and spend more on the grad schools." ND professors are generally accessible and approachable, especially those who teach small classes. As students move up within their individual majors, they tend to know their professors even better. "Most people have good working relationships with their professors," said one student. Getting good grades is not overly difficult, "if you do the work," of which there always seems to be a lot. "Sometimes the workload interferes with the social setting," said one undergrad. "We spend so much time related to academics." Another student said, "There are lots of motivated students here and

lots of pressure, but most of it is self-imposed."

God in the Classroom?

"Religion and God definitely do come up a lot," said one student. "Religion is continually around you on a day-to-day basis, but it's not oppressive." Crucifixes hang in every classroom and building on campus, and all students at Notre Dame are required to take theology, "but the theology which is taught is not specifically Catholic," pointed out one non-religious undergrad. The student went on to say "taking theology is really good for a lot of students who have never been exposed to religion in this way."

Students say that lots of people at Notre Dame are religious, but label their peers as "fairly open" and the school's priests as "fairly liberal." Approximately 85 percent of the ND population is Catholic, with about 60 percent actively practicing. There is a chapel in every dorm where mass is held five days a week. One student warned that incoming freshmen might be put off by the prominence of their classmates' religious faith, but "the majority of students are not gung-ho about religion." Nevertheless, students say that the non-religious or non-Catholics miss out on certain aspects of ND culture, such as going to mass in the dorms on Sunday—they "have to find other ways to participate in the ND family."

The South Bend Social Scene

Like at many colleges, the weekend at Notre Dame begins on Thursday, when many students head out to bars. Friday night usually brings dorm parties with beer and friends, in anticipation of the next day's football game. About half the undergraduate population hits the tailgate before the game on Saturday, after which students usually spend a low-key evening hanging out with friends or studying, even after victories. "Everyone stands the whole game, so we get really tired by the end," explained one student. Sunday is a day for homework, inter-hall sports, and mass in the evening. Students said they actually drink more during the non–football seasons, "but [drinking] isn't a big deal and there's not a lot of pressure to drink," said one undergrad. Those students whose "crappy fakes" cannot get them into bars tend to hit off-campus parties or drink in the dorms (there are no frats). Although students report that the administration is rather lenient regarding alcohol, it is apparently not so lax about visiting hours. ND's parietals dictate that students cannot be in the room of members of the opposite sex after midnight Sunday to Thursday and 2 A.M. Friday to Saturday. Students caught breaking the rules are sentenced to community service or kicked off-campus; expulsion is the punishment if one is caught having sex. "That's where you see the strict adherence to Catholic tradition," said one student. "It's not forced down your throat, but this place is definitely a Catholic institution."

> "Religion is continually around you on a day-to-day basis, but it's not oppressive."

Students admitted that beyond partying, there is really "not that much to do . . . South Bend leaves a little to be desired." The Student Union Board organizes movies and barbecues on a regular basis and plans major events like An Tostal, ND's spring festival. There are two or three school-sponsored concerts each semester with bands such as Third Eye Blind and Aerosmith.

A superficial look around the Notre Dame campus would give the impression that the school is populated by yuppies, according to one undergrad. "But once you get to know people you see that there's more diversity," said another student. "There are a lot of hidden talents you'd never know people had just by looking at all the North Face and Abercrombie & Fitch." Another student said, "Everyone gets homogenized . . . you just need to peel back the layers." But students said there definitely is an identifiable stereotype: "white, suburban, conservative, Midwestern, and preppy," listed one undergrad. Some people are more vocally dissatisfied with ND's lack of diversity. "Yes, all the different races are represented, but the large majority is Catholic

and white, and I would like to see more of a mix."

Gay and lesbian rights have recently become a huge issue on campus, as the administration "struggles with how to treat everybody equally and still retain the school's Catholic nature," according to one student. The issue is whether to add sexual orientation to Notre Dame's legal nondiscrimination clause. There is only a handful of openly gay people on campus, which is not surprising given the level of homophobia that students notice pervading the campus atmosphere. In general, the student body is "fairly conservative . . . most people yearn for the Reagan years." But the campus rarely gets politicized over national issues, as immediate campus concerns tend to take precedence.

Dorm Community
Eighty-five percent of Notre Dame students live on campus. Dorm unity abounds, adding to the strong sense of community with regular social functions and inter-hall sports. "It becomes almost like a frat," said one student. "Dorm life is the source of all my close friends." Everyone is randomly assigned to roommates and dorms (which are single-sex) at the beginning of freshman year, and most end up living in doubles. Approximately half of the senior class moves off-campus into apartment complexes, and those who don't all get singles. The competition to be one of the six RAs in every dorm is stiff because these select seniors become the leaders of the dorm community. Although social life seems to revolve around the dorms, students said that the dining hall is "the place to go to see and to be seen." Undergrads can choose a 14- or 21-meal plan option with $200 for the other food outlets—such as the Burger King—located all over campus. Generally, the dining hall food is "not bad, although it gets repetitive."

Life Outside of Class
Notre Dame students have plenty of activities and clubs to join, ranging from the College Democrats to the "Right to Life" group to various service clubs. But above all, sports seem to dominate students' free time. About 90 percent of ND students were varsity athletes in high school,

according to one undergrad. Thus they come out in full force to join the inter-hall contact football league, as well as the lacrosse, soccer, baseball, hockey, and boxing teams. "Recreation sports are overarching," said one student. "Exercise in general is big . . . lots of people work out." A recently finished sports center houses three basketball courts and a weight-suspended track for student use.

In addition to inter-hall leagues and personal training, sports occupy the time of a large majority of the student body off the playing field, as well. An estimated 95 percent of students hold season tickets to ND football games, which are a huge source of unity and pride. "People here really love [football]," said one student. "Going to games is one way to demonstrate your love for the university, and it's a big rally-ing point for the community." Other varsity sports are well recognized, too; men's basketball, hockey, women's basketball, and women's soccer—a national power-house—all bring out crowds for their games. But, the general feeling is that football traditionally overshadows everything else at Notre Dame. "A lot of kids work really hard, and sometimes that just gets swept under the rug," said one under-grad. Regardless, students have enormous pride in the historic success of the football program, a pride that manifests itself in an array of traditions, including well-attended pep rallies. "It's appealing to me," said one student, "because people here have a really strong sense of the school. This translates into an enormous sense of unity and pride." —*Liz Kukura and Staff*

FYI

The three best things about attending Notre Dame are "the tailgates before every football game is the perfect combination of absolute chaos and the best party of your life, the breaks during the semester right when you are really starting to burn out, and the incredibly close community created in the dorms which leads to really close events like dorm masses and dances."

The three worst things about attending Notre Dame are "the competition, the lack of diversity, and the sweeping under the rug of real issues and problems on campus."

The three things every student should do before graduating from Notre Dame are "to streak through the second floor of the library during exam week, party nonstop from Friday afternoon until Saturday afternoon after the football game, and tour the Golden Dome."

One thing I wish I knew before coming here is "people should know that Notre Dame football games (home games) only happen six weekends out of the year. They are fun while they last but no one should come here simply because of them."

Valparaiso University

Address: Kretzmann Hall;
Valparaiso, IN 46383
Phone: 219-464-5011
E-mail address:
undergrad_admissions
@valpo.edu
Web site URL:
www.valpo.edu
Founded: 1859
Private or Public: private
Religious affiliation:
Lutheran
Location: small city
**Undergraduate
enrollment:** 2,970
Total enrollment: 3,650
Percent Male / Female:
47% / 53%
Percent Minority: 8%

Percent African-American:
3%
Percent Asian: 2%
Percent Hispanic: 2%
Percent Native-American:
0.5%
**Percent in-state / out-of-
state:** 36% / 64%
Percent Pub HS: 80%
Number of Applicants:
3,494
Percent Accepted: 78%
**Percent Accepted who
enroll:** 28%
Entering: 751
Transfers: 72
Application Deadline:
rolling
Mean SAT: 592 V, 601 M

Mean ACT: 26
Middle 50% SAT range:
530–660 V,
530–660 M
Middle 50% ACT range:
24–29
3 Most popular majors:
nursing, education, English
Retention: 89%
Graduation rate: 68%
On-campus housing: 93%
Fraternities: 21%
Sororities: 2100%
Library: 673,800 volumes
Tuition and Fees:
$17,636 in; $17,636 out
Room and Board: $4,660
Financial aid, first-year:
85%

Until a few years ago, when its basketball team catapulted into the Sweet Sixteen of the NCAA playoffs, few people outside the Midwest knew about Valparaiso University. Valpo, as it is affectionately called by students, is a small private Lutheran school in northeastern Indiana.

VU prides itself on the absence of TAs. The students are overwhelmingly pleased with the dedication of their professors who teach all undergraduate classes, including labs and language sections. One student reported that the "faculty tend to be very receptive to individual pursuits and are very welcoming." Students must take 124 credits, including three theology classes, and in their opinion, too many general education requirements. The average class size is 20 students with some classes made up of as little as 10 or 15 people. Christ College was established as an honors program for the humanities that focuses on writing skills. One complaint about Valpo's curriculum is that many theology classes tend to be focused on Christian doctrine and echo the administration's position on certain issues. Except for some engineering classes, which are known to be difficult, the workload at Valpo is not considered very demanding.

To Party or Not to Party

Officially, Valpo is a dry campus, although non-drinkers mentioned that they often feel left out of the social scene. With few exceptions, only fraternities are allowed to live off campus while sororities are housed in dorms. Freshman dorms are considered "decent" and RAs are available for help and advice in all dorms. Most dorms are single-sex by floor. An extremely unpopular university regulation is the enforcement of visiting hours for all members of the opposite sex, which mandates that no visitors are allowed in the dorms after midnight on weekdays and 2 in the morning on weekends.

Students report that frat parties draw sizable crowds on the weekends, but undergrads also like to hang out at the Student Center. Many complained about the lack of alternatives in town, but one student suggested that a lot of people are simply unaware of all the resources Valparaiso, Indiana, has to offer since the university does not encourage interaction with the community. The most obvious example of that interaction is that though VU students are required to have a meal plan for six semesters, students often frequent local restaurants. Two popular places nearby are Al's Diner and the Night

Owl coffee shop. In addition, many freshmen go home for weekends—and, as one student pointed out, Chicago is not too far away.

> **"Faculty tend to be very receptive to individual pursuits and are very welcoming."**

Extracurricular activities flourish at Valpo. They range from traditional newspapers, Student Senate, a student-run radio station, community service organizations, to the more bizarre Jonathan Rivera Fan Club. Founded a couple of years ago by Jonathan's roommate, Jonathan's fan club has become an official organization complete with buttons and T-shirts.

Basketball is definitely the most popular sport at Valpo, and student-only sections make for easy access to games. Other varsity sports are not as popular but intramural sports remain a great alternative for most students.

Incoming freshmen be warned: VU undergraduates report that they are part of an extremely homogenous student body. The stereotypical Valpo student is Christian, white, from the Midwest, and middle to upper-class. In addition, the university has a reputation for being homophobic and not very receptive to interracial dating.

The majority of students are satisfied with the academic and social life at Valpo. If you are looking for a small university with an extraordinarily dedicated faculty, be sure to give Valpo a closer look.
—*Sarah DeBergalis and Staff*

FYI

The three best things about attending Valparaiso University are "the faculty, the frats, and the classes."

The three worst things about attending Valparaiso University are "Valparaiso, Indiana; the diversity; and the requirements."

The three things every student should do before graduating from Valparaiso University are "to attend a basketball game, to join an organization, and to go to Chicago for the weekend."

One thing I'd like to have known before coming here is "what life is like in rural Indiana."

W a b a s h   C o l l e g e

Address: PO Box 352; Crawfordsville, IN 47933
Phone: 765-361-6225
E-mail address: admissions@wabash.edu
Web site URL: www.wabash.edu
Founded: 1832
Private or Public: private
Religious affiliation: Independent
Location: small city
Undergraduate enrollment: 861
Total enrollment: 861
Percent Male/Female: 100%/0%
Percent Minority: 13%

Percent African-American: 5%
Percent Asian: 3%
Percent Hispanic: 5%
Percent Native-American: NA
Percent in-state/out-of-state: 74%/26%
Percent Pub HS: 91%
Number of Applicants: 894
Percent Accepted: 75%
Percent Accepted who enroll: 44%
Entering: 297
Transfers: 5
Application Deadline: 1 Mar
Mean SAT: 576 V, 598 M

Mean ACT: 25
Middle 50% SAT range: 520–630 V, 540–650 M
Middle 50% ACT range: NA
3 Most popular majors: history, economics, psychology
Retention: 81%
Graduation rate: 69%
On-campus housing: 99%
Fraternities: 70%
Sororities: NA
Library: 253,024 volumes
Tuition and Fees: $17,275 in; $17,275 out
Room and Board: $5,435
Financial aid, first-year: 100%

Wabash College is rich in history, tradition, and financial endowments. As one of the few remaining all-male colleges in the United States, Wabash thrives on spirited students and exceptionally loyal alumni. "People who come here support it until they die," claimed one Wabash student.

Hard-Core Curriculum

Based on a strong core curriculum, academics are rigorous at Wabash. "There are not many classes that you can blow off," one student reported. Undergraduates must take courses in the natural sciences, math, a foreign language, English composition, literature, and fine arts, regardless of their major. Sophomores must take Cultures and Traditions, a course that studies the philosophies and political ideas of various cultures in the same period in history. "It's quite politically correct, but you learn a lot," one student said. To graduate, all Wabash seniors must pass "comps," a daylong series of oral and written exams administered by professors in the student's major.

Students report that the religion and economics departments are particularly strong. The philosophy department benefits from a prestigious faculty that includes well-known philosopher William Placher. English majors say their department has a particularly cohesive faculty that works well together as a team. Art and music, however, do not fare as well in students' opinions. Many Wabash students are on a pre-professional track and hope to enroll in law or medical school after graduation; as a result, the college is reportedly strong in the premed sciences such as biology and chemistry.

In addition to strong academics in the classroom, Wabash also offers its students the chance to study abroad or obtain various internship positions through a wide range of off-campus study opportunities and an extensive alumni network.

Super-Small Classes

Wabash's size allows not only for small classes (the largest class, a popular classics lecture, enrolls about 110), but also for maximum student-faculty interaction. Most Wabash professors live within walking distance of the campus and often eat lunch or talk informally with their students. Professors routinely give out their home phone numbers to their classes, and students say they are comfortable calling them at home for help. Students cite this open communication and sense of friendship with faculty as one of the best aspects of Wabash. The sense of community often endures long after graduation.

Wabash students also benefit from the new fine arts center on campus, which includes a large art gallery, a new auditorium, classrooms equipped with modern audiovisual equipment, and practice rooms with pianos. Salter Hall, located in the arts center, is reportedly one of the most acoustically sound halls in the state of Indiana. The recently renovated Detchon Center houses the classics and foreign-language departments, a computer center, and several new classrooms. According to students, Detchon is "a good place to study." For serious study, students go to the Lilly Library, also recently modernized, where "it is always quiet, no matter what," according to one sophomore.

No Woman, No Cry?—The Social Scene

Although Wabash is an all-male school, most students say they find no shortage of female company. Many attend social events at Purdue and Indiana University, both less than 90 minutes away. One student, however, pointed out that the lack of women, combined with the un-happening surroundings of Crawfordsville (a town of 15,000 in which "Wal-mart serves as the social epicenter"), can make the Wabash experience socially isolating in relation to the outside world. In his assessment of the social situation at Wabash, he continued, "We are encapsulated in this tiny microcosm filled with testosterone, and the result is a return to the primordial instincts of aggression and survival." But the capsule also serves as a social safe haven, a tightly knit community where "all students feel somewhat connected to one another." In this sense, Wabash can resemble a "huge male-bonding fest."

Nowhere is this more apparent than in Wabash's fraternities, which dominate the campus social scene. Rush starts during spring visitation for high school seniors and resumes as soon as freshmen arrive on campus. Beer drinking is a central activity on Greek Row and throughout Wabash, despite the college's "Gentleman Rule" that says each Wabash undergrad must "behave like a gentleman on- and off-campus at all times." One student warned that this is a "very wet campus, one of the wettest I've seen."

"People who come here support it until they die"

The largest campus-wide event happens each fall when the Wabash Little Giants and their archrival DePauw University compete for the Monon Bell in the oldest football rivalry west of the Allegheny Mountains. In 1993, the 100th anniversary game was nationally televised and covered in *Sports Illustrated*. Homecoming week features special events such as the Chapel Sing, in which pledge brothers assemble in front of the chapel to sing the school song. Whichever group yells and sings the loudest wins the competition, as judged by the Sphinx Club, an exclusive club whose members perform community service, promote school spirit, and symbolize "the essence of a Wabash man." The competition is more tiring than it sounds, for Wabash has the longest school song in the nation; pledges must exercise their vocal cords for over 45 minutes!

Other sports events take place in a somewhat more subdued manner, although student participation in sports remains high. "It's really hard to be cut [from a team] here, so lots of people can participate no matter what their skill or experience level," explained one junior. The swim team and the football team usually draw the most student support, as does the well-ranked cross-country team. Other teams, however, have less impressive records, and in the words of one student, "This is definitely not a jock school." Wabash students also participate in intramural sports ranging from touch football to bowling. The athletic facilities are "in need of an upgrade," according to one student, although another allows that the facilities are "not bad for Division III."

Students also participate in extracurriculars from the *Bachelor*, a widely read weekly newspaper, to the student-run radio station WNDY—the Giant. There is also a strong theater program that produces many plays throughout the year.

Food Fights

Despite the administration's reported efforts to "diversify the food scene," Wabash students report that the food, while edible, is certainly not what you would eat if you had a choice. Although each of the many fraternity houses has its own in-house cook, food in the houses is reportedly not much better than in the cafeterias. The required plan of 19 meals per week has been a recent point of contention between students and the administration, and many students want a more flexible (and less expensive) plan. Nonetheless, off-campus restaurants and bars offer a break from dining hall food. The Silver Dollar Bar currently reigns as students' favorite local bar. Little Mexico and Joe's, a bar and grill, also draw many away from dining halls.

Living Arrangements

The large majority of Wabash students live in fraternity houses during their four years at the college. But among the campus dorms, students cite the recently renovated Martindale and the quiet Wolcott Hall as most desirable, while dorms such as Grant are less coveted. One floor in Morris Hall was recently designated as dry in an effort to reduce peer pressure and provide a quiet haven for nondrinkers. Space reportedly abounds in all Wabash dorms except those with single rooms.

The campus is self-contained, with a mix of architectural styles. Despite the mix, however, one student said, "The buildings here are very square; they really all look the same." With generous funding from graduates, Wabash is able to maintain first-rate facilities and provide financial aid to a large percentage of students, a major draw for out-of-staters in need of financial assistance.

Although about three-fourths of the student body hails from Indiana, many different nationalities and races comprise the student population. Many students feel, however, that the campus is not diverse enough. The administration has reportedly stepped up its minority and international recruitment efforts. One student described the campus as filled with "lots of liberals in search of a well-rounded education." Others, however, say the prevailing conservative political climate can, at times, lead to closed-mindedness and stereotyping, especially in relation to such issues as feminism and homosexuality.

In spite of these complaints about the lack of diversity at Wabash, many are proud of the solid education, strong heritage, and fierce loyalty that come with being a Wabash man. "It's hard to explain, but after coming here, I wouldn't go back to a co-ed university," one Wabash transfer student said. —*Susanna Chu and Staff*

FYI

The three best things about attending Wabash are great financial aid, spacious dorm rooms, and not having to worry about what girls think of you every second

The three worst things about attending Wabash are "how large an Indiana student body population there is, the Gentlemen Rule, the lack of female company

The three things that every student should do before graduating from Wabash are hang out at the Silver Dollar Bar, attend the Wabash/DePauw game, branch out and go to a social event of some sort at another nearby school

One thing I'd like to have known before coming here is how easy it is to get stuck in the tiny world of Wabash and forget about what happens outside

Iowa

Cornell College

Address: 600 First Street West; Mount Vernon, IA 52314-1098

Phone: 319-895-4477

E-mail address: admissions @cornell-iowa.edu

Web site URL: www. cornell-iowa.edu

Founded: 1853

Private or Public: private

Religious affiliation: Methodist

Location: rural

Undergraduate enrollment: 946

Total enrollment: 946

Percent Male/Female: 43%/59%

Percent Minority: 7%

Percent African-American: 2%

Percent Asian: 1%

Percent Hispanic: 3%

Percent Native-American: 1%

Percent in-state/out-of-state: 74%/26%

Percent Pub HS: 85%

Number of Applicants: 1,102

Percent Accepted: 72%

Percent Accepted who enroll: 34%

Entering: 269

Transfers: NA

Application Deadline: 1 Feb

Mean SAT: 565 V, 579 M

Mean ACT: 25

Middle 50% SAT range: 520–650 V, 530–630 M

Middle 50% ACT range: 22–28

3 Most popular majors: psychology, economics, English

Retention: 82%

Graduation rate: 56%

On-campus housing: 86%

Fraternities: 30%

Sororities: 3200%

Library: 172,000 volumes

Tuition and Fees: $19,570 in; $19,570 out

Room and Board: $5,410

Financial aid, first-year: 90%

Imagine starting and ending a class in just one month. It sounds impossible, but for Cornell College students, month-long classes are a reality. The small Mount Vernon, Iowa, college operates on a block system whereby students enroll in just one class at a time. While many other colleges and universities divide their academic years into fall and spring semesters, Cornell's system is comprised of nine blocks, each for three and a half weeks. Many students describe the short class periods as "intense," but insist that they are "manageable."

Block Scheduling

The nine blocks are spread from late August until early May. Students typically enroll in a class for eight of the nine blocks, with the leftover block becoming three and a half weeks of vacation time. However, particularly ambitious students can enroll in courses throughout all nine blocks. In such cases, the ninth block course can be taken for free. Because the winter recess is currently just one week and students do not have a spring vacation, there has been a call on campus to change the system to eight blocks, adding a spring break and lengthening the winter vacation.

All students must take four blocks of a foreign language (although testing out is possible), one of fine arts, one of math, two of physical science, and three of humanities. There are also requirements in writing and physical education. Students who choose to double major try to fulfill the requirements in the first two years through introductory-level courses, leaving their final two years for more intense and upper-level study in their chosen fields. Although many students bubble with delight over the block system, some undergrads admit that it is difficult to fit a year's worth of a language into less than a month, and that a more "conventional" approach for teaching foreign languages would be more effective.

> **Not having to plan a semester full of classes in advance allows students much more time to decide on a major.**

Not having to plan a semester full of classes in advance allows students much more time to decide on a major. In the past, many students have chosen to become triple or quadruple majors. However, this past year Cornell limited students to two majors, with the hope of fostering a basic liberal arts education while requiring its graduates to have a sharper focus.

All of the block courses are taught for five days a week, some meeting twice a day. Classes begin on the first Monday of each month and continue until the final Wednesday of that month. According to one sophomore, "The block system lets you focus on one thing. Some nights you have a lot of stuff to do, but other nights you won't have a damn thing, which is nice." Another student described the average amount of homework per night as "around one hour."

Besides the unique block system, many students choose Cornell because of its impressive student-faculty interaction. Enrollment in most classes is capped at 25, the average class size is just 15, and all courses are taught by professors. Many students express a high level of comfort with all of their professors; home visits with profs are not uncommon.

Special Programs
Students name the sciences, especially biology, as the best departments. Cornell's special 3–2 engineering program allows students to complete three years of selected courses at Cornell and then transfer to Washington University in St. Louis to earn a joint B.A.-M.S. degree from the two schools. Cornell also has an early-acceptance pre-dental program associated with the nearby University of Iowa. After completing their sophomore year

and taking the Dental Achievement Test, students who are accepted into the program are assured a place in the U of I School of Dentistry after graduation. Another popular area of study is religion. Many students cited such religion courses as Epistles of Paul, The Idea of God, and The Question of Faith as some of the more stimulating courses at the college.

Many students choose to study abroad during their time at Cornell. One of the most popular Cornell-sponsored programs occurs during the fifth block, which begins after New Year's. The program consists of a trip to England for the entire length of the block to study and travel. Many students praise the creative nature of the program, calling it a "very good trip." Students may also study abroad for a year or a semester through programs of the Associated Colleges of the Midwest or by joining an approved program from another university.

Social Associations
Although the college has no Greek system, it has local groups called associations. One such association is Phi Beta Kappa, the nation's oldest scholastic honorary society. The groups are referred to by their shortened names, often Greek letters, such as the "Gammas." The associations sponsor most of the on-campus parties, including the Axetoberfest put on by the "Axes" at a farm just outside Mount Vernon in the middle of October. Pledging for the associations (six men's and six women's) occurs in the spring for freshmen and in the fall for sophomores, climaxing during the four-day break between the first and second (fall) or seventh and eighth (spring) blocks.

Besides participating in the social associations, many students choose to visit one of the two local bars or go to the University of Iowa campus in Iowa City. One student described both of the bars as "cool," but "very different from each other; Joe's is more for the athletic types and the more social-life conscious, while Randall's crowd is more mixed." Both of the bars allow anyone 19 years of age and older to enter, but you must be 21 to drink.

Although Cornell is situated in the small town of Mount Vernon, few students seem to mind the quiet setting. One student from Chicago said, "Coming to Mount Vernon was a big change in that it was more rural, but once you get yourself a group of friends, you're pretty much set." Another student complained that "it takes more effort to find stuff to do on the weekends," but overall students are happy with the friendly town. According to one student, "The campus makes up the town. We keep a lot of the businesses running and they really suffer during the summer."

Moreover, Cornell is within 20 miles of both Cedar Rapids and Iowa City. The University of Iowa provides added resources, such as library materials. One ju-

nior explained that although there "is not much microfilm or microfiche at the Cornell library, students can go to Iowa City for a lot of their research."

Cornell continues to make its mark among the numerous small midwestern colleges because of the block system. This system allows undergrads to study subjects with a degree of attention unmatched at other schools, yet still be exposed to many different people and their ideas due to the constant changeover of classes. According to students, the constant change at Cornell provides for a stimulating and exciting four years.— *William Chen and Staff*

FYI

The three best things about attending Cornell are "the block system, the student-faculty interaction, and our social associations."

The three worst things about attending Cornell are "our locale, the emphasis on one course for an entire block, and our less than okay research facilities."

The three things every student should do before graduating from Cornell are "go biking in Mount Vernon, pledge an association, and study abroad."

One thing I'd like to have known before coming here is "how much I like Mount Vernon."

Grinnell College

Address: PO Box 805; Grinnell, IA 50112
Phone: 515-269-3600
E-mail address: askgrin@grinnell.edu
Web site URL: www.grinnell.edu
Founded: 1846
Private or Public: private
Religious affiliation: none
Location: small town
Undergraduate enrollment: 1,299
Total enrollment: 1,299
Percent Male/Female: 45%/55%
Percent Minority: 13%
Percent African-American: 3%

Percent Asian: 5%
Percent Hispanic: 4%
Percent Native-American: 0.5%
Percent in-state/out-of-state: 14%/86%
Percent Pub HS: 78%
Number of Applicants: 1,816
Percent Accepted: 65%
Percent Accepted who enroll: 28%
Entering: 325
Transfers: 28
Application Deadline: 20 Jan
Mean SAT: 669 V, 659 M
Mean ACT: 29

Middle 50% SAT range: 630–730 V, 610–710 M
Middle 50% ACT range: 27–31
3 Most popular majors: anthropology, biology, economics
Retention: 92%
Graduation rate: 82%
On-campus housing: 100%
Fraternities: NA
Sororities: NA
Library: 393,583 volumes
Tuition and Fees: $20,500 in; $20,500 out
Room and Board: $5,820
Financial aid, first-year: 91%

Nestled between the bridges of Madison Country and baseball's field of dreams lies Grinnell, Iowa, a rural, "not exactly Manhattan," town

that boasts rows of corn and a gas station that, although once called Always Open, has been renamed Almost Always Open. Don't let the town's obscure location and small size fool you, however; it's in this town that you can find Grinnell College, a liberal arts college that 1300 Birkenstock-clad students call home. Despite its remote geography, these laid-back but dedicated Grinnellians flock to Grinnell because it offers challenging academics, eccentric opportunities, hard-core partying, and yeah . . . the six week winter vacation.

A Recipe for Sleep Deprivation

This six-week vacation serves as a respite from the intense academic load that Grinnell's students endure. Students claim that Grinnell has "the second highest workload in the country." The 100 pages of reading that some classes demand per night has convinced one Grinnellian that "the workload is like the third level of hell." Despite the massive amount of work, students enjoy their academic experiences.

One defining mark of this academic experience is the freshman tutorial. All freshmen enroll in a tutorial where they can hone their writing. Past tutorials have surveyed topics like "Inside Star Trek" and "Music & Nature." With class sizes limited to 12 students, the tutorials provide freshmen a lot of advice on how to improve their writing and analytical skills.

The class sizes don't increase after the freshman tutorial, however. While some classes like Intro to Psychology have 60–100 students, students report that most of their classes range between 2 and 25 students. They also promise that as topics narrow and levels advance, class size decreases.

In addition to small classes, students enjoy close contact with great faculty. One student proclaimed that her professor was a "goddess," yet the professors are approachable and considerate. "I had to drop one of my classes because I was having health problems. The professor was incredibly kind to me and said he hoped I'd be able to re-take the class next year." There are no TAs, but there are "mentors" who have taken the class before and help grade and tutor.

Students insist that no slacker major exists at Grinnell. All majors require dedi-

cated work, but Bio/Chem and other science majors are especially challenging. Students claim that education concentrators and theatre majors put in some serious hours too. But not all classes are as intense as organic chemistry. Students can choose to take Exco classes, non-credit courses in which members of the Grinnell community or Grinnell students teach on random subjects. One student was delighted to have taken Yoing for Pleasure, a class that uncovered the secrets of yo-yos.

Where Have All the Grinnellians Gone?

Although one student announced, "We are the *royalty* of procrastination," students eventually have to hit the books and find a place to study. If you live in a single, the quiet of your room may be ideal. Burling Library offers a "really cozy" place to study. An added incentive to Burling is the opportunity to take a study break and contribute graffiti on the basement's bathroom walls. Students say that "not only does the administration not care about the graffiti, they actually encourage it."

> Students can join SCA (Society for Creative Anachronism), Free the Planet (an environmental group), Dagorhir (a blue-foam-sword fighting group), the Campus Monarchists (the group that proposed building a moat around North Campus . . . their project was denied funding), and the Vegan Coop.

For those who prefer background noise and a social atmosphere, the Forum Grill is a good place to whip out the books. The Forum Grill is located in one of the campus' two student centers: the Forum and the Harris Center. Students can go to the Forum to buy food ("you can get Ben and Jerry's nearly any time of day"), peruse the art gallery, play the grand piano, have a small meeting in the reserved rooms, or visit the Student Government offices. Harris provides students with a concert hall for parties and musicians, a TV lounge with couches, and a game room with pool and foosball tables.

Other notable areas on campus are the recently completed Robert Noyce Science Center and a Bucksbaum Center for the Arts, which student consider "two great additions." Students love the fact that "no two buildings really match." The Fine Arts building, for example, is shaped in a circular pattern "reminiscent of a nautilus shell" while the Goodnow building looks more like "a stone castle from the European Middle Ages." The architectural diversity is welcome since otherwise "you feel trapped in the middle of cornfields."

While off-campus housing is cheaper, most students opt to live on campus. While there's "no exposed plumbing, no dripping asbestos," the suites are "not exactly hotel quality." Students can choose from Cleveland, "the smoking dorm;" Read, "the non-smokers' dorm;" Loose, the dorm with the coziest main lounge; Younker, "the party place;" and Norris, the air-conditioned building. The campus is divided into two areas: "jocks live on North campus" and "alternatives live on South campus." Between the two areas are the ever-popular Bob's Underground Café, an enclosed loggia, and a dining hall.

The dining hall is "nothing to write home about," but students say that the food is getting better ever since Hungarian Noodlebake has been removed from the menu. Students also recommend avoiding the mozzarella sticks. Bob's Underground, the Pub, Pizza Hut, Pag's (an Italian eatery), Saint Rest's (a coffee house), and Café Phoeniz (the ritzy restaurant) are more popular places to dine.

When They're Not Studying

Despite the inordinate amount of reading and work required of the average Grinnell student, extracurriculars are popular and eccentric. Students can join SCA (Society for Creative Anachronism), Free the Planet (an environmental group), Dagorhir (a blue-foam-sword fighting group), the Campus Monarchists (the group that proposed building a moat around North Campus . . . their project was denied funding), and the Vegan Coop. Traditional extracurricular activities are available too: community service, the literary magazine, a comic magazine, a weekly paper, and the symphonic band, to name a few. The Grinnell Singers, an audition-only group, is also popular. All these groups tend to take the place of a Greek system, and students appreciate the absence of fraternities and sororities.

Grinnell students are generally stereotyped as "liberal, gay, pot-smoking activists." The liberal attitude, students say, is a stark contrast to the conservative mid-west town that surrounds the campus. Passionate liberalism makes for a charged political environment, and therefore the Campus Democrats is a popular club. Students attest to the fact that there are "no (out of the closet) Republicans."

Sports don't draw huge crowds. While the intramural football, ultimate frisbee, and rugby teams are relatively popular on campus, the varsity football team went undefeated last year and few people knew or celebrated it. Spectators at varsity events tend to be friends of the athletes.

After grueling weeks of activities and schoolwork, students relieve stress by partying hard on the weekends. Due to a lax alcohol and drug policy and the free beer at Harris parties, drinking is quite pervasive. It's not uncommon to spot a "Has anyone seen my bong" sign drifting around campus. Other activities are also available, thanks to the yearly activity fee required of each student. This fee funds free performances of groups like the Russian National Ballet and Second City. Other campus activities include house parties that are off-campus, Waltz (the semester formal), Disco (the yearly disco dance), the Drunken Titular Head Festival (an independent movie festival), Mary B. James (the annual cross-dressing party), Alice in Wonderland (a music festival with live bands), and the 10/10 progressive drinking party.

"Intense!" best describes this liberal college in Iowa. Whether it's the grueling academic life, the offbeat clubs, the creative organizations, the political aura that drapes over campus, or the big-time partying, Grinnell offers an educational experience of the utmost caliber. —*Marti Page*

FYI

The three best things about attending Grinnell are "the people, the freedom students are given, and the great academics."

The three worst things about attending Grinnell are "the stress, the pseudo-openmindness, and the dining hall food."

The three things that every student should do before graduating from Grinnell are "contributing to the graffiti in Burling Library, explore the steam tunnels, and go to a Mary B. James cross-dressing dance."

One thing I'd like to have known before coming here is "that you really need a car to get out of these cornfields."

Iowa State University

Address: 100 Alumni Hall; Ames, IA 50011-2011

Phone: 515-294-5836

E-mail address: admissions@iastate.edu

Web site URL: www.iastate.edu

Founded: 1858

Private or Public: public

Religious affiliation: none

Location: suburban

Undergraduate enrollment: 21,503

Total enrollment: 25,384

Percent Male/Female: 55%/45%

Percent Minority: 8%

Percent African-American: 3%

Percent Asian: 3%

Percent Hispanic: 1%

Percent Native-American: 0.5%

Percent in-state/out-of-state: 83%/17%

Percent Pub HS: NA

Number of Applicants: 12,172

Percent Accepted: 88%

Percent Accepted who enroll: 38%

Entering: 4,085

Transfers: 2,262

Application Deadline: 21 Aug

Mean SAT: 590 V, 610 M

Mean ACT: 25

Middle 50% SAT range: 520–660 V, 550–690 M

Middle 50% ACT range: 21–27

3 Most popular majors: elementary education, mechanical engineering, civil engineering

Retention: 84%

Graduation rate: 62%

On-campus housing: 34%

Fraternities: 16%

Sororities: 16%

Library: 2,000,000 volumes

Tuition and Fees: $3,132 in; $9,974 out

Room and Board: $4,171

Financial aid, first-year: 75%

Squirrels scamper across the copper roofs, leaves float between Greco-Roman pillars, and students steal kisses as the campanile (clock tower) begins to strike 12. In the 1920s, traditions such as kissing under the clock tower, or "campaniling," were sacred, the fraternity and sorority systems were strong, and most of the students had similar backgrounds and came from Iowa. Today, traditions such as campaniling and the friendly midwestern atmosphere remain, but Iowa State has changed with the times. The popularity of fraternities and sororities has steadily declined, and the administration is making a concerted effort to create a more diverse student body on a campus already known for strong academic and extracurricular activities.

Across the Board

Iowa State's undergrads are divided into seven different colleges: agriculture, business, design, education, engineering, family and consumer sciences, and liberal arts and sciences. Those who have already made career decisions can apply to the college of their choice. Those who are undecided are welcome as well; they simply apply and sort out their plans with an advisor after they arrive on campus. Although most students at Iowa State take academics seriously, they admit that the workload, course requirements, and academic experience vary greatly depending on the college and the individual. Classes can range in size from 8 to 400, and in subject from introductory theater to soil management to poultry nutrition.

The engineering and architecture programs are popular, and one student said, "the agriculture program here is as good as it gets." Many in-staters come to the university to learn how to manage the vast farms that fill some of the most fertile land in the nation. With hog and cattle management facilities and genetic research farms located throughout the state and the fact that farming is big business in Iowa, there's little doubt why students give it such high marks.

Where to Lay Your Head

Most freshmen live in residence halls on campus. Friley reportedly is the second-largest college dorm in the country, and the modern Towers is said to be comfortable but distant from the center of campus. Some complain about the extra blocks in their early-morning dazed rush to class. Despite the availability of campus housing, a large portion of the student body lives off-campus with the more lax regulations and greater privacy that the Greek system offers.

> **"Iowa has more to offer than just corn."**

Students in the residence halls and the Greek system are the most involved in the campus social scene. Although the fraternities host many of the campus parties, students report that "pressure to rush remains within the Greek system." Those not interested in the fraternities or sororities have other options. Memorial Union offers not only reading rooms for quiet study but also a bowling alley, pool tables, and video games. It also houses the Maintenance Shop, a campus bar that sponsors concerts ranging from blues to alternative rock, along with comedy shows and poetry readings.

The shopping area (known as Campus Town), restaurants and bars of Ames (population 47,200) offer students some off-campus entertainment. Café Baudelaire tempts many students with Middle - Eastern and Indian food, unusual drinks, and bands who perform in the window. Establishments like People's Bar and Grille and Underwhere attract the 21-and-over crowd.

Sports and Fun

Athletic contests at Iowa State are social occasions for both Iowa State students and the Ames community. The basketball team, a success in the Big Eight athletic conference, draws the widest student and community support. The future of Cyclone basketball did look shaky when Hilton Coliseum, like much of Iowa, lay submerged under 14 feet of floodwater in the summer of 1993, but with strong community support, the stadium and other water-damaged buildings were repaired.

Students rave about the new recreation center, which offers extensive aerobic and weight lifting facilities as well as basketball courts and playing field for club and intramural sports. The recreation center even organizes trips for students interested in activities such as rock climbing or horseback riding.

VEISHEA is HUGE

VEISHEA (pronounced "vee-sha"), one of the largest student-run festivals in the nation, is also one of the most popular annual events on campus. About 400 students work together to plan and organize this campus and community celebration that includes a musical production, food fair, and a battle of the bands, and culminates in a parade with floats, balloons, and athletic events. The average Iowa State student is from small-town Iowa, but the universtiy also attracts many students from midwestern cities such as Chicago and Minneapolis. The administration has recently made efforts to attract more minority and international students. As the minority population at Iowa State has begun to grow, some tension has developed; according to undergrads, some members of the community and student body were never really prepared for diversity. Some minority students say they sometimes feel invisible and that they "only want equality." After a recent boycott of an African-American history class whose professor made what some students felt were racist remarks, many organizations and departments implemented changes designed to improve race relations. The student government, for example, planned an international student week with cultural activities, lectures, dancing, and Global Food Fest.

An Administration that's Truly in Touch

One of the best aspects of Iowa State, students say, is the university's flexibility. According to one student, there's no better example of this than the school's agricul-ture program, which manages to stay up to date in its research and in giving hands-on experience to its students. But whether you're looking for an education integrated seamlessly into the practicality of farming, or you're challenged by the abstract fundamentals of mathematics, students say their school has it all. As one student quipped, "Iowa has more to offer than just corn." —*Madhu Pocha and Staff*

FYI

The three best things about Iowa State are "how many people are involved in extracurriculars, the agriculture program is awesome, and the people here are friendly."

The three worst things about Iowa State are"the Greeks are in decline, it's too homogeneous, and some classes are too huge."

The three things that every student should do before graduating from Iowa State are "participate in VEISHEA, attend a basketball game, and do intramurals."

One thing I wish I knew before coming here is "how often people make fun of us about corn!"

University of Iowa

Address: 107 Calvin Hall; Iowa City, IA 52242-1396
Phone: 319-335-3847
E-mail address: admissions@uiowa.edu
Web site URL: www.uiowa.edu
Founded: 1847
Private or Public: public
Religious affiliation: none
Location: small city
Undergraduate enrollment: 18,770
Total enrollment: 28,837
Percent Male/Female: 46%/54%
Percent Minority: 8%
Percent African-American: 2%

Percent Asian: 3%
Percent Hispanic: 2%
Percent Native-American: 0.5%
Percent in-state/out-of-state: 72%/28%
Percent Pub HS: 89%
Number of Applicants: 11,358
Percent Accepted: 83%
Percent Accepted who enroll: 41%
Entering: 3,859
Transfers: 1,318
Application Deadline: 15 May
Mean SAT: NA
Mean ACT: NA

Middle 50% SAT range: 520–660 V, 540–660 M
Middle 50% ACT range: 22–27
3 Most popular majors: psychology, communications studies, English
Retention: 82%
Graduation rate: 64%
On-campus housing: NA
Fraternities: 12%
Sororities: 12%
Library: NA
Tuition and Fees: $3,128 in; $10,890 out
Room and Board: $4,594
Financial aid, first-year: NA

Set in the relatively small college town of Iowa City, the University of Iowa provides both a quality Big Ten education and a "surprisingly nice tuition bill," according to one pleased student. The home of the Hawkeyes combines a thriving social scene with strong academics. When asked what set the University of Iowa apart from other schools, a senior simply replied, "We're the best!" and expressed his sympathies for those who did not have the good fortune or foresight to attend the university themselves.

No Corn and a Huge Mall?

"The biggest myth about our school is that it's in the middle of the cornfields," said a senior marketing major. "If you drive out ten minutes, you can see cornfields, but there are no farms on campus. Nobody believes it until they see it, and then they're like, 'Wow, cool town.'" While most students expressed positive feelings about Iowa City, which is home to many movie theaters, restaurants, pizza places, coffee shops, bars, and is just two miles from Coral Ridge Mall, the third-largest in the Midwest, one student complained that "after four years here, you certainly realize this town is pretty boring."

The reason for boredom among a minority of students is the widespread drinking on campus; U of I students are typically known as "educated drinkers." While many school-organized activities are available, such as frequent lectures (recent lecturers include Maya Angelou and Adam Carolla and Dr. Drew from MTV's Loveline), rock concerts, and special pre-screening of movies such as The Game, the typical weekend involves "drinking it alive and well in the binge-drinking capital of the Midwest. There is a bar for everyone in Iowa City," described one student. He went on to explain that 19-and-over bars and dance clubs such as The Field House and The Union Bar give students their "first taste of barstool sub-culture" while sports bars such as the Sports Column or Mondo's are great for "cheering on the Hawks with buddies." The liberal and pot-smoking crowd tend to hang out at places such as the Sanctuary or The Mill. And while the Hawkeye wrestling team has won almost every national title for the past twenty years, tailgates associated with the football team play the important role on weekends. In some cases, the tailgates have even overshadowed the sport. One freshman reported seeing "many drunk and hungover people sitting outside and drinking near where a football game was many hours after a game."

Stepping Up

A few years ago, the university received an $800,000 federal grant from the Robert Wood Johnson Foundation for their Stepping Up University/Community Action Partnership to Reduce High-Risk Drinking Project. In recent years the entire campus has maintained a campaign against binge drinking. In response to an alcohol-related student death a few years ago during a Greek rush, the administration has put the frats under heavy pressure, while

"most sororities went dry years ago," according to the university president. Parties are still prevalent, however; popular ones include the Beta Blue Hawaii, '70s parties, and margarita party nights.

What's Wrong with Chicago Suburbans?

Many students joke that their school should be called the University of Illinois at Iowa because of the large number of students from suburban Chicago. Some find that the mixing between these students and those from rural Iowa as well as the large percentage of gays and lesbians in Iowa City creates a great deal of school diversity. But others complain about the lack of racial diversity. But students agree that everyone from students to professors to residents of Iowa City are very friendly. "Everyone says hi whether you know them or not," said one senior.

Don't Hate Us 'cuz We're Beautiful

U of Is campus is gorgeous, as the school is built around the beautiful gold-domed former Iowa capital building. The Iowa River runs through the middle of campus, splitting the graduate and undergraduate buildings; the west side contains the university hospital, the third-largest teaching hospital in the nation. While this causes a severe shortage in parking spaces, as one senior put it, "those are the sacrifices you make for beauty." As for the size of campus, one student praised its compactness, stating that "everything is within walking distance," while another praised the three different bus lines linking the different parts of campus. Many students sit in the Pentacrest, the center of campus, to study or meet people, and even in the middle of the night, students feel safe walking alone.

> "Everyone says hi whether you know him or not."

Most students live off campus in privately owned apartment buildings, but the dorms are almost all air-conditioned and have nice, large rooms. Each residential hall has its own personality, ranging from

Burge, David Letterman's number one party dorm, to Rienow and Slater, the jock dorms, to Stanley, the quiet dorm. An RA system is in effect, but "if you don't tick them off, they won't mess with you," said one student. Dining hall food is generally considered decent, although a freshman recalled asking an upperclassman how dinner was and receiving the response, "It was good, but I feel sick."

Streaking and Religious Studies

U of I also has relatively small classes (most are under 50 students, with large lectures split into 20-person discussion sections). Students also benefit from professor and TA attention during office hours. One student mentioned that the business classes utilize advanced technology and multimedia to make learning interesting. U of I boasts one of the nation's best writing programs, while the graduate students who attend the highly reputed Writer's Workshop where Kurt Vonnegut once worked "pass much of their knowledge to undergrads." Students also mentioned that the physics, Russian, astronomy, and political science departments were outstanding. The political science, English, and creative writing TAs are reportedly awesome, while the science TAs are known to be a bit lacking. However, that may stem from the fact that most U of I students are humanities-oriented. When asked to name the most heinous thing about classes, most students mentioned

"waking up for morning classes." Some U of I classes begin as early as 7:30 A.M.

When asked about professors, students praised such interesting and humorous teachers as Judeo-Christian Tradition professor Jay Holstein, who once claimed that he would retire if a student streaked during his class (a male student did precisely that a few months later, and Holstein explained that he had meant a female student).

Almost everyone is involved in at least one of the 350-plus student organizations, which include Habitat for Humanity, African American World Studies Association, American Medical Women's Association, Gay Lesbian Bisexual Transgender Union, and Campus Crusade for Christ. Most students are athletic, and "almost every athletic team is in the hunt for the Big Ten title," raved one senior. Aside from the reputedly strong club and intramural teams, students also go in droves to play pickup basketball games in the Field House; alums who have visited campus recently include NBA point guard B. J. Armstrong, formerly of the world-champion Chicago Bulls. Many students also have jobs or volunteer.

All in all, the University of Iowa is a happy, thriving community. Most students find the friendly, open environment, great bargain education, and charming college town and campus a comfortable and interesting place to spend four years. —*Jennifer Wang and Staff*

FYI

The three best things about attending U of Iowa are "you get to meet a lot of different kinds of people, the wide selection of things to study, the friendly atmosphere."

The three worst things about attending U of Iowa are "bad parking, huge classes, science TAs."

The three things every student should do before graduating from U of Iowa are "study, party, then party some more."

One thing I'd like to have known before coming here is "how much students here drink and have sex."

Kansas

Kansas State University

Address: 119 Anderson Hall; Manhattan, KS 66506
Phone: 785-532-6250
E-mail address: kstate@ksu.edu
Web site URL: www.ksu.edu
Founded: 1863
Private or Public: public
Religious affiliation: none
Location: suburban
Undergraduate enrollment: 17,809
Total enrollment: 20,306
Percent Male / Female: 53% / 47%
Percent Minority: 7%
Percent African-American: 3%

Percent Asian: 1%
Percent Hispanic: 2%
Percent Native-American: 0.5%
Percent in-state / out-of-state: 91% / 9%
Percent Pub HS: NA
Number of Applicants: 10,457
Percent Accepted: 65%
Percent Accepted who enroll: 52%
Entering: 3,504
Transfers: 1,771
Application Deadline: rolling
Mean SAT: NA
Mean ACT: 23

Middle 50% SAT range: NA
Middle 50% ACT range: NA
3 Most popular majors: animal science, journalism, mechanical engineering
Retention: 77%
Graduation rate: 45%
On-campus housing: 28%
Fraternities: 20%
Sororities: 20%
Library: 1,400,000 volumes
Tuition and Fees: $2,592 in; $9,195 out
Room and Board: $3,950
Financial aid, first-year: NA

Known to its fans as the "Happy Purple Place," K-State overflows with school spirit. One student summed up the energy by saying, "Everyone here has at least six purple shirts, and they're not afraid to wear them!" Kansas State University has a centralized campus about 1.5 miles long, set amid the Flint Hills of northeast Kansas. Consisting largely of limestone buildings covered with ivy, students are quick to point out the beauty and variety of the gardens and shrubbery around campus that are largely due to the extensive horticultural program. True to its location in the American heartland, KSU exemplifies the typical all-American college.

K-State is located in Manhattan, Kansas, a town that thrives on the vitality and the business the students bring. When the students leave for the summer, a large number of pizza places and other college oriented businesses close. Manhattan is very supportive of the school and its students and the residents proudly display K-State's colors and symbols. In fact, the town firetrucks are emblazoned with three foot tall Powercats in honor of the school mascot, Willy the Wildcat. However, due to the town's relatively small size, many students often travel as far as once a week to Lawrence (45 minutes away) to shop, and at least twice a month to Kansas City (2 hours away).

Not Just Farmers and Country Music

K-State was originally an agricultural college, and while some students complain that the school retains an unfair image as being filled with "farmers, hicks, and country music," others are proud of the distinction that the agricultural programs have brought to the university. The academic programs are divided into nine colleges, and while the College of Agriculture is just one of these, it provides some of the most distinctive majors that K-State offers. Among these are baking and milling (officially known as grain science and industry), which prepares its students for jobs with grain processing companies, such as Kellogg's. Leadership Studies, another unique program created in 1997, deals with the theory and practical application of leadership abilities and skills.

Another prestigious program at K-State is the Architectural College, to which students must apply to directly upon entering the university. According to one architecture major, students in the program are expected to put in at least 20 hours a week in the studio. Many report that they virtually live in the studio, which is equipped with strategically placed vending machines for microwaveable meals. Architecture, along with milling, veterinary science, and engineering are known as "weed-out majors" in which the first two years of study are particularly demanding and time consuming in order to limit the enrollment.

Nuclear Engineering 501: Atomic Gut

K-State actually runs its own small nuclear reactor. Located on campus, this unit is used to power the campus. It is also used to show how nuclear power works as part of an infamous gut class: Introduction to Nuclear Engineering, a course some students say is graded purely on attendance. Other reportedly easy classes include Music Literature Lab, Introduction to Applied Architecture, and Impact of Technology on Society.

Kansas State freshmen find that their first semester schedule is largely predetermined by a set of mandatory core classes. Because the registration process is based on seniority, upperclassmen report few problems getting into the classes they want, while sophomores and second-semester freshmen have a much harder time. Students find the advising system cumbersome and unhelpful and the advisors uninformative and inflexible, and thus the academic advising system is not well liked. Some students even choose to circumvent the advising system, claiming "it's easier to guide yourself."

Groovin' with the Profs

Professors at K-State get rave reviews for being "very open, accessible, and friendly," often distributing their home phone numbers in class. "You're just as likely to see your professor in a bar on Saturday night as on campus," one student claimed. Another student dubbed many of the professors "closet hippies." "They talk to you like human beings. We've got 27 year-old professors; you cannot beat that!" said one undergrad. Many professors reportedly also have a sense of humor. One freshman remembered when her professor, who always wore jeans and a white shirt, came to the last day of class "wearing plaid pants, a polka-dot shirt, and showed slides of David Hasselhoff (of *Baywatch* fame) and himself in a play from his days in college."

Teaching assistants are common in math and science, but rare in other subjects. One textiles major claimed that in four years she had only one TA, although an engineering major had them in about half of his classes. The TAs assist, rather than lead, classes, serving primarily as lab facilitators. Some TAs received poor reviews by students, largely based on their poor grasp of the English language. Running on a semester system, K-State academic requirements include two English composition classes, psychology and sociology, college algebra, history, macro and micro economics, and human development. There is no language requirement, and a physical education requirement was dropped in 1997. Class size varies by college, but the average lecture consists of about 250 students while discussion classes enroll from 20 to 40 students.

While most students find a car unnecessary on campus, those who live off campus complain about the parking situation. Some drivers report at least an hour's wait for a space in the student parking lots, although the faculty lots have "plenty of empty spaces." Students often park instead at their fraternity or sorority houses and then walk to class from there. Bicycles are very popular, but can be ridden only around the periphery of campus.

Study Habits

Students cite Turtle Creek as a favorite spot to hit the books, or just spend a lazy

Sunday afternoon. Located about 10 minutes from campus by car, this large lake is where the crew team rows. Students also use the creek to swim and water ski, and some hike on the extensive trail system surrounding it. Many students also study at the Manhattan City Park, or in the shade of the large trees on campus. The campus libraries close at midnight, so late-night studiers crowd coffee shops in Manhattan, as well as the Village Inn, the only 24-hour restaurant in Manhattan known for its comfy booths, milk shakes, and fried chicken for the sleep deprived.

Life on Campus

While a large portion of K-State upperclassmen prefer to live in apartments off campus, few students complain about the dorms. Most dorms are L-shaped buildings with two wings of double rooms. Each floor determines its own quiet hours and rules, although the top floor of each building is designated as an "intensive study" floor with longer quiet hours. Each building is about eight stories high, with an elevator at the apex of the "L." There is 24-hour visitation on single-sex floors, but males must always be escorted when on female floors.

Dorm rooms are fairly large, with air conditioning and a three-panel window. One freshman reported that she and her roommate fit a loft, two desks, a couch, and a coffee table into their room. The lighting is more than sufficient—as one student said, "Turn that puppy on and you're blind!"

> **"The Greek system is very strong at K-State, but students agree that participation is far from essential."**

Students say they feel safe on campus, and additional outdoor lighting was recently installed. Safety phones are located throughout campus and an escort service will walk students home upon request.

Undergrads are less enthusiastic about campus food, although a salad bar, a grill, vegetarian, and vegan options are available. Students can choose between a standard meal plan or a debit system that deducts the cost of each meal from an ac-count. Some favorite eateries off-campus include Rock-a-Belly Deli, Habachi Head (Cajun), and Pizza Shuttle.

Kabillion Activities

On-campus activities are extensive. "There are kabillions of them!" one student professed. *The Collegian*, the school newspaper, and the marching band are both popular. Societies based on interests and majors also abound. Although it rarely snows in Kansas, the university has a ski club a well as a rock-climbing club. The Landane Lecture Series brings one speaker to campus each month: recent speakers have included Henry Kissinger and Colin Powell.

The university recently renovated Farrell Library, the Student Union, and the sports complexes. The library, previously criticized for its small size, is now "huge." Study space abounds in a modern, comfortable environment. The Student Union, a.k.a. the Onion, houses a bowling alley in the basement, places to study, to watch TV, arcades, a pool table, a cafeteria-style restaurant, and a sit-own restaurant. Every other Tuesday a large crowd gathers in the Onion to watch *South Park*. *Jerry Springer* is also popular, as are *The Simpsons* and *The X-Files*.

Working Out the Wildcat Way

Athletics are very popular at K-State. Athletes and non-athletes alike call the recreational center the "Taj Mahal" of sports complexes. Even the football stadium has recently been expanded to increase seating. "Everyone attends football games," said one fan. At games, Willy the Wildcat often spells KSU with his body, while fans scream the letters. At every touchdown or field goal, the fans point to the end zone and scream, "Good for another wildcat!"

A large number of students are involved in the intramural sports program. Frisbee and golf arc extremely popular. "Powder puff" football (women's flag football) is also a favorite, as is wallyball (a variation of volleyball played in a racquetball court).

After Hours

Kansas State University is officially a dry campus, but some students say drinking is popular. While most claim that being underage is no problem, security officers hand out many citations for MIPs (Minor in Possession) each week, and this deters a significant portion of the under-21 crowd. The social life for most students revolves around Aggieville, an off-campus strip that houses 37 bars in a two block radius. Underclassmen tend to congregate at the dance bars, particularly a club nicknamed "Kiddie Junction." Upperclassmen find seclusion in the quieter jazz bars, particularly Auntie Mae's. "Everyone in the bars are smoking Marlboro or Camel lights," one student said. Although chain smoking is popular, students rarely light up on campus. Some students report that marijuana is present on campus, but others claim it is rare or underground.

K-State is one of the few schools where traditional dating is common, especially "Coke-date" (an informal study session over Cokes at a coffee shop). These low-key dates relieve the pressure of a "first date" environment, but provide an alternative to Aggieville. Most students feel that the gay population is not visible on campus, but homosexuality is generally accepted. Ethnic diversity on campus has improved over recent years, but is still behind when compared to other universities. Students seem unconcerned, saying the school is remarkably diverse for its location.

The Greek Life

The Greek system is very strong at K-State, but students agree that participation is far from essential. While undergrads tend to move in either Greek or non-Greek circles, there exists no hostility between the groups. First-year sorority members live in dorms, while men live in their fraternity houses all four years. Annual theme parties include: the Festival of Gluttony, where students ride a waterslide from a barn roof; Patty Murphy (a party named after a fraternity member who allegedly drank himself to death during prohibition), which features tombstones and hot tubs as decorations; and the Mud Bowl, a beach volleyball tournament to raise money for Alzheimer's research. The largest event of the year, however, is homecoming. Planning begins in the spring for the following year's game. Fraternities and sororities team up to compete in float building, body pyramid building, parade, and chanting contests, and winners are announced at the homecoming football game.

K-State is . . .

Students report that their classmates generally have a "happy-go-lucky" attitude and a "polite and social" demeanor. The dress is preppy and casual, the mood is friendly. "People that I've never met before open doors for me," recounted one student. Others echo this sentiment by saying that school spirit and friendliness are the two attributes that most clearly define Kansas State University's personality. —*Cynthia Matthews and Staff*

FYI
The three best things about attending K-State are "the professors, the sports, and the people."
The three worst things about attending K-State are "the city (or lack thereof), the bureaucracy, and the escorts on the women's floors."
The three things that every student should do before graduating from K-State are "to go to the Festival of Gluttony, to play IMs, and to go to Turtle Creek."
One thing I'd like to have known before coming here is "that cars were so important. If you don't have one, you need to know someone who does!"

University of Kansas

Address: KU Visitor Center,
1502 Iowa State;
Lawrence, KS 66045
Phone: 785-864-3911
E-mail address:
adm@ukans.edu
Web site URL:
www.ukans.edu
Founded: 1866
Private or Public: public
Religious affiliation:
none
Location: suburban
**Undergraduate
enrollment:** 19,477
Total enrollment: 27,567
Percent Male / Female:
48% / 52%
Percent Minority: 10%

Percent African-American:
3%
Percent Asian: 3%
Percent Hispanic: 3%
Percent Native-American:
1%
**Percent in-state / out-of-
state:** 72% / 28%
Percent Pub HS: NA
Number of Applicants:
8,409
Percent Accepted: 69%
**Percent Accepted who
enroll:** 67%
Entering: 3,878
Transfers: 2,190
Application Deadline:
1 Apr
Mean SAT: NA

Mean ACT: 24
Middle 50% SAT range: NA
Middle 50% ACT range:
21–27
3 Most popular majors:
biological sciences,
psychology, business
Retention: 78%
Graduation rate: 50%
On-campus housing: 48%
Fraternities: 19%
Sororities: 21%
Library: 3,500,000
volumes
Tuition and Fees:
$2,725 in; $9,493 out
Room and Board: $4,114
Financial aid, first-year:
39%

B uilt into the side of a mountain, the
University of Kansas gives its students plenty of exercise trekking to
classes. As one student put it, "You can
tell what year students are by the size of
their calves." "KU calves" are only one of
many characteristics that distinguish this
public, Midwestern school, well-known
for its nationally ranked basketball team.

The University of Kansas is generally
considered "easy to get into, but hard to
stay in." While not as selective as such
state schools as the University of Michigan, Ann Arbor or the University of North
Carolina, Chapel Hill, KU provides a top-
quality education at a reasonable price.
The university some students describe as
a "good deal" is notable for its strong commitment to the liberal arts, mirrored by
the large percentage of students enrolled
in the program. All students in the school
of liberal arts must meet a core group of
requirements that include Western and
non-Western civilization classes as well as
prove proficiency in a foreign language.
Outside of liberal arts, the requirements
vary dramatically from program to program. The fine arts school, for example,
has musical performance requirements.

Recently, the university increased its efforts to recruit more academically talented students. The school's Honors College offers selected undergrads small
seminar classes taught by actual professors. Class sizes are limited to 30 students
and even freshmen in the Honors College
have access to these classes. The Honors
College professors earn higher reviews on
average than the majority of university
faculty. As one freshman raved, "My history teacher is the bomb!"

Overall, students are pleased with the
range of majors and classes available under the liberal arts program. Introductory
classes tend to be large and taught by
graduate teaching assistants (GTAs), especially in math and science, while upper-
level courses are smaller and taught by
professors. Several teachers and classes
received great reviews. In particular, Dr.
Dennis Dailey's class on human sexuality
is very popular. Academics are seen as
challenging, but never overwhelming.
Foreign languages have a reputation for
being difficult. "Some people avoid liberal
arts just to avoid the foreign language requirement," one student said. But, students report that many easy, "gut" classes
can be found in the art history and child
development departments. Some students have grievances with the grading
scale used by professors. "The grading

scale is not uniform at all. A 94 percent can be an A in one class or a B in another." Despite this, undergrads generally find professors friendly and accessible, although it can take some effort to get to know them.

> **"The drink of choice is 'whatever you can get your hands on.'"**

What is the typical KU student like? While there is no predominant stereotype, students describe their classmates as attractive and fairly preppy or alternative in style. The school is rather homogeneous: students are mainly Caucasian, Christian, heterosexual Midwesterners. However, the university has a fairly tolerant and liberal reputation. Nicknamed "Gay U." by some, the university has a substantial gay and lesbian community. Overall, racial diversity is improving at the school due to the concerted effort of undergraduate admissions in recruiting minority students.

Party School
Ranked as the number eight party school in the nation by the Princeton Review, KU has a social life one student described as "very happening." Rush, or "going Greek," is a popular and painless but fairly competitive process. With a large Greek scene, a party can always be found, the majority of them open to non-Greeks as well. For many freshmen experiencing freedom for the first time, drinking is a popular weekend activity. Though KU is a dry campus, some students say alcohol is easy to find, the drink of choice being "whatever you can get your hands on." However, many options exist for non-drinkers at KU. Kansas City is a popular weekend destination for upperclassmen, and several good dance clubs, such as Bleachers, surround the campus. The "Day on the Hill" music festival held every spring attracts big-name bands like They Might Be Giants. Another popular pastime is dating, which students unanimously described as "big," along with casual sex. On a related note, legend has it that the large, bronze Jayhawk statue in the center of campus will fly away if a virgin ever graduates from KU.

Kansas Livin'
Undergrads describe the tree-filled KU campus as "gorgeous." The buildings are an eclectic mix of collegiate-style architecture and modern structures like Wesco Hall, where many English classes are held. Situated in the heart of the campus, the patio and stairs that surround Wesco Hall are known as "Wesco Beach," a popular hangout before, after, or even during classes. Overall, students say they feel very safe on campus. Security does not seem to be much of an issue in the quiet town of Lawrence.

Campus facilities, for the most part, are in excellent condition. Although some students complained that the dorms are "old and crappy," renovations of all the dorms are underway. The university is moving toward "suite" style dorms like Templin, which contain suites of four or more students who share a common living room and bathroom. Many upperclassmen choose to live off campus, but one senior described the renovated dorms as "the best place to live." Naismith Hall, run by Holiday Inn, is considered very nice, as are the scholarship halls reserved for Honors College students. Described as "a community within a community," the scholarship halls require students to share the responsibilities of chores and cooking.

Most students at KU do not make their own food, but instead eat their meals in the dining halls. Many rate the dining hall food average to below-average, with "recycled menus" being the major complaint. The most variety and the best food reportedly is available at "Mrs. E's", the largest dining hall on campus. Vegan and vegetarian options are always available. For those tired of dining hall food, popular restaurants await in Lawrence, including Papa Keno's ("pizza to die for"), La Familia (Mexican), and Java Break (coffee shop).

"Something for Everyone"
With more than 400 campus organizations, "there's something for everyone here," one student said. KU even has a Dr. Seuss Club, whose members proudly affirm their affinity for green eggs and ham. Writing for the *University Daily Kansas*, the campus newspaper, is a popular extracurricular for many aspiring journalists.

By far the greatest pastime for KU students is watching their beloved Jayhawks basketball team on the court. KU b-ball games are an event in themselves. To kick off the season, KU coach Roy Williams organizes a midnight pep rally and exhibition for the fans, affectionately termed "Late Night with Roy Williams." Students demonstrate their KU spirit by camping out days in advance to get prime seats for the games, held in the always-packed Allen Field House. Chants of "Rock Chalk, Jayhawk, KU" can be heard at any sporting event, showing the ever-present spirit of KU fans.

KU fans love not only their team but also their school. When asked if they would pick KU again as their college choice, all students interviewed responded with an enthusiastic "Yes!" Quality academics combined with exciting sports and an active Greek scene make KU an attractive choice. —*Madhu Pocha and Staff*

FYI

The three best things about attending the University of Kansas are "the bars, the hottie frat boys, and the basketball team."

The three worst things about attending the University of Kansas are "the bars, the hottie frat boys with attitudes, and the hills that smokers can't walk up."

The three things that every student should do before graduating from the University of Kansas are "attend a KU game, dance/wade in the Chi Omega Fountain, go to O Street."

One thing I'd like to have known before coming here is "Everyone has a significant other!"

Kentucky

Centre College

Address: 600 West Walnut Street; Danville, KY 40422
Phone: 606-238-5350
E-mail address: admission@centre.edu
Web site URL: www.centre.edu
Founded: 1819
Private or Public: private
Religious affiliation: Presbyterian
Location: rural
Undergraduate enrollment: 1,015
Total enrollment: 1,015
Percent Male / Female: 49% / 51%
Percent Minority: 5%

Percent African-American: 3%
Percent Asian: 0.5%
Percent Hispanic: 0.5%
Percent Native-American: 0.5%
Percent in-state / out-of-state: 64% / 36%
Percent Pub HS: 80%
Number of Applicants: 1,142
Percent Accepted: 86%
Percent Accepted who enroll: 26%
Entering: 253
Transfers: 29
Application Deadline: 1 Feb
Mean SAT: 608 V, 602 M

Mean ACT: 27
Middle 50% SAT range: 570–690 V, 580–680 M
Middle 50% ACT range: 25–30
3 Most popular majors: English, economics, history
Retention: 87%
Graduation rate: 64%
On-campus housing: 100%
Fraternities: 62%
Sororities: 69%
Library: 270,000 volumes
Tuition and Fees: $21,350 in; $21,350 out
Room and Board: $5,300
Financial aid, first-year: 61%

Rock concerts for credit. Semesters in England or France. No class on Wednesdays. Centre is not just your typical small-town school.

Campus Tour

Welcome to Centre College, a small yet academically challenging school located in Danville, Kentucky. Let me show you around. On your left you will find Greek Park, the biggest collection of Centre's many fraternities and sororities. Greek life is central to the Centre social scene, but you will learn more about that when the weekend comes. On your right you can find the Norton Center for the Arts, which houses a great performing arts program. Look up ahead—there is a collection of freshman dorms. Almost everyone lives on campus at Centre, but freshmen live in single-sex dorms, with men and women on opposite sides of the campus. There are no visitation hours until after the winter homecoming freshman year,

after which guests are restricted until midnight on weekdays and 2:00 A.M. on the weekends. Don't worry, though; students agree that these visitation rules are "easy to break" and "never enforced."

> **"I can't imagine a school more dominated by Greek organizations."**

I hope that you've noticed by now that this campus "is beautiful and small," with most everything within easy walking distance. Take a good look, because students here agree that you will be spending most of your time on campus. One of students' biggest complaints is the city of Danville. Danville is notorious for its lack of bars and good restaurants—with only fast food to feed a hungry student. There are not many friendships between Centre students and Danville "townies," and one student went so far as to complain that she was "tired of being leered at by rednecks in pickup trucks and workers who hang around Wal-Mart."

Saturday Night Fever
Danville may not be loved, but students still get off campus, especially when the weekend arrives. Many students go out to dinner or go shopping with friends in nearby Lexington, which helps make up for the dullness of Danville. Since Boyle County is dry, students have to drive at least a half an hour away to pick up alcohol for the weekend. However, most students find that this does not bother them and gives them a welcome chance to get off campus. In fact, one student loved that in Danville "there aren't any bars, so on-campus parties are bigger."

Once you are ready to party, you will almost definitely want to head to the fraternity houses. One student said, "I can't imagine a school more dominated by Greek organizations." Most students welcome the Greek system, which sponsors a number of campus events, as an easy way to meet people and make friends. With about two-thirds of students in a fraternity or sorority, many students attend chapter meetings on Sundays and happily participate in the wide array of Greek rivalries and traditions. Centre has a "liberal drinking policy," which provides for a variety of theme parties each week (such as Dekes of Hazard and the Catholic School Girl party) that spice up the social scene.

To add to the social scene, Centre has a few crazy and popular traditions. The most famous adventure is to "Run the Flame." Tradition holds that "before you graduate, you must strip down to your birthday suit and run around the Flame (a flame-shaped statue in the middle of campus) and back to your clothes before getting caught with a $100 fine." Most fraternities and sororities have their own traditions and rivalries. One fraternity brings the portrait of "Dead Fred" (Frederick Vinson, a Supreme Court Chief Justice and Centre graduate) to every sporting event. Nearing its 200th birthday, Centre has accumulated its share of tradition.

First Day of Classes
There is a strong consensus that Centre is academically very challenging. Students rated the classes from "very hard," to "tough and demanding," to "harder than what everyone said." Don't get too worried, though. The hard work that students put in doesn't come without its rewards. Centre's size allows for small classes— none with more than 35 students. Most of the "accessible" and "really amazing" professors at Centre have Ph.D.'s, and they are also known for the personal attention that they give to students. There is a general sentiment that the classes at Centre are hard, but the "many new outlooks on life" that students receive make the schoolwork worthwhile.

In order to help students stay committed to this liberal arts education, Centre has a unique Convocation program. From a wide variety of options, students are required to attend 12 art performances (ranging from renowned lecturers to Broadway shows). Students feel that this was a welcome opportunity to broaden their horizons, and one pondered, "I sometimes wonder where else you can get credits for going to see Art Garfunkel." Centre also has a fairly dense general education requirement, for which students must complete 115 course hours in areas outside their major. These include a variety of subjects—from philosophy to economics—and one student warned against the challenge of the religion courses.

Small School: Cozy or Nosy?
With an undergraduate population of a little over a thousand students, Centre encapsulates most of the typical benefits and grievances of a small school. Students agree that the biggest benefit of a small school is "the great friendships you make." The large amount of on-campus activity leads to a strong student community at Centre. The small class sizes, short walking distances, and low levels of peer pressure lead students to love Centre's cozy feel. However, this compact feeling also leads to one of the students' biggest complaints—the lack of privacy. One student said that it seemed like "everyone knows everything about you and what you have done" and that "the gossip spreads to easily."

Another dynamic familiar to many college campuses is the dating scene. Relationships are divided between the "typical random hookup and long-term-boyfriend dating scene." One student claimed that there is a "constant complaint" that "casual dating is virtually unheard of." Students learn to adapt their lives to these small-school hazards and enjoy the wide variety of activities that Centre offers.

Getting Involved

To make up for the problems of being a small school, Centre offers both the opportunity for close friendships and after-school activities that are open to students. Most students are involved in sports, whether through varsity sports or the popular intramural program. Although some sports draw low fan levels, the Centre Colonel fans get "rowdy" at the football and basketball games. Centre's soccer team is also known for both being talented and having "cute guys."

Many students agreed that Centre does not have a particularly active political atmosphere, although it does have the largest chapters of both Democrats and Republicans in the state. Most students are considered mildly conservative, and political activism seems to take the form of private debate or assisting larger campaigns in nearby Lexington. Students did get excited when Centre hosted the vice-presidential debate in 2000 between Sen. Joe Lieberman and Dick Cheney. This brought national attention and hype to Centre's usually calm campus.

Bye-Bye, Danville; Hello, World

One of Centre's strongest and mostly widely praised attributes is its study abroad program. Almost 60% of students study abroad. Every fall and spring trimester, Centre sends 20 students to Regent's College in London and 20 others to study in Strasbourg, France. Many biology majors go to South America during the winter term to see plant and animal life firsthand. Students unanimously praise the study abroad program and recommend that all students who attend Centre take advantage of this opportunity. Centre bends over backward to help students explore the world. One student loved the lack of a financial burden to study abroad—"Centre foots the bill; we pay the plane ticket."

While Centre provides all of the advantages and disadvantages of a small school, its unique study abroad program and strong liberal arts education make it stand out. But what students learn most during their time at Centre is how to develop strong friendships and grow as individuals within a warm community.—*Adam Rein*

FYI

The three best things about attending Centre College are "studying abroad, liquor runs, and the incredible people that populate the place."

The three worst things about attending Centre College are "attempts to curtail Greek excitement, the cliques, the liquor runs."

The three things every student should do before graduating from Centre are "run the Flame, swim in the Norton fountain, and dance on the Deke pool table."

One thing I'd like to have known before coming here is "you need a car!"

University of Kentucky

Address: 100 W.D.
Funkhouser Building;
Lexington, KY 40506
Phone: 606-257-2000
E-mail address:
admissio@pop.uky.edu
Web site URL: www.uky.edu
Founded: 1865
Private or Public: public
Religious affiliation: none
Location: urban
**Undergraduate
enrollment:** 16,841
Total enrollment: 23,540
Percent Male / Female:
49% / 51%
Percent Minority: 8%
Percent African-American:
5%

Percent Asian: 2%
Percent Hispanic: 0.5%
Percent Native-American:
0.5%
**Percent in-state / out-of-
state:** 81% / 19%
Percent Pub HS: NA
Number of Applicants:
8,320
Percent Accepted:
73%
**Percent Accepted who
enroll:** 44%
Entering: 2,681
Transfers: 2,202
Application Deadline:
15 Feb
Mean SAT: NA
Mean ACT: 25

Middle 50% SAT range: NA
Middle 50% ACT range:
22–27
3 Most popular majors:
accounting, biology,
psychology
Retention: 78%
Graduation rate: 48%
On-campus housing:
30%
Fraternities: 15%
Sororities: 15%
Library: 2,800,000
volumes
Tuition and Fees:
$3,782 in; $10,002 out
Room and Board: $3,722
Financial aid, first-year:
53%

Recently, the University of Kentucky set an ambitious goal for itself: to become a top twenty research university. This goal has noticeably reshaped the campus: renovating buildings, reshaping the attitudes of the students, and even restructuring entire departments, causing considerable and often difficult transitions. Yet students seem optimistic about the future of UK. "They are finally getting their act together. Instead of just talking about progress, we're actually seeing some."

Quest for Excellence

The academics of UK have been a major issue, and a major motivator for the University's goal to become a top 20 institution. Since the University stated its goal, students have reported an increase in professor-undergraduate interaction. "Before, the professors only cared about working with graduate students . . . now it seems like professors and undergraduates really work together." UK is divided into five colleges, to which students apply directly: architecture, engineering, arts and sciences, business and economics, or communications. Students say the programs in agriculture, architecture and the

sciences are top-notch, and the pharmacy program is also one of the best in the nation. Students reported that the strongest departments are Communications and Health Sciences, while math and the "hard sciences" like physics and chemistry are the toughest classes. UK has introductory courses ranging in size from 50 to 150 people.

Students from Lexington Community College also take classes at UK, and this is beneficial for many students living in the Lexington area. Students can take general instruction courses at L.C.C. where there is "better interaction with the instructors" and then move on to UK. Many undergraduates also choose UK because of their strong financial aid program. Freshman who do well on the PSAT and become National Merit Finalists can earn a full ride. As a result, more and more eligible students are choosing to accept UK's offer to pay for tuition, room, and board.

There is very little difference between freshmen and upperclassmen on-campus housing at UK. "Upperclassmen are less likely to be in one of the Towers on South campus, but all the dorms are about the same." Still, some students complained that although the housing is about equal for upperclassmen and freshmen, it's all pretty bad. The campus dorms are either single-sex or co-ed by floor and regulations regarding opposite-sex visitation are strictly enforced.

Construction, Construction, Everywhere

In order to achieve their goal to become a top research university, UK embarked on a spree of construction on campus, to the point where it seems like "someone dropped a construction crew and told them to fix everything and build everywhere." Recently completed was the $50 million construction of the WT Young Library, which is one of the "best networked libraries in the entire U.S." However, the construction can be a "nuisance." Some students also complain that certain projects are "really a waste of money." For example, UK has recently started using expensive brick signs that say "University of Kentucky" at all intersections which some students find pointless and annoying.

But the main reason to move off campus, according to students, is the food. "A lot of students complain that they could never possibly eat the amount of food they're charged for on their meal cards," one undergraduate said. Some don't bother with the meal plan at all. Popular off-campus eating options include mostly fast-food restaurants, such as Kentucky Fried Chicken and Long John Silver's. "It's really hard to eat healthy," one student complained.

Not Entirely Greek

The University of Kentucky draws students from over one hundred countries. Students felt the University was very open to diversity. Although some students reported that a Greek stereotype dominates the image of the average student—"the standard frat boys, sorority chicks, jocks etc."—most students felt that this is not exactly the truth. Most non-Greek students did not feel left out at all, and in fact, "some of the office bearers of the Student Body don't belong to any Greek houses."

Back Woods Kind of Guys

Although there is always a Greek event every weekend on campus, there are plenty of other things to do. The party scene is just as big on campus as it is off campus, and very popular. It's also diverse. "Some people are really into drinking and partying every weekend/day, but others do it sparingly, or don't drink at all. There is a wide band of attitudes and beliefs." Still, the cult of moonshine isn't entirely dead, and "lots of back woods kinda guys go here . . . there is a lot of drinking and drugs."

> **"Still, the cult of moonshine isn't entirely dead," and "lots of back woods kinda guys go here . . . there is a lot of drinking and drugs."**

The surroundings offer other options for use of free time. Many students noted the sharp contrast between the city of Lexington and the surrounding hills. "It's more city than country," one junior said of Lexington, "but one of the best things about UK is being able to go just ten miles off-campus and end up on a beautiful hillside or horse farm." Yet, some students rarely leave campus except to go home—"most everything is within three miles of campus. People go to malls, parks, libraries, etc." But for the adventure-seekers, the greater Kentucky offers plenty of escapes from campus: to "Louisville for cool night life, Beckley for skiing, Cumberland for water sports." Students even go to Cincinnati to see either the Bengals or the Reds. "They are all pretty near and quite inexpensive."

And, of course, Basketball

Even outside basketball, UK has a strong athletic tradition. One student wrote that "not only are students and faculty fans, but most of the state is fanatical about UK athletics." Though there may be other sports at the University of Kentucky (there are twenty-two Division I sports) the sport that excites the campus and state the most is obviously basketball. The UK Wildcats have "the best (record) of all the NCAA basketball teams." Spirits at these games are high. Tickets to basketball and football games are free to students, and the games always have huge attendance. Even though many students go to the games, one student complained that "we don't have pep rallies very often which is another issue."

From the shadow of the basketball team, UK's football is really starting to make a name for itself. In 1998, the sophomore quarterback Tim Couch won the Heisman Trophy and was then recruited to play for the Cleveland Browns. Plus, in line with the recent construction on campus, twenty thousand seats have been added to the stadium, making it a circular stadium that seats almost fifty thousand.

When extracurricular energy at UK isn't devoted entirely to basketball, students manage to get involved with other activities. The school newspaper, the *Kentucky Colonel*, covers life both at UK and in Lexington. Political activity among UK students is relatively low except during campus or national elections, when the Young Republicans and Young Democrats hold rallies on campus for their candidates. Other Activities range from waterskiing to UKLUG (Linux Users Group) to outreach programs. Although there are over two hundred organizations on campus, one student complained that the community service is not very popular on campus. "That really bothers me. [There is a] lot of apathy here."

Oh the Places You'll Go

Change is really apparent at UK. "It is really growing," said one student, "and with the new mission to be a top 20 research school, lots of world class research is being done here. You can really go far here if you try." So as UK gets closer and closer to reaching its goal, the question is: What next? —*Nicole Jabaily*

FYI
The three best things about attending the University of Kentucky are "girls . . . man . . . awesome girls; inexpensive living, and the feeling of belonging to UK basketball religion."
The three worst things about attending the University of Kentucky are "no skiing resort nearby even though you see a lot of snow, people prefering Stanford students over you at your job just because you're from UK, and being thought a redneck or hilly-billy."
The three things that every student should do before graduating the University of Kentucky are "get drunk with Bourbon, get bankrupt at Keeneland, and go rafting at Cumberland."
One thing I'd like to have known before coming here is that "the rest of my high school, which is also in Lexington, Kentucky would also be here."

Louisiana

Louisiana State University

Address: 110 Thomas Boyd Hall; Baton Rouge, LA 70803
Phone: 225-388-1175
E-mail address: lsuadmit@lsu.edu
Web site URL: www.lsu.edu
Founded: 1855
Private or Public: public
Religious affiliation: none
Location: urban
Undergraduate enrollment: 24,771
Total enrollment: NA
Percent Male/Female: 47%/53%
Percent Minority: 16%
Percent African-American: 9%

Percent Asian: 4%
Percent Hispanic: 2%
Percent Native-American: 0.5%
Percent in-state/out-of-state: 91%/9%
Percent Pub HS: NA
Number of Applicants: 9,661
Percent Accepted: 82%
Percent Accepted who enroll: 65%
Entering: 5,187
Transfers: 1,322
Application Deadline: 1 May
Mean SAT: NA
Mean ACT: NA

Middle 50% SAT range: NA
Middle 50% ACT range: 21–26
3 Most popular majors: business management, engineering, education
Retention: 83%
Graduation rate: 48%
On-campus housing: NA
Fraternities: 12%
Sororities: 15%
Library: NA
Tuition and Fees: $2,881 in; $7,081 out
Room and Board: $4,130
Financial aid, first-year: NA

LSU students say that when it comes to their school and sports, they bleed purple and gold. In the words of one student—"Football is king here!" Last season when rumors spread that not all students would be guaranteed tickets to the games, there were mini-riots, protests, and demonstrations. Said one student, "Maybe it's a southern thing, maybe it's a Louisiana thing, but that's just how it is."

Academics: Not Always First Priority

Like most big schools, Louisiana offers its students a great deal in terms of academic diversity, with majors spanning the humanities and the sciences. But as many students are quick to say, "Yeah, academics are a priority, but they're not always first priority." Indeed, some students resent what they feel are the school's overly lax academic standards—"It's way too easy to get into LSU. A lot of people

come in that just want to screw around, and that makes it hard for the rest of us." Many hard-core studiers can be found among the ranks of engineering majors, reportedly among the hardest LSU has to offer. Graphic design and photography were described as "considerably less challenging."

But for all students, getting into classes is reportedly a big problem. One senior called the registration process "painful . . . involving lots of time wasted standing in line." Another student exclaimed, "Thank God we only do it twice a year!" Once registered, however, students generally have few complaints. Class sizes were described as "decent," requirements "do-able," and grading "fair—though not uniform throughout majors."

In light of the student body's mammoth proportions, however, one student did lament that it was all too easy for students to slip through the cracks. "TAs do most of the grading so the teacher doesn't really learn how you do work, and the TA doesn't associate a face with the name," he complained. Indeed, in attending such a large school, students commonly complain that the administration is often inefficient and seldom very helpful. Concerning LSU bureaucracy, one student said, "It's hell, as evidenced by the joke told to every arriving freshman who's been given the LSU runaround—you've just taken and passed LSU 1001."

Another student was quick to counter, however, that "professors are genuinely concerned about you and what you learn, if you take the time to approach them." LSU reportedly has an overabundance of instructors from foreign countries, however, which as one student commented, makes for some "interesting classroom experiences." One senior recommended that students should "just ask around and find out who speaks plainly."

The Sophomore Run from Residential Life

One student reported that "the dorms tend to have a high turnover rate." And based on what student say about on-campus housing, it is not hard to see why. An average freshman dorm room was described by one student as "small, ugly," resembling a "mental institution." Strict visitation restrictions and "crazy card access rules" also contributed to students' overall dissatisfaction with residential life; visitors of the opposite sex are not allowed after a certain time, and they must be checked in and escorted by a resident at all times. In spite of the downside to dorm life, however, most students would agree living on campus first year is important in forging friendships and getting a little taste of the typical college experience. But as one student was quick to add—"After first year run—just run away from residential life."

First years can choose from a variety of dorms, which students say all have distinct personalities. One student broke them down into four categories—"There are the honor's dorms, the slacker dorms, the freak dorms, and the frat and sorority dorms." Another student characterized them by gender. "The girl dorms are a bit snobby. Guy dorms are laid back." For girls, East Laville and Evangeline are said to be "awesome"; for guys, top picks include McVoy and West Laville, both "surrounded by all girls' dorms." About Kirby-Smith, a notoriously bad guy dorm, one student commented, "Apparently the inhabitants don't know much about personal hygiene."

Many upperclassmen move into apartments on campus after their first year. Typical accommodations are described as "nice, but small and very expensive." Each comes equipped with its own kitchen, washer/dryer, and living area. The several apartment complexes near campus are also popular options, especially because many of them fall on a city bus route. Buses run every 8 minutes or so, and off-campus dwellers report using them quite frequently in order to get back to campus. One student praised the setup as "very convenient."

"Tiger Town"

Students say that Baton Rouge, or "Tiger Town," as it is affectionately called, "looks more like a town than a city." One sophomore complained, "It's not like Boston or Seattle where it has a huge downtown area and you can walk everywhere. You've got to have a car here—everything's 10 minutes away." And with the dearth of adequate campus parking, owning a car can prove problematic. The school has been making efforts to improve the situation, but as one student pointed out, even this new parking is not always accessible. "They're building new lots all the time, but the lots are out in Egypt compared to where your classes are."

> **"Everybody loves Mike the Tiger."**

School food was described as "awful." Students out looking for alternatives can find them at any one of the numerous local eateries. Don's Seafood, Nympha's, and Pasttimes (pizza) are among the more popular student choices. The student union also offers a variety of fast food places as well, with everything from McDonald's to Chick Fil-A and Pizza Hut.

"Getting Sloppy"

Drinking is a popular pastime at LSU, especially on weekends when "getting sloppy" (local slang for "getting drunk") is the thing to do. "It's involved in about 75% of what we do," said one student. Popular local bars include the Caterie and the Varsity. On campus as well, alcohol abounds at parties thrown by frats and in the dorms. Students also rave about street parties, when everyone living on a certain street "closes off this street just off-campus, and everyone from LSU is invited to party out in the street all night." One such street party, traditionally held around Halloween, is especially fun, students say. During the fall, students spend their time hopping from tailgate party to tailgate party before and after football games. In fact, football game days are the only days when students are allowed to drink openly on campus. All other days of the year, students say, on-campus drinkers risk the wrath of the administration. But generally, the school tends to be "tougher on the frats because of a high-profile student death related to alcohol a couple years ago."

When asked, LSU students agree that their school merits its reputation as a party school. Interestingly though, in light of this school-wide penchant to party and drink, it is surprising to note that most students would also agree that non-drinkers "don't really feel so out-of-it on campus." Many students would say that you don't have to drink at parties— "there's only pressure to drink within the Greek system—otherwise those who don't want to drink don't have to." Another student added, "I don't drink, and I have lots of fun. You can go out or not go out. It's all about the crowd you prefer."

Certainly the Greeks do dominate aspects of campus life, but those students who don't care much for the party or frat scene can find their kicks in any number of other areas. People with cars will often take road trips to New Orleans, a massive "breeding ground of culture," only an hour's drive away. Locally, the music scene is a major draw. Many local hangouts feature live bands 7 nights a week. "That good old grunge sound tends to be pretty popular here," said one student. "This is one city rebelling against the mainstream."

But closer to the mainstream is where most LSU students would fall, politically. The student body tends to be very conservative. Said one student, "Sure we have our crazies and left-wing nuts, but overall, we're pretty conventional and tradition-oriented." In accordance with the school's very political atmosphere, recent campus visitors have included former president George Bush Sr. and William F. Buckley Jr. One student even recalled that in his political science classes, three former state governors delivered guest lectures in the time frame of one semester. The typical student was described as a white, middle to upper class Republican, with most coming to LSU from within the state. One senior described the typical student wardrobe—"Most people are from Louisiana, so odds are they are wearing Structure or Abercrombie. And girls love those black pants."

Rooting for the Home Team

But politically conservative or not, one area in which all LSU students can stand united is in the sports arena. Students will often rave about their Saturday nights in Death Valley, a popular nickname for Tiger Stadium, where students go to watch football games en masse. One senior described the atmosphere at games— "LSU fans are the craziest I have ever seen. Anytime we score a touchdown, the student section throws their cups in the air whether they're full or empty. The band sits by the student section and plays and dances with the students—it's insane!" Before every football game, the cheerleaders parade Mike the Tiger, the school mascot, around the stadium in his cage and try to make him growl. All students agree he is the symbol of school unity, a sentiment that moved one student to exclaim, "Everybody loves Mike the Tiger. And if you ask every person, you'll get 30,000 different opinions on everything except that."

Football is undoubtedly the dominant sport, but other team sports enjoy their own measures of success as well. The basketball and baseball teams are particularly popular and generally perform very well at the national level. The LSU basketball team was ranked 15th in the nation last year, and the baseball team, after winning 4 national titles in the 1990s, ranked third.

Sports are definitely a high priority for

students at this school. Most report that their free time is spent either going to the various games or playing sports games themselves. School intramurals see high student participation, with rugby and flag football being especially popular.

Other school extracurriculars with mass appeal include the LSU student government and the school's daily newspaper, the *Daily Reveille*. Many students report working part-time on the side as well.

And as at most large schools, students can find a niche virtually anywhere, and no two students will have the same college experience. This variety is what appealed most to one student, who praised LSU's "multitude of atmospheres." "You can find virtually any type of environment on campus—a study environment, a social one, quiet, loud, fun, serious—it's all there at the same time. That's what makes LSU such a great place." Prospectives would do well to look for their own niches and would undoubtedly be able to find one at LSU. —*Jane H. Hong*

FYI

The three best things about attending Louisiana State are "the school spirit, the beautiful campus, and the support from the Baton Rouge community."

The three worst things about attending Louisiana State are "the parking lots that get taken over by football fans, the gross dorms, how registration is a hassle."

The three things every student should do before graduating from Louisiana State are "eat at the Chimes, sit on the Parade Grounds at night, go to at least one football game."

One thing I wish I had known before coming here is "you're just a number—no one is going to help you find out all the rules and regulations."

Tulane University

Address: 6823 St. Charles Avenue; New Orleans, LA 70118-5680
Phone: 504-865-5731
E-mail address: undergrad.admission@tulane.edu
Web site URL: www.tulane.edu
Founded: 1834
Private or Public: private
Religious affiliation: none
Location: urban
Undergraduate enrollment: 7,163
Total enrollment: 11,438
Percent Male/Female: 47%/53%
Percent Minority: 13%

Percent African-American: 4%
Percent Asian: 5%
Percent Hispanic: 3%
Percent Native-American: 0.5%
Percent in-state/out-of-state: 34%/66%
Percent Pub HS: 65%
Number of Applicants: 8,388
Percent Accepted: 78%
Percent Accepted who enroll: 25%
Entering: 1,632
Transfers: 164
Application Deadline: 15 Jan
Mean SAT: 651 V, 640 M
Mean ACT: 29

Middle 50% SAT range: 600–703 V, 591–690 M
Middle 50% ACT range: NA
3 Most popular majors: social sciences, engineering, business
Retention: 90%
Graduation rate: 78%
On-campus housing: 90%
Fraternities: 16%
Sororities: 19%
Library: 1,300,050 volumes
Tuition and Fees: $25,390 in; $25,390 out
Room and Board: $6,908
Financial aid, first-year: 62%

When Tulane University initially built its library, there was one slight miscalculation. The engineers did not account for the fact that there were going to be books in the library. As a result, the building has sunk somewhat with the weight of the books. Although their library now leans slightly, Tulane students are still able to take advantage of the space to study. Tulane students work hard to meet tough academic standards, but they also take plenty of time to enjoy their community in New Orleans.

The Curriculum

Academically, Tulane has several colleges to suit the academic needs of its undergraduates. These include the University College, designed to accommodate older students returning to school; Tulane College for men; and Newcomb College for women. Although male and female students apply to different colleges within the university, this separation only applies to the registration process. All academic classes are open to all students regardless of their particular college. Students interested in more specialized programs can also apply to the engineering school or architecture schools.

Students are required to fulfill numerous general education requirements. One undergrad noted that, "despite these requirements, many students are able to use AP credits to get out of them." Those in the specialized schools at Tulane are required to take core classes within their respective colleges along with electives, which are taken alongside classmates in Tulane-Newcomb. Students declare majors in their sophomore year. In terms of class size, some introductory classes can be large, but most classes enroll about 20 students. As one student noted, "the administration is good about keeping classes small." Tulane students say they generally are content with their professors, although some dislike the stringent attendance policy enforced in class. Of her foreign-language class, one student said, "you are allowed three misses, and I've already missed five. For every miss after those first three, one point gets taken off your final grade!" Although some students feel "bogged down by the work," many report that the academic program at Tulane is "conquerable."

Swinging Social Scene

Although Tulane is often considered as one of the best universities, academically, in the Southeast, some students believe that the social life is "much more important." According to one student, "In New Orleans and on campus, drinking rules the social activities here." At Tulane, students are allowed to drink in their dorm rooms. One undergrad reported that the legal drinking age is not always an obstacle because "fake IDs are easy to get and the bars usually don't care. I went to a bar with the ID of someone who looked nothing like me and I got in, no problem."

The Greek tradition is strong at Tulane. "Frat parties are open to whoever wants to go, although I think they are pretty lame," said one undergrad. Social activities, such as those planned by the Tulane University Campus Productions (TUCP), an organization that sponsors large screenings of movies and live shows, gets rave reviews from students. Students can also head over to the University Center (UC), which houses a pub, arcade, radio and TV stations, and various restaurants. Recently, Kevin Spacey and Spike Lee came to speak on-campus.

New Orleans Fun

Of course, many students are quick to point out that there is always New Orleans itself "if you want to have a good time." For $1.25, students can take the St. Charles streetcar right into the city. Many students find themselves "drinking the night away" in the French Quarter ("the Quarter") on famous Bourbon Street. Restaurants abound in New Orleans, although some tend to be expensive. Students on a tighter budget, "can always chow some food from Cucos," explained one undergrad. Some upperclassmen have cars, but the high cost of a parking permit and the cheap trolley fare into town deters most students from keeping a car on campus. One cannot talk about New Orleans and not mention Mardi Gras. The celebrations last about two weeks. There are daily parades before Mardi Gras and nine of them on Mardi Gras. People from all over the country come to New Orleans to try to collect beads, which is "almost always accomplished by stripping." "Alcohol flows freely and people go wild."

Tulane students agree that dating is prevalent on campus. As one student reported, "There are some brutally hot people here!" New Orleans also offers plenty for romantics to do, like taking "a carriage ride around the French Quarter." One student added that, "all of the dorms had sex orientation, but they ran out of free condoms."

Several students complained that Tulane lacks a diverse student body. According to one student, "it looks like all the guys just walked out of Structure, and all the girls just came out of Express." Another student noted that "there seems to be a lack of African-American students and it bothers me more and more."

Nightmare Housing

Housing at Tulane draws mixed reviews. Freshman living is reportedly the worst. Upon seeing her freshman dorm, one student said, "No way! No! I'm not living here." The two primary freshman dorms are Sharp and Monroe. Just mentioning these names provoked one student to exclaim, "Nightmare!" Collectively, the two dorms are labeled "the projects" and complaints center on the age and poor maintenance of the buildings. Specific complaints about the current state of these dorms include "experiencing projectile vomit on the walls" and "calcium deposits in the showers that causes them to flood." In addition, one student reported that "the elevators are always broken and I live on the twelfth floor!"

> **Tulane students work hard to meet tough academic standards, but they also take plenty of time to enjoy their community in New Orleans."**

There are, however, some popular dorms on-campus. The honors dorm, Butler, is considered quite "respectable," and the all-women's dorm, Josephine Louise, is "just beautiful." Mayer Residences consist of suites and some super singles and students refer to Mayer as being "superb." Willow Hall, which includes two special projects, was opened this year. These projects are the Urban Village and Leadership Village. Students get into these "villages" by application and once a member, they can benefit from classes that are offered specifically for them. "Some people have two-story rooms" in Willow that are "incredibly luxurious and beautiful." Students report sophomore dorms are much

cleaner and more expansive. The dorms have air-conditioning, although one student said that in some cases, it was "not functional." RAs live on each hall, although students report that "RAs are not very strict" and the regulations are "fairly relaxed." Despite the poor quality of freshman dorms, social life is much better compared to upperclassmen dorms. Many upperclassmen choose to live off campus, and often find cheaper rates than the cost of university housing.

Food at Tulane is reportedly "low quality, though they try hard," said one undergrad. Another added that the dining services at Tulane are run by the Marriott, "so it's respectable." There are currently five campus dining facilities: the UC, der Rathskeller, Bruff Commons, the Drawing Board and TU Deli. UC has Taco Bell, Subway and Pizza Hut and Bruff Commons has Sbarro among the options they present. All freshmen must purchase a meal plan through the university. Though one student noted that, "the dining halls are on par with the best high school cafeterias in the nation," others complain about the cost of the meal plan. Meals are purchased before school starts and "food is really pricey." The dining hall hours have become a lot more flexible in the recent years. Deli and Taco Bell are open until 11 PM and Bruff Commons serves a Late Night Meal from 10.30 PM till midnight which is popular among students. There are vegetarian options, but "it seems to be the same veggie thing every day," said one undergrad. Though the dining halls are clean, one upperclassman said the dining hall "is definitely not someplace you could sit in all day and hang out because it is a very enclosed and drab sort of atmosphere."

The Garden District

The Tulane campus is not situated in the heart of New Orleans, but in the neighboring Garden District. The Garden District is "the wealthy, beautiful part of the city" and home to famed author Anne Rice, whom Tulane students often report seeing on campus. The campus is divided into two different areas: "The front half is pretty, with open grassy areas and Romanesque and Gothic architecture. The back half, though, looks like trashy '70s."

Many undergrads consider the campus beautiful, but some feel "there is too much construction going on." "Bring a bike," suggested one undergrad. "Roller blades are not the best here because the sidewalks are all torn up." Students say that they feel moderately safe on campus. As one student said, "You can't go out by yourself at night. You go five blocks and you are in the ghetto. It's as if the Garden District is a facade of mansions hiding what is really there."

Tulane students also find some time to get involved in extracurricular activities. Students cite the service organization CACTUS, as well as various religious organizations, particularly Jewish groups, as very strong and active.

Sporting events are fairly popular. Although Tulane usually has "sucky teams," according to one student, the recent emergence of Tulane football, which capped an undefeated season in 1998 with a Liberty Bowl victory, has drawn notice around the country. Football games themselves are quite an event. The games are played in the New Orleans Superdome and "ac-

cording to some southern tradition, everybody dresses up for them." The football games are popular, with tickets included in Tulane's tuition. School spirit runs high, with the new school mascot, Riptide, the pelican, leading the way. For those who do not want to commit to varsity sports, there are plenty of club sports and intramurals for students. Reilly Recreation Center offers students a variety of choices including yoga and dance classes, indoor and outdoor pools, squash and tennis courts, and a fitness center.

Tulane definitely holds up its reputation as a party school, but students also stress strong academics. Students from the North are particularly struck by Tulane's southern charm. As one senior reflected, "My years have been truly awesome and I have met a lot of really great people from all over the world. I don't know what makes one college better than another, but Tulane has a great mix of being in a really cool city, yet having its own campus at the same time." —*Jeff Kaplow and Staff*

FYI
The three best things about attending Tulane are "the location, excellent faculty who give personal attention, and Mardi Gras."
The three worst things about attending Tulane are "freshman dorms, the Greek system is emphasized too much, and lack of student community/ camaraderie."
The three things that every student should do before graduating from Tulane are "attend Mardi Gras celebrations, get involved in All-nighter events, explore New Orleans' restaurants."
One thing I would like to have known before coming here is "how bad and unpredictable the weather is."

Maine

Bates College

Address: 23 Campus Avenue; Lewiston, ME 04240-6098
Phone: 207-786-6000
E-mail address: admissions@bates.edu
Web site URL: www.bates.edu
Founded: 1855
Private or Public: private
Religious affiliation: none
Location: small city
Undergraduate enrollment: 1,706
Total enrollment: 1,706
Percent Male/Female: 49%/51%
Percent Minority: 8%

Percent African-American: 2%
Percent Asian: 4%
Percent Hispanic: 1%
Percent Native-American: 0.5%
Percent in-state/out-of-state: 12%/88%
Percent Pub HS: 60%
Number of Applicants: 3,860
Percent Accepted: 33%
Percent Accepted who enroll: 38%
Entering: 479
Transfers: 1
Application Deadline: 15 Jan
Mean SAT: 660 V, 660 M

Mean ACT: NA
Middle 50% SAT range: 630–700 V, 630–700 M
Middle 50% ACT range: NA
3 Most popular majors: psychology, biology, English
Retention: 93%
Graduation rate: 87%
On-campus housing: 100%
Fraternities: NA
Sororities: NA
Library: 499,777 volumes
Tuition and Fees: 32,650 total expenses
Room and Board: NA
Financial aid, first-year: 44%

"The professors are more available than most students' parents" said one undergrad, "we get to see more snow than the Olympic ski team" added another and "you can see the world, travelling to a different country every year, and make up a major for it" noted a third. All three are referring to the opportunities they have at Bates College in Lewiston, Maine.

Tons of Options

Students cite "professors' commitment to each individual regardless of class size" as the most exciting aspect of Bates academics. Professors teach all classes and there are no TAs. "I love seeing professors outside of class who know me by name and being able to discuss topics other than class with them" said one sophomore. Biology, English and political science are regarded among the strongest departments. Most students agree that

neuroscience and biochemistry are the hardest majors.

Students can also choose to have a secondary concentration, the Bates name for a minor. Although secondary concentrations are not yet available in all departments, students are happy with this aspect of the curriculum, which was added several years ago. The toughest classes are organic chemistry and "Math Camp," whereas intro-level geology and psychology are the popular gut courses. Most classes tend to enroll between 15 and 25 although their sizes can vary, according to major. One senior said, "I've had theatre classes with 8 people, and intro psych with over 100." Students report that Bates offers "tons" of special programs. "Go away to a foreign country your freshman year! I went to Japan, with no prior study in Japanese," recommended one sophomore. Finally, Bates offers a "3–2" program in which students get their

B.A.s in engineering in three years at Bates, and go on to get Masters in two years at either Dartmouth or Columbia.

Bates students are required to take five humanities courses, with three of the five relating to each other in a "cluster." Three social science courses are also required along with three science classes, two of which must be related and one in quantitative reasoning. Students can use AP credits to fulfill some of these requirements. There is also a four-credit physical education requirement that can be fulfilled by playing a varsity sport or with classes such as Scuba Diving, Swing Dancing or Bowling. Students refer to these requirements as "pretty easy to fulfill, important and not so strict." With regard to grading, "most professors have forgotten the first letter of the alphabet" said one student. Another one added that "there's this fairytale about someone graduating with a 4.0 long long ago, but that is all it is, a fairy tale."

The Best Idea Since Sliced Bread

As one student defined it, Bates' Short Term program, which occurs during the last week in April and the month of May, is the "best thing since sliced bread." Bates students choose from a wide array of opportunities in selecting and planning Short Terms. Students must attend two short terms during their time at Bates, in which they take one class that meets three to five times a week. Some majors have required short term classes such as "Cell Hell" for biology majors. This is a cellular molecular biology class that meets four times a week and has two lab periods. Most students, however, get to leave campus for Short Term. Last year, students went to Jamaica for African-American studies, to Sri Lanka for an anthropology class, to Utah to study Native American art, and to Mexico to study women in Mexican nationalism. Others stayed in Lewiston for International Debt negotiations or Perspectives on Education. Batseys refer to the Short Term as "the best thing about Bates, academically." One junior adds "the class offerings *rock* and it's *such* a fun 5 weeks—reward for all the hard work over the year."

Food and Sleep: the Necessities of Life

Most Bates students choose to live on campus, where they have guaranteed housing for four years. They can choose to live in dorms or in one of the thirteen on-campus Victorian "houses." Houses are quieter and smaller than dorms and they provide a more intimate and family-like atmosphere. Freshmen are grouped in Freshman Centers, clusters of usually 12 freshmen and their Junior Advisor (JA) who live in the same section in a house or dorm and share the faculty advisor. "JAs definitely want to be your friend; mine is now one of my closest friends" said one sophomore. The many housing options available after freshman year are "co-ed, single-sex, chem-free dorms/houses, theme houses, mixed with freshmen or not mixed with freshmen." It's "almost exclusively seniors who live off campus." "The Village" is the newest dorm built in 1994 and it's "like a hotel." It consists of three separate buildings and a social hall in the center and has "awesome" rooms, some of which even have lofts.

> **"Short-term is the best idea since sliced bread."**

Students are really happy with dining hall food. You are either "on or off" the meal plan and "if you're on, you can go as often as you want and eat as much as you want." They refer to it as "the best college food I've had; huge selection and good quality." Commons, the main dining hall, is the center of campus life and a "great place to socialize." One problem is that there is not enough space for all the students, so it is "way overcrowded." "Just don't go on peak hours and things are fine" recommends one student. The Den is a campus restaurant that hosts "Terrace Parties" sponsored by various student groups. The student-run on-campus coffeehouse, the Ronj, named for its orange walls, is a popular hangout at late night hours and on Saturday afternoons. Although students usually don't leave campus to eat, Chopsticks receives credit as a great restaurant off-campus.

Paul Newman and St. Patrick

The administration "tries not to get involved with alcohol but encourages non-alcohol related activities." Party hosts need to have permission from the administration in the form of "blue slips" and they are also required to check IDs. "Underage people still drink all the time, but they do have to be slightly more smart about it." Drug use on campus consists mostly of marijuana. Some popular parties of the school year are the Halloween Party, the 80s Party and "Lick-It" which is sponsored by the GLBA—the Gay Lesbian Bisexual Alliance. Most students' comments on Lick-It are along the lines of "it's *crazy*" and "it is a "must" every year." Random hook-ups are quite common at Bates. "You're either randomly hooking up or you are married" says one senior. "It's cold, people need to stay warm" notes another. The President's Gala, a formal dinner-dance held by the college president for students and faculty, is another popular event. "The concert series are also great: free jazz, classical, and types of music you've never heard before," says one sophomore. Recent performers at Bates have included Indigo Girls, Wyclef Jean, Dar Williams and Ani DiFranco. On Paul Newman Day, students try to drink 24 beers in 24 hours and carry on their normal activities, usually unsuccessfully. This tradition is derived from the movie *Cool Hand Luke*, in which Paul Newman had to eat 50 eggs in one hour. On St. Patrick's Day, the rugby team sponsors the "Puddle Jump," which involves getting dunked in the ice-covered Lake Andrews.

Outside of Class

"Everyone does something" at Bates. The most popular extracurricular activities are the Outing Club, which has "a ton of members" and various sports. "Debate is elite" and volunteering opportunities are made possible through the community service house and several school-sponsored organizations. Some of the more unusual groups are Strange Bedfellows, an improv comedy group, and Club Meat, a meat appreciation club to counter the vocal vegetarian population. Writing for the weekly *Bates Student* or hosting a radio show on WRBC, the campus radio station, are among the other possibilities. "You can really do anything, and if it's not here yet, it's easy to start it and get funding."

In its first few years as a varsity sport, crew is one of the most popular teams. People also enjoy soccer games because the soccer team buys beer for the fans before games. Students are generally proud of Bates athletics. Besides varsity sports, a lot of people enjoy the laid-back atmosphere of intramurals. "Everybody is working out all the time," one student said. The Underhill Ice Arena, completed in 1995, includes an ice rink and the Davis Fitness Center with new cardiovascular equipment. Merill Gym has weights, squash and racquetball courts and a "great" indoor pool.

Students find the Bates campus "really pretty with red brick buildings and lots of trees." In the center lies "the Puddle" (Lake Andrews), the scene for the famous "Puddle Jump." Pettingill Hall, the new building for the social sciences, is "gorgeous with waterfalls in the 3-story glass atrium overlooking Lake Andrews and state-of-the-art with tons of computers and comfy places to study." One student referred to it as the "most incredible building I've seen on any college campus." Contrary to students' positive feelings about their campus, many believe that the area around campus *sucks*." There is "*no* reason to do *anything* in Lewiston, besides go to CVS or Walmart." Most students refer to Lewiston as "the worst aspect of Bates." Portland and Freeport, both 40 minutes away, "are a blast but they are somewhat of a commitment." Students agree that it helps to have a car or know someone who does; a lot of upperclassmen have cars.

Although the Bates student mostly consists of "fit, preppy, friendly kids looking like models in the LL Bean catalogue," diversity has been increasing in the recent years. Regardless of background, Bates students share a similar trait. "Everyone's friendly here, you can walk through the dorms, find an open door and go meet people" noted one junior. Most Batseys agree that this friendly atmosphere, various academic offerings, and fun traditions such as the Puddle Jump and Paul Newman Day "make the trip up to Lewiston, Maine worthwhile." —*Engin Yenidunya*

FYI

The three best things about attending Bates are "academic calendar (so many vacations, Short Term), friendly atmosphere on campus, there's always someone I can bum a cigarette off."

The three worst things about attending Bates are "New Englanders that can't find Texas on a map, we see more snow than the Olympic ski team, and Lewiston."

The three things that every student should do before graduating from Bates are "try the Puddle Jump, complete Newman Day, attend Lick-It."

One thing I would like to have known before coming here is "small schools are small and although it can be a huge benefit, there are also some consequences."

Bowdoin College

Address: 5000 College Station; Brunswick, ME 04011
Phone: 207-725-3100
E-mail address: admissions-lit@plar.bowdoin.edu
Web site URL: www.bowdoin.edu
Founded: 1794
Private or Public: private
Religious affiliation: none
Location: suburban
Undergraduate enrollment: 1,600
Total enrollment: 1,600
Percent Male / Female: 48% / 52%
Percent Minority: 13%

Percent African-American: 2%
Percent Asian: 7%
Percent Hispanic: 3%
Percent Native-American: 0.5%
Percent in-state / out-of-state: 86% / 14%
Percent Pub HS: 59%
Number of Applicants: 3,942
Percent Accepted: 32%
Percent Accepted who enroll: 37%
Entering: 464
Transfers: 33
Application Deadline: 1 Jan
Mean SAT: 670 V, 670 M

Mean ACT: NA
Middle 50% SAT range: 640–720 V, 640–710 M
Middle 50% ACT range: NA
3 Most popular majors: government / legal studies, biology, history
Retention: 92%
Graduation rate: 84%
On-campus housing: 100%
Fraternities: NA
Sororities: NA
Library: 870,000 volumes
Tuition and Fees: $25,890 in; $25,890 out
Room and Board: $6,760
Financial aid, first-year: 40%

It's two o'clock in the morning and you have nothing to do. Where do you go? If you are a Bowdoin College student, you take a late-night trip to the Freeport L. L. Bean outlet, which is open 24 hours a day and serves free coffee, in addition to having the latest in sleeping bags, tents, and other camping equipment. At Bowdoin, a small liberal arts college in Maine, students take advantage of a strong academic program set against a beautiful New England backdrop.

Academics with a Personal Touch

Bowdoin offers strong programs in both the sciences and the humanities. The environmental science program is renowned, as is the government/legal studies program.

Students are generally "hardworking," and one said he doesn't "know anyone who isn't a double major or working on an honors project." Bowdoin also provides special programs for particularly directed students, including a five-year J.D. program, in which participants spend three at Bowdoin and two at Columbia Law School.

In order to graduate, everyone must complete two courses in each of four distributional groups: natural sciences, social sciences, humanities, and non-Eurocentric studies. "You do it by accident," said one student; freshmen shouldn't worry since they will probably complete their requirements "without even trying" by senior year. Students must take "nine classes, more or less," within their major, and though they aren't required to complete a senior project, many students choose to do a project for honors in their major.

Professors switch classes every semester, so it is often specific professors who are popular rather than particular classes. All classes are taught by professors, who have a reputation for being friendly and interested in their students. "I've had dinner and lunch at my profs' houses and they've thrown parties and other things," reported one senior. Class sizes are usually pretty small, which helps to foster an environment where personal attention is valued.

School-Run Frats

Because the last of Bowdoin's fraternities was phased out in the spring of 2000, much of campus social life now centers around the new social houses, which one student called "basically school-run frats." Each of the six freshman dorms is affiliated with one of the six social houses, which is "a great way for freshmen to meet a variety of upperclassmen." Parties can be either campus-wide or for affiliated students only. Upperclassmen also party in campus apartments and off-campus houses and local bars. There is an on-campus pub that regularly brings in bands and other entertainment.

> "Nearly everyone is from New England."

Other campus-wide activities include movies every weekend and lectures every Friday. However, one student complained that "most social alternatives end when the parties start." Both Brunswick and nearby Portland offer a variety of restaurants, but Boston, the nearest big city, is a few hours away. One student called Portland "not huge, but cute," which makes it a popular weekend destination for students. Cars are "common" and can be parked on campus for a few dollars a semester.

Housing Choices

All freshmen live in the Bricks, six brick dorms located around the Quad, mostly in two-room doubles and triples. The Bricks are coed, with mixed single-sex and coed halls. Senior residential advisors live on each floor. After freshman year, students have a lot of housing options, including dorms, social houses, and school-owned apartments. Many end up living in Coles Tower, by far "the tallest building on campus," in which students live with as few as 4 and as many as 16 of their closest friends. Students who want their own kitchens can live in the campus apartments, and non-drinkers have Wellness House, a dorm that is substance-free and has quiet hours. In addition, lots of upperclassmen live off campus, either in Brunswick apartments or houses, "because it is cheaper."

The majority of Bowdoin students spend their junior year studying elsewhere, either in a foreign country or in a different part of the United States. "They have a ton of programs," raved one student, including everything from engineering exchanges with Caltech, Dartmouth, and Columbia to joint programs with fellow Maine colleges Colby and Bates that can take you as far away as South Africa

Good Eats

Most students give Bowdoin's food a high rating. There is "lots of veggie stuff," and at the beginning of every year the school treats its students to a traditional dinner of Maine lobster. The dining halls are "all newly renovated and nice." Freshmen are on a full meal plan, but upperclassmen have the option of choosing a plan with fewer meals or having a declining balance. Students can also use their dining hall points at on-campus convenience stores.

Extracurricular Both Inside and Outside

The Outing Club is Bowdoin's largest student organization and "sponsors four or five trips every weekend," including overnights and full weekend trips. They also rent out camping equipment to students, including everything from kayaks and life jackets to tents. While it might be the largest club, the Outing Club is by no means the only thing happening in Bowdoin's extracurricular scene. "It seems like there is a club for everything," remarked one student. Bowdoin has its own radio station, which features alternatives to mainstream popular music, and its own cable television network, which airs a soap opera called *The Tower* and televises sports games. For aspiring journalists, there is the *Bowdoin Orient*, which is published weekly.

Bowdoin athletics are part of NCAA Division III and definitely "a big thing on campus." Most students participate in some form of athletics, whether at the varsity, club, or intramural level. "Every social house has its own intramural team and so do some of the freshmen dorms." There are also pickup games of volleyball and basketball almost every weekend at the gym. During the chilly Maine winters, many students flock to watch Polar Bear hockey, the school's most popular spectator sport, along with soccer and club rugby—especially when facing the school's rivals, Bates and Colby.

A Lack of Diversity but Abundance of Tradition

Diversity is not Bowdoin's strongest point. The college has a "mostly white campus," and "nearly everyone is from New En-gland." One student described his classmates as "faux crunchy," and there are a ton of people clad in Patagonia and North Face during the Maine winters. As for the lack of diversity, one student said he "is not too bothered. It is Maine after all."

Bowdoin does, however, have its share of history and tradition. The school was founded in 1794, "as an alternative for students who didn't want to go to Harvard." Harriet Beecher Stowe wrote *Uncle Tom's Cabin* at this small liberal arts college, and both Nathaniel Hawthorne and Henry Wadsworth Longfellow rank on its roster of famous alumni. In the very recent past, Bowdoin has undergone a multitude of changes, including a new science center, converting to the social house system, and welcoming a new college president for the 2001–2002 academic year. With every new addition, Bowdoin has proved that the college can keep pace with the future without losing sight of its past.
—*Pamela Boykoff*

FYI

The three best things about attending Bowdoin are "the location, the people, the inexpensive off-campus housing on the ocean."

The three worst things about attending Bowdoin are "a lack of sunlight in the winter, academically sub-par prep school kids, half of the freshman floors are single-sex."

The three things that every student should do before graduating from Bowdoin are "go to L. L. Bean at two in the morning, go to Popham Beach, and visit Arcadia National Park."

One thing I'd like to have known before coming here is "how useful bringing a car can be for easier access to Maine's resources."

Colby College

Address: 4800 Mayflower Hill, Lunder House; Waterville, ME 04901	**Percent Asian:** 5%	**Middle 50% SAT range:** 610–690 V,
Phone: 207-872-3168	**Percent Hispanic:** 2%	610–700 M
E-mail address: admissions@colby.edu	**Percent Native-American:** 0.5%	**Middle 50% ACT range:** 26–30
Web site URL: www.colby.edu	**Percent in-state / out-of-state:** 11%/89%	**3 Most popular majors:** biology, English, economics
Founded: 1813	**Percent Pub HS:** 61%	**Retention:** 91%
Private or Public: private	**Number of Applicants:** 4,363	**Graduation rate:** 89%
Religious affiliation: none	**Percent Accepted:** 33%	**On-campus housing:** 100%
Location: small city	**Percent Accepted who enroll:** 34%	**Fraternities:** NA
Undergraduate enrollment: 1,764	**Entering:** 489	**Sororities:** NA
Total enrollment: 1,764	**Transfers:** 10	**Library:** 924,900 volumes
Percent Male / Female: 48%/52%	**Application Deadline:** 15 Jan	**Tuition and Fees:** 32,750 total expenses
Percent Minority: 11%	**Mean SAT:** 660 V, 660 M	**Room and Board:** NA
Percent African-American: 3%	**Mean ACT:** 28	**Financial aid, first-year:** 39%

"**M**aine—the Way Life Should Be." It's a popular T-shirt slogan in the state of Maine, and students at Colby seem to agree. Colby kids speak with enthusiasm about lots of things: their professors, their campus, and most of all, their fellow students. "I have never felt more at home than I do here," raves one sophomore. "I actually get homesick for Colby when I'm on vacation at my real home." What is it about Colby that inspires such affection? There seem to be several answers to this question.

Despite chilly winters and perpetual student consumption of hot chocolate, this small liberal arts college is known for providing, as one student explains, a "warm, comfortable atmosphere for students who are serious about learning how to think and learning how to live." Colby's small size (about 450–500 a class) encourages students to form a close-knit community, which allows "tons of opportunities to not only get involved, but take on positions of leadership," and intimate class settings with professors described as "both personal and personable." The secluded campus in Waterville, Maine, is "one of Colby's best attributes," featuring redbrick Georgian architecture, duck ponds, and

sprawling lawns that "look beautiful in every season." Another student pointed out that, "from the leaf-pile frolicking in the fall, to the first snowball fight of the winter, to the pickup Frisbee games in spring, you cannot help but love this New England atmosphere." Even those from the West Coast find the Maine appeal hard to deny.

Getting the Job Done

While some report that "it's definitely possible to slack off here and still get by," most Colby students are committed to making the most of their learning opportunities. One junior noted that "if you're not self-motivated, which most people here are, then the professors will motivate you. They have a way of doing that—it's almost eerie." Academics in general at Colby, like the students, are described as "fairly well-rounded." Students give the English, political science, and psychology departments particularly high marks, and developments in the science curriculum have many students talking. Colby also has the Olin Science Center, which boasts state-of-the-art laboratories equipped with the latest technology, a research greenhouse, computer classrooms, a new science library, and laboratories designed for collaborative student-faculty research. The biology department has also enjoyed a long-standing tradition of excellence.

Colby has a somewhat unique set of course requirements that draws comments ranging from "no big deal—it's stuff you'd take anyway" to "confusing and a pain in the butt." Courses are divided into six "Areas," and students must complete one credit in all but Area V, in which two credits are required. Area I encompasses the arts; Area II, historical studies; Area III, literature; Area IV consists of classes in quantitative reasoning; Area V, the natural sciences, and one of the two required credits must be a class that involves laboratory work; and Area VI covers the social sciences. Other requirements include one course that covers issues of diversity, and some feel that this requirement is a "lame attempt on the part of the administration to compensate for the fact that our school is rather homogeneous." The physical education requirement has been recently revised, and now involves students participating in Colby's "Wellness Program." This program requires students to complete four credits, which can be met by participating in wellness seminars, fitness classes, varsity athletics, or club sports. Starting with the Class of 2002, students have to fulfill their wellness requirement in their freshman year. "Rumor has it if you don't, then you set up chairs for graduation but I am not sure if that is actually true."

Students are expected to declare a major by the end of freshman year, but a sophomore cautions that "this stresses too many people out unnecessarily—it's really easy just to fill out 'Undeclared.'" Unique to Colby is the "Jan Plan," which gets very high marks among the student body. The Jan Plan is a break from the traditional semester system during the month of January, when students can pursue personal projects of interest, take classes for full credit, intern with local businesses, and even travel nationally or abroad. While the school offers a wide range of courses, some students complain that the offerings are "too traditional." But most feel that what they sacrifice in terms of class diversity by attending a small school pales in comparison to the benefits: intimate classes, individual attention,

and a strong sense of belonging in an academic community.

A Winter Wonderland

While the strong academic program is certainly a draw, most students would agree that the campus life is the best part of Colby. Students describe their peers as "friendly and outgoing," and "fun-seeking, rugged types." Most Colby kids are fond of the outdoors, and are thrilled to take advantage of their location by going skiing, sledding, or hiking. Prior to the start of freshman year, many students participate in COOT (Colby Outdoor Outing Trips), which are described as a great way to meet people and assimilate into the Colby community. The Outing Club is one of Colby's largest and most popular organizations; it offers expeditions such as backpacking along the scenic Maine coast, loans equipment to all interested students, and even maintains a 17-mile stretch of the Appalachian Trail. One junior remarked gratefully that, "if I didn't have the Outing Club, I don't know what I'd do. It keeps me sane." Indeed, it appears that to be truly happy at Colby, one must appreciate the natural part of the outdoors and not expect too much else from outside the campus borders.

Waterville does inspire some affection for its "quaint country stores" and "New England charm," but received generally low marks for catering to student needs and providing nighttime recreation. "You can buy beer in town," noted one student, "but that's about as far as the town's contribution to the social life goes."

Social life on-campus centers on the housing program, which follows the "Commons" system. The campus is divided into four Commons, each one containing several residence halls, dining halls, and student lounges. At the intersection of the four Commons lies the student union, which contains the post office, snack bars, and space for speakers and parties. Each Commons has its own Commons Council and budget to sponsor activities for residents, and this also creates good leadership opportunities for those interested in self-government.

Dorms were given decent reviews on the whole. Most rooms in the Commons are two-room doubles with one bedroom and a common area. There are some singles, but as one student points out, "would you rather share a bedroom and living room with a friend, or live in a two-by-nothing cubicle alone? Singles are not in very high demand here." Housing has undergone some improvement. After fraternities were abolished in 1984, the frat houses were converted into on-campus housing with larger rooms and central locations. Also, the school recently constructed three new dorms, which feature larger suites. The most recent addition to the housing options is the "Senior Apartments" that are only available to seniors. They are "absolutely amazing by normal standards—not just by campus living standards." Each apartment has a fully equipped kitchen, a living room, at least one bathroom, and bedrooms.

> **"Every so often there are benefits to the cold weather, like when the boilers break and classes are canceled!"**

Most students stay on campus all four years, if nothing else because the administration requires them to apply to live off campus, and off-campus housing is in short supply. But because nearly all social life revolves around the campus, most find living at Colby more desirable anyway. "At first I was disappointed and annoyed that I couldn't live off campus senior year," recalls one student. "But now I realize that I spend all my time here anyway, so it probably would have been more of an inconvenience than anything else!"

Cutting Through the Red Tape

Off-campus housing policy isn't the only problem students have with the Colby administration. One issue frequently mentioned is difficulty with financial aid. "The financial aid office is abysmal," griped one student. "They seem to thrive on alienating and confusing us." Some point to the school's problems with financial aid as one reason the student body has remained so homogeneous. "Why does it seem like almost everyone here is an L. L.

Bean–wearing, Jeep Cherokee–driving, well-to-do preppy northeastern WASP?" wondered one freshman. Not all students agree that the student body is so extremely uniform, however. Two-thirds of students come from public schools, and an increasing amount are beginning to arrive from areas outside the Northeast. It also appears that the administration is pushing for more diversity, though "somewhat unsuccessfully," according to a few. One noteworthy step Colby has taken is its huge capital campaign called the Campaign for Colby, which aimed to raise 100 million dollars by the end of 1999, but actually exceeded its goals and raised more than 150 million dollars. The money raised will be focused on improving financial-aid packages for students. "Colby has a long way to go," reasoned one student, "but is definitely moving in the right direction."

"White Mules Rule!"

While Colby's mascot, the white mule, may be puzzling to some, the enthusiasm for school athletics is definitely clear. Nearly all students participate in some form of athletics, be it varsity teams, intramural sports (called I-plays), or working out in the recently renovated athletic center. School spirit abounds, especially when major teams go head-to-head with rivals Bates or Bowdoin.

Administration has tightened its alcohol policy last year. "Alcohol no longer seems to flow freely." "Since the hosts are held responsible for all the incidents occurring at their parties, seniors really don't want to host parties. So the campus has engaged in all-school events." There is a party in the student center every weekend sponsored by the school. Usually, there are parties on both Friday and Saturday nights every weekend. At these parties, people of legal drinking age can usually buy alcohol from kegs once they show their ID's. "As a result in the crackdown on alcohol, drinking is mainly done in rooms." "One thing though—people really do go to the school parties . . ."

For those not wishing to engage in "mass alcohol consumption," Colby does have a couple of "chem-free" dorms, which are much appreciated by their residents. The school has also begun to sponsor better and more frequent campus-wide events, although the traditional ones remain the most popular. Such traditions include Homecoming weekend and the Junior/Senior formal, which are always big draws. And only Colby students get to look forward to the First Night of Loudness, which takes place in the fall, and the Last Night of Loudness, occurring in the spring. Both are immensely popular parties that feature hit singers or bands. Guests in previous years included Jewel, the Indigo Girls, and the Beastie Boys.

"If you're thinking about Colby," one student offered, "you can't ignore the snow factor, you just can't. It's a surpris-ingly large part of life here." True, Maine winters are not for everyone, but "every so often there are benefits, like when the boilers break and classes are canceled!" Weather conditions aside, most students find Colby College to be a tremendously rewarding place to spend four years. Perhaps most important, they feel like they are truly part of a community. "When I was sick and had to spend a few days in the health center," one student recalls, "my professor actually came and visited me to fill me in on what had taken place in our class discussions. I think it was at that moment that I knew I had really come to the right place." —*Rachel Grand and Staff*

FYI

The three best things about attending Colby are "beautiful campus, close-knit community, we have a funny mascot."

The three worst things about attending Colby are "no real diversity, pretty far from a major city, the administration."

The three things that every student should do before graduating from Colby are "go back-packing, play on a team and beat Bowdoin and Bates at least once, take a wild challenge during Jan Plan."

One thing I would like to have known before coming here is "when they say people work hard and party hard, they really mean it."

College of the Atlantic

Address: 105 Eden Street; Bar Harbor, ME 04609
Phone: 207-288-5015
E-mail address: inquiry@ecology.coa.edu
Web site URL: www.coa.edu
Founded: 1969
Private or Public: private
Religious affiliation: none
Location: suburban
Undergraduate enrollment: 288
Total enrollment: 288
Percent Male/Female: 34%/66%
Percent Minority: 3%
Percent African-American: 0.5%

Percent Asian: 1%
Percent Hispanic: 0.5%
Percent Native-American: 0.5%
Percent in-state/out-of-state: NA
Percent Pub HS: 75%
Number of Applicants: 234
Percent Accepted: 73%
Percent Accepted who enroll: 44%
Entering: 75
Transfers: 0
Application Deadline: 1 Mar
Mean SAT: 650 V, 630 M

Mean ACT: 28
Middle 50% SAT range: NA
Middle 50% ACT range: NA
3 Most popular majors: human ecology, marine biology, arts and design
Retention: 75%
Graduation rate: 58%
On-campus housing: NA
Fraternities: NA
Sororities: NA
Library: NA
Tuition and Fees: $19,485 in; $19,485 out
Room and Board: $5,400
Financial aid, first-year: 71%

"Before COA was COA, it was a mission. A mission to teach people how to make the world a better place. When the college was founded in 1969, its original name was going to be "Acadia Peace College." COA's idealistic roots are still apparent today.

A Single Degree

College of the Atlantic awards one undergraduate degree: the Bachelor of Arts in Human Ecology. Within this degree, students create their own curricula by concentrating in one or more of the following: public policy, marine studies, environmental science, natural history museum studies, design, teacher education, landscape and building architecture, and selected humanities studies. "Each of the 275 students here has a different definition of human ecology," said several students. Academic offerings are divided into the three areas of Environmental Science, Arts and Design, and Human Studies. COA has the trimester academic calendar: there are three terms of 10 weeks during which students usually take three classes. They are not allowed to take more than four classes each term. A common feeling is that the term is "six weeks of a fine workload and four of hell where all the final projects are due." COA has a "looooooong" winter break starts with Thanksgiving and going until the first week of January.

During their time at COA, each student is required to take two courses in each of the three areas of Environmental Sciences, Arts and Design, and Human Studies, a Human Ecology Core course, one Quantitative Reasoning course, and one Writing course. Students also have to write a Human Ecology Essay, do an internship, participate in 40 hours of community service, and complete a Final Project. Most students agree that the requirements are "pretty lenient."

For the required internship, which is usually done in the junior year, students forfeit regular classes for a term, and instead do an internship for three course credits. "Some people live on campus and intern at a nearby organization, whereas others travel to other parts of the US and the world for different opportunities."

"Wherever you want to go, whatever you want to do, it's up to you," said one student. "The Yucatan Term" that runs from December to March is an option, "popular with some students," In this program, a group of COA students and professors travel to the city of Meridan in Mexico's Yucatan region and hold three classes there. COA has established exchange programs with two universities, one in Uruguay and the other in the Czech Republic.

Students can also transfer credits from other colleges' transfer programs. COA students also get ample research opportunities. "We have two field houses and our own farm. Tell me which other school has these?" Mount Desert Rock and Great Duck Islands are "popular hangouts" for various land and sea bird species as well as for seals, dolphins, porpoises, and whales. Beech Hill Farm offers activities such as organic farming, winter gardening, soil maintenance, seed and plant collections.

COA students have nothing but praise for their professors. "We are extremely lucky to have a faculty so devoted to the idea of human ecology," said one senior. "They are really good about meeting with students outside of class, and allowing room for the integration of courses," added another student. Most professors are well published and respected in their fields. A few visiting professors also teach classes each term. COA's small size has its pluses—"you're not just a faceless number lost among the hoards." It also has its minuses, a major one being its course offerings: "There are many terms when I feel that there aren't enough classes being taught. But there is usually some amazing class I love to take." Another student complained that, "getting into classes can be a problem, a lot of the courses are limited to a very small size." "There are sometimes really cool classes, like photography, that everyone wants to take," but due to size limitations, they cannot.

Substance-free and Meat-free

The five dorms at COA are Blair-Tyson, Seafox, Ryles, Cottage House, and Peach House. Seafox, which is the substance-free form, is right next to the ocean and has the best view. Its neighbor, Ryles, is the party dorm. Ryles and Peach House are also known as the "hippie houses." Blair-Tyson is very new, has a "modern look overall" and mostly has singles. In the dorms, floors and bathrooms are usually coed and RAs are "cool as long as you clean up after yourself." "Different students like different houses or dorms for their particular needs, wants and likes," one junior explained. Overall, students are happy with their dorms. Compared to other schools, "rooms are considerably larger and most have furniture that is in good condition." Only first-year students are guaranteed on-campus housing. International students and transfers have priority for on-campus housing among upperclassmen but usually the dorms fill up before they get a chance. Therefore, living in off-campus apartments or houses is a "necessity" for almost all upperclassmen. Almost all students agree that they like living in town.

The meal plan is "expensive" but the food is reputed to be "the best of the best." Students refer to the food as "very new-age and phoo-phooish" and agree that there is "definitely something for vegans and veggies, not always for normal meat guys." A meat-lover noted that, "people in the kitchen probably use tweezers when handling the meat." Another student added, "meat: they give an honest effort, but if you are afraid of eating meat, how can you prepare it?" The only on-campus dining facility is the cafeteria named "Take A Break" referred to as "Tab" in everyday COA language. "Tab is open 5 days a week, otherwise all of the dorms have kitchens and students feed themselves on the weekend." Some students voice concerns about the short dining hall hours: "the cafeteria is only open for two and a half hours for breakfast and lunch and an hour and a half for dinner." Several explicitly stated that the hours are "kind of lame" or that "they suck."

Social Life! Love Life?

"Usually a student meets people within their first term here, and they can meet a lot of people, but after the first term the social circles tighten, and it is rare to become friends with someone you weren't friends with in the beginning," acknowledged one student. "[COA] tries for organized activities but it is not always successful with such a small student body." Still, not all students complained about the social life. One sophomore explained that there are often "neat people speaking on campus, movies and dances" and a few local bands "play here every once in a while." "I heard that Phish played here before they were huge," added one student. The campus-wide organized activities are "okay, they usually don't pull a huge crowd, but those that go enjoy them." The Tab also serves as the venue for contra dancing classes after dinner and yoga classes are offered in the student lounge.

Parties usually take place in people's houses in town where under and upperclassmen mix "as there aren't enough people for too many parties anyway." This means that, "sometimes there are different parties, but for the most part you will find the same people at the same parties." However, there have been some cool theme parties such as the "80's party and the disco night." Another student felt that the smallness served to bring people together: "Since there are not a tremendous amount of people on the island, different groups mix more here than they might elsewhere." Kegs are not allowed on campus. The administration's alcohol policy is "it's fine as long as we don't see the bottle or smell the alcohol." Students repot that marijuana is "the dominant drug on campus."

Besides attending parties, COA students fill their weekends with a variety of activities. Reel Pizza in town is a place that "a lot of COA students frequent." Run by former COA students, Reel Pizza has frequent independent movie screenings and offers a "cozy atmosphere" with reclining couches and beanbags. In order to escape the isolation of COA, students recommend a car "if you want to go anywhere." They warn that public transportation is not available. Students especially find cars handy, "when it's cold in the winter," so you can leave campus." If you don't have a car, you will most certainly have a friend with one since, "probably about half the people have cars." On the other hand, "another 1/5 don't know how to drive."

The love life at COA varies. Most people have significant others instead of random hook-ups. "We're too small a college for one-night stand," noted one student. Furthermore, "rumor spreads incredibly fast and you'd end up in the same classes as the other person anyway." One thing that almost everyone mentioned is that "there are not enough males on this campus." There are "more than twice as many girls as there are guys." This could benefit COA men. However, one student pointed out that although "there are plenty of attractive women, they're usually dating each other." Lesbian couples are visible at COA, but "I don't know of any gay males here." The general consensus seemed to be that, "there isn't a lot of sex at COA, the few people who have sex have it a lot, but there just aren't that many people who get action." So, many students turn to long-distance relationships to cope.

COA Active

Hiking is the most popular activity among COA students. All students get a free membership to the local YMCA where they go to swim, play basketball or use the fitness center. Volleyball and soccer become popular sports when the weather conditions improve. Men and women's soccer teams are called "the Black Flies because we don't stink, we suck." However, one student reported that with "the coldest days of winter comes a strong wave of knitting mania. Most people start going around campus with knitting needles and yarn in their hands. It lasts a couple of weeks and then flies away." Free Tibet is one of the popular activist organizations on campus: "There are more Tibetan prayer flags on campus than there are American ones." Social Environmental Action (SEA) is another one of them. Allied Whale is an organization that catalogues all humpback whales that live in the North Atlantic and are also involved with seal stranding.

Pot-smoking Crunchy Tree-Huggers

"I hate to say it, but the stereotypical COA student is a hippie," admitted one junior. Some phrases that students used to describe the stereotypical COA student are "crunchy tree-hugger, vegan/vegetarian,

middle class, white, overly idealistic, pot-smoking, usually female, spiritual person." Some students said that there is "a real sense of community." However, they also mentioned that the student body is "too homogenous." There is "very little ethnic or cultural diversity." Several students complained about "students being prejudiced towards people taking opposite stances even though most of them desperately try not to seem or sound like it." Another one added, "There is non-traditional segregation. If you are somehow not environmentally conscious or friendly, or if you throw a bottle in the trash and not recycle, you are evil and treated accordingly." Fashion at COA is stereotypical of tree-huggers: "Most people here wear Carharts. To class, they wear whatever they have on, or have had on for the last week. There are some "mainstream" people here this year, who dress semi-trendy, but most of them are leaving next year." Although students expressed interest in diversity, one student felt that such a population just wasn't "attracted to COA."

Mount, Desert and Island

COA is located on Mount Desert Island, in the town of Bar Harbor, Maine. "The location speaks for itself; how can you get more isolated than a place that combines "mount," "desert" and "island?" However, this is the case in the cold months of Maine. The island becomes a heaven for tourists in the summer and, especially, in the fall. Bar Harbor is a summer tourist town. The restaurants reinforce that idea when many close at the end of the season, although "some good places stay open." Many recommend Jordan's, "an awesome breakfast place that has award-winning blueberry pancakes." One student warned, "if you like big movie theaters and city life, stay away from Bar Harbor."

> **"We're too small a college for one-night stands." "There are plenty of attractive women, but they're usually dating each other."**

Almost all students "love" campus because it is "pretty, unique, small cozy and right by the ocean." One student praised that, "there are a bunch of great spots to get away, do some work, or whatever. Having the ocean border one side of campus is a definite plus." One student described the bay as "the biggest eye-catcher, along with trees and lobster boats." Acadia National Park next to the school "definitely adds to the campus life." One student said that "the surrounding area is the campus life, without it COA wouldn't be special." Turrets, an administrative office building with two large classrooms, is a gorgeous old stone building with wooden hand carved stair banisters and lavishly detailed ceilings. A new building was recently constructed for the Natural History Museum. Safety on campus is not an issue at all: "There is nowhere safer. At night the campus is like an empty city where everyone left their lights on."

COA's unique location on Mount Desert Island provides incredible opportunities for the study of human ecology. Interdisciplinary studies flourish at COA due to its academic flexibility and professors' willingness to integrate courses. If the idea of studying human ecology excites you, why not consider coming to COA and sharing your enthusiasm with fellow students and brilliant professors? —*Engin Yenidunya*

FYI

The three best things about attending COA are "the students, your closeness to your professors, self-directed curriculum."

The three worst things about attending COA are "the lack of diversity among students, a lack of needed (or wanted) courses, and the fact that Bar Harbor isn't much of a town during the winter."

The three things that every student should do before graduating from COA are "hike every square inch of Mount Desert Island, complete the Bar Island Swim (a 1/3 mile swim to the closest island in the fall, find something to be an activist for and send a school wide e-mail vouching for your cause."

One thing I would like to have known before coming here is "how negatively people who are the opposite of crunchy would be received."

University of Maine / Orono

Address: 5713 Chadbourne Hall; Orono, ME 04469-5713

Phone: 207-581-1561

E-mail address: um-admit@umaine.edu

Web site URL: www.umaine.edu

Founded: 186

Private or Public: public

Religious affiliation: none

Location: NA

Undergraduate enrollment: 7,882

Total enrollment: 9,945

Percent Male/Female: 45%/55%

Percent Minority: 5%

Percent African-American: 1%

Percent Asian: 1%

Percent Hispanic: 1%

Percent Native-American: 2%

Percent in-state/out-of-state: 85%/15%

Percent Pub HS: NA

Number of Applicants: 4,568

Percent Accepted: 85%

Percent Accepted who enroll: 42%

Entering: 1,611

Transfers: 477

Application Deadline: rolling

Mean SAT: 539 V, 542 M

Mean ACT: 21

Middle 50% SAT range: 480–590 V, 480–600 M

Middle 50% ACT range: NA

3 Most popular majors: elementary education, business, nursing

Retention: 80%

Graduation rate: 53%

On-campus housing: 84%

Fraternities: 14%

Sororities: 6%

Library: 792,402 volumes

Tuition and Fees: $4,656 in; $11,946 out

Room and Board: $5,256

Financial aid, first-year: NA

Best-selling horror author and University of Maine at Orono alum Stephen King probably didn't get his ideas from the four years he spent at the school's campus, which students described as idyllic. Both the campus itself and the general area are "beautiful," while somewhat isolated, students said, and even during winter hikes "across the mall"—a central green resembling a football field—they still often pause to admire the beauty of the forested landscape. Because the nearest metropolitan center, Boston, is four hours away by car, the university offers many on-campus social events and sponsors extremely popular yearly trips to Montreal and Quebec, where students bond, in one upperclassman's words, "by club-hopping, intoxication (legal drinking age in Canada is 18) and the intense ignorance of the French language." Nearby Arcadia National Park and Baxter State Park also topped the list of "must-sees," especially for wilderness-loving students.

It's a Small World after All

Although more than 7,000 undergraduates and almost 2,000 graduate students are enrolled at the University of Maine, many students find the campus community tight-knit and extremely friendly. One said the size is just right, "large enough that I never get bored but small enough that I don't feel like just a number." That sense of community results from a shared sense of school spirit that pervades every aspect of life at the University of Maine, inside and outside the classroom. Students regularly join the school's mascot, Bananas the black bear, in enthusiastically cheering at the "incredible" hockey games, where five students, campus celebrities known as the "Naked Five," paint MAINE on their chests and run around the arena when the team scores. In 2000, a group of women joined them for the first time, spelling BEARS, inaugurating what one of the participants hopes will become a new tradition. "Even the most timid student will get swept up in the excitement of school rivalries, especially while watching the University of Maine's hockey, basketball and football teams," one upperclassman promised, adding that he attends most games even though he is not a sports enthusiast.

Students uninterested in sports, though, can still find plenty to do on and around the campus. Celebrities visit the University of Maine frequently, and some recent guests are Stephen King, Hillary Clinton, the Violent Femmes and the Dave Matthews Band. Honor societies and clubs cater to almost every interest, including environmental and outing clubs, cheering clubs, a marching band and more eclectic groups like a campus branch of the Society for Creative Anachronism—dedicated to re-enacting medieval and Renaissance celebrations. A popular freshman carnival held every fall prepares students for dorm theme parties marking events like Mardi Gras and Halloween, charity balls and the spring "Bumstock" celebration, a week-long concert of local bands modeled on the legendary Woodstock. Another popular community-building event is the "Ritual of the Boot," a rite of passage at the popular in-town Oronoka restaurant for Maine students turning 21. The ceremony involves drinking beer from a boot-shaped pitcher and posing for snapshots that are posted on the Oronka's walls. Students who break the boot while drinking, though, have to pay for it, prompting one to make the sage suggestion, "Bring your credit cards for insurance." One student did caution, though, that those who do not enjoy parties will sometimes find their on-campus social options limited.

A Hard Day's Work

Life at Orono isn't all fun and games, though. In fact, the University of Maine, one of New England's best-kept academic secrets, boasts several widely esteemed academic programs, offers a wide range of honors classes and is particularly strong in engineering and music. Physics and math programs are extremely competitive, and the school is a national center for sensor research. One student did complain, though, that some prominent professors are at the University of Maine primarily to research and regard "teaching only as a side requirement."

Students applying to University of Maine must choose between its five colleges: liberal arts and sciences; engineering; education, public policy and health; education and human development; and natural sciences, forestry and agriculture.

Because each school has its own specific academic requirements, transferring between colleges is difficult, although all five share university-wide core requirements mandating classes in arts and humanities, math, science and ethics. A wide range of small honors classes and labs complement the large introductory lectures, and all students develop individual courses of study in their senior year as part of the required "Senior Capstone Experience." Students in the honors program must write a senior thesis. The campus' "huge" Fogler library, the largest in Maine, boasts 950,000 volumes and owns a specialized collection, housed in a separate branch in nearby Walpole, of 12,000 volumes dealing with marine studies. Other special collections include the library's "Canadiana" and lumbering and logging archives. Convenient networking services in almost every room also make research easier.

Urban Legends

Opened in 1868 as State College of Agriculture and the Mechanic Arts with only 12 students and two faculty members, the University of Maine has enjoyed a long and colorful history. Legend has it that three dead construction workers from early in the century remain beneath the concrete of one building's steps, but students differed on which building. Another popular story states that the original mascot, a live black bear cub kept in one of the fraternity house's basements most of the year, had to be replaced by a costumed performer after attacking the University of Connecticut husky at a basketball game. Students said they did not know whether Stephen King heard—or invented—these stories as an undergraduate. Many students believe the school's greatest legend is King himself, who graduated in 1970 with a B.S. in English, three years before the publication of *Carrie* made him famous, and still attends basketball games and visits campus frequently. King met his wife, Tabitha, in the stacks of the Fogler Library, where they both worked as students.

Bon Appétit

Many students said the quality of the school's dining hall food pleasantly surprised them and expressed satisfaction with campus meal plans. Popular features include a full "beans and greens" vegetarian program and the ability to transfer meal plan funds to campus snack bars, markets and convenience stores and local restaurants, including pizzerias that deliver as well as the school-owned Bears' Den and M.C. Fernald's. Different meal plans allow students to have from 7 to 19 dining hall meals a week and from $50 to $500 in transferable meal funding. Special meal plans are also available for commuters. Some students also said they appreciate the flexibility of a "grab-'n-go" dining hall policy that allows them to eat their meals on the run.

> One upperclassman promised, "Even the most timid student will get swept up in the excitement of school rivalries, especially while watching the University of Maine's hockey, basketball and football teams."

But dining halls are hardly the only haunts of hungry University of Maine students, as a number of inexpensive restaurants are on or near the campus. Students with cars frequently visit the mall in nearby Bangor, with a variety of restaurants, while others take advantage of the on-campus Taco Bell and Pizza Hut. Numerous pizza houses, almost all of which deliver, are in Orono, and students said two of the most popular are Pat's Pizza and Pizza Dome. Two clubs, Jeddy's and Margarita's, were also highly recommended. For students who prefer to stay in, individual dorms sometimes provide extra food, giving out snacks during finals and on some other occasions throughout the year.

Home, Sweet Home

Some students did remark on the lack of diversity among the student body, less than four percent of which is made up of ethnic minorities, but most were not perturbed by it. Theme housing, including a "chem-free dorm" where no drugs and alcohol are served, an all-female dorm and the "S-cubed" dorm for science students, as well as the availability of on-campus apartments, mean that most students end up happy with their living arrangements. "The community is close-knit enough that meeting people with your general interests is never a problem," one student said. Freshmen are mixed with upperclassmen in the dorms, which many students found a good thing, saying it broadened their social horizons. Students must live on-campus as freshmen and are free to commute or move off-campus afterward, but most don't. "I never thought that I would choose to spend four years in a dorm," one senior remarked. For most, the strong campus-wide sense of community and school spirit is enough to keep them in Orono. Besides, no one wants to miss the chance to see Stephen King if he happens to turn up. —*Erik Johnson*

FYI

The three best things about attending the University of Maine at Orono are "the beautiful location, strong academic programs, and tight-knit campus community."

The three worst things about attending the University of Maine are "frigid winters, remote location, and lack of cultural diversity."

The three things that every student should do before graduating from the University of Maine are "visit as many parts of Maine as you can, go on the seven hour sojourn to Quebec and Montreal and attend a hockey game."

One thing I'd like to have known before coming here is "how cold 10 below really is!"

Maryland

Goucher College

Address: 1021 Dulaney Valley Road; Baltimore, MD 21204-2794
Phone: 410-337-6100
E-mail address: admission@goucher.edu
Web site URL: www.goucher.edu
Founded: 1885
Private or Public: private
Religious affiliation: none
Location: suburban
Undergraduate enrollment: 1,114
Total enrollment: 1,303
Percent Male/Female: 28%/72%
Percent Minority: 15%
Percent African-American: 9%

Percent Asian: 2%
Percent Hispanic: 3%
Percent Native-American: 0.5%
Percent in-state/out-of-state: 41%/59%
Percent Pub HS: 64%
Number of Applicants: 2,121
Percent Accepted: 83%
Percent Accepted who enroll: 18%
Entering: 317
Transfers: 31
Application Deadline: 1 Feb
Mean SAT: 600 V, 570 M
Mean ACT: 26

Middle 50% SAT range: 550–660 V, 520–630 M
Middle 50% ACT range: 21–28
3 Most popular majors: psychology, biological sciences, English
Retention: 82%
Graduation rate: 58%
On-campus housing: 85%
Fraternities: NA
Sororities: NA
Library: 290,000 volumes
Tuition and Fees: $20,485 in; $20,485 out
Room and Board: $7,380
Financial aid, first-year: 64%

For students who enjoy both the beauty of a hilly campus and the convenience and excitement of living in a city, Goucher College may be the perfect school. A small liberal arts college located about eight miles from the center of Baltimore and an hour from Washington, D.C., Goucher is secluded by woods from the city but close enough so that students have easy access to what city life has to offer. One student described the verdant wooded campus as "absolutely beautiful . . . with the ability to escape if small-campus life gets too overwhelming." With a relatively small student body of approximately 1,200 students, Goucher is able to provide a close-knit community with an ideal place to live and learn.

Small Classes, Better Learning

Although students at Goucher have to fulfill a number of requirements, many agree that this is essential for a well-rounded education. All students are expected to complete at least three semesters of a foreign language or test out of the requirement by showing proficiency on a placement exam. In addition, students must take one semester each of math, social science, a natural science, and art and two different half-semester physical education classes. Goucher students must also demonstrate "writing proficiency" and "computer proficiency in major" prior to graduation. Exploring New Frontiers is a one-course program that all freshmen must participate in. Since all Frontiers classes meet at the same time and all papers are due at the same time, the program provides an opportunity for the freshmen to bond. In order to help students make the adjustments to college life, freshmen are also required to take a non-credit course, Wellness and Transitions. It is more of a discussion course than a class, and topics include alcohol, sex, date rape, and other major issues on campus. Consisting of about 15 to 20 freshman, the class meets three times a week for 50-minute intervals. Though some students complain about this requirement, many have found it beneficial in the end because it encourages student bonding and student awareness.

Perhaps one of the more enjoyable and beneficial requirements is the "off-campus experience," which can be satisfied by either studying abroad or obtaining an internship within a student's major. Students have the opportunity to participate in an exchange program with Exeter, a university in England, and one student per class is given a scholarship to study at Oxford for a year. Many students choose to intern in Washington, D.C., or Baltimore as well as in the local community.

At this liberal arts school, learning takes place in an intimate environment where students call their professors by their first names. One student commented, "I've really been surprised about how much I enjoy the small classes and really getting to know your professor." Although some introductory courses or required courses may have up to 70 students, class sizes tend to hover around 15 students for most courses. As one student said, "They are just big enough so there is a diverse amount of people in the class, but small enough that you can feel comfortable expressing your views and opinions." Although there are no teaching assistants at Goucher, there are supplementary instructors (SIs)—undergrads who have already taken the class and done well.

The workload at Goucher is described as "steady," but the student's major and course selection play a major role in this. Pre-med and natural science majors are known for being relatively tough, whereas the communications and management majors give students a little more free time. Other popular majors include English, dance, and psychology. On the one hand, some of the easier courses at Goucher include Math 100 ("Math for Plants") and several of the education courses (although they can be time-consuming). Cell biology and expository writing, on the other hand, are "notoriously difficult." For students with a strong desire to learn, Goucher boasts an honors

college, the option to create your own major, and the 3 + 2 engineering program with nearby Johns Hopkins University. In the words of one satisfied student, "The academics are phenomenal at Goucher. Students should feel prepared to go out into the world if they used the education to the best of their abilities."

No Greeks at Goucher

When Goucher students are not busy studying, they have no trouble finding fun and interesting ways to occupy their time. One student remarked, "It is incredibly easy to get involved in activities, events, and organizations on this campus. Therefore, it is incredibly easy to meet people." At Goucher, the students create a close community, with no big divisions between classes. Although self-segregation and cliques exist on campus, the small size and liberal attitude of the school diminish the importance of cliques. One student remarked, "The population is very liberal and open-minded, which is really nice . . . although I wish there were minority students." Goucher students dress casually, with typical clothing ranging "from pajamas to Banana Republic."

> "The people are great and the campus is beautiful. I would recommend this school to anyone."

Although the school is only 30% male, one girl says, "I don't think it's a problem because there are plenty of other campuses around here and there are plenty of ways to meet people." Hanging out on campus, stopping by local malls and movie theaters, and visiting nearby schools such as Johns Hopkins, Towson State, Loyola, and Morgan State are all popular options among Goucher students. Many are glad that there is no Greek system at the college, but those who are into frat parties can easily find them on neighboring campuses. On the weekends, students who have cars may head off to Washington, D.C., Annapolis, or Fell's Point, the club section of Baltimore, for concerts, mini-golfing, hiking, clubbing, bars, shopping, or just getting off campus for a little while. Other students have just as much fun hanging out in people's rooms on campus, having interesting conversations, and renting movies. There is also a shuttle that transports students to and from Towson, where they can go to another popular hangout, the Gopher Hole. Also known as the "G-Hole," this hangout is a non-alcoholic pub that shows movies, has an open mike, and hosts live bands.

Activities abound on campus, and students can get involved in groups such as the Bowling Congregation, a game show club, and a belly-dancing club. Several respected organizations are B-GLAD (a gay/lesbian alliance), UMOJA (an African alliance), Lotus (which promotes Asian Pacific enrichment), Hillel (a Jewish community), the *Quindecim* (the student newspaper), and a cappella singing groups. One of the larger and more active groups on campus is CAUSE (Community Auxiliary Service), which provides volunteers for Habitat for Humanity, local soup kitchens, and Parents Anonymous, a child abuse prevention program. Another option is the Student Activities Association, which helps to plan and organize campus activities and events. Recent speakers on campus include Hillary Clinton (who happened to visit on the day the Monica Lewinsky scandal broke) and Dorothy Allison.

Get Into Goucher (GIG) Day is one of the biggest events of the year at Goucher. On GIG Day, which takes place in the spring semester, classes are canceled and there is a big carnival with faculty, staff, and community members all invited for "rides, food, and a good time." Another campus-wide event is the Pumpkin Bowl, a day of friendly competition between dorms, which follows Spirit Week on the weekend before Halloween. Several semiformal dances are planned during the year, including the Blind Date Ball and Gala.

Renovated Dorms

With all of the activities and studying that Goucher do, they need somewhere to catch up on their rest. As one student put it, "The rooms all over campus tend to be big." Some of the newly renovated dorms, such as the Heubeck dorms, have air-conditioning and are considered to be the best. The Stimson dorms, however, are not nearly as nice and are affectionately referred to as "the Ghetto dorms." There are also foreign language dorms, non-smoking housing, and 24-hour quiet housing available to students. Goucher provides an RA system for every house, but students do not have to worry about overly strict residential advisors. "The RAs are usually understanding. They don't want to write you up, but they expect you to help them achieve that," commented one student. Approximately 15% of the students choose to live off campus, either at home or in nearby apartments.

Those who do not live on campus can choose whether or not they want to sign up for a school meal plan, which has been described as "expensive and mandatory" for students who live in campus housing. However, the dining facilities are "very clean, with great hours," and "something is always open." "There are lots of happy vegetarians at Goucher," said one student who wishes that there were some additional meat dishes. The kosher dining hall is also "a huge plus." When students get tired of the dining halls, there are plenty of choices for food off campus, including Paper Moon Diner, which has "good food, great service, and [is] a really cool-looking place." Louie's Café, Bubba's Breakaway, and Golden Gate Noodle House are other popular places to eat. As one student summarized, "The food is great. . . . I've eaten much worse and of course better, but it was better than I expected."

The Goucher community can look forward to the completion of numerous renovations that are currently under way. They include air-conditioning in the dorms, new academic buildings, a new student center, a new track and stadium, and expansion of the alumni house. The most popular teams on campus are soccer, basketball, and lacrosse. Athletic facilities are good, and a decent number of students participate in intramural sports.

A School for Anyone

As one student concisely put it, "I love Goucher. The people are great and the campus is beautiful. I would recommend "this school to anyone." With classes that "really get you to become open-minded," Goucher is the picture of a liberal arts college that is "too beautiful not to enjoy." —*Robert Wong*

FYI

The three best things about attending Goucher are "the intimacy, the campus, and being close to Baltimore."

The three worst things about attending Goucher are "the lack of student diversity, the lack of faculty diversity, and academic stress."

The three things that every student should do before graduating from Goucher are "get involved in extracurriculars, study abroad, and go camping in the woods."

One thing I'd like to have known before coming here is "how useful a car would be."

Johns Hopkins University

Address: 3400 North Charles Street; Baltimore, MD 21218
Phone: 410-516-8171
E-mail address: gotojhu@jhu.edu
Web site URL: www.jhu.edu
Founded: 1876
Private or Public: private
Religious affiliation: none
Location: urban
Undergraduate enrollment: 3,910
Total enrollment: 5,022
Percent Male/Female: 59%/41%
Percent Minority: 28%
Percent African-American: 6%
Percent Asian: 19%

Percent Hispanic: 2%
Percent Native-American: 0.5%
Percent in-state/out-of-state: 13%/87%
Percent Pub HS: 61%
Number of Applicants: 9,499
Percent Accepted: 33%
Percent Accepted who enroll: 32%
Entering: 1,012
Transfers: 98
Application Deadline: 1 Jan
Mean SAT: 670 V, 700 M
Mean ACT: 31
Middle 50% SAT range: 620–730 V, 660–760 M

Middle 50% ACT range: 26–33
3 Most popular majors: biology, biomedical engineering, international studies
Retention: 95%
Graduation rate: 83%
On-campus housing: 99%
Fraternities: 30%
Sororities: 20%
Library: 3,200,000 volumes
Tuition and Fees: $24,930 in; $24,930 out
Room and Board: $7,870
Financial aid, first-year: 50%

Do you want to go to a school where students say, "Of course the academics here are awesome; that's the reputation and this school doesn't disappoint!"? If so, Johns Hopkins is just the place for you. Just watch out for the seal in Gilman Hall—the legend is that if you step on it, you'll never graduate.

The Dreaded "Throat"

Undergraduates at Johns Hopkins are divided into two schools: the School of Arts and Sciences and the George William Carlyle Whiting School of Engineering. Requirements for students are pretty loose—you must take humanities and science courses, but there is no official core curriculum. "It's cool because you're not forced to take a stupid English class that everyone hates," said one pre-med major.

An English class might be a welcome break in a schedule of difficult science classes, however. Hopkins' Physiological Foundations was rated one of the hardest classes in the nation last year. And while psychology, sociology and political science are considered slacker majors, biology and biomedical engineering are the highly competitive "throats"—campus slang for cutthroat classes. Unbeknownst to many, international relations—for which there are many special programs—is a popular major as well.

Getting into the classes of your choice is not too hard at Hopkins. Upperclassmen get priority for the most popular classes, but younger students are usually not disappointed with their options. The one major complaint among students is class size. "Class size is horrible if you're a science major because this is a science and engineering school. It gets better as you progress into upper-level classes, though," commented one senior. "My main problem with class size is that it just isn't conducive to asking questions," remarked another student. Another issue that Hopkins students take to heart is the "lack of grade inflation": "The average here is still a B or B– and that is a lot lower than at a lot of the Ivy League schools." There is no complaint about the breadth of classes, though: "Hopkins is good in a lot of departments, so it's not hard to find a good class to take."

There *Is* a Social Life

The student stereotype is definitely one of pre-med geekiness, but that is far from the truth. Hopkins brings together "a great mix of people from all walks of life." This diversity does not hinder the educational process; in fact, "people actually tend to want to teach each other about their own lives." Most students feel that it is easy to meet people as long as you go out and make the effort. "Friends change all the time and you never know when you'll meet a new one," said one junior, sounding more like an encouraging mother than a student. As for being more than just friends, one upperclassman remarked, "If you look hard enough there is a significant other for you here, but people don't really date; they do end up together, though."

> **"The average here is still a B or B– and that is a lot lower than at a lot of the Ivy League schools."**

Each weekend, there are a number of exciting events, as well as dances and movie nights, which Hopkins makes a conscious effort to provide as alternatives to studying or drinking. Frat parties, however, seem to be the main attractions for underclassmen. "The frats are the main weekend retreat as well as the place to get hammered for underage drinkers," admitted one underage student. The general consensus amongst JHU students is that the best frats are SAE and Wawa, while the best sorority is Kappa Alpha Theta. "It's

not hard to rush and the people in it are pretty nice," said one non-Greek. According to students, the best parties "would have to be the SAE Front and Back Nine as well as the FOAM party. Also, the Sip Ep Purple Sky Red Haze. And . . . every Wawa party is crazy fun with a ton of people." Upperclassmen tend to go to house parties with their friends or to go out to Fell's Point, the club section of Baltimore.

There have been a few problems with alcohol in the past few years, so recently the administration has been cracking down on underage drinking. Officially, no alcohol is allowed on campus except at the campus bar, which only serves on Thursdays and is strictly monitored and operated.

Living and Eating

All freshmen and sophomores are required to live on campus unless they have some medical reason not to or they live in a frat house. The freshmen dorms are small and for the most part are not air-conditioned. There are residential advisors in the houses, which have about 30 residents each. "The RAs are typically not strict as long as you don't piss them off," elaborated one sophomore. There are substance-free dorms, and there is an all-girl as well as an all-guy dorm. All the different dorms, however, share most of the same qualities, except that some are dorm-style while some are suite-style. In the buildings, the floors are coed, with unisex bathrooms. There is a no-alcohol policy, but otherwise, there are no restrictions. Students are generally satisfied with their dorms: "I was happy in the dorms because I got to meet a ton of people and it seemed like a big family."

After sophomore year, all juniors and seniors live off campus in apartments or private housing. "It's easy to rent a place and it is not bad for a city," said one senior. Generally, how far away from campus you live and how nice your housing accommodations are will determine your rent price. The whole campus is small enough that students can say, "I love that you can leave your apartment/dorm ten minutes before class and still get to the building that's all the way across campus." With an abundance of "Hop Cops," on-campus security is not seen as a problem by students at Hopkins. Immediately off campus is okay, too, but students report that if you get too far away, things may get scary. There have been some reported muggings, but "Baltimore is a city, for goodness' sake." The plus side of going to school in a big city is that there are plenty of places off campus to go. "People leave campus, but sometimes they are stuck on the whole Inner Harbor idea. They need to venture off the beaten path a little," advised a senior. "There's the whole city of Baltimore at your fingertips and not enough Hopkins students take part in it," added another student.

The dining experience leaves much to be desired, but Hopkins students do survive the first two years without too much pain. There are plenty of vegetarian options, but nothing spectacular, according to many. The main complaint with the meal plan is that the meals cannot be used anywhere but in the cafeterias, and once a particular meal has passed, you cannot use the meal credit later. Most students at Hopkins are so busy with classes, work, and extracurricular activities that the cafeteria can an eat-quickly-and-run place. For those who choose to go off the meal plan after their first year, there are plenty of good restaurants surrounding the campus. A popular place to take a date is a fondue restaurant in Towson called the Melting Pot.

Life Away from Books

Most people are involved in several extracurricular activities. The most popular clubs are religious groups and community service groups. Of course, there are also many sports teams and a cappella groups such as the Allnighters, who went to the national a cappella championships last year. "There's a lot of stuff to do for any type of person," said one student who is heavily involved in Circle K, one of the big community service groups on campus.

In sports, men's lacrosse is *the* team to watch. There is an incredible amount of support and spirit for the lax team, the college's sole Division I team. The other sports teams at Hopkins are Division III, and while some have won titles recently, "they usually don't mean much because they're DIII." Sports are a popular pastime on campus, with plenty of pickup games of basketball and Ultimate Frisbee. Intramural sports are fun and a good number of people get involved.

In general, students do not have much to complain about and truly appreciate all the academic opportunities available to them at Johns Hopkins. While some may have a problem with the social life among Hopkins' competitive undergrads, all you really need is "an outgoing personality and a fun-loving outlook" and there will be no problems, assured one undergrad.
—*Victoria Yen*

FYI
The three best things about attending Johns Hopkins are "the great pre-med program, the lacrosse team, and Spring Fair in April."
The three worst things about attending Johns Hopkins are "Baltimore can sometimes be scary, grading is tough, and there is no coasting class-wise."
The three things that every student should do before graduating from Johns Hopkins are "visit Fell's Point during the day for some great food, go to the Baltimore Museum of Art because it's right there, and check out the stores in Hampden and Mount Vernon."
One thing I'd like to have known before coming here is "it's really not as cutthroat an environment as people make it out to be."

St. John's College

Address: PO Box 2800; Annapolis, MD 21404
Phone: 410-626-2522
E-mail address: admissions@sjca.edu
Web site URL: www.sjca.edu
Founded: 1696
Private or Public: private
Religious affiliation: none
Location: small city
Undergraduate enrollment: 454
Total enrollment: 516
Percent Male/Female: 52%/48%
Percent Minority: 5%
Percent African-American: 0.5%

Percent Asian: 2%
Percent Hispanic: 2%
Percent Native-American: 0.5%
Percent in-state/out-of-state: 17%/83%
Percent Pub HS: 65%
Number of Applicants: 446
Percent Accepted: 78%
Percent Accepted who enroll: 38%
Entering: 134
Transfers: 11
Application Deadline: rolling
Mean SAT: NA
Mean ACT: NA

Middle 50% SAT range: 660–750 V, 580–680 M
Middle 50% ACT range: NA
3 Most popular majors: liberal arts only major
Retention: 80%
Graduation rate: 77%
On-campus housing: 100%
Fraternities: NA
Sororities: NA
Library: 100,000 volumes
Tuition and Fees: $24,770 in; $24,770 out
Room and Board: $6,576
Financial aid, first-year: 45%

"This school is a legend by itself. It is distinctly different," is how a student describes St. John's. With a different purpose and a different method in education, St. John's, the third oldest college in the United States, has been teaching its students through the "St. John's method" since 1696.

Tutors and Fellow Students

St. John's has a different approach and a different language in education. The curriculum is "the Program," and the professors are "tutors." "We call our professors here "tutors" because they guide us along a path as opposed to instructing us," explains a student. What makes the college different from others is its Program, which is based on the Great Books of Western Society. However, music, math and science also constitute a major part of students' curricula. But, even math is taught through Great Books; "Reading Newton in the original text is how we learn calculus," describes a student. The Great Books Program doesn't have any electives; it is all required: four years of mathematics, one and a half years of Greek, one half year of French, one half year of Shakespearean poetry, one half year of modern poetry,

three years of Laboratory Science, one year of Music, four years of Seminar, one major essay at the end of each year, and one year of freshman chorus. All freshmen gather weekly to sing. However, there are also Preceptorials, or specialized classes on one particular work. Preceptorials can only be taken in junior and senior years, offering different subjects, from Aristotle to Joyce, Faulkner to William James.

No Grading

There are no tests and students' papers aren't graded. Students receive a grade for their work in a semester, which is a combination of papers and class. Class participation is considered "the quality and caliber of what one says, its tone, and how one treats confusion, difficulty in understanding himself and in others." Tutorials and Labs have around 14 students with one tutor, and seminars average about twenty students and two tutors. Students enjoy this method of education, though the reading load can be tremendous.

Everyone is called Mr. or Ms. in class, including the tutor. A student describes the classes as "egalitarian," even with world-renowned tutors such as Eva Brann, Laurence Berns, A.P. David, Joe

Sachs. Also, the weekly Friday night lectures host visitors from philosophy departments of other schools such as Stanly Fish, Robert Pinsky, and Robert Fagles.

Students have a close relationship with their tutors: they play sports together, tutors are invited to student parties, and they have dinners together regularly. Students find the tutors interesting and "cool." As an example, one student gives one of his seminar tutors, who was the first person to clone garlic. Even though all the classes have a tutor, some science and music courses also have assistants, who help with the technical set-up.

Older Students, Less Underage Problems

Parties are regularly organized and attended. The average St John's student is older than the college mean; therefore, underage drinking is less of a problem than elsewhere. However, underage drinking, if caught, is dealt severely. Coffee-shop parties, which take place twice a month at the basement of McDowell hall, are very popular. The Great Hall, an 18th century ballroom that doubles as the main classroom, hosts formal balls every month. Swing-dances, the Pink Triangle Society Cross-dress parties, and the annual Seducers and Corrupters party, make up a colorful social life for students. However, Lola's is probably the greatest theme party: A casino night. "There's live music, gambling, (blackjack, poker and roulette) dancing and a couple of bars. It's a great time. Some of our tutors will deal blackjack. It's a lot of fun," a student describes Lola's, also adding "We are allowed to hold this event because our school charter is older than that of the state of Maryland." Kegs are allowed on campus. The Senior Prank, which is based on kidnapping students from class and spending the evening drinking, is popular among students.

Reality Bites

Croquet Weekend, of *Sports Illustrated* and National Public Radio fame, is the weekend of the annual croquet match against the naval academy. A coffee-shop party takes place the previous night. The day of the match itself is ". . . and all day lawn party with people wearing sun dresses and linen suits." A cotillion dance takes place after the match where Godiva chocolates with the St. John's seal on them are served with champagne. A student-run group, Reality, whose central activity is Reality Weekend, organizes Lola's, Croquet Day and the coffee-shop parties. Juniors organize Reality Weekend as a celebration for graduating seniors. Beer, live music, a three-day film festival beer and Spartan Madball are the key features of the Reality weekend. Rules of Spartan Madball are having no shoes, no weapons and no vehicles. The goal is to run the ball through the goal on a field with no boundaries. Spartan Madball, played once a year, resembles rugby.

Ideas Are What Counts

Even though there are some drawbacks of having a small community, St. John's students enjoy it. It is easy to get to know people since everyone is open and eager in discussing and sharing opinions. But, racially and ethnically, the student body is very homogeneous. "Our joke is that you can describe a third of the student body by saying 'oh, he's a tall, skinny, white guy.' But that matters very little, since the ideas are what count, and there is a huge range of ideas people here hold," is how one student describes his peers. Another student relates that even when they are drunk, their discussion subject is most probably Aristotle.

> **"Reading Newton in the original text is how we learn calculus," describes a student.**

Most upperclassmen live off campus. All freshmen are required to live on campus, and the floors are single sex except for two dorms on campus. "The Resident Assistants' main goal is to take care of you, not be a policeman." Humphreys, a freshman dorm, is well liked and Chase-Stone, an upper-class dorm, with its hardwood floors and high ceilings are favorable like Humphreys, is also highly desirable. Another freshman dorm is Randall—famous for its clanking pipes and small rooms. Paca-Carroll is the "quiet dorm."

Historic Grounds

McDowell Hall, the main classroom building, is an 18th century colonial Governor's mansion. Lafayette danced in the Great Hall of McDowell Hall when he visited Annapolis after the American Revolution. The Liberty Tree on front campus, which was cut down after Hurricane Floyd, was the meeting place for the Sons of Liberty of Maryland of the American Revolution. Humphreys Hall was a hospital and a morgue, and Pinkney Hall was a barracks during the Civil War. Newly built is the gym with a suspended track around the ceiling.

Overall, the campus is small and is characterized by its colonial red brick buildings. It is a safe campus, situated in a safe city, Annapolis. The quad is the place to meet on lazy Sundays. Even though there are some eating out options in Annapolis, DC and Baltimore offer superior restaurants.

Students find the food on campus moderate. There are three meal plans: 5, 14 or 21 meals per week and it is mandatory to be enrolled in one of them. The dining hall offers many options to vegetarian students. The Little Campus, recently closed down, was students' eat-out choice for over thirty years. Now, Harry Browne's is their new preference. Student also enjoy sushi at Nikko or Joss.

The Sports Triangle

People are engaged in many activities on campus; therefore, most stay in Annapolis rather than going to DC or to Baltimore. Students in Project Politae work for Habitat for Humanity, St. John's Chorus sings, the elected Delegate Council distributes funds to student activities, and the Student Committee on Instruction discusses Program issues are active organizations. Mabel the Swimming Wonder Monkey is a different organization that "watches and heckles bad movies." Melee is another organization where students are involved with medieval arts and crafts as well as rubber sword fighting.

Fencing, Crew, and Croquet are the only three varsity sports of the college, and students are proud of their success, and were the National Intercollegiate Croquet Champions for the third year in 2000. All other sports are played as intramurals. Nearby golf courts and a swimming pool are available to students.

Students are proud to be a part of the St. John's tradition as well as of its history and are happy to study in a unique educational environment. "St. Johns is totally incomparable. This place is unique, and it is what I always wanted." —*Yakut Seyhanli*

FYI
The three best things about attending St. John's are "the Program, the thinking, and discussing."
The three worst things about attending St. John's are "news traveling fast, the Program—makes one realize how many more books s/he wants to read and how little time one has
The three things that every student should do before graduating from St. John's are "going to a Coffee shop party, picking a fight in Melee club and listen to a senior oral."
One thing I'd like to have known before coming to St. John's is "its math and lab programs are intense."

United States Naval Academy

Address: 117 Decatur Road; Annapolis, MD 21402-5017
Phone: 410-293-4361
E-mail address: NA
Web site URL: www.usna.edu
Founded: 1845
Private or Public: public
Religious affiliation: none
Location: suburban
Undergraduate enrollment: 4,040
Total enrollment: 4,040
Percent Male/Female: 85%/15%
Percent Minority: 18%
Percent African-American: 6%

Percent Asian: 4%
Percent Hispanic: 7%
Percent Native-American: 1%
Percent in-state/out-of-state: 5%/95%
Percent Pub HS: 60%
Number of Applicants: 10,145
Percent Accepted: 15%
Percent Accepted who enroll: 82%
Entering: 1,232
Transfers: 0
Application Deadline: 31 Jan
Mean SAT: 638 V, 666 M
Mean ACT: NA

Middle 50% SAT range: 500–620 V, 600–700 M
Middle 50% ACT range: NA
3 Most popular majors: political science, economics, oceanography
Retention: 86%
Graduation rate: 80%
On-campus housing: 100%
Fraternities: NA
Sororities: NA
Library: 470,000 volumes
Tuition and Fees: midshipmen receive full tuition, room and board
Room and Board: NA
Financial aid, first-year: NA

Sink or swim? In one of the Physical Readiness Tests (PRTs) that United States Naval Academy students must pass, students must jump off of a ten-meter platform into a diving well. The situation is analogous to the leap that these same students made in deciding to attend the Naval Academy: it is a difficult decision to make, and, once your toes are lined up at the edge of a platform 30 feet above water, the move to commit follows with a precipitous descent into the watery world of the midshipman, or "middie" as Naval Academy students refer to themselves.

One of the major enticements to take the plunge at one of the government service academies is the promise of a salary of almost $550 a month from the time you matriculate—i.e., free education. As with most government offers, however, there is a hook: in obtaining a degree from the United States Naval Academy you are promising at least five years of your life to active duty in either the United States Navy or Marine Corps.

Plebe Life
First-year students, or "plebes" (shortened from the word "plebeian"), are immersed completely in the spartan lifestyle of the academy. The requirements in every spec-

trum of plebe life are numerous. One student remarked, "This place is all about requirements." Plebes are expected to take two semesters of chemistry and calculus, as well as classes dealing with naval history and ethics. Students are also expected to maintain certain body-weight standards and participate in a rigorous physical regimen including either varsity athletics or intramural competition in swimming, boxing, wrestling, judo, weight training, hand-to-hand combat, and other activities.

The students generally see these requirements as providing them with a "base for any Academy grad to pursue virtually any graduate work regardless of the degree you receive here." However, some students say that the requisites also can be a pain, because they "don't leave you with many options." There is a strict honor code that all students must adhere to regarding their academic and personal lives. Students say it works well and everyone follows it.

Free Time
The social options are often as rigid as the academic options, as plebes are only allowed "liberty" (free time) between Saturday's noon formation and 11 P.M. that evening. Many plebes choose to spend this time "sleeping, sleeping, sleeping,"

while others choose to visit their sponsor families (Annapolis families that provide surrogate homes to middies) or watch television.

> **"Shoes gotta be shiny, clothes folded, beds made, and doors kept open so that inspectors can spot-check us with their white gloves."**

As middies move up in the ranks from plebe year, they begin to enjoy extended liberty. Hours are extended on the weekends, and gradually, by the time students reach fourth-year status, life reaches the normalcy of "a student at most any other undergraduate institution."

The limits imposed on socializing are numerous, however. Middies are not allowed to "fraternize" or have sex with other students and there is definitely "a stigma attached to dating other mids." Since the male-female ratio at the USNA is better than five to one "you basically have to go into town for any kind of relationship." A student must also be "sat" or satisfactory in the area of academics in order to have liberty. Those students with a sub-2.0 GPA, or more than two D grades in any classes, lose their liberty privileges and must spend their weekends studying.

Those who must hit the books usually go to the sole library on-campus, Nimitz, which has over half a million volumes, or for the more socially inclined, Dahgren Hall at the Drydock Restaurant. Academics at the academy are intense, but students generally have a lot of cooperative help to offer one another. One student remarked, "There's a real strong sense of 'let's get each other through this purgatory.'"

Dorm Details

When evening studies in Nimitz have drawn to a close, students return to Ban-

croft Hall, the huge dormitory that houses all of the academy's 4,000-plus students, and which is also known as "Mother B." Bancroft hall is currently undergoing renovation, which are expected to be completed by 2008. The current rooms were described as either "saunas" or "meat lockers" since the facility lacks air-conditioning. The rooming options were also described as "nonexistent." Every student has a personal computer, and is connected to the campus-wide data network, but phones are allowed only "in rare cases." "Shoes gotta be shiny, clothes folded, beds made, and doors kept open so that inspectors can spot-check us with their white gloves." The dorms are coed "like an apartment building," and "learning to live in close quarters with both sexes can be a challenge, but it works . . . of course there are strict rules of decency," one middie reported.

With the strict honor code of the Naval Academy, theft of property is "never a problem," and with Marines and Department of Defense police patrolling the campus, students agreed that the campus is very safe.

A major facet of the USNA is the school spirit that the administration helps foster with "spontaneous, but mandatory" pep rallies. During "Army Week," the week before the big football game against their West Point archrivals, "chaos, pandemonium, and stress relief" are the results of massive school spirit.

Overall, students at the United States Naval Academy are well aware of the fact that they lead a "non-traditional college life" in a "none too diverse" and "extremely conservative" setting, but they balance the current situation with the eventual payoff. Said one third-year student, when asked what advice he would give to high school seniors, "Be sure it is what you want, and be prepared to make many sacrifices. But, oh, is it worth it when you get that diploma."—*Vladimir Cole and Staff*

FYI
The three best things about attending USNA are "the discipline, the free education, and the physical regime."
The three worst things about attending USNA are "the lack of personal space, lack of personal time, and lack of personal choice."
The three things that every student should do before graduating are "live up Army Week, make sure your room is ready for inspection, and don't get caught with another middie."
One thing I'd like to have known before coming is "how rigorous training can be."

University of Maryland / College Park

Address: College Park, MD 20742-5235
Phone: 301-314-8385
E-mail address: um-admit@uga.umd.edu
Web site URL: www.maryland.edu
Founded: 1856
Private or Public: public
Religious affiliation: none
Location: suburban
Undergraduate enrollment: 24,717
Total enrollment: 33,006
Percent Male/Female: 51%/49%
Percent Minority: 34%
Percent African-American: 14%

Percent Asian: 14%
Percent Hispanic: 5%
Percent Native-American: 0.5%
Percent in-state/out-of-state: 74%/26%
Percent Pub HS: NA
Number of Applicants: 18,807
Percent Accepted: 54%
Percent Accepted who enroll: 38%
Entering: 3,937
Transfers: NA
Application Deadline: 15 Feb
Mean SAT: NA
Mean ACT: NA

Middle 50% SAT range: 560–660 V, 580–680 M
Middle 50% ACT range: NA
3 Most popular majors: criminology and criminal justice, psychology, accounting
Retention: 88%
Graduation rate: 31%
On-campus housing: 80%
Fraternities: 9%
Sororities: 11%
Library: 3,500,000 volumes
Tuition and Fees: $4,939 in; $11,827 out
Room and Board: $7,258
Financial aid, first-year: 46%

As it moves up in national rankings, University of Maryland has become one of the most highly respected state schools in the country. With its improvements in academic departments, further development of honors programs, proximity to Washington D. C. (nine short miles away) and a lively social scene, Maryland offers its students "a good time and a great education. "

Academics

University of Maryland prides itself in offering a liberal arts education, having extensive core requirements in addition to requirements for one's major. These include two writing courses, one math class, and a "diversity" course, in addition to twelve distributional courses in the humanities, math and sciences, and social sciences and history. Most find taking classes in a variety of disciplines to be a great experience, especially if "you don't know what you want to major in. "

The preprofessional departments are extremely respected at Maryland, particularly engineering, life sciences, journalism, and business, while the humanities tend to be weaker. Many students find class sizes

to decrease as one begins to take upper level courses. "It doesn't really matter if there are 100–1500 students in the intro classes, but in my advanced courses there are only 10–20 students in them, one with several professors working with us; it's really amazing," one student described. Maryland offers everything from gut courses like Bowling and Sex Education to honors seminars. However, Business 110 with Professor Nickels attracts quite a following; "It's practically a requirement for the diploma," one student joked. Voted Professor of the Year in three different years, Nickels offers his legendary "happiness speech" on how to be happy in this course, getting incredible reviews from his students.

An option for incoming freshmen is the variety of honors programs available. Beginning with the College Scholars Program, which is a 2-year program specific to a particular subject, Scholars live with other Scholars and enjoy smaller classes. However, depending on the particular subject the programs vary in strength. "I didn't get that much out of it," said one student who partook in the Government College Scholars Program, "though I know others who really enjoyed their program." The University Honors Program, which is more difficult to get into, has gotten great reviews from a majority of students as a way to get a challenging curriculum for the first two years of college. "It could not be better. The classes were small and the professors were really motivated and interested in teaching," one honors student said about the program.

Facilities

Maryland offers two major libraries for student studying: McKeldin (the graduate library) and Hornbake (the undergraduate library). More serious studiers choose McKeldin, while the upper levels of Hornbake are usually suitable as well. However, the basement of Hornbake tends to be more social.

> "Habitat for Humanity has been one of the greatest things I have been a part of here. We have been doing demolition and reconstruction on rundown housing in a low income Baltimore neighborhood."

Other facilities include the Maryland Center for Performing Arts, which opened in 1999, and the Recreation Center, a 125 million dollar athletic complex that has "everything" and is open for all students. In addition to the new plant life building and Computer Science building, there are plans to build a new Student Center.

Residential areas at Maryland are separated into North and South Campus. Although living on campus is never compulsory, the majority does live on campus. There has been an increase in the amount of juniors and seniors who opt to live on campus, causing a housing shortage for freshmen, who mostly live in North campus, often in triples due to the housing problem. The dorms on North Campus, which are considered "not too bad but a little on the small side," are a great social environment for freshmen to meet fellow classmates. The majority of upperclassmen live in the apartments and suites of South Campus, often enjoying single bedrooms and spacious living space. While most dorms are coed, other living options include athletic housing, language housing, special honors housing, and substance free housing.

Food

While one student described the food as "terrible," another said that it "could be worse." Most students do recommend "North Woods" eatery on North campus, an all-you-can-eat buffet, which offers food that is "more healthy and much less greasy. " There is always the option of eating out at Papa John's, Taco Bell, Denny's, WaWa, the Bagel Place, or other late night places around campus.

College Park

"College Park isn't really a college town but we really don't need one with DC so close and everything else happening on campus," one student noted, summing up the role of College Park in the lives of Maryland students. Although the town offers Cornerstone, Bentley's and Santa Fe Café, three popular bars, most go to Washington D. C. on the weekends or stay on campus. Security around campus is said to be very good with a solid police presence and good lighting.

Outside of Academics

Although its students tend to be from Maryland, New Jersey, and New York, that does not mean they are not diverse. Coming from all parts of the political spectrum, students are known to be tolerant, making minorities and the gay and lesbian community feel generally comfortable and supported.

The variety of extracurricular activities including a juggling club, a Baha'i Club, a healthy intramural sports program, and a skydiving club, and a wide variety of ethnic organizations are just a few of the many organizations that are on campus. "Habitat for Humanity has been one of the greatest things I have been a part of here. We have been doing demolition and reconstruction on rundown housing in a low income Baltimore neighborhood," one student said. He continued, "I feel like I'm really helping out the community." The daily newspaper, the *Diamondback*, has wide readership among Maryland students as does the literary magazine, *Stylist*, and various ethnic magazines. While the Greek scene is present on campus, involving 10% of the student population, it is no longer the major force on campus as it used to be. Students find that "Maryland is big enough for everybody to find a niche and people they like." One thing that does unify the student body is athletics, particularly football and basketball. With both teams extremely strong the past few years, school spirit and student participation have been overwhelming with such events as the "Midnight Madness" in October when students sleep over at the gym to celebrate the beginning of basketball season and Homecoming. Soccer, lacrosse, and field hockey events are also well attended by students. Besides athletic events, Maryland students have the "All Niter," a fall festival at the Student Union and "Art Attack," an all day music event in the spring, where bands like George Clinton's P-Funk play. Besides these school-sponsored events, there are always parties going on particularly, between Thursday and Saturday night. While drinking is rather heavy on campus, the administration has continued its no-keg policies in attempts to crack down on excessive drinking, while "the actual implementation of the policies is really pretty lax." Marijuana, the most popular drug on campus, is "present, but not overly so."

As the University of Maryland is consistently improving in its image as a nationally respected university, "it is still the only place I know where you can have amazing school spirit, (my buddies and I are always waiting for basketball tickets a couple hours before the game), a great social life (there's always something to do) and still get a solid diploma at the end too." —*Jessica Morgan*

FYI
The three best things about the University of Maryland are "The beautiful campus, honors program, and being close to Washington D.C. "
The three worst things about the University of Maryland are "Parking, College Park, and bureaucracy. "
The three things that every student should do before graduating are "Attend *every* basketball game, go to "Art Attack," and rub Testodoe's (a turtle) nose before an exam.
One thing I'd like to have known before coming to the University of Maryland is "how amazing watching basketball can be. "

Massachusetts

Address: Campus Box 2231, PO Box 5000; Amherst, MA 01002
Phone: 413-542-2328
E-mail address: admissions@amherst.edu
Web site URL: www.amherst.edu
Founded: 1821
Private or Public: private
Religious affiliation: none
Location: small city
Undergraduate enrollment: 1,664
Total enrollment: 1,664
Percent Male / Female: 52% / 48%
Percent Minority: 26%
Percent African-American: 6%

Percent Asian: 12%
Percent Hispanic: 7%
Percent Native-American: 0.5%
Percent in-state / out-of-state: 14% / 86%
Percent Pub HS: 57%
Number of Applicants: 5,198
Percent Accepted: 19%
Percent Accepted who enroll: 42%
Entering: 423
Transfers: 5
Application Deadline: 31 Dec
Mean SAT: 700 V, 697 M
Mean ACT: 30

Middle 50% SAT range: 650–760 V, 650–740 M
Middle 50% ACT range: 27–33
3 Most popular majors: English, political science, psychology
Retention: 97%
Graduation rate: 96%
On-campus housing: 100%
Fraternities: NA
Sororities: NA
Library: 889,989 volumes
Tuition and Fees: $25,222 in; $25,222 out
Room and Board: $6,560
Financial aid, first-year: 43%

The squirrels at Amherst College have been known to throw acorns at students with terrifyingly accurate precision. Fortunately, they are the one and only hazard of the Amherst campus. Set in the quaint, picturesque, friendly town of Amherst, Massachusetts, Amherst College has a familial quality to it. With a total enrollment of only about 1,600, students know the face, if not the name, of almost every other student at the school.

Intimate Academics

"Overall, the thing that satisfies me most about Amherst is the professors," says one sophomore. Professors at Amherst are generally extremely approachable and described as "inspiring and very dedicated to making you a better student." Students say profs are "very eager to help you and encourage you." Since Amherst does not have graduate students, professors teach all of the classes and most of the discussion sections.

Class sizes are also learning-conducive. Most sections have between 20 and 25 people, and lecture classes normally enroll about 45 students. When 70 students crowd into a class, students complain about it being too large.

Because of the intimate academic atmosphere, many students are able to build close relationships with their professors, even going out to dinner or taking trips to Boston with them. Professors are known to befriend their students. (Of course, professors may not always be so beloved. Rumor has it that the Amherst grad who wrote the screenplay for the movie Dead Poets Society included the name of his English professor as the author of a particularly disagreeable and pompous introduction to a textbook.)

The only required class for all Amherst students is a semester-long freshman seminar. Freshmen choose from a list of 15 interdisciplinary classes such as Reading Paris and Imagining Landscape. Otherwise, students are free to choose whichever classes they wish—as long as their faculty advisor approves the schedule. Students preregister for classes and have two weeks at the beginning of the semester to make changes to their schedules. A faculty advisor is assigned to each freshman, but students can choose their own advisors once they declare their major. Classes also can be taken with the pass-fail option, although few choose to use it.

Students can design their own interdisciplinary majors and cross-register for courses in the Five-College consortium, which includes neighbors Smith College, University of Massachusetts at Amherst, Mount Holyoke, and Hampshire College. Students from any of these five colleges can take classes offered at the other schools for credit. Some male students have been known to take classes at the two women's colleges, Smith and Mount Holyoke, for nonacademic reasons.

"The amount of reading and the expectations of the professors are huge," said one English major. Amherst is a reading-and-writing-oriented school. No matter what your major, you will have to write papers. Even science classes require them.

Tales of Beer

According to students, the Amherst social life revolves mainly around drinking. "The administration turns a blind eye to underage drinking, just as long as you're not in Amherst town and don't make the school look bad," said one sophomore. "Getting drunk turns into a status thing. People brag about getting drunk in class. People do it because everyone else does." Another student agreed: "Hanging out at Amherst means getting together and drinking." Although there are non-drinkers, "the niche is very small," one student said.

Especially for Amherst women, dating can present something of a problem. Everyone agrees that it is much easier for the guys to find available girls due to the proximity of Smith and Mount Holyoke. Many Amherst guys seem to believe the saying, "Smith to bed, Mount Holyoke to wed, Amherst girls to talk to." "We're [the guys'] lab partners," complained one

Amherst female. "People don't date much. There are lots more random hookups," an Amherst male added.

Even for those who don't drink or date, there is plenty to do at Amherst on the weekends besides catch up on reading and admire the scenery. Amherst is a college town, and the surrounding area caters to college students. An abundance of restaurants, movie theaters, fast-food restaurants, pharmacy stores, bookstores, and other shops along with a nearby mall and supermarket, are accessible on foot or by bus. A free bus system links the five colleges in the consortium.

Life in the Dorms

The administration allows only 50 seniors to live off-campus each year. All other students must live on-campus, where housing is quite plentiful. Freshman year is spent in the freshman dorms, the only housing with single-sex floors and single-sex bathrooms. Each floor has a resident counselor to perform such duties as giving study-break parties. After freshman year, students choose their own roommates and, through a draw, pick their own rooms. There are no dorms designated specifically for sophomores, juniors, or seniors, but many dorms primarily house members of a particular class. Residents say dorm rooms are in decent, livable condition, but they are by no means luxurious or new.

Other housing options include "social dorms" and theme houses for various cultures such as the Asian-American house. All Amherst students buy a meal plan for the school's dining hall. Students are satisfied, but not thrilled, about the quality of their food. Vegetarian dishes and a salad bar are offered at every meal. However, even a nonvegetarian agreed that "there are no decent vegetarian options."

Outside the Classroom

Almost everyone at Amherst participates in one or two extracurricular activities. Faculty advisors encourage their students to get involved by making sure their class schedules are not so time-consuming that they prevent them from having outside interests. Among the activities available are five a cappella singing groups, underground fraternities and sororities (officially banned by the administration), and various religious and ethnic groups. Though some students participate in community-service activities, such activities are not extremely popular.

> Some male students have been known to take classes at the two women's colleges, Smith and Mount Holyoke, for nonacademic reasons.

Complaints about the Amherst administration by various student groups are not uncommon. "The administration, especially the president, neither listens to nor respects students, especially minority students. They want to make Amherst into one unified, unrealistic, colorblind society. But it's not just the minorities; most kids on-campus feel the administration does not listen to them," said one Asian sophomore.

Amherst students from every background, though, agree that their classmates are on the whole very friendly. While some complain about the school's academically intense atmosphere, competitiveness is not pervasive; instead students tend to be "closet grade-hounds" who describe Amherst as a warm and caring place. —*Sherry Tsai and staff*

FYI

The three best things about attending Amherst are "the helpful professors, the small science courses, and the relaxed social scene."

The three worst things about attending Amherst are "the fact that you've met everyone by sophomore year, the cold, how busy most people are."

The three things that every student should do before graduating are "get a slice at Antonio's, get a cup of coffee at The Black Sheep, make a friend at one of the other colleges nearby."

One thing I'd like to have known before coming here is "that everybody knows everybody else's business."

Babson College

Address: Admisssions Office; Mustard Hall; Babson Park, MA 02457-0310	**Percent African-American:** 2%	**Mean ACT:** NA
Phone: 781-239-5522	**Percent Asian:** 6%	**Middle 50% SAT range:** 540–630 V, 590–670 M
E-mail address: ugradadmission@babson.edu	**Percent Hispanic:** 4%	
	Percent Native-American: 0.5%	**Middle 50% ACT range:** NA
Web site URL: www.babson.edu	**Percent in-state / out-of-state:** 64% / 36%	**3 Most popular majors:** finance, marketing, economics
Founded: 1919	**Percent Pub HS:** 50%	**Retention:** 91%
Private or Public: private	**Number of Applicants:** 2,582	**Graduation rate:** 62%
Religious affiliation: none	**Percent Accepted:** 45%	**On-campus housing:** 96%
Location: suburban	**Percent Accepted who enroll:** 35%	**Fraternities:** 12%
Undergraduate enrollment: 1,701	**Entering:** 414	**Sororities:** 11%
Total enrollment: 1,701	**Transfers:** 47	**Library:** 130,000 volumes
Percent Male / Female: 64% / 39%	**Application Deadline:** 1 Feb	**Tuition and Fees:** $21,952 in; $21,952 out
Percent Minority: 13%	**Mean SAT:** 566 V, 608 M	**Room and Board:** $8,746
		Financial aid, first-year: 45%

Babson College students often say, "If you want to go into business, it's an excellent school, the best." The real world agrees; Babson is consistently rated one of the best business schools in the country and students say that if you know what you want to do, it's the place for you.

Born into Money

Most of the students complain about the heavy workload they face from the start of their freshman year. Students start their business education with foundations classes. FME, Foundation through Management Experience, the special program for freshmen, includes introductions to accounting, marketing, business and information systems. After these introductory level courses, which are also known as the "boot camp," second-term freshmen actually lay their hands on money and start a small business of their own. After devising different plans for forming a business during the first semester, the class chooses from these plans and proceeds to enact some in the second term. With the use of a loan from the school, students in the past have set up calendar and cookie companies and even a "flow glow" company, which did special-event decorating. In their second year, students get to choose a company like Tommy Hilfiger, Timberland or Royal Caribbean and analyze the firm in detail. During this "Intermediate Management" they go to the plant and prepare a presentation of the company. In their last two years, they specialize in one area of study. Internships during these years help the students get acquainted with the business world. While the library provides good research resources, students also use the VAX computer network for online information about jobs and internships.

Marketing is one of the most popular majors and students note that "finance is coming up strong." Entrepreneurial studies is another strong major and is ranked highly nationally. Babson also has a program with Wellesley College, so students can take Russian and Italian classes at Wellesley.

Students are impressed by and satisfied with the faculty. Since the number of students in class usually varies between 20 and 25, students interact with professors in almost all of their classes. "The professors care about you," says one student, pointing out their accessibility as an especially strong point. Even though there are no TAs in classes, students have mentors who help students with the questions they might have about classes and also serve as advisors. Starting freshman year, when students participate in the Freshman Year Experience, faculty advisors and advisees get together at the movies or over a dinner to get to know each other better.

The Suites and the City

Social life in Babson is mostly described as "the Suites and the City." Suites, which are larger and more comfortable compared to dormitories, are mostly occupied by fraternity members and sports players. Five dormitories out of fourteen are air-conditioned; many have single-sex floors. Each dorm has a common lounge where students can relax on comfortable couches and play air hockey or foosball. All dorms have laundry rooms and kitchens and are all centrally located. Seniors have priority for singles and suites.

> **"Babson is trying to differentiate itself from other business schools."**

Students say the parties in the suites are the best parties at Babson. There are also 3 semi-formal parties every year, as well as theme parties including fall weekend, Oktoberfest, and Harvest. There are also weekly parties sponsored by CAB, Campus Activities Board and by the Knight Auditorium. Even though drinking is not a problem in suite parties the school is very strict about the drinking age. As long as you are not seen by an RA (one of whom lives on every floor of the dorms), students say there aren't any real problems with drinking. Many students party at Boston College and Boston University as well. This involvement with other colleges is also a result of the male to female ratio, which is roughly 7:3. The lower ratio of females to males on campus makes it "a challenge for men to get laid," students complained.

Students enjoy the location of the College. Boston is easily accessible with the T, commuter rail, and buses. Still many students have cars since they find the hours of the public transportation inconvenient on weekends. This creates a parking problem. For the freshman, the situation is even worse: their parking lot is further away from the center of the campus.

The area where Babson is located is one of the richest areas of the country; the expense of going out explains why students find it "easy not to be social." Off-campus housing is available, but the rents of near-by apartments are high. Therefore some students end up finding apartments away from the school, which requires them to get cars.

Student Body on Safe Grounds

Students say the Babson population is segregated. The percentage of foreign students is not high. Foreigners mostly associate with themselves, as do sports players and Greeks. Some have complained of many cliques within the student body.

Students socialize in Reynold, a popular spot for lunch. Both cold and hot dishes as well as fast-food from restaurants like Pizza Hut can be purchased. For dinner, however, many prefer going to Trim. It is the dining hall of the college (the catering service is from Marriott) and students appreciate the variety of the dishes served. Of course, you can always go to Wellesley to eat out—or to have a coffee at Starbucks. Another popular place on campus is Rodger's Pub, which is named after Roger Babson, the founder of the college. Roger Babson was a prohibitionist and many students say he must have "rolled over in his grave when his name was given to the pub."

Although the number of student organizations is not very high, many work efficiently and are popular among the students. These include Student Board, Campus Activity Board (CAB), Entrepreneurship Club, Marketing and Philosophy Clubs and the sports clubs, especially men's soccer and basketball, women's field hockey and lacrosse. CAB, for instance, doesn't only plan the weekly dances, but also arranges for speakers to come to Babson, and most students are pleased with their choices, pining only for their hero—"if they could get Bill Gates!"

Students also enjoy the safety of the campus. Students don't report any concerns about going out at any time during the night. Going to Sorenson Center, the center for theatre and fine arts, coming from Wellesley, or from the PepsiCo Pavilion Gym—which provides students with an indoor pool, track, squash, racquetball courts, a weight room, three basketball courts, and a dance/aerobics center—is not a problem at all.

Babson's Effort

"Babson is trying to differentiate itself from other business schools," commented one student. Students observe that the college is changing its curriculum and its methods every year. In the last few years, students have been concentrating more on team-teaching and enjoy seeing how accounting, business and team-teaching fit together.

Also, each freshman class now chooses a council, made up of respresentatives from their class, who prepare certain resolutions concerning their year. Students find this useful and believe these resolutions also add to the improvement of the college, of the social life, and of their year.

Besides the city students are here for one reason: getting into the real world fast. Even though the business world is competitive, they know that their Babson education is a great advantage. "It's the best, and is still going strong." —*Yakut Seyhanli.*

FYI
The three best things about attending Babson are "specialized education, preparing for the real world, proximity to the city."
The three worst things about attending Babson are "female to male ratio, an expensive environment, the sports."
The three things that every student should do before graduating from Babson are "Go to the city, take road trips, live in a suite."
One thing I'd like to have known before coming here is "the heavy workload of the freshman year."

Boston College

Address: 140 Commonwealth Avenue, Devlin Hall 208; Chestnut Hill, MA 02467-3809
Phone: 617-552-3100
E-mail address: ugradmis@bc.edu
Web site URL: www.bc.edu
Founded: 1863
Private or Public: private
Religious affiliation: Roman Catholic / Jesuit
Location: suburban
Undergraduate enrollment: 9,190
Total enrollment: 9,344
Percent Male / Female: 47% / 53%
Percent Minority: 18%

Percent African-American: 4%
Percent Asian: 8%
Percent Hispanic: 5%
Percent Native-American: 0.5%
Percent in-state / out-of-state: 27% / 73%
Percent Pub HS: 58%
Number of Applicants: 19,746
Percent Accepted: 35%
Percent Accepted who enroll: 33%
Entering: 2,284
Transfers: 507
Application Deadline: 15 Jan
Mean SAT: NA
Mean ACT: NA

Middle 50% SAT range: 590–680 V, 610–690 M
Middle 50% ACT range: NA
3 Most popular majors: English, finance, psychology
Retention: 94%
Graduation rate: 81%
On-campus housing: 98%
Fraternities: NA
Sororities: NA
Library: 1,400,000 volumes
Tuition and Fees: $23,520 in; $23,520 out
Room and Board: $8,510
Financial aid, first-year: 48%

Mobs of Boston College students run around their beautiful campus every spring, tracing hidden clues to find their prize. The prize? It's not the prestige of winning some freshman orientation activity, nor a pot of gold (or scholarship money), but a much-coveted ticket to one of the most popular dances at BC: Middlemarch. According to BC students, Middlemarch is "possibly the best college dance in the States." Only the lucky few who successfully complete the scavenger hunt gain entrance to this mysterious event.

Boston College, a Jesuit school located about six miles outside downtown Boston, offers its students a balance of popular parties and a rigorous core curriculum and of an open suburban setting with the convenience of nearby Boston.

The Core Academics

Boston College consists of several undergraduate programs: the College of Arts and Sciences, the Wallace E. Carroll School of Management, the Lynch School of Education, and the School of Nursing. Students enroll in one school but can take elective classes from other schools. Some of the most popular majors and classes,

such as finance and accounting, fall under the School of Management. English, political science, and economics are popular in the Arts and Sciences. Students agree that classes in the pre-med arena, such as organic chemistry and biochemistry, are exceedingly difficult.

All four colleges of Boston College share a core program that requires coursework in a myriad of subject areas. The College of Arts and Sciences, for example, requires 15 core courses including writing, literature, arts, mathematics, history, philosophy, social sciences, natural science, theology, and cultural diversity. Many students complain about the stringency of the core requirements, even though one student confesses, "These classes are great for my personal development."

Students agree that the best part of BC academics is the teacher–student relationship. One student praised the professors of two of his favorite classes, Philosophy of the Person and Modern European History: "Both my teachers for these two classes knew the subject inside and out. They made learning the subject fun; they showed that they cared for their students, and were always available outside of class for any extra help." One freshman already had stories to tell about a professor who threw a pizza party for the class at the end of the year. He raved, "The good professor–student relationship makes BC an academically resourceful institution."

A Note on Being Catholic

When asked about the Catholic presence at the school, one student said, "I used to see the Jesuits on my way to classes last year." The Catholic influence seems to be felt more in the academics than the social life: one student felt that "some class offerings have Catholic undertones." Moreover, Jesuit priests teach some of the classes. One student claims, "The school teaches students how to be a human through its Jesuit education."

Go, Eagles! The Sports Scene at BC

As at many colleges, football is big at BC. During football season, there are "always tons of tailgates going on, parties left and right, parties at night." Notre Dame is BC's big rival, and some students make the trek out to Indiana for the big game. Hockey is also popular at BC, maybe "bigger than football," according to one student. Every year, the Eagles hockey team plays in the Fleet Center. One student recalls proudly one game from last season: "In the NCAA championship (Frozen Four), we had an adrenaline-rushing game against North Dakota, and although we couldn't bring the trophy back to the school, our patriotism to the team never cooled off." Basketball is also up there on the popularity list.

The athletic facility is complete and accessible for students who remain on the sidelines of the games. The Flynn Recreation Complex, affectionately called the Plex, is fully equipped with treadmills, bikes, weights, track, tennis courts, squash court, swimming pool, and a basketball and volleyball court. Some dorms also have their own weight rooms.

Food and Living

When it comes to the living situation at BC, your luck depends mostly on your year. According to one student, "About half of the freshmen class have to suffer the tragedy of living on the Newton campus." Although freshmen get accustomed to living in the Newton campus and enjoy the benefits of a small and tight-knit community, one student complains, "Every student should know that if you live in Newton, it takes an extra hour in traveling time to get anywhere." One hour might be an exaggeration, but the students in Newton do have to take a shuttle bus to get to classes on Middle Campus. "The bus ride itself is only about five minutes long," says one student, "but they need to stand outside to wait for the bus to come—even when it's snowing heavily. Also, if you live on the main campus, you can go back to your room between classes, but otherwise, you'd have to bring all your books and be prepared to be out for the entire day."

> "The good professor–student relationship makes BC an academically resourceful institution."

The rooms on the Newton campus are also notoriously small. Sophomore years and beyond, however, students may find themselves winning the lottery for comfortable rooms with kitchens and private bathrooms. Housing is usually guaranteed for three years, and many students choose to stay on campus. A fair number live off campus or study abroad their junior year. High-rise apartments with kitchens are available for upperclassman. Also popular are the modulars, called "mods" for short. Mods are small town houses located in the center of campus and are famous for their popular parties.

Most BC students seem to be satisfied by the food. "Considering the amount they have to make, the food at BC is high-quality," says one student. Students have a few dining halls from which to choose for every meal. The Lyons Dining Hall, called the Rat, is popular for lunch. Particularly popular plates are made-to-order steak and cheese, London broil, and dessert.

The Weekends

BC might not be known as *the* party school, but there is definitely enough partying going on. According to many, the school's social life centers on drinking and clubbing. The "weekend" starts on either Thursday or Friday, with partying on campus. The administration has announced a zero-tolerance alcohol policy and the BC Police Department is out on weekends to enforce the policy. Students nevertheless find it pretty easy to encounter their bottles of liquor, usually through upperclassmen. One student even claims, "I don't know if it's possible not to drink at this school, especially if you are on a sport team."

The spotlight of campus partying is in the mods. Students feel that the mods fill the social niche left open by the lack of a Greek system. One sophomore warns, "Mod parties can be elitist." For the freshmen without IDs, however, "mod-hopping" is the only way of getting access to alcohol.

These parties may also be the ideal place for hooking up, which occurs frequently, according to some students. "People do date, but hookups are more popular," said one student. Another student added, "There is a lot of sex at this school. That's not even the question." When they get tired of campus, students take advantage of the proximity of Boston. Boston has a lot of clubs, according to BC students, but the bars are strict about the drinking age. The city also offers cultural activities, a wealth of shopping malls, movie theaters, and concerts. Students can also work at part-time jobs or internships in the city.

The Melting Pot Versus the Clam Chowder

According to some students, Boston looks more like New England clam chowder (that is, white) than a melting pot and the same holds somewhat true for BC. One student who had grown up in a very diverse neighborhood said he experienced a "total culture shock when I came to BC because I had never been around so many white people before." These students stress, nevertheless, that racial problems or conflicts on campus are rare. Minority students can "make their voices heard to the community" through the school's cultural organizations. Activities such as the Asian Caucus attract a lot of students. About BC, one student concluded, "It's fairy easy to meet people here if you go out there and try."—*Mariko Hirose*

FYI

The three best things about attending Boston College are "the locale, the parties, and the faculty."

The three worst things about attending Boston College are "the size of the dorms and the housing lottery, the T system, and the lack of universal ID card access to all the dorms on the campus."

The three things every student should do before graduating from Boston College are "scream and go wild at 11:00 P.M. during the finals week, go to Middlemarch, and learn the difference between the B and D lines on the T."

One thing I'd like to have known before coming here is that "applying to study abroad can be a tedious process."

Boston University

Address: 121 Bay State Road; Boston, MA 02215
Phone: 617-353-2300
E-mail address: admissions@bu.edu
Web site URL: www.bu.edu
Founded: 1839
Private or Public: private
Religious affiliation: none
Location: urban
Undergraduate enrollment: 15,469
Total enrollment: 28,487
Percent Male/Female: 40%/60%
Percent Minority: 22%
Percent African-American: 3%

Percent Asian: 12%
Percent Hispanic: 6%
Percent Native-American: 0.5%
Percent in-state/out-of-state: 25%/75%
Percent Pub HS: 72%
Number of Applicants: 28,090
Percent Accepted: 55%
Percent Accepted who enroll: 27%
Entering: 4,225
Transfers: 557
Application Deadline: 1 Jan
Mean SAT: 636 V, 640 M
Mean ACT: 28

Middle 50% SAT range: NA
Middle 50% ACT range: NA
3 Most popular majors: soc. Sciences, bus. Adm./commerce/mgmt., mass communications
Retention: 85%
Graduation rate: 66%
On-campus housing: 100%
Fraternities: 5%
Sororities: 7%
Library: 2,100,000 volumes
Tuition and Fees: $25,044 in; $25,044 out
Room and Board: $8,450
Financial aid, first-year: 58%

I t's 5:30 on Friday night and your classes are over for the week. You think about your weekend plans—you could go clubbing in Landesdown, take a walk down to Fenway Park for a Red Sox game, or just go window-shopping on Newbury Street. For Boston University students, these options are just part of another normal weekend at school.

Big City, Big School

Students say that Boston University is unique in its location and size: you are in the heart of the city, with Fenway Park in one backyard and Newbury Street, famous for its shops, in another. Anything that isn't within walking distance, said one student, "is just a short T ride away." The T, Boston's underground mass transit system, has seven stops on or near campus and goes almost anywhere in Boston for one dollar. With a total student body of 30,000 students, BU is one of the largest and most diverse campuses in the nation. "You're always seeing a new face, even in your own dorm," said one freshman.

The trade-off for living in the heart of Boston, according to some students, is a lack of cohesive school spirit and campus community. BU does plan student-oriented events such as concerts, hypnotist shows,

and dances like the Back Bay Ball, a winter formal. However, some find that these events are poorly advertised, and others would simply rather go out in Boston.

Another trade-off that BU students make hinges on safety. The BU administration is strict on issues such as alcohol use and dorm living. The dormitory-style housing in Warren Towers, Shelton, and the brand-new Student Village is guarded, meaning that students must swipe their IDs to get past the guard. Non-resident students have to be signed in by a resident after 8:00 P.M., visitors aren't allowed in after 1:00 A.M. Overnight guests must also be signed in and registered with the resident advisor. "It's a pain," said one freshman, "but you get used to it. Being in downtown Boston, it does make you feel safer." The alcohol policy is similarly strict. There is a no-tolerance policy for underage drinking, and punishment for violations can be as harsh as eviction from university housing. Students of legal age may only keep up to one six pack plus one liter of alcohol in their rooms. "There's a major effort to stop underage drinking," said one student. "You hear all the stories in [the student newspaper] the *Daily Free Press* about people getting caught by undercover cops." Since the security system prevents large parties in the dorms, some students venture off campus to drink. However, most clubs are 19 and over, and carrying a fake ID has heavy consequences, both legally and with the BU administration. Despite the precautions, one student said, "people who want to drink do. Everyone knows an upperclassman who will buy for them or knows people elsewhere in Boston where they can go. But if you don't drink, it's easy to avoid [alcohol]."

Academics

Boston University's academic offerings match the scale of its surroundings and student population. Freshmen apply to 25 undergraduate schools ranging from the traditional, like the College of Engineering, the College of Arts and Sciences, and the College of General Studies, to the more experimental, like the University Professors Program, in which students create their own cross-disciplinary majors. The College of Communication is among the best in the nation, and students who enroll in it have access to their own radio and TV stations, not to mention the advantage of being at "ground zero for media internships." Students consider the School of Management, which was recently renovated, and the College of Engineering to be especially challenging. The large number of schools at BU gives students the advantage of being able to transfer from a school without transferring from the university. While it depends on which school you're trying to go to and when ("going from College of Arts and Sciences to College of Engineering in your senior year is going to be difficult"), students appreciate the flexibility the system allows.

Students say that you shouldn't expect to be overloaded with work freshman year, but that the amount of time you spend studying depends on what college you choose. Upperclassmen warn that "by far the first year is the lightest course load and it just intensifies from there." Luckily, most believe time spent on academics is well worth it. As one sophomore put it, "I feel that I will graduate with a strong background in my field." If you need incentive to go to class, BU has several well-known professors. Elie Wiesel, winner of the 1986 Nobel Peace Prize, is a professor of philosophy and religion in the College of Arts and Sciences. One student says, "Professor Kean in the School of Management seems to be the guy to get! His classes fill up amazingly fast and people try to move into his class quickly. I've known of people who sit on the stairs of his classroom just to hear his lecture."

As for getting into classes, students register by a process called Telreg each semester. Seniors get first dibs, followed by juniors, sophomores, and freshmen, respectively. While classes occasionally fill up, professors are usually flexible and "willing to add you into the class during the first weeks if there is physical room in the class to fit you."

The Freshman Experience

Moving away from home is intimidating enough for some freshmen. Now imagine moving into the second-largest non-military residence in the U.S. This would be Warren Towers, the 1,700-student dorm in which 80% of all freshman live. It is divided into three towers and 14 floors. Students can choose to live on theme floors according to their college or to be assigned randomly to floors, which are single-sex. Each floor has an RA who is "there for your problems, if you need to talk." RAs also are responsible for the floor and "are supposed to turn you in for doing anything wrong, but most of them don't really care." Most freshmen will share with a roommate in "decent-sized, if not spacious," rooms and share bathrooms with the floor. There are the usual restrictions on halogen lamps and heating appliances, but BU will allow the rental of special fridge-and-microwave combinations. The roommate pairing process "is not a science. All they want to know is if you smoke and if you mind if your roommate smokes." With so many inhabitants, it's easy enough to get away from your roommate if it doesn't work out.

After freshman year, many students prefer to move into smaller residence halls or school-owned brownstones. Apartment- and suite-style housing is available, as is theme housing. The brownstones along Bay State Road are considered to be among the "prettiest" places to live, and many are language houses or theme residences, like the Dean's House, Classics House, and the Limited Parietal House. There is also a Wellness House, for students who prefer substance-free living.

> **"You're always seeing a new face, even in your own dorm."**

Students describe the dining halls as "very impressive." There are six dining plans to choose from, each made up of meals, dining points, and convenience points. Meals can be used at any of the five residence dining halls or the kosher dining hall. Dining points can be used to purchase additional meals at the dining halls, at the food court at the George Sherman Union, or for Domino's delivery. Convenience points are like a debit system; you can add convenience points to your account and use them in the Campus Convenience stores, for laundry, or in vending machines. "There are plenty of choices no matter what you like to eat. It's the same thing all the time, but it's good food!" said one student.

Playtime in Beantown

In their downtime, students at BU have all of Boston as their playground. Some students take advantage of all the city has to offer, including concerts, shows, clubs, shopping, and food. Since the Greek system at BU is "almost non-existent," students hit the MIT frat houses, which are practically on campus, for parties described as the "wildest and closest in the city." Aside from going out, students also find a wide variety of extracurricular activities to take part in. According to one student, "There is a club for anything imaginable and it is easy to start a club yourself." The student newspaper, the *Daily Free Press*, has a large presence on campus; other activities include singing groups, the drama stage troupe, and community service organizations. For those more athletically inclined, there are intramural sports and pickup games at the Shed, a sports complex with an indoor track, rock-climbing wall, beach volleyball courts, and batting cage. Students also work out at the Harold C. Case Physical Education Center, commonly known as Case Gym, which boasts an ice-skating rink, a swimming pool, and fitness rooms.

Despite all Boston has to offer, more than one student said that his favorite weekend activity is "catching up on sleep." One senior said, "Even with everything Boston has to offer, people still complain there's nothing to do."

No Typical BU Student

Boston University prides itself on its diverse population, of students who come from all 50 states and 125 countries. "There's a big emphasis on foreign students here," says one student. "I had a roommate from Kenya freshman year, which probably isn't typical at other schools." However, despite the cultural diversity, one student said, "everyone here is from the upper middle to upper class. There's a lot of money on campus." Many students also noted that ethnic groups tend to self-segregate, especially in the dining halls: "Ethnic groups tend to form their own social circles, but it doesn't create tension and doesn't mean people don't socialize outside those groups." Another student described the environment as "highly tolerant. I think being in the city, you become used to differences between people."

As for the BU student stereotype, "the school is way too large for that." There are some stereotypes as far as individual colleges go, for example, "rich types in the School of Management, nerds with pocket protectors in the College of Engineering. But of course it's not really serious—you'll find all sorts of people in every school."

As BU is a big school in a big city, students find themselves with tons of choices both academically and socially. While it's very possible to get lost in the shuffle, most students find their college years here exciting and fulfilling. —*Emily Hendrick*

FYI

The three best things about attending BU are "there are students and people from all over the place; the T (Boston's subway system) is easily accessible; it's close to the city."

The three worst things about attending BU are "the crazy security they have in all the dorms, not enough school spirit, especially since we don't have a football team; shuttle buses run irregularly."

The three things that every student should do before graduating from BU are "explore everything about Boston . . . visit museums, walk around, go clubbing, shopping . . . ; live at the Student Village or Bay State; go to a Red Sox game."

One thing I'd like to have known before coming here is "how bad we are ripped off on everything, in the convenience store, with housing, washing machines, food prices, etc."

Brandeis University

Address: 415 South Street; Waltham, MA 02454

Phone: 781-736-3500

E-mail address: sendinfo@brandeis.edu

Web site URL: www.brandeis.edu

Founded: 1948

Private or Public: private

Religious affiliation: none

Location: suburban

Undergraduate enrollment: 3,040

Total enrollment: 4,527

Percent Male / Female: 44% / 56%

Percent Minority: 16%

Percent African-American: 2%

Percent Asian: 10%

Percent Hispanic: 3%

Percent Native-American: 0.5%

Percent in-state / out-of-state: 27% / 73%

Percent Pub HS: 70%

Number of Applicants: 5,792

Percent Accepted: 52%

Percent Accepted who enroll: 27%

Entering: 794

Transfers: 51

Application Deadline: 31 Jan

Mean SAT: 660 V, 660 M

Mean ACT: NA

Middle 50% SAT range: 610–710 V, 610–710 M

Middle 50% ACT range: NA

3 Most popular majors: psychology, biology, economics

Retention: 89%

Graduation rate: 73%

On-campus housing: 99%

Fraternities: NA

Sororities: NA

Library: 1,000,000 volumes

Tuition and Fees: $25,174 in; $25,174 out

Room and Board: $7,040

Financial aid, first-year: 45%

When people think of colleges in Boston, Harvard and MIT instantly come to mind. However, what some people don't know is that the most exciting college town in the nation is also graced with the presence of a younger establishment named Brandeis University. Founded as recently as 1948, Brandeis has quickly earned an outstanding reputation as a university with great devotion not only to maintaining stellar undergraduate academics but also to being a leading research university. Distinct from its Boston counterparts, Brandeis also quickly earned the reputation of being the most Jewish college in the country.

Watch Out, Pre-Meds

Brandeis students seem to have few complaints when it comes to academics. There are a good deal of course requirements, including freshman writing seminars, three semesters of language courses, and a gym class. Students have to take 32 hours of credit from "clusters" such as medicine and social policy. However, students say that these requirements are "very open" and that it is "really convenient" to satisfy them. One freshman expressed that "it ends up just happening that you fulfill everything."

The majority of classes at Brandeis are relatively small in size. Aside from entry-level lectures in subjects such as chemistry that often top 300 people per class, students generally agree that most classes have approximately 20 students. Despite small class sizes, it is easy to be placed in the classes that you want; and even if you request to be in one of the higher-level, more popular classes, the school "will basically get you in." The small class size at Brandeis facilitates attention from professors, which in turn leads to academic rigor. However, intense schoolwork is a small price to pay for establishing relationships with some of Brandeis' faculty. Professors at Brandeis have included the late Eleanor Roosevelt and Morrie Schwartz, who has been immortalized by the bestselling book *Tuesdays with Morrie*. Currently, the Brandeis faculty includes notables like attorney Anita Hill.

Students at Brandeis feel that the typical class is difficult and demanding. While it seems that economics and political science tend to be the "slacker" majors, students who are taking the pre-med sequence and are pursuing majors in science claim that it is "the hardest thing in the world" and that there is simply a "ton of work." For example, one freshman interested in the pre-med program said that her introductory chemistry class probably lost about half of its students due to the intense workload. Fortunately, the students have a positive outlook on Brandeis' rigorous academics. Small class size, intimacy with world-renowned professors, and reasonable course requirements led one Brandeis student, when asked if she is pleased with the school's academics, to affirm wholeheartedly, "Oh yeah, definitely."

Looking for Fun? Go to Boston . . . or at Least Get off Campus

While "the Deis," as it's known as by students, is a haven in the world of academia, the campus' social atmosphere does not seem quite up to par. As one freshman said, "You've got to really search for something going on campus." Students tend to look toward Boston for entertainment on the weekend (which typically starts on Thursday night). The Deis is located in Waltham, Massachusetts, about 10 to 20 minutes from Boston. This proximity allows students to spend typically one night a weekend there hitting the clubs. However, underage students beware—it is common knowledge around campus that if you plan on dancing the night away at a club, you need an ID.

However, there is a lot more to do in Boston than go clubbing. Many students frequent Faneuil Hall or Harvard Square to meet students from other colleges. The commute to Boston is easy for most because the majority of students in this wealthy student body have cars. Yet students also note that those without cars needn't worry, because the Bran-van will be glad to take you into the city. The "Bran-van," aside from having a cute name, is a school-funded vehicle whose purpose is to take students anywhere on or off campus. In addition, it saves students the trouble of choosing a designated driver.

What also drives students away from the grounds of Brandeis on weekends is the fact that a large percentage of upperclassmen live off campus. Moreover, fraternities are also not on campus—in fact, Greek organizations are not even recognized by the Deis (although many disguise themselves as official clubs in order to receive funding from the university). Despite the lack of recognition from the university, fraternities play a large role in the social life at Brandeis. Not only do they throw parties such as formals and black-tie events, but they also have their own tables in the dining halls and the members form strong cliques. As one student stated bluntly, "If you want a life and you're a guy, definitely join a frat . . . [it's] definitely not necessary for girls." Unfortunately, because Brandeis does not regulate frats, it also does not regulate hazing. While there are no hazing horror stories to report, it is well known that "pledging is a pain in the ass."

Fortunately, to say that there is nothing to do on the Brandeis campus on weekends would be an exaggeration. Recently the school has sponsored concerts with popular musicians such as Less than Jake and Tracy Chapman. Students also look forward to concerts by their own acappella groups, which are "amazing and award-winning." Students also partake in notoriously drunken parties in senior housing, although if a quieter, sober evening is more your thing, Cholmondeley's is great for a cup of coffee and an open mike for local artists. All in all, students refer to weekends on campus as "hit or miss," but if it's a miss, there's always Boston.

"Brandeis Goggles"?

In reference to the girls at Brandeis, one male student jokingly said, "Nine out of ten Jewish girls are pretty, and the last tenth go to Brandeis." Brandeis girls have similar feelings for their male counterparts—as one female put it, "There are not a lot of attractive people here." This lack of hotties on campus has caused many students to wear Brandeis goggles. Similar to beer goggles, "Brandeis goggles" have the effect of reminding the wearers that beauty is relative, and therefore, they must lower their standards. It is these Brandeis goggles that students claim cause the great number of hookups on campus.

If goggles aren't the reason, it could be the booze that leads to the large number of hookups at the Deis. Moreover, students say that there is a significant presence of both marijuana and ecstasy on campus. All three substances are reportedly easy to obtain, but students maintain that there isn't a serious drug abuse problem at the school and drinking is far from a social necessity. However, at the same time, the campus and the Waltham police seem very indifferent to underage alcohol consumption, and one freshman noted that at parties she could just show any ID, no matter how old it said she was, and be allowed to enter.

Despite the school's relatively lax alcohol policy, freshmen are compelled to live in what are called "dry quads," where liquor is a no-no. Students are also not allowed to smoke cigarettes if they are within 25 feet of a dormitory. Failure to obide by these rules leads to written citations, which appear to many to be just a slap on the wrist, but students also say it is not a good idea to accumulate too many of these. These seemingly rigid rules for freshmen are not very strictly adhered to. One freshman pointed out that despite the dry quad she lives in, "I have a bottle of Amaretto and Smirnoff in my closet right now."

Sweet Buildings

The physical aspects of the Deis are very popular among the students. The school is relatively small, which means its never a "hassle to get around." Furthermore, the architecture is interesting. For example, the theater building is shaped like a top hat and the music building looks like a grand piano. To represent the religious tolerance on which Brandeis was founded, there are three separate houses of worship right next to each other. And interestingly enough, the sanctuaries have been constructed in such a way that at no time can any one of the buildings cast a shadow on another.

Perhaps the most dominant and "gorgeous" structure on campus is the university's first building, the Castle. Currently used as a residential building, the Castle has rooms that are widely coveted by students. In particular, pre-meds desire rooms in the Castle because the university has deemed it a quiet building, where residing students devote most of their time to their studies.

> **"It's not like I only see white, Jewish kids, but there are a lot of them."**

Students are also very proud of their gym, the Joseph P. and Clara Ford Athletic and Recreation Complex. This gigantic facility has recently served as a practice center for the Boston Celtics, and although sports are not a very prominent aspect of campus life, a lot of students do spend time at the gym either staying in shape or playing intramurals. There are no contact sports at Brandeis, as demanded by the people who funded the construction of the gymnasium. With no football, the students typically cheer on the Brandeis Judges at baseball and basketball games.

A Jewish University

Although Brandeis has a predominantly Jewish population, the school is much more diverse than many people expect. Fifteen percent of students are minorities, and this number seems to increase more and more each year, as evidenced by this year's freshman class, which has the greatest number of minority students and the fewest number of Jews in the school's history. Fortunately, students at Brandeis seem to avoid self-segregation, and as one student happily pointed out, "I hang out with totally mixed people." Furthermore, aside from the problems with looks, students are very happy with one another. One student confessed, "I wasn't really expecting to meet a lot of cool people here, but I really did." Another student added, "Everyone is just really friendly."

Despite Brandeis' increased efforts to diversify the student body, Judaism still plays a major role on the campus. As one student observed, "It's not like I only see white, Jewish kids, but there are a lot of them." Brandeis was founded on tolerance, and the community is without doubt very accepting and liberal. This atmosphere allows the university to focus its attention on academics and maintain its growing reputation as one of the better research universities in the country.
—*Jonathan Levy*

FYI

The three best things about attending Brandeis are "the friendly atmosphere, the exercise you can get from such a hilly campus, and the proximity to Boston."

The three worst things about attending Brandeis are "the food, the lack of student diversity, and the expense of tuition."

The three things that every student should do before graduating from Brandeis are "drink the punch at a fraternity party, study abroad, and party at Pachanga, Brandeis' international-style dance club."

One thing I'd like to have known before coming here is "not to waste classes—only take stuff you're interested in."

Clark University

Address: 950 Main Street; Worcester, MA 01610-1477
Phone: 508-793-7431
E-mail address: admissions@admissions.clarku.edu
Web site URL: www.clarku.edu
Founded: 1887
Private or Public: private
Religious affiliation: none
Location: urban
Undergraduate enrollment: 2,013
Total enrollment: 3,003
Percent Male/Female: 40%/60%
Percent Minority: 11%

Percent African-American: 3%
Percent Asian: 4%
Percent Hispanic: 3%
Percent Native-American: 0.5%
Percent in-state/out-of-state: 55%/45%
Percent Pub HS: 80%
Number of Applicants: 3,231
Percent Accepted: 73%
Percent Accepted who enroll: 21%
Entering: 487
Transfers: 43
Application Deadline: 1 Feb
Mean SAT: 574 V, 566 M
Mean ACT: 25

Middle 50% SAT range: 520–630 V, 520–620 M
Middle 50% ACT range: 22–28
3 Most popular majors: psychology, biology, economics
Retention: 87%
Graduation rate: 65%
On-campus housing: 95%
Fraternities: NA
Sororities: NA
Library: 560,836 volumes
Tuition and Fees: $22,620 in; $22,620 out
Room and Board: $4,350
Financial aid, first-year: 79%

Cluttering the Clark University campus are posters that display a large pea pod with different colored peas inside. Underneath it reads, "Categorizing people isn't something we do here." This diversity is what draws many students to Clark. Clark students, for example, enjoy music that ranges from Grateful Dead to country to the newest hip-hop. Clark also boasts the third largest population of international students.

Freudian Slip

A few years ago, a statue of Freud was erected in Red Square, the center of campus. This statue inspired many debates among the students of Clark. But Clark students are proud that their university was the only campus where Freud ever spoke and his presence on campus brought attention to Clark's psychology department, a popular department with the students. Students also have the opportunity to explore many other departments, because they are required to fulfill a program consisting of classes in eight perspectives: aesthetic, historical, values, language, science, formal analysis, verbal expression, and comparative.

Other popular departments include the new Center for Holocaust Studies, and the interdisciplinary Communications and Culture major. One very popular professor is Prof. Turner, who is one of the geography department's most respected faculty members. One of Turner's students said, "He is a big part of the reason I chose to minor in geography. Everyone should take a class with him." Students also gave good reviews to Creative Actor and Medical Ethics classes. Although non-art majors regard art as a slacker major, one art student reported that "art classes are much more time consuming and demanding than any other classes I've taken."

The difficulty of classes is hard to generalize. Some lower level classes are grueling while some upper level classes seem quite basic. Some students, claim that academic variety is sacrificed due to Clark's small size. This small size, however, allows students to interact with their professors more intimately. Students say that professors are down to earth, very understanding, and incredibly approachable. Some professors even incorporate dinners into their classes. Students should be warned, however, that Clark has its share of professors with heavy accents. TA's do not teach classes, but they are there to help.

The Study Abroad Department at Clark is very popular; most students go away during their spring semester of junior year. Popular destinations include Scotland, London, Spain, Africa and Japan. For those who want to try out being abroad for a shorter amount of time, Clark also participates with The College of the Holy Cross in a month-long May term in Luxembourg.

You Can Do What You Want To Do

Clark's social life is what you make of it. The weekend begins on Thursday since many students don't have class on Fridays. The Clark Student Activities Board brings entertainment on campus, ranging from bands and comedians to even hypnotists. The Clark University Film Society shows over thirty screenings each semester. Two theatrical groups, The Clark University Players Society and Clark on Drama, coordinate productions throughout the year. One of the most popular groups on campus is the improv troupe called the "Peapod Squad." Empty seats at their shows are hard to find! There are also two a cappella groups, the Counterpoints (all female) and the Clark Bars (coed), which perform on and off campus.

For such an academically motivated school, Clark has an inviting party scene. On weekends, underclassmen flock to crowded parties at upperclassmen inhabited off-campus houses. Kegs are very common at these parties. Of-age and resourceful underage students frequent the local bars like Scarlet O'Hara's. One underclassman admits, "my social life is limited because I do not have a fake ID."

Clark's alcohol policy is relatively lenient. Freshman dorms are dry and no kegs are allowed in campus housing. Students who are 21 are free to drink yet no open containers are permitted in public. While campus police enforce this policy, they are not as strict as the Worcester Police. One student said, "Due to the school's location, the school police seem to focus more on safety and less on alcohol policies."

The alcohol's presence at Clark is magnified on Spree Day. Spree Day is usually held in April as a celebration of the coming of Spring. The date is selected and kept secret by a committee of upperclassmen until that day when they interrupt students' slumber by banging on garbage cans and yelling. Classes are canceled that day as students and staff flock to the Campus Green, which transforms into a carnival. Musical groups have played in the past, as well. By five o' clock, most students retire to their rooms to pass out.

Dorms

Campus housing is mandatory only for freshmen and sophomores, but two thirds of the student body live on campus all four years. Freshmen usually live together in a first-year residence hall, yet some freshmen can live in dorms with upperclassmen. In general, freshmen halls are louder and more exciting than their upper class counterparts. Rooms in the freshman halls, Wright and Bullock, are reportedly small but acceptable, and the better social life in these buildings make the cramped living worth while. A senior commented that living in a freshmen hall was "the highlight of my four years." Resident Advisors (RA's) in freshmen halls try to be your friend but often seem more like police that strictly enforce quiet hours.

Maywood Hall seems to be the most desirable of the upperclassmen dorms. Maywood is the newest residence hall, and its apartment-like 4 to 6 person suites consist of bedrooms, a common room, and private bathroom. Unfortunately for freshmen, they are not allowed in Maywood. In addition to the traditional dorms, students can live in theme houses like the Quiet House, the Year-Round House, and the Substance Free House.

Freshmen and sophomores living in dorms must be on a meal plan. The meal plan consists of boards (individual meals) and flex dollars which give students an account to spend as they choose. Students can eat either in the dining hall or at the Bistro, a deli that offers sandwiches, salads, and grill food made to order. Food in the dining hall is mediocre, but always suspiciously better when parents and prospective students are around. However, the variety of choices are good, and there is a special vegetarian/vegan section. The sandwich counter is a favorite of many students. The draw of the dining halls is not necessarily the food however; it's a great place to "sit with friends and talk and laugh a lot." Students are not rushed in and out, and meal times are considered a social gathering.

Little "Brick" Different

Clark's campus is very compact: a "far" walk on campus takes less than 10 minutes. Most of the buildings are fairly modern and constructed with brick. The Goddard Library (named after Robert Goddard, creator of the rocket) is a strangely shaped building, which supposedly looks like an open book from an aerial view. The library's strange shape makes for many interesting hiding places. According to *Rolling Stone* magazine, the Goddard Library was Jerry Garcia's favorite place to trip (an important consideration for any prospective student). At the center of campus is Red Square that, due to reconstruction, is no longer red. Right next to Red Square is the Campus Green, a very social place in warm weather where people read, lay out, or play frisbee.

> **According to *Rolling Stone* magazine, the Goddard Library was Jerry Garcia's favorite place to trip.**

Dana Commons is the student union and offers a place to email, play pingpong, shoot pool, watch movies, hold meetings, or eat at the Moonlight Cafe. The Moonlight Cafe is open late on weekends and also accepts flex dollars. The University Center (UC) is home to meeting rooms, the dining hall and Bistro, the mailroom, and the general store. The UC is at the center of campus and is a popular meeting place.

Wormtown

Worcester, is a sizeable industrial city in the middle of Massachusetts, and unfortunately, Clark sits in one of its less desirable areas. As in any big city, safety is a concern at Clark and thus students are encouraged to stay in groups and take advantage of the foot and car escort services. The key to staying safe at Clark is to use common sense and lots of caution.

While many students complain about Worcester, the city has its attractive points. The Worcester Centrum is a large concert arena, which hosts shows ranging from Eminem to Metallica. Worcester has many bars, a few dance clubs, and interesting international restaurants like Thai Cha Da, Dalat, House of India, Cactus Pete's and Tortilla Sam's. No trip to Clark would be complete without a trip to Tatnuck Bookseller and a meal at Wendy's Clark Brunch. Wendy's is a popular

Clarkie hang-out and is very social. Breakfast is served all day and Annie, the owner and cook, knows the students by names and loves to talk with them.

Worcester's location is close to nature trails, skiing, and Boston. Although Clark provides a shuttle to and from Boston, many students feel that cars are a necessity. Those without cars often borrow friends' cars or resort to begging for rides.

Extracurricular Activities

Clark prides itself on its abundance of clubs and extracurricular activities. Groups range from the Bisexual, Lesbian and Gay Association (BILAGA), Caribbean American Students Association, the Animal Rights Group, and MASSPIRG (an environmental group). Some clubs sponsor activities such as speakers and discussions. Religion on campus is not overly visible, but Hillel and the Clark Christian Fellowship do exist and help to create a religious community. Also, Clark students are fairly community service oriented. MASSPIRG works closely with the community in environmental contexts and a newly formed group, Rotoract, is based solely on community service.

Many student athletes said that the Clark athletics are under appreciated and under funded. Clark is a Division III university that actively recruits athletes, but it does not offer sports scholarships. The men's basketball team and women's soccer teams are the most popular among fans. The softball team, the women's soccer team, and the men's soccer team have all received NCAA tournament bids. Clark has no football team, which tends to prevent any swelling of school spirit. Despite lack of outside appreciation, however, one junior athlete says that "among athletes, everyone is very close and dedicated and driven by a sincere love of the game."

Intramurals are popular, and sometimes becomes relatively competitive. Pick up sports like basketball, soccer and Frisbee bring out lots of Clarkies. The student body is fairly health conscious, making the fitness center (with cardiovascular equipment and weights) often very crowded.

Good Things Come in Small Packages

Whether it's a chat with the cook at Wendy's, a quiet evening hidden in Goddard Library, or a frolic on Spree day, Clark provides a small, but delightful, community. While sometimes the town of Worcester can be daunting, Clarkies find that their little peapod is a great place to spend their four years of college. —*Jessica Bondell*

FYI
The three best things about attending Clark are "the diversity of students, small classes, and great professors."
The three worst things about attending Clark are "the high costs, Worcester, and lack of school spirit."
The three things every student should do before graduating from Clark are "get something pierced, eat at Wendy's Clark Brunch, and take a nap on the green."
One thing I'd like to have known before coming here is "how small the school feels after a few short years."

The College of the Holy Cross

Address: 1 College Street; Worcester, MA 01610-2395
Phone: 508-793-2443
E-mail address: admissions@holycross.edu
Web site URL: www.holycross.edu
Founded: 1843
Private or Public: private
Religious affiliation: Jesuit
Location: small city
Undergraduate enrollment: 2,778
Total enrollment: 2,778
Percent Male/Female: 48%/52%
Percent Minority: 12%

Percent African-American: 3%
Percent Asian: 3%
Percent Hispanic: 5%
Percent Native-American: 0.5%
Percent in-state/out-of-state: 35%/65%
Percent Pub HS: 45%
Number of Applicants: 4,836
Percent Accepted: 44%
Percent Accepted who enroll: 34%
Entering: 721
Transfers: 14
Application Deadline: 15 Jan
Mean SAT: 631 V, 629 M

Mean ACT: NA
Middle 50% SAT range: 550–670 V, 550–670 M
Middle 50% ACT range: NA
3 Most popular majors: English, psychology, economics
Retention: 95%
Graduation rate: 93%
On-campus housing: 100%
Fraternities: NA
Sororities: NA
Library: 561,970 volumes
Tuition and Fees: $23,815 in; $23,815 out
Room and Board: $7,540
Financial aid, first-year: 50%

Steeped in tradition and Jesuit ideals, the College of the Holy Cross offers students a strong liberal arts education in a close-knit, nurturing setting.

Intense Academics

Holy Cross offers students a rigorous liberal arts education, grounded in competition between students and close interaction with professors. Through distributional requirements, the school attempts to make its students as well-rounded as possible. Students must take one class in religion, history, philosophy, literature, the arts, math, science (or two classes in either math or science), and two classes in the social sciences. Students generally find the requirements beneficial, and many take advantage of their AP credit to wave survey courses. Most students at Holy Cross take their classes very seriously, and competition for good grades is intense. In addition, grading is extremely difficult. According to one freshman, "There are no easy majors, and there is no grade inflation at all. I heard that there hasn't been a 4.0 in ten years." The competition is balanced by open access to professors, who tend to be genuinely interested in students' academic careers

and active in helping them to do well. One student raves that "I have yet to meet a professor who wasn't interested in the success of his students." Furthermore, TAs never teach classes, and the small size of classes (usually between 12 and 24 students) provides for an intimate, more engaging learning environment.

Students interested in a freshman year more concentrated in the humanities can apply to the First Year Program. Every year 160 students enroll in the program, which includes a fifteen-person seminar and an emphasis on philosophy and the pursuit of truth and knowledge. These students develop a sense of family with their fellow classmates and eight professors. The students all live together in the same dorm, Hanselman Hall, and they participate in extra meetings and extracurricular activities. Of FYPpers, as student in the program are called, one student says, "I have yet to meet one who's normal; they are really quirky people." Holy Cross's other special program is a highly selective honors program in which students can enroll at the beginning of junior year. Under the guidance of two faculty advisors, fourth-year students in the program devote a quarter of their time to a research project in their major field. In addition to the special academic programs, the administration supplements the educational experience by bringing in guest speakers and lecturers. As one student stated, "there's a different lecture every night."

Student Body: Homogenous but Connected

While for many students, the student body is the most attractive aspect of Holy Cross, for others it is the most in need of diversification. The student population is predominantly white, Irish-Catholic, and many feel that this adds to the closeness of the students as "we all have a lot in common in the way of previous experiences. Students can relate to each other pretty well." Other students regret "how homogenous it is," citing the overwhelming presence of white students clad in Abercrombie & Fitch clothing. "If you love hanging around with white, Irish Catholics," remarked one student, "come on down." These students point out that most Holy Cross students cannot relate to minorities. Generally, however, students feel comfortable and are not bothered by the seeming lack of diversity. They say that there is more racial diversity on campus than one would think, given the stereotype, and they recognize that the administration is taking steps to diversify the student body.

Beyond racial limits, students have other problems with the lack of diversity. "There is a problem with homophobia here," said one student. In response to this problem, students have started three support and activist groups for gay students. Other students complain of the lack of creative diversity: "Artists and creative writers would make life a little more interesting."

The unifying and most noticeable quality of the students, however, is not their ethnicity, but rather their personal drive and their intense motivation in all of their pursuits. A universal quality of the students is that they seem to thrive under stress. "I don't really know any slackers," says one student. Whether it's academics, athletics, or extracurriculars, Holy Cross

students truly strive for excellence in achievement.

Social Scene

Despite the administration's efforts to curb drinking on campus, it is still "the major part of social life" at Holy Cross. A typical Saturday night for students begins with having a couple of beers in someone's dorm room and then going to Caro Street to hit one off-campus drinking party after another. Students do not see drinking as a problem, but rather as a good balance to the overwhelming workload. "There is a lot of partying," says a freshman at Holy Cross, "but we do a ridiculous amount of work as well." The school is cracking down on drinking, however, and students complain of strict regulations and intrusive police intervention: "The administration is by far the worst part of HC. Their alcohol policies include hiring off-duty police officers to arrest students who party off campus." The regulations have done little to stop students from spending their weekend as they want. Still, upperclassmen warn that "the partying culture can fool a naive freshman into thinking that HC is only about drinking."

For those not intrigued by off-campus parties, the school provides events every weekend to keep campus life fun. "Students can always find something to do," emphasized one student. Movies, guest speakers, shows, and concerts are almost always weekend options. The school has an annual Opportunity Knocks dance, in which students set their roommates up on blind dates. The student Center, Hogan, boasts a bookstore, a popular coffee spot, Cool Beans, and a deli, Crossroads, where students often gather to study or just hang out. Next to Crossroads is the campus pub, where good bands often play. The pub is limited to those over 21, and they are very strict about having ID. Another big part of the social life is the ultimate Frisbee league, which students take very seriously. Every night, two teams square off on the fields; as one spectator stated, "it's a big deal." Students stress that it is generally easy to meet people if you get involved in sports or extracurriculars, and social groups are pretty flexible, although "it gets kind of cliquey around activity groups." Students note that there is no permanent dating scene, "just random one-night-stand hookups." There are also no fraternities or sororities, but sports teams such as soccer and rugby team houses become substitutes for the Greek system.

> **"There is a lot of partying," says a freshman at Holy Cross, "but we do a ridiculous amount of work too."**

Though Worcester is by no means a college town, venturing into the city can expand students' social options. Some students complain of the lack of a bar scene and say flat out that "Worcester sucks, there is no night life at all," while others praise the vast array of restaurants and shopping malls. One student calls Worcester "the diner capital of the Northeast." Worcester also has some good clubs such as The Source, which is especially fun on Thursday nights. The Palladium is reportedly "a great place to check out some great bands," and the Centrum is a larger venue for bigger concerts and events. Without a car, however, it is difficult to get off campus and into Worcester. The problems that students have with Worcester are often with the media portraying the students as party animals or with the police: "they exist only to nail HC students."

Campus Life

The most striking aspect of the campus at Holy Cross is how "pristine" it looks, according to students. On the outskirts of Worcester and separated from the city by a large iron fence, the campus is set on a hill, with the dorms, administration buildings, classroom buildings, and the Hart Center (the athletic center) rising respectively above students as they glance up the hill. The campus greenery is impressive, and "it seems that the grass is cut every other day." One student remarked that "the physical plant guys must be obsessive-compulsive." The Hart Center was recently remodeled to include a Wellness Center with state-of-the-art fitness

equipment. The athletic facilities also include an Olympic-size swimming pool, a basketball court, and a hockey rink which of which most Holy Cross students make use. Beyond the 25 varsity sports such as the championship level women's basketball team, students can participate in one of the 17 club sports or work out in the gym. Most people do some kind of physical activity at Holy Cross.

Overall Students agree that the dormitories are comfortable. Freshmen and sophomores get doubles with two desks, two beds which can be lofted, Ethernet, and cable television. Wheeler is the oldest dorm on campus and is known as the party dorm. "Kids are really friendly there," said one student. Students in the First Year Program all live in Hanselman Hall, one of the best dorms. Juniors and seniors have the option of moving off campus, but most stay on campus and live in Alumni and Carlin, dorms with all quads with two big bedrooms and a large common room. Students can choose in any year to enter substance-free housing in Loyola, which "has really nice rooms and facilities." Dorms are coed, with alternating male and female floors. For safety purposes, a key-card is required to get into the dorm buildings and into the hallways. In other words, guys cannot get into female floors without the permission of the girls on the floor. As one student noted, however, "the doors are often propped open, and if they're not, you just wait a few minutes until someone goes out the door."

Dining at Holy Cross is decent, and there is one gigantic dining hall named Kimball. Students choose between all-you-can-eat dining hall food upstairs in Kimball and a food court downstairs. There is also a campus restaurant, but a good reason is usually needed for meal transfer. Students can also go off campus to eat in one of the city's many restaurants.

Campus life at Holy Cross is made complete by student involvement in extracurricular activities. Beyond academics and athletic activities, students are active in everything from the campus newspaper—the Crusader—to the Mock trial team and Model United Nations. "Pretty much everyone is involved in extracurriculars," said one student. As with their studies, students are "really dedicated" to their outside activities, and they are often defined by what they participate in. Their friends become those whom they associate with in these activities. While there is not much political activism at the college, volunteerism and outreach to the city are very popular. There are several community programs, and "the Jesuit ideal of service really does live in the hearts of HC students." With an education and philosophy rooted in Jesuit ideals and the closeness between students, "HC is a place where you can get very involved," a setting in which determined and talented students will undoubtedly thrive. —*Chiraag Bains*

FYI

The three best things about attending Holy Cross are: "the professors, the beautiful campus, and the connection with my classmates."

The three worst things about attending Holy Cross are: "Worcester residents, Worcester, and Mount St. James."

The three things that every student should do before graduating are: "check out Caro Street on a Saturday night, go to the Opportunity Knocks dance, and play a good game of dorm Assassins."

One thing I'd like to have known before coming here is: "you are stuck on campus freshman and sophomore year unless you know someone with a car."

Hampshire College

Address: 893 West Street; Amherst, MA 01002	**Percent African-American:** 4%	**Mean ACT:** NA
Phone: 413-559-5471	**Percent Asian:** 4%	**Middle 50% SAT range:** 610–720 V, 550–650 M
E-mail address: admissions@hampshire .edu	**Percent Hispanic:** 3% **Percent Native-American:** 0.5%	**Middle 50% ACT range:** 27–31
Web site URL: www.hampshire.edu	**Percent in-state / out-of-state:** 17%/83%	**3 Most popular majors:** art, theater creative writing
Founded: 1965	**Percent Pub HS:** 54%	**Retention:** 77%
Private or Public: private	**Number of Applicants:** 1,774	**Graduation rate:** 38%
Religious affiliation: none	**Percent Accepted:** 61%	**On-campus housing:** 99%
Location: rural	**Percent Accepted who enroll:** 28%	**Fraternities:** NA
Undergraduate enrollment: 1,162	**Entering:** 297	**Sororities:** NA
Total enrollment: 1,162	**Transfers:** 111	**Library:** 110,000 volumes
Percent Male / Female: 44%/56%	**Application Deadline:** 1 Feb	**Tuition and Fees:** $2,500 in; $2,500 out
Percent Minority: 12%	**Mean SAT:** 647 V, 592 M	**Room and Board:** $6,622 **Financial aid, first-year:** 53%

If you ever thought that you were born in the wrong era, that you would have been better off growing up in the liberal days of the 1960s, then Hampshire College is likely for you. Hampshire and its students defy classification and are as liberal as can be imagined. However, underlying this environment of seemingly little responsibility is an academic plan that requires an immense amount of individual care and attention.

A Unique Education

Hampshire students benefit from several unique features of the college; namely, its focus on individual learning, the absence of tests and grades, and the college's membership in the Massachusetts Five College Consortium. Hampshire students engage in an individualized course of study as soon as they arrive on-campus. The academic structure of Hampshire consists of three divisions. Students must complete work in each division to graduate. First, students must complete coursework in the four schools of Division 1: humanities and arts, natural science, social science, and cognitive science. In those four schools, students can complete coursework either through formal classes or by doing projects. "It's possible to graduate Hampshire without ever taking a class," said one student.

Division 2 requirements constitute the coursework that makes up a students major. Students pick an advisor with whom they work on a portfolio of their projects and research. Projects can take the form of internships, artistic creations, classwork, or study abroad. Once a student has completed Division 2, he moves on to Division 3, in which the student completes the equivalent of a senior thesis or project in his or her concentration. Students normally work on their Division 3 project for an entire year, consulting constantly with faculty members. One student noted that "all the professors here are very willing to work and they know their fields of study incredibly well." In place of grades, students at Hampshire receive detailed critiques of their work.

Hampshire's small size and liberal bent on academia creates an environment in which individual learning is encouraged. As a result, however, departments are scattered and often lack focus and resources. To compensate, Hampshire is a member of the Five College Consortium, and shares resources with Smith College, Mount Holyoke College, Amherst College, and the University of Massachusetts at Amherst. "Hampshire might not have the depth of the fields, but the Five College system makes up for it. We have access to their classes, resources, and professors, and a bus runs through the Five College circuit every half hour," said one student; another student found that most Hampshire students take advantage of the consortium.

The uniqueness of Hampshire's academic structure has received both praise and criticism from students. "It takes a really unique kid to do well here, because it's so easy to do nothing and stick around for eight years, as a lot of kids do," said one student. "You have to have an immense drive and take a real responsibility for getting an education. No one here is going to hand anything to you." For those students who do take that responsibility, however, the experience can be very rewarding. "It's the best educational idea I've ever heard," said one student. "It's basically laissez-faire applied to a college. I've never seen anyplace like it, and you learn so much more here about everything academic and nonacademic than at a conventional school because you design your entire education."

Social Life

The social scene at Hampshire is just as liberal as the academic scene. According to one student's estimate, half the Hampshire population is made up of "hippies," meaning "they don't bathe, they have dreadlocks and listen to the Grateful Dead." Vegetarians and vegans make up a majority of the population, and recreational drug use is not unheard of. Students at Hampshire get along incredibly well and, according to one student, "everything here is okay as long as you believe in it. No one is unapproachable." The campus is increasingly diverse, and there is little to no racial or sexual-orientation tension. Minorities feel very comfortable on-campus. "Everyone at Hampshire seems to be bisexual. It's a running joke," said one student. Religion is not very big at Hampshire, but there is a predominance of Jews. "The Yiddish Book Center is based at Hampshire," said one student, "I suppose that draws a lot of Jews here. It's really the only active religion. Atheism is second to Judaism."

The Hampshire administration contributes to this cooperative, permissive atmosphere. "The administration really does not comment. If it does not harm anyone, then they think it's okay," said one student. "Officially they would have to condemn it, but we don't really have rules. We go by community standards and campus norms."

Some of those norms would not be

norms at any other school. The most popular club on-campus is the Bondage and
S&M club, and the most popular event
each year is the Drag Ball, for which students dress in drag and local drag queens
come and perform. And Hampshire Halloween was named by *Rolling Stone* as
one of the best parties of the year.

Student interests range from the mainstream to the fringe. "This might be the
only place that you'll hear the Grateful
Dead, Miles Davis, and hardcore Gothic
music simultaneously while watching
Dawson's Creek and obscure German art
films in one night," said one student.

Living it Up

Housing at Hampshire offers a large number of options. Students can live in dorms
or modular housing. Dorms have mostly
singles, and students are guaranteed
rooms there. In the dorms, there are several theme halls, including lesbian and
gay, clothing-optional, substance-free, and
study-intensive options. Mods offer greater
diversity. There are five mods, each of
which has its own characteristic population. For example, the hippies on-campus
live in Endfield while the more academically oriented students stay in Greenwich. All students must live on-campus
for the entirety of their Hampshire education. "The dorms are very social. All the
bathrooms and halls are coed," said one
student. "People love living in dorms."
There are residential assistants in the two
dorms who, according to one student,
"are supposed to carry out the policies of
the housing office, but don't really care
what you do."

The housing buildings like the other
buildings on-campus, are described by
students as "ugly." However, the setting of
the school is idyllic. Hampshire is situated
on what used to be an apple orchard and
is surrounded by woods. The administration is currently building a student center,
and is constantly improving classroom
and academic work space. The building
for which Hampshire is known, however,
is its "Yurt," a Mongolian shack made of
animal skins. The building, which started
out as a former Hampshire student's Division 3 project, currently boasts heat and
an Internet connection.

All students in dorms and many students living in mods eat at Saga, the large
cafeteria on-campus, whose food is provided by Marriot. The food gets poor ratings from students: "The motto here is,
Saga: where food goes to die." However,
Saga does offer a large array of options,
including many vegetarian and vegan
dishes. "They know their audience well,"
said one student. The nearby presence of
the other member colleges of the consortium led to an abundance of restaurants
catering to college students, so there are a
large number of businesses that deliver
food until 3 or 4 in the morning.

> According to one student's esti-
> mate, half the Hampshire popula-
> tion is made up of "hippies,"
> meaning "they don't bathe, they
> have dreadlocks and listen to the
> Grateful Dead."

On weekends, Hampshire students often split their time between Hampshire
proper and the nearby towns of Northampton, Amherst, and, two hours away,
Boston. On-campus, students often go to
the Ash Auditorium, a large cultural center
that has hosted the likes of Blonde Red-
head and Lou Barlow of Sebadoh in the recent past. Mods also throw parties almost
every weekend. Students often go into
Amherst, Northampton, and Boston for a
wider offering of social options. However,
there is little social mingling between the
Consortium colleges. "You have your
friends from the classes you take at other
schools, but that's about it," said one student. "Most of the time, you'll just see them
in Amherst or Boston on the weekends
anyway." There are often fraternity parties
at UMass, but Hampshire students "would
never even think of going."

Since the fraternity scene is obviously
not an option at Hampshire, students have
to find other ways to keep themselves
busy. Two campus newspapers, Omen and
Foreword, are well-read on-campus, and
the Hampshire Community Council works
to "determine policy as much as student
organizations can." The most popular activities on-campus are theater and music.

Theater students tend to stick together and hang out on weekends. Musicians, however, wander from group to group. "There are some pretty amazing musicians here, and everyone is willing to play with everyone else," said one student. "There are no organized, formal bands. You make your own, put up a poster, and get a lot of responses." Musicians frequently play in four or five groups simultaneously.

The focus on arts leaves little room for athletics on-campus. "Athletics are sort of looked down upon here, but, as with everything else, no one really cares," said one student. Hampshire is part of the New England Small Schools League and competes against other schools with less than 1,500 students in ultimate Frisbee and basketball. "Ultimate is immense here, our basketball team is a joke, and football is nonexistent," said one student. "But watch out as you walk on-campus. I've gotten hit by at least 100 Frisbees in my two years here."

Students at Hampshire revel in their freedom and uniqueness. They are able to create an idiosyncratic social and academic scene while drawing on the academic offerings of four other schools and the cultural offerings of two nearby towns and one nearby city. If you are self-motivated and interested in learning more outside the classroom than inside, Hampshire is likely for you. —*Alan Schoenfeld and staff*

FYI

The three best things about attending Hampshire are "very understanding professors, 850 acre campus yet nothing is farther than a 2.5 minute walk, Yiddish Book Center"

The three worst things about attending Hampshire are "optional showering and optional smell, excessive pot smoking, and (relatedly) lack of Visine in school book store, which happens to sell lesbian and gay porn but no straight porn."

The three things that every student should do before graduating from Hampshire are "spend a lot of time at the Hampshire Tree, fall asleep in Farnklin-Patterson Hall, sample the delicate fare of SAGA."

One thing I'd like to have known before coming here is "despite the fact that Amherst is close, civilization is far, far away."

Harvard University

Address: Byerly Hill, 8 Garden Street; Cambridge, MA 02138
Phone: 617-495-1551
E-mail address: college@fas.harvard.edu
Web site URL: fas.harvard.edu
Founded: 1636
Private or Public: private
Religious affiliation: none
Location: urban
Undergraduate enrollment: 6,684
Total enrollment: 18,103
Percent Male/Female: 54%/46%
Percent Minority: 34%

Percent African-American: 8%
Percent Asian: 17%
Percent Hispanic: 8%
Percent Native-American: 0.5%
Percent in-state/out-of-state: 16%/84%
Percent Pub HS: 65%
Number of Applicants: 18,161
Percent Accepted: 11%
Percent Accepted who enroll: 79%
Entering: 1,634
Transfers: 79
Application Deadline: 1 Jan
Mean SAT: NA
Mean ACT: NA

Middle 50% SAT range: 700–800 V, 700–790 M
Middle 50% ACT range: 30–34
3 Most popular majors: government, economics, biology
Retention: 96%
Graduation rate: 97%
On-campus housing: 100%
Fraternities: NA
Sororities: NA
Library: 13,000,000 volumes
Tuition and Fees: $25,128 in; $25,128 out
Room and Board: $7,982
Financial aid, first-year: 52%

"I have a roommate who had a day in New York named after her for a community service project she did."

"I started a junior high summer school, and I really learned a lot hiring teachers and staff."

"My friend ran a culinary academy."

For every Harvard student, there exists a story of a remarkable feat; the extraordinary becomes cliché in Cambridge, Massachusetts, where Harvard attracts the intellectual elite of every generation. To attend Harvard, according to one student, is "to be surrounded by people who are amazing." But according to another Harvard student, or Cantab, students' awareness of their excellence causes them to see Harvard as "the be-all and end-all of academic experience"; to incoming freshmen, "the 'I'm going to Harvard' thing is a pretty big deal." However, regardless of the "Harvard name," the achievements of Harvard's world-renowned faculty and alumni, as well as its honored traditions, continue to woo prospective students to Harvard Yard.

Academic Richness

Benefiting from Harvard's academics largely depends on self-motivation and teaching fellows (TFs), graduate students pursuing their Ph.D.s. One student noted that "while TFs are meant only as a supplementary resource to professors' lectures, all one-on-one interaction happens with them. So, it's really important that you find enthusiastic TFs." Lectures are where "professors speak; you listen," one undergrad said, "and discussion sections are where you work through the material."

When professors speak, students generally listen, because the professors are nearly all world-renowned. As undergrads, students can take African-American studies from Henry Louis Gates or Introductory Economics from former presidential economic advisor Martin Feldstein. Lectures might enroll "several hundred students or only seventeen; the numbers really depend on the level of the course and the popularity of the professor," noted an undergrad. The smaller classes are mandatory freshman expository writing courses, seminars, and language classes. These "smaller courses are harder to get into, and sometimes people get locked out," one student said. After undergrads declare their concentration (Harvard's term for a major), "it's easier to get into smaller classes within your concentration," one sophomore noted. Even biology and chemistry, notorious for large classes at other institutions, offer small upper-level courses to interested students. Each concentration offers not only unique information, but a distinctive method of instruction as well; Music 51, taught by John Stewart, uses "an approach to teaching that has been cultivated within the music department," as a part of which students write and perform original compositions as final projects.

In order to help students find classes like Music 51, Harvard has the "Q-Guide" and "Shopping Period." The "Q-Guide," officially the "Harvard University Course Evaluation Guide," is a catalog compiled by students that rates different characteristics of a course, such as the professor, readings, lectures, and overall competitive atmosphere. Shopping Period is a week at the beginning of each semester during which students can sit in on different classes before deciding what to take.

In contrast to the academic flexibility provided by Shopping Period, Harvard requires students to demonstrate proficiency in a foreign language, pass a statistics exam, and complete a freshman expository writing course. During sophomore year students usually take a "tutorial," which is a seminar that brings students and professors closer together within each department. If a student wants to graduate with honors, and most do, taking these "tutorials" in addition to writing a senior thesis is required.

Before graduating, Harvard students must also complete a core curriculum. Undergrads take courses in 8 out of 10 core disciplines, including courses in literature and humanities, natural sciences, foreign cultures, and social analysis. There are students who "enjoy fulfilling the core requirements," noted an undergraduate, "because it gives you an opportunity to take a class you'd never really take unless you had to." Many respect the theory behind the core curriculum, which is to introduce students to intellectual perspectives of a variety of departments.

Some, though, disdain the core; one senior considers core classes "watered-down versions of various subjects" where students are "half-interested" and "not reading or participating."

> One student noted a "bland normalcy" where "you can't wear anything too crazy to parties or you'll be the 'crazy person.'"

Perhaps the most common gripe from Harvard students is the school's final exam schedule. Instead of taking place before winter break in December, final exams do not occur until students return in January. Thus each year undergrads leave campus for the holidays with unfinished papers and final exams hanging over them. This may seem like a nightmare, but one student noted, "It's really not that bad. We have a two-week reading period after break, and that's usually enough time to catch up on reading, so you don't feel burdened over break."

"So Much Stuff" or "Bland Normalcy"?

Students claim that the classroom is just one arena for their education. "About half of our time is spent on academics and the other half is for extracurricular activities," one undergrad remarked. The list of Harvard student organizations is extensive, and students can do anything from writing for a travel guidebook to acting in a theater troupe. One student reported, "There's so much stuff you can do that it would be a waste not to pursue some of it." Students also noted the range of interests. "You can pretty much find someone with an interest in anything," a student observed, "and usually an 'interest' means they've written a book or something." Getting involved in Harvard's organizations, publications in particular, can require "comping," the application process students complete to demonstrate their skill and commitment to an organization. Other extracurricular activities include a cappella groups, crew (particularly popular among freshmen), and community service. Most service groups work under

Phillips Brooks House, where "there are a hundred different projects that constantly are looking for eager volunteers." Students take a keen interest in what their fellows create; one senior commented, "The weekend'll come, and I'll be with my friends like, 'Oh, you're doing a show; you're doing a show; I'm doing a show,' and we'll all go to each other's shows."

Each group, though, "has its own self-contained social scene—band parties, magazine parties." All open parties "must be officially registered" with Harvard, and on-campus parties are disbanded by cops at 1:00. Because most parties occur in "Harvard space," many seem alike. One student noted a "bland normalcy" where "you can't wear anything too crazy to parties or you'll be the 'crazy person.'" "Black pants" and "North Face jackets" predominate, and "80's pop, like 'Come-on, Eileen,'" crowds out "alternative" genres. "If you can't handle a little pressure to conform," said one student, "don't come to Harvard."

A small but growing Greek scene offers a different set of social options. A member of a fraternity said, "We fill a social need." Perhaps this "social need" is best defined as a longing for a "typical" college experience of "beer-pong and partying and hanging out," though fraternities at Harvard also offer "faculty dinners and Haunted Houses for neighborhood kids." Many Harvard fraternity brothers "wouldn't have thought they would join fraternities" in high school, and Sigma Chi especially is "very diverse." Finals clubs, societies comprised of chosen seniors, host parties and various social events as well. Still, "Harvard is not a party school at all. There are some who probably never go out," and students looking for a party scene tend to seek it "in nearby Boston and at MIT."

Cantabs often take the twenty-minute T (subway) ride to Boston's museums, symphonies, restaurants, and clubs. A freshman acknowledged, "Whether or not you go into Boston a lot, it's great to know that it's there." Students who don't want to venture as far can also find plenty to do around Cambridge. Harvard Square is home to various shops, bookstores, cafés, and restaurants, in addition to the "many interesting entertainers that frequent the newsstand," one student said, referring to the center of Harvard Square. Although most bars near Harvard are strict about IDs, one will reportedly "let you in with a note from your mother that says you're 21."

After most freshmen spend their first year living in suites on Harvard Yard, upperclassmen form "blocking groups" with up to 16 friends. Each group is randomly assigned to 1 of 12 houses, where the students live for their remaining three years, except for the few students who live off-campus. Each house, which ranges architecturally from traditional to modern, has its own dining room, library, computer room, and special facilities like darkrooms or recording studios. Dining options at Harvard also include Annenberg (where most freshmen eat) and several cafés around campus, such as William James Hall Cafe, the Greenhouse (which now delivers pizza), and Conroy Commons. Freshmen often socialize at Loker Commons, located downstairs from Annenberg at the heart of Harvard Yard, where there is a food court, pool tables, and cable TV. At these cafés and at various campus stores, students can purchase items with Crimson Cash, a debit account set up using students' Harvard IDs.

Outside of Loker Commons and dining halls, students run into friends at Harvard's libraries. Most study at Lamont Library, while Widener is "more of a research place." Students also often study together and "do a lot of group work for economics, statistics, and science courses"; one freshman noted that "everyone works really hard, and group work is encouraged in certain courses."

There is no question that a Harvard diploma can lead to many opportunities. However, one alumna stressed that graduates still must prove themselves just like everyone else; though an undergrad who works hard at Harvard usually has the skills to succeed in any field. While students report that it is easy to become isolated in such an intense, intellectual atmosphere, most still appreciate the benefits of the Harvard experience. One freshman said Harvard "has been the best experience of my life—the tradition, the education, the people—it has been incredible so far." The talented student body, exciting metropolitan location, and inspiring faculty, imbue Harvard with unsurpassable intellectual excitement and energy. One proud student understandably asked, "If you get into Harvard, why would you ever go anywhere else?"
—*Brian Abaluck and Leslie Kane*

FYI

The three best things about Harvard are "diversity, the number of opportunities on campus for extracurriculars, caliber of students."

The three worst things about Harvard are "the administration cracking down on fun, the adjustment period—now you're the small fish in a big pond—tuition bills."

The three things that every student should do before graduating from Harvard are "urinate on the John Harvard statue, have sex in Widener Library, do *not* kiss the John Harvard statue."

One thing I'd like to have known before coming here is "don't be scared of the professors."

Massachusetts Institute of Technology

Address: 77 Massachusetts Avenue Room 3-108; Cambridge, MA 02139
Phone: 617-253-4791
E-mail address: admissions@mit.edu
Web site URL: web.mit.edu
Founded: 1861
Private or Public: private
Religious affiliation: none
Location: urban
Undergraduate enrollment: 4,292
Total enrollment: 9,947
Percent Male/Female: 59%/41%
Percent Minority: 47%
Percent African-American: 6%
Percent Asian: 28%

Percent Hispanic: 11%
Percent Native-American: 2%
Percent in-state/out-of-state: 10%/90%
Percent Pub HS: 70%
Number of Applicants: 9,136
Percent Accepted: 19%
Percent Accepted who enroll: 60%
Entering: 1,048
Transfers: 37
Application Deadline: 1 Jan
Mean SAT: 706 V, 753 M
Mean ACT: 31
Middle 50% SAT range: 660–760 V, 730–800 M

Middle 50% ACT range: 30–33
3 Most popular majors: electrical engineering, computer science, mechanical engineering
Retention: 97%
Graduation rate: 81%
On-campus housing: 99%
Fraternities: 48%
Sororities: 25%
Library: 2,400,000 volumes
Tuition and Fees: $26,746 in; $26,746 out
Room and Board: $7,175
Financial aid, first-year: 60%

During the month of January, the majority of MIT students return to campus for one of the activities that make their university a unique one. Classes don't start until February, but few students miss the Independent Activities Period (IAP), when faculty and fellow students offer four weeks of fun, creative, and educational programs to the MIT community. Activities range from a workshop on how to create your own bonsai to a lecture and tour of the Boron Neutron Capture Therapy (BNCT) at the MIT Research Reactor. According to one MIT underclassman, "IAP is one of the most anticipated events of the year." The program gives both students and faculty an opportunity to show off and to share their intellectual passions in a laid-back and enjoyable atmosphere.

Intense Academics

MIT has earned a reputation for intense academics, which is, by all accounts, an accurate one. Students here are passionate about math, science, and technology. Out of an undergraduate population of less than 5,000 for the 1999–2000 academic year, 2,011 students were enrolled in engineering studies. Students are expected to test the limits of their abilities in the quest for new knowledge, and in return, they are rewarded with an education that is "at the top in the world."

Students come from all over the world to Cambridge in order to learn from and do research with leaders in math and science. "There are famous inventors, Nobel Prize winners and start-up owners in practically every field of study at MIT," said one student. The 923 full-time faculty members include 10 Nobel Prize winners, 4 Kyoto Prize winners, and 2 Pulitzer Prize winners. Professors teach most classes, so even freshmen have the opportunity to "listen to famous professors." Teaching assistants head smaller recitation sections, which meet once a week.

No student would call the workload light. "It will not be an easy four years here for you. The sooner you realize that the better off you will be," said one junior. Students complain about "lots of homework, especially problem sets," and all-night study sessions are not uncommon. All classes taken during freshman year are pass/fail in order to give students time to adjust to the level of work. Students are perpetually complaining about being "hosed," MIT slang for overwhelmed with work, which is derived from the analogy "getting an MIT education is like drinking from a fire hose." However, one student reveals, "The workload is what you make it to be," and by choosing an easier major or settling for lower grades student can lighten their burdens.

> **"Contrary to popular media belief, most people on campus do not drink like fish."**

Every MIT student must take a core group of math and science classes, including two semesters of calculus, two of physics, one semester of biology, and one of chemistry, plus a lab requirement. One student says fulfilling these requirements has been "not bad at all," and many students get a lot of the core out of the way freshman year. Science and math requirements are, however, "just part of the bargain." Students are also required to take eight humanities, arts, and social sciences classes, and four semesters of physical education (Ping-Pong counts) and complete a writing requirement. MIT does its best to make humanities classes interesting and practical. "In my writing class, we put all the stuff we wrote into an on-line magazine," raved one freshman. Others complain that eight humanities classes are "a little constraining" and take up time that could be devoted to courses within a major.

All students are required to complete a major at MIT. Most popular are electrical engineering and computer science, which enroll approximately one-fourth of all students. For students looking for the hard road, physics is supposed to be the most difficult major, whereas and management is reputably the easiest. Nevertheless, "you will be challenged regardless of the major you choose," and students warn that there are hard classes in every major. MIT students also have the option of double-majoring, adding a minor, or graduating in five years with a master's degree.

Introductory classes are usually large, around 200 to 400 students. Freshmen who want more individualized attention

have the option of participating in the Experimental Study Group (ESG), in which first-year students are taught in small groups by professors and upperclassmen and the format is either a discussion-based seminar or a tutorial. Once introductory courses are out of the way, class size shrinks and can "range from 2 to 80 depending on the major." Students have the opportunity to cross-register at Harvard or Wellesley if MIT doesn't offer a class they're interested in.

One of the jewels of the MIT academic curriculum is the Undergraduate Research Opportunities Program (UROP). It fosters research partnerships between undergraduates and MIT faculty, encouraging students to become involved at the forefront of developments in science and technology. "If you are interested in submersing yourself in cutting-edge research, MIT is the place to be," said one upperclassman. Students can participate for academic credit or pay, but many join as volunteers and often work on UROP projects over the summer, as well as during the school year. The program allows MIT students to apply what they learn in the classroom to real scientific problems.

Nights in the City

When it is time to put the books away, MIT students know how to have a good time. There is a Greek system on campus, with 26 fraternities and sororities. Usually there is a fraternity party "at least once a week," but these parties are often "by invitation only." Students also frequent the active club scene, dancing the night away with students from Boston's other universities. There are local bars, but you need an ID, and "everything closes at two in the morning." While in recent years techies have gained a reputation for heavy drinking, many students feel it is an unwarranted one. "Contrary to popular media belief, most people on campus do not drink like fish," said one student, and non-drinkers are not ostracized or excluded from the social scene.

Both Boston and Cambridge provide a multitude of alternatives to the party scene. There are movies, restaurants, and coffee shops, all accessible through Boston's system of public transportation and students often venture out into the city. "People go off campus all the time to eat, especially on the weekends, " taking advantage of the restaurants in the North End or along Newbury Street. In the beginning, many students do "a lot of touristy stuff," said one freshman, like visiting the Museum of Fine Arts or shopping at Quincy Market. Most students do not have cars because parking is hard to find in Boston and public transportation makes them unnecessary.

How to Avoid Work: IMs and Hacking

Intramural sports are "very popular" at MIT, and each year hundreds of teams compete in everything from pool to water polo, with teams usually organized by living group. Intercollegiate sports are less popular, but about 20% of the campus participate at the varsity level in at least one sport. The rowing and fencing teams are "very strong," as are the pistol and rifle teams. Few people attend the football games, however, and "the opposing teams' fans often outnumber our fans."

MIT students traditionally show off their creativity and daring through performing hacks, "which are clever, nondestructive practical jokes on campus." Famous hacks of the past include placing a replica of a police car, complete with flashing lights, on top of the MIT dome and changing the inscription in Lobby 7 to read: "Established for Advancement and Development of Science, Its Application to Industry, the Arts, Entertainment and Hacking." Hacks are always performed with a spirit of mischief and fun, and students frown upon any prank that damages property or offends students.

The Housing Scene

MIT undergrads get to choose their housing starting freshman year. When new students first arrive, they are put in temporary dorm housing for orientation, which is followed by a four-day period when students can rush fraternities and sororities and attend events at the various dorms. Since MIT students choose where they live, each dorm is unique and it is the "personality that sets individual dorms apart," rather than location or setup. By the time classes start, students are set in permanent housing either in fraternities or sororities or in a dorm through "a lottery system run by a computer."

The typical freshman dorm room is a double or a triple, and "most of them are very nice." All the dorms are coed, except for McCormick Hall, which is the all-girl residence. There is a residential advisor, usually a graduate student, on every floor of the dorms. "RAs are generally very laid-back," said one student. Most students live on-campus all four years, because "rent can be quite expensive in the area." On-campus living also means on-campus dining, and the food ratings range anywhere from "average" to "sucky." In the words of one freshman, "I've seen better and I've seen worse."

Passionate Students

When asked what sets MIT apart, many reply that the student body possesses a passion and intensity for learning found in few other places. "The ultimate thing that differentiates MIT from other schools is that we are nerds, some of us big nerds, and we are proud of it." On a campus where students take science and math seriously, both buildings and majors are labeled with numbers (for example, Computer Science and Electrical Engineering is called course 6), and the words "fun" and "math" are not mutually exclusive. While many students profess a love/hate relationship with the school, they also say that if they could go back in time, they would choose MIT all over again. —*Pamela Boykoff*

FYI

The three best things about attending MIT are "strong academics and research opportunities, pass/no record first year, and the location."

The three worst things about attending MIT are "expensive tuition, a lot of work, and some bad faculty."

The three things that every MIT student should do before graduating are "develop a true love for calling things by numbers rather than names; take 6.001, the Structure and Interpretation of Computer Programs class; and hate the school but gradually learn to love it."

One thing I'd like to have known before coming here is "there is definitely no room for slackers."

Mount Holyoke College

Address: 50 College Street;
South Hadley, MA 01075
Phone: 413-538-2023
E-mail address:
admissions@mtholyoke
.edu
Web site URL:
www.mtholyoke.edu
Founded: 1837
Private or Public: private
Religious affiliation: none
Location: suburban
**Undergraduate
enrollment:** 1,879
Total enrollment: 1,879
Percent Male / Female:
0% / 100%
Percent Minority: 20%
Percent African-American:
5%

Percent Asian: 9%
Percent Hispanic: 5%
Percent Native-American:
0.5%
**Percent in-state / out-of-
state:** 20% / 80%
Percent Pub HS: 62%
Number of Applicants:
2,435
Percent Accepted:
60%
**Percent Accepted who
enroll:** 39%
Entering: 563
Transfers: 59
Application Deadline:
15 Jan
Mean SAT: 626 V,
602 M
Mean ACT: 27

Middle 50% SAT range:
600–660 V,
570–650 M
Middle 50% ACT range:
25–29
3 Most popular majors:
biology, English, social
sciences
Retention: 94%
Graduation rate: 79%
On-campus housing:
99%
Fraternities: NA
Sororities: 10%
Library: 653,613 volumes
Tuition and Fees:
$24,354 in; $24,354 out
Room and Board: $7,110
Financial aid, first-year:
66%

P icture a small, liberal arts college for women, dedicated to excellence, and tucked into the small, picturesque New England town of South Hadley, Massachusetts. The close-knit community allows the women of Mount Holyoke to build lasting, meaningful relationships with professors and peers as well as strengthen their independence and individuality. However, this quaint and peaceful community exists within the broader world of the Five-College Consortium that unites Mount Holyoke with Smith College, the University of Massachusetts/Amherst, Amherst College, and Hampshire College. The consortium gives the Mount Holyoke students access to the academic resources and social activities of five colleges.

Small but Intense

Academics at Mount Holyoke are almost universally described as extremely rigorous. Students are required to take distribution requirements consisting of three classes in the humanities, two in math or science (one with lab), two in social science, one in foreign language, one "multicultural" course, and six credits of physical

education. The amount of time that the requirements take up, particularly the hefty PE requirement, is sometimes a hassle, but on the whole, most Mount Holyoke women enjoy the diverse requirements; one student explained that they "got me to think harder about what I was doing before I declared my major."

Some of the most popular majors are reportedly psychology, English, chemistry, and biology. While one student claimed that "all of the departments are strong," some claim that the classics major is the least popular. Students say that class size varies a lot, and large classes tend to be science lectures, Intro Psych, and other introductory classes that fulfill distribution requirements. However, most of these larger classes only enroll 50 to 60 students, while most upper-level classes have less than 20. One student said that "the classes are tiny, and students participate (whether they want to or not) in class."

Professors at Mount Holyoke are "fun, accessible, and just generally awesome." There are a few TAs, but students say that all of the teaching is done by professors; TAs may aid in labs or lead help sections, or language fellows may teach the discussion part of language classes and leave the teaching of the class to a professor. Some famous faculty include prizewinning poet Mary Jo Salter, National Security Advisor Tony Lake, author Beverly Tatum (*Why Are All the Black Kids Sitting Together in the Cafeteria?*), and statistician George Cobb. Even high-profile professors are described as extremely friendly and accommodating, a factor to which many students attribute their decision in choosing Mount Holyoke.

In addition to everything that Mount Holyoke has to offer its students academically, students also have access to everything that the Five-College Consortium has to offer. The consortium forms a larger collegiate grouping in which all of the members benefit from the resources of the others. Any student at Mount Holyoke can take classes at these other institutions and get credit for them, and students also can use any of the other four colleges' library systems and benefit from other academic offerings such as lectures and special programs.

Living Among Women

One student summed up the visual appearance of the Mount Holyoke campus by saying "This is what I grew up thinking colleges were supposed to look like." Women at Mount Holyoke consistently rave about their campus, dubbing it the "most beautiful campus in the country." It has trees, grass, two lakes, a waterfall on the north end of campus, and old redbrick buildings with ivy on them everywhere. Students describe the campus as fairly self-contained, and very safe, because of its location in tiny South Hadley. One of the most distinctive buildings on-campus is the library, which students admire both for its impressive architecture, and for how conducive it is to getting work done; students can choose either to hide away in the silence of the stacks and study on comfy sofas, or they can sit together in meeting rooms for more informal, group studying.

Since students are required to live on-campus for all four years unless they have special permission, most live in the dorms, which are reportedly quite nice. Most students prefer the older dorms, such as

Pearsons and the Rockies, because they are more beautiful and have unique features, like windowseats; newer dorms, though, are often more spacious. Dorms consist of mainly double and single rooms, and all seniors and most juniors get singles. Every dorm is single-sex, since Mount Holyoke is an all-women's school, but there are no restricted hours for guests, male or female, in the dorms. The only rule is that guests must be escorted up and down the stairs in the escalators by a resident student. Each floor has one single-sex bathroom on it, and each dorm has a nonsmoking floor or two. There are also "quiet hours" between 11 P.M. and 8 A.M. on weekdays, and there are two floors on-campus that are official "quiet floors" for "people who want peace 24 hours a day."

> **"Lots of women have boyfriends elsewhere. Others have girlfriends here. Some have both."**

Every dorm also has a dining hall, and a full meal plan is included in tuition. Students say that, although the same menu is served at each location, the smaller the dorm, the better the food tends to be. There are vegetarian and vegan options at every meal, which are reportedly tastier than the nonvegetarian dishes. Students like to order in pizza or eat at some of the many restaurants and delis in South Hadley or in nearby Amherst or Northampton. However, since all meals have already been paid for with tuition, students generally only go out on weekends or when they have an off-campus class in Amherst or Northampton.

Outside of Class

Mount Holyoke women "do an amazing amount of extracurricular work, whether it be community service, college government, or campus organizations." Despite the heavy academic workload, most students reportedly find a lot of time to spend on the vast number of groups open to them. There are lots of political organizations to become involved in, several publications, including a student newspaper called the Mount Holyoke News and a variety of literary magazines, and a very active Student Government Association. Musically inclined students can join the Glee Club, or one of two English Handbell Choirs. Mount Holyoke also has a program called Free Theater that allows students to produce shows independent from the theater department and thus encourages experimental works and participation by nontheater majors. A more unusual, though popular, group on-campus is the Lunar Howling Society, in which a group of women "go out and hoot at the full moon once a month." One student said that she had "never heard anyone complain about the lack of organizations to join!"

Sports are also an option for athletic Mount Holyoke students. The biggest rival school is nearby Smith. Students say that the two schools have a "great relationship and a healthy competition." The most popular and competitive varsity teams are said to be field hockey, crew, lacrosse, and basketball. In addition to these, there is also a very successful rugby team; the team, though only a club team, has "a huge cult following." There are also a number of intramural sports in which any student can participate, and the athletic facilities—including the gym, pool, dance studios, workout rooms, weight machines, tennis courts, and a huge equestrian center—are open to anyone and reportedly very extensive.

Social life at Mount Holyoke is a bit more low-key than at many colleges, but nonetheless can be very satisfying. Some students claim that to have any fun at all, students must either own a car to get off-campus to parties at Amherst or UMass, or else have enough patience to wait for the free bus service that runs between campuses and neighboring towns. However, others say that Mount Holyoke is such a close-knit community that its students have fun with their friends at smaller gatherings on weekends in the dorms, or at larger, campus parties such as Vegas Night and the Sophomore Semi-Formal. There is no Greek system at Mount Holyoke, which most students appreciate. Students say that the small size of their campus is enough to bring people together.

The Mount Holyoke administration is extremely anti-drinking, with stringent rules against having kegs in the dorms.

One student claimed that Mount Holyoke could be "the driest campus in the nation." But others reported that, while the drinking scene might not be comparable to that of Animal House, it is not totally nonexistent, and if people want to drink, they would be able to obtain alcohol, and many frequently do. Mount Holyoke students throw parties, like most college students, which often attract students from the other schools in the surrounding area. Not all students party or drink by any means, but those who want to have big parties do. They just have to be very discreet about their alcohol consumption, due to the strict regulations.

Students report that the campus is fairly open to sexual or romantic relationships of any kind. One student summed it up by saying "lots of women have boyfriends elsewhere. Others have girlfriends here. Some have both." While there are obviously no guys in classes, they are in no short supply, since there are several large co-ed colleges nearby, and there are always lots of male visitors around, especially on weekends. Students are quite accepting of the lesbian and bisexual students, and True Colors (also known as LBTA-Lesbian, Bisexual, Transgender Alliance) has a very strong presence on-campus.

Students at Mount Holyoke are fairly liberal in general, and described as extremely politically active, but the campus admittedly does house some more conservative types as well, including members of the College Republicans organization. The student body is also described as incredibly diverse, hailing from all over the U.S. and the rest of the world, although most do come from the Northeast.

Students at Mount Holyoke love their school for the great balance it gives them. At Mount Holyoke, they find an extremely rigorous academic program with a lot of outlets for extracurricular activity. They also find a small, supportive community of women that is right near a large population of other college-age men and women. Lastly, they find a contained college in a small town, but have access to the social and academic resources of the Amherst/Northampton area. At Mount Holyoke, many women feel that they truly have the best of both worlds. —*Lisa E. Smith and Staff*

FYI

The three best things about attending Mount Holyoke are "the professors, the campus, and the way people are really committed to their activities."

The three worst things about attending Mount Holyoke are "the size, the girls who have money and flaunt it, the self-righteousness of some people."

The three things that every student should do before graduating are "watch a rugby game, talk to Tony Lake about military stuff, play an IM."

One thing I'd like to have known before coming here is "how funky-smelling girls bathrooms can be."

Northeastern University

Address: 360 Huntington Avenue; 150 Richards Hall; Boston, MA 02115
Phone: 617-373-2200
E-mail address: admissions@neu.edu
Web site URL: www.neu.edu
Founded: 1898
Private or Public: private
Religious affiliation: none
Location: urban
Undergraduate enrollment: 12,183
Total enrollment: 26,869
Percent Male/Female: 51%/49%
Percent Minority: 17%
Percent African-American: 6%

Percent Asian: 7%
Percent Hispanic: 3%
Percent Native-American: 0.5%
Percent in-state/out-of-state: 46%/54%
Percent Pub HS: NA
Number of Applicants: 16,418
Percent Accepted: 62%
Percent Accepted who enroll: 24%
Entering: 2,395
Transfers: 1,334
Application Deadline: 1 Mar
Mean SAT: 540 V, 552 M
Mean ACT: 23

Middle 50% SAT range: 510–600 V, 520–620 M
Middle 50% ACT range: 22–26
3 Most popular majors: business, engineering, criminal justice
Retention: 81%
Graduation rate: 44%
On-campus housing: 75%
Fraternities: 1%
Sororities: 1%
Library: 1,100,000 volumes
Tuition and Fees: $15,688 in; $15,688 out
Room and Board: $5,740
Financial aid, first-year: 73%

Looking for a school that combines fast paced academics with real-life experience—all located in metropolitan Boston? If so, then Northeastern, with its unique "co-op" program may be the school for you. But, as students warn, this program is not for everyone even "if the school can be."

The Trimester System

Students who attend Northeastern can usually plan on being in school for an average of five years since about 95% of the undergraduate population take advantage of the "co-op" program. Although the program differs for each major, students take either a 3 or 6 month "co-op" paid internship each year in their field of interest and work instead of attending classes during those months. Freshmen who choose not

to participate in the co-op take a freshman English class and other introductory courses. Students say that the co-op program is one of the best and most unique things about Northeastern, but one freshman warns, "If you don't wanna take co-op, then don't come here."

Because of the way the co-op program is structured, classes are set up in a trimester system as opposed to the traditional semester system. This can be both an advantage to those students who like to take a variety of courses, but also a disadvantage because "the classes move at a really fast pace." This system will most likely be replaced by the semester system in either 2001 or 2002, a possibility which has caused jubilation among some students and drawn complaints from others who are worried about how it will affect their co-op experience. Most likely, the new system will make for fewer, but longer co-ops experiences.

Majors that can be applied to real world experiences are popular for students at Northeastern. It is no surprise that both the business and criminal justice programs are considered strong. Some students reported that they offer the most interesting and most well-paid internship opportunities. Comparatively, the English and Math departments tend not to be so strong. Class sizes range from about 20 to over 200, but the majority of classes reportedly have only 25 to 30 people. Students say that professors are friendly and helpful. "They know me," says one student. Another offered a tip for dealing with professors and the administration at large schools like Northeastern: "Get your point across and be actively involved."

Big City Living

Most students agree that one of the best things about Northeastern is living in the city. Located in downtown Boston, the campus is in close proximity to just about everything one could need. However, that is not to say that there is not enough happening on Northeastern's campus that one would have to leave it to find excitement. The Carl S. Ell Student Center is a popular hangout for upperclassmen and freshmen alike. The school bookstore is connected to the Center, which houses the offices of many campus organizations in addition to offering a cafeteria, a study room, and a lounge. For more serious studying, there is the Snell Library, which is described as "huge," and "great."

As far as campus living goes, freshmen generally live in one of three dorms, although on-campus housing is optional due to the large number of commuter students. Dorm rooms are "like prison cells," according to one student. Stetson East and Stetson West are considered to be the worst, while Kennedy Hall, the honors dorm, is considered one of the best. Students may also opt to live in Coe Hall, a wellness dorm, or Rothman, an international dorm. Most dorms are coed by hall with single sex bathrooms. There is currently a new dorm under construction.

Upperclassman housing is determined

through a lottery system and "if you don't get housing have fun finding a place in Boston for a reasonable price," said one student. One of the downsides of city living is that dorm residents must have their cards swiped by an attendant and sign in guests 24/7, even if their visitors are just students from another dorm. All campus dorms are also staffed with residential advisors. According to students, the RAs are generally a mixed bag with some wanting to be your friend and others who are strict about alcohol policies.

Again, because of the university's urban location, there are innumerable food options around campus. Undergraduates can choose from 3 different meal plans, but freshmen must have at least 10 meals per week. Students may also choose to have money put on their Husky Card, which allows them to eat at many local establishments—something that makes many cafeteria-weary students happy. Local favorites include Pizzeria Uno, Chicken Lou's, and Au Bon Pain, as well as Marche's at the nearby Prudential Center and numerous take-out and fast food restaurants on adjoining Huntington Avenue.

Uh, Football Team?

When asked about the Husky football team, one student giggled and innocently asked, "Do we even have a football team?" Undoubtedly, the football team has a less-than-illustrious record, finishing 10th in the Atlantic 10 conference in 1999. Hockey reportedly receives more support, especially at the game against the University of New Hampshire and at the Bean Pot Tournament with across-town rivals Boston College, Boston University, and Harvard. Men's and women's crew have also posted strong seasons in the past. Still, students say that school spirit at Northeastern is not incredibly strong, partly due to the popularity of the co-op program, which detracts attention from other aspects of Northeastern including their often lackluster sports teams.

Intramural sports are popular, however, and varsity athletes and non-varsity athletes alike use the facilities at the Marino and Cabot Centers. Non-athletes can also participate in various cultural clubs, dramatic and musical events, or write for various publications including the literary magazine, *The Spectrum*.

Boston Night Life

Weekends at Northeastern start on Thursday nights, and there is no end to the variety of entertainment options available in Boston. Most freshmen frequent nearby clubs and parties, while upperclassmen attend apartment parties and bars. Underclassmen agree that while being underage does pose a problem, it does not stop them from drinking, though the university is stepping up its efforts to crack down on underage drinking with a stronger campus police presence.

> **"If you don't wanna take co-op, don't come here."**

Students say that "there are a ton of random hook-ups mostly because kids from BC, BU, and Emerson all mix at clubs, etc." In addition to parties, the city of Boston also offers alternatives such as theater, dance and symphony concerts by such acclaimed orchestras as the Boston Pops. Cambridge and Harvard Square are other popular destinations. When students just want to hang out, they tend to "hang out with friends in dorm rooms," and when the weather is nice people can lounge on the "beautifully landscaped campus" or hop on the "T," which runs right through the middle of campus. The "T" is Boston's subway system and goes just about everywhere in Boston.

At Northeastern, "There is no stereotype. Everything goes." It is a relatively diverse campus, ethnically and culturally, although some feel that it is not as diverse geographically. The majority of students come from the Northeast and as one Ohio resident griped, "People wonder why I don't have a southern accent. When I meet other people from the Midwest, we have an automatic bond." According to one student, though "the school is diverse as a whole, you don't see as much mixing as you should." Many students feel that there are lots of cliques on campus. Nevertheless, the atmosphere tends to be liberal, and the gay and lesbian population is generally accepted by students and the administration alike. Most students come from middle-class backgrounds, and work-study is a popular form of employment on campus.

Northeastern is a fast-paced career-oriented university, and with its innovative co-op program, students get cutting edge work experience combined with a rigorous education. The city of Boston offers unlimited opportunities in work, cuisine, and entertainment, and the proximity of the university to the "T" is invaluable. But prospective students should be warned that Northeastern is a university for those who know what they want and are not afraid to go after it, since it may be easy for the less determined to become lost in the fast shuffle of city and university life. —*Melissa Merritt*

FYI
The three best things about attending Northeastern are "the city, the co-op program, and lots of offerings in every field."
The three worst things about attending Northeastern are "the size, the poorly organized administration, and the trimester system."
The three things that every student should do before graduating from Northeastern are "to do the co-op, to explore Boston, and to voice your opinion to the administration."
One thing I'd like to have known before coming here is "how the trimester system really works."

Simmons College

Address: 300 The Fenway;
Boston, MA 02115
Phone: 617-521-2051
E-mail address:
ugadm@simmons.edu
Web site URL:
www.simmons.edu
Founded: 1899
Private or Public: private
Religious affiliation:
none
Location: urban
**Undergraduate
enrollment:** 1,235
Total enrollment: NA
Percent Male / Female:
0% / 100%
Percent Minority: 16%
Percent African-American:
6%

Percent Asian: 6%
Percent Hispanic: 3%
Percent Native-American:
0.5%
**Percent in-state / out-of-
state:** 60% / 40%
Percent Pub HS: NA
Number of Applicants:
1,184
Percent Accepted:
72%
**Percent Accepted who
enroll:** 32%
Entering: 271
Transfers: 52
Application Deadline:
1 Feb
Mean SAT: 546 V,
537 M
Mean ACT: 24

Middle 50% SAT range:
510–590 V,
500–540 M
Middle 50% ACT range:
21–28
3 Most popular majors:
education,
communications, business
Retention: 82%
Graduation rate: 71%
On-campus housing: 90%
Fraternities: NA
Sororities: NA
Library: NA
Tuition and Fees:
$20,134 in; $20,134 out
Room and Board: $8,046
Financial aid, first-year:
85%

The 1999–2000 school year marked the 100th anniversary of Simmons College. To mark the event, the faculty compiled a CD-ROM, which they will took on a Centennial Road Show, bringing the anniversary to all of those alumni who would otherwise be unable to make the celebration. The Road Show was an indication of just how far Simmons had come, and how far its alumnae have gone. The anniversary provided good opportunity for Simmons to marvel at one hundred years of giving young women the preparation needed for success in this world.

Heavy on the Science

Simmons' greatest academic strength lies in its science departments. The physical therapy department offers a six-year doctorate program. Nursing majors benefit from internships at area hospitals, including one that is across the street from the college. Some majors require a hospital internship to graduate. The abundance of student interns reflects the pre-professional goals of the women here. Many students describe themselves as pre-something, including its fair share of pre-meds. Unfortunately, some students find that the strength of the science departments is balanced by a weakness in other areas. "If you are coming to Simmons to be a science or management major, great. If you are coming to Simmons for a liberal arts education, not so great." In addition to management, students also consider communications and education to be strong non-science majors.

The small size of Simmons makes it easy to get small classes. As freshmen, a student might find herself in a Spanish class with just four other people, including the professor. If a large lecture course is more up their alley, introductory courses—particularly in the sciences—often see more than one hundred women in a class. In either large lecture or small seminar, students find the professors to be personable and accessible, both in the office and at home. One professor "took [her] entire class out to a movie and a nice dinner—all expenses paid."

Simmons' small size also makes it possible for underclassmen to get into upperclassmen seminars. "Classes are fairly easy to get into if you are willing to go find a teacher and make some requests." On the flip side, a Simmons curriculum also includes several required courses. Students must attain intermediate skill in a foreign language by taking three semester of language. Freshmen take a multicultural English course. By graduation, all students will also have been in seven "modes of inquiry" and in four physical education classes of their choice, ranging from yoga to tennis.

Simmons offers several term abroad programs. Students say Cordoba, Spain draws many Simmons students as a destination for both semester long and short-term courses. A photography course in Paris and Marine Biology in Puerto Rico are offered, as well.

Living in Beantown

The city of Boston has become the playground for the women of Simmons College. The actual college campus consists of two buildings for classes and a residence area that consists of redbrick dorms surrounding a grassy courtyard. Another college campus sits between the residential and academic buildings and the city of Boston fills up the rest of the surrounding space.

> One student describes the dining hall food as "good, actually, I've had much worse."

"One of the best things about Simmons is the residents campus: it is beautiful." The quadrangle "makes you feel like you're not in the city." Once inside the dorms, the rooms can be described as small, but nice. One student divides the dorms into two groups: "hotel dorms" and "ghetto dorms." The moniker "hotel dorm" is usually reserved for those dorms that have been recently been renovated, like Dix and South Halls. The college plans on eventually renovating all nine of its dormitories. All of the dorms have RAs that keep the peace and, although none of the dorms are known as quiet dorms, all of the dorms have quiet areas. Bartol, one of the two dining halls, is conveniently located near the residence halls.

A seven-minute walk separates the academic buildings from the residential buildings. The two main classroom buildings—the aptly named Main College Building and the simply named Science

Building—have nice lecture halls and the MCB has been recently renovated. The school's other dining hall, The Fens cafeteria, is located in the MCB. The Beatley library is also situated in the academic part of the campus. Beatley provides a nice place to work on group projects and to study, although some describe it as "scary."

The location of the campus puts it in close proximity to all of the happening places in Beantown. Only a few blocks separate the MCB from Fenway Park and Kenmore Square. The T takes students almost anywhere in Boston (making the daunting task of pahking the cah unnecessary); the T stop is only a hop, skip, and a jump away from the MCB.

Social Life (?)

The weekend plans of most Simmons' students depend on what is happening in Boston. Due to a lack of men and strict alcohol/noise regulations, parties on Simmons campus are rare occurrences. If students stay in on the weekend, they'll usually rent a movie. When they want to go out, they look to Boston. "There's a lot of stuff to do in Boston: go to coffee houses with friends, shop on Newbury or at the Cambridgeside Galleria Mall, go to the science museum and catch a planatarium show, go to the aquarium, or just go see a movie." When looking for a little bit more debauchery, the women of Simmons often go to parties at "larger schools like MIT, BU, Wentworth, and, sometimes, Harvard."

The few social events that happen on Simmons' campus are more appreciated because of their scarcity. Each dorm holds mixers and students look forward to the Mr. Simmons pageant each spring. Students can cut a rug at the Sadie Hawkins Dance and the Valentines' Day Dance. And after four years of college, seniors get to bring their parents in for the Father/Daughter and Mother/Daughter weekends.

Happenings on Campus

The Campus Activities Board brings special acts to campus every week, "everything from hypnotists to a capella singing groups, usually they are free and provide some entertainment on campus." Student groups range from the usual—the Colleges of the Fenway Orchestra, student government and hall council—to the unusual (or just unusually named)—"Cunt." In addition, the college requires students to perform community service.

For the athletes who don't play a varsity sport, intramurals become an outlet for athletic enthusiasm. The school has a program called Leap, in which many different sports and other classes are offered, like aerobics, dance, learning to dive, and Alaskan dog sledding. Non-varsity athletes will also find that they have easy access to gym facilities, which are described as nice. The gym, which is located in the residential area, contains Nautilus equipment, a "gorgeous" pool, and a suspended track for student use.

Wining and Dining
Even with the luxury of living in America's seafood Mecca, students don't find their dining hall food to be all that bad. One student describes the food as "good, actually, I've had much worse." Of course, even the best dormitory food gets a little old after a while; luckily, students at Simmons have the culinary delights of Boston right at their fingertips. The city boasts such popular restaurants as the Cheese Cake Factory, Brown Sugar, Vinny Testa's, and Bertucci's. On campus, Quadside café offers "yummy junk food" and doubles as a popular late night hangout.

The lack of male students on campus provides a unique experience for the ladies of Simmons. "It is definitely a different experience than coed. You become much more independent and head strong, and you receive a better education because your degree is not compared with a male's." Students also note that the absence of the male gender results in a student body that does not have to worry about competition for guys. "It's pretty comfortable in the sense that you don't really have to worry about what you look like hanging around the dorms or even going to class for that matter." Most importantly, this small school in the heart of Boston provides a nurturing environment where women can learn, grow, and experience life. Simmons is just the first stop for these women who will be prepared to go out and make a difference in this world. —*Kenneth Tseng*

FYI
The three best things about attending Simmons are "Boston, the friendly people, and the Physical Therapy Doctorates Program."
The three worst things about attending Simmons are "All girls, all girls, all girls."
The three things that every student should do before graduating from Simmons are "see a Red Sox game, visit the Museum of Fine Arts, and go to the Valentine's Day Ball at the top of the Prudential Building."
One thing I'd like to have known before coming here is "save more money, especially quarters."

Smith College

Address: 7 College Lane; Northampton, MA 01063
Phone: 413-585-2500
E-mail address: admission@smith.edu
Web site URL: www.smith.edu
Founded: 1871
Private or Public: private
Religious affiliation: none
Location: suburban
Undergraduate enrollment: 2,665
Total enrollment: 2,778
Percent Male/Female: 0%/100%
Percent Minority: 18%

Percent African-American: 4%
Percent Asian: 9%
Percent Hispanic: 4%
Percent Native-American: 0.5%
Percent in-state/out-of-state: 21%/79%
Percent Pub HS: 68%
Number of Applicants: 2,998
Percent Accepted: 56%
Percent Accepted who enroll: 40%
Entering: 667
Transfers: 110
Application Deadline: 15 Jan
Mean SAT: NA
Mean ACT: NA

Middle 50% SAT range: 600–710 V, 580–670 M
Middle 50% ACT range: 25–29
3 Most popular majors: government, psychology, English
Retention: 88%
Graduation rate: 77%
On-campus housing: 100%
Fraternities: NA
Sororities: NA
Library: 1,200,000 volumes
Tuition and Fees: $22,622 in; $22,622 out
Room and Board: $7,820
Financial aid, first-year: 59%

Walk around the picturesque town of Northampton, Massachusetts, and you will inevitably spot a proud Smithie wearing a T-shirt that reads, "It's not a girls' school without men—it's a women's school without boys." While some treasure the experience of college without men, students inevitably questioned why she decided to "condemn herself to life without the opposite sex." While the value of an all-women's college will always be debated among Smithies, there is no doubt that Smith's inspiring academic program and involved community provide an incomparable college experience.

Academics

Academic life at Smith is marked by a great degree of freedom. Having no distribution requirements allows for much exploration, but it also puts much responsibility on undergraduates to chart and plan their own education. Opinions vary on how challenging courses are at Smith. One student guaranteed that "every course is difficult—this is Smith." Other students, however, said that each class is what each student makes of it. One senior commented that "how

much useful information you learn has nothing to do with the difficulty of the course," and that the difficulty of a class "depends entirely on the professor."

Students applaud the teachers for their accessibility, explaining that the accessibility of professors "really adds to Smith's close-knit feel." One student explained how she meets with professors: "I e-mail them, call them, or go to their office hours. I sometimes drop in on my favorite profs, Kiki Smith (costume design) and Ernie Alleva (philosophy), just to say hi." Part of this personal attention can be attributed to the intimate class settings. All classes are taught by professors, and most of the classes are very small. The few larger classes are very uncommon, according to one sophomore who said that "when one of my classes had 150 students, people were surprised."

Smith boasts particularly strong English, government, women's studies, and art history departments, but also because of its involvement in the Pioneer Valley's Five-College Consortium. Students from Smith College, Hampshire College, Mount Holyoke College, Amherst College, and the University of Massachusetts at Amherst can hop on one of the consortium's complimentary buses and attend classes at any of the five schools. Students appreciate the broad spectrum of classes that this cooperative of schools offers, and "almost everybody" has "thoroughly explored the entire Five College area," making friends at the other four schools. This program is especially appreciated because of the opportunity to pursue the sciences, one of Smith's weaker programs, at other schools that have more developed facilities.

Northampton Life

Life in Northampton provides a refuge from the tedium of studying. Downtown "NoHo" is within a three-minute walk from campus. The proximity to town allows students to frequent Pearl Street, where there are many little shops and restaurants. Fun retreats in NoHo include the Fire and Water Vegetarian Cafe, Bart's Ice Cream, the Haymarket coffeehouse, and local bars. For a great meal, students often choose Jake's No Frills Dining and Spaghetti Freddy's. One student commented that "Northampton is an interesting place to walk around, but it's frustrating to shop unless you have a lot of money." Also accessible to students at Smith is adventure in Amherst, where students can take buses. Because movies are shown in Amherst every weekend, many students enjoy making the quick trip.

Students say that they feel safe in the area around Smith, possibly a result of a great campus security. One student commented that "they're nice and respond pretty quickly, and they will give you a ride across campus if you don't feel safe walking home at night." Another student noted how "walking home at night, I've often seen campus security pass me two or three times."

According to several students' estimates, as high as 50% of the students have had some lesbian experience by the time they graduate.

Smithies are currently observing changes to their 125-acre campus. A new stu-

dent center is under construction, but one student complained that to build the new facility, "they had to tear down two houses, and housing is getting really cramped." Other highlights on-campus are the Lyman Plant House, complete with Botanic Gardens, an art museum complete with more than 24,000 works, a new Bass Science Building, the Young Science Laboratory, and the Nielson Library. Students interested in using the school's athletic facilities can enjoy 25 acres of playing fields, an all-weather track, crew facilities and a boathouse, lighted tennis courts, riding facilities, and a three-building complex called the Ainsworth Gymnasium.

Utilizing these facilities are 14 varsity sports, which are "pretty popular, but not to the point of fanaticism." Crew and rugby and lacrosse attract a surprising number of participants, one student said, and large crowds gather to watch competitions against rivals like Wellesley and Mount Holyoke.

Housing and Social Life

The Smith housing situation is unique. Instead of huge dorms, Smithies live in houses, each one with access to a kitchen and dining room. These houses coordinate social activities, ranging from formal dinners to afternoon teas. When in such close quarters, students cement close friendships. One student noted that "your house becomes like a big extended family, even if there are 90 or 100 students living there!" Because of the enthusiasm for the house system, very few Smithies live off-campus. Each house also has its own dining hall, or shares one with another house.

Opportunities for activities abound at Smith. One student boasted that "everybody at Smith is involved in something, whether it is sports or community service or ethnic or identity groups or music or theater or art." In each of these categories there is some sort of organization, ranging from the Nosotras for Latina students to the Korean-American Students of Smith to the Service Organizations of Smith (SOS) to the Sazanami Club to the Smiffenpoofs, the oldest female a cappella group in the nation. Basically, "if you can think of it, there's probably a club for it at Smith." Smithies are characterized by their great political awareness and activism, according to one student who also said that "Smithies are really enthusiastic about feminism and gay rights." According to several students' estimates, as high as 50% of the students have had some lesbian experience by the time they graduate. Students cite both the environment and the self-selected student body. Students are also interested in race issues, and marking their desire for a diverse student body was the inauguration of Ruth J. Simmons, the college's first African-American president.

There is always something for people to do at Smith. For the politically minded, there are frequent lectures and debates. For those interested in fine arts, there is always a movie or play or dance or concert. A concert hall attracts names like Fiona Apple, Squirrel Nut Zippers, and Ladysmith Black Mambazo. Smith also, despite the fact that it is an all-women's school, has a party scene like most co-ed schools; the typical weekend at Smith includes parties, "almost every Friday and Saturday involving beer, deafening music, blinding lights, smoke, and drunk UMass frat boys."

Traditions

When it comes to traditions, one student commented that "you'd be surprised at what some of those Smithies have thought up over the years!!!" Students celebrate Otelia Cromwell Day, the birthday of the first black student to graduate from Smith, by organizing various lectures and workshops that address minority issues. Mountain Day, a day that the president spontaneously announces in October, is also an appreciated Smith tradition. Quad Riot elicits excitement among students who emerge from their rooms and launch a barrage of attacks using personal-hygiene products.

Despite the absence of men on-campus, Smithies have a great time. Their activities, clubs, sports, organizations, and classes provide innumerable opportunities to explore. Going to Smith is all about exploration, and it is a great place to pursue new things while securing close-knit friendships. —*Marti Page and staff*

FYI
The three best things about attending Smith College are "its housing experience and tradition, its support for international students, and having no curriculum."
The three worst things about attending Smith College are "the small bar and club scene, having no men, and its not much flavored food."
The three things you should do before graduating from Smith College are "join the quad riot, attend the immorality ball, and study in the island."
One thing I'd like to have known before coming to Smith College is "how strenuous the work load is."

Tufts University

Address: Bendetson Hall; Medford, MA 02155
Phone: 617-627-3170
E-mail address: uadmiss_inquiry@infonet.tufts.edu
Web site URL: www.tufts.edu
Founded: 1852
Private or Public: private
Religious affiliation: none
Location: suburban
Undergraduate enrollment: 4,977
Total enrollment: 8,742
Percent Male/Female: 47%/53%
Percent Minority: 26%

Percent African-American: 6%
Percent Asian: 13%
Percent Hispanic: 6%
Percent Native-American: 0.5%
Percent in-state/out-of-state: 25%/75%
Percent Pub HS: 59%
Number of Applicants: 13,471
Percent Accepted: 32%
Percent Accepted who enroll: 31%
Entering: 1,347
Transfers: 134
Application Deadline: 1 Jan
Mean SAT: NA
Mean ACT: NA

Middle 50% SAT range: 610–710 V, 640–720 M
Middle 50% ACT range: 27–30
3 Most popular majors: international relations, English, biology
Retention: 95%
Graduation rate: 76%
On-campus housing: 99%
Fraternities: 15%
Sororities: 3%
Library: 900,000 volumes
Tuition and Fees: $24,751 in; $24,751 out
Room and Board: $7,375
Financial aid, first-year: 37%

Tufts University, situated on a suburban hilltop overlooking Boston, in many ways has the best of both worlds. Only a few miles outside of the city, students can take advantage of Boston's theaters, restaurants, nightclubs, stores, and concerts by taking the T, Boston's subway system. But while Tufts benefits from its proximity to Boston, it remains a contained and almost secluded campus in the suburb of Medford. The campus itself has open lawns and trees, and is quiet, since no major roads cut through it. Tufts students experience the richness of a big city in a quiet, suburban community.

Academics

Academics at Tufts are tough, but most students feel that they are up to the challenge. Undergrads apply to either the School of Engineering or the School of Liberal Arts, both of which mandate very stringent "distribution" requirements. Students in the liberal arts program must take two courses in each of five areas: natural sciences, mathematics, fine arts, humanities, and social sciences; six semesters of foreign language or culture;

and also one class that completes the World Civilizations requirement, which is a class in a non-Western discipline. Engineering students must take the language and World Civilizations requirement, as well as two semesters of English composition and writing. Many students find these requirements excessive and "a pain in the neck." However, standardized test scores may be used to waive some of these requirements, which "gives us a little more freedom," and some students also say "it's easy to find courses that fulfill more than one requirement."

Class sizes at Tufts are large for introductory lectures, around 100 to 200 students, but more specific courses, such as upper-level courses for your major, generally enroll around 20 people. Classes are always taught by professors; TAs often lead recitations sections and labs for the larger courses. Classes like English, foreign languages, and philosophy are reported to be kept small in order to encourage "interaction and discussion." Sometimes students can get closed out of classes during registration, when students are assigned registration times and classes fill on a first come, first served basis. Students say they get into most of their top-choice classes with no problem, and even if you are closed out, "speaking to the professor and showing genuine enthusiasm generally gets you in." Freshmen also go through a weeklong orientation, which helps them to choose classes for the upcoming fall.

Some of the most popular majors at Tufts are international relations, economics, biology, and psychology. Many students who major in international relations go on to Tufts' world-renowned graduate school, the Fletcher School of International Law and Diplomacy. International relations majors, as well as language majors, have the opportunity to go abroad their junior year to places like Ghana, England, France, and Spain, and about a third of all juniors end up taking advantage of these programs. Since there is no major for pre-med students at Tufts, many who wish to go on to medical school major in biology. Premeds are reported to be "hard-core competitive," not only in academics, but in terms of "anything else they think that med schools might look at." People in other areas of study also may foster this sense of competition, but in general "people aren't competitive with anyone but themselves," said one undergrad. Students say that there are times when people will study on Friday nights, but those same people might end up going out and partying on a weeknight. Tufts students tend to think that although "academics are definitely the prevailing concern," they have found a balance between intense, never-ending studying and complete abandon.

Uphill and Downhill

Freshmen at Tufts are required to live on-campus, and generally sophomores also live in the dorms. Some of the dorms are large buildings with long hallways of double and single rooms, while others are smaller and organized into suites. Housing is divided into two campus areas, Uphill and Downhill, with Uphill nearer to classes and Downhill nearer the Campus Center. Some students criticize the dorms for their "lack of maintenance," but say that they "each have their charm." West Hall, a big Gothic-style dorm in the middle

of campus, is considered one of the best due to its prime location and nice rooms. Wren Hall, one of the dorms arranged into suites, on the other hand, is described as "maze-like and anti-social," and is said to have very small rooms. Dorms are co-ed, but floors are divided into single-sex sections. In addition, there is one all-female dorm on-campus, but it does not restrict visiting hours for males.

Other rooming options include off-campus housing, Greek housing, or cultural houses. A large number of juniors and seniors choose to live off-campus, often in group houses near campus. These houses often throw good parties, and although rent is expensive, one student said she liked "being part of a neighborhood and having our own little community." There are also several Greek houses, and cultural houses such as the Russian house, Asian-American house, and African-American house. Students like the atmosphere of these cultural houses, but claim that the "worst thing about them is the distance to the Campus Center."

Dining options at Tufts are quite good. Freshmen are required to purchase a full meal plan, which they sometimes "aren't too thrilled about," but after that, the options include a full meal plan or partial plans of 14 meals per week, 150 or 95 meals per semester, or the "point system." Points can be used in any of the campus dining halls, in the Campus Center, and in several restaurants and coffee shops off-campus. Since there is so much choice, students say they are quite satisfied with their options, "especially after you visit your friends at other colleges." The two large dining halls on-campus, Carmichael and Dewick MacPhie, serve traditional dining hall fare, and generally have a lot of different options at each meal, even though "from week to week you find the same meals being served over and over." Hodgdon, also small, is praised for its stir-fry and rotisserie chicken and allows students to order food to go. The Campus Center has several shops for sandwiches, subs, pizza, and snacks. Students almost universally praise campus food, both in quality and variety, but they also tend to eat out a lot. Some students say they order take-out "all the time," and also go into

Harvard Square or the North End in Boston for meals on the weekends.

Busy and Content

When asked how much time Tufts students spend on extracurriculars, one student enthusiastically responded, "Most!" Undergraduates produce a variety of publications, including the Tufts Daily; the Observer, Tufts' oldest paper, which comes out every Thursday; and Zamboni, a humorous paper that satirizes the other two more serious papers and is published about once a month. There are also several literary journals, such as Queen's Head, and literary magazines for specific ethnic groups, such as the Asian-American Voices. Tufts also offers extensive opportunities for students to get involved in traditional activities such as singing groups, ballroom dance, and student government, as well as some more unusual groups like the Monty Python Society. In addition, the Leonard Carmichael Society is an umbrella organization for over 30 community service groups on-campus, and is entirely student-run. As one student reported, "Most students are actively involved in at least one extracurricular activity, if not more."

> Tufts also has a large population of international students, but one student said undergrads tend to be "very cliquey in terms of geographic origin."

Sports at Tufts are not such a big deal, since the school competes in Division III (except for the sailing team that is the top-ranked national team), and students say that the school is "not that great in sports at all." Students do muster up a lot of school spirit at times, though, particularly when the situation involves basketball or their mascot, Jumbo the elephant. Tufts varsity basketball games always draw a large crowd, especially when the team makes the championships, where Tufts pride is at its highest. As for Jumbo, one student said "it seems that the mascot being an elephant had a lot to do with swinging some students' preference toward Tufts." Intramurals are fairly extensive at

Tufts, involving "every sport you could possibly hope for!" Facilities are not large, but there is a new intramural gym, Chase gymnasium, and undergrads say the facilities are always open for the entire student body. In addition to traditional sports, the Tufts Mountain Club, which owns a lodge in New Hampshire, is also a popular activity, offering outings in rock climbing, kayaking, hiking, and camping.

Social life at Tufts offers a wide variety of options. On weeknights, students who want a break from their studying can find others to go out to coffee shops or the Campus Center, just to hang out. On weekends, there are always parties and dances, often held by student organizations. The Programming Board is in charge of big social events on-campus, and fraternities, while not particularly a large force, do organize house parties every weekend. The T and buses make transportation into Boston so easy that many students, especially upperclassmen, wander off-campus for weekend entertainment at clubs, theaters, restaurants, and other attractions. In Medford itself, which "used to be pretty dead, but is now coming into its own," there are a lot of CD and clothing stores, restaurants, and bars.

Officially, the Tufts administration has designated the campus drug-free, and kegs are not allowed. In reality, though, some students say there is a small, but quiet, drug scene, and beer is plentiful at frat parties and on-campus parties alike. Undergrads say that most of their peers drink, and that "people who drink tend to drink a lot." Some students harshly criticize Tufts' dating scene, which many regard as practically nonexistent. Relationships are nearly always "short and sex-oriented," or long-distance; "a lot of people have girl/boyfriends from home, so if you are looking for anything long-term . . . forget it!"

The Tufts student body contains a healthy mix of ethnic backgrounds, though some students criticize its lack of diversity. The majority of students are from New England and New York, but there is representation from all 50 states. Tufts also has a large population of international students, but one student said undergrads tend to be "very cliquey in terms of geographic origin." Some also feel that

Tufts is lacking in economic diversity and in African-American students. Tufts has many organizations and cultural houses for minority students to help foster a strong community. The student body tends to be "mostly politically liberal, and almost completely socially liberal," although there are a small number of active conservatives. Although students tend not to show their school spirit in huge outbursts of support at giant sporting events, and may criticize things about their school, "most students enjoy being here at Tufts and would be proud to say they are a student here."

Students find Tufts to be a school with very high academic standards and a plethora of outside activities. In addition, Tufts is ideally located for "people who like to have access to the big-city activities that Boston offers, but still like to come home to a quiet place in a neighborhood with families living in houses all around." —*Lisa E. Smith*

FYI

The three best things about attending Tufts are "its being close to Boston, the intercultural week and the study abroad opportunities."

The three worst things about attending Tufts are "lack of housing options, its small size, and lack of computers."

The three things you should do before graduating from Tufts are "participating in the Naked Quad run, watching the city from the library's roof at night, and going abroad."

One thing students would like to have known before coming to Tufts is "the prominent place of the Greek system in social life."

University of Massachusetts / Amherst

Address: Amherst, MA 01003-0120
Phone: 431-545-0222
E-mail address: mail@admissions.umass.edu
Web site URL: www.umass.edu
Founded: 1863
Private or Public: public
Religious affiliation: none
Location: suburban
Undergraduate enrollment: 18,619
Total enrollment: 23,932
Percent Male/Female: 50%/50%
Percent Minority: 16%
Percent African-American: 5%

Percent Asian: 6%
Percent Hispanic: 4%
Percent Native-American: 0.5%
Percent in-state/out-of-state: 75%/25%
Percent Pub HS: 89%
Number of Applicants: 19,914
Percent Accepted: 69%
Percent Accepted who enroll: 30%
Entering: 4,060
Transfers: 1,794
Application Deadline: 1 Feb
Mean SAT: 558 V, 566 M
Mean ACT: NA
Middle 50% SAT range: 510–620 V, 520–620 M

Middle 50% ACT range: NA
3 Most popular majors: communications, psychology, hotel/restaurant/travel administration
Retention: 79%
Graduation rate: 34%
On-campus housing: 96%
Fraternities: 6%
Sororities: 4%
Library: 2,800,000 volumes
Tuition and Fees: $5,212 in; $13,254 out
Room and Board: $4,790
Financial aid, first-year: 60%

Nestled in the pleasant college town of Amherst is a public university that was once labeled "ZooMass." True to its label, the campus was marked by extended party weekends, great basketball, and a reputation as New England's party school. While life at the UMass now has increasing academic prestige, vestiges of this reputation remain: its basketball and football teams still enjoy national prestige, and it maintains its party-school image. UMass today boasts an award-winning faculty and updated facilities, enabling it to attract students who want both fun and academic promise.

Academics

UMass academics provide opportunities for every interest. With bachelors degrees offered in over 90 areas, students enjoy a selection of every conceivable major, ranging from building materials and wood technology to sports management to business writing. Those students who desire to pursue an uncovered subject are free to explore a self-designed major.

Whatever their major, students must fulfill some graduation requirements, most notably the Social World requirements. The Social World requirements entail classes in six disciplines including literature, the arts, history, the social and behavioral sciences, and the natural sciences. Students must also fulfill certain writing requirements. They are required to enroll in a "College Writing" class freshman and junior years. Students benefit from the small, seminar-style writing courses that are limited to 25 students. The writing class taken junior year must be specific to the student's elected major. Many students complain about these requirements, but others acknowledge that the class requirements are "stuff you'd be taking, or at least should know anyway."

Students affirm the difficulty of many of the courses offered at UMass. While students report that slacker classes exist (especially in the physical education courses and "those courses that cover stuff you already know"), the general opinion about classes is that they are tough. One freshman declared that "all my classes are impossible" while another complained that "any course toward your major is hard." Despite these reports, many students feel that classes are "tough enough to keep you on your toes, but not always tough enough to fail you."

Earning particularly high ratings from students is the English department where the faculty stars include John Edgar Wideman (a two-time winner of the PEN Faulkner Award and a recipient of a MacArthur Genius Award) and James Tate (the 1992 Pulitzer Prize winner for Ameri-

can poetry). Students also give favorable marks to the economics department, the School of Management, the School of Food and Natural Resources, and the School for Humanities and Fine Arts.

The science departments have expanded rapidly, thanks to new building facilities like the recently constructed Knowles Engineering Building, the Silvio Conte Center for Polymer Research, and the University Marine Station at Gloucester. UMass has it all, from the classic chemistry lab to the unique Agricultural Experimental Station at Waltham.

> There are plenty of unique organizations, according to a freshman who claimed, "We have [an organization] for everything you can think of, and if there isn't one, you can start one!"

For the student who desires to explore another subject in which UMass does not specialize, students have a varied selection of classes from other institutions. UMass is a member of the Five-College Consortium, an intercollegiate academic program that permits students from UMass, Smith, Mount Holyoke, Amherst, and Hampshire to take classes at any of the other schools. Students also have the option to enroll in international exchange programs and join in various internships for credit. Student who graduate from high school with high SAT scores and class ranks are invited into the UMass honors program. Ultimately, students say that UMass provides them with opportunities that "can typically be found only at private schools."

The College Town

Undergrads speak highly of Amherst, a "bustling college town" in the historic Pioneer Valley of western Massachusetts. Students report that they feel safe when walking around campus, but security still provides a bus that circles the 1,400-acre campus every 15 minutes. For no cost, the bus provides transportation to the neighboring schools, the mall, and distant parts of the campus. The northern portion of campus is characterized by its Georgian and colonial architectural styles while the southern part is more modern. All freshmen and sophomores are guaranteed on-campus housing. Freshmen like the fact that there is no distinct or separate freshman dorm because they can learn from the upperclassmen with whom they are intermingled. Most floors are co-ed, but there are special floors like the 24-hour quiet floor and some single-sex floors for women. Students do warn against dorms in the "Sylvan Area," and are confident that dorms will be even better "as soon as the new furniture is put in." Once students reach their junior year, many choose to live off-campus.

In these dorms are DCs (Dining Commons) where students enjoy a varied palette of foods. The food "isn't actually that bad," and there are options even for the vegetarian and vegan. The DCs are close and convenient, especially those that have the extended eating hours. Many students enjoy the food at the school's most popular hangout, the Blue Wall.

Social Life

UMass was not given the title "ZooMass" for no reason; any weekend invariably includes parties at one of the 20 fraternities or sororities located on or near campus. Underage drinking, however, is strictly regulated by campus police and the administration's hard-line approach. One of the things that makes UMass so exciting are other creative opportunities on the weekends. The campus center has a program called SEV (Something Every Friday) that offers, of course, something every Friday. Recent "somethings" have included hypnosis, improv comedy, ice skating, and movies. Movie selection is good, students claim. One weekend, for example, the campus center played Armeggedon and There's Something About Mary. UMass has frequent concerts with such famous names as Korn, U2, Tori Amos, Natalie Merchant, and Bob Dylan. Weekends include some sleep and some study too; and with study comes the need for study breaks. One student related one creative study break: "Sixty of us were sledding down the hill behind my building last night. We stayed there going crazy until 1 A.M."

Athletics and other extracurricular activities make UMass even more exciting. Sports have traditionally played a key role on the UMass campus. Their particularly strong basketball and football teams are popular, and games are well attended. There are plenty of unique organizations, according to a freshman who claimed, "We have [an organization] for everything you can think of, and if there isn't one, you can start one!" One student noted that she and her friends were starting a "fratosorority."

Students attend the university to take advantage of both the excitement and the academic rigor of the school. Academic opportunity, a variety of extracurricular activities, the symbiotic relationship of the Five-College Consortium, and a legacy for partying combine to make UMass at Amherst a great school. —*Marti Page and staff*

FYI

The three best things about attending Umass at Amherst are "being a part of the 5 college consortium, Durfee Gardens, and diverse student body."

The three worst things about attending Umass at Amherst are "drinking policies, the food and too many TA's for classes."

The three things that every student should do before graduating from Umass at Amherst are "visiting the Durfee conservatory, riding the elevators in the library without getting sick and taking a class from one of the four other colleges."

One thing I'd like to have known before coming to Umass at Amherst is "the school has very high standards."

W e l l e s l e y   C o l l e g e

Address: 106 Central Street; Wellesley, MA 02481-8203
Phone: 781-283-2270
E-mail address: admission@wellesley.edu
Web site URL: www.wellesley.edu
Founded: 1870
Private or Public: private
Religious affiliation: none
Location: suburban
Undergraduate enrollment: 2,290
Total enrollment: 2,290
Percent Male / Female: 0% / 100%
Percent Minority: 37%
Percent African-American: 7%

Percent Asian: 23%
Percent Hispanic: 6%
Percent Native-American: 0.5%
Percent in-state / out-of-state: 18% / 82%
Percent Pub HS: 60%
Number of Applicants: 2,862
Percent Accepted: 46%
Percent Accepted who enroll: 46%
Entering: 603
Transfers: 23
Application Deadline: 15 Jan
Mean SAT: 678 V, 671 M
Mean ACT: 29

Middle 50% SAT range: 630–720 V, 630–720 M
Middle 50% ACT range: 28–31
3 Most popular majors: economics, psychology, English
Retention: 95%
Graduation rate: 90%
On-campus housing: 100%
Fraternities: NA
Sororities: NA
Library: 728,000 volumes
Tuition and Fees: $23,320 in; $23,320 out
Room and Board: $7,234
Financial aid, first-year: 51%

On the Sunday before the first day of classes, Wellesley women come together on this "Flower Sunday" in the Wellesley chapel and have a day of reflection. On a beautiful day in the middle of the fall semester, all of the Wellesley women gather for a college-wide picnic. Wellesley College is a tradition-filled school whose traditions are not kept merely for the sake of tradition, but rather, because they are examples of the sense of community that the women of Wellesley share. Located in the relaxed, tightly-knit, suburban town of Wellesley, Massachusetts, an even stronger community rests within the walls of the college. Wellesley women are united by their common sense of drive. At Wellesley, the women know what they want and are driven to achieve it.

The Wellesley Voice

Wellesley is unusual not only because it is an all-women's college, but also because of the women who go there. Its student body is described as "intense, intelligent, beautiful, and international." As a women's college, students feel encouraged to find their own voice. Their professors want them to really find themselves in everything they do—from the outside activities that they pursue to their coursework. As one freshman commented, "It's nothing like high school. My professors really want to know what I think, how I express those thoughts, and how I can develop myself as a person."

Although the academic environment at Wellesley is very intense, the students there are supportive of each other; "Wellesley is very much a community." Thanks to the way the school is organized, Wellesley women become a part of an extensive nurturing network. For instance, frosh can talk to their "big sister" (an upperclasswoman who helps first-years adjust), the head of their dorm floor, the dorm house president, a first-coordinator, or a head of their dorm.

Wellesley is a very liberal and "politically correct" place. Although all of its students are very accepting of one another's differences, some say that the political correctness can get a bit ridiculous. One student complained that her dorm was not able to call a dance the "Holiday Ball" in order not to offend those who don't celebrate any of the December holidays.

Intensity

Wellesley is not a place to kick back. "'Slackers at Wellesley' is a total oxymoron." According to students, the school's women are all "intensely driven." In everything they do, Wellesley women push themselves, not because they are forced to, but because they want to. Most are actively involved in two, three, four, and even five activities at one time, saying "we want to make the most of our time here."

The administration has recently imposed some new academic regulations to toughen the academic rigor of the school. Students entering after the fall of 1997 are required to fulfill a new set of distribution requirements. They must take one class from each of the following areas: language and literature; the arts (visual arts, music, theater, film, and video); social and behavioral analysis; natural or physical science, with lab; and mathematical modeling/problem solving. For those students that are not oriented toward math and the sciences, there are courses available that are intended for non-majors. But some science and math majors complain that there are not enough nonmajor humanities and social sciences classes. Although the strict requirements have earned the school a nickname "HELLesley," most say "they aren't too hard to fulfill." In addition to the new distribution policy, students must now take 34 instead of 32 credits in order to graduate.

Academic life is rigorous and "sometimes you feel like the endless stream of work will never end, but in the end, it's entirely worth it." Although there is "tons of work, it's manageable." The rigors of Wellesley, most students say, is worth the sacrifices that they must make. One freshman noted, "I look at some of the seniors and see how articulately they relay ideas. It's what Wellesely does to a timid and somewhat quiet first-year student like myself." Further, to lessen the stress on students around final exam time, Wellesley allows students to schedule their own exams to ensure that they aren't too overwhelmed.

Students are generally very satisfied with their courses. They love the small size of the classes, many of which are typically under 25 people, because they encourage students to become articulate, and discussion is especially lively in the upper-level classes. Only a few introductory classes are taught in large lectures. Touted departments include economics, political science, and art history, while African studies, women's studies, and sociology are reportedly less popular. Professors are said to be generally very "supportive and nurturing" while pushing students "to develop our ideas and selves." One senior raved, "Some professors will have the class over for dinner. They are so considerate and sincere."

"It's nothing like high school. My professors really want to know what I think, how I express those thoughts, and how I can develop myself as a person."

While Wellesley College itself is small and limited in the number of classes that it can offer, the number of classes available to its students is immense. As part of a 12-college consortium with nearby schools such as MIT, Harvard, and Mount Holyoke, students are able to take classes that are not offered on-campus at any one of the other consortium schools. One upper-class science major said, "It's great. I can take advanced science classes that aren't offered by Wellesley and have the resources of all the other schools open to me."

Total Freedom?

As an all-women's school, the absence of "boys" makes the Wellesley experience drastically different from most other colleges. For many, it's "theoretically a blessing" not having to worry about what we wear or how to act to attract a guy's attentions. "I chose Wellesley because it'd let me concentrate on my education rather than what I look like at two in the morning." Many consider it to be "Total Freedom" because there aren't any guys around.

Many Wellesley women believe that attending an all-women's college transforms them and their education. "I marvel at how confident and articulate the upper-class women are," one first year student said. "They know their stuff and have no trouble and no qualms in stating their opinion." Discussion and debate were cited to be at a very high level. One student explained, "I think that at co-ed institutions, women don't have the same opportunities to develop this self-consciousness about their abilities as women. The most important thing I'm getting out of my Wellesley education is the knowledge that as a woman, I have the opportunity and ability to do whatever I put my mind to. Period. It's what the Wellesley experience is."

Social Scene

The social scene at Wellesley generates the greatest number of complaints by students. To have a social life "takes a lot of effort at Wellesley." One student explained that "Wellesley is self-contained except for the town of Wellesley, where the only thing most students go for is the CVS pharmacy there." It is popular for women to go off-campus on weekend, since reportedly "campus parties are usually rather sad." Boston is one popular and easily accessible destination. The college runs a bus or "Love Truck" between Boston and Wellesley that leaves every hour from both destinations and costs only a few dollars. It makes stops at Harvard Square, MIT's "Frat Row," and, at scheduled times, the Museum of Fine Arts in Boston. "First-years cannot have cars, and without the bus, we'd be stranded here," one frosh emphasized. Some Wellesley women felt that it was difficult to meet "decent" non-Wellesley students because the only chance they have to mix with others is at off-campus parties on the weekends.

However, many students do enjoy staying on campus. One frosh's roommate was "shocked about the fact that there are plenty of people who stay in on the weekends." On weekend nights, a lot of people hang out in their friends' rooms; "there's no pressure to go out and party if you don't want to." Also many people have friends from other schools stay over with them during the weekends, to such an ex-

tent that the "campus looks co-ed on weekends."

Wellesley's own social scene currently includes four social clubs that each have a theme: TZE (art and music), ZA (literary), Phi Sigma (lectures), and the Shakespeare Society, which puts on two of the Bard's plays each year.

The basic unit of social and residential life at Wellesley, though, is the dorms—whether they are old and Gothic or modern. The three modern dorms, though seemingly out of place on the Wellesley campus, feature rooms with built-in dressers, shelves, and closets, although some students prefer the exterior beauty and spacious rooms of the older dorms. The dorms all house members of every class, which students say makes campus life more cohesive, since freshmen and seniors live side by side in the residences.

The food at Wellesley generally gets high marks. One upperclasswoman noted that she had been to several other colleges and "their food was not nearly as good as ours." In addition, the dining halls have very flexible hours; they are open continuously from 7 A.M. to 8 P.M., and are located in each dorm complex. There are also no restrictions on how much one can eat. "The food system here is great!" said one student. I can get food whenever I want it."

The Tradition of Wellesley

Wellesley women say that the school's famous alumnae have inspired them. Hillary Clinton, Nora Ephron, Lynn Shurr, Cokie Roberts, Diane Sawyer, and Madeline Albright are just a few of the women that got their start at Wellesley. "It's intimidating, but also inspiring to know that I'm carrying on the tradition that these women have established. But I know that I have everything available to get to the same places that these women have." —*Melissa Lau and staff*

FYI

The three best things about attending Wellesley are "the professors, the prestige, and the educational atmosphere."

The three worst things about attending Wellesley are "an all female environment which encourages cattiness (competition and anal-retentiveness), preprofessional atmosphere, an administration that gets out of touch for such a small school."

The three things that every student should do before graduating from Wellesley are "go to the dyke ball, skinny dip in Lake Waban, go to a volleyball game."

One thing I'd like to have known before coming here is "you have to work harder than they tell you to find some sort of social life that you can fit into."

Wheaton College

Address: Wheaton College; Norton, MA 02766
Phone: 508-286-8251
E-mail address: admissions @wheatoncollege.edu
Web site URL: www.wheatoncollege.edu
Founded: 1834
Private or Public: private
Religious affiliation: none
Location: suburban
Undergraduate enrollment: 1,500
Total enrollment: 1,500
Percent Male/Female: 37%/63%
Percent Minority: 11%
Percent African-American: 4%

Percent Asian: 3%
Percent Hispanic: 3%
Percent Native-American: 0.5%
Percent in-state/out-of-state: 38%/62%
Percent Pub HS: 61%
Number of Applicants: 2,463
Percent Accepted: 71%
Percent Accepted who enroll: 24%
Entering: 427
Transfers: 21
Application Deadline: 1 Feb
Mean SAT: 610 V, 590 M
Mean ACT: 26

Middle 50% SAT range: 570–640 V, 550–680 M
Middle 50% ACT range: 22–28
3 Most popular majors: psychology, economics, sociology
Retention: 85%
Graduation rate: 70%
On-campus housing: 100%
Fraternities: NA
Sororities: NA
Library: 371,071 volumes
Tuition and Fees: $23,150 in; $23,150 out
Room and Board: $6,730
Financial aid, first-year: 63%

Since 1921, Wheaton students have observed the school's Honor Code. First-year students arrive on-campus and are led into the college's chapel for a discussion of the policy—which allows tests to be taken unproctored and relies on each individual to be completely truthful. At the end of four years, seniors again convene in the chapel—this time just before graduation—to sign out of the Honor Code. Wheaton's small size allows such advantages as the Honor Code as well as personal relationships with professors. However, it also prevents students from getting lost in the crowd or preserving their anonymity.

Wheaton College is a focal point of the sleepy town of Norton. "We would like our own town," said a senior. Thirty-five minutes from Boston and twenty minutes from Providence, Wheaton appears to be too isolated and picturesque to be situated between two thriving urban centers. Only 1,400 students populate Wheaton's campus—which resembles an overgrown prep school.

The college is divided into New and Old campuses by Peacock Pond. New Campus was developed ten years ago when Wheaton, formerly an all-girls school, became co-educational. New Campus features dining halls Chase Square (which has a saute line and a variety of hot meals) and Chase Round (which has fast-food offerings such as grilled cheese, pizza, and fried foods). Old Campus invites diners to Emerson.

Real-World Academics

Academic departments at Wheaton adopt a supportive approach. Professors' offices are often located directly across from their classrooms, and class sizes allow for individual attention. Students say that the sciences have a good reputation and are known for doing a large amount of fieldwork. The average upper-level class in any subject has from 17 to 22 students, while introductory classes usually top off at 70. "All classes are taught by professors," said a student. "There are TAs, but they simply help the professors." The school is also making a push toward technology-oriented classrooms.

Popular majors are psychology, Hispanic studies, political science, English, and biology. Students do not have to declare a major until junior year. Wheaton requires a general education program beginning with a first-year seminar to aquaint freshmen with each other and orient them toward their liberal arts education. Additionally, the college requires students to take a semester each of a lab science, natural science, physical education (unless involved in a competitive sport), English, and a year of a foreign language. To fulfill the rest of the general education requirement, students choose from a variety of courses including multicultural and math and logic offerings. Wheaton also requires students to have a "second transcript," detailing real-world work experience earned while at the school. The college pushes the value of internships constantly, students say. Students can also design their own majors. "It lets people focus more on their interests," said a senior. "It's good for people who want to go to grad school."

Playing Around

Outside classes, sports are a big focus. Wheaton boasts the Haas Center, completed in 1992, which features an indoor track, a swimming pool with underwater speakers for the synchronized swimming team, and other state-of-the-art facilities. Varsity games—especially against rivals Brandeis and Babson—are often well-attended. A sophomore said that a recent game against Brandeis' soccer team was played in the pouring rain "but there were tons of people who just came anyway. It was a mudfest." There are also intramural sports ranging from ultimate Frisbee to flag football and club sports such as golf and rugby that compete against area schools.

> "All classes are taught by professors," said a student. "There are TAs, but they simply help the professors."

The various sports teams are the most popular extracurricular activities at Wheaton, although other groups draw strong followings. Student government is said to be competitive; a senior noted that "it gets pretty heated around election time." There are also two a cappella groups, the Whims and the Wheatones, and such far-ranging activities as Students for a Free Tibet.

Residential Life

The Wheaton community maintains its intimacy in part because 98 percent of the 1,400 students live on-campus. There is little alternative housing in Norton, and the school limits the number of seniors who may live off-campus. The dorm rooms are generally small, though students say it is better to live on Old, rather than New, Campus. The jewel among the dorms is Keefe Hall, located near an old favorite, Gebbie Hall. Keefe features spacious three-to-six-person suites and an elevator.

Floors in most dorms are single-sex by room. However, there is an all-male floor and an all-female dorm as well as a substance-free dorm and a twenty-four hour quiet dorm. Eight to ten people can also create theme houses, such as "Athletes Against Alcohol," which might be based on a community service program. A panel chooses the best theme ideas and awards the houses to the chosen groups of students.

Where's the Party?

Students commonly mingle in the Balfour-Hood Center, which contains a dance studio, cafe, mailboxes, weight room, video arcade, and Ping-Pong table. School dances or performances are often held in the Center's Atrium. Wheaton weekends tend to be quiet. The school has adopted a policy that students cannot be seen with alcohol or it will be confiscated. Most of the big parties are given by the school, since there are no fraternities or sororities, and people are carefully carded. "It's not a drastic policy," said one student. "Parties tend to be small and quiet. It's a mature atmosphere." Students who are over 21 can have a beer at the Loft, the school's bar, and others come to see comedians or various performances. According to one student, "there's also a great student-run coffee shop called the Lyon's Den," where musicians and comedians perform. Many Wheaton students use the weekends to catch up on work or hang out with friends.

In nearly all aspects of campus life, Wheaton students maintain that "how much you get involved is how much you get out of it," said a sophomore. Academics, sports, and extracurricular activities are encouraged by the school community. Students say that professors are often seen cheering on soccer teams and that the president of the school often takes strolls around campus. —*Kara Miller and staff*

FYI

The three best things about attending Wheaton are "sautes, accessible professors, and pleasant peers."

The three worst things about attending Wheaton are "more and more dorm-crowding, the female/male ratio, and the price."

The three things that every student should do before graduating from Wheaton are "build a boat for the Build-Your-Own-Boat Race, find something fun to do in Norton, and take a psychology class."

One thing I'd like to have known before coming here is "how important it is to develop a taste for coffee."

Williams College

Address: 988 Main Street, PO Box 487; Williamstown, MA 01267

Phone: 413-597-2211

E-mail address: admissions@williams.edu

Web site URL: www.williams.edu

Founded: 1793

Private or Public: private

Religious affiliation: none

Location: small city

Undergraduate enrollment: 2,052

Total enrollment: 2,162

Percent Male/Female: 51%/49%

Percent Minority: 23%

Percent African-American: 7%

Percent Asian: 9%

Percent Hispanic: 6%

Percent Native-American: 0.5%

Percent in-state/out-of-state: 14%/86%

Percent Pub HS: 57%

Number of Applicants: 5,007

Percent Accepted: 23%

Percent Accepted who enroll: 47%

Entering: 544

Transfers: 9

Application Deadline: 1 Jan

Mean SAT: 701 V, 700 M

Mean ACT: NA

Middle 50% SAT range: 650–760 V, 660–750 M

Middle 50% ACT range: NA

3 Most popular majors: economics, history, English

Retention: 98%

Graduation rate: 94%

On-campus housing: 100%

Fraternities: NA

Sororities: NA

Library: 934,755 volumes

Tuition and Fees: $24,790 in; $24,790 out

Room and Board: $6,730

Financial aid, first-year: 44%

Does the idea of enjoying doughnuts and apple cider on a mountaintop with friends on a beautiful fall day appeal to you? When you picture the ideal college setting in your mind, does it encompass intimate and lively class discussions led by brilliant yet accessible professors? Could you learn to become fervently enthusiastic at the sight of a purple cow? If your answers to the above questions are yes, you may want to give Williams College a closer look.

A World of Opportunity

"Williams is so amazing, I cannot imagine myself anywhere else," gushed one freshman. Indeed, Williams does seem to have so much to offer its students. It is undoubtedly a top-notch academic institution, and students rave about the accessibility of the professors and the benefits of the small class sizes. The school takes its role as a leading liberal arts college quite seriously, and "values the student-faculty relationships excessively." Professors are described as "easy to get to know," and even make an effort to learn all of their students' names so they can greet them in passing outside of class. Professors often give students their home phone numbers as well. Students point out that "the difference between Williams and your average research university is that instead of being concerned with fitting in everything they want to talk about, the professors here make sure that you are getting everything you want out of the class." Nearly all intro-level lectures, such as Psychology 101, have under 150 students, and upper-level classes range from about 30 in a class to fewer than 10. Lively class discussion is encouraged; as one student said: "The professors love it when a good fight breaks out."

There is also an excellent support system for those feeling they need a bit of help on the side. Each department has its own peer tutoring program, and Teaching Assistants, although few in number, do exist. They do not teach any courses, but rather assist the professors and are present at every class. Each student is also assigned an academic advisor, who is a good resource throughout the four years. For a school of such small size, Williams has a good deal to offer in the way of academics. The English, economics, and history departments are reputedly strong, and the natural sciences are also given good reviews, with the caveat that they require a lot of lab time. Williams does have its share of gut courses, especially in the sciences: Physics 100 ("Funhundred") and Geology 166: Climates through Time (the classic "Rocks for Jocks") are perennial favorites. But even these courses offer challenge, and the typical Williams student will seek it. Most students seem to be "academically well-rounded; you see a lot of double-majors."

To fulfill the distribution requirement, students must obtain at least three credits in each of three divisions. Division One is comprised of languages, including English, and the arts; Division Two includes history, philosophy, religion, and the social sciences; Division Three covers mathematics and the natural sciences. The requirement is generally thought of as "painless," and "the courses are ones that you would want to take anyway." Williams

does maintain its swimming test and PE requirement, but these too are fairly easy to fulfill, as is the "Peoples and Cultures" one-course requirement, which is usually met by taking an anthropology course. One benefit of attending a small college is the lack of competition to enroll in certain courses. Students report that it is rare to be closed out of a class, although some courses do give preferential status to upperclassmen. Registration has been made simple through Williams' computerized UNIX "self-reg" program, which is reportedly convenient and easy to use. The college calendar is designed on a 4-1-4 system, meaning that students take four courses in the fall and the spring, but engage in Winter Study for the month of January. During Winter Study, students have the option of taking a single course (for credit or for fun), working at an internship, or creating an independent-study program of their own. Many look forward to Winter Study as a break from the academic routine and a chance to devote themselves to one thing in a way they don't otherwise have time to do. Other study options available to Williams students are the Williams-Mystic program, which allows students to pursue American maritime studies in Mystic, Connecticut, for a semester; the Williams-Oxford exchange with Exeter College in Oxford, England, for a year; or the 12-College Exchange, where students can spend a semester or a year at one of the other schools in the program.

Size Does Matter

While the academic offerings at Williams are comparable to those at larger institutions, this school's small student body sets it apart in a number of ways. Many students find that they can recognize almost everyone in their class by the end of freshman year, and this has its ups and downs. One female student explained that "being in such a small class does have its drawbacks, but none that I didn't expect when I chose to come here." Frequently mentioned gripes include limited social options, lack of privacy, and a good deal of gossip. "Gossip here is inevitable because everyone knows whom everyone else is talking about," remarked one student. "You may have heard of Six Degrees of Separation . . . at Williams, we have one degree," commented another.

> "You may have heard of Six Degrees of Separation . . . at Williams, we have one degree."

However, the intimate atmosphere fosters a sense of community that indeed drew many students to Williams in the first place. There are several annual events that students always look forward to: Mountain Day, where the entire student body treks up to a mountain and then gets apple cider and doughnuts; a barbecue on Convocation, and a couple of semiformal dances. Being in a graduating class of about 500 also makes for an interesting dating scene. There is not much formal dating at Williams; as is common in other colleges, people tend either to engage in random hookups, or to settle into longlasting relationships. Unique to Williams, however, seems to be the phenomenon of students being incredibly eager to jump to conclusions about the relationships of others. One sophomore lamented that "you walk across the street with someone, and all of a sudden, you're thought of as a couple!"

Living in Style

The housing at Williams was given high marks across the board. Freshmen generally live in either Frosh Quad or Berkshire Quad, and are split into entryways of about 20 freshman each with two Junior Advisors (JAs). Because the JAs are not given any benefits by the school for their services, they are more eager to become friends with their advisees than to crack down on rules in the dorms, and are described as "awesome" and "great to have around." Housing definitely serves as a big social unit freshman year. Most frosh live in doubles, but some do get singles. Upperclassmen can often secure singles off of small hallways with a large common room at the end, an arrangement whose success can be measured by the overwhelming majority of students who choose to live on-campus all four years. While some of the housing is spread out or a bit removed from the center of campus, students feel that "making the walk is never a chore, because it is so beautiful here!" And whatever dorm one is in, the view from the window is sure to be a gorgeous one.

Work Hard, Play Hard

The old college cliché still seems to thrive at Williams. While devoted to challenging academics during the week, Ephs (named for school founder Colonel Ephrain Williams) waste no time in having fun when Thursday night rolls around. Thursday is usually dance night at the Log, a Williams-owned multipurpose space close to central campus. Since the abolition of fraternities in the 1970s, students have been left to their own devices to find parties on the weekends, but "there always seems to be something going on." Sports teams often provide social units and hold parties, so being on a team has its advantages. However, it seems that "most parties open to everyone at around 11:00." Alcohol is often a presence, but there is little report of drugs or even cigarettes. And there are a fair amount of students who don't drink; "the campus is very accepting of that." Many students pointed to the fact that Williams is a very "health-conscious" campus, perhaps stemming from the large percentage of undergraduates who participate in athletics. Sports are very popular, and football and basketball games are always well attended, especially if against archrival Amherst College. Purple Cow fanatics will cheer on their teams in the worst of New England weather. The school spirit at Williams is hard to ignore, and often lasts long after graduation. This leads to a strong alumni network that has proved very helpful to recent graduates of the school searching for jobs beyond the "Purple Bubble."

For those not interested in sports, Williams also has a lot to offer in the way of extracurriculars. Said one sophomore, "the school really wants everyone to become involved, so they give the students every opportunity to become leaders." Aspiring thespians can take part in one of the ten theatrical productions each year, or join the Cap and Bells dramatic society, whose alumni roster includes Stephen Sondheim. A cappella singing groups are popular, as are dance troupes. Williams has an excellent outdoor club, which offers trips to the nearby Berkshire Mountains. The college council is also active and well respected. As one freshman put it, "Everyone here does some form of something." Once a student finds his or her niche, the small student body allows for many leadership opportunities: "Williams creates an environment where the individual can really shine." The school seems to have struck an important balance between emphasis on the individual and a strong sense of community.

Looking Ahead
Williams seems to be constantly looking for ways to improve student life, and this has led to some renovations and constructions that students believe will add a lot to the campus. Goodrich, a new student center, has just been completed and includes a coffee bar and performance space. Alumni have also recently donated $20 million that will be used over the next four years to refurbish performing arts facilities.

Of course, there is still room for improvement. The campus is not as diverse as many would like, although students remark that the administration does seem to be trying to remedy this. The image of the preppy athlete still dominates, and walking around the campus, one notices a "preponderance of J. Crew model lookalikes." However, the political scene is described as slightly left of the center, and alternate lifestyles, while not the norm, are generally accepted with ease.

"Williams is an amazing place, but I think some people are disappointed when they realize the location isn't exactly a hub of excitement and culture," pointed out one freshman. The largest student dissatisfaction appears to be with Williamstown itself, a sleepy New England town with only two commercial streets. Some students wish that there were more off-campus dining options, as Pappa Charlie's deli is the "only place suited to a student's budget." The college has a couple of art museums, including the highly reputed Clark Art Institute. There is also a movie theater on Spring Street, although students note that it plays mostly "random independent flicks." The students who are happiest at Williams seem to be the ones who are content to have their lives revolve around the campus. But with all the sports, arts, and other diversions, you would be hard-pressed to claim that there is nothing to do. And most Ephs would agree that the best part of Williams is the people: "everyone here can surprise you in some way." Perhaps most important of all, Williams students are happy. "I cannot always pin a reason on it," said one junior, "but I don't think a day goes by when I don't stop, look around, and smile."—*Rachel Grand and Staff*

FYI

The three best things about attending Williams are "quaint Williamstown, sports life, and personal attention on all levels."

The three worst things about attending Williams are "the rumor mill, not having enough time to spend taking advantage of everything Williams offers, and the 'health-conscious' attitudes."

The three things that every student should do before graduating from Williams are "have a huge snowball fight, visit the Berkshires, and start ordering from the J. Crew catalog."

One thing I'd like to have known before coming here is "how much of an advantage you get by way of personal attention at a smaller school."

Worcester Polytechnic Institute

Address: 100 Institute Road; Worcester, MA 01609
Phone: 508-831-5286
E-mail address: admissions@wpi.edu
Web site URL: www.wpi.edu
Founded: 1865
Private or Public: private
Religious affiliation: none
Location: suburban
Undergraduate enrollment: 2,737
Total enrollment: 3,742
Percent Male / Female: 78% / 22%
Percent Minority: 13%
Percent African-American: 2%

Percent Asian: 7%
Percent Hispanic: 3%
Percent Native-American: 0.5%
Percent in-state / out-of-state: 50% / 50%
Percent Pub HS: 79%
Number of Applicants: 3,244
Percent Accepted: 79%
Percent Accepted who enroll: 26%
Entering: 662
Transfers: 114
Application Deadline: 1 Feb
Mean SAT: 620 V, 660 M
Mean ACT: NA

Middle 50% SAT range: 560–660 V, 620–700 M
Middle 50% ACT range: NA
3 Most popular majors: mechanical engineering, electrical engineering, computer science
Retention: 91%
Graduation rate: 58%
On-campus housing: 96%
Fraternities: 31%
Sororities: 38%
Library: 350,000 volumes
Tuition and Fees: $22,158 in; $22,158 out
Room and Board: $6,912
Financial aid, first-year: 73%

Where can a serious science or engineering student get lots of hands-on project experience, jump into vibrant campus extra-curriculars and really get a taste for the fun-filled scenic Northeast? At "WPI," Worcester Polytechnic Institute, of course. Founded in 1865 at Worcester, Massachusetts, WPI is the nation's third oldest engineering school and emphasizes a hands-on, practical approach to learning.

Learn by Doing

The WPI academic calendar consists of four seven-week quarters and a summer quarter. Students will take three courses per quarter, giving them a more intense focus on the subject matter. This quarter system draws mixed reviews, with some students convinced that "it allows you to concentrate more on each class" and others citing it as one of the worst features of WPI.

Mechanical Engineering remains the number one major at WPI. Web-minded Bill Gates wannabes are filling up the Electrical & Computer Engineering and Computer Science departments, making them the second and third most popular majors. Students at WPI enjoy their courses—"My favorite class was Anatomy. The professor was so cool, he'd just do all sorts of things, like make up songs about the bones!"— and class size is "perfect, IMHO (In My Humble Opinion)!" Introductory level courses, particularly in biology, will be large lectures (around 200 students). Students say advanced courses can have as few as eight per class, however.

The personalities of teachers came up several times as a WPI plus, "The professors are wicked nice!" gushed one student. Still, students better beware of "whole departments that basically don't speak English," laughed one Biotechnology major. Students warn especially of teaching assistants in the Russian department and then teaching assistants *and* professors in the Math department who may be English-challenged.

As members of the Worcester Consortium, WPI students can take classes at nine other area colleges including Holy Cross, Assumption, Clark and Worcester State. Although it is not common to do so, WPI students who have elected to dual-enroll find the humanities classes at neighboring schools "rewarding" and "very good."

All undergraduates at WPI participate in WPI Plan. The WPI Plan involves three comprehensive projects, each combining classroom learning with hands-on experience off campus. The first, the Sufficiency, focuses on the humanities and arts. WPIers choose a sequence of five humanities courses and complete a project on a theme arising from the five. Topics have ranged from the love affair between Antony and Cleopatra to the impact of radio astronomy on the development of cosmology. Students generally finish Sufficiency papers in their sophomore year, and the papers are usually twenty to twenty-five pages long.

Part Two of the Plan, the Interdisciplinary Qualifying Project (IQP), means multi-disciplinary teams of students work with professionals for a seven-week quarter. Teams solve thought-provoking technology and society problems. With project centers in London, Bangkok, Venice, Australia and Puerto Rico, many WPI students elect to go abroad during their IQP term. In the past, IQP projects have examined tourism in Puerto Rico or the biological effects of marine organisms in Venetian canals.

Part Three, the Major Qualifying Project (MQP) is the longest and most intense; students devote their time to research or problems directly related to their major.

Girls and Greeks

With twelve fraternities and two sororities, WPI has a strong Greek system, which students admit dominate the social scene. Thirty-five percent of the undergraduate men and forty percent of the women undergraduates at WPI are Greek members. But even those who are part of some of the major mixing find it tiresome. Laments one sorority girl, "I wish I had known how strained the social scene was—how much it would revolve around Greek life." WPI students concede that in a heavily male-dominated population (78% male, 22% female) not being Greek may leave the guys feeling more left out than the gals.

Still, many insist, "Greek life is important if you want to have a really active social life." The rush process is traditional

and brief, lasting for a few weeks before Thanksgiving Break in November. Fraternities tend to build their membership around "common interests." For example, WPIers can consistently refer you to "the soccer frat," "the football frat," and "the drug frat." Speaking of drugs and alcohol, this is not a campus where "serious" drugs are a presence. Students report the occasional recreational use of marijuana, 'shrooms, speed, but they are not a centerpiece of the social action. As for alcohol, WPI is a place where "people can party like crazy on weekend and still pass all their classes," says one student. Most underclassmen head to off-campus apartment parties, or frat parties (if they know someone and can get on the "list"). However, girls say the pressure to drink is fairly relaxed. "I know a lot of guys in frats who don't drink, and its cool," one student said. "People respect that."

> "My favorite class was Anatomy. The professor was so cool, he'd just do all sorts of things, like make up songs about the bones!"

Friendships are strong at WPI. Some students credit the nature of their project-based schoolwork and then shared common interests ("Engineering!") for bringing this student body together. "More than friends," however, is a different issue altogether. Guys don't like the 80/20 guy/girl ratio. This leads many of the male population to go a-hunting elsewhere on weekends, particularly at Holy Cross or Assumption where the ratio is the opposite.

Living Large

Virtually all freshmen at WPI live on campus in dorms. Although WPI began a five-year program to fully renovate the majority of its residence halls in 1996, the food that they serve is still "really bad!" Poor food convinces many students to live off campus. Rent for living off-campus is reasonable, and "some apartments are closer than the dorms!" Owning a car is "useful, but not necessary" since WPI maintains a free late-night escort service,

SNAPS, for students' safety in not-so-safe Worcester. Limited availability of parking spaces is a complaint.

Those legitimately over twenty-one ("if you're not over twenty-one, don't even try") enjoy the bar scene in downtown Worcester, a fifteen minute walk from campus. Especially popular are The Leatrim on Thursday nights ("Everybody goes. It's like a club/bar on Thursday nights, but every other night of the week, its just a dive bar,") and bars The Irish Stein and The Firehouse.

Finding Friends

When asked to enumerate the student stereotype at WPI, responses were: "Smart kids, big egos, somewhat geeky." Students don't become so engrossed in their work, however, that they don't have time to join one of WPI's 130 organizations. Students at WPI love being involved because it offers a great way to make friends.

Students also enjoy their school traditions. One tradition, The Skull, is alive and well. Skull is a senior honor society, which "taps" 10–15 juniors every spring. Activities of the organization are highly secretive, but students are very aware of their presence and prestige. When asked what its like, one WPI student responded, ". . . a couple of my best friends are members, yet they swear secrecy and don't tell much about it." Another student confirmed that "Skull is top-secret. Details are hard to come by." So, what is clear? We do know Skull owns and meets in an old windowless building on the corner of campus and pledges "wear long yellow ribbons every day like pledge pins, and they get shorter and shorter as they get closer to being initiated." Hey, isn't this a movie? —*Ann Sun*

FYI
The three best things about attending WPI are "Pretty good campus, good reputation, great travel and project opportunities."
The three worst things about attending WPI are "incompetent math instructors, $10 for a parking decal but there are no places to park after 9am, and no liberal arts."
The three things every student should do before graduating from WPI are "see Bancroft tower, join a club . . . or several, and take classes not directly related to your major (at Holy Cross, etc.)."
One thing I wish I had known before coming to WPI is "How strained the social scene really is."

Michigan

Address: 611 East Porter Street; Albion, MI 49224
Phone: 517-629-0321
E-mail address: admissions@albion.edu
Web site URL: www.albion.edu
Founded: 1835
Private or Public: private
Religious affiliation: Methodist
Location: urban
Undergraduate enrollment: 1,543
Total enrollment: 1,543
Percent Male / Female: 41%/59%
Percent Minority: 8%
Percent African-American: 4%

Percent Asian: 2%
Percent Hispanic: 1%
Percent Native-American: 0.5%
Percent in-state / out-of-state: 16%/84%
Percent Pub HS: NA
Number of Applicants: 1,413
Percent Accepted: 84%
Percent Accepted who enroll: 35%
Entering: 412
Transfers: 25
Application Deadline: 1 Apr
Mean SAT: 580 V, 590 M
Mean ACT: 25

Middle 50% SAT range: 520–630 V, 530–640 M
Middle 50% ACT range: NA
3 Most popular majors: bus./marleting, biological / life sciences, social sciences / history
Retention: 84%
Graduation rate: 711%
On-campus housing: 100%
Fraternities: 45%
Sororities: 44%
Library: 316,335 volumes
Tuition and Fees: $18,952 in; $18,952 out
Room and Board: $5,404
Financial aid, first-year: 64%

During their first night on campus, Albion freshmen sing "Io Triumphe," the school song. At least, tradition says they should. How many freshmen actually participate in this linguistically challenging tradition? Well, if not all of them, they'll have four years to figure it out. Besides having learned "Io Triumphe," future graduates of Albion will have experienced going to school in a small-town environment, with a close-knit student body, in a friendly midwestern atmosphere.

Academic to the Core

Because of its relatively small student body, Albion provides an excellent opportunity for students to get to know their professors. Class size averages about 20, and the largest lecture classes run at about 40 or 50. Teaching assistants don't exist at Albion, although undergraduate student assistants sometimes lead the discussion sections. Most students at Albion find their professors challenging but friendly, often taking their classes out onto the Quad when the weather is warm. One student said, "I've gone to a couple of my professors' houses for dinner. They open their homes and it really helps you get in touch with your instructor." "Many [professors] become your friends and people you can talk to about stuff outside of academics," said another. One history major said, "The best class I have taken is Colonial American History because unlike a typical history, the structure of the class was different and a lot of fun. We had a variety of discussion groups, including one similar to the format of Jerry Springer." The administration pays attention to the attitudes of students toward their professors: at the end of each term, students evaluate non-tenured professors, and the administration takes these evaluations into consideration.

Besides classes required for their major, Albion students also need to get class credit in several different cores: a gender core credit, an environmental credit, a race credit, a lab science, and a non-lab science. However, crafty students can choose classes that count toward both their core and their major. One communications major explained, "[I took] Race and Ethnicity, . . . a 300 level sociology class, which covered core for me. It really helped me to understand how race and ethnicity impact all of our lives, no matter what our background." But, of course even students taking core classes outside of their major still appreciate the idea behind the core classes: "to promote diversity and get students more in tune with all aspects of culture." Most undergrads will find the classes helpful and a diversion from classes for their major. At the very least, said one student, "I didn't mind the core requirements at all."

Albion's Gerstacker Program in Professional Management and the Gerald R. Ford Institute for Public Service offer internships for political science and business majors. For those majoring in other fields, there are other people at Albion College who help students get started finding great internships. One female student exclaims, "Albion gives great internships! Most of my friends have spent a semester elsewhere, either in cities like NYC, Philly, New Orleans, or abroad in Vienna, London, Paris, or Heidelberg." These internships not only allow a brief escape into the real world but also build valuable resumé experience; some students are able to parlay their internships into jobs after graduation.

Wasted Away Again in Margaritaville

Even the best students need a little time to relax; when asked about the coolest thing a professor had ever done in class, one student replied, "Canceled it!" After a week of demanding classes, Albion students know how to kick back and relax.

For some students, the weekend festivities start Wednesday night, when many Albion students can be found at one of the local bars. One student states, "Everyone goes out [on Wednesday] because typically there are not early Thursday morning classes. You don't have to be twenty-one to get into the bars, so there are people from all classes there . . . it's a good time." For the unfortunate souls who do have Thursday morning classes, there are parties on the official weekend, too. Fraternities throw theme parties: "Jimmy Buffet Bash, Hawaiian Party, Toga Night, Graffiti Party are just some of them." How do you get into these fraternity parties? "Show up at the door!" says one partygoer. Unlike at some larger schools, most fraternity parties at Albion are open to everyone on campus. One sorority sister says, "People here are really friendly and always encourage underclassmen to go out to the frats/house parties. It is very easy to get to know people." Several organizations on campus try to get together formal dances, although most students agree that these events, except perhaps the Valentine's Day formal, are not very popular.

Aside from the fraternity parties, students say weekends in Albion are somewhat dull. Popular off-campus weekend destinations include the nearby city of Jackson (a popular place to go on dates), Michigan State and the University of Michigan (less than one hour from Albion), and home. Referring to a new student center, one fun-seeking student says, "The college is trying to encourage students to stay on campus during the weekends, but their attempts have not been popular."

> "It's great to go to sporting events here because you actually know a lot of the athletes!"

For those spending their weekends in Albion, the city has two bars, including the popular Cascarelli's (sometimes called "Relly's"), a movie theater with free admission on Wednesdays, a Big K, a grocery store, and a couple restaurants. Many students also spend the weekends hanging out with friends in their rooms, watching movies, catching up on homework, or sleeping.

What's a Briton?

Many students come to Albion for the chance to play intercollegiate sports. Because it is a Division III school, almost anybody who wants to can join the team. While being a Division III school takes off a little bit of the stress of intercollegiate athletics, the competitive Briton spirit is still there. One volleyball player says, "It is stressful at the same time as fun."

Going to watch sports can be exciting at a smaller school, too. "It's great to go to sporting events here," says a student, "because you actually know a lot of the athletes! They are your friends, your classmates, or they live down the hall. Typical games have lots of students for that very reason." Another student says, "A typical basketball game is similar to those in high school. There is a student section with guys in matching t-shirts (known as Kresge Krazys) cheering on the team and aggravating the refs."

Many athletes also participate in intramural sporting events, putting together teams of their sorority sisters, friends, or floormates. In addition, many students are looking forward to the planned upgrade in the fitness facility, including the addition of more cardiovascular equipment.

Movin' On Up

All freshmen live in either Wesley Hall or Seaton Hall their first year, with most of the freshmen being housed in Wesley. Both residence halls have community bathrooms. One former Wesley resident says of her living experience, "The rooms are small and the furniture is old and not very good. The dorm is clean and well taken care of." As sophomores, many students move into Whitehouse or Twin Towers, both of which have double rooms connected by a bathroom. All students must live on campus, although options include living in one of the campus fraternity houses or some college-owned apartments, in addition to the main dorms. Student residential advisors and residence hall directors are available in every dorm to help students adjust to college life, and most students find the RAs to be friendly and knowledgeable.

Most hungry Britons take their meals at Baldwin, the only dining facility on campus. Few students complain about the quality of food, and some even enjoy the grilled chicken, vegetable soup, and homemade bread. Besides Baldwin, the only other place to get food on campus is the Taco Bell eat shop, which also sells burgers and chicken tenders. But the dearth of places to get food isn't all that bad, considering the size of the campus. Students report that walking to classes only takes five minutes. And for those who can't live without their store-bought junk food, the campus provides shuttle buses that go downtown and to the bigger surrounding cities. Or, as an alternative, "there is always someone you know that has a car," says one student.

Comedy Central

As one female undergrad puts it, "Albion does a great job of keeping us entertained! They try really hard to bring in big-name speakers, musicians, et cetera." Recent visitors to campus have included singer Shawn Colvin, comedienne Paula Poundstone, authors Howard Zinn and Stephen Jay Gould, boxer Rubin "The Hurricane" Carter, and a hypnotist. In addition, students participate in over 120 student organizations, ranging from the school newspaper, to community service groups, to Section 41—the role-playing game organization.

Many students also participate in the Greek system at Albion. One sorority officer explains, "[Getting into a sorority or fraternity is] not very hard. The recruitment structure is very open and allows for a variety of people to join." Her sorority sister adds, "If you make a point to hang out with the house you like and get to know them, it's not hard at all to get a bid." Many students who have joined the Greek system say being Greek gives them an opportunity to become more involved on campus and in the community.

But do not forget that students who choose not to pledge a sorority or fraternity can still get into the parties. One female student says, "If you choose NOT to go Greek, it's not a big deal. People intermix a LOT."

And that feeling of people intermixing is everywhere at Albion. For some students, being at a small school can be stifling. "I don't like knowing a lot of people on campus," says one student, "and would rather have gone to a bigger school where I could meet someone new every day." The relatively small student body also makes it harder to randomly hook up with people at parties. But for most students, the sense of community at Albion makes the difference. "I feel that it is perfect to get to know a lot of people and also it is easy to get involved in the activities available," says one senior. "If I don't know a person by their name, I almost always rec-ognize them walking through campus, from a class or a job or something." One student says, "Everyone here is outgoing and friendly . . . people here say hi to you just because. I like walking around campus and seeing my friends and being able to call my professors at home to ask them a question about class." She goes on to sum up the Albion experience, "Small classes, good food, and a well-balanced work/play ethic." —*Kenneth Tseng*

FYI

The three best things about Albion are "the small campus, the professors here are amazing, and the way the word *Liberal* in our Liberal Arts Education is more 'real' than most other liberal arts schools."

The three worst things about Albion are "the town of Albion is rather empty, the school is very expensive (and the price keeps rising), and there is not a lot of off-campus living offered, even for [upperclassmen.]"

The three things every student should do before graduating from Albion are "paint the rock, go off campus for a semester, and go through recruitment to join a fraternity or sorority."

One thing I'd like to have known before coming here is "I don't think anything that anyone can tell you, because you will not understand until you get to college and start living on your own. It is a whole lifestyle change, and the difficulty [in adjusting] really depends on the person. I wish I knew how hard it would have been for me, personally, but I also do not think that I would have listened to my dad or anyone else who had tried to tell me."

Alma College

Address: 614 West Superior Street; Alma, MI 48801
Phone: 517-463-7139
E-mail address: admissions@alma.edu
Web site URL: www.alma.edu
Founded: 1886
Private or Public: private
Religious affiliation: Presbyterian
Location: small city
Undergraduate enrollment: 1,350
Total enrollment: 1,350
Percent Male/Female: 43%/57%
Percent Minority: 5%

Percent African-American: 2%
Percent Asian: 0.5%
Percent Hispanic: 2%
Percent Native-American: 0.5%
Percent in-state/out-of-state: 96%/4%
Percent Pub HS: 93%
Number of Applicants: 1,366
Percent Accepted: 83%
Percent Accepted who enroll: 30%
Entering: 339
Transfers: 38
Application Deadline: 1 Mar
Mean SAT: NA

Mean ACT: 25
Middle 50% SAT range: NA
Middle 50% ACT range: 22–28
3 Most popular majors: business administration, biology, education
Retention: 89%
Graduation rate: 70%
On-campus housing: 90%
Fraternities: 24%
Sororities: 23%
Library: 230,398 volumes
Tuition and Fees: $21,748 in; $21,748 out
Room and Board: $5,726
Financial aid, first-year: 97%

The Alma College campus is a pleasant place—"The buildings are red and white brick, not Gothic or modern" and have "a nice feel." The MacIntyre Plaza has a garden and chairs, and there are trees and flowers everywhere. Both the beauty and the idyllic solitude of the campus reflect what students describe as an isolated, cozy place to receive a liberal arts education.

A Well-Rounded Education

Students at Alma take 168 credits, normally 46 courses, to earn a degree, and along with selecting an area of concentration, they must complete a range of general-education requirements. These include courses in Basic Skills, a year of English and one semester of mathematics, and courses fulfilling requirements in Historical Perspectives, Fine Arts and Humanities, Social Sciences, and Life and Physical Sciences. Before finishing these courses, students must do lab work in the sciences, and take courses in creative or performing arts, religion or philosophy, and literature. Creative and performing arts classes take advantage of the extensive and beautiful Heritage Center and the "theater and dance departments, which are strong for a school of Alma's size." The performing arts requirement can be accomplished with anything from piano lessons, to highland dance classes, a reflection of the school's Scottish heritage.

The academic calendar includes a month-long spring term after the traditional spring semester. Everyone must complete two spring terms, usually after sophomore and junior years. One course must be a designated "S" course, which usually involves travel. Classes meet every day and can be "highly intense," but one junior noted that the homework load is usually about the same as that of four courses during the regular semester. Offerings are generally creative: one student's rhetoric class traveled to Detroit to help prisoners write essays, while another class visited African-American churches throughout the area. Some students spend the term interning in journalism in Washington, D.C., traveling with the education department to London schools, or going to Australia with the business club.

"No Easy Way Out"

Student opinions on the level of academic intensity vary. One sophomore said that the workload was comparable to other schools, while a junior said that everyone has "a ton of work." All students agree that professors push the students, who are generally from the top of their high school classes. "Students are at college because they want to go, not [because they] have to go. Everyone is academically-oriented and

career driven," said one senior. "Everyone is used to being the best and tries to do it again," although no one feels that the school is dog-eat-dog or has unfriendly competition. Grading is "tough, but not impossible," and some of the toughest work happens in introductory courses because "every department has weeder courses . . . to keep classes small."

Alma's strongest programs include the sciences (especially biology), education, and business. Exercise and Health Science (EHS) is a popular option, especially for those aspiring to medical school. A new wing, which includes a cadaver lab, opened in the physical education building in December 1997 to accommodate the growing interest in EHS. Students have few complaints about any one department, although traditional majors such as philosophy and mathematics are quite small.

> **"Once you are on campus you have to study because there's nothing else to do."**

Class size at Alma usually averages around 20 students, and the largest course on-campus has about 65 students. Most professors "work to facilitate discussion" and "work really hard to know students." They give out e-mail addresses, home phone numbers, and hold office hours. One junior reported that students could even send e-mail to the college president and expect an answer. Students had no problems getting into classes (a talk with the professor of a closed class usually does the trick,) but one undergrad explained that at a school as small as Alma not every course is offered every semester. Another noted the need for greater diversity in the curriculum, citing the limited course offerings in areas such as Jewish religion and women's studies.

"Cheers"

Alma college is a small college in a small town, and students report that they know almost everyone. The students have nicknamed the school Cheers, "because everyone knows everyone's name." Students even said that they have specific spots in the dining hall where everyone knows they sit. Cliques are "inevitable" and the school is sometimes "too small," but most students are happy with this atmosphere, and picked Alma because of it. "It is a big, friendly, teddy-bear place," said one junior.

The students within the "Alma Bubble" are fairly homogenous, mostly white, middle class, and from suburbs north of Detroit, or from small towns surrounding Alma. Few students are from other states or ethnic groups, and the school is working hard to recruit a more diverse student body. Although the student body has a reputation for being conservative, one student reported that he was "not looked down on for being liberal." The Young Republicans are active on-campus, but "if you come in right wing and uptight, you cannot leave that way." Although minority recruitment is a somewhat touchy issue, "most people realize that the campus would be more interesting and have more flair [if it were more diverse]." Homosexuality is also fairly accepted; a popular female art professor is openly married to another woman.

Quiet Campus

Students describe Alma as very quiet on the weekends. Alma is "an hour away from everything, and once you're on campus you have to study because there's nothing else to do." Although the college has a sizable number of Greeks, and though there are parties most weekends, students feel little pressure to rush or drink. Fraternity parties are small affairs compared to those at nearby Central Michigan University or Michigan State, partially because the administration owns the houses, and "the dean of students will go to every fraternity party more than once [to check it out]." Dorm parties occur, but students are careful "not to draw attention to it."

Many students leave campus for socializing, partially because "they want a change of environment from studying so hard." One senior estimated that she left campus two weekends out of every month. Popular destinations include CMU and MSU, along with Mount Pleasant, which has "better restaurants," a casino, and several popular bars, including Wayside, which features swing dancing.

On weekends, a main force on-campus is ACUB, or Alma College Union Board. ACUB sponsors coffeehouses with live music on Friday nights, and brings concerts, films, and other events to campus, which are generally "very well-attended." Sororities throw formals throughout the year, and homecoming involves a week of celebration and draws many alums back to campus.

Comfortable Living

Alma dorms earn few complaints. Freshmen and sophomores usually live on main campus, in one of four dorms, two all-male and two all-female. All of the rooms are fairly similar, and "bigger than a lot of schools." The administration is in the process of upgrading all of the rooms, wiring them for the Internet, and adding new furniture and carpeting. Juniors and seniors can move to South Complex, which is further from the classroom buildings and "more like an apartment complex." Theme housing is also available, and fraternities and sororities have limited residential space.

Marriot provides all of Alma's meals, although the main dining hall, Hamilton Commons, retains the nickname Saga, after the company that once provided food. The food is described as very good, with hot food, a grill, a salad bar, deserts, vegetarian items, and a deli at every meal. Students can also take Munch Money to Scottie's, a convenience store, or Joe's, a popular hangout that serves hamburgers. Also, the dining hall staff is very "nutrition-oriented" and displays nutritional information above all the foods served.

Sports and Honors Societies

Almost everyone at Alma is involved in extracurricular activities, and students point out that they have a large number of organizations for the school's size, probably more than 100. Of that number, only 20 to 25 are social, and most of the others are connected with some academic discipline. "Most people strive to be a part of [honorary] societies," said one senior. There is also a strong Model UN team and several popular Christian organizations.

Almost half of the student body is involved in varsity athletics. Because most athletes can be on full teams, intramurals are less popular, although the school plans to build a new IM facility beginning in the spring of 2000. School spirit runs high at Alma, and football and soccer games are well attended. One cheerleader said, "Our away-game crowd is often bigger than [the opposing team's] home crowd."

Alma College is admittedly a small college in a very small town. But the isolation of the "Alma Bubble" is not necessarily a turnoff. Students feel that their education is well-rounded and solid, and that their community is friendly. One spirited junior even said, "It's a bubble because it's so perfect!"—*Bethany Lacina*

FYI

The three best things about attending Alma are, "the accessibility of the administration, the academics, especially the dance and theater departments, and the Spring Term."

The three worst things about attending Alma are, "the Alma Bubble, the prevalence of cliques, and the lack of social activities/opportunities at Alma and its towns."

The three things that every student should do before graduating Alma are "trying to stay on campus for some weekends, revel in the school's athletic spirit, and get involved in a honorary society."

One thing I'd like to have known before coming here is "how small it really is!"

K a l a m a z o o   C o l l e g e

Address: 1200 Academy Street; Kalamazoo, MI 49006
Phone: 616-337-7166
E-mail address: admission@kzoo.edu
Web site URL: www.kzoo.edu
Founded: 1833
Private or Public: private
Religious affiliation: none
Location: small city
Undergraduate enrollment: 1,367
Total enrollment: 1,367
Percent Male/Female: 44%/56%
Percent Minority: 9%
Percent African-American: 3%

Percent Asian: 4%
Percent Hispanic: 1%
Percent Native-American: 0.5%
Percent in-state/out-of-state: 70%/30%
Percent Pub HS: 85%
Number of Applicants: 1,410
Percent Accepted: 77%
Percent Accepted who enroll: 34%
Entering: 370
Transfers: 18
Application Deadline: 1 Feb
Mean SAT: 640 V, 622 M
Mean ACT: 27

Middle 50% SAT range: 590–690 V, 570–670 M
Middle 50% ACT range: 24–29
3 Most popular majors: economics, biology, political science
Retention: 89%
Graduation rate: 71%
On-campus housing: 99%
Fraternities: NA
Sororities: NA
Library: 300,978 volumes
Tuition and Fees: $19,834 in; $19,834 out
Room and Board: $5,961
Financial aid, first-year: 97%

What is an ideal liberal arts school? Maybe it is one that would offer more than the generic promise of small class size and a well-rounded education. Students at Kalamazoo College in western Michigan think their K-Plan does just that. Before graduation, they will be exposed to traditional, experiential, and foreign education, in a friendly environment.

Special K

Under Kalamazoo's K-Plan, students are required to take courses across the liberal arts and sciences, including emphasis on the "K" Foundations of written expression, oral expression, quantitative reasoning, and information and computer literacy. Also, five quarters of physical education are mandatory. Few students are bothered by these requirements because, as one junior said, "You can go Rollerblading three times a week and call it PE."

Students are also encouraged to complete a quarter of Career Development, usually as an off-campus internship. Course credit is not granted, but 85 percent of students still participate. They keep a journal for the school, and the work experience is recorded on their transcript. Also optional, but very common among juniors, is foreign study, taken during either both the fall and winter quarters, or over the spring quarter. While students can travel to every continent and innumerable countries, the most popular program is in Madrid, "where the school sends all the Spanish students who don't really speak Spanish." Seniors complete a SIP (Senior Individualized Project), an original thesis that must be defended before a panel of faculty from the student's major.

In addition to all of this, a freshmen writing seminar is mandatory, as well as 25 LAC (liberal arts colloquium) credits, which can be fulfilled through attendance of on-campus cultural events, such as Kalamazoo Symphony Chamber Orchestra concerts, scholarly lectures, and professional theater productions. Students enjoy the LAC credit requirement, and one student said, "I had them done before the end of sophomore year. Lots [of the events] are really interesting." There are some recent modifications to the K-Plan. All graduates will now be completing a Web portfolio, which is an online record of school and work experiences, which one student sees as a "fairly simple" requirement. The administration has also eliminated on-campus classes in the summer, and Career Development now usually happens the summer after sophomore year, instead of in the spring. Motivating factors for this change included the chance to allow more continual involvement in extracurricular activities. Other students have pointed out that the new calendar has made class scheduling, especially in the sciences, more difficult.

Academically Intense

Kalamazoo academics are generally described as "very intense." One chemistry major said, "You can just go to class and get Bs, but you really have to put work in to get As." "Stress levels are high here," noted another student, partially because classes move quickly to fit material into a quarter rather than a semester. Foreign languages are especially difficult to master in the limited time frame. Kalamazoo is well-known for its biological sciences, and pre-med, pre-law and the natural science majors are the "hard-core stressed-out people." Pre-meds also have the largest classes, with introductory science courses averaging around 60 students. According to some students, the administration favors the science programs. "They have the most spending and the most scholarships available," said one biology major. A sociology major complained that his department is understaffed by comparison.

Faculty in Flux

Most students like their professors, and say they are "cool people," but are concerned with the administration's handling of faculty, particularly with the high faculty turnover in recent years. This turnover is due partially to administrative initiatives, and partially to lower-than-average faculty salaries. A senior chemistry major noted that the department has been dismantled except for one teacher, and is now made up of temporary faculty. Despite these difficulties, however, teaching assistants exist only to oversee introductory labs, and native speakers are used as TAs in language labs. A French major, with a German and Chinese double minor, exclaimed about the TAs: "I cannot tell you how helpful it is [to have a native speaker]."

Still Liberal Heaven?

Kalamazoo's community has long been marked by its liberality, though its population remains fairly homogenous. Most of the students are white, upper-middle-class Michigan residents. Although, one senior said, there are two groups, "one that pays full tuition, and the other receives a whole lot of aid." The school is working to bring more minorities to both the student body and the faculty through a new staff position devoted to diversity initiatives and the student organization CORD (Coalition on Race and Diversity).

Politically, most students lean to the left. "Lots of people wear gay pride rainbows on their backpacks and everyone wears a ribbon on AIDS Day." The most popular extracurricular activities on-campus are those related to liberal causes. Respected groups include the Black Student Organization (BSO), Envirorg (the Environmental Organization), and the Non-Violent Students Association. Students celebrate "Coming Out Day," and "Pentagon Day," when the military and war in general are protested with slogans such as "Beer, not bombs." Community service is also popular, with a strong Habitat for Humanity chapter. Students also participate in a wide range of non-social action groups in the performing arts, various academic groups, and even a Society for Creative Anachronism, a group that celebrates all things medieval. One student said, "Most people are involved in at least a couple of things.".

A Varied Social Life

Social life at Kalamazoo is not that of a typical party school. One junior said, "Freshmen tend to party, while upperclassmen chill out a bit more and have dinner parties with wine." School sponsored formals, held about once a quarter, are poorly attended and "are most fun if you get drunk before you go—most people go that way." In the absence of fraternities, most parties are held by students who live off-campus, by some of the sports teams, or as small gatherings in dorm rooms. Students report little pressure to drink, especially after freshmen year, and there are always alternative cultural activities on-campus. The quarterly theater productions and the improvisational group Monkapult, for example, are very popular. The city of Kalamazoo adds little to the school's social life and students tend to live in "the K Bubble," venturing out only for road trips to Chicago or Detroit.

Although Kalamazoo is small, few are willing to characterize it as cliquey. "People have their own groups of friends, but I've met new people even into my senior year," said one student. Athletic teams, especially the men's and women's swim teams, are known for being elitist, but few other extracurricular activities dominate a person's social life. One sophomore said she would be "comfortable asking anyone to do something for her." Another student was more cautious, saying, "If you survive the smallness of Kalamazoo the first year, you'll love it."

> **"Lots of people wear gay pride rainbows on their backpack and everyone wears a ribbon on AIDS Day."**

Students tend to be unenthusiastic about athletics. Few people attend sporting events, even for successful teams like swimming and tennis, both the male and female squads. Pickup soccer and ultimate Frisbee games ("the most popular sport on-campus") dot the Quad. Kalamazoo alums are even known to bring their disks back to campus over homecoming to play the school's long-standing Frisbee golf course.

Ghet-Trow and the Great Dorms

The housing policy at Kalamazoo has just undergone a major change; recently, for the first time, seniors could live off-campus. Many seniors have taken advantage of relatively inexpensive apartments in historical homes surrounding campus. One senior said, "I walk into the dining hall and see only 10 people I know [because so many are off-campus]." Students living on-campus are fairly enthusiastic about the dorms, all of which are co-ed. One junior said that they are "the best thing at K. They're socially conducive, because you live, work, and play with the same people." Two dormitories contain suites, and the others have a mixture of doubles, quads, and some singles. All the dorms have been remodeled in the last two years, including the replacement of carpets with bare tile floors. Harmon is "a good size and social," while Trowbridge, the oldest of the dormitories, earns the nickname Ghet-Trow (from "ghetto") for its large size and convoluted layout.

The K meal plan ranges from ten meals a week to a carte blanche, and includes money that can be used at Quadstop, a '50s-style restaurant in the student center, "which is good for studying when you don't really want to study." The one dining hall on-campus, Hicks Center, which has

been recently remodeled, and students are pleased with the facilities, though the food is "all the same . . . normal dining hall food."

Kalamazoo College naturally stands out among many small schools, with its uniquely close-knit community and the K-Plan. It offers a strong, thorough academic experience with a comfortable college lifestyle. —*Bethany Lacina*

FYI

The three best things about attending Kalamazoo are, "its academic K-Plan, CORD, and the close-knit community."

The three worst things about attending Kalamazoo are, "the intensity of academics because of the quarter system, the high faculty turn-over, and the smallness of the school."

The three things that every student should do before graduating Kalamazoo are "participate in Career Development, go abroad, and participate in social activism or community work."

One thing I'd like to have known before coming here is "that I would rarely see a professor twice over the years because they come and go so quickly."

Michigan State University

Address: 250 Administration Building, MSU; East Lansing, MI 48824	**Percent African-American:** 9%	**Middle 50% SAT range:** 490–610 V, 490–630 M
Phone: 517-355-8332	**Percent Asian:** 4%	**Middle 50% ACT range:** 21–26
E-mail address: admis@msu.edu	**Percent Hispanic:** 2% **Percent Native-American:** 0.5%	**3 Most popular majors:** business-marketing, psychology, acounting
Web site URL: www.msu.edu	**Percent in-state / out-of-state:** 94% / 6%	**Retention:** 88%
Founded: 1855	**Percent Pub HS:** NA	**Graduation rate:** 69%
Private or Public: public	**Number of Applicants:** 22,623	**On-campus housing:** 98%
Religious affiliation: none	**Percent Accepted:** 71%	**Fraternities:** 9%
Location: small city	**Percent Accepted who enroll:** 41%	**Sororities:** 9%
Undergraduate enrollment: 33,966	**Entering:** 6,528	**Library:** 4,200,000 volumes
Total enrollment: 43,571	**Transfers:** 2,596	**Tuition and Fees:** $5,590 in; $12,992 out
Percent Male / Female: 48% / 52%	**Application Deadline:** 30 Jul	**Room and Board:** $4,298
Percent Minority: 16%	**Mean SAT:** 563 V, 547 M **Mean ACT:** 24	**Financial aid, first-year:** 42%

You are standing in an oval stadium. You look all around and can't find a single empty seat. Thousands of people are on their feet, screaming for blood. At the bottom of the stadium, a chariot drives across the length of the field. A puffy man wearing green-and-white armor marches side to side in front

of the stands. Soon after, you hear the crushing of bones and the yells of the people beside you. But you are not an extra on the set of *Gladiator* or *Ben-Hur*. You are somewhere much more exciting. You are taking part in one of the greatest events in sports: you are at a Michigan State football game. When you turn to ask the guy standing next to you what he thinks about all of this, he responds, "The best, awesome."

The More the Merrier
Michigan State University is one of the biggest universities in the country. Inevitably, students take the occasional large lecture class. More important, though, being one of the biggest colleges in the country provides a lot of opportunities.

The university is divided into 15 colleges, including the College of Education, the College of Engineering, and the College of Arts and Letters. For the aspiring politician, MSU offers James Madison College, a college dedicated to teaching public affairs. For the aspiring teacher, MSU lets students apply to the College of Education as undergraduates. For the aspiring inventor, one computer science major warned, "The [engineering] classes themselves can be a little dull, but I think that's a result of engineering professors in general being dull." And for the people still looking for things to do, the College of Arts and Letters provides a great liberal arts education. Not surprisingly, many undecided MSU students choose to be in the College of Arts and Letters. As one student in the program said, "The College of Arts and Letters . . . seems to run smoothly, but it doesn't exactly have a small-school-within-a-big-school feel."

The honors college gives students the smaller-school feel some students prefer. As one student put it, "The honors college cuts through a lot of the red tape." An honors option teaching assistant invited her entire class to her apartment and cooked dinner for them. Students in the honors college also benefit from guaranteed research opportunity with professors in their major. Most students will find their professors accessible and even fun-loving people. One student said the coolest thing his professor had ever done was watch an English "futbol" game while lecturing, and another student said his professor "poured liquid nitrogen across the physics department halls." On a more normal day, students have dinner with their professors or meet them at other times of the day just to chat.

Many students find that they enjoy taking the occasional large lecture class. In an Intro to Psychology class one male student said that he enjoyed doing an observational study: "Groups monitored behavior in places like elevators and supermarkets—going to the place, introducing an unnatural element, and observing people's reactions." A female student said that the professor in Intro to Psych made the really large lecture seem small. The best incentive for going to a big school like MSU seems to be the diversity of people. One student said, "I'm currently taking a teacher education class that is very thought-provoking. We talk about all these controversial issues and there are a bunch of really weird kids in my class, so it makes discussion extremely interesting."

Eat, Drink, and Be Merry
For the college students who come to MSU because of its party school reputation, they will likely be able to find what they are looking for. Typical of the party experiences of many a college partier, one wise sophomore said, "Most of the freshmen try to find these huge house parties where the kegs are always empty." According to another sophomore, most freshman who drink go to off-campus parties and frat houses and dance clubs. Where do these ingenious young freshmen go later on in their college career? "I think upperclassmen go to the same places that freshmen do; they just pretend that it's cooler."

Students say that only a small percentage of MSU students join frats or sororities. Unfortunately, getting into a frat party still isn't any easier than at other schools; to get into Greek parties, one guy said, "you either have to (a) know someone in the frat or (b) bring a lot of girls with you to the party." However, another undergrad pointed out, "Greek parties don't really go down like they used to." Students looking for the proverbial random hookup can usually find those. A female student reported, "My roommate last year was a big partier, and she didn't randomly hook up with anyone at all last year, but her friend hooked with like six guys in three months."

But an MSU social life does not have to revolve around drinking or random hookups. Every weekend, MSU opens up the Campus Center, where the school takes two or three buildings in the middle of the campus and hosts activities and free movies in some of the lecture halls. Students who want to go out to eat can choose from the multitude of chain restaurants in East Lansing. Mongolian Barbeque attracts many student diners, as well as El Azteco, Panchero's, Ruby Tuesday's, Beggar's Banquet, and others.

For those looking for something a little more high-class (or someplace to go when parents are in town), the State Room at the Kellogg Center draws a lot of alumni. The Homecoming Ball gives students a chance to put on their formal wear, but other than that night, tuxedos and other evening wear usually spend most of their time in the closet. The college also attracts many performing artists, both collegiate and professional. One student remembered her experience with theater at MSU: "I went to see *Titanic* [an off-Broadway non-MSU play] at the Wharton Center, which discouraged me from seeing any other plays. It was bad." But that student did have a good experience with some stars of a higher caliber when she met Martin Sheen, Julia Louis-Dreyfus, Alfrie Woodard, and Rob Reiner at a Diane Byrum rally. The student's male friends reported that Julia Louis-Dreyfus is much better-looking in person than on television.

Like many college students around the country, MSU students also look forward to weekends as a chance to catch up on sleep and reading. And the undergrads have no problem with just relaxing. One male student said, "I have the most fun at little ten-people shindigs where I know all the people there and we are all just kicking back and having fun."

Marry Me!

MSU legend has it that if you kiss someone near the Beaumont Tower, you'll get married to that person. Of course most college freshmen are not ready to take that plunge, and that's totally okay since MSU offers great opportunities to meet people. Most of the freshmen live on campus during their first year. Except for James Madison students, most of those freshmen live in the Brody Complex. Experiences in each of the dorms differ. One

female student who lived in Hubbard freshman year expressed great disgust at that Hall: "I hated Hubbard! The girls on my floor were totally anti-social, my roommate was an alcoholic, and my RA was never there." She said she enjoyed her new dorm—Wilson Hall—a lot more. A male undergrad reported that Mason Hall dorms were "nice," and a Bryan Hall resident said that he had a very large room. James Madison freshmen live in the very nice Case Hall, in suites of four people, with two bedrooms connected by a bathroom.

> **"Greek parties don't really go down like they used to."**

Instead of resident assistants, MSU offers mentors for students living in the dorms. The mentors are MSU students, usually undergrads, who are responsible for keeping order on each of the floors. One dorm resident says, "Mentors are a good resource, and only enforce the 'rules' (with a few exceptions, like alcohol) when there's a complaint." People living in the dormitories usually take their meals in the cafeteria on the first floor of the residence hall, affectionately called the "caf." Caf diners enjoy the Vegetarian Vegetable Soup and the perennial college favorite chicken fingers. Freshmen on the meal plan can usually also be found at the Union or the International Center, or they can get the cafeteria food to-go at the Caf-II-Go.

Students who want to burn off the calories from the caf can exercise at any one of the three IM buildings on campus free of charge. They can also go to the weight rooms in the residence halls, although they pay a small maintenance fee for that convenience. For students who prefer jogging to running on a treadmill, one female student recommended going to see all the gardens on the far south side of the campus. "Most people don't even know they're there and they are so great! There is a children's garden with a bunch of fun colors and toys in it and a rose garden that is just amazing!"

Sparty

Michigan State boasts one of the best college sports programs in the country. The Spartans are perennial contenders for national titles and Big Ten titles. In addition to very successful teams, MSU students come out in force to support the MSU football, basketball, and hockey teams. The crowds can be counted on to be loud and energetic. One undergraduate football fan says, "The atmosphere is electric, especially during a game against a good opponent. I once gave high fives to three rows' worth of people I didn't even know after a touchdown." And every year students eagerly await the big game against cross-state rival U of M. They even have a tradition of guarding Sparty—the MSU mascot—an entire week before the U of M game.

For the athletes who didn't make it onto MSU's Division I teams, they can always play any number of intramural sports, from soccer, to volleyball, to air force football. However, one male athlete warned, "Coed intramurals are pretty sweet for hanging out with the ladies, but if you are competitive, you should keep to the non-coed sports."

In addition to intramurals, students also participate in a lot of extracurricular activities, from community service to the Society for Creative Anachronism. Among the benefits of going to a big school is definitely the wide range of extracurriculars. One female student tutors a Chinese grad student in conversational English and gives campus tours through the Student Alumni Foundation. Another student helps seventh-grade kids in the local school district understand the importance of college and the potential they possess for the future.

Yes! Michigan!

Most MSU students come from in-state, so they know what to expect when it comes to Michigan winters. What they might not expect is the size of the campus: it is big. One benefit to attending such a large school is the chance to meet lots of people; as one student said, "It is just a sweet all-around environment." One downside, though, is all the walking students say they have to do to get around campus. One upperclassman would offer this little piece of advice for new Spartans: "The first year at college anywhere is the coldest winter anyone ever experiences because you have to walk everywhere and no one's used to that. The one thing I would recommend for anyone who plans on coming here is a good pair of tennis shoes, because you're gonna have a whole bunch of walking to do."

—*Kenneth Tseng*

FYI

The three best things about attending MSU are "the study abroad program, good campus-run events, and Big Ten athletics."

The three worst things about attending MSU are "the long walks to class (on the largest college campus in the country), the social life is centered around alcohol, limited access to the largest porno collection in the world."

The three things that every student should do before graduating from MSU are "go to at least one football game and sit in the student section, eat at the Peanut Barrel, walk on the Spartan stadium field."

One thing I'd like to have known before coming here is "when you go to an in-state school with a lot of your high school friends, you have to make the extra effort to get to know new people and make new friends. Otherwise, a year later, you're still hanging out with the kids from high school."

University of Michigan

Address: 1220 Student Activities Building; Ann Arbor, MI 48109-1316
Phone: 734-764-7433
E-mail address: ugadmiss@umich.edu
Web site URL: www.umich.edu
Founded: 1817
Private or Public: public
Religious affiliation: none
Location: urban
Undergraduate enrollment: 24,493
Total enrollment: 36,450
Percent Male/Female: 50%/50%
Percent Minority: 25%

Percent African-American: 8%
Percent Asian: 12%
Percent Hispanic: 4%
Percent Native-American: 0.5%
Percent in-state/out-of-state: 72%/28%
Percent Pub HS: 80%
Number of Applicants: 21,132
Percent Accepted: 64%
Percent Accepted who enroll: 41%
Entering: 5,559
Transfers: 1,074
Application Deadline: 1 Feb
Mean SAT: NA
Mean ACT: NA

Middle 50% SAT range: 560–670 V, 600–710 M
Middle 50% ACT range: 25–30
3 Most popular majors: psychology, business administration, mechanical engineering
Retention: 95%
Graduation rate: 57%
On-campus housing: 97%
Fraternities: 18%
Sororities: 18%
Library: 6,500,000 volumes
Tuition and Fees: $6,735 in; $20,455 out
Room and Board: $5,614
Financial aid, first-year: 36%

Every year during freshman orientation, new University of Michigan students walk through the fountain in front of Rackham Auditorium. Over the next four years, these U of M students will get the full college experience. From top-notch academics to football games in the Big House, U of M and Ann Arbor provide a great place for students to learn a lot and still experience the simpler pleasures of being at college. After graduation, new University of Michigan alumni pass through the same fountain, but with a new sense of the world, and several years of a quality education under their belts.

The Leaders and Best

Right after they tell you about their football program, most U of M students will tell you about the excellence of their academic programs. Indeed, the Wolverines of U of M are the "leaders and best"—as the fight song "Hail to the Victors" says—both on the athletic fields and in the classrooms or labs. As one student says, "Students [at] Michigan look forward to a high quality education with tons of opportunities in any subject imaginable."

The scope of U of M's academics is seen in the number of colleges or schools within the larger university—13, to be exact. The colleges include nursing, dental, drama, engineering, business, and the College of Literature, Science and the Arts (LSA)—the largest of the 13 schools. While students may feel like they are just a number within the large university or even LSA, "the University of Michigan is a good place to grow up and learn about standing out among thousands of other students." Undergrads can also choose from a number of special academic programs within their colleges. The Undergraduate Research Opportunity Program (UROP) is for freshmen and sophomores who are looking to get exposed to lab research. As one student describes it, "[UROP] allows students to work with professors [who help] them with their research and learning practical knowledge about these sorts of things to apply later down the line." As another student puts it, "Ten hours of work equal one credit." Students in the honors college enroll in more rigorous classes and enjoy increased access to professors. Students in the Residential College program all live in the same dorm freshman year. Residential

College classes (in which non-enrolled students can cross-register) are small, and the program allows some students to create their own concentration and propose their own majors, if the major cannot be found elsewhere in the university.

Another of the larger schools within the university, the Engineering School, is tucked away on scenic North Campus. One engineering student says, "[Engineering] is much harder than the normal college of LSA. We tease our friends for being in that [college] because the engineers always have homework while the LSA people go out and party on Tuesday, Wednesday, and Thursday nights." Students throughout the school list psychology, kinesiology, and communications as the easiest majors. Regardless of a class's difficulty level, all of the students laud the variety of academic resources that are available to them at U of M. Knowledgeable and nationally respected faculty teach everything from Roman Sports, to Mammalian Reproductive Endocrinology, to Great Books of China. And students complete projects ranging from analyzing the color composition of *Terminator 2: Judgment Day* to writing 15-page research reports on "how many high school boy track athletes are involved with the culture of the NFL, MLB, NBA, as opposed to high school girl athletes." But even the best college students need the occasional break from academics; one student describes the coolest thing his professor ever did: "let us out early." Nonetheless, most of the time, students at U of M eagerly discover the wealth of knowledge their school provides. As one student says, "For two huge bags under your eyes, you get one heckuvan education."

Double Occupancy

Almost all freshmen live on campus their first year at the University of Michigan. And almost all sophomores move out of the dorms the next year. Most look for their own apartment because they want more space, although one South Quad resident—who has lived there for two years—described his living conditions as pretty decent: "Loud but great. Laundry facilities, food, nice-sized rooms. Can't ask for much more from a dorm." A Burs-ley resident described Bursley as "kinda dark and drab, but everyone sort of develops a bond together because it is on North Campus; plus the food is better there." One Markley denizen described it as being "loud" and having "crappy food." The same student, now living in a house off campus, described his new living conditions as "good food. Quiet." The quality of food—or lack thereof—is a common complaint at U of M (as at most college campuses), although one undergrad who moved off campus his second year admitted to occasionally going to the dorms "because I am too lazy to cook for myself." Each of the dorms is also equipped with a residential advisor for the benefit of the freshmen. Most people report, however, that like wolverines, the RAs won't bother you unless you bother them.

Wolverines at Play

The weekend begins Friday afternoon for most U of M students, when many spend their time just hanging out or doing some sort of physical activity. The Central Campus Recreation Building (CCRB) attracts hordes of weekend warriors, prompting some students to complain that it can get crowded. However, most agree that the facilities are pretty good; the CCRB has "a huge weight room, about 15 racquetball courts, about four basketball courts, an indoor track, a few volleyball courts, etc." Other weekend warriors head out to the intramural fields to play flag football, soccer, broomball, or a variety of other sports; some houses have their own intramural teams, while other teams are made up of just a bunch of friends out for a good time. And of course you can always find a pickup game to be found, whether your sport is "football, soccer, softball, basketball, chestnut throwing into a small plastic cup on the sidewalk."

Saturday afternoons in the fall are set aside for University of Michigan football games in Ann Arbor. With a stadium that holds more than 100,000 people, games are always big events. As they progress from freshmen to seniors, students move closer to the front of the student sections. Michigan fans have been known to throw marshmallows at opposing fans or do a variety of waves, ranging in speed from slow to fast. One girl said, "Sometimes my friends and I will make jungle animal noises during a 'key play.'" And with the largest group of alumni in the world, U of M games are sure to be packed with fans who come from all over to watch their Michigan Wolverines take on the rest of the Big Ten Conference and the country—usually with great success. Michigan is consistently a contender for the Big Ten football title, and the season often culminates in a heated game against archrival Ohio State or state rival Michigan State University. Basketball and hockey games are well attended, too.

With more than 650 registered student organizations, U of M offers many options for extracurricular life. Some students write for the *Michigan Daily* newspaper, others are active in groups such as the AIESEC ("largest student-run non-profit organization in the world that sends people abroad to work and receives those from other countries and finds them jobs here"), a cappella singing groups, K-Grams ("we wrote pen pal [letters] to elementary school students"), pre-professional societies, or the Society of Assassins ("they play with Nerf guns"). And students are always free to start their own organizations if they feel there is a void in the extracurricular scene.

Drama is also a popular activity among students. The Gilbert and Sullivan Society puts on musicals twice a year, and many other groups put on their own performances as well. If casual performances or beat poetry is more your thing, one student recommends dropping by the Frieze building: "One of the coolest things that goes on here is the Basement Arts theater. Not a lot of people know about this. Anyone can come, and it is just a little tiny theater, with couches and pillows for people to sit on and watch. People read poetry, sing, dance, act, [do] comedy acts—I always feel so happy at the end of the show."

House Party

Most students follow similar laid-back schedules on Friday and Saturday nights. One student said a typical weekend night "is spent telling stories and chilling up til' about twelve, when you might head out looking for something to do. The night could end anywhere from about one to five. Mine was spent in typical college pointless fashion by sitting on the porch roof of my house along with about twenty other people doing everything from tying a dollar bill to a string, putting it on the corner, and watching people walk by and try to pick it up to just sitting outside waving to the people and just mainly being social."

"It's better than I could have dreamed."

There's always a party for those who want more structure in their social lives. Some of the theme parties described by U of M students include foam dances, candy necklace dances, popular beach dances, and "ahhh, never mind—they're pretty much all the same." Those looking to use their tux or evening gown might stop by Kappa Delta Phi's Charity Ball, the Inteflex I-Ball, or the AAA Lunar New Year Formal. Frat parties can be difficult to get into for non-Greeks. According to one girl, the trick to getting into frat parties is "wear a hoochie top and act like you're drunk if you're a girl, and all the frat guys will think they can score, so they'll let you in." For guys, "if you walk by and have a large group of girls, they let you in no problem; otherwise you have to be on a list." Fraternities and sororities provide their members with many leadership and community service opportunities and always help get you "on the list."

A-Squared

As a female student puts it, "Ann Arbor is a fun place to be for college. It gives you some of the sanity of the Midwest while exposing you to some crazy artsy-fartsy stuff." Whether it's movies, food, good company, or famous people that students are after, Ann Arbor usually has the answer. Students overwhelmingly recommend Jimmy John's as a great place to get subs, and others single out Mongolian BBQ as a nice place to take dates. In addition, the city is full of bars and coffee shops where students can enjoy the company of their friends or even strangers.

The Student Union offers pool table rentals at reasonable prices, has a few fast-food restaurants and a bookstore in the basement, and is often the site of meetings for different campus organizations. Hill Auditorium consistently hosts popular guest speakers or performers. Recent visitors to the campus include Wyclef Jean, Ben Harper, Jim Breuer, the president of the Czech Republic, and Lisa Ling. And every year during spring finals, Michigan students can see several thousand of their fellow students running through the streets—naked—in the Naked Mile.

The advantages of coming to the university are numerous. When one Michigan resident was asked why he would choose U of M if he were a high school senior again, he replied, "C'mon. The tuition, baby." For other students, the balance of life at Michigan draws them: they can take top-notch classes in the morning, relax in Palmer Field or Nichols Arboretum during the afternoon, and still hit the Blind Pig (a bar) at night. But mostly it's the college atmosphere that almost all students enjoy here: "It's better than I could have dreamed. You can learn a lot about life outside of classes; that's what I appreciate the most. Not to mention being in the greatest college town in the country."

—*Kenneth Tseng*

FYI
The three best things about attending U of M are "the high academic standards, football, and a nice college town."
The three worst things about attending U of M are "the impersonal nature of large classes, the campuses being split up, the undergrads that live in my neighborhood trash it."
The three things that every student should do before graduating from U of M are "go to a football game (because U of M fans are the craziest), go to the top of the Burton Bell Tower and see the sky-view of campus, and ride the pumas outside of the natural science museum."
One thing I'd like to have known before coming here is "that you shouldn't listen to your honors academic advisors."

Minnesota

Address: 100 South College Street; Northfield, MN 55057
Phone: 507-646-4190
E-mail address: admissions @acs.carleton.edu
Web site URL: www.carleton.edu
Founded: 1866
Private or Public: private
Religious affiliation: none
Location: rural
Undergraduate enrollment: 1,882
Total enrollment: 1,882
Percent Male/Female: 47%/53%
Percent Minority: 16%

Percent African-American: 3%
Percent Asian: 9%
Percent Hispanic: 3%
Percent Native-American: 0.5%
Percent in-state/out-of-state: 23%/77%
Percent Pub HS: 76%
Number of Applicants: 3,457
Percent Accepted: 46%
Percent Accepted who enroll: 32%
Entering: 510
Transfers: 29
Application Deadline: 15 Jan
Mean SAT: NA
Mean ACT: NA

Middle 50% SAT range: 650–740 V, 640–720 M
Middle 50% ACT range: 28–32
3 Most popular majors: biology, English, economics
Retention: 95%
Graduation rate: 81%
On-campus housing: 100%
Fraternities: NA
Sororities: NA
Library: 530,000 volumes
Tuition and Fees: $23,469 in; $23,469 out
Room and Board: $4,761
Financial aid, first-year: 54%

A small liberal arts college in northern Minnesota, Carleton College combines an exciting academic atmosphere and an involved student body. The typical Carletonian, many students agree, "would be upset by the idea of being typical." Everyone, however, "has a way of not taking Carleton [or themselves] too seriously." While students admit that Carleton is "a bit too homogeneous on first look," most are quick to say that each person at Carleton comes from a very interesting, diverse background.

Classes and Comps

Academics at Carleton are exciting, fast-paced due to the trimester system, and challenging. Professors are known as accessible and engaging. One student said, "I've had great conversations with professors, been to their houses for dinner, and even dog-sat for the tennis coach last summer." Each Carleton student must ful-fill requirements in distributional categories for a liberal arts degree. Students must take courses in four groups (arts and literature, math and science, social sciences, and humanities). Students are generally complimentary of the requirements, and as one student explained, "They get you taking classes you would normally not consider taking . . . [and] you only get stuck taking bad classes if you don't think at all about how you'll fulfill them." In addition, students must also fulfill both foreign language and physical education requirements.

All students must also write "comps" for their majors. Generally, a comp involves a 30-page paper, but some majors allow individual projects in lieu of the paper. Usually, students take a class in their senior year entirely devoted to discussing and writing their comp. Despite the fact that academics are taken very seriously, most Carleton students will quickly remind you that there is always room for fun on campus. A great example is that at 10:00 PM on the night before exams everyone on campus takes a break for "Primal Scream"—people rush outside and let out a collective scream, which can be heard echoing across the campus.

Stay Inside, 'Cause It's Cold Out There

Students live in a variety of dorms or houses on or off campus. All students live together, although two of the nine dorms are reserved for upperclassmen only. Incoming students are assigned to dorms for their freshman year, but upperclassmen choose their rooms in order of class. This means that the best dorms usually fill up with seniors (and, strangely enough, freshmen); however, there is no class elitism on campus. As one senior notes, "The fellow freshmen on my floor my first year were meaner to me than the seniors." Floors are coed, except the one or two floors per year reserved as single-sex. Floor residents decide whether bathrooms will be coed or not.

Carleton is currently in the process of building a new academic and dining building, affectionately known as Linguistics and Linguini on campus. There are currently two other dining halls and a snack bar. "The food itself isn't great," one student explained, but the dining halls are nice, "there's variety," and it's a good chance to catch up with friends after a busy day.

Bubbles and a German Poet

Carleton is full of tradition, starting the first Friday of classes. At the opening convocation (or convo.), a semireligious weekly event with a guest lecturer, the professors all enter in full commencement attire and the seniors blow bubbles down at them from the balcony. One senior noted, "I have two big bubble blowers handed down to me from past generations." He explained, "It's a way to signal to the freshmen, whatever you do, don't take anything too seriously here." Another important Carleton tradition involves the bust of the German poet Friedrich von Schiller. In the '60s, a group of students stole a plaster bust of Schiller and then brought it to prominent campus

events and ran Schiller across the stage. Since then, the bust has often been stolen again. A few years ago, the plaster bust was traded in for a marble bust at a secret meeting with the president of the college in the middle of a secluded field. Schiller has been on *Air Force One*, has traveled to Mexico, and, of course, has been to all commencement ceremonies.

> While there is a conservative minority, the college is very liberal and conservatives "might feel a little isolated."

Carletonians also claim that everyone should experience the tunnels connecting all of the buildings on campus. They were officially closed in 1991. Murals in the tunnels include Alice in Wonderland, Pink Floyd album covers, and the Yellow Brick Road. The water tower is also painted on occasion—as one student put it, "Paint the tower and get caught, you face a fine. Escape detection, and face fame." The tower has been orange, blue, "Skeeched" (Skeech being the nickname of the president of the college), and Clintoned (on the occasion of Bill Clinton's visit for commencement last May).

Frisbee, Parties, and More Frisbee

Despite the heavy course load, one student admitted, "Carls don't want to give up the things they love doing." Students are quick to say that school spirit exists at Carleton, but it generally involves the school itself or "antagonizing our cross-town rival, St. Olaf," as opposed to cheering for sports teams. While Carleton is a Division III school and does no recruiting, there are still many opportunities for sports, especially Frisbee. There are Frisbee teams at all levels of competition, from intramurals (each dorm floor has a team) to the nationally ranked women's varsity team and CUT, the men's team. There is also a new recreation center, complete with a rock-climbing wall, and the 800-foot Arboretum, with nature trails, streams, and wildlife.

There are a wide variety of extracurricular activities at Carleton. The Reformed Druids of North America were actually founded at Carleton in 1963 to protest the school's religious requirement. There are also a cappella groups, a popular dance group called Ebony II, the newspaper, the *Carletonian*, and many religious and special-interest groups. Some of the more interesting clubs include a cricket club and Chelsea 1117, in which a group of people meet at 11:17 P.M. and perform mini-scenes written by other students.

One student identified two types of weekends at Carleton—the busy weekend and the fun weekend. On the busy weekend, "you need a two-week break to catch up on your work, but you've got until Monday." The fun weekend, however, involves partying and maybe some studying, preferably mutually exclusive of each other. Social life is pretty big on campus, and there is never a shortage of things to do on the weekend. Most events are free, and students can attend movies presented by the student organization SUMO, parties, or other performances. There are a significant amount of parties, and drugs and alcohol can be found "if you want them." The Twin Cities are nearby and there is enough transportation to get there easily, but one student added that people would go there more often "if Carleton was more boring."

A large number of students do community service, and activism is very popular—while there is a conservative minority, the college is very liberal and conservatives "might feel a little isolated." One senior even noted that "people post jokes about conservative views on campus, because the majority of the campus [is liberal]." When Charleton Heston came in the fall of 2000, students were there to greet him with tombstones, black clothing, and shoes representing each child killed by gun violence in Minnesota in the past year. But activism extends far beyond political views. One senior created a holiday in the spring of 1999 called International Saisal Mohyuddin Day—a day in May when there are various concerts and other activities and t-shirts are sold to raise money for various charities.

Carleton offers both a challenging academic environment and a very active, involved social and extracurricular life. As one student put it, "Carleton is better, more interesting, more friendly, and more fun than I had ever imagined it to be."

—Jessamyn Blau

FYI

The three best things about attending Carleton are "the people—this place has the best people I've ever met—from professors to janitors to students, the easygoing atmosphere, and the Frisbee games, of course."

The three worst things about attending Carleton are "the weather here is the worst, sports teams are really not followed, and oh yeah, the weather here is the worst."

The three things that every student should do before graduating from Carleton are "try a gyro pizza if you're not a vegetarian, go in the tunnels, and visit the Arboretum."

One thing I'd like to have known before coming here is "that the academics would be harder than I expected."

Gustavus Adolphus College

Address: 800 West College
Avenue; St. Peter, MN
56082-1498
Phone: 507-933-7676
E-mail address:
admission@gac.edu
Web site URL: www.gac.edu
Founded: 1862
Private or Public: private
Religious affiliation:
Lutheran
Location: suburban
**Undergraduate
enrollment:** 2,500
Total enrollment: 2,500
Percent Male / Female:
44% / 56%
Percent Minority: 5%
Percent African-American:
1%

Percent Asian: 3%
Percent Hispanic: 0.5%
Percent Native-American:
0.5%
**Percent in-state / out-of-
state:** 71% / 29%
Percent Pub HS: 92%
Number of Applicants:
1,993
Percent Accepted:
79%
**Percent Accepted who
enroll:** 42%
Entering: 654
Transfers: 25
Application Deadline:
1 Apr
Mean SAT: 610 V,
613 M
Mean ACT: 26

Middle 50% SAT range:
560–670 V,
560–670 M
Middle 50% ACT range:
23–29
3 Most popular majors:
biology, psychology,
communication studies
Retention: 91%
Graduation rate: 76%
On-campus housing:
100%
Fraternities: 25%
Sororities: 22%
Library: 260,758 volumes
Tuition and Fees:
$18,250 in; $18,250 out
Room and Board: $4,605
Financial aid, first-year:
90%

The infamous winters of Minnesota might be expected to engender equally cold social environments, yet nothing could be more false about Gustavus Adolphus College. With excellent academics and a high rate of extracurricular participation, this liberal arts school has a lot to offer its Gustie population—not the least of which is an invitation to the Nobel Conferences held at the college each year.

Unique Curriculum

Gustavus requirements include a personal fitness credit, two human behavior/sociology credits, three writing credits, and one credit in religious studies. Students find the requirements one of the strong points of their college. The school runs on a 4-1-4 schedule, with four classes taken in the fall, one class during a short winter session called J-term, and four more classes during the spring semester. Incoming frosh select a first-semester class, described as a seminar-style "first step into college" course reserved strictly for first-year students. The professor of a student's seminar serves as his or her freshman faculty advisor.

Biology is reportedly the strongest and

most popular major at Gustavus. Political science and psychology are popular as well. The biology department guards against overcrowding in introductory courses by splitting classes into two sections of approximately 80 people each (chemistry and psychology do the same). TAs assist students in lab classes, but professors do most of the formal teaching. Students relish the relationships with their professors, who often invite students over for dinner or organize opportunities to conduct research. Professors are also known to have saved students "outregistered" from a class. Registration usually works out for most people, although one undergrad said, "you may have to do a bit of finagling here and there." Frosh register over the phone before they arrive at school, while other students (with priority to upperclassmen) do so during a fourday period at the beginning of the semester. Academics are definitely competitive at Gustavus, but the "really good balance" that exists makes success an "achievable goal," one student said.

A Hilltop Campus

The self-contained campus is situated on top of a hill within the small town of St.

Peter and includes a blend of older buildings and newer ones erected in the 1960s. Students in certain dorms enjoy a view of the Minnesota River Valley. The Arboretum, located on the west side of campus, attracts students looking for a "neat place to go watch the stars at night." St. Peter provides some off-campus housing but is "not much of a metropolis by any means," according to one student. Larger nearby cities include Mankato, a 10-minute drive away, and Minneapolis–St. Paul, less than two hours away. The Safety and Security department provides effective 24-hour security, Night Hosts guard the entryways from the hours of 8 P.M. to 3 A.M., and an escort service is available for students walking through campus at late hours. "I've never felt unsafe on campus," one female student said.

All first-year students are required to live on-campus. The North End is a reputed center for jocks and major party life, while those more interested in a quiet, academic, and artsy environment prefer the South End. The nine campus dorms are co-ed by floor or, in some cases, by section. Norelius Hall houses frosh and sophomores, and Wahlstrom includes students from all four classes. Dorms have "a lot of community to them," and are often the site of casual socializing or studying. The International House attracts international students and those interested in foreign studies. Collegiate Fellows and Head Residents (similar to RAs) offer a peer-support network. Off-campus houses are available in St. Peter and are close enough so that "off-campus students don't feel isolated."

The College Dining Room (CDR) is the central cafeteria on-campus. According to one student, "When you get the chicken strips, you realize someone loves you. When you get the tuna melt, you know Domino's is always a phone call away." The meal plan is mandatory for first- and second-year students, most of whom live on-campus. An additional option includes the flex plan, which gives students either $75, $100, or $200 to spend as they wish. Students looking for snacks find them at the campus Canteen shop.

The three-floor Gustavus Adolphus campus library, Folke Bernadette, is equipped with computer labs, audio-visual resources, a relatively broad selection of research materials, and an interlibrary loan connection with Mankato State University. Conference rooms also are available for social studying. The newly constructed Olin Hall is a center for math, computer science, and physics, and also has an observatory. The Nobel Hall of Science was renovated just a few years ago, and the King and Queen of Sweden were present during the opening of a new wing.

Golden Gusties

A large number of students participate in intramurals and form teams according to dorm or social group affiliations. Choirs and bands also draw large numbers of students. Future journalists and publishers write for the Gustavian Weekly, the primary school newspaper released every Friday, and the biannual Fire Thorne literary magazine. A number of students also support the Gustavian college yearbook. While students here generally shy away from political activism, they often engage in community service through the Meaningful Activities for Gusties in Community (MAGIC) student group, which connects undergrads with various community programs. Some students have worked with mental health patients, and the Study Buddies Program allows undergrads the opportunity to tutor area high school students. Less traditional groups include the Gustavus Sauna Society, which meets regularly in the athletic center saunas.

> According to one student, "People would like to see dating happen more often."

Gustavus Adolphus athletes maintain especially strong traditions in gymnastics and hockey, with the former team winning the national championship four out of the last five years. The new Lund Athletic Center houses all the athletic facilities, such as an ice arena, five racquetball courts, and an indoor track. One student mentioned how "people joke that Lund looks like a country club." The Golden Gustie mascot, Gus the Lion, inspires devoted fans (especially during hockey games) to dress in gold and black, including wigs. Many alumni return during homecoming, which features a dancing debut by the first-year hockey players during the football half-time.

The Campus Activities Board and the Student Activities Office organize most of the social activities on-campus, and the Peer Assistance group promotes parties that advocate "healthy lifestyles." Two big parties are the President's Ball, a formal held each year in a rented hall in the Twin Cities, and Earth Jam, a spring festival featuring multiple bands, which one student called "a very small version of Lolla-palooza." Christmas in Christ Chapel attracts people interested in hearing seasonal music from the student choirs and orchestras. Gustavus provides a dj in the Dive student center every Friday and Saturday night, and the Campus Activities Board also sponsors one or two concerts a year. Greek participation increases during rush time, but few students describe the Greeks as especially influential in campus social life, although they hold many of the parties on campus. In keeping with the casual social scene, dating is said to be fairly low-key and usually in the context of friendships. According to one stu-dent, "People would like to see dating happen more often."

Most Gusties are natives of either Min-nesota or the greater Midwest. Students describe their classmates as "not terribly diverse" and feel that a population of white, midwestern students "can get a little frustrating at times." In response to the lim-ited diversity, the Diversity and Affirmation Committee recently held a "Building Bridges" conference aimed at developing a more minority-friendly environment at Gustavus. The college has support groups for Asian and African-American students, but some report that the Hispanic support network is weak. The gay, lesbian, and bi-sexual students on-campus strongly pro-mote Coming Out Week and dedicate time to increasing student awareness on-campus.

"Everyone has a lot of Gusty pride," one student said. Gusties proudly speak of their academic standing, competitive sports teams, congenial atmosphere, and prime access to the annual Nobel Confer-ences. Future Gustavus students not only need winter coats and flannel sheets, but also a "get-involved attitude" to maintain the strong Gusty tradition. —*Tahia Rey-naga*

FYI

The three best things about attending Gustavus Adolphus are "cool people, winter session, and professors who are on your side."

The three worst things about attending Gustavus Adolphus are "sometimes unrecognizable food, a few cocky athletes, and frostbite."

The three things that every student should do before graduating from Gustavus Adolphus are "go to the President's Ball, go to earth Jam, and go to the Nobel Conferences."

One thing I'd like to have known before coming here is "that you need to talk your way into some classes."

Macalester College

Address: 1600 Grand Avenue; St. Paul, MN 55105-1899
Phone: 651-696-6357
E-mail address: admissions @macalester.edu
Web site URL: www.macalester.edu
Founded: 1874
Private or Public: private
Religious affiliation: Presbyterian
Location: urban
Undergraduate enrollment: 1,794
Total enrollment: 1,794
Percent Male / Female: 42% / 58%
Percent Minority: 13%

Percent African-American: 4%
Percent Asian: 5%
Percent Hispanic: 3%
Percent Native-American: 0.5%
Percent in-state / out-of-state: 29% / 71%
Percent Pub HS: 67%
Number of Applicants: 3,161
Percent Accepted: 53%
Percent Accepted who enroll: 27%
Entering: 460
Transfers: 31
Application Deadline: 15 Jan
Mean SAT: 664 V, 650 M

Mean ACT: 29
Middle 50% SAT range: 630–720 V, 610–700 M
Middle 50% ACT range: 27–31
3 Most popular majors: psychology, biology, economics
Retention: 90%
Graduation rate: 77%
On-campus housing: 100%
Fraternities: NA
Sororities: NA
Library: 477,908 volumes
Tuition and Fees: $20,688 in; $20,688 out
Room and Board: $5,760
Financial aid, first-year: 74%

L eave no stone unturned, leave no establishment unquestioned. Macalester students are wickedly proud of their uncanny knack for questioning, injecting, inspecting, detecting, and selecting every possible establishment in society. Every course from economics to Spanish to history is taught with a race, class, gender, or sexuality spin. As one student said, "even in the hard sciences, there are classes like 'Biology and the female body/reproduction.'"

Small Class Sizes

Macalester uses its small size of 1600 students to its advantage in the classroom. All the classes are small and one junior noted that her largest class ever had twenty-seven students in it. Most classes have less than twenty students, and it is not uncommon to have less than ten. This small population fosters close teacher student relationships, though the class size can be a problem for freshmen trying to get into classes.

Until very recently, Macalester offered a J-term: a time to take an exploratory class during the month of January in between the two semesters. During this time, students could take anti-establishment courses like "Cursing and Swearing." Two years ago it was eliminated, and now it is a shadow of its former self. The dorms are still open, if the students make arrangements in advance, but no classes are offered directly through Macalester. Now students can use the time to pursue internships, conduct independent studies, or take courses at some of the other schools in the Twin Cities.

As with many colleges and universities around the country, Macalester has its fair share of grade inflation. A's and B's abound, while C's are "reserved for personal vendettas or total slackers." As one student said, "There's a few crusaders trying to curb it (grade inflation) but everyone just ends up hating them."

From Kosovo to Rothko

The Macalester campus does not remain faithful to a set building type. Situated over four blocks, it sports reminiscent, red brick buildings with white trim and chic, modern, glassy structures, creating an impressive skyline that compliments the fall colors. The newest architectural dilemma on campus is the student union.

A new student union will be ready by April 2001, but in the meantime, Macs are without a formal student union. These students are able to make do, though, as the chapel has been turned into a student lounge at lunch and dances are held in the field house in socks—shoes are forbidden. One student complained that, "the place where our union used to be looks like Kosovo. When it is finished, it will look like Rothko." Yet some students are excited about the new building and its advertised amenities like a post office, lecture hall, and innovative dining facilities.

Currently, all students on the meal plan dine at Kagin Commons. Non-first year students can choose between 12 and 19 meals per week. Vegetarian and vegan options come with every meal, and the Hebrew House in Kirk Hall offers bi-weekly Shabbat dinners. The food drew poor marks from the students. Unfortunately, it is not even a matter of getting used to the Macalester cuisine: "The food was great my first year, but I detest it now because it is always the same," explained one student.

> Macalester students are wickedly proud of their uncanny knack for questioning, injecting, inspecting, detecting, and selecting every possible establishment in society.

Macalester has a variety of housing options, ranging from the six-story Dupre Hall to the charming, antiquated Wallace to the aptly named (or unnamed, rather) New Hall, the newest and nameless building on campus. All freshmen and sophomores must live on campus. However, Macalester does not have enough housing for everyone. Seniors get first dibs on the remaining space and many juniors are left to fend for themselves in off-campus housing. Finding apartments is often difficult, and some people end up living far from campus.

One of the Twin Cities' wealthiest residential neighborhoods surrounds Macalester. A small shopping area with a mix of eclectic shops and coffee places is conveniently situated right off campus. Trans-portation is made easy with an excellent and inexpensive bus system. Since Macalester is located directly between Minneapolis and St. Paul, students can experience the best of both of cities. The Twin Cities have no lack of clubs and shows, and they are home to nationally renowned icons like the Mall of America and Prairie Home Companion.

Internationalism

Macalester students say they're known for being "smart, but badly dressed" and are generally proud of this distinction. Because of the trend at Macalester to question everything that has to do with the establishment, women are often stereotyped as ultra-feminist: no make-up, no dresses. And everyone who is politically verbal is considered liberal. The few conservative students on campus are generally quiet, and socialism is an accepted ideal. Macalester currently enrolls students from seventy-six different countries despite its small size. One famous alumnus includes Secretary General of the United Nations Kofi Annan.

The student body is small, intimate, but some feel that this can get cliquish at times. Others disagree, saying the small atmosphere is a great way to get to know people well. Because of the size of the student body, news travels quickly. One student mourned that this "can be a real molestation when you do something stupid or get a bad reputation."

Hippie Holdout

Macalester students pride themselves in their political and social awareness. In many ways, wrote one student, Macalester is a "hippie holdout because students hold protests and vigils for darn near everything." Community service is especially big at Macalester. It has a program called MACTION, a popular community service group. MACTION organizes one-time community service events, but no continuing projects. The Queer Union (QU) is a "really awesome and high profile" group for gays, lesbians, and bisexuals. QU is involved with promoting HIV and AIDS awareness on campus. It reportedly used to organize a mass coming-out party on Parents' Weekend, but the administration convinced its members to change this tradition. Regardless of the group, people usually have some kind of issue. Other popular groups on campus include Macnaked, a group that holds random Frisbee tournaments at midnight, and Fresh Concepts, the "funniest improv group on campus."

Although most people partake in activities, varsity sports are not as popular here as elsewhere. The football team never wins, and football players in general have a bad reputation. Students equate them with bad high school memories: "We were all oppressed by them in high school, and the tables are definitely turned here." The most popular team on campus is a toss up between men's soccer and women's soccer. At soccer games, bagpipes sound every time the soccer team scores a goal. Women's soccer made headlines when it won the NCAAIII championship in 1998.

For students, who do not play sports, or the bagpipes, there are plenty of "fun athletic cheers" to urge their team on and upset their opponents. Several students mentioned the cheer, "Drink blood, smoke crack, worship Satan . . . GO MAC!"

Colonial Rematch

Aside from varsity sports, intramurals abound. Soccer seems to be the most popular sport intramural. A favorite nonvarsity event is the annual Colonial Rematch. Every fall at Macalester, the European students take on the African students in the ultimate payback for imperialism. The European students, varsity players from Denmark, Germany, or Spain gather in earnest, while the African team shows up, having never practiced, and delay the game half an hour while they "run around the field with flags, take pictures, yell a lot and practice other forms of quite amusing intimidation."

The Greek system has been banished from the Macalester campus, but students generally agree that the Greeks would feel left out anyway. For the Greek-seeker, sports teams often have houses off campus that act as similar communities. But for most students, the parties are quite sufficient without Greeks. Students rave about the biannual QU dances. One senior claims, "people get naked and dance on the tables long after the lights come on. Nothing like it." Another phenomenon on campus is the "progressive" floor-wide party, where each room offers a different kind of drink. Students go from one room to the next drinking, partying, and dancing in the various ambiences.

Drinking is big on campus, and visible, but most people feel that it is done in moderation. Alcohol is permitted, provided it is in a private room, but rumors now circulate that the administration wants to make Macalester a dry campus. Pot is definitely the drug of choice, but harder drugs are not accepted. Still, as one student put it, choosing not to drink is "generally respected, if you're a unrespectable person." The same applies for other drugs. Still, Macalester is not a party school. For better or worse, many people spend the entire weekend studying in the libraries.

Yet despite this, Macalester students are overwhelmingly happy with their college selection. When asked whether, knowing what she knows now, she would choose Macalester again, one senior said, "I would choose this school in a heartbeat." —Nicole Jabaily

FYI
The three best things about attending Macalester are "internationalism, small class sizes, and guys in kilts."
The three worst things about attending Macalester are "the career development center, the rate at which gossip travels, and the Minnesota winter."
The three things every student should do before graduating from Macalester are "ring the sex bell, study abroad, and attend the Queer Union dances."
One thing Iíd like to have known before coming here is that "students are extremely politically active."

St. John's University / College of St. Benedict

Address: PO Box 7155; Collegeville, MN 56321-7155
Phone: 320-363-2195
E-mail address: admissions@csbsju.edu
Web site URL: www.csbsju.edu
Founded: 1857
Private or Public: private
Religious affiliation: Roman Catholic / Benedictine
Location: small city
Undergraduate enrollment: 3,803
Total enrollment: 3,932
Percent Male / Female: 99% / 1%
Percent Minority: 3%

Percent African-American: 0.5%
Percent Asian: 1%
Percent Hispanic: 0.5%
Percent Native-American: 0.5%
Percent in-state / out-of-state: 86% / 14%
Percent Pub HS: 76%
Number of Applicants: 1,119
Percent Accepted: 85%
Percent Accepted who enroll: 50%
Entering: 475
Transfers: 100
Application Deadline: 1 Feb
Mean SAT: 578 V, 582 M
Mean ACT: 25

Middle 50% SAT range: 520–640 V, 540–660 M
Middle 50% ACT range: 23–27
3 Most popular majors: management, biology, psychology
Retention: 90%
Graduation rate: 75%
On-campus housing: 98%
Fraternities: NA
Sororities: NA
Library: 569,410 volumes
Tuition and Fees: $16,687 in; $16,687 out
Room and Board: $4,930
Financial aid, first-year: 92%

St. John's University for men, and its sister campus, the College of St. Benedict for women, give the word "teamwork" a new meaning. Located in northern Minnesota, these two campuses are four miles apart, but are close in every other aspect. "Community" is the byword at St. John's/St. Ben's, beginning with academics. The faculty is approachable, and professors get to know students on a personal level. "If you are having a bad day, the professor will ask you why you're not being yourself," one St. Ben's sophomore said.

To graduate, students must satisfy many liberal arts requirements, including fine arts classes. In addition, all undergrads must take at least six "flagged" courses, which emphasize either writing, discussion, quantitative analysis, gender issues, or global topics. The theology department earns student praise, and courses emphasizing gender development and differences are also popular. The school enjoys a lofty reputation in Minnesota: "not that money's everything, but you see a lot of their graduates doing really well around here," one student proudly proclaimed.

The Benefits of the J-Term

Students are also quick to praise the "J-term," a three-week January semester during which they enroll in a single class. "It's a nice transition period, instead of jumping right back into things after Christmas break," one Johnnie said. Many use the J-term to study in other parts of the world. St. John's and St. Ben's offer programs in a broad range of locations, including Cairo, Rome, London, Spain, Greece, China, El Paso, and New York City. Those who opt to stay on-campus for J-term can choose from any number of unconventional courses, including Detective Fiction and Books You've Always Wanted to Read.

The town of "St. Joc" contains a number of popular bars, including Sal's and Loso's (aka "The Middie"). The current favorite of most Johnnies is the LaPlayette (affectionately dubbed "The La"), known for its Taco Tuesday nights. For movies or a good meal, students usually head to the small city of St. Cloud, about a ten-minute drive from either campus. A car is not necessary for a social life; the "great" busing system, which runs until 2 A.M. every night, connects the campuses to St. Joe. Campus hangouts include the pub in the Sexton Commons, a huge new student center on the St. John's campus. The St. Ben's library is also quite a social scene on weeknights—a sharp contrast to the studious atmosphere of the St. John's library.

The Watab Mixer and Pine Stock

Both campuses are large, scenic, and secluded. With a definite sense of privacy, a small island in the middle of Lake Watab is host to the year's two biggest parties: the Watab mixer and Pine Stock. The Joint Events Council, which sets up guest speakers and other campus programs, arranges for a band to play at these parties. Notable guests have included Soul Asylum, Blues Traveler, and the Jayhawks.

Unlike the celebrated "Dead Poets Society look" of St. John's, St. Benedict has modern architecture—with the noticeable exception of the library. "It sticks out like a sore thumb," said one Bennie, which is not to say Gothic architecture does not have its place on-campus; students affirm that Abbey Church at St. John's is "a beautiful, beautiful building. It's just breathtaking, really."

Catholic Influence, Not Rule

St. Ben's students say there is not a bad dorm to be found on their relatively young campus. Lucky seniors end up in the West Apartments, whose units feature a kitchen, large living room, and two spacious double bedrooms. Johnnies usually vie in the annual housing lottery for the Menton Court, site of 11 luxurious suites of four singles and a large bathroom. Dorms are the only place where Bennies and Johnnies live separate lives—but according to one Johnnie, "They don't do bed checks or anything." Students who live on-campus have a full meal plan, which allows them to eat in either the large commons or a smaller dining hall. Those who live off-campus or in the West Apartments can charge meals on a dining hall account if they wish.

A large portion of the students are children of St. John's/St. Ben's alumni, which some say enhances the sense of community. Most students hail from Minnesota, and an overwhelming majority are Roman

Catholic. Out-of-staters and non-Catholics are nonetheless welcome. "It's a very warm, supportive place—people readily accept you for who you are," one New Yorker said.

> "It's a very warm, supportive place—people readily accept you for who you are," one New Yorker said.

St. John's and St. Ben's are private schools in the middle of small college towns, and townsfolk repeatedly stereotype the students as "rich and preppy." Locals have griped about the late-night partying, but town-gown relations are reportedly "just fine. We don't have more quibbles than the next college town." If anything, they are on the upswing: VISTO, a student volunteer group, does a lot of charity work in the town, particularly around Christmastime. A core council consisting of town residents and students also works to improve community relations.

VISTO is one of many strong extracurricular clubs and organizations at St. John's and St. Ben's. Both campuses have active student governments, and the Joint Events Council has members from both colleges. The schools support chapters of Greenpeace and ROTC, along with several bands, a cappella groups, and choirs. The radio station, KJNB, is popular among students and locals and often has listener call-in shows. Campus publications include the Record at St. John's and the Independent at St. Benedict's; both are biweeklies and they come out on alternate weeks. The brand-new Haehn Campus Center at St. Ben's boosts extracurricular life even more with its restaurants, intramural and varsity gyms, conference/banquet rooms, and a dance floor. Students consider themselves politically active, and although a sizeable liberal contingent exists, the majority of students at both schools have a conservative slant.

Football Fever

The most popular activities, in terms of sheer numbers and spirit, are without a doubt home football games. A perennial Division III powerhouse led by coach John Gagliardi (who made the cover of Sports Illustrated this year), the Johnnies finished the season undefeated, going 9–0. Students usually pack each game, but biggest is the game against the archrival college of St. Thomas. "The St. Thomas games can be violent affairs," a senior quipped. Intramural sports, some of which take place in Warner Palaestra, are also popular. The Palaestra gym features an eight-lane pool, an indoor track, racquet-ball courts, and a sauna. Also the new fa-cilities at the Haehn Center are available to students.

Tradition thrives at St. John's and St. Benedict's. The week before Thanksgiving break, the campus sits down for a large turkey meal together, and before Christ-mas, students gather for the lighting of an enormous tree in the Great Hall. With generation after generation of families at-tending the schools, along with close inter-action between the two campuses and a friendly face everywhere you turn, it's no wonder St. John's and St. Benedict's are a team to be reckoned with. Said one stu-dent, "Life here actually is a cliche—it's community-oriented, everyone really looks out for each other, and I cannot imagine going to school anywhere else."

—*William Chen and Staff*

FYI

The three best things about attending St. John's/St. Benedict are "caring professors, great dorms, fun football."

The three worst things about attending St. John's/St. Benedict are "town-gown problems, boring weekends, and snow."

The three things that every student should do before graduating St. John's/St. Benedict are "go to the Watab mixer, take a religion course, and drink at The La."

One thing I'd like to have known before coming here is "classes that others consider inter-esting I find dull."

St. Olaf College

Address: 1520 St. Olaf Ave, Northfield, MN 55087
Phone: 507-646-3025
E-mail address: admissions@stolaf.edu
Web site URL: www.stolaf.edu
Founded: 1874
Private or Public: private
Religious affiliation: Evangelical Lutheran Church of America
Location: small city
Undergraduate enrollment: 2,998
Total enrollment: 2,998
Percent Male / Female: 41% / 59%
Percent Minority: 6%

Percent African-American: 1%
Percent Asian: 3%
Percent Hispanic: 1%
Percent Native-American: 0.5%
Percent in-state / out-of-state: 49% / 51%
Percent Pub HS: 87%
Number of Applicants: 2,359
Percent Accepted: 76%
Percent Accepted who enroll: 42%
Entering: 766
Transfers: 37
Application Deadline: 1 Feb
Mean SAT: 635 V, 634 M
Mean ACT: 26.7

Middle 50% SAT range: 580–680 V, 570–680 M
Middle 50% ACT range: 24–29
3 Most popular majors: biology, engineering, economics
Retention: 94%
Graduation rate: 77%
On-campus housing: 100%
Fraternities: NA
Sororities: NA
Library: 502,954 volumes
Tuition and Fees: $18,250 in; $18,250 out
Room and Board: $4,320
Financial aid, first-year: 61%

Despite a small campus and fairly homogeneous student body, St. Olaf undergrads love their school. Oles haunt Manitou Heights, known to students as "the Hill," on which the entire campus is situated in Northfield, Minnesota.

An Ole's Education

St. Olaf is a liberal arts college, so there are a number of general education requirements that constitute about one-third of the total credits a student must have to graduate. Students don't seem to mind, however—as one noted, "There are hundreds of classes that fulfill the requirements . . . you want specialization, go to a state school." Popular majors include economics, psychology, biology, and music. The pre-med program is also big, and science majors are considered the hardest. Students say that professors are very engaging and "are generally interesting people." One Latin professor is known for "throwing chalk at students that fall asleep in class," and one student added that his philosophy professor "regularly calls out to God for mercy in class." There is a low faculty–student ratio, and most describe their relationship with professors as "intellectually intimate." Students say that the natural science departments are very good, while the theater department has suffered layoffs.

January brings an Interim term, when each student takes one class for the month. As one put it, Interim offers interesting courses while allowing "plenty of free time to party and sleep." St. Olaf also organizes a special program called "the Great Conversation" that lasts two years. The program, according to one student, covers "just about all the classics of literature from ancient Greece to the present." The students in the program form a special bond because they are also housed together freshman year.

Fat Squirrels, Castles, and Fram Fram

St. Olaf is located on a hill in Northfield, Minnesota, a city the college shares with its cross-town rival, Carleton College. Students often admit that they feel like they are in a "bubble" and that many "never really seem to know what's going on outside of St. Olaf." One student defined the typical St. Olaf undergrad as a person who "shops only at J.Crew, is a devout Lutheran, is of average height with blond hair, blue eyes, and a last name ending in 'son.'" Most agree, however, that this atmosphere fosters a large sense of community. As one student noted, "Everyone smiles at you as you walk across campus and from the first day you feel very welcome." Another Ole, however, warned that "there are circumstances where I feel very uncomfortable because I am not religious, particularly because I am not Lutheran." Students do say that diversity is probably lacking on campus, although one sophomore said that there is nothing missing at St. Olaf except "trained monkeys to carry books for you." Northfield is "an adorable town with a lot to offer," said one student. It is easy to walk from campus into town, and the trip to Minneapolis/St. Paul is about 40 minutes long.

Most Oles will mention "Um Ya Ya" as a definition of their school. It is actually the chorus of the school's fight song, which, students claim, is the only fight song in the country that is a waltz. Students also laud their battle cry, "Fram Fram," which means "Forward, Forward." Oles love their campus, and one student said that if you stood in the middle of it you'd see "students, hundred-year-old trees, ivy-covered limestone buildings, and fat squirrels." Students agree that the buildings are beautiful, especially Holland Hall, which "looks like a fairy-tale castle, complete with a turret." Most claim that there is a ghost story for just about every building. In one such tale, a girl reportedly committed suicide and a printer located in the room where she died once started spewing out pages of her diary. Some students also claim that the women on campus have been rated #2 in the nation by *Playboy* magazine, although others say that this is a myth.

Incoming freshmen live in one of five halls on single-sex floors. Each freshman also has a junior counselor (who are the equivalents of a residential advisors, whom St. Olaf also has for upperclassmen), with one JC for every 20 freshmen. The main concern is safety, so most JCs and RAs aren't "overly strict, and most are well liked." Some rules are strictly enforced, however, including the no-drinking policy, a no-smoking policy in public areas, respect during quiet hours, and "intervisitation" hours between men's and women's floors. Freshmen are assigned to certain dorms, but in later years there is a lottery for each class. St. Olaf also has honor houses, where, "in return for the right to live in the house," students work together to complete a community service project. There are also many language houses.

Students eat in the new Buntrock Commons, which was dedicated in November 1999. All on-campus students must be on a meal plan—underclassmen get 21 meals a week, and seniors have the option of 14 meals a week plus money to spend on food in other eateries. Students agree the food is pretty good, though one noted, "There's always some crazy-looking stuff that I try to stay away from." There are vegetarian options as well, although somes say that "unless you are starving, you shouldn't attempt to go through that line."

From Books to Buntrock Commons

Despite a lack of diversity in the student body, the college still has a "global perspective." A majority of students study abroad, often through one of St. Olaf's many programs. Students also do a lot of community service at local hospitals and nursing homes. Extra curricular activities are important and include student government, church organizations, and choral groups. Most students are involved in one or more outside projects, although one noted that "most of the time, science and math majors will spend much less time on [extra-curricular activities] than other majors." Some of the biggest organizations on campus are Fellowship of Christian Athletes, the student government, and GLOW, the gay rights group. Many prominent celebrities visit campus as well, including recent guests Ben Stein and Bill Bradley.

Music is a very important part of St. Olaf, and the campus has recently attracted the likes of Busta Rhymes, Semisonic, and Citizen King. There are also other concerts, dance, choral groups, and bands. Many students look forward to the Christmas Festival, when all of the choral groups and orchestras perform. Choral groups are especially popular on campus, and according to one student, "There is always someone singing no matter where you are."

> **"In a college full of students who still think in terms of high school, we have to have some sort of prom."**

St. Olaf is a Division III school, but there are a lot of athletic opportunities. A number of students play varsity sports, and others join intramurals that range from football to broomball. Athletic Oles benefit from a track, a field house, and a pool. These facilities are, as one student put it, "not necessarily brand-new, but we've got everything a person needs." One student also said that while sports aren't the main focus on campus, the school fight song, "Um Ya Ya," is still a big tradition.

St. Olaf is officially a dry campus, meaning that there is no alcohol allowed. But, students admit, there is the opportunity for underage drinkers to have a good time and to "make a big point to let everyone know that that's exactly what they're doing." Students mention the President's Ball as a popular annual party. One undergrad said, "In a college full of students who still think in terms of high school, we have to have some sort of prom." Since the construction of Buntrock Commons, students have also benefited from the Lion's Pause, a student-run "no-study zone," with a TV and games, a café that sells food like pizza bagels and ice cream, a video game room, pool tables, dart machines, and a club that holds dances and concerts every semester.

All Oles agree that St. Olaf definitely creates a good atmosphere and provides a strong liberal arts education. While many agree that diversity is "something this college needs to improve," the tight-knit student body maintains a global outlook. "People are so accepting here," one student said, and "everyone, no matter what they believe in or where they come from, will fit in." What else would you expect from a school with a waltz as its fight song? —*Jessamyn Blau*

FYI

The three best things about attending St. Olaf are "the Christmas Festival, the beautiful campus, and the dining hall meals—really!"

The three worst things about attending St. Olaf are "the winters, if you're not from around here, the dry-campus rule, and a lack of diversity, unless you prefer white middle-class midwesterners."

The three things that every student should do before graduating from St. Olaf are "eat some good Norwegian food, listen to the wonderful music, and go tray sledding down the Hill."

One thing I'd like to have known before coming here is "that a lack of sports spirit doesn't mean a lack of school spirit."

University of Minnesota

Address: 240 Williamson Hall, 231 Pillsbury Drive SE; Minneapolis, MN 55455-0115
Phone: 612-625-2008
E-mail address: admissions@tc.umn.edu
Web site URL: www.umn.edu/tc
Founded: 1851
Private or Public: public
Religious affiliation: none
Location: urban
Undergraduate enrollment: 26,968
Total enrollment: 45,361
Percent Male/Female: 48%/52%
Percent Minority: 15%

Percent African-American: 4%
Percent Asian: 8%
Percent Hispanic: 2%
Percent Native-American: 0.5%
Percent in-state/out-of-state: 74%/26%
Percent Pub HS: NA
Number of Applicants: 15,319
Percent Accepted: 73%
Percent Accepted who enroll: 46%
Entering: 5,141
Transfers: 2,107
Application Deadline: 15 Dec
Mean SAT: NA
Mean ACT: 25

Middle 50% SAT range: 540–660 V, 550–670 M
Middle 50% ACT range: 22–27
3 Most popular majors: engineering, social sciences, buisiness
Retention: 82%
Graduation rate: 51%
On-campus housing: NA
Fraternities: 6%
Sororities: 6%
Library: 6,000,000 volumes
Tuition and Fees: $4,649 in; $12,789 out
Room and Board: $4,494
Financial aid, first-year: NA

L ocated on the banks of the Mississippi River, under the shadows of Minneapolis skyscrapers, is the University of Minnesota. The Twin Cities campus is the largest of Minnesota's state universities. With nearly 23,000 undergraduate students and a total enrollment of about 37,000, the U of M can be overwhelming at times. According to students, the size of this university is both its greatest strength and its greatest weakness.

Lots of Options

Such a large university affords a multitude of academic options. There are six undergraduate colleges: the College of Agriculture, College of Liberal Arts, College of Human Ecology, College of Natural Resources, General College, and the Institute of Technology. Students cite many programs in each college as particularly strong, including economics, political science, history, journalism, and engineering. Engineering provides a unique opportunity for its majors, who have the option of alternating three months of classwork with three months of real-world work experience. Students say this special program is an example of the university's attempt to give them an edge in the competitive job market. In addition, an Honors College offers highly motivated and talented students smaller classes and more interaction with professors. Those in the Honors College cite class size as their primary reason for choosing the special program. Classes in the rest of the university have a reputation for being notoriously large. Some are so big that they use television monitors. But introductory courses are the largest, so as classes become more specialized, the average class size drops.

Classes are organized around a trimester system, and students have both cheers and jeers for this schedule. Several undergrads complained that they cannot always cover material in enough depth under the trimester system. According to one student, "Classes feel scrunched together at times." The accelerated pace of the calendar, however, allows students to take more classes than a semester system allows. For some students, the opportunity to explore unfamiliar subjects and new areas of study more than make up for any flaws in the current system.

Huge U of M

The huge student population of the U of M is also reflected in the expanse of the campus. Located in the heart of Minneapolis, the university is separated into East and West Banks. The East Bank is the main campus, while the West Bank is home to the university's business school. The agriculture school is in nearby St. Paul. Commenting on the spread-out campus, one freshman said, "I've been here two quarters and I've only seen probably a third of the school." The main downtown campus (East Bank) is an eclectic mix of old and new buildings that span a wide range of architectural styles. The Mall, a centrally located grassy area, is a prized spot for meeting and people-watching, and a green escape from the concrete jungle that comprises much of the university. The large number of campus parking lots is a necessity at a university where nearly 90 percent of the students live off-campus.

> **"I've only seen probably a third of the school."**

The small percentage of students who live on-campus describe dorm life as "fun" and "a great place to meet people and make friends." The average freshman dorm room is quite large with single beds, no bunking necessary. Students on each floor must share a common bathroom. Besides the eight residential dorms, students have a plentiful supply of off-campus housing to choose from. The most popular locales include Dinkytown and Stadium Village. Many students find that off-campus living is generally cheaper, and the money saved by living off-campus is very important to cash-strapped undergrads.

On or Off?

The high percentage of off-campus students does affect U of M social life, which can feel "fragmented." Most of the excitement on weekends centers on frat parties, sporting events, and bar-hopping. For most freshmen, the Greek scene is where the fun is. The percentage of U of M undergrads involved with the Greek system is small, but the actual number of students who belong to frats and sororities is quite large. As a result, frat parties dominate weekends at the U of M.

All sorority houses are now dry and many of the fraternity houses are following suit. This policy has met with mixed reviews from students, Greek and non-Greek alike. Upperclassmen tend to prefer local bars and clubs like Bullwinkles', Foul Play, the Gopher Hole, Sally's, and Sgt. Preston's. Students of all classes can be found at basketball and hockey games. Both sports are extremely popular and strong at this Big Ten school. Basketball and hockey are also the most popular intramurals at the school, but intramural sports make up only a small fraction of the more than 500 undergraduate organizations. Overall, students report that it's hard not to find a group to join among the hundreds on-campus.

U of M students find plenty of entertainment in the city of Minneapolis. Common destinations include the Walker Art Gallery designed by the famous architect Frank Gehry; the Metrodome, home of the Minnesota Twins baseball team; and the Target Center, site of Timberwolves NBA games. The Mall of America, the nation's largest enclosed shopping center, is in nearby Bloomington. For intrepid U of M shoppers, this gargantuan mall is a regular weekend destination.

Like the Mall of America, the University of Minnesota's size is its most distinguishing characteristic. It gives the university an economically and ethnically diverse student body, an extensive choice of majors, courses, and extracurricular activities, and a varied social scene. Students agree that the University of Minnesota is both exciting and overwhelming, but if you choose to come here, do not forget to pack a parka—Minnesota winters are vicious. —*William Chen and Staff*

FYI

The three best things about attending U of M are "the picturesque surroundings; the people; and the student center."

The three worst things about attending U of M are "the size of the campus; the split between campuses; and the stench around the farm."

The three things that every student should do before graduating from U of M are "visit the Mall of America; eat cheese, we've got a lot of it; and go out on one of the thousand lakes."

One thing I'd like to have known before coming here is "how incredibly big this place is."

Mississippi

Millsaps College

Address: 1701 North State Street; Jackson, MS 39210
Phone: 601-974-1050
E-mail address: admissions@millsaps.edu
Web site URL: www.millsaps.edu
Founded: 1890
Private or Public: private
Religious affiliation: United Methodist
Location: urban
Undergraduate enrollment: 1,191
Total enrollment: 1,191
Percent Male / Female: 45% / 55%
Percent Minority: 13%

Percent African-American: 9%
Percent Asian: 3%
Percent Hispanic: 0.5%
Percent Native-American: 0.5%
Percent in-state / out-of-state: 49% / 51%
Percent Pub HS: 64%
Number of Applicants: 912
Percent Accepted: 87%
Percent Accepted who enroll: 36%
Entering: 284
Transfers: NA
Application Deadline: 1 Jul
Mean SAT: 600 V, 580 M
Mean ACT: 27

Middle 50% SAT range: 550–650 V, 530–620 M
Middle 50% ACT range: 24–29
3 Most popular majors: business administration, English, biology
Retention: 85%
Graduation rate: 62%
On-campus housing: 96%
Fraternities: 59%
Sororities: 61%
Library: 200,302 volumes
Tuition and Fees: $15,029 in; $15,029 out
Room and Board: $6,106
Financial aid, first-year: 98%

Entrenched Ivy League–style behind a sturdy iron fence, manned gates, and a conservative history, Millsaps College seems an incongruity in the middle of Mississippi's bustling political and social capital, Jackson. All around the college, the city of Jackson tempts students to enjoy its concerts, plays, shopping, and fertile work environment, but within the iron gates the campus life is busily quiet and beautifully serene.

Jackson, Miss.

Truth be told, Millsaps is not in one of Jackson's most prestigious or beautiful neighborhoods, but some students see their proximity to the problems of a big city as "a real opportunity for community service work. Jackson's only as much as you make of it, and luckily, there is a lot of opportunity to do good in the city." The Mississippi Opera Association, Mississippi Symphony Orchestra, New Stage Theater, Jackson Zoo, and a planetarium add to the incentive to explore beyond the comfortable confines of the college. Jackson also hosts the USA International Ballet Competition every four years (the next is scheduled for June 2002).

Within the iron fence, students enjoy the amenities of an impeccably sculpted campus, which one student described as "spotless," another as "small, nice, isolated," and another as "distractingly romantic." A valley-like depression, called the bowl, is in the center of this Greek Revival campus; students flock to the bowl on nice days (the average annual temperature in Jackson is 64 degrees) and in between classes to socialize, toss Frisbees, sit and chat, eat lunch, and chill on the manicured lawn.

Old Southern Competition

The laid-back look of the campus can be misleading, however. Students at Millsaps study more than they will casually admit: "Actually, this place is hard as hell—some of us study all the time just to survive." The founders of this Methodist Church–affiliated college may not have intended a study environment of hellish intensity, but the students must be able to handle the competitive pressures of a small community and a liberal arts education, where students tend to agree that academics are first, and extracurriculars an afterthought.

Students cite the life sciences as the most popular majors, with biology topping the popularity and difficulty lists. A large number of Millsaps students are pre-med, and many others study business administration. Registration is a painless process at Millsaps, and classes generally enroll fewer than 20 students. Teaching is done mostly by doctorate-holding professors, although Millsaps does have a teaching apprenticeship program that allows students interested in education to assist in some teaching duties. Professors are "extremely accessible," said one student, and other students remarked that professors sometimes invite their classes to dinner.

Students must satisfy a core curriculum consisting of one mandatory first-year class, Introduction to Liberal Studies, and one fourth-year mandatory class, Reflections on Liberal Studies. The other eight courses can be taken from a range of disciplines, all of them focusing on a high degree of cross-relevancy. More than half of Millsaps freshmen opt for the challenging Heritage Program, a four-course series stressing interdisciplinary learning.

When students need to cram, they head to Millsaps' main library, the Millsaps-Wilson Library, or to Olin Hall, the science building. Dorm rooms, which are typically doubles (with a limited number of singles) are also favorite study spots, since many of them have views overlooking the beautiful bowl.

Greek or Geek

Despite the intense academics, Millsaps students find plenty outside of the academic sphere to keep them busy. Over half of the campus decides to go Greek, explaining why one student felt "there's too much pressure to rush." Since all freshmen and sophomores must live on-campus (with the exception of married students

and those who commute from home), Greek activity draws students from the center of campus to Frat Row, where the weeknight party scene is the biggest. Millsaps has six fraternities and six sororities, but no theme, athletic, or special language houses. In addition to the Greek scene, students often involve themselves in extracurricular activities related to their major. Popular options include the Millsaps chapter of the American Chemical Society for pre-meds, and the Millsaps Computer Club for computer science majors. Other popular organizations are Habitat and Circle K, a community service group.

Students who live close by (most students are from Mississippi and the surrounding states) usually go home for the weekend, and others seek out private parties, frat parties, and activities in Jackson. In recent years, however, the student affairs office has brought free concerts to campus and organized other activities in an effort to keep students at Millsaps on weekends. Another major social activity is Major Madness, a weeklong spring festival of bands, Greek events, and general good times.

The obvious alternative to the outdoor and social Greek life is the dorms. Millsaps has both coed and single-sex dorms, which residents generally describe as sufficient, although some complained about communal showers.

Millsaps Dining Hall Services offers 21- and 14-meal plans that can be used both at the main cafeteria, or "the Caf," as students call it, and at Acy's Place, a campus institution where students have enjoyed traditional college sandwich-and-fries fare for almost 40 years now. Student satisfaction with Millsaps food seems low: one student remarked, "the spicy beef pie is the hard way out of final exams." To satisfy their late-night junk-food cravings, students head to the Waffle House, or that other center of fine southern fast food dining, Krystal, both of which are open 24 hours.

Millsaps sports don't generate a lot of student support, even though the Division III football team is successful against rivals Trinity, Sewanee, and Rhodes. To promote student athleticism and boost school spirit, the administration has spent over $17 million in 2000 for the construction of the Maurice H. Hall Activities

Center ("the PAC"), a new gym and fitness center that includes an indoor workout facility, a basketball court, an indoor track, an outdoor pool, racquetball and handball courts as well as a student plaza for outdoor events such as concerts and parties.

> **Over half of the campus decides to go Greek, explaining why one student felt "there's too much pressure to rush."**

Overall, students say they are satisfied with their choice of Millsaps, and the value of the education they are getting. Millsaps accepts the common application, and follows a need-blind admissions policy. One student specifically mentioned that the generous scholarship aid packages Millsaps offers were a major incentive to admission, and others appreciate the proximity of their homes in the South. Said one student, "Sure, you could pay more for worse weather and more stress, but why?" —*Jeff Kaplow and Staff*

FYI

The three best things about attending Millsaps are "our pretty campus, the friendly professors, and the financial aid."

The three worst things about attending Millsaps are "ridiculously hard work, low quality area, and odd housing policy."

The three things that every student should do before graduating from Millsaps are "take a road-trip to New Orleans, laugh at your premed friends (assuming you're not pre-med), and hand in a paper on time."

One thing I'd like to have known before coming here is "to avoid anything that sounds fancy in the dining hall."

Mississippi State University

Address: PO Box 6305; Mississippi State, MS 39762
Phone: 662-325-2224
E-mail address: admit @admissions.msstate.edu
Web site URL: www.msstate.edu
Founded: 1878
Private or Public: public
Religious affiliation: none
Location: rural
Undergraduate enrollment: 12,879
Total enrollment: 16,076
Percent Male/Female: 55%/45%
Percent Minority: 20%
Percent African-American: 18%

Percent Asian: 1%
Percent Hispanic: 0.5%
Percent Native-American: 0.5%
Percent in-state/out-of-state: 82%/18%
Percent Pub HS: NA
Number of Applicants: 5,949
Percent Accepted: 70%
Percent Accepted who enroll: 48%
Entering: 2,024
Transfers: 1,453
Application Deadline: 1 Aug
Mean SAT: NA
Mean ACT: 24
Middle 50% SAT range: NA

Middle 50% ACT range: 19–27
3 Most popular majors: elemntary education, marketing, business administration
Retention: 78%
Graduation rate: 41%
On-campus housing: 85%
Fraternities: 8%
Sororities: 8%
Library: 1,422,763 volumes
Tuition and Fees: $3,017 in; $6,119 out
Room and Board: $4,835
Financial aid, first-year: 81%

Longtime rivals of Mississippi State University like to stereotype it as an institution filled with country bumpkins, but MSU is a far cry from its rivals' slander. MSU's unusual academic programs and warmhearted students attract a diverse population from all over the country.

The Programs

Students report that academics at MSU are strong, with architecture, veterinary science, agriculture, and engineering among the most notable departments. Yet, in addition to these majors, MSU offers smaller, more unusual programs. The professional golf management (PGM), retail floristry, turf-grass management, and landscape architecture programs attract focused students from across the nation. Students also make use of MSU's large co-op program to get "real life" training or job experience. Although certain majors require a co-op experience, many students take co-op jobs to earn extra money or simply to get away from the classroom for a while.

Most MSU undergrads spend their first two years fulfilling a core curriculum, which includes courses in the natural sciences, English composition, humanities, and social sciences, in addition to three hours in computer literacy, a junior or senior writing class, and speech. Students generally agree that the core is not a burden, although one student said speech is unpopular. "Many students are terrified to speak in public," she explained. Upperclassmen report that overall, MSU academics are not too demanding and that plenty of "blow-off" and fun courses, in areas such as military science, floral design, arts and crafts, horseback riding, tennis, and aerobics, ease the academic load. One highly recommended course is Dr. Hank Flick's interviewing and communications class, which has been known to involve such activities as reading a Dr. Seuss book on a fountain in the middle of campus to fulfill a "social norm violation" assignment. Dr. Sandra Harpole's physics class is also popular for its outstanding, "magic show–like" demonstrations.

Dynamics of the Class

Introductory classes tend to be large (around 250 students), while upper-level courses are small (around 15 students). Professors teach most courses, while TAs lead discussion sections and labs. In general, professors are eager to get to know their students if students take the initiative: many undergrads describe student-faculty relations as "great." One student recalled that all of her professors sent her get-well cards when she had her tonsils removed.

Registration occurs during the preceding term for upperclassmen and during the summer for incoming freshmen, and students agree that in most cases they have no trouble registering for desired classes. Dedicated students with either a high GPA or high ACT scores not only get preference during registration but also may qualify for the honors program, which offers smaller, more intense, and occasionally more unusual classes (for example, wine-tasting, for students 21 and over). Honors students rave about the program, claiming that they enjoy MSU's best dorms, professors, and facilities. Honors courses and honors forum discussions are not completely exclusive; regular students who avidly want to enroll in them can do so with permission from the honors director. As one student explained, "Accommodations are often made."

Extracurricular Activities

Outside of the classroom, students participate in a number of extracurricular activities. One student explained that the easiest way to get involved is to join one of the Student Association committees, which plan the majority of the school-affiliated social events. Other groups include the Black Friars theater group, an association for players of Dungeon and Dragons–style role-playing games, and pre-professional fraternities for students in such fields as music and engineering. Students with journalistic aspirations can work on the biweekly student newspaper, *The Reflector*. The administration also encourages students to help out with freshman orientation and recruitment. When the weather is warm, students play Frisbee on the Drill Field. Another campus hangout is the student center, which has a movie theater, a bowling alley, and numerous video games.

When students want to hit the books, they often go to Mitchell Memorial Library for quiet studying. Students describe the structure as "massive," containing almost everything they could ever need academically. When undergrads prefer to study in groups, they usually go to each other's rooms, apartments, Allen Hall, or McCool Hall.

Dorms are in good condition at MSU, yet only about one-third of the student body, mostly freshmen, lives on-campus. The two honors dorms, one for freshmen and one for upperclassmen, are coed by wing and are considered the best. MSU also has 12 single-sex non-honors dorms. Most freshmen live on campus because, as one student explained, "living on-campus your first year allows you to meet your social crowd."

Instead of purchasing a meal plan, MSU students buy a Money Mate card, from which they deduct the cost of each meal they eat. Students can use their Money Mate cards at either the cafeteria, which serves only breakfast and lunch, or the food court, which houses various fast-food restaurants like Taco Bell and Great Wall of China. When students want variety, they go off-campus to the popular Bulldog Deli, Oby's, and the Cotton District Grill.

The Social Scene

Because in-state students often go home on weekends, campus parties are more common during the week. About one-fifth of MSU students belong to the Greek system, but independents say that there is no pressure to rush: because the school is relatively small, almost everyone knows a fraternity member, so invitations to Greek parties are easy to get. Since the administration enacted a dry-campus policy, drinking has become less prevalent at campus parties. "It doesn't matter if you are 19, 21, or 50—you can't have alcohol on-campus," one student explained. Any frat caught with alcohol at one of its parties will be put on probation. Even with this stringent policy, however, students report that MSU still has its share of drinkers at Greek "swaps" or mixers, and private parties given by students living off-campus. Most MSU students also have cars, so nearby bars such as Doug's, Rick's, and Mulligan's are also easily accessible. On-campus, the main social event of the year is the Super Bulldog Weekend, which involves homecoming-type festivities and a weekend of parties centered on the baseball team. All students, as well as many alumni and town-folk, join this campus celebration.

Sports, both varsity and intramural, are popular at MSU. Students are filled with pride for their nationally ranked baseball team, and because MSU has the largest campus baseball facility in the United States, the school hosts divisional championships every year. Football and basketball games are also well attended, especially against archrival University of Mississippi. (Until recently, students substituted "Go to Hell, Ole Miss" for the "amen" at the end of the prayer at every football game.) During varsity games, Bulldogs fans try to sneak cowbells into the stadium and ring them while rooting for their team, even though the bells have been outlawed by the Southeastern Conference. Sports teams garner so much support that motor homes filled with fans roll into town on home-game Thursdays. The Sanderson Center, a 150,000-square-foot recreational facility that houses state-of-the-art athletic facilities for student and administrative use, is at the heart of MSU's large intramural sports program.

> **During varsity games, Bulldogs fans try to sneak cowbells into the stadium and ring them while rooting for their team, even though the bells have been outlawed by the Southeastern Conference.**

The majority of MSU students come from Mississippi, and according to undergrads, the general political climate is conservative. Fraternities and sororities are racially segregated and the campus has no active gay or lesbian groups, which some students attribute to the school's location in the Bible Belt. As one student explained, "We'll be nice to gays, but they will not be accepted." Furthermore, drugs and pre-marital sex are generally not discussed on-campus. Some students are active in campus and state politics, although they say they tend to hold conservative views regardless of their party affiliation. As one student explained, "If you're from the North, it's culture shock."

MSU is located in Starkville, Mississippi, which students described as "not a very happening place." Starkville is a quiet, conservative town, yet Starkville residents often attend MSU athletic games and campus activities. The undergrads call the campus beautiful and feel that it is generally safe. University police and a student escort service ensure security on-campus.

Recently, MSU has grown increasingly serious about its academics, boosting its efforts to recruit the brightest students in Mississippi. Yet undergrads report that the greatest asset of their university is the friendliness of the student body. According to one student, many undergrads go on to attend MSU graduate school simply because they don't want to leave the students and teachers of their undergraduate years. "You must visit the campus and discover the great southern hospitality for yourself," she said, "for nowhere else except at MSU will you always find a smiling stranger who readily says 'hi' to all."—*Jeff Kaplow and Staff*

FYI

The three best things about attending MSU are "intramural play, Money Mate cards, and the co-op opportunities."

The three worst things about attending MSU are "Starkville, partying only during the week, and Northern culture shock."

The three things that every student should do before graduating from MSU are "enjoy Super Bulldog Weekend, ring a cowbell, and appreciate southern hospitality."

One thing I'd like to have known before coming here is "how strange it is that we party during the week."

University of Mississippi

Address: 145 Martindale Center; PO Box 1848; University, MS 38677
Phone: 662-915-7226
E-mail address: NA
Web site URL: www.olemiss.edu
Founded: 1844
Private or Public: public
Religious affiliation: none
Location: rural
Undergraduate enrollment: 9,222
Total enrollment: 10,280
Percent Male/Female: 45%/55%
Percent Minority: 12%
Percent African-American: 10%

Percent Asian: 1%
Percent Hispanic: 0.5%
Percent Native-American: 0.5%
Percent in-state/out-of-state: 67%/33%
Percent Pub HS: 70%
Number of Applicants: 4,196
Percent Accepted: 76%
Percent Accepted who enroll: 57%
Entering: 1,826
Transfers: 983
Application Deadline: 1 Aug
Mean SAT: NA
Mean ACT: 23
Middle 50% SAT range: NA

Middle 50% ACT range: 20–28
3 Most popular majors: general business, biological science, accounting
Retention: 76%
Graduation rate: 28%
On-campus housing: 95%
Fraternities: 25%
Sororities: 32%
Library: 1,000,000 volumes
Tuition and Fees: $3,053 in; $6,155 out
Room and Board: $3,414
Financial aid, first-year: 33%

As visitors step onto the campus of the university affectionately known as "Ole Miss," they cannot help but be reminded of a historical tradition that include belles, chivalry, and classic southern hospitality that many students on-campus praise with enthusiasm.

A Stronger Academic Program?

In addition to a nationally ranked pharmacy program and the recent addition of an extensive acoustics lab, Ole Miss offers strong humanities departments. One English major reported, "I haven't had an

English class I didn't enjoy." The university has invested a "ton of money to make the academic program here stronger." Such investments include revamping the science departments, and so far students say the engineering program has seen the most marked improvement. Although business is a popular major at Ole Miss, some students say the program could be more challenging.

For undergrads "seeking a greater academic challenge," Ole Miss has also opened a new honors college, thanks to a sizable donation from alumnus James Barkdale, the CEO and president of Netscape. Undergraduates praised the McDonnell-Barkdale Honors College for its academic rigor, small class sizes of 15, and the enthusiasm of its professors. One student noted that "most importantly, this program also creates a close knit community among the students, because certain dorm floors are devoted to students within the Honors College."

One of the biggest complaints from students is the "excessive class size" at Ole Miss. Many required classes are "simply too big." Although most classes enroll fewer than 30 students, one senior reported that his seminar, which he felt should have had no more than 20 students, had around 50. In these situations, professors are helped by TAs, which "helps a little in curbing class size."

Ole Miss is one of three schools in the nation to offer a department of Southern Region Studies, which includes such classes as Southern Fiction, Folk Art, and the History of the Blues. Undergrads even have access to B. B. King's blues record collection, which was recently donated to the university. Another popular resource is the Sarah Isom Center for Women's Studies, which conducts classes and seminars that focus on women's issues.

Rebel Tradition

The University of Mississippi is keenly influenced by long-standing southern traditions and a lively sense of community that encompasses the surrounding town of Oxford in northern Mississippi. The school band still plays "Dixie" and students still wave the "Rebel" flag at sporting events. Ole Miss students see such traditions as evidence, not of intolerance, but of strong school spirit. As one student said, "We are just incredibly excited to be a part of traditional school pride here." In fact, the university is attempting to distance itself from its history of prejudice.

One example of this effort was the decision to revamp the school mascot, replacing the image of Colonel Reb as a southern plantation owner with a new Colonel Reb decked out in school colors with a football jersey and helmet. Undergrads at the University of Mississippi enjoy "hollering for our teams!" Before most football games, students reportedly partake in "grove-ing," a practice of extensive mingling during tailgate parties.

Afraid to "jinx" their teams, fans stand during all four quarters of home football games, sitting only during halftime. Huge crowds attended "the Game" against the university's ultimate rival, Mississippi State. As one student said, "For the bigger games, people start parking their trailer homes on Thursday in anticipation for game Saturday!"

> **"This is just a prime example of the conservative bent on-campus."**

Ole Miss students sometimes complain that from sports to religious associations, "it is hard to get involved with other organizations as people tend to form cliques quickly and introductions are made more difficult." Another student added, "I only know two or three people in a few random groups, largely because they tend to hang out only by themselves."

Party, Party, Party!

Students at the University of Mississippi pride themselves in being able to have a good time "no matter the circumstances. We may lose a game, but we never lose a party. Our football might not be best in the (SEC) division, but we can party harder than you can," one undergrad said. Greek life at the University of Mississippi is an "integral part of life here." As one student reported, "Greeks basically run the school."

Fraternities and sororities are very large organizations, and it is not uncommon to see alumni return for weekend Greek parties. Another student particularly noted that "husbands bring their wives and you see forty-year-olds passed out on the floor! It gets a bit ridiculous."

Although kegs are not "technically allowed on-campus," students report that "they are prevalent in many social situations." Fraternity houses are off-campus so they do not have to worry about such regulations. As one student pointed out, "It's supposed to be a dry campus, but the last party I went to had 12 kegs." While Ole Miss does not publicly condone drinking, one student said that drinking "goes on, they know it, we know it . . . we just have an understanding, that's all."

Students who do not join fraternities are not left out of social interaction. As one student explained, "There are so many frat boys here that it's not hard to find a friend that'll get you into a party or invite you to go hang with the guys." For students not interested in Greek life or the party scene, the university sponsors lectures and trips on weekends. Other opportunities range from hearing visitors like comedian Adam Sandler speak, visiting William Faulkner's house, or playing pickup basketball games with professors "as long as you are willing to participate." If Greek life gets old, Memphis is only a 45-minute drive from campus and, as one undergrad explained, "it is not totally unheard of for students to head out of town for a weekend getaway."

Conservative Housing Policy

The University of Mississippi abides by Mississippi state law forbidding co-ed housing in state dormitories. According to one student, "This is just a prime example of the conservative bent on-campus." On weekdays, visiting hours for the opposite sex end at midnight, while weekend hours are extended to "only 1 A.M." Although students have clamored for an open 24-hour visiting policy, they say the proposal has been "quickly shot down" by campus administration.

While dorm restrictions reduce opportunities for both sexes to intermingle, students generally are content with housing options. Dorm residents say the rooms are "ample for the number of people living in them." For the most part, only freshmen live in the dorms because "sophomore year, everyone migrates to the frat houses." Most upper-class students rent apartments close to campus," one undergrad said. Cars are reportedly not essential for students living on (or close to) campus. One student said, "You can usually hitch a ride from a friend who has a car, so there isn't really a problem getting around unless you want to go somewhere without your friend or you have no friends at all!"

Undergrads at the University of Mississippi are attracted to a vibrant tradition of school spirit and southern pride. Students receive a solid education in both academics and social interaction. As one student said, "This place is what college should be . . . you work hard and play a thousand times harder." —*Jeff Kaplow and Staff*

FYI
The three best things about attending Ole Miss are "the school's tradition and spirit, a friendly student body, and the off-campus party scene."
The three worst things about attending Ole Miss are "the conservative housing policies, the Rebel Burgers in the dining halls, and overcrowded classrooms."
The three things every student should do before graduating from Ole Miss are "work out at Ole Miss Fit, the student rec center, go to The Game, and "grove" at as many tailgates as possible."
One thing I wish I'd known before coming to Ole Miss is "the administrations overly conservative policies."

Missouri

University of Missouri / Kansas City

Address: 5100 Rockhill Road, 101 AC; Kansas City, MO 64110
Phone: 816-235-1111
E-mail address: admit@umkc.edu
Web site URL: www.umkc.edu
Founded: 1929
Private or Public: public
Religious affiliation: none
Location: urban
Undergraduate enrollment: 5,400
Total enrollment: NA
Percent Male / Female: 42%/58%
Percent Minority: 24%

Percent African-American: 12%
Percent Asian: 7%
Percent Hispanic: 4%
Percent Native-American: 0.5%
Percent in-state / out-of-state: 80%/20%
Percent Pub HS: NA
Number of Applicants: 2,583
Percent Accepted: 68%
Percent Accepted who enroll: 39%
Entering: 685
Transfers: NA
Application Deadline: 1 Apr
Mean SAT: NA

Mean ACT: 24
Middle 50% SAT range: NA
Middle 50% ACT range: 21–27
3 Most popular majors: psychology, computer science, liberal arts
Retention: 73%
Graduation rate: 19%
On-campus housing: 6%
Fraternities: 18%
Sororities: 18%
Library: NA
Tuition and Fees: $3,852 in; $10,387 out
Room and Board: $4,865
Financial aid, first-year: 54%

Despite the stereotype, "University of Missouri at Kansas City is not a hick school." In fact, Kansas City is one of the fastest growing cities in America. Located in the heartland of America, UMKC offers an affordable education in an urban setting.

Known as the "artsy" of the UM universities, UMKC may not draw as many out-of-state students as some other state schools, but it still offers a diverse student body. What it lacks in geographical diversity, it makes up for in its students' wide-ranging backgrounds and interests. A large percentage of UMKC students are part-time or returning students, many of them having to balance their studies with jobs or families.

Ambitious Academics
As can be expected with an older student body, UMKC is known for its excellent pre-professional programs and tends to attract students who are career-oriented. Specifically, the dual-degree programs that offer a B.A. or B.S. degree in conjunction with a degree in medicine, law, dentistry, or education, cater to ambitious and focused students.

The College of Arts and Sciences is comprised of fifteen departments ranging from traditional majors such as English and History to more unusual departments such as Military Science. Computer Science and Psychology are two of the most popular departments. Requirements vary according to major. Overall, the requirements for B.S. and B.A. degrees are similar except that a B.S. degree requires a total of 60 hours in math and science credits. In general, students must complete a minimum of 26 semester hours and a minimum of 12 semester hours in their respective majors. Double and combined majors are also available.

UMKC students must comply with a

unique Missouri law that requires students to complete courses about the U.S. Constitution and the Missouri State Constitution. Though most appreciate the former requirement, some out-of-staters complain about the latter.

Students who wish to intensify their academic experience can participate in a special honors program that encompasses much more than their requisite honors classes. Honors students have their own publications—*The Undergraduate Review* and *The Onner's Gazette*—and have access to special honors facilities. The program itself centers on a weekly one-hour colloquium offered every semester. Honors in all classes meet with the faculty and distinguished guest lecturers to discuss a wide range of subjects.

With a professor to student ratio of 1:12, UMKC prides itself on its small class sizes. Hence, though UMKC is a research institution, students are not bogged down in huge classes with little student-professor interaction. "At UMKC you don't feel like a number. The professors I have encountered are extremely accessible," one student said. The one complaint students did have concerned the intensity of work. "I didn't expect my American Studies course to be so intensive. I am enjoying it though," one freshman said.

Kasey the Kangaroo

How UMKC came to have a Kangaroo as its mascot is a question that has been pondered for years. Although UMKC officially got the idea for its mascot from two kangaroos adopted by the Kansas City Zoo back in 1936–37, the kangaroo was probably adopted largely because of Disney's "Kasey the Kangaroo's" popularity. Apparently, "Kasey" seemed the perfect mascot for a school called "KC."

> "Coming to UMKC from New York City, I was shocked to see how friendly Kansas City is. People on the street will stop to say hello or good morning."

The kangaroo is a prominent symbol. First-years arriving in the fall are greeted by organizations at the Roo Fair, a one-day activities fair that introduces students to UMKC's more than 200 organizations. Some of the many organizations range from *U-News*, the weekly student newspaper, to *KCUR*, UMKC's public radio station, one of the first educational radio stations in the state. But even with the wide range of activities, students wishing to start new organizations will find the Student Life Office extremely helpful. With over a dozen fraternities and sororities, Greek life undoubtedly plays a role on campus as well. But, according to students, "if Greek is not your thing, that's okay too."

For the athletically inclined, UMKC is a NCAA Division I affiliate. Part of the Mid-Continent Conference, the school offers a wide range of varsity teams for both men and women. Women participate in basketball, golf, tennis, volleyball, cross-country, track and field, and softball. Men compete in basketball, golf, tennis, cross-country, track and field, rifle, and soccer.

Even if they don't take part in varsity athletics, most students come out to cheer for their favorite teams. Among the biggest events of the year is the basketball game against Kansas State University, one of UMKC's traditional rivals. During this game, the UMKC stands are often packed, and the Kangaroos go wild. For less hardcore athletes, UMKC offers a wide range of intramural sports at Swinney Recreational Center.

Campus Living or Apartment Style?

Despite the bustling on-campus extracurricular life, less than 10% of students actually live on campus. The one on-campus dorm is "Residence Hall" with approximately 330 students living within its walls. The rest of the student masses live off campus. For non-Missouri natives, the availability of cheap local housing is one of UMKC's greatest draws. "Coming from out of state I was worried at first about finding a place. It turned out to be the easiest part of coming to college," one student said.

To facilitate student searches for off-campus housing, UMKC has its own real estate office. It helps students find nearby university-owned rentals while the Welcome Center has listings of non-University-owned property. Students describe the rentals as relatively inexpensive and extremely convenient. The Twin Oaks Apartment complex is popular among students. Located on the west side of campus, its proximity to UMKC makes it a favorite.

Small Town Friendliness

Contrary to popular belief, Kansas City is truly a bustling city with the friendly atmosphere of a small town. "Coming to UMKC from New York City, I was shocked to see how friendly Kansas City is. People on the street will stop to say hello or good morning," one student said. Located in one of Kansas City's most happening neighborhoods, UMKC offers its students a lively off-campus social life. Close by are the popular 51st Street Coffeehouse, Main Street eateries, and area parks and museums. Less than a fifteen-minute walk from campus is the Country Club Plaza shopping and restaurant district. With its Mexican architecture and numerous fountains,

the Plaza area is quite a "site." For students wishing to splurge, the Plaza houses such upscale stores as Ralph Lauren and Tiffany's. Lots of students also frequent Abercrombie and Fitch, the Gap, and The Limited. Also nearby is the Cheesecake Factory, a popular restaurant among UMKC students. Within minutes of campus, Westport has many bars featuring live bands, and is the place to be for nightlife. Students would agree that social life in Kansas City is great because it is safe as well as relatively inexpensive. Unlike students at other urban schools, UMKC students report that they don't have to worry so much about safety during a night out on the town.

With its abundance of activities on and off campus, it's no wonder UMKC students have so much school spirit. They rave about UMKC life both inside the classroom and out. As one student said, "I just hate the thought of graduation." —*Alyssa Blair Greenwald*

FYI
The three best things about attending UMKC are "Kansas City, affordable living, and the arts department."
The three worst things about attending UMKC are "Kansas City, requirements, and the intense work."
The three things that every student should do before graduating from UMKC are "to explore haunted Epperson House Hall, be Kasey the Kangaroo, attend a UMKC-KSU game."
One thing I'd like to have known before coming here is "that there are so many local students."

University of Missouri / Columbia

Address: 230 Jesse Hall; Columbia, MO 65211
Phone: 573-882-7786
E-mail address: MU4U@missouri.edu
Web site URL: www.missouri.edu
Founded: 1893
Private or Public: public
Religious affiliation: none
Location: suburban
Undergraduate enrollment: 17,811
Total enrollment: 22,483
Percent Male/Female: 49%/51%
Percent Minority: 9%
Percent African-American: 6%

Percent Asian: 2%
Percent Hispanic: 1%
Percent Native-American: NA
Percent in-state/out-of-state: 88%/12%
Percent Pub HS: NA
Number of Applicants: 9,091
Percent Accepted: 90%
Percent Accepted who enroll: 48%
Entering: 3,932
Transfers: 1,592
Application Deadline: 1 May
Mean SAT: NA
Mean ACT: 25
Middle 50% SAT range: NA

Middle 50% ACT range: 24–29
3 Most popular majors: business administration, biological sciences, psychology
Retention: 83%
Graduation rate: 28%
On-campus housing: 83%
Fraternities: 23%
Sororities: 25%
Library: 4,500,000 volumes
Tuition and Fees: $4,726 in; $12,895 out
Room and Board: $3,815
Financial aid, first-year: 57%

L ike many large state schools, the University of Missouri is defined by an active frat life and a relatively loose attitude toward academic life. At the same time, the sheer immensity of a state institution guarantees that students can find something to fit their interests. A closer look reveals some local color peeping through the State U mask.

Mizzou Curriculum

Students consider academics at Mizzou "average to moderately difficult." The undergraduate core curriculum includes a three-year language requirement and two writing-intensive courses, the hardest of the requirements to fill. Two of the more prominent academic programs are the Minority Achievement Program, which offers workshops to promote further education and teach effective study habits, and the extensive study-abroad program. The journalism school is the most recognized department that the university has to offer and is the main source of the small out-of-state diversity on-campus. Undergrads report that along with the psychology department, the journalism school is the most popular. Some of the hardest classes

are in the sciences, including University Physics, "the roughest course they offer here," one student said. One of the more popular courses is Human Sexuality, which has a more laid-back reputation. Professors teach lecture classes and TAs teach the smaller sections, but as one student explained, "many of the TAs are foreign and hard to understand, so you end up learning the most from books."

Academics are not a great source of stress for many Mizzou students. As one undergrad said, "Even during finals week, people don't seem very flipped out." People study in the two main libraries on-campus, the law library and Ellis, which are some of the biggest libraries in the state. Several new campus facilities are in the works, including a new wing for the chemistry building and a new cafeteria. The athletic facilities are particularly popular. One student called them "excellent, with at least six basketball courts and even a climbing wall."

Landscapes, Frats, Food

"The prettiest part of campus has to be the main quad with the pillars. There are always students out there having fun," another undergrad reported. The University of Missouri's huge campus is a big part of the surrounding town of Columbia. Students say it is a safe environment with "enough to offer," including a mall, restaurants, and the Blue Note, a local dance club and bar. The residents of this college town are friendly and take advantage of the facilities on-campus. The town also plays an important role in student housing.

According to students, off-campus living is cheaper than staying in the dorms, and shuttles connect off-campus apartment buildings to different parts of campus. Off-campus residents say it is not necessary to have a car, although it is convenient for trips to the nearest big cities.

On-campus living is more convenient, with doubles and singles and community bathrooms. Suites of two bedrooms with a shared bathroom are also available, but these go mainly to the juniors and seniors. One student explained, "The rooms are boring, with thin cement walls and lofts or cots, but at least there aren't any bunk beds." Juniors and seniors get the best housing, and the best dorm is one of the only all-women dorms on-campus—Johnston Wolpers—which one student said "looks like a hotel" and has air-conditioning. Most of the other dorms are coed with single-sex floors. Each floor of the residential halls has a residential advisor as part of a bigger advising system that first-year students find particularly helpful.

> There is a lot of spirit behind the Tigers, especially the men's basketball team, which draws a full crowd for every game.

Other housing options include theme houses, language houses, and fraternity and sorority houses. The campus has a large Greek community, and their housing is, as one student described, "mansion-like."

Students who live on-campus choose a meal plan of 7, 14, or 21 meals a week. Food can also be charged on student ID cards at the Brady Commons student union, which has Chik-Fil-A, Taco Bell, Pizza Hut, and Burger King outlets. The dining hall food does not get rave reviews, but is generally considered "acceptable," and there are always vegetarian options. Most students eat off-campus in town a couple of times a week, with options from the cheapest and favorite Taco Bell to the nicer and popular El Maguay Mexican restaurant. Some students find local coffee shops also offer a good place to study.

The university also offers an "E-Z Charge" to its students, which gives each student $400 of credit to spend each month. It is accepted at the bookstore, dining halls, campus convenience stores, Brady Food Court, and Memorial Union Food Court. "You end up buying everything you want on it at an extremely over inflated price. Don't get it—it's very addictive," one student advised.

Athletics and Associations

Athletics play a big role in Mizzou life. There is a lot of spirit behind the Tigers, especially the men's basketball team, which draws a full crowd for every game. Kansas University is the rival that draws the most student animosity on-campus. Intramural sports are popular among extracurriculars. Options range from volleyball and basketball—which are some of the more popular—to the rock-climbing club that makes use of the climbing wall in the campus athletic complex. The meteorology club, the roller hockey club, and Peaceworks, an environmental awareness group, attract interest, as do many minority groups on-campus, from the Asian American Association (AAA) to the Romanian Student Association to LUBRASA for Luso Brazilian students. Students do not consider Mizzou's undergraduate population diverse, although support networks for minority students include the ethnic clubs and other groups such as the Black Culture Center and the Black Collegiates. Another significant and controversial minority group on-campus is the Triangle Coalition for gay and lesbian students. Most student groups are funded by the Missouri Student Association, MSA, the student government. The MSA, however, is "known as a joke rather than as an important student force," according to one student.

Campus Events

Students involved with the MSA work to organize movies, concerts, speakers, tutoring, rides, and advice opportunities. It has brought in such celebrities as George Stephanopoulos, and organized barn dances—including its own version of the popular MTV program Singled Out for Valentine's Day. Other big social events revolve around basketball games, such as big pep rallies before the games and other parties put on by the fraternities. One of the biggest events of the year is homecoming for the big football game each fall. The university has rules against kegs on-campus, but the administration has a reputation for being relatively lax with the frat houses. There are also rules about drug use on-campus, but some students say they are not well enforced. Other activities include the yearbook, the *Savitar*, and the *Maneater*, the bi-weekly newspaper. Performance opportunities on-campus also abound, with theater, singing, and orchestral student performing groups.

The student body is considered rather conservative by many undergrads, more so than the surrounding town. Diversity continues to be an issue for students on-campus, as the majority are white Missouri natives. Different programs have been introduced to promote diversity and raise the academic level of the school. The Bright Flight program and the Curator Scholarships both offer opportunities to students with good ACT scores and class rank. The Conley Scholars Program is also a unique academic opportunity for incoming students. It guarantees four years in the University of Missouri Medical school without taking the MCATs. In general, the campus, while large, is full of what students agree are "friendly" people.
—*William Chen and Staff*

FYI

The three best things about attending the University of Missouri are "tons of opportunities to perform, the journalism school, and the Tigers."

The three worst things about attending the University of Missouri are "E-Z Charge system, Missouri natives are everywhere, and how expensive on-campus living is."

The three things that every student should do before graduating from the University of Missouri are "go to MSA events, go Greek, and drive to St. Louis to party."

One thing I'd like to have known before coming here is "that people don't stress too much about their academics."

Washington University

Address: Campus Box 1089, One Brookings Drive; St. Louis, MO 63130-4899
Phone: 314-935-6000
E-mail address: admissions@wustl.edu
Web site URL: www.wustl.edu
Founded: 1853
Private or Public: private
Religious affiliation: none
Location: suburban
Undergraduate enrollment: 5,993
Total enrollment: 12,088
Percent Male/Female: 50%/50%
Percent Minority: 22%

Percent African-American: 7%
Percent Asian: 12%
Percent Hispanic: 2%
Percent Native-American: 0.5%
Percent in-state/out-of-state: 14%/86%
Percent Pub HS: 67%
Number of Applicants: 17,109
Percent Accepted: 34%
Percent Accepted who enroll: 24%
Entering: 1,384
Transfers: 187
Application Deadline: 15 Jan
Mean SAT: NA
Mean ACT: NA

Middle 50% SAT range: 620–710 V, 650–730 M
Middle 50% ACT range: 28–32
3 Most popular majors: psychology, biology, engineering
Retention: 96%
Graduation rate: 86%
On-campus housing: 99%
Fraternities: 25%
Sororities: 27%
Library: 3,350,122 volumes
Tuition and Fees: $24,745 in; $24,745 out
Room and Board: $7,724
Financial aid, first-year: 58%

U ndergrads dot the grassy quad with notebooks in their hands and smiles on their faces. Few landscapes are more picturesque, but at Washington University this is the daily scene. There is an incredible energy in the air as students seize every opportunity to explore life from the safe haven of their St. Louis school. Like the city that hosts the college, Wash U is a lively, stimulating place that combines midwestern values and intellectual curiosity.

Pre-Med—Everyone?

According to its students, "Wash U is tough—really tough." Prospective students apply to one of five undergraduate colleges: the College of Arts and Sciences, the School of Engineering and Applied Sciences, the School of Art, the School of Architecture, and the John M. Olin School of Business. The school of business is notoriously easier than the other four schools, while students in the School of Engineering and Applied Sciences and the School of Architecture reportedly "never sleep." Despite the discrepancies, a comprehensive set of distributional requirements and rigorous programs of study in all five colleges require "a lot of work in

order to do well." Math and science are known to be the most difficult and biology and psychology the two most popular majors.

With such a reputable medical school, it seems that "everyone and their brother comes into Wash U pre-med," but they are quickly scared off by the difficulty of the introductory chemistry classes. Popular classes include Cultural Anthropology and Intro to Biological Evolution, and students often recall giving standing ovations to their "phenomenal professors" for lectures in these classes.

Although Wash U may be difficult, students generally feel that the extensive support system will prevent anyone from falling through the cracks: "The university genuinely wants us to do well, and there is so much support it is unbelievable." Professors teach all classes, with the exception of the Freshman Writing Class, for which graduate students lead sections. Undergrads claim their teaching assistants are "helpful," but one student said that there's "little point getting help from the TAs when I can go visit my professor just as easily. The staff is absolutely astounding."

The flexibility of the Wash U academic

departments is cherished by its students. Frequently undergrads will complete a major in one school while minoring, double-minoring, or even triple-minoring in subjects directed by other schools. The variety of majors and classes is "almost overwhelming," and it is extraordinarily easy for students to design their own major if the standard fare does not satisfy expectations. One senior reported that the "opportunities and facilities continually amaze me and everyone's enthusiasm is so encouraging, you want to do well for more than just a grade."

Overcommitment and General Enthusiasm

"I think you'd be hard pressed to find a student who is not involved in at least one extracurricular," claimed one student at Wash U. With hundreds of clubs and student organizations ranging from Skydiving to Chess, Wash U students are overwhelmed with opportunities to get involved, and almost all students seize this opportunity. In fact, freshmen must quickly learn how to say no because, according to one student, "If you did a tenth of everything you could possibly do, you'd never sleep."

The most popular activities include intramural sports (although on the collegiate level women's basketball is the only sport that catches attention), Campus Y (the community service organization), several a cappella and improv comedy groups, and the Congress of the South 40 (the student governing body). Extensive student involvement in all activities is what makes Wash U's extracurricular programs so dynamic. Furthermore, the city of St. Louis provides many opportunities for internships and work. In such an energetic environment, the "possibilities are endless."

Play Hard on Frat Row

"Very wet on weekends and dry as a bone on weeknights," Washington University is best described as the quintessential work-hard, play-hard environment. New students quickly learn that frat row is the place to be every Friday and Saturday night—for everyone. Given their proximity to the headquarters of Anheuser-Busch, Wash U students claim a fondness for a certain golden brew and report no difficulty in obtaining alcohol at any age—however, they are also quick to defend the right to abstain. One student observed that "many underclassmen, particularly guys, do a lot of drinking at the frats," but, when questioned, another male underclassman hailed the fraternities for the amount of respect they give to those who choose not to drink. Dry parties are also known to be well-attended frat events.

In a school where 30% of the student body belong to one of 11 fraternities or 5 sororities, Wash U maintains a fun environment that is open and inviting. Deferred rush gives students the chance to relax into Greek life before joining, and one underclassman praised the sororities' inclusiveness: "They are great! They don't haze at all and have a genuine focus on philanthropic work—unlike so many other schools I know."

Frat parties are known to be hookup events, but many students were surprised at how many committed couples there are. "I get the impression that people are looking to meet someone special," said a female freshman. Homosexual and interracial couples are not commonplace at Wash U, although no one seems to object to them in principle.

Off frat row, popular parties include W.I.L.D., Walk-In Lay-Down, a campus-wide party held on the first and last Friday of the year, featuring both local and nationally recognized bands. The Spin Doctors and They Might Be Giants have been recent performers. W.I.L.D. is one of "the few times almost all students socialize together"—beginning around noon and going until late in the night. In addition, the School of Architecture hosts a biannual "Bauhaus" party that is another popular event, and Thursday night at the Rat (short for "Rathskeller"—an underground bar and restaurant) is the kickoff to every weekend for fun seekers.

You Go to School Where?

Once students discover that Washington University is in Missouri, not a Pacific northwestern state, they learn to love the city of St. Louis. The clubs, bars, and music of downtown lure upperclassmen who own cars, and even those who depend on public transportation find St. Louis incredibly accessible and appealing. A 15-minute walk from campus, the Loop is known for its inexpensive shops and restaurants and as an "offbeat, college-town-like" section of St. Louis. Forest Park, one of the nation's largest public parks, borders campus and provides students with bike trails, wide open greens, and outdoor attractions.

> **"Everyone and their brother comes into Wash U pre-med."**

Getting people to leave campus tends to be a problem, however. Known as "the most beautiful campus anywhere," and the only school that actually looks like its brochure, Wash U is the place where students want to be. Its Gothic architecture and "incredible quadrangles" are often the site of pickup football games, picnic lunches, and study sessions.

Hotels and Turkey Sandwiches
Located on the South 40 (the center of student activity on campus), the dorms of Wash U are considered to be "just as beautiful as the rest of campus." However, housing crunches during the past year have resulted in two new dorm buildings that students say are "more hotel-like than a college dorm should be." Air-conditioned, carpeted rooms and "maid service for the bathrooms" make the decision to leave

campus a difficult one for upperclassmen, and the university has had to offer "incentives" including free telephone and Ethernet service to lure students away from the crowded housing system.

Washington University's dining services are praised by some, while others consider the food "pricey" and "lacking in variety." "I have had more turkey sandwiches here than I ever expected to eat in my life," claimed one sophomore. Generally, it is believed that "the food could be better, but no one is starving," and it is possible to get good cheap food.

Abercrombie and Fitch Poster Children
Esteemed as having a "moderate to very attractive" student body, Wash U prides itself on its well-dressed students. Although, in general, the population is upper-middle-class, Wash U is too big to be defined by one stereotype, and students genuinely appreciate the diversity on campus. There are a number of students from metropolitan areas like Chicago and New York, but Wash U also attracts students from other parts of the country and the world—creating an extremely diverse, sophisticated atmosphere. "The people" are universally hailed as what makes Wash U so special. To the surprise of many new students, "everyone is involved in everything and incredibly energetic about what they are doing." Students, faculty, and neighbors are all "so unbelievably friendly" that even with its other strengths, most students believe that Wash U's greatest asset is its midwestern charm. —*Emily Barton*

FYI
The three best things about attending Wash U are "W.I.L.D., the proximity of Forest Park, and the amazing architecture on campus."
The three worst things about attending Wash U are "people thinking you go to school in either Washington, D.C., or Washington State, dining hall food, of course, and the recent crackdown on alcohol."
The three things that every student should do before graduating from Wash U are "take Cultual Anthropology, study (or, um, other things) on the roof of Olin Library, and go to the top of the Arch."
One thing I'd like to have known before coming here is "that the city of St. Louis can offer so much!"

Montana

Address: Lodge 103;
Missoula, MT 59812-
0002
Phone: 406-243-6266
E-mail address:
admiss@selway.umt.edu
Web site URL:
www.umt.edu
Founded: 1893
Private or Public: public
Religious affiliation:
none
Location: small city
**Undergraduate
enrollment:** 10,357
Total enrollment:
12,208
Percent Male/Female:
47%/53%
Percent Minority: 5%

Percent African-American:
0.5%
Percent Asian: 0.5%
Percent Hispanic: 1%
Percent Native-American:
3%
**Percent in-state/out-of-
state:** 74%/26%
Percent Pub HS: 70%
Number of Applicants:
3,384
Percent Accepted: 84%
**Percent Accepted who
enroll:** 62%
Entering: 1,760
Transfers: 1,019
Application Deadline:
rolling
Mean SAT: NA
Mean ACT: 23

Middle 50% SAT range:
480–590 V,
470–590 M
Middle 50% ACT range:
20–25
3 Most popular majors:
business, education,
medical sciences
Retention: 77%
Graduation rate: 39%
On-campus housing:
80%
Fraternities: 5%
Sororities: 4%
Library: 570,287 volumes
Tuition and Fees:
$2,910 in; $8,020 out
Room and Board: $4,400
Financial aid, first-year:
45%

If a large, open green the size of two football fields, filled with ardent Frisbee players and engaged artists, is your idea of college life, perhaps a closer look at Big Sky country is in order. At one end of the "oval," as the campus green is called, stands stately Main Hall. Directly behind the tower of Main Hall, the peak of Mt. Sentinel reminds one of the natural beauty of the area. This mix of academic buildings and untouched natural wonders is what makes the University of Montana special.

A Montana Education

While the varied callings of their beautiful environment tempt Montana students, undergrads here are serious about their academics. The university features a general education requirement for all liberal arts students. Everyone must graduate with "competency" in three major areas: writing composition, math, and foreign language. Luckily, there are approximately 75 classes to choose from in each category. Students must also take two classes in each of six categories: expressive studies, such as studio art, dance, or music; literary/artistic studies, such as English or art history; historical/cultural studies; social sciences, ethical and human values; and natural sciences. Students have mostly positive attitudes toward the general education requirements, although some say they already learned the material in high school. One student said, "The requirements are beneficial. I came to school with one major in mind and the General Education Program opened my eyes to the fact that I could take other classes and not get hindered."

Popular majors include business, education, forestry, wildlife biology, environmental studies, and creative writing. Some of these majors may be pursued by taking classes at other schools in the university besides the liberal arts school. Students can apply to these schools separately during the admissions process. Montana's schools include the School of Pharmacy, the School of Education, the School of Allied Health, the School of Journalism, and the School of Business. In addition, the Davidson Honors College is a small liberal arts college within the university. To be accepted and remain a member of the honors college, a student must have finished freshman year, maintain a certain GPA, and participate in volunteer service. All classes in the honors college are small, with no more than 20 to 25 people.

As many sometimes tire of the long and cold Montana winters, studying abroad is a popular option. Students can travel with University of Montana faculty to such countries as France, Spain, Germany, Australia, Mexico, New Zealand, and many East Asian countries while living in the homes of native families.

Men and women at the University of Montana say that their classes range from 300-person introductory lectures to smaller classes of up to 25 students. "The difficulty of the course work depends on how much you apply yourself," said one student. Those who wish to study intensely do so in Mansfield Library or the study rooms in the University Center, while anyone who wants an atmosphere more conducive to socializing can study in the first floor of the library or the study lounges in each residence hall.

Students find faculty to be relatively accessible, although their approachability varies with professors and programs. Almost all classes are taught by professors, although some introductory classes such as math, English, and psychology are sometimes taught by teaching assistants. While registering for classes at large state universities can be a hassle, the university has moved to make the process easier for students. In order to register for their classes, Montana Grizzlies find the Dial-a-Bear Registration system very satisfactory. It is "definitely a positive," said one student. The system dictates that students meet with their appointed advisors prior to registering, then call up the system to see if they've gotten into the classes they wanted. Registration goes smoothly, with 27 phone lines allocated to the process.

Each semester, priority switches from those with last names in the first half of the alphabet to those in the last half so that registration is fair. Students said they often get their first picks, regardless.

Life at UM

On-campus living is mandatory for all freshmen. All of the dorms at the University of Montana are located within a ten-minute walk, at most, of major classroom buildings. Students say the main difference between the dorms is that some have been renovated and some not. Even the non-renovated dorms are reputed to be "not bad" by students familiar with the typical college dormitory. The newest dorm is an upperclassman dorm, Pantzer Hall, built in 1995. Pantzer consists of suites in an almost apartment-like setting. Turner Hall (an all-female dorm), Elrod (an all-male dorm), Jesse and Aber (the two high-rise dorms), and a dorm for married students are also available for on-campus living. Some dorms have substance-free floors or floors reserved for students in the Honors College.

All dorms include a laundry room, game room, and lounge in which students can come together to study, watch TV, or just hang out. Each floor has an RA, who can be a sophomore, junior, or senior. The RA serves as a liaison to University administration, an enforcer of rules, a counselor, and a resource for information in campus life. RAs, in conjunction with the student organization Peers Reaching Out, present information on sex, drugs, drinking, assault, stress management, and other pertinent topics at the beginning of the year. The degree to which underage drinking rules are enforced depends on the individual RA, although students generally feel the alcohol policy on-campus is relatively strict. Students also said that there is a definite drug scene on-campus, including marijuana.

Many upperclassmen move off-campus to apartments in Missoula, which are accessible to campus by walking or bicycling, or by public buses, which are free to all students with their university ID. Many bring cars to campus, which allows them to find apartments farther from central campus. These apartments have the advantage of being cheaper than those in the heart of Missoula. Students can also live in the fraternity and sorority houses—although these houses are not very large and are not the most popular housing option on-campus, according to students.

Students who live on-campus are required to purchase the meal plan, and many say the food isn't bad. "While the cooking isn't like Mom's, overall it's by far the best college food I've had," said one transfer student. The university has one main dining hall, nicknamed "the Zoo." Students can also use their meal plan at Mama Zula's Pizzeria and the Country Store, or use "Bear Bucks" at Copper Commons cafeteria or Cafe Bristo in the University Center. For off-campus eating and coffee students frequent eateries and fast-food outlets in Missoula. Favorite coffee places include BoJangle's, which has live entertainment and poetry readings, and Cybershack, where you can enjoy a cup of joe while e-mailing your best friend from home. Popular Missoula restaurants include the Depot (for fancy fare), Food for Thought, Finigan's, and Pizza Pipeline.

On weekends students tend to spend their days either engaged in outdoor activity, indoor sports, or studying. With the amazing natural environment, students always have something to do. The nearest ski area is 15 to 30 minutes by car, and those enrolled at the university are given special discounts. In the fall and spring, students enjoy hiking, biking, jogging. Besides skiing, winter activities include trips to the indoor gym facilities of the Adams Center, Shriver Gymnasium, or the Rec Annex to use climbing walls, weight rooms, basketball courts, racquetball courts, exercise rooms, wrestling rooms, and more.

> "The nearest ski area is 15 to 30 minutes by car, and those enrolled at the university are given special discounts."

Besides these weekend activities, other sports activities are also actively pursued. Intramurals are popular, especially softball, soccer, and basketball. Varsity sports are also a big deal at the university. The women's soccer team is very successful, women's basketball has gone to the league tournament for the past three years, and the football team recently won the championship.

Having Fun
One big event of the year is the Montana/Montana State football game. For this game and for all others, the 20,000-capacity Washington-Grizzly Stadium is packed—this is a pretty amazing feat considering that the whole university has less than 15,000 students and the town of Missoula only 50,000 residents. Homecoming weekend, with floats and all draws a crowd. The Forrester's Ball, in which the gym is changed into a mining town, is also popular; party-goers enter the ball through a mine shaft and all drinks or food must be purchased for the price of a kiss.

Other extracurricular activities include Peers Reaching Out, Advocates (a group of student ambassadors to the University), ASUM (the student government), the choir, the band, Greek activities, dance and theater productions, and writing for the *Kaimon* (the university paper that comes out Tuesday through Friday).

On weekend evenings, students either go out to bars, to off-campus parties, or to the alcohol-free Nite Kourt events sponsored by a student organization, Residence Life. These events usually take place once a month and can include free use of the game room, a comedian, a Velcro obstacle course, or a mix and mingle event. University Productions also sponsors small concerts twice a month. Fraternities used to be more of a force at U of M, but since the campus went dry in October of 1996, their parties have died down.

Many other changes are also in the works or have recently taken place, although these are more structural in nature. The Field House was transformed into the Adams Center after a large-scale renovation project in 1999, which included the building of an auxiliary gym, improved seating, a new weight room, and a new training center among others. The completion of the Gallagher Business Building in 1996 provided business students with a spacious home. Renovations in the University Center provided space for more eateries, study lounges, student organization offices, a game room, the women's center, a bank, a post office, a hair salon, a computer store, a travel agency, and a ballroom. Remodeling of the University Theater has benefited both the university and the Missoula community.

Big Sky, Small Town

The university and the town of Missoula are very connected and, as students attest, have an "excellent" relationship. Students see shows at the Montana Repertory Theater or visit the Southgate Mall, while Missoula residents come and see theater and dance productions at the university theater or sporting events at the Adams Center. Many students enjoy Missoula so much that they spend the summer there rafting, kayaking, and hiking.

While most of the undergrads are from Montana, many students come from other parts of the country as well as other parts of the world. The atmosphere is described as liberal, yet diverse, ranging from "cowboys to tree-huggers." The campus has a small minority population and a small but active lesbian/gay population as well. All students interviewed said that the school possessed a great deal of spirit and, as one student said, "You'll see the same student at a sporting event and at an art show. The environment is one of 'pat me on the back, [and I'll] pat you on the back.'" —*Staff*

FYI
The three best things about attending Montana are, "big mountains, laid back people, lots of trails to run on."
The three worst things about attending Montana are "lousy weather, the traffic downtown, loud train whistle."
The three things that every student should do before graduating from Montana are, "smell the fresh air, especially if you're from the east coast, travel abroad, and try the velcro obstacle course."
One thing I'd like to have known before coming here is "how anti-fraternity the administration is."

Nebraska

Creighton University

Address: 200 California Plaza; Omaha, NE 68178-0055
Phone: 402-280-2703
E-mail address: admissions @creighton.edu
Web site URL: www.creighton.edu
Founded: 1878
Private or Public: private
Religious affiliation: Jesuit
Location: urban
Undergraduate enrollment: 3,976
Total enrollment: 6,292
Percent Male/Female: 41%/59%
Percent Minority: 18%

Percent African-American: 3%
Percent Asian: 11%
Percent Hispanic: 3%
Percent Native-American: 1%
Percent in-state/out-of-state: 46%/54%
Percent Pub HS: 53%
Number of Applicants: 3,112
Percent Accepted: 91%
Percent Accepted who enroll: 30%
Entering: 855
Transfers: 147
Application Deadline: 1 Aug
Mean SAT: NA
Mean ACT: 25

Middle 50% SAT range: 520–630 V, 520–650 M
Middle 50% ACT range: 23–28
3 Most popular majors: health professions, business, medical sciences
Retention: 85%
Graduation rate: 57%
On-campus housing: 100%
Fraternities: 26%
Sororities: 25%
Library: 780,000 volumes
Tuition and Fees: $14,910 in; $14,910 out
Room and Board: $5,782
Financial aid, first-year: 60%

When asked to name their favorite aspect of Creighton, students agree on one: the size of the school. They say the small size of the campus and classes make it "easy to get to know your professors and people around you." One student remarked, "When you're in a smaller situation, you're more apt to work in teams." Thanks to its size, a student choosing Creighton can expect a warm atmosphere to go along with a rigorous academic program.

Close Interaction

The relatively small enrollment at Creighton makes small classes and close faculty-student interaction possible. Freshman introductory classes like chemistry and psychology hold between 40 and 60 students, while upper-level classes rarely enroll more than 20. Students say the abundance of personal attention from the faculty is one of Creighton's strong points

and many delight in the fact that their professors actually know their names.

Creighton has three undergraduate schools: the College of Arts and Sciences, the business school, and the nursing school. The business school attracts many students, and the nursing school is said to be "excellent and pretty demanding." Within the College of Arts and Sciences, biology, chemistry, psychology, and education are the most popular majors—each gets high praise. Students have a hard time naming "worst departments," and besides complaints about the lack of a music program, they say they are generally "pretty satisfied" with Creighton's existing majors and departments.

Those interested in the health fields are particularly satisfied at Creighton. According to one student, "If you're interested in health professions, this is the school for you." A great number of students are interested in medicine, dentistry, and nursing.

One student praised the concentration of the student body in the sciences, saying that it allowed him to be "surrounded by people with the same focus, which is important." Many of those who don't go on to medical or dentistry school do graduate work in the sciences.

Academics are described as "competitive" and "challenging, but nothing overly demanding." One student said there are "definitely not any [guts] in the sciences, and most classes are writing-intensive anyway." Another mentioned a gymnastics class as a gut, but on the whole students seem to agree that there are few easy courses.

A Demanding Core Curriculum
A rigid core curriculum exists in the arts and sciences school, which one student said provides "a good base in just about anything." One drawback is that "you're not going to like all the classes you're going to take." To graduate, students must complete 128 credit hours, with 64 of them going toward the core. The core itself is comprised of six classes in theology/philosophy/ethics; six in Culture, Ideas, and Civilizations; two in the natural sciences; two in the behavioral sciences; and five in Skills (English, math, communications). In addition, two intro-level language classes or one higher-level language class is required. The business and nursing schools have different requirements, but all Creighton students, regardless of school, must complete the theology requirement. Some students felt six classes devoted to religion is "a little excessive," while others criticized some of the views taught as "really biased and lame." Defenders of the requirement pointed out that other religions besides Catholicism are covered and maintained that "religion is never forced on anyone."

One disadvantage of Creighton's small size is its small library. A frustrated student complained that "for major research, you have to go elsewhere." To supplement its limited collection, the three-story Reinhart Library participates in an interlibrary loan system, allowing students to gain access to any book in any college within a week or two. Students also praised the librarians for going out of their way to help.

All freshmen and sophomores must live on campus. Of the four dorms, three are coed by floor and the fourth, Deglman, is all-female. One student recommended Deglman to incoming first-year women because "people really get to know each other there." Swanson, "the loudest and dirtiest" dorm, is also the biggest and is known as the party dorm. Another housing option is the small Creighton House, where everyone has his or her own room and takes turns cooking meals. Students also can request to live in specified floors known as the Wellness Community or the Study Community. Study Community floors are meant to be quieter than normal floors, while Wellness Community floors are supposedly substance-free. One freshman living there described the policy as a "joke," however, "because people have beers in their fridges."

For the first two years, undergrads must buy a meal plan. Students eat either in the two main cafeterias or in the Student Center, which houses some fast-food places such as Taco Bell and Godfather's Pizza. When Creighton students want to escape what some feel is the "gross" on-campus food, they frequent such off-campus eateries as Austin's Steakhouse, the Garden Cafe, and TGI Friday's.

Filling Those Extra Hours
Also at the Student Center are fireside chats, held weekly by school president Father Morrison, and Java Joint, coffeehouse sessions where students play blues and drink coffee. On warmer days the grassy mall in the center of campus replaces the Student Center as the main hangout. The mall, which still has train tracks on it from the days trains ran through the campus, is the site of one of the biggest parties of the year. During the first week of the fall term, a stage is set up and a reggae band is brought in for Jamaican Jam. Another popular event is called Dim Wand, the name of a hypnotist who comes to hypnotize the students in his audience. Another unusual, popular activity is The Price Is Right, for which Creighton buses students to the nearby Civic Center to compete in their own version of the television game show. Prizes include trips to New York City, mountain bikes, and color TVs.

Regarding social life, one student reported that "there is always something to do," while another added the corollary that "there's not much to do if you're under 21." Off campus, students like to frequent the historic part of Omaha known as Old Market, where bars, restaurants, and shops line quaint cobblestone streets. Other things to do on a weekend include going to the movies, the bowling alley, or frat parties.

> "Students felt six classes devoted to religion is 'a little excessive,' while others criticized some of the views taught as 'really biased and lame.'"

About one-third of Creighton students participate in the Greek system, but students report there is no pressure to join and no stigma against the non-Greek. Most frat parties are open to all, so independents do not feel excluded. Although some students say Omaha has a high underage drinking rate, the school administration upholds a strict alcohol policy.

Many students also participate in community service activities, especially Habitat for Humanity. With organizations such as Habitat, students take service trips across the country during their vacations. Students also go on weekend spiritual retreats. Those interested in journalism write for the weekly newspaper, the *Creightonian*, or work for JTV, the student-run television station. Those with a literary bent work on *Windows*, a quarterly literary magazine.

Students also participate in Division I sports and intramurals. Creighton has no football team, but as one student said, "soccer and baseball rock here." The women's softball team and the tennis team also do well. Creighton Blue Jay athletes practice and play in the Kiewit Athletic Center, while nonathletes use the Fitness Center connected to the Student Center. "Practically everyone does intramurals," said one undergrad, with volleyball, basketball, and soccer among the most popular.

Many undergrads do not consider Creighton's student body diverse; most people come from the Midwest and only a small percentage come from foreign countries. One student saw the homogeneity as a boost for campus clubs: Multicultural activities are a "big thing just because the school is not very diverse." Regarding the political scene, one undergrad said the campus is "not a political hotbed," adding that views were largely right-leaning. The lack of a pronounced lesbian/gay community at Creighton is consistent with this assessment.

When asked what they would tell high school students thinking of applying to Creighton, students advised a visit to the campus, "because if you don't like Omaha, you will be miserable for a while." Undergrads say the city is boring, and some lament that the campus is "not really pretty because it's in downtown." One good thing about the campus is that it's safe. Students say they feel very safe on campus because "Creighton spares no expense" on security. Guards are said to be "always driving around looking for things to do," and will even drive students anywhere within reason at night. In general, however, students said they would tell high school seniors to apply to Creighton simply because "you get your money's worth" through its tough academic program and lots of personal attention. —*Santosh Aravind and staff*

FYI
The three best things about attending Creighton are "it's easy to get to know your professors, it's the place to be if you're interested in service to others, and we get cool Spring Fling performers like Third Eye Blind, Smashmouth, Goo Goo Dolls, New Radicals, Bush, and Moby."
The three worst things about attending Creighton are "rumors spread quickly, people are cliquish, and lack of school spirit."
The three things that every student should do before graduating from Creighton are "go to the Henry Doorly Zoo (*very* cool rainforest exhibit), go see a Huskers game, and experience a tornado."
One thing I'd like to have known before coming here is "that there's basically no nightlife. Everything closes before midnight."

University of Nebraska / Lincoln

Address: 1410 Q Street; Lincoln, NE 68588-0417
Phone: 402-472-2023
E-mail address: nuhusker@unl.edu
Web site URL: www.unl.edu
Founded: 1869
Private or Public: public
Religious affiliation: none
Location: small city
Undergraduate enrollment: 17,741
Total enrollment: 22,142
Percent Male/Female: 53%/47%
Percent Minority: 7%
Percent African-American: 2%

Percent Asian: 2%
Percent Hispanic: 2%
Percent Native-American: 0.5%
Percent in-state/out-of-state: 74%/26%
Percent Pub HS: NA
Number of Applicants: 6,977
Percent Accepted: 92%
Percent Accepted who enroll: 57%
Entering: 3,673
Transfers: NA
Application Deadline: 30 Jun
Mean SAT: NA
Mean ACT: NA

Middle 50% SAT range: 500–630 V, 510–660 M
Middle 50% ACT range: 21–27
3 Most popular majors: NA
Retention: 79%
Graduation rate: 45%
On-campus housing: NA
Fraternities: 18%
Sororities: 16%
Library: 2,278,154 volumes
Tuition and Fees: $3,278 in; $7,785 out
Room and Board: $4,070
Financial aid, first-year: 61%

With three national titles in the past ten years, University of Nebraska at Lincoln Cornhuskers pride themselves on their football dynasty. While many other large state universities boast of powerhouse programs and dedicated fans, those unfamiliar with Nebraska cannot fully appreciate the magnitude of Husker spirit. Said one student "It's like religion here, on game days Memorial Stadium becomes the third largest city in Nebraska, and if by chance we lose the entire state needs anti-depressants!" Another noted that "At Nebraska there are four seasons of sport. In the fall is football season. The winter is football recruiting season, followed by spring football practice. Lastly comes summer and general anticipation of the coming fall! Isn't it great?"

Colleges, TAs, and Honors

While most UNL students will tell you that the football team is close to perfection, many feel that university academics are in need of some more coaching. Nebraska is divided into nine different academic colleges: the College of Agricultural Sciences & Natural Resources, the College of Arch- itecture, the College of Arts & Sciences, the College of Business Administration, the College of Engineering & Technology, the College of Fine & Performing Arts, the College of Human Resources & Family Sciences, the College of Journalism & Mass Communication, and the Teacher's College. Each college offers a variety of majors totaling 149 in all, and ranging from Grazing Livestock Systems to Pre-Nuclear Medicine. Students feel that the large selection of majors encourages everyone to find a course of study they enjoy, but also note that overly easy majors abound. Slackers avoid any hard sciences, but find refuge in the Communication Studies, Business Administration, and Fishery and Wildlife departments. Grading is known to be "a little too nice to the student," and one student summed up the workload by saying, "It's definitely harder than high-school, but never unreasonable."

Big lecture classes at UNL seldom exceed an enrollment of 150, and students seem content with class sizes. Said one junior, "at the lower levels the classes are small enough to get to know the teacher but too big to know everybody in the class; but as you get more into your major the numbers go down." Students report that professors are friendly and accessible, but only to students who make the effort to meet them. Conversely, students are critical of TAs, many of whom cannot speak English. One sophomore estimated that ten percent of Nebraska's TAs aren't capable of teaching class, and two others mentioned that they are failing classes specifically because their TAs do not understand English. Said one: "If my TA didn't understand a word on my exam he would count it wrong."

On the upside, Huskers seeking a more challenging academic environment may choose to participate in the University Honors Program. Incoming freshmen are considered for the program based on their ACT/SAT scores, and their high school grades and curriculum. Once enrolled, they enjoy smaller classes and work directly with top faculty members. The program culminates in a senior thesis, and along the way honors students have access to special housing in Neihardt Hall and exclusive honors computer centers.

Dry? Who's Dry?
Because most UNL students live in Nebraska, many report going home on weekends to visit with high school friends and to get laundry done. Others caution that this does not mean UNL is a boring place to be once classes end. On the contrary, Huskers find each other extremely friendly and enjoy their social scene. Officially, UNL is a dry campus, but students don't have much difficulty in finding alcohol. Because of the dry campus rule, most underclassmen choose to party in off-campus apartments or at the fraternity houses, while upperclassmen frequent the bars of downtown Lincoln. The Greek system maintains such a strong presence on campus that many students consider the campus stereotype to be that everyone is Greek. Fraternities host many of the year's biggest parties, with themes such as "Gilligan's Island" and "Grease." Those who aren't members of a fraternity or sorority don't seem to mind their social alternatives however, and the Greek system isn't considered exclusive by non-Greeks.

Nebraska's size affords students with a wealth of clubs and extracurricular organizations in which to participate. Govern-

mental and political organizations, ethnic clubs, and sports and recreational teams provide Huskers with outlets for every kind of creative, athletic or community service oriented student.

Once again, football's role in the social scene at UNL cannot be understated. Nothing brings out the Nebraska faithful in greater numbers than a Saturday morning tailgate, as Huskers of all ages intermingle in support of their common cause. As one female student noted, "I don't even especially like football, but going to a Husker home game is an experience not to be missed."

Dorming and Dining
UNL requires its freshmen to live in one of the 12 university residence halls, but students don't have many complaints about dorm-room quality. All residence halls are either single-sex or coed by floor, and provide students with amenities such as high-speed Internet access, cable, and air-conditioning. Different residence halls make up larger communities, which feature dining and laundry facilities, computer labs, and recreational areas. Halls are staffed by RAs, who help younger students with academic questions and encourage dorm residents to get involved in different campus activities. Different halls cater to different groups of students and hold somewhat different reputations. Abel and Sandoz accommodate mostly freshman students. Sandoz is all female, while Abel is coed and known as the party dorm. Cather and Pound are coed halls reserved for upper-class students, and offer their residents laundry and computer facilities on every floor. Love Hall offers its 46 female residents a co-op atmosphere in which they share household responsibilities and costs.

> "I don't even especially like football, but going to a Husker home game is an experience not to be missed."

One student summed up dining at Nebraska by saying "to be honest, it's a far cry from mom's home-cooking, but it's bearable." Dining hall food is labeled as "boring," and students make comments like "how many times in a week do they expect us to eat spaghetti?" On the plus side, Huskers on a meal plan have the option of eating at any one of the campus' dining halls, and their Student ID cards double as charge cards for between-meal snacks. Vegetarian options are plentiful, yet equally unimaginative. For those who wish to eat out, downtown Lincoln offers virtually every type of fare, from fast food to popular restaurants like Old Chicago and Carlos O'Kelley's. One particular section of the city, known as the Haymarket, is especially liked by students, who mention it as a great place to take a date on a stroll or for a cup of coffee at The Mill.

Two Campuses, One Union

UNL's campus is divided into two sections. Most departments reside on City Campus, while the agriculture and home economics schools inhabit East Campus. Shuttle buses run between the two sections, but students are often labeled as either "frat boys or sorority girls" on City and "hicks" on East. Active students enjoy the Lee Sapp Recreational Center for its indoor climbing wall, racquetball and basketball courts, weight room and two indoor tracks. They can also watch the men's and women's varsity basketball teams take on their Big 12 rivals in the Devaney Sports Center. Students looking for a cultural experience can also benefit from the Lied Center for Performing Arts, a 150,000 square foot performance house that has hosted such notables as the Philadelphia Orchestra and the Broadway musical "Les Miserables."

The university's social center is undoubtedly the Nebraska Union, which contains the University Bookstore and the offices of the school paper the *Daily Nebraskan*. Renovated and expanded in 1998, the Union now contains a convenience store, big-screen television lounge and game room in its basement, and an art lounge, computer room, copy shop and large auditorium on its first and second floors. These new additions combined with a popular food court make the Union one of UNL's most popular attractions.

Cornhusker Spirit!

When asked what building on their campus is most impressive, Huskers routinely answer "Memorial Stadium, of course!" With the addition of $40 million worth of skyboxes for the 1999 football season, Memorial Stadium is the pride of many a Nebraskan, just like the team itself. While football may be a rallying point for school spirit, Huskers are quick to add that "Pride in this school comes from living in such a clean, safe, and beautiful environment . . . football just helps us express our feelings!" If enjoying their football prowess is truly an indication of how Huskers delight in their school, then the University of Nebraska is certainly a great place to be. —*Robert Berschinski*

FYI
The three best things about attending the University of Nebraska are "Husker Spirit, small town students, and the student to teacher ratio."
The three worst things about attending the University of Nebraska are "Cold Nebraska winters, the parking situation, and the separate campuses."
The three things that every student should do before graduating from the University of Nebraska are "go to a Husker game, meet new people, and realize that the greatest days of your life will be spent at UNL."
One thing I'd like to have known before coming here is "I would have liked to have seen more of the dorms before I had to choose one."

Nevada

University of Nevada / Reno

Address: Mail Stop 120;
  Reno, NV 8957
Phone: 775-784-6865
E-mail address:
  unrug@unr.edu
Web site URL: www.unr.edu
Founded: 1874
Private or Public: public
Religious affiliation:
  none
Location: small city
**Undergraduate
  enrollment:** 8,818
Total enrollment: 12,532
Percent Male/Female:
  45%/55%
Percent Minority: 15%
Percent African-American:
  2%

Percent Asian: 6%
Percent Hispanic: 5%
Percent Native-American:
  2%
**Percent in-state/out-of-
  state:** 80%/20%
Percent Pub HS: 93%
Number of Applicants:
  2,903
Percent Accepted:
  91%
**Percent Accepted who
  enroll:** 59%
Entering: 1,548
Transfers: 953
Application Deadline:
  rolling
Mean SAT: 518 V, 525 M
Mean ACT: 22

Middle 50% SAT range:
  460–570 V,
  470–580 M
Middle 50% ACT range:
  20–25
3 Most popular majors:
  elementary education,
  psychology, biology
Retention: 78%
Graduation rate: 44%
On-campus housing: 49%
Fraternities: 9%
Sororities: 6%
Library: 956,282 volumes
Tuition and Fees:
  $2,454 in; $9,434 out
Room and Board: $5,400
Financial aid, first-year:
  70%

Picture a university with a low-key atmosphere and very reasonable tuition set against the mountains of Nevada. This is UNR, a Nevada state university that educates both fraternity brothers and senior citizens alike.

Oodles of Colleges

Ten colleges comprise UNR: agriculture, arts and sciences, business administration, education, engineering, human and community sciences, college of extended studies, journalism, mining, and nursing. Students select their college as sophomores, but they can take classes in any field regardless of their year. The School of Journalism, among the strongest of all the colleges, maintains a faculty including Pulitzer Prize-winning alumni. The School of Engineering also draws raves from students: "Engineering, especially mechanical engineering, is just great. All of my teachers have been really interesting."

A newly implemented core curriculum includes "Western Traditions." All students must complete classes that, together, present a broad overview of Western history, philosophy, and literature. One student complained that Western Tradition classes demand "way too much reading, sometimes 200 or 300 plus pages a week." Another student believed that "understanding our Western tradition is important for anyone living in a Western society like ours." Aside from Western traditions, students must take two to three upper-level, interdisciplinary "Capstone" courses.

Students herald the UNR Honors Program. Honors students have smaller classes; one student said that her psychology honors class had only 30 students, as opposed to the typical 150. Honors students may choose to live in honors housing, which lodges men and women in different buildings, claims 24-hour quiet periods, and offers restored buildings with "very comfortable" suites. Only honors students can graduate with Greek distinction of either magna cum laude or summa cum laude.

An Older Student Body

The average age of the UNR student is 26, and the undergraduate population includes a large number of people from the community, including senior citizens and those who have returned to school several years after high school. Many UNR students work during the day and commute at night. Older undergrads reportedly "make other students work harder because they tend to ruin class curves." However, older students "have real-world knowledge of what we're only seeing in the classroom," explains one engineering major. "I mostly benefit from having them here."

> **"Many UNR students work during the day and commute at night."**

Despite its proximity to many strip clubs only one county away, UNR attracts a rather conservative student body. "Most of the people who have political interests are Republicans," explains one junior. Students at UNR are also ethnically and racially homogeneous. "My high school was more diverse," complained one student. Most students are Nevada natives or Californians looking to "escape the UC system," as one said. (Through a "good neighbor" policy, Californians can attend UNR for a lower tuition than they would pay at a University of California school.) Regardless of age, most UNR students choose to live off campus; even freshmen are not required to live on campus. Those who stay on campus live in the Manzanita, Juniper, Canada, Nye, White Pine, or Lincoln dorms.

Students describe the campus as "pretty and clean." The redbrick buildings and bell tower on the main quad draw praise from students: "The older brick buildings are a refreshing change from the '70s and '80s concrete you see everywhere else."

'Thletes and Greeks

Huge, beer-laden tailgates and rowdiness accompany football games, which are always well attended. The swim team usually wins its conference, and the boxing team is nationally recognized. UNR has recently joined the Big West division, home of archrival University of Nevada/Las Vegas. Intramural sports are popular as well.

Despite small membership, fraternities and sororities maintain a strong social presence. Greek parties are popular, and non-Greeks can attain invitations easily. Because of alcohol regulations, dorm parties are rare, but parties in apartments around campus are common. The campus coffeehouse and local bowling alleys offer non-drinking options. However, commuters tend to participate in life less than those living at UNR, and older students normally avoid the UNR party scene. Many students believe that "a fake ID is a must." Local bars like the Beer Barrel and Little Waldorf are popular hangouts, while casinos attract student gamblers. Concerts with local bands always bring in large numbers, while some students frequent nearby Lake Tahoe and its ski slopes.

UNR has an exciting social scene, and its reputation is growing as its low tuition brings out-of-staters to the campus. Students say they're pleased to be getting such a well-rounded education in a relaxed setting. —*Brian Abaluck and Staff*

FYI
The three best things about attending UNR are "the low cost of tuition, the flexibility of class scheduling, and the many colleges."

The three worst things about attending UNR are "the disunited student body, the lack of diversity, and the lack of campus-sponsored activity."

The three things every student should do before graduating from UNR are "go to Lake Tahoe for a weekend, go to a football game against the University of Nevada/Las Vegas, and get some real-world experience."

One thing I wish I'd known before coming to UNR is "the strongly Republican bent of the student body."

New Hampshire

Dartmouth College

Address: 6016 McNutt Hall; Hanover, NH 03755
Phone: 603-646-2875
E-mail address: admissions.office@dartmouth.edu
Web site URL: www.dartmouth.edu
Founded: 1769
Private or Public: private
Religious affiliation: none
Location: rural
Undergraduate enrollment: 3,998
Total enrollment: 5,308
Percent Male / Female: 52% / 48%
Percent Minority: 22%
Percent African-American: 5%

Percent Asian: 10%
Percent Hispanic: 5%
Percent Native-American: 2%
Percent in-state / out-of-state: 3% / 97%
Percent Pub HS: 66%
Number of Applicants: 10,259
Percent Accepted: 21%
Percent Accepted who enroll: 50%
Entering: 1,056
Transfers: 25
Application Deadline: 1 Apr
Mean SAT: 713 V, 713 M
Mean ACT: NA

Middle 50% SAT range: 670–770 V, 680–760 M
Middle 50% ACT range: 28–33
3 Most popular majors: biology, government, economics
Retention: NA
Graduation rate: 94%
On-campus housing: 100%
Fraternities: 48%
Sororities: 40%
Library: NA
Tuition and Fees: $25,653 in; $25,653 out
Room and Board: $7,557
Financial aid, first-year: NA

O n the edge of New Hampshire, bordering Vermont, lies a small college town along the Connecticut River. The students at this college in Hanover have access to more outdoor activities than one can imagine. They can be routinely found canoeing, kayaking, and swimming on the river during the spring and summer months and ice-skating on the pond during the winter. Surrounded by beautiful mountains to the north, this college even has its own ski lodge and slopes, open to its students. In the autumn, leaf-peepers flock here to admire the colorful foliage and hike along the Appalachian Trail. With so much beauty in their world, one wonders how these students are able to take it all in and still have time to study. To outsiders, this picturesque setting may appear to be an unlikely location to host an institution of higher learning. To those who've been here and who've studied here, this is the *perfect* place.

Welcome to Dartmouth.

Green Ivy

You know how everyone you know in high school—guidance counselors, teachers, parents, and the like—tells you that college is going to be easier than high school? Well, the students at Dartmouth College don't seem to agree. Many students commented that classes are rigorous and fast-paced and the "workload is pretty steep," since each quarter is only 10 weeks long. This unique academic schedule, known as the Dartmouth Plan, divides the school year into fall, winter, spring, and summer quarters. Students choose to study during any three of the four terms each year and are required to remain on campus for three terms during their first and last years, as well as during their sophomore summer. One perk of the system, however, is that they only enroll in three courses per term.

All of the classes at Dartmouth are taught by professors, and students praise the "close interaction" and attention they receive. However, some lament the fact that the new administration has recently placed a greater emphasis on research rather than teaching. The result is that "newer profs really suck in comparison to the older profs, who still believe that they are teachers first and researchers second." Teaching assistants are usually students who have previously enrolled in a particular class and help the professor grade papers. The quality of the TA can vary greatly; luckily, many classes don't even make use of them.

Several students singled out Education 20: Educational Issues in Contemporary Society as a "life-changing" course, "one of those hardest classes you'll ever love." It is enormously popular every year, drawing over 200 students and a wait-list for enrollment. Guest speakers from all facets of education are invited to lecture on various issues; past speakers include inner-city teachers, school superintendents, and even the student-body president of a local high school. The education department faculty is known for holding "lively and fun, interactive courses." Prof. Andrew Garrod impressed his students by learning the names of all 200 students in his lecture and ran the class like a "discussion seminar, calling on students by name."

Other prominent professors include psych professor Rogers Elliott, who has "been here forever," English professor Peter Saccio, who can "make anybody love Shakespeare," Thomas Cormen, a popular and "brilliant computer scientist," and psych professor Robert Kleck, whose experiments have been repeated on *Oprah*. John Rassias in the French and Italian departments is well known for developing new methods of teaching language, in which students meet in a small group with a professor or TA during a "drill" session,

a "fast-paced daily speaking practice session" that promotes quick thinking.

One biology major commented that "it's a lot harder to get an A in science and math courses than in English and history." A history major corroborated this claim by admitting that "there is some grade inflation in the humanities." Though Dartmouth academic departments are strong all-around, international relations, biology, chemistry, dance, and foreign languages are tops.

One of Dartmouth's strengths is its commitment to study abroad programs. To fulfill the foreign language requirement, students can opt to go on an LSA (Language Study Abroad), in which they take classes abroad, studying with both Dartmouth and local professors while living with host families. Another option is to participate in one of over 40 different FSPs (Foreign Study Programs), where students will explore a particular field in an ideal location for study. For instance, there are programs in coral reef ecology in Jamaica, rain forest ecology in Costa Rica, and colonial literature in Trinidad, to name just a few.

Life's a Party; Drink It Up!

In Hanover, "people tend to drink at the frats on weekends. Aside from that, they do whatever it is that people do," observed one student. The college sponsors various social alternatives to partying on Webster Avenue (aka Frat Row), such as dance parties, fun fairs, and fake casinos, but with poor attendance these "haven't exactly been all that the administration had hoped." There are no bars in Hanover, though it does have a dance club called Poison Ivy, which students don't seem to care for. There's no doubt about it—the social life at Dartmouth revolves around the Greek system, which became the inspiration for the 1978 film *Animal House*, co-written by Dartmouth alumnus Christian Miller, '62. Today, Theta Delta Chi hosts a toga party each spring.

"The whole *Animal House* rep is not entirely false," noted one student; "a lot of people drink a lot of alcohol every weekend," though another is quick to claim that "we're no better or worse than any other college in the nation." At Dartmouth, 60% of the eligible undergraduate population (non-freshmen) are members of a Greek house. Underage drinking is prevalent on campus and never a problem for those who wish to drink, though they may encounter a limited selection—"you must like beast from the keg," one senior warned. With regard to peer pressure to drink, one sorority member said, "If you're willing to hang out with drinkers and just not drink, people love you. If you aren't comfortable being around people who are drinking, though, I could see there being problems." A male student corroborated this claim by observing, "Non-drinkers may feel out of place."

Two years ago, the administration launched the Student Life Initiative, an attempt at "reimagining the campus environment" in terms of social and residential life. So far, in an effort to reform the Greek organizations, permanent taps and large refrigeration units have already been eliminated, while stricter drug and alcohol policies are still under consideration. The college hopes to de-emphasize Greek life by organizing and building new residential dorm "clusters," groups of dormitory buildings connected by common areas, which they hope will foster a sense of community and continuity as the center of a student's residential life experience.

Perhaps these clusters will also help revive the dormant love lives of Dartmouth students. "When you don't have time to sleep, do you really think you are going to have time to date?" asked one senior. Most students agree that not a lot of dating goes on. Granted, there are a few successful relationships and "virtually married couples," but the majority of students don't go out on dates. Even if they wanted to go out, the fact that they live in Hanover doesn't help their cause. "There really isn't anywhere to go unless you have a car, because the closest activities are twenty minutes away," one student complained.

Students also blame the Greek system, because it fosters the kind of environment where guys are able to just stay at their house and wait for the girls to go to their parties. "Then, these little nerdy high school boys never learn about asking girls out, the girls get frustrated, and everyone just vents their sexual frustration through random hookups," a senior said. Random hookups are so prevalent that students often describe relationships on campus as "six degrees of hookup," meaning everybody knows everybody else through, at most, six different hookup occasions.

The college hosts four big weekend events each year, one during each semester. In the fall, during Homecoming weekend, freshmen build a 70-tier bonfire in the center of the Green and then take part in the Freshmen Sweep, where they run around the fire the same number of times as their class year—the Class of '05 will run 105 laps. Winter term brings Winter Carnival, and along with it come free ski days at the Dartmouth Skiway, sledding on the golf course, a polar bear swim at Occum Pond, and the construction of a snow sculpture on the Green.

The Green Key Society, an organization that works on various community service projects at Dartmouth and in Hanover, hosts Green Key weekend in the spring term, when bands will often come to campus for an all-day party. Summer term has Tubestock, which is the highlight of the sophomore summer. During this event, the Connecticut River gets filled with students with inner tubes, floats, or whatever inflatable devices they happen to find.

Students say dance troupes and a cappella singing groups are quite popular, although the Dartmouth Outing Club (DOC) has the most members of any student organization on campus. Some project that approximately 80% of the undergraduate population have gone on a trip with the DOC. After spending so much time with the naturel world, it's no wonder that these students often find themselves streaking and swimming au naturel. "People are very open about nudity and sexuality, but not really in a disgusting way," said a biology major. The Ledyard Challenge consists of jumping into the Connecticut River at the Ledyard Canoe Club, swimming across to Vermont, and running back across the bridge to the club—all done naked and without getting caught.

Closet Nerds

At Dartmouth, "the thing everyone is always remarking on is how smart they never guessed their classmates were." To an outsider, the students here never appear to study much, and yet they still do well in their courses. But the students know that this is because all the studying is done independently, behind closed doors. "They don't engage in boasting games of who has more work to do, but rather act like the three hundred pages of dense science reading and the twenty-page paper they did last night were nothing. It's poor form here to complain about how much work you have to do," warned a senior.

Students describe the typical Dartmouth student as a white upper-class prep-schooler from "just outside of Boston" who wears a North Face jacket over an Abercrombie shirt and Gap jeans. A sophomore observed that "there is a BIG line between [socioeconomic] classes here, noticeable in who joins the Greek system" and to which house they belong. In terms of diversity, a history major commented, "It's somewhat homogenous, but not really, probably whiter than most Ivies." Indeed, three-quarters of the student population are Caucasian, though students say the school has been actively recruiting more Native American and international students recently. One complaint voiced by students is that "there is a lot of conformity once students arrive here. Everyone comes in with lofty aspirations and unique traits, but leaves 'Dartmouthized.'"

For a school full of "nerds in high school who tried to cover for being smart by being jocks," sports don't seem to attract much fan support at games, except for the football games during Homecoming weekend. The administration keeps pushing Harvard as the principal rival, though students say that "you can never get a seat at a Dartmouth-Princeton game and the biggest hijinks always occur at these games." The most popular and well attended games are for Dartmouth's ice hockey team, which is one of the best in the country. Women's ice hockey, field hockey, and lacrosse also fare well in their leagues.

For the rest of the students, the Kresge Fitness Center is, as one student put it bluntly, "surprisingly bad." The facility does not have adequate equipment or machinery to accommodate the enormous demand by students, strange in light of the fact that Dartmouth requires its students to pass a swim test in order to graduate and also has a mandatory three-term physical education requirement. Many students also participate in intramurals, putting together teams made up of groups of friends, club members, or frat brothers.

The Big Green

Students describe the Dartmouth campus as "classic New England—red-brick buildings" covered in ivy, situated among open green spaces and lots of trees. All of the buildings are centered on the town Green, enclosed by Baker Library at one end and the Hopkins Arts Center at the other. Also noteworthy are Kiewit, the nine-story underground computer center, and Berry Library, a new addition to famous Baker Library. Berry contains a large collection of books, as well as "a lot of great study spaces," and a media center capable of creating all types of interesting projects.

The "River" dorms and the Choates (which students refer to as the "Chetto") house most of the freshmen, since they have smaller doubles and an ugly facade, which makes them undesirable to upperclassmen. The River dorms in particular are the farthest from central campus, forcing students who live there to "walk twenty minutes uphill every day just to eat." In terms of location, one upperclassmen said, "Mass Row is where it's at"—step outside these dorms and you're in front of the dining hall and classrooms. Others flock to the East Wheelock cluster, which is Dartmouth's experiment to replicate the residential experience found in Harvard's House system and Yale's Residential Colleges. To promote bonding among students, the cluster hosts special activities, panel discussions, and even trips to Boston and Montreal throughout the school year. Though farther from the dining halls, the cluster features its own snack bar, which serves the same "full range of grill food as one of the dining halls." The rooms in East Wheelock are much larger, with two to four singles attached to a common room and a private bathroom.

All of the dorms at Dartmouth are coed; a few have single-sex floors, but most floors are coed (with single-sex bathrooms). Students say that only about 10% of the population choose to move off-campus and most off-campus housing is so close that "they're practically still on campus." One alternative to Dartmouth housing is a fraternity, sorority, or coed house. Because Hanover is a small town, you won't find any apartment complexes near campus, although students will often rent a house with a group of five or six friends, the cost of which is comparable to what they would pay for boarding at Dartmouth otherwise. One bonus, however, is that they get to give their house a cool name like the "Love Shack" or the "River Ranch."

At Dartmouth, everyone always talks about "how smart they never guessed their classmates were."

Safety on campus has generally never been an issue. Being in such a rural location, "you're more likely to be attacked by a rabid squirrel than be the victim of a crime." Another student echoed these feelings by adding, "There's hardly any crime, and when there is, it's usually on big weekends when tons of people pour into Hanover and it's harder to keep track of outsiders." This mind-set, as well as safety procedures and precautions, may be about to change. In January 2001, two Dartmouth professors were the victims of a double homicide, which took place in their home, just four miles from the center of campus. Still, students appear confident that this is not the beginning of a crime trend of any sort. The last murder that occurred in Dartmouth was in 1991, the one before that in 1948.

The on-campus meal plan received relatively high marks from students, who, after freshmen year, have a choice of meal plans ranging from $450 to $1,200 (with $750 as the typical plan). The four main dining halls (each with a different atmosphere and focus) are cafeteria-style, so that you pay only for what you eat. "It's great because you're not restricted to eating during certain hours and food is available from seven A.M. to one A.M. every day," raved a sophomore. Among students, Homeplate, where healthy food is served, is a favorite. In addition to the dining halls, students are welcome to use their cards to eat at various other smaller cafés on campus, such as Collis Cafe, which serves excellent homemade fruit smoothies, stir-fry, omelets, and baked goods, and the Big Green Bean, a coffeehouse. Despite this, one student felt that "we do not have enough places to eat—every night the dining halls are packed." For off-campus fare, EBA's (Everything But Anchovies') pizza is a late-night staple, delivered until 2:15 A.M. Students also recommend Panda House, which is relatively inexpensive for going out with friends.

The Good Life

Oh, the places you'll go after Dartmouth. Theodor Geisel graduated in 1925 and went on to become a popular children's book writer, under the pseudonym "Dr. Seuss." Dr. Seuss is remembered on the freshmen outdoor orientation trips sponsored by the DOC, when the Moosilauke Lodge crew serves green eggs and ham for breakfast on the last day. The college also counts Daniel Webster, poet Robert Frost, former vice president Nelson Rockefeller, and former U.S. Surgeon General C. Everett Coop among its notable alumni. Today, Dartmouth graduates are involved in government, law, medicine, banking, and consulting. A diploma from Dartmouth is often seen as a ticket to the good life.

Students at Dartmouth bleed green. One lamented, "Four years is not enough time to do all there is to do here. I'm a senior, and the mere thought of leaving makes me want to break down and cry." In the famous Dartmouth College Case argued before the U.S. Supreme Court, Daniel Webster remarked, "It is but a small school, sir, and yet there are those who love it . . ." And love it they do.—*Christopher Au*

FYI
The three best things about attending Dartmouth are "the incredible professors, blitzmail system (pager, phone, IM, and E-mail all in one!), and the endless opportunities to study abroad."
The three worst things about attending Dartmouth are "isolation from the world, picking classes, because the registrar's office always makes mistakes and they never know the criteria for getting into each department's courses, and Mud Season (when all the snow melts and there's mud for about a month)."

The three things every student should do before graduating from Dartmouth are "hike around the gorgeous mountains with the Dartmouth Outing Club (DOC), participate in a Foreign Study Program (FSP), run around the Homecoming bonfire as a freshman."

One thing I'd like to have known before coming here is "to bring some funky or sketchy clothes, because a lot of parties are themed and you'll always find a use for anything from a thrift shop."

University of New Hampshire

Address: 4 Garrison Avenue; Durham, NH 03824
Phone: 603-862-1360
E-mail address: admissions@unh.edu
Web site URL: www.unh.edu
Founded: 1866
Private or Public: public
Religious affiliation: none
Location: rural
Undergraduate enrollment: 10,215
Total enrollment: 12,454
Percent Male/Female: 41%/59%
Percent Minority: 3%

Percent African-American: 0.5%
Percent Asian: 1%
Percent Hispanic: 0.5%
Percent Native-American: 0.5%
Percent in-state/out-of-state: 60%/40%
Percent Pub HS: 84%
Number of Applicants: 8,833
Percent Accepted: 81%
Percent Accepted who enroll: 36%
Entering: 2,573
Transfers: 702
Application Deadline: 15 Feb
Mean SAT: 554 V, 560 M
Mean ACT: NA

Middle 50% SAT range: 510–600 V, 510–610 M
Middle 50% ACT range: NA
3 Most popular majors: psychology, business, biology
Retention: 82%
Graduation rate: 49%
On-campus housing: NA
Fraternities: 10%
Sororities: 10%
Library: 1,000,000 volumes
Tuition and Fees: $7,395 in; $16,465 out
Room and Board: $5,154
Financial aid, first-year: 35%

Set in the beautiful White Mountains, the University of New Hampshire boasts a "laid-back and casual atmosphere." Professors are approachable and students praise campus life. "There are a ton of different people here so everyone can find a group that they fit in with," explained one undergrad. But UNH isn't just peaceful mountain vistas. "The students go crazy for hockey," said one student. "We put on curly wigs and face paint. Every time a goal is scored for us, a song starts overhead, and people wave their hands in the air; it's a real fun time." UNH provides a dynamic balance between a laid-back environment in a rural New England town with warm, passionate people, and a lot of fun.

Another Business Major?

Students at UNH agreed that classes are "what you make of them." Business is the most popular major on campus. "Many business majors at UNH either chose business because they couldn't think of anything else, or because they dropped their first major and ended up in business," explained one undergrad. Students also praised the English department, and said the engineering department is "one of the world's best kept secrets." Students who do choose engineering find that the major is incredibly demanding. "They do a really thorough job teaching—you are initially told that it may take you five years to complete the major," said one undergrad.

Regardless of which major students choose, General Education (GenEd) requirements force undergrads to take classes in eight specific knowledge areas. One sophomore complained, "Personally, I feel they're stupid, and I'd rather not deal with them. I'm taking a mythology course I'll never use." But some students do feel that GenEds serve their intended purpose. "They can be a pain in the butt to schedule, but they break the monotony of taking major classes. I would have perished if I were stuck doing only math and computer science classes at UNH and not taken other interesting classes, like theatre and English," acknowledged one undergrad. Introductory GenEd classes are usually the largest on campus, but class size wasn't viewed as a problem by most, since more advanced courses are generally quite small.

Students consider their instructors very approachable. Professors encourage their students to get to know them better, making themselves available in person and through email. "I am in some pretty big classes, but you can still get to know the professors," said one undergrad. UNH has other resources for academic help, including a writing center, where graduate students assist undergrads with essays and other assignments.

Students study mostly in libraries and their dorm rooms. In 1998, UNH opened the newly renovated multi-million dollar Diamond Library, which is "so nice, it makes you want to study." In addition, there are a number of specialized branch libraries, such as the Bio-Sciences Library in Kendall Hall, which offer good places to study if the dorm gets too loud.

Eating and Sleeping

UNH sprawls over nearly 200 acres of land, featuring courtyards, grassy areas, and a traditional New England feel. The campus is split into four regions with three dorm areas and one area of on-campus apartments. Underclassmen usually live in the dorms, where there are two Residential Advisors (RAs) per floor. RAs are not disciplinarians, but they enforce some rules and seek help when students are in trouble. "My RA is strict when she needs to be," said one undergrad, "but she definitely has time to be our friend." The largest dorm on campus is Stoke Hall, housing nearly 600 students. Stoke, like other dorms, has outdoor volleyball and basketball courts, a new recreation room with a ping-pong table, a snack bar, and a 24 hour quiet study lounge. Mini-dorms, six small themed houses in a circular drive, offer an alternative housing option. Students apply for mini-dorms based on special interests such as the creative and performing arts, out-

door experience, academic awareness, or science and engineering. The themes allow students to immerse themselves in a particular interest and get to know others students with similar ideas.

Many upperclassmen chose not to live in the dorms. The school owns three on-campus apartment buildings: Gabbs, Woodside and Forest Park Apartments. Students can also choose to move off campus, either to a fraternity or sorority house, to Durham, or nearby towns. However, those who bring cars warn of "Parking Services and their psycho ticket-giving lackeys" and the difficulty in finding parking. Explained one undergrad, "the parking situation for commuters has almost come down to a blood sport!"

> "The whole campus turns into a pack of animals clutching beers and running all over the town of Durham."

Students love chickwiches, which are available at one of the 3 dining halls on campus. One student explained, "It's like a hamburger, except with chicken." The food is described as "pretty fattening," but students admit there is a decent variety, and vegetarians say they have plenty of choice in the dining hall. Freshmen are required to have a meal plan, which includes 19 meals per week. Students can also use their meal plan to get up to $5 toward food at the Memorial Union Building (MUB), the student union center, instead of eating a meal in one of the dining halls. MUB has some classic fast food chains, such as Papa Gino's Pizza, Taco Bell and DeAngelo's Subs. During lunch and prime time, transfer meals can be eaten at the Wildcattesen, a food court under one of the dining halls. There, students can eat pizza, subs, or even made-to-order Asian food.

Small Town Living

UNH is located in Durham, a typical New England small town with a non-student population of around 13,000. "Durham is a small 'main street' town," explained one undergrad. "There are two bars, a few take out-pizza places, two restaurants, two coffee, shops, one grocery store . . . you get the picture." There are some common student hangouts in Durham, including Mike Libby's bar, where every Tuesday night is nickel draft night. "Vegetarians should definitely try a falafel at Aladdin's Pocket, located inside the Laundromat," said one undergrad. The Licker Store, an ice cream and coffee shop, is also popular with students, featuring "really good iced coffee shakes," and a day-old bin full of muffins and pastries for the student on a budget. Students who find the town dull have many other options. Undergrads hang out at the MUB, and an on-campus movie theater plays 3 or 4 movies a week. Students also enjoy the newly renovated Whittenmore Center, a sports complex with basketball courts, indoor running tracks, and exercise equipment.

UNH students pride themselves on being active, and with regard to extracurricular activities, "there is something for everyone." Clubs range from singing groups and community service, to an Outing Club, which takes trips white water rafting and hiking. The student-run radio station, WUNH, is a 6000-watt non-commercial radio station that plays music before it hits the mainstream. And, thanks to the Internet, WUNH has "listeners in Australia, Finland, Florida, and Boston." For live entertainment, students turn to the Paul Creative Arts Center, where student theater and music groups frequently perform.

For those who still want to get off campus, the school provides a free bus service, Wildcat Transit, which takes students to the city of Portsmouth, only 10 minutes away. In the warm months, students go hiking or head to the beach, and in the winter, UNH is perfectly located for the weekend skier. There are numerous local ski resorts, and Killington, one of the country's best ski resorts, is less than 3 hours away.

Weekends start on Thursday nights. UNH tries to maintain a dry campus, so parties involving alcohol are at fraternities or off-campus apartments. "The authorities are pretty strict about drugs and alcohol in the dorms," said one student, "but no one gets caught if it's at a party." The frat scene is loud with music and dancing, and those who want to go to a "chill party," head to house parties in Newmarket or hang out in the Gables, the on-campus apartments. School sponsored activities, such as hypnotists, outdoor movies, game shows, and swing dancing lessons, are popular, and national bands often stop at UNH arena, including such headliners as the Dave Matthews Band.

Hockey is a great unifier on campus. Quite simply, "hockey rules." Even those who hate the sport admit that everyone at UNH gets involved during hockey season. "The whole campus turns into a pack of animals clutching beers and running all over the town of Durham," explained one undergrad. "They have huge bonfires and go insane. It's interesting to watch." In recent years, the Wildcats have contended for the NCAA title, and UNH fans often lead the Hockey East Conference in attendance. Bizarre traditions accompany the general pandemonium during the games. "During every game, after our first goal, someone throws a big fish on the ice," explained one student.

The flying fish at hockey games might seem out of place in a peaceful New England town like Durham, but UNH is more than just a laid-back atmosphere and great skiing. Students pursue their academic and social lives with the same spirit they throw at the opposing hockey team. In and out of the classroom, UNH offers exciting opportunities which student body, a spirited and friendly group, take full advantage of. —*Ashleigh Hegedus*

FYI

The three best things about attending University of New Hampshire are "small classes with lots of individual attention and instruction, fifteen minutes from the ocean and forty-five minutes from the mountains, and chickwiches."

The three worst things about attending University of New Hampshire are "not enough parking, the price of tuition, and crazy weather."

The three things that every student should experience before graduating from University of New Hampshire are "nickel draft night at Libby's Bar, sex on Wagon Hill, at least one hockey game."

One thing I'd liked to have known before coming here is "that knowing your way around Windows will not prepare you for Computer Science classes."

New Jersey

Address: PO Box 7718;
Ewing, NJ 08628-0718
Phone: 609-771-2131
E-mail address:
admiss@vm.tcnj.edu
Web site URL:
www.tcnj.edu
Founded: 1855
Private or Public: public
Religious affiliation: none
Location: suburban
**Undergraduate
enrollment:** 5,930
Total enrollment: 6,711
Percent Male/Female:
40%/60%
Percent Minority: 16%
Percent African-American:
6%

Percent Asian: 4%
Percent Hispanic: 5%
Percent Native-American:
0.5%
**Percent in-state/out-of-
state:** 95%/5%
Percent Pub HS: 65%
Number of Applicants:
5,755
Percent Accepted:
55%
**Percent Accepted who
enroll:** 38%
Entering: 1,209
Transfers: 94
Application Deadline:
rolling
Mean SAT: NA
Mean ACT: NA

Middle 50% SAT range:
560–650 V,
580–670 M
Middle 50% ACT range:
NA
3 Most popular majors:
business, elementary
education, English
Retention: 93%
Graduation rate: 76%
On-campus housing: NA
Fraternities: 17%
Sororities: 17%
Library: NA
Tuition and Fees:
$5,685 in; $9,002 out
Room and Board: $6,330
Financial aid, first-year:
94%

The name has changed from Trenton State College to The College of New Jersey, but the school's academics and affordability have remained the same. The first public college founded in New Jersey continues to impress its students with its strong academics and variety of opportunities.

No Babying Here

TCNJ students are quick to praise the academics and stress that expectations are high. "They don't baby you, even though it is a state school," one student said. Undergraduates call the curriculum "rigorous," "thorough," and "highly competitive," although one student admitted that academics are not everyone's top priority. Qualified students seeking an extra challenge can enroll in TCNJ's honors program. One student warned, however, that "the honors students are separated from the general student population as freshmen and thus are never fully integrated into campus life." Other educational opportunities include the International and National Exchange Programs for those wishing to travel and learn in different settings. For students interested in pursuing a career in medicine, TCNJ offers a seven-year medical program that includes three years at TCNJ and four years at UMDNJ (the University of Medicine and Dentistry of New Jersey). A similar program for law and justice students is offered in conjunction with the Rutgers School of Criminal Justice.

TCNJ is known for its education department. "The college was founded on making teachers," said one student. Other popular majors include biology and English. Several students remarked that the art department is among the least popular. Regardless of their major, all students must complete several requirements, including interdisciplinary courses, English/public speaking classes, and math. One student described the requirements as "bearable," but another complained that the required three semesters of a foreign language "just add to the workload." Students also note that the mandatory classes fill up quickly, making it hard to fulfill the requirements.

Classes, even at the intro level, are small at TCNJ; few undergrads have classes larger than 30 students, and higher-level courses are even smaller. Although intro classes are small, one student said that the entry-level courses are not among the most exciting. "Math 101—lots of people I know have composed the most wonderful poetry during such classes." Students praise the fact that only "quality" professors teach undergraduates, and say that student-faculty interaction is good due to the size of the classes.

The Campus
The students commend the facilities as well, describing them as "really clean" and "well kept." Undergrads study (or write poetry, as the case may be) in the Roscoe L. West Library, a multilevel research facility described as "expansive." The campus has a variety of architectural styles that one student called "a mismatch of architectural trends. The original structures are really quite beautiful, but some of the later buildings are just mistakes." Many students mentioned the prevalence of construction around campus. The school recently completed renovations to the Social Science Building and Packer Hall, which houses athletics, the aquatic Center, and the Wellness Center. Plans to renovate the library are currently underway.

Students describe the campus, located in suburban Ewing, New Jersey, as "self-contained." The trees, large lawns, and lakes (complete with "tons of geese") on campus create an environment that is much different from urban Trenton. The security measures on campus, which include the student security patrol, emergency police phones, and pedestrian escort service, remind the students that they are not isolated in suburbia. Students describe the security measures as "effective" and note that they "keep problems to a minimum." Nearly all freshmen and sophomores live on campus because they are guaranteed housing. Many upperclassmen decide to live off campus in affordable apartments a short drive away. The

fraternities and sororities also have off-campus housing for upperclassmen.

How We're Livin'
All freshmen are housed in Travers-Wolfe Towers, while most seniors on campus live in Community Commons, which offers carpeted doubles with private bathrooms. Several students mentioned that the worst dorm is Centennial because it is old. TCNJ also offers special-interest housing, such as honors and music dorms. Some dorms are coed by floor; others have mixed halls. CAs (Community Advisors) live on every floor. Along with the Ambassadors (who help organize some activities), the CAs make up the counseling system at TCNJ.

> Students describe the campus, located in suburban Ewing, New Jersey, as "self-contained."

Two of the three campus dining areas are in Travers-Wolfe Towers and the Commons. The Student Center offers a variety of meal choices as well; it contains a Taco Bell, a salad bar, a deli, and a snack bar. The dining halls offer vegetarian options, but one student described them simply as "pasta, dry and stale." Another student complained that there is little variety, especially on weekends, when the Student Center is closed. Undergrads often eat off campus at chain restaurants such as the Olive Garden, Ground Round, and Burger King, as well as the diners on nearby Route 1.

Abounding Activities
Extracurricularly, TCNJ has a lot to offer. Because many people come to TCNJ to study music, there are many small music ensembles on campus, as well as the symphony, the concert band, and the TCNJ Chorale. Students can join over 140 clubs, including the fencing club and the Frisbee club. They can also write for the *Signal*, the weekly campus newspaper. For those interested in intramural sports, volleyball and football are among the most popular.

TCNJ does not disappoint serious athletes, either. The college has 21 varsity sports, many of which are among the best in the NCAA Division III. Women's field hockey, softball, and cross-country are consistently strong teams, while the men's wrestling and tennis teams also have impressive records. Students describe the athletic facilities as "outstanding": Packer Hall houses the pool and basketball courts, while the football team plays in the lighted, Astroturf-surfaced stadium.

On the social side, some students feel that opportunities at TCNJ are narrow. Students hang out in the Student Center or in the lounges in their residential buildings. The big social events on campus include homecoming and the semiformal. On other weekends, students can go to frat parties, which are all off campus. Since most Greek parties are open to all, students feel that the Greek system at TCNJ is "a good way to meet people." Another option on the weekends is the "Rat" (short for Rathskeller), the campus bar that often hosts live bands and serves beer to those with valid IDs. Although one student described TCNJ as "definitely not a dry campus," students generally don't feel that drinking is a large problem. For variety, some students make the relatively short drives to Princeton or Rutgers Universities, while others make the roughly hour-long drive to New York City or Philadelphia. TCNJ's location makes it helpful, if not necessary, to have a car. Since students are not guaranteed parking until their junior year, many depend on upperclassmen for transportation off campus.

Who We Are

Many undergrads notice a lack of diversity within the student population. Although there are some minority fraternities and other minority clubs, the actual minority population is small. One student said that there is "absolutely no diversity, although the administration would have you believe so." Another student commented that "there is talk about diversity, but the people don't really mix." Over 90 percent of the students come from New Jersey. With TCNJ's continued high rankings in various publications, however, students from nearby states (such as Pennsylvania and New York) have begun to take advantage of TCNJ's opportunities.

Many students cited TCNJ's value and affordability as reasons to attend the college. "It's a great school . . . a great opportunity, and it provides students with a lasting education," said one TCNJ advocate. Realistically, TCNJ students know that they will not find "the culture of New York" in suburban Ewing, New Jersey, but they believe that the quality of the academics and the "friendly, close-knit" campus make the experience worthwhile.—*Abby Rubin and Staff*

FYI

The three best things about attending TCNJ are "it's close to my home, the chance to live with all your classmates freshman year, and the education department."

The three worst things about attending TCNJ are "the fact that we can't have cars till we are juniors, the New Jersey heavy student population, and there is not that much to do on Friday nights."

The three things that every student should do before graduating from TCNJ are "head into either New York or Philly, shoot some hoops at Packer, and go to the Rat."

One thing I'd like to have known before coming here are "Ewing isn't the greatest place to spend four years."

Drew University

Address: Madison, NJ 07940-1493	**Percent African-American:** 4%	**Middle 50% SAT range:** 550–670 V, 550–660 M
Phone: 973-408-DREW	**Percent Asian:** 6%	
E-mail address: cadm@drew.edu	**Percent Hispanic:** 5%	**Middle 50% ACT range:** NA
Web site URL: www.drew.edu	**Percent Native-American:** 0.5%	**3 Most popular majors:** political science,
Founded: 1866	**Percent in-state / out-of-state:** 55% / 45%	psychology, English
Private or Public: private	**Percent Pub HS:** 64%	**Retention:** 87%
Religious affiliation: Methodist	**Number of Applicants:** 2,400	**Graduation rate:** 74%
Location: suburban	**Percent Accepted:** 75%	**On-campus housing:** 96%
Undergraduate enrollment: 1,421	**Percent Accepted who enroll:** 23%	**Fraternities:** NA
Total enrollment: 2,127	**Entering:** 405	**Sororities:** NA
	Transfers: 11	**Library:** 420,000 volumes
Percent Male / Female: 42% / 58%	**Application Deadline:** 15 Jun	**Tuition and Fees:** $23,008 in; $23,008 out
Percent Minority: 16%	**Mean SAT:** 625 V, 617 M	**Room and Board:** $6,564
	Mean ACT: NA	**Financial aid, first-year:** 65%

Hailed more than once by the Princeton Review as one of America's "Top Ten Most Beautiful College Campuses," Drew University breaks the stereotype of "ugly New Jersey and its turnpike." With its majestic trees and winding paths, the school has earned the nickname "University in the Forest." Students say stepping on campus is like entering a different world, leaving all kinds of urban ugliness and commercial eyesores behind. Yet Drew offers the best of all worlds, occupying a prime location in Madison, New Jersey, just 30 minutes from the skyscrapers of New York City and less than an hour from the sands of the Jersey shore.

Academic Breadth and Depth

In an effort to ensure both "breadth and depth" in education, Drew University requires its students to complete both a major and a minor. General requirements include two courses in four distribution groups: natural and mathematical sciences, social sciences, humanities, and arts and literature. In addition, there is a writing and foreign language requirement. Most students agree that fulfilling them is "not too much of a chore." Another student remarked with regret, "At first they

[the requirements] seem really annoying, but now that I'm done with them, I wish I had taken the time to enjoy them more."

True to the school's liberal arts roots, popular majors at Drew include theater, psychology, and English, but students refrain from sticking their school into a mold. "It's a good mix of arts and sciences, not just a science or English school." Indeed, science majors report "excellent facilities," and one physics major went so far as to say "Drew's physics department is the reason I came here."

Students of all majors praise their school's "warm and caring" faculty. As one student boasted, "Here the professors are concerned about each student—they care about you instead of their master's degree or their book publishing. You're a name to them, not a number." Another student simply said, "Academically, I have no complaints."

Special Stuff

Although the majority of students do come from the New York/New Jersey area, Drew offers a number of special academic programs that draw students from beyond the bounds of metro New York. Particularly popular is the school's 7-year accelerated medical program, conducted in conjunction with the University of Medicine and Dentistry School of New Jersey. Students accepted to this program complete college in three years and proceed directly onto medical school without having to go through the hassle of the application process. Similar pre-professional programs are available in the fields of law, business, and teaching. The school has a highly developed study abroad program, as well. One student estimated that roughly half of the student population participates in these international seminars, month-long programs in January and June that allow students to study in places from Ireland, to Egypt, to France.

Specifically for freshmen, the First-Year Seminar Program offers students the opportunity to study a topic in depth with small classes consisting of 12 to 16 people. The professors leading these seminars also serve as the students' faculty advisors, giving frosh a headstart on building relationships with their instructors. Student feedback on the seminars ranged from good to bad: one first-year described the selection of topics as "anything a kid would ever want to know," while another grumbled that they "only seem interesting until you get to class." In recent years, seminar topics have included the History of New York City, the NCAA and the Student Athlete, and Images of Women in Quebec Literature.

Another very popular Drew program is the Computer and Knowledge Initiative Program through which all students receive a free personal computer, software, and printer upon entering Drew as a freshman. Students praise the free stuff as "awesome—the best!"—an enthusiasm compounded by the fact that these computers are the students' to keep after graduation. Network access in the dorms adds convenience to students' lives and makes for a well-connected student body.

Small School Living
Most students live on campus for all four years, since decent housing in surrounding Madison tends to be expensive and hard-to-find. But there are few complaints since dorms are generally livable. Housing options range from single-sex suites to coed floors of singles. Every dorm has a Residential Adviser (RA) on every floor (usually an undergraduate), and a Residential Director (RD) in charge of everything (usually a graduate student). Students can also opt to live in one of seven theme houses. Among the more popular are La Casa, a Hispanic-American dorm; The Earth House, concentrating on environmental concerns; and Umoja House, the African-American house.

Campus food is described as "pretty good." The vegan line, though repetitive, is edible, and there is a grill room and stir-fry bar for students tired of regular lunch-line fare. Students can either eat at Commons, the only campus dining hall, or use "points" to buy munchies at the snack bar or The Space, both located in the University Center. The Other End is another well-frequented campus eatery. On weekends, the coffee shop-type establishment hosts bands, and students can sit and sip coffee while enjoying the mellow ambiance.

"More than Its Fair Share of Weirdos"
Students count their school's small size as both a blessing and a curse. As one student explained, "It's great because you get to know people, but it's ridiculous—if there's someone new on campus, you'll know." Though small, however, the student body reportedly does not lack variety. Said one student, "It is a liberal arts school, so you get more than your fair share of weirdos, but it's still a college so you get every type of person." Apparently the variety works though—different types of people are generally said to "mix pretty well." "There are definite groups, but they're not really exclusive," observed one student. One area in which the school's size can hurt, however, is the dating scene. "There are so few people, so there's not much choice," complained one sophomore male.

> Drew University breaks the stereotype of "ugly New Jersey and its turnpike."

The school's small size takes its toll on the social life in other ways, as well. "There's always something happening—it's just hard to find it sometimes," said one student. Added to the fact that the school has no fraternities and sororities, upperclassman dorms are the primary sites for bacchanalian blowouts. Recent changes in the administration's alcohol policy are reportedly hindering dorm party success, however, as the school cracks down on campus drinking. Thus far, it seems its attempts are working. Many students report that nowadays, parties are often moved to off-campus venues in an effort to dodge the new university regulations.

The Roads of Jersey

Students describe Madison, New Jersey, as "not a college town at all." "Small and quaintly residential," it offers students little more than basic necessities, like a supermarket, a movie theater, and CVS Pharmacy. Sweet Dreams coffee shop is a notable exception, named by student after student as the best place to take a date near campus. Nearby Morristown, with its wider selection of eateries and bigger movie theater, is a fast 5-minute drive for students with cars or friends with cars. On weekends, too, many students with cars will head for New York City, 30 miles west of campus. But since only juniors and seniors are allowed to have cars on campus, underclassmen often have to find their own fun around campus.

Drew students report that there is no shortage of school-sponsored events. Drama tends to be very popular, and student productions are well-attended. Most non-student plays are held at the recently rebuilt S. M. Kirby Shakespeare Theater, while most student performances take place in the Commons theater. Drew is also home to the annual New Jersey Shakespeare festival, celebrating the Bard and his greatest works. Visitors flock from all over the state to attend this May event. Drew students take a lot of joy in the prestige the event brings to their school. "It's great because a lot of times students can get really involved in planning and preparations for it," said one student.

There's More to Life . . .

Drew athletics are a popular extracurricular activity, thanks to what one student called the school's "phenomenal" facilities. Although Drew has no football team, other sports like soccer and those on the intramural level draw considerable student support and substantial participation. For the not-so-athletically inclined, Drew offers a host of musical, literary, and service groups. Popular a capella singing groups include On a Different Note and 36 Madison Avenue, or "MadAv." Campus publications like the literary magazine, *Insanity's Force*, and the weekly newspaper, *The Acorn*, give students the opportunity to display their journalistic talents. Community service organizations, especially environmental concerns groups, also enjoy high student participation.

As one student concluded, "Many people are here because they have to be—they don't really think about it and just go through the motions, and because Drew's a very liberal school with lots of freedom, it's easy to just stay that way. But I'd warn everyone not to squander the experience—there's just too much out there to waste time. And what better place to spend your four short college years than Drew?" —*Jane H. Hong*

FYI

The three best things about attending Drew are "the small classes, the personalized attention, and the gorgeous campus."

The three worst things about attending Drew are "there's not much to do on the weekends, the fact that you need to be a junior to have a car, and there's no Greek life."

The three things that every student should do before graduating from Drew are "to take a road trip to the city, to study abroad, and to go to Sweet Dreams Café with a date."

One thing I'd like to have known before coming here is "how small the school is."

Princeton University

Address: Princeton University; Princeton, NJ 08544-0430	**Percent Asian:** 12%	**Middle 50% SAT range:**
	Percent Hispanic: 6%	680–770 V,
	Percent Native-American:	680–770 M
Phone: 609-258-3060	1%	**Middle 50% ACT range:**
E-mail address: NA	**Percent in-state / out-of-**	NA
Web site URL:	**state:** 16%/84%	**3 Most popular majors:**
www.princeton.edu	**Percent Pub HS:** 60%	history, economics, politics
Founded: 1746	**Number of Applicants:**	**Retention:** 98%
Private or Public: private	14,875	**Graduation rate:** 90%
Religious affiliation: none	**Percent Accepted:**	**On-campus housing:** 97%
Location: suburban	11%	**Fraternities:** NA
Undergraduate	**Percent Accepted who**	**Sororities:** NA
enrollment: 4,556	enroll: 68%	**Library:** 5,000,000
Total enrollment: 6,200	**Entering:** 1,150	volumes
Percent Male / Female:	**Transfers:** NA	**Tuition and Fees:**
53%/47%	**Application Deadline:**	$25,805 in; $25,805 out
Percent Minority: 26%	1 May	**Room and Board:** $7,206
Percent African-American:	**Mean SAT:** NA	**Financial aid, first-year:**
7%	**Mean ACT:** NA	NA

A "Gothic paradise," Princeton University has one of the most striking campuses in the nation. Manicured lawns, stone buildings bedecked with ivy—the way one might envision Princeton is not so far from the reality. Located in an upscale New Jersey suburb, the enclosed campus is hailed by students as exceptionally safe. "I feel comfortable walking by myself nearly everywhere," one student reported. Although the surrounding town of Princeton is not especially lively, the university's prime location is ideal. New York City and Philadelphia, two favorite destinations among Princetonians, are each less than an hour's train ride away. There is much more to Princeton, however, than a pretty facade. Students agree that the school's real gem lies in the wealth of its academic offerings.

World-Class Academics

At the center of the university's reputation for excellence is its distinguished faculty. "Absolutely amazing scholars teach here," said one junior. "Virtually every professor is a forerunner in his or her field." Lecturers include Nobel Prize winners, prominent politicians, cutting-edge journalists, and even a former president of France. Literary masters Toni Morrison and Joyce Carol Oates head the university's outstanding creative writing program. In addition to being accomplished, professors are also extremely accessible. Princetonians in all departments have close relationships with faculty. Because the university's graduate program is relatively small (there are approximately double the number of undergrads as grads), professors actively and energetically delve into undergraduate teaching. An economics major said, "Unlike at many other Ivy Leagues, undergrads here are number one in the eyes of the faculty, and the professors make you feel it." Another student agreed: "The professors here don't want to just be lecturers. They want to interact with us, hear our viewpoints, and learn from us as well."

Even first-year students enjoy the advantages of close student-faculty relations. Freshman Seminars offer students the opportunity to work in a small group setting (roughly 12 to 15 students) on innovative topics. Of the 50 or so seminars offered each year, recent topics have included Blasphemy and Pornography as well as Extraterrestrial Life and Literature. Princetonians agree that although academics are rigorous, competition is far from cutthroat. A comparative literature major explains, "Students here are surprisingly laid-back—everyone has a thousand interests outside of studying. But if you're not careful, the workload can really creep up behind you and give you a swift kick in the ass."

To graduate, all students must take a minimum of 30 courses in seven distributional areas: Epistemology and Cognition, Ethical Thought and Moral Values, Historical Values, Literature and the Arts, Social Analysis, Quantitative Reasoning, and Science and Technology. Much to the dismay of humanities students, two semesters of a lab science as well as a semester of math are also mandatory. Those who dread the hard sciences, however, can take "softer," statistics-oriented social science courses such as Election Statistics. Further requirements include a one-semester writing class, a junior essay, a senior thesis, and proficiency in a foreign language.

Although the quality of academics is high across the board, students praise the highly selective Woodrow Wilson School of Public and International Affairs as exceptional. Providing participants with hands-on experience in government and policy-making, the "Woody Woo" program, as it is commonly called, culminates in a project in which students propose a solution to a global problem. Other popular majors (or "concentrations") include economics, English, history, politics, and engineering. For those whose interests lie beyond a single field, "certificate" programs (similar to minors) are offered. Students agree that the most strenuous majors are those in the School of Engineering (SE). In addition to taking rigorous upper-level science courses in their first year, SE students, approximately one-sixth of the student body, must complete 36 courses to graduate as opposed to the standard 30. "You hardly run into engineering students," one junior said. "They're almost always locked up in a library or a laboratory."

Courses at Princeton range from elementary to overwhelming. "Shake and Bake" (Earthquakes and Volcanoes) and "Nuts and Sluts" (Abnormal Psychology) are notorious guts, while a course on The Divine Comedy is described by one sophomore as "Dante's next level of Hell."

Virtually all courses, however, are reading-intensive. "Professors assign more pages to read than there are seconds in a day," one sophomore joked. Dedicated Princetonians from all academic backgrounds may also opt for the Humanities Cycle, an intensive yearlong sequence (begun in the second semester of freshman year) that covers the great works of Western thought. Consisting of three seminars and two lectures, the cycle was hailed by one participant as "an amazing experience. It provides you with one-on-one interaction with the best professors on campus." However, students warn that the program is not for the faint at heart; it is "a massive time commitment" and "definitely limits your opportunities to explore other fields and activities."

Learning at Princeton reaches far beyond the classroom. Not-for-credit sophomore workshops offer second-year students the opportunity to explore such unconventional topics as Architecture and Ethnicity and Transvestitism and Performance. These classes meet three to five times per semester and frequently involve field trips throughout the Northeast (all expenses are covered by the university). Also popular are college-sponsored Meistro dinners in which students dine with prominent artists and scholars.

Talent Reaches Beyond the Classroom

"The most wonderful thing about Princeton students," one politics major reflected, "is that each person is amazingly talented as well as intelligent. I'm constantly being surprised by the depth of people's interests—it's really cool to discover that my next-door neighbor is not only a Westinghouse scholar, but also an amazing poet or that a girl in my history class used to dance with a professional ballet company." Students can express these diverse talents through over 200 student-run organizations ranging from intramural sports and student government to science-fiction discussion groups. With the largest membership of any association on campus, the Student Volunteer Council connects students with community service projects in neighboring Trenton and Newark. Performance opportunities also abound. For the musically inclined, there are twelve a cappella groups (which take advantage of the campus's Gothic architecture each weekend by hosting mini-performances known as "arch sings"), a glee club, a variety of bands, and an orchestra. All of these groups benefit from the luxurious new practice spaces provided by the recently completed Woolworth complex. On a more dramatic note, favorites among thespians and audiences alike include the Triangle Club, a one-of-a-kind musical comedy ensemble, "side-splitting" improv comedians Quipfire!, and the Princeton Shakespeare Company. Dance companies Body Hype and Expressions similarly draw sold-out crowds.

Although some students say support for Princeton varsity teams is "pathetic" (partially due to the fact that Palmer Stadium is "literally crumbling at the seams"), students grab their furniture to fuel the bonfire traditionally lit after the Tiger football team defeats both Yale and Harvard. Another annual ritual is the Cane Spree, a day of competition between freshmen and sophomores that culminates in mud wrestling.

Where We Live, Eat, and Other Important Details . . .

Princeton freshmen and sophomores live in one of five residential colleges—Rockefeller, Mathey, Butler, Wilson, and Forbes. Although slightly removed from the other colleges, Forbes is said to have the best double rooms as well as the best food on campus. However, getting good housing in this college is simply the luck of the draw: a number of first-year students in Forbes are housed in "the most run-down rooms on campus," known as "Freshman Slums."

Overall, students report that the food served in the college dining halls is "pretty decent," featuring grill items and many vegetarian options at every meal. Juniors and seniors can choose to remain in the residential colleges and act as mentors for younger students, but the majority choose to move to upperclassmen housing ("Almost no one moves off campus," one junior said). Upperclassmen, however, do not eat in the college dining halls. They may join one of 12 "eating clubs" (by far the most popular option), join a co-op in which students prepare meals for each other, or declare themselves "independent" and cook for themselves.

Although the eating clubs exist for the functional purpose of feeding juniors and seniors, they also dominate Princeton's social scene. Prospect Avenue, the site of all 12 clubs, simply called the "Street" by students, is the heart of the school's social life. The clubs are in former mansions and are all equipped with dining rooms, computer labs, and areas for large social events (only officers are permitted to live in the clubs). Meals are prepared by chefs, and the food is reported to be "exceptional." The more ritzy clubs, such as the Ivy, even have waiters.

> **"Virtually every professor is a fore-runner in his or her field."**

Club membership begins the second semester of sophomore year. Each club has a distinct identity. Cap and Gown is athletic, Tairus is "artsy," Ivy is "exclusive," while Tiger Inn is "all about alcohol." Due to these generalizations, said one sophomore, "people tend to identify you by your club." Seven of the clubs are non-selective; students simply "sign in" with a group of friends and are assigned to a particular club by lottery. The other five clubs select members through "bicker," a process similar to Greek rush ("It's basically a lot of interviews and a lot of beer," one student said). For those who choose to undergo this process, bicker can be a source of stress. According to one junior, "If you aren't in the same eating club as your friends, you basically can't spend time with them at any meals." Those who have their heart set on one particular club can bicker multiple times. "You can usually get in the second or third time around," one undergrad reported.

Let the Weekend Begin

Weekends at Princeton begin Thursday nights at the "Street" and center on parties at the eating clubs. The majority of these events are not restricted to members, although some clubs distribute a limited number of passes when featuring particularly popular bands or DJs in order to prevent overcrowding. "Even if you can't get into a particular party, you'll still see everyone you know and have a good time. It's the Street that people go to rather than a specific club," one student insisted. Alcohol is readily available and is a central feature of these parties, but students report little pressure to drink. Beer is served in the basement or "tap room," of each club and is removed from the dancing and socializing that takes place on the main level. "It's great," declared one student. "If you want, you can just go to a party and dance and have a wonderful time without coming into contact with alcohol. On the dance floor, you can't tell who has been drinking and who hasn't." Friday nights at Princeton are much tamer, known across campus as "culture night." Students take a break from partying to enjoy the university's numerous student productions and concerts. The more adventurous travel to nearby New York City to visit friends, go clubbing, or join college-sponsored excursions to Broadway shows. Among the biggest events of the year are the House parties, a three-day-long extravaganza hosted by the eating clubs. One student explained, "It's like a three-day-long prom," involving a semiformal, a formal, and a day of lawn parties. "People take it really seriously because you have the same date for three days straight. You can feel the tension mount about five weeks beforehand."

Population Breakdown

Although over half of Princeton students receive some form of financial aid, many students insist that the university has a very upper-middle-class feel. "People have preconceived notions about Princeton—that it's exclusive and run by some ole' boys network. It's not like that at all," said one student. "There are people here from every class and every background." Other students find the campus to be lacking in ethnic diversity. One sophomore said, "The student body tends to be more diverse with regards to nationality than to race." But Princetonians tend to agree that the breadth of student interests and talents helps diminish whatever homogeneity exists among the campus' socioeconomic population.

Princeton offers students the opportunity to learn from some of today's most prominent scholars in a secluded environment that can sometimes feel more like a community than a world-class institution. Students are encouraged to consider the Princeton experience for themselves.
—*Lauren Rivera and Staff*

FYI
The three best things about attending Princeton are "the school's focus on undergraduates, eating clubs where people drink every Thursday and Saturday night, and the residential college system."
The three worst things about attending Princeton are "the not-so-diverse student body, some dorms are really old and gross, the oh-so-boring residential town of Princeton."
The three things every student should do before graduating from Princeton are "to go to the 'Street' on dean's date (the day before finals start), to take a class with Professor Uwe Reinhardt, and to eat dinner at the Ivy Eating Club."
One thing I'd like to have known before coming here is "how homogeneous the student body can sometimes be."

Rutgers, The State University of New Jersey

Address: 65 Davidson Road #202; Piscataway, NJ 08854-8097

Phone: 732-932-INFO

E-mail address: admissions@asb-ugadm.rutgers.edu

Web site URL: www.rutgers.edu

Founded: 1766

Private or Public: public

Religious affiliation: none

Location: suburban

Undergraduate enrollment: 10,894

Total enrollment: 48,341

Percent Male / Female: 49% / 51%

Percent Minority: 37%

Percent African-American: 7%

Percent Asian: 20%

Percent Hispanic: 9%

Percent Native-American: 0.5%

Percent in-state / out-of-state: 90% / 10%

Percent Pub HS: NA

Number of Applicants: 20,441

Percent Accepted: 48%

Percent Accepted who enroll: 25%

Entering: 2,462

Transfers: 6,546

Application Deadline: rolling

Mean SAT: NA

Mean ACT: NA

Middle 50% SAT range: 540–640 V, 560–670 M

Middle 50% ACT range: NA

3 Most popular majors: psychology, biology, economics

Retention: 89%

Graduation rate: 42%

On-campus housing: 52%

Fraternities: 8%

Sororities: 5%

Library: 6,200,000 volumes

Tuition and Fees: $6,052 in; $10,982 out

Room and Board: $6,098

Financial aid, first-year: 52%

Study nerds. Partiers. Slackers. Jocks. Every type of student is to be found at Rutgers, where diversity is key. Said one student, "Don't believe it when someone tells you that he's the typical Rutgers student because there is no such thing."

Rutgers University encompasses ten undergraduate colleges: Rutgers; Cook; Douglass; Livingston; the College of Pharmacy; Mason Gross School of Arts; the College of Engineering; the School of Business; the School of Communication, Information, and Library Studies (SCILS); and University College.

Each college maintains a distinctive personality within the larger university. Rutgers College, the largest and most competitive school, focuses on liberal arts. Its colonial College Avenue campus is said to be the social center of the university. Cook College, known for its many "wide open spaces," centers on the agricultural and life sciences. Only females reside on Douglass' beautifully bucolic campus, home of the nation's largest all-women's college. Austerely-styled Livingston, the newest college, offers liberal arts with a social-issues focus while University College accommodates the nontraditional returning and adult students. The university's five remaining schools offer specialized programs in fine arts, pharmacy, engineering, business, and communications.

Despite its notorious reputation as an "easy school," Rutgers succeeds in luring some of New Jersey's best students with generous scholarships, special honors, and pre-professional programs. And many Rutgers students would agree that "state school or not, Rutgers shouldn't be anyone's back-up college."

Rutgers—Not a BS School

Students agree that doing well at Rutgers requires a fair amount of work. One freshman lamented that the school's academic program is "vastly underestimated." "You can't just fool around here. A lot of people don't realize that and are rudely awakened freshman year when they get all Ds," added another student. General academic requirements vary from college to college. Rutgers College is generally considered the most rigorous, requiring students to complete both a major and a minor. Other requisites for Rutgers College include two expository writing classes, commonly called "Expos," and two courses in each of six academic disciplines. Other colleges typically demand less of their enrollees. Livingston, in particular, is known as the "easiest college to get into and graduate from."

Across the board, most students say that Rutgers sciences are more difficult than the humanities. Engineering was commonly named the hardest major with one student commenting on the unusually high dropout rate of engineering majors from the program. "It seems like everyone who starts out as an engineering major ends up switching after freshman year." So-called gut majors include psychology and communications.

Size Does Matter

Students love Rutgers' big-school atmosphere. "Nothing beats big schools. You just have so much to choose from—so many classes, friends, clubs and things to join." Still, most students would also agree that attending a large school has its disadvantages. One student complained that Rutgers' enormous size made her feel like "just another number" among the ranks of the near-25,000 undergraduate population. "I just don't feel like anyone really cares about the individual student. I barely even know my own professors, much less the administration." Other student grievances include jam-packed introductory lecture courses and "an annoying time trying to get into the classes that you want."

At Rutgers, students register for classes over the phone. Many would agree that although this system adds convenience to the harrowing process, it can also be a nuisance. One freshman complained, "The whole automated thing is great and all, but you have to call at like 6 A.M. to ensure that the classes you want are still open." As a last-ditch resort, though, many students opt to get into closed classes by obtaining special permission. "It's a hassle, but it's worth it," noted one student.

In the words of one Rutgers senior, "Your Rutgers academic experience all depends on how you approach it. If you have motivation and a thirst for knowledge, you'll learn a lot. If you don't care and choose to sleep during classes, then you won't. It's as simple as that."

The Alcohol Culture

In line with Rutgers' reputation as a major party school, many students admit that partying is definitely a priority. Frosh are particularly notorious, typically spending their weekends "looking for parties and trying to get drunk." After dark, they flock to frat houses lured by the promise of free beer. Indeed despite the administration's strong efforts to reduce the campus alcohol presence, drinking remains a popular student pastime. For those who choose not to take part in the alcohol scene, both the university and downtown New Brunswick offer a host of fun alternatives.

Students with access to cars can find their kicks off-campus, journeying to either New York City or Philadelphia or trekking downtown to enjoy the cultural nightlife there. A short walk from College Avenue campus, lower New Brunswick is the quintessential college town, attracting students with its variety of cafes, restaurants, and theaters. Off-campus wanderers are warned not to wander too far, though, since parts of downtown can be dangerous.

Campus Life

Students agree that life on campus can be a lot of fun. "There are so many people here—it's wonderful!" gushed one student. Most freshmen live on campus their first year, supervised by dorm preceptors (residential advisors) who have been called everything from "awesome" to "anal."

Depending on their college affiliations, students can live in a variety of dorms ranging from the College Avenue river dorms to the Livingston quads, which one student called "reminiscent of the Projects." Other residential options include off-campus and university-sponsored special-interest housing. The average dorm room was described as "small and plain—pretty much what you would expect." The Easton Avenue apartments, housing a modern gym and parking garage, are a notable exception. "Everyone drools over them," said one student.

One thing that few Rutgers students would not salivate over, however, is the school food. "The cafeterias may be sanitary, but the food's just no good," complained one student. The ever-popular "grease trucks" perennially circling campus offer hungry students an alternative, serving up fat-filled favorites like greasy hamburgers and oily onion rings. "I feel my arteries close up every time I see a truck drive by," joked one student.

Students can also find other fast food fare at the student center, a popular hangout with ATMS, computer labs, and places for groups to socialize and study. For more quiet study sessions, many students opt for the multi-level Alexander Library, also located on College Avenue campus. "It's absolutely huge and scary—I love it," said one frequent visitor.

There's More to Life . . .

Offering a variety of activities from a cappella singing groups to competitive ballroom dance teams, Rutgers boasts a seemingly endless list of extracurricular offerings. "Although at first a lot of people feel overwhelmed by all the choices, everyone seems to find their place eventually in at least one campus group," said one student. Among the university's better-known organizations are the college's daily newspaper, *The Targum*, the weekly *Rutgers Review*, and the Rutgers College Program Council, the group (RCPC) responsible for bringing a lot of bands and speakers to campus.

> "We're not just a bunch of NYU rejects."

The university's plethora of racial and ethnic groups also enjoys mass involvement, representing various elements of the eclectic minority population. But they remain controversial in many students' eyes. According to one ex-member, they "perpetuate racially segregated groups" at a school infamous for its racially divided atmosphere." "The idea behind the groups is great, but in practice, they're little more than social groups," observed one student. "Rutgers would be better without them."

Sports, on the other hand, make few waves among the Rutgers student population. "No one even seems to care about them," remarked one student. A fair number of students regularly attend varsity games, but according to one student, they only go "to laugh at the athletes for being as bad as they are." In spite of the school teams' normally less-than-stellar playing, Rutgers has its share of noteworthy athletes in certain areas with members of the track and men's soccer teams regularly achieving recognition on the national level.

No doubt, students can still find excellent athletic facilities at Rutgers. The Sonny Werblin Recreational Center is particularly popular among students from all over the campus. Oftentimes, students will opt out on their own gyms and make the long trek to Busch campus just to use the Center's modern equipment. Complete with two swimming pools, an impressive weight room, and modern courts, the Center is like a "Jack LaLanne times two."

State School? So What?

Rutgers students are proud to be part of such a large, diverse, and stimulating environment. Said one student, "Yeah, Rutgers is a state school. Yeah, Rutgers is a public school. So what? That doesn't make it a bad school." Another student put it more sarcastically, "A lot of people don't realize that you actually have to study here. We're not just a bunch of NYU rejects." So, what does that mean to prospectives? As one senior advised, "Before visiting Rutgers, remind your potentially misinformed self that people who go to state schools aren't necessarily second-rate students." —*Jane H. Hong and Staff*

FYI

The three best things about attending Rutgers are "the school's location between New York City and Philadelphia, the diversity of the student body, it's inexpensive."

The three worst things about attending Rutgers are "it's in Jersey!, having to ride buses to classes because they're so far away, R.U. Screw—getting caught up in administrative red-tape, getting lost on the huge campus, being treated like a number rather than a person—basically all the bad things that come with attending a really big school."

The three things that every student should do before graduating from Rutgers are "take Theater Appreciation, visit all the different campuses, have a 'fat-cat' (i.e. a double cheeseburger with french fries on top) from a grease truck."

One thing I'd like to have known before coming here is "how impossible parking is . . ."

Seton Hall University

Address: Enrollment Services Office; 400 South Orange Avenue; South Orange, NJ 07079
Phone: 973-761-9332
E-mail address: thehall@shu.edu
Web site URL: www.shu.edu
Founded: 1856
Private or Public: private
Religious affiliation: Catholic
Location: suburban
Undergraduate enrollment: 4,801
Total enrollment: NA
Percent Male / Female: 45%/55%
Percent Minority: 28%

Percent African-American: 12%
Percent Asian: 6%
Percent Hispanic: 9%
Percent Native-American: 0.5%
Percent in-state / out-of-state: 83%/17%
Percent Pub HS: 68%
Number of Applicants: 4,941
Percent Accepted: 76%
Percent Accepted who enroll: 29%
Entering: 1,084
Transfers: 287
Application Deadline: 1 May
Mean SAT: 522 V, 530 M
Mean ACT: 23

Middle 50% SAT range: 480–580 V, 480–580 M
Middle 50% ACT range: 20–26
3 Most popular majors: communications, biology, criminal justice
Retention: 84%
Graduation rate: 38%
On-campus housing: 60%
Fraternities: 15%
Sororities: 12%
Library: 459,458 volumes
Tuition and Fees: $18,290 in; $18,290 out
Room and Board: $7,722
Financial aid, first-year: 72%

At Seton Hall University, two traditions dominate the school: Catholicism and men's basketball. Despite the large number of commuters, students at the Hall enjoy a sense of community and a busy social life with active fraternity and sorority life. Between hanging out on the campus green, satisfying late-night munchies at the Maplewood Diner, and spending weekends in New York City, students combine the best of both worlds with a small campus in suburbia located near a major metropolitan city.

Academic Life

The Seton Hall academic program retains its religious foundation. Although the core curricula vary among the five different schools—the College of Arts and Sciences, the W. Paul Stillman School of Business, the College of Education and Human Services, the College of Nursing, and the School of Theology—they all include six credits in religion. In addition, all freshmen take a course in time management and study skills. Students comment that the core curriculum requirements are not difficult to fulfill and provide a nice academic sampler. "I didn't have any problems taking my requirements and major

classes. I'm going to graduate in four years and I only had to take 18 credits one semester," said one student.

Classes are generally kept very small. Although some freshman intro classes approach 100 students, most classes enroll approximately 20 to 40. Because many classes have a size limit, students trying to register for popular classes encounter some difficulties. Registration is by class in order of seniority, in random alphabetical order for each class. "If you're a freshman whose last name is at the bottom of the registration, a lot of times you won't get the classes you need," remarked one student. However, students toward the top of the waiting list usually get into the class within the first week. In extreme cases, deans ask the professors to increase class sizes to allow more students from the waiting lists into the courses.

Despite these efforts, students sometimes remain shut out of required classes. As one student explained, "A lot of times people are here more than four years because they can't get the classes they need, and some are only offered in spring or in fall." Students also complain about a shortage of teachers for the popular communication classes.

In addition to communications, business-related subjects, nursing, and secondary education are also very popular majors. The sciences are not. "Seton Hall University is not really a science school. If you want to be a doctor, you don't come here. We are known for our law and business schools," said one student.

Classes are taught by professors, although some teaching assistants help run science labs. Priests teach classes with a religious base. Students are relatively satisfied with the interaction with faculty, noting that most professors keep accessible office hours and will give students their home phone numbers.

Location, Location, Location

Seton Hall's location in South Orange, New Jersey (except the Law School, which is in Newark), is a major factor in some students' decision to attend. A majority of students are from the Northeast and like the school's closeness to home, especially since approximately 40 percent of the students are commuters. Furthermore, students can enjoy a taste of the cultural offerings of the Big Apple with SHU's close proximity to New York City. Although students feel safe on the actual campus, students noted that while the adjacent village of South Orange is also safe, the other side of campus goes into Newark, which can be dangerous. Despite the feeling of safety in South Orange, one student remarked that South Orange "doesn't like the fact that it is a college town." Campus security is extremely effective, according to students. There are pedestrian escorts, gatekeepers at the two entrances, and constant patrols. In addition, due to a rape three years ago in a dorm, dorm security measures have been beefed up. Students carry ID badges that they must show at the front desk of any dorm, and must sign in any visitors.

A Mix of Old and New

The campus is enclosed by a fence and contains a mix of old and new buildings. Since the campus is small and self-contained, students feel it fosters a sense of community. Said one, "You won't get lost in the shuffle here." Students enjoy the benefits of a small campus, such as not having to wake up too early to get to classes. The main buildings are centered on a green where many parties are held in the spring. Spring is a favorite time for students because the campus is abloom with flowers and people migrate outdoors. "People live and sleep on the green in spring," said one student. Throughout the year, undergrads can also be found hanging out in the student center with its organizational offices, the cafeteria, and the fraternity and sorority Greek room.

When it comes to studying, students prefer the $20 million Walsh Library. The third and fourth floors of the library contain over 400 study carrels and many group-study rooms, providing students with plenty of space for hard-core and social studying.

> Between hanging out on the campus green, satisfying late-night munchies at the Maplewood Diner, and spending weekends in New York City, students combine the best of both worlds with a small campus in suburbia located near a major metropolitan city.

A new business and education building that is home to the psychology department opened recently. An addition to the Brennan Recreation Center is currently under way, although students are reportedly satisfied with the current gym facilities. All Seton Hall students have free access to its weight room, Olympic-size swimming pool, indoor track, weight and exercise equipment, and many aerobic classes such as step, slide, and abdominals.

Although many people commute from home, the majority of students opt to live in campus residential halls. Freshmen live together in a freshman dorm that is coed by wing. Upperclassmen live in dorms that are coed by hall. Students report that the best dorm is Xavier, which features private bathrooms (shared by two doubles) and wall-to-wall carpeting. Older halls, such as the freshman dorm and Aquinas Hall, are the least popular. There are many options in dormitory living, such as nonsmoking floors, substance-free floors, single rooms, modern-language floors, all-female Neumann Hall, and Ora Manor—university-owned apartments for upperclassmen. Although the university does not permit official fraternity houses, many Greeks opt to live together in off-campus housing.

Students report that the RAs are active with the freshmen to help them in their adjustment to SHU. All underclassmen except freshmen can serve as RAs. RAs hold monthly meetings and sponsor different events like pizza and ice cream parties.

SHU has only one cafeteria, but it resembles a mall food court with its stands for Carvel, Kentucky Fried Chicken, Pizza Hut, Taco Bell, a bagel place, and Healthy Food Choice. "When I first started out, there were no franchises. Since I've been here, it's gotten better. But some people complain because it's fattening," one student said. Students can opt to enter varying amounts of money into their declining balances for meal plans, and commuters have special options as well. Vegetarian options are available. Although the cafeteria is open until 1 A.M., students are more likely to satisfy their late-night munchie attacks by visiting the Maplewood Diner or by ordering take-out from Village Pizza, El Greco's, a Chinese restaurant, or Cluck U. chicken.

The Social Scene

The large number of commuters affects SHU in its extracurricular and social activities. One commuter reported that she felt somewhat isolated at first and found it difficult to get involved in activities since club meetings are conducted at night. However, the university has made efforts to accommodate the commuters by establishing a commuter lounge and a commuter council. Each month, the commuter council raffles off a great parking spot—a coveted item at a school notorious for inadequate parking facilities.

Despite the occasional difficulties, both commuters and residents get involved in a wide array of activities. Extracurriculars include intramural sports; the weekly student newspaper the *Setonian*; the yearbook, *The Galleon*; gospel choir; the radio station; the Student Government Association (SGA); and a pep band for basketball games. The diverse student body of Seton Hall has many special-interest organiza-tions like the Women's Resource Center, Black Student Union, African Student Leadership Coalition, Latino organizations Adelante and Caribe, and a Filipino group. A Student Activities Board sponsors movies and other campus events and the university SHUttle van provides transport-ation to local malls and movie theaters.

Community service is an important aspect of Seton Hall campus life. Entering freshmen even have a community service requirement for graduation. Students can be found providing gifts and putting on a Christmas show for underprivileged children in events like "Joy to the Children" and "Deck the Halls."

Sports and More

With Division I status for teams, SHU Pirates events are a popular spectator sport. Since there is no football team, fall sports are dominated by the men's and women's soccer games. Come winter, students are off to the Continental Airlines Arena to watch the men's basketball team face off against big rival Rutgers and out-of-state competition like St. John's and George-town. Basketball season is a social time, with the Midnight Madness pep rally before the first game. Many students attend the games and can be found painting their faces blue and white in support of the Pirates, but support for the team reportedly varies with the team's record.

Beyond basketball, Greek life is a dominant social force. "For the size of the campus, we have a pretty high percentage of students who are Greek," observed one student. Big events include formals and the fall Greek Week competition between the fraternities and sororities. Although the Greek parties and activities are not exclusive events, one student admitted that it is difficult to know where and when these events are if you are not part of Greek life. According to another student, the administration is not too friendly toward the Greeks because "they are the biggest suppliers of alcohol." Last year, a dean called the South Orange police to warn them about a fraternity party being planned, which the cops subsequently busted.

As a response to the Greek system, the university has been trying to sponsor other no-alcohol campus events such as a weekly coffeehouse with poetry readings, bands, or comedians. Other popular campus events include the Pirate Queen and King Contest, the SGA Halloween Party, Parents Weekend in March, the Senior Formal, and University Day in the fall with booths on the green and a university mass.

The fact that SHU is a Catholic university affects the school: priests teach classes and there are religion course requirements. As one student said, "When morals come into question, Catholic standards are applied." One student reported that a roommate was fined for cohabitation because the visitor logs revealed that a member of the opposite sex had spent the night. Furthermore, the administration refuses to recognize a proposed gay and lesbian organization. However, if you are looking for a sound education to supplement your religious background, Seton Hall could be just the choice for you.
—*Katie Lindgren and Staff*

FYI

The three best things about attending Seton Hall are "the commuter lounge, SGA Halloween Party, and watching the Pirates in action."

The three worst things about attending Seton Hall are "commuter school issues, no football team, and a sometimes stifling Catholic tradition."

The three things that every student should do before graduating from Seton Hall are "go clubbing in New York City, participate in Greek Week, and get psyched for Midnight Madness."

One thing I'd like to have known before coming here is "how much of an effort the SHU administration makes to keep students happy."

Stevens Institute of Technology

Address: Castle Point on Hudson; Hoboken, NJ 07030
Phone: 201-216-5194
E-mail address: admissions@stevens-tech.edu
Web site URL: www.stevens-tech.edu
Founded: 1870
Private or Public: private
Religious affiliation: none
Location: small city
Undergraduate enrollment: 1,550
Total enrollment: 3,248
Percent Male/Female: 78%/22%
Percent Minority: 40%

Percent African-American: 5%
Percent Asian: 22%
Percent Hispanic: 12%
Percent Native-American: 0.5%
Percent in-state/out-of-state: 65%/35%
Percent Pub HS: NA
Number of Applicants: 2,205
Percent Accepted: 67%
Percent Accepted who enroll: 29%
Entering: 428
Transfers: 94
Application Deadline: 20 Aug
Mean SAT: 620 V, 680 M
Mean ACT: NA

Middle 50% SAT range: 560–680 V, 640–740 M
Middle 50% ACT range: NA
3 Most popular majors: engineering, computer science, chemical biology
Retention: 85%
Graduation rate: 27%
On-campus housing: 76%
Fraternities: 30%
Sororities: 35%
Library: NA
Tuition and Fees: $20,890 in; $20,890 out
Room and Board: $7,280
Financial aid, first-year: 60%

What makes Stevens different from other science and technology schools? In the words of one student—"the city of course!" Situated along the Hudson River, the Stevens campus maintains its 55-acre presence in Hoboken, New Jersey, just across the river from the wonders of New York City's downtown Manhattan. This metropolitan location affords Stevens students unparalleled opportunities through easy access to the city and its numerous resources.

Just for Engineers?

Stevens offers a variety of majors ranging from physics to American history, but as one student quipped, "you don't come here to study English." Most students consider Stevens a school mainly for wannabe engineers where the vast majority of students opt to major and ultimately pursue careers in engineering-related fields. Other popular majors include computer science and chemical biology, programs that most students would describe as "pretty good."

Not surprisingly, the Stevens curriculum aims primarily to accommodate engineering majors, requiring all students to complete courses typically expected of engineers-in-training. While this works out well for would-be engineers, those students outside the majority field are not always so happy about their school's seemingly narrow focus. As one non-engineering major complained, "I'm getting an engineering education when I should be getting a chem-bio education. What chem-bio major needs four semesters of calculus?"

Indeed many students would agree that Stevens has some stiff requirements. Unlike freshmen at most other schools, Stevens freshmen are not allowed to choose their own classes. Instead, they follow a schedule of required courses in calculus, computer science, physics, general chemistry, humanities, and physical education with honors students typically allowed some class choice. After first year, students have a great deal more freedom, but are still expected to meet other general academic requirements, which include four semesters of calculus, six semesters of physical education, and eight semesters of humanities.

Students often joke about Stevens' humanities courses, commonly referred to as "Hum." "The whole range of humanities here falls under a one-syllable title—kinda tells you something, doesn't it?" remarked one student. Even so, most students would agree that while humanities classes at Stevens are not-all-that-challenging,

they are likewise not easy-As. "They're not hard as long as you do the work," said one student. Stevens students also have the option of taking humanities classes at New York University through the NYU-Stevens cross-registration program. Because of their hectic schedules, however, some students find it difficult to take advantage of the program. "It's just too big a hassle," one student put it bluntly.

> **"We probably have the best view of any college in the world, and we totally take it for granted."**

In addition to its regular academic programs, Stevens offers a number of accelerated pre-professional programs that enable students interested in medicine, dentistry, and law to earn both a Bachelor's and a professional degree in seven years. Another popular program is the "Co-op," a five-year plan that allows students to spend three to six semesters working at such global companies as Lucent and General Electric as well as at a number of local companies. Participation proves advantageous to students in that it reduces one's courseload without costing an extra year of tuition and gives them a chance to earn pay ($7,000 a year on average) while gaining valuable work experience. Stevens places 100% of its Co-op applicants, and about 40% of students are currently involved in the program.

Overall, most students would agree that academics at Stevens are "pretty demanding," a rigor compounded by heavy courseloads. The graduation requirement of 135 to 150 credits (which differs with major) results in students taking an average of 19 to 21 credits, the equivalent of 5 or 6 classes, per semester. "Everyone studies. You can't do well otherwise," warned one student.

A lot of students choose to do their work in the Stevens library, which one freshman described as "a nice, quiet place to study." It apparently lacks the resources needed for research, however. "It has like 3 books—all from the 1970s or before," complained one student. The situation has gotten better, though, with a new program available on-line that, for a fee, allows students to request needed publications directly from publishing companies. "It's really convenient," said one frequent user.

A Room with a View

Residential students can live in one of the school's five dorms or, if involved with one of the twelve Greek groups on campus, in a house on Fraternity Row. Frosh usually live in single-sex dorms, made up mostly of doubles. After their first year, students can request dorms with housing assignments made on a first-come, first-serve basis. Upperclassmen have their choice of dorms and room set-ups with many opting to double-up in Technology Hall, the only dorm with amenities like air-conditioning, carpeting, and private bathrooms. Many rooms facing the river offer beautiful views of the New York City skyline, but as one student said, "No one really cares about rooms with views. It's sad—we probably have the best view of any college in the world, and we totally take it for granted."

Although Stevens is primarily a residential school, the campus can look pretty empty on weekends as many New Jersey students head home. For some of the weekend campus-dwellers, the Stevens social life "revolves around New York City," just a $1.50 PATH train ride away. Typical activities for city-goers include shopping, clubbing, and "just wandering around the city streets." For those students who prefer to stay closer to campus, fraternity parties are always an option. Currently, about one-third of students are involved in Greek life, but as one non-member explained, "Parties are a lot of fun even if you're not in a frat, and there's no pressure to drink if you don't like that sort of thing."

Another popular destination any day of the week is Washington Street, just a two-block walk from campus. Students can choose from a wide variety of eatables with everything from Chinese take-out to "pizza places out-the-wazoo." "Every other place is a food joint," said one frequent visitor, "and everything else is a bar." Indeed Hoboken is notorious for its abundance of pubs. One student claimed that Hoboken was known for having the "highest density

of bars in the country." "It's great if you're 21 or have a fake ID, but only if you're into that kind of thing," added another student.

Out-of-Class

Most students would agree that Stevens has a "fairly social atmosphere, but only for those who choose to take part in it." Women reportedly have an easier time getting dates, which is not surprising in light of the lopsided male-female ratio. One female student protested however, "The guys here snag us the minute we arrive— we don't even have time to breathe." Faced with a dearth of females, Stevens men tend to find dates at other colleges or back in their hometowns. A typical date entails "eating out—it always beats campus food," remarked one student. In general, students describe the food at Stevens as "just plain nasty," a situation ameliorated by the many dorm kitchens available for student use. "A lot of us make our own food," said one student.

As for extracurricular involvement, many students call it "limited" with those "students who get involved tending to get very involved." More than 50 student organizations are registered at Stevens. The more popular ones among them are WCPR, Stevens' own radio station; *The Stute*, Stevens' weekly newspaper; the Black Student Union (BSU) and the Indian Undergraduate Association (IUA), two of the more vocal ethnic groups on campus.

Although Stevens has no football team, varsity and intramural sports remain popular. The $13 million Charles V. Schaefer Jr. Athletic Center offers sports aficionados and dilettantes alike access to a fitness center, pool, squash court, and four-court gymnasium.

Students on Stevens

Stevens students agree that their school lacks school spirit, a chronic condition that led to their inclusion in the Princeton Review's ranking of the top-ten "unhappiest college students in the United States." Many students would dispute this title, however, with one student emphatically declaring "I love it here, and if I had to go back and do it all again, I'd definitely come to Stevens." Student feelings vary overall, ranging from an intense hatred to a passionate love for Stevens.

So, in light of such conflicting messages, what advice would current students give to prospectives? As in the words of one wise senior: "What else can you do? You should visit the campus, of course, but when you do, close your eyes to how pretty Hoboken is, ignore the view, forget what everybody else tells you, and really ask yourself, '*Would I be happy here?*' Do that and I guarantee you'll find your answer." —*Jane H. Hong*

FYI

The three best things about attending Stevens are "free laptops for freshmen, small classes, the integration of computers into classroom learning."

The three worst things about attending Stevens are "it's so small you can't avoid people you don't like, administrative red-tape, poor lab equipment."

The three things that every student should do before graduating from Stevens are "go to New York City, go to Castle Point and look at the NY skyline, watch the lights of the Empire State Building go out at 12 midnight."

One thing I'd like to have known before coming here is "just how bad the Humanities department is."

New Mexico

New Mexico State University

Address: Box 30001; MSC 3A; Las Cruces, NM 88003-8001
Phone: 505-646-3121
E-mail address: admissions@nmsu.edu
Web site URL: www.nmsu.edu
Founded: 1888
Private or Public: public
Religious affiliation: none
Location: urban
Undergraduate enrollment: 12,831
Total enrollment: 15,449
Percent Male/Female: 47%/53%
Percent Minority: 45%

Percent African-American: 2%
Percent Asian: 2%
Percent Hispanic: 38%
Percent Native-American: 3%
Percent in-state/out-of-state: 75%/25%
Percent Pub HS: NA
Number of Applicants: 6,624
Percent Accepted: 68%
Percent Accepted who enroll: 51%
Entering: 2,266
Transfers: 670
Application Deadline: July
Mean SAT: NA
Mean ACT: 21

Middle 50% SAT range: NA
Middle 50% ACT range: 18–23
3 Most popular majors: elementary teacher education, education, marketing
Retention: 72%
Graduation rate: 44%
On-campus housing: 50%
Fraternities: 4%
Sororities: 3%
Library: 1,032,970 volumes
Tuition and Fees: $2,502 in; $8,166 out
Room and Board: $3,726
Financial aid, first-year: NA

W hile the rest of the country braves the winter cold, students at New Mexico State University sunbathe on the well-kept, palm-tree-lined lawn of a spacious campus that provides an oasis in the middle of the desert. Located in the southern part of the state, and only 45 minutes from the Mexican border, NMSU attracts students looking for a quality education and a relaxed atmosphere.

The six undergraduate colleges at NMSU (business administration, education, human and community services, arts and sciences, agriculture, and engineering) offer an abundance of academic programs. A number of students attend NMSU for the highly respected agriculture department, but the engineering program also receives attention for its research in geothermal and wind energy. "NMSU is not known as the 'liberal arts school' in the state—that credit goes to University of New Mexico," said one senior. "We're more known for our 'ag' and applied sciences schools." Not sur-

prisingly, NMSU ranks high in the volume of engineering research and development that goes on there, compared to other schools of its size. The engineering college consists of several facilities, including a brand-new $15 million research complex and the soon to be completed Center for Sustainable Arid Land, appropriate for the dry New Mexico climate.

The "limited use" of graduate students as TAs contributes to a strong level of interaction between undergrads and professors. Most upper-level courses average 20 to 30 students. Instead of giving preference during registration, the university uses a lottery based on the first letter of the student's last name, so that all students have a fair shot at obtaining the courses they want. (Crimson Scholar honor students and disabled students, however, have priority over all other undergrads.) One student described NMSU academics as "taxing, but not overwhelming." For those who do find the course load too arduous, physical education classes are known for their easy requirements.

Southwest Charm
The campus architecture, with slanted flat-top roofs, red tile, and Navajo white stucco, accentuates the southwestern atmosphere at NMSU. Students agree that the campus looks attractive "except in February, when a lot of the grass looks dead." Favorite places to study include campus lawns and the two university libraries. The New Library, completed a few years ago, houses the arts, education, and humanities resources. The older Branson Library includes information on business, agriculture, and the sciences. "It's usually not hard to find a quiet place to study," one student said.

Because of the wide range of university housing, a high percentage of students live on campus. Several apartment buildings are open to students with at least sophomore status. To accommodate nontraditional students with spouses and/or children, NMSU also offers family student housing units with two bedrooms, a bath, kitchen, and indoor/outdoor living space. The majority of undergrads, however, choose the standard university dorms. Rules forbid drinking in all of the dorms except for Alumni, which is reportedly the party dorm.

Better Dine Out
University dining receives less than favorable reviews. Out of approximately 13,000 undergrads, only about 1,300 purchase a meal plan. One student government representative said that the administration may bring in outside companies once the present food service contract expires. Currently, the dining system consists of one dining hall serving standard cafeteria fare and eight "satellite" stations that serve snack foods and drinks.

> **"We're more known for our 'ag' and applied sciences schools."**

A number of campus groups work to generate a social scene at NMSU. The Cor-

bett Center, a popular hangout during the day, includes a small art gallery, a movie theater, and the campus bookstore as well as a dining hall and a game room. Several student organizations such as the student government and the biweekly Round-Up newspaper use the recently expanded center as a meeting area. The Association of Students–New Mexico State University (ASNMSU) organizes a book swap at the beginning of each semester and screens current movies on Sundays, among other activities. Recent entertainers to visit the campus have included Garth Brooks, Pearl Jam, and Salt 'n' Pepa. Fraternities organize parties on most weekends, but students say that only a very small portion of NMSU undergrads join the Greek system.

Sports Haven
Aggie athletics receive enthusiastic support from the NMSU community. Men's basketball remains the number one draw as the team consistently fights for the top spot in the NCAA. The women's volleyball team has seen similar success in intercollegiate competition. NMSU football also gets "a lot of hype," one student said. Once named Sports Illustrated's "worst college football team," the program has grown with a change in coaching staff. Now, the program challenges rival University of Texas/El Paso in the annual football showdown. Besides intercollegiate sports, NMSU offers intramural volleyball, soccer, touch football, and other outdoor sports. At the Activities Center, students often borrow sporting equipment (such as canoes, tents, bicycles, and rock-climbing gear) to experience the New Mexico landscape on their own.

Undergrads generally agree that Las Cruces is a great college town. Students frequent its night spots, especially Cowboys, a country-western dance club. On Mondays, disco night at the Rock Island Bar usually attracts a number of partygoers. Some favorite restaurants include Little Nellie's and Chopi's, both restaurants in Old Mesilla along the Rio Grande River.

Although students report a low crime rate in Las Cruces, NMSU stresses the need for continued safety and provides a dependable security system that includes emergency phones and security patrols around the area. When Las Cruces starts to seem stifling, students often escape to dance clubs in El Paso or to bars across the border in Mexico.

The friendly attitude pervasive at New Mexico State distinguishes this school from other universities. "You don't have to walk around with your head down. You can't help meeting people here," one stu-

dent said. The beautiful weather allows students to roam the campus, and as another student said, this makes the dating scene "pretty happening."

Regardless of the stifling heat of the New Mexico desert surrounding Las Cruces, students say NMSU's combination of work and leisure makes the climate just perfect.
—*Brian Abaluck and Staff*

FYI

The three best things about attending NMSU are "sunny weather, the awesome party scene, and the hot girls."

The three worst things about attending NMSU are "a social scene that depends of alcohol too much, no major cities nearby, and not well known."

The three things every student should do before graduating is "make the trip to Lake Havasu for spring break, head down to Mexico for a tequila party, and go country line dancing at Cowboys if you've never done it."

One thing that I'd like to have known before coming here is "the non-tech areas are not very strong and most people are very pre-professional."

University of New Mexico

Address: Student Services Center 150; Albuquerque, NM 87131-2046
Phone: 505-277-2446
E-mail address: apply@unm.edu
Web site URL: www.unm.edu
Founded: 1889
Private or Public: public
Religious affiliation: none
Location: urban
Undergraduate enrollment: 16,133
Total enrollment: 23,770
Percent Male / Female: 43%/57%
Percent Minority: 45%
Percent African-American: 3%

Percent Asian: 3%
Percent Hispanic: 33%
Percent Native-American: 6%
Percent in-state / out-of-state: 83%/17%
Percent Pub HS: NA
Number of Applicants: 4,346
Percent Accepted: 92%
Percent Accepted who enroll: 67%
Entering: 2,687
Transfers: 1,481
Application Deadline: 15 Jul
Mean SAT: 543 V, 533 M
Mean ACT: 22

Middle 50% SAT range: 480–600 V, 470–590 M
Middle 50% ACT range: 19–25
3 Most popular majors: university studies, elementary teacher education, psychology
Retention: 70%
Graduation rate: NA
On-campus housing: NA
Fraternities: 5%
Sororities: 4%
Library: 2,200,000 volumes
Tuition and Fees: $2,430 in; $9,172 out
Room and Board: $4,800
Financial aid, first-year: 41%

Situated in the center of Albuquerque, the University of New Mexico is a different kind of state school. Most members of the student body live off campus, and many are returning students who have full-time jobs. The school has a cul-

tural and social diversity that almost any university would be hard-pressed to rival.

Light Academics

One student described UNM academics as "fairly easy," but another said, "It depends on what you want to get of it." The biology, geology, and photography departments have earned the most praise from undergrads, while some report that the math and music departments need improvement. Students can take courses in the university graduate schools, but priority for all classes goes to graduate students and upperclassmen, making it a problem sometimes to get the classes you want, according to a sophomore. Although pre-professionalism abounds at UNM, undergraduates agree that the college still has a strong liberal arts program.

Monster Courses

Students sometimes complain about class sizes, which can be as big as 500 students in introductory classes. Most courses are taught by professors, but graduate students teach some introductory-level courses. Undergrads report that faculty-student interaction can be very good when the student takes the initiative. The academic environment is quite laid-back and not intensely competitive, according to one senior. Qualified students with high GPAs are eligible for enrollment in an honors program that offers special seminars that emphasize reading, discusstion, and writing.

UNM students seem satisfied with the university facilities. The six libraries, especially Zimmerman Library and the technical libraries, are the best places for quiet study. A grassy area under the trees by the duck pond is another relaxing place to get work done. A favorite spot for social study is the Cellar, a pizza place located in the basement of one of the dorms, where there's also a game room. Another popular UNM hangout is the Student Union Building (SUB), which has a courtyard and a ballroom. In town, students enjoy hanging out in several of Albuquerque's cafés, including the Double Rainbow, and in various bookstore cafes.

Social Events? Go Greek

Since few UNM students live on campus, most parties happen in off-campus houses. Only a small number join fraternities, but frat parties are extremely popular. The biggest fraternity party of the year, the Can You Bring bash, requires all guests to bring a can of food to be given to the Albuquerque poor. On campus, UNM offers at least 600 clubs, according to one student, including theater, music groups, community service, and the *Daily Lobo*, a highly praised student newspaper.

A Place to Hang My Hat

Campus housing is said to be quite good. The best (and most expensive) dorms are the Student Residence Centers (SRCs), which are apartments with private bathrooms and kitchens. In contrast, in the Eldorado dorm, 100 women share two communal bathrooms. One student stated, Even though Eldorado isn't the greatest dorm, it's still a place to hang my hat.

> **Many UNM undergrads study part-time and are older than the average college age; the average age of the freshman class is 20.**

The architecture is typical New Mexico–style, and students emphasize that the school's setting in the Sandia Mountains is simply gorgeous. Safety is a growing concern on UNM's compus, but escorts are available 24 hours a day. UNM has one central cafeteria, and students report that the food is unpopular. Many students choose to cook for themselves, and there is no scarcity of alternative off-campus eateries. Frontier, a 24-hour food shop, is one of the favorite places to eat off campus, and Albuquerque also offers a wide variety of Mexican restaurants.

Howling Lobos

Sports are big at UNM, whose mascot is El Lobo, Spanish for the wolf. Students are especially proud of their basketball team, which won the Western Athletic Conference championship in 1994. The Lobos' biggest rival is neighboring New Mexico State University, and it is a tradition for the Lobos to howl at their opponents before every basketball game. The volleyball and tennis teams have also had successful seasons recently. UNM's athletic facilities include the on-campus Johnson Center, which has, according to one student, everything you can imagine in terms of sports equipment, as well as the football stadium and another recently built gym in downtown Albuquerque. Club sports and intramurals are popular, particularly skiing. In fact, one undergraduate said that many people make their schedules around the time they can go skiing.

Some students call life in Albuquerque slow, but another praised the town's good theaters, which host symphony concerts, dance shows, and Broadway productions. Since most students live in town or grew up in the community, town-gown relations are warm and friendly. For students who feel the need to escape, beautiful and culturally rich Santa Fe is only two hours away, as is the famous Taos ski resort.

Diversity University

The UNM student body is a diverse ethnic mix. The number of minority students, particularly Latinos, gave one sophomore the impression that here, whites are a minority, although another student said he had expected the Latino population to be even larger. UNM is, in fact, a bilingual school, and many courses are taught in Spanish as well as in English. One international student said that there is a strong minority support network, and that the campus has centers for all minorities, including gay and lesbian students, who reportedly are accepted by the rest of the student body. Undergrads also seem to have an open attitude toward drugs. According to one, you can frequently smell people smoking pot on campus. Many UNM undergrads study part-time and are older than the average college age; the average age of freshmen is 20.

Size: Asset or Problem?

The size of the university is a problem for some and an asset for others. On the one hand, a student complained, in a large university like this you end up being a number. On the other hand, UNM's size puts many resources at students' disposal. The key to the University of New Mexico, as one student remarked, is that it has a lot to offer, and you have to decide what you want to get out of it. The university's relaxed atmosphere, its extensive resources, and the socially and culturally diverse student body give undergrads great freedom to shape their education according to their interests, and provide them with great opportunities for a solid education.
—Kurtland Ma and Staff

FYI
The three best thing about attending UNM are "the awesome cultural diversity, all the hard partying that goes on here during the weekends, and the pretty campus."
The three worst things about attending UNM are "the town of Albuquerque, feeling like this place is too big, and many people's focus on life after college instead of life during it (many older and off-campus students)."
The three things every student should do before graduating are "go skiing at Taos as often as you can (it's so cheap as a student), go drive through the desert at 100 mph, and you gotta go to the UNM vs. NMSU football game."
One thing that I'd like to have known before coming here is "how easy it is to get the bad habits of slacking and sleeping really late here."

New York

Address: 1 South Avenue; Garden City, NY 11530
Phone: 516-877-3050
E-mail address: admissions @adlibv.adelphi.edu
Web site URL: www.adelphi.edu
Founded: 1896
Private or Public: private
Religious affiliation: none
Location: urban
Undergraduate enrollment: 2,774
Total enrollment: 7,003
Percent Male/Female: 33%/67%
Percent Minority: 21%
Percent African-American: 12%

Percent Asian: 6%
Percent Hispanic: 3%
Percent Native-American: NA
Percent in-state/out-of-state: 92%/8%
Percent Pub HS: 83%
Number of Applicants: 1,420
Percent Accepted: 78%
Percent Accepted who enroll: 29%
Entering: 321
Transfers: NA
Application Deadline: rolling
Mean SAT: 490 V, 490 M
Mean ACT: NA

Middle 50% SAT range: 410–540 V, 460–588 M
Middle 50% ACT range: NA
3 Most popular majors: business-management, education, nursing
Retention: 74%
Graduation rate: 34%
On-campus housing: 41%
Fraternities: NA
Sororities: NA
Library: 480,000 volumes
Tuition and Fees: $14,000
Room and Board: $6,850
Financial aid, first-year: 87%

Located on Long Island, with a student body composed primarily of commuters, Adelphi offers a unique college experience geared mostly toward students who reside nearby and plan to either live at home or visit home often. One enthusiastic student claimed that "even as a commuter, you can still get a full college experience from Adelphi, spending long hours at the library, or just hanging around campus." And if your idea of a full college experience is an intimate environment, both socially and academically, where you can cheer for a great basketball team, experience a level of independence, and yet still be able to go home for a home-cooked meal, Adelphi may be just the place for you. If, however, you want to go farther from home and stay on campus during weekends, enjoying yourself at Adelphi might require a little bit of an adjustment and frequent trips into New York City.

Intimacy and Choices

Adelphi consists of several different schools for undergraduates. Besides the College of Arts and Sciences, there are also individual schools for education, business, nursing, social work, and psychology. Students must indicate which college they are applying to on the college application. Requirements vary depending on your college and your major. Students in the College of Arts and Sciences must fulfill general education requirements, which force students to take at least six credits in arts, natural sciences and mathematics, humanities and languages, and social sciences. However, one student admitted that although the requirements were "a pain in the neck and I complain about them now," the skills acquired in the classes will likely help in the future, "so it all pays off in the end."

One student cited the "small classes

and personal attention" as the best aspects of Adelphi academics. However, this intimacy has recently been jeopardized by an increase in enrollment, which has led to overcrowding in some classes and sections. However, overcrowding tends to be significant only in introductory classes and classes with especially popular professors. Many of Adelphi's classes are still small enough to foster "great group discussions," even if they are not quite so intimate. Overall, students reported that they were happy with professors. Dr. Salvadore Primeggia, a sociology professor, got rave reviews for being enthusiastic, "talking to students as equals," and getting everyone involved in class discussions. As one student enthusiastically exclaimed, "I have never been in a more exciting class!" Although not all professors inspired such praise, students agreed that they all were fairly accessible and that they "make an effort to accommodate students" even if their office hours are "few and far between."

> **"Even as a commuter, you can still get a full college experience from Adelphi."**

Students cited nursing, business, and education as the most popular majors. The theater department is reportedly also large. Business, social work, education, and theater are considered by some to be the most competitive and intense majors. Science classes, especially biology, tend to be dominated by pre-med students and are therefore considered difficult and competitive as well. However, if you are thinking about a major in one of these areas, you need not be intimidated by their reputations. Speaking about her education classes, one student said that although they were sometimes very time-consuming, they were "enjoyable" and "don't necessarily feel like work." And students can always make use of Adelphi's "excellent resources to obtain help," which, besides professors, include a learning center and tutors. Said one student, "[Adelphi] has a lot to offer, including direction if you don't

know what you want to do with your life." Advisors, professors, and other staff are always readily available for advice, "plus there are so many electives that if you don't know what you want, you can take a course that may spring some interest."

And You Thought Your Menopausal Mother Had a Hormonal Imbalance. . . .

One notable aspect of Adelphi is the disproportionate number of female to male students. In certain classes, notably those in education, nursing, and English, there may be no males at all. One student felt that the ratio was a major disadvantage to the school, stating that although "the guys love it, because there are so many girls to choose from, the girls hate it because all the guys you meet, you either become friends with and aren't attracted to or you are attracted to but find out they are attracted to someone else." However, these difficulties must work themselves out somehow, because, according to students, "there is a lot of random hooking up" and even some dating.

Another aspect of Adelphi social life that one should take into consideration before applying is that of those undergraduates who live on campus, many go home on weekends, leaving the school "a ghost town come Thursday nights." One student lamented that "there is nothing to do on the weekends." However, with a large mall nearby, students can find solace and drown their sorrows and boredom in the latest Banana Republic and Kenneth Cole fashions. There is even a shuttle bus that goes back and forth to the mall and bus terminals. And if shopping fails, New York City is also only a 30-minute train ride away. Adelphi bar nights can provide a break from weekend boredom. These fraternity- or sorority-sponsored events are held at various bars, which are primarily populated by Adelphi students for the night, allowing students to interact with "the same people you see in your classes all week, only now they're drunker." However, according to one student, even these "get tiring after a while," since you are constantly seeing the same people.

Running into familiar faces is a natural product of the small undergraduate population. A negative consequence of Adelphi's small size is that "*everyone* knows your business. If you get drunk and do something stupid, then the next day everyone knows what you did and you feel like an ass." According to students, those who aspire to get drunk and make fools of themselves will not have any problem doing so at Adelphi. Although it is officially a dry campus, one student explained that people often drink in dorms anyway and that alcohol plays "a major role" in the social scene. Although students are put on probation if they get caught, this is rarely an issue. Being underage is reportedly "not a problem," either, because the bouncers at the Adelphi bars will usually let you in. Light drug use plays a small role in the social scene as well. According to one student, "People smoke and drink in the dorms and no one really cares."

Don't Judge a School by Its (Longgisland) Accent
The majority of Adelphi students come from the tristate area, especially Long Island, and they are primarily white. However, it would be wrong to stereotype the school based on these demographics. While some complain that lack of diversity is a problem, others claim that Adelphi is "very diverse" and that there are "a lot of foreign students." One student claimed that although many minority groups tend to hang out together, "it is not because they don't get along with other white people." Whether the diversity is great enough may be a matter of opinion, but as one student said, "Diversity or no diversity, Adelphi is a very inviting place to all races and genders." And apparently to all sexualities as well, since the attitude toward homosexuals is reportedly "pretty accepting," although one student admitted that it may be difficult to hide one's homosexuality for long because, due to the small size of the campus, "news travels fast."

A sense of community is strongest among residents at Adelphi. However, commuter students feel ties to Adelphi as well. This sense of community and school spirit stems mostly from a common sense of pride in Adelphi's basketball and lacrosse teams, which draw big crowds and are a major component of student life. Basketball even sparks a tradition

known as "midnight madness," which involves students' participating in silly games to win prizes up until midnight, when the basketball teams come out, marking the official start of the basketball season. According to one student, midnight madness "shows school unity because everyone is there."

Students report that there is not much extracurricular involvement outside of sports. While sororities and fraternities are the largest organizations, Greek life is not really that big, and some students complain that Greek pride is something that is conspicuously lacking in the Adelphi community. Besides sororities and fraternities, students may also choose to become involved in student government or publications such as the *Delphian*, a weekly newspaper, or *Ascent*, a literary magazine. However, many students are too busy working to pay for their Adelphi education to become heavily involved in other pursuits.

For the most part, students are happy with the campus and housing. Campus is described as small and homey, allowing students to travel across it in very little time. It's is also very "floral," which makes it especially beautiful in the springtime, as one student enthusiastically pointed out. Garden City, the wealthy suburban town that's home to Adelphi, also got positive reactions from students. It is described as "beautiful" and has much to offer students, including nearby malls, restaurants, bars, and close proximity to Manhattan. Students also agree that they feel very safe at Adelphi and have "no problem walking across campus alone at night." If someone did feel unsafe, there are blue security lights posted around campus that students can press to notify security. One major complaint, however, is that there are inadequate parking spaces, a major inconvenience at a school where many students commute. Overcrowding has also become a problem in dorms lately due to a rise in enrollment. The administration has only recently begun planning construction to solve this problem.

Many students are satisfied with their experience at Adelphi. They enjoy the intimacy of the academic and social environment and the beauty of their suburban campus. Others really appreciate the school's close proximity to home. However, students admit that Adelphi is not for everyone and that those who live far from Adelphi or who do not wish to go home on the weekends should carefully consider their choice before deciding on Adelphi.—*Elyssa Berg*

FYI

The three best things about attending Adelphi are "the Long Island accents, close-knit community, small classes."

The three worst things about attending Adelphi are "the Long Island accents, no parties, core requirements."

The three things every student should do before graduating from Adelphi are "go to an Adelphi bar night, take a class with Dr. Primeggia, go to a least one midnight madness."

One thing I'd like to have known before coming here is "how the commuter lifestyle kills the social scene."

Alfred University

Address: Saxon Drive; Alfred, NY 14802-1205
Phone: 607-871-2115
E-mail address: admwww@alfred.edu
Web site URL: www.alfred.edu
Founded: 1836
Private or Public: private
Religious affiliation: none
Location: rural
Undergraduate enrollment: 2,112
Total enrollment: 2,435
Percent Male/Female: 50%/50%
Percent Minority: 9%
Percent African-American: 3%
Percent Asian: 2%

Percent Hispanic: 4%
Percent Native-American: NA
Percent in-state/out-of-state: 70%/30%
Percent Pub HS: NA
Number of Applicants: 1,954
Percent Accepted: 81%
Percent Accepted who enroll: 35%
Entering: 556
Transfers: 110
Application Deadline: 1 Feb
Mean SAT: 567 V, 564 M
Mean ACT: 23
Middle 50% SAT range: 530–620 V, 520–630 M

Middle 50% ACT range: 23–28
3 Most popular majors: art and design, ceramic engineering, materials science
Retention: 83%
Graduation rate: 65%
On-campus housing: 95%
Fraternities: 15%
Sororities: 8%
Library: 231,629 volumes
Tuition and Fees: $21,036 in; $21,036 out
Room and Board: $7,582
Financial aid, first-year: 83%

"If you want a bustling city life, Alfred University is not the place to be. But for everything else a college student needs, it's great," boasted one Alfred student. True to his words, Alfred University, located in upstate New York, is small-town school. Yet, what it lacks in big city glamour, it makes up for with rolling pastures and a close-knit community. Its nationally recognized ceramic engineering department doesn't hurt, either.

Not Your Typical Curriculum

Academics at Alfred are truly unique and diverse. Popular majors range from the less common, such as athletic training, to more typical offerings such as computer science and mechanical engineering. Students at Alfred tend to have a wide array of academic interests. Classes are described as challenging, and students agree good grades are not so easy to come by, although requirements and difficulty do vary by major. The only course all students are required to take is physical education. "I guess they want us all to be fit," one student said, trying to rationalize this requirement.

One of the strongest and most popular majors at Alfred is ceramic engineering.

Not only is Alfred nationally recognized for its faculty in this department, but the school also makes available many co-op opportunities for majors to pursue their interests in this field. Indeed, the program is so good, many students say they came to Alfred because of it. Other strong departments include the arts, computer science, business, English, and history. The music department, on the other hand, tends not to receive such rave reviews due to its limited course selection.

In addition to its regular academic programs, Alfred offers a special honors program for qualified students. This program provides academically ambitious students more access to the best professors at the university. Honors students have the opportunity to delve into certain fields in more depth than they would have studying under the normal program.

As a small school in a small town, it is not surprising that Alfred gets good reviews for its small class sizes. The average class enrolls only about 15 students, and professors teach not only all lectures, but conduct all discussion sections as well. The small-scale learning environment fosters a supportive environment, and many students note that they felt close to their professors. The close-knit community also proves advantageous in that it allows for students to participate more confidently in their education. In fact, it is not unusual to find professor-student interactions even outside the classroom. Professors and students are often seen meeting for a meal or coffee in a local eatery. At Alfred, learning is not confined to the classroom.

The two libraries on campus also receive acclaim from students. Of the two, Herrick Memorial tends to be the more popular study place, and is often crowded. The other library, Scholes, has the largest ceramic engineering research collection in the world.

In addition to these excellent libraries, Alfred boasts many new classroom buildings. Olin is a fairly recent business building, and the Miller Performing Arts Center and Glass Science Laboratory are both new additions to the campus. Binns-Merrill Hall and Kanakadea Hall, housing the ceramics and human studies departments, respectively, are also being renovated. This is not unusual for Alfred, which tends always to be on the cutting edge. "Our campus is constantly being remodeled—it's great!" boasted one student.

Northern Exposure

Northern Exposure, a late 1980s TV show depicting life in the boonies, is rumored to be based on Alfred. Most students would agree that life in the boonies is part of the Alfred experience. First-year students at Alfred live in special freshman dorms, usually in doubles, coed by floor. Barresi is one popular freshman dorm, whereas Tefft tends to be less popular. Upperclassmen select rooms by lottery and have a wide array of choices open to them ranging from suites to campus apartments with full-size kitchens. In addition, a large number of students live off campus in sorority or fraternity houses.

Food is not horrible, and students may eat in either of the campus's two dining halls—Powell, located in the campus center, or Ade. Alfred changed its dining services a few years ago, and students say they are benefiting from it. Many students opt to eat at off-campus eateries, as well. Popular spots include the Collegiate, The Dill Pickle, Little Sicily's, and Alfred Pizza and Sub Shop.

Extracurricular Life in the Boonies

Alfred University is an extremely health-conscious school, so it is no surprise that sports are very popular. Alfred is a Division III school and cannot offer athletic scholarships, but the school still manages to have great athletic competition. The lacrosse team is very good, having made the Division III NCAAs twice in the last four years.

> "If you want a bustling city life, Alfred University is not the place to be. Yet for everything else a college student needs, it's great."

School spirit at athletic events is extremely high, as many an Alfred student comes out to support the Saxon Warriors. The school's athletic facilities are described as "fairly good" and are open to all students free of charge. These include squash courts, basketball courts, a swimming pool, and a weight room. For those not as athletically inclined, intramurals are popular, including everything from squash to basketball.

In addition to sports, other popular campus activities include participating in the college newspaper, the *Fiatlux*, which is distributed bi-weekly. Other journalistic venues include literary magazines such as the *Alfred Review* and the *Poasis*. Students describe both of these magazines as "bizarre but interesting." Other popular extracurriculars include the school radio station and a world-traveled jazz band. Greek life also holds a strong presence on campus, and according to students, is the "be-all and end-all" of campus social life. Alcohol is also big, and binge drinking is perceived as a problem by some. However, despite the predominance of alcohol, students say they do not feel pressure to drink.

Located in such a rural community, Alfred sponsors many on-campus activities. One in particular is Hot Dog Day, the campus's biggest weekend of the year featuring parades, non-stop partying, live bands, and "a lot of fun."

Although many of the students come from New York, Alfred draws in a wide range of students from all sorts of backgrounds. In this small town, these students band together and experience what has been described as "a great four years." Said one student, "Although Alfred isn't for everyone, if you can handle small town life, do give it a try. You won't be disappointed."—*Alyssa Blair Greenwald and Staff*

FYI

The three best things about attending Alfred are "the small classes, the parties, and the ceramic engineering department."

The three worst things about attending Alfred are "the bad weather, the binge drinking, and the fact that SUNY Alfred is right across the street."

The three things every student should do before graduating from Alfred are "to hang out in Hornell, to get pizza from Alex's, and to go the Collegiate Restaurant."

One thing I'd like to have known before coming to Alfred is "how small a town Alfred really is."

Bard College

Address: Hopson Cottage, Bard College; Annandale-on-Hudson, NY 12504

Phone: 914-758-7472

E-mail address: admissions@bard.edu

Web site URL: www.bard.edu

Founded: 1860

Private or Public: private

Religious affiliation: none

Location: rural

Undergraduate enrollment: 1,233

Total enrollment: 1,427

Percent Male/Female: 41%/59%

Percent Minority: 0%

Percent African-American: NA

Percent Asian: NA

Percent Hispanic: NA

Percent Native-American: NA

Percent in-state/out-of-state: 24%/76%

Percent Pub HS: 60%

Number of Applicants: 2,508

Percent Accepted: 47%

Percent Accepted who enroll: 28%

Entering: 335

Transfers: 36

Application Deadline: 15 Jan

Mean SAT: 650 V, 610 M

Mean ACT: NA

Middle 50% SAT range: 530–700 V, 540–670 M

Middle 50% ACT range: NA

3 Most popular majors: literature, fine arts, social sciences

Retention: 83%

Graduation rate: 65%

On-campus housing: 99%

Fraternities: NA

Sororities: NA

Library: 260,000 volumes

Tuition and Fees: $24,000 in; $24,000 out

Room and Board: $7,220

Financial aid, first-year: 58%

If an annual drag queen contest, known simply as "The Drag Race," is something you're looking for in a school, perhaps Bard is the place to be. Set in the lush, beautiful, Hudson River Valley, Bard College is by far one of the most naturally pretty campuses around. Bard students take advantage of this serene setting to engage in a variety of artistic and academic adventures.

Arts Abound
While all Bard students have to take at least one lab course and one science/mathematics course, students are quick to get those requirements out of the way to delve into the arts and humanities. Bard students are also required to take courses in foreign language, social and historical studies, literary texts and linguistics, and philosophy classes. According to one student, "the requirements are really fair and really easy to manage as long as you don't slack." While the school's majority is made of artists, it is actually the concentrations in art that are the most difficult. Majors in photography, film, painting and sculpture find that there is simply "a lot of work and a lot of time involved."

Difficulty aside, Bard students enjoy small classes, which seem to diminish in size as students progress in their studies. One junior reported that his largest class had 21 students. As for getting into classes themselves, students actually appeal to their professors explaining why they want to take that class. While it is naturally a system easiest for seniors, another students said that "it's actually pretty easy if you plan. I've rarely had difficulty in getting into my classes." Students are universally pleased with the chance to work closely with faculty in their small classes and find their professors easily accessible and willing to help. Some classes are indeed challenging, but as one student remarked on the Bard experience, "it's as hard as you make it and the professors are able to match that."

Social Life?
Although Bard makes use of its beautiful, pastoral setting, it is also quite remote, limiting social life. As one student said, "You either party at bars, or go to campus parties, or just hang out in the dorms."

When students aren't living it up at local joints like Stony Creek or Pongo, they can be found on campus, partaking in the various movies, concerts, or lectures that are constantly happening. Bard students particularly like the annual theme parties, such as the Silk Party, an S&M Bonanza, and the annual Drag Race. Moreover, national and local bands perform quite frequently. Many students also like to use the Bard Student Center, which has a multipurpose room, a computer room, two study rooms, a post office, the bookstore, and two key features, an ATM, and a room full of La-Z-Boy seats and a television.

Legendary toga parties and "Animal House"-like behavior is an anomaly at Bard. There is no Greek system at Bard. As one junior put it, "I have some friends who drink beer and are athletic, and that's about as close as it gets." Without a Greek system, however, the students at Bard still have enough parties to go to. Alcohol and drugs are definitely present on campus, with one student estimating that "about 70% of the student smoke cigarettes, you can't avoid it." Alcohol is also part of the social scene with the administrative stance being that it is their job to "protect, not enforce."

Have Wheels, Will Travel
What makes up a typical Bard student? Well, according to a sophomore, it's "impossible. We have rich hippies and lazy jocks. We're mostly middle ground; there are a lot of free spirits who are still hardworking." The Bard population is relatively diverse, although one junior commented that "Bard's small, so it can start to get homogeneous." Although most students don't fit into a general schema, it is clear that a sizeable percentage of students have cars. Cars are "very necessary. There is nothing in walking distance besides the campus, so you have to drive at least three to four miles to get to local towns."

Close Quarters
One student described his freshman dorm room as "extremely small and cramped . . . with another person." The housing situation at Bard is not looked on with particularly glowing eyes. The school was once so tight for housing that it actually had students living in emergency trailer housing. Despite these sub-par conditions, there

are some nice living arrangements on campus. These include Super Cruger and Keen, two new and modern dorms, as well as Manor, an old mansion. Manor is definitely considered on of the best places to live, although as one resident said, "it's a little removed from central campus." All dorms have RA's, who "have to enforce some rules, but usually let people do what they want." Students looking for variations on dorm housing can choose to live in quiet dorms, a co-op or a number of small two-story houses owned by Bard. Many upperclassmen move off campus because they feel housing is "mediocre. It's expensive, and you might get a good room or not. Nothing's sure." For those who do live off campus, Tivoli and Red Hook are popular complexes and, when compared to dorm housing, are either less expensive or the same price for a lot more."

The dining system at Bard is also seen as rather poor. One student simply said, "it's expensive, and it's pretty bad." However, students agree that there is a lot of food available and a lot of choice, just not very good quality. One sophomore complains, "there's lots of starch." Bard has one dining hall, Kline, where most students go. Vegetarians and vegans never feel left out as there are "plenty of options." The dining hall itself is not really a very social setting; students tend to rush in, eat, and leave. For those looking to have some stimulating dinner time conversation, they have the choice of either going to Down the Road in the student center, or going out to eat. Within a 20 minute radius of campus, Bard students frequent a variety of restaurants, which, according to a senior, "are pretty varied for such a small place." Favorite places include Osaka, Panada, Stony Creek, The Rotisserie, and the Red Hook Diner.

Outside of Class

While it is certainly easy to get involved in extracurricular activities at Bard, few students seem to take advantage of it. One student described Bard as having "enormous amounts of small organizations, which are easy to join. But most people are just too lazy to do it." Furthermore, given the artistic inclination of its students, there is clearly little a focus on athletic activities. There are a variety of clubs that engage in artistic expression as well as prominent feminist and women's rights groups. Also active are ethnic and cultural clubs such as the African Students Organization, Asian American Students Organization and the Central European Students Organization While community service is not as popular at Bard, it is the school's hope that within two years, at least 50% of the campus will be involved in some kind of volunteer work. Also, for a school with almost three-fourths of its students on some kind of financial aids, most Bard students work through student employment. For the more active students, there is a strong intramural sports following, with softball, ruby, soccer, basketball, and tennis, making up the most popular teams. While the school does compete intercollegiately, there is little school spirit for these events. Rugby is the only sport at Bard with a real following.

> There is no Greek system at Bard. As one junior put it, "I have some friends who drink beer and are athletic, and that's about as close as it gets."

The students of Bard love the location on a "gorgeous piece of land in the Hudson Valley filled with historical sties and wonderful landscaping." At the same time, they love the hour and a half drive away from New York City, where there is a wealth of social opportunities. Bard is a truly stunning place for those geared toward the humanities. As one student put it, "Bard gives you the freedom to figure out what you need." —*Shu-Ping Shen*

FYI

The three best things about attending Bard are "freedom, the natural environment, and the faculty."

The three worst things about attending Bard are "food, housing, and expensive tuition."

The three things that every student should do before graduating from Bard are "go abroad, take advantage of famous faculty, and meet the president."

One thing I'd like to have known before coming here is "how remote Bard really is."

Barnard College

Address: 3009 Broadway; New York, NY 10027	**Percent Asian:** 23%	**Middle 50% SAT range:** 620–710 V, 610–690 M
Phone: 212-854-2014	**Percent Hispanic:** 6%	
E-mail address: admissions@barnard.edu	**Percent Native-American:** 0.5%	**Middle 50% ACT range:** 26–30
Web site URL: www.barnard.edu	**Percent in-state / out-of-state:** 39%/61%	**3 Most popular majors:** English, psychology, political science
Founded: 1889	**Percent Pub HS:** 58%	**Retention:** 94%
Private or Public: private	**Number of Applicants:** 3,883	**Graduation rate:** 65%
Religious affiliation: none	**Percent Accepted:** 37%	**On-campus housing:** 95%
Location: urban	**Percent Accepted who enroll:** 39%	**Fraternities:** NA
Undergraduate enrollment: 2,294	**Entering:** 558	**Sororities:** NA
Total enrollment: 2,294	**Transfers:** NA	**Library:** 180,000 volumes
Percent Male / Female: 0%/100%	**Application Deadline:** 15 Jan	**Tuition and Fees:** $23,056 in; $23,056 out
Percent Minority: 34%	**Mean SAT:** 671 V, 652 M	**Room and Board:** $9,358
Percent African-American: 4%	**Mean ACT:** 29	**Financial aid, first-year:** 46%

B arnard College offers its students the best of three worlds. As a women's college, it creates an environment that supports and empowers women. As an affiliate of Columbia University, it offers all the resources and prestige of an Ivy League institution. Lastly, as an urban school, it provides students with easy access to all the attractions and distractions of New York City, "the ultimate college town."

Academics

Clearly Barnard is not your typical women's college. According to one student, Barnard is "only as much of a women's college as you want it to be." Indeed, many students would agree the school has a defined coed environment though only women may matriculate. As one student explained, "Most classes have men in them, though there tend to be fewer in Barnard classes." Barnard women also have the option of cross-registering for classes at Columbia and vice versa. Depending on their major, some Barnard women end up taking almost all of their classes at Columbia, while others may go four years without taking one. "It's so great because you have the power to choose. The decision to cross-register is all up to the individual," said one student.

Barnard's core class requirements are designed to give students a broad academic overview, and many Barnard women would agree that they do just that. According to some students, however, the requirements can get ridiculous at times. One junior called the physical education requirement "absolutely absurd because people should be able to choose whether they want to be fit and not be forced to take class" and the two required semesters of lab the "bane of my existence because lab work is so time-consuming." As a liberal arts school, students say Barnard's English and political science majors are particularly strong. Sociology is reportedly among the school's easier majors as the requirements are less intensive. But above all, as more than one student emphasized, "Barnard is by no means a slacker school—everyone here works and works hard."

Students feel privileged to learn under the guidance of Barnard's exceptional faculty, raving about their "totally amazing" professors. The faculty's availability and approachability were said to foster close professor-student relationships. The school attracts its share of famous instructors including Holocaust survivor, Elie Wiesel, who was on campus recently, giving a series of lectures. And both

Barnard and Columbia students alike vie for places in Professor Thurman's (actress Uma Thurman's father) Indo-Tibetan Studies courses.

City Living

Due to exorbitant city rents, most Barnard students live in dorms for all four years. Students can choose to live in either Barnard or Columbia housing and can choose how many people they want to live with. Single-sex and coed floors are also available. School dorms are described as "generally pretty clean and decently sized," with the exception of Reid and Brooks, both described as "really old." On the whole, though, since the majority of dorms were recently renovated, there tend to be few complaints about housing.

There is an RA system for freshmen. The typical RA was described as "pretty helpful," but "not all that important, to put it truthfully." First-years live in the Quad, which is comprised of four, connected dorms. Students living in the Quad have to remain on the meal plan, whereas those living elsewhere usually do not, since many suites have kitchens. Students generally agree that being on the meal plan and having to consume school food is not terrible. The dining services are said to offer adequate vegan and kosher options. Price, not taste, is the biggest concern. "Food is just horrendously overpriced," said one student.

Alternative fare is easy to find. The school's neighborhood of Morningside Heights offers students a host of dining options, from the cheap and quick to the more expensive sit-down meals. Noteworthy among local establishments are Tom's Diner (of late *Seinfeld* fame); Ollie's, a popular Asian noodle shop; and Café Pertutti, famous for its wonderful pastas. Students looking for more authentic ethnic cuisine or more extensive menus can find them in New York City's Chinatown, Koreatown, or Little Italy—all just a $1.50 subway ride away.

Morningside Heights, New York City

Barnard occupies a small campus just across the street from Columbia in uptown Manhattan's Morningside Heights. Most students would say the local area is "pretty safe" despite its location on the outskirts of Harlem. Still, they would warn against walking alone at night. Escort services are available, though according to one student, "not too many students use it." The neighborhood was described as "calm, even kinda boring." According to one student, "It's a great place to live because everything you could possibly need can be found within a 12-block radius."

> **"Barnard is only as much of a women's college as you want it to be."**

Because of Barnard's location in New York City, students agree there is never a shortage of things to do. Any day of the week, great shopping, famous sites, and great theater are minutes from campus. According to some Barnard women, a typical Friday night inevitably involves "bar-hopping or clubbing somewhere downtown." Getting alcohol is reportedly not a problem, especially since fake IDs are easily obtainable. Weekend frat and suite parties at Columbia are also popular, especially among the first-years. Drugs do not have a sizable presence on campus, though as one student said, "they're definitely there and widely used by some." Considering Barnard's prevalent alcohol culture, one junior warned that the school can be "socially difficult" for non-drinkers. But whether on campus or in the city, most students are able "to find our niches and amuse ourselves."

A Bastion of Independence

On the whole, Barnard tends to be a very self-focused environment. "It's a real fend-for-yourself kind of atmosphere," one student said. "As a result, it can sometimes be a very cold place because the city dilutes a specific Barnard campus identity." Students tend to be cliquey, which contributes to the common student complaint that the school lacks community. Cliques also tend to divide along ethnic lines.

Still, students are quick to identify causes which bring Barnard women together. Every year, the school hosts a march entitled "Take Back the Night" which seeks to empower women against violence and abuse. Started during the 1960s civil rights movement, the march enjoys high participation even today as Barnard and Columbia students alike come together for a common cause.

The Student Stereotype

Extracurricular life at Barnard is closely tied to Columbia. Most organizations allow members from both schools. Varsity sports are also joint enterprises. Intramural sports at Barnard such as rugby and crew enjoy a more modest popularity. One senior described Barnard women as "fairly apathetic" and complained that "it's hard to get people out for clubs." Moreover, lots of students opt to join city organizations instead of school-sponsored ones, another factor in lower extracurricular participation.

Among school groups, ethnic organizations like the Latino and Korean student associations are especially popular. This fact seems to contradict the stereotype of a typical Barnard student—"a Caucasian girl clad in the latest fashion, cell phone in one hand, cigarette in the other." Students are proud of their school's great ethnic diversity although one student did complain that the school seemed to have a "preponderance of Valley Girl types." Lesbian groups also have an obvious presence on campus. "I don't think there are necessarily more lesbians here than at other places—they're just a lot more active and visible here," said one student.

In Columbia's Shadow?

Barnard College has been affiliated with Columbia University for more than a century. Even after all that time, however, tensions between the two schools reportedly still run pretty high. Barnard undergrads report that Columbia students oftentimes begrudge them as being a "drain on Columbia's resources." According to one student, many Columbia students "think Barnard women are less intelligent and that Columbia doesn't get a higher ranking because of Barnard's lower admission standards." A well-known saying among Columbia men reflects this attitude: "Barnard women to bed, Columbia women to wed." One junior would refute this sentiment, however. "I know a lot of Barnard girls who were accepted to both schools and chose Barnard over Columbia. And I also have friends who transferred to Barnard from Columbia." Others echo her response. "Some people think Barnard is full of dumb lesbians who want to feed off Columbia, but in actuality, only a select few ignorant people actually express that attitude." Concluded one student, "We stand in no one's shadow, including Columbia's. Barnard is a terrific school in its own right." And with a campus in one of the world's most exciting cities, Barnard is as exceptional a women's school as one can get, offering its students a supportive yet challenging environment amidst the metropolitan madness. —*Jane H. Hong*

FYI
The three best things about attending Barnard are "the personal attention, the great-faculty–student interaction, and its location in the city."
The three worst things about attending Barnard are "the stereotypes of Barnard students as dumb lesbians, the affiliation with Columbia, and the lack of community."
The three things that every student should do before graduating from Barnard are "to take a women's history class; to march in 'Take Back the Night'; and to go downtown and see a Broadway show."
One thing I'd like to have known before coming here is "how independent everyone here is."

The City University of New York System

The City University of New York (CUNY-pronounced "kyoony"), underwent radical revision on November 22, 1999 that its Chancellor Matthew Goldstein hopes will "redefine and substantially broaden the view of the role and promise of a public urban university." On that date, New York State Board of Regents approved CUNY's Master Plan Amendment proposal to remove remedial courses from the baccalaureate curriculum and demand demonstration of basic skills through the SAT, ACT, or Regents Exams. It also revamped its intra-system transfer policies and got a $97 million boost from the 1999–2000 state budget. Through these changes, CUNY hopes to improve its academic image, strength of its offerings, and retention and success of its students. Whether Goldstein's plans will be successful or headed for a fall, only time will tell.

Variety and Different Focus

CUNY is the third-largest university system in the world with 200,000 students on 21 campuses (10 undergraduate, 6 community colleges, 1 technical, 4 graduate) throughout the five boroughs of New York. An additional 150,000 part-time and continuing-education adult students attend a CUNY school. Its student body reflects the city's ethnic diversity: 32% of students are black, 31% white, 25% Hispanic and 12% Asian. Although the differences among colleges are immense, nearly all the students interviewed by the Insider's Guide mentioned the word "bureaucratic." As one student said, the colleges are "run by the city of New York, so basically . . . anyone you deal with at the administrative level gives you the same attitude you would expect at the Department of Motor Vehicles."

A Good Deal

Despite the dissatisfaction with the administration, however, most CUNY students feel they're getting a good education and a good deal. The huge variety of night courses attracts a large population of students who work during the day. All of this is available at a price made more reasonable by the fact that most students are from New York and can live at home, which is "a big reason" many students choose CUNY schools. According to one undergrad, "Most students I know here work and are from families where that's necessary." Understandably, most students take up to six years to graduate and the graduation rate is low.

Each school has its individual strengths. "[Each college] has different concentrations," one student said. "Hunter has a big nursing school; at Queens, it's English; at Baruch, it's business; and The City College covers the technical areas: engineering and computer science." According to students, these individual strengths help them decide which school to attend. "If a student lives in Brooklyn, and wants to be an English major, it's not that big a commute—he'll go to Queens," one student explained.

Grab Bag

Campus environments vary as well. Students describe the colleges in Manhattan as more fast-paced and urban than those in the other boroughs; they are also considered "more liberal" and "free." According to one undergrad, some students from suburban Long Island "come to Queens and are in awe of it—if they went to Manhattan, they'd have a heart attack. The culture is different in Long Island: you really don't see anyone with a shaved head and nose ring walking around the other campuses." Students in Manhattan say, "It's Manhattan"—in the middle of everything, creating an extremely diverse and exciting environment.

Admissions criteria depend on the individual school. Spaces in the community colleges are guaranteed to New York students who have earned a high school diploma, while the four-year schools maintain more selective admissions policies. Students are required to have a cumulative academic average (CAA) of 80, a measurement that incorporates grades only from "academic" subjects such as math, English, science, foreign language, and history.

> As one student said, the colleges are "run by the city of New York, so basically . . . anyone you deal with at the administrative level gives you the same attitude you would expect at the Department of Motor Vehicles."

Overall, students praise the faculty as one of the CUNY system's greatest assets. "We have a lot of really fine teachers here," one student said. Others described their professors as "gifted people as well as gentle and giving teachers," and "excellent, and nationally renowned."

New York City serves as both CUNY's campus and its source of extracurricular activities: A CUNY ID can get a student discounts at many museums, galleries, and theaters around town. One student even claimed that "if you make arrangements, there's hardly a museum in the city that won't let you in for free." However, this does not prevent some CUNY schools from having strong extracurriculars, including newspapers, clubs, and student government.

Students generally agree that the CUNY system provides a solid education for people of all ages, interests, schedules, and backgrounds. General Colin Powell and Jerry Seinfeld are two of many distinguished alumni of the CUNY system as is the current Chancellor Goldstein. The colleges are reportedly "malleable to the individual student's ambitions" and meet the changing needs of a remarkably diverse population. According to one student, "Overall, the administration is pretty unpopular, but the teaching is informative if you choose the right courses—it's a good education." *—Seung Lee and Staff*

City University of New York / City College

Address: 160 Convent Avenue; New York, NY 10031	**Percent Asian:** 11%	**Middle 50% SAT range:** 450–490 V, 600–630 M
Phone: 212-650-6977	**Percent Hispanic:** 30%	**Middle 50% ACT range:** NA
E-mail address: admissions @admin.ccny.cuny.edu	**Percent Native-American:** 0.5%	**3 Most popular majors:** electrical engineering, computer science, psychology
Web site URL: ccny.cuny.edu	**Percent in-state / out-of-state:** 90%/10%	
Founded: 1847	**Percent Pub HS:** 85%	**Retention:** 83%
Private or Public: public	**Number of Applicants:** 3,298	**Graduation rate:** 14%
Religious affiliation: none	**Percent Accepted:** 46%	**On-campus housing:** 0%
Location: urban		**Fraternities:** 3%
Undergraduate enrollment: 8,041	**Percent Accepted who enroll:** 54%	**Sororities:** NA
Total enrollment: 12,093	**Entering:** 828	**Library:** 1,200,000 volumes
Percent Male / Female: 48%/52%	**Transfers:** NA	**Tuition and Fees:** $3,402 in; $7,002 out
Percent Minority: 76%	**Application Deadline:** rolling	**Room and Board:** NA
Percent African-American: 34%	**Mean SAT:** NA	**Financial aid, first-year:** NA
	Mean ACT: NA	

Located in Harlem and intersected by busy city streets, the City College of New York (CCNY) is an institution whose assets include New York City itself. Although CCNY has no campus housing, its academic offerings are considerably more diverse than those of most other CUNY schools. CCNY provides students with a good education at a great price that attracts commuters from all five boroughs of New York City.

Academics

Undergrads report that CCNY has a number of strong departments, including English, political science, and history. One student said, "The caliber of the teaching staff is excellent." However, CCNY has not been unaffected by recent cuts to CUNY's budgets. While film, media, and music have grown recently, that has come at the expense of dance and theater. Pressed by diminishing funds, the college president, herself an anthropologist, recently threatened to eliminate the anthropology department. Only when she learned she risked losing her place in the American Association of Anthropology did she preserve the department, although one anthropology major said, "It is not a very strong department." Undergraduates and graduate students take classes together.

Most students agreed that CCNY is strongest in, and best known for, the sciences and engineering. One student said, "[CCNY] boasts about all the money it has for research."

The engineering school is separate from the school of liberal arts, and has its own building. One special engineering program is the Program for Retention of Engineering Students (the PRES Program), which provides tutoring and counseling for minority engineering students.

Another special academic program is the seven-year B.S./M.D. program in the Sophie-Davis School of Biomedical Education. Sophie-Davis has a selective admissions policy and a preset medical curriculum. Students must sacrifice the freedom to choose their classes, and must commit to working for at least a year in the community after receiving their medical degree. In exchange, they get an affordable path to an M.D.

The liberal arts school also has special programs, including the Honors Program and the Scholars Program. Students who are admitted into the Honors Program based on placement-test results have special Honors advisors and receive priority in course registration. Students in the Scholars Program, which is similar to the Honors Program, have special class sections and receive academic scholarships.

Regardless of the program they choose, all CCNY undergraduates must fulfill course requirements in the sciences, social sciences, English, a foreign language, math, art, music, and physical education. Required classes include English 110 (Freshman Composition), World Civilization, and World Humanities. Students also must pass proficiency tests in math, reading, writing, and speech. Some students report that the academic requirements are ultimately beneficial, though one science major said, "I don't want to take any of these non-science courses because they are boring." Another student complained about the required Freshman Orientation, a semester-long, pass/fail course "worth zero credits."

Many introductory courses are lecture classes of a few hundred people. However, students reported that professors teach nearly all classes. "I haven't experienced graduate students teaching classes, which is what I expected." A freshman said, "I only see the TA when the prof gives a test."

Weekly review sections called recitations supplement many large classes. More advanced classes, as well as Honors and Scholars sections, often number 20 to 25 students. While professors are usually given high marks, some are difficult to understand. One student said, "I've had professors with thick accents. Sometimes they were very hard to understand and I wished that they had slowed down."

Undergrads report that CCNY has a number of good, quiet places to study if you know where to look. Unfortunately, many consider the main library, officially called the Morris Raphael Cohen Library, too noisy for serious studying. The North Academic Center (the NAC), a central building where most classrooms are located, is said to be a better destination when it's time to really hit the books. The air-conditioned science library in the

Robert E. Marshak Building and the music library in Shepherd Hall are also generally good places to get work done. The writing center in Townshend Harris Hall, where all students can get assistance with papers from writing tutors, is quiet as well.

Mixin' It Up

As one student said about CCNY, "There is such a mix of people here." Outside of class, students are involved in a variety of cultural and ethnic clubs, a major reason minority students say they feel so comfortable on campus. New York City also contributes to this feeling of comfort. A student from Sweden said, "One thing I like about New York is that no matter who you are, you fit in."

> **"There is such a mix of people here."**

The diverse student body also has diverse interests. Although CCNY has no dorms and students live off campus, the week has designated club hours for extracurricular activities. Students participate in a number of extracurricular activities, including drama club, the Government and Law Society, the very active Day and Evening Student Governments (day and evening students have separate student governments, even though the two groups are closely affiliated), and the Frederick Douglass Society, a speech and debate club. CCNY, which is very much a "working-class school," has many political students who are inclined toward activism. Students protest rising tuition, budget cuts, and the bureaucratic administration, which "can be a pain sometimes." The Student Coalition is a prominent activist undergraduate organization that organizes demonstrations and petitions.

Some students devote their time to the three student newspapers: the *Campus*, a monthly that is the general school paper; the *Paper*, an African-American publication; and *Nightwatch*, which is aimed at evening students. The newspapers are generally "well respected," though one student expressed doubt that they are free to print what they wish. "The student newspapers have no controversy. They in-

clude things like letters from the president. When you work on the school paper, there are eyes on you."

The college has no football team, but students rally around the basketball, baseball, volleyball, and lacrosse teams instead. Popular intramural programs in soccer, swimming, volleyball, and basketball, which often are played during club hours, are "well run and easy to sign up for." The Herman Goldman Center for Sports and Recreation, a new outdoor sports complex, recently opened to student praise.

Where is everyone?

There are comparatively few campus social events, mainly because CCNY is a commuter school. One student said, "I don't even interact that much with people. They have parties here but I don't want to come back to school and then leave the area at 3 A.M." There are a few fraternities and sororities with houses, but they are focused on service more than on parties.

When they find themselves with free time, students just hang out more than anything else, one undergrad said. Popular hangout spots include a few restaurants near campus. The surrounding neighborhood has its advantages and disadvantages. One woman said, "[The neighborhood] has a bad reputation, but while I wouldn't want to walk alone there late at night, there are many things there that I like to do." Another student described the neighborhood as "very neighborhoody."

CCNY's campus, a mixture of modern and Gothic architecture, also offers students many options. The eight-story North Academic Center houses classrooms, the student center and lounge, and a ballroom. One student said, "Everything's there." Many students use the student lounge and center to study or to hang out. There is also an on-campus theater and an art building that shows exhibits. Students complained that there are not enough computers and that the gym is open at odd hours.

Safety First

CCNY has the feel of a real campus in the middle of the city; as one undergrad said, "Since all buildings face inward, it seems like a real campus." Nonetheless, CCNY is in an urban location, and campus security is not lacking. The entrances of all campus buildings are well guarded, and everyone must present an ID before entering a building. A computerized door system using swipe cards was recently installed as a new safety measure. One student added "A CCNY shuttle is offered if you miss the last bus home, or security will personally drive you to the train station."

Some CCNY students have part-time jobs or children and see CCNY as a place to get a college degree and a better job. However, others are there to learn; one student called CCNY "a mind-stimulating place." CCNY's lack of dorms and location in New York City have the drawback of causing a reported lack in traditional school spirit. Nevertheless, CCNY's solid academic programs and low tuition make it a bargain. —*Billy Rahm and Staff*

FYI
The three best things about attending CCNY are "the city (of course), the sciences, and the diversity of people."
The three worst things about attending CCNY are "the sense of security (the lack thereof), the outrageous living expenses, and the fact that everyone commutes."
The three things that every student should do before graduating from CCNY are "see a Yankees game, play basketball on a mid-Saturday morning, and try the local diners."
One thing I'd like to have known before coming here is "that the lack of dorms takes away from that 'college' feeling."

City University of New York / Hunter College

Address: 695 Park Avenue; New York, NY 10021
Phone: 212-772-4490
E-mail address: admissions @hunter.ccny.edu
Web site URL: hunter.ccny.edu
Founded: 1870
Private or Public: public
Religious affiliation: none
Location: urban
Undergraduate enrollment: 14,426
Total enrollment: 15,251
Percent Male/Female: 29%/71%
Percent Minority: 58%
Percent African-American: 20%

Percent Asian: 14%
Percent Hispanic: 23%
Percent Native-American: 0.5%
Percent in-state/out-of-state: 97%/3%
Percent Pub HS: NA
Number of Applicants: 6,986
Percent Accepted: 42%
Percent Accepted who enroll: 54%
Entering: 1,584
Transfers: 0
Application Deadline: 15 Jan
Mean SAT: 485 V, 490 M
Mean ACT: NA

Middle 50% SAT range: 420–540 V, 430–540 M
Middle 50% ACT range: NA
3 Most popular majors: psychology, sociology, English
Retention: 79%
Graduation rate: 19%
On-campus housing: 1%
Fraternities: 1%
Sororities: 1%
Library: 600,000 volumes
Tuition and Fees: $3,347 in; $6,547 out
Room and Board: $1,900
Financial aid, first-year: 77%

Located in the heart of a great cultural center, Hunter College in New York City has an extremely diverse undergraduate community, dedicated professors at the top of their fields, and solid educational opportunities.

Academic Opportunities
Students cite nursing, education, and the performing arts as the best departments at Hunter, with English and communications also garnering high praise. The honors program offers interdisciplinary courses

to qualified students, which allows them to devote less attention to core requirements and more to their majors. Hunter also offers study-abroad programs in Europe, Africa, Asia, South America, and the Caribbean, with Europe the most popular destination.

The college's distribution requirements include one lab science, several courses in the humanities, music, sociology, or economics, and four semesters of a language. Few students complain about these requirements. Classes can be as large as 300 in the sciences and introductory lectures, and as small as ten in the upper-division and honors classes. Evening sessions are popular at Hunter, especially among the many students holding day jobs.

Students say professors are supportive and "treat us as human beings." At least 50 percent of the staff are adjunct professors, whom students say are outstanding. Students don't have as much access to these professors, however, because adjuncts have neither on-campus phone numbers or offices. For the most part, students say they must make appointments to see their professors. "The professors are there but students have to make the effort to get help," claimed one undergraduate. TAs do not lead sections or teach classes.

Commuter School

Hunter's main academic buildings are uptown, on East 68th Street, but the only dorm is on 25th Street. A shuttle bus runs from the dorm to the campus every hour, and public transportation is abundant. First- and second-year students generally remain at the school for the whole day. Between classes, they hang out or study in the cafeterias, hallways, lounges, or club offices. Although Hunter is primarily a commuter school, students say it's easier to meet classmates and become involved in campus life if they live in the dorm, which houses about 400 people. Most of the dorm residents are in the nursing, physical therapy, athletics, or honors programs. With no meal plan, students are forced either to dine in the neighborhood's numerous eateries or, as most prefer, prepare food for themselves in the kitchens located on every dorm floor. Each dorm room has the added convenience of a sink. Many undergrads go to Hunter's library to study. As one sophomore put it, the quiet is "like a cemetery." Commuter students generally opt to study at home.

New York City provides students with countless options for entertainment including, but hardly limited to, world-famous theaters, restaurants, and museums. Campus parties are rare, and students say drinking is rare as well. Sororities and fraternities play a minor role in campus life, occupying no houses and performing charity work as their main activity. Cultural clubs organize some social events such as dances and rallies. RAs on each floor of the dorm sponsor activities each month, ranging from a papier-mâché night to a game night.

Politically Active

The fact that most Hunter students hail from New York, New Jersey, or Connecticut does not at all imply a homogeneous student body. According to one student, "It's incredible; everyone's completely different, yet they live together in harmony." Another student called Hunter a "mini-NYC." Many students are politically active, especially concerning issues of racism, feminism, abortion rights, the environment, gay and lesbian rights, and AIDS. The student branch of New York Public Interest Resource Group (PIRG) gets students involved in both environmental and campus issues. The active student senate represents academic departments, school interests, and students at large. One student said anyone can join the senate, although not everyone gets to vote. The teachers who are involved are said to be "top-notch."

> **"It's incredible; everyone's completely different, yet they live together in harmony."**

Although sports are not a big priority on campus, both basketball games and wrestling matches are well attended. Intramurals such as volleyball are also quite popular. Hunter's athletic facilities receive positive reviews despite the complaint that, as one student put it, "they're hidden in the basement." Students read the

Hunter Envoy, a biweekly newspaper, as well as other student publications. Ethnic organizations (such as the Asian-American, Caribbean, Greek, Puerto Rican, and African-American clubs) are very popular, as are dance groups, choir, jazz band, and theater clubs. The student-run Shakespeare Society also produces a full play and a collection of scenes once a semester. No classes are held during Dean's Hours every Tuesday from 2 to 3 P.M. and every Wednesday from 1 to 3 P.M. so that student clubs and organizations can hold meetings.

The City

The Hunter campus is truly part of the city. According to one student, "At times it's good because you're involved with the real world, but you also miss out on the things a private university in the city can offer, like a campus and unity." One undergraduate said there's "not really a campus, just some buildings together, and the dorm is by itself." Many students work full-time and consider school a "part-time thing." The city provides easy access to work and job openings.

"The school is involved with the community, and the community is involved with the school," one student said. The area around Hunter is a commercial district, so it's busy, and students assert that they "blend in." The school has taken measures to ensure student security, including emergency phones and guards that one undergrad reported "roam around a lot." Each dorm resident is generally allowed no more than two guests at a time.

According to one student, "The teachers are at the top of their fields and really want to teach, but they're not teaching under the best conditions." Students are managing all the same, however. As one undergraduate pointed out, "It is a city school, and the tuition is still low."

One student warned incoming freshmen to "make sure you're on top of your education and getting what you want. No one's going to help you unless you ask for help." Another student suggested that if you're looking for a structured program and lots of guidance, Hunter might not be the best choice. But Hunter students seem satisfied. "We get a much richer experience because of the huge diversity in terms of nationality and also in terms of age," one said. "This diversity gives a unique flavor to Hunter College." In fact, many undergrads see Hunter as a working model of the real world. —*Staff*

FYI

The three best things about attending Hunter are "the campus, the location, and again, the location. How can anyone top the upper East side?"

The three worst things about attending Hunter are "the high cost of living, the lack of school unity, and the lack of academic structure."

The three things that every student should do before graduating from Hunter are "see a student production, get out of the city at least once, and do part-time work as a street vendor or a cabbie."

One thing I'd like to have known before coming here is "that cafes are the best place to study."

City University of New York / Queens College

Address: 65-30 Kissena Boulevard, Kiely Hall, Room 217; Flushing, NY 11367-1597
Phone: 718-997-5614
E-mail address: NA
Web site URL: qc.edu
Founded: 1937
Private or Public: public
Religious affiliation: none
Location: urban
Undergraduate enrollment: 11,041
Total enrollment: 15,686
Percent Male/Female: 37%/63%
Percent Minority: 43%
Percent African-American: 10%

Percent Asian: 16%
Percent Hispanic: 16%
Percent Native-American: 0.5%
Percent in-state/out-of-state: 99%/1%
Percent Pub HS: 67%
Number of Applicants: 4,635
Percent Accepted: 49%
Percent Accepted who enroll: 35%
Entering: 802
Transfers: 1,209
Application Deadline: 1 Jan
Mean SAT: 544 V, 555 M
Mean ACT: NA

Middle 50% SAT range: 450–560 V, 480–580 M
Middle 50% ACT range: NA
3 Most popular majors: accounting, sociology, psychology
Retention: 82%
Graduation rate: 38%
On-campus housing: 0%
Fraternities: 1%
Sororities: 1%
Library: 489,096 volumes
Tuition and Fees: $3,393 in; $6,993 out
Room and Board: NA
Financial aid, first-year: 50%

Take 76 acres of gently rolling grassy hills, plop down a handful of student-filled buildings and some fountains, roll in the spired skyline of the largest and busiest city in America, and you get Queens College. Students claim that Queens College has the finest professors and the nicest campus of any CUNY school. Just as the college uniquely accommodates itself to both city and nature lovers, it stretches to fit a wide range of academic needs, from honors seminars with renowned professors to catch-up work in algebra.

Academic Options

All Queens College undergrads must fulfill the Liberal Arts and Science Area Requirements (LASAR), which divide the college curriculum into seven areas. Students take introductory courses in each area, many of which are large lecture classes. Although the lectures generally do not break down into smaller discussion sections as they do at some other colleges, students agree that the professors are very accessible. "At the first class, one famous professor gave us his home phone number," reported one junior.

Outside of introductory courses, students can expect an average class size of 20 to 40 people. ("That's not to say all 40 show up," one junior said.) Some students complain that these small courses fill up too easily. According to one, "I knew some guys who had to take an extra year to graduate because they couldn't get what they needed for their majors." Music students enter the renowned Aaron Copland School of Music, which features a rotating staff of prominent modern composers.

Special academic programs at Queens include an honors sequence in the Western tradition comprising 16 courses centered on a selection of "Great Books," an honors sequence in math and the sciences, and honors programs in business and journalism. Students consider the latter two an especially good value, with extra-small classes, full scholarships, summer internships in New York (which help establish impressive resumes and important connections), and, in the business program, a class with the president of Queens College. One business honors student said, "The most I've ever had in a class is 20 people, and honors students can register before the rush, so I always get my courses."

Queens reaches out to everyone, however, not just the academic elite. Its SEEK program (Search for Education, Elevation, and Knowledge) is designed for students who might have missed a few essential high school courses or who aren't ready for a standard college curriculum. Available only to New Yorkers, SEEK provides personal academic counselors who help students schedule the necessary college prep classes that will enable them to begin the LASAR sequence and eventually earn a bachelor's degree. According to one student, "If it weren't for SEEK, I wouldn't be in college." Other flexible academic features at Queens include evening classes and Fresh Start, a bachelor's program for anyone who's been out of school for more than three years.

Campus Life, Commuter School

Since Queens College is a commuter school (there are no dorms; most students live with their parents), many students leave the campus after classes. To encourage undergrads to spend a little extra time on campus, however, the administration schedules "free hours" in midday, during which no classes are held. During this time, one student said, "Everyone goes to the cafeteria or the student union," which features a pizza parlor, Dunkin' Donuts, TCBY, Taco Bell Express, and a kosher kitchen. "There are a lot of cliques in the student union," one student said. "You can pretty much map out who's going to sit where." But the union also is the headquarters for more than 175 extracurricular clubs and organizations, along with Thursday night club-hosted parties, frequent guest lectures, a wide-screen TV, and a formidable collection of pool tables.

Students agree that taking part in the social life at Queens requires some initiative; despite the large number of clubs, many events are poorly advertised.

"Queens reaches out to everyone."

Many Queens College students laugh at the mention of athletics. The campus has a gym and playing fields; in fact, new facilities recently were built for softball, soccer, and lacrosse. Only the fans are missing. As one team member said, "If we get 20 people to come see a game, that's a great turnout." Those who use the gym say it's fine, but a little old. The biggest problem, one student reported, is that there's "no ventilation in the gym. In the hot weather, I almost passed out a few times."

Recently, articles in the *QC Quad*, the weekly campus paper, reported on the university's proposed plans to cut some of Queens' smaller departments and consolidate them with similar programs at other CUNY schools. Although students taking classes in one of these departments were concerned that they might have to commute as far as the Bronx or Staten Island, Queens is not the only school in the CUNY system that has had budget problems in recent years.

Queens offers an inexpensive, flexible education with a wealth of impressive professors, many of whom earned their degrees from the most prestigious schools in the country. Sure, traditional "school spirit" is a foreign concept at this unique school, but if you're looking for a solid education, no matter what your background, grab a subway token and take a look at Queens. —*Susanna Chu and Staff*

FYI
The three best things about attending Queens College are "the great professors, the terrific backdrop, and the laid-back atmosphere."
The three worst things about attending Queens College are "everyone commutes, so there's no sense of community, and it's harder to meet people."
The three things that every student should do before graduating from Queens College are "go bar hopping in the City, go to a Broadway play, go to a few campus parties."
One thing I'd like to have known before coming here is "how rural the place seems. Definitely not a city life."

Clarkson University

Address: Box 5605;
Potsdam, NY 13699
Phone: 315-268-6479
E-mail address:
admissions@clarkson.edu
Web site URL:
www.clarkson.edu
Founded: 1896
Private or Public: private
Religious affiliation: none
Location: NA
**Undergraduate
enrollment:** 2,532
Total enrollment: 2,902
Percent Male/Female:
74%/26%
Percent Minority: 8%
Percent African-American:
3%

Percent Asian: 2%
Percent Hispanic: 2%
Percent Native-American:
0.5%
**Percent in-state/out-of-
state:** 73%/27%
Percent Pub HS: 91%
Number of Applicants:
2,551
Percent Accepted:
83%
**Percent Accepted who
enroll:** 33%
Entering: 707
Transfers: 143
Application Deadline:
15 Mar
Mean SAT: 575 V, 626 M
Mean ACT: NA

Middle 50% SAT range:
520–620 V,
560–660 M
Middle 50% ACT range:
NA
3 Most popular majors:
civ. eng., mech. Eng.,
management
Retention: 85%
Graduation rate: 72%
On-campus housing: 98%
Fraternities: 17%
Sororities: 17%
Library: 237,251 volumes
Tuition and Fees:
$20,225 in; $20,225 out
Room and Board: $7,484
Financial aid, first-year:
96%

C onstant ice storms and snow fail to dampen the enthusiasm of Clarkson students in the classroom, laboratory, or in their myriad other activities. Dedication to a rigorous training in engineering or business and management is what brought Clarkson students to this small and technologically-developed campus in Potsdam, New York. Rising to the challenges of a demanding set of courses while taking time to enjoy college life to its fullest characterizes Clarkson students as they prepare for a definite set of goals in the field of engineering and business management.

The Workload

Although few students describe their workload as impossible, many clearly approach their undergraduate courses as a graduate training program. Students major in such diverse fields as finance, management and engineering, computer science, biology, aeronautical engineering, and civil and environmental engineering. While one student commented that the "engineering facilities are good, but as far as other majors, there are some complaints," the school does not deny that "engineering makes up the bulk of the student body." Clarkson accordingly is equipped

for such technologically challenging areas of study, with a "very network-oriented" campus connecting computers at many different laboratories and work spaces, such as the new Center for Advanced Materials Processing (CAMP). The school has recently received high honors from the Accreditation Board for Engineering and Technology (ABET).

To prepare them for any major in the field of engineering or business, first-year students at Clarkson are required to take courses in inorganic chemistry, physics, calculus, and two liberal studies classes known as Great Ideas in Western Civilization. During their remaining three years, all students are required to take two more liberal studies courses in addition to mathematics electives such as statistics, linear algebra, and microeconomics. Even with these requirements, students are able to take some free electives.

Clarkson professors participate in research for government, military, and civil departments such as NASA, conduct experiments in zero gravity welding for the new international space station, explore high-temperature deposits, aircraft structures, and even treatments for breast cancer. Students praise profs such as Jim Peploski in chemistry, Amy Zander in civil engineering, and M. Sathyamoorthy in aeronautical engineering for their teaching as well as for being "very easygoing and fun in general." Liberal studies professor Wes Craven even developed the idea for the Nightmare on Elm Street movies based on Elm Street in Potsdam. One senior stated, "I can't think of any professors that I didn't like" and regretted not getting to know all of his professors. While first-year classes in areas such as chemistry can have up to 200 students, after freshman year the classes get "pretty small, but still big enough to get to know people," one student said. With most classes enrolling around 30 students, the school creates "a small, intimate environment . . . with a lot to offer." Departments also host faculty-student socials to enhance contact.

What They Do

But avidly reading and exploring projects in the lab is only part of the Clarkson University experience. "Everyone's involved in something . . . anything that you can think of, we have someone doing it," one student said. The Pep Band, the Clarkson Integrator, the Flying Club, Amateur Radio, the Garage Club, the Environmental Club, and community service projects such as the Red Cross, Coed National Service Organization, Pets for People, and the Food Bank comprise some of the over 160 organizations and clubs that Clarkson students participate in, despite their challenging workloads. Jobs and research projects, however, often take the lion's share of many students' spare time.

While campus social life at Clarkson once was dominated by the Greek societies, the university has recently "toned down" the Greek system after a drinking-related fatality. The administration has installed a Greek Affairs Manager. According to one senior, students want to have fun, but "on the side of caution." Clarkson is officially a dry campus with no kegs allowed and stiff penalties for drinking among students under 21. "So freshmen can no longer place empty beer bottles in their windows," one junior joked. Another agreed that Clarkson is a "conservative school . . . taking a conservative stance." While the Greek parties are still well attended, students agree that you "don't have to be Greek to get things done."

Naturally, "come Friday, everyone wants to blow off steam," and for those who do not participate in Greek societies, the school manages to keep weekends exciting as well. Guest lecturers are invited to give talks on topics ranging from UFOs to wildlife photography to alumni networking and information about the engineering industry and management. A recent year-long series of activities with the theme "Victorian Era to Star Trek Era" included parties, time capsules containing CD-ROMs of student e-mails, and guest lectures. The Clarkson Union Board is a student organization that puts on nonalcoholic "midnights" with music, magicians, and comedians. The school also sponsors dances and Honor Society formal events. Many students find recreation in the vast outdoor spaces of Potsdam like hiking and skiing. "If you keep your eyes open, opportunities present themselves," one student said.

> "The best hockey and pep band in the East!"

As for dating, the "ratio favors the women, but Potsdam State is not far away," one sophomore commented. Students agree that the characteristic social environment at Clarkson on the weekend is large groups of students hanging out together to watch a movie or go downtown. Potsdam has quite a few bars and coffeehouses that host jazz and blues groups. "There's more than enough to do here," one junior reported. Potsdam is close to Adirondack Park, Lake Placid, Lake Ottawa, and Montreal, a popular destination for students in search of a larger party scene. But time for excursions out of the Potsdam area is limited, and most students stay close to campus.

Food at Clarkson receives the most critical reviews. "The tacos seem to give some GI trouble. They taste good, but it's a time bomb," one senior reported. The campus has numerous dining centers. Some are cafeteria style, while others have more of a fast-food setting, such as the new Cheel Center. Potsdam has local pizza restaurants, fast food, a family restaurant, and a '50s-style diner where "it's really fun to watch them cook on the grill," said one student customer.

The school administration is reluctant, some students reported, to allow undergrads to move off campus except for economic reasons or residence in a Greek house. Most dorms are coed, except for freshman dorms. All dorms have cable TV and each room has a computer network connection. Also available are university-run apartments where students can live on campus without being on the meal plan. The campus used to be separated into Hill and Downtown halves, but current construction is aimed at consolidating the campus. From dorms, classes are generally a five- to ten-minute walk, although "some lazy bums actually drive to class! But there is no reason," said one junior. A shuttle bus connects the Clarkson campus, downtown Potsdam, and Potsdam State University. The administration recently installed blue-light security phones, and students generally walk in groups, although there have not been many crime-related incidents. "It's probably the safest place in the world, unless the squirrels get rabies," said one city-bred student.

Sports at Clarkson centers on hockey, Clarkson's only Division I sport. "If you're not a hockey fan when you start, you are when you leave," assured one enthusiastic senior. Engaged in a prolonged rivalry with nearby St. Lawrence, the hockey team is "almost mythical on campus," according to students. Extensive recruiting has created "a little animosity" between the hockey team and the rest of the student body in terms of privileges, one student said, but school spirit seems to override these concerns as the games at the Cheel Center are always well attended. We have "the best hockey and pep band in the East!" one band member exclaimed. Another student added, "The pep band has a high opinion of themselves." The baseball team has also performed well over the past few years. For nonvarsity athletes, intramurals and gym classes are very popular at Clarkson.

The Student Body

Many Clarkson students have lower- to upper-middle-class-backgrounds, and the school gives a great deal of financial aid. "I didn't expect as much as I got," said one junior. Undergrads say the student body is racially homogeneous and generally "moderate Republican." One senior found it "surprising . . . that [there] are no major rifts. Everybody gets along pretty well."

Clarkson students agree that "everyone is here because they like it." The intense academic focus leads those who dislike the school or the academic orientation to leave early in their college career. "The reputation is very good, and you can get a lot out of this place if you want to . . . and we're all very proud of Clarkson," said one student. Devotion to their selected tracks of study and loyalty to their school are the hallmarks of this spirited student body as its members prepare for the real world and enjoy their college years to their fullest. —*Eric Weiss and Staff*

FYI
The three best things about attending Clarkson are "the friends, the challenging academics, and Potsdam."
The three worst things about attending Clarkson are "how the teachers are difficult to understand, the weather, and Potsdam."
The three things every student should do before graduating from Clarkson are "to go to Duffs, attend a hockey game, and pull a prank."
On thing I wish I had known before coming here is "how difficult the Chemical Engineering program was."

Colgate University

Address: 13 Oak Drive; Hamilton, NY 13346-1383
Phone: 315-228-7401
E-mail address: admission @mail.colgate.edu
Web site URL: www.colgate.edu
Founded: 1819
Private or Public: private
Religious affiliation: none
Location: rural
Undergraduate enrollment: 2,866
Total enrollment: 2,876
Percent Male / Female: 48%/52%
Percent Minority: 14%

Percent African-American: 5%
Percent Asian: 5%
Percent Hispanic: 3%
Percent Native-American: 0.5%
Percent in-state / out-of-state: 32%/68%
Percent Pub HS: 71%
Number of Applicants: 5,590
Percent Accepted: 42%
Percent Accepted who enroll: 32%
Entering: 751
Transfers: 9
Application Deadline: 15 Jan
Mean SAT: 644 V, 651 M

Mean ACT: 29
Middle 50% SAT range: 600–690 V, 610–700 M
Middle 50% ACT range: 28–32
3 Most popular majors: economics, English, history
Retention: 97%
Graduation rate: 89%
On-campus housing: 100%
Fraternities: 33%
Sororities: 31%
Library: 615,940 volumes
Tuition and Fees: $25,740 in; $25,740 out
Room and Board: $6,330
Financial aid, first-year: 41%

L ooking for a small school with an incredible amount of choices? Colgate is probably the only school that can claim 13 as its lucky number. Thirteen Baptist men with 13 prayers and $13 founded Colgate in 1819. Located in Hamilton, New York, with close to 3,000 undergraduates, Colgate has grown from humble beginnings into a small liberal arts institution with a big reputation.

"You Have to Take a Swim Test"

With 49 concentration (major) choices, Colgate offers a very diverse academic program. All freshmen choose a seminar class for which they receive credit. The topics run the gamut from biology to global change to philosophy. Each class has roughly 20 students and the seminar professor becomes the student's faculty advisor until the spring of sophomore year, at which point each student chooses his or her major. Freshmen are enthusiastic about the seminar program because it allows them to interact with their advisee group regularly. They also have the opportunity to create a good relationship with their advisor in and out of the classroom. Colgate requires 32 credits to graduate.

Students must take two classes in each of three distribution areas: social sciences, natural sciences, and humanities. In addition, there is a four-credit physical education requirement as well as a mandatory swim test. One student explained, "You have to take the swim test, or else they make you set up all the chairs for graduation. That's a lot of chairs."

Colgate also offers a multitude of study abroad programs, as well as unique short-term abroad opportunities. These trips apply classroom concepts in more realistic settings. If you study Japanese, you can take advantage of the one-month program in Japan called Living in the Religious Heritage of Japan; or if you are interested in the classics, Colgate offers the Material Culture of Rome and Pompeii trips for beginning classics students. There are also several other similar trips, and Colgate students find them highly accessible and enjoyable.

All in all, the students find the workload "difficult, but manageable" and average three hours of work a night. Class size is small, with most enrolling between 20 and 40 students. There is only one class with more than 100 students. Students cite economics, astrophysics, and upper-level calculus as the most painful classes at Colgate. Students reportedly "love our professors." They say that the professors are intelligent, amiable, and approachable. One student recalls an instance when her professor took her out to lunch and discussed Oprah with her. Many others have been invited over to professors' homes for dinner or study breaks.

Besides good professors, Colgate students have the chance to listen to great speakers. In the past, speakers such as Jesse Jackson, Mikhail Gorbachev, and Bill Cosby have graced the Colgate campus to speak to students.

It's Beautiful

One reason speakers might be happy to visit Colgate is that its campus is gorgeous. It is situated on top of what is fondly known as Cardiac Hill. The majority of freshmen dorms are on the top of the hill, while the fraternities, upperclassmen housing, and restaurants are on the bottom of the hill. Many students joke that a significant part of every student's life is negotiating the daily trek up the Hill. The picturesque landscape is full of lush greenery and the academic buildings overlook Moraine Lake. In terms of architectural beauty, students list Persson Hall and the chapel as two of the most noteworthy buildings on campus. Persson has a glass walkway that gives a magnificent view of the campus and the lake. The chapel is the most prominent building seen from the quad, and is an attractive place for students to lie out and study in the sun.

So, Where Do I Live?

There are roughly seven freshmen dorms each year. Most dorms are coed but single sex by floor with two or three people per room. One dorm, Andrews, has suites with common rooms for three to four people. The rooms come with bunk beds, dressers, desks, and either a closet or a wardrobe. East, another dorm, is substance-free, while West is considered the party dorm.

Students are sent roommate preference forms before their freshman year, and for the most part, students are happy with their first-year rooms and roommate assignments. There is also a Residential Advisor program for freshmen which pairs groups of students with an upperclassman who watches over them during their freshman year. The function of an RA is to help students move in, deal with roommates, and enforce no-alcohol-in-room policies. Reportedly, RAs are strict with regulations, but "if you leave your door closed they'll leave you alone."

After freshman year there are multiple housing options. There are special-interest houses such as the Asian Interest House, the Harlem Renaissance Center, and the Ecology House as well as dorms. Sophomores tend to stay in the dorms, while juniors often move into on-campus Colgate apartments, and seniors enter a lottery to live off campus.

"Tasty, but Dangerous"

The food at Colgate is not four-star quality, but it serves its purpose. Students advise staying away from most meat and shepherd's pie. One student commented that the cheesesteaks and pizza are "tasty, but dangerous because they come back to haunt you later." Freshmen and sophomores use a 19-meals-per-week plan, while most juniors and seniors who live in rooms with kitchenettes tend to make their own food. Students report that the dining halls are clean and welcoming, and that students can just sit in them and talk for hours over coffee. There are plenty of seats and food is served until 6:30 P.M. The dining halls also do an adequate job of providing variety and alternate options for vegetarians and vegans. Students say that there are not many off-campus restaurants, but among the most notable is Sushi Blues, while the best coffee shop is on campus and is called the Barge.

Homogeneous

Students report that the one word to describe the student body is "homogeneous." The average Colgate student is white, preppy, athletic, wealthy, and drives a Jeep Grand Cherokee. Many people drive, although parking availability is a problem. One student commented on the general economic status of the student body by describing the parking lot as "looking like a showroom." The wardrobe of choice also resembles a showroom and showcases primarily J. Crew, Banana Republic, and Abercrombie and Fitch.

In general, the students are happy with the student body. People are pretty laid back and sociable. They gather together with friends to watch *Party of Five*, *Ally McBeal*, *Friends*, *The Simpsons*, and *Dawson's Creek*. Phish, the Grateful Dead, R & B, and funk can be heard blasting out of dorm rooms. While there is not much ethnic diversity at Colgate, minorities are not complaining to heavily.

"Oh Yeah, People Can Get Play"

Colgate students go out Monday, Wednesday, Thursday, and Friday nights. Until ten years ago, there were no classes on Tuesday or Thursday, so students were able to go out and party on Monday and Wednesday nights. Though there are now classes on Tuesday and Thursday, they tend to be low-key so the tradition of weekday partying is kept alive, if in slightly modified form.

> **"The social scene at Colgate revolves around the Greek system and bars."**

The social scene at Colgate revolves around the Greek system and bars. Since the bars tend to stringently check IDs, most freshmen spend their nights at fraternity parties. Due to the administration's newer and stricter policies on alcohol, all fraternity parties must be catered by an outside service. As a result, frats have to pay a substantial amount of money to throw a party, and consequently, the door fees for such parties have risen to around $5. Upperclassmen often spend their evenings in one of the three popular bars down the hill: the Jug, Risky Business, and the Hour Glass.

Although the Greek system has a large role socially at Colgate, there is no real pressure for everyone to join. Non-Greeks do not tend to feel left out because the frat parties are open to all students. Students rush fraternities and sororities in their sophomore year. It is not hard to rush, and

it does not involve hazing. The most popular frat is Sigma Chi and the most popular sorority is Kappa. Frats also throw big, annual theme parties such as Beta Beach and Derby Days. Beta Beach is a pool party in the middle of winter, and Derby Days are a week-long series of athletic and drinking events.

There is not much of a dating scene at Colgate; instead, there is a much wider occurrence of random hookups. Students say that the student body "is hot, and you can get a lot of play."

Spare Time

Colgate has many extracurricular organizations that students join in their spare time. Some of the most respected are Outdoor Ed, Student Government, the Link Program, and Sidekick. Outdoor Ed sponsors adventure trips in the area, the Link program supplies juniors and seniors work with a seminar professor to help advise groups of freshmen, and Sidekick pairs Colgate students with disadvantaged elementary school children. There is also a popular improvisational comedy group called Charred Goosebeaks and a radio show called *Sunday Night Procrastination*. Few students work actual jobs.

Da Jocks

The most popular teams at Colgate are football, hockey, and basketball. The football team, the Red Raiders, won the Patriot League 2 years ago. Most students attend the football games and many alumni return for them as well. There is a strong sense of school spirit, and most students will even travel to away games in order to support their teams. The gym facilities are also excellent, and many students take advantage of the weight room and tracks. The Greek system is involved in organizing intramural games, and students are enthusiastic about these as well.

Colgate is a serious academic institution with a relaxed, party atmosphere. Students who want a gorgeous campus set in the cozy hills of Hamilton, New York, and who are up for the academic challenge, should definitely put Colgate at the top of their list.—*Dana Peck and Staff*

FYI
The three best things about attending Colgate are "the parties, the people, and the amazing faculty."
The three worst things about attending Colgate are "the 'sameness,' the amount of work, and the class size (professors always know when you're not there)."
The three things that every student should do before graduating from Colgate are "to hear a famous speaker, to study abroad, and to get a good fake ID."
One thing I'd like to have known before coming here is "that there's a huge hill separating campus and where everyone hangs out!"

Columbia University

Address: 1130 Amsterdam Avenue MC 2807; New York, NY 10027
Phone: 212-854-2522
E-mail address: ugrad-admiss@columbia.edu
Web site URL: www.columbia.edu
Founded: 1754
Private or Public: private
Religious affiliation: none
Location: urban
Undergraduate enrollment: 3,913
Total enrollment: 21,857
Percent Male/Female: 49%/51%
Percent Minority: 34%

Percent African-American: 10%
Percent Asian: 16%
Percent Hispanic: 7%
Percent Native-American: 0.5%
Percent in-state/out-of-state: NA
Percent Pub HS: NA
Number of Applicants: 13,013
Percent Accepted: 14%
Percent Accepted who enroll: 55%
Entering: 964
Transfers: NA
Application Deadline: 1 Jan
Mean SAT: 663 V, 672 M

Mean ACT: NA
Middle 50% SAT range: NA
Middle 50% ACT range: NA
3 Most popular majors: English, political science, history
Retention: 93%
Graduation rate: 88%
On-campus housing: 99%
Fraternities: 19%
Sororities: 25%
Library: 2,000,000 volumes
Tuition and Fees: $24,974 in; $24,974 out
Room and Board: $7,732
Financial aid, first-year: NA

Are you bored by the idea of spending the next four years in Small Town, USA, where your college is the entire town? Would you like to live in a city where art and theater are at your fingertips and the night life rages into the morning hours? Check out New York's Columbia University where students have the advantages of both an Ivy League education and life in the big city.

One of the first things prospective students learn about Columbia is the school's strict core curriculum requirement, which many seem to feel is both a blessing and a curse. All students must take the yearlong Literature Humanities, and Contemporary Civilization classes, as well as Arts Humanities, Music Humanities, and Logic & Rhetoric, which are each semester-long courses. Everyone must also take at least two classes in a related subject area, which fulfill the Major Cultures requirement (for example: Latin American Civilizations and History of Harlem, or Asian Texts and Japanese Film), three classes for the science requirement (two of which must be in sequence), and pass the foreign language requirement.

Although students are not unanimous in their like or dislike of the requirements, the core is certainly something that everyone complains about. "At first I was really annoyed [by the core] because I wasn't particularly interested in some of the classes," said one student. "It sounds lame, but I really am becoming more well-rounded because of it." One concern about the core curriculum is that there are so many sections of each course being taught each semester, it is difficult to establish uniform grading policies and to regulate the quality of the teachers. Graduate students, who generally receive mixed reviews, also teach some core classes.

However, students are enthusiastic about their professors, who are reportedly very accessible. One student was disappointed with a TA for Arts Humanities who had no appreciation for the material, but said that her music professor made up for it. "He is a world-renowned musician, had written books and composed. But after I didn't do well on the exam, he spent 45 minutes humming with me in his office to help me remember a piece."

Beyond the core curriculum, students are impressed with Columbia's wide course offerings, especially considering the small size of the undergraduate population. Political science, economics, and English rank among the most popular majors, while foreign-language majors are less common. Classes at Columbia tend to be small, except for a few introductory classes such as economics. "There is generally no problem getting into classes except freshman year, when they pre-register you for your core classes," said one student. "I couldn't fit in any of the other things I wanted to take."

Unlike many colleges, students are not actually required to declare a major, but can instead choose to concentrate in a specific area or areas. Theoretically, this allows students more freedom to take advantage of the liberal arts environment, but in many departments the concentration is only two or three classes less than a major, and therefore most people—with the exception of some premeds—choose to declare a major anyway. One student complained about the lack of academic guidance she has received. "There are no advisors until after you declare your major, and even then the administration isn't very friendly or helpful," she said. "There's also a lot of red tape."

Life in the Big City

Although location is always a factor in the college search, prospective Columbia students should think twice as hard about the school's environs. "Life at Columbia totally revolves around being a part of New York City," said one student. New York is the "city that never sleeps," and the weekends and sometimes the weekdays represent just that. A subway stop directly on campus makes it easy for people to leave the Upper West Side and venture over to the East Side or downtown. In *Time Out New York*, the *Village Voice*, and other newspapers and magazines, Columbia undergrads find huge numbers of movie, club, gallery, theater, and restaurant listings. Favorite activities include an afternoon at the Museum of Modern Art (free admission with your student ID) or a walk/ride in Central Park. "There is so much to take advantage of," said one student, "and Columbia does a good job of getting students involved in the city." One drawback to the college's location, however, is New York City's high cost of living. This is especially true for students who frequent downtown clubs and bars. But there are cheaper regularly scheduled movies, as well as concerts and plays on campus.

Columbia's urban setting greatly influences the college social life. "There is less campus life than at other schools because we're right in the city," explained one undergrad. Students tend to drink at bars, rather than attend campus parties, which are busted pretty easily by the NYPD. Although some head to other sections of the city to party, several bars in the Columbia vicinity cater to college students, including the West End, which attracts a sporty crowd, Cannon's, the Heights, 1020, and Soha. Some say a fake ID is useful, and many students have them because the bars are really strict. Although Columbia does have a Greek system, frat life is small and often looked down upon, while sororities are even less popular.

Drugs are popular but isolated at Columbia. "If you get into drugs, it's really easy to get them," said one student. "But the drug scene is not necessarily centered on campus. It's easy to go to parties in Brooklyn or to raves downtown," said another, "and no one knows what you do when you go off campus."

Clubbing is also popular among some Columbia students ("a night at Twilo is literally an all-night experience"). Students are quick to point out, though, that drinking and drugs are by no means the only things to do.

The Typical Columbia Student

The general consensus is that there is no typical student at Columbia. One student describes a division between those who choose Columbia for New York City—they are into the scene, hit the bars every weekend, dress well, and seem really superficial, and those students who choose Columbia for its Ivy League Status—lost sheep who try really hard to be sophisticated. One undergrad described the student body as cliquey, while another said more generally: "We have a diverse student body, not just ethnically or politically but also according to interests, which is not always so good because it's hard to find one thing for the student body to focus on."

Despite this seeming lack of unity, however, students said it is not hard to meet people, especially during freshman year. "Your core classes are small with all freshmen, so you know everyone," explained one undergrad, plus the communal atmosphere in dorms and the dining hall social life really helps. Freshman year is also the only year students are required to buy a university meal plan (most upperclassmen choose not to). On-campus food options include the one dining hall, John Jay, a grocery store called J.J.'s Place, and several fast-food vendors where students can arrange to have meal plan points. Dining hall food received average marks, with weekend brunches being the favorite meals.

The majority of Columbia students live on campus all four years (housing is guaranteed). "The dorms range from really good to pretty bad," said one student. The newest dorm is East Campus: twenty stories high with views of the East and West Rivers, suites for five students configured like three-bedroom apartments with a common room, bathroom, and kitchen (and fridge). This is quite a contrast to some of Columbia's older dorms, "But the worst dorms are no worse than what I've seen at other colleges," said one student. Columbia has an RA system on each floor of its dorms, but RAs are reported to be not too strict, as long as students do not abuse their privileges. The administration has restrictions on alcohol, drugs, cooking equipment, and incense, as well as scheduled quiet time in the dorms, but students say that nothing is too strictly enforced.

"There are so many things to worry about security-wise at Columbia that the students have a lot of freedom in other areas," explained one undergrad. Students said that being safe at Columbia is all about using common sense and being careful in the city, especially in the Morningside Heights area where the campus is located, running approximately from 110th to 120th Street. "Columbia is in the middle of the city, but it's closed off so there is a feeling of a campus," explained one student. The only major complaint about the physical plan was the current shortage of places for students to meet. The student center was recently torn down to make way for construction of a new center, the Alfred Lerner Hall, due for completion in the fall of 2000. It will include a more upscale restaurant, a black box theater, offices for campus organizations, study space, computer labs, a print shop, an auditorium, and a game room.

Beyond Academics

Extracurricular activity is a big part of life at Columbia. "Few people just go to school," said one undergrad. "If you have an interest in something, chances are you can find a group that you'll fit into." Visible groups on campus include a number of religious and cultural groups. Political activists are also prominent on campus with poster campaigns about issues outside Columbia, especially around election time. "You can't be on College Walk without getting accosted by the ISO [Independent Socialists Organization, one prominent political group]," joked one undergrad. Columbia's active gay and lesbian community has a big presence on campus as well. "For a campus that is fairly conservative, we have a tight-knit gay community with tons of activity," said one undergrad. "If you're comfortable with yourself, then it's totally comfortable to be out at Columbia . . . People don't get away with making homophobic remarks—it just doesn't fly."

Opportunities for creative students include theater and music groups, as well as literary magazines and Columbia's daily newspaper, the Spectator. Student editors can apply for a position as a Writing Fellow and get paid and receive credit for helping other students with their papers. "Community service is also popular because we live in a neighborhood where there are a lot of opportunities to help," explained one student. Community Impact organizes programs in which students volunteer to tutor in Harlem schools, to care for children of homeless people so they can look for jobs, or to clean parks in nearby neighborhoods. Community Outreach day is an annual event when students devote a Saturday to cleaning the city; last year over 1,000 members of the Columbia community participated.

Columbia is not known for athletics, although the student body is fairly active, both in club sports and on an individual level. Popular club sports include those for tae kwon do, ultimate Frisbee, rugby, and archery. The fencing and swimming teams stand out as two of the most consistently successful teams, although football is the only team people actually go to watch. One student said, "There is no school spirit here, except maybe at the homecoming football game." Columbia does actively recruit, although not heavily enough, in the opinion of one athlete. However, teams do play a prominent role in the campus social life—members of a team tend to eat and hang out together a lot.

Sharing Columbia

Columbia students have the opportunity of taking classes at Barnard, which was once Columbia's sister school and still remains all-female. Students from both schools interact frequently, often living and taking classes together. Some students complained that the relationship between the colleges makes for weird tension between females at Columbia and Barnard. "Some girls at Columbia think they're superior, and some girls at Barnard antagonize Columbia students," said one undergrad. Said another student, "Classes at Barnard don't have to be all-female, but many are. I've heard that the atmosphere in some classes is sexist against men . . . it's weird because there's no separate school for men, just for women."

> **"Life at Columbia totally revolves around being a part of New York City."**

Another unique characteristic of life on campus is the presence of a large number of graduate students. "There are a lot of older people around," said one student. "And there's not much interaction between grad students and undergrads outside of the classroom. There's almost some tension about it because a lot of the university is geared to the grad schools."

"I think Columbia would be ideal for grad school, when you know better what you want when you have a life established," said one undergrad. "It's rough being an undergraduate here, especially freshman year, because it's not an outright friendly environment." "[Columbia] is a very sophisticated school . . . You have to be driven, have a goal, and be ready to pursue your own path."—*Liz Kukura and Staff*

FYI
The three best things about attending Columbia are "the sex ratio—with Barnard, and then Columbia being half female, this is a great place to be a single guy, New York City, and the Core Curriculum."
The three worst things about attending Columbia are "the lack of on-campus social life (though this is improving), the lack of trees, and the fact that you need 124 points (5.5 classes per semester) to graduate."
The three things every student should do before graduating from Columbia are "to hook up in the library stacks, go to the roof of Butler Library at night . . . you can see all the way down to the World Trade Center, and do the 'Trinity' [basically, making your way from Cannon's Pub, to the West End, to the Amsterdam Cafe, local bars, all in one night]."
One thing I wish I knew before coming here is "that Columbians are rather independent people."

Cooper Union for the Advancement of Science and Art

Address: 30 Cooper Square; New York, NY 10003
Phone: 212-353-4120
E-mail address: admissions@cooper.edu
Web site URL: www.cooper.edu
Founded: 1859
Private or Public: private
Religious affiliation: none
Location: urban
Undergraduate enrollment: 845
Total enrollment: 907
Percent Male / Female: 66% / 34%
Percent Minority: 39%
Percent African-American: 5%

Percent Asian: 25%
Percent Hispanic: 8%
Percent Native-American: 0.5%
Percent in-state / out-of-state: 63% / 37%
Percent Pub HS: 70%
Number of Applicants: 2,216
Percent Accepted: 13%
Percent Accepted who enroll: 69%
Entering: NA
Transfers: 33
Application Deadline: varies
Mean SAT: 690 V, 740 M
Mean ACT: NA

Middle 50% SAT range: 620–720 V, 700–780 M
Middle 50% ACT range: NA
3 Most popular majors: fine art, electrical engineering, mechanical engineering
Retention: 91%
Graduation rate: 78%
On-campus housing: 22%
Fraternities: 2%
Sororities: 1%
Library: 97,000 volumes
Tuition and Fees: $8,800 in; $8,800 out
Room and Board: $10,000
Financial aid, first-year: 100%

Set in the fast-paced, heart-pounding Big Apple, Cooper Union (CU or Cooper) is a place where innovation and diligence are the staples of life. Graced with the legacy of historical figures such as Abraham Lincoln and Thomas Edison, Cooper is no stranger to fame or ingenuity. Its concentrated emphasis on the undergraduate experience in the areas of engineering, art, and architecture are bolstered by a rare financial advantage: full-tuition scholarship for all students.

Serious Stuff

"Academics is the number one thing at Cooper," says one senior who characterizes his peers as energetic, inquisitive intellectuals who believe that there is always more than one solution to any question. With academic requirements ranging from calculus, physics, and chemistry to engineering and the humanities, the challenging and highly structured curriculum of Cooper Union reflects a commitment to build students' analytical and problem-solving skills. Class size typically ranges from 6 to 23, and this close-knit environment demands a considerable amount of dedication, enthusiasm, and participation from the student body. One freshman said, "With almost no lecture classes, this is the place where they really work your noodle." With few "free nap" classes, students become fully absorbed, often hands-on, in original projects that ultimately yield significant rewards in broadening their thinking about the connection between real-world situations and theoretical learning.

The grading system is designed in such a way that those who devote the time and effort will get grades that "honestly reflect their perseverance through the thinking hurdles along the way." Several upperclassmen dismiss the notion that there are professors that give no As. There seems to be a consensus at CU that "the instructors are fully aware of how much time people need to spend in finding 'a different angle' of thinking."

While Cooper is not a liberal arts college by any measure, students of all concentrations (majors) are required to take four years of humanities classes such as introductory courses to the plays of Shakespeare or studies in literature. This shift from solely science-centered programs to a more diverse broad-based education was the result of student action in 1997. Many undergraduates felt that their only contacts were the 20 or 30 other people in their major and that they lacked the kind of learning alternatives that other college students enjoyed. The administration's quick response in improving this situation clearly demonstrates its desire to provide Cooper students with a more integrated undergraduate experience.

> **"If you really do know what you want, and your parents have no problem with a free education, Cooper is the place to be."**

Moreover, CU is consciously making an effort to highlight the importance of its bond with the surrounding community by taking full advantage of the cultural events available in New York.

Who's Teaching?

Professors, who are passionate about their areas of research, are not only approachable, but actively seek out means to stimulate their students and increase the pulse of academic life. Some leading researchers in their respective fields include Emanuel Kondopirakis (mathematics), Fred Siegel (humanities expert on American cities), John Bove (organic chemistry), Toby Cumberbatch (electronics), Irv Brazinsky (thermodynamics). "Cooper has a very interactive environment between students and professors, who are more like your contemporaries." "You really learn about what it's like to use the information they teach you in the classroom and apply it in life," says one junior. Another sophomore said, "I was really surprised when I found out last year that there is only one section offered per subject. This way, we have the opportunity to regularly communicate with even the most well-known professors. This just doesn't happen at other technology-oriented schools where TAs lead the ma-

jority of classes." A number of upperclassmen agree that they have had a number of awe-inspiring discussions in classrooms and with professors in which all their years of learning at Cooper seemed to "just come together and fit perfectly like a jigsaw puzzle. It was amazing."

Mingling with the NYC Crowd

"Freshman year is relatively less intensive and more all-nighter oriented," remarks one junior. Compared to the progressively accumulating workloads of juniors and seniors, freshmen have relatively little work since they must first fulfill graduation requirements within well-defined schedules. Although it is great to live on campus and move to the beat of the East Village's vibrant night life, being underage has its disadvantages in New York City, where there is strict enforcement of the underage drinking law. Nevertheless, a freshman states that "people are always able to find their niche in club parties, fraternity/sorority gatherings, semi-formals, alumni dinners, and somewhere within the large number of other entertainment options NYC has to offer."

Since many Cooper students share the belief that its student body is pretty homogeneous, socially, they tend to mingle with the general college population in the area. As a result, relationships between Cooper and non-Cooper students are quite common. Furthermore, free parties such as the Halloween and St. Patrick's Day celebrations are wonderful opportunities to introduce oneself to the intriguingly diverse and animated 18-to-23 crowd of New York. Students also say there is very little evidence of substance abuse at Cooper besides the continuous doses of coffee that pervade every other college environment during times of stress.

Any Time to Spare?

Despite its serious focus on academics, most Cooper students are encouraged to become involved in at least one extracurricular activity. People at CU become very active beyond the classroom setting mainly because they are sincerely excited about expanding the horizon of their interests. One senior said, "It is not easy to continually devote a large part of time to extracurriculars, especially as the years go on, but everyone, even those who commute, manage to find time to take part in the Club Hour," a designated time for the meeting of undergraduate groups. The variety of organizations at CU is just as abundant as at any other college, striving to provide for interests in a number of areas. Groups such as Renaissance, the Chinese Student Association (CSA), the African-American student organization (Onyx), and the Jewish student organization (Kesher), regularly sponsor trips to concerts at the Lincoln Center, movies and lecture events, and other social activities. Professional societies in such fields as mathematics, architecture, and mechanical, chemical, and electrical engineering often host lectures and other learning opportunities outside the classroom. "A large number of people also work in industry while attending class as further study enrichment," reported one junior.

Sports at Cooper Union are very much like at other colleges. CU does actively recruit athletes, as it believes that physical competitions also enhance the mental capacity of its students while infusing the campus with a greater sense of school pride. Cooper students are equally proud of their men's tennis team as they are of their intellectual abilities. Athletes are not stereotyped in any way, although it is traditional that "freshmen athletes are covered with shaving cream, sticky sugary liquid, and paint if they fall asleep after their first road trip." Despite the inconvenience of participating in sports when one is not on a team, the Hewitt gym is always available to anyone eager for a good workout, and a pool is accessible at the Asser-Levy facility within walking distance from the center of campus.

A "Citified" Experience

Cooper's campus is what students describe as "citified." There has been contin-

ual debate about how advantageous the locale of CU really is. There are those that claim that "the city detracts from campus life, since there are so many other things someone can do in New York." Others complain that CU really "has no campus in the sense that there is little greenery." However, one advantage is that the buildings are very close to one another, making travel from class to class a breeze. Student consensus is that security has improved considerably in recent years.

With rental rates at a premium in the city, living arrangements at Cooper are cheap according to students and comparatively sophisticated or even luxurious. One sophomore commented, "The average freshman suite is a single-sex apartment with its own kitchen and bathroom. All the buildings and suites are air-conditioned and are pretty well kept by the Cooper custodial staff." Privacy and convenience are some notable qualities of CU's dormitories, and housing is guaranteed for all those who are not within commuting distance. "People get along very well and voluntary segregation really doesn't exist in the dorms," says one senior. On the other hand, the situation in the dining halls is not as pleasant. Although there are some satisfying vegetarian options, tasty would not usually be an honest description of the provisions "except for wrapped food, which can also be easily transported." Nonetheless, Pizzaria Uno, BBQs, Peking Duck House, and a notable combination of other cultural cuisine are available within walking distance of the school.

On the whole, CU students advocate that "there aren't that many other places that offer one of the best undergraduate experiences in engineering, art, or architecture. If you really do know what you want, and your parents have no problem with a free education, Cooper is the place to be." —*Roletta Chen and Staff*

FYI

The three best things about attending Cooper Union are "the full-tuition scholarships for all, New York City, and the amazing professors."

The three worst things about attending Cooper Union are "the intense course load, lack of campus, and being underage in New York City."

The three things every student should do before graduating from Cooper Union are "to dance at Twilo, to study with world-renown researchers, and to explore the Village."

One thing I'd like to have known before coming here is "how much work it would be."

Cornell University

Address: 410 Thurston Avenue; Ithaca, NY 14850-2488
Phone: 607-255-0659
E-mail address: admissions@cornell.edu
Web site URL: www.cornell.edu
Founded: 1865
Private or Public: private
Religious affiliation: none
Location: rural
Undergraduate enrollment: 13,639
Total enrollment: 18,914
Percent Male / Female: 52% / 48%
Percent Minority: 27%
Percent African-American: 4%

Percent Asian: 16%
Percent Hispanic: 6%
Percent Native-American: 0.5%
Percent in-state / out-of-state: 43% / 57%
Percent Pub HS: NA
Number of Applicants: 19,949
Percent Accepted: 33%
Percent Accepted who enroll: 48%
Entering: 3,136
Transfers: NA
Application Deadline: 1 Jan
Mean SAT: 660 V, 695 M
Mean ACT: NA

Middle 50% SAT range: 620–710 V, 650–750 M
Middle 50% ACT range: NA
3 Most popular majors: social sciences, ecvonomics / business, biological sciences
Retention: 93%
Graduation rate: 81%
On-campus housing: 96%
Fraternities: 24%
Sororities: 21%
Library: 5,800,000 volumes
Tuition and Fees: $23,848 in; $23,848 out
Room and Board: $7,827
Financial aid, first-year: 52%

"I t's moo-licious and moo-tricious," reads the caption. A newly developed carbonated milk-based drink—the first of its kind—E-Moo is anticipated to be the next big thing in nutritious beverages. Cornellians are proud that such a novel creation was birthed at their university, where classroom academics meet real-life application every day to produce a variety of fun and novel ideas.

The Pressure is Intense

At Cornell, the academic pressure is intense. "It's a competitive atmosphere—I definitely feel the crunch," admitted one student, "although the academic opportunities are tremendous." Indeed, Cornell offers something for everyone, with seven undergraduate schools that range from agriculture to hotel management. Arts and Sciences as well as the School of Engineering are generally considered the most rigorous, while the Hotel School is known to be the least rigorous. Said one student, "Hotellies have one paper to write a semester, and spend the rest of the time getting dressed up and eating cookies." Although the school's most popular ma-

jors are psychology, biology, and government, students are required to fulfill distribution requirements that cover all ranges of the academic spectrum. Arts and Sciences students must take nine courses: five from the social sciences/history and humanities/arts, and four from the physical and biological sciences. Each student must also be proficient in a foreign language, although most fulfill this with advanced placement credit from high school. Finally, every Cornellian must pass a swim test and take at least two PE classes. Most students end up taking a PE class every semester; Cornell offers everything from figure skating to archery in its physical education department.

With over 13,000 undergraduates, Cornell's introductory classes are huge—often with hundreds of students. One student explains, "My Intro Psych class has about 1,500 people in it—but the professor is so outstanding he keeps everyone interested." Some students find the TAs frustrating. One student complained, "Half of the time I don't think my TA speaks English." Smaller classes, however, are fairly easy to find if you put forth the effort. Said one student, "Out of my four classes, three are under twenty students, and I'm only a freshman."

Most students spend their time studying in one of Cornell's fifteen libraries. As one student said, "The Law Library is so quiet, breathing is loud." The best places to study are Uris and Olin, and many students rave about the view from the Uris lounge, described as a "good place to pretend you're studying." Regardless of where they study, students report that they feel the pressure to do well. "Sometimes, I feel like I can barely keep up," admitted one student. "The work just never stops."

Wining and Dining

Living at Cornell is as varied as the academic program it offers. Soon all freshmen will live on the quieter North Campus, which is undergoing $65 million in renovations. West Campus, where most Cornellians live, is described as "crazy." Said one student, "It's like a non-stop party. There are always people running around or screaming out their windows." Despite the reputation of West Campus, most students choose to live in a Greek house or in nearby Collegetown. Those who live off campus, however, soon begin to crave Cornell's "unbelievable" food service, which is run in part by the hotel school. Each part of campus has its own cafeteria, which offers everything from pizzerias to ice cream parlors. Sunday brunch is especially popular: raves one student, "It's probably the best meal I've ever had in my life."

Greek Chic

Cornell boasts 52 fraternities and 13 sororities. Although most students claim there is "no pressure" to rush, the presence of the Greeks pervades social life. From Delta Delta Delta and AOPi's annual "Green Eggs and Kegs" homecoming party to after-hours fiestas that do not begin until the wee hours of the morning, Cornell students are never without a party. Some of these parties, however, carry on without alcohol with a new administration policy which forces parties to be catered and students to be ID'd at the door. Despite these new regulations, many students report that drinking is

available if you are interested in participating. As one student admitted, "I haven't had a problem getting drunk, although they are trying to make it a bit difficult."

> **"Hotellies have one paper to write a semester, and spend the rest of the time getting dressed up and eating cookies."**

For those not into Greek life, other social opportunities are plentiful, although as one student complained, "the parties . . . instigate the moral abysses into which the entire community sinks." Nevertheless, those wishing to ignore Greek life can take in a movie at the Cornell cinema, or the over-21 crowd can visit one of college town's many dance clubs, such as Republica and the Palms. The biggest party of the year, Slope Day, is an annual event replete with food and live music. It's also the "one day the administration looks the other way with regard to drinking." Indeed, as one student admits, "Cornell students do drink a lot—although I know a lot who don't. It's totally your option." Drug use is reported to be about "average in comparison to other schools," with the most popular substance being marijuana.

How We Fill Our Time

Most students at Cornell take part in at least one of the school's many extracurricular activities. The most popular are the student publications, including the *Cornell Daily Sun*, which boasts such prominent alumni as E. B. White. Theater performances are also popular, as are a cappella groups and improv comedy groups. Many students also take part in community service groups, which work with run-down sections of the Ithaca community.

Sports also take up a large part of life at Cornell. On Saturdays, "everyone goes to the football game" to cheer on Big Red. When hockey season rolls around, the fans become more rabid: one student reported that camping out overnight for tickets is not uncommon. Intramural sports are also popular, drawing a large number of students out of their rooms to play flag football, hockey, and basketball. The more daring may even try Cornell's large rock-climbing wall.

Neither Snow nor Rain . . .

Students described Cornell's campus as "beautiful, but isolated," especially during the fall, where "the trees are just magnificent." The winters, however, are less popular. They are long and cold, and as one student put it, "God's revenge on someone!" The weather is often described as "Ithacating—some sort of rain, snow, or sleet, with constantly gray skies."

Despite the ambiguity, Cornellians refuse to stay in, and they report that security is "never a problem." The university runs escort services to walk students home late at night, as well as littering the campus with emergency blue-light phones. When out, Cornellians reported that they see "mostly New Yorkers," probably because of Cornell's state-funded schools (Cornell is a half public, half private institution). One student, however, complained, "More than half of my classmates must be from Long Island!"

Cornellians take pride in their school. "I came here and fell in love with the campus," said one student. Cornell is a place where "almost anyone can find a niche." Gushed one student, "The mix of work and play here is outstanding. I couldn't imagine myself anywhere else in the world." —*Staff*

FYI

The three best things about attending Cornell are "the huge variety of classes to take, there are tons of different kinds of people to meet, and it's in a beautiful and natural setting."

The three worst things about attending Cornell are "the winter weather, the huge-ass campus is very spread apart, and New York City is a 5-hour drive away."

The three things that every student should do before graduating from Cornell are "eat ice cream from the Cornell Dairy, slide down the slope on a cafeteria tray during the winter, and swim in the gorges during the summer."

One thing I'd like to have known before coming here is "how far it is from everywhere else!"

Eastman School of Music

Address: 26 Gibbs Street; Rochester, NY 14604-2599

Phone: 716-274-1060

E-mail address: esmadmit @uhura.cc.rochester.edu

Web site URL: www .rochester.edu/eastman

Founded: 1921

Private or Public: private

Religious affiliation: none

Location: urban

Undergraduate enrollment: 503

Total enrollment: 825

Percent Male/Female: 45%/55%

Percent Minority: 12%

Percent African-American: 3%

Percent Asian: 2%

Percent Hispanic: 7%

Percent Native-American: NA

Percent in-state/out-of-state: 17%/83%

Percent Pub HS: NA

Number of Applicants: 899

Percent Accepted: 29%

Percent Accepted who enroll: 47%

Entering: 122

Transfers: 0

Application Deadline: 1 Jan

Mean SAT: 600 V, 650 M

Mean ACT: NA

Middle 50% SAT range: NA

Middle 50% ACT range: NA

3 Most popular majors: music performance, music education, music composition

Retention: 89%

Graduation rate: 72%

On-campus housing: 98%

Fraternities: 13%

Sororities: 11%

Library: 500,000 volumes

Tuition and Fees: $20,320 in; $20,320 out

Room and Board: $7,512

Financial aid, first-year: 70%

Do you love music? Not just as a hobby, but as your life? Do you love music enough to practice until you get calluses from playing your instrument for so long? Enough to sing not just in the shower, but for hours at a time? If you do, you probably already know about this world-renowned music school. At the Eastman School of Music, serious musicians can immerse themselves in an environment where everyone thinks about, listens to, or plays music 24 hours a day.

Learning about Music

Eastman provides its students with a rigorous and thorough musical education as well as a solid humanities background. Most students are performance majors (the technical name is "applied music"). The next most popular majors are music education, composition, and theory. The performance major requires three years of theory, two years of music history, covering everything from Gregorian chants to contemporary music, and, of course, weekly lessons. Performance majors must be competent piano players regardless of their chosen instrument. All performance majors must take Piano 101 and 102, or test out of this requirement. Eastman also has a humanities requirement, which can be filled with courses in literature, history, languages, philosophy, or a combination of these. Eastman students are serious about their humanities classes as well as their music, and classes are not easy. As one undergrad explained, "It seems like either you do really well or you completely fail." By senior year, most of Eastman's requirements are out of the way, and students have more flexible schedules that allow them to audition for jobs or graduate school.

Because Eastman is part of the University of Rochester, students have access to the university's libraries and other facilities. Some of the humanities classes are held on the U of R campus, although as one student said, "You can make it all four years without leaving this campus." The reason many like to stay on the Eastman campus is the 15- to 20-minute bus ride to the U of R.

Students who apply to Eastman can ask to work with a particular professor, and many apply to the school primarily to do just that. One student, for example, said he met his cello teacher at a summer music camp and decided to go to Eastman so he could continue to study with her. Some popular professors include clarinetist Kenneth Grant, pianist Barry Snyder, and flautist Bonita Boyd. The members of the Cleveland String Quartet also teach at Eastman and attract many to their classes and concerts. Students have substantial contact with faculty members, both in lessons and in other contexts like chamber groups.

Living and Breathing Music

Everything at Eastman revolves around music. The musical motif on campus is inescapable; the snack bar is called the Orchestra Pit and the newspaper is called Clef Notes. Students rave about their "access to music on hand anytime." They can go to concerts every night if they want to; Eastman's calendar is filled with student and faculty performances by soloists and groups in the Eastman Theater, concerts every other week by the Rochester Philharmonic Orchestra (Eastman students get free tickets), and limitless other performances. Eastman's Sibley Library also has an enormous music collection (the second-largest in the nation), including books, manuscripts, and recordings of "just about everything," one student said. Whenever undergrads want to listen to music but just can't find a concert to go to, they can always listen to their favorite symphony or opera at the library. Students who want to participate in athletics, student government, and other nonmusical extracurricular activities can journey over to the University of Rochester campus.

> **"It's not like a big old party school."**

For those with the energy to play for more than the three to six hours they're expected to practice each day, there are plenty of opportunities to perform. Some students give several recitals a year, while others only do one in their four years at school. Many undergrads participate in chamber orchestras, quartets, or other small ensembles, either for credit or for fun. Jazz bands and string quartets are in constant demand at local restaurants and bars. Traveling Broadway shows that come to Rochester sometimes need a player to fill in and look to Eastman students for help. Students also have many chances to play at church services, weddings, and other special events.

Few Distractions

The Eastman campus is small, with just three buildings located in the heart of downtown Rochester: Eastman Commons, a classroom building, and Sibley Library. The food at the cafeteria is "pretty normal," according to one student. "You know, it's got a salad and pasta bar, burgers and fries, and a frozen yogurt machine." In the dorm, freshmen live in doubles, and all upperclassmen have singles. Moving off campus is a popular option for juniors and seniors, but freshmen and sophomores are required to live on campus. Many students prefer the dorm because the surrounding neighborhood reportedly "isn't the greatest." Dorm life exposes students to an environment where everyone knows everyone else and has the same interests, so life can get a little boring. For those who need to get away, popular options include the Rochester Club, which features jazz every Friday night, and the Spaghetti Warehouse. Students also like to hang out and "go crazy" at nearby dance clubs in downtown Rochester.

Campus social life is somewhat limited.

As one student explained, "It's not like a big old party school." For those who favor the Greek scene, there is one all-male fraternity, one sorority, and one coed fraternity. The all-male and all-female groups each have a floor of the 14-story Eastman Commons to themselves. The all-male fraternity sponsors most of the parties, while the other Greek groups focus on community service work. Eastman has two annual formals, one in the fall and one in the spring. Small parties in the dorm are common; one student remarked that the delivery truck from a local liquor store is frequently spotted outside the dorm. Students don't seem to mind the low-key social scene; as one sophomore pointed out, "The fewer distractions, the easier it is to concentrate on practicing—which is good, I guess."

Freshmen typically arrive at Eastman from all corners of the world with visions of their names in lights. Each dreams of being the next great viola player, soprano soloist, or jazz pianist. These dreams become transformed over the next few years into more realistic aspirations. One junior explained that it doesn't matter to her whether she ends up as the soloist with a major symphony or a player in a community orchestra: "As long as I'm playing, that's cool with me." —*Susanna Chu and staff*

FYI
The three best things about attending Eastman are "the faculty, the caliber of the students, and the connections you build."
The three worst things about attending Eastman are "Rochester, the competitiveness, and the gloomy weather."
The three things that every student should do before graduating from Eastman are "attend a seminar by a world-famous musician, play every instrument once, and go see Niagara Falls."
One thing I'd like to have known before coming here is "how competitive people are."

Eugene Lang College of the New School University

Address: 65 West 11th Street; New York, NY 10011
Phone: 212-229-5665
E-mail address: lang@newschool.edu
Web site URL: www.newschool.edu
Founded: 1919
Private or Public: private
Religious affiliation: none
Location: urban
Undergraduate enrollment: 436
Total enrollment: 436
Percent Male/Female: NA
Percent Minority: 23%
Percent African-American: 7%

Percent Asian: 4%
Percent Hispanic: 11%
Percent Native-American: 0.5%
Percent in-state/out-of-state: 42%/58%
Percent Pub HS: 40%
Number of Applicants: 503
Percent Accepted: 60%
Percent Accepted who enroll: 37%
Entering: 110
Transfers: 84
Application Deadline: 1 Feb
Mean SAT: 610 V, 580 M
Mean ACT: 27

Middle 50% SAT range: 519–654 V, 529–664 M
Middle 50% ACT range: 21–27
3 Most popular majors: writing, cultural studies, psychology
Retention: 73%
Graduation rate: NA
On-campus housing: 80%
Fraternities: NA
Sororities: NA
Library: NA
Tuition and Fees: $19,104 in; $19,104 out
Room and Board: $9,005
Financial aid, first-year: 72%

Situated in the heart of New York City, Eugene Lang College is the undergraduate, liberal arts college of New School University, formerly known as the New School for Social Research. Founded in 1973 as the Seminar College of the New School for Social Research, Lang acquired its current name when philanthropist Eugene Lang and his family donated $5 million to the school in 1985. Despite the name change, seminars that range in size from 5 to 15 students remain the basis of the educational experience at Lang.

It's All Up to You

Lang is a small college, which enrolls over 500 students and offers a strong liberal arts education. The New School University is comprised of Actors Studio Drama School, Eugene Lang College, Graduate Faculty, Mannes College of Music, Milano Graduate School, The New School, and Parsons School of Design. It also has affiliated programs with Benjamin N. Cardozo School of Law, Dial Cyberspace Campus, Educated Citizen Project, Jazz & Contemporary Music/New School University BFA Program, and Joffrey Ballet School/New School University BFA Program in Dance.

It is obviously a bit confusing to try to make sense of how all these schools interact, but students can take classes at the other schools to a certain level.

Courses at Lang itself are divided into five broad areas of concentration: literature, writing and the arts; social and historical inquiry; mind, nature and value; urban studies; and cultural studies. Students use these areas as the basis for designing their own majors. "You don't actually design your major all by yourself; there are certain paths you can take like gender studies, queer theory or education under cultural studies" said one student. Since most classes at Lang are interdisciplinary, students say that they get exposed to many different subjects rather than sticking with a single one.

Lang's strength is in the social sciences. Students looking for hardcore science courses and lab facilities have to enroll in courses at Cooper Union and transfer their credits. Many students also take classes at Parsons School of Design that is also under New School University. Juniors and seniors can also take graduate classes at the Milano Graduate School. Seminars, often taught by famous professors or by published authors in the case of the writing program, can be very demanding and usually involve several writing assignments. Although, in the past, students could have a casual attitude about attending classes, this year, administration has started enforcing an attendance policy: the professor has the right to fail students who miss three classes throughout the semester. However, one student commented, "This is not the way it works in practice. The professor usually lowers your grade instead of failing you."

Students complain about the small number of full-time faculty members and the big "turnover of professors." Since most professors are only "visiting," they are "here for one term and disappear the next." Overall, students have praise for their professors: "I have had some incredible professors who have helped me make important decisions affecting my life." Students see their interactions with professors as one of the major benefits of attending Lang. "I can call all of my professors at home," on student exclaimed. Students are also positive about the advising system: "My advisers did really advise me—about academic issues as well as about my personal life." One student went as far to say, "I probably would not be in New York right now if it wasn't for my advisors. That's how close you can get to them." Lang has a study abroad program with the University of Amsterdam, but that is the "only official study abroad option." Many students still go to different countries for a term or an entire year.

> "Survival in New York City is a big part of the Lang experience."

Registration is the "biggest pain!" There is no phone or online system for registration. One senior explained, "Starting with the seniors, each class meets in a big room and registers for classes. It is total chaos." Since all classes are capped at 15 students, "you may end up registering for classes totally different from the ones you had in mind if you are unlucky in the registration draw." Students can add and drop classes after registration, which usually brings them "closer to their initial set of desired courses." Administrators, however, usually known to students on a first-name basis, receive very good overall reviews for their responsiveness and willingness to help.

New York, New York
Most Lang students are self-defined urbanites. For those who aren't, adjusting to life in New York City is the biggest challenge. Social life centers on clubs and cafés in Greenwich Village as well as other parts of the city. "Parks are also great in the spring," said one enthusiastic junior. Most students agree that "You can either fall through the cracks or benefit from everything the area has to offer."

Students think of the student body as a reflection of New York City: diverse, liberal and composed of strong individuals. "One thing we don't have at Lang are conservatives—we are a fairly progressive bunch," noted one sophomore. However, despite the progressiveness, "the political activism of the Seminar College days has faded away."

> "I can call all of my professors at home."

Formal extracurricular activities and sports programs do not exist at Lang. "There are not many sports fans here." Those who are into sports can participate in Cooper Union's small intramural sports program. Lang in the City is a college-sponsored program that offers students discounted tickets to performances, movies and art events, but "is not used by many students." One student explained, "You don't go through the school, you create your own independent life." Lang's Internship Coordinator helps place students in internships with employers in the city. Professors' connections also help in getting high-quality internships. "We even get credit for internships; they are an incredible experience. They allow you to bring theory and practice together," said a senior.

A Single Building
Eugene Lang is situated in a five-story building that contains classrooms, study rooms and a small cafeteria. One student

said, "we, at least, don't have to walk for miles to get from one class to the other." However, students taking classes at Parsons or at the Milano Graduate School have to walk "a couple of streets." Lang's library is part of a three-school consortium with the libraries of Cooper Union and New York University, giving students access to nearly 3.3 million volumes.

One housing option for Lang students are the three residence halls within walking distance of the school building: Loeb Hall, Marlton House and Union Square. Rooms vary in size and type depending on the building. The dorms do not belong entirely to Lang; students share them with students from Parsons School of Design and Mannes College of Music, which are also schools under the New School University. Space is guaranteed to freshmen and first-year transfer students but others are often forced to enter the painful search for apartments in New York city: "I would not recommend the dorms, but then, I would not recommend looking for an apartment in your first year in New York either," noted one student. "The moment you move to an apartment, your social life is totally independent from the school." These "New Yorkers" do have to commute to school.

Lang combines a strong liberal arts education and small seminars with the opportunities of the most urban setting possible. This combination leads Lang students to build their potentials in their time here and leave Lang as independent thinkers and as "individuals."—*Engin Yenidunya*

FYI

The three best things about attending Eugene Lang are "your close relationship to your professors, being in the City, and very small class sizes."

The three worst things about attending Eugene Lang are "the registration process, the terrible dorms, and you can get lost in New York."

The three things that every student should do before graduating from Eugene Lang are "enjoy New York City, do an internship, and study abroad."

One thing I would like to have known before coming here is "that dining halls are almost non-existent."

Fordham University

Address: Thebaud Hall; Bronx, NY 10458-9993	**Percent Asian:** 4%	**Middle 50% SAT range:** 540–640 V,
Phone: 718-817-1000	**Percent Hispanic:** 12%	520–610 M
E-mail address: enroll@fordham.edu	**Percent Native-American:** 0.5%	**Middle 50% ACT range:** 23–28
Web site URL: www.fordham.edu	**Percent in-state / out-of-state:** 67%/33%	**3 Most popular majors:** business administration,
Founded: 1841	**Percent Pub HS:** 34%	psychology,
Private or Public: private	**Number of Applicants:** 8,600	communications
Religious affiliation: Catholic	**Percent Accepted:** 62%	**Retention:** 88%
Location: urban	**Percent Accepted who**	**Graduation rate:** 59%
Undergraduate enrollment: 6,407	**enroll:** 30%	**On-campus housing:** 50%
Total enrollment: 6,407	**Entering:** 1,584	**Fraternities:** NA
Percent Male / Female: 41%/59%	**Transfers:** NA	**Sororities:** NA
Percent Minority: 22%	**Application Deadline:** 1 Feb	**Library:** 1,600,000 volumes
Percent African-American: 5%	**Mean SAT:** 589 V, 574 M	**Tuition and Fees:** $20,660 in; $20,660 out
	Mean ACT: 25	**Room and Board:** $8,310
		Financial aid, first-year: 73%

Be it the wide lawns and Gothic architecture in the Bronx, or the towering 20-floor complex in the heart of Manhattan, the two campuses of Fordham University give its students both the rushed atmosphere and rare calmness that New York City can offer.

Two Campuses, Like Curriculums

Students at Fordham University attend either Fordham College at Rose Hill, which is the College of Business Administration, or else Fordham College at Lincoln Center. While the two campuses, Rose Hill and Lincoln Center, are both physically and characteristically separate, the schools share a core curriculum. The Core is an extensive list of requirements of courses ranging in rhetoric, theology, and philosophy, to social and natural sciences. While many students see the curriculum as a good basis for the study of liberal arts, more than one student described the program as having "an emphasis on what's Western. The philosophy classes can be very dogmatic." Fordham is also a Jesuit school and thus has a theology requirement. While the study of religion is not the school's driving force, one junior said that, "some theology classes, such as 'Faith and Critical Reasoning' seem to be attempts to convert your Christianity. I'm not such a fan of that."

Advanced students may choose to join the Honors program, which is made up of a group of specific classes of very interdisciplinary material, including either a Junior term either abroad, an internship, or directed reading. For all students, a Fordham education is topped off with a Senior Seminar in Values and Moral Choices. Despite the program's Western leanings, Fordham students must also take at least one class in Global Studies, and American Pluralism, which emphasizes ethnicity, race, and class in the United States. The Lincoln Center campus also offers a unique Bachelor of Fine Arts in Dance in combination with the Alvin Ailey Dance Center.

Classes are reportedly quite easy to get into and are generally quite small. One student said, "I've been lucky enough to never have more than 25 students in my classes." Humanities-based classes are popular, and many students major in English. Science classes are reportedly tough, and are almost exclusively taught at the Rose Hill campus, which according to one Lincoln Center student, "is extremely aggravating." Whatever inconveniences there may be, Fordham students are extremely happy with their professors. TA's are rare except in laboratory settings, and often in conjunction with another professor. What some students find upsetting about their classes is the fact that "a lot of students aren't interested. They see class as something they have to get over." Regardless, Fordham boasts an excellent academic reputation rooted in Jesuit tradition.

Social Life?

Perhaps because of its location in a city where there are almost too many things to do, many students report that "social life on campus is pretty scant. We're in New York, after all." Regardless, there is a Weekend Activities Committee, which has brought the Indigo Girls to campus and shows movies on Tuesdays and Thursdays. As a result of this lack of campus life, one on-campus student stated, "You better make friends right in the beginning. Those friends are the ones who you'll end up hanging out with all the time." One sophomore stated that "a lot of kids at Fordham are from around here, so they already have friends and don't bother too much with social life here." Fordham students make the most of their location, often going to theater and museums in the city and participating in the bar and club scene both in the Bronx and in Manhattan.

> **"Social life on campus is pretty scant. We're in New York, after all."**

The student body itself is statistically diverse, but many students see diversity only in the numbers. Fordham attracts many commuter students, and according to one student, "A lot of the commuters are the minority students and, as a result, there's not always a lot of racial interaction." Perhaps social lifestyle most differentiates the two campuses of Fordham. Students at Rose Hill claim that there is little sex on campus, while the students in Manhattan simply say, "there is a lot of sex, and not always within the student body." Additionally, while the lesbian and gay community of Rose Hill is quite small, one student described Lincoln Center as "just exuding gayness." Thus, depending on the campus, the lifestyle at Fordham can either be both calm and wild.

A Dee-luxe Apartment in the Sky

Rose Hill students who choose to live on campus usually aim for Alumni Court North and South, the two newer dorms on campus. Students also have the option of living in the Residential College of Queen's Court. Many students, though, do choose to live off campus. Meanwhile, in Manhattan, students literally live in a 20-floor apartment building with large suites containing bathrooms and kitchens. According to one sophomore, though, "it gets pretty tight because lots of people like it." At both campuses, the major grievance with housing is the enforced restrictions. There is a strict sign in policy, and students may not have guests of opposite sex stay in their rooms. Additionally, any guests who do come to stay must look for a new place soon, because they are allowed a two-night maximum. All residence halls have RA's, who the students describe as very active. As one student put it, "The RA's are great. They monitor the building and make the dorms a good living situation."

Gothic and Modern

The greatest physical difference between the Rose Hill and Lincoln Center campuses are their distinct architectural styles. While Rose Hill boasts sprawling lawns and very traditional Gothic architecture, Lincoln Center is comprised of three buildings, all very modern. Within these different buildings, however, the same goals are met at the two campuses. In the Bronx, there is the Vince T. Lombardi Athletic Center and McGinley Hall, the student Union, which houses two cafeterias and Dagger John's Pub. In Manhattan, students take advantage of the aptly-named Fitness and Exercise Center, and frequent the Lowenstein Center for food, which includes going to bar Blarney's. As for food, students often purchase a meal plan, although opinions on the campus food range from "good" to "very bad, except on turkey night." Of course, the area provides a wealth of restaurants and students often cook for themselves as well.

Outside of Class

Fordham students, when not in class, can often be found doing community service, ranging from organized activity through Kiwanis-sponsored Circle K, the POTS Soup Kitchen, or finding such opportunities independently, be it at one of New York's hospitals or the Red Cross. There are a number of clubs at both campuses, ranging from ethnic clubs such as Molino, which emphasizes African culture, to academically related groups, such as the Pre-Law Society. Varsity sports are on campus, but, according to one student, "There's not a whole lot of support for the Rams." For students in need of physical activity, without the rigor of the varsity level, there are both intramural and club sports, ranging from lacrosse to an intramural screaming contest.

Fordham University and New York City provide its students with a lot of real world experience as well as a solid liberal arts education. As one student said, "Sometimes I feel more real when I go into the city. I see a lot more than when I'm cooped up studying all the time." With a range of academic and extra-curricular possibilities, students at Fordham love their school and enjoy their status as "New York City's Jesuit University." —*Shu-Ping Shen and Staff*

FYI

The three best things about attending Fordham are "location, small size, and teacher-student relation."

The three worst things about attending Fordham are "no campus life, slightly oppressive Jesuit atmosphere, and small size."

The three things that every student should do before graduation from Fordham are "work in New York City, live on top floor, get in touch with you Club Kid side."

One thing I'd like to have known before coming here is "most of the campus is female."

Hamilton College

Address: 198 College Hill Road; Clinton, NY 13323
Phone: 315-859-4421
E-mail address: admission@hamilton.edu
Web site URL: www.hamilton.edu
Founded: 1812
Private or Public: private
Religious affiliation: none
Location: rural
Undergraduate enrollment: 1,712
Total enrollment: 1,712
Percent Male/Female: 51%/49%
Percent Minority: 12%
Percent African-American: 3%

Percent Asian: 4%
Percent Hispanic: 4%
Percent Native-American: 0.5%
Percent in-state/out-of-state: 44%/56%
Percent Pub HS: 62%
Number of Applicants: 3,909
Percent Accepted: 42%
Percent Accepted who enroll: 30%
Entering: 500
Transfers: 17
Application Deadline: 15 Jan
Mean SAT: NA
Mean ACT: NA

Middle 50% SAT range: 550–670 V, 580–670 M
Middle 50% ACT range: NA
3 Most popular majors: economics, government, English
Retention: 92%
Graduation rate: 85%
On-campus housing: 100%
Fraternities: 38%
Sororities: 21%
Library: 538,377 volumes
Tuition and Fees: $25,050 in; $25,050 out
Room and Board: $6,200
Financial aid, first-year: 62%

Imagine yourself on an intimate campus, in the middle of green grassy hills, where everyone knows your name and TA's do not exist. Nestled in quiet upstate New York, Hamilton sits on top of a hill with countryside views that stretch for miles. But beauty is not the only thing that distinguishes Hamilton. Students extol their educational experience at this prestigious liberal arts college as well.

Small Classes With Energetic Professors

When students enter Hamilton as freshmen, they are required to take two classes in four different distributional groups: mathematics and science, the arts, historical studies and social sciences, and humanities and languages. A course in ethical issues is also required and students must take either a language or a class on culture to fulfill the cultural diversity requirement. Students must also take 3 six-week PE classes (varsity athletes only take 2), ranging from scuba diving to badminton.

Students praise both their teachers and small classes. "The biggest class I have ever been in is 70 students, and that was only because it was an introductory class." If you are in a class of 70, you will have sections and meet with a professor in groups of no more than 20. Most classes are capped at 25, however, with a given quantity of freshman, sophomores, juniors and seniors allowed in each section. Although classes fill up quickly, students report that if they go and talk with the professor, they will probably be admitted. Every class is taught by a full-fledged professor." At Hamilton there are no TA's, and every professor on the faculty has a Ph.D." Since Hamilton has no graduate students, the professors focus all their time on undergraduate teaching, and they are said to be very accessible. "I even had one professor who brought doughnuts and coffee to class for our 8:30 A.M. class."

When it comes to majors, chemistry, history and public policy are notorious for keeping students up late at nights. If you want the easy way out, major in communications. Popular majors include economics, English, history, geology and psychology, and students love the anthropology and sociology departments. If you are a geology major, Hamilton has a program where you can go to Antarctica. "Chemistry classes, especially organic, are impossible here." But there are some "gut" classes available to fulfill the mathematics/science requirement, one being "A

Physicists View of Nature." As one student puts it "you can definitely make it through without doing a ton of work. It's up to you." Most Hamilton students are happy with their educational experience.

A Dazzling Isolated Campus
All Hamilton students laud their beautiful campus. The campus is split into two parts: North Campus (nicknamed "the white side") and South Campus (nicknamed "the dark side"). The North Campus hosts beautiful traditional buildings described by one student as "more Ivy League than the Ivy League itself." Between the buildings there are expansive green lawns, where many students play Frisbee. The not so popular South Campus, formerly Kirkland, the women's college, is home to the "artsy" population and is known for its "hideous" 60's style buildings made out of gray cement. These buildings won an award for their Cubist style.

Although Hamilton students love the beauty of their school, many complain about its isolation. "We are in the middle of nowhere." Clinton, the town students live in, has few shops, and only 3 bars. Many students travel to Syracuse, 45 minutes away, to fulfill their shopping needs, or to the small mall and movie theatre 10 minutes away. Freshmen are not allowed to have cars, but after first year about 70% of the students drive. Most students see having a car as essential to escaping the tiny town of Clinton. The weather is another factor that Hamilton students complain about. Winter in Clinton begins in November and ends in late March. "If you aren't into cold weather, than you will not dig the conditions here."

Students at Hamilton are very happy with their living accommodations. In 1995, fraternity houses were banned and the school bought the houses from the fraternities, renovating them and making them into dorms. Although it created upheaval in the years following, students from all classes live together in the same dorms, and the upperclassmen singles are huge. Students can live on single-sex floors if they wish, although the coed floors are known to be much cooler. Freshman, sophomores and most juniors are required to live on campus and all ex-

cept for freshmen's rooms are assigned by a lottery system. Seniors and juniors who pull a low lottery number can live off campus. Freshmen are assigned resident advisors, who help them adjust to college life.

> **"If you aren't into cold weather, than you will not dig the conditions here."**

The most popular places to live include Roger's Estate, Eels House, Woolcott House, which are all old frat houses. Many students who live in Bundy, a sophomore dorm, complain about its location and the trek to classes in the cold weather, as the dorm is situated at the bottom of the hill.

Homogeneous Hamilton
Hamilton definitely lives up to its reputation as being a very homogenous, white, upper-middle class school. One student states "everyone here is wealthy, wears Patagonia, J. Crew, North Face and Abercrombie, and drives a Jeep Grand Cherokee. There is a little underlying granola as well." Although the administration is trying to recruit minorities, they still constitute a very small percentage of the student body and many students note the lack of diversity on campus. There is also racial segregation, especially noticeable in the dining halls. Interracial couples on campus are not common, and there is not a large homosexual population either. As far as the rest of the dating scene in concerned, students report there are not many long-term relationships at Hamilton, "just a lot of random hookups." Another common characteristic students note is "how nice everyone is here." One thing that Hamilton does have is good financial aid. There are merit scholarships as well as purely financial grants. One student remarked "if you need the money and are qualified to come, Hamilton will give it to you."

Dining and Night Life
All Hamilton Students living on campus must be on the meal plan. Freshman and sophomores must be on the full meal plan, and juniors and seniors can opt for

the 14-meal-a-week plan. The Diner, one of the places on campus where the meal plan can be used, has a jukeboxes and good food. They make fresh cheeseburgers and let students place orders. The other dining halls are said to be clean, and the food decent. They also have a stir fry bar in which they cook the food in front of you. Many noted that the vegetarian options "could be a lot better."

When dining off campus, many students go to Zebb's for hamburgers or to the Adirondack coffee shop. The VT (Village Tavern) is the most popular bar in town, and a major hangout for upperclassmen and underclassmen with ID. Otherwise students party in rooms or go to fraternity parties, which have to be held in students rooms since there are no frat houses anymore. There are some theme parties, such as "Mardi Gras," "Heaven and Hell," and "Pimps and Hoes" that have huge turnouts. There are also some sororities on campus, though none of them are national, and they have never had separate housing. Greek life is more of a deal for the guys on campus, but people in general do not feel excluded if they are not a part of Greek life.

Hamilton also lives up to its reputation as somewhat of a party school. Getting alcohol is definitely not a problem, and some students report that people who don't drink sometimes feel uncomfortable. The administration is pretty relaxed on its alcohol policy, although it does require that all people planning to throw a party with mass quantities of alcohol attend a two-hour lecture about abusing alcohol. After the lecture they are given a pass so that they can serve. Pot is also fairly easy to find on campus, though most students reject other more hard core drugs.

"Most of the weekend life is on campus, as there is not much to do off, and the school does a great job at providing entertainment." This year the band Dispatch has visited the campus, as well as other groups such as an African drumming group. The five a cappella singing groups at Hamilton also have huge turnouts for their shows. The school even provides popular free movies on the weekends. The "Great Names Lecture Series" has brought names like Margaret Thatcher and Desmond Tutu to campus. In the realm of extracurriculars, one of the most popular organizations on campus is The Outdoor Club, which has climbing and backpacking trips to destinations including Ecuador. Community service and writing for the weekly newspaper, *The Spectator*, are popular as well. Every Sunday night in the winter is "Sunday Night Skiing" night, and many students board busses to go night skiing. Many students participate in intramural and varsity athletics, and the turnout for varsity events is said to be fair. The biggest game of the year is the first ice hockey game. Continuing the tradition of "Citrus Ball," all Hamilton students throw oranges to the opposing team's goalie after Hamilton scores the first goal.

Overall, Hamilton students are very content with their educational experience. The small student body and rural setting can be both very intimate and at times isolating. However, most students seem to be happy with the academic and social opportunities available to them and equally happy with their choice to attend Hamilton. Just remember to bring a good winter coat for the cold winters and good hiking boots for the hill climbing you will be doing. —*Carolyn Grace and Staff*

FYI

The three best things about attending Hamilton are "great professors, huge, beautiful campus, and the variety of extracurriculars."

The three worst things about attending Hamilton are "Clinton, no frat houses, snow in November."

The three things that every student should do before graduating Hamilton are "go skiing in Adirondacks, attend one of the huge theme parties, go to Turning Stone Casino."

One thing I'd like to have known before coming here is "how necessary cars can really be."

Hobart and William Smith College

Address: 629 South Main Street; Geneva, NY 14456
Phone: 800-852-2256 (Hobart) 800-245-0100 (William Smith)
E-mail address: hoadm@hws.edu
Web site URL: www.hws.edu
Founded: 1822
Private or Public: private
Religious affiliation: none
Location: small city
Undergraduate enrollment: 1,823
Total enrollment: 1,823
Percent Male/Female: 48%/52%

Percent Minority: 13%
Percent African-American: 6%
Percent Asian: 2%
Percent Hispanic: 4%
Percent Native-American: 0.5%
Percent in-state/out-of-state: 50%/50%
Percent Pub HS: 65%
Number of Applicants: 2,634
Percent Accepted: 75%
Percent Accepted who enroll: 25%
Entering: 501
Transfers: 35
Application Deadline: 15 Feb
Mean SAT: NA

Mean ACT: NA
Middle 50% SAT range: 530–620 V, 530–620 M
Middle 50% ACT range: NA
3 Most popular majors: English, economics, psychology
Retention: 87%
Graduation rate: 83%
On-campus housing: 100%
Fraternities: 20%
Sororities: NA
Library: 350,000 volumes
Tuition and Fees: $24,342 in; $24,342 out
Room and Board: $6,882
Financial aid, first-year: 66%

L ocated on exquisite Seneca Lake, Hobart and William Smith Colleges (HWS) offer students a unique package of comfort and academics. Both Hobart, the men's college, and William Smith, the women's college, have their own deans, masters, athletic teams, student governments, and admissions staffs, but the two colleges share a single campus, faculty, classes, and dorm system.

Together but Apart

This "coordinate system" of different administrations but common experience mainly draws praise from students. Many women consider the numerous support groups, the women's studies program, and the general focus on women's issues "empowering." However, some males feel that the coordinate system benefits only women, and some are convinced that HWS should place "more emphasis on the coming together of the sexes than on each sex finding its own strength." But regardless, Hobart men leave college sensitive to women's issues and problems.

A Carefully Groomed Campus

Nature has endowed HWS well with Seneca Lake, and HWS administrators have carefully built and maintained the campus. The appearance of Hobart and William Smith Colleges is "addictive" and "breathtaking." One student explained, "I knew I was coming here as soon as I set foot on campus." Not only is the campus beautiful, but it is also "incredibly well kept."

How picturesque is Seneca Lake? According to legend, all the buildings that have been built between the "Lady of the Lake" statue and Seneca Lake have burned to the ground because the Lady of the Lake will not allow any object to obscure her gorgeous view.

Geneva, New York, home of HWS, is not a college town. One student joked, "Hobart would be perfect if it were in Ithaca." The Seneca Lake area does, however, have its benefits: there are numerous wineries in the area that offer wine tasting to those who are of age.

Living

In general, students like their dorms. Yet, one senior complains that "the housing situation sucks" because of Hobart and William Smith's strict limitations for off-campus living. But students are generally happy with on-campus options. Freshmen live in standard, comfortable dorms. But upperclassmen can now live in luxurious condominiums. According to one pleased student, "The condos are nicer than my house." Other options such as theme houses and the field house, where students till their own land, offer unique living arrangements.

Hobart and William Smith students like their dining hall food in general. The quality is mediocre, but "the variety is amazing," said one senior. Outside of the dining halls, students can snack at The Cellar, Cafe Cabana (downtown), or Just Cookies and Pies (which, paradoxically, serves top-notch sandwiches also). Spinnakers and Ports offer more upscale, gourmet meals.

Typical Students?

Two traits characterize the typical student at Hobart and William Smith: "well-off" and "friendly." Yes, "80 percent of the campus dresses in J.Crew," said one student, but the other 20 percent feel little pressure to conform. Most of the students are Caucasian and hail from New England and the Mid-Atlantic suburbs. Some feel that "Hobart is not as diverse as it could be," but Hobart is now making a large-scale effort to attract and support minority students. The fact that minorities comprise 20 percent of the class of 2001 indicates that minority-recruiting efforts have succeeded. While some say that students still segregate themselves to some degree, one senior said, "Your group changes from where you come from [and what ethnic group you are] to where you are or where you are going." However, one Hispanic freshman believes, "Some people here can be so close-minded at times it is not even funny." The gay and lesbian population is small, but accepted. The Gay, Lesbian, Bisexual Friends Network provides support to homosexual students and awareness to others

Greek life at Hobart plays a major role in social life. Also, the condos provide more than enough space for room parties.

In general, alcohol is readily available, and HWS can be "a real weed-fest," though most feel that drugs are no more or less prevalent at HWS than at other colleges. Random hookups are common, but "long-term relationships are difficult."

Extracurriculars

In extracurriculars, students range from "apathetic" to "fanatical," with the mean skewed towards the "apathetic" end of the spectrum. However, student government, especially William Smith's Congress, affects life directly and powerfully. "Geneva Heroes" brings Hobart and William Smith students together with area eighth graders to perform community service.

> "Each student does something deviant. Last year, one girl ate an earthworm, lots of people did stripteases, and some guy stole a fire hydrant and brought it to class."

Academics at Hobart are what one makes of them. The year is divided into three trimesters, allowing students to take few classes at once. In political science, English, women's studies, and biology, Hobart and William Smith excel. Hobart students rave about the accessibility and excellence of their professors. Jack Harris, one well-loved professor, spices his sociology class with "Deviance Day," where "each student does something deviant. Last year, one girl ate an earthworm, lots of people did stripteases, and some guy stole a fire hydrant and brought it to class."

A new science building provides science majors with excellent facilities. Physics, however, is a weak point. Additionally, Hobart and William Smith send hundreds of students abroad each trimester. The destination list is huge for such a small school, and professors accompany students to some foreign locations.

Still, Hobart and William Smith seem to attract "a lot of kids who had all the opportunities in the world in high school, but only took advantages of a few of them." HWS changes most of these people, but nevertheless fails to inspire some.—*Brian Abaluck and Staff*

FYI
The three best things about attending HWS are "that it's two different schools, but they're really together, so it's coed."
The three worst things about attending HWS are "Geneva, the lack of anything constructive to do, and the apathy of the student body."
The three things that every student should do before graduating from HWS are "piss off someone of the 'opposing' gender, tell a tourist the 'Lady of the Lake' legend, and throw a party in your condo."
One thing I'd like to have known before coming here is "how much emphasis there would be on gender differences."

Hofstra University

Address: 100 Hofstra University; Hempstead, NY 11549
Phone: 516-463-4700
E-mail address: hofstra@hofstra.edu
Web site URL: www.hofstra.edu
Founded: 1935
Private or Public: private
Religious affiliation: none
Location: suburban
Undergraduate enrollment: 9,173
Total enrollment: 12,439
Percent Male/Female: 46%/54%
Percent Minority: 20%
Percent African-American: 8%

Percent Asian: 5%
Percent Hispanic: 6%
Percent Native-American: 0.5%
Percent in-state/out-of-state: 85%/15%
Percent Pub HS: 70%
Number of Applicants: 7,893
Percent Accepted: 55%
Percent Accepted who enroll: 44%
Entering: 1,906
Transfers: 1,447
Application Deadline: rolling
Mean SAT: 543 V, 549 M
Mean ACT: 24

Middle 50% SAT range: 500–580 V, 500–590 M
Middle 50% ACT range: 21–26
3 Most popular majors: psychology, accounting, marketing
Retention: 78%
Graduation rate: 42%
On-campus housing: 37%
Fraternities: 10%
Sororities: 10%
Library: 1,400,000 volumes
Tuition and Fees: $14,512 in; $14,512 out
Room and Board: $7,060
Financial aid, first-year: 71%

Nestled in the flower-filled city of Hempstead, New York, home of the annual Daffodil Festival, is a campus that students guarantee is "incredibly gorgeous." Its campus, couple with its "comparably affordable" tuition, draws both local and international students.

Hitting the Books

Hofstra offers classes that span the spectrum of subjects and levels of difficulty. As long as students meet the foreign language requirement and the core requirements in math, social science, humanities, cross-cultural studies, and natural science, they may participate in an academic honors program or one of several study abroad programs. Students find that computer sci-

ence, engineering, biochemistry, business and math are more difficult than "*the* slacker major": physical education. While P.E. majors' "backpacks aren't always full," other classes generate workloads that range from "one hour per week per class to a couple hours per day per class."

Regardless of their major, however, students can have free time "if you're efficient with your time." Many find that the best place to study is the Axinn Library, but others opt for their rooms, the student center, dorm lounges, or, for the half of the student body that commutes, home. Recently, students are sticking around campus a little more, thanks in part to the new modern chemistry building and modern business building.

In addition to Hofstra's great class offerings, students rave about their school's small classes. Class sizes range from a couple of people to a maximum of 65. While the small class size increases contact and fosters conversation with the professors, some students complain that the limited class size forces the administration to cap certain classes based on seniority. Sometimes, however, students who personally speak with professors manage to "weasel" their way into classes.

Life On and Off Campus

While half of Hofstra's student body commutes, the other half lives in dorms that "aren't too bad." The New Complex, the newest residence hall on campus, offers students the choice between singles or suites, as well as providing lounges and laundry facilities on each floor. While most rooms in the fifteen-story Tower are singles, students complain that the bathrooms "aren't that clean" and that the singles "are closets!" Larger rooms in Nassau, Suffolk, Colonial Square, and The Netherlands are slightly more distant from campus. Students generally prefer Nassau and Suffolk over the other two options. These dorms are all equipped with a kitchen, a TV lounge, and laundry rooms. Students have the choice of living on single-sex floors, smoke-free floors, and alcohol free floors in the dorms. The administration's alcohol policy is supposedly enforced by each dorm's Resident Advisor (RA), but RAs are reputed to let some things slide.

Nearby are a variety of restaurants that are included in students' meal plans. Students are free to choose from seven restaurants on campus, including Bits 'n' Bites, the Hofstra Deli, and the cafeteria in the student center that stays open until 2 A.M. Students who want to venture off campus to eat can choose from "quick food" places like McDonald's, Checker's, Friendly's, Burger King, Subway, and 7–11, or from restaurants like Hooters or TGI Fridays, or the "excellent cuisine" of Vincent's Italian Restaurant. For an even greater selection, students can make the 15 minute trek into New York City. Coffee shops, like the popular Witch's Brew, also provide a mellow place for students to hang out.

The off-campus scene in the city of Hempstead isn't something students rave about. While safety "isn't really a problem," most learn not to walk into downtown Hempstead at night. Most students have cars which make shopping at the Roosevelt Field Mall and off-campus partying popular. One student claimed that "if you meet someone from Hofstra, it's usually not on campus."

> **"Everyone here drives a Beamer or a Mercedes in his or her Polo or Hilfiger outfit."**

The administration does make an effort to offer fun on-campus events, In addition to the on-campus movie theater, there are often special events like lectures and seminars. Students enjoy the selection of movies that the on-campus theatre offers, but they complain that the screen is too small and that the sound quality is poor. The administration brings in quite a few bands and performers as well, including Billy Joel, George Clinton, Eve 6, Mighty Mighty Bosstones, Busta Rhymes, and Third-Eye-Blind. Off campus parties are popular, and students enjoy such on-campus parties as the Freak Formal on Halloween, the Scrufest, the basketball team's Midnight Madness, and Homecoming. Because "Greek life dominates," there are always frat parties to choose from as well.

The Student Body

While students generally consider their classmates to be "pretty friendly," impressions of the diversity on campus seem to differ. One student claimed, "we have students of every race, religion and color;" another thought that "there's a little more diversity than my high school, but that's not saying much;" and another student criticized the fact that "everyone here is rich." Diversity, he claimed, was hindered by the fact that "Everyone here drives a Beamer or a Mercedes in his Polo or Hilfiger outfit."

Students certainly have a diverse selection of extracurricular activities to choose from. Hofstra is the nation's only school to have a ROYGBIV (acronym for the colors of the rainbow) club, where students can color in coloring books. More demanding commitments include the symphonic band, the accounting club, the school newspaper, *The Chronicle*, theatre groups, students government, and intramural sports. Students frequent the Hofstra Recreation Center to stay in shape and have fun. The Rec Center houses basketball courts, a track, a pool, classrooms for karate and an "increasing number" of classes, and "basically, all your gym stuff."

Sports teams are "becoming" more popular, thanks to the new 5,000-seat basketball arena. In addition to the solid basketball team, Hofstra's men's lacrosse and football are popular. Women's athletics are becoming increasingly popular as well. Also popular on campus is the Hofstra Greek life. Social life at Hofstra is shaped by fraternity and sorority parties and events. There's no great pressure to join a frat or sorority, and students regard the pledging process as "fun." Students claim that these parties are better than those at Hofstra USA—the school's own nightclub. Carding is strictly enforced at Hofstra USA, but when frats or sororities host parties at neighboring bars, students say the carding policies tend to be more lenient.

Hofstra students, whether commuting or residing in the dorms, enjoy their school. Its small campus and friendly student body make this university a fun place to "get a great education but not for a lot of money." —*Marti Page and Staff*

FYI
The three best things about attending Hofstra are "the price, the atmosphere, and its great reputation."
The three worst things about attending Hofstra are "the Tower, the fact that you need a car, and the commute."
The three things that everyone must do before graduating from Hofstra are "*actually learn what you're majoring in*, go to the Freak Formal, and go to Vincent's Italian restaurant."
One thing I'd like to have known before coming here is "that you need a car."

The Juilliard School

Address: 60 Lincoln Center Plaza; New York, NY 10023-6588
Phone: 212-799-5000
E-mail address: NA
Web site URL: NA
Founded: 1905
Private or Public: private
Religious affiliation: none
Location: urban
Undergraduate enrollment: 468
Total enrollment: 770
Percent Male/Female: 49%/51%
Percent Minority: 25%
Percent African-American: 8%

Percent Asian: 14%
Percent Hispanic: 3%
Percent Native-American: NA
Percent in-state/out-of-state: NA
Percent Pub HS: NA
Number of Applicants: 1,176
Percent Accepted: 11%
Percent Accepted who enroll: 81%
Entering: 104
Transfers: NA
Application Deadline: 1 Dec
Mean SAT: NA

Mean ACT: NA
Middle 50% SAT range: NA
Middle 50% ACT range: NA
3 Most popular majors: music, dance, drama
Retention: NA
Graduation rate: NA
On-campus housing: 100%
Fraternities: NA
Sororities: NA
Library: 73,000 volumes
Tuition and Fees: $16,600 in; $16,600 out
Room and Board: $6,850
Financial aid, first-year: 91%

Iigh above the taxi crowded streets of midtown Manhattan stand two buildings where the sounds of violins, singing, and clarinets drown out the noise of automobiles down below. The buildings belong to Juilliard—you might have heard of it. The buildings once housed Robin Williams, Patti Lupone, and

Wynton Marsalis—you might have heard of them. The buildings now house the next generation of performers—you will hear of them.

Twentieth Floor. Please Exit the Elevator Now for . . .

One of the school's towers at Lincoln Center houses the classrooms, libraries, practice rooms, performance spaces, and the administration of the school. Inside these walls, students train with the premier teachers in the area of concentration—and they train hard. Students are out of their rooms from early in the morning until at least ten at night training, practicing, rehearsing, attending classes, and trying to grab a meal in between.

Juilliard students are enrolled in one of three programs: music, drama, or dance. Within each student's area of concentration, the faculty is respected professionals and experts in their field. "If you're good," one student noted, "you can get a good professor. It doesn't matter how old you are." Students are not just taught their skill; they are driven to master it. "The training is so beneficial. They have a lot of money, so they can offer a lot," said one sophomore. Students within each of the programs are a community unto themselves. But within these communities, "especially with casting," a drama student complained, "the directors already know who they want before the audition. It's not based on your ability in the audition, it's already predetermined."

In addition to classes in their concentration, students are required to take one humanities course per term. A musician praised the humanities course as a break from the music and taught her to "open her mind to new ideas" instead of "worrying about her concerto." But, one dancer described the courses as "poorly thought up." He continued: "They are trying to get you to look inside yourself, and it doesn't work." For example, when reading Homer's *Odyssey*, a class of students was asked, "how does this make you feel?" They disliked this attempt to personalize the interpretation of classical works and lamented its pointlessness. Juilliard students desiring a more diverse curriculum are permitted to enroll in classes at Columbia.

However, few students take advantage of this opportunity because, as one musician pointed out, "it takes a lot of time!" Most students simply cannot fit the time consuming uptown commute into their busy schedules.

Inside the Community of Artists

There is nothing ordinary about living in Lincoln Center. Students praise the hotel-like atmosphere with two great—and particularly appropriate—views of the Hudson River and Broadway. First year students are required to live in the residence hall, and this helps to foster a sense of community within the school. "We're like a family," one musician described. All of the rooms in the high rise are suites shared by up to seven students. Some students complained about the reliability of the phone system within these suites, noting that "at certain times in the night you try to call out and you can't—it just happens randomly." Regardless of the occasional communication glitch, students were enthusiastic about living with their talented peers. One musician remembers: "I played a Bach piece and my roommate choreographed a dance to it. It was really beautiful." Life in the residence hall inspires creativity in many.

And what about New York City? Some students wanted to escape the city and complained that they did not have "a real campus," while others appreciated Lincoln Center's "prime location." The Center's proximity to Central Park and the Metropolitan Opera Company provides students with the opportunity to escape into nature and attend a world-class production in the same evening. Attending professional performances inspires the students. One student remembers a particularly moving musical performance: "The way that they performed, it made me forget that I was at a performance. It made me think of my own performance and how I can make audiences feel the same." Even though the students embrace professional performances for inspiration, some lament their twenty-four hour days, which does not allow for much time to take full advantage of Manhattan. When students are not recovering from their tiring weekdays or trying to learn from master performers, they frequent local restaurants and bars where, one drama student noted, "ID is not a problem." Inside the residence tower, there are "community assistants" to help plan events for the floor and the entire building from Sushi Night to a St. Patrick's Day Party.

> **"The emphasis here is on the process—how to do it properly, not just whether you can do it."**

Juilliard students believe that there is a misconception that their school is cutthroat. "Before coming here there were all these horror stories like razor-blades between piano keys," one musician noted. "Actually," another musician continued, "people here are pretty normal. Ultimately it is a great place—people are really nice." The students are supportive of each other, and they have great respect for each other's talents. Because they spend so much time practicing and training, "it's kind of hard to meet people outside of your department. There isn't much time. It's pretty closed off." Students on campus are accepting of interracial and same sex relationships, but some girls complained that there are "not enough straight guys to go around for all of the girls."

Despite the Manhattan backdrop and Lincoln Center accommodations, Juilliard stills falls victim to the ills of institutional food. One student warned: "Stick to the salad bar—it's safe. Veggie burgers and sandwiches are fine. But any of the cooked food . . ." The students' busy lifestyle makes it hard to eat healthy. When "they give you half an hour to eat, all you can do is grab a slice of pizza and a coke." Students are concerned that eating disorders are not addressed, particularly among the dancers. One student called for a "class on nutrition."

Above and Beyond Lincoln Center

Does everyone at Juilliard become a celebrity? Well, that depends on whether or not you want to be famous. One dancer noted, "There are some people who say, 'I'm going to make it.' But I don't consider them artists. They are not here to do what they love, but to be a star." Certainly, the name Juilliard will open doors after graduation, and the extensive alumni network provides great opportunities to graduates. One drama student claimed "We know each and every person who has graduated: what they are doing, if they've got a job, if they don't have a job, even how long their contracts are for." If nothing else, students are prepared to fight their way to the top through mastery and application of their talents.

When Juilliard showcases its talent, New York listens. Students feel that the school puts an emphasis on "getting into a company" after graduation. Students are encouraged to excel as individual performers in the context of a supportive community. In addition to being able to present themselves effectively, graduates are equipped with skills to teach their art to aspiring students. "There is no pressure on becoming famous. There is immense pressure on becoming an artist, and artists aren't famous until they're dead," one student said.

Juilliard recently renovated its Lila Acheson Wallace Library. The collection now includes more than 50,000 scores; 20,000 books on music, dance, and drama; 15,000 sound recordings, and 500 videocassettes. In April 1999, The Campaign for Juilliard was announced: Over the next five years, one hundred million dollars will be spent on a wide range of projects to better prepare Juilliard students for the demands of the next century. These include efforts to expand and enrich the curriculum, increases in scholarship aid and faculty salaries, commissions to produce new artistic works, and the renovation and enhancement of the school's Lincoln Center buildings.

Juilliard's focus is intense. Students warn prospectives: "You need to know what you're doing before you go into a school that is so one-dimensional." But, it is precisely this focus which allows students to turn their talent into mastery.
—*Jason Friedrichs and Staff*

Manhattanville College

Address: 2900 Purchase Street; Purchase, NY 10577
Phone: 914-323-5464
E-mail address: admissions@mville.edu
Web site URL: www.manhattanville.edu
Founded: 1841
Private or Public: private
Religious affiliation: none
Location: suburban
Undergraduate enrollment: 1,509
Total enrollment: 1,895
Percent Male/Female: 34%/66%
Percent Minority: 26%

Percent African-American: 7%
Percent Asian: 4%
Percent Hispanic: 14%
Percent Native-American: 0.5%
Percent in-state/out-of-state: 62%/38%
Percent Pub HS: NA
Number of Applicants: 1,803
Percent Accepted: 66%
Percent Accepted who enroll: 33%
Entering: 387
Transfers: 200
Application Deadline: rolling
Mean SAT: 510 V, 520 M

Mean ACT: NA
Middle 50% SAT range: 500–599 V, 500–599 M
Middle 50% ACT range: NA
3 Most popular majors: psychology, management, political science
Retention: 80%
Graduation rate: 53%
On-campus housing: 68%
Fraternities: NA
Sororities: NA
Library: 280,000 volumes
Tuition and Fees: $18,860 in; $18,860 out
Room and Board: $8,000
Financial aid, first-year: 88%

Situated in the town of Purchase in the suburbs of New York City, Manhattanville College combines solid academics with a small, personal atmosphere of learning. The prevailing philosophy of Manhattanville is to offer the utmost challenge to its students in an environment that is enjoyable and personal, to prepare them for life beyond college.

Manhattanville's Departments

Students report that the strongest departments are psychology, political science, English, history, music, and dance, while the weakest are chemistry and physics. According to one undergrad, "Some students have to go to SUNY/Purchase to take physics." Classes usually average 15 to 20 students, and rarely exceed 35. Professors are readily accessible and are reportedly eager to talk with their students. All lecture classes are taught by professors, while student instructors, or SIs, lead review sessions. Manhattanville offers study-abroad programs in Florence, Paris, London, and other cities. A new program called CSTEP (Collegiate Science and Technology Entrance Program) offers qualified high school seniors and Manhattanville students lectures in scientific and technological areas, as well as field trips and conventions that offer opportunities to speak with business representatives. Students can also apply for internships with nearby companies such as Pepsico, IBM, and the Nestle Corporation. Students say these internships sometimes result in full-time employment after graduation. Many undergrads, however, aspire to continue their education in graduate programs in law, medicine, and other fields.

Manhattanville students are required to take a writing course, eight credits in math and science, six credits in the arts, three credits each in humanities and the social sciences, and six credits in "global perspectives." Classes in Western and non-Western culture can be waived if a student majors or minors in a foreign language. All freshmen take a yearlong preceptorial class, in which they read and write about a wide range of classical literature. Students generally agree that at first these requirements seem to be a "hassle," but say that in the end they expand their knowledge and contribute to a strong liberal arts education.

Manhattanville also has a unique "portfolio system" designed to track students' progress through their college years. Students meet with their individual faculty advisors in the beginning of their freshman year to create a four-year course list. Each subsequent spring, students then place a written self-examination and an example of the work they have accomplished during that school year in their portfolios, where it will later be reviewed by a committee of faculty members and administrators.

Campus Life

Manhattanville dorms are reportedly comfortable and well-kept. Two of the most popular dorms, Tenney and Spellman, were recently renovated, and even Damman, generally regarded as the worst dorm, has undergone renovation. All four dorms are co-ed by suite or room. Spellman houses predominantly freshmen, while Founders houses juniors and seniors. A portion of Tenney Hall is an intercultural center that is home to many of the international students on campus. The center offers multicultural meetings, lectures, and events. Most students live on campus, and those who do not usually commute.

For those who live on campus, the college meal plan allows them to get food at the cafeteria or the Cafe. The cafeteria serves everything from stir-fry, salad, and vegetarian food to hot entrees like chicken and pasta. The Cafe offers more opportunities for snacking, with such choices as grilled sandwiches, pizzas, and burgers. Students use a meal card to "charge" food during designated "equivalency hours."

Most Manhattanville students come from the tristate area of New York, New Jersey, and Connecticut, and many go home on weekends. There is no Greek system at Manhattanville, and campus social life on the weekends is traditionally slow. Some students are trying to compensate for this with a Clubs Council, which meets every week to organize weekend events. Also, students regularly hold parties in their rooms. One student joked that, if worse comes to worst, "you can follow the rugby team, and there is a party around them all the time."

Although the reportedly conservative administration has a strict policy against kegs on campus, in recent years students have been allowed to organize registered "pub nights" in response to the growing popularity of the nearby bars in town like O'Henry's and JB's. The newly formed Monday Night Football pub night keeps students on campus to watch televised football games and to drink at the Pavillion, the student center. The best parties of the year are the Fall and Spring formals and the Quad Jam. Following the Spring Formal, the Quad Jam is a daylong party where students can "drink, dance, and play games" to the music of up to ten bands. Entertainment on campus also includes occasional movie marathons and Sunday nights at the Coffee House, where people read poetry, play the guitar, or listen to performances given by visiting bands. During the week, students socialize at the Pavillion while picking up their mail or going to the bookstore.

> "The personal attention we get is sometimes overwhelming."

Sports-minded students can find outlets in club and intramural sports. The most popular club sport is rugby, while football, soccer, and lacrosse dominate in intramurals. Other students get involved in clubs such as LASO (the Latin American Student Organization) and the BSU (the Black Student's Union). Students also write for Touchstone, the campus newspaper, or the student literary magazine. Undergrads report that there is not much interaction between the students and the surrounding community, and community service is not popular at Manhattanville. According to one student, the college and the town "try to stay out of each other's way." Once a semester, however, a campuswide drive collects clothes, books, and toys for the needy in the area.

Students report that the administration is generally responsive to their complaints and needs. After a recent incident involving racially motivated vandalism, the administration immediately tightened campus security and also organized a discussion forum to address students' feelings and proposed solutions. Some undergrads believe the college should install a new outdoor lighting system for improved safety.

The student body is fairly diverse and politically liberal. Many students describe their classmates as politically aware without being very politically active.

According to students, Manhattanville College is an excellent place to receive a good education and lots of personal attention. Undergrads can find both tranquility and excitement by dividing their time between suburban campus life and visits to nearby New York City. This excitment will soon be added to. The New York Rangers are building their practice arena on campus, and the school is starting a hockey team. Students enjoy the quality of life at Manhattanville, and the opportunities it provides. As one student remarked, "If you want to be in control of your future, come to Manhattanville." —*Ann Zeidner and Staff*

FYI

The three best things about attending Manhattanville are "the people, the location, and the personal attention."

The three worst things about attending Manhattanville are "the sparcity of classes, the lack of weekend social events, and the strict administration."

The three things that every student should do before graduating from Manhattanville are "watch the Super Bowl at the Pavillion, figure out if anyone else likes the portfolio system, and meet a hockey player."

One thing I'd like to have known before coming here is "just how much attention one gets."

New York University

Address: 22 Washington Square North; New York, NY 10011-9191
Phone: 212-998-4500
E-mail address: NA
Web site URL: www.nyu.edu
Founded: 1861
Private or Public: private
Religious affiliation: none
Location: urban
Undergraduate enrollment: 18,204
Total enrollment: 37,124
Percent Male/Female: 40%/60%
Percent Minority: 31%
Percent African-American: 6%
Percent Asian: 17%

Percent Hispanic: 7%
Percent Native-American: 0.5%
Percent in-state/out-of-state: 52%/48%
Percent Pub HS: 71%
Number of Applicants: 28,794
Percent Accepted: 32%
Percent Accepted who enroll: 38%
Entering: 3,492
Transfers: 904
Application Deadline: 15 Jan
Mean SAT: NA
Mean ACT: NA
Middle 50% SAT range: 620–710 V, 610–710 M

Middle 50% ACT range: 28–31
3 Most popular majors: visual and perofrming arts, business, social sciences
Retention: 88%
Graduation rate: 72%
On-campus housing: 84%
Fraternities: 7%
Sororities: 6%
Library: 3,000,000 volumes
Tuition and Fees: $23,456 in; $23,456 out
Room and Board: $8,676
Financial aid, first-year: 63%

Located near the Greenwich Village, NYU provides students the opportunity to frequent myriad nightclubs and cafes, walk right through the scene of a movie being filmed, or just hang out and listen to music in Washington Square Park. "The city is within us," one student proudly proclaimed.

Diversity Sums It All Up

Mention NYU, and instantly you hear of NYC, which everyone simply refers to as "the city." Often regarded as the college's best feature, the city is about as diverse as they come. Anything you're looking for, the city's got. NYU dorms and class buildings are integrated into the city—providing easy access to the theatre, the arts, the world's leading business center (Wall Street), and hundreds of restaurants. "It's the real world, with all types of people with various backgrounds and interests," remarked one student. Added another, "New York City will challenge the way you think and view the world. As they say, 'if you can make it here, you can make it anywhere.'"

NYU has a student body representative of the city's diversity. Students come from all over the U.S. and the globe. With six separate undergraduate schools ranging from traditional academic areas to colleges devoted to the arts, social work, or music, NYU reflects the multitude of cultures represented in the Village. Each maintains its own personality and academic requirements. NYU's version of the small liberal arts college, the College of Arts and Sciences, requires students to take courses under the Morse Academic Plan (MAP) with the intention of providing a well-rounded liberal arts education. Requirements are not universally loved. "They take a long time to wade through," remarked one undergrad. "And with the amount of money we're paying, we should be able to take what we want."

The Gallatin Division of NYU takes a different approach, however. Referred to as the "create your own major" division, work is self-paced and credits are earned as academic work is completed. Professional schools include the Stern School of Business; the School of Education, Health, Nursing, and Arts Professions; and the School of Social Work. Among these, the most selective are the Tisch School of the

Arts and the Film School. As one student put it, "they have excellent education in drama, film, and dancing. They have Academy Award winners working there." NYU also offers a wide range of study abroad options. An example is the "Freshman Year in Florence" Program that allows students to spend their first year in Florence, start their college lives in a smaller community, and to study the Renaissance at its origin.

As one of the largest private universities in the nation, NYU is inundated with lecture courses that are inordinately large. Little personal attention is provided "unless you *really* make an effort to track someone down" and graduate students teach many classes, including most of the freshmen writing courses. The close-knit, pleasant atmosphere of smaller, enclosed campuses is absent here. "You can get lost in such a large university," said one student.

Living in the City

While NYU is concentrated in one of the nicer and safer areas of NYC, there is no clear delineation between campus and Greenwich Village. The quality of dorms vary, but residents are generally pleased. Some are apartment-style and have private bathrooms, and "although you have to clean them, they are a huge advantage." Many are renovated apartment buildings and residential hotels. Others—including Rubin, Weinstein, and Hayden—are more traditional, and house many freshmen. The Weinstein cafeteria has TVs playing, and students can touch the TV screen to request a video from the NYU music video station. Hayden Hall is located right on Washington Square Park and is known as a bit of a "creepy dorm" because it is so old. Third Avenue North is a dorm that is considered "in between" the good and the bad, though its dining hall "kind of has a fifties twist to it." Carlyle is considered good because of the apartment-style rooms, but it is bit of a walk from campus. Although Goddard is traditional, many students like it for its proximity to most classes. Broome Street is "supposed to be huge in terms of space, but 10 or 11 people share one kitchen and two bathrooms." One of the noisier dorms is Brittany, which houses many students from Tisch.

Regarding food, one freshman admitted, "It started off great, but now it gets kind of boring." At meals, cereal, a salad bar, hamburgers, hot dogs, turkey burgers, and three entrees are always present. But whatever cuisine you crave that the dining halls can't provide, you can find in the city. "There's at *least* a couple eateries anywhere you walk." One area, referred to as "the Four corners," has a café at each corner, including the Café Figgaro—a vegetarian place popularly known for its falafels. Though admittedly, "it can be very, very expensive to attend NYU—there are numerous forms of financial aid, merit scholarships, and work-study programs, but living in the city can put a hole in your pocket."

Events Actually *On*-Campus

There are many activities on campus, but like the academics, "it's easy to get lost in the shuffle here." Students said that being part of an organization helps to ease the feeling. Popular on campus are the Political Spectrum, Peers' Ears, and the Sexual Health Advisory. A daily newspaper, the *Washington Square News* is also continually seeking writers, as are literary magazines and cultural publications. Students for Social Equality, a politically based group, is also popular among students. But if none of the existing organizations particularly strikes one's interest, creating a new one is not regarded as a difficult task. "If you have an idea and you have people willing to do it, NYU will give you funding," one undergrad pointed out.

> "It's the real world, with all types of people with various backgrounds and interests . . . anything you want, it's got."

NYU's Cantor Film Center hosts several film screenings and festivals every year that bring acclaimed directors, writers, and film critics to campus. Recent examples include *Rendezvous with French Cinema 2001* and the screening of Ang Lee's *Crouching Tiger, Hidden Dragon*. Despite all the efforts to bring activities on campus, NYU's social life revolves around the city. Students frequent local clubs, from jazz clubs like Boo Radley to dance clubs like the Wetlands. With no major Greek life, few parties are actually held on campus grounds. In fact, no place on campus is really large enough to throw a traditional dance or party. However, the offerings are plentiful off campus, and many students choose to spend much of their leisure time there. You can find parties with nonstop action 'til 4 A.M. You can find quaint little coffee shops dimly lit. You can find comfortable outdoor cafes with views of the New York masses walking by.

But with no clear definition of a campus and undergraduate students spread far apart, there is little school spirit. There is very little focus on organized athletics, though club sports include ballroom dancing and racquetball. "Just look at the name," one student point out, referring to the NYU Violets, "and you can tell why." For those seeking to work out, however, the Jerome S. Coles Sports Center maintains stellar facilities, including an Olympic-size pool, an additional dive pool, a track, and tennis courts. The Coles Center also organizes classes for the NYU community that range from golf to martial arts, belly dancing to indoor climbing, and fitness to ballroom dancing.

Given its location, security is tight in campus buildings. Students use their ID cards to get into campus buildings, and 24-hour security guards monitor all dorms. But most feel safe in Greenwich Village and East Village. The increased activity at night around the NYU neighborhood also provides security in anonymity, giving the impression that the areas around campus are a safe place to walk. "The lights come alive at night," one student remarked. Although undergrads sometimes complain about losing IDs and consequently being locked out of their own dorms, one explained that "it's just important to be alert and to use common sense when living in New York City as in any place!" Doing so opens many doors—the city is at the students' fingertips, and all recommend that good use be made of this opportunity to melt into the country's most populous and most vibrant city.

—*William Chen and Staff*

The three best things about attending NYU are "New York City, the diversity of student body, and the rich environment that allows for hands-on learning and a dynamic social life."
The three worst things about attending NYU are "no clear delineation of a campus, the large number of students, the hefty price tag on education."
The three things that every student should do before graduating from NYU are "take advantage of the city and have fun, get work experience, and decide for yourself what's important for you to do before graduating!"
One thing I'd like to have known before coming here is "that the city is not as dangerous and 'scary' as many believe it to be."

Parsons School of Design

Address: 66 Fifth Avenue; New York, NY 10011-8878
Phone: 212-229-8910
E-mail address: parsadm@newschool.edu
Web site URL: www.parsons.edu
Founded: 1896
Private or Public: private
Religious affiliation: none
Location: urban
Undergraduate enrollment: 2,322
Total enrollment: 2,600
Percent Male/Female: 28%/72%
Percent Minority: 30%

Percent African-American: 4%
Percent Asian: 17%
Percent Hispanic: 8%
Percent Native-American: 0.5%
Percent in-state/out-of-state: 52%/48%
Percent Pub HS: NA
Number of Applicants: 1,313
Percent Accepted: 42%
Percent Accepted who enroll: 54%
Entering: 300
Transfers: 327
Application Deadline: rolling
Mean SAT: NA

Mean ACT: NA
Middle 50% SAT range: 480–600 V, 460–580 M
Middle 50% ACT range: 20–25
3 Most popular majors: design, fashion, illustration
Retention: NA
Graduation rate: NA
On-campus housing: NA
Fraternities: NA
Sororities: NA
Library: 17,000 volumes
Tuition and Fees: $21,420 in; $21,420 out
Room and Board: $8,857
Financial aid, first-year: 85%

In the heart of New York, in downtown Greenwich Village, students are finding their way through the challenge of Parsons and the excitement of the city. One student says, "We have access to all kinds of facilities and events in the city that has offerings from all over the world. Even beyond what the city can give us, the university offers information and facilities for those interested in learning."

The City as Campus

New York city is one of the most dynamic cities of the world, offering many centers for culture, design, communications, architecture and business. The campus, located in Greenwich, is at the heart of Manhattan's artistic life. Parsons has a main building along with three residence halls in walking distance of the Greenwich Village campus. Loeb Residence Hall houses mostly freshmen and provides its residents access to an art studio, a reading room, a lounge and laundry room. The other two residence halls, The Marlton House and Union Square, are for those above 19 years of age. These two halls offer singles, doubles and some suits.

As for other resources, Parsons provides its students with links to New York University's and Cooper Union's libraries. Many students also take an advantage of the Parsons study abroad programs. France, Israel, the Netherlands, Great Britain and Sweden are destinations offered to students, and many choose to go to Paris. The Paris campus consists of a couple of dorms within the walking distance of the main building.

Not Only Fashion Design

Parsons New York also offers different areas of study. There are three four-year undergraduate art and design degree options: BFA, the Bachelor of Fine Arts, BBA, the Bachelor of Business Administration and the five year BA/BFA degree. The Bachelor of Business Administration requires the completion of a specific curriculum in design marketing. The five-year dual degree offers students a complete studio art or design major along with a liberal arts education.

Since Parsons is a part of the New School system, students always have the option of choosing electives from the New School for Social Research. The first year is the "Foundation Year" and the courses offered, which are basics of drawing and design, are the "Foundation Courses." The Foundation program is also offered as a part of non-degree programs. The freshmen take classes in small sections, with 15 to 20 students, often taught by professionals in the field of the class. The class offerings are constantly evolving and new programs are being added as a result of changing trends and job opportunities in the design world.

Parsons challenges all students and weeds out slackers. "The workload is too heavy. Many of the people usually drop out the first year and some more drop out the following years," comments a student. Fashion and product design are considered the hardest majors. Design marketing isn't as challenging as fashion and product design.

> "The workload is too heavy. Many of the people usually drop out the first year and some more drop out the following years."

There also are four affiliate schools that offer two-year programs and whose graduates continue their education at Parsons, to complete their bachelor's degree. One is in Paris, France, the others are in the Dominican Republic, Kanazawa, Japan and in Seoul, South Korea. Students studying in France take French Language classes, a part of the core curriculum. The aim of this core curriculum, which also includes Liberal Studies courses that offer classes on the intellectual and historical aspects of France, is to help students become more independent in their environment.

It Takes Two to Tango

The students enjoy their time in the city but many have money issues. "You have to pay a lot to either rent an apartment or live outside Manhattan and take the subway. Parsons is a very expensive school," a student says. This may explain another comment of students. Students find Parsons to be always concerned with teaching about marketing your designs and making money. Students say that it is a "School of Design" and not a "School of Art." One student explains, "Anyone who doesn't like to make money upon graduation or anyone who is really interested in fine arts and learning skills and crafts should stay away!"

The social life for Parsons students is not on campus or at school but rather in the city. Being underage can cause great problems since it narrows down many of the clubbing options. However, almost all have found ways to solve the problem. The social life takes place outside of school, and since there is no campus, people have other lives. "I feel like a working adult here, because I live in an apartment and go to school everyday like my office and come home and I have a completely different social life."

Designers Lead the Way

Many famous and successful designers, artists and employers of huge companies live in New York and visit Parsons all the time. The teachers are all professionals in their fields and many are working designers in Manhattan. "They just teach part-time which is very cool." Students have great connections through their savvy teachers, which allow many students to obtain outstanding and competitive internships.

As long as managing to find the balance between the New York City life and the work, students are happy to be a part of the lively, energetic city, with its Museum of Modern Art, the Guggenheim, the Whitney and many other art shops. But since art has been said to imitate life, New York and Parsons are guaranteed to produce many complex masterpieces.—*Yakut Seyhanli and Staff*

FYI

The three best things about attending Parsons are "being in the City, having great internship options, and the study abroad option in Paris."

The three worst things about attending Parsons are "having great expenses, many people around you doing drugs, and the City."

The three things you should do before graduating from Parsons are "doing a great internship, take advantage of all the City has to offer to you, and do a study abroad."

One thing students would like to have known before coming to Parsons is "how important it is to manage your time."

Rensselaer Polytechnic Institute

Address: 110 8th Street; Troy, NY 12180-3590	**Percent Native-American:** 0.5%	**Middle 50% ACT range:** 24–29
Phone: 518-276-6216	**Percent in-state / out-of-state:** 51%/49%	**3 Most popular majors:** general engineering, management, computer science
E-mail address: admissions@rpi.edu	**Percent Pub HS:** 79%	
Web site URL: www.rpi.edu	**Number of Applicants:** 5,264	
Founded: 1824		**Retention:** 92%
Private or Public: private	**Percent Accepted:** 78%	**Graduation rate:** 44%
Religious affiliation: none	**Percent Accepted who enroll:** 32%	**On-campus housing:** 57%
Location: suburban		**Fraternities:** 32%
Undergraduate enrollment: 4,867	**Entering:** 1,323	**Sororities:** 30%
Total enrollment: 6,560	**Transfers:** NA	**Library:** 440,000 volumes
Percent Male / Female: 76%/24%	**Application Deadline:** 1 Jan	**Tuition and Fees:** $22,955 in; $22,955 out
Percent Minority: 20%	**Mean SAT:** 607 V, 659 M	**Room and Board:** $4,250
Percent African-American: 4%	**Mean ACT:** 27	**Financial aid, first-year:** 76%
Percent Asian: 11%	**Middle 50% SAT range:** 560–660 V, 620–710 M	
Percent Hispanic: 4%		

Imagine going to a school that boasts alumni like Washington Roebling, who built the Brooklyn Bridge, and George W. Ferris, creator of the Ferris wheel, as well as National Hockey League players Adam Oates, Daren Puppa, and Joey Juneau. Not only known for being a great technology school, Rensselaer Polytechnic Institute is also recognized for its Division I hockey team.

A Ton of Work

Undergraduates at RPI are able to choose their majors from among the Schools of Architecture, Humanities and Social Sciences, Management and Technology, Engineering, and Science. The school also offers a program in information technology (IT), a relatively new degree, created in response to the industry's need for IT professionals. Although the five schools of RPI offer a diverse range of strong academic programs, Rensselaer does have a primary focus on engineering, which is generally considered the toughest major, while "management and information technology are the slacker majors." The difficulty of the engineering major can be partially attributed to the challenging requirements, among which Differential Equations ("Diffy Screw"), Introduction to Engineering Analysis, and Data Structures and Algorithms are reportedly the toughest. Regardless of major, all students must fulfill the distribution requirements that include courses in humanities and social sciences.

Class sizes vary between 30 and 40 people, although there are some larger intro classes. While getting into classes is not usually difficult, there are sometimes problems with overcrowded computer science and engineering classes. Students also complain it's often difficult to understand their teaching assistants' foreign accents. Students always feel that they have a "ton of work," but as one sophomore said, "Academics are quite good; they are what made me choose RPI."

De-stressing

Besides knowing how to work hard, students at Rensselaer also know how to fraternize and have a lot of fun. There are 30+ frats and 4 officially recognized sororities that are popular on campus, though students report feeling no pressure to rush. Although alcohol is not supposed to be in the dorms and kegs are not allowed on campus, the administration is reportedly not very strict about drinking, and being underage is not generally considered an issue. "The frat boys stamp underage drinkers on the hand when you walk into parties, but you can still get drinks." Some of the most popular parties are annual frat parties, including Phi Kappa Alpha's Shoot the Dog, which has the slogan: "If you don't come to this party, we'll shoot this dog." Alpha Epsilon Pi's golf party invites students to "go through different rooms and each room is a different 'hole' [where a host] serves a different drink. And if you get through the 18 drinks you finish with a Jack Daniel's."

If downing alcohol or going to parties is not your idea of relaxing, the campus hosts movie nights three times a week that show first-run films, and occasionally host advance screenplays—an "awesome and cheap alternative." And there is always something going on at the Student Union, which is a popular hangout with wireless Ethernet. Those interested in theater can go to the Playhouse to see plays, while those eager to see famous performers head to the Field. RPI has a history of great concerts and recent big performers include Pearl Jam, Alanis Morisette, Korn, and Third Eye Blind. Af-

ter a long week, however, many students prefer just to chill with their friends. As expressed by one freshman, "I love the people on this campus most—they make it what it is . . . nothing else. RPI isn't in the best place, but as a student body, we make do with what we have."

Sleeping and Eating, When Time Permits

Freshmen, unless they are commuters, are required to live in dorms, and most report being satisfied with this situation. "I feel the general on-campus living situation is pretty good," remarked one freshman. The average freshman dorm has two students per room, a lounge, a computer lab, and a laundry room. Upperclassmen dorms are nicer and have air-conditioning and heating. While some floors are coed, bathrooms are always unisex. Suite situations are also unisex. The best freshman dorm on campus is Barton Hall—"it's like a Hilton there, literally. It cost over a million dollars to renovate." Otherwise, there is not much difference between the freshman dorms, except that Cary Hall is all-male. Residential advisors live on every floor of every freshman dorm and get along well with the students. After freshman year, many students live off campus due to lower costs of living there. Off-campus housing costs approximately one-third to one-half the price of living on campus, and many apartments are only a short walk from school.

The campus meal plans are very versatile and try to suit the individual student. Based on their choice of meal plan, students may have unlimited visits to the dining hall. They can also get RADs or MADs (Rensselaer or Marriott Advantage Dollars) to pay for food at some of the mini-stores on campus. Besides the three largest dining halls, Commons, Bar-H, and Russell-Sage, there are many fast-food options at the Student Union. There is even a Ben and Jerry's on campus.

Some undergrads recommend that you buy your own food after freshman year from the local Price Chopper, which can save half the amount spent on meal plans. Also a couple of blocks away from the campus are a Friendly's, a Popeye's, and a Taco Bell. For good, cheap pizza, two favorites among RPI students are NY Pizza and Hoosick Pizza. There are also plenty of restaurants in downtown Troy. For a meal with that special someone, there is both an Olive Garden and Macaroni Grill about a 15-minute drive away in Albany.

Attention, Females

The student stereotype of RPI is "that we are all computer-loving nerds." "On one level," one student admitted, "it is true." Students have greatly differing opinions about campus diversity. Some students feel that there is a "good racial/ethnic mix," while others call the student body "homogeneous and disappointingly normal and cliquey and preppy." However, most males agree that the 3 to 1 male to female ratio "really sucks." Females, on the other hand, have a great time taking advantage of this: "Because there are three or four guys to every girl, girls who wouldn't normally have a lot of guys after them suddenly get a ton of attention from guys." Another related comment is that there is not enough sex. An interesting t-shirt on campus says, "Sex Kills—Come to RPI and Live Forever."

More than Classes and Parties

Many students at RPI also find time to be involved in various extracurriculars and sports. This involvement comes in different forms, ranging from writing for the *Poly*, the daily newspaper, and joining the *X-Files* Club, to driving for the RPI ambulance and waltzing away with the Ballroom Dance Club. All types of extracurricular clubs exist at RPI, including community service groups such as APO and Circle K and ethnic organizations,

such as the Black Students' Alliance and Alianza Latina.

Although the school actively recruits hockey, football, and basketball players, hockey is the most popular sport, because it is the only Division I team at RPI. There is a lot of spirit for the hockey team; even before school starts in the fall, students line up by the hundreds, if not the thousands, around the Student Union to get the best seats for the upcoming hockey season. Rensselaer's very active pep band also does special cheers for the hockey team. The Big Red Freakout, where "everybody dresses up and paints their faces and everything in red," is the biggest hockey game of the year and one of the biggest annual schoolwide events. For those who want to do more than cheer but don't play on a team, there is a new gym students call the "iGym" because it is made out of clear blue glass like the popular iMac computer. Intramurals are also extremely popular at RPI.

> **"I love the people on their campus most."**

If you decide that RPI is the school for you, just watch out for West Hall. Rumored to be haunted, the building, which has a morgue in the basement, used to be a Civil War hospital. Apparently, "it's falling down the hill that it's on." But that's the only thing about the school that seems to be falling down. As one freshman remarked, "The school's only going to get better . . . so I guess I'm in the right place. After all, 'why not change the world' is a motto of students here at RPI." —*Victoria Yen*

FYI

The three best things about attending RPI are "the school spirit surrounding hockey season, the top-notch engineering program, and getting that diploma."

The three worst things about attending RPI are "the lack of enough women, the focus on engineering, if you're not an engineering student, and language barriers with TAs."

The three things that every student should do before graduating from RPI are "go to the Big Red Freakout—or at least one other hockey game—drop something down the 10-story CII (Center for Industrial Innovation) stairwell, and go to at least one event in Troy Music Hall."

One thing I'd like to have known before coming here is "that being a female at RPI has its advantages."

Rochester Institute of Technology

Address: 60 Lomb Memorial Drive; Rochester, NY 14623
Phone: 716-475-6631
E-mail address: admissions@rit.edu
Web site URL: www.rit.edu
Founded: 1829
Private or Public: private
Religious affiliation: none
Location: rural
Undergraduate enrollment: 9,902
Total enrollment: 15,000
Percent Male/Female: 66%/34%
Percent Minority: 14%

Percent African-American: 5%
Percent Asian: 5%
Percent Hispanic: 3%
Percent Native-American: 0.5%
Percent in-state/out-of-state: 52%/48%
Percent Pub HS: 80%
Number of Applicants: 7,497
Percent Accepted: 77%
Percent Accepted who enroll: 38%
Entering: 2,197
Transfers: NA
Application Deadline: 15 Mar
Mean SAT: NA
Mean ACT: NA

Middle 50% SAT range: 520–620 V, 560–660 M
Middle 50% ACT range: 22–28
3 Most popular majors: photography, information technology, mechanical engineering
Retention: 84%
Graduation rate: NA
On-campus housing: 60%
Fraternities: 10%
Sororities: 5%
Library: 360,000 volumes
Tuition and Fees: $17,637 in; $17,637 out
Room and Board: $6,852
Financial aid, first-year: 80%

"**B**rick, brick, brick, brick, lots of brick." That's how most students describe RIT's campus. No wonder that the family, alumni, and student weekend is known as the Brick City Festival. Every building is made of red brick at this university, which offers a strong education combined with valuable training for the workplace.

Academics You Can Actually Use

The single word that describes RIT academics best is "pre-professional." The main focus here is on life after graduation. As one student described it, "We actually learn stuff that we'll use later on in life." Upon application, students choose to enroll in one of the six colleges that focus on applied science and technology, business, science, engineering, imaging arts and sciences, and liberal arts, respectively. Deaf students may also enroll in the renowned National Technical Institute for the Deaf (NTID). Because they must make a commitment so early on, "most freshmen arrive with their majors and even careers in their minds."

Both the photography department and the engineering programs receive high praise from students, while NTID is the world's largest mainstream college program for the deaf and hearing-impaired. This institute provides sign-language interpreters in every classroom and laboratory to give 1,100 students with impaired hearing a first-rate, fully integrated college experience.

The academic requirements at RIT consist of "a general core of classes and a core of classes inside the major." Although some engineering and science majors say that "liberal arts is an easy major," in general most agree that "no major is particularly easy." Class size varies depending on the level of the course. Students say the majority of classes tend to be 40 students or less, with some larger intro classes. Laboratory classes are "usually around 10 or so."

Although the majority of students seem to be happy with most professors and describe them as "extremely knowledgeable about their subject areas" and "more than willing to help out their students," one student did confess that "there are always a few not-so-good ones around." Most professors are "easy to contact and get along with." There are "hardly any TAs," and they are "used primarily for grading."

RIT's quarterly system creates a fast-paced schedule. Generally, undergraduates think that "RIT provides great academic instruction." In most majors, students combine classroom education and work experience through RIT's very popular cooperative education program (Co-op). These students take five years to complete their degrees, and in their last two years they spend four of the eight quarters working full-time in a firm. Students describe the benefits of Co-op as "gaining valuable experience in the workplace, being able to apply what you learn in your courses, having an advantage over other job candidates, and helping finance your education." The company assignments for Co-op are based on students' interests and career choices. AT&T, General Motors, Texas Instruments, Xerox, and IBM are just some of the corporate employers.

Residential Life—Many Options to Choose From

Freshmen are required to live in the dorms, which students say are "in good shape" and are coed either by floor or by door. Most have doubles, and some have singles. A number of the dorms have recently been renovated, and the new rooms have full air-conditioning and heating, more closets and floor space, and jacks for phone, cable, and network connections. After freshman year, the three housing options are living in the dorms, living in on-campus apartments, and going off campus. A number of hearing students also choose to live in the "NTID dorms," specifically designed for the deaf and hearing-impaired. Four on-campus apartment complexes all have the convenience of bus service and the advantage of an active social scene. RIT also has special-interest housing options consisting of Art, Community Service, Computer Science, Engineering, Photo, Unity, and International Houses, where students with similar interests live together on a designated floor. The Greeks also live together in either the dorms, the apartments, or their own houses.

Where Do They Eat?

There are three places to eat on campus. Gracie's, the "all-you-can-eat buffet-style dining hall" that offers with a wide range of options; the Commons, a restaurant-style dining hall; and the Student Alumni Center cafeteria. The RITskeller, beneath the cafeteria, has a full bar that serves alcoholic drinks to staff, faculty, and students who are over 21. The Commons also houses a coffee stop called the College Grind. Off campus, Nick Tahoe's in Rochester, which is open 24 hours, is a student favorite. The restaurant is known as "the home of the original Garbage Plate." According to one student, these plates make "a good two A.M. I-need-to-study meal." There are also "corner stores" in the tunnels under the dorms where students can buy snacks. These tunnels are also favorite places to socialize because they have pool tables and arcade games. Crossroads, which recently opened on campus, has a dining area as well as a market.

Who Are These People?

"Deaf, hearing, white, black, Asian, Indian, foreign, musician, artist, engineer—we've got it all," commented one undergraduate about the student body. "The only stereotype is that we don't have any school spirit," another one added. There is a wide-enough variety of students on campus that anyone should be able to find plenty of people with similar interests. While some groups form right away and remain constant, most students find their groups changing throughout their years at RIT. One point that all students agreed on is that the student body "needs more women," although they admit the male–female ratio has recently been improving . . . slowly. Despite these extremes in the student body, one student claimed that "people start to look and act alike at the end of senior year, as if they were coming from the same factory."

Which Way Is the Party?

The Greeks throw parties, and there are smaller parties in the dorms in addition to apartment parties. Alcohol is completely banned from dorms and frat houses and may only be served in apartments. But non-drinkers say they do not feel excluded at any of the parties anyway. Fraternities and sororities are not dominant in the social scene, and their parties are open to non-members. Their houses are located on the Quarter Mile, the famous path from the dorms to the academic buildings. One student explained that there are "lots of random hookups among frats and sororities."

> **"We are good at grades, not sports."**

Most other social events are held at the Student Alumni Union. The College Activities Board shows current movies on the weekends; "concerts and lectures are also common." As one student said, "You do have to know where to look, but the events are out there." Upperclassmen also go off campus to local bars like the Creek. About 10 minutes from campus, Rochester offers bars, clubs, restaurants, concerts, and movies. Having a car or knowing someone with a car helps a lot when you want to go off campus. Although many students consider cars essential, "they are by no means required to have fun at RIT."

When They Are Not Studying!

The Rochester Wargamers Association and Guild (RWAG) is the largest student club on campus, "because they count anyone who comes to their meetings as members." The members play role-playing games and different card games. The RIT Formula SAE Team is another popular organization, which designs, builds, and then races its own cars. In 1998, the Rochester Cannabis Coalition was a controversial club; they were denied official recognition and use of student government funds because they supported education about cannabis, an illegal drug. Although some students use soft drugs, the drug scene is not extremely popular at Rochester.

RIT's varsity teams do not attract huge crowds. Men's and women's hockey are the most popular teams, with "very, very enthusiastic fans." The basketball teams follow the hockey teams in terms of popularity. One student stated that "the general RIT population couldn't care less about how the sports teams are doing." Another undergraduate said, "We are good at grades, not sports." Despite this lack of support for varsity sports, intramural sports are often played and attract large participation.

RIT is for the career-oriented student who has already made certain decisions about the future. And this planning pays off. Firms are ready to grab RIT students upon graduation because of the high quality of their education and the workplace experience that they have already gained through Co-op. What most of these career-oriented students discover, though, after four or five years, is that "they didn't actually expect to enjoy RIT so much!"

—Engin Yenidunya

FYI
The three best things about attending RIT are "the Co-op program, the student diversity, the pre-professional academics."
The three worst things about attending RIT are "the lack of school spirit, the workload, the dining hall hamburgers."
The three things that every student should do before graduating from RIT are "grab a Garbage Plate at Nick Tahoe's, explore Rochester, try to benefit from the diversity of the student body."
One thing I'd like to have known before coming here is "how much brick there is—it's everywhere."

S a r a h   L a w r e n c e   C o l l e g e

Address: One Mead Way; Bronxville, NY 10708-5999
Phone: 914-395-2510
E-mail address: slcadmit@slc.edu
Web site URL: www.slc.edu
Founded: 1926
Private or Public: private
Religious affiliation: none
Location: suburban
Undergraduate enrollment: 1,178
Total enrollment: 1,495
Percent Male/Female: 20%/80%
Percent Minority: 16%
Percent African-American: 6%

Percent Asian: 5%
Percent Hispanic: 4%
Percent Native-American: 0.5%
Percent in-state/out-of-state: 25%/75%
Percent Pub HS: 65%
Number of Applicants: 2,070
Percent Accepted: 43%
Percent Accepted who enroll: 31%
Entering: 278
Transfers: 28
Application Deadline: 1 Feb
Mean SAT: 640 V, 570 M
Mean ACT: 25

Middle 50% SAT range: 590–700 V, 520–610 M
Middle 50% ACT range: 23–28
3 Most popular majors: writing, theater, literature
Retention: 92%
Graduation rate: 63%
On-campus housing: 95%
Fraternities: NA
Sororities: NA
Library: 288,000 volumes
Tuition and Fees: $25,406 in; $25,406 out
Room and Board: $7,991
Financial aid, first-year: 48%

For those who dare to take the road less traveled, Sarah Lawrence offers a supportive learning environment. In a peaceful suburb of New York City, this small liberal arts college caters to students interested in shaping their own educational experience.

Serious Students

The curriculum at Sarah Lawrence College consists of three courses per semester, each of which requires an independent project. Course registration requires an interview process: students interview teachers to find out about the course material and expectations, while professors decide whether the students are right for their class. According to one student, the process is "not too difficult, but can sometimes be a problem with very popular classes." All first-year students must take a freshman studies course, and individual meetings with the professor of this course take place weekly. By graduation, all students must have taken one course in three of the following four disciplines: humanities, creative arts, social sciences/history, and natural sciences/math. Aside from these requirements, students are free to choose from a diverse course list. Art courses are especially popular, but one student reported that the art facilities don't measure up to the level of student interest. Writing and psychology are also popular departments.

In their first two years at Sarah Lawrence, students choose a faculty advisor to help them design their program of study. Students meet with their advisor, or "don," once a week during their freshman year and biweekly thereafter. Student-faculty relations extend beyond these routine meetings and classes, however. Many students say they even "hang out with their teachers." This strong relationship is bolstered by the small seminar courses that dominate the departments at Sarah Lawrence. Seminar sizes generally range from 12 to 18 students. The college offers some lecture courses, however. While they are taught by professors, there are some TAs, who are available primarily for students who need extra help.

Students at Sarah Lawrence say they are "passionate about learning," and they appreciate the college's emphasis on the learning process instead of on grades. Unless students ask for letter grades in their courses, they receive only written evaluations detailing their performance. The de-emphasis on grades makes the academic atmosphere "not competitive at all," one student said. Special academic programs at Sarah Lawrence include independent-study projects, study abroad, and a continuing education program for students of nontraditional age.

Outside Involvement

Research for classes can be done at the college's Esther Raushenbush Library, although one student said "it doesn't have a great selection of anything . . . students do research there because there isn't anywhere else." Despite its reportedly limited resources, the library is a comfortable place for quiet study, especially the "pillow room," which is so comfortable that some students can barely stop themselves from falling asleep in it. One of the reasons cited for this is the building's poor lighting. For better lighting, some people choose to study in their dorm rooms or in empty classrooms.

"Unless students ask for letter grades in their courses, they receive only written evaluations detailing their performance."

Some students live off campus, but most choose to live on campus because off-campus housing tends to be expensive. Housing options at Sarah Lawrence range from single-sex and coed dormitories to quiet houses where no one is allowed to make any noise that can be heard outside the door. Much of the student housing shares building space with offices and classrooms; campus residents recommend living in one of the newer, more standard dorms "if you want to have a social life." Some of the rooms are considered "very pretty" while others are categorized as "generic dorm rooms." Dining options are not quite as varied. First-year students are required to eat on the school's meal plan, either in the school's main cafeteria or the health-food bar. The third dining option is a fast-food restaurant, the Pub. Dinner is also a good time for socializing, since many students hang out at the dining halls. Students also praise the dining halls for offering ample vegetarian options, and they say that "it's much easier to be a vegetarian than an omnivore at SLC."

One undergrad described the Sarah Lawrence student body as "diverse in every way I can possibly think of." Many students come from the East and West Coasts, although demographics are fairly scattered. While students admit there is some truth to the Sarah Lawrence stereotype of the "radical, black-clad lesbian," they agree that this is not an accurate portrait of the entire student body. Originally a women's college, Sarah Lawrence went co-ed in 1968, and has even attracted a few conservatives into its fold. In general, however, students lean toward the political left. Sarah Lawrence has a fairly large and accepted gay and lesbian population, and gay issues are at the forefront of discussion. Ethnic minorities are also well represented on campus with active minority-student groups such as the Black Student Union.

Extracurricular Activities

Extracurricular activities at Sarah Lawrence reflect a wide range of student interests. Despite one student's negative appraisal ("there's not much to do ever, and a lot less on weeknights"), there does seem to be a lot going on. Student government is very big. Improvisational comedy groups are available for the more light-hearted; one student described them as a group "who think they're humorous." Many of the activities at Sarah Lawrence have artistic themes—writing is one of the major modes of expression. The *Sarah Lawrence Review* and *Dark Phrases* are student-written literary and poetic compilations. Another is a semi-regular newspaper called *The Phoenix*. Student-run concerts are fertile ground for aspiring musicians. Throughout the week, guest lecturers and poetry readings are held by student organizations. Although "there aren't lot of places to hang out on campus," one student said, undergrads congregate in dorm rooms or the student-run coffeehouse, Javahouse, which raises money for scholarships.

On weekends, students go into New York City or to local bars like the Spinning Wheel. On campus, there are movies and a dance every Saturday night. All campus parties are initiated by students and must be registered with college administrators. According to one student, the administration takes a position on alcohol that is "officially discouraging, but in actual practice doesn't care." Some students say that the administration has been taking a stricter stance recently, but that room searches are not allowed unless they receive a complaint. The students themselves have quite lenient attitudes toward alcohol and drug consumption. Even if they do not spend their free time "drinking or doing some kind of chemicals," one student said, they are tolerant of those who do.

Some other activities that students rate highly are gay/lesbian/bisexual Coming Out Week, and the Deb Ball, which began as a debutante ball for the prim Sarah Lawrence women of decades past, but has since become a less "proper" tradition. The annual Bacchanalia, a spring festival of bands, beer, and dancing, also earns student praise.

Campus response to sports varies. Some students claim that "A few people do them, but they're no big deal for the rest of campus," while others enthusiastically support varsity sports, particularly hockey. Students have enjoyed the new Campbell Sports Center and the announced construction of Leckonby Football Stadium. Sarah Lawrence also has varsity men's and women's tennis, crew, cross-country, and equestrian teams, and it sponsors a number of intramural sports.

The Sarah Lawrence campus is self-contained and situated within a quiet suburb of New York. Students call the campus "very beautiful;" it's surrounded by trees, rocks, lots of hills, and, strangely enough, skunks. The relationship between the college and the affluent, rather conservative community of Bronxville, however, is "a bit of a conflicting situation," according to one undergrad, who felt that local residents "aren't too pleased with the students who go here." The benefit of living in such a wealthy enclave is that crime is minimal. Security guards patrol the area, but security measures are generally unobtrusive. The school also provides emergency phones and escort services. Students keep their doors and windows locked to guard against theft, but one student reported that the crime is "nothing comparable to other schools I've seen or been to."

For students entering Sarah Lawrence, advice from those on the inside is "If you're a very curious person, then Sarah Lawrence would probably be a good place." Students are generally independent in their academic pursuits, so if that is what you have in mind, Sarah Lawrence can make all the difference. —*Billy Rahm and Staff*

FYI
The three best things about attending St. Lawrence are "the contact with the professors, the de-emphasis on grades, and the diverse student body."
The three worst things about attending St. Lawrence are "the cold winters, occasional housing problems, and the lack of choices for places to study."
The three things that every student should do before graduating from St. Lawrence are "check out Javahouse, go to a hockey game, and explore New York City."
One thing I'd like to have known before coming to St. Lawrence is "that school spirit is so low."

Skidmore College

Address: 815 North Broadway; Saratoga Springs, NY 12866
Phone: 800-867-6007
E-mail address: admissions@skidmore.edu
Web site URL: www.skidmore.edu
Founded: 1802
Private or Public: private
Religious affiliation: none
Location: suburban
Undergraduate enrollment: 2,540
Total enrollment: 2,540
Percent Male/Female: 40%/60%
Percent Minority: 11%
Percent African-American: 2%

Percent Asian: 3%
Percent Hispanic: 5%
Percent Native-American: 0.5%
Percent in-state/out-of-state: 27%/73%
Percent Pub HS: 60%
Number of Applicants: 5,414
Percent Accepted: 49%
Percent Accepted who enroll: 25%
Entering: 647
Transfers: NA
Application Deadline: 15 Jan
Mean SAT: 606 V, 605 M
Mean ACT: 23

Middle 50% SAT range: 560–650 V, 560–650 M
Middle 50% ACT range: 23–28
3 Most popular majors: English, business, psychology
Retention: 89%
Graduation rate: 69%
On-campus housing: 80%
Fraternities: NA
Sororities: NA
Library: 410,000 volumes
Tuition and Fees: $25,475 in; $25,475 out
Room and Board: $7,270
Financial aid, first-year: 39%

About half a mile from downtown Saratoga, on the peak of a hill lies "a beautiful campus" despite its "somewhat ugly 60's style buildings." Skidmore College offers a fine liberal arts education for its small population. However, academics are far from the only thing on its students' minds. They also rave about the attractiveness of the student body, a great social scene and town, and thriving extracurricular organizations.

Academics

Skidmore is definitely a school for humanities-oriented students. In addition to the requirements of their respective majors, all Skidmore students have core course requirements, including two Liberal Studies, two society, two arts, two science and one non-Western course. One junior praised the core requirements, saying "they allow for a broad range of study in many disciplines before specializing in a major." Another junior said that though "the LS1 course encompassed everything" and was "useful," it was "a little boring." More bluntly, explained a senior, "the core requirements are fairly easy and the major requirements are all intense. Most people

do a double major or a major and minor in two unrelated fields. Slackers only have one major so they don't have to do as much."

Classes are small, averaging about 15 students a class and there aren't any TAs. "If you have a group of people who love what they're doing, it can be really stimulating," said a computer science major. One senior said that "grading is very easy, and all in all, classes are fairly laid back and students get involved." However, business classes are known to be quite intense and demanding. Study abroad programs, summer programs, and co-ops with other schools are also available for students to participate in.

Skidmore professors are great, say students. "I firmly believe that the Skidmore faculty are some of the most inspiring and hard-working professors in higher education. The best part is seeing how much every professor loves what he or she does, and seeing students get really involved in a great discussion," said one student. Popular teachers include English professor Tom Lewis, who won an Emmy award for a documentary on American highways, English professor Stephen

Millhauser, who recently won a Pulitzer Prize, and Sheldon Solomon, who among other habits, drinks too much coffee, wears shorts in the dead of winter, and "is a genius." Raved a junior, "We have several notable professors in virtually every department. You don't realize how many important people teach at Skidmore until you look around. It's pretty amazing." Best of all, "there's a close relationship between faculty and students. Faculty often make themselves available outside of their office hours," said a pleased sophomore.

Social Life

Despite the lack of Greek life at Skidmore, these kids know how to party come weekend time. Explained a senior, "Freshmen tend to stay to the dorms with small parties or they head on down to the campus housing where juniors and seniors live." As for the upperclassmen, a junior joked that they, in turn, go and look for the freshmen, in addition to parties, bars, and concerts. One popular party mentioned in particular was the Diva Night. "There are plenty of social alternatives, but people usually just want to get drunk," said one student. It's too bad, because "there is a ridiculous amount of organized activities on campus. If you can make it to every campus activity, you'll end up failing out of school and going broke. But at least you'll have a great time in the process," a junior quipped. But even discounting the on-campus bar, being underage is not a problem. Despite the fact that kegs are not allowed on campus, one student boasted, that it "very rarely stops us." Indeed, students reported that there is quite a bit of drug and alcohol use; one student even gave the statistic that over 86 percent of students "use that stuff."

"There are more random hook-ups than there are bricks in this school—the hookups usually lead to relationships, so I have no objections to that," said one student. This isn't a problem for male students, as one raved, "the female population is gorgeous, I've had friends come up and visit, then declare they are transferring after seeing the wildlife at one party." Female students also agreed that the student population is plenty attractive at their school. Furthermore, students all said that it is very easy to meet people at Skidmore, and while there are quite a few cliques, they are easy to get into and change often.

> **"There are more random hook-ups than there are bricks in this school."**

There are plenty of places for students to take dates and to chow in general. While dining hall food isn't too bad and Skidmore offers quite a few vegetarian options, the multitude of great restaurants in Saratoga are a much better option. Students mentioned The Saratoga Brew Pub and Maestro's as great date restaurants. Summed up one senior expertly, "Esperanto, the Brew Pub, and The Parting Glass are all good places to bet a quick bite, and the latter two serve great pints. Great food is found at Scallions, Wheatfields, and Lillian's." A Skidmore professor owns Esperanto, and one junior recommended the doughboys there as being particularly scrumptious.

90210-esque?

As for the students themselves, as one junior put it, the population is filled with "rich, spoiled brats." A little less scathingly, one senior said, "the student stereotype is that everyone is rich. Most people wear designer casual wear to class. People are shunned for wearing Gap. Even the school bus is white. Everyone is very into looking good, so there is a good amount of working out and staying in shape." The general consensus was that the student body is "way too homogeneous," and that "more internationalism and racial diversity" is needed at Skidmore. One junior said that the stereotypical student is a "pretty, shallow, rich, white girl from Long Island." However, another student countered that there are many homosexual and interracial couples, and that "everything is accepted at Skidmore."

Especially popular are the a cappella singing groups on campus. One senior said, "Everyone loves the music groups. The Bandersnachers are gods in the eyes of some people." Most students, if not in a cappella groups, are involved with other forms of performance art. Students mentioned The Wombats, Sketchies, and the orchestra as popular organizations. Community service is "not super popular, but a lot of people do volunteer." The school is quite community oriented, said one sophomore, "Most concerts are open to the public for free and volunteering clubs often get involved with local children and local issues."

Intramurals are also big, although varsity sports are not popular—probably because Skidmore does not have a football team. "The school does not support the athletic teams, and therefore they don't play well. It's a shame," lamented one student. Athletes all live on south campus because it is closer to the gym. One junior complained about frequently malfunctioning treadmills at the gym, but mentioned that there is a pool, tennis courts, and a public golf course in town.

Campus and Dorms

Aside from problems finding parking, students love the campus and town, which they say is gorgeous, though not exactly hopping. On the flip side, students always feel safe and have no security issues. "The campus is right up against a forest and the outskirts of the city are on the other side," described one student. One senior did complain, however, that the school needed more "open grass space."

Students love their dorms, even describing freshman year housing fondly. "There are only two bad dorms and they are Moore and Skidmore hall. Skidmore hall is as far south on campus as possible," said one student. However, warned a junior, "Your sophomore year can be bad if you get a bad lottery number—you could end up in Moore Hall, an off-campus dorm." A senior said that Moore is about a five-minute ride by car and that "pretty much you are stuck there sophomore year unless you have a good room number." Students tend to prefer North Campus to South, "but all the dorms are far more accommodating than anywhere else I've been," praised one student.

Nonetheless, many students live off-campus, especially seniors, "though there are some juniors and a handful of sophomores. Usually people want to be close to the heart of the campus to know what's going on," said a senior. The dorms have a great many restrictions, but most of them are enforced with an "if the RA didn't see it, I didn't do it" state of mind, said one student.

Other buildings of note are the music building, which was given by the Filenes family, and a "gigantic" art museum being built near the gym.

All in all, Skidmore is a fun place that provides a complete education for students who don't mind a small school atmosphere. As one senior summed up, "I would choose Skidmore again any day, the education is good and the people are all really chill. The atmosphere is great on campus and if you can't get laid here you need to seek professional help."—*Jennifer Wang and Staff*

FYI
The three best things about attending Skidmore College are "that the male/female ratio is 40/60, the small classes, and the fun professors."
The three worst things about attending Skidmore College are "the small town, how you can't do much without a car, and the small selection of guys."
The three things that every student should do before graduating from Skidmore College are "to go bar-hopping in Saratoga, get involved in as much as you can without killing yourself, have sex in the north woods."
One thing I'd like to have known before coming here is "the right way to pick up a woman."

St. Bonaventure University

Address: PO Box D; St. Bonaventure, NY 14778
Phone: 716-375-2400
E-mail address: admissions@sbu.edu
Web site URL: www.sbu.edu
Founded: 1858
Private or Public: private
Religious affiliation: Franciscan
Location: rural
Undergraduate enrollment: 2,116
Total enrollment: 2,822
Percent Male / Female: 48% / 52%
Percent Minority: 3%
Percent African-American: 1%

Percent Asian: 0.5%
Percent Hispanic: 0.5%
Percent Native-American: 0.5%
Percent in-state / out-of-state: 77% / 23%
Percent Pub HS: 68%
Number of Applicants: 1,840
Percent Accepted: 90%
Percent Accepted who enroll: 33%
Entering: 543
Transfers: NA
Application Deadline: 1 Apr
Mean SAT: 532 V, 532 M
Mean ACT: 23

Middle 50% SAT range: 470–570 V, 460–560 M
Middle 50% ACT range: 16–22
3 Most popular majors: education, journalism, accounting
Retention: 83%
Graduation rate: 51%
On-campus housing: 98%
Fraternities: NA
Sororities: NA
Library: 270,000 volumes
Tuition and Fees: $15,140 in; $15,140 out
Room and Board: $5,790
Financial aid, first-year: 75%

One student at St. Bonaventure University described both the advantages and the disadvantages of attending this small, liberal arts–oriented, Catholic university when he said, "Everyone knows everybody else. You go out on the town on a Friday night and you'll probably see one of the priests wherever you are. It's no big deal to see him at a bar. You just say, 'Hey, Father,' and then you go on with whatever you're doing. He might even come over and join you."

Out of necessity, St. Bonaventure is a fairly self-contained and close-knit community. Set in the Allegheny Mountains, the campus is quite isolated. The nearby working-class town of Olean (population 25,000) has few attractions for the college crowd. As one student said, "You see a lot of trees." Buffalo, the nearest big city, is an hour away and easily accessible if your friend owns a car.

St. Bonaventure undergrads enroll in one of four schools: arts, sciences, business, or education. Students consider education and accounting among the strongest and most popular majors. The philosophy and English departments also earn praise, but some describe the science departments as merely "adequate."

Know Your Profs

In keeping with its liberal arts emphasis, St. Bonaventure requires undergrads to take a large number of core courses, including three theology courses, three philosophy courses, and additional courses in English, math, and science. Enrollment in these required classes usually exceeds 50, but students report that overall the average class size is closer to 20. Some upper-level courses even have as few as 2 to 5 students.

Undergraduates generally consider their professors accessible. Because of the small class sizes, professors know their students by name. To give motivated students a wider range of academic options, St. Bonaventure allows undergrads who qualify to take supplementary seminars as part of an honors program.

The Saints and the Spooks

One of the most popular courses at St. Bonaventure deals with theology and the occult. Detached observers can speculate all they want about why demonic possession and exorcism hold such fascination for St. Bonaventure students, but the students themselves simply flock to the "Spooks" class. Only so many can flock at once, however, because Father Trabold requests that the front row of seats be reserved for visiting "spirits."

St. Bonaventure recently started a four-year Environmental Studies program with course work in environmental ecology, chemistry, biology, and engineering in addition to liberal arts course work. A program requires its students to participate in an internship in the field. The school's proximity to Allegheny State Park aids student research and hands-on experience. The biochemistry program is quite popular as well. The fine arts are now more appealing thanks to the new $7 million Quick Fine Arts Center.

Life and Dorms

Housing at St. Bonaventure ranges from dorms to campus apartments to off-campus accommodations. Undergrads agree that Devereux is the dorm best suited for partying and least conducive to studying, despite the small, attractive rooms. Doyle offers a quieter atmosphere. Most of the dorms are coed by floor. Newly built are the Townhouses, the first phase of a three-part project. The Townhouses offer seniors and grad students modern facilities for a more independent lifestyle. Freshmen are concentrated in single-sex dorms.

Some students describe St. Bonaventure as "a mostly white, middle-class, Catholic university" and complain of the relatively homogeneous student body.

St. Bonaventure students have a new outlook on the food. The Reilly Center, the recently remodeled student center, provides them with a more attractive dining atmosphere. In addition, they can charge everything in the Reilly Center on their meal cards, including food at the Taco Bell. When undergrads need a break, they either run to S&G, considered the best and cheapest place to eat off campus, or the recently remodeled New Moon Cafe, a coffee shop where acoustic musicians set the mood.

Sports Crazy

Sports, especially intramurals, are some of the most popular extracurriculars on campus. Basketball fans are thrilled about the improvement in the Bonnies' current record; basketball is reportedly "a big to-do" at St. Bonaventure. Spirited fans are often spotted "acting like animals," dressing up like the visiting team's coaches and throwing newspapers on the court. The baseball team has a new coach and an improving record. Hockey is another popular sport, but watch out: after the first goal of every game, St. Bonaventure fans reportedly throw seafood onto the ice. In addition, skiing and snowboarding are "a good way to get rid of those mid-semester blues," since the Holiday Valley Ski Resort in the Allegheny Mountains is just a 15-minute drive from campus and the campus ski club receives student discounts. In fact, St. Bonaventure students are so interested in sports that courses are offered in both basketball and tennis coaching.

Aside from sports, St. Bonaventure students can get involved with the weekly newspaper, the *BonaVenture;* a literary magazine; a theater group; and various other clubs. The Campus Ministry is one of the largest student organizations, and its popular Big Brother/Big Sister program allows students to volunteer in the surrounding low-income community.

The Party Places

St. Bonaventure has no Greek system, but the weekend parties still have defined admission. The on-campus parties are generally held by upperclassmen and are limited to their friends and sports teams. Off-campus parties, though less frequent, feature open admission and wild and crazy fun for all. The most popular annual event is the school-sponsored Spring Weekend, which features outdoor concerts by bands such as Blues Traveler, and accompanying parties. Off campus, students frequent the bars in Olean, such as Mad Dogs, the Burton, the Other Place, and the Hickey. During the week, movies, bands, and Wednesday-night comedians who "aren't that funny" are some of the on-campus nighttime social options.

Some students describe St. Bonaventure as "a mostly white, middle-class, Catholic university" and complain of the relatively homogeneous student body. Most undergrads come from New York or the New England area.

St. Bonaventure undergrads readily admit that they are part of a small community in less-than-cosmopolitan surroundings, but most are quick to say how satisfied they are. Students praise St. Bonaventure's open, accepting community. As one student said, "Friends of mine who come and visit from other colleges can't believe how easygoing and friendly everyone is here. Colleges with fraternities don't have the same open-door policy we have. Knowing everyone, since it's such a small school, really makes school comfortable and easy." St. Bonaventure is a fine choice for anyone seeking a small, reasonably priced liberal arts college with a Catholic emphasis and a close-knit atmosphere. —*Neel Gandhi and Staff*

FYI

The three best things about attending St. Bonaventure are "the close friendships, the faculty, and the intramurals."

The three worst things about attending St. Bonaventure are "the poor science department, its isolated location, and the cold."

The three things that every student should do before graduating from St. Bonaventure are "play on an intramural team, go skiing, and have fun on Spring Weekend!"

One thing I'd like to have known before coming here is "that you really need a car to go anywhere off campus."

St. Lawrence University

Address: Canton, NY 13617
Phone: 315-229-5261
E-mail address: admissions@stlawu.edu
Web site URL: www.stlawu.edu
Founded: 1856
Private or Public: private
Religious affiliation: none
Location: rural
Undergraduate enrollment: 1,851
Total enrollment: 2,031
Percent Male/Female: 49%/51%
Percent Minority: 6%
Percent African-American: 2%

Percent Asian: 1%
Percent Hispanic: 2%
Percent Native-American: 0.5%
Percent in-state/out-of-state: 51%/49%
Percent Pub HS: 68%
Number of Applicants: 2,235
Percent Accepted: 74%
Percent Accepted who enroll: 35%
Entering: 575
Transfers: 58
Application Deadline: 15 Feb
Mean SAT: 557 V, 561 M
Mean ACT: 24

Middle 50% SAT range: 510–610 V, 520–620 M
Middle 50% ACT range: 22–27
3 Most popular majors: English, psychology, economics
Retention: 83%
Graduation rate: 75%
On-campus housing: 94%
Fraternities: 18%
Sororities: 29%
Library: 470,000 volumes
Tuition and Fees: $23,095 in; $23,095 out
Room and Board: $7,205
Financial aid, first-year: 85%

Tucked into a corner of the Adirondacks, in a small town in New York near the Canadian border, sits St. Lawrence University, just small enough to fit into the little town, but big enough for its students to call it home. The relatively small size of SLU allows the formation of a close-knit community, both within the student body and between the students and faculty. The rural location affords opportunities for outdoor activities and gives the campus its beautiful backdrop, the pride of many a SLU student. Even though many students complain about the huge piles of snow in the cold winter months, most agree that the warmth of the friendly people around them more than makes up for the weather.

Studying at SLU

Academics at St. Lawrence are described as difficult at times, but, as one student said, "you don't have to be doing work ALL the time." Some of the most popular departments include economics, psychology, and biology, with geology cited as a less popular subject. Because of the small size of SLU, students benefit from small class sizes and they enjoy close contact with professors right from the start of their freshman year; students reported that essentially all classes enroll between 20 and 25 students, are taught exclusively by professors, and have a TA or two to give extra help to students that need it. Small class size rarely results in students being shut out of classes they want to take, though. One student said, "registration usually is pretty hectic . . . students line in front of the registrar's office and wait for hours to get classes, but then everybody usually gets the ones they want in the end."

St. Lawrence's academic program includes a fair number of required courses: undergrads must take courses in two out of three groups: modern languages, math or computer-related, and fine arts or music. They also are required to take at least one class each in the humanities, social sciences, and lab science, and one class which relates to a non-Western culture. Opinions of these requirements vary from "a hassle" to "a good way to get us to start exploring different departments." In addition, freshmen participate in First Year Program, a year-long course devoted to developing oral and written communication skills, taken with other students from the same dorm. While many students acknowledge the benefits of FYP, others complain about how the course runs the whole year and often conflicts with other desired courses.

When students at St. Lawrence want to study, they often head for Owen D. Young library, the main library on campus. ODY is a fairly modern building; and although its aesthetic merits are often debated, most agree that the recent renovation has made the atmosphere on the inside is cheerful and stimulating. However, the lively atmosphere also frequently inspires conversation, and many students describe ODY as more of a social place than a studious one. For hard-core, serious studying, Madill, the science library, is your best bet.

Living and Eating

Housing at SLU is mainly in dorms, although there are also off-campus options such as Greek and theme housing and athletic suites. The dorms are mostly set up in traditional singles and doubles, and are coed, but some dorms also offer the option of suites with kitchens, mostly for upperclassmen. Students cite Sykes as one of the best dorms, with Whitman as the best dorm for freshmen. On the other hand, Lee and Rebert halls are said to be the worst, although even in those less desirable dorms, rooms are reportedly spacious and nicely furnished. Almost universally, students praise their dorms, whether they live in the best or worst location, for the sense of community fostered there.

As upperclassmen, students at St. Lawrence have more housing options, although finding an off-campus apartment isn't really one of them, since available apartments are extremely scarce in Canton. However, many upperclassmen choose to live in Greek houses, which lie just at the edge of campus; one student living in her sorority house described her experience by saying it is "very home-like, and there is always something to do." Theme housing is another alternative to dorms available after freshman year, and such houses include a house for environmentalists, for people who enjoy outdoor activities, and for cultural groups and international students.

> However, students complain that campus security and Canton police strongly frown upon student alcohol use, which is not allowed on campus.

SLU students tend to give their meal plan and dining options high ratings. There are three on-campus eating establishments: Dana Dining Hall (a traditional cafeteria), Northstar Pub, and Jack's Snack Shop (a deli). The pub has more of a relaxed atmosphere where students go to hang out and relax, and the food there is considered the best of the options on campus, particularly the chicken wrap sandwiches. Jack's Snack Shop, on the other hand, is the place to go if you need to pick up a quick bite, and is frequented by students in between classes. There are two meal plans available to students, the 21-meal plan, which is only accepted at Dana, and a declining-balance plan which is accepted at all three on-campus locations. While students favor the declining-balance plan because of its flexibility, most agree that it is impossible not to run out of money before the end of the semester, and so that plan is better for students who are not eating all of their meals on campus.

When students get tired of the places to eat on campus, or just want to treat themselves, they look to the restaurants in the town of Canton. For quick meals, there are the standard chains: McDonald's, Burger King, and Pizza Hut, and also A-1 Oriental Kitchen, which is a popular delivery choice. Other restaurants in Canton include Sergie's Pizza, which has pizza and Italian food, Jerek Subs, and The Lobster House; the Cactus Grill, a Mexican restaurant located in nearby Potsdam, is also frequented by many St. Lawrence students.

Life after Studying

Students at St. Lawrence spend a lot of time on extracurricular activities, and there is "always something to get involved in." One of the most active groups on campus seems to be the Outing Club, which goes on lots of trips and does other activities together. A recently-founded karate club, which is student-run and student-taught, is growing rapidly, an example of the ample opportunity to start new organizations if you are interested. Many students also spend their time working for *The Hill*, the main weekly publication of St. Lawrence.

Sports are also an option at St. Lawrence, both for fans and athletes. Varsity soccer and hockey are the most popular, with rugby and lacrosse games also drawing crowds. School spirit peaks at the time of the Clarkson-SLU hockey game, and the long-time rivalry draws huge crowds. Students say that you have to get tickets at least a week in advance if you don't want to stand up to watch the game, but that it is one of the highlights of the year that cannot be missed. Sports are not limited only to varsity athletes, though, as St. Lawrence has a wide variety of intramural teams which allow people of all levels the opportunity to play. In addition, the athletic facilities are described as "great, and always available to everybody." Recently the hockey rink was renovated, and a new outdoor track and football stadium were built, and with a new recreation complex in the works, facilities at SLU are in tip-top shape.

Unfortunately, the social life and weekend plans are definitely limited by the small student body and Canton. Some things that students do when they are hanging out or partying include shooting pool, going to see a movie (with a discount for showing a student ID), going to see a band playing at Java House, or going to a frat party. However, students complain that campus security and Canton police strongly frown upon student alcohol use, which is not allowed on campus. On top of that, on-campus and off-campus parties alike tend to get shut down soon after they begin. Thus, most students say that they spend a lot of time hanging out in bars in Canton with their friends, or taking trips on the weekend to Ottawa, the capital of Canada, or to Syracuse, both which are within a few hours driving distance.

Even though there may be downsides to living in a remote, rural town, students at St. Lawrence agree that the beauty of their campus and the surrounding area is worth it. The architecture of the university, a mixture of old and modern buildings, the quaintness of the town of Canton, and the beauty of the mountains and forests make St. Lawrence a scenic and pleasant place. If you are looking for a school with a fast-paced, urban environment and a restaurant and club for every night of the week, SLU may not be for you; however, if you want a school with a tightly-knit community of professors and students, set in a beautiful landscape offering a place to hike or just sit and contemplate, St. Lawrence University is the one. —*Lisa Smith*

FYI

The three best things about attending St. Lawrence are "the friendly people, small classes, with lots of individual attention, and beautiful snow-lined mountains."

The three worst things about attending St. Lawrence are "the cold weather, lack of things to do off-campus, and the remote isolation of Canton."

The three things that every student should do before graduating from St. Lawrence are "climbing the bell tower and ringing the church bells, participate in a big snowball fight, and going on a trip with the outing club."

One thing I'd like to have known before coming here is "how cold it really gets."

State University of New York System

Comprising more than 64 schools, the State University of New York is one of the largest state university programs in the nation. One of the greatest benefits of SUNY, according to students, is its diversity. With undergraduate populations ranging from 9,000 to 16,000, the four university centers—Albany, Binghamton, Buffalo, and Stony Brook—are the largest and wealthiest SUNY campuses. SUNY's 13 smaller university colleges focus on the arts and sciences. They include locations in Brockport, Buffalo College, Cortland, Empire State, Fredonia, Geneseo, New Paltz, Old Westbury, Oneonta, Oswego, Plattsburgh, Potsdam, and Purchase, New York. Thirty SUNY schools are community colleges, and various other colleges which specialize in different areas. There are six colleges of technology, four health science centers, five statutory colleges associated with private schools like Alfred and Cornell Universities, as well as several schools offering special programs in technology, optometry, maritime science, environmental science, and forestry.

The Different Flavors of SUNY Schools

Besides offering a wide variety of academic programs, SUNY schools differ greatly in size, location, and competitive flavor. Considering the many choices available, some students may find it difficult to decide which school is right for them, but SUNY has responded to this concern by simplifying the application process. Forty-nine schools use SUNY's common application, allowing students to apply to several schools with just one form.

The SUNY schools are diverse in many ways, but SUNY students share a common bond as over 90 percent of them come from New York. One reason for the high percentage of in-state students is the low in-state tuition cost. Economical as it is, however, some students nevertheless find that it is becoming more and more difficult to pay for tuition. In recent years especially, tuition assistance programs (TAPs) have been significantly reduced as a result of state budget cuts. These cuts have affected not only the cost of a SUNY education, but, in some cases, also the size and quality of various academic programs within the system.

Despite rising costs, though, students still agree that, with their wide range of affordable educational options, SUNY schools are a great deal for New York residents. The following four articles describe SUNY's centers in Albany, Binghamton, Buffalo, and Stony Brook, New York.

—*Steven Hayhurst and Staff*

State University of New York / Albany

Address: 1400 Washington Avenue; Albany, NY 12222
Phone: 518-442-5435
E-mail address: ugadmissions@albany.edu
Web site URL: www.albany.edu
Founded: 1844
Private or Public: public
Religious affiliation: none
Location: suburban
Undergraduate enrollment: 11,002
Total enrollment: 16,616
Percent Male/Female: 51%/49%
Percent Minority: 24%
Percent African-American: 9%

Percent Asian: 8%
Percent Hispanic: 6%
Percent Native-American: 0.5%
Percent in-state/out-of-state: 97%/3%
Percent Pub HS: NA
Number of Applicants: 15,312
Percent Accepted: 61%
Percent Accepted who enroll: 24%
Entering: 2,281
Transfers: NA
Application Deadline: 1 Mar
Mean SAT: 558 V, 566 M
Mean ACT: NA

Middle 50% SAT range: 500–600 V, 520–610 M
Middle 50% ACT range: NA
3 Most popular majors: English, psychology, business
Retention: 85%
Graduation rate: 52%
On-campus housing: 58%
Fraternities: 15%
Sororities: 15%
Library: 1,800,000 volumes
Tuition and Fees: $4,338 in; $9,238 out
Room and Board: $5,828
Financial aid, first-year: 58%

SUNY Albany lies at the heart of the state's SUNY system. Located in New York's bustling capital city, the school provides a sound academic environment that will not strain the student budget.

Unforgiving Requirements

Strict course requirements, however, do strain students' schedules. All undergraduates must take two courses each in humanities and arts, social science, and natural science, as well as two writing-intensive classes. "It's those writing classes that are particularly annoying," one junior said, complaining about the number of assignments. Other requirements include a cultural and historical perspective class and a class in human diversity. These interdisciplinary classes combine the social sciences and the humanities. Particularly driven students can also participate in the General Education Honors Program, which centers on small discussion sections with professors.

Although upper-level courses usually enroll around 30 students, introductory lectures max out at 400. Professors are not inaccessible, however, and under-

graduates remain the school's focus. Students apply to a particular school after their freshman year. The schools of business and criminal justice tend to be the most selective. Applicants must take a placement test, submit a writing sample, and meet a minimum grade-point average. Albany features many strong academic departments, most notably in psychology and English. Students also say the political science program, assisted by the backdrop of the state government scene in Albany, is excellent.

A Divided Campus

"Campus" is a misnomer of sorts for SUNY Albany. The university actually has two campuses, one uptown, one downtown. The uptown campus is the school's true center, containing most of the student housing and academic buildings. Four quads—Dutch, Colonial, State, and Indian—form the corners of the uptown campus's square design, enclosing an open area around a fountain known as "The Podium." Various dorms and special-interest halls are contained within the quads.

Students insist that despite the dorms' identical appearance, each has its distinct personality. Perhaps this is because students are free to live with peers who share their interests. Wellness Hall, for example, stresses health and exercise and has Nautilus machines. One of the quads is reserved for first-year students only. "It's comforting knowing that everyone you live with is entering the same situation," one freshman said. Other special-interest options include Math Hall, Science Hall, and Substance-Free Hall. Those few undergraduates living on the uptown campus often complain about the accommodations, which generally take the form of either suites with private bathrooms or doubles with hall bathrooms. Downtown campus, about a ten-minute walk away, wins in the looks category with ivy-covered brick buildings as opposed to the "gray and dreary" structures of uptown. Many students move off campus after their first or second year. The school owns off-campus housing called Freedom Quad, where many graduate students reside.

A New York Crowd

So many New Yorkers make the trek upstate for school that a Long Island-based rock radio station, WDRE, now broadcasts its signal in Albany. Because a large portion of the undergraduate population comes from the melting pots of New York City and Long Island, the campus is ethnically if not geographically diverse.

> **Albany offers much more than a great educational bang for your tuition buck.**

According to students, the nearly 30 frats and sororities are a significant force at SUNY Albany. Rushing is a popular undergraduate activity, although students generally do not feel pressured to participate. The Greeks are the primary campus source of parties and alcohol. "I'm glad you don't have to be a full-fledged member to attend their parties," said one sophomore. Albany's several bars and pubs provide an alternative to the Greek night life for the 21-and-over crowd—the Lamp Post, Peabody's, and Washington's Tavern are perennial student favorites.

Albany students report feeling content with the school's food policy—mainly because they can charge purchases at Taco Bell, Nathan's, and Pizza Hut to their meal accounts. When students spend time in the city, it is mainly for food or to socialize at the bars.

Despite the popularity of political science as a major, the school student government reportedly lacks mass student appeal. The Student Association organizes some annual social events, such as the year-end "Party in the Park" and Fallfest, both of which feature live music, dancing, and plenty of food. The student newspaper, *The Albany Student Press*, comes out twice a week and draws enthusiastic undergraduate participation. Unfortunately, the same cannot be said for varsity sports, but students have glowing praise for the school's recently built "tremendous" sports complex, where many work out in their spare time. Students also have no complaints about the security and safety of the school. An escort service and shuttle van serve as alternatives to late-night walking. Abundant emergency phones throughout campus also work to put students at ease.

All things considered, Albany offers much more than a great educational bang for your tuition buck. Its satisfied student body and sound academics would make it a great deal in any state of the union.
—*Ann Zeidner and Staff*

FYI
The three best things about attending SUNY Albany are "the dorms are all really close to one another, it's easy to meet people here, and the variety of night life—there are lots of clubs and bars in the area."
The three worst things about attending SUNY Albany are "the coed bathrooms in some dorms, the SNOW, and sometimes it's hard to get all the classes you want."
The three things every student should do before graduating from SUNY Albany are "to take a road trip to Canada, to visit Lake George, and to go out and experience the Albany night life."
One thing I'd like to have known before coming here is "it's TOO easy to have fun here—which makes it hard to do much else."

State University of New York / Binghamton

Address: PO Box 6000; Binghamton, NY 13902-6001
Phone: 607-777-2171
E-mail address: admit@binghamton.edu
Web site URL: www.binghamton.edu
Founded: 1946
Private or Public: public
Religious affiliation: none
Location: suburban
Undergraduate enrollment: 9,710
Total enrollment: 12,564
Percent Male / Female: 47%/53%
Percent Minority: 29%
Percent African-American: 5%

Percent Asian: 17%
Percent Hispanic: 6%
Percent Native-American: 0.5%
Percent in-state / out-of-state: 96%/4%
Percent Pub HS: 85%
Number of Applicants: 16,386
Percent Accepted: 42%
Percent Accepted who enroll: 30%
Entering: 2,050
Transfers: 726
Application Deadline: 15 Jan
Mean SAT: 585 V, 616 M
Mean ACT: NA

Middle 50% SAT range: 540–640 V, 570–660 M
Middle 50% ACT range: NA
3 Most popular majors: management, English, biology
Retention: 91%
Graduation rate: 70%
On-campus housing: 98%
Fraternities: 18%
Sororities: 14%
Library: 1,700,000 volumes
Tuition and Fees: $4,416 in; $9,316 out
Room and Board: $5,516
Financial aid, first-year: 65%

O ver their four college years, SUNY Binghamton students learn to appreciate Binghamton life's small pleasures—jaunts through the rain, midnight food runs, good movies on free cable. And although many upperclassmen admit their school can get pretty monotonous—"there's nothing to do out here in the middle of nowhere!"—most would agree that it gets better as it goes. Even those students who reported loathing the school their freshman year would now offer this caution to their predecessors: "If you want to transfer out of this place, transfer out quick because this school really grows on you. Everything—the place, the people, even the never-ending rain—it all gets better as time goes on. Trust me, if you stay here, you'll hate your first year but love the rest."

The Ivy of the SUNYs

Binghamton is widely recognized as one of the most academically competitive SUNYs, attracting many of New York's best with its affordable quality education. The university comprises five undergraduate schools catering to a wide range of interests: the Harpur College of Arts and Sciences, the Decker School of Nursing, the School of Management, the School of Education and Human Development, and the Thomas J. Watson School of Engineering and Applied Science.

Graduation requirements vary with school and program. Generally, though, most majors have to fulfill one course credit in each of four core areas: the arts, pluralism, global, and communications. In addition, all students must earn two physed credits and satisfy a writing requirement. Many students agree with the general education requirements and think them great in theory but typically hate them in practice. Said one senior, "Requirements are good in the sense that they encourage students to get a broad view of things, but they're kind of a waste of time too."

And if there's one thing Binghamton students lack, it's enough time in the day. One student emphasized, "Binghamton may be easy enough to get into, but it's really hard to stay in." Students of all majors claim to grapple with "substantial" workloads, but engineering, management, and science (especially pre-med) majors reportedly suffer the heaviest loads.

Class sizes at Binghamton follow traditional college patterns—huge introductory courses of up-to-several hundred students with numbers generally shrinking as classes become more specialized in the upper levels. Teaching is generally rated as average. One student remarked, "Some professors don't even really seem to like teaching, but then there are those that make you really love your classes. I guess it's that way at most schools." TAs often co-teach and lead discussion sections for lower-level courses, becoming fewer-and-far-between at the higher levels.

Students conveniently register for classes via computer, a process which one sophomore described as "very easy and great in that I can register from home if I wanted to." Because class availability follows a pecking order dictated by seniority and major, frosh sometimes find themselves having a hard time getting into the classes they want. But, according to one experienced senior, "If you know what you're doing, you can pretty much petition and beg your way into any class." In several instances, though, the classrooms themselves have lacked the space to accommodate enrollees. Faced with a shortage of seats, many students ended up sitting through class without desks or chairs. One student voiced his concern: "It's like you're paying money to sit on the floor. That's just not right."

In years past as well, students have had to deal with similar shortages in housing. One year, in fact, the situation was so bad that some freshmen were forced to take up temporary quarters in floor TV common rooms because there were no permanent rooms available. Despite occasional problems, however, most students seem pretty content with their on-campus housing. One student described the dorms as "totally decent" with "relatively big and clean" rooms.

Community Life
Undergrads live in one of five "communities," each of which includes several coed dorms and a central building housing a dining hall. Each community has a distinctive character and stereotype attached to it. Newing College is the Greek-dominated party dorm. Hinman is the quiet haven for hardcore studiers. Dickinson is racially and ethnically diverse, while College-in-the-Woods (CIW) is notorious for abundant drug use. The fifth dorm, the graduate community, is restricted to juniors and seniors. The summer before freshman year, incoming frosh are asked to indicate their first and second community choices on a preference sheet, and in most cases, they are assigned to one of the two. After freshman year, students can choose to remain in their communities, move to another, or move off campus. Apartments are generally "cheap and easy-to-find," but students without cars may find transportation a problem.

Most communities have libraries where students can do work, but the main Bartle library is also a popular study spot. Late-night studiers seeking for a quiet atmosphere can find it in the "tombs," a popular nickname for a scary tomb-esque section of Bartle's main lobby.

In Pursuit of the Freshman 15
After stressful study sessions, Binghamton students grab much-needed sustenance at Snax or the Night Owl, open until midnight and 1 A.M. respectively. Students can charge these purchases to their meal plans.

At mealtimes, Bing students have the option to eat in the community dining halls or at the mini-mall, which sells typical food-court fare like Taco Bell, Chinese food, pasta, and a char-grill. School food was described as "decent but pretty repetitive" with the same entrees offered again and again. "How many ways are there to prepare chicken?" wondered one student. "And amazingly, no matter how they make it, it all tastes *exactly the same.*"

For students looking to escape campus food, Binghamton's main throughway, Bethel Parkway, is a hungry man's heaven. Dozens of eateries ranging from dirt-cheap grease to pricier four-star cuisine dot this long asphalt strip. Perenially popular options include TGI Friday's, Olive Garden, Denny's, and Tony's—great food at a bargain. No. 5 was said to be a good place to take a date. Local Binghamton also attracts students with its many sports bars and handful of clubs. Some clubs will periodically hold "SUNY nights," which one student described as "a good way to meet other people in the university."

The Self-Contained Brain

Seen from the air, the Binghamton campus is arranged in a circle, which students have affectionately dubbed "the Brain." Wooded mountains enclose the campus, creating a valley of sorts; this valley tends to keep clouds in, above school grounds, resulting in lots of rain and snow. "Don't forget to bring an umbrella," advised one student.

Just a short walk from campus is a nature preserve spanning 117-acres. "It's a great place to take a date," said one sophomore guy. Other students flock there to escape the noisy campus construction currently in process. "I mean, it'll be great when the campus union is renovated and those new dorms are done, but for now, I'm just looking to get away from the racket," said one student.

Because Binghamton's campus is so isolated and self-contained, most students would agree that cars are a necessary evil for off-campus treks. "Cars are great because of the freedom they give, but parking is a drag," said one car-owner. Not only are parking spaces on campus limited, but the lots are often inconveniently located. Newing College's three parking lots are commonly referred to as "heaven," "purgatory," and "hell," with "hell" being the farthest and "heaven" the closest distance away.

> "For a school without a football team, we have a ton of really big and buff guys."

Cars also prove convenient when Bing students just want some "away time." While New York City, a 3-hour drive, may be a bit far for a road trip, major college-towns Syracuse and Ithaca are both less than an hour away, making for a good day or weekend getaway.

Weekend Fun

Back on campus, Greeks tend to dominate social life. The party scene revolves around the frats, which regularly throw weekend bashes. Alcohol abounds at these events; for $3, attendees can drink as much as they want. Considering the abundance of inebriated guys and girls in attendance at these parties, it is not surprising that here are where most random hook-ups occur. Some people will go with dates, but it's less common.

For students not into the partying and drinking scenes, the university offers a host of other social options. Movie showings, student productions, guest lectures, and dances are just a few of the alternatives. The campus pub is also another fun hangout, with a bowling alley, arcade, and billiards.

Surprising Diversity

Binghamton has no football team, a reality that undoubtedly contributes to the general absence of school spirit among the student body. Despite that empty pocket, however, intramurals or "co-recs" are pretty popular, especially soccer and rugby. The university athletic facilities are divided between the East and West Gymnasiums. East Gym is generally considered the better of the two, but unlike West Gym, is not free. Remarked one student, "For a school without a football team, we have a ton of really big and buff guys."

In addition to intramurals and recreational sports, lots of students report heavy involvement in campus extracurricular groups. The student association, Binghamton's answer to student government, is generally recognized as pretty popular. Cultural organizations also enjoy high student participation, not surprising in light of the school's diverse student makeup. Music-minded students can perform in school musical groups like the orchestra and wind ensemble, and journalistic or literary minds can write for one of the many campus publications. Binghamton students hold a variety of interests, and club offerings reflect this wide range.

Indeed Binghamton's student body can be surprisingly diverse and eclectic considering Binghamton is a state school full of mostly New Yorkers. Even within the state, though, certain regions are said to be over-represented—Long Island in particular. For some this can be a drawback, as one student complained, "There are too many students from Long Island, Westchester, and New York City. There aren't even that many from upstate New York!" But all things considered, Binghamton would qualify as a wise college choice for Yankee and non-Yankee alike, offering an excellent education for the money and a diversity rarely found at state institutions. —*Jane H. Hong and Staff*

FYI

The three best things about attending SUNY/Binghamton are "the people—they're awesome!, the cost, and the scenery's beautiful."

The three worst things about attending SUNY/Binghamton are "the administration—it's disorganized and has some poorly trained staff, the lack of parking, and the apathetic professors."

The three things that every student should do before graduating from SUNY/Binghamton are "go the Highest Point with that special someone, go to Denny's at 3:30 A.M., get lost at the nature preserve."

One thing I'd like to have known before coming here is "that I would need a car. Oh, and to bring an umbrella because it never stops raining here!"

State University of New York / Buffalo

Address: 1300 Elmwood Avenue; Buffalo, NY 14222
Phone: 716-878-4017
E-mail address: admission@buffalostate.edu
Web site URL: www.buffalostate.edu
Founded: 1846
Private or Public: public
Religious affiliation: none
Location: suburban
Undergraduate enrollment: 8,762
Total enrollment: 23,429
Percent Male/Female: 42%/58%
Percent Minority: 16%
Percent African-American: 11%

Percent Asian: 1%
Percent Hispanic: 3%
Percent Native-American: 0.5%
Percent in-state/out-of-state: 98%/2%
Percent Pub HS: NA
Number of Applicants: 6,568
Percent Accepted: 60%
Percent Accepted who enroll: 31%
Entering: 1,219
Transfers: NA
Application Deadline: rolling
Mean SAT: 561 V, 584 M
Mean ACT: 25

Middle 50% SAT range: 430–530 V, 430–530 M
Middle 50% ACT range: 18–21
3 Most popular majors: psychology, business administration, health-related professions
Retention: 82%
Graduation rate: 31%
On-campus housing: 22%
Fraternities: 1%
Sororities: 1%
Library: 3,000,000 volumes
Tuition and Fees: $3,909 in; $3,909 out
Room and Board: $5,170
Financial aid, first-year: 55%

In 1846, University at Buffalo was a private medical school consisting of a few lecture rooms in an old church. As the years went by, the university slowly expanded by adding a school of pharmacy, a law school, a dental school, a school of arts and science, a school of management, and numerous other offerings. After becoming part of the SUNY system in 1962, the school grew rapidly and split into a North Campus and South Campus. Today's Buffalo students have the pleasure of attending not only the largest public university in New York, but in all of New England as well. Size is one of the school's most unique characteristics;

SUNY Buffalo boasts the largest faculty in the SUNY system and the greatest number of degree programs.

Big Options

"This school has just about every single major you can think of." Buffalo offers a wide variety of majors as well as the option of double majoring or minoring in a subject. As one student notes, "Having a second major or a minor can be pretty common." Those who do not wish to follow a traditional major program have the freedom of designing their own major. One sophomore gladly noted, "Although the requirements for graduation vary by major, there is no physical education requirement." When asked about the academic environment at Buffalo, one student replied by saying, "It is a big engineering and science school." Some of the strongest programs at Buffalo include the engineering and pharmacy departments, which rank among the best in the SUNY system.

Students agreed that the science, engineering, and computer science courses, as well as pre-med classes, tend to be on the more difficult side. One student commented, "Your workload depends on which classes you take. If you are pre-med, prepare to lose some sleep." For those who are searching for classes that do not require too much work, several recommended courses are Methods of Inquiry and Psychology 101.

According to one student, "Registration is primarily done through a phone system called BIRD, while some people take advantage of the newly introduced online registration." The large student body creates some difficulties during registration period. As one student complained, "The Internet becomes very slow and classes fill up quickly. It is extremely hard to get the class you want, or when you want it." Priority is given to students who have received more credits, so in general seniors get first pick while freshmen hope there will still be empty slots when it is their turn. "Getting into some classes can be real tough for freshmen," said one student. There is a broad range in class size, ranging from small seminars of about ten students to introductory lectures with over five hundred students.

Although developing a relationship with the professor is harder in the lecture classes, students can get to know them by visiting during weekly office hours, which every teacher holds. Students can also receive help by attending the smaller recitations led by graduate-student TAs. Students are happy with the majority of their professors. As one student said, "My English teacher played the guitar and sang to us." However, "sometimes you will find a teacher that is hard to understand or does not really know English, especially in the math department." As a response to the general academic environment, one student replied, "I hate work, but I love to learn."

Social Life

When the week of classes is over, students have fun by doing almost whatever they want. Fraternities on South Campus, bars on Main Street, and dorms are popular sites for those looking for parties. Although alcohol is allowed for those above 21, "it is usually consumed by mostly minors." For non-drinkers, there are plenty of other options, such as a movie theatre, a symphony orchestra, concerts, or just hanging out with friends. During Fall Fest and Spring Fest, popular bands perform at North Campus for the students. After attending one of the on campus concerts, one student proudly exclaimed, "I saw Busta Rhymes!" Students can easily attend local Buffalo Bills or Sabres games or travel about twenty minutes north to Canada. As one student commented, "UB has a ton of organized activities from clubs to specific dorm arranged activities. There is always something to do."

> **"While in Buffalo,"** one student said, **"you must eat the Buffalo wings! You just have to eat them, they _are_ that good."**

At Buffalo, the large student body makes it possible for almost anyone to find a group of friends that share their interests. As one student put it, "I found it very easy to meet people. There is always room for one more in a group. Most of my friends were made through friends, dorm, and classes." One negative aspect of the size of UB is that people must make a conscious effort to keep up contacts. With many students, "groups form right away, but can change in an instant."

How Is Life on Campus?

Since UB is part of the SUNY system, nearly all of the students are New York State residents. Despite a large number of middle class people from Rochester and Long Island, there is a great amount of ethnic and religious diversity. Although there were mixed opinions among students about the necessity of a car, there was a general consensus that they were helpful. While one student claimed "you need one like you need air to breathe," another stated that they "aren't needed but are a big bonus."

Buffalo is the only SUNY school that does not require freshmen to live on campus, so those who live near by often commute. With such a large student body, a good number of people also choose to stay off campus. One student commented, "The rent is decent, and proximity is not bad either." There are RAs for everyone living in dorms, regardless of their year. They are generally nice but "won't hesitate to turn you in if they have to." Students live on coed floors with single sex bathrooms. UB helps bring together people of similar interests by offering themed housing, which in turn creates different personalities for different dorms. The living situations have been improving recently with the addition of the Hadley Village Undergraduate Apartments, the Flickinger Court Graduate Apartments, and South Lake Village Apartments.

I'm Getting Hungry . . .

Students feel safe while on Buffalo's large campus and often visit the surrounding areas for entertainment. Many places are within walking distance, and several malls are less than a twenty-minute drive away. UB students enjoy eating out once in a while and can pick from a large number of choices, including Starbucks, Red Lobster, and Olive Garden. Students with a tongue for fast food enjoy visiting Taco Bell, Burger King, and Campus Pizza & Italian Specialties. Duffs, a local restaurant where chicken wings are served, cannot be missed according to several students. "While in Buffalo," one student said, "you must eat the Buffalo wings! You just have to eat them, they *are* that good."

While eating under the university's meal plan, students have several places they can enjoy all-you-can-eat dining hall food. Although some students have complained about the inconvenient designated meal times, there are plenty of vegetarian options and meal plans can be used at other locations. There are definitely noticeable cliques in the dining halls, where people can often be found chatting long after they have finished their meals.

How About A Pick-Up Game?

Basketball and football are big sports at UB. Even though the Division IA football team does not have a winning reputation, one spirited student remarked, "I don't miss a home game." On campus, there is much more to sports than the varsity teams. The athletic facilities are good, including a new football stadium and a natatorium that has hosted the World University Games and the Empire State Games in the past. For people who do not play sports for a team, it is easy to find a pick-up game. Each year, over 9,000 UB students take a break from their work and participate in club sports or intramurals.

The city of Buffalo has much to offer to the university and its students. The size of the school allows people to choose their own education and have a great time along the way. When approached with the idea of going back and choosing a college again, one undergraduate enthusiastically replied, "I would definitely choose UB. I love it!" —*Robert Wong and Staff*

FYI

The three best things about attending UB are "the size of the school, the freedom, and always having something to do."

The three worst things about attending UB are "the size of the school, the weather, and early classes."

The three things that every student should do before graduating from UB are "have Buffalo wings at Duffs, keep in touch with their friends, and do their homework and learn something."

One thing I'd like to have known before coming here is "I wish someone would have told me how useful a car is here."

State University of New York / Stony Brook

Address: Stony Brook, NY 11794	**Percent Asian:** 22%	**Middle 50% SAT range:** 490–590 V,
Phone: 631-632-6868	**Percent Hispanic:** 7%	520–640 M
E-mail address: admiss @mail.vpsa.sunysb.edu	**Percent Native-American:** 0.5%	**Middle 50% ACT range:** NA
Web site URL: www.sunysb.edu	**Percent in-state/out-of-state:** 95%/5%	**3 Most popular majors:** psychology, biology, business management
Founded: 1957	**Percent Pub HS:** NA	**Retention:** 82%
Private or Public: public	**Number of Applicants:** 14,892	**Graduation rate:** 56%
Religious affiliation: none	**Percent Accepted:** 58%	**On-campus housing:** 78%
Location: suburban	**Percent Accepted who enroll:** 26%	**Fraternities:** 15%
Undergraduate enrollment: 12,690	**Entering:** 2,248	**Sororities:** 11%
Total enrollment: 19,128	**Transfers:** 1,269	**Library:** 2,000,000 volumes
Percent Male/Female: 47%/53%	**Application Deadline:** 10 Jul	**Tuition and Fees:** $3,975 in; $8,875 out
Percent Minority: 39%	**Mean SAT:** 560 V, 600 M	**Room and Board:** $6,222
Percent African-American: 9%	**Mean ACT:** NA	**Financial aid, first-year:** 61%

Nearly half a century ago, SUNY Stony Brook was founded in 1956 to produce math and science teachers and become one of the finest research universities in the nation. Although initially located in Oyster Bay, Long Island, in 1962 the university was relocated to a 480-acre area in Stony Brook, approximately 60 miles outside of Manhattan. The university has grown to include a College of Arts and Sciences, a College of Engineering and Applied Sciences, a school of management, a medical school, a dental school, and a hospital. The university has greatly increased the quality of its reputation, and the Carnegie Foundation now considers Stony Brook one of the top 70 research schools in the United States. With over 1,100 acres and 70 academic departments, Stony Brook is one of the few major nationally ranked schools situated on Long Island.

Dedicated Students

Stony Brook students are happy with their academic environment. In the words of one student, "I'm extremely satisfied at a university like Stony Brook." While running on a semester system, Stony Brook requires students to take their Diversified Education Curriculum. In order to satisfy this, students must take one course each in American pluralism, European history, non-Western history, fine arts, humanities, math, technology, and writing. In addition, two courses must be completed in the natural sciences and the social and behavioral sciences. The one-year foreign language requirement can be satisfied with a score of 75 or higher on the appropriate New York State Regents examination.

Students describe the university as having excellent professors and a good working environment. All school faculty members are involved in teaching, as well as research. Some of the more notable members of the faculty include Nobel laureate physics professor C.N. Yang and mathematics professor John Milnor, winner of the prestigious Fields Medal. Another important resource for Stony Brook students to take advantage of are the seminars offered by professors on field studies and the environment of jobs in their field.

At Stony Brook, students can expect to find large lectures in introductory courses, but the professors keep the class interested in the material. One student recalled how his physics professor would perform entertaining experiments in class that demonstrated the principles they were studying. Although the introductory biology and psychology classes may each enroll nearly five hundred students, more advanced seminars tend to be much smaller with approximately twenty students per class. Each lecture is broken down into much smaller recitations led by TAs that facilitate learning through more one-on-one interaction. The only problem students noted was that several TAs have trouble with their English.

Students agreed that the engineering and science classes tended to offer the greatest workload and most competition. However, this does not pose a problem for Stony Brook students since the school is great in those areas and "everyone seems dedicated to their work." Although more students choose to major in the technical fields, a large number of people study liberal arts. This can be partially attributed to the DEC, which allows students to explore different areas of study. Another option that students make use of is majoring in a second subject. In the words of one student, "I couldn't be more satisfied with this school's academics."

Living at Stony Brook

With 26 residential halls, Stony Brook is the largest residential campus in the SUNY system. Students have the choice of living in corridor-style dorms or suite-style dorms. The corridor dorms allow students to live in singles or doubles along a hallway and share common areas, bathrooms and cooking areas. In suites, four to six students share two to three bedrooms, a common area, and a private bathroom. The university offers special living options, such as 24-hour quiet hour dorms and substance free rooms for students who wish to live in areas without alcohol or tobacco. Aside from the residential halls, two different on-campus apartment complexes are available for graduate students, families and married couples. Six computing centers are provided for the convenience of students. More athletically inclined students can attend the seven athletic centers at Stony Brook, which are open seven days a week.

At the athletic centers, Stony Brook residents have the option of taking aerobics classes, lifting weights, using Nautilus equipment, or training on state-of-the-art Cybex circuit machines.

"You can find it ALL."

Each year, the Department of Residential Programs holds hundreds of educational and social events for Stony Brook students. Some of the more popular annual events include Roth Quad Regatta (students, faculty and staff design their own boats and race them across Roth Pond), Spirit Night (music, fireworks and a skit to show school pride), Homecoming (a parade, football game, and crowning of the King and Queen), and Ultimate Spring Blast (a week of carnivals, shows, fireworks, food, and fun). The school also sponsors diversity themed months, during which cultural, social and educational activities are used to celebrate a different group each month.

Outside of the Classroom

Security is important at Stony Brook, and the university does a good job of making students feel safe on campus. University Police Officers patrol the campus at all hours and check IDs at the main gate after midnight, when the campus is closed to students who do not have Stony Brook identification or prior permission. All residence halls are locked 24 hours a day, and only students who live in a hall have the access card to get in. The campus is well lit at night and "blue-light phones" placed throughout the campus allow students to call for help from anywhere. Another useful option is the free Walk Service Program, which lets students call for two people with walkie-talkies to escort them to their destination.

Stony Brook offers twenty intercollegiate varsity sports for its students, ten for men and ten for women. The Stony Brook Seawolves' athletic success can be seen by their rise from NCAA Division III. After a ten year process that began in 1989, Stony Brook has recently completed a full upgrade of its athletic program to Division I level. The most popular teams on campus are the basketball and soccer teams, which both draw large crowds as they begin making their name in Division I.

For students who wish to have some fun off campus, public transportation is a popular option. The Stony Brook station of the Long Island Rail Road is on campus, allowing students to travel to other parts of Long Island, as well as into New York City. On campus and off campus buses can be used to get to nearby malls and towns, such as Port Jefferson, the Smithhaven Mall, and Stony Brook Village. The Port Jefferson Ferry lies just a few minutes away, giving students the ability to travel across Long Island Sound to Bridgeport, Connecticut.

Many students choose to go home over the weekend, making the school known for being a "suitcase" college. However, the students who stick around campus do not have any trouble finding ways to have fun. The student union has planned activities every night, and school-organized movies and concerts give students even more options to choose from. Other hangouts include fraternities, sororities, bars, clubs, and "The Spot" (a nightclub where bands come and play). Most students are satisfied with the social alternatives and can almost always find something amusing to do either on or off campus.

What's for Dinner?

Stony Brook's meal plan received positive reviews from its students, who felt that "the school has a good selection of just about everything." Students can choose from over 25 options, including a Pizza Hut, Burger King, Deng Lee's Chinese, Wrap-a-bles, and a made-to-order grill. A Kosher-dining hall is available, as well as low sodium, fat and cholesterol free selections. The meal plan is required for first year students, except for those living in cooking suites. For students who want a change of taste, there are also many nearby places to find something good to eat. Some campus favorites include local diners, Red Lobster, and Boulder Creek.

Although the majority of Stony Brook students are from the southern portion of New York State, the student body still offers a wide range of diversity. Many different ethnic groups are well represented; however, there is some tendency for groups to self-segregate. When asked if any particular style of clothing or genre of music stood out at the school, one student replied, "You can find it ALL." The strong academic program and public school tuition combine to make Stony Brook a school that no one should skip over.

—Robert Wong and Staff

FYI

The three best things about attending Stony Brook are "the professors, the working environment, and the science and engineering departments."

The three worst things about attending Stony Brook are "the campus, too many commuters, and non science departments could be stronger."

The three things that every student should do before graduating from Stony Brook are "take advantage of professors' seminars, go to Spirit Night, and make some close friendships."

One thing I'd like to have known before coming here is "that there would be so many Long Islanders here."

Syracuse University

Address: 201 Tolley Administration Building; Syracuse, NY 13244
Phone: 315-443-3611
E-mail address: orange@syr.edu
Web site URL: www.syracuse.edu
Founded: 1870
Private or Public: private
Religious affiliation: none
Location: urban
Undergraduate enrollment: 10,685
Total enrollment: 14,557
Percent Male / Female: 46%/54%
Percent Minority: 16%
Percent African-American: 7%

Percent Asian: 4%
Percent Hispanic: 4%
Percent Native-American: 0.5%
Percent in-state / out-of-state: 44%/56%
Percent Pub HS: 80%
Number of Applicants: 12,663
Percent Accepted: 59%
Percent Accepted who enroll: 37%
Entering: 2,752
Transfers: NA
Application Deadline: 15 Jan
Mean SAT: NA
Mean ACT: NA

Middle 50% SAT range: 540–640 V, 560–660 M
Middle 50% ACT range: NA
3 Most popular majors: information management and technology, architecture, psychology
Retention: NA
Graduation rate: 56%
On-campus housing: 72%
Fraternities: 17%
Sororities: 23%
Library: 3,100,000 volumes
Tuition and Fees: $20,816 in; $20,816 out
Room and Board: $8,750
Financial aid, first-year: 62%

Snow on Commencement Day? Sounds like a fantasy, huh? Well, not at Syracuse. Members of Syracuse University's Class of 1997 witnessed snow on their Commencement Day. Snow that starts in November and continues through March or April does not seem to change the undergrads' studying or partying patterns. And certainly, snow does not keep hard-core fans of the nationally ranked football team from filling up the Dome to see the Orangemen play.

Academics: So Many Options

The academic experiences of Syracuse students vary a lot due to Syracuse's twelve different undergraduate schools and colleges. These separate schools specialize in education, architecture, arts and sciences, engineering and computer science, social work, management, nursing, human development, visual and performing arts, information studies, law, and public communications; and each has its own requirements. In particular, the Newhouse School of Public Communications is considered one of the best communications schools in the U.S., and it is the most prestigious school of the university.

Many students, though, are enrolled in the College of Arts and Sciences, which provides a basic liberal arts education. The distribution requirements in this college consist of four courses in both of the social science groups, natural sciences and math, and humanities. Students can also take classes from other schools within the university. For this reason, coming to Syracuse undecided in major is not a problem; students can enter one of the schools after developing an interest in that area in the introductory classes. Transferring to Newhouse, though, is more difficult compared to the other schools and requires a higher GPA.

In each of the schools at Syracuse, professors teach most of the classes, and students seem happy with the professors overall. Opinions on professors vary from "I haven't had any professors I didn't like" to "I have had amazing professors and not so exciting ones." Students also report that professors are usually accessible, although one student added that "it is sometimes hard to get to know them on an individual basis." Also, TAs who teach the sections generally receive good reviews from the students. As students report: "They know what they are doing" and "it is easier for them to relate to the students because of the small age difference." Some students, though, have had problems with a few of their TAs' accents.

Class size varies among the schools. The largest class at Newhouse consists of 75 people, while some intro classes in the Arts and Sciences can reach 200. Classes that enroll more than 100 students meet in smaller groups of 20 for discussions. The upper-level classes, in contrast, are smaller in size. Most students consider engineering and architecture the most difficult majors. Several students identify science, calculus, and management courses as "pretty tough for non-majors." One favorite class among students is the half-semester course called Freshman Forum, which consists of 15 freshmen meeting with an advisor and "provides an opportunity to get to know the campus and the things going on."

To Drink or Not to Drink . . .

Partying is a major "concern" for many undergraduates at Syracuse. As one student said, "You could call Syracuse a party school, but there is the other side as well." The non-alcoholic and non-partying social options have been improving. A senior commented that "there were not so many social alternatives before as there are now." Those who are not into partying choose to hang out in one of the numerous coffeehouses in the surrounding area or attend events sponsored by different school organizations.

One thing that all students agree on is that "the parties are there if you want it." Greek and house parties are the two main options, although the Greeks are becoming more and more exclusive because of the university's banning of alcohol on campus. One student reported that there are "rumors that the chancellor is trying to get rid of all the Greeks." And there is evidence to support that claim: more than ten fraternities and sororities "are gone" for various reasons since he assumed his position. Since the Greeks are limiting access of non-members, a student advises "if you want alcohol, go to the houses." Walking down Euclid Street en route to the house parties is a "big freshman thing." For some, "the best parties are the house swing parties, where there is swing music and the atmosphere is great." Syracuse also has tons of entertainment besides parties. The School of Music organizes concerts on a regular basis. There are also famous bands and musicians who have concerts on campus and different events draw interesting speakers to campus.

For entertainment or other purposes, everyone seems to agree that cars are extremely useful at Syracuse. As one student reports, "You can get off-campus jobs and you can get around much easier." Buses operate between the campus and downtown, but cars are definitely "better." "Having a car allows you to do more interesting things and have more fun." However, students warn that parking is a serious problem.

No Stereotypes

Although almost half of the students at Syracuse are from New York state, everyone here mentions the diversity. They agree that "there is no stereotypical Syracuse student." There is a mix of upper class and middle-class, and although different ethnicities are represented, students report that people from these groups tend to stick together. "Generally, cliques are evident [on campus]," said one student. Cliques also form among groups of students who share majors because "they see each other all the time and share common interests."

According to several people, Coming Out Week was a time when "the homosexuals' voices were heard a little louder than people would like to hear." A lot of people are "very close-minded about this issue." Others find it "great that gays and lesbians have formed a union to educate people." The fraternity brothers and sorority sisters also tend to stick together all the time, and freshmen that live in the same dorm usually hang out with each other, as well.

Bed and Breakfast: Living and Food

There are several living options at Syracuse. All freshmen and sophomores have to live on campus. On-campus options include dorms and university-owned apartments on South Campus. Dorm rooms can be singles, open doubles, or split doubles, and for the most part students have the opportunity to choose the dorm and the type of room that they want to stay in. The dorms differ in that some are coed by floor, others by wing and by door. There are also quiet lifestyle and wellness floors that are alcohol- and drug-free. Each floor sets its own standards, which can concern anything from quiet hours to bathroom rules. Students are assigned RAs, and they report that most RAs are "friendly and want to be your friend." In some cases, "juniors and seniors get a sophomore RA, which creates strange situations." After sophomore year, many students choose to live off campus.

> **"There is no stereotypical Syracuse student."**

Syracuse students offer different opinions on food. "Food sucks," say some while others say "food is pretty good overall." The quality of food differs depending on the dining hall. Most dorms or their neighboring dorms have dining halls. There are two food courts on campus with favorite options such as Burger King, Taco Bell, Sbarro's and Dunkin' Donuts. Marshall Street, which is right beside the campus, is also popular during lunch breaks, with several pizza places, cafés, and ethnic restaurants.

And onto the Campus . . .

The university is located on a hill that overlooks downtown Syracuse, a medium-sized city that is a twenty-minute walk away. As one student said, "It is not urban, it is not suburban. It is somewhere in between." Students cite the "huge" mall nearby as popular because it includes a large-screen movie theater. On campus, the "Mount" is an area where several freshman dorms are located. Students report that the 120 stairs from the main quad to the Mount create a serious challenge in icy winter conditions. At the center of campus is the "beautiful" Quad surrounded by academic buildings that are a part of the College of Arts and Sciences. The other

schools are pretty separated from one another, but no distance requires "more than a fifteen-minute walk." Not long ago, a new law school building was added that now serves as the main building of the College of Law.

The Schine Student Center is also a popular hangout for students. They pass through there during the day, stop by to quickly check their e-mail, or enjoy lunch in the food court. It includes a large auditorium, a gallery, a food court, a game room, and several lounges and meeting rooms. The university bookstore and offices of several student organizations are also in this building. For the studious, the main library, Bird, has more than 2 million volumes. Those who find "studying in the dorm difficult" often visit the Carnegie Library or the Moon Library. Some students also enjoy spending time in the Lowe Art Gallery and the Sculpture Court. Interested students can see both amateur and professional theater productions year-round at the Syracuse Stage.

The Orangemen

Sports are really big at Syracuse. All women's and men's varsity teams are NCAA Division I, and many are nationally ranked. The 50,000-seat Carrier Dome is home for the football, basketball, soccer, and lacrosse teams and is the largest domed stadium on a college campus. Football, basketball and lacrosse are the three most popular sports that also attract local crowds. Even if varsity sports are not your thing, Archbold and Flanagan Gymnasiums provide plenty of opportunities to be involved in sports. Intramurals are "well organized and attract many people," and floors usually form their own teams or students sign up in the gym to join other teams. If you have been looking for just the right combination of sports, academics, and fun, consider Syracuse. It may be the perfect school for you! —*Engin Yenidunya*

FYI
The three best things about attending Syracuse University are "the great sports, it's tons of fun, and all the snow."
The three worst things about attending Syracuse University are "the cold, the need for a car, and the cliques."
The three things every student should do before graduating are "to paint yourself orange, party like mad on the weekends, and to watch a game in the Carrier Dome."
One thing I'd like to have known before coming here is "how much snow Syracuse gets."

Union College

Address: Schenectady, NY 12308
Phone: 518-388-6112
E-mail address: admissions@union.edu
Web site URL: www.union.edu
Founded: 1795
Private or Public: private
Religious affiliation: none
Location: small city
Undergraduate enrollment: 2,112
Total enrollment: 2,191
Percent Male/Female: 52%/48%
Percent Minority: 14%
Percent African-American: 4%

Percent Asian: 5%
Percent Hispanic: 4%
Percent Native-American: 0.5%
Percent in-state/out-of-state: 49%/51%
Percent Pub HS: 69%
Number of Applicants: 3,761
Percent Accepted: 46%
Percent Accepted who enroll: 31%
Entering: 535
Transfers: 34
Application Deadline: 1 Feb
Mean SAT: NA
Mean ACT: NA

Middle 50% SAT range: 560–650 V, 580–670 M
Middle 50% ACT range: NA
3 Most popular majors: psychology, economics, political science
Retention: 94%
Graduation rate: 83%
On-campus housing: 99%
Fraternities: 33%
Sororities: 26%
Library: 293,253 volumes
Tuition and Fees: $24,099 in; $24,099 out
Room and Board: $6,474
Financial aid, first-year: 58%

The Idol, a Chinese sculpture of lions and cubs, was donated by a Union alumnus who wanted to give something back to his alma mater. The administration did not find the Idol so aesthetically pleasing and relegated it to the basement of a building on campus. Upon receiving the news that the donor would be visiting, the university prominently displayed the sculpture in front of West Dorm. After the alumnus left, some students took it upon themselves to improve the Idol by painting it. The Idol has since moved several times, but the tradition of painting this sculpture has remained at Union. A sports team, a fraternity, or just a group of boisterous students can paint the Idol with their names, letters of their Greek organization, or just about any other decoration imaginable. In the spring, the Idol tends to change color more than once an evening.

Three Times Fun

Academic life is intense at Union. One freshman claimed, "I've never worked so hard just to keep up," while a sophomore said, "It's difficult to get an A, but a B or C is no problem." Union keeps class sizes small, with approximately 40 students in an introductory course, and as little as 10 or fewer in upper-level classes. This type of educational setting allows students to have extensive contact with professors and get to know them well. Students find their instructors quite accessible, a necessity at an institution like Union where there are no teaching assistants.

Union runs on a trimester system. Students have three separate segments of study as opposed to two in the traditional semester system. School starts two weeks later than most colleges, includes a Christmas break of six or seven weeks, and does not end till the middle of June. Students generally take three classes per trimester and are usually in class only on Monday, Wednesday, and Friday. Most students are in favor of this system because "it allows us to really concentrate and spread out our work." But, the trimester system also means that at times there are only 10 weeks to complete a course that usually requires 15 weeks. The administration is considering a change to a semester schedule in the future just for this reason.

In addition to completing 36 classes, Union students also need to fulfill the General Education Curriculum (GenEd), which includes two history courses, two sciences with labs, one introductory course in the social sciences, and either demonstration of foreign-language proficiency or a term abroad. All freshmen must take the Freshman Preceptorial, a class that includes a lot of reading and "basically teaches you how to write." Union also requires a number of Writing Across the Curriculum courses (WACs), which emphasize writing in several departments. Because class registration is done by person instead of with computers, it can be time-consuming and difficult to get into a class. Undergrads in different majors experience a range of academic expectations. Those interested in engineering reportedly have a more difficult and heavier course load than psychology or political science majors do, which can be for "slackers." Some of the most common majors are biology, psychology, and engineering. The engineering school has a well-respected program in conjunction with General Electric that offers students access to latest technology. One of the most popular classes is a study of the Holocaust taught by Professor Berg, an expert in the field. Most students try to take this course before they graduate, making it one of Union's largest classes, enrolling approximately 200 students. Professor Baker, a world-famous biomedical ethicist, is another distinguished member of the Union faculty.

There are a number of special academic opportunities at Union. Students can study in York, England, through a program sponsored by the English department, learn about various medical systems of the world while traveling to Europe and East Asia, or participate in a marine biology program in Maine. In addition, Union offers a seven-year combined medical school degree in conjunction with Albany Medical School as well as a five-year MBA program. Undergrads also have the opportunity to create their own major within a department.

Greek Life and Alcohol

Two things dominate the social life at Union: Greek life and alcohol. This aspect of Union hits first year students particularly hard. One sophomore summed up the situation, "If you like to drink and party, Union is the place for you. If you don't like to drink, you could be bored." Another student said, "I spent my first se-

mester drunk three or four nights a week." Union is "the mother of all fraternities." Considering the 26 fraternities and 6 sororities that exist in a school of only 2,000 people, it is safe to say that Union's Greek system is huge. The Greek scene "rules the social life at Union." One unofficial Union graduation requirement is the "campus crawl," which involves stopping by all the fraternities in one night and having a beer at each one. For the most part, fraternity parties are free and are open to everyone, which prevents non-Greeks from feeling alienated. Freshmen are not allowed to rush until the second trimester. Some Hellenic organizations are more selective than others, although anyone who wants to join will be able to at least get into one of the "nerd frats."

The university recognizes the drinking problem on campus and is trying to crack down on alcohol consumption. One moderately successful solution attempted was an alcohol awareness week during which a semiformal dance was held and all the fraternities were closed for the week. But non-drinkers say they can fit in at Union. According to one such student, "There are so many social alternatives on campus, especially since the Student Activities Office is creating more options."

Preppy is Popular

When walking around campus, students often feel as if they have stepped into a J. Crew catalog. Dressing well is important to most Union students, and preppy is definitely the popular look. Most students come from wealthy backgrounds. Jeep Grand Cherokees and BMWs fill Union's parking lots. One student was amazed by how many "really smart people" there are at Union and how everyone "has something intriguing about him or her." However, there is not much geographical or ethnic diversity among its largely conservative students. Most students are from the Northeast, especially New York and Massachusetts. Few students come from outside the Mid-Atlantic and New England states, and even fewer are internationals. Minority students often self-segregate, a tendency that is especially apparent in the dining hall, where different ethnic groups cluster at separate tables. Interracial as well as homosexual couples are rare at Union. Union can be difficult for those on financial aid because most scholarships do not cover the expenses of the academic materials, which carry inflated price tags due to a monopoly of the book market.

After a hard day of work and play, students head home to dorms that students find satisfactory. The university consistently tries to improve the living conditions through renovations, and there are many options available. Several large, co-ed dormitories such as West, Fox, and Davidson have the reputation as party dorms. Webster, the coed, substance-free dorm; Richmond, the all-female dorm equipped with night security; and South, the all-male dorm, reportedly provide quieter living arrangements for those who like sleep. Many dorms have alternating smoke-free floors at every other level. Members of fraternities or sororities can live in their respective houses. Non-Greeks who seek a sense of camaraderie can choose to live in a theme house, where residents share similar interests. Housing is guaranteed only through junior year, leading some seniors to find accommodation off campus.

Union students unanimously describe their ivy-covered walls, French-style architecture buildings, and arched doorways as "beautiful." Many admit that Union's striking, 204-year-old campus is what drew them to the school. However, its location in Schenectady, New York, does not provide much choice in entertainment. Without access to a car, the selection of off-campus activities is meager. Although freshman cannot have cars, an estimated 85 percent of upperclassman have their own transportation in order to take advantage of the bars, clubs, and shopping in Albany, which is about a half-hour drive from campus. Students generally feel secure on the campus, although some express concern while off campus. One undergrad commented, "You don't want to go off campus alone." Many students take an active stance in trying to improve the community. They get involved in various community service programs such as Big Brothers, Big Sisters, or tutoring for elementary schoolchildren.

There are many places to study, including North Colonnade, an all-night study facility, the Nott Memorial, the only 16-sided figure in the Western Hemisphere, which contains an art gallery and a huge study lounge where "you can hear a pin drop." Few students utilize the Schaeffer Library for studying. Union students who do not require silence for their studies can go to the Reamer Campus Center, where they will always to be able to find an empty room for group studying among the number of study lounges that the facility houses. One student cannot even imagine Union without the always busy campus center. Jackson Gardens is a great hiding spot to spend a lazy Sunday either reading or just hanging out.

Most students agree that the dining hall fare leaves something to be desired. There are two main dining halls on campus, West Dining Hall and Upperclass Dining Hall. The reportedly "horrible" West Dining Hall caters to freshmen while Upperclass has a much better reputation among the students and is exclusively for those who have completed their first year. One student recommends "sticking to the staples like the salad, sandwich, or bagel bars." The meal plan, which can range from 7 to 15 meals per week, also includes a Validine card, a debit card with a $200 balance that can be used to buy food at a number of on-campus eateries with options such as deli, pizza, or grill. Since Marriott runs all dining options, there are no chain restaurants on campus, forcing students off campus to get their fast-food fill. The university recently implemented a common lunch period so that all students are out of class for lunch at the same time. This has caused some controversy because of the crowding it causes in dining halls.

Pucks Flying

Union students are quite busy during the week participating in over 70 clubs and activities. There is something for everyone. Activities include the Ballroom Dance Club, a cappella singing groups, an Outing Club for those who like to hike and ski, and even a Skydiving Club for those adventurous students who want to add excitement to their college experience. Writing for the *Concordiensis*, a weekly newspaper, or the *Idol*, a popular literary magazine, are two other alternatives. Drama students are attracted to the Mountebacks, the longest continually run college theater troupe.

> **"When walking around campus, students often feel as if they have stepped into a J. Crew catalog."**

Hockey, Union's only Division I sport, is also the only sport to draw a large following of spectators and fans. The Flying Dutchmen get the biggest turnout for their rowdy games against rivals Rochester Polytechnic Institute and Hamilton College. The team usually does well, until they play "the big teams, like some of the Ivies." The football team, although it does not garner the following of the hockey team, has been quite successful recently, along with the swim team and the crew team, a club sport hoping to gain varsity status. Intramurals are not hugely popular among Union students, despite several interesting choices including squash, broomball, and tennis. The facilities for athletes are more than adequate. The newly renovated Alumni Gym has a huge drawing, and many students work out there New weight-lifting equipment, tennis and squash courts, as well as a pool combine to make the gym a top-notch exercise facility.

Union students display their uniquely fun-loving side through an on-campus tradition that "everyone must do at least once before graduating." The Naked Nott Run requires a student, most likely drunk, to disrobe and run nude around the Nott Memorial Building, usually while it is snowing. Spirited students as well as serious academics and an active party scene combine to make Union College a unique institution of higher learning. And students would agree that Union is an amazing place. —*Naomi Schoenbaum and Staff*

FYI
The three best things about attending Union College are "Jackson Gardens, the small size, and it has good places to study."
The three worst things about attending Union College are "walking around the Nott, which is like a wind tunnel in the winter, and the lack of a variety of things to do."
The three things that every student should do before graduating from Union College are "take an art class, paint the Idol, and take a term abroad."
One thing I'd like to have known before coming here is "the town is really dead. You have to find your own way of doing things."

United States Military Academy

Address: 606 Thayer Road; West Point, NY 10996-1797
Phone: 914-938-4041
E-mail address: admissions@usma.edu
Web site URL: www.usma.edu
Founded: 1802
Private or Public: public
Religious affiliation: none
Location: rural
Undergraduate enrollment: 4,209
Total enrollment: 4,209
Percent Male/Female: 85%/15%
Percent Minority: 17%
Percent African-American: 7%
Percent Asian: 5%

Percent Hispanic: 4%
Percent Native-American: 0.5%
Percent in-state/out-of-state: 92%/8%
Percent Pub HS: NA
Number of Applicants: 12,442
Percent Accepted: 15%
Percent Accepted who enroll: 63%
Entering: 1,192
Transfers: NA
Application Deadline: 21 Mar
Mean SAT: 627 V, 641 M
Mean ACT: NA
Middle 50% SAT range: 570–660 V, 590–680 M

Middle 50% ACT range: 26–30
3 Most popular majors: economics, political science-international politics, mechanical engineering-general engineering
Retention: NA
Graduation rate: 78%
On-campus housing: 100%
Fraternities: NA
Sororities: NA
Library: 500,000 volumes
Tuition and Fees: tuition, room and board paid for by the U.S. Government
Room and Board: NA
Financial aid, first-year: NA

There is no wussy orientation program for incoming "college" freshmen of the United States Military Academy. The opening weeks of training for cadets, affectionately known as the "Beast," are mandatory for all incoming students and future military officers. Students endure long hikes, target practice, and the gas chamber. One student reminisced, saying, "the Beast was the most intense six weeks of my life." It is during this time that the most cadets are apt to drop out. For the 90% or so who do survive, the United States Military Academy, known as West Point, is four years of free "education with a purpose" that ultimately requires the cadet to pledge allegiance to the flag for several years after graduation in exchange for this world class training.

GI Joe Hits the Books

Academics, above all else, are the top priority for cadets at West Point. The course load, while including such traditional subjects such as writing skills, psychology, foreign language, economics, politics, and geography; also includes in the later two years of studying focus on such subjects as math and science while giving the cadets a bit more leeway in terms of electives.

Far and away the most popular major on campus is engineering. Engineering math courses are rigorous in terms of both workload and grading. Civil and mechanical engineering top the list as the most popular of the engineering subspecialties and earned high marks from the cadets. Slacker majors at West Point are nearly non-existent. While the political science and history departments are routinely praised, science and engineering, being the main focus of study, cause the most consternation and exasperation. One cadet stated that his physics and chemistry courses were "ludicrously hard." Some of the least favorite of West Point's requirements are the physical education classes that include such fear inspiring names as "boxing." According to one cadet, who put it quite succinctly, "PE just sucks."

But fear not future cadets, for the academy provides a Center for Enhanced Performance that improves cadets reading skills, speaking abilities, and study habits. Professors are also readily available to help upon request. One student recalls meeting with a physics professor for a late night study session the night before an exam.

Class sizes, ranging from 16 and 20 students, are as small and accommodating as the most prestigious American liberal arts institutions. Smaller class sizes facilitate open discussion and help encourage cadets to ask questions when the material presented is particularly difficult.

The library, although disparaged by some students, is currently undergoing renovations to be completed in 2002, just in time for West Point's Bicentennial.

"This Ain't No Party, Soldier"

Perhaps the most drastic change that comes with military life is the alteration in the social lives of the cadets. The main credo of any nascent cadet is, "Get the hell away from Post," Post being the affectionate term for the academy. Life at the academy is strictly regimented with designated times for everything from extracurriculars to movie times. Intramurals are popular options with most cadets since the campus is chock full of sports enthusiasts. However, waking up at 6 A.M. everyday for roll call tends to drain the cadets.

Dining hall food at this verdant redoubt on the Hudson tends to draw mediocre reviews from most students. A perk of the experience, at least for upperclassmen, used to be the fact that first years, a.k.a. "Plebes," must serve their elders. The first two meals of the day were nerve-wracking for plebes as they were generally expected, at these meals, to remain at the beck and call of the other cadets. Dinner was generally more relaxed (and was optional), allowing cadets time to kick back and gossip about the day's events. The potentially angst-ridden plebe would also be happy to know that breakfast and lunch are optional on weekends, providing a brief respite from the upperclassmen. There has been a recent push on campus and by the administration to reduce the level of hazing that occurs at the academy. "The way plebes were treated changed about three years ago into a more orderly

and professional method parallel to the Army's structure that involved each class (2001–2004) being assigned a rank and responsibilities instead of the 3 upperclassmen just hazing the plebes like it was before," said one cadet.

On-campus dating is sparse thanks in part to the fact that strict regulations exist concerning male/female interactions. Another possible factor contributing to this paucity of "lovin'" may be the fact that, according to one cadet, the women at West Point "ain't nothing to rave about." However, according to some female cadets, being in the minority, they can always find a date on campus. Unfortunately for the sexually deprived senior, West Point forbids seniors from dating plebes. Some cadets attempt to maintain their relationships from high school. The other cadets provide them with the moniker, "2% Club." Simply put, of those who attempt to maintain their relationships from high school, only about 2% are successful.

Obviously, at West Point, no Greek system exists. The camaraderie provided for students by the Greek System at other universities is fulfilled by the military regimentation—"training, sleeping, eating, learning together"—the sense that everyone is in it together.

> "The camaraderie is fulfilled by the sense that everyone is in it together."

Character development and education are what inspires most cadets. "Not everything about this place is great, but everything helps to make us better leaders, no matter how much it may suck. I'm glad I'm here." While this may sound a bit contrived, West Pointers insist that they are not brainwashed. "You just have to accept the fact that this lifestyle is nothing like that of the typical college student."

The typical college lifestyle? We all know that means raucous binge drinking right? Not at West Point. The administration keeps a tight ship allowing only those legally able to drink to do so on Post. So for those 18-year-olds that love "alky shoot" or the "beer funnel," you'd better stay away.

Dorm lifestyle at West Point is also somewhat different from the typical college experience. The rooms, of course, are small and all basically look alike. Cadets must keep their rooms in tiptop condition owing to the frequent inspections that occur throughout the year. Companies, a military type unit, are comprised of around 120 cadets. Throughout the year these cadets work to overcome and adapt to the hardships of military lifestyle. As a result, close friendships are formed. One cadet's advice is to "quickly adapt." Those slow to adapt to the military lifestyle are often left feeling lonely and abandoned.

As previously mentioned, leaving Post is a popular option for cadets. Only seniors can leave on weekends but everyone, with permission, can head into town on the weekends. Popular destinations, outside of the local region, include Boston, New York City, and in some isolated instances, Washington, DC However, the majority of cadets remain on campus during the weekends. Frequently, movies are shown in academy halls throughout the weekend at specified times.

Sports are also extraordinarily popular on campus. Varsity games are frequently attended by cadets and pick-up games can always be found on campus. Attendance at football games is mandatory. The Academy has a 40,000-seat stadium. Mandatory attendance is not a problem for cadets because, simply put, everyone is into athletics. Personal fitness is virtue on this campus and encouraged by the administration—hence the popularity of sports. The Army, in fact, requires that cadets participate in intramural activities. Clubs are also popular on campus and range from martial arts to film forums.

The campus itself is dominated by Gothic architecture with a smattering of recently renovated buildings. Renovations continue in preparation for West Point's 200th birthday in 2002. Construction has dominated campus in recent years, but most cadets are not fazed, believing the renovations will greatly improve the efficiency of the campus. "There are lots of renovations and the landscape is massively changing. They're building a new gym, a really nice walk, some of the buildings are being renovated. Right now it looks like a big construction area, but by 2002, it will be NICE."

Nach der Schule

During the first two summers of their West Point Careers, cadets must attend Camp Buckner. The level of training is intense and prepares them well for future combat. After that, they may be stationed at any location within the United States. Again, adjustment and adaptation is the key to success at West Point.

After graduation, West Point cadets are required to serve six years in the United States Army. Many graduates generally look forward to this period of growth and maturation, calling it an incredible learning experience. The cadets are commissioned into the army as 2nd Lieutenants.

Overall, the benefits of a West Point education are tremendous but the adjustments numerous. Graduates wax romantic about their days at "The Point." The academics are rigorous but only for those who successfully navigate the extraordinarily competitive appointment and acceptance progress. This institution forever changes the hearts and minds of its graduates. —*Sean McBride and Staff*

FYI
The three best things about attending West Point are "the camaraderie, the regimentation, and the sports."
The three worst things about attending West Point are "the 6 A.M. wake up call, the regimentation, and Physics."
The three things that every student should do before graduating from West Point are "go bar-hopping in town, attend an Army-Navy Game, and get an awesome post."
One thing I'd like to have known before coming here is "the difficulty of adapting to the military lifestyle."

University of Rochester

Address: PO Box 270251; Rochester, NY 14627-0001	**Percent African-American:** 5%	**Middle 50% SAT range:** 600–700 V, 630–710 M
Phone: 716-275-3221	**Percent Asian:** 12%	
E-mail address: admit @admissions.rochester.edu	**Percent Hispanic:** 4%	**Middle 50% ACT range:** 27–32
	Percent Native-American: 0.5%	**3 Most popular majors:** biological sciences, engineering, psychology
Web site URL: www.rochester.edu	**Percent in-state/out-of-state:** 54%/46%	
Founded: 1850	**Percent Pub HS:** NA	**Retention:** 93%
Private or Public: private	**Number of Applicants:** 8,652	**Graduation rate:** 65%
Religious affiliation: none	**Percent Accepted:** 66%	**On-campus housing:** 100%
Location: suburban	**Percent Accepted who enroll:** 19%	**Fraternities:** 20%
Undergraduate enrollment: 4,445		**Sororities:** 14%
	Entering: 1,087	**Library:** 2,800,000 volumes
Total enrollment: 8,451	**Transfers:** 242	**Tuition and Fees:** $23,730 in; $23,730 out
Percent Male/Female: 52%/48%	**Application Deadline:** 31 Jan	**Room and Board:** $7,740
Percent Minority: 22%	**Mean SAT:** 638 V, 688 M	**Financial aid, first-year:** 66%
	Mean ACT: 28	

Graffiti is not really against school regulations. You do not always have to trudge through snow to get to class in the Northeast. It is not really that frosty during the winter in upstate New York—in fact, sometimes it gets pretty hot. How could all of this be true in the dead of winter at the University of Rochester, an academically exceptional school, on ice? The Tunnel that connects numerous academic buildings on campus underground becomes the primary route of choice during snowy winter months on campus. The Tunnel also pays a price for its popularity as students often leave their mark upon its walls.

Academics Win Out

Academics are reportedly a high priority among UR students. As one sophomore reflected, "if it is ever a choice of academics versus participating in extracurricular activities of any sort, academics will always win out." Special programs at the University of Rochester attract students from across the nation. One of the most popular programs is the Rochester Early Medical Scholars (REMS), a program that guarantees talented students a place in the university's medical school upon completion of their undergraduate education at Rochester. Students at the Eastman School of Music within the university boast about superb performance facilities and one of North America's most comprehensive academic music libraries.

> "They've got lots of brick and ivy, which I always thought a proper college should have. But, more importantly, they have that and plenty of beer."

The University of Rochester offers undergraduates the option to participate in either the regular curriculum of the school or the Honors program. Some subjects such as Philosophy, History, and the Practice of Non-Violence are offered at the "Quest" level, meaning that they are intense courses that strongly emphasize collaboration between students and professors. Students apply for these classes, and take no more than one per term. Personal interaction between students and professors is fostered in a smaller class setting. However, students who want to take advantage of these courses are required to apply in order to take classes at this level. Additionally, the University of Rochester offers the "Take Five" Scholars Program. This program grants undergraduates the opportunity to stay at Rochester for a fifth year, tuition-free, in order to take courses that supplement their regular course requirements.

The housing system at Rochester is highly specialized. Incoming freshmen are given very long, "often tedious," questionnaires to complete. Students have the option to apply for special-interest housing. The possibilities for special-interest housing are numerous, including medieval houses, drama houses, community service dorms, and athletic dorms. Within such diverse housing options, students may also select international floors, language floors, computer interest floors, music floors, or even quiet study floors. While many of the dorm buildings have been newly renovated many students seem to agree that single-sex dorms still remain the worst. As one freshman female asked, "Can you just imagine a bunch of guys grouped together? It is so sloppy and awful!" Despite these specific housing options, students at Rochester do not believe that they miss out on meeting people of diverse backgrounds and tastes even though the University of Rochester draws a large percentage of students from New York State.

The social scene at the University of Rochester reportedly "revolves around alcohol—drinking underage here is never a problem." The campus has a Greek system whose fraternities and sororities are the scene of many weekend social functions. One student noted that "they've got lots of brick and ivy, which I always thought a proper college should have. But, more importantly, they have that and plenty of beer." Parties can be "either quiet drinking parties or lively dances." In terms of the university's response to underage drinking, many students believe that "UR has more of a 'don't ask, don't see, don't tell' policy." The University does sponsor movies on the

weekends, albeit not first-run. Still other students simply opt to "just hang out" in the student center designed by master architect I. M. Pei (perhaps best known for his pyramid sculpture at the Grand Louvre in Paris). Though some students find the immediate area surrounding the campus "dull and gray," recent concerts by Jewel and the Verve Pipe are "testimony to the fact that Rochester is what you make it."

Students at Rochester participate in numerous extracurricular organizations on campus. There are over 100 student organizations registered at Rochester, ranging from cultural associations to gaming clubs, gay/lesbian coalitions to conservative unions, literary magazines to newspaper publications. The a cappella singing groups such as the Yellowjackets and SWINGSHOT!? are also very popular. Students say that undergraduates take advantage of numerous community service opportunities on campus, which draws over 70 percent of the UR student body. During the annual Wilson Day, the freshman class gather together to go out into the city of Rochester and volunteer their time for the day.

Athletics at UR do not seem to draw much student support. In fact, many athletes themselves grumble at the lack of enthusiasm and school spirit, stating, "It would be great if once in a while fans would actually come to root for our side!" What does draw student involvement are the intramural games on campus. Undergraduates reportedly "flock to the fields to compete against one another." Some of the most popular intramural sports include soccer, ultimate Frisbee, and even crew.

Though it may get cold in the winter, students at the University of Rochester keep warm together in the Tunnel beneath the campus. With strong academics and an active student body, Rochester provides an environment where students feel comfortable sharing their talents, thoughts, and ideas, and learning from one another. —*Melissa Chan and Staff*

FYI
The three best things about attending Rochester are "the snow (assuming you love snow), a beautiful campus, and top notch academics."
The three worst things about attending Rochester are "the food, the cold, and the single-sex housing."
The three things every student should do before graduating from Rochester are "to sled with the food trays, play snow touch football, and lick the flagpoles."
One thing I'd like to have known before coming here is "it's really, really cold."

Vassar College

Address: Box 10, 124 Raymond Ave.; Poughkeepsie, NY 12604
Phone: 914-437-7300
E-mail address: admissions@vassar.edu
Web site URL: www.vassar.edu
Founded: 1861
Private or Public: private
Religious affiliation: none
Location: suburban
Undergraduate enrollment: 2,317
Total enrollment: 2,317
Percent Male/Female: 43%/57%
Percent Minority: 20%

Percent African-American: 5%
Percent Asian: 9%
Percent Hispanic: 5%
Percent Native-American: 0.5%
Percent in-state/out-of-state: 70%/30%
Percent Pub HS: 60%
Number of Applicants: 4,777
Percent Accepted: 43%
Percent Accepted who enroll: 31%
Entering: 640
Transfers: 25
Application Deadline: 1 Jan
Mean SAT: 677 V, 654 M

Mean ACT: 30
Middle 50% SAT range: 640–730 V, 610–700 M
Middle 50% ACT range: NA
3 Most popular majors: English, psychology, political science
Retention: 96%
Graduation rate: 87%
On-campus housing: 98%
Fraternities: NA
Sororities: NA
Library: 900,000 volumes
Tuition and Fees: $24,030 in; $24,030 out
Room and Board: $6,770
Financial aid, first-year: 53%

Vassar College is eclectic. Once a women's college where pearls and gloves were required at daily tea, Vassar has come a long way. It became coed in 1968, but traces of its early days can still be found in the hallways of the original dorms, which were originally built seven feet wide to accommodate the hoop skirts characteristic of 19th-century women's fashion. Throughout the years, Vassar's strong commitment not only to academics but also to the idea of open-mindedness and tolerance has endured. Its atmosphere is distinct, composed of liberals and conservatives, homosexuals and hippies, aesthetes and scientists, feminists and communists, interest and apathy.

Academics

Students give their professors uniformly high marks. A philosophy major said that the "quality of the professors is the most attractive feature of Vassar." Given the small size of the school, there is a great deal of student-faculty interaction, and almost all professors are highly accessible; in fact, the majority of them live on campus. Often faculty go out of their way to demonstrate their devotion to students— a sophomore noted that his professor once invited him to dinner to continue a discussion. Another student was excited about the fact that Maya Angelou was a visiting professor.

Classes at Vassar are small and intense: most enroll fewer than 25 students. TAs do not teach any classes, and most people feel there is a genuine focus on the individual student. Registration is done on the Internet, and most students feel it is a breeze. Some do complain, however, that because many classes have capped enrollments, it becomes difficult and often impossible to get into them.

While Vassar has some basic requirements, students describe the curriculum as "open," "self-structured," and "empowering." First-year students must take a small, writing-intensive course, but have the freedom to choose from a wide range of possibilities in several departments. Students must also fulfill a quantitative (natural or social science) requirement and demonstrate proficiency in a foreign language, either through two semesters of language at Vassar or high scores on placement, SAT II, or AP tests.

English, cognitive science, and art history are named among the best departments at Vassar, and one student said the film and drama departments are on the rise. In addition to standard majors, Vassar has several interdisciplinary majors and also the option to design your own area of concentration. In general, chemistry courses are reputed to be unusually difficult, and most believe there are no standout gut courses. An extremely popular class that "almost every Vassar student has taken," according to one undergrad, is Drugs, Culture and Society.

Vassar offers a number of unique academic programs. One opportunity that students take advantage of is field work, an internship arranged through a specific academic department; the four-hour weekly time commitment is worth half a credit per semester. The choice of internships is unlimited, many of them are local, and transportation is often provided. Junior Year Abroad is another popular program, with approximately one-third of juniors participating. Candidates for study abroad face strict GPA and language requirements, which do not discourage students with strong interest. Established Vassar programs are located in many European countries, such as France, England, Spain, and Germany, but students have the option to choose their own (often exotic) destination and create an individualized program of study.

Facilities

Ranging from Gothic to modern, even the architecture at Vassar is eclectic. Students are generally happy with Vassar's facilities and describe Thompson Library as "beautiful and amazing—it looks like a cathedral." With a collection of about 750,000 volumes, sizeable for a small liberal arts college, the library is more than adequate for most people's needs. Hardworking Vassar students can find a great place to study in the quiet nooks of the library that "are nice places to work where you can't be disturbed." The library recently reopened after a 2-year renovation project.

Almost all Vassar students spend their four years living on campus in one of the nine dorms. After their first year living in a double, students are guaranteed singles. The most popular dorms are Cushing and Jewitt, the largest dorm, known for its distinctive tower. Main has wide hallways, large windows, and an ideal central location, according to residents. The most un-

popular dorm, Noyes, which one student said "is really a Motel Fifty," is said to be less comfortable and ugly. All dorms are co-ed save one: Strong, in keeping with Vassar tradition, is an all-female dorm. Many juniors and seniors live in the coveted Terrace Apartments (TAs) or Town Houses (THs), which can be either single-sex or coed. Each dorm is equipped with a parlor, TV room, game room, and laundry room. In addition, because a member of the famous Steinway family was once a student at Vassar, a Steinway grand piano can be found in every dorm. "There is definitely a sense of community within each dorm," reported one student. This community, which includes Student Fellows (advisors to freshmen who provide support rather than discipline) and House Fellows (professors who live in dorms, offer advice and guidance, and organize occasional study breaks), makes it easy for the Vassar student to build lasting relationships and complete the transition from high school to college.

Vassar's All-Campus Dining Center, known as AC/DC, garners criticism from the student body. Despite the fact that "there are a lot of options, especially for vegetarians and vegans," many students either don't really care about the food ("It's okay—nothing special") or dislike it ("It's kinda gross"). One student noted that improvements are being made to dining fare. The Retreat, an on-campus snack bar, is more popular, offering a wide variety of food and a convenient location. All students living on campus (except those in Terrace Apartments or Town Houses) are required to be on the meal plan, and most don't venture into Poughkeepsie to eat out. When they do, favorite eateries include the Mill House Panda (good Chinese food), Saigon Cafe, and Pizzeria Uno.

Trashed and Bashed

Despite the absence of Greek organizations, students say alcohol is both accessible and widely consumed. After all, Vassar was founded in 1861 by a brewer. Keg parties are commonly held in dorms, and must be registered with the university. Students generally agree that the administration's enforcement of the drug and alcohol policy is, in a word, "lax." Matthew's Mug, the on-campus bar, is open all week and is extremely popular. Aula, the campus dance club, is also a hot spot with students. Social nightlife at Vassar is often said to "revolve around the Mug and Aula." The Campus Activities Office, Vassar Student Association (VSA), and Vassar Campus Entertainment (VICE) organize many campuswide events, as do various student organizations and clubs. Also, each dorm throws a "campus party" during the year—another indication of the strong residential community at Vassar. The Homo Hop, the biggest and most popular dance of the year, is sponsored by one of the most vocal groups on campus, BiGaLa (the bisexual, gay, and lesbian organization). Teetotalers and nonpartyers can go to the weekend Blodgett film series, a play or concert on campus, a movie in town, or take the train to New York City, less than two hours away.

Passionate About Their Beliefs

Athletics definitely are not the first thing that comes to mind when thinking of Vassar College. While students do participate in an extensive intramural system, varsity athletes and school spirit are in short supply. The exceptions to this are excellent men's and women's volleyball teams, and competitive field hockey and lacrosse. Popular intramurals include rugby and ultimate Frisbee. The mascot, not surprisingly, is the Brewer.

> "In general, Vassar students are extremely tolerant and decidedly liberal."

If athletics are not Vassar's strong suit, the arts certainly are. According to one student, "There is a new production almost every weekend—theater at Vassar is intense." A strong interest in the dramatic arts isn't where it ends. Other arts-related campus activities include several bands, a gospel choir, more a cappella singing groups than any other college its size, improvisational theater groups, and a widely admired radio station. In addition, Vassar has an active outing club, the Black Student Union, Asian Student Alliance, Korean Student Alliance, a literary magazine,

and BiGaLa, among myriad other activities.

While Vassar students generally are active, one junior said that before she came to Vassar, students appeared to be genuinely interested in the community. "Now that I'm here," she lamented, "I don't think so anymore." Political activism is virtually nonexistent. A senior film studies major attributed the absence of activism to the lack of ideological tension: "Vassar is a place where most students share common beliefs—there is little tension here." Nevertheless, there is definitely a strong sense of social activism: students are concerned about such topics as gay rights, reproductive rights, and women's issues. The campus weekly, the *Miscellany News*, often publishes politically oriented articles, and students can keep up with national headlines in a small-scale daily newspaper, the *Vassar Daily*.

Vassar's campus is "beautiful," with two lakes and a golf course on the grounds. It is self-contained, separated from Poughkeepsie by a guarded gate, which creates a highly isolated atmosphere. Security is not a problem: all buildings are locked and an ID is required for entrance. There is a campus patrol, and emergency phones can be found all over the campus. Many students feel that Poughkeepsie is basically dead: "There's not much to do, there's no culture; all you can do is go to the mall." One student mentioned that "it's easy to get away—you just need a car." Town-gown relations are severely strained, and there is "resentment in the Poughkeepsie community," one student said. A junior psychology major mentioned the efforts of a select few Vassar students in their attempt to foster a positive relationship between the school and town, but expressed discouragement due to the "general sense of apathy at this place."

Vassar students hail from almost every state and several foreign countries, but the majority are from New York and California. Many students also noted the lack of cultural diversity. While one senior said the student body was "pretty homogeneous," he added that the "administration is working hard" to recruit minorities. Minority students at Vassar have a strong support network in the campus ethnic organizations and the Multicultural Center.

A common complaint is that the male to female ratio is a bit unbalanced: approximately 40 percent male, 60 percent female. Again, the administration is making efforts to attract more males, and based on recent matriculation rates, its initiatives have been successful. Students say the Vassar stereotype encompasses "freaks, homosexuals, eccentrics, and Deadheads," and the fashion prototype is "long hair, vintage clothing, and body piercings." In general, Vassar students are extremely tolerant and decidedly liberal.

"People here are passionate not only about their classes but about their beliefs," reported one student. "That's what I love about this place." Vassar students are proud of their school's genuine commitment to academics, the beauty of their secluded campus in Poughkeepsie, and the feeling of acceptance and freedom that pervades their environment. "It's empowering," one sophomore asserted. Vassar College is eclectic. In step with Vassar's lasting sense of tradition, afternoon tea is still served in Rose Parlor, only pearls and gloves are no longer required.

—*Siddhartha Shukla and Staff*

FYI

The three best things about attending Vassar are "the small classes, the beautiful campus, and the liberal attitude of the students."

The three worst things about attending Vassar are "there's very little to do on campus after 10 P.M., Poughkeepsie is the armpit of the world, and it's hard to find men to date (but easy to find women to date)."

The three things every student should do before graduating are "spend a weekend in New York City, eat at the Acropolis diner, go to the Mug—our one and only dance club."

One thing I'd like to have known before coming here is "how hard it is to keep yourself entertained in Poughkeepsie."

Wells College

Address: Route 90; Aurora, NY 13026
Phone: 315-364-3264
E-mail address: admissions@wells.edu
Web site URL: www.wells.edu
Founded: 1868
Private or Public: private
Religious affiliation: none
Location: rural
Undergraduate enrollment: 385
Total enrollment: 385
Percent Male/Female: 0%/100%
Percent Minority: 13%
Percent African-American: 4%

Percent Asian: 6%
Percent Hispanic: 2%
Percent Native-American: 0.5%
Percent in-state/out-of-state: 63%/37%
Percent Pub HS: 92%
Number of Applicants: 410
Percent Accepted: 90%
Percent Accepted who enroll: 37%
Entering: 135
Transfers: 32
Application Deadline: 1 Mar
Mean SAT: 580 V, 540 M
Mean ACT: 24

Middle 50% SAT range: 520–630 V, 490–600 M
Middle 50% ACT range: 22–27
3 Most popular majors: biological and chemical sciences, English, visual and performing arts
Retention: 80%
Graduation rate: 68%
On-campus housing: 99%
Fraternities: NA
Sororities: NA
Library: 248,130 volumes
Tuition and Fees: $12,300 in; $12,300 out
Room and Board: $6,100
Financial aid, first-year: 88%

Wells students are enthusiastic about their small community in Aurora, New York. Fairly compact and surrounded by Cayuga Lake and rolling hills, the rural campus boasts waterfalls, hiking trails, and small gardens. Students describe the campus as "wooded and peaceful." They rave about their interaction with professors, the history and traditions of Wells women, and the strong alumnae support.

Stellar Interaction

Students cite interaction with faculty as one of the best things about Wells. "They teach brilliantly and interactively. The faculty make the college experience worthwhile," one senior said. Students describe Wells as a tight-knit community where students are treated "with respect and understanding by professors." Undergrads report that they get to know their professors quite well, and it is not uncommon to go over to their houses for dinner, to babysit, or just hang out in their offices.

The range of academic possibilities is extensive and students have the option to create their own class or major. All students must fulfill distribution requirements by enrolling in courses in foreign language, formal reasoning, arts and humanities, natural and social sciences, wellness, and physical education. In addition, as part of the liberal arts curriculum, students must take a group of courses whose theme is "Learning for the 21st Century." Priority for registration is given by class, beginning with seniors. With the exception of creative writing and computer classes, students report that there is usually no problem getting into classes. Notoriously popular classes include Human Sexuality and Women and Sex in Early Modern Europe. Courses are described as rigorous, and one senior said, "Classes are rough and getting As is getting tougher." Another student called the grading "tough, but fair."

Small-town Living

The town of Aurora is about 25 minutes north of Ithaca, and students wanting a change from the typical Wells social scene generally go to Cornell University or Ithaca College on weekends. Students also go to Syracuse for women's studies lectures or other campus events. "Many first-years start at Wells thinking that it's going to be like a huge school. They see all the images of what a college is like and when Wells doesn't fit all that, they freak out," said one student. As one student explained, the people that Wells are right for are the ones who see that, in fact, Wells is

different—a small, all-female community, who "because of our location in the middle of nowhere are forced to come up with our own fun, thus creating very strong friendship bonds." Some activities Wells students create includes organizing dances such as Mainly '80s or Disco Dodge, playing sports on campus, and going to the Morgan Opera House in Aurora for plays. There are no sororities on campus and while students say alcohol is not hard to obtain, they also advocate there is no pressure to drink.

A Place for Self-Expression

Students describe Wells as a great place for self-expression and exploration. In speaking of student support for the lesbian and bisexual students on campus, one undergrad described the campus community as "very supportive of people's lives." Wells' minority population is small. Many students at Wells are from instate or the Northeast. Further, there are minority clubs and cultural activities on campus for support and learning, such as the United Women of Color and the American Indians in Science.

Home Is Where the Heart Is

Many dorms are actually old homes, each with their own unique feel. There are four residence halls, and a fifth is currently being renovated. Glen Park is the old home of Henry Wells, who founded Wells Seminary in 1868 for the "gift of female education." Students say it has a "homey feel," with a large, central kitchen, three floors of rooms, and a spiral staircase winding through the middle. Each room is different, but many have high ceilings and wooden floors. Leach is a more typical dorm, with three floors of rooms and a large central lounge. Dodge, a dorm built in the '60s, draws the most complaints for its age, but also inspires fierce loyalty from those that live there. Although it has smaller rooms, upperclasswomen can obtain singles in rooms meant to be doubles. Dodge hosts one of the biggest campus events, the Disco Dodge, in the fall.

Almost all students live on campus, since they need special permission to live off campus. First-year students are assigned "sisters" from each of the three other classes to provide guidance and friendship. There is also an RA system in the dorms. Recent renovations to the ever popular Weld House, a dorm used by students of all years, has provided Wells students with expanded Internet access, two 24-hour computing labs, and a network connection in every room. The renovations to Weld are part of a general $2.4 million dollar technology upgrade currently going on around the campus. Wells' students, by the end of the renovations, will possess the most up-to-date computer software and hardware with a student-computer ratio of 3:1.

> **"Students describe Wells as a great place for self-expression and exploration."**

Students must buy a meal plan of 19 meals per week. During the week, meals are served in one dining hall, though the Somner Student Center provides weekend brunch and Saturday dinner. Somner Center is open daily until midnight and the meal plan allots each student $50 a semester to spend there (they can also pay cash). Students say the dining hall has a huge salad bar, a deli bar, and for hot food, a meat line and a wellness/vegetarian line. Undergrads report that vegetarians usually have no problem finding something to eat.

Active Women

Sports at Wells have been improving. Wells recently joined the All Women's College Conference (AWCC) and now offers students the opportunity to participate on the field hockey, lacrosse, swimming, and soccer teams among others. Other athletic options include intramural basketball and volleyball, and there is a golf course on campus for student use, as well.

Rife with Tradition

Wells is famous for its traditions. Students are divided into odd/even classes depending on year of graduation for such events as the Odd/Even basketball game. Other traditions include the Junior Blast, where first-years hide the juniors' beds and leave clues about where to find them. Fall and spring weekend festivities feature bonfires and concerts, which in the past have drawn such acts as the SpinDoctors. Other traditions include a countdown of the last hundred days of senior year; seniors mark the first day of the countdown with a champagne breakfast and wear of their graduation robes. Bells are rung from Main tower to celebrate everything from the first snowfall to the marriage of a Wells woman.

Wells is noted for its consistent and strong alumnae support, and students praise the opportunities this support provides for leadership and internships. Wells offers a leadership week where alumnae help match students with internships in January for credit. One student said, "Our alumnae network is really amazing and it's one of the things that I think makes Wells women so successful. Alumnae feel indebted to the school and give by way of internships, which I think is one of the reasons why Wells women have such high graduate school acceptance rates."

Wells is not right for everyone, but for the student who seeks a school with strong academic roots and many opportunities to participate in tradition and form lasting friendships, Wells is a strong community. One student said, "This tiny school has a unique all-female environment. The atmosphere on campus is supportive and open—people can be who they want to be. I wouldn't trade my Wells experience for the world!"—*Laura Chaukin and Staff*

FYI
The three best things about attending Wells are "the small class sizes, the personal relationship with professors, and the internship opportunities."
The three worst things about attending Wells are "the weather—'I slid to class today,' the relative isolation, and the small library."
The three things that every student should do before graduating from Wells are "to take a women's studies class, to study abroad (popular destinations include England, Italy, Spain, and the Dominican Republic), and to JUMP IN THE LAKE."
One thing I'd like to have known before coming here is " the rich history of the area."

Yeshiva University

Address: 500 West 185 Street; New York, NY 10033-3201
Phone: 212-960-5277
E-mail address: admission@yu1.yu.edu
Web site URL: www.yu.edu
Founded: 1886
Private or Public: private
Religious affiliation: none
Location: urban
Undergraduate enrollment: 2,119
Total enrollment: 4,989
Percent Male/Female: 58%/42%
Percent Minority: 0%
Percent African-American: NA

Percent Asian: NA
Percent Hispanic: NA
Percent Native-American: NA
Percent in-state/out-of-state: 52%/48%
Percent Pub HS: 3%
Number of Applicants: 1,354
Percent Accepted: 84%
Percent Accepted who enroll: 69%
Entering: 788
Transfers: 71
Application Deadline: 15 Feb
Mean SAT: NA
Mean ACT: NA

Middle 50% SAT range: 510–630 V, 560–680 M
Middle 50% ACT range: NA
3 Most popular majors: psychology, accounting, pre-med
Retention: 84%
Graduation rate: 49%
On-campus housing: 100%
Fraternities: NA
Sororities: NA
Library: 960,000 volumes
Tuition and Fees: $14,920 in; $14,920 out
Room and Board: NA
Financial aid, first-year: 75%

Picture this—a sociology class begins with an admitted gang member lecturing on the hardships of daily life on the street, at a school that also requires its students to participate in programs of Jewish studies in the original Hebrew and Aramaic. Not possible, you say? Take SOC 1116, the Sociology of Deviance, at Yeshiva University and one day you may have one of the head gang members of the Latin Kings presenting the lecture.

A Rigorous Combination

As undergraduates, students at Yeshiva University pursue a full program of Jewish studies while taking college courses in the liberal arts, sciences, and business. Divided into Yeshiva College for men and Stern College for women, the university also includes the undergraduate Sy Syms School of Business, the Belz School of Music, Isaac Breuer College of Hebraic Studies, Irving I. Stone Beit Midrash Program, James Striar School of General Jewish Studies, and Yeshiva Program/Mazer School of Talmudic Studies. Most freshmen do not begin their years as Yeshiva students on campus in New York City. Instead, with the S. Daniel Abraham Israel Program, freshmen who want to spend a

year in Israel and concentrate on Jewish studies take courses at any one of more than 30 Israeli institutions. Upon their return sophomore year, however, the students must satisfy the university's requirements in three years instead of four— however, this does not seem to be much of a problem. As one student says, "I feel that the requirements are interesting and they help serve in providing a well-rounded education."

The Programs and Classes

Students explore diverse interests within 40 majors and may tailor their studies through concentrations and joint degree programs or by adding a minor. Yeshiva University is for all majors—from engineering to English. The school has a very respectable honors program that stresses writing and critical analysis, cultural enrichment, research, internships, and individual mentoring, along with a joint program with Columbia Engineering. Workload varies depending on your major, but overall "it's not too bad—except if you are pre-med."

Some classes are held very late in the day, and because Yeshiva is such a small school, popular classes close out quickly. However, this limited class size leaves little room for complaints about student–faculty relationships. Students are able to have very personal relationships with their professors. "I am very happy with my professors; they all love to teach," comments one student. And from another: "Professors are always willing to help a student strive for more knowledge." Such an enriching experience with faculty may be difficult to find elsewhere but is hard to miss at Yeshiva.

A Prime Location

While the campus is very small, Yeshiva has some beautiful buildings, ranging in style from Gothic to modern. Being smack in the middle of Manhattan gives the campus a different feel from the classic "grass and trees" atmosphere of many other schools. As evidenced by one student's complaint that "I wish there was more grass . . . all we have is one patch of grass," greenery is minimal. However, students also note that New York City's Central Park is a favorite destination. And of course, on those freezing cold, snowy days of winter, "walking to a class is never a problem."

> "The school has a closeness—all students feel as one not only because they are all Jewish but also because they are always ready to lend a hand to each other."

New York City offers the best of everything—from Broadway theater to kosher dining, from Manhattan's museums to the richest resources in Jewish history and culture outside of Israel. For the motivated and career-oriented students of Yeshiva, unsurpassed opportunities for internships and jobs on Wall Street and in the offices of the world's leading corporations and international organizations are just minutes away. The midtown Manhattan area where Stern College is located has all the attractions of downtown New York City literally at the students' doorstep. The Washington Heights area of Yeshiva College, however, has some crime problems. Campus security is known to

be tight, though, and a van escort service operates nightly.

Not Just Religion

Most students have part-time jobs, but they still find time to "do everything on the weekends—concerts, clubs, bars, sporting events, chill in Central Park." Undergraduates on the Main Campus participate in intercollegiate and intramural sports and physical education classes in the Max Stern Athletic Center, which houses a gym, the six-lane Benjamin Gottesman Pool, exercise and steam rooms, a track, areas for fencing and wrestling, and a lounge/recreation area. Intercollegiate sports include basketball, cross-country, fencing, golf, tennis, volleyball, and wrestling, while intramural athletics include basketball, floor hockey, karate, softball, and running.

Though school spirit could be stronger, most students are proud of their school's athletics: "The facilities are great and are always open, almost everyone plays on intramural teams, and there are tons of pickup sports games." There are also over 30 clubs and organizations, ranging from chess club and environmental society to philanthropic society and student government. Community service is big at YU, where many students visit the sick in a neighboring hospital and the chess club runs goodwill events to help those who are less fortunate.

Live Somewhere, but Eat?

The average freshman dorm at Yeshiva is a nicely sized square, and most students are happy with their living conditions, with the exception that they are "shoved in the middle of nowhere land." After freshman year, students can stay in the dorms (where there are residential advisors on each floor who are "awesome—they are very friendly and easygoing") or get an apartment. For those who remain in the dorms, Rubin dorm is *the* place to be. It is not only the newest but also "smack-dab in the middle of campus," making it close to all the main student attractions on campus: the cafeteria, gym, pool, sauna, steam room, track, and cafeteria store.

The harshest criticism of dorm life by the students comes as a result of a terrible meal plan "that we don't want, but there is no other option—we can't eat pizza or order out every day." Many students feel that they are ripped off for non-nutritious, overpriced food. One exasperated sophomore explained the dearth of dining choices by noting, "Vegetarians would not be able to survive—they are better off eating the tables for fiber." While the dining halls are clean, the hours are not suitable for many: "Whenever you actually need the store to be open, it isn't."

The best thing about not wanting to eat in the dining halls, however, is the desire and the opportunity to explore the whole city for other dining options. Manhattan has thousands of wonderful, easily accessible restaurants. A place often frequented by Yeshiva students is Timeout, "the official YU pizzeria." And it seems that everyone at Yeshiva and Stern has been to Dougies and Pizza Cave.

The Down and the Dirty

The student body at YU is composed of middle-class to wealthy students who wear very preppie clothing. Abercrombie, J.Crew, Gap, Structure, and Banana Republic are the common brands found on the campus, where "most students are fit and sexy." Although virtually all students are Jewish, many enjoy the diversity found within this homogeneous group. As one student noted, "The school has a closeness—all students feel as one not only because they are all Jewish but also because they are always ready to lend a hand to each other. There are many different types of Jews from all over the world; all these cultures come together to form a melting pot known as Yeshiva University." This very friendly campus, where people are always willing to be your friends, does not have a problem with drugs. "You can honestly say that drugs are not found on campus," says one student. Of course, because Yeshiva and Stern separate the men and the women, there are no random hookups on campus, though dates are very common. There is also "no sex, no STDs, no alcohol, no kegs, and no Greek anything." This makes for some nice clean fun, although students at Yeshiva still pride themselves on great private-apartment parties. —*Victoria Yen*

FYI
The three best things about attending Yeshiva are "the opportunity to study in Israel, the location in New York City, and the combination of both religious and secular studies."
The three worst things about attending Yeshiva are "the expense of living in the city, the heavy workload, and the poor facilities at Stern."
The three things that every student should do before graduating from Yeshiva are "go to Israel to learn; go to Grandma's Cookie Jar, a bakery on campus (the homemade chocolate chip cookies are *so* good); and take part in some of the charitable events—coat drives, charity auctions, peanut butter and jelly sandwich makings—that the students at the school offer to the community."
One thing I'd like to have known before coming here is "just how many married students I'd meet."

North Carolina

Davidson College

Address: PO Box 1737; Davidson, NC 28036
Phone: 704-892-2230
E-mail address: admissions@davidson.edu
Web site URL: www.davidson.edu
Founded: 1837
Private or Public: private
Religious affiliation: Presbyterian
Location: suburban
Undergraduate enrollment: 1,652
Total enrollment: 1,623
Percent Male/Female: 50%/50%
Percent Minority: 0%

Percent African-American: NA
Percent Asian: NA
Percent Hispanic: NA
Percent Native-American: NA
Percent in-state/out-of-state: 23%/77%
Percent Pub HS: 51%
Number of Applicants: 2,824
Percent Accepted: 38%
Percent Accepted who enroll: 42%
Entering: 455
Transfers: 11
Application Deadline: 2 Jan
Mean SAT: 658 V, 662 M

Mean ACT: 29
Middle 50% SAT range: 610–710 V, 610–700 M
Middle 50% ACT range: NA
3 Most popular majors: biology, English, history
Retention: 95%
Graduation rate: 90%
On-campus housing: 100%
Fraternities: 50%
Sororities: NA
Library: 440,000 volumes
Tuition and Fees: $22,228 in; $22,228 out
Room and Board: $6,340
Financial aid, first-year: 35%

Nestled quietly in North Carolina, Davidson College offers a challenging liberal arts education with an environment that is "really tranquil and beautiful." Often considered the "Pomona of the South," Davidson, a Presbyterian school 20 miles outside of Charlotte, is a close community of dedicated students and faculty.

Challenging Academics

Describing academics, one student said, "the professors want you to do well." Although students find the academics at Davidson rigorous, they have nothing but compliments for their accessible professors. Because classes are generally 20–30 students with no lectures and no TAs, Davidson students enjoy individual atten-

tion from professors genuinely interested in teaching, not just research. "They are really personal and are always sure to learn your name. If you're not doing well in their class they'll be sure that you get all the extra help you need," one student said.

Help from professors proves useful in tackling the challenging academics at Davidson. "The work is really tough, but doable," said one undergrad. "It can be really stressful. I work a lot more here than I did in high school." While Davidson students may be working a little harder than those at other schools, most agree that "the effort is really worth it and everyone else is working just as much so it feels like we're in it together."

Davidson prides itself in giving its students a liberal arts education. Like most schools, there are a variety of requirements in order to insure that students, at the very least, "learn a little about a lot of different topics." With required courses in English, Social Science, History, Religion and Philosophy, Mathematics, and Art, most students enjoy "taking classes they really wouldn't take the time to look at." However, as one physics major stated, "I really didn't want to take the required Religion course and that's one less class I could take of something else." In addition to major requirements, there are P.E. requirements as well. While some students feel weighed down by the large amount of required courses, the options Davidson offers make fulfilling the necessary courses much easier. "There is really a fair amount of flexibility with the academic requirements and you can do things like water skiing to fulfill the PE requirements," one student said.

> "People leave their keys in their car with the engine running, rooms are left unlocked, and twenty dollars would be left on the ground and would not be touched. That's nice to know."

Davidson offers a wide variety of respected majors as well as minors. This small southern school is particularly known for its premed program with one of the most popular majors being chemistry. "It seems like everyone here is premed," one student noticed. But despite the challenges that come with the premed curriculum, "everybody is so nice, not cutthroat like at other schools." English is considered one of the easier majors, "because while we [science majors] are slaving away in the labs every afternoon, they are playing Frisbee on the grass."

A Close Community

"You can strike a conversation with anyone here and people I don't even know say hi to me all the time," said one freshman. Descriptions of Davidson inevitably include the honor code and Southern hospitality. An integral part of the campus, the honor code impacts all parts of life. As one student described, "The Honor Code basically says that we must not cheat, lie, or steal and should report anybody who does. I've never seen anybody do any of that the whole time I've been here. People leave their keys in their car with the engine running, rooms are left unlocked, and twenty dollars would be left on the ground and would not be touched. That's nice to know."

There are complaints, however, about the homogeneity of the student body. "Everybody here is Christian, white, and either from North or South Carolina." While recruitment of international students and enrollment of students from other states is increasing, there is still a lack of diversity. Nevertheless, this lack of diversity does not keep the Davidson campus from having a diverse array of activities for its students. Besides writing for *The Davidsonian*, or *Libertas*, students are also involved in such organizations as Learn and Serve, a community service organization, the Dahn Hak Club, which teaches ancient Korean holistic medicine, or the Ultimate Frisbee Team. Additionally, the Intervarsity Christian Fellowship is very popular. Because Davidson is a Presbyterian school, most students are religious, and Christianity plays an integral role on campus. There are also 11 varsity sports for men and 10 for women at this Division I school, with Davidson remaining very competitive. The wide variety of activities is endless. "Its not hard to find something you like to do, what is difficult is choosing among all the possibilities and if there isn't a club for what you want to do, you can just start it up yourself," said one student.

Patterson Court

Centered on Patterson Court, a semicircle of houses and fraternities are generally considered the focal point of the Davidson social scene. Greek life is rather small; only a small number of men join the fraternities. Moreover, the administration has been deeply involved to insure there is no hazing. "In the fraternities here you must still pledge and be chosen by the fraternity brothers in order to join, but drinking isn't really a big part of the scene. There are a lot of guys who don't drink at all, then there are others who are big party animals." For women, there are eating houses, each with its own character. Approximately 86% of women end up joining one of the eating houses. While the food is thought to be "less greasy than Commons, there is a lot less choice, which is annoying." Eating house membership is done by lottery, which most consider is "really fair. You can also transfer easily if you want." Eating houses, fraternities, and the Black Student Coalition sponsor social functions, but non-members are also welcome. While some eating houses offer themed formals like "Heaven and Hell," the school administration sponsors independent social functions and formals that many students attend. The Grey College Union also sponsors performances by musicians and comedians as well as other events. Some recent performers presented by the Union include Hootie and the Blowfish, the Indigo Girls, and Chuck Davis and the African Dance Ensemble.

Davidson students certainly aren't lacking in spirit. Football games are very popular, particularly because of the team's recent good record, basketball games are also well attended. Besides going to Patterson Court, Union or attending sports events, some students drive 20 minutes to Charlotte, which "has some good restaurants and clubs."

Posh Living

"I loved the freshman housing," one sophomore said. While the freshman rooms are rather small and most of the furniture is built-in, "you get to meet so many people and there is such hall bonding." Most freshmen live in Richardson Hall living on five single sex floors. Others live in Belk Hall, which supposedly sports even smaller rooms. Sophomores live in "Sophomore City," comprised of three identical dorms. "I like the dorms except I live down the hill in Erwin, which is a 10 minute walk to classes," one sophomore said. Ninety-five percent of students live on campus, with rooms determined by lottery. There is no special interest housing and fraternities are non-residential. Nevertheless, by senior year, "you get these great suites with a living room and a kitchen."

The Town of Davidson

There are mixed feelings about Davidson, the town. Most students find it to be spirited and cute. With places like Ben and Jerry's, Summit, a coffee shop, and a Soda Shop, Davidson offers a few hangouts a very short walk from campus. But having only one main street, the town "can be really boring and if you don't have a car, it can feel restrictive."

One student said, "I chose Davidson College for its small town atmosphere, small teacher-student ratio, its value of service, its reputation of honor, and, above all, the amazing education the college offers. The atmosphere at Davidson is like no other I've experienced." While providing students with the best in faculty, facilities, and education, Davidson fosters a caring environment where students feel comfortable trying new things and continuing on with things they enjoy. Whether that be varsity sports, intramural athletics, religious fellowship, singing groups, visual arts, or dancing wildly on Patterson Court, Davidson offers it all. "Davidson is a place where you are assured to be challenged, not only academically but spiritually and socially as well." —*Jessica Morgan and Staff*

FYI
The three best things about Davidson are "the honor code, friendliness, and the academic challenge."
The three worst things about Davidson are "being far from a major city, lack of diversity, and lack of choice of eating house food."
The three things that every student should do before graduating from Davidson are "go to professors' office hours, go crazy on Patterson Court, and learn to throw a frisbee."
One thing I'd like to have known before coming here is "how hard I'd be working."

Duke University

Address: 2138 Campus Drive; Durham, NC 27708	**Percent African-American:** 9%	**Middle 50% SAT range:** 640–740 V, 660–760 M
Phone: 919-684-3214	**Percent Asian:** 13%	**Middle 50% ACT range:** 29–33
E-mail address: askduke @admiss.duke.edu	**Percent Hispanic:** 4% **Percent Native-American:** 0.5%	**3 Most popular majors:** biology, economics, psychology
Web site URL: www.duke.edu	**Percent in-state/out-of-state:** 14%/86%	**Retention:** 96%
Founded: 1838	**Percent Pub HS:** 66%	**Graduation rate:** 87%
Private or Public: private	**Number of Applicants:** 13,407	**On-campus housing:** 84%
Religious affiliation: none	**Percent Accepted:** 28%	**Fraternities:** NA
Location: urban	**Percent Accepted who enroll:** 43%	**Sororities:** NA
Undergraduate enrollment: 6,368	**Entering:** 1,630	**Library:** 4,500,000 volumes
Total enrollment: 11,589	**Transfers:** 97	**Tuition and Fees:** $25,630 in; $25,630 out
Percent Male/Female: 52%/48%	**Application Deadline:** 2 Jan **Mean SAT:** NA	**Room and Board:** $7,387
Percent Minority: 27%	**Mean ACT:** 30	**Financial aid, first-year:** 44%

K nown for its excellent academics, athletics, and party scene, Duke offers "an incredibly well rounded experience." Sometimes referred to as the "Ivy of the South," Duke offers the same rigorous academics and distinguished faculty as many of its northern cousins but "with a better basketball team and better weather." Although intense about their academics, students mostly compete with themselves and mutually support one another. This intensity and camaraderie are carried over to basketball, the second passion of Duke students. At Duke, students push themselves to the limit intellectually and socially, making the most of their time in the "Gothic Wonderland" that is Duke.

Y2K, Duke Style

Duke has recently instituted changes to its curriculum, making the academic requirements more stringent. The new Curriculum 2000, as these changes are officially termed, was launched in the fall of 2000 and affected all incoming freshmen. It requires that students take at least three classes in each of four areas of knowledge, which include arts and literatures, civilizations, social sciences, and natural sciences and mathematics. At least two of these classes must expose students to two different modes of inquiry and three focused inquiries. Under the new Curriculum 2000, students must also fulfill a writing and research requirement and must prove competency in a foreign language. Some of the freshmen affected by these new requirements were "not big fans" of the changes. One student said that the curriculum forces you to take classes you do not really want to take and allows much less flexibility. However, another freshman pointed out that even with the more restricting Curriculum 2000, there are no specific classes that are required, so the options are pretty open.

One area where options definitely abound is in picking a major. Students can choose from 38 existing majors, or, if they cannot find a something that matches their interests, they can opt for the alternative Program II. Program II allows students to pick their own topic and design an individualized curriculum with the help of a faculty advisor. Freshmen may also choose to apply to the FOCUS Program, a first-semester program that takes an interdisciplinary approach to 1 of about 20 themes. The students are in small seminar classes of about 10 to 15 students, with some of the university's most distinguished professors. One freshman said that while it was a rewarding experience, prospective applicants to the program should "know what they're getting into. It's a lot of work, and you have to be very dedicated."

For the most part, the workload depends on a student's major. For the many pre-med students and those majoring in engineering, the workload can be pretty demanding, even "overwhelming." However, those in other majors, especially such "slacker" majors as sociology, history, religion, and cultural anthropology, generally find the workload much more reasonable. Yet even pre-med students can balance their schedules by taking such gut courses as Introduction to Jazz, Introduction to Geology, or even Social Dancing.

Despite Duke's reputation as a distinguished research university for graduate work, undergraduates do not feel marginalized and professors generally get rave reviews from students. Said one student, "The professors make everything come to life, even in lecture classes." The legendary James Bonk, a professor of chemistry for over 40 years, is reportedly so great that students go to Chem 11L (aka Bonkistry) lectures even though it is possible to learn the material without going to class. The professors are "extremely accessible." They are eager to get to know their students and encourage students to meet with them, even outside of office hours.

Abercrombie, Fitch, and Duke

So you may wonder what Duke students are like. While most agree that there is no "typical" Duke student, there are some characteristics that seem to apply to the population as a whole. For one, the students are passionate about what they do, fully embracing the motto "work hard, play hard." "In everything, whether it's in classes, in debates, or at basketball games, everyone here is always intense," said one student. Another student stated that the student body was "overwhelmingly very attractive." Or, as a more modest student put it, "I'm not grossed out when I look around or anything." The reality of the situation may depend on personal opinion, but there is at least a consensus on one thing: most people at Duke care about their appearance. One student commented, "Everyone looks like they walked out of an Abercrombie and Fitch ad." The gym gets a lot of use, since everyone is "ridiculously healthy." Most people get dressed up to go to classes; girls generally wear skirts and sweater sets, and guys don khakis and button-down shirts. However, do not mistake a concern for appearance with superficiality, a characteristic that is not at all common to the Duke population. Students are routinely surprised with how "incredibly impressive" their peers are. Many people have rare and special talents, and you "constantly meet people who have done things that blow your mind."

Some students complain that Duke is a little *too* much like an Abercrombie and Fitch ad, with its homogeneity, but others praise the school for its attempts at recruiting people of diverse ethnic and socioeconomic backgrounds. While there may be a stereotype of "wealthy white kids who drive expensive cars," one student asserts, "Duke is not a school full of snotty little rich kids. A lot of students are on financial aid and work study." The geographic, ethnic, and socioeconomic diversity "makes [the school] a lot more interesting." However, despite the improved diversity, many still find that self-segregation is a problem. Although students say there is a lack of racial or ethnic tension, there is also a lack of interaction. This segregation even extends to housing, with many minority students choosing to live on Central Campus. However, people do defy this stereotype, choosing to interact with people of all ethnicities, so "it really depends on the person."

What Would You Do for Basketball Tickets?

Another thing that Duke students have in common is "amazing school spirit," which stems mostly from Duke's highly successful basketball team. Said one student, "If you're not at a game, you're watching it in your room." Students take their basketball seriously, which is manifested by Krzyzewskiville, or K-ville, a yearly tradition. Named after the basketball coach, *K-ville* refers to the tent city that springs up as students camp out to get tickets to choice home games. Students come days before school reopens to pitch their tent, and they camp out, or "tent," for weeks, enduring snow, 20-degree weather, and frequent "tent checks" in the middle of the night, which ensure that at least one person is in the tent at all times. The tenters are so hard-core that one student recalled receiving death threats after moving to the front of the line after discovering a loophole in the rules. At basketball games, the energy is "like nothing you've ever felt before." Some paint their bodies from head to toe in blue and white and others dress only in saran wrap. Basketball helps create a sense of community among Duke students. As one said, "You just warm up when people mention Duke. When you're away from school, and you see someone who goes to Duke, you just get a flood of emotion." Another student expressed similar sentiments, claiming, "We all love each other by association with Duke." (Just as long as you don't try to steal someone's tent spot, that is!)

Here a Greek, There a Greek . . .

The social scene is, for the most part, dominated by the Greek system. However, the excitement of toga parties and other such fraternity-sponsored theme parties is not limited to members of the fraternity. The organizations generally have a welcoming attitude, so those who are not in a fraternity or sorority do not feel left out. A student who does not wish to go to a frat party may opt instead to go to one of the bars on campus, which include Tap House and Hideaway, the latter of which "you can get served at with an ID that says you're 38." However, one student commented that Duke "does not exceed its reputation as a party school." This is due, in part, to a recent crackdown on underage drinking. East Campus, where freshmen live, is now completely dry. Distribution of alcohol has also become more tightly controlled. Kegs must be purchased through the university, and parties must have university-approved bartenders. However, despite these new regulations, it is "not at all" difficult for underage students to obtain alcohol. You just have to be "a little bit quieter" about it and not walk around with open drinks. Students often drink in their rooms before going out or get other people to get them drinks.

Joining a fraternity or sorority is not essential for making friends, either. Most people tend to stick by their friends from freshman year. One student said that 90% of his friends were from his freshman dorm. People tend to form a close circle of friends that can be cliquish at times. However, according to one student, "Everyone's open to meeting new people," although it may be easier to meet people in classes than it is in a social setting. Those who do choose to join a fraternity or sorority may find that it governs their social life. There are strong ties to fraternities and some students commented that there is limited mixing between guys in different fraternities and between the Greeks and non-Greeks. While the fraternity members are very accepting at parties, they tend to be aloof from the general population otherwise. Sorority members however, are not as exclusive, partially because the sorority members do not live together, as do the frat brothers.

> "In everything, whether it's in classes, in debates, or at basketball games, everyone here is always intense."

Okay, so you have friends, but what if you need something more? One lonely freshman lamented that a lot of girls come to Duke with boyfriends from back home, while the guys are notably unattached. However, prospective Duke students may be relieved to know that commitments are hardly a problem among the upperclassmen. In fact, the scarcity of them might be the only concern. Because of the intense commitment that Duke students have to their academics and extracurricular obligations, there is, "unfortunately," little time left over for dating. Casual hookups seem to be the only alternative to serious relationships. As far as same-sex relationships go, one student commented that there does not seem to be a large population of homosexuals at Duke, but that the general attitude is accepting. In fact, Duke Chapel just recently authorized same-sex marriages, which met with a loud student response, from both those who supported the decision and those who opposed it.

At Home in a "Gothic Wonderland"

Duke's sprawling campus, comprised of Gothic architecture and beautiful stonework, is set in the middle of a large wooded area. Students have nicknamed it the "Gothic Wonderland." One student said that the campus gives you "a spiritual feeling, whether you're religious or not," and that the "gorgeous" campus alone was enough to make her come to Duke. All freshmen live on East Campus. The housing is "decently sized," although only a couple of dorms have air-conditioning, and you have to pay a lot extra for it. Upperclassmen live on either Central Campus or West Campus, which is coveted for its close proximity to classes and also because it is ground zero for parties. A majority of seniors tend to move off campus. One of the advantages of being in a fraternity is guaranteed housing on West Campus, in the section of a dorm that is designated for the particular fraternity. A student may also choose to rush Selective Housing groups, which are coed and have certain themes, such as the Arts Dorm, Women's Studies Dorm, or multicultural Prism dorm. This also guarantees housing on West Campus. Most freshmen like the arrangement, claiming that the all-freshman East Campus makes the atmosphere "less intimidating." The only real complaint about the campus is that because it is so spread out, it is necessary to take a bus or car to get to classes, and both parking and the bus system are "major issues."

Students generally feel safe on campus, although they do not say the same about the surrounding city of Durham. What does Durham have to offer college life? Well . . . "plenty of opportunities for community service," as one student said. And although the beauty of the campus allows you to "walk around without a care in the world," many students do not do this, in-

stead choosing to involve themselves in such activities as Habitat for Humanity and tutoring in public schools. Other popular extracurricular activities include student government, a cappella groups, and intramural sports. Protest groups, such as Students Against Sweatshops, are also prevalent, and one student complained about them, stating, "A lot of it is protest just to protest."

Students do occasionally head off campus to see a movie, eat dinner, or go to a bar on weekends. Especially popular is Satisfactions, or "Satties," as it is also known, a restaurant/bar that is a big Thursday night hangout. Parizade and Georgia's are also major party destinations. Although these places are strict about carding, you only need to be 18 to get in. Those with cars may also take a short ride to Chapel Hill, which is a more active college town.

Although the bars of Durham may offer a change of pace from the frat-dominated social scene, many students do not find it necessary to go out to eat. With a flexible meal plan that allows students to use points to buy food from such places as McDonald's, Breyers, or the Loop, students can often satisfy their cravings on campus. And if students can't find what they want from any of the options on campus, they can get food delivered from almost any restaurant in Duke's vicinity.

All in all, Duke students tend to be well rounded, and although they are intense about their academics, they do not let it consume their lives. They are able to find a balance between studying, partying, and extracurricular interests. The unique combination of rigorous academics, extraordinary school spirit, and abundant parties, all encased within the lush Duke campus, creates "an incredible experience" that cannot be replicated at other schools.—*Elyssa Berg*

FYI

The three best things about attending Duke are "the attractive student body, the dynamic professors, and the kick-ass Greek scene."

The three worst things about attending Duke are "Durham, the bus system, and the ratio of random hookups to actual dating."

The three things every student should do before graduating from Duke are "tent, fool around in Duke Gardens, and climb the dome on top of Baldwin Auditorium."

One thing I'd like to have known before coming here is "how absolutely hard-core some of the pre-med students are."

North Carolina School of the Arts

Address: 1533 South Main Street; Winston-Salem, NC 27117
Phone: 336-770-3291
E-mail address: admissions@ncarts.edu
Web site URL: www.ncarts.edu
Founded: 1965
Private or Public: public
Religious affiliation: none
Location: small city
Undergraduate enrollment: 700
Total enrollment: 918
Percent Male/Female: 61%/39%
Percent Minority: 13%
Percent African-American: 8%

Percent Asian: 2%
Percent Hispanic: 2%
Percent Native-American: 0.5%
Percent in-state/out-of-state: 50%/50%
Percent Pub HS: 95%
Number of Applicants: 629
Percent Accepted: 47%
Percent Accepted who enroll: 60%
Entering: 176
Transfers: 138
Application Deadline: 1 Mar
Mean SAT: 560 V, 521 M
Mean ACT: NA

Middle 50% SAT range: 520–620 V, 480–600 M
Middle 50% ACT range: 20–26
3 Most popular majors: filmmaking, theater design/production, music
Retention: 69%
Graduation rate: 35%
On-campus housing: NA
Fraternities: NA
Sororities: NA
Library: 190,000 volumes
Tuition and Fees: $2,655 in; $11,283 out
Room and Board: $4,686
Financial aid, first-year: 63%

A haven for talented and dedicated young performers, aspiring film-makers, and theater production buffs, North Carolina School of the Arts (NCSA) is anything but a traditional college. With its highly selective admissions policy and hard-core artistic atmosphere, artists who end up at NCSA have to be intensely devoted to their fields. With no sports and no time for extracurriculars, NCSA is virtually all arts, all the time.

Lights, Camera, Acting!

NCSA is divided into six schools: Modern Dance and Ballet, Drama, Filmmaking, Music, Theater Design and Production (known as D&P), and Visual Arts. Students can apply to and enter only one of the six schools. All six have excellent reputations and get rave reviews from students: dance students praise the drama program, acting students can't stop talking about the dedicated D&Pers, and so on.

Along with courses for training in their field of art, first-year students have to take classes from a general curriculum known as general studies, or GS, but the classes are helpful since, as one D&Per explains,

"They relate to your major. An art student will take history of art, or a drama student will find it helpful to take English classes, whereas a scene builder is better off taking math." If the mention of the m-word invokes chills in your scene-building body, never fear. GS classes are "pretty easy," according to a second-year D&P major who is not a big fan of mathematics.

Most students find the faculty at GS to be good, but as one student observes, "Some of them just don't want to be there. They'd rather be where people care more about regular academics, because students here don't really care about general studies classes. They want to be completely focused on their art." Other students describe GS classes as "disappointingly unchallenging" and "not very worthwhile." A first-year acting student, however, says that he at least enjoys the classes as "a good change of pace."

Academic classes may take the backseat at NCSA, but don't be fooled—they may not be cracking textbooks and pulling all-nighters for papers, but students are worked to the bone in their artistic training and are expected to dedicate themselves seriously to their art. In fact, during second year the faculty "cuts," or dismisses, any students they judge to be unprepared for the level of dedication required for success at the school. If you ever wanted a chance to test your dedication as an artist, NCSA is it, and there is no warm-up period—it's intense from day one. "It's hard to get in, and hard to stay in," says a D&P lighting design major. "Freshman year especially they hammer you with a lot of work. It's tough." Dancers typically have classes from 8:00 A.M. to 5:00 P.M., and actors train from 9:00 A.M. to 6:00 P.M. If you think that's bad, check this out: D&Pers often pull "triple crews," working from 8:00 A.M. to 11:00 P.M. on a set. For NCSA students who are this passionate about their art, the intensity of the training is a heaven of hell.

Weak-Ends: Dead on Arrival

With the heavy workload during the week, NCSA students look forward to a more relaxing weekend schedule. Partying happens mainly off campus, since the school's alcohol policy is fairly strict. Furthermore, most students choose to live off campus after their first year because of cheap rents and lackluster dorms. Like the overall social scene, parties are pretty chill. D&P students have a traditional Friday night party called "Beers": each year two to four off-campus houses volunteer to alternate hosting the parties. A drama student describes them as "the same people at the same houses, drinking. Basically everyone who goes out drinks." There are also a few theme parties every once in a while, such as a recent '80s party. Students with ID hang out at the 1st Street Drafthouse, which a fourth-year D&P student describes as "*the* hangout—the only place you can go every night and find people out." Every student stresses that a car is a must-have, if possible, in Winston-Salem.

The Student Activities Committee does plan some events, such as a recent first attempt at a Winter Ball, but they're generally not very popular. "Student activities [don't] work at all, because [they're] really badly run," criticizes one student. One successful school-organized event is Beaux Arts, a weekend-long party before gradua-

tion. It includes special events and bands during the week, a carnival on Saturday, and a semiformal dance at the end of the week. One student describes it as "a lot of fun. We get to dress up, though it seems like the point is to wear the least amount of clothes possible." In addition to Beaux Arts, there are roughly 200 student performances each year.

Sketchy Meat

A common sentiment among students is that on weekends, the NCSA campus itself is dead. "A lot of people leave, since half the students are from North Carolina," says a fourth-year student. "There's no incentive to stay, so people just pack up." Winston-Salem also earns less-than-ecstatic reviews. "There's not a whole lot to do there," says one student. "It's a typical small southern city." Students describe Winston-Salem as "sketchy" and "shady," though the NCSA campus is described as safe. People usually venture off campus to eat, another activity for which a car comes in handy. Despite a snack bar and a cafeteria loaded with vegetarian options, "the food here is nasty. I don't eat the meat they cook here—it doesn't look right," says one student.

Artistic Integrity, Artistic Intensity

Because students spend so much time working with classmates in their own schools, they also tend to socialize primarily with them, too. Each school definitely has a stereotype, and there isn't much mixing between them. Also, with only about 700 undergrads, NCSA is "*very* small," adding to the competition within the schools, which one dance student describes as "pretty intense. Even if you're all friends, in the arts, you have to compete for parts, and in the end, for a job." Despite the competition, students are impressed with their classmates. "There's so much talent here, it's amazing," says a second-year student. "I never expected it." One student adds, "Everyone has the notion that people here are super artsy-fartsy . . . and they are. But it's not a bad thing. There are so many different types of people here, and it's okay to be different. That's the best thing about it." Students agree that they have a diverse group of peers.

Hot Student Bodies

The student body at NCSA is also above-average in terms of looks, partly because of the inherent attractiveness of dancers and actors. "Every single dancer is beautiful," says a ballerina, "and drama guys are hot." Even with the abundant hotties, one student admits, "It's hard to date somebody and work with them, and also since it's such a small school, nobody wants to date. They'd rather be good friends." Another student says that despite the dating shortage, "there is probably more sex than usual here. There are also a lot of gay people. It's a very good environment for someone who's gay—kind of like a gay oasis in the middle of the city."

Students have mixed reactions to the younger faces that sometimes appear on campus, those of the seventh through twelfth graders who attend NCSA High School. "They try to keep us as separate from them as possible, but generally people don't like it," says a dance student. Another student says, "At times it's pretty awful, but they're not allowed in our area at all. There are some benefits, like in our productions—there's a wider range of talent." A first-year drama student who happens to be dating a girl at the high school added, "At first I thought it was kind of stupid, but now I think it's all right."

"Everyone has the notion that people here are super-artsy-fartsy . . . and they are."

The annoying high schoolers and the usually lifeless weekend scene are a small price to pay for the NCSA experience. As one actor puts it, "My classes are really what's keeping me alive. They've given me a new respect for the art of acting, and this school has really improved me as a person. It's really exhilarating." Other students agree that the high level of professionalism and talent in this select community of dedicated artists makes NCSA as worthwhile as it is unique.

—*Patricia Stringel*

FYI

The three best things about attending NCSA are "the talent and dedication of the artists here, the quality of the programs, and the focused environment."

The three worst things about attending NCSA are "the lack of social life, the annoying high school kids, and the egotistical artists."

The three things every student should do before graduating from NCSA are "go see other departments' performances, go to Beaux Arts, and have a beer at 1st Street Drafthouse."

One thing I'd like to have known before coming here is "the slightly lame social scene, or lack thereof."

North Carolina State University

Address: Box 7103; Raleigh, NC 27695
Phone: 919-515-2434
E-mail address: undergrad_admissions@ncsu.edu
Web site URL: www.ncsu.edu
Founded: 1887
Private or Public: public
Religious affiliation: none
Location: urban
Undergraduate enrollment: 19,337
Total enrollment: 28,011
Percent Male / Female: 60%/40%
Percent Minority: 18%
Percent African-American: 10%
Percent Asian: 5%

Percent Hispanic: 2%
Percent Native-American: 0.5%
Percent in-state / out-of-state: 92%/8%
Percent Pub HS: 91%
Number of Applicants: 12,227
Percent Accepted: 62%
Percent Accepted who enroll: 47%
Entering: 3,553
Transfers: 1,085
Application Deadline: 1 Feb
Mean SAT: 577 V, 602 M
Mean ACT: 25
Middle 50% SAT range: 530–620 V, 550–650 M

Middle 50% ACT range: 22–27
3 Most popular majors: business management, electrical engineering, communications
Retention: 88%
Graduation rate: 65%
On-campus housing: 75%
Fraternities: 10%
Sororities: 9%
Library: 2,820,312 volumes
Tuition and Fees: $2,414 in; $11,580 out
Room and Board: $4,540
Financial aid, first-year: 42%

North Carolina State University is a school so large that few students have trouble finding a program that suits their interests. The school is especially well-regarded for its agriculture, architecture, and engineering schools. NC State is also the single largest research institution in North Carolina. Undergraduates claim that the size of the university is not overwhelming, and that it even has a relaxed and slow-paced environment.

The campus is located in Raleigh, the capital of North Carolina, and although it is definitely not a quintessential "college town," the city contains many rich cultural offerings such as the Museum of Natural History, the State Museum of Art, a repertory theater, and a symphony. Students tend to remain close to the campus, however, and spend most of their off-campus time on Hillsborough Street, which offers a variety of clubs, bars, bookstores, cinemas, and restaurants.

Heavy Workload

Freshman and sophomores must fulfill the requirements of their individual majors. Among the range of majors, engineering,

business, and pre-med are three of the most popular. Students ofter find the workload to be a little heavier than they initially expected. The School of Design is heighly respected and the engineering program attracts many out-of-state students who see NC State as a bargain compared to other private technology institutes. Engineering students seem to appreciate the wide variety of classes (14 different engineering tracks) offered in this department. One undergraduate described the academic setting as "both challenging and laid-back, yet without either cutthroat intensity or total laziness."

Parties Are Out of Control

Students say the laid-back environment of the school is conducive to an extensive social life. While some students feel that there is litte else to the social scene except drinking, others opt to go bowling or take advantage of Raleigh's museums and shops. Drinking is common among undergrads, and the alcohol policy is basically "ignored," according to one student. The administration is attempting to regulate off-campus drinking, since, as another student argued, "It makes the university look bad when [the students] trash residential areas." Fraternities often are held responsible for partying gone out of control. The Greek system at NC State is fairly large, but one student said, "You don't have to be in a fraternity or sorority to have a social life." Fraternities hold many parties, including the State Lawn Party in the fall, which attracts students from neighboring colleges such as Duke and Carolina.

Students at NC State take part in many extracurricular activities as well. Intramural sports are reportedly the most popular, especially among fraternity and sorority members. Religious groups, such as the Campus Crusade for Christ, and volunteer organizations like Habitat for Humanity have chapters on campus. At the performing arts center, a number of student theater groups give an average of two performances each per year.

The Union Activities Board also sponsors programs and activities in the Union Student Center, such as musical and theater production and debates that address current political, social, and economic issues. The board is divided into roughly a dozen committees, including the Entertainment Committee, which invites outside speakers. The Union Student Center is also a general meeting place for such organizations as the student literary magazine, the *Windover* yearbook, and the radio station. The campus also has two newspapers: the *Technician* and the *Nubian Message*, an African-American publication founded recently.

Diversity?

Some students voice concerns about the limited diversity among undergraduates, as well as the fact that different ethnic groups tend to isolate themselves from one another. The university administration reportedly is attempting to increase the diversity of the student population. Presently, about more than 80 percent of undergraduates come from North Carolina, and male students outnumber females. There are, however, international students from 97 different countries and an increasing percentage of minority students. The school has a wide variety of ethnic organization, and the Black Stu-

dent Board of the Union Activities Board sponsors an annual Pan-American festival that spans several days. Nevertheless, one student remarked, "When you walk into a class or dining hall, you can definitely tell what the racial situation is."

Generally, students seem to be tolerant of differences in beliefs and ethnicity, but this tolerance is not boundless. In particular, gay and lesbian student organizations have been, in the words of one graduate, "challenged by hatred and intolerance on campus." Anti-gay slurs have been spray-painted in the "free expression tunnel," a tunnel on campus where students are allowed to express their opinions with spray paint. Although NC State reportedly is working on incorporating sexual orientation into its non-discrimination policy, the school is, according to one student, "far behind."

Students report that NC State is dominated by conservative attitudes and beliefs, although many undergrads are not politically active. Popular political groups include the Young Republicans and student government, which organizes debate forums with the Union Activities Board. One student lamented the low voter turnout for the student government elections.

Varsity sports are a vital part of life at NC State. Most NC State athletic teams consider UNC–Chapel Hill their biggest rival. Both the basketball team and the football team have often been nationally ranked in the past and enjoy widespread support from students and alumni alike. Students commonly camp out overnight for football tickets, and the games themselves, along with the tailgates, turn the athletic events into social gatherings. Students report that school spirit is abundant, expecially in the annual football game against UNC. In the case of an NC State victory, celebrating crowds of students have been known to bring traffic to a halt on Hillsborough Street.

Sick of Brick

The university houses freshmen in one of 19 coed and single-sex residence halls across campus. Freshmen are guaranteed housing, and in the last few years the university has been able to guarantee housing to all undergrads. Housing is divided into four sectors: East Campus, which is NC State's orginal campus; West Campus, considered to be the most social; Lee and Sullivan, which are coed and have what some residents call "lax" regulations; and Center Campus, which consists of single-sex dorms. There are also theme dorms, including Alex International (in which international students room with American students for a cross-cultural experience), Arts and Creative Living (for students interested in fine arts), and High Technology (with computer hookups to the university mainframe in every room). Many of the dorms across campus do not have air-conditioning, but a few have been converted from hotels.

The campus itself is dominated by colonial brick buildings, and as one student said, "You will get sick of brick very fast." There is even a quad paved in brick called Brick Yard. Incongruous to the overall architecture is Harrelson Hall, whose circular structure stands out among the rest of the campus buildings. The campus has a wooded area for hiking and a hill called Court of the Carolinas, which is a popular site for picnics, sunbathing in the spring, and sledding in the winter.

> **Generally, students seem to be tolerant of differences in beliefs and ethnicity, but this tolerance is not boundless.**

Although the NC State campus might seem intimidating to students from small towns, undergrads say that they feel safe. The university provides an escort service along with other security measures. The citizen of Raleigh also have organized groups concerned with public safety and city awareness.

Despite some prevalent political views and similar geographic orgins, the NC State student body is too large to be homogeneous. Combining academics with a lively social scene and southern hospitality, NC State is attractive, expecially for in-state students. As one undergrad put it, "The lifestyle here is perfect!"—*Reid Lerner and Staff*

FYI
The three best things about attending NC State are "the crazy parties, the huge research facilities, and the fact that I am close to home."
The three worst things about attending NC State are "how this place can swallow you up, the dependence on alcohol for a good time, and the self-segregation that takes place."
The three things that every student should do before graduating from NC State are "chant loudly for NC State against UNC–Chapel Hill at the games, write for one of the papers, and hit the frat scene."
One thing I'd like to have known before coming here is "how this place is sometimes like a scene from *Animal House*."

University of North Carolina/Chapel Hill

Address: Campus Box 2200, Jackson Hall; Chapel Hill, NC 27599
Phone: 919-966-3621
E-mail address: uadm@email.unc.edu
Web site URL: www.unc.edu
Founded: 1789
Private or Public: public
Religious affiliation: none
Location: suburban
Undergraduate enrollment: 14,969
Total enrollment: 24,439
Percent Male/Female: 39%/61%
Percent Minority: 18%
Percent African-American: 11%

Percent Asian: 5%
Percent Hispanic: 1%
Percent Native-American: 0.5%
Percent in-state/out-of-state: 73%/27%
Percent Pub HS: 86%
Number of Applicants: 16,022
Percent Accepted: 39%
Percent Accepted who enroll: 55%
Entering: 3,396
Transfers: 1,244
Application Deadline: 15 Jan
Mean SAT: 610 V, 611 M
Mean ACT: NA

Middle 50% SAT range: 550–680 V, 560–670 M
Middle 50% ACT range: 24–30
3 Most popular majors: biology, business, psychology
Retention: 82%
Graduation rate: 62%
On-campus housing: 40%
Fraternities: 18%
Sororities: 18%
Library: 4,000,000 volumes
Tuition and Fees: $2,364 in; $11,530 out
Room and Board: $5,740
Financial aid, first-year: 26%

If you're looking for a school where there's tons of tradition, intelligent and fun-loving people, awesome athletics, and high-quality education, the University of North Carolina/Chapel Hill is the place for you. In the middle of a friendly town and distinguished by "gorgeous grassy quads, oak trees, and red-brick buildings," UNC entices students to fall in love with its campus and easygoing atmosphere. Says one student, "It's something you have to come to Chapel Hill and experience—it brings a smile to your face!"

Learn It All

Students at UNC/Chapel Hill get a broad education, regardless of what they choose to major in. "I think it's wonderful to be able to learn about things outside your concentration," says one student when asked about the general college requirements. In the spirit of a liberal arts education, students have "perspectives" to fill from different disciplines (i.e., math, science, philosophy, art, etc.) during their freshman and sophomore years. "They're a great way to expose students to a broader range of knowledge," according to one business major. Students must then declare their majors by the end of their sophomore years. Business and all science majors are competitive at UNC. Psychology is also popular, journalism and business are known to have good departments, and communication studies is labeled an easy major.

Class sizes vary according to level and subject. An introductory biology or economics course might enroll as many as 400, while English, foreign language, and math classes will generally have fewer than 30 students. Larger classes usually meet for weekly recitations of 15 to 20 students. "Getting into a class has never been a problem for me. Any student who demonstrates genuine interest in the course should have no trouble getting into it."

Even though UNC students may seem to be all fun and games, you'd be surprised at the amount of studying they have to do: "The workload is pretty challenging and there's a lot of pressure to do well." But the key is to take on a manageable course load. Tar Heels learn to "break it up over the semester and keep their work balanced with play. People here work hard *and* play hard!"

Professors and teaching assistants at UNC are "knowledgeable and interesting." One journalism major says, "I've had terrific professors and TAs during my time here." There seems to be a consensus among the students that if you seek the instructors out, they can be very resourceful. They're quite personable as well. Deb Aikat, professor of Electronic Information Sources, "uses a digital camera to capture everyone's face at the beginning of the semester. From then on, he knows everyone's name." Another well-known professor at Chapel Hill is Chuck Stone in the journalism school. He was the first nationally syndicated black columnist and was also a White House correspondent for ABC News.

Grade inflation has been an issue of concern at UNC recently. Some students say "professors are generally reluctant to give out A's," while many professors claim that inflation definitely exists. Although some attribute the higher average GPAs to the rising quality of the entering classes, many professors think that's no excuse and feel that they should raise the standards. However, many Tar Heels feel that any A's they get "are definitely well deserved."

As for special academic programs, "there are tons!" The honors program, the Burch Fellows Program, and the numerous study abroad programs are just a few. The Burch Fellows Program sends students to do self-designed research around the world. Some Fellows of the past have worked with "flying doctors" in Kenya, traveled to Northern Ireland to study conflict resolution, and worked at a camp for the deaf in Minnesota. "You can find so many different programs that provide the chance to study in a place you never dreamed of going to before at Chapel Hill."

It's Time to Get Your Groove On!

You'll never have a problem finding something to do at this school. Students, whether part of the Greek scene or not, "have a great social life." Although only 20% of the student body is Greek, they still have a visible presence on campus. Says

one sorority sister, "I think it's partly because of the fact that Greeks are so active, involved, and inclusive of the rest of the campus." Indeed, non-Greeks say that they don't feel left out of the social scene—"I'm not Greek and my social life is perfectly fine," says one student. Drinking is just as common as at most other colleges, although there has been a recent move to reduce it. The ALE is a prominent force at UNC to enforce drinking rules and catch fake ID users. "If you're not 21, it's hard to get into most of the bars uptown, unless there are mixers or special 18 and up nights . . . but that's not really a big deal because the uptown scene is focused on upperclassmen anyway."

Students at Chapel Hill get dressed up for the annual fraternity and sorority formals. In addition, there are theme parties throughout the year like the '70s, '80s, toga, beach, and luau parties. And you can't forget the infamous Halloween bash all along Franklin Street. People come from all over the state for this happenin' party.

But parties aren't everything at Chapel Hill. Students will often just use the weekends to "hang out with friends, sleep, and catch up on work." As for campus-wide organized activities, you'll find movies at the Union, lots of lectures with the different organizations all over campus, and tons of bands playing at the local concert hall. Vertical Horizon played on campus recently as well. Dating is a big part of UNC social life, but the 60-to-40 female to male ratio makes it an enviable challenge for the men. "Way too many gorgeous people around!" and "There are a lot of beautiful girls here" are just a couple of the comments students at UNC make about the attractiveness of the student body.

The Tar Heel

There seem to be mixed feelings about the diversity of the students at UNC/Chapel Hill. One student commented that "ethnically and personality-wise, the school is very diverse." Others think that the minority presence on campus is lacking. The school has been getting an increasing percentage of minority students each year, but some students also feel that "ethnic polarization exists." Since UNC is a state school, "so many people are all from the same geographical area... the South," comments one out-of-stater. With more than 80% of the undergraduate population from in-state, some out-of-state students say that it's hard to rush for the frats and sororities just because they "didn't have the connections the in-staters had."

The typical Tar Heel is "intelligent, involved, social, and incredibly friendly." Students come from both wealthy and middle-class homes and usually wear jeans and t-shirts to class. Most people participate in organized activities, with community service being one of the more popular extracurriculars.

The Sports Authority

Sports are also a very important part of the Tar Heel life. "This is a sports-crazed school," says one student. With 75% of undergraduates participating in intramural sports, numerous club sports, and Division I varsity sports, UNC students are on the whole "very fit." Students are great about attending games and cheering their teams on, especially when they're playing archrival Duke. Men's basketball and women's soccer are among the more popular teams at UNC, with basketball consistently among the top 10 and soccer winning the national championship recently. After basketball victories, the tradition is to have "huge, raging bonfire parties on Franklin Street." Sports at this school aren't just for the jocks, however. The gym facilities include tennis courts, swimming pools, and golf courses and are available for even the non-athletes who just want to stay fit and have some fun.

Living at Chapel Hill

Most students at Chapel Hill feel safe on campus. "Usually the only crime we have is theft that occurs when students don't lock their dorm doors," says one student. Tar Heels love the gorgeous homes, inviting streets, and friendly neighborhoods surrounding the campus. Movie theaters, restaurants, and shops draw students to Franklin Street. Some popular local restaurants are Cosmic Cantina, Hector's, Time Out Chicken, and Pepper's Pizza. As for on-campus dining, students seem to be pretty satisfied with services. Freshmen are not required to have a plan, but most

do since eating in the dining halls is a good way to socialize with others. Students are "okay" with the system and say that the dining halls are clean, although some "wish that they were open later."

> "I love Carolina . . . the people, the atmosphere, the classes, Chapel Hill, just life in general!"

UNC has a North, Middle, and South Campus. South Campus is relatively isolated, but since it's home to almost 50% of the on-campus residents, "it's a great setting to meet other people." North and Middle Campus predominantly house upperclassmen, transfers, and graduate students. Freshman suites are "pretty small but adequate." Residential advisors watch out for all of the freshmen, and "it really depends on who you get, but for the most part they're pretty cool." Some students live on coed floors, and undergrads can also choose to live in one of the theme houses, such as the Spanish House or the Women's Issues House. Many upperclassmen move off campus after their sophomore year, but "it's not abnormal to stay on campus all four years." Off-campus housing is "affordable and within walking distance," says one student. But regardless of where you live, there's a "real sense of community here at Chapel Hill."

Sweet Carolina

As the first state university in the U.S., UNC/Chapel Hill has many traditions. One student recounted the myth about "the Old Well," which stands in the heart of the campus: "It's said that drinking out of the Old Well on the first day of classes will earn you all As." Another landmark at Chapel Hill is the tree called "Davie Poplar." Students say that the tree has been around almost as long as the university and "as long as this tree stands, so shall the university!" Having been struck by lightning, today it is held up by a rod. "And just in case it does come down, there is always Davie Poplar Jr. and Davie Poplar III!"

Many students at UNC say they "wouldn't trade going to UNC for anything." With never-ending parties, hard-core academics, some of the best athletes in the nation, and the "friendly Carolina smile," Chapel Hill students know how to balance their fun with work. "There is no place I would rather be than here," says one enthusiastic Tar Heel. "I love Carolina . . . the people, the atmosphere, the classes, Chapel Hill, just life in general!"—*Jane Pak*

FYI

The three best things about attending UNC/Chapel Hill are "the variety of student organizations; basketball is HUGE and adds a lot to school spirit; and the campus is really easy to navigate."

The three worst things about attending UNC/Chapel Hill are "it's easy to get lost in the crowd, the majority of students are from in-state, so there's not as much diversity, and the advising system is really ineffective."

The three things that every student should do before graduating from UNC/Chapel Hill are "go to the UNC–Duke basketball game, spend Halloween on Franklin Street (the wildest party in the state!), and climb the Morehead-Patterson Bell Tower during your senior year."

One thing I'd like to have known before coming here is "that South Campus is the best place for freshmen to live because that's where most of the freshman bonding goes on."

Wake Forest University

Address: Winston-Salem, NC 27109	**Percent Hispanic:** 0.5%	**Middle 50% SAT range:** 600–690 V,
Phone: 336-758-5201	**Percent Native-American:** 0.5%	610–700 M
E-mail address: NA	**Percent in-state / out-of-**	**Middle 50% ACT range:** NA
Web site URL: www.wfu.edu	**state:** 30% / 70%	**3 Most popular majors:**
Founded: 1834	**Percent Pub HS:** 70%	business, psychology,
Private or Public: private	**Number of Applicants:**	biology
Religious affiliation: none	4,982	**Retention:** 93%
Location: suburban	**Percent Accepted:**	**Graduation rate:** 70%
Undergraduate	49%	**On-campus housing:** 100%
enrollment: 3,847	**Percent Accepted who**	**Fraternities:** 37%
Total enrollment: 5,892	**enroll:** 40%	**Sororities:** 51%
Percent Male / Female:	**Entering:** 979	**Library:** 1,300,000
49% / 51%	**Transfers:** 279	volumes
Percent Minority: 11%	**Application Deadline:**	**Tuition and Fees:** $21,420
Percent African-American:	15 Jan	**Room and Board:** $5,900
8%	**Mean SAT:** NA	**Financial aid, first-year:**
Percent Asian: 2%	**Mean ACT:** NA	25%

Tucked away in North Carolina, a state known for UNC/Chapel Hill and Duke, is another, smaller university that prides itself on both academic and social intimacy. With an undergraduate population of about 4,000, students at Wake Forest University feel that they receive a level of personal attention missing at their larger counterparts. Rallying behind their nationally renowned basketball team, Wake Forest students, despite their small numbers, make a lot of noise and are known to be one of the most spirited student bodies around.

Get Ready to Work

Wake Forest's small size provides its students with wonderful perks. Class sizes typically range from 20 to 40 students, and even the largest introductory lectures rarely enroll more than 100 people. These small classes allow professors to develop personal relationships with their students, and students love the attention.

This is not hard to believe, considering these small classes have been taught by professors such as Maya Angelou. Teaching assistants instruct very few classes, and instruction rather than research seems to be the main priority among all of the professors. One enthusiastic freshman exclaimed, "The teachers here are awesome, and I feel like I've really connected with a lot of them." When the weather is nice, as it often seems to be in North Carolina, many professors opt to get out of the classroom and hold class outside on what has been called "a nice and landscaped, green campus."

To enjoy the benefits of having such intimate classes taught by wonderful professors, Wake Forest students put forth a lot of effort to be prepared for class. Professors usually know their students personally and demand a lot of them. Participation is a must, and as one frustrated student said, "You just can't get away with stuff like not doing the reading, because of the small classes." However, Wake Forest students agree that they'd much rather get to know their professors than hide away in a large lecture hall. Moreover, many students say that if you want to avoid Wake's academic rigor, you should major in either politics or economics. You can also take off from Wake Forest for a term and participate in one of their many abroad programs in London, Tokyo, Venice, or Vienna. Conversely, students warn that if you major in philosophy, chemistry, or biology, you might as well "move your dorm room to the library."

> **"This is a work-hard, play-hard type of place."**

The only real complaint that Wake Forest students have about academics pertains to course requirements. Students have to take three classes in each of the following four areas: literature and arts, natural sciences and math, history, philosophy, and religion, and social and behavioral sciences. Freshmen must also take first-year seminar courses but have a variety of topics from which to choose. While the Wake Forest curriculum does ensure a liberal arts education, some students find these requirements to be excessive. One freshman feared that she would "be filling divisionals even after sophomore year." However, in general, students are in love with academic life at Wake Forest and revel in developing relationships with devoted professors who are experts in their fields.

Thank You, Sir. May I Have Another?

The social scene at Wake Forest revolves around the Greek system. As one sorority sister exclaimed, "Greek life is simply huge." Another student remarked that "athletes don't pledge, but pretty much everyone else does." In actuality, 50% of the student body pledge to either a fraternity or a sorority, and an estimated 85% rush at least one of the organizations. Interestingly, fraternities at Wake Forest do not actually have houses. Instead, they have what are called "lounges," or halls located in the basements of the dormitories. Weekends usually consist of what are called "hall crawls," where groups of friends go drinking and partying from one fraternity lounge to another.

Students feel that if you do pledge a sorority or fraternity, it is tough to avoid alcohol. One pledge stated, "Drinking is just a big aspect of Greek life." It is because of this drinking, one female noted, that "Wake Forest is not so much of a dating school as it is a drunken hookup school." However, the university does have a "kind of tight" alcohol policy, which students say resulted from a drunk-driving accident. If caught drinking underage, students can be fined, and repeat offenders can be kicked off campus. Yet students feel it is very difficult to get in this kind of trouble, as the majority of residential advisors "don't typically care about drinking." Other students note that there are many social alternatives to Greek life. Intramural sports and community service groups occupy a lot of students' time, and although many say the city of Winston-Salem is not too exciting, it does have a number of popular restaurants. Furthermore, concerts, comedy shows, and plays are constantly held on campus.

Surprisingly, for a school that is so academically demanding, many students often begin to "go out" on Wednesday nights. Yet students do not spend much time recuperating from "hall crawling," as they are up early studying the next morning. As one student said, "This is a work-hard, play-hard type of place."

Good Southern Living

The majority of students are pleased with their style of life at Wake Forest. Freshman rooms are described as "tiny, but big enough" and are scattered among the on-campus dorms. Many sophomores remain on campus but make an effort to live in the dorm of their particular fraternity lounge. Students are very enthusiastic about dorm life and say "it creates great friendships." Juniors and seniors are more likely to live off campus in one of the many condominium complexes that surround the university or in one of Wake Forest's theme houses. However, the majority of students are so content with campus housing, they live there for all four years. Adding to this happiness is the fact that students are allowed cars for all four years and, while many do have automobiles, others note that it is easy to get by without one. Furthermore, campus athletic facilities are all top-of-the-line, and the new Benson Center provides a great place for students to hang out.

The food at Wake Forest is considered good, but students do complain about the lack of variety in dining. Unfortunately, just as the food at Wake Forest lacks assortment, so does its student body. While students do not tend to form cliques or self-segregate, diversity is an issue on campus. One freshman characterized the majority of her student body as being "preppy, white, and Republican." The university does recognize this as one of its faults and is making concerted efforts to attract minority students. In the meantime, however, Wake retains what one student called "a 'WASPy' reputation."

The Spirit of the Demon Deacons

Perhaps the most exciting time of the year at Wake Forest is basketball season. Known as the Demon Deacons, the Wake Forest basketball team is consistently ranked in the top 25 in the nation and has graduated members who go on to play professionally, including NBA star Tim Duncan. Such a high level of competition brings the students out to cheer on their Deacons en masse. One avid fan said, "Hoops is just awesome and everyone has extreme team spirit." After victories, students run back to their campus and do what they call "rolling the quad." This consists of covering Wake Forest's absolutely gorgeous campus with rolls of toilet paper. However, even when the basketball team is not in season, Wake Forest provides constant excitement for its students, and its high academic standards make it one of the best universities in the country. —*Jonathan Levy*

FYI
The three best things about attending Wake Forest are "home basketball games, the small class sizes, and hall crawling."
The three worst things about attending Wake Forest are "Winston-Salem can be a bore; the prevalence of alcohol, if that's not your thing; and too few parking spaces."
The three things that every student should do before graduating from Wake Forest are "streak the quad, go to a home basketball game, and see the great state of North Carolina."
One thing I'd like to have known before coming here is "that such smart people can party so hard."

North Dakota

University of North Dakota

Address: Enrollment Services; Box 813; Grand Forks, ND 58202
Phone: 701-777-4463
E-mail address: enrolser @sage.und.nodak.edu
Web site URL: www.und.edu
Founded: 1883
Private or Public: public
Religious affiliation: none
Location: small city
Undergraduate enrollment: 8,680
Total enrollment: 10,590
Percent Male / Female: 50% / 50%
Percent Minority: 6%
Percent African-American: 0.5%

Percent Asian: 1%
Percent Hispanic: 1%
Percent Native-American: 3%
Percent in-state / out-of-state: 66% / 34%
Percent Pub HS: NA
Number of Applicants: 2,928
Percent Accepted: 70%
Percent Accepted who enroll: 86%
Entering: 1,754
Transfers: 665
Application Deadline: rolling
Mean SAT: 559 V, 562 M
Mean ACT: 23

Middle 50% SAT range: 480–630 V, 510–630 M
Middle 50% ACT range: 19–24
3 Most popular majors: nursing, business, criminal justice
Retention: 75%
Graduation rate: 46%
On-campus housing: 60%
Fraternities: 13%
Sororities: 9%
Library: 176,259 volumes
Tuition and Fees: $2,956 in; $7,098 out
Room and Board: $3,406
Financial aid, first-year: 61%

Providing an affordable, first-rate education in a safe and comforting environment, the University of North Dakota is hailed by its students as "a wonderful place filled with opportunity and encouragement." In the "pleasant" but sometimes "boring" town of Grand Forks, UND attracts students from across the country because of its exceptional aeronautics program. With such offerings as a Burger King in the student union, a nationally ranked hockey team, and sponsored performances by country music stars, students enjoy their time at UND despite the below-zero temperatures and abundance of snow.

Pre-professional Focus with Liberal Arts Foundations

Noted for its outstanding pre-professional programs as well as its liberal arts emphasis, the academics at UND are appreciated by students as "challenging but supportive." Engineering and pre-med are considered most difficult, while the aeronautics program is thought to be "easy but kind of expensive." Other reputable degrees include nursing, communication, and physical therapy. General education requirements mandate that all students take two composition classes and complete a certain number of classes in humanities and sociology departments.

Students believe their class sizes to be "much smaller than other big universities," with intro classes rarely exceeding 150 students and most classes numbering 15 to 25. The staff is thought to be "very supportive and accessible" as well as "quite knowledgeable and informative." Science lectures break down into lab sections, and professors are "always willing to help."

Furthermore, students claim no difficulty getting into their desired classes.

White Winters and a Colorful Campus

Every spring the university makes a great effort to brighten campus, planting thousands of flowers and giving the place a "really green look." While the winters, according to one, are "way too cold" and many complain that the school does not properly equip the students with means to fight the cold (few tunnels and car plug-ins), most students generally enjoy campus living. Swanson is known to be the nicest dorm, with bathrooms in every suite, and few undergrads complain about their rooms. Nevertheless, most upperclassmen live off campus. "If you are not involved in a fraternity or sorority and have the option of getting off campus, there is little keeping you on campus," remarked one junior.

> **"So many girls are way too interested in marriage."**

While the school itself is "very nice," "the town sucks," claimed a freshman. "It is so boring and flat and ugly." The town and the school come together every year for Spring Fling. Traditionally, a band played on the town green while students partied; however, recently the concert has been moved onto campus, and now "everyone just stays on the green and parties."

Athletics Above All

Although it may be best known for its athletic teams, the University of North Dakota offers countless other extracurricular opportunities to students. In fact, many groups have great difficulty sustaining membership because of the sheer number of possibilities. Pre-professional organizations report the highest levels of membership, as extracurricular involvement reflects student motivation and academic enrichment. In addition, many students work and "run out of time for extracurriculars," said one junior. The most popular activities include intramural and club sports, and others find time for literary or theatrical pursuits.

Regardless, students and community members rally around athletic events. With all students receiving free passes to games, the school pride at UND is evident in almost all athletic events. The Hyslop Athletic Center offers classes and exercise facilities to students wishing to release some tension and stress after class. Everything from dance classes, to swimming, to aerobics is offered in this Division I training center.

Booze and Marriage

Students have varied opinions about the social climate of UND. Many praise the "close-knit community feeling" that the campus and town provide, while believing the students to be "some of the friendliest people you could ever meet." Others, however, find their school to be "very limited in social opportunities." "The campus is very cliquey," reported one sophomore girl. "Everywhere you go you see the same people doing the same thing and everyone talks way too much." Still others find UND to be very preppy in comparison to its more agriculturally oriented interstate rival North Dakota State.

Most agree that drinking is big at UND. "It is so cold during the winter and generally pretty boring in the middle of nowhere, so there is nothing else to do," remarked one senior. Greek life is popular but hardly necessary to have a good time. Athletic events are as much social events as demonstrations of school spirit, with "everyone wasted every weekend."

Above all, UND's affordable education and liberal off-campus housing opportunities attract many students who are married or interested in getting married soon. Some undergraduate males complain that "so many girls are way too interested in marriage" but approve of the social opportunities nonetheless. It is fairly uncommon to find interracial or homosexual couples in the fairly homogeneous white middle-class student body, although the 10% Club was recently formed to promote the acceptance of homosexuality on campus.

For whatever reason they chose to come, most students are genuinely happy with their life at UND and enjoy an intimate but nationally conscious college experience. —*Emily Barton*

FYI

The three best things about attending UND are "the convenience of getting to classes on the small campus, the wide range of cultural activities, and the great professors."

The three worst things about attending UND are "the cold, the town of Grand Forks, and a somewhat limited curriculum."

The three things that every student should do before graduating from UND are "go to a hockey game, eat a red pepper, and get wasted at Spring Fling."

One thing I'd like to have known before coming here is "just how cold the winter can get."

Ohio

Antioch College

Address: 795 Livermore Street; Yellow Spring, OH 45387
Phone: 937-767-6400
E-mail address: admissions @antiochcollege.edu
Web site URL: www.college.anitoch.edu
Founded: 1852
Private or Public: private
Religious affiliation: none
Location: rural
Undergraduate enrollment: 595
Total enrollment: 624
Percent Male/Female: 34%/66%
Percent Minority: 12%
Percent African-American: 6%

Percent Asian: 2%
Percent Hispanic: 3%
Percent Native-American: 1%
Percent in-state/out-of-state: NA
Percent Pub HS: NA
Number of Applicants: 465
Percent Accepted: 85%
Percent Accepted who enroll: 30%
Entering: 119
Transfers: NA
Application Deadline: rolling
Mean SAT: 509 V, 495 M
Mean ACT: 24

Middle 50% SAT range: 540–670 V, 520–600 M
Middle 50% ACT range: 25–28
3 Most popular majors: psychology, visual arts and literature/creative writing
Retention: 74%
Graduation rate: 60%
On-campus housing: 100%
Fraternities: NA
Sororities: NA
Library: 300,000 volumes
Tuition and Fees: $21,628 in; $21,628 out
Room and Board: $4,176
Financial aid, first-year: 73%

Peace studies in Tibet. Brazilian rain forest ecology. The circus. Students at Antioch regularly participate in such eclectic programs—and all for credit! Co-op credit, that is.

Interesting Academics

One of the many distinctive features of Antioch College is its co-op program, which requires students to take classes on campus for two of the four terms each year (fall, winter, spring, summer), and go on co-ops, which are similar to work-study programs, for the other two. Students have high praise for the co-op program; in fact, many cite it as their main reason for attending Antioch. "It gives me credit and experience doing real things," said one student. Antioch recently switched from a semester to a trimester system, which changes the number of course and co-op credits required of each student. First-year students generally spend the fall and winter terms on campus, and then do co-ops in the spring and summer. After the first year, students can design their own program of work and study, choosing when they will be on campus and when they will be on co-op. The co-op office is filled with resources and information about students' experiences on co-ops from previous years. Students are assigned a co-op advisor, but many find their specific program advisor to be more helpful.

Students can choose to go on virtually any co-op they like, although at least one must include studying a culture other than one's own. Many students fulfill this requirement by doing a co-op overseas; however, it is possible to do a domestic field program, such as examining the African-American experience in the Deep South. Most students try to relate their co-op to their major, but this connection is not required. Undergrads can study peace processes in the Middle East, work at a center for missing children in Minnesota, or run the lights and electronics for a circus, as one student recently did. While students thoroughly enjoy the Antioch co-op experience, they warn that it is intense. "Antioch is a full-year commitment," explained one student. "You don't have summers free, because you are either studying or on co-op." Consequently, it is "easy to get off track from a four-year plan," said one second-year student. "It's common to spend five years here."

Academics at Antioch are generally strong, although students are more attracted to the co-op program than to specific departments. Nonetheless, psychology environmental science, communications, and women's studies are all well regarded, while the education and music departments are said to be weaker. Students must demonstrate competence in a foreign language, and either pass or place out of a quantitative reasoning course. Students can pre-register for up to three classes over the summer. The small student-faculty ratio allows for a "very personalized education," according to one second-year student. Most classes enroll 10 to 15 students. "The largest class I've heard of had 40 people," said one student.

Campus Facilities

While the co-op program receives praise, students are less enthusiastic about the facilities on campus. Most of the facilities are reportedly "old and decrepit, but still useful," said one student. The Olive Kettering Library "looks ancient and smells of old books," according to one first-year. The librarians are said to be helpful, although students agree that the library needs new resources. The periodicals holdings are extensive, but students find the collection of newer books to be rather limited, which some attribute to financial limitations. "The library has been enlarged five times and we still need another, but there is no money," one student complained. Consequently, students tend to study in their rooms, or take a 20-minute car ride to the largest nearby library at Wright State University. Other buildings on campus, however, have been renovated recently, including South Hall (home to the co-op office and library), a computer center for students with learning disabilities, and various classrooms.

The majority of Antioch students live on campus. Dorms vary widely in terms of facilities and themes. Presidents dorm has mostly singles, permits alcohol inside, is quiet, smoke-free, and has hall kitchens. West does not have kitchens, but permits smoking. Birch is widely known as a party dorm; North houses primarily first-years and transfers; and Units is a new group of dorms supposedly "so clean they're sterile," in the words of one North resident. Spalt has different language halls, and is located in the International Building, which has classrooms downstairs from the dorm rooms. Some dorms are single-sex, and since there are more women than men at Antioch, there are more all-female than all-male dorms. Like many other buildings at Antioch, the dorms generally are "run-down, but safe," one student said. Most dorms do not have phone connections for each room; residents share one common phone per hall instead. In addition, each hall also has its own common area.

Unusual Social Life

Because of the co-op program, only half of the Antioch student population is on campus at any given time. There are no varsity sports at Antioch, but intramurals such as softball and Frisbee are popular. Politically, the student body is decidedly liberal, and extracurriculars include animal-rights and environmental organizations, as well as a Winnie-the-Pooh support group established solely as "an excuse to act silly and make people feel good," in the words of one member. Media enthusiasts can write for Antioch's weekly paper, *The Record*, or work at one of the two radio stations on campus—WYSO (the official school station) or AntiWatt (a smaller, pirate station). The Lesbian, Gay, and Bisexual Center (LGBC) is extremely popular; one student said it sometimes seems as if "about half of campus is homosexual." The center sponsors dances and potlucks, among other activities.

Frequenting the Caf

The LGBC is located in the Student Union, which also houses the women's center, a TV and video lounge, practice rooms for bands, and a space to hold dances. The cafeteria, known as "the Caf," is also located in the Student Union, as is the C-Shop, the campus coffee shop. The food on campus is reportedly "not bad"—good news for first-years and transfers, who are required to buy a full plan of 19 meals per week. The Caf offers a plethora of options for vegans and vegetarians, including a tabbouleh and hummus bar. The C-shop is popular, but serves only snack foods. Off campus, students eat at Haha's Pizza, Sunrise Cafe, and Carol's Kitchen. The Tavern, reportedly one of the oldest standing buildings in Ohio, as well as Current Cuisine and Chill Lights, also earn student praise.

> **"What is mainstream here makes us freaks to the rest of the world."**

Parties happen almost every night, according to one second-year, but Friday is considered the biggest social night. A first-year described a typical weekend as "go out Friday, sleep Saturday, homework Sunday." Antioch students tend to have small get-togethers in each other's rooms, or go to dances held in the student union every Wednesday and Saturday. To get away from the small town of Yellow Springs, students can travel to Dayton for clubbing. The Wellness Center, which exists to improve students' mental and physical well-being, also sponsors dances and shows movies every Friday. Social activity at Antioch often has a political edge: the annual Drag Ball Halloween dance, for example, has led to an entire weekend focused on gender issues, with speakers brought in by the Wellness Center. Div dances, which bring together students from the on-campus and co-op divisions, take place at the end of each quarter.

Sexuality Taken Seriously
The Antioch administration made national headlines with its sexual harassment policy, requiring students to request permission from their partners before engaging in any sexual act. Although the policy has disappeared from the headlines, students still "joke about the hooking-up policy, though it's nice to have as a

backup," said one first-year. Another student praised the sexual harassment policy for its ability to "open up the community" and make issues like safer sex more prominent. "All bathrooms now have safe-sex packages with everything you could ever need, so there is really no excuse for not having safer sex here," she said.

Regarding alcohol and other drugs, the administration is "lax, to say the least," according to one second-year. Students report that the main security issue is bike theft, and that the security guards tend to "baby-sit," rather than enforce alcohol rules.

Student Body
Antioch's Community Council, which consists of elected student and faculty members, sponsors weekly community meetings open to all staff, faculty, students, and administrators. The meetings are a time to "voice concerns, make proposals to the community government, or just hang out and eat ice cream," said one council representative.

Students at Antioch describe themselves as "radical," which is probably not an exaggeration. A liberal school tends to have liberal students, and Antioch students are "honest, if nothing else," said one first-year. While Antioch draws applicants from most of the continental U.S. and partakes in an exchange program with Kyoto-Seika University, a sister college in Japan, students reported that the majority of their classmates are white. The general opinion at Antioch, according to a second-year, is "whatever goes, goes, as long as you're cool and respectful." To put that in perspective, she added that "what is mainstream here makes us freaks to the rest of the world." Antioch students are content with their "freakish" community. While one student admitted that the constant moving between co-ops and campus is "tiring," she added that the frequent change meant that "there are always different people on campus, which is exciting." The unusual opportunity for free expression in personal life and in academics may be "too unique" for some, one student warned, but for those who can handle it, the Antioch experience is unparalleled. —*Staff*

The three best things about Antioch are "the co-op program, the opportunity to get hands-on experience, small class size."

The three worst things about Antioch are "the decrepit buildings, the poorly stocked library, and an unconventional schedule."

The three things that every student should do before graduating from Antioch are "go on some exotic co-op, go to the a Div dance, and go clubbing in Dayton."

One thing I wish I'd known before coming here is "how the co-op schedule makes it hard to always be at school at the same time my friends are."

Bowling Green State University

Address: 110 McFall Center; Bowling Green, OH 43403
Phone: 419-372-2086
E-mail address: admissions@bgnet.bgsu.edu
Web site URL: www.bgsu.edu/welcome
Founded: 1910
Private or Public: public
Religious affiliation: none
Location: rural
Undergraduate enrollment: 15,040
Total enrollment: NA
Percent Male/Female: 43%/57%
Percent Minority: 7%
Percent African-American: 4%

Percent Asian: 1%
Percent Hispanic: 2%
Percent Native-American: 0%
Percent in-state/out-of-state: 92%/8%
Percent Pub HS: NA
Number of Applicants: 9,483
Percent Accepted: 92%
Percent Accepted who enroll: 42%
Entering: 3,664
Transfers: NA
Application Deadline: 15 Jul
Mean SAT: 552 V, 523 M
Mean ACT: 22

Middle 50% SAT range: 460–570 V, 460–570 M
Middle 50% ACT range: 19–25
3 Most popular majors: education, business and nursing
Retention: 78%
Graduation rate: 26%
On-campus housing: NA
Fraternities: 15%
Sororities: 11%
Library: 4,200,000 volumes
Tuition and Fees: $3,870 in; $9,158 out
Room and Board: $4,392
Financial aid, first-year: 55%

While for one weekend each year, it is the internationally revered home of the World Tractor Pulling Championships, the town of Bowling Green is perhaps best revealed through its offering of a solid and dynamic liberal arts education to the students of Bowling Green State University.

An Academic Myriad

With over 160 majors including everything from Glass, Popular Culture, and Fiber/Fabric to the more commonly seen Humanities, Arts, and Sciences, it is rare to find a student who cannot find a personal course of study at BGSU. While almost all academic programs are regarded as strong and marketable, the most popular majors among undergraduates are biology, psychology, and the renown and competitive education program. Several options are available to fulfill each student's needs, including self-designed majors, double majoring, an honors program, and several pre-professional programs. Getting into classes is not typically regarded as a problem. One student noted that being shut out is particularly unlikely "if you get on waiting lists immediately and actually talk to people to get strings pulled." Another student liked the fact that he could easily take classes outside his major, such as dance and theater. Students generally praise most of their professors, even when they have problems communicating with them. "My English teacher barely speaks English," said one undergraduate. "We are always asking him to repeat what was said and say it slower, but he's a good sport about it." Another undergraduate was impressed by the fact that her professors "remembered [her] name, and who I was." Students noted several creative assignments, including everything from "stand in front of a mirror naked and watch yourself" to "just relax for the weekend."

The Living Experience
The rules at BGSU dictate that freshman and sophomores are required to either live on campus or with their parents, although the general consensus is that "everyone gets around them." Almost 60% of BGSU students live off campus, as apartments are widely available close to campus. Rent can be rather high, though students say the experience is worth it. For those students who live on campus, coed dorms of single and double rooms are the norm. However, special housing for honors students, musicians, and other special interest groups are available, as well as housing in any of the 35 fraternities and sororities. Every dorm has its definite set of rules, and while some halls strictly enforce these regulations, others barely acknowledge their presence. Each student living in a residence hall is required to purchase a meal plan (students in the Anderson or Bromfield halls are exempted) which can be used at any dining hall on campus, as well as at a local convenience store. But as one student observed, "A box of Lucky Charms costs over five bucks!" The Sundial has been noted as "the best place to eat, but it's mass chaos at mealtime."

Students tend to be pleased with the overall experience and appearance of campus. The trees and landscape are frequently praised, and while the weather is notorious for being bitter cold, students note that the fall and winter seasons enhance the natural beauty of the area. The student union, a main center of activity on campus, is being closed as a new, improved facility is to be opened in two years that will accommodate the massive growth the school has experienced since the original building was built in 1958. An old cemetery marks the middle of campus, a landmark which most students find interesting and compelling. There is a myth regarding the ghost of a woman who haunts Hanna Hall, "Supposedly," one student reported, "the ghost must be invited to every theater production or something bad will happen during the play, so every year they personally invite her."

> "Supposedly," one student reported, "the ghost must be invited to every theater production or something bad will happen during the play, so every year they personally invite her."

The town of Bowling Green integrates with parts of the university, and undergraduates say that the relations between the town and school are comfortable and friendly. Most students work, be it on or off campus, which when combined with the great number of commuters makes for definite frustration with the lack of space in the parking lots. One student noted that sometimes it took him over half an hour to get to his car from his residence hall. Students who work exceptionally late hours can apply for special permits which allow them to park nearer their dorm. During the nighttime hours, some tend to be wary of the apparent lack of security and lighting while others commented that they did indeed feel safe on campus.

When Friday Comes . . .
For BGSU students, weekends can mean almost anything: partying at a frat or private apartment, clubbing in either Bowling Green or nearby Toledo, working out at the gym (a greatly acclaimed facility) or playing intramurals, going to a football or hockey game, seeing a show, going home, taking a road trip, working, or most likely, a mixture of many of the above. While Bowling Green is a dry campus and the residential halls strictly enforce the rules, undergraduates observe that being underage isn't really a problem, with the help of a fake ID or an older friend.

The Greek system tends to be somewhat prominent, as one student noted, "God, if I see another toga I'll scream!" But, students repeat that it is definitely not an overpowering social force. Many students are involved in Bowling Green's 180 registered student organizations, which include everything from religious and cultural groups to honor societies, music groups, political and public speaking forums, and drama. Marching band and Greek activities are regarded as the most popular extracurriculars. BGSU actively recruits athletes, with football, basketball, and hockey as the most popular sports. "There is a good amount of school spirit, and it's nice to see it," one undergraduate noted. "However, it's not overdone." Most students attend the annual football game against rival school University of Toledo, where one student insists "You must get your picture taken with Freddy and Freida Falcon!"

When describing the student population, most regard their peers and laid back and typically friendly. "There is a stereotype of the khaki wearing prep here, but honestly, no one really cares," noted one undergraduate. Diversity is "present, but very minor," although multicultural organizations on campus thrive. Bowling Green is a high quality university with a great number of opportunities, be it academic, extracurricular, social, or just plain everyday living. "Our colors may be poop and orange," exclaimed one student, "but we're really cool, I promise!" —*Amanda Ambroza*

FYI

The three best things about attending Bowling Green are "the tree-laden landscape, the town is interesting and integrated with the campus, and the friendly people."

The three worst things about attending Bowling Green are "there's rarely enough parking, the frigid cold, and water that's much less than tasty."

The three things that every student should do before graduating from Bowling Green are "ride the elevators in University Hall and try to make it out alive, go to football and hockey games, and walk on the right side of the seal."

One thing I'd like to have known before coming here is "the legend of the ghost because it scares the begebers out of me."

Case Western Reserve University

Address: 103 Tomlinson Hall, 10900 Euclid Avenue; Cleveland, OH 44106-7055
Phone: 216-368-4450
E-mail address: admission@po.cwru.edu
Web site URL: www.cwru.edu
Founded: 1826
Private or Public: private
Religious affiliation: none
Location: urban
Undergraduate enrollment: 3,286
Total enrollment: 9,601
Percent Male/Female: 61%/39%
Percent Minority: NA

Percent African-American: 5%
Percent Asian: 13%
Percent Hispanic: 2%
Percent Native-American: 0.5%
Percent in-state/out-of-state: 39%/61%
Percent Pub HS: 70%
Number of Applicants: 4,380
Percent Accepted: 72%
Percent Accepted who enroll: 24%
Entering: 765
Transfers: 81
Application Deadline: 1 Feb
Mean SAT: NA
Mean ACT: NA

Middle 50% SAT range: 590–710 V, 630–730 M
Middle 50% ACT range: 26–31
3 Most popular majors: biology, psychology, management
Retention: 92%
Graduation rate: 73%
On-campus housing: 85%
Fraternities: 33%
Sororities: 19%
Library: 2,015,763 volumes
Tuition and Fees: $20,260 in; $20,260 out
Room and Board: $5,815
Financial aid, first-year: 92%

May I have your attention please? The faculty, students, and staff of Case Western would like to furnish you with the following message:

NO, WE ARE NOT
A MILITARY ACADEMY.

You got that, Private?

You see, that's not "Reserve" in the sense of "National Reserve Corps" but more along the lines of "Northwest Reserve Land Act of 1787." Back then Ohio was a territory of the state of Connecticut, and the Western Reserve College was founded in 1826 with that connection in mind. After countless mutations and name changes, CWRU today still retains most of the intensity and high expectations of its East Coast brethren, but its midwestern location lends it a neighborly character that makes Case Western a truly unique experience. According to many Case students, "that whole GI thing" is only the first of many misconceptions about the school.

Homework, Sweet Homework

Academically, Case is about as hard-charging as they come. Engineering and the sciences loom large, due to Case's position as a top scientific research institution, and these fields set the brisk pace of academics. Many students are quick to agree that "all rumors about the workload are absolutely true." In short, Case offers a bruising curriculum in the sciences. One junior observed, "Many freshmen come in thinking they want to be doctors, fail Bio 110, and then don't know what to do." The management major is a common place of refuge for burned-out scientists.

On the other hand, Case works remarkably hard to guide students around these academic pitfalls, offering free tutoring and a "learning assistant" in each dorm. The shining light of this movement is one Dr. Ignacio Ocasio, known as "Doc Oc," who teaches Intro Chemistry with tireless energy. Legend has it that Doc Oc learns the name of each student in his large class on the first day. He spends almost all of his time making sure every student passes chemistry, offering extra help and even hosting a call-in TV show, with a studio audience, for students with homework

questions. "He's just really interested in teaching," says one sophomore. Doc Oc is not typical of all Case professors of course. General opinions of the faculty varied widely, from complaints about poor teaching to the thoughts of one biomedical engineering major: "[Professors] are incredibly approachable and nice to the students—much different from what one would expect from a research institution . . . students go out drinking with their profs and advisors all the time." Generally, professors are said to be friendly and accessible to those who can work up the nerve to go seek them out.

Beyond the rigors of engineering, Case Western offers a wide variety of classes in its College of Arts and Sciences. Still, many students feel that Case "is not a place for English majors" and segregation between the Case School of Engineering on the north side of campus, which merged with Western Reserve University in 1967, and the south side is still apparent. Engineers expressed both bitterness and plaintive yearning toward their liberal arts brethren, decrying their "easy" workload but secretly wishing that the stringent engineering program allowed them to interact more with students in the liberal arts curriculum.

Everybody's Working for the Weekend

"I make sure I do at least one fun thing on the weekends," promises one junior, a double major and varsity softball player. Many Case students complain that the immense workload can quickly reduce social life to a sad, sad condition. Some students either have little interest in partying or simply can't find the time. One student offers the following breakdown: of the 3,200 or so CWRU undergrads, about 2,000 don't ever go out to parties, leaving the same crowd of 1,000 to appear at every party, every weekend. This makes Case feel much smaller than it really is.

This legion of party goers corresponds roughly to Case's fraternity and sorority population, and Case's biggest parties are Greek parties. Case's 18 fraternities and 5 sororities (the disparity reflects less a lack of interest in sororities than the large male majority on campus) comprise the core of social involvement at Case. In addition to hosting parties, fraternities and sororities run extensive community service programs and organize Greek Week, a kind of bacchanalian Olympics, which is the high point of spring semester. Fraternity and sorority rush is considered an integral part of the freshman experience and an important way to get to know fellow students. While most feel that the fraternities are laid-back and inviting, the sororities, on the other hand, are pegged with a "formal rush" process, a procrustean affair in which the group of rushees is pared down successively over a week based on a series of nightly parties. The most sought-after fraternities seem to be SAE, Phi Kappa Psi, and DKE. The top sorority, by an overwhelming majority, is Phi Mu.

> **"You'd have to really be obnoxious to get written up."**

Those not interested in Greek life are urged to make the most of orientation week, when students are most open to meeting new people. There are also a number of clubs, many, such as the Biology Club and Chemical Engineering Society, associated with academic majors. The Chemical Engineering Society hosts a popular "kegs on the quad" event about one Friday afternoon per month. CWRU hosts a number of quirkier undergraduate organizations, such as the Heavy Industry Club and a nationally renowned trivia bowl team. Strosacker Hall, although its name is certainly the most ridiculed on campus, offers the most popular alternative to the party scene with its weekend movie screenings.

Drinking is the most prevalent activity at Case parties, although non-drinkers abound both within and without the Greek scene. "Most of us can't afford the recovery time," explained one sorority member. Although the university officially frowns on underage drinking, most feel that those who want to drink don't have any trouble quenching their thirst. One senior assured, "You don't have to drink, because there is a lot to do when your school's in the middle of a big city."

Hellooooo, Cleveland

Home of baseball's Indians, the famous Warehouse district, and the Rock and Roll Hall of Fame, Cleveland is not an altogether unexciting place to live. Case is the centerpiece of University Circle, a square mile with the greatest concentration of cultural and educational institutions in the country. Severance Hall, home of the Cleveland Symphony Orchestra, and the Cleveland Museum of Art, both extremely highly recommended by students, are on campus. "There are very few places like this in the entire world, really," said one senior. The flats area, accessible by car, features nightclubs popular with Case students.

As for the living conditions themselves, most freshmen live in doubles on coed floors with upperclassmen. A few experimental freshmen-only theme floors have sprung up in recent years, however. Living on Freshman Experience floors, available by application only, is seen as the most fun way to spend freshman year. Each floor has a resident assistant and a learning assistant. Each dorm also has a faculty advisor. The RAs are responsible for making students feel at home and acting as the first line of discipline. However, RAs are not generally known to get in the way of a good time. One RA even admitted, "You'd have to really be obnoxious to get written up."

After freshman year, many Greeks move into their fraternities and sororities, while "dormies" shuffle off to nicer rooms on the south side of campus. Students must live on campus until they turn 21 or get married. Many seniors and (presumably) newlyweds move to Little Italy, a nearby neighborhood with nice apartments and a 24-hour doughnut shop.

And What About the Students?

According to many students, the most remarkable thing about their classmates is their humility and friendliness, which takes some of the edge off the academic competitiveness of the place. "While everyone is striving for good grades," said one junior, "they still take time out to help each other do well." A senior proclaimed, "The people who go here are the coolest, most down-to-earth people you will ever meet. Case has done well to be a semielite school and still not be snobbish at all." Through its generous merit scholarships and financial aid programs, Case attracts many high-achieving students who would otherwise possibly choose more well known schools. Case students' inherent drive to succeed sets the serious aca-

demic tone of the school. "Everyone here seems to be pre-something," observed one senior. "This place is full of aspirations." Armed with hard-earned CWRU degrees, students head into the real world to find their wishes often easily answered. —*Charles Umiker*

FYI
The three best things about CWRU are "the education and the prestige of the professors, it's a fairly mediocre-size school—not too big, not too small—so everyone can excel in a particular area, and they're very generous with financial aid."
The three worst things about CWRU are "the high crime rate (security isn't as tight as it should be), professors are mostly motivated by the funding for their research and not so much by teaching, and the lack of resources in the career placement office for finding a job after graduation."
The three things that every student should do before graduating from CWRU are "hang out with Doc Oc, go through fraternity or sorority rush, see the Cleveland Symphony."
One thing I'd like to have known before coming here is "how hard it would be."

The College of Wooster

Address: Galpin Hall; Wooster, OH 44691	**Percent African-American:** 4%	**Middle 50% SAT range:** 520–640 V, 520–640 M
Phone: 330-263-2322; 800-877-9905	**Percent Asian:** 1%	**Middle 50% ACT range:** 23–28
E-mail address: admissions @acs.wooster.edu	**Percent Hispanic:** 1% **Percent Native-American:** 0%	**3 Most popular majors:** English, biology, economics
Web site URL: www.wooster.edu	**Percent in-state / out-of-state:** 45%/55%	**Retention:** 82%
Founded: 1866	**Percent Pub HS:** 76%	**Graduation rate:** 68%
Private or Public: private	**Number of Applicants:** 2,093	**On-campus housing:** 100%
Religious affiliation: Presbyterian	**Percent Accepted:** 86%	**Fraternities:** 20%
Location: small city	**Percent Accepted who enroll:** 28%	**Sororities:** 15%
Undergraduate enrollment: 1,696	**Entering:** 507 **Transfers:** 17	**Library:** 860,000 volumes
Total enrollment: 1,747	**Application Deadline:** 15 Feb	**Tuition and Fees:** $19,230 in; $19,230 out
Percent Male / Female: 48%/52%	**Mean SAT:** NA	**Room and Board:** $5,070
Percent Minority: 6%	**Mean ACT:** NA	**Financial aid, first-year:** 65%

D o not let the relaxed, pastoral setting of The College of Wooster fool you. At the core of this idyllic campus is an intense academic program featuring small classes and professors "who rock." Located in the rural northern Ohio town of Wooster, the college seems to have something unique to offer for just about everyone—from its Bagpipe Band

representing Wooster's rich Scottish tradition to the independent study program required of juniors and seniors.

Gettin' Tough
The College of Wooster requires its students to take a fairly extensive set of core courses, but they are generally described as easy to complete. "You just have to re-

member to do them!" Students need three courses in the social sciences and/or history, three courses in math and/or science, and three courses in literature, philosophy, and/ or the arts. Students must also take a first-year seminar, pass a writing requirement, complete two courses in a foreign language, and do a religion course, as well. The sciences are reportedly the hardest majors, while communications and history are supposedly the easiest. English, music, biology, and chemistry all receive good reviews. Chemistry majors can enjoy a newly renovated building, and all science majors can take advantage of the two-year-old science library. Students interested in engineering also have the option of participating in Wooster's 3+2 program, in which students finish their last two years at another school.

Both juniors and seniors take part in Wooster's independent study (IS) program within their majors. During junior year, students spend one semester fulfilling the requirements of the program, while seniors spend their entire year doing so. Getting into classes is generally not a problem, though one freshman warned that getting into lower-level language courses and non-lab science classes can sometimes be challenging. Most students also seem very happy with their professors and cite the small class sizes of about 15–20 students as a huge asset. Overall the workload is said to be "tolerable," with students describing themselves as "well-worked."

Student Life

Generally people at Wooster study in their rooms, but some take advantage of the library, Andrews, to study. Lowry, the student center is reportedly busy as well, but the snack bar area is said to "need a major face lift." Dorms were described as "pretty nice." Freshmen live in all but four of the dorms, which house solely upperclassmen. Some of the more popular freshmen dorms include Armington, Stevenson, and Bissman—but they're all fairly loud and are considered party dorms. Nicer dorms include Luce and Kenarden for sophomores, juniors, and seniors because they are newer and have carpeting and air conditioning. Program dorms are also popular. After freshman year, students have to enter a room draw or apply to the special program dorms, which include languages, smoke-free, chemical free (no alcohol), and a quiet dorm. Students can also move off campus or into one of the small houses owned by the university, although housing is guaranteed all four years.

> "We don't worship jocks or fraternities, and we aren't all tree huggers. I guess we defy some of the stereotypes and that differentiates us from a lot of schools."

Students generally go to Lowry, the main dining hall, for meals, or try and find some better food off campus. The on-campus meal plan is a 21 meal per week plan, and the dining hall offers open hours from 7 A.M. to 7 P.M. However, the food is "not great" ("the cookies are good"), so many students look elsewhere to find better food. Matsos, a Greek restaurant, The Old Jaol, and Woogle's, a bagel shop, all offer a change of menu. Wooster, being a small town, does not offer much in the way of late-night hangouts. "We need a Starbucks or something that can stay open until 12 A.M. or 1."

Social Scene

One of the big social scenes on campus is the Greek system. The Greeks throw many of the weekend parties and being underage is not perceived as a problem for most students. Generally, there is much to do on campus over the weekend from "seeing plays and going to concerts to dancing and drinking." Campus-wide parties include the 70's/80's Dance, 20's Prohibition Party, Bacchanalia and Spring Fest. The latter two are considered to be the biggest social events of the year, and students camp out in the cornfields to party and listen to various bands.

However, partying is not the only thing going at Wooster on the weekends. There are many active extracurricular clubs such as Let's Dance—a swing dance club, the Art Club and numerous others, including club sports. Students seem to agree that what the town of Wooster lacks in things to do, the college seems to make up for with movies, seminars, and productions over the weekends.

While they don't play a huge role at Wooster, athletics are nonetheless well respected, with both the football and baseball teams consistently posting winning seasons. Perhaps one of Wooster's most unique traditions is the Bagpipe Band, which, fully clad in kilts and knee socks, accompanies the football team onto the field and plays during the games. In addition, the college has its very own 18-hole golf course and boasts a new weight room "with state-of-the-art Cybex weights, treadmills, bikes, and stairmasters. It's really nice." One thing that the school lacks, however, is an adequate field house, and many students express hope that a new one will be built in the near future.

Little Diversity

Most students at Wooster hail from Ohio and the Northeast, but there is also a significant international contingent. This is about where the diversity at Wooster ends though, as most students are white and come from a middle-class background. The student body tends to be self-segregating with students sitting with their own groups in dining halls. Although the school is fairly homogenous, one student commented that "our largest minorities are Indians and Pakistanis, and not much else. However, diversity is improving." Minorities actively participate in various cultural clubs such as the Black Students Association and Student Allies of Sexual Minorities. Other campus-wide organizations include *The Voice*, the student newspaper, the Outdoor Club, and the Wooster Volunteer Network.

In general, The College of Wooster provides an intense academic experience for students who know how to get what they want and who are not afraid to work hard to get it. A typical Wooster student stereotype is hard to describe. Perhaps one student said it best when he said, "We don't worship jocks or fraternities, and we aren't all tree huggers. I guess we defy some of the stereotypes and that differentiates us from a lot of schools." —*Melissa J. Merritt*

FYI

The three best things about attending The College of Wooster are "the faculty, the students, and the community."

The three worst things about attending The College of Wooster are "its location, the academic registration process, and the food."

The three things that every student should do before graduating from The College of Wooster are "use the bathroom at the Underground, eat at the Old Jaol, and study abroad."

One thing I'd like to have known before coming here is "how the registration process works."

Denison University

Address: Box H; Granville, OH 43023
Phone: 740-587-6276
E-mail address: admissions@denison.edu
Web site URL: www.denison.edu
Founded: 1831
Private or Public: private
Religious affiliation: none
Location: suburban
Undergraduate enrollment: 2,156
Total enrollment: 2,156
Percent Male/Female: 46%/54%
Percent Minority: 9%
Percent African-American: 4%

Percent Asian: 3%
Percent Hispanic: 2%
Percent Native-American: 0%
Percent in-state/out-of-state: 37%/63%
Percent Pub HS: 69%
Number of Applicants: 2,821
Percent Accepted: 76%
Percent Accepted who enroll: 29%
Entering: 622
Transfers: 15
Application Deadline: 1 Feb
Mean SAT: 604 V, 600 M
Mean ACT: 26

Middle 50% SAT range: 550–650 V, 550–640 M
Middle 50% ACT range: 24–29
3 Most popular majors: communications, economics and english
Retention: 87%
Graduation rate: 68%
On-campus housing: 98%
Fraternities: 31%
Sororities: 32%
Library: 340,000 volumes
Tuition and Fees: $20,680 in; $20,680 out
Room and Board: $5,760
Financial aid, first-year: 53%

Located on a hill in the middle of Ohio, surrounded by hills and big trees, full of squirrels running about, harboring a bioreserve, Denison inspires descriptions of "peaceful" and "beautiful." Aside from their spectacular surroundings, Denison students describe a demanding courseload and a social life dominated by Greeks.

Broadening Horizons

Students say Denison offers a broad but comprehensive liberal arts education. The General Education Requirements (GER) include two years of a foreign language and distribution courses that span a range of categories including philosophy, math, and science. "The requirements can be burden, especially if you want to have a double major," a student commented. Environmental studies, biochemistry, computer science, and biology are considered to be the hardest majors, while political science, music and economics are relatively easy. Still, many students find themselves overwhelmed with work, and don't report any lazy Sundays. Even though preprofessional students don't have their own majors, programs are offered to these students that include special advi-

sors and related clubs. These include the pre-med, pre-vet and pre-law clubs.

Students usually find it easy to get into classes, even though most classes are capped at 15 to 20 people, but "some studio art classes are hard to get in," one student complained.

Pleasing Professors

Students are pleased with their professors, noting that many of them are well-known in their fields: "The microbiology professor worked on the Viking program to determine if there was life on Mars." "I had a class of ten people and towards the middle of the semester, people stopped participating and the discussions weren't very good, so the professor had us over to his house for dinner and a "therapy session" so we could make the class better," recalled a student. Another said, "We had an medieval feast in my Anglo-Saxon English class. An English professor invited our class to his house for a movie and dinner." Students emphasize that professors try to make students think constantly and not memorize in "everywhere but the chemistry department." Also, the speakers that visit the school are enjoyed by many Denison students. Among recent visitors was scientist Keith Campbell, who cloned "Dolly" the sheep. TA's are useful for students in that "they add to professors' help but don't replace it." The biggest complaint about academics is that "grading is harsh."

Greeks and their beer

"If you are not obnoxious then being underage is not a problem," commented one student. Upperclassmen parties are common, but not as popular as the fraternity and sorority parties that take place off-campus. The two bars in Granville are also popular with upperclassmen. "D-Day (Derby days) is a great activity," students say, complimenting their drinking festival. At keg parties, everyone pays for a mug and is bussed out to a field where there are many kegs waiting for them. Drugs are not as common as drinks: "Marijuana is popular, but there are strict rules against it. Beer rules here." There are two formal parties per year which are the only occasions people get dressed up for, unless you are part of the Greek system. As for relationships, "There is a lot of sex, but homosexuals and interracial couples are frowned upon," says one student.

Besides beer . . .

Non-drinkers, characterized as mostly "sports people", also find things to do. Other social activities on campus include lectures, movies, and dances. Students feel "you have to search out the fun activities but they do actually exist." Student organizations like the juggling club add color to the social life on campus. Community service is also very popular. Nevertheless, many find the life outside the university "dull." There aren't many options for dining or shopping in Granville. Pizza Hut and Taco Bell are the most common dining places to go to outside of the Denison meal plan, which students must purchase. "I would never recommend anyone attending Denison University unless you like to live in the same room eating the same horrible food for four straight year," one student said. The cafeterias are noted for their crowded lines although "the cafeteria people are some of the nicest people you have ever met." The limited public transportation to any nearby cities like Columbus makes cars a must for many.

Inn Denison?

The freshmen dorms aren't a big complaint at Denison; students note that "the nightmare starts later," when you realize that you are phased out of off-campus housing. Students feel stranded by these kind of restrictions: "Their reasoning is that they believe on campus living is a significant determinant in having a fruitful Denison career while in reality it is to force all students into paying the school for residential expenses as well as the costly meal plan." Also, a housing lottery results in many juniors staying in freshmen dorms. Shorney is known as "the Ghetto" while the Sunset dorms are apartments, air conditioned and the biggest dorms on campus. Students believe that instead of building new dorms, the administration should allow more off-campus housing.

Wealthy and homogeneous

Many complain of the cliques that form right away. However, "it's still true that a couple bottles of beer always open up the way for new friendships." The typical Denison student is characterized as rich and preppy. Abercrombie, J.Crew and North Face are the uniforms of many. "Wealth is prevalent," is a common comment, and most of the students seem to have come from "wealthy east-coast boarding schools."

> **Abercrombie, J.Crew and North Face are the uniforms of many.**

Students report geographic, but not ethnic, diversity. The student body is very athletic. Swimming and lacrosse recruit heavily while "football doesn't matter that much. The lacrosse team made the final four last year and men and women's swim teams are strong competitors for the national championships."

Enjoy the peace

Despite the difficult class-work, students seem to be happy with their choice of college. With its peaceful campus and wild Greek parties, Denison is indeed a place to be enjoyed. —*Yakut Seyhanli*

FYI
Three best things about attending Denison are "small classes, caring professors and the May Term internship program."
Three worst things about attending Denison are "limits on off-campus housing, transportation, housing lottery."
Three things that every student should do before graduating from Denison are "walk up the hill from Mitchell center in the middle of winter, get lost in the library stacks, do at least one May Term internship."
One thing I'd like to have known before coming here is "that there's a lack of social activities off-campus around Granville."

Kent State University

Address: PO Box 5190; Kent, OH 44242-0001
Phone: 330-672-2444
E-mail address: kentadm @admissions.kent.edu
Web site URL: www.kent.edu /admissions/app_opt.html
Founded: 1910
Private or Public: public
Religious affiliation: none
Location: suburban
Undergraduate enrollment: 17,275
Total enrollment: 21,653
Percent Male/Female: 41%/59%
Percent Minority: 11%
Percent African-American: 8%

Percent Asian: 1%
Percent Hispanic: 1%
Percent Native-American: 0.5%
Percent in-state/out-of-state: 94%/6%
Percent Pub HS: NA
Number of Applicants: 8,594
Percent Accepted: 92%
Percent Accepted who enroll: 43%
Entering: 3,414
Transfers: 913
Application Deadline: 15 Mar
Mean SAT: 510 V, 503 M
Mean ACT: 21

Middle 50% SAT range: 450–560 V, 440–560 M
Middle 50% ACT range: 18–23
3 Most popular majors: nursing, psychology, architecture
Retention: 72%
Graduation rate: 43%
On-campus housing: NA
Fraternities: 19%
Sororities: 11%
Library: 2,077,369 volumes
Tuition and Fees: $5,014 in; $9,918 out
Room and Board: $4,530
Financial aid, first-year: NA

Kent State University will live on forever as the site of intense Vietnam War protest, which exploded into the shooting of four students on May 4th, 1970. Kent State, however, doesn't try to keep the event under wraps. In fact, the University just inaugurated a memorial for the four students. Additionally, students at Kent are able to study conflict management and dispute resolution. This non-traditional subject matter is representative of the various academic opportunities that surround the Golden Eagles.

Academics Abounds
Students at Kent State have a wide arrange of school from which they choose a course of study. Aside from a traditional College of Liberal Arts and Sciences, Kent State also hosts the College of Fine and Professional Arts, the School of Nursing, a College of Education, and a College of Business Administration, among others. The College of Education and the Fine Arts program are considered quite strong. Regardless of major, however, students are allowed to take classes in any of Kent's colleges. As part of the Kent experience, students are required to fulfill Liberal Education Requirements (LERs), which consist of courses from all fields, including humanities, fine arts, social sciences and basic sciences. Student opinion is split on these requirements. One sophomore said that "we have to take 39 LERs, which are supposed to make us well-rounded students, but that means I have to take a lot more of these annoying classes when I really would like to delve into my major." Another student, how-

ever, said that "they can be kinda fun and relatively easy, so I don't mind them too much." Students are cautious about the nursing and architecture programs, both of which have notorious reputations for being difficult.

For those who seek a greater academic challenge, there is an Honors College, which allows students to take more advanced classes as a freshman. One freshman said, "instead of having to go through basic English 1 and 2, I was able to jump right into a more in-depth literature class." Being part of the Honors program, as another student described, "affords more attention from the professors. You're not as anonymous." Freshman in the Honors College get to take smaller classes, although class size does not appear to be a major problem at Kent. Most classes range from 25 to 30 students, while larger classes, as one senior said "rarely exceed 75 students or so." TA's are definitely present on campus, but rarely teach classes above the introductory level, particularly in the English, Foreign Language, and some science departments. The academic options at Kent are quite varied and as one student put it, "if you choose the right classes, academics are great. There are a lot of classes offered."

Where to Go For a Good Time

Kent not only offers plenty of classes, but there are many social options as well. Though many join fraternities, one junior explained that "life is still pretty balanced. There's no real pressure to go Greek." Aside from Greek life, the Student Center serves as a social center, housing a concert hall in the basement, pool tables, and plenty of restaurants. Additionally, as one student stated, "A lot of the student organizations are based there, so it can get really social." Various departments organize lectures open to students of any discipline and there is a pretty lively music scene. The University recently had George Clinton and the Psychedelic Funk play at its Homecoming. Students on campus find it quite easy to meet each other. As a freshman said, "this school is pretty large, which can be an adjustment for some people, but it's easy to meet people from all sorts of background." As for off-campus fun, there is a "big strip one block

away with bars and restaurants," described one senior. There, students profit from the food at Ray's Place and the $3 pizzas at The Loft. On the weekends, students generally stay on campus, even students from nearby Cleveland.

Why Leave?

Students have good reason to stay on campus since it is, simply put, "very beautiful." The campus covers several blocks with "several hills, nice landscaping, and these wonderful trees that are naturally there. Front Campus is one the prettiest spots and is right by the fashion museum," described one freshman. The campus boasts a recently built wellness center, where students partake in aerobics, yoga, and various fitness classes. Students can get around campus very easily thanks to KSU Bus service, which one student called "a very intricate and efficient system." Safety on campus is a very minor issue; students are quick to mention the security escort service, which students find particularly useful on late nights coming home from the library.

> "If you're in a double, it's pretty small; if you're in a single, it's really really small."

Coming home, however, does not necessarily mean returning to the lap of luxury. As one student described the dorms, "If you're in a double, it's pretty small; if you're in a single it's really really small." Freshmen are not required to live on campus, although most do. Freshman generally choose from Terrace Dorm, which is coed, or the single sex dorms, Prentice and Dunbar, for women and men respectively. Students in the Honors College get to live in Honors Housing, which tends to be better. There are strict visitor policies; officials emphasize that visitors must be escorted at all times. Students who might not want to deal with these policies move off campus. There are many apartment complexes in the surrounding area, most of which are served directly by the Kent bus system, making them extremely convenient.

On-campus dining is described as "pretty good. We have a lot of options here." All students are given a Flash Card from the beginning, which then serves as a debit system for all the food establishments on campus, which includes a McDonald's and Friendly's in the Student Center. For those in search of a more fancy meal, Mario's is one of the few restaurants where students can sit down and be waited on. Kent State has not been described as terribly vegetarian friendly, but it has, according to students, improved its selection in recent years. While on campus students rarely go off campus to eat, one student cited The Pufferbelly as "very worth going to."

Socially Conscious Students

The Kent State student body is very involved in social causes, mostly through community service. The strong Greek system recently staged a Build-a-Playground Campaign, in which they went to a local elementary school and built a playground set in one day. The school also has a strong America Reads program. Students can find pretty much anything at Kent, ranging from the Christian Coalition to the Neo-Pagan Coalition, or the more prominent chapter of Amnesty International and the Lesbian, Gay, Bisexual

Union. Students can get involved in physical activity either through personal workout at the wellness center, or else join intramural and club teams, among which the Green Dragon Kung Fu Club is quite popular. Varsity sports do not play a central role in student life. As one student described it, "There is plenty of school spirit, although that doesn't mean our teams are that great. Our football team just won its first game and the season's almost over." Regardless, the male and female Basketball teams are both well-regarded especially due to recent success in NCAA tournaments.

Kent State offers it students many academic and social opportunities. Furthermore, the school strongly emphasizes diversity and has been attempting to improve the its racial makeup. The school also fosters many artistic endeavors. For example, a large community of published writers live and work at Kent, a situation which one student described as being "a great opportunity if students take the initiative to do something with it." Kent, while still greatly tied to its past history, has evolved since May 4th, 1970, and maintains a very dynamic and socially minded student body. —*Shu-Ping Shen*

FYI
The three best things about attending Kent State are "graduating, amount of student activities available, and the computer labs."
The three worst things about attending Kent State are "parking, consistency from you advisors, and the almost too political nature of the campus."
The three things that every student should do before graduating from Kent State are "go to Brady's Café, visit the Fashion Museum, and check out some musical event."
One thing that I'd like to have known before coming here is "the variety of majors that were available."

K e n y o n   C o l l e g e

Address: Ransom Hall;
Kenyon College; Gambier,
OH 43022
Phone: 740-427-5776
E-mail address:
admissions@kenyon.edu
Web site URL:
www.kenyon.edu
Founded: 1824
Private or Public: private
Religious affiliation: none
Location: rural
**Undergraduate
enrollment:** 1,574
Total enrollment: 1,574
Percent Male / Female:
44% / 56%
Percent Minority: 10%
Percent African-American:
4%

Percent Asian: 3%
Percent Hispanic: 3%
Percent Native-American:
NA
**Percent in-state / out-of-
state:** 20% / 80%
Percent Pub HS: 76%
Number of Applicants:
2,420
Percent Accepted:
68%
**Percent Accepted who
enroll:** 28%
Entering: 459
Transfers: 3
Application Deadline:
1 Feb
Mean SAT: 666 V,
634 M
Mean ACT: 29

Middle 50% SAT range:
610–710 V,
580–690 M
Middle 50% ACT range:
27–31
3 Most popular majors:
English, psychology,
political science
Retention: 93%
Graduation rate: 82%
On-campus housing: 100%
Fraternities: 35%
Sororities: 4%
Library: 1,000,000
volumes
Tuition and Fees:
$24,680 in; $24,680 out
Room and Board: $4,160
Financial aid, first-year:
41%

L ooking for a close-knit community? There is no clear line where the town of Gambier ends and Kenyon College begins. Students drink coffee with one another at the Red Door Café, they check their mail next to residents at the Gambier Post Office, and they congregate on the town green. The strong connection between town and college isn't so surprising considering that Kenyon students outnumber full-time Gambier inhabitants 3 to 1. In fact, setting is one of the most unique attractions of this small liberal arts college.

Academics 101

Every Kenyon student is required to take one unit (two semesters) from each of the four academic divisions: the fine arts, humanities, natural sciences, and social sciences. Students also have to complete a major and have the additional option of completing a minor or concentration. Nine different concentrations are offered, each an interdisciplinary group of courses, ranging from law and society to environmental studies. While Kenyon maintains a strong tradition of liberal arts (English is the most popular major), the sciences are particularly challenging, and a number of

students do go on to medical school. History, however, is not regarded as challenging; one student said, "Slackers: history, hard majors: everything else."

Classes at Kenyon tended to be small, and the largest, Biology, Genetics and Development, enrolls around 80 students. There are some very unique classes offered, including Drinking Culture: The Anthropology of Alcohol Use, Uncanny Love Stories: Theories of Love in German Literature from the Enlightenment to the Present, and Fieldwork: Rural Life, a research-based sociology course that takes as its subjects the residents in nearby rural Knox County. The small size of the school can, however, translate into limited course offerings. "As a senior, if you are in a small department, you don't have much choice as far as classes go," complained one Russian major.

The Personal Touch

The attentive nature of Kenyon professors overshadow many of the students' academics. One student loves that "all class are taught by professors" and teaching assistants help out only in language classes, where they supplement the professors' instruction. Personal interaction between faculty and students extends even beyond the classroom, since many professors reside in Gambier. According to a senior, professors "often invite me to their homes for dinner or small parties." Many professors are also known for their quirky and unorthodox lecture styles. "My chemistry professor keeps describing an atom as a chicken sitting an egg," said one amused, but puzzled, freshman.

Whether in their dorms or Olin Chalmers Library, Kenyon students do a great deal of studying. One underclassman calls the course load "a ton of work, but manageable," while another warns that it is hard to hide in a class of only 10 people. Students caution that you have to watch out for classes that sound easy but turn out to be quite difficult. Looking to fulfill their fine arts requirement, many students take a dance class only to find that "it requires a ton of reading." In addition to their upper-level classes, all seniors must complete a senior exercise in their major, ranging from a research paper to an exam or multimedia presentation.

On Campus: The Only Option

All Kenyon students must live on campus for all four years. The housing options "vary greatly," ranging from traditional dorm rooms, to apartments, to fraternity and sorority houses. All of the freshmen live together on the north side of campus, which includes an area known as the "Freshman Quad," and there is reportedly "no typical" freshman room, with singles, doubles, and triples, coed by hall or floor, available. However, some freshmen are stuck with "huge dividers" in their rooms, put there in an attempt to portion off areas for each roommate.

> "As a senior, if you are in a small department, you don't have much choice as far as classes go."

Housing for upperclassmen is determined by a lottery, which one student calls "a weird-ass system that nobody understands." After freshman year, students can choose to live in specialized dorms, such a single-sex buildings or ones with substance-free floors. Some of the most sought-after upperclassman housing is the Woodland Cottages, a set of on-campus apartments that include their own kitchens.

Finding good food can be a "little difficult," especially if you are a vegetarian or vegan. There is the Granary, however, which always serves a creative vegetarian option. There are only two dining halls on campus, but students have "unlimited" access and are welcome to as many meals a day as they like. "The hours are good; the main dining hall is open all day till seven-thirty at night." But since students live on campus all four years, most feel they are "stuck" with the food.

Scenic Living

There are advantages to attending college in rural Ohio. Students describe the town and its residents as "scenic and very friendly." Plus, it does not take that long to figure out your way around. Most students at Kenyon don't seem to mind that they are in the middle of nowhere. However, except for a handful of restaurants and the campus bookstore, there are very few options for shopping or entertainment in Gambier. A free shuttle runs every day to the nearby town of Mount Vernon, which has a Wal-Mart, some shops, and a movie theater, and once a week students can take an hour-long bus ride to Columbus, the state capital, for five dollars. Still most of the students spend their free time on the Kenyon campus, engaging in activities organized by the students or the college.

Diving In

The most dedicated athletes at Kenyon are found in the water; the men's swimming and diving team holds 21 straight national championships—an NCAA record for longest national winning streak in any sport or division—and the women's team holds 17. As members of the NCAA Division III, the Kenyon Lords and Ladies compete in North Coast Athletic Conference, against schools like Denison, Oberlin, and Wooster. There is also a strong intramural and club program, which includes sports like Ultimate Frisbee and rugby. Even if you have never been involved in a particular sport before, "the team will teach you how to play," said one freshman rugby player. Sports also contribute to the social scene at Kenyon, where students meet one another through athletics and different teams throw parties for the campus at large.

Outside of sports, Kenyon has the traditional assortment of student extracurriculars. Every year the students are introduced to the different clubs at "an activity that closes down the main street in Gambier. You can walk around for hours." Publications include the *Kenyon Collegian*, Kenyon's weekly newspaper, published both in print and on-line, and the *Kenyon Observer*, a journal in which Kenyon students express their opinions about pressing issues in politics and culture. Kenyon has an active student government and a campus senate, composed of students, faculty, and administrators. Students can also get involved in the community, becoming members of the local fire department or volunteering as tutors in the public schools.

Trying to Diversify

According to the *Kenyon Profile*, "The College has made a concentrated effort to diversify its student body in recent years." About a third of Kenyon students come from the Midwest, and the great majority are white. One student says the campus "is diverse not ethnically, but socially," while another notes that it seems like a pretty even division between those who attended public school and private school. Many agree that there is no typical Kenyon student, while there may be a typical Kenyon look. Most students are "nicely dressed, wearing J. Crew, Banana Republic, Abercrombie."

Kenyon is very welcoming toward its gay and lesbian population. "People are pretty accepting of others' lifestyle choices," said one student. Many call the campus "promiscuous" and note that there are "a lot of random hookups." Students don't really date, but there are long-term relationships and lots of sex.

Leave the Books Behind

Since the majority of students don't have classes on Thursday, Wednesday night is a party night at Kenyon, as are the typical Friday and Saturday evenings. The scene is a mixture of frat parties, on-campus parties, and, for the upperclassmen, the two bars on campus. Freshmen "have to watch out for security, but the upperclassmen will still serve them alcohol." The Greek scene is "big for guys and nonexistent for girls," but parties are open to all and a wide variety of students attend. Theme parties every year include "One Item of Clothing" and "Shock Your Mama," hosted in honor of the champion swim team. All parties have to be registered with security, and lately the administration has been "cracking down" on underage drinking, breaking up some gatherings.

For those not in the mood to party or who prefer not to drink, there are always movies "three or four times a week" and a variety of activities, ranging from scavenger hunts to dinners hosted by campus organizations. The college hosts "late-night non-alcoholic" programs, and a lot of students spend time hanging out in one another's rooms or in Gambier. The college hosts a formal every year, and some of the frats host semiformal dances as well. Students consider the campus "extremely safe" and feel comfortable at night in Gambier.

Rural Ohio might not be everyone's dream college setting, but for Kenyon students, living in Gambier helps make their college experience worthwhile. This unique environment fosters the education, the relationships, and the growth that students cherish in their four years at Kenyon. —*Pamela Boykoff*

FYI

The three best things about attending Kenyon are "the people are friendly, the professors, and the beer."

The three worst things about attending Kenyon are "the food, rumors spread quickly, and you are in the middle of nowhere."

The three things every student should do before graduating from Kenyon are "pass your senior comps, jump off *the* bridge, and take an English class."

One thing I'd like to have known before coming here is "that it is gray all winter."

Miami University

Address: 201 South
Campus Avenue Bldg.;
Oxford, OH 45056
Phone: 513-529-2531
E-mail address:
admission@muohio.edu
Web site URL:
www.muohio.edu
Founded: 1809
Private or Public:
public
Religious affiliation:
none
Location: suburban
**Undergraduate
enrollment:** 14,803
Total enrollment: 16,328
Percent Male/Female:
45%/55%
Percent Minority: 8%

Percent African-American:
4%
Percent Asian: 2%
Percent Hispanic: 2%
Percent Native-American:
0%
**Percent in-state/out-of-
state:** 73%/27%
Percent Pub HS: NA
Number of Applicants:
11,862
Percent Accepted: 78%
**Percent Accepted who
enroll:** 37%
Entering: 3,423
Transfers: NA
Application Deadline:
31 Jan
Mean SAT: NA
Mean ACT: NA

Middle 50% SAT range:
540–630 V,
560–650 M
Middle 50% ACT range:
27–31
3 Most popular majors:
marketing, elementary
education and zoology
Retention: 90%
Graduation rate: 62%
On-campus housing: 100%
Fraternities: 24%
Sororities: 27%
Library: 2,100,000
volumes
Tuition and Fees:
$4,766 in; $11,226 out
Room and Board: $5,070
Financial aid, first-year:
34%

If your vision of college life combines serious academics with an active social scene set against a backdrop of colonial-style redbrick buildings and beautifully designed courtyards, you might want to consider a visit to Oxford, Ohio, home of Miami University of Ohio.

Oxford Academia

During the week, academics are very important to the majority of Miami students. As one student said, "Miami is filled with people who make sure they get their work done before they go out." The academic requirement for students is the Miami Plan, which aims to give students a strong liberal arts foundation and consists of foundation courses in English, humanities, social sciences, natural sciences, fine arts, and formal reasoning. In addition to this curriculum, further study must be done in an area outside of the chosen major, and a senior project or seminar must be completed. While the Miami Plan certainly gives students broad exposure to a variety of academic disciplines, many students find the requirements stifling. They feel that they take classes they do not want to take, only to fulfill a requirement. Students register for classes by phone,

and though priority for scheduling is given to upperclassmen, most students do not have problems getting the classes they want.

Miami University is divided into six schools: arts and sciences, applied science, education, business, fine arts, and allied professions. The business school in particular garners rave reviews from students, as do many science and business classes in general. One major unique to Miami University is paper science, which prepares students in the study of the production of paper. Students placed elementary education and communications as among the easier majors offered. In addition to liberal arts majors, pre-professional programs are offered in law and medicine. Among the distinctive academic programs Miami offers are the University Honors Program, which features community service projects and a seminar format of instruction; the School of Interdisciplinary Studies, which allows students to create their own majors and a study-abroad program at the university's campus in Luxembourg. This program allows students to live with a local family, travel independently in Europe, and complete Miami requirements all at once.

Students generally seem extremely happy with academics at Miami of Ohio. While classes are said to be challenging, most students feel the level of instruction is excellent. With the exception of some introductory courses, classes are generally small, with an average range from 15 to 30, and students feel that student-faulty interaction is outstanding.

A Whole New World

Facilities on campus are in superb condition. Many students find King Library, the main library, perfect for researching and studying. In addition, libraries for science, music, and art and architecture are easily accessible and well-used. Other well-maintained facilities include the Outdoor Pursuit Center, which hosts outdoor adventure trips, and the Recreational Sports Center, which as one student put it, "has everything anyone could ever want in an athletic facility, from whirlpools to climbing walls as well as an indoor soccer complex."

Students at Miami love their idyllic campus setting. One building in particular that catches their attention is Upham, where to get to classes, they can walk through a beautifully designed archway. Ancient Miami folklore also says that if two people kiss under this archway at midnight, they will undoubtedly get married. But, not all folklore is so optimistic. Many students walking on the slant walk, a particular sidewalk with the school emblem engraved in it, avoid stepping on the school seal because doing so is a precursor to failing all your exams. Students also appreciate how well kept their campus is. "I would feel bad dropping a gum wrapper because it's so clean!" said one freshman.

Students must live in dorms during their first year, but after freshman year many Miami students choose to live off campus. Dorms are situated in different quads on campus: North, South, East, and Central. In addition there is a Western Campus, which many students feel is secluded from the rest of the university. Besides dorms, which are coed by floor, there are also three all-male dorms and seven all-female dorms. Among the student-rated best dorms are MacCracken and Hamilton, all-female dorms that women can move in to as sophomores.

Most feel that their dorms are adequate but not great. Food options abound at Miami, where most students are happy with the food quality and variety. Students seem content with eating at either the dining halls or the student center.

Pass the Feta Cheese

With over 300 student-run organizations, Miami has a lot to offer for those looking to be involved in extracurricular activities. Among these organizations are the *Miami Student*, a biweekly publication said to be the oldest college newspaper in the nation, and the Campus Activities Council. Students in fraternities and sororities also help in the leadership and organization of these groups. Many students are also involved with club sports and intramurals, such as flag football and rugby. However, students complain of a lack of spirit for their college varsity teams. While some attend football games, the crowd is said to be "calm" rather than loud. Students claim some of the best teams at Miami are the men's swimming and ice hockey units.

> **"Miami is filled with people who make sure they get their work done before they go out."**

While students generally agree that they are studious during the week, the Miami weekend scene is a thriving one. The Greek system is the center of social life on campus. However, freshmen do not rush until second semester of freshman year, leaving some feeling left out during first semester. Many students feel that joining a sorority or fraternity is the key to having a vibrant social life because it is easy to meet people at fraternity-sponsored social events. Although there are many campus-run activities like concerts and lectures, most feel that these are overshadowed by the Greek scene. Some of these events include Green Beer Day, where all beer is dyed green in honor of St. Patrick's Day, and the many "Grab a Date" dances, where fraternity or sorority members scurry around to pick dates for the evening. Many students also spend their leisure time on Uptown, a brick road lined with many restaurants, bars, and dance clubs. Some popular bars in town include Mack and Joe's, First Run, and Hole in the Wall. On campus, students must live according to the administration's strict "three strikes" policy. Here, if a student receives three alcohol violations, he or she is suspended from school. Despite administrative efforts, drinking is still quite prevalent at Miami. Students say, however, non-drinkers will not have a problem with the campus social scene provided they are comfortable with the party scene itself. In addition to all these social events on campus, some students also take occasional trips to Cincinnati or Dayton for movies, special events, or a more varied social scene.

While diversity is slowly increasing at Miami, students say "that's not saying much." One student described diversity at Miami as being "diversity between what Abercrombie sweater you're wearing." Indeed, most students who attend Miami come from white, upper-middle-class, conservative families. Most students also come from Ohio or other Midwestern states. Students agree that homosexual couples and interracial couples are not condoned by a large part of the student body, and students with a more liberal view than most Miami students tend to live on Western Campus. Students feel that the Miami student body is friendly overall. However, some out-of-state students find it harder to find their niche because so many in-state students already arrive with friends from home and connections at the school. Many students suggest the Greek system as the fastest way to meet friends. Also, male freshmen seem to find it more difficult to make ties with upperclassmen. One student cited a "respect factor" expected of freshmen men to male upperclassmen.

Miami students also seem to take pride in their appearance. Students wear dressy clothing pretty regularly, giving support to the description of Miami as "J. Crew U," full of "black pant girls and khaki boys." Many also put in the effort to keep fit. As one student put it, "Any time of day you'll see people running, and the Rec Center's always busy." Perhaps due to these efforts, males and females both agree that the campus is not the only thing that looks good at Miami. While there are more females than males on campus, females describe the stereotypical Miami male as a "player just looking for a good time" instead of a serious commitment.

Although student spirit for the Redhawks athletic teams is fledgling at best, students have pride in their school. Miami alumni, happy with their college experience, give large donations to the school each year. Both the alumni and the current students believe that a beautiful campus, excellent undergraduate instruction, and students who take pride in themselves all combine to create a fulfilling college experience.—*Roseanne Pereira and Staff*

FYI
The three best things about Miami are "the small classes, the Greek scene, and the beautiful campus."
The three worst things about Miami are "the lack of diversity, lack of school spirit, and conservatism."
One thing you should do before you graduate from Miami is "drink some green beer on St. Patrick's Day."
One thing I'd like to have known before coming here is "most students are from Ohio."

Oberlin College

Address: 101 North
Professor Street; Oberlin,
OH 44074
Phone: 440-775-8411
E-mail address: college
.admissions@oberlin.edu
Web site URL:
www.oberlin.edu
Founded: 1833
Private or Public: private
Religious affiliation: none
Location: rural
**Undergraduate
enrollment:** 2,932
Total enrollment: 2,932
Percent Male / Female:
41% / 59%
Percent Minority: 22%
Percent African-American:
8%

Percent Asian: 9%
Percent Hispanic: 4%
Percent Native-American:
1%
**Percent in-state / out-of-
state:** 5% / 95%
Percent Pub HS: 66%
Number of Applicants:
4,504
Percent Accepted:
54%
**Percent Accepted who
enroll:** 30%
Entering: 730
Transfers: 91
Application Deadline:
15 Jan
Mean SAT: 671 V,
637 M
Mean ACT: 28

Middle 50% SAT range:
610–720 V,
590–680 M
Middle 50% ACT range:
26–31
3 Most popular majors:
english, history and biology
Retention: 89%
Graduation rate: 59%
On-campus housing:
100%
Fraternities: 0%
Sororities: 0%
Library: 1,200,000
volumes
Tuition and Fees:
$23,174 in; $23,174 out
Room and Board: $6,238
Financial aid, first-year:
53%

Oberlin has a "brilliantly progressive history." It was the first college to graduate students regardless of race and the first to graduate women and men in the same programs. In 1970, Oberlin became the first college to house men and women in the same dorms and made the cover of *Life* magazine for it. Oberlin students have always been politically progressive and active and proud of it. This progressiveness is evident in all aspects of Obies' lives, from academics to extracurriculars, from housing to parties.

Academics

Academic requirements at Oberlin involve nine credits from each of three areas: arts/humanities, social sciences, and natural sciences, in addition to nine credits of cultural diversity classes, one class with writing proficiency, and one class with quantitative proficiency. Students say that the administration is "pretty lenient. The college is respectful of different students' interests and ability to plan the most appropriate schedule for themselves." Several students said that they were "glad that the cultural diversity requirement exists." Class size averages around 22 and only

about four courses each semester have more than 100 students. All courses are taught by professors; there are "very few TAs and they do not do much." One student recommended "seeking out the really great professors," and another one added, "I should've talked to upperclass students from the beginning to get advice on which professors are best." Professors "often assign, or are open to, non-traditional methods of evaluation: performances, portfolios, group papers, and projects are fairly common—this is great, because it keeps you stimulated, thinking in multiple ways." An example of the close student–faculty interaction is the Professor Beers event, sponsored by the college; if a professor and student show up together, they get free popcorn, beer, or soda.

Getting into classes is "not a problem if you know how to work it." One student said, "Registering on-line, you'll probably only get half the classes you want. The trick is to write the professor early and signal your interest, get on the waiting lists, and come to class each time until somebody else drops it." Obies aren't cutthroat competitive about grades, which is "refreshing, although most do care somewhat about their GPA. If you like, you can take a class (or all your classes) pass/fail and get a written evaluation instead."

Oberlin is well known for its prestigious music conservatory, which attracts world-renowned musicians and conductors (students as well as professors) to the campus. Besides being a union of talent for those taking part in its programs, the Conservatory, or "the Con," as it is referred to in Obie-speak, is a great resource for the entire college community, as it enables them to attend some great concerts and be surrounded by amazing musicians.

Drag Ball and Safer Sex

Drugs and alcohol are definitely present on campus: TGIF at 4:30 on Fridays, which involves beer and music on the central green, is one of the clearest signs that Oberlin students like a good time. Pressure to drink is low and non-drinkers do not feel left out; "People tend to respect others' decisions regarding drugs and alcohol." Being underage is "definitely not a problem," and residential advisors are "unlikely to turn anybody in; neither are campus officers." The administration's policy on alcohol is "don't ask; don't tell." Certain parties have to be registered, but "if you don't act stupid or too loud, they won't bust your door down." Kegs are allowed on campus for registered parties, although "most keggers are off campus."

The largest and best party of the year is, "without a doubt, Drag Ball, a celebration by all of sexual freedom and expression." Safer Sex Night is "a smaller party than Drag Ball, but just as uniquely Oberlin." Despite the existence of Safer Sex Night, several students noted that there is "not nearly enough sex" on campus: "If you want sex, it's there for the getting. If you are looking for something more long-term, you will have to work on it more." Dates at Oberlin "consist of getting coffee." Besides the parties, campus-wide organized activities are "pretty good—we have an eclectic film society; a lot of good speakers come. Recent concerts include Angelique Kidjo, the Afro-Cuban All-Stars, Bela Fleck, Amiri Baraka. Students often organize thematic lecture or film series, and these are "generally excellent."

The Stereotypical Obie?

Attractive people are "lacking in the traditional sense of the word; people here are individuals. I think most people here had a hard time fitting in in high school or chose not to." Another student noted, "There is not one stereotype here; I've identified at least six stereotypical Obies: the Connie (superbusy prodigy, always-working Conservatory student), the crunchy granola hippie, the pomo (perenially critical and always wearing black), the outrageous pink-haired rebel, the obsessive activist, the straitlaced future physicist, etcetera." There is no stereotypical Obie dress, although "Birkenstocks are pretty common." One student explained, "People like to show their individuality, so clothing trends rarely take hold."

Oberlin is "very culturally diverse, especially for a small liberal arts college. We come from all 50 states, numerous countries, and all sorts of childhoods." Other students noted, "I wish we were more socioeconomically diverse" and that "Oberlin needs more class and racial diversity." Within this diverse community, Obies "definitely tend to self-segregate: co-ops attract lots of white hippie types, and some program houses draw many of the people of color. Oberlin does have a problem with people hanging around similar people all the time." One junior mentioned that there are "a lot of rich people who like to pretend they're not," and another referred to "rich liberals who won't recognize their own contradictions."

Let's Bond As We Bake Bread

The average freshman dorm room is "a double, boxy, pretty standard unless you luck out and get placed in Tank Co-op, Baldwin, [or] Talcott." Sophomores can apply for an on-campus single, a room in a housing co-op, a quad, etc. Each dorm votes on whether it wants the floors and bathrooms to be coed. In co-ops, bathrooms are generally coed. There is one female-only house and one male-only ("and stereotypically jock") house. The language and program houses (such as La Casa Hispanica, French, German, Russian, Third World, and African Heritage Houses) are "good for building a thematic community and practicing a foreign language." The eight popular housing co-ops serve one-third of the student body; they are cheaper and "good for fun and community." Students run them, order the food, cook it, clean up, and plan fun events; each co-oper puts in a certain amount of work. Said one student: "There is great community in the co-ops . . . you get a unique bonding experience when you bake bread with someone every week. Some serve meat; some don't—each has a different personality." Lunch and dinner are served every day, breakfast sometimes. "It's a lot of fun and a great way to meet people. Co-op life features extra-fancy gourmet and/or thematic meals twice a week, occasional picnics, weekly pizza-and-beer, and the occasional naked cleanup crew."

Only juniors and seniors can live off campus, and "slightly more than half do. Most everyone lives within a half-mile of campus. There are apartments, run-down houses, parts of houses, fancy houses, near and far ones, everything." The dining alternative to the co-ops is the Campus Dining Services (CDS), which provides "typical okay institutional food, served at several dining facilities: a monolithic facility on North Campus, a smaller facility on South Campus, a fast-food and packaged-staples option in the student union, and the two best halls, Talcott and Lord Saunders."

Get Out of the Bubble
Community service is a popular and effective way to get off campus, with mentoring and tutoring being the primary volunteer activities. One student said, "Like many colleges, Oberlin has a 'bubble'—get out and help out. Oberlin is a demographic blip in one of the poorest counties in Ohio." There are more than 100 chartered student organizations, ranging from the Oberlin College Can Consortium Steel Drum Band, to the Pottery Co-op, to student publications, to political groups. "Rumor has it that a few Republicans reside here, but they're few and far between; Nader is a local hero." Environmental and political groups, especially socialist, are among the popular organizations on campus. People are identified by what they do: "A person involved in Ohio PIRG is known

as a PIRGer or a socialist is known as a socialist."

> **"You get a unique bonding experience when you bake bread with someone every week."**

When asked about the football team, one junior commented, "Our team has won one game since I've been a student here and I think that was the first win in a few years." Other teams are more successful and more supported, however: "Men's and women's Ultimate Frisbee teams are fantastic and our women's lacrosse team rocks. Our coed ice hockey team is great, too." The sports facilities, open for everybody's use, are "fantastic: there are 23 playing fields, indoor and outdoor tracks, a nearly Olympic-sized swimming pool, weight machines, open courts, gym, sauna; it's all here and in great condition."

A Crazy Quilt
The Oberlin campus is "very flat. There is no sign of a hill." The architecture varies "wildly by building, making the campus look like a crazy quilt, but I like the effect. [There are] some very old buildings, some very modern and new, some ugly and institutional, many beautiful." Tappan Square in the middle of campus is where "people stroll around both from the college and the town, hanging out on park benches and playing on the bandstand. The ephemeral albino squirrel might make an appearance. Somebody might be painting one of three free-speech stones with a political slogan, [news of an] upcoming concert, or [a] happy-birthday wish." Wilder Student Union houses the dance club, the 'Sco, in its basement and the offices of almost every student group. It is a popular spot for small groups to meet and study. The new Environmental Studies Center is "our pride and joy." It is "groundbreaking in terms of sustainable architecture and is a beautiful example of 'green design.'" A brand-new science building is currently being constructed that will be finished in 2002 and will house biology and chemistry departments.

Most people don't have cars, but "you

need one to get off campus." The surrounding area is three blocks of downtown that one student described as "really cute and quaint." Interesting off-campus places include "Adam's Corn Maze, various caves and quarries that you'll find by word-of-mouth, little waffle houses and greasy spoons, the occasional ugly mall." The area around campus has "a lot of vivid personality, especially the small towns." Mostly people go clubbing in Cleveland or go out to eat at a nearby restaurant. There are some county and state parks nearby, and the Outing Club often organizes weekend or fall/spring break trips to other parks and preserves. One student noted that "the surrounding area doesn't add to campus life, but it'll add to *your*

life. You can survive the whole time staying on campus, but your experience will be much richer—and have much more real-world perspective—if you venture off campus to explore, talk with people, do community service, or just get away."

With its Conservatory, politically active student body and progressive history, the opportunity to live in co-ops, and the strong academics, which allows for creative evaluation methods, Oberlin offers a unique experience. "It's not an experience that everyone would enjoy, though," warned one junior. "But if this sounds good to you, then Oberlin might be the place where you'll spend the best four years of your life." —*Engin Yenidunya*

FYI

The three best things about attending Oberlin are "the varying architectural styles that make the campus really pretty, the politically active and progressive student body, Professor Beers."

The three worst things about attending Oberlin are "the relative lack of socioeconomic diversity, tuition, rich liberals who won't recognize their own contradictions."

The three things that every student should do before graduating from Oberlin are "dress in drag and do the runway at Drag Ball, see tons of Conservatory concerts—so much talent, so close by—spend at least one semester in the co-op dining experience."

One thing I would like to have known before coming here is "there are more 'peculiar' people here, I believe, than at most other colleges."

Ohio State University

Address: Third Floor Lincoln Tower; 1800 Cannon Drive; Columbus, OH 43210
Phone: 614-292-5995
E-mail address: oafa@fa.adm.ohiostate.edu
Web site URL: www.osu.edu
Founded: 1870
Private or Public: public
Religious affiliation: none
Location: urban
Undergraduate enrollment: 36,252
Total enrollment: 48,278
Percent Male/Female: 52%/48%
Percent Minority: 15%

Percent African-American: 8%
Percent Asian: 5%
Percent Hispanic: 2%
Percent Native-American: 0%
Percent in-state/out-of-state: 89%/11%
Percent Pub HS: 87%
Number of Applicants: 18,952
Percent Accepted: 79%
Percent Accepted who enroll: 41%
Entering: 6,139
Transfers: 1,715
Application Deadline: 15 Feb
Mean SAT: 557 V, 573 M
Mean ACT: 24

Middle 50% SAT range: 503–627 V, 511–647 M
Middle 50% ACT range: 21–27
3 Most popular majors: English, communications and marketing
Retention: 82%
Graduation rate: 57%
On-campus housing: 100%
Fraternities: 8%
Sororities: 8%
Library: 5,100,000 volumes
Tuition and Fees: $3,879 in; $11,448 out
Room and Board: $5,289
Financial aid, first-year: 53%

Looking for that Big Ten college experience, replete with an enormous student body, endless academic possibilities, and tons of school pride? Ohio State University, located in Columbus, might be just the place for you.

Size Matters

With an undergraduate population of over 42,000, there is no denying that OSU is HUGE. Offering 177 majors and over 10,000 courses, the school has something for everyone. Engineering, history, and business are all described as being popular majors, with psychology and business reportedly as the easiest. "Everyone who's a sucker takes psych," said one sophomore. Organic Chemistry is almost unanimously declared the toughest class at OSU, with statistics, economics, and honors science classes also considered difficult. All students must complete the General Education Curriculum, or GEC, which varies from major to major. Most majors require a combination including a foreign language, physical science, and biology sequence. While some students appreciate the liberal arts approach, others are not so thrilled. "It's hell!" griped one student. Undergrads are generally happy with the quality of their professors, though many complain that their teaching assistants have "English issues."

OSU students also have the opportunity to apply to the honors program, a rigorous curriculum for academically competitive students. Students in the honors program benefit from priority in scheduling, smaller class sizes, and generally a more intimate environment within the university. While scheduling is no problem for athletes and honor students, it can sometimes be a problem for others, depending on the class. In an attempt to make registration easier, OSU has implemented an on-line course registration system, where students may also view course availability and waiting lists.

Living and Eating

All freshmen at OSU must live in the dorms unless they are living at home. There are three main areas of campus in which students can choose to live, each with its own personality. South Campus is the social end of campus, with older dorms and two-person suites. North Campus is quieter and the dorms are generally thought to be nicer, with air-conditioned, two- and four-person suites. West Campus contains the two Towers, Lincoln and Merrill, which house "jocks and honor students." Housing can be either coed or single-sex, depending on floor and dorm. For students looking for an alternative to normal dorm life, there are many different types of theme housing. Humanities, engineering, agriculture, international, and arts are just a few of the possibilities. Steeb Hall houses freshmen who wish to participate in a First Year Experience leadership program.

All three main areas of campus contain their own cafeteria. Most students seem to agree that the food is just plain "bad," and many choose not to have a meal plan at all. Those who do can choose a plan with 8, 10, 14, or 19 meals per week. Sprouts, in South Commons, is the only vegetarian dining hall, and few other on-campus alternatives exist. The university is attempting to expand the meal program, though they have not met with success so far. Most juniors and seniors choose to live off campus and take advantage of the plethora of restaurants up and down High Street. Ample housing exists in the areas surrounding Ohio State, and students say to "expect to pay more the closer you are" to the middle of the sprawling campus.

Buckeyes and Booze

Make no mistake about it: Ohio State Buckeyes like to party. With over 50,000 total students, you can bet that there is always something going on. Underclassmen tend to frequent the clubs and bars on High Street such as the Spot and Not Al Too's. Frat parties are another popular diversion, as OSU supports an active Greek scene. Being underage is not perceived as a problem by most students, and as one student stated, "If you want alcohol you can get it." For those looking for alternatives to the party scene, there are plenty. With over 500 registered student organizations, "everyone's in something." From environmental groups to Starfish, the Jewish Center's community service organization, the options are as diverse as the student body. Each dorm, as well as many clubs and groups, has its own intramural teams, ranging from basketball to inner tube water polo. The Wexner Center for the Arts, located on campus, frequently has performances and exhibitions, and the Ohio Union, OSU's student center, often sponsors speakers, as well as providing space to study and places to eat.

> ### "Sometimes it pisses me off it's so big!"

Buckeyes do not generally just limit themselves to the campus area but take advantage of nearby shops, restaurants, and movies. Downtown Columbus and the Short North are only a short 10-minute bus ride away straight down High Street. With the inaugural season of pro hockey in Columbus in 2000–2001, Blue Jackets games attract large crowds of students and Columbus residents alike to the new Arena District in the heart of downtown. Bucca de Beppo, Lemongrass, and Haiku are all popular downtown restaurants. Closer to campus, the Lennox Town Center boasts a 24-screen movie theater, several restaurants such as Don Pablo's, Champps, and Johnny Rockets, as well as a Barnes and Noble, Target, and Old Navy.

An Urban Campus

Although for years the stretch of High Street near campus was run-down, with seedy bars and riddled with graffiti, recent efforts by the Gateway project to revive the area have proven to be successful. The smaller stores are disappearing and giving way to Starbucks, Urban Outfitters, and Steak and Shake, and the overall safety and appearance of the area is greatly improving. Most students say they feel safe on campus, and as one student commented, "OSU does a good job at trying to keep people safe."

Though there is no true stereotype for a student body so large, most say it is mostly middle-class, and over 90% of the students are from Ohio. As one student said, "OSU could be more diverse for having so many people." With its sprawling, flat campus, getting around without a car

is easy, though for students living off campus a car is almost a necessity. The university is centered around the Oval, a large, grassy open space in the middle of campus. For some, it is their favorite hangout to play Frisbee, read, or socialize. However, for those making the trek across the Oval to get to class, it also becomes a big pain. "Sometimes it pisses me off it's so big!" complained one student.

"Rabid Football Fans" and TBDBITL

Ohio State students are not just passionate about their football; they're "rabid," commented one student gleefully. The Game, the annual football contest between Ohio State and Michigan, their bitter Big Ten rival to the north, inspires an entire week of partying and spirit activities. The OSU Marching Band, an impressive group of several hundred musicians, is widely hailed among Buckeyes as "The Best Damn Band In The Land," or TBD-BITL, as a popular bumper sticker reads. Their formation of the script "Ohio" during halftime is a widely lauded Buckeye tradition. However, OSU is not just about football. The men's basketball team made a Final Four bid in 1999 and has boasted winning seasons since, playing in the brand-new Schottenstein Center. The women's gymnastics, synchronized swimming, and rowing teams have also met with successful seasons recently. But Buckeyes need not be varsity athletes to participate in athletics. Intermurals are popular, and Larkins Hall is a huge recreational facility open to all students. Containing five swimming pools, multiple gymnasiums, and weight rooms, the facility has become outdated, and plans are in the works to raze the entire thing and build an all-new, state-of-the-art center.

Though most students who choose to attend OSU are well aware of its immense size, many are still shocked when they see how big it really is. However, size does not always mean anonymity. Said one student: "The diverse opportunities, people, and points of view are available because it's such a big place. I didn't expect how easy it would be to make the school feel small. I'm not a faceless, nameless number. I'm a person!" —*Melissa J. Merritt*

FYI

The three best things about attending Ohio State are "the size, the football games, and there is something for everyone here."

The three worst things about attending Ohio State are "it's huge, so you can't find anyone to answer your question; the curve in the science classes; and the fact that most of my TAs don't speak English and some of my professors seem like they would rather be in lab than teaching."

The three things that every student should do before graduating from Ohio State are "jump into Mirror Lake the Thursday before the Michigan game, go to a Michigan game, go to at least one really wild party."

One thing I'd like to have known before coming here is "I'm not as smart or athletic as I thought I was."

Ohio University

Address: 120 Chubb Hall; Athens, OH 45701
Phone: 740-593-4100
E-mail address: frshinfo@ohiou.edu
Web site URL: www.ohiou.edu
Founded: 1804
Private or Public: public
Religious affiliation: none
Location: suburban
Undergraduate enrollment: 16,619
Total enrollment: 19,189
Percent Male/Female: 45%/55%
Percent Minority: 6%
Percent African-American: 4%
Percent Asian: 1%

Percent Hispanic: 1%
Percent Native-American: 0%
Percent in-state/out-of-state: 96%/4%
Percent Pub HS: 84%
Number of Applicants: 12,722
Percent Accepted: 74%
Percent Accepted who enroll: 37%
Entering: 3,483
Transfers: 504
Application Deadline: 15 Feb
Mean SAT: 555 V, 551 M
Mean ACT: 24
Middle 50% SAT range: 500–600 V, 510–600 M

Middle 50% ACT range: 21–26
3 Most popular majors: business, biological science and communication
Retention: 85%
Graduation rate: 43%
On-campus housing: 100%
Fraternities: 11%
Sororities: 16%
Library: 2,100,000 volumes
Tuition and Fees: $4,530 in; $9,531 out
Room and Board: $5,076
Financial aid, first-year: NA

Colorful flower beds, rolling hills, and lush trees characterize the campus of Ohio University. Many students cite the cobblestone streets, acres of green grass, and small surrounding community as factors in their decision to attend OU. This large state school has more to offer than just charming scenery, however. For many of the students roaming the picturesque campus, academics are the first consideration.

Challenging and Fast-paced

Students view OU's academic curriculum as challenging and fast-paced. In addition, most say that the choice of classes is diverse enough to satisfy almost anyone's interests. Undergrads consider the college of journalism among the best departments, and telecommunications, one of the most popular majors. To ensure a well-rounded education, the university requires all students to fulfill three "tier" requirements before graduation. Tier One consists of math and English courses taken during the first year. Tier Two requires 30 credit hours in the following five subject areas: applied sciences and technology, humanities and fine arts, natural sciences and mathematics, social sciences, and third world cultures. Students cite the third world cultures requirement as especially thought provoking, since it deals with issues beyond more traditional, Western civilization courses. The third tier consists of an English composition course taken during junior year. The most popular courses fill up quickly, so some students have to settle for their second-choice classes in order to meet the requirements on time.

Class size at OU ranges from 20 students in small seminars to about 300 in lecture courses. Professors teach the large lecture courses and reportedly are receptive to students' questions. Aside from handling the smaller lecture discussion sections, TAs teach most lower-level English courses, which students tend to enjoy. One freshman described his English course as "the most fun course I've taken yet."

Where You'll Live

Dorms at OU promote interaction among all levels of undergraduates. The seven freshman dorms allow frosh to get to know each other during their first year, while the other three classes mix in several upperclass dorms. Single-sex and coed housing are available to accommodate student preferences. Bryan Hall is especially popular for its kitchen, laundry facilities, and quiet location. Residents consider the other dorms comfortable and spacious, although some recommend bringing a carpet to avoid "cold floors in the morning."

While Alden Library is considered the best place for quiet study or research at OU, in warm weather many students take their books outside and engage in some social studying on the college green. A sort of outdoor student union, the green is also a favorite spot for organizational meetings, picnics, or just plain hanging out between classes. The Baker Student Center is another popular destination for students looking to blow off steam. It houses a bowling alley and billiard room, and is the site of social events sponsored by the University Program Council. During the winter, students relieve stress by sledding down Jefferson Hill.

With more than 20 bars and dance clubs in Athens, drinking at OU is a common weekend activity. The Athens police department guards against underage drinking, however, by placing officers in bars. Apart from off-campus drinking, there are many university-sponsored activities through out the year. OU's annual Halloween celebration is the largest campus party, attracting 30,000 students from colleges all over Ohio. To prepare for the celebration, the OU administration closes off Athens's main street, and students cover the town with Halloween decorations and posters. On Halloween night, students dress in costumes and party up and down the streets of Athens.

The Greek system at OU is strong, with most students calling it the backbone of OU's social scene. With such a large student population, fraternities and sororities provide a more personal environment conducive to socializing. "There really isn't pressure to rush," one freshman said, "but it is encouraged because it's how you meet people."

> **During the winter, students relieve stress by sledding down Jefferson Hill.**

As for sports, the OU Bobcats are traditionally strong in hockey; Bird Arena is always standing-room-only during hockey games. On the other hand, OU's football squad is not as successful. Although many fans turn out to cheer for the team in the first half of home games, the crowd usually disperses after the nationally acclaimed marching band finishes its halftime show. Even during games against the Miami University Redskins, OU's biggest football rival, crowds are scarce. Intramurals don't draw much support.

OU has earned itself a party-school reputation, but with such a large student body, there are just as many students who choose a less rigorous social scene as those who go out every night. Nevertheless, students at OU are a spirited group, and this spirit shows itself in the many activities that they engage in, from studying to partying.

No matter how students decide to spend their four years at OU, the fact is that most are happy with their education and college experiences when they graduate. As one senior put it, "OU is a school I can be proud of."—*Santush Aravind and Staff*

FYI
The three best things about OU are "games against our rivals, freshman English, and having the Baker Student Union."
The three worst things about OU are "our crummy football team, the tier system, and our party-school rep."
The three things that every student should do before graduating from OU are "sled down Jefferson Hill, hit the Athens bar scene, and really dress up for Halloween."
One thing I'd like to have known coming here is "how much I would hate to leave this place."

Ohio Wesleyan University

Address: 61 South Sandusky Street; Delaware, OH 43015
Phone: 740-368-3020
E-mail address: owuadmit@cc.owu.edu
Web site URL: www.owu.edu
Founded: 1842
Private or Public: private
Religious affiliation: Methodist
Location: suburban
Undergraduate enrollment: 1,873
Total enrollment: 1,873
Percent Male/Female: 49%/51%
Percent Minority: 7%

Percent African-American: 4%
Percent Asian: 2%
Percent Hispanic: 1%
Percent Native-American: 0%
Percent in-state/out-of-state: 37%/63%
Percent Pub HS: 71%
Number of Applicants: 2,021
Percent Accepted: 85%
Percent Accepted who enroll: 30%
Entering: 515
Transfers: 515
Application Deadline: rolling
Mean SAT: 593 V, 619 M

Mean ACT: 26
Middle 50% SAT range: NA
Middle 50% ACT range: NA
3 Most popular majors: zoology, psychology and economics/management
Retention: 81%
Graduation rate: 58%
On-campus housing: 99%
Fraternities: 50%
Sororities: 30%
Library: 490,000 volumes
Tuition and Fees: $20,940 in; $20,940 out
Room and Board: $6,560
Financial aid, first-year: 73%

Just fifteen minutes outside of Columbus, Ohio, is the small town of Delaware, which is home to the even smaller Ohio Wesleyan University. With a population of almost two thousand people, Ohio Wesleyan creates a supportive and personal environment. As one student said, "I feel like I know all of campus, if not by name, by face." These feelings of comfort and community extend into all realms of campus life.

Where Everybody Knows Your Name

Academics at OWU are highly praised by students who love their small classes and caring professors. As one sophomore put it, the professors are "obviously here because they want to be here." Students applaud that professors know them by their first names, give out home phone numbers, entertain them and picnics or din-

ners, and just generally "work with you to make sure you get what you want out of a class." This creates an atmosphere where students feel supported by their professors.

The university, as a whole, is reportedly committed to helping students excel. For example, the Writing Resources Center is open Monday through Friday with the purpose of helping all students become "more confident, effective writers." One undergrad says, "The step-by-step help I received at the Writing Resource Center improved my writing dramatically." Another mentioned that while "They won't write the paper for you, they will help with any stage of the writing process." This is only one of the many academic support systems that OWU provides for its students. However, students do note that they do have problems with the administration when it comes to "implementing and supporting [other] student services."

Academically, OWU is a liberal arts college that exposes its students to a wide range of academic disciplines. To ensure a well-rounded education, the college requires Freshman English (or the equivalent in the form of standardized test scores), two semesters of a foreign language (or suitable proficiency test scores), one course in fine arts, three in the social sciences, three in the natural sciences, three in the humanities, plus at least 15 "above-110 classes." Also required are three writing-intensive courses and a course that deals with non-European culture. While students have mixed views on these requirements, as one particular student complained about the language requirement, most feel that it directs rather than limits their course schedule. They find that there are enough courses available to make it easy to find a class that you are interested in that also fulfills a requirement. While most majors are considered difficult, students cited the sciences as having the most difficult majors, and sociology as one of the easiest majors. Most students say it is easier to be admitted to Ohio Wesleyan than to stay there. As one junior put it, "I lose friends every year who just can't make the grade."

Let's Go . . . Battling Bishops!!!
Yes it's true. The Battling Bishop was featured as one of the worst college mascots in the nation by *Time* magazine. However, this doesn't stop the students of OWU from competing and winning in many athletics activities. While it is said that the spirit is especially high for lacrosse and men's soccer, which has won the NCAA Division III championship in nine of the last fifteen years, no sport is without support. That also goes for club and intramural competition, as the university embraces the idea that "there's something for everyone at OWU."

And for those of us who lack certain hand-eye or foot-eye coordination, OWU has a multitude of other activities ranging from academic honor societies to service clubs to the See America Club. Student actors are able to participate through the strong theatre program in numerous pro-

ductions throughout the year. For the writers of the university, there is both a school newspaper, the *Transcript*, and a campus literary magazine, the *Owl*. Amongst the larger community service activities are the efforts of the Delaware Initiative and Columbus Initiative.

Chow and Chambers
Students at OWU describe the food as "not bad" and "edible." Students can use their meal card at any cafeteria, dining hall and Thompson's, an on-campus grocery store that has convenience items and the all-important ice cream. Students generally eat at one of the dorm dining halls or the Campus Center, which during weekday lunchtime is reportedly extremely packed.

Students have a wide variety of options regarding their housing, including an all-female dorm (Hayes Hall), co-ed dorms and Welch, which prohibits loud noise and alcohol and requires a 3.0 GPA for admittance. While Stuyvesant and Smith are named as two of the best coed dorms, students say that everyone regards their one dorm as the best, and Stuy and Smith just happen to house more students. In addition, 50 percent of men and 30 percent of women are involved in the Greek system and choose to live in their respective houses after freshman year.

> "It is because of the students and our social lives that Ohio Wesleyan is a school worth attending."

The campus itself is described as having a "New Englandish" appeal with a variety of limestone, old stone, and brick buildings. It also encompasses over 200 acres of "lush landscaping and tree-lined walkways." Many of the older academic buildings' designs give hints of prior purposes. One undergraduate goes as far as to say, "Almost every building here was once something else," such as a hotel or Methodist church.

Finding a Niche
As most OWU students study hard on the weekdays, they feel proud in their ability to party come the weekend. A typical weekend schedule has been described as

"Friday, party; Saturday, sleep late, maybe take in a sporting event, then party; Sunday, work." Students believe that they use the same intense focus for academics during the week as for partying on weekends. Students also like to designate Wednesday as a party night, in order to break up the workweek. However, while it may seem that drinking is prevalent on party nights, non-drinkers will not feel uncomfortable at OWU as long as they can be comfortable being around other people who do drink. Drugs, on the other hand, are not "big in the frats," as one student said, but can be found for those who are interested.

While many students choose to go to the "Hill," where fraternity houses are, on weekends, there exist many alternative campus hangouts. Popular amongst the student population, the Grub Pub entertains with comedians and musical groups. And for still more comic relief, one can do no better than turning to the Battling Bishops for finely tuned improv skills. Still, there are also frequent film screenings in the Philips Auditorium as well as the Coffee House. Students also report that hanging out in the dorm rooms is a common occurrence. In addition, off-campus housing has recently become the site of many weekend parties.

Yet, while there are a multitude of options, some students are dismayed by the lack social life "because you are constantly seeing the same people." But this can also be helpful as it helps incoming students find their niche: Wherever you go, you will recognize a friendly face. The quaint town of Delaware also adds to the comfort and intimacy of the student body. It provides some small shops and restaurants, and if students want big city excitement, they need to only travel as far as Columbus.

It Just Makes You All Warm and Fuzzy Inside

Students describe their peers as open-minded and accepting of both homosexual and interracial couples. While some students complain about the lack of diversity, one student said that the diversity is "good, but that the international students tend to be cliquey with one another." In fact, despite the name Ohio Wesleyan, over half the population comes from out of state. The school has even established scholarships for students from different geographical backgrounds within the United States. Although Ohio Wesleyan shares thee many benefits of being small schools, it does have some drawbacks. As one student noted, "Everyone you run around with socially will know lots about you;" so breaking out of constricting cliques can be difficult.

However, most students attend Ohio Wesleyan because they believe that the positive aspects of a small college far outweigh the negatives. Overall, students seem to credit themselves and their peers as the reason for attending the university. One student said, "It is because of the students and our social lives that Ohio Wesleyan is a school worth attending." The students at OWU are friendly, open-minded, hardworking, and fun people who want to experience their lives to the fullest. They work hard and party hard. Moreover, they value that the same peers, who they can carry on a thoughtful discussion with during the academic week, are the same people that they can dance the night away with on the weekends.
—*Marissa Wagner*

FYI

The three best things about attending Ohio Wesleyan are "incredible and caring people, a unified campus and the ability to participate in any organization."

The three worst things about Ohio Wesleyan are "no low-fat and low-sodium foods, the isolation, and the Housing Department."

The three things to do before graduation are "to take a semester abroad, be in the Delta Zeta JelloTug-O-War, and live in a SLU (small living unit)."

One thing I'd like to have known before coming here is "the language requirement and the isolation."

University of Cincinnati

Address: PO Box 210063;
Cincinnati, OH 45221-
0091
Phone: 513-556-1100
E-mail address:
admissions@uc.edu
Web site URL: www.uc.edu
Founded: 1819
Private or Public: public
Religious affiliation:
none
Location: urban
Undergraduate
enrollment: 20,656
Total enrollment: NA
Percent Male / Female:
52% / 48%
Percent Minority: 18%
Percent African-American:
14%
Percent Asian: 3%

Percent Hispanic: 1%
Percent Native-American:
0%
Percent in-state / out-of-
state: 94% / 6%
Percent Pub HS: NA
Number of Applicants:
10,704
Percent Accepted: 86%
Percent Accepted who
enroll: 29%
Entering: 3,068
Transfers: NA
Application Deadline:
31 Jul
Mean SAT: 548 V,
556 M
Mean ACT: 23
Middle 50% SAT range:
480–600 V,
480–620 M

Middle 50% ACT range:
20–26
3 Most popular majors:
communication arts,
psychology and
accounting
Retention: 70%
Graduation rate:
NA
On-campus housing:
29%
Fraternities: 23%
Sororities: 14%
Library: 1,800,000
volumes
Tuition and Fees:
$4,026 in; $11,532 out
Room and Board:
$5,958
Financial aid, first-year:
58%

With a "very compact" campus, a majority of students living off campus, an enormous spectrum of interests, and "good school spirit at the Bearcats games," the University of Cincinnati contains many elements that combine to form the uniquely "urban but fairly quiet" atmosphere of the school.

The Social Spectrum

The wide variety that characterizes almost every aspect of the university begins with the social options facing each student at UC. On one hand, the "Greek societies lead the party scene," especially at the beginning of each quarter, when frats throw large open parties. Other popular fraternity events include the Sigma Alpha Epsilon Wedding Party, where everyone dresses in secondhand wedding clothes, and the infamous Paddy Murphy Week, which one student explained as an annual "weeklong party in honor of the SAE brother, Paddy Murphy, who tried to rid the world of alcohol during Prohibition, by drinking as much as he could, and died in the process." Aside from these large parties thrown by the Greek societies,

many students shy away from the scene, saying that "there is so much else to do, I would never waste my time at a frat house" and insisting that SAE in fact stands for "Same Assholes Everywhere."

Despite some apparent tensions between social groups, UC students seem to "always unite at the Bearcats games." The men's basketball team is popular both with students and locals, especially around the time of year near the Crosstown Shootout with rival Xavier University. "You can wait in line for five days to get tickets," one student claimed. For the nonvarsity athletes, UC offers club and intramural teams, all with "excellent facilities, but better ones for the varsity teams," as well as workout rooms, indoor tracks, and other fitness facilities. Each dorm also contains a weight room.

There is extensive construction and renovations occurring on campus. The expanded and renovated 93.2 million dollar CCM Village for the Conservatory of Music has just been completed as well as the Vontz Center for Molecular Studies. In fact University of Cincinnati has been designated "as one of the 20 'most distinguished campuses' in Europe and America" in 1999.

If You're Afraid of Heights, Um . . .

The five dormitories—two coed, one all-female, and two all-male—are all eleven-to-twelve-story skyscrapers. Each dorm contains a kitchenette and lounge per floor, as well as a main-lobby lounge, laundry facilities, a computer room, meeting rooms, and a weight room. Sawyer, "the best dorm on campus," goes to lucky upperclassmen who get a kitchen, bathroom, and common room in each suite. Students sound fairly happy with the living space, but they tend to complain about the height of the buildings and "the largest cockroach in the world," rumored to live in Daniels. On-campus living could get even better, students said, because "they plan to cover the campus with turf . . . someday we might actually have grass." The administration has taken action to increase the amount of "open space," by razing several building and replacing them with parks. "Its nice to look out the window and see grass instead of a big ugly building," one student said.

> Despite definite positive reviews about the co-op program, some students have criticized the academics at UC for being "frustratingly simple at lower levels."

The small percentage of on-campus residents "get pretty tight but don't explore the city as much as the off-campus livers," said one student. A common complaint is that "Cincinnati requires a car for college life." Most students wander beyond the realm of the university to frequent off-campus bars and coffeehouses, in the nearby trendy Clifton area, and the more culture-hungry students find intrigue at various theaters, concerts, symphonies, films, and art shows that the city has to offer. "Cincinnati's not so bad," claimed a second-year student from outside Ohio. "If you look hard enough, you can find stuff here, it's just a really different atmosphere

from, say, New York—much smaller scale." Students inclined to disagree tend to head up to other nearby colleges, such as Ohio State or Miami, when things at UC slow down.

Academics: Divided Opinions

Students must enroll in one of the academic schools—the School of Business, School of Engineering, Cincinnati Conservatory of Music (CCM), College of Arts and Sciences, or College of Design, Art, Architecture, and Planning (DAAP). Overall, students seem happy about academic options, facilities, and instruction. "The best part is that we only have one real requirement: a year of freshman English," one undergrad said. Students who join the co-op program rave about the experience. The program provides for a work-study job that includes paid internships with local businesses, "invaluable hands-on" experience, and many future contacts. Despite definite positive reviews about the co-op program, some students have criticized the academics at UC for being "frustratingly simple at lower levels." "Registration is the worst," said one student. "I never get the classes I want." Now, students can register on-line, "which makes the process a lot easier." Another student explained that "if you want good classes, you have to fight for them, but it's not that hard. I think whether you get professors or TAs, though, kind of depends on what department you're in and how lucky you are."

Overall, students agree that UC is a big enough school that "you can find a little of everything." Students say the News Record, a triweekly newspaper, has good stories. Another place where students often reach a consensus involves the food: "It sucks." "It's disgusting." "Don't do it, man." But again, there are always a few students who insist that "it's edible."

In a school large enough for a good amount of diversity, "the personality of this school seems really schizophrenic at times, but that's just because there are so many different aspects to everything. If you are looking for it somewhere, it's probably somewhere at UC. —*Lisa Barrett and Staff*

FYI
The three best things about UC are "the co-op program, the honors program, and diversity."
The three worst things about UC are "the food, registration, and the intro classes."
The three things that every student should do before graduating are "eat out, um, eat out, and eat out again."
One thing I'd like to have known before coming here is that "you are really on your own because it is such a big school."

Wittenberg University

Address: PO Box 720; Springfield, OH 45501
Phone: 937-327-6314
E-mail address: admissions @wittenberg.edu
Web site URL: www.wittenberg.edu
Founded: 1845
Private or Public: private
Religious affiliation: none
Location: small city
Undergraduate enrollment: 2,036
Total enrollment: 2,105
Percent Male/Female: 44%/56%
Percent Minority: 11%
Percent African-American: 8%

Percent Asian: 1%
Percent Hispanic: 1%
Percent Native-American: 0.5%
Percent in-state/out-of-state: 66%/34%
Percent Pub HS: 75%
Number of Applicants: 2,390
Percent Accepted: 88%
Percent Accepted who enroll: 29%
Entering: 620
Transfers: 35
Application Deadline: 15 Mar
Mean SAT: 560 V, 565 M
Mean ACT: 25

Middle 50% SAT range: 535–620 V, 540–630 M
Middle 50% ACT range: NA
3 Most popular majors: business, biology, education
Retention: 85%
Graduation rate: 71%
On-campus housing: 95%
Fraternities: 15%
Sororities: 35%
Library: 340,000 volumes
Tuition and Fees: $21,640 in; $21,640 out
Room and Board: $5,374
Financial aid, first-year: 75%

At Wittenberg University, the freedoms of a liberal arts education are combined with a conservative background based in Wittenberg's Evangelical Lutheran Church affiliation, a mix that students at Wittenberg find "supportive" and "just plain perfect."

Wittenberg's small student population is an asset in the eyes of most students. "Our size really makes it easy to get to know people. In fact, you can't escape it. From my first day on campus people I didn't know were saying hi to me," one student said. Other students were slightly less enthusiastic about the fact that their classmates knew all the details of those inevitable freshman-year mistakes. As one student put it, "Word travels fast, real fast."

Wittenberg Wisdom
Deadlines approach even more quickly. "We aren't some Ivy League, but we're no slackers either. I'd say we're as East Coast, academically, as an Ohio University can

get." Wittenberg grants scholarships based on academic merit, but not athletic ability. Students whose grades fall below 2.3 are given a semester to repair their grades before the administration suspends them.

Some students describe the course offerings at Wittenberg as "run of the mill," but the individual attention students receive is "truly above average." "I've never had a teaching assistant teach any of my classes," said one student, "and I've found my professors extremely approachable when it comes to scheduling appointments." Class sizes cater to this same idea, with a class of 40 students occurring "rarely, and even then only in the premed and intro science classes." Most classes enroll fewer than 20 students.

Pre-laws, Pre-meds, Pre-requisites
Popular departments at Wittenberg include biology, geology, and psychology, with numerous pre-med and pre-law

students as well. The Wittenberg education is founded on prerequisites in each of seven areas: Integrated Learning; Natural World; Social Institutions; the Fine, Performing, and Literary Arts; Religious and Philosophical Inquiry; Western Historical Perspectives; and Non-Western Cultures. Students also have to fulfill requirements in the two co-curricular areas of physical activity (which can be fulfilled through either intercollegiate athletics or various health and fitness courses) and community service, which requires sophomores to complete 30 hours of community service over the course of one term.

> **"From my first day on campus people I didn't know were saying hi to me."**

The campus facilities vary from "newly renovated and modern" to "built in the sixties and seventies and definitely showing it." Myers Hall, the original Wittenberg building of 1846, still stands and today houses Wittenberg's honor students. Dorms are coed, but floors are single-sex, and students can visit the opposite-sex floors only until 12:30 A.M. Students are required to live on campus for the first two years, after which time all but a few move off campus. Students complain that the dorms are surrounded by low income housing, making the off campus housing a more attractive option.

BYOB

Fraternity and sorority members, who make up approximately one-third of the campus population, live off campus in one of Wittenberg's 11 Greek houses (6 sororities and 5 fraternities), where much of the school's nightlife is centered. Alcohol is allowed only in the rooms of students 21 and over, and fraternity parties, instead of providing kegs, are BYOB. Keg parties can be found at private student houses off campus and out of the jurisdiction of university policy. The Ringside Cafe, which has a weekly college night, is a popular student hangout and many students say they drink, on average, four times per week. The town of Springfield "kinda sucks," one candid student remarked, because "we are the fast-food mecca of America." Students who want to find some serious grub often have to hunt long and hard before they find a cool hangout like Springfield's Mike and Rosey's Restaurant.

The student union, however, with its Marriott-catered food and flexible meal plans, is a popular hangout for the social studier and hungry student. The second floor of the union has a la carte food service open until 1 A.M., as well as a bar.

Students are heavily involved in a wide range of extracurriculars. Intercollegiate sports, especially against rivals Denison, Ohio Wesleyan, and Oberlin, are popular draws, as are various intramurals, rock climbing, spelunking, and water skiing on the nearby Springfield reservoir. To get away from campus, students often visit the "neat little hippie town" of Yellow Springs, a 15-minute drive from campus. When students want to relax on campus they head to the Hollow, a grassy vale that is filled with sledders throughout the winter. Warm weather invites sunbathing, picnicking, and Frisbee-tossing to the Hollow.

When spring approaches, the Hollow is also home to a weekend of music, drinking, and general stress relief called Wittstock. Past Wittstock performers have included Hootie and the Blowfish and 10,000 Maniacs, while some students "just go for the carnival aspect of it."

Recent changes to campus life have been minimal. Wittenberg switched from a trimester to semester system three years ago, and the new university president, Baird Tipson, "runs things pretty smoothly," one student said. Perhaps the homogeneity of the university is responsible for the smooth aspect of campus life. The population is predominantly Caucasian, and alternative lifestyles, such as homosexuality, are "kept on the down low . . . we don't discuss it much, and perhaps it's better that way."

Regardless of general student attitudes toward minority groups, undergrads described the atmosphere as "supportive," "intensely friendly," even "homey." Just one warning before you decide to make "Sprinklefield" your home away from home: "be prepared for the wet." —*Vladimir Cole and Staff*

FYI

The three best things about attending Wittenberg are "small class size accompanied by personal attention by professors, friendly and aesthetically pleasing campus, and off-campus housing for juniors and seniors in the immediate campus area."

The three worst things about attending Wittenberg are "the new parking lot that eliminated the Frisbee golf fields, some residence halls outdated and inadequate parking, and no paper towels in the bathrooms."

The three things that every student should do before graduating from Wittenberg are "go abroad, visit the Career Placement and Development Office, and take advantage of exit meetings."

One thing I'd like to have known before coming here is "that tuition increases 4% every year."

Oklahoma

Oklahoma State University

Address: 324 Student Union; Stillwater, OK 74078
Phone: 405-744-6858
E-mail address: admit@okstate.edu
Web site URL: www.okstate.edu
Founded: 1890
Private or Public: public
Religious affiliation: none
Location: small city
Undergraduate enrollment: 16,159
Total enrollment: 19,350
Percent Male / Female: 53%/47%
Percent Minority: 15%
Percent African-American: 3%

Percent Asian: 2%
Percent Hispanic: 2%
Percent Native-American: 8%
Percent in-state / out-of-state: 88%/12%
Percent Pub HS: NA
Number of Applicants: 5,716
Percent Accepted: 89%
Percent Accepted who enroll: 58%
Entering: 2,929
Transfers: 2,089
Application Deadline: rolling
Mean SAT: 569 V, 576 M
Mean ACT: 24

Middle 50% SAT range: 495–620 V, 500–640 M
Middle 50% ACT range: 21–27
3 Most popular majors: marketing, finance, accounting
Retention: 82%
Graduation rate: 43%
On-campus housing: 34%
Fraternities: 7%
Sororities: 8%
Library: 1,900,000 volumes
Tuition and Fees: $2,578 in; $7,168 out
Room and Board: $4,536
Financial aid, first-year: 44%

Although outsiders tend to characterize Oklahoma State as simply an agricultural university, one student pointed out that "the Ag school is actually the fourth smallest on campus." Oklahoma State has shed its "hick" image and now boasts top-rated undergraduate business and engineering programs. In fact, *Business Week* has recently ranked the accounting program among the top 15 in the United States.

A Building Program
Not surprisingly, the administration has worked to supplement OSU's rising academic reputation with first-rate campus facilities. Willard Hall, previously an undergraduate dorm, underwent extensive renovations and now houses the education department. Since the 1997–98 school year, the new $17.3 million Food Technology Center has been in use, and in 1998 officials completed the construction of a $27.5 million engineering lab. Only a few years ago, the university also celebrated the opening of an advanced telecommunications building, which NASA uses to broadcast educational programs to high schools across the country.

Open Doors, Open Arms
Students are generally satisfied with the faculty at OSU. "Our professors don't just have office hours," one junior said. "They pretty much have an open-door policy where we can go in anytime." The most significant praise, however, went to OSU president James Halligan and his administration for establishing themselves as "the most student-oriented people on campus, even more so than the professors." A number of new programs, focusing specifically on undergraduates, have improved the quality of life at OSU. For example, the administration recently increased the number of senior professors that teach in-

troductory courses and reduced the university's traditional reliance upon graduate TAs.

OSU rewards its most gifted students by offering a strong honors program. Students have the option to enroll in either the general honors program or an honors program in their particular major. All enjoy similar privileges: special housing in Parker Honors Hall, use of a special honors study lounge and computer lab located on the fifth floor of the Edmon Low Library, priority enrollment for all courses (even before graduating seniors), and extended library checkout privileges equivalent to those of graduate students. Non-honors students report that quality attention is also paid to their needs as well—most classes enroll only about 20 to 40 students, although introductory lecture courses such as chemistry attract up to 300 undergrads. The university also sponsors study-abroad programs and internship opportunities with OSU alumni.

Academic requirements vary within each major, but all students must take introductory courses in political science, American government, English, and American history. Despite the strong focus on academic excellence at OSU, students say the wine-tasting class or "any leisure and health elective" can provide a brief respite from the rigors of academic life.

Home, Sweet Home

The frosh-dominated Kerr-Drummon dorm is said to be the most popular on campus. In addition to the special honors housing, OSU also provides a special athletic dorm, Bennett Hall, with modern amenities to appease its athletes, who must live on campus all four years at OSU. Interested students can sign up to live on special foreign language or "major" floors. Each college cafeteria also serves its own special theme food; student favorites include the Italian, Mexican, and bakery items. Strict rules concerning curfews and alcohol, however, have motivated many upperclassmen to move off campus after their mandatory freshman year on campus.

Wide World of Sports

Many students participate in intramural sports at OSU. "We have traditional sports, like football and soccer, but we also have

things like Frisbee or Ping-Pong," one student said. Students can also become involved in various student government and planning committees designed to enhance the quality of academic and social life on campus. The Student Activities Board recently sponsored visits from speakers as varied as former First Lady Barbara Bush and sex therapist Dr. Ruth Westheimer.

The OSU homecoming festivities, said to be the third largest in the nation, represent the most spirited campus-wide event. Fraternities and sororities spend over a month prior to the big weekend "completely covering their houses with decorations" in a style usually reserved for parade floats. The Harvest Carnival is also an integral part of Homecoming, and several groups sponsor entertainment activities or food booths for the event.

School spirit for OSU athletics increased substantially two years ago when the men's basketball team reached the Final Four of the NCAA championship tournament. This recent boost to the athletic program only added to prior OSU victories, including the Cowboy football team's success against the University of Oklahoma Sooners for the first time in 19 years during the fall 1995 season. The women's basketball, men's baseball, and wrestling teams are reportedly successful as well. Pistol Pete, the OSU mascot, and other fans are also celebrating the renovation of Gallagher Iba Arena (formerly notorious for its limited seating capacity during basketball season), which will now accommodate 6,000 additional fans.

The focus on physical fitness extends beyond the athletic teams, however, to include all members of the OSU community. The Wellness Center is available to those who wish to follow a holistic approach to self-improvement by addressing emotional, spiritual, and physical health. For old-fashioned, heart-pumping exercise, the Colvin Center has basketball and racquetball courts, a rock climbing wall, aerobics classes, a swimming pool, weightlifting equipment, and other fitness outlets for both the serious athlete and occasional health-minded undergraduate.

"Not Greek or Geek"

No single group dominates the campus social scene. Fraternities and sororities are popular, but students agree that the campus attitude is "not a 'Greek or geek' thing at all." Parties sponsored by Greeks are open only to members and their invited guests. Students looking for a party scene leave the dry OSU campus for Tumbleweeds, a country-western dance bar, or Eskimo Joe's, a combination bar and restaurant. Some traditional party events during the year include the campus-wide festivities over the OSU–Oklahoma University football game weekend and the more clandestine "Field of Dreams," a bash held out in the Oklahoma countryside. Alcohol is "socially accepted" as a large part of the OSU party scene, but students contend that "no one ever brags about or offers drugs and they are definitely not done in public, even at parties." For those seeking other weekend opportunities, Tulsa and Oklahoma City are just a little over an hour from the OSU campus.

Who Are We?

Students consider their classmates fairly "open-minded, considering their background," one undergrad said. Most students are white, come from in-state rural areas, and are largely conservative. The percentage of minority students is low, but these students reportedly receive the respect of other undergrads and attention from administrators hoping to increase diversity on campus. Generally, undergrads are "laid-back, not artistically expressive, and do not dress up for class." Other than local university issues, students are described as apathetic when it comes to political activity. One senior noted how a

Stillwater city proposal to completely ban open alcohol containers or alcohol consumption on the streets, even for those over 21, passed because of poor student turnout at the city polls.

This redbrick, Georgian-style campus is in the midst of the Stillwater community and has no significant problems with security or safety. OSU reportedly ranks as the safest school in the Big 12 conference. Nevertheless, well-lit, emergency phones dot the campus, and security officers patrol the area 24 hours a day. When asked about the surrounding community, one student said, "The population of Stillwater is small, so you have that hometown atmosphere, though we're still big enough for a Super Wal-Mart."

> **The OSU homecoming festivities, said to be the third largest in the nation, represent the most spirited campus-wide event.**

Academics and extracurriculars provide challenging opportunities without stifling the relaxed attitude of the majority of students. Undoubtedly, the small-town, country atmosphere attracts a number of students to OSU. As one student said, "Anyone interested in the university should visit the campus. We don't put on a show for visitors—all the students and staff members are friendly every day. And that just makes all the difference in the world."—*Kurtland Ma and Staff*

FYI

The three best things about attending OSU are "the friendly attitude on campus, the student-focused administration, and the Greek scene."

The three worst things about attending OSU are "living in Stillwater, sometimes tough academics, and a conservative environment."

The three things that every student should do before graduating from OSU are "participate in Homecoming, go to Tumbleweeds, and watch the Sooners."

One thing I'd like to have known before coming here is "how much school spirit there is."

Oral Roberts University

Address: 7777 South Lewis Ave; Tulsa, OK 74171
Phone: 918-496-6518
E-mail address: admissions@oru.edu
Web site URL: www.oru.edu
Founded: 1963
Private or Public: private
Religious affiliation: none
Location: suburban
Undergraduate enrollment: 3,064
Total enrollment: 3,682
Percent Male/Female: 42%/58%
Percent Minority: 24%
Percent African-American: 16%
Percent Asian: 2%
Percent Hispanic: 5%

Percent Native-American: 1%
Percent in-state/out-of-state: 50%/50%
Percent Pub HS: NA
Number of Applicants: 1,567
Percent Accepted: 70%
Percent Accepted who enroll: 71%
Entering: 780
Transfers: 442
Application Deadline: rolling
Mean SAT: 538 V, 523 M
Mean ACT: 23
Middle 50% SAT range: 490–610 V, 470–600 M

Middle 50% ACT range: 20–26
3 Most popular majors: elementary teacher education, telecommunications, business/accounting
Retention: 80%
Graduation rate: 44%
On-campus housing: 70%
Fraternities: NA
Sororities: NA
Library: 750,000 volumes
Tuition and Fees: $11,650 in; $11,650 out
Room and Board: $5,076
Financial aid, first-year: NA

Glistening in gold and silver, the Oral Roberts University Prayer Tower rises 250 feet toward heaven, exemplifying the school's commitment to religious excellence and perseverance. People worship inside the tower 24 hours a day, 365 days a year, and a prayer line receives telephone calls from across the nation. From the tower's observation deck, visitors behold a panorama encompassing all of ORU's other architectural wonders, including the 4,500-seat Christ Chapel and a 50-foot sculpture of praying hands.

Religious Rules

In 1963, Oral Roberts claimed to receive a vision from God calling for a university to be built in Tulsa. Roberts promptly obeyed and founded Oral Roberts University. Not surprisingly, religion influences student life, both in and out of the classroom. The university holds mandatory chapel services twice a week for all students. The campus dress code stipulates, with exceptions for Fridays and Saturdays, shirts and ties for males, and modest skirts for females. (In recent years, however, the code has relaxed to allow casual but appropriate attire for both sexes after

4 P.M.) When students apply, they must sign a statement agreeing to follow an honor code that forbids drinking, smoking, cheating, and premarital sex. All female students have a midnight curfew, and male students must observe the same curfew for their first two years.

> In pursuit of excellence in mind, body, and spirit, ORU requires all students to participate in sports.

ORU requires students who are not living with their families to live on campus, but few students see this requirement as a burden because the dorms provide pleasant accommodations. Extensive renovations of the dorms are currently under way, and a food court including fast-food restaurants is also planned. Students live in single-sex wings that serve as social substitutes for sororities and fraternities. Although dancing remains forbidden on campus, each wing hosts clambakes and other events. Most students who choose to attend ORU do not mind the rules; in fact, one undergrad explained that "living a Christian life here has made me stronger, and, frankly, I wouldn't want to live amidst the grease of secular life."

Academic Resources

Academically, many students gain communications experience by working for ORU's television station or for the national Abundant Life Prayer Group. The Learning Resource Center is the primary academic facility on campus, with 4.5 acres of libraries, classrooms, and labs. The Center, like all the dorm rooms, is hard-wired with a closed-circuit TV system so students can watch different educational programs as well as 26 channels offered on cable. The administration blocks out some channels, such as MTV, because they are deemed inconsistent with ORU's religious spirit. Sermons are also occasionally shown, which give the observer a taste of what one student called ORU's specialty—"Charismatic Christianity." Many students report that the theology program is excellent, despite one undergrad's complaint that "there's not much serious questioning or confrontation." In recent years, the education department also has earned praise from students. The business school, located in a building that one observer described as "futuristic in a sixties sense," is popular because it instructs young capitalists on how to combine morality and economics.

In pursuit of excellence in mind, body, and spirit, ORU requires all students to participate in sports. Many play intramurals, and attendance at varsity games is high. Last year, in an effort to invigorate the sports program, ORU changed the name of its teams from the Titans to the Golden Eagles. All ORU teams play in Division I, and the basketball and golf teams usually bring the most victories. The Tulsa community uses ORU's basketball arena, the Maybee Center, for everything from local sports to graduations and concerts. Major performers such as Garth Brooks have performed there in recent years.

Students generally agree that ORU has changed for the better. Four years ago, the 75-year-old Oral Roberts stepped down as president of the university and passed the post on to his son, Richard Roberts. Students describe the younger Roberts as highly approachable and popular on campus. Enrollment continues to increase, and if you are seeking a spiritual, as well as an academic, collegiate experience, you may be one of the growing number of applicants considering Oral Roberts University.—*Brian Abaluck and Staff*

FYI

The three best things about attending ORU are "the theology program, being a part of a group of people with a shared value system, and having to participate in the sports program."

The three worst things about attending ORU are "the censorship of television channels like MTV, mandatory chapel services, and the lack of alternative extracurricular opportunities."

The three things that every student should do before graduating from ORU are "play intramurals, go to prayer group regularly, and take advantage of the city of Tulsa."

One thing I'd like to have known before coming here is "just how little people challenge their own religious beliefs."

University of Oklahoma

Address: 1000 Asp Avenue;
Norman, OK 73019-4076
Phone: 800-234-6868
E-mail address:
admrec@ouou.edu
Web site URL: www.ou.edu
Founded: 1890
Private or Public: public
Religious affiliation: none
Location: small city
**Undergraduate
enrollment:** 16,990
Total enrollment: 21,339
Percent Male/Female:
52%/48%
Percent Minority: 25%
Percent African-American:
7%
Percent Asian: 6%

Percent Hispanic: 4%
Percent Native-American:
8%
**Percent in-state/out-of-
state:** 21%/79%
Percent Pub HS: NA
Number of Applicants:
6,384
Percent Accepted: 89%
**Percent Accepted who
enroll:** 58%
Entering: 3,298
Transfers: 1,485
Application Deadline:
15 Jul
Mean SAT: NA
Mean ACT: 24.5
Middle 50% SAT range:
NA

Middle 50% ACT range:
21–27
3 Most popular majors:
management and
information systems,
psychology, journalism
Retention: 80%
Graduation rate: 48%
On-campus housing: 80%
Fraternities: 19%
Sororities: 20%
Library: 4,107,132
volumes
Tuition and Fees:
$2,456 in; $6,791 out
Room and Board: $4,384
Financial aid, first-year:
75%

You are driving in your car with five of your best, rowdiest buddies squished into the backseat. The radio is blasting country-western music as you race along I-35 at breakneck speed. Once you arrive in Dallas, the party has just begun as you, along with over 100,000 other fans, pile into the Cotton Bowl for some good ole-fashioned Sooner Tradition. The weekend rounds out with parties destined to turn Dallas, Texas, into the party town it was meant to be, and you leave with the knowledge that the return trip is just another year away.

Sound like a description from a college admissions brochure? Not likely, since the true life of the University of Oklahoma student reaches beyond academics and university regulations and into a strong social realm. Social life is "what makes OU, OU" as one student said, and football is often the main event. The famous OU–Texas game is the high point of the season—the biggest game against the biggest rival, where the majority of Sooner fans attend and the rest watch on television as they party at home. "Our team right now isn't the best we have ever had, but we still sell the stadium out every weekend," one senior noted, and every student we spoke with named football games as one of the best weekend activities.

A New Academic Agenda

OU president David Boren has been particularly working to enhance the quality of academic instruction and the state of classroom facilities. In fact, this former senator teaches "one of the best classes at OU," a university-required course on American government in which Boren draws from his own political career. Another popular professor, "Dr. Indestructo," excites students in his Introductory Physics class by drinking liquid nitrogen, exploding objects, and "often even endangering his own well-being." Other popular majors include business, political science, and English, which draw rave reviews from many students. Humanities and social sciences have been improving, and the university launched an international and area studies program during the 1997–98 school year. As one senior noted, "These frosh are really lucky to be able to enjoy the benefits of academic improvements for the next couple of years."

President Boren has also been working to attract a growing number of National Merit Scholars to the university. These scholars have a great deal that includes full tuition, early enrollment, smaller classes, and annual recognition at the halftime of a football game, when they line up from end zone to end zone. These honors students are also allowed to register for classes before the rest of the student body.

OU classroom facilities are praised for their "good sound systems and modern computer projection systems," indispensable in large lecture courses in a variety of areas including the sciences and art history. The Sam Noble Museum of Natural History, which displays artifacts of Oklahoma and the Midwest, is also a resource that students take advantage of and was opened in the summer of 1999.

Happenings on Campus

Fraternities and sororities dominate social life at OU. Independent students can gain access to some Greek parties with friends who are members. Many view Greek life as "a great way to meet lots of people," but others criticize the Greek system as "exclusive." Drinking is common; one student said, "If you come here, you'd better bring a good liver." However, many students prefer nights of bowling or movies to drinking.

Though the administration aspires to attract minorities, OU students often consider themselves homogeneous. One student from the Midwest called Oklahoma "the Buckle of the Bible Belt" and noted the powerful Christian presence on campus. Another student lamented, "I've been looking for a drug scene all year, but haven't found one."

> **Scholars and athletes reportedly get along "remarkably well, largely because we both get special treatment here," said one sophomore.**

Intramurals are the major extracurricular activities at OU. A wide range of sports are available ranging from the traditional football, basketball, softball, and baseball to the ever-interesting ooze-ball (a form of volleyball played on a muddy court hosed down by the Norman Fire Department) and "pickleball" (coed touch football).

The Sooner Tradition

The Sooner Tradition embodies a culture of strong school spirit and outstanding varsity athletics. Those who question the importance of football need only look to the 75,000-seat Memorial Stadium, home of Sooner football, located at the dead center of campus. Though the football program has struggled since the departure of shoot-from-the-hip coach Barry Switzer, outstanding facilities and strong alumni economic support "should one day restore glory" to Sooner football tradition. Students have also proven themselves to be more than fair-weather sports by making football games sell-outs.

The OU Environment

Students express overall satisfaction with the OU campus. OU architecture is a mix of stone Gothic and colonial redbrick, which one student described as "Gothic Cherokee." The addition of new sidewalks and gardens, "always well kept," have also bettered the campus in recent years. Dorms are newly renovated and modern in design. Unfortunately, to the dismay of many students, "the sculpture of a blue Mustang horse with freakish, red-glowing eyes" mars campus aesthetics. Passing by this large statue, students wonder why the "eerie and idiosyncratic" horse is present.

The city of Norman, located 20 minutes from Oklahoma City, surrounds the university and is "obviously geared toward OU students." McDonald's, Taco Bell, the Olive Garden, Don Pablo's, and a handful of coffeehouses thrive around the university. Twenty-four-hour restaurants such as Denny's and the Kettle are popular places for social studying.

On-Campus Dining Options

The only cafeteria open to all students at the University of Oklahoma is the Couch Cafeteria, which, according to one student, "looks exactly like an airline terminal—complete with flags." Students find the food mediocre, though varied. Couch offers Sooner Sports Grill's hamburgers and wings and make-your-own stir-fry as well as an assortment of daily specials. The meal plan includes "Dining Sense," which gives students a debit card to purchase food from surrounding restaurants and convenience stores.

First Come, First Served

Freshmen who choose not to live at home must live on campus. The two most desirable dorms, Walker Tower and Adams, are arranged in suites of two double bedrooms joined by a bathroom and are slightly larger than most other dorm rooms. Other residence halls have singles with communal bathrooms at each end of the hall. Housing is assigned on a first-come, first-served basis, so those wishing to avoid the unpopular Cross Center with its "crumbling walls and bad plumbing" must make housing decisions quickly. Dorms are coed by floor freshman year and coed by suite in upperclassman dorms. The university limits coed visitation in the freshman dorms; all visitors must be out of students' rooms by midnight on weeknights and 2:00 A.M. on weekends in order to avoid citations and fines. Freshman floors also have RAs, who serve not only as academic advisors, but as social organizers.

The Wilkinson Complex is a group of dorms offering large rooms and exclusive access to the Jefferson Cafeteria and is largely available to athletes and honors students. The recent $500,000 renovation has made the Jefferson Cafeteria an "excellent facility with really gourmet fare." The Jefferson Cafeteria also hosts the popular "Seafood and Steak Night" every Wednesday night. Scholars and athletes reportedly get along "remarkably well, largely because we both get special treatment here," said one sophomore.

Students define the University of Oklahoma in terms of tradition. The majority of students are from in state or the Midwest, and many of the current undergrads were preceded at OU by their parents. The Sooner Tradition creates a culture of massive school spirit and ensures exciting sporting events. Just try not to forget that this is the "friendly South" in the fourth quarter of a close OU–Texas game!
—*Brian Abaluck and Staff*

FYI
The three best things about attending OU are "the football games, the charm, and warm spring afternoons outside."
The three worst things about attending OU are "fraternities, sororities, and the people who populate them."
The three things that every student should do before graduating are "go to the Texas–Oklahoma football game, play pickleball, date a cheerleader."
One thing I'd like to have known before coming here is "how tough the science classes would be."

The University of Tulsa

Address: 600 South College Avenue; Tulsa, OK 74104
Phone: 918-631-2307
E-mail address: admission@utulsa.edu
Web site URL: www.utulsa.edu
Founded: 1884
Private or Public: private
Religious affiliation: Presbyterian
Location: urban
Undergraduate enrollment: 2,866
Total enrollment: 4,236
Percent Male/Female: 48%/52%
Percent Minority: 19%
Percent African-American: 8%

Percent Asian: 2%
Percent Hispanic: 3%
Percent Native-American: 6%
Percent in-state/out-of-state: 66%/34%
Percent Pub HS: 85%
Number of Applicants: 2,037
Percent Accepted: 80%
Percent Accepted who enroll: 38%
Entering: 615
Transfers: 612
Application Deadline: 1 Mar
Mean SAT: 610 V, 605 M
Mean ACT: 25

Middle 50% SAT range: 540–670 V, 40–680 M
Middle 50% ACT range: 23–29
3 Most popular majors: finance, accounting, psychology
Retention: 75%
Graduation rate: 32%
On-campus housing: 100%
Fraternities: 12%
Sororities: 13%
Library: 800,000 volumes
Tuition and Fees: $13,480 in; $13,480 out
Room and Board: $4,660
Financial aid, first-year: 59%

People come to the University of Tulsa for the same reason they come to Tulsa itself: TU offers diversity, beauty, and opportunity in the heartland of America. TU's relatively high rate of acceptance does not mean the curriculum lacks vigor; in fact, students say the university offers a challenging, world-class education.

A Top Priority

TU's commitment to academic excellence reaches many programs. The College of Engineering and Applied Sciences is considered preeminent worldwide, particularly for its petroleum research and chemical engineering programs. The English department is recognized nationally as a center of James Joyce scholarship. The department publishes the *James Joyce Quarterly*, an academic journal with international circulation, and the McFarlin Library houses a special collection that features Joyce's writings along with 20th-century Anglo-Irish, American, and Native American literature.

Students consider the university's commitment to a strong academic program a top priority. The university curriculum, called the Tulsa Curriculum, provides a solid foundation in the liberal arts. The Tulsa Curriculum is divided into three parts: the core curriculum, the general curriculum, and the major area of concentration. The core curriculum focuses on reasoning, writing, math, and language courses. In order to fill the general curriculum requirements, students must take two courses in each of four blocks: Artistic Imagination, which includes literature and art courses; Social Inquiry, which studies the nature and behavior of the individual and group; Comparative and Historical Interpretation, which includes classes on religion, politics, economics, and culture; and Scientific Investigation, which consists of classes in the experimental and natural sciences.

Undergraduates note the strength of many of TU's departments. The School of Business is particularly impressive, with strong programs in marketing and communication. Additionally, with the current emphasis on computers and technology, TU's Management Information Systems (MIS) program is very popular among undergraduates. Students do say, however, that programs in music, theater, and economics are lacking, and the TU Honors program also gets mixed reviews: some students find it rewarding, while others believe it needs improvement. All agree, however, that the small class size and personal attention given to students by professors makes Tulsa's academic program attractive. One senior says, "I have been here for four years and have never been taught by a teaching assistant and have never been in a class with more than 35 students."

All Work and No Play?

Of course, life at TU is not all work and no play. There are a number of activities in which to get involved and meet other people. The largest organization at TU, the Student Association, is responsible for coordinating various student activities and community service projects. Undergraduates also enjoy writing for TU's newspaper, *The Collegian*, or managing the student-run radio station, the Underground. Students also spend time in many of the different ethnic organizations on campus.

> "TU students love to have fun, finding a party is never a problem."

Perhaps the best way to meet other people at TU is through the Greek system. Fraternities and sororities host parties almost every weekend. While drinking is officially forbidden, enforcement is lenient and most would describe TU as a wet campus. By going Greek, freshmen have an easy way to go to great parties such as Snake-in-the-Grass and Pike Fest, meet a lot of new people quickly, and make many new friends. If the Greek scene is not for you, however, don't worry. There are plenty of other alternatives. When the Student Association is not sponsoring a dance or party, you can find them throughout the dorms. As one student puts it, "TU students love to have fun, finding a party is never a problem." Also, it is quite common to hang out with friends at JR's or at the Hut.

Students also take advantage of the city's entertainment. The city boasts a nationally renowned ballet corp, an opera company, a philharmonic, and several theater groups. The Gilcrease and Philbrook are popular museums. Reportedly, the Gilcrease Museum has the largest collection of Western American art in the world. Tulsa also boasts several festivals during the year, including Octoberfest, Reggaefest, and Mayfest.

Students take their dates out to one of the city's restaurants, such as the Metro Diner, or they frequent malls such as Woodland Hills, Promenade, and Southroads. Free university shuttle service provides transportation to all of these places as well as to movie theaters around the city. And, at the end of 1998, two 20-screen movie theaters were built in Tulsa, one of which is very close to campus.

Where We Hang

When students hang out on campus, they usually spend time in the Allen Chapman Activities Center (ACAC), one of the university's two libraries, or their dorms. ACAC features the Hurricane Hut (a restaurant that serves as a center for beer guzzling), as well as meeting halls and study rooms. Many undergraduates like to study on the green lawns surrounding the churchlike McFarlin Library or inside the law library, which is open 24 hours.

Although housing is reportedly comfortable, with dorm rooms including air conditioning, cable, and computer connections, a large percentage of the student body chooses to live off campus or in fraternity or sorority houses. Many believe the food, which some diners call "unappetizing" and "monotonous," has driven students off campus.

There are five dorms on the TU campus: Lottie Jane, John Maybee, Twin Towers, Tower West, and Lafortune. Tower West and Lafortune are coed by suite, while Lottie Jane and John Maybee are single-sex. Twin Towers offers newer, smaller rooms, and is coed by floor. Housing in the area can be found cheaply, and the university just completed in the spring of 1997 the University Square Apartments for those wanting the benefits of apartment living without having to move off campus. While most agree housing at TU is not a problem, they complain about a lack of parking. And although the new shuttle service is helpful, most students agree a car is very important.

What students at the University of Tulsa

really enjoy about their school is its size. The approximately 4,200 undergraduates are just enough to establish a diverse community while keeping a family-like environment. Tulsa is also known for its commitment to athletics. Sports are popular, although some students think TU places too much emphasis and funding on the sports program. Men's basketball is thought to be the biggest sport, and a new Convocation Center is being built for the basketball games. The football team plays in Skelly Stadium and is usually heavily supported at games. TU has a wide variety of men's and women's sports in everything from tennis to golf. Students not wanting to play a varsity sport take advantage of the popular intramural program.

A small, private school in America's heartland, the University of Tulsa is proud to provide its students with a solid liberal arts education. Prospective students are encouraged to take advantage of Tulsa Time, the University's program for prospective students to visit the campus, ask questions, and experience life at TU. As one student said, "When you have a degree from TU, people pay attention." If you are looking for a beautiful, active, and fun university in a great city with a strong academic program, then the University of Tulsa is definitely for you.—*Brian Abaluck and Staff*

FYI

The three best things about attending TU are "the quality of the faculty, the gorgeous campus, and low cost of entertainment."

The three worst things about attending TU are "the ill-equipped career services center, the cliques, and the poor equipment in the Computer Supported Writing Center."

The three things every student should do before graduating from TU are "take at least one class from Dr. Joseph Kestner, visit the Alexander Hogue Gallery, and do an internship at one of the publications."

One thing I wish I'd known before coming is "how humid the summers are."

Oregon

Lewis and Clark College

Address: 615 SW Palatine Hill Road; Portland, OR 97219
Phone: 503-768-7040
E-mail address: admissions@lclark.edu
Web site URL: www.lclark.edu
Founded: 1867
Private or Public: private
Religious affiliation: none
Location: suburban
Undergraduate enrollment: 1,743
Total enrollment: 3,203
Percent Male/Female: 41%/59%
Percent Minority: 11%

Percent African-American: 0.5%
Percent Asian: 7%
Percent Hispanic: 3%
Percent Native-American: 0.5%
Percent in-state/out-of-state: 30%/70%
Percent Pub HS: 72%
Number of Applicants: 3,008
Percent Accepted: 69%
Percent Accepted who enroll: 25%
Entering: 521
Transfers: 69
Application Deadline: 1 Feb
Mean SAT: NA
Mean ACT: NA

Middle 50% SAT range: 580–680 V, 570–660 M
Middle 50% ACT range: 25–29
3 Most popular majors: English, biology, sociology
Retention: 80%
Graduation rate: 59%
On-campus housing: 99%
Fraternities: NA
Sororities: NA
Library: 175,854 volumes
Tuition and Fees: $20,326 in; $20,326 out
Room and Board: $6,220
Financial aid, first-year: 85%

Not far from the city of Portland, Oregon, students at Lewis and Clark College carry on blissfully on a wooded estate with a spectacular view of Mt. Hood in the distance. Small classes, a close-knit community, and a love for the great outdoors draw a diverse student body to this oasis in the Pacific Northwest where outdoor activities are never too far away.

Attentive Academics

Lewis and Clark is known for its strong academic departments that lavish students with personal attention. Favorite majors include international affairs, biology, business, English, and sociology/anthropology. Classes generally enroll around 20 students, although some introductory courses can enroll between 40 and 60 students. Small class size allows undergraduates the opportunity to "become closer with professors," who are known to take keen interest in their students. One student described her professors as, "approachable, friendly, and involved in the academic careers of their students." Another student added, "Professors at LC do not try to push their ideas onto you. They are well educated and want to see you grow with the expertise they can provide in their field." There are no TAs at Lewis and Clark. Students feel that academics are "challenging." However, one undergrad explained that students "enjoy the challenge because they respect the professors and feel intellectually rewarded by their classroom experience."

As part of the liberal arts requirement, incoming freshmen are required to take Inventing America, a survey course covering American history and philosophy. The class is apparently "hated by most freshmen." However, one undergrad explained that "Inventing America can be an amazing class with the right professor, which is pure luck because all different types of professors teach it (including psychology, biology, math, etc.)."

Many students flock to Lewis and Clark for its renowned international affairs and language departments. Students also report these departments as being the "most demanding academically." Many students double major with whatever language they are taking. Students praise the extensive study-abroad programs, which allow them to travel and implement their newly acquired language skills. Over half of all Lewis and Clark undergrads go abroad before they graduate. They can choose among programs in Germany, France, and England, as well as those in more exotic places such as India and Argentina. Lewis and Clark also allows students to study in Washington, D.C., while completing an internship with a government bureau or private company. For one student, working in Washington "provided me with work experience while I went to school at the same time."

> Students feel that they are "mostly liberals, who are upstarts seeking change and newness in the world."

When Lewis and Clark students need to hit the books, they use the "totally awesome" Watzek Library. Watzek has a wide array of resources including an interlibrary exchange program, which allows students to borrow from other libraries if their own does not have what they need. There are study rooms for group study, long tables, and private carrels with computer hookups that allow students to check their e-mail from a laptop instead of waiting in line at the computer center. "Everyone goes" to the library, said one student, "which makes it a pretty social place."

Since the mid-1990s, a number of construction projects have revamped the Lewis and Clark campus. The size of Watzek Library was doubled and a center for the humanities and arts was finished in 1996. The Templeton Center was restructured, bringing the "headquarters for student activities closer together, which is a

plus," according to one undergrad. Students also rate the weight room as "a step up." A new arts and humanities building and music building were completed in 1998.

No Greek Scene? Thank God

There is no Greek system at Lewis and Clark, but students do not seem to miss it. One student explained that it was "a big part of why people come to LC." The Greeks were removed from campus in the early 1970s with a donor's amendment. Apparently, the donor would not give the school her fortune unless they promised to prohibit Greek houses, install an all-women's dorm, and serve ice cream at every meal!

Despite the lack of a Greek scene, Lewis and Clark is not lacking in social events on the weekends. Although this is not a "major party school," many students partake in a drink or a joint or two over the weekend. Dating does occur at Lewis and Clark, though, how often depends on which student is asked. Random hookups also occur frequently; students do warn that with a small campus, the social scene can seem "filled with rumors" at times, but people are "mostly laid-back about romance here."

Lewis and Clark is technically a dry campus, but apparently this policy does not stop anyone from drinking. Although students report that campus police will "write up" students and repeat offenders may find themselves before a peer review committee, it does not happen very often. However, due to this policy, most large parties are held off campus. Lewis and Clark students are lax when it comes to drugs and alcohol. One student explained that "it is easy to drink and smoke here, though it is not done in excess too often." Marijuana is the most prevalent drug found on campus, although drugs like LSD and mushrooms are also in use to an extent.

Students report spending their weekends doing numerous activities on and off campus. Popular hangouts on campus include two student-run cafes, the Rusty Nail and the Platform, which host music events regularly. Many students enjoy the big-screen movies presented every Saturday night in Council Chambers by the Students Organized for Activities (SOFA).

Many students report they enjoy just "relaxing with friends on-campus." Since Lewis and Clark's campus is located in a suburban neighborhood (which means there is nowhere to go "just off campus"), many students venture into Portland for nighttime activities. Undergrads describe Portland as "a great city where the people are always friendly despite all the rain." There are numerous clubs, pubs, bars, and restaurants that students enjoy going to, including Fulton Pub, Buffalo Gap, and Seges. In addition, Powell's is also a popular Portland gathering spot for Lewis and Clark students. It is the largest independent bookstore in America and apparently has "good readings on Friday nights." Portland also has a growing swing and rave scene as well. However, students complain that fun in Portland only lasts so long because "everything closes very early, like 10 P.M. on the weekends."

Many a Rainy Day

Fortunately or unfortunately, depending on whom one asks, there are many rainy days on the Lewis and Clark campus. The LC campus is not a place to be without an umbrella, which drives some students nuts. Yet, other students appreciate the weather because campus is like "a huge, wet garden." Green is certainly the most appropriate adjective for the campus, which has a rose garden, lots of trees and grassy lawns, and cobblestone paths, not to mention the "spectacular" view of Mt. Hood. The charm of a lush campus "makes students love Lewis and Clark despite the impossible rain."

Freshmen and sophomores are required to live on campus, although many students consider this requirement restrictive and overly expensive. Some go so far as to equate living on campus to "hell on earth." Although others feel that "it is hard to meet new people when you move off campus and you are closer to the campus facilities on campus." Students who live on campus are usually housed in dorm rooms in groups of two, four, or six (known as a "six-pack"). Room size and amenities vary from dorm to dorm. Most dorms are coed by floor (because residents of each floor share a bathroom) and some have language theme floors. While students rate

Copeland as the best dorm, Platt Howard (also known as "the projects") is consistently called the worst. Copeland is known across campus for throwing parties and is generally acknowledged as the most social dorm. Hartsfeld, which offers some suites, is preferred by upperclassmen who remain on campus; the atmosphere is peaceful, which allows for better studying. For those who do not mind the walk, the luxurious Stewart dormitories, about 10 minutes from the center of campus, have walk-in closets and large rooms, although they reportedly lack the social atmosphere of Copeland. Lewis and Clark has one all-female dorm, commonly referred to as "the convent."

The main dining hall at Lewis and Clark is in the Templeton College Center, nicknamed "the Bon" (pronounced as "Bone") for the catering company, Bon Appetite. Students living on campus must purchase a meal plan that includes at least 14 meals per week. The food is considered "pretty good," for college food. Students say that Bon Appetite, which is considered the best food service in the Northwest, offers a variety of options for each meal. Pizza, salad, and sandwiches are popular choices. Several vegetarians, of whom there are many at LC, reported that they cater well to their needs. Students who have Flex points, which are purchased at the beginning of the school year, can use them at the Trail Room, a grill on the floor below the Bon. Students rarely venture off campus for a meal, as there is little choice in the residential neighborhood surrounding the school. Domino's Pizza does deliver, but most students save their money for quality meals in downtown Portland.

It is generally agreed that there is a "big schism" between people who live on and off campus after sophomore year. Since the campus is surrounded by a suburban residential area, housing is often more affordable off campus than on. A large number of upperclassmen choose to move out of the dorms and into "cheap and plentiful" apartments or houses with friends. For those who live farther away from campus there are shuttle buses run by the college. Many students have cars, but caution that one has to be careful to avoid parking tickets.

Trail Blazers

Many students fear that Lewis and Clark will soon be stereotyped by their most famous graduate, Monica Lewinsky. In reality, students say that "there are a lot of rich rids rebelling" at LC. The school does make up for its "nonexistent" racial diversity with a good number of international students and a diversity within the students' backgrounds and interests. Students feel that they are "mostly liberals, who are upstarts seeking change and newness in the world." However, others pessimistically believe that "everyone here pretends to be hippie and liberal while content to buy their Tommy gear and be apathetic to global and environmental causes." Generally, undergrads feel that "most students accept people for who they are and are supportive of people of different races, religions, and sexual orientations."

The student body of Lewis and Clark has low school spirit. What spirit there is for varsity athletics is "mostly athletes supporting their friends and other athletes." This does not mean, however, that Lewis and Clark students swear off athletics altogether. In fact, intramural sports are some of the most popular activities on campus, especially volleyball, skiing, soccer, crew, rugby, lacrosse, and sailing. Students who aren't as into school-sponsored athletics enjoy taking advantage of their natural surroundings by participating in outdoor activities. Hiking, rock climbing, mountain biking, and skiing are popular sports. One student suggested that Lewis and Clark students are passionate about "outdoorsy" activities since "the Nalgene bottle clipped onto a backpack with a carabiner is the biggest fashion statement here." Students can reach the Oregon coast in two hours and the Columbia River Gorge in about an hour's drive. Both are apparently "breathtaking, even on a drizzly day." For the nonathletes, there is the campus TV station, LCTV, and radio station, KLC. Various green clubs are also reportedly popular. Aspiring writers can join either, the *Pioneer Log* or *Sacajawea's Voice*, the two campus newspapers.

Even at a college without tremendous school spirit, the Lewis and Clark mascot, the Pioneer, is an appropriate representative of the school. An attitude typical of Lewis and Clark is apparent in one of the school's mottoes: "Do not follow where the path may lead, go instead where there is no path and blaze a trail." Although students rally around the fact that their school is actually a close-knit community, "people here like to do their own things, and Lewis and Clark's free-minded attitude encourages this." Students at Lewis and Clark are individuals who "blaze their own trails," but who will come together to support their community. Many students believe that Lewis and Clark offers them the best of all worlds—a solid liberal arts education in a community of outdoors lovers.—*Alison Pulaski and Staff*

FYI

The three best things about attending Lewis and Clarke are "the small classes, the fact that professors listen to you, and that everything is green."

The three worst things about attending Lewis and Clarke are "the isolation of being off campus, that everyone thinks that kids here are like Monica Lewinski (alumnus), that Monica Lewinski no longer attends."

The three things that every student should do before graduating are "go to Portland, hike around Mt. Hood, and go somewhere weird to study abroad."

One thing I'd like to have known before coming here is "how many inches ice cream can add to your waistline."

Oregon State University

Address: 10 Kerr Administration Building; Corvallis, OR 97331-2106
Phone: 541-737-4411
E-mail address: osuadmit@orst.edu
Web site URL: osu.orst.edu
Founded: 1868
Private or Public: public
Religious affiliation: none
Location: suburban
Undergraduate enrollment: 12,554
Total enrollment: 14,336
Percent Male / Female: 54% / 46%
Percent Minority: 13%
Percent African-American: 1%
Percent Asian: 8%

Percent Hispanic: 3%
Percent Native-American: 1%
Percent in-state / out-of-state: 82% / 18%
Percent Pub HS: NA
Number of Applicants: 6,494
Percent Accepted: 91%
Percent Accepted who enroll: 48%
Entering: 2,846
Transfers: 1,373
Application Deadline: 1 Mar
Mean SAT: 534 V, 551 M
Mean ACT: 23
Middle 50% SAT range: 480–590 V, 490–610 M

Middle 50% ACT range: 20–26
3 Most popular majors: business administration, liberal studies, exercise and sport science
Retention: 79%
Graduation rate: 28%
On-campus housing: 95%
Fraternities: 22%
Sororities: 19%
Library: 1,000,000 volumes
Tuition and Fees: $3,549 in; $12,393 out
Room and Board: $5,394
Financial aid, first-year: 65%

When Oregonians think of Oregon State University, many classify it as a fraternity-dominated party school. Although the school recognizes a whopping 26 fraternities and 13 sororities, students there will quickly point out that OSU has much more to offer than just frat parties, including the small-town environment of Corvallis, the beautiful setting of the campus, a strong academic curriculum, and an active student body.

Small-Town Life

Corvallis, Oregon, is a town of about 30,000 people situated 15 miles off Oregon's main freeway, Interstate 5. A few students describe Corvallis as "quiet and a little boring," but most undergrads love the town's slow pace and quaint feel. Corvallis really caters to the students and their needs, with "a little downtown surrounding the campus," one undergrad noted. Indeed, there are enough pizza joints, coffee shops, and bars just off campus to satisfy any college student. Because of the university and technology/computer firms in the area, Corvallis attracts a large number of educated professionals and is definitely "not a hick town" as some people might think. One town spot that all students are familiar

with is "the Ette," a grocery store some say is known for its cheap prices and high volume sales of Busch Light.

Oregon is famous for its outdoor opportunities, and Corvallis doesn't disappoint. Many students go camping on long weekends in the spring and fall, make frequent trips to the Cascades for downhill skiing, or take off for the scenic Oregon coast, which is only 45 minutes away. When students miss the action of the big city, many travel to the lively club and bar scene of Portland, just an hour and a half to the north. Lots of students have cars, so transportation usually is not a problem, even for those who don't own a car.

Another benefit to small-town life is safety. Car break-ins and other petty thefts are almost unheard of in Corvallis, and most students report feeling "completely safe." One female undergraduate, however, said that she feels secure during the day on campus, but around the off-campus houses and fraternities at night is "a little more sketchy."

"Bac Core"

Oregon State's Baccalaureate Curriculum (Bac Core) requires all students to take classes in a variety of fields before burying themselves in their major. One engineering student admitted that the core's emphasis on writing and liberal arts "is actually pretty good stuff." Other students agreed that the course requirements are "fair," although possibly a bit too easy. According to one student, "If you passed fourth grade, you'll get an A."

Outside of the core, students have rave reviews for their classes and programs. Despite a student body of almost 15,000, undergrads rarely have problems getting in to the classes they want to take. Some departments, such as English and the arts, offer many small classes (20 people or fewer). One student said its easy to "get involved in your classes, outside of class" through such activities as plays and art shows. Oregon State is known for its topnotch engineering and agriculture departments, but the other majors get their share of attention. One forestry student praised his department, noting that the TAs and professors were knowledgeable and the location of the classrooms near a forest helps in learning. Undergrads call the workload "decent," although it can pile up and become a burden just like at any other college. Classes are challenging, but not impossible: one student suggested that "if you go to class and do some reading, then you're fine." Common complaints about the occasional unhelpful TA or professor with a thick foreign accent exist here, but students say they are satisfied overall.

To Rush or Not to Rush, That Is the Question

So just how big is the frat scene at Oregon State? Twenty-six fraternities and 13 sororities are a lot, but only about 25 percent of students actually pledge. Different houses hold functions from Thursday through Saturday, and these parties (some of them are themed) reportedly are "creative, well-decorated, and pretty fun," even for non–frat types. As a result, people up and down Oregon know OSU for its lively party scene and big bashes. These parties can get pretty wild: one female undergrad reported seeing "naked guys running around at parties all the time." Non-Greeks say they "associate, but don't totally hang out" with the fraternities, and usually no friction occurs between these two groups. Because the fraternities tend

to be a bit choosy, pledges describe the rushing process as "somewhat difficult," but well worth it once they're accepted into the frat of their choice.

> Classes are challenging, but not impossible: one student suggested that "if you go to class and do some reading, then you're fine."

Although not everybody participates in the fraternity circuit, it can seem as if all students partake in heavy drinking. Stores around campus card regularly, but a large number of students are over 21 or have fake IDs. One student described many of her classmates as "drunks," and others agreed that the unofficial mascot of OSU would be a beer mug. Unfortunately, nondrinkers can feel out of place in this environment. But breathe easy, fearful parents: according to students, OSU is "definitely more of a drinking school than a drug school," and drug usage is considered peripheral.

As an alternative to the drinking and fraternity scene, the Student Council keeps activities running for students' enjoyment, including formal dances, tailgates, and special events like Dad's Weekend. Students at OSU are "very friendly," and most have an easy time meeting other people and making new friends. Not many students join clubs or other extracurricular activities, however, claiming that they are plenty busy with jobs, academics, and partying. Formal dating does not have a strong presence here, and one student described the dating scene as, "People do it, but they're not in the majority."

Beaver Believers

Sports and athletics are a major part of life at OSU. The grassy fields and state-of-the-art gyms provide venues for intramural sports or just working out. Students form their own IM teams, so often the competition is between numerous fraternities and a few "GDIs" (independents).

Despite the perennial losing records of many OSU varsity teams, students still have school spirit. "People are way more into women's sports," one undergrad reported, "especially women's basketball."

Football games are a fun place to socialize, but students consider basketball the most popular sport. The biggest sports event of the year is the football "Civil War" game against archrival University of Oregon, when thousands of "Beaver Believers" (OSU alumnus) descend upon Parker Stadium for a game that's always packed and competitive. But throughout the year, whenever OSU gets that occasional win, "the school goes nuts."

Photogenic Campus

All students at OSU have great things to say about the physical campus. It is large and spread out with "old, beautiful brick buildings" and plenty of open spaces. Careful attention is paid to the landscaping, with thick grassy fields, bushes, flowers, lamps, and benches to highlight the grounds.

Reviews of the campus housing, however, are less enthusiastic. Freshmen who choose to live on campus are housed in dorm rooms with two people per room and about 40 per floor, which are described as "old and a little crowded." Students can choose to live in single-sex, coed, or "quiet" dorms. Upperclassmen, whose dorms are traditionally bigger, also have the option of "wellness" dorms like Sackett that prohibit drinking, smoking, and other drugs. After freshman year, many students move off campus, choosing to rent houses and apartments in town. Dining hall food does not elicit rave reviews, so many students opt for the mall-style food courts in the Memorial Union, where fast-food joints such as Burger King, Taco Bell, and Subway accept points from the meal system.

The student center, better known as Memorial Union, or "MU," to students, is a popular and beloved hangout. Students go there "all the time" to use its rooms for napping, studying, or meeting people. The building, which adjoins the campus bookstore and cafeteria, also contains the student agencies and even a bowling alley and game room in the basement.

Overall, students agree that Oregon State is much more than just a typical fraternity party school. Among the challenging academics, beautiful location and campus, and a hearty and sometimes wild social life, undergrads find their niche easily. As a result, one said, "most students love it here."—*Johny Swagerty and Staff*

FYI

The three best things about attending OSU are "the parties, the people, and the beauty of the place."

The three worst things about attending OSU are "the housing, people drinking way too much, and the required classes."

The three things that every student should do before graduating are "bring your father to campus for Dad's weekend, especially if he's an alum, take a road-trip, weak sports teams."

One thing I'd like to have known before coming here is "that it rains all the time in Oregon."

Reed College

Address: 3203 Southeast Woodstock Boulevard; Portland, OR 97202-8199
Phone: 503-777-7511
E-mail address: admission@reed.edu
Web site URL: www.reed.edu
Founded: 1909
Private or Public: private
Religious affiliation: none
Location: suburban
Undergraduate enrollment: 1,353
Total enrollment: 1,353
Percent Male/Female: 44%/56%
Percent Minority: 11%
Percent African-American: 1%

Percent Asian: 6%
Percent Hispanic: 3%
Percent Native-American: 1%
Percent in-state/out-of-state: 15%/85%
Percent Pub HS: 62%
Number of Applicants: 2,018
Percent Accepted: 68%
Percent Accepted who enroll: 24%
Entering: 337
Transfers: 45
Application Deadline: 15 Jan
Mean SAT: 690 V, 654 M
Mean ACT: 29

Middle 50% SAT range: 640–730 V, 610–700 M
Middle 50% ACT range: NA
3 Most popular majors: biology, English, psychology
Retention: 88%
Graduation rate: 65%
On-campus housing: 98%
Fraternities: NA
Sororities: NA
Library: 450,000 volumes
Tuition and Fees: $24,990 in; $24,990 out
Room and Board: $6,820
Financial aid, first-year: 48%

When asked to describe the typical Reedie, many students come up with one word: "strange." "People who wouldn't fit in anywhere else fit in at Reed," said one student. "Everyone's wacky here—and most people are wonderful." Many students at Reed say that they can't believe that they would love another school nearly as well. "Reed is as unique as its students. Actually, that is probably because the students make the school."

Amazing Academics

Academics at Reed are excellent, intense, and "amazing." "Don't come here if you want lots of free time, or if you're not serious about learning," said one student. Every student's academic career at Reed begins with "Hume 110," a required freshman intensive reading and writing course. All sections have 18 or fewer students, and the swift pace and high standards set the tone for the rest of a student's time at Reed. "It gives us all a common experience, and it's a great introduction to college," one sophomore said. In order to complete a Reed degree, students are also required to take two courses in each of four distribution groups and one year of a

lab science. "The requirements are pretty easy, although the science part is hard on us humanities majors," said one student.

Popular majors include biology, English, and psychology. Reed's commitment to academic freedom includes allowing students to design their own course of study, and interdisciplinary majors are also very popular. Students can be even more creative with their coursework during "Paideia," a 10-day period before spring semester where students take noncredit courses in such areas as bagel-making and underwater basket-weaving. Academics at Reed become even more difficult junior year, when students are required to pass qualifying exams in their major, although students report that few fail. Senior year, Reedies must complete a thesis and defend it in front of their advisor and three other professors from their department. "It's probably the hardest thing I've ever had to do," said one student. "But it was also incredibly rewarding." Even in the midst of their toughest classes, however, Reed students have the help of their excellent faculty. "The professors here are amazing," said a senior. "They're always willing to help." "Professors are personable and open-minded," said another. Classes at Reed are fairly small and always taught by professors, and classes with more than 30 students are considered large. "Classes are hard, but no one really cares," said one student. "Everyone has the same amount of work." Students say that academics form such a large part of life at Reed that "studying all the time isn't all that bad."

Time to Relax

Despite all their work, students at Reed still find time to relax. "People say they study all the time, but no one really does," said one student. Students say that the college cliché is that "students study hard and party hard" is doubly true at Reed. "It's hard for some students to handle," said one Reedie. "Everything is intense here." One of the school's nicknames is "Weed," and students report that marijuana use is fairly common. "People can't do too much and keep up with their classes, but a lot of people dabble," one student said. Other drugs are also common, as is drinking, but students say that there is little pressure to partake: "Reed is a very 'do your own thing' school." The social life is generally fairly casual. Students report that there is not a lot of dating. "People either hang out or have sex," said one undergrad. Downtown Portland is nearby, and many students who need a break from life at Reed go to the city for dinner or dancing. "Portland's great," said one student. "It has everything." Another student complained, however, that "everything seems to close at 10 P.M."

> "We have a great assortment of hippies, Goths, punks, skaters, skids, and just plain weirdos."

Even with everything else that they have to do, Reedies still seem to find time for extracurricular activities. Students say participation is "irregular." Some people are really into it, and some could care less. "Academics are the first priority for pretty much everyone," said one junior. For students who choose to participate, there are many campus groups, and if they don't find what they want, they can "just start it themselves." Community service through SEEDS (Students for Education Empow-

erment and Direct Service) and other organizations is very popular. Students can also choose to work for the newspaper, the *Quest*, or for the campus radio station. Other activities are as unusual as the students who participate in them, and range from the Fetish Student Union and the wine-tasting club to more conventional choices such as the Feminist Student Union and the French Club. Sports at Reed are played "the Reed way"—for fun, not for competition. "Few people are very serious about sports, but lots of people enjoy them," said one student. "It's a great way to relax," said another.

The Reed Campus

Reed students describe their campus as "lovely." "Most of it's right out of Dead Poets Society," said one sophomore. The 28 dorms are "generally nice." Old Dorm Block is described as "beautiful," and Anna Mann House as "luxurious." Even the notorious Asylum Block was recently renovated, and now it is "very livable if you can stand the aesthetic ugliness." One sophomore, however, found Asylum Block so unattractive that she chose to move off campus rather than live there. "I've seen Asylum rooms, and these are worse," she said. Students generally live in suites. Other living options include the Woodstock language houses and student-chosen theme houses. Students are not required to live on campus after their freshman year, and many choose to move off. "The dorms are kind of shabby. It's just not worth it," said one student. Housing around campus is reasonably priced and not difficult to find. Campus residents are required to have a meal plan. Students say that the dining hall has a variety of foods with plentiful vegetarian and vegan entrees but "it's mostly really gross." "They try, and it keeps getting better, but it will take a lot of improvement," one student said. "Most people stick to the Ben & Jerry's Ice Cream and a few other selected items." Reed students are liberal and politically active. "Our unofficial slogan is 'communism, atheism, and free love,'" said one sophomore. "There is just a little communism, a whole lot of atheism, and hardly any free love unless you get lucky at the winter formal." "A lot of people here were considered different in high school," said another. "We have a great assortment of hippies, Goths, punks, skaters, skids, and just plain weirdos." In this diverse community, students are united by their dedication to academics and by their "open minds." Students say, however, that they would like to see more ethnic and cultural diversity at Reed, which many think is lacking, despite the school's dedication to academic diversity.

Students warn that "Reed isn't for everyone." Although most Reedies are dedicated to their school, they realize that the very characteristics that make them love it might turn others off. Therefore, they advise high school students looking at Reed to be careful. "Be sure to visit first," said one senior. "If you love it on sight, like I did, you'll probably never lose that love." For those who take the plunge, Reed provides a "supportive environment, both academically and emotionally." "School is life and life is school here," said one student. For those who feel at home at Reed, however, both school and life are challenging and satisfying.—*Kathryn Eigen and Staff*

FYI

The three best things about attending Reed are "small classes, senior theses, and really chill people."

The three worst things about attending Reed are "potheads, people who seem to think they're in the sixties and the Man is out to get them, and food that only tastes good to potheads."

The three things that every student should do before graduating are "go to the Winter Formal, talk to lots of people about politics, and read on your own."

One thing I'd like to have known before coming here is "strange people are cool."

University of Oregon

Address: 240 Oregon Hall; Eugene, OR 97403
Phone: 541-346-3201
E-mail address: darkwing. uoregon.edu/admit
Web site URL: www.uoregon.edu
Founded: 1876
Private or Public: public
Religious affiliation: none
Location: urban
Undergraduate enrollment: 13,610
Total enrollment: 16,716
Percent Male/Female: 47%/53%
Percent Minority: 12%

Percent African-American: 2%
Percent Asian: 6%
Percent Hispanic: 3%
Percent Native-American: 1%
Percent in-state/out-of-state: 73%/27%
Percent Pub HS: 80%
Number of Applicants: 7,157
Percent Accepted: 90%
Percent Accepted who enroll: 37%
Entering: 2,422
Transfers: 1,371
Application Deadline: 1 Feb
Mean SAT: 558 V, 552 M

Mean ACT: NA
Middle 50% SAT range: NA
Middle 50% ACT range: NA
3 Most popular majors: business, journalism, psychology
Retention: 82%
Graduation rate: 59%
On-campus housing: 64%
Fraternities: 11%
Sororities: 11%
Library: 2,366,626 volumes
Tuition and Fees: $3,810 in; $13,197 out
Room and Board: $5,350
Financial aid, first-year: 45%

Set by the Willamette River and the Cascade Mountains, the University of Oregon's 250-acre campus offers its students the vast resources of a public university along with the individual attention given by a midsize institution. The combination of well-regarded academics, diverse extracurricular opportunities, and lush, green surroundings make Oregon an amazing place to spend four years.

Academics

In addition to major requirements, most students find the general distribution requirements, or academic "clusters," to be very rewarding. By taking classes outside his major to fulfill the requirement, one student said, "I never would have taken some of the classes I ended up really enjoying." Although most introductory courses are large, students say that professors are very accessible. "You just need to make an effort and the professor would be happy to meet with you," said one freshman. To contrast this large size, all English and math courses are capped at 30 students per class. Classes become much smaller in upper division courses; some classes have no more than four students. Although the majority of majors offered at UO are respected, the preprofessional programs are particularly well regarded; Business, Journalism, and Architecture boast superb faculty and strong reputations. One academic option for freshmen is the Clarks Honors College, a liberal arts program for first-year students, which offers small classes, individual attention from top-notch professors, and a workload emphasizing writing, verbal skills, and critical thinking. With the best professors of the university at their disposal (including UO's president), honors students say it is most definitely worth the work.

> ". . . it will not be long before UO reclaims its rank as the most wired college by Yahoo!"

Extracurriculars Abound

With ferocious spirit, the Ducks are a force to be reckoned with on the track, field, or elsewhere. Varsity athletics play an important role for students, with track and field, basketball, and football teams drawing the biggest crowds. Besides going to the soon to be renovated Autzen Stadium to see the Ducks fight it out against archival Oregon State, students are heavily involved in intramural sports, community service, and political action. "We don't just talk, we do something," one student said about activism on campus. As the sixth largest source of Peace Corps volunteers, UO also boasts over 250 active student organizations ranging from the *Oregon Daily Emerald*, the daily newspaper, to a variety

of political interest groups heavily involved in local and national politics. The community internship program, which entails working in Eugene for academic credit, is a combination of community service and work experience. "There is something here for everyone. It is just a matter of finding your thing," one student noted, showing the diversity of the UO campus.

A Social Niche for Everyone

Besides extracurricular activities, UO students like to party. The Greek scene is prominent with 15 fraternities and 11 sororities. In contrast to the Greeks, there is a high contingency of alternative or hippie crowds, sometimes referred to as the granolas. Drug use is apparent, although marijuana is predominant, mushrooms and LSD are present as well. Many students, however, have no problem finding a niche between these two extremes and, in the end, everyone has a group of friends. Sometimes students go to Eugene for the weekend because it is a "fun, liberal place," but apparently "dead" at night, encouraging some to stay on campus. Students are extremely happy with campus security; with good lighting, call boxes, and Safe Rides program, students have no problem walking around late at night.

Dorms and Dining

Freshmen who choose to live on campus stay in either in Bean Hall, Hamilton, or Walton Dorms. Bean, known for being "small and dark," exclusively houses freshmen, while Hamilton and Walton house a mixture of freshmen and upperclassmen. Students have the choice of single-sex, coed, athletic, or "academic pursuit" dorms, allowing students of all lifestyles to live comfortably. In addition to meeting fellow students through dorms and classes, Freshman Interest Groups (FIG) led by upperclassmen bring students together in groups of 15 to 30 students who share the same academic interests. "It was a great way to meet people and see if other people are going through the same thing you are academically or otherwise," one student said.

Many sophomores remain on campus living in Hamilton, Walton, or Carson. Because Carson also houses graduate students, undergraduates claim it is a much quieter area of campus. Another option is Riley dorm, where 75% of the residents are international students. "It's a great place to live. You get to meet and hang out with people from all over the world," one American student said. While students who live on campus must have a meal plan, the variety of places to get food makes it "doable." As junior year rolls around, the majority of students move off campus to nearby apartments. Rather than having a meal plan, many upperclassmen eat at the Erb Memorial Union (EMU), the student center, between classes. There, students can use their meal plan to purchase food from Subway, Jamba Juice, and Pizza Hut, or specialty food at the "Market Place," which offers different types of food every day. "Without fail, I go the EMU on Tuesdays for Indian and Wednesdays for Mexican," one student said.

Getting a Face Lift

While UO is already a well respected institution, its campus is still changing for the better. The science research buildings, home to two American Cancer Researchers, were recently renovated, while the gym has just undergone the first phase of remodeling. Now equipped with a new fitness center, indoor rock climbing wall and an astro turf field, students can now utilize the new facilities for intramural and physical classes. In addition, more renovations of the gym will soon be completed, as well as the stadium and Gilbert Hall in the near future. Great strides are also being made with the computer system on campus. With the purchase of new internet servers, and internet connections in every classroom and dorm, it will not be long before UO reclaims its rank as the most wired college by Yahoo! By bringing together a great faculty, developing facilities, and a smaller student body in comparison to other public institutions, UO is a well regarded school offering a solid liberal arts education. —*Jessica Morgan*

FYI
The three best things about attending University of Oregon are, "the Ducks, the tolerance, and the EMU."
The three worst things about attending University of Oregon are, "rain, um, rain, and, um, rain."
The three things that every student should do before graduating are, "go to a football game, listen to your parents, and buy an umbrella."
One thing I'd like to have known before coming here is, "How much you can get out of any class if you just show some initiative and talk to the professor."

Willamette University

Address: 900 State Street; Salem, OR 97301
Phone: 503-370-6303
E-mail address: undergrad-admission@willamette.edu
Web site URL: www.willamette.edu
Founded: 1842
Private or Public: private
Religious affiliation: none
Location: small city
Undergraduate enrollment: 1,598
Total enrollment: 2,365
Percent Male/Female: 45%/55%
Percent Minority: 13%
Percent African-American: 2%

Percent Asian: 6%
Percent Hispanic: 4%
Percent Native-American: 1%
Percent in-state/out-of-state: 50%/50%
Percent Pub HS: 81%
Number of Applicants: 1,541
Percent Accepted: 90%
Percent Accepted who enroll: 26%
Entering: 363
Transfers: 68
Application Deadline: 1 Feb
Mean SAT: 600 V, 610 M
Mean ACT: 27

Middle 50% SAT range: 540–660 V, 540–650 M
Middle 50% ACT range: 24–29
3 Most popular majors: biology, business economics, English
Retention: 88%
Graduation rate: 74%
On-campus housing: 95%
Fraternities: 28%
Sororities: 22%
Library: 280,000 volumes
Tuition and Fees: $21,821 in; $21,821 out
Room and Board: $5,700
Financial aid, first-year: 85%

In the heart of downtown Salem, Oregon, surrounded by office and state government buildings, one finds the oasis of Willamette University. The campus, with lush greenery, historic redbrick structures, and a stream crossing through it, complements a unique university where academic fervor mixes with an intimate, friendly, and fun student body.

Professors Who Care

Willamette University, the oldest university west of the Mississippi, has a reputation for strong academics. With Oregon's seat of government right across the street, it's no surprise that political science is one of the most popular majors. Following the recent completion of the Olin Science Center, more and more students are choosing to specialize in the natural sciences, especially biology and chemistry. In addition, strong departments at this liberal arts institution include economics, psychology, and English.

Students across the board rave about the quality of the academic experience here. The average class size consists of about 25 students, and one undergraduate commented that a 35-student lecture constitutes "a really big class." As many seminars and upper division classes only enroll eight to ten students, undergraduates report that "we can do so much more within our classes," such as long discussions, special projects, guest speakers, and even field trips. Classes are challenging but not overwhelming, and students are able to adjust to the rigorous atmosphere after their first year. For a university of its size, Willamette offers an incredible number of courses, and students can only complain that they don't have time to take all the classes they would like.

One of the most remarkable features of the university is the degree to which professors care about and are involved with their students. For better or worse, professors keep track of undergrads and follow their progress. As one student explained, "If the professor notices you have missed a few classes, or that your grade is slipping, he will definitely take you aside to talk about what's going on with you and try to find a solution." Professors reportedly "know their stuff well," and one student reverently referred to his history professor as "ferocious—the smartest guy I've ever met." In general, professors are both very well respected and well liked.

"Drying Out" the Campus

Dominating the social scene recently is the administration's move to make Willamette a completely dry campus. Suddenly, alcohol is no longer served at on-campus functions, and students risk punishment if they are caught with alcoholic beverages. Even the fraternities, which are located on campus, now host dry parties.

> **"If the professor notices you have missed a few classes, or that your grade is slipping, he will definitely take you aside to talk about what's going on."**

However, this administrative action has not halted the social life at Willamette. More parties are now thrown off campus, in the apartments or houses of students, and upperclassmen frequent the handful of bars in close proximity. Occasionally, undergraduates will make the trek to Portland, 45 minutes away, to hit the bar and club scene there. On campus, the University sponsors one to two formal dances per semester, new release films played in school auditoriums, and events such as Art Attack, a weeklong celebration of the arts, and WUstock, a popular homecoming celebration. Five fraternities and three sororities are located at Willamette, but non-Greeks report that they do not feel excluded. Salem, a town of about 90,000, is not known for a "bumpin'" weekend scene. Besides the few bars immediately around campus, students say entertainment in Salem is limited to the movies and bowling but praise the quality of nearby movie theaters and bowling alleys.

Students at Willamette are serious about their extracurricular activities as well. At such a small school, almost every student plays some kind of sport, with a surprising number involved at the varsity level. Football, soccer, basketball, and track are popular among undergraduates, but a wide range of varsity sports are available. School spirit "depends on the season," although the men's basketball team recently won an NAIA division championship. At every basketball game, fans fill the auditorium to sing the favorite "Ooh ah Bearcats" song. A plethora of other extracurricular activities are also available, with most students participating in some club or group. The debate team, outdoors groups, and volunteer organizations are most popular, and students speculate that sports or volunteering is the most commonly participated activity.

Campus and Facilities

Students say it's easy to get hooked on what many people consider Willamette's greatest attribute: its "picturesque," "stunning," "quaint and beautiful" campus. Some undergrads also describe the campus as "red and green—there are red bricks and green trees and lawns." The grounds are so well kept that students wonder just how much money the University spends on groundskeeping. Squirrels abound, and ducks paddle around Mill Stream, which runs right through campus.

The other University buildings and facilities are a source of pride for students and administration alike. Students hit the books in 24-hour study rooms at the Mark O. Hatfield Library or in open classrooms around campus. When they feel like taking a study break, they drag their books to the Bistro, a student-run coffee shop. Many students, especially those who live in the West Campus, "away from the frats," find it quiet enough to study in their dorm rooms or in the student lounges.

Students name Doney the best dorm because it's quiet, but other dorms are considered comfortable as well. Kaneko, a new dorm built by Willamette's sister school, the nearby Tokyo International University of America, is equipped with tennis courts, a swimming pool, air-conditioning, and tinted windows; the dorm is a "regular Hilton." Freshmen and sophomores are required to live on campus, but about half of juniors and seniors choose to move off campus to nearby West Salem. Of them, most are very satisfied with the apartments and houses available, the safety of the neighborhood, and the increased opportunities "to find something to do."

Willamette students are from mostly conservative, white, upper-middle-class backgrounds, although in recent years the campus has become increasingly diverse. Students realize that the student body is fairly homogenous but do not report that this takes away from their overall experience there. One undergraduate reported that the campus was "pretty diverse" compared to the state of Oregon itself, but Japanese students from TIUA add an international perspective both in and out of the classroom.

How Do You Say "Willamette"?

Students all agree that the intimacy between students, the faculty, and the administration distinguishes Willamette from other universities. There is a "close camaraderie" between students in the small school, and everyone feels like they know a lot of their classmates, "but in a good way." Professors genuinely care about the students in their classes, and even the administration exudes a feeling of intimacy and compassion toward undergraduates.

Willamette students generally are very content with their college choice. Students only really complain about the price of attending the school, which indicates something of the happiness of students there. Just listen to a Willamette student's spirited cry when an outsider mispronounces the school's name: "It's Wil-*lam*-ette, dammit!"—*Johnny Swagerty*

FYI

The three best things about attending Williamette are "small and intimate classes, the attractiveness of the main campus, and the friendships formed on campus."

The three worst things about attending Williamette are "high cost of attending, lack of party/social oppurtunities, and the rain in Oregon."

The three things that every student should do before graduating are "visit the Star Trees, take rhetoric class, and be 'Mill-Streamed,' when you are thrown in the Mill Stream fully clothed on a special occasion."

One thing I'd like to have known before coming here is "that there is a much higher percentage of girls to guys."

Pennsylvania

Allegheny College

Address: Meadville, PA 16335
Phone: 814-332-4351
E-mail address: admiss@admin.alleg.edu
Web site URL: www.alleg.edu
Founded: 1815
Private or Public: private
Religious affiliation: United Methodist
Location: rural
Undergraduate enrollment: 1,897
Total enrollment: 1,897
Percent Male / Female: 47% / 53%
Percent Minority: 5%
Percent African-American: 2%

Percent Asian: 2%
Percent Hispanic: 1%
Percent Native-American: 0%
Percent in-state / out-of-state: 58% / 42%
Percent Pub HS: 80%
Number of Applicants: 2,947
Percent Accepted: 82%
Percent Accepted who enroll: 22%
Entering: 532
Transfers: NA
Application Deadline: 15 Feb
Mean SAT: 591 V, 589 M
Mean ACT: 25

Middle 50% SAT range: 545–640 V, 540–630 M
Middle 50% ACT range: 23–28
3 Most popular majors: psychology, biology, and English
Retention: 87%
Graduation rate: 62%
On-campus housing: 100%
Fraternities: 14%
Sororities: 22%
Library: 650,000 volumes
Tuition and Fees: $20,410 in; $20,410 out
Room and Board: $4,970
Financial aid, first-year: 83%

W alking through the 72 acres of western Pennsylvania that form Allegheny College, a visitor would be likely to first notice the sheer beauty of the campus. One student described Allegheny as "beautiful . . . picturesque, very distinguished . . . very much like out of a movie," with its grass, walkways, and old buildings. But the college's setting is definitely not its only source of appeal. Students agree that Allegheny's carefully tailored liberal arts curriculum and scientific and athletic excellence are among its major draws.

Academics: Liberal Arts and a Common Bond

In addition to the demands of individual departments, Allegheny has a unique sequence of graduation requirements. All freshmen choose a "Freshman Seminar" from among the more than 30 offered each year. Past options have included Cre-

ativity and Problem Solving, Anthropology and Dance, and Biotechnology. Each student's seminar professor becomes his or her advisor for at least two years. All sophomores take Writing in the Liberal Arts seminars. The more than 20 annual section choices in this program have included Films of Ingmar Bergman and Woody Allen, Political Economy, and The Revolutionary Mind. During their junior and senior years, students pursue a major, a minor, and a Senior Project in their major field. The project, or "Comp," must include a Junior Seminar, independent research, and an oral defense. Students' majors must be in one of three divisions (Humanities/Arts, Natural Sciences, and Social Sciences), accompanied by a minor in another area, and at least two courses completed in a third. With all of these requirements, plus a physical education requirement, students are left with about 13 to 15 free course slots for electives. Students generally do not mind Allegheny's requirements: "It's a liberal arts school," one sophomore pointed out, "so you expect to do that when you come here." According to students, the hardest—and often the best—classes are in the sciences, and one of the college's proudest recent achievements is a new science building. Concerns about a pro-science bias came to the forefront when, in budget cuts, the college eliminated several humanities majors and minors including classics, Greek, and sociology/anthropology. Not everyone agrees with the student who complained, "The facilities for the humanities are really run-down." However, many students feel that it is a better college for science majors than people who want to focus on the humanities.

Some of Allegheny's academic features, however, cut across departmental lines. Besides the special requirements, Allegheny academics features small class sizes, close student-professor relationships, and an almost complete absence of graduate student teaching assistants. Classes usually are not difficult to get into, and students tend to participate in class. Allegheny students report that the college is academically intense. "I have time to myself on the weekends a little," says one junior communication arts major, "but I don't think I could ever have one day and not do any work."

Student Life

In addition to the beauty of the campus, a typical visitor to Allegheny would notice rap music booming out of dorm room windows and students walking to class in jeans and baseball caps. One student described the typical Allegheny student as "WASP, very J.Crew, loafers, well dressed, good socioeconomic background, bio or chem major, partier," and from Pennsylvania or the surrounding states. Most students are socially conservative, and some students see a link between Allegheny's small number of minority students and students' attitudes about race and sexual orientation.

"You need to get involved to really experience Allegheny," reported one junior. "There is a group for every interest and if you don't find one, you can start your own." Many student groups are housed in

the student center, which is also a popular hangout. Most people are involved in at least one activity, with sports being a particularly major focus. Allegheny does not give sports scholarships, but "for a Division III small, private school," one student said, "they're among the best on the East Coast," particularly in football and women's soccer. The new gym offers excellent facilities and many students participate in intramurals.

> "You're friends with everybody, you walk down the street and say hi to people. . . . It's like a family," one student said.

When asked what freshmen do on the weekends, one junior replied, "hope that they can get beer, and drink in their rooms without the RAs catching them, or go out to house parties and stand around a keg in a crowded basement hoping to get drunk, while being grossly overcharged for their cup." Upperclassmen tend to socialize at bars and invitation-only parties. Drinking and rowdiness are not permitted in dorms, and kegs are allowed only with a party permit. Fraternity parties, which do not serve alcohol and are usually open to all students, are also a big draw. While there is some hostility between Greeks and non-Greeks, students say the year-long rush process is open and friendly. School-sponsored events such as the annual Springfest and weekly movies and lectures are also major activities. These, along with plays and cultural events, are among the options for those who choose not to drink, a choice that one student reports is possible, and even common, but can be difficult.

Students report a certain amount of apathy toward social events at Allegheny. One sophomore said "People are more into just getting their degrees," while one junior said that most people are not particularly thrilled with the social alternatives "but no one has any clue how to make it better." Small-town Meadville, Pennsylvania, offers movie theaters and restaurants, but not much else for the college crowd. Students often go home or to

Pittsburgh (an hour and a half away and home to many students) on the weekends. Some students also report a certain "cliquey" quality to the Allegheny community, and some complain about the "gossip mill." One sophomore called Allegheny's social scene "high schoolish."

Allegheny students cite the school's size as one of its major assets and flaws. "I never expected to know everyone either by name or face on campus," reported one junior. Its size limits students' options, but encourages student-professor interaction. "You're friends with everybody, you walk down the street and say hi to people. . . . It's like a family," one student said. Depending on the student, four years at Allegheny can seem a long time to spend in such a closed-in environment or can provide a challenging, exciting experience in a picturesque setting.—*Jessica Champagne and Staff*

FYI

The three best things about attending Allegheny are "small classes, nice campus, good science programs."

The three worst things about attending Allegheny are "low access to alcohol, sometimes slow social scene, budget cutting."

The three things that every student should do before graduating from Allegheny are "go tube-sledding, visit Philadelphia, come up with a false rumor about yourself and see how far it travels."

One thing I'd like to have known before coming here is "that I wouldn't be going and getting trashed very often."

Bryn Mawr College

Address: 101 N. Merion Avenue; Bryn Mawr, PA 19010-2899
Phone: 610-526-5152
E-mail address: admissions@brynmawr.edu
Web site URL: www.brynmawr.edu
Founded: 1885
Private or Public: private
Religious affiliation: none
Location: suburban
Undergraduate enrollment: 1,301
Total enrollment: 1,779
Percent Male / Female: 0% / 100%
Percent Minority: 25%

Percent African-American: 4%
Percent Asian: 17%
Percent Hispanic: 3%
Percent Native-American: 0.5%
Percent in-state / out-of-state: 18% / 82%
Percent Pub HS: 73%
Number of Applicants: 1,596
Percent Accepted: 59%
Percent Accepted who enroll: 34%
Entering: 321
Transfers: 8
Application Deadline: 15 Jan
Mean SAT: 670 V, 640 M
Mean ACT: NA

Middle 50% SAT range: 610–710 V, 600–680 M
Middle 50% ACT range: NA
3 Most popular majors: English, math, biology
Retention: 95%
Graduation rate: 81%
On-campus housing: 99%
Fraternities: NA
Sororities: NA
Library: 1,062,594 volumes
Tuition and Fees: $23,360 in; $23,360 out
Room and Board: $8,100
Financial aid, first-year: 56%

Right outside of Philly, easily available profs that actually care about undergrads, a party scene that covers four colleges, and traditions to boot. There's only one college that meets these exciting criteria: Bryn Mawr. Located on Philly's swanky Main Line, Bryn Mawr College combines a healthy social life with an incredibly intense intellectual life. Being a single-sex university doesn't faze Bryn

Mawr women: "At Bryn Mawr we're a community of women—empowered, beautiful, and intelligent."

No Slackers

Academics at Bryn Mawr are described by one sophomore as a "ton of work"and are the number one priority for Byrn Mawr students. Bryn Mawr stresses a core set of academic standards that include a Freshman Liberal Studies Seminar sponsored by the English department, three humanities requirements, two social science courses, and three courses in the natural sciences. Unfortunately for students not inclined to the sciences, this includes two labs. The Freshman Seminar focuses, as most universities like to do, on the students writing. According to one student, there are no "gut" majors. Every field of study is challenging in its own unique way. But those classes with particularly mean reputations include organic chemistry and Elementary Greek and Latin. Greek students, according to student legend, "eat, sleep, and dream Greek."

Class size at Bryn Mawr is generally small. The intro courses tend to be larger, but generally class size runs between 20 and 50 students. Classes also include some students from surrounding schools such as Haverford. Preregistration is key and students have a ten-day shopping period during which they decide their upcoming semester schedule. Upperclassmen are not given preference in registration. Bryn Mawr uses a lottery system to determine whether or not students make it into the class of their choice. Bryn Mawr registrars try to accommodate students and are generally described as "helpful, courteous, and accommodating." Seniors, however, do receive preference if the course is a requirement for their major.

Professors here are "awesome." "I once had a major test coming up. I didn't feel prepared at all so I called up my professor. She sat down with me and went over the work. It was wonderful." This kind of faculty dedication is not uncommon at a small school such as Bryn Mawr. Professors readily hand out their home phone numbers and e-mail addresses. Often, they burn the midnight oil long past office hours to accommodate a student in need. Lucky students have even set up lunch dates with their professors to discuss the latest math theorem or that Byron poem that was difficult to understand. As for the TAs, so often feared by students at large research universities, they are present on campus and do assist in teaching. All classes are, however, taught by professors.

With such stress placed on academics at Bryn Mawr, one would think that there is an intense feeling of competition. According to one student, "Competition is not a problem at Bryn Mawr. We're all in this together." The honor code also helps to discourage competition. The honor code prevents students from discussing tests and grades outside of class. The code also allows for unproctored exams and plays an integral role within the school community.

Slackers, although lacking at Bryn Mawr, will be happy to know that grades are not sent home to parents. Every student's academic file is kept confidential. This adds to the feeling of "independence" that many freshman say "they absolutely love."

Social Life: Crazy, Sexy, Cool

Thanks to brother school Haverford, Bryn Mawr women do enjoy the "traditional" college experience. Although there are some parties at Bryn Mawr, Bryn Mawrians often head into Philly (UPenn, Drexel), Swarthmore, and Haverford to party on the weekends. Haverford, the main party locale, is a mere mile away. It is easily within walking distance of the campus and a bus runs between the two schools every fifteen minutes. A lot of individuals head into Philly for "College Day," which is sponsored by other Philadelphia area colleges in addition to Bryn Mawr and includes parties, concerts, and general merriment.

Bryn Mawr's alcohol policy follows Pennsylvania Law. If you're 21 you can have a wet party or alcohol in the room. Nevertheless, underage students who desire alcohol can easily aquire it. In general, Bryn Mawr students are fairly responsible drinkers. As for the non-drinkers, the school sponsors several bashes annually including the Fall Bash and the semi-formal Pallas Athena.

Beyond the normal party scene, Philadelphia offers myriad activities for the culturally minded student. The Ben Franklin Parkway in Philadelphia has a ton of museums and other cosmopolitan activities for the burgeoning aesthete. The Society Hill Area, including South Street, is also a popular destination for the Bryn Mawr student. The Hill offers several artsy movie theatres and South Street is known for its trendy shops and restaurants.

On campus hangouts include the "Campus Center." The Center boasts a small café where students frequently congregate. It also sponsors a Performing Arts Series along with dances and little concerts.

Dating at Bryn Mawr received mixed responses. While dating certainly isn't the dominant form of social activity, students do "see" other students from neighboring Haverford and Penn. Some girls have serious boyfriends off campus and at home. There is also an active Rainbow Alliance on campus and issues of sexuality are freely discussed at Bryn Mawr. As one student puts it, "single sex doesn't mean no sex."

Incoming students to the college are welcomed at the beginning of the term with freshman orientation. Each freshman is assigned to a Customs Group during "Customs Week," known at other colleges as Orientation Week. Two sophomores lead these inchoate Bryn Mawr groups and act as valuable resources for the new students. The Customs Groups established during the first week provide a social foundation for the incoming class. Freshmen can often be seen with their group heading to meals or other activities.

Living It and Loving It

Living at college is probably one of the major concerns of incoming students. Bryn Mawr's campus is full of beautiful old Gothic dorms, in a style that rivals Princeton and Yale. The rooms themselves are fairly large by college standards and 70% of them are singles that are "greatly appreciated" by freshmen looking for a nap after a particularly trying test. The school guarantees housing for all four years. Nevertheless, some upperclassmen choose to live off campus. There has been a recently built facility known as Glen Meade that was once a house owned by the school, which now serves as student housing. Although the large majority of students do live on or near campus, Bryn Mawr also has a few commuters.

> **"Students at Bryn Mawr, unlike other schools, are not cliquish."**

What about the individuals whom you'll be sharing your lives with for the next four years? Students at Bryn Mawr, unlike other schools, are not cliquish. While some in the country characterize Bryn Mawr as a bastion of liberalism and feminism most students are quick to discount that myth. There is a definite ethnic and geographical diversity present on campus that helps to combat stereotypes present in the media and the society at large.

Bringing guys into this community, specifically the dorms, has never been a problem. Male visitors are expected to abide by the honor code and students are, of course, responsible for the behavior of their guests. It is expected that roommates will notify each other when a guy spends the night. It is the students themselves who decide on the coed status of the bathroom on their floor at the beginning of the year. In other words, many choose to have coed bathrooms to accommodate boyfriends and friends.

The social lives in the dorms are enhanced by the presence of upperclassmen in all dorms. No dorms at Bryn Mawr are specifically reserved for freshman. Hall Advisors help to monitor the girls but are there only in an advisory capacity.

The campus itself is verdant and quaint. Everything is confined to a large rectangular area and all buildings are contained within this area. Bryn Mawr, the town, is a wealthy suburb of Philadelphia that contains numerous coffee shops and small commercial outlets. Town/gown relations are positive as the town actively supports Bryn Mawr students in their social outreach efforts.

Students are apt to hang out in their dorm rooms but do often venture into the town proper to socialize at Starbucks or Xandos. During most of the weekdays students are either studying or shopping in the city. While some students do dine off campus the food on campus is "really good, especially the all beef hamburgers." There are four dining halls on campus including one in Brecken Dorm. A lot of Haverford boys also eat at Byrn Mawr. On weekends, however, students tend to venture into Philadelphia to eat or they can easily order pizza and Chinese food from local restaurants.

Extracurriculars and Traditions

Students are often dedicated to extracurriculars and Byrn Mawr is no exception. The Student Self-Government Association is a popular and well-respected organization on campus. Students also actively participate in Christian Fellowship, Jewish Fellowship, as well as cultural and academic groups.

But perhaps what makes Bryn Mawr what it is today is its Traditions; Traditions with a capital "T." The Traditions are four events conducted each year. They are mostly for the freshman but are heavily attended by upperclassmen as well. Parade Night is the first of these traditions, designed to welcome freshman into the Bryn Mawr community. Lantern Night is also an all-school extravaganza. Each class holds up a lantern of a distinct color used to identify the class. Rumor has it that the girl whose lantern burns out first will be the first in the class to earn her PhD. Hell Week, a time honored parody of sorority rushes, is also wildly popular among sophomores and freshman. "The Hellers" (the sophomores), are each assigned a freshman. For the remainder of the week the freshman must do the every bidding of the sophomore. Luckily for the freshman, sympathetic juniors rescue them from the nefarious grip of the sophomores by providing them with little treats and respites during the week. Lastly in May, the college president rides into campus on a horse to open up May Day celebrations. The president then delivers a speech, which is then followed by a Maypole Dance. The girls then proceed to buckle down for final exams.

A Final Word

Students rave about the benefits of having in a single-sex education. Single-sex education "provides girls with an opportunity to gain confidence" and students tend to "feel a lot more confident in [their] academic abilities" after only a year.—*Sean McBride*

FYI

The three best things about attending Bryn Mawr are "the traditions, friends, and the professors."

The three worst things about attending Bryn Mawr are "the massive amount of work, the lab requirements for science courses, and the stress."

The three things every student should do before graduating from Bryn Mawr are "to ring the Taylor Bell, go abroad, and party in Philly."

One thing I wish I knew before coming here is "there are so many vegan dishes in the dining hall!"

Bucknell University

Address: Freas Hall;
Lewisburg, PA 17837
Phone: 570-577-1101
E-mail address:
admissions@bucknell.edu
Web site URL:
www.bucknell.edu
Founded: 1846
Private or Public:
private
Religious affiliation: none
Location: rural
**Undergraduate
enrollment:** 3,370
Total enrollment: 3,506
Percent Male / Female:
52% / 48%
Percent Minority: 11%
Percent African-American:
3%

Percent Asian: 4%
Percent Hispanic: 3%
Percent Native-American:
0.5%
**Percent in-state / out-of-
state:** 33% / 67%
Percent Pub HS: NA
Number of Applicants:
7,011
Percent Accepted:
44%
**Percent Accepted who
enroll:** 29%
Entering: 889
Transfers: 22
Application Deadline:
1 Jan
Mean SAT: 614 V,
637 M
Mean ACT: NA

Middle 50% SAT range:
570–650 V,
590–680 M
Middle 50% ACT range:
26–29
3 Most popular majors:
business administration,
biology, economics
Retention: 94%
Graduation rate: 89%
On-campus housing:
100%
Fraternities: 36%
Sororities: 43%
Library: 670,000 volumes
Tuition and Fees:
$22,881 in; $22,881 out
Room and Board: $5,469
Financial aid, first-year:
50%

Situated in the rustic setting of Pennsylvania in the small town of Lewisburg, which one student described as the epitome of small-town America, lies Bucknell University. Although Bucknell is isolated from the hustle and bustle of a city, students find plenty to do on campus, and remark that the lack of off-campus activities actually adds to the university's strong feeling of community. One sophomore said, "Yeah, Bucknell is small, but I don't think it's ever constricting."

Work Hard

Bucknell has strong engineering and business programs. Other popular majors include psychology, biology, and political science, and many students choose to double-minor. The only large classes, enrolling up to 100 people, tend to be introductory ones that range in difficulty; a junior said, "It completely depends on your major: Intro to Sociology is an easy A, but Intro to Psych is hard because they try to weed people out for the major." The majority of classes are small, with the average size around 20 to 30 students; some classes may have as few as 8 students.

As for the liberal arts requirements students have to meet, one student remarked,

"I love them—we have a very diverse curriculum," while another sophomore felt that "the requirements are too easy," especially since they do not include foreign language. First-year students must complete an English and a math course, and sophomores must take two lab sciences; other requirements outside of those for departmental majors include four courses in the humanities, two in the social sciences, and the completion of three writing courses. First-year students also take a seminar to work on foundational skills, which "introduce you to a higher way of thinking, writing, analyzing, and arguing," and which they will need in the coming years at Bucknell.

First-year students can apply to a special Residential College seminar program in which they live in Smith Hall, recognized as one of the nicer dorms on campus, on a floor with others in the same program: the Environmental College; the International College; the Arts College; the Social Justice College; and the Humanities College.

As far as getting the classes you want, one student said, "It's not a problem except for the last 10 percent who register; everyone else pretty much gets their first choice of classes and first choice time slots." All classes are taught by professors, with TAs available for extra help and discussion sections. Most students are happy with their professors, and find that many go out of their way for undergrads. One sophomore reported, "One professor came up to my room one day and just hung out and talked about my paper. Most of the profs will meet you over lunch if you need help; I haven't had a professor yet who was opposed to helping out."

Play Even Harder
The weekend starts on Wednesday for Bucknell students and lasts all the way through Sunday, with the main focus on the Greek system. Recently, the administration has begun enforcing a strict policy against underage and excessive drinking. One student explained, "You get fined $50 if you're found drunk. The second time it's a $100 fine and a year of probation. The third time you lose off-campus privileges, you have to write letters to the administration, and go to a class; there's also a fine of $150 per person in a house hosting a party with underage drinking." Despite the steep penalties, some students find ways of getting around the rules and describe the weekend as "the partying time."

> "Bucknell is small. But I don't think it's ever constricting."

The Greek system plays a large part of social life at Bucknell. Students are not allowed to rush until their sophomore year, which most Greek members feel is a good thing, since they get to look around more, and aren't "just thrown in somewhere." One student described bid day, the day when students find out which fraternities or sororities have accepted them, as "the best day of my life here." Students consider the annual House Party at the end of the spring the best party of the year; one student said, "They basically block the campus off from the outside world for two days at the end of April and every frat holds a party." One student not involved with the Greek system said, "It's tough not to be [in a fraternity/sorority], it depends

on your personality, but if you're strong enough, you can do it." The administration provides social alternatives to those not involved with Greek life, such as movies every Wednesday and Saturday, concerts, comedians, and drama shows. The university also sponsors two big concerts each year, one in the fall and one in the spring.

Your New Home
Bucknell students are satisfied with their living situations on the whole, and most stay on campus all four years. Smith Hall, home of the residential college programs, is considered one of the best first-year dorms, while juniors seek out rooms in Hunt Hall. Students generally are satisfied with freshman housing, and after that, as one student commented, "If you're lucky, and you are one of 200 out of 900 that get good room pick numbers, the rooms are big and pretty nice. Otherwise you get stuck in a dingle (a single with two people), which has about an 8'×15' floor space after all of the immobile [built in] furniture."

About half of the dorms are air-conditioned and all except one are coed. Dorms have mixed and single-sex halls, but as one sophomore remarked, "the closest you'll get to same-sex housing is a wing [of a dorm]." The "sorority dorm" is the only all-female dorm, and sorority members are usually required to live there for a semester or a year, since the sororities don't have official houses. There are also special housing options such as the residential colleges, one substance-free house, called "Calvin and Hobbes," and Bucknell West, also called the mods, which "look like trailer houses" and have kitchens and family rooms; one junior said of the mods, "they're nice but far away."

Bucknell students have four places to eat on campus: the Bison, an a la carte grill, a sub shop, Larison Dining Hall, the Terrace Room, which serves sandwiches and grilled items, and the "Caf," the main dining hall. One student remarked that the atmosphere of the dining hall is "somewhat cliquey, frosh all sit on one side; all the minorities sit in the same spot; the sororities sit in the middle." According to one senior, "They require you to have a meal plan if you live on campus, but they have many different packages, so you can usually find one that suits your eating habits. Freshmen are automatically given a 19-meals-a-week plan." What does one do when the dining hall just doesn't cut it? "There are some great little delis in town; there's this one called Five Points, they have the weirdest combinations of food, the Champion [sandwich] is the best!" said one student. Other popular eateries are Vinari's, the Italian Terrace, BJ's, 7th St. Cafe, and the Bison.

Outside of Class

Bucknell offers a wide range of activities for students, from student government to community service clubs. Bucknell is a very athletic campus, with many students participating in club and varsity sports, as well as intramurals. One student said, "The gym has very nice athletic facilities, but the pool is kind of crummy. We also have a golf course." The most popular teams are the well-supported men's and women's basketball teams and the football team. While the administration is trying to get more students out to the football games by offering free season passes to all students, many already have a lot of team spirit for their Bisons.

What makes a Bucknell student? "There are two kinds, there are all the J. Crew junkies and the rest are the pocket-protector boys," one student said. The campus has a very small minority population that is reportedly not very well integrated into campus life. According to one junior the minority situation is "okay, but we definitely should increase it." Bucknell does provide a student resource center that includes a minority affairs division, and a cultural house for students who choose to live with other minorities.

Walking by the dorms on any given day, you would probably hear the Dave Matthews Band blaring from the radio and see *Friends* on the tube. Although students agree that the campus is pretty uniform, they find that the "sense of community makes the school really close." One sophomore remarked of her classmates, "Everyone's really really friendly; it's not even funny."

Despite its remote location Bucknell students are happy there, finding that the secluded and enclosed nature of the school helps foster the sense of community that makes Bucknell an exciting and enriching place to live and learn.—*Katherina Payne and Staff*

FYI

The three best things about attending Bucknell are "class size, social scene, and the excellent professors.

The three worst things about attending Bucknell are "sometimes too small of a campus, registering for classes is inefficient, location."

The three things that every student shoud do before graduating are "get drunk and hook up, utilize the alumni and professors to make connections in your field, and to live off-campus so you know what the responsibility is like."

One thing I'd like to have known before coming here is "that the social scene was so Greek-dominated!"

Carnegie Mellon University

Address: 5000 Forbes Avenue; Pittsburg, PA 15213
Phone: 412-268-2082
E-mail address: admit@andrew.cmu.edu
Web site URL: www.cmu.edu
Founded: 1900
Private or Public: private
Religious affiliation: none
Location: urban
Undergraduate enrollment: 5,050
Total enrollment: 7,912
Percent Male/Female: 65%/35%
Percent Minority: 36%
Percent African-American: 5%

Percent Asian: 25%
Percent Hispanic: 6%
Percent Native-American: 0%
Percent in-state/out-of-state: 17%/83%
Percent Pub HS: NA
Number of Applicants: 13,187
Percent Accepted: 42%
Percent Accepted who enroll: 23%
Entering: 1,274
Transfers: 49
Application Deadline: 1 Jan
Mean SAT: 651 V, 710 M
Mean ACT: 29
Middle 50% SAT range: 590–710 V, 660–750 M

Middle 50% ACT range: 27–32
3 Most popular majors: computer science, business administration and electrical and computer engineering
Retention: 92%
Graduation rate: 58%
On-campus housing: 100%
Fraternities: 15%
Sororities: 13%
Library: 935,888 volumes
Tuition and Fees: $22,100 in; $22,100 out
Room and Board: $6,810
Financial aid, first-year: 59%

Carnegie Mellon students are sometimes affectionately referred to as "the freaks and geeks," according to one sophomore, because the school is known for its unusually strong fine arts, computer science, and engineering programs. This is not surprising considering that it is the first university in the world to have its own wireless computing network (which began in October 1999 in partnership with Lucent Technologies), as well as the first to award an undergraduate degree in drama (1917). The expression "freaks and geeks" isn't necessarily a bad thing—"everybody here is really nice. Even when they're studying their [butts] off, they're all really civil and there's never academic competition," said one freshman. In any case, students agree that the academics at their Pittsburgh-located school are challenging but incredible, that the social life is good if you know where to look, and most importantly—if it floats your boat, you can major in bagpipes.

Computers, Art, and More Computers

CMU is very computer-oriented; "a techie school all the way," said a sophomore, but he added that "there are many wonderful arts programs." Just keep in mind that "No matter what field you are in you *will* be a computer addict before you leave," warned a business and ethics, history, and public policy double major. The academic requirements differ between the five undergraduate schools; that is, the Mellon College of Science, the Carnegie Institute of Technology, the College of Fine Arts, the College of Humanities and Social Sciences, and the School of Computer Science. "Each school has a different 'core curriculum,' as does every major," explained a German and business double major. These core classes are not the most enjoyable: "I have always hated GenEd classes—I think they're boring and easy, presenting no challenge to anyone and offering only a little information," described a sophomore. Students agreed that the workload was quite heavy, especially in computer science, math, and engineering classes, but that slacker majors and classes did exist. Slacker majors mentioned included Music Performance, Psychology, English, and Modern Languages. Some of the specialized majors, especially the Robotics minor in Computer Science and Human-Computer Interactions, earned praise from students. Also mentioned was the five-year Masters program where "you start prepping for your Master's while you're still an undergrad, and then [in the fifth year] you student-teach and do other Master's classes. Then you graduate with a Master's in your field *and* with a teaching certification," explained one student.

Classes' sizes tend towards the extremes, from as small as five to fifteen people in discussion sections and recitations, but with lecture courses ranging up to the 300s. However, lecture classes are still small enough that students can ask questions of the professors if necessary. One student said that "a lot of professors are famous for research in their fields, but to us unenlightened, we wouldn't know the difference." Students did agree that the computer science and history profs are superb. In particular, Peter Stearns, who is the Head of the History Department and Dean of Humanities and Social Sciences, "is an awesome historian—he knows so much and can put it in language that is easily understood," gushed one sophomore.

Student participation in classes, however, is not the best—"People here tend to be pretty apathetic," described a chemical engineering major. "In recitations, most people go just because they feel that they would be wasting their money should they not go. In lectures, half the class is asleep." Indeed, "profs who randomly call students from the roll tend to discover just how many people are asleep," said an electrical and computer engineering and computer science double major. Also, "there aren't enough TA's that speak English," complained a sophomore. Grading tends to be "pretty tough," but most professors grade on a curve, and will only curve students' grades up but not down. Student opinion on academics could be best summed up by one student's rave: "Rigorous, interesting, and just what I was looking for when I came here. Overall thumbs *way up.*"

The Girls Got it Good
One legend at CMU exemplifies the imbalance between males and females at CMU: "a few years back—the number of years ranges—there was supposedly a survey done of all students in Computer Science. It was found that there were more Daves

enrolled than females," described a sophomore. And despite the prevalence of wealthy kids, students all mentioned the diversity of the student population. An architecture student gushed, "we have students that dress, act, and have totally different personalities! That's what makes CMU so great!" Students pointed to CMU diversity especially in terms of sexuality—"It's a fairly gay-positive campus, with huge support from the administration," explained a member of cmuOUT. He also said that "there are also great deal of Asian—including Indian—and white interracial couples."

Unfortunately, mourned one sophomore who voiced the opinion of many CMU students, "In terms of attractive people, our campus is pretty limited. There's not really enough girls to go around, but, if I were a girl, I probably wouldn't want to date most of the freaky and dorky guys here either. So, in general, not many of us get play. It sucks to be us." It seems that most students definitely put academics above social life.

> **"APATHY! APATHY! A-P-A-...**
> **nevermind..."**

Furthermore, students said that social groups that formed during freshman orientation never quite seemed to break apart. One junior said that CMU "is very, very cliquish—especially among ethnic groups." Indeed, at dining halls (which serve awful meals—students warn future freshmen to get as small a dining plan as possible), tables are comprised either of "cliques or loners," said a sophomore. Not much dating goes on, and one information decision systems major said that "all of the sex is casual and fleeting."

However, frats and sororities are not hard to rush—"Rush is mainly going to the different houses and playing games," explained one freshman. Cool frats and sororities mentioned were Kappa Kappa Gamma, Phi Kappa Theta, and Theta Xi. Unfortunately, "parties suck... crappy beer, bad music," complained a student. Most freshmen only have the option of frat parties on weekends, explained one upperclassman, because they don't know enough people to go to other parties. Another junior said that upperclassmen tend to go to private parties or clubs and bars, while a sophomore concurred and added that they also go to raves. One student said that "There is a lot of binge drinking and a good bit of drug use, mostly weed." Kegs are allowed on-campus into the non-dry frat houses, but no alcohol is allowed in students' rooms. Cool theme parties include the jungle party, the swing party, and the beach party.

Most students who wish to stay sober on the weekends "watch movies in Mc-Conomy, the campus auditorium/movie theater with a kick-[butt] sound system." Other students opt to "go off-campus or simply play computer games," said a computer science major. Campus-organized activities are widely attended when they do occur. One sophomore mentioned the Spring Carnival in particular: "For three days the entire campus goes nuts with an actual carnival on one of the big parking lots. There are many activities, the highlights being carnival booths, buggy, and the mobot (mobile robot) competition." Buggy, explained an activites coordinator, involves the following: "Take a five-foot-long bullet, cut it in half. Put it on wheels, put a person inside. Attach a bar at a sixty-degree angle from the ground, and push it around campus along a course that goes both uphill and downhill, around sharp turns. Make it a race."

Safe, Beautiful, and Good Eating

"I love Pittsburgh, this is a beautiful and safe campus," declared one pleased freshman. Added another student, "the campus is small, which is nice, because you can walk everywhere. It's very pleasant and has beautiful yellow brick buildings. However, unless it's a really nice day, you won't see anyone hanging out outside—we're notorious for hanging out in computer clusters!"

Despite the beautiful campus, most students move off-campus after freshman year, even though most students thought freshman-year dorms were fine. Specifically, students say that Mudge, a converted mansion, is the best dorm, with suite-style, spacious rooms, and a gorgeous courtyard. Donner is "a dungeon, with small dingy rooms and shared bathrooms." One reason for the migration to off-campus housing, as one sophomore explained it, is that "it's difficult to get any unless you know people already there, at least sophomore year." Another sophomore said of off-campus housing that it is because "it's usually cheaper than living in the dorms, and you get *way* more space and freedom. Dorms have RAs, but they're "cool." However, one major complaint made by a junior was that "there is no place to study here! You'd think they would have more open spaces!"

Good places to eat off-campus include the Pirmanti Brothers, Lu-Lu's House Of Noodles, and The Union Grill Mad-Mex—there are plenty of great low-price restaurants on Craig Street, right near campus. For dates, students head over to Station Square, an area with nice restaurants.

Apathy Prevails

Varsity sports are definitely not a big thing at CMU—"People are too lazy. Only about five people go to football games," said a freshman. However, intramurals are pretty popular among students. Also well liked are the comedic organizations, KGB and CIA, which compete against one another. A sophomore mentioned that "there are quite a few hard-core community service organizations on campus." Also well respected is the International Relations Organization, Mayur (the Southeast Asian organization), and the campus newspaper. Most people participate in extracurricular activities, but people are identified more by their majors, especially the computer science majors, who, according to a junior, are known to play Quake 24/7.

A common cheer heard at the school that might reflect CMU and its students' wits and interests best is "APATHY! APA-THY! A-P-A- . . . nevermind . . ." If building robots beats football, if being on the cutting-edge of incredible technology is as important as being in a great arts program for you, then CMU is definitely the place to go. As one student put it, "I have several friends who are double majoring in Art and Computer Science and are amazingly talented in both. It makes for an interesting mix to have some of the most creative and some of the most boring people all in the same school."—*Jennifer Wang*

FYI
The three best things about attending Carnegie Mellon are "the weird relationship between the fine arts and engineers, living in Pittsburgh, and 24-hour computer clusters."
The three worst things about attending Carnegie Mellon are "the shortage of available women, the food on campus sucks, and student apathy."
The three things that every student should do before graduating from Carnegie Mellon are "to get away from the computer, sneak into the steam tunnels one night, participate in buggy and Spring Carnival."
One thing that I'd like to have known before coming here is "how boring, unimaginative and apathetic so many people are—there are a lot of cool people, but there are a lot of people who just love to code all day and have no social life or social skills."

D i c k i n s o n   C o l l e g e

Address: PO Box 1773; Carlisle, PA 17013-2896
Phone: 717-245-1231
E-mail address: admit@dickinson.edu
Web site URL: www.dickinson.edu
Founded: 1773
Private or Public: private
Religious affiliation: none
Location: suburban
Undergraduate enrollment: 2,024
Total enrollment: 2,024
Percent Male/Female: 40%/60%
Percent Minority: 7%

Percent African-American: 1%
Percent Asian: 3%
Percent Hispanic: 2%
Percent Native-American: 0.5%
Percent in-state/out-of-state: 46%/54%
Percent Pub HS: 75%
Number of Applicants: 3,434
Percent Accepted: 64%
Percent Accepted who enroll: 28%
Entering: 620
Transfers: 10
Application Deadline: 1 Feb
Mean SAT: NA

Mean ACT: NA
Middle 50% SAT range: 560–650 V, 550–640 M
Middle 50% ACT range: NA
3 Most popular majors: modern languages, political science, English
Retention: 89%
Graduation rate: 75%
On-campus housing: 100%
Fraternities: 31%
Sororities: 29%
Library: 452,632 volumes
Tuition and Fees: $24,475 in; $24,475 out
Room and Board: $6,450
Financial aid, first-year: 84%

Dickinson, a small liberal arts college located in suburban Pennsylvania, has much more to offer than its pastoral campus suggests. It provides students with an atmosphere of hard work and partying and a diverse educational background.

Dickinson is known for its foreign-language and political science departments. Many students opt to major in political science with the hope of eventual admission to the college's highly ranked law school.

Small, Intimate Classes

Students praise Dickinson's student-faculty ratio. The average class size is 15 to 30 students, except for several popular introductory-level courses in the science departments. All classes are taught by professors. These professors all live on Dickinson's campus and frequently invite students to their homes for meals. One student reported that some professors can even be spotted at college parties.

Students must fulfill distribution requirements outside their majors. Undergrads must take courses in philosophy, religion or environmental studies, the social sciences, the natural sciences (including lab courses), a foreign language, comparative civilizations, physical education, and a literature course in English or a foreign language. To help fulfill these requirements, some students seek out the rare "easy-A" courses such as introductory courses in psychology, lighting, and art history. While some students find these requirements "a hassle because you have to take courses you wouldn't ordinarily take," most students agree that the requirements end up making them "well-rounded." One student reported, "You have to work hard in all your classes. Dickinson has a lot more course work than a lot of other schools." All freshmen take the Freshman Seminar, an introduction to all aspects of college life, from improving one's writing to learning to make full use of the university's facilities. To further supplement the variety of classes, Dickinson allows students to design their own majors under supervision of an academic panel that reviews their course schedules every semester.

In addition to the programs offered on the Dickinson campus, students can choose to spend a semester or year abroad at a wide variety of affliated programs around the world. Programs in most European countries, Africa, Asia, and South and Central America offer the opportunity either to take classes pertaining to the student's major, or to "integrate themselves into an entirely different culture by means of host families and internship programs." Students nearly universally praised the study-abroad options at Dickinson, one going so far as to deem study-abroad "the shining jewel in Dickinson's crown."

> The traditional residential halls "give more sense of community. They're louder and more fun," according to one undergrad.

For quiet study on campus, some students recommend the Spahr Library, although one senior called it the center of "the campus social scene." With the recent addition of the Waidner wing, the library is much larger, brighter, and more comfortable, with new furniture, computer facilities, and outlets and internet ports to accommodate laptop users. In addition, the library is also more research-friendly, since the stacks were enlarged

making more materials easily accessible to students

When they are not in the mood for the library, students opt to study in their dorm rooms or the lounge areas in academic buildings; for group studying, comfortable chairs in the spacious basement of the student union are popular.

"The Hub" of Social Life
The student union building houses the Hub cafeteria, a place to eat, study, and socialize. As one student said, "Everyone at Dickinson eats at exactly the same time, so you can find anyone at the Hub at noon." The food is largely praised, and recent renovations that shortened lines and lessened crowding in the cafeteria have improved students' opinions. A flex plan, allowing students to purchase 16 meals a week with extra points for the cafeteria and snack bar, is an alternative to the traditional required 21-meal-a-week plan. Those students looking for a break from the cafeteria turn to the Backdoor Cafe, a small local restaurant within walking distance of the campus, which is popular for its pizza and lasagna. Another area restaurant and bar frequented by students is the Gingerbread Man.

Fun Stuff
According to one senior, "everyone is involved" in several extracurricular activities, ranging from the choir and drama club to the student senate. Each foreign-language department has its own club. Concerts and plays are held in Schlechter auditorium and Rubendall Recital Hall. Student publications include the yearbook, the *Microcosm*, and the weekly *Dickinsonian* newspaper. Literary magazines come and go; as one student explained, many times the magazines "fizzle out" after several issues. One junior reported that due to Dickinson's small size, there is only "a limited amount of talent and leadership" in the student body and frequently, activities are run by "the same people over and over again, just like it was in high school."

The Kline Athletic Center is a top-notch fitness center that, according to one student, has "all the resources, if you want them." The Kline Center has a new wing which houses all-new aerobic equipment and a huge nautilus and free-weight system. Students also praise the gym for the extensive aerobics schedule and impressive track.

The most popular varsity teams are football and swimming. Except for homecoming (when alumni return) there is not a lot of support or school spirit for the teams. Intramural teams are quite popular and can be used to fulfill the physical education requirement. Soccer, basketball, and volleyball draw the most participants, especially those athletes who "don't feel like putting in all the time required for a varsity sport," one student said.

Where Sleeping Options Abound

Dorm life is "decent," according to Dickinson residents. The campus is divided into quads and traditional dorms. While the dorms have kitchens and are coed, quads are smaller and have new carpeting. The latter, as Student Directed Learning Centers, allow for theme housing including multicultural and equality groups, language houses, volunteer groups, ROTC members, and fraternities and sororities. The traditional residential halls "give more sense of community. They're louder and more fun," according to one undergrad. Another student praised Adams Hall for its large halls and secluded nature. Some criticize Morgan for its "maze-like quality." Most students live on campus for four years, an advantage one student praised because it "allows me to focus on my work alone. I don't have to deal with rent and apartments this early on."

Drink Until You Puke

Social life at Dickinson revolves around drinking. As one student said, "They don't call it 'Drinkinson' for nothing." Greek life at Dickinson is quite prevalent. Although some independents feel the Greeks are condescending, the Greeks themselves "don't see independents as losers or anything," said one student. There is reportedly a great deal of tension, however, between the administration and the Greeks. Since the administration's crackdown due to the death of a student during rush week several years ago, Greek life is seen as "going

downhill." According to one student, "The fraternities and sororities do positive things for the community, too. We're not like Animal House or anything."

For those not interested in Greek life, there are several popular bars in Carlisle. The G-man, Fast Eddie's, and the Blessed Oliver Plunckett attract a student crowd. To provide alternatives to alcohol-centered social events, the Campus Activities Board sponsors concerts, shows movies, and brings in performers ranging from hypnotists and magicians to comedians and singers such as Harry Connick, Jr. However, some students report that, despite the plethora of non-Greek activites available on- and off-campus, a large number of students leave Carlisle and "head for more fertile cultural areas on the weekends."

Town-Gown Blues

Carlisle, the quaint neighboring town, has "two bad malls and a bowling alley that closes at 5 P.M.," reported one undergrad. Some students sense a strong anti-Dickinson sentiment among the residents of Carlisle. As one student explained, "A lot of the people see us as 'little rich kids,' but they don't realize how much business we pull for them." While many students complain that "there's nothing to do" at Dickinson, one advised that "there actually is a lot to do if you know where to look." Students occasionally travel to Harrisburg and the factory outlets in Reading. As one student said, "If you want to do stuff, you really need a car."

Dickinson's campus of limestone buildings is considered safe, an attribute the college takes measures to maintain. Dickinson requires keys and electronic key tags for entry into the dorms and provides a student patrol system. Dickinson even provides a shuttle from the campus to and from one of the most popular bars to "make sure all the drunk kids make it home safely," said one student. Although some students complain about the small size, suburban atmosphere, and upper-middle-class white-student stereotype at Dickinson, others find the size an advantage. "Even though I know a lot of people at this school, I'm constantly meeting new people," one junior remarked.

Upon graduating, Dickinson students traditionally march through the front door of the oldest building on campus. Students see this as a sign that Dickinson has opened the door to the world for them. In that world, Dickinson graduates can reminisce about four years at a college with minimal diversity but rich in a friendly, small-school atmosphere.—*Alexandra Rethore*

FYI

The three best things about attending Dickinson are "the beautiful limestone buildings and the landscape, the approachable professors, and the people you meet here."

The three worst things about attending Dickinson are "strict rules on partying, lack of housing, the town of Carlisle."

The three things that everyone should do before graduating from Dickinson are "study in front of the warm fireplace in the library, take a professor out to eat, lay out on Morgan Field during a sunny spring day."

One thing I'd like to have known before coming here is "how much you need a car."

Drexel University

Address: 3141 Chestnut Street; Philadelphia, PA 19104
Phone: 215-895-2400
E-mail address: undergrad-admissions @mail.drexel.edu
Web site URL: www.drexel.edu
Founded: 1891
Private or Public: private
Religious affiliation: none
Location: urban
Undergraduate enrollment: 8,902
Total enrollment: 10,455
Percent Male/Female: 64%/36%
Percent Minority: 15%

Percent African-American: 1%
Percent Asian: 12%
Percent Hispanic: 2%
Percent Native-American: 0%
Percent in-state/out-of-state: 56%/44%
Percent Pub HS: NA
Number of Applicants: 9,303
Percent Accepted: 69%
Percent Accepted who enroll: 33%
Entering: 2,118
Transfers: NA
Application Deadline: 1 Mar
Mean SAT: 553 V, 578 M
Mean ACT: NA

Middle 50% SAT range: 500–600 V, 520–630 M
Middle 50% ACT range: NA
3 Most popular majors: electrical engineering, mechanical engineering and finance
Retention: 84%
Graduation rate: 50%
On-campus housing: 100%
Fraternities: 8%
Sororities: 5%
Library: 500,000 volumes
Tuition and Fees: $24,280 in; $24,280 out
Room and Board: $7,950
Financial aid, first-year: 79%

The word students most commonly use to describe a Drexel education is "practical." Drexel students alternate classroom learning with full-time jobs and internships during their co-op semesters.

The Curriculum

"When you're comparing Drexel to other schools, think of the real-world experience Drexel offers," one senior advised. For up to three semesters during their sophomore and junior years, Drexel students leave the classroom for internships at various companies. Each internship lasts about six months and pays, on average, about $10,000. The largest co-op employers include SmithKline Beecham, Lockheed Martin, ARCO Chemical Company, PECO Energy Company, and E. I. DuPont de Nemours & Co., Inc. One senior business major who spent a semester at a steel company and two semesters at an investment banking firm explained, "It gives you good exposure at a very young age." According to students, many internships lead to employment offers.

Drexel is divided into six colleges: the College of Arts and Sciences, the College of Business and Administration, the College of Design Art, the College of Engineering, the College of Information Science and Technology, and the College of Evening and Professional Studies. However, the engineering school predominates and offers better facilities than the other schools. One freshman complained, "Ninety percent of my money goes to the engineering school even though I am not an engineering student." However, many feel that the school derives its reputation from engineering and therefore benefits all students by maintaining excellence in engineering.

And all fields of engineering, from computer to civil, are highly regarded. The architecture program draws raves from most who participate. As a result of the co-op program, business majors report satisfaction with their learning experience at Drexel. However, humanities majors often feel they have been given the "Drexel Shaft" and find the overly technical library content useless.

Campus and People

The Drexel campus itself is at best "functional" and at worst "ugly," students report. Drexel houses students in five dorms. However, many undergrads commute or choose to live off campus. The living arrangements are generally "livable but unspectacular." Yet, students writhe at the mention of dining hall food. Several students suggest that just going to the dining hall is a hopeless endeavor. One student argued, "Don't buy a meal plan. You'll regret it." Philadelphia offers plenty of eating options for the student who does not use Drexel's cafeteria.

The campus has a diverse population, but compared to surrounding areas of Philadelphia, the African-American population on campus is small. Drinking is common, but one student complained that "Drexel parties are lame."

Philadelphia

Drexel offers both the risks and opportunities of urban living. More than one non-Philadelphia native bemoaned Drexel's location and even the city of Philadelphia itself. One student quoted the Sherman Edwards musical 1776 to describe the city and his experience at Drexel: "Nothing's ever solved in foul, fetid, fuming, foggy, filthy Philadelphia." However, the consensus is that Philadelphia is a net positive. There is crime on campus, but emergency phones and an escort service have increased safety at Drexel, and crime has declined citywide over the past few years. The city offers a huge spectrum of recreational activities. One student frequents the Hindi music clubs, while another takes a noncredit class offered at the Philadelphia Art Museum. Many Drexel students attend fraternity parties at Temple and the University of Pennsylvania, while others party at the city's many clubs. South Street, only a few blocks from campus, offers a strong alternative scene.

> "When you're comparing Drexel to other schools, think of the real-world experience Drexel offers," one senior advised.

For the focused preprofessional, Drexel can be a firm stepping-stone into well-paying and satisfying employment.
—*Brian Abaluck and staff*

FYI

The three best things about attending Drexel are "Philadelphia, the internships, and the facilities."

The three worst things about attending Drexel are "the workload, those oh-so-exciting parties, and humanities classes."

The three things that every student should do before graduating are "visit the Art Museum, go to Independence Mall, dance at the clubs on Delaware Avenue."

One thing I'd like to have known before coming here is "that you need ID if you're under 21 to do a bunch of things."

Franklin and Marshall College

Address: PO Box 3003; Lancaster PA 17604-3003
Phone: 717-291-3953
E-mail address: admission@fandm.edu
Web site URL: www.fandm.edu
Founded: 1787
Private or Public: private
Religious affiliation: none
Location: suburban
Undergraduate enrollment: 1,862
Total enrollment: 1,862
Percent Male/Female: 50%/50%
Percent Minority: 11%
Percent African-American: 3%

Percent Asian: 5%
Percent Hispanic: 3%
Percent Native-American: 0%
Percent in-state/out-of-state: 36%/64%
Percent Pub HS: NA
Number of Applicants: 3,926
Percent Accepted: 54%
Percent Accepted who enroll: 24%
Entering: 509
Transfers: NA
Application Deadline: 1 Feb
Mean SAT: 623 V, 635 M
Mean ACT: 27

Middle 50% SAT range: 570–670 V, 590–680 M
Middle 50% ACT range: 24–31
3 Most popular majors: government, biology, and business
Retention: 95%
Graduation rate: 73%
On-campus housing: 100%
Fraternities: 40%
Sororities: 30%
Library: 390,000 volumes
Tuition and Fees: $23,720 in; $23,720 out
Room and Board: $5,730
Financial aid, first-year: 47%

If enthusiasm is what you are looking for, Franklin and Marshall is the place to find it. Students dedicate themselves to all aspects of college life. Many chose the college for a challenging course load, and that is what the school delivers. But their dedication extends far beyond the classroom. From helping in the community to enjoying themselves on the weekends, F&M students enjoy keeping themselves busy. Nestled in the picturesque town of Lancaster, this small liberal arts college prides itself on both academic excellence and rigor, combined with a healthy taste for amusement.

STUDY, STUDY, STUDY!

"Classes are hard," F&M students unanimously chime. When asked what an easy major is at F&M, one senior replied "I don't think that there is one." But, F&M is a college designed to be tough, and the students rise to the challenge posed by their inspiring professors. "I have tons of reading to do every night. Some people don't do all of the reading . . . but those are the students who only get average grades."

A self-proclaimed liberal arts college, F&M's focus has long been on the sciences. "The school has pretty good facilities for being [so] small," one senior reported. Students say F&M's computer facilities are excellent, with Ethernet connections available in all public areas, such as libraries and classrooms, and in most of the dorms—"my whole life is on the Web," one student boasted. While the science complex was renovated recently, the school is currently trying to help the arts programs with renovations and expansions. The arts "deserve better," one student said.

Many students choose F&M for the premed program. Students "don't always survive the premed program, but that's what they come for," said one undergrad. "I have sympathy for the premeds," one junior commented. "They hammer themselves." Departments such as English, classics, and psychology are also quite strong.

Distribution requirements consist of courses in at least three different areas, such as Knowledge and Belief, Foreign Study, and Social Science. Two semesters of foreign language also are required.

Class sizes are small at F&M, topping off at around 20 to 25 students, so some freshmen have trouble getting into the classes they want. Many feel that the close rapport with professors and the small, discussion-intensive sections far outweigh any problems with registration. F&M professors, including Howard Kaye and Carol Auster in sociology, Sanford Pinsker in English, and Curtis Bentzel in German, earn student praise for their dedication and desire to teach. They "seem to want to be here [and] . . . treat you like you're smart," one student said. By the time you graduate, one student was happy to report, you're "close to one if not close to a bunch." It is not unusual for students to eat dinner or baby-sit at their professors' houses. Many students remain in close contact with professors even after graduation. One junior exclaimed in praise of his profs, "If you give them an inch, they'll give you a ton!"

Franklin and Marshall students are quick to point out that their college is not entirely a machine that grinds their faces into the books. Instead, they characterize the college as a place "that is really academically rigorous and then parties like at any other school." Extracurriculars provide the main chance to meet other people, and if "one is not involved, it makes it harder," one student reported. Popular activities to which students devote a great deal of time and energy include the drama society, known as the Green Room; the weekly newspaper, the *College Reporter*; the radio station, WFNM; the Student Congress; Minority Integration Program; and the College Entertainment Committee. Various community service programs connected with F&M's new Community and Public Service Institute and the America Reads Program also attract wide participation. Students involved in these campus activities, as well as in work-study programs, consider themselves "some really dedicated individuals."

Outside the Classroom . . .

Much of the F&M social scene is dominated by Greek societies, which although not officially recognized by the college, involve the majority of the student body. Weekends consist of "frat parties, frats, and more frats," according to one senior. Although much town-gown tension stems from the Greek houses' loud parties and initiation rituals, which one member said get "pretty rough," students seem to find

that the independence of the Greek societies from the college has pulled a lot of the tension away from the school. At the same time, students agree that membership or non-membership defines them. Campus cliques center on Greek membership and reportedly turn the dining hall experience into a "'Dining Hall Culture." One student warned, "You don't just sit anywhere . . . like high school."

For those who dislike the Greek system and the many parties dominated by drinking, "there really isn't much left to do [but] . . . sit around and complain," one senior groaned. Another summarized the F&M college work ethic as "kill yourself working during the week and kill yourself drinking on the weekend."

To provide an alternative for those uninterested in Greek activities, the school sponsors parties, such as the Blizzard Bash and Around the World, movies, lectures, and an occasional comedian. Recent guests include Kwaisi Infume, Maya Angelou, John Updike, Newt Gingrich, Billy Joel, and the Dave Matthews Band. A popular campus hangout is Ben's Underground, which has a publike atmosphere where students can eat snacks and play pool or versions of supermarket bingo and The Dating Game.

> Frat parties are the center of social life on weekends, and "the parties are a lot of drinking and some dancing and hooking up. That's about it."

As for real dating, one experienced senior reported that "there isn't really much to do in Lancaster, so the dating scene is very limited." Frat parties are the center of social life on weekends, and "the parties are a lot of drinking and some dancing and hooking up. That's about it." Another student agreed that the social scene was "hookup central," with very few steady couples populating the campus.

The town of Lancaster gets mixed reviews from students. Some like its quaint affability while others lament that "Lancaster sucks . . . nothing to do." The town has a dance club for students over 18, a 24-hour bowling alley, as well as many restaurants and coffeehouses, such as the popular Fred and Mary's and the Cafe Angst. Philadelphia and Baltimore, as well as the closer malls and outlets, offer more excitement for students who have cars, but some claimed that there was too much work to allow frequent excursions.

Food at F&M gets the same sort of tempered criticism as it does everywhere. In the dining hall, suggested one grumpy student, avoid everything. Another exclaimed, "Some of their creations are just amazing!" such as the orange cheese sauce and "ratatouille." The options for vegetarians are mainly salad and pasta, and according to one student "it's bad, it's bad pasta." But, students gladly use their meal credit for snacks and sandwiches at the college Common Ground, and food in Lancaster is rated highly, with many pizza spots, chain and local restaurants, and a Farmer's Market for fresh vegetables.

Dorm life at F&M is almost universally praised. First-year students and sophomores are required to live in the dorms, with mostly coed floors, although students can request single-sex housing. Dorm life is supervised by RAs—residents call them "tools of the administration"— but this does not seriously hamper social life. The dorms are reported to be very spacious and convenient, with phone and Internet connections, but many juniors and seniors move off campus, where the housing is "pretty good," although security is less tight outside the perimeters of the campus security patrols. As for safety, walking at night "could be dangerous if people are stupid," but students generally walk in groups, especially to and from off-campus locales.

Enthusiastic participation in athletics or attendance at sporting events are not priorities at F&M. The football and basketball teams are popular and their games are fairly well-attended, especially by certain Fummers who paint their faces blue and do push-ups for every Diplomat touchdown. But overall, the teams are not a central rallying point for school spirit, which, on the whole, is rated very low— "people are really negative about the school . . . very cynical in general."

F&M is a Division III college and does not give athletic scholarships. For those not on teams, club sports and intramurals are popular. The new Athletic Sports and Fitness Center (ASFC) is good for many exercise-hungry students.

While F&M students generally think of themselves as nonpolitical and "pretty apathetic," many are also fairly conservative in their views on social issues. The student population is "more diverse than people give it credit for," but one student admitted that racial minorities are seldom fully integrated into the mainstream of the student body. However, the small minority groups are active and outspoken, with the Black Student Union acclaimed for being the only really politically active forum on campus.

While the challenges of the social environment make some F&M students "a little bitter," the intelligent cynicism of the student body seems to fit well with the mission of the school as a place of devotion to rigorous academics. Franklin and Marshall is a perfect fit for those students with an enthusiastic desire to educate themselves, to better their community, and to make time for a healthy social life as well. The requirements for students both in and out of the classroom are intense, and the process of rising to meet these challenges breeds a healthy dedication to all aspects of college life.—*Erik Weiss and staff*

FYI

The three best things about attending Franklin and Marshall are "good classes, crazy partying, and air-conditioned dorms."

The three worst things about attending Franklin and Marshall are "you can't touch the trees, there's not much to do except drink, and Lancaster is not so exciting."

The three things that every student should do before graduating are "have Chinese food at that place in the student center, go to the Farmer's Market, and make a stir-fry."

One thing I'd like to have known before coming here is "that people judge you by your fraternity."

Gettysburg College

Address: Eisenhower House; Gettysburg College; Gettysburg, PA 17325-1484
Phone: 717-337-6100
E-mail address: admiss@gettysburg.edu
Web site URL: www.gettysburg.edu
Founded: 1832
Private or Public: private
Religious affiliation: Lutheran
Location: rural
Undergraduate enrollment: 2,123
Total enrollment: 2,123
Percent Male/Female: 48%/52%
Percent Minority: 3%

Percent African-American: 1%
Percent Asian: 1%
Percent Hispanic: 1%
Percent Native-American: 0%
Percent in-state/out-of-state: 26%/74%
Percent Pub HS: 76%
Number of Applicants: 3,641
Percent Accepted: 73%
Percent Accepted who enroll: 24%
Entering: 638
Transfers: NA
Application Deadline: 15 Feb
Mean SAT: 595 V, 600 M
Mean ACT: 25

Middle 50% SAT range: 550–630 V, 560–645 M
Middle 50% ACT range: 24–28
3 Most popular majors: business administration/management, psychology, and political science
Retention: 87%
Graduation rate: 74%
On-campus housing: 100%
Fraternities: 31%
Sororities: 25%
Library: 340,000 volumes
Tuition and Fees: $23,112 in; $23,112 out
Room and Board: $5,346
Financial aid, first-year: 59%

Six score and sixteen years ago, President Abraham Lincoln issued his famous address in Gettysburg, Pennsylvania. Today, the town is the site of Gettysburg College, a top-notch, small liberal arts school. Gettysburg has a student population committed to learning and a devoted faculty adept at its facilitation.

Academics at Gettysburg are centered on a traditional liberal arts core. While the school frequently adjusts the core requirements, one student compared them to the distribution requirements he had in high school, including math, English, hard science, and social science. Students also stressed that the requirements still leave them with ample room to form their schedules. As one student summed up, "Some [required classes] are eye-openers, but others are a pain."

The most popular majors at Gettysburg according to students are history, management, and psychology. All of these departments have strong faculty, according to students. Some consider management the least difficult major.

Individual Attention

Whatever one's major, one sure thing at Gettysburg College is small classes. Even popular introductory courses seldom have more than 50 students, and most upper-level courses have between 10 and 15 students. Classes of this size make it easy for student-faculty interaction. One student said, "My professors have even called me to see how things were going." Another added, "When I was in freshman year, one of my professors invited our class to her house for a cookout. It was a lot of fun and made us feel less homesick." Since Gettysburg is a small school, courses are also small, but few students report being shut out of any class. For courses with capped enrollments, seniors and majors get priority.

The Gettysburg campus itself presents students with a panoply of architectural styles. One of the oldest buildings, Pennsylvania Hall, was built in 1837, while the newest, a residential complex known as the Quarry Suites, is brand new for the year 2000. In addition, a new science building is also currently under construction. The most notable building is Glatfelter Hall, a liberal arts classroom building built like a medieval castle. Like many small colleges set apart from urban areas, the Gettysburg campus is self-contained. Students consider Gettysburg one of the safest campuses in America. The main drawback is the dearth of off-campus attractions within walking distance.

Musselman Library, built just a little over a decade ago, is universally praised by students as both a place to find materials and a place to study. As one student said, "Everyone goes to the library." Another added, "I also have my own personal 'hiding' place to do work. . . . I won't reveal it 'cause then others will realize how quiet it is and it won't be quiet anymore!" The other advantage of campus facilities is that almost all buildings are air-conditioned.

> **Regarding the alcohol policy, one student responded, "The college's policy toward alcohol is similar to that of other colleges: they do not support underage drinking and will not allow kegs on campus, but they realize what goes on in the world of college."**

Housing at Gettysburg is based on seniority. While not everyone lives on campus, almost all students live in Gettysburg housing—either dorms or apartments in town owned by the university. Freshmen are all required to live on campus, and generally receive the smallest rooms. All dorms have live-in residential assistants, usually juniors and seniors, who serve both as counselors and disciplinarians. In addition, upperclassmen have the option of fraternity or sorority housing, choosing from approximately 11 fraternities and 5 sororities.

Fantastic Food

There is a central dining hall at Gettysburg, called Servo, as well as a fast-food take-out service called Cafe 101, more popularly referred to as The Bullet Hole. Students are upbeat about the food. "In all honesty, the food here is really great. Honest!" one student said. Freshmen must purchase a 20-meal-per-week plan; upperclassmen can choose fewer meals per week or go off the plan altogether. Students also frequent Mamma Venturi's Pizzeria (often called Mamma V's) and the Pizza House.

Intramural sports are popular at Gettysburg, as are choirs, political organizations, and community-service organizations. Aspiring writers can join the weekly newspaper, the *Gettysburgian*, a biannual literary magazine, the *Mercury*, or the yearbook, the *Spectrum*.

Facets of Social Life

According to students, the social scene at Gettysburg truly has two faces. On the one hand, approximately half the students are involved in the Greek system, and reportedly rely heavily on fraternity and sorority houses to provide them with social activities. Independent students spend time at the Junction, a campus social center that features live bands, and a number of off-campus hangouts such as the Lincoln Diner, known for its ice cream, and the local movie theater. Regarding the alcohol policy, one student responded, "The college's policy toward alcohol is similar to that of other colleges: they do not support underage drinking and will not allow kegs on campus, but they realize what goes on in the world of college."

In general, Gettysburg students classify themselves as middle- and upper-class, clean-cut, conservative, but not politically active, and from the East Coast. However, one student hastened to point out that there is some economic diversity: "About half of us are on work-study programs, [and] not wealthy; that's just the stereotype." Students claim their peers are generally laid-back and tolerant—one of the reasons many are glad they chose Gettysburg College. —*David Oppenheim and Staff*

FYI

The three best things about attending Gettysburg are "extensive extracurricular opportunities, small classes, and the small-town environment."

The three worst things about attending Gettysburg are "high cost, the relative lack of things to do in the town of Gettysburg, and Safety and Security are really strict, even about little things like parking tickets."

The three things every student should do before graduating from Gettysburg are "visit the battlefields and learn at least a little bit about the battle, attend the Don't Break the Seal party at Mamma V's (free drinks until someone goes to the bathroom), and attend a sporting event and cheer on the Bullets."

The one thing I'd have liked to know before coming here is "how big the Greek system is."

H a v e r f o r d   C o l l e g e

Address: 370 Lancaster Avenue; Haverford, PA 19041-1392
Phone: 610-896-1350
E-mail address: Admitme@haverford.edu
Web site URL: www.haverford.edu
Founded: 1833
Private or Public: private
Religious affiliation: none
Location: suburban
Undergraduate enrollment: 1,118
Total enrollment: 1,118
Percent Male / Female: 47% / 53%
Percent Minority: 20%

Percent African-American: 5%
Percent Asian: 9%
Percent Hispanic: 5%
Percent Native-American: 0.5%
Percent in-state / out-of-state: 18% / 82%
Percent Pub HS: 54%
Number of Applicants: 2,650
Percent Accepted: 33%
Percent Accepted who enroll: 35%
Entering: 302
Transfers: 3
Application Deadline: 15 Jan
Mean SAT: NA

Mean ACT: NA
Middle 50% SAT range: 640–740 V, 630–720 M
Middle 50% ACT range: NA
3 Most popular majors: biology, English, psychology
Retention: 97%
Graduation rate: 88%
On-campus housing: 100%
Fraternities: NA
Sororities: NA
Library: 513,500 volumes
Tuition and Fees: $24,940 in; $24,940 out
Room and Board: $7,910
Financial aid, first-year: 34%

Imagine a top-ranked college where the professors know your name. At Haverford, instructors not only know your name, but have "baked bread, held class in their houses, and come to my soccer games," explained one student. Professors who invite students into their homes only reflect the cohesiveness of the college as a whole. Haverford's honor code is another reflection of close-knit college life. Under the code, a student may arrange with his teacher to take an exam in his own room, and hand it in later. Undergrads say that the honor code attracts a certain type of student who wants the responsibility and respect that comes along with the code. One student said, "I was doing laundry, and I noticed a dollar bill taped on to a washing machine with a little note that said, 'If you put quarters in this machine and forgot to run it, here's your dollar back'. This is the type of behavior that often occurs at Haverford. Everyone respects each other so much that no one even considers taking money if it's not theirs."

Academic Intimacy

Students cited Haverford's small size (only about 1,200 students) as one of its most attractive features. "I think I'm getting a better education here than I would at a bigger school," said one undergrad. "I like learning from someone who knows who I am." Students said "classes are generally small—but not as small as they tell you on the tours." The largest classes might have up to 100 students in them, and the smallest range from 7 to 12 students. One undergrad said her 65-person introductory chemistry course "doesn't even feel like a huge class—the teacher knows and remembers everyone's names." Students also praised the responsiveness of their professors outside the classroom. "I've always been able to schedule an appointment with my professor," explained one student, "either by speaking to him after class or by e-mail—I've never had to wait more than a day to meet with him."

Many "'fords," as students call themselves, were also attracted to the school because of its academic reputation. Remarkably, though, the honor code prohibits students from discussing their grades. Competition is "taboo," but students are "constantly challenged." "People are stressed," explained one senior, "they often think and talk about work. It's easy to lose perspective and become unaware of the outside world."

Haverford offers students the opportunity to try out classes at the beginning of each term. During a two-week-long "shopping period" at the start of the semester, students are encouraged to attend any classes in which they are interested. One student praised the system saying, "It gives us a chance to sample courses, and it helps to prevent students from getting stuck taking courses they hate." English and biology are the most popular majors, and both involve a heavy workload. According to one bio major, "Haverford earns its reputation of being a top-notch intensive biology program. The workload can be overwhelming, and is designed to drill the knowledge and understanding of concepts into you."

Haverford's small size doesn't affect its class offerings—students have the option of taking classes at Bryn Mawr, the University of Pennsylvania, or Swarthmore. Haverford and Bryn Mawr are especially close, and "before graduating, every student should take at least one class at Bryn Mawr." Additionally, Haverford offers a large study-abroad program. "There are programs on all continents (excluding Antarctica)," said one student. "If you want to go there and are an average Haverford student, the college will help you get there."

Welcome Freshmen

According to one freshman, "Haverford is the perfect place to get over homesickness." Their customs group immediately integrates students into the Haverford community. Led by two upperclassmen, called "customs people," the customs group consists of about 12 "frosh" in the same hall and helps ease the transition into Haverford life. Because freshmen live with their customs group, they often go to meals and other events together, sometimes becoming so close that students describe the group as their "family" and their customs people as their "surrogate parents." Freshmen also have an upper class advisor (UCA) and faculty advisors, who help them in choosing classes each semester, but one student said, "it's generally easier to meet with your UCA because his door is always open."

Freshmen live in one of three dorms: Gunmere, "made of cinder block, so it is

kind of like a jail cell"; Barclay, with many doubles and a few singles; or the HCA, Haverford College Apartments, where four students share a two-bedroom apartment. The apartments have the advantage of a kitchen and living room, although they are nearly a half-mile from campus. A student in one of the dorms reported, "I'm at most 400 feet from my farthest class." Most upperclassmen opt to live in the on-campus apartments or in themed houses.

> The Haverford community is sometimes nicknamed the "Haver-bubble" since "it is such an honest place, it doesn't seem like the real world."

The meal plan (20 meals per week) is required for freshmen only. The dining center (DC) is being redone, and students said it is a lot more aesthetically pleasing. Students also praised the dining options available to them, including their new Edy's ice cream machines. On Fridays, students enjoy Pastabilities, where six chefs cook made-to-order pasta.

Sports and the Social Scene

"People at Haverford seem pretty apathetic about sports unless they happen to play one," one student remarked. "The stands at the soccer games normally don't have more than 30 students in them, usually less, and often a good number of them are from the other school. The school doesn't have a football team, let alone a suitable stadium. My high school's football field had more bleacher space, and our team was awful." Haverford competes in NCAA Division III sports, and each student must complete a requirement of 6 half-semesters of sports by the end of their sophomore year.

Weekends start on Thursday nights, although some students complained, "Friday nights are dull." One student explained, "the student body would fall down in exhaustion if there were big parties on Thursday, Friday, and Saturday nights, so the social committee decided not to plan parties on Friday nights." There is always a campus-wide dance on Saturday night, and most students stop by after attending smaller get-togethers. Popular theme dances include La Fiesta, featuring Spanish and Mexican music, and the Drag Ball, sponsored by the Gay and Lesbian Organization. "It's really interesting to see how many students actually do dress up for them," commented one student.

At Haverford, JSAAPP, the Joint Student-Administration Alcohol Policy Panel is a representative body of students and administration who meet to discuss violations of the alcohol policy. "The alcohol policy pretty much trusts us to drink responsibly," explained one student. "The college will not bust anyone for drinking, regardless of their age."

Haverford itself is located in a small town; however, there is plenty to do off campus. Students travel to Philadelphia, which is 20 minutes away by train, and visit a number of other nearby colleges, including Bryn Mawr, St. Joseph's and Villanova. Freshmen aren't allowed to have cars, but restaurants, such as Ruby's diner and Peace O' Pizza, as well as ice cream parlors and a mini-mall, lie within a 10 to 15-minute walk from campus.

Haver-bubble

Students admitted that Haverford students tend to look very similar. "Haver-ford is not especially diverse," explained one student. "There has been an effort to recruit minority students, but it is still not totally effective. There isn't a wide showing of international students, and that explains why there are only two major ethnic clubs—the Asian Association and the African-American/Latino Club." A large proportion of the school is "white, upper-middle class, and from the east coast," although one undergrad argued that "Haverford students are not racially diverse, but they have diverse interests like sports, the arts and community service." Most Haverford students identified themselves as "politically liberal."

Regardless of their interests and background, students felt that the honor code leads to greater respect between members of the community. "Everyone's nice," said one undergrad. "They say 'hi' to you even if you don't know them." The Haverford community is sometimes nicknamed the "Haver-bubble" since "it is such an honest place, it doesn't seem like the real world." One freshman said, "People ask me if I will be ready for the real world when I leave Haverford. I don't know, but I'm just going to enjoy my four years here."—*Ashleigh Hegedus*

FYI

The three best things about attending Haverford are "the great professors, they really get to know you; the honor code; and the beautiful campus, close to Philadelphia."

The three worst things about attending Haverford are "lack of public recognition, homogeneous student body, and it's small size and limited choices of classes and extracurricular activities."

The three things that every student should do before graduating from Haverford are "get locked in the library and play dark tag; eat breadsticks at Skeeter's, the student run, on-campus pizza joint; and climb on the field house tin roof."

One thing I'd like to have known before coming here is "Friday nights are sooo dead here."

Lafayette College

Address: 118 Markle Hall; Easton, PA 18042
Phone: 610-330-5100
E-mail address: admissions@lafayette.edu
Web site URL: www.lafayette.edu
Founded: 1826
Private or Public: private
Religious affiliation: Presbyterian
Location: suburban
Undergraduate enrollment: 2,244
Total enrollment: 2,244
Percent Male/Female: 54%/46%
Percent Minority: 7%
Percent African-American: 4%

Percent Asian: 1%
Percent Hispanic: 2%
Percent Native-American: 0%
Percent in-state/out-of-state: 28%/72%
Percent Pub HS: NA
Number of Applicants: 4,478
Percent Accepted: 54%
Percent Accepted who enroll: 25%
Entering: 605
Transfers: NA
Application Deadline: 1 Jan
Mean SAT: 600 V, 623 M
Mean ACT: 25

Middle 50% SAT range: 550–640 V, 570–670 M
Middle 50% ACT range: NA
3 Most popular majors: engineering, economics/business and government/law
Retention: 91%
Graduation rate: 78%
On-campus housing: 100%
Fraternities: 38%
Sororities: 45%
Library: 480,000 volumes
Tuition and Fees: $22,844 in; $22,844 out
Room and Board: $7,106
Financial aid, first-year: 49%

Once described as a sleepy and traditional small liberal arts college, Lafayette is challenging those conceptions. Lafayette students take advantage of popular engineering and business programs, while the campus is glimmering with newly completed dorms, labs, and the massive Kirby Sports Complex. The extremely athletic student body come alive to see their Lafayette Leopards compete with archrival Lehigh, while almost everyone on campus takes part in a variety of intramurals. A vibrant social life and a beautiful parklike campus in Easton, Pennsylvania, add to the Lafayette experience, and more than anything else, Lafayette students value the "family atmosphere" their school offers.

The Core Curriculum

Academics at Lafayette are by no means a free-for-all. All first-semester freshmen must complete a core class called a First-Year Seminar (FYS), a writing-intensive class capped at 16 students. FYS topics cover a wide and untraditional variety of subjects; recent offerings have included Popular Culture, Women Detectives, and The Appeal of Evil in Western Culture. All students also must take College Writing (English 110) either freshman or sophomore year, while second-semester sophomores are required to enroll in a Values And Science/Technology seminar. VAST seminars explore issues in modern science in a writing-intensive format; recent courses have included Computers and Society, Science in Literature, and Technology and the City. In addition to completing requirements for their majors, all students are required to meet distribution requirements in humanities/social sciences, natural sciences, mathematics, and writing, while many are required to take a course dealing with a foreign culture. While engineering and science students are reputed to have the most difficulty meeting all their requirements, most students feel that meeting their requirements and taking the required courses within their major is manageable. Most Lafayette students carry a load of four courses per semester, though many engineering and science students must enroll in five classes at once.

The Academic Picture

Perhaps the aspect of academics that students at Lafayette College value most is the small class size and close contact with approachable, supportive professors. Classes generally enroll around 15 to 20 students, while popular introductory-level classes can enroll 60 or 70. Professors teach all classes; teaching assistants only supervise labs. Students rave about the accessibility of their professors. A junior recounts, "I was going to drop my electrical engineering class, but a professor who didn't even teach the course offered to help me. He tutored me for two hours every other night, and with his help, I made it through the class." Students say that they value getting to know their professors well but complain that as a result, they cannot go unnoticed when absent from class.

Lafayette offers a traditional liberal arts curriculum, with about 40 individual majors from which students can choose. Setting Lafayette apart from many similar liberal arts institutions is the exceptionally strong and popular engineering program. Students praise the "outstanding" engineering faculty and the "state-of-the-art" facilities. Another popular field of study is economics and business, which is well known for its large selection of courses relevant to the "real world." Chemistry, physics, and biochemistry students can now take advantage of the brand-new multimillion-dollar Hugel Science Center. One undergrad warns that only those who are "seriously into programming" should consider the computer science major. Students generally describe grading as "fair," while a junior complains that professors of more advanced courses tend to phase out any beneficial curve. Courses considered easy include Elementary Public Speaking, A Chemical Perspective ("Baby Chemistry"), and several basic music classes ("Clapping for Credit"). Organic chemistry and certain physics offerings are reputed to be among the most difficult classes at Lafayette. Students report experiencing little trouble registering for and getting into their desired classes, and many Lafayette juniors take advantage of a growing number of opportunities to study abroad.

Campus Distractions

Students describe the Lafayette campus, sitting atop a hill overlooking the convergence of two rivers, as "incredibly picturesque." Many new and renovated buildings provide comfortable, luxurious spots for students to live, study, and hang out. Of the dorms, newly constructed Keefe Hall garnered praise for its air-conditioning and "hotel-like" atmosphere, while South College is known as a big party hall. Many undergrads rush fraternities and sororities, but freshmen must wait a full year before they may rush.

The main library on campus, Skillman Library, is a serious place for everything from nightly course work (which students say averages two to four hours) to cramming for finals. Though Skillman closes at midnight, the library contains an all-night study lounge.

In addition to the post office and activity rooms, several dining options exist in Farinon, the student center. The upstairs dining hall is popular for meals, while students fulfill their junk-food cravings in the downstairs snack bar. Gilbert's, a popular new coffeehouse, is a big draw thanks to its late-night food, nice atmosphere, and open-mike nights. Outside of Farinon, the dining room in Marquis Hall is praised for the made-to-order Asian food. Most undergrads describe the food as "fair to okay," while a junior complains that the menus are "annoyingly repetitive." Domino's is always a phone call away, but for the more adventurous, popular off-campus eating destinations include Campus Pizza, Morici's (Italian), Don Pablo's (Mexican), and the Olive Garden. For those over 21, Porter's is a popular hangout. Many Lafayette students have cars, and the college also operates a weekend bus system to and from the Lehigh Valley Mall (a 20-minute drive from campus).

> "I was going to drop my electrical engineering class, but a professor who didn't even teach the course offered to help me. He tutored me for two hours every other night, and with his help, I made it through the class."

Since tiny Easton has little entertainment to offer, undergrads generally spend their time on campus. The Lafayette Activities Forum (LAF) sponsors films, concerts, and other activities, while the Williams Center for the Arts brings in many performers throughout the year. The student government and the daily newspaper (the *Lafayette*) are among the most popular extracurriculars. Many students also join the Lafayette Investment Club, a haven for budding Wall Street tycoons that invests a small portion of the college's endowment.

Social life generally centers on frat parties, and although Lafayette retains its reputation as a "party school," students report that Greek life plays a less important role on campus than it has in the past. Lafayette's alcohol policy has become stricter in recent years and includes a ban on kegs. Fraternities dominate the social scene, but all students are welcome at most parties, and undergrads generally don't feel pressure to rush.

As for dating, both men and women at Lafayette agree that "there are nearly as many people dating as there are people who are just randomly hooking up on a one-time, no-relationship basis. . . . I think we're pretty big into committed relationships." One disadvantage of the small student body is that there just are not that many new people to meet and date after a while.

An Athlete's Paradise

Lafayette undergrads unanimously describe the student body as "athletic." Varsity sports attract a large following, with the football and men's basketball teams drawing the largest crowds. The most anticipated sports event of the year is the football game that pits the Lafayette Leopards against their archrivals from nearby Lehigh. At a less competitive level, intramurals are extremely popular and include, in addition to the usual sports, activities such as chess, mini-golf, croquet, and card games. Teams are drawn from fraternities, residence halls, and groups such as the International Students Association. Athletes and non-athletes alike take advantage of Lafayette's impressive new Kirby Sports Complex. An undergrad explains that "if you want to meet someone in the afternoon, go to the gym. Everyone's there." Students have free access to Kirby's facilities, including the basketball, squash, tennis, and racquetball courts, swimming pool, and hockey rink, and the gym, which stays open until 2:00 A.M. on weeknights, truly serves as "one of the social centers of campus."

The Student Body

Lafayette students describe their classmates as generally white, Christian, straight, middle-class preppies from Pennsylvania, New Jersey, or New York who wear clothes from Abercrombie and Fitch, the North Face, and the Gap. There are few minority students at Lafayette; however, a junior reports that the campus is becoming more diverse. The African Black Cultural Club (ABC) and the Hillel House attract a number of undergrads. Many students say that the lack of diversity is their main complaint about Lafayette.

According to one undergrad, "Lafayette's small size really made the transition from high school a lot easier. It's so easy to meet people here, and soon everybody knows each other." Everyone at Lafayette seems to form a tight web of social bonds, from fraternities, to sports teams, to members of a First-Year Seminar who are still friendly after two years. While some see the college's small size as an obstacle to meeting new people, most students agree that the intimate feel of Lafayette unites them and gives rise to an overwhelming sense of school spirit. Add to that spirit a stunning campus and a group of caring, supportive professors, and you can see why most Lafayette students wouldn't think of being anywhere else.—*Justin Albstein*

FYI
The three best things about attending Lafayette are "the people are really friendly; the professors are totally open to talking about anything; classes prepare you for the real world."
The three worst things about attending Lafayette are "administration and paperwork; it's impossible to find parking—there's a city ordinance that mandates you have to move your car every 72 hours—there's never enough time to do everything you want to do!"
The three things that every student should do before graduating from Lafayette are "rush fraternity, visit the Crayola Crayon factory—you can see it from campus—go to a Lafayette–Lehigh football game."
One thing I'd like to have known before coming here is "don't be afraid to get involved with everything."

Lehigh University

Address: 27 Memorial Drive West; Bethlehem, PA 18015
Phone: 610-758-3100
E-mail address: inado@lehigh.edu
Web site URL: www.lehigh.edu
Founded: 1865
Private or Public: private
Religious affiliation: none
Location: suburban
Undergraduate enrollment: 4,487
Total enrollment: 6,316
Percent Male/Female: 60%/40%
Percent Minority: 11%
Percent African-American: 3%

Percent Asian: 5%
Percent Hispanic: 3%
Percent Native-American: 0%
Percent in-state/out-of-state: 27%/73%
Percent Pub HS: NA
Number of Applicants: 8,384
Percent Accepted: 52%
Percent Accepted who enroll: 26%
Entering: 1,134
Transfers: 130
Application Deadline: 15 Jan
Mean SAT: 605 V, 640 M
Mean ACT: NA

Middle 50% SAT range: 559–651 V, 592–688 M
Middle 50% ACT range: NA
3 Most popular majors: finance, mechanical engineering and civil engineering
Retention: 94%
Graduation rate: 66%
On-campus housing: 100%
Fraternities: 41%
Sororities: 43%
Library: 1.3 million volumes
Tuition and Fees: $23,150 in; $23,150 out
Room and Board: $6,630
Financial aid, first-year: 54%

On the side of a mountain in the town of Bethlehem lies Lehigh University, with the fraternities at the top of the hill and the classrooms at the bottom. Some students wonder if this configuration says something about their priorities. Although Lehigh has a very active Greek system, students are more than satisfied with the academics as well. According to one student, "The most unique quality of Lehigh is that students party hard and study hard."

Academics

Lehigh, whose team name changed recently from the Engineers to the Hawks, is known for its excellent engineering school; however, the university also has fine schools of business and arts and sciences. Each school has its own set of requirements, but all first-year students are required to take English 1 and English 2. First-year students in the engineering school also must take physics, chemistry, and one elective. Class size ranges from 200 to 300 people in introductory lecture courses to around 30 people in upper-level classes. All courses are taught by professors, with TAs leading only weekly recitation sections. For an "easy A," some students recommend "religion courses" and Human Sexuality.

For students looking for a challenge, Lehigh offers special programs such as the Five-Year Plan, in which engineering students can earn a bachelor's and a master's degree in five years. In addition to this opportunity, any undergraduate may take classes in the graduate school by petitioning the graduate committee and gaining permission from the instructor.

Dorms and Surroundings

Students at Lehigh say they are quite satisfied with their housing options. Only freshmen are required to live on campus, but the majority of undergraduates remain on campus all four years. The most desirable places to live include campus apartments in Trembley and the freshman dorm known as "M&M" (McClinton and Marshall). Most dorms are coed by floor. For upperclassmen who do choose to live off campus, fraternity and sorority houses are popular options.

As for the food, students are as satisfied as they can be with food that isn't home cooking. Lehigh has five dining halls, including three traditional cafeterias, a food court with a Burger King and a deli, and a shop where students can take out bag lunches. For breakfast they can make their own omelets or waffles every day of the week. When dinner rolls around, many students would suggest forgoing the meat in favor of the safer pasta.

Social Life and Student Body

"When you are not studying, you are drinking. And when you drink, you drink a lot," said one Lehigh student. Undergrads say Greek life is basically the be-all and end-all at Lehigh; about half of them join one of the 26 fraternities and 8 sororities. Students look forward to the annual Greek Week, which occurs in the spring, and is a week filled with toga races, eating contests, and other competitions. The Lehigh/Lafayette game is one of the biggest rivalries, providing the occasion for some of the best parties. "During Lehigh/Lafayette they have sunrise cocktails every morning before classes; even the teachers are trashed the whole week. There are huge parties every night," one student said. The administration has recently made an unpopular move to regulate the size of parties. One freshman explained, "There is a new regulation limiting the number of people attending parties. Before 12:00 you must be on the 50-person guest list, and then an extra 50 people are allowed to enter after 12:00, but they have to sign an 'uninvited' guest list."

When life on the Hill becomes monotonous, students attend campus comedy acts, movies, and concerts. If students need to get away, they do not have far to go to find the big city; New York is only a two-hour drive, and Philadelphia is just 90 minutes away.

Lehigh students participate in all sorts of extracurriculars, ranging from varsity sports to community service to drama. Popular sports include football, wrestling, crew, and basketball. Students say that football is not only the dominant sport, but also dominates the social atmosphere. Games prompt an array of tailgates and early morning cocktail parties, and foster healthy school spirit.

For students who are less athletically inclined, intramurals offer competition without the pressure of organized varsity sports. Beyond the sports fields, Lehigh offers choir, drama, the *Brown and White* (a biweekly newspaper), an orchestra, and many opportunities for community service.

Through its community service programs Lehigh has been making an attempt to improve relations with the neighboring towns of Bethlehem and Allentown. For example, with STAR Academy, a popular tutoring program, Lehigh students act as mentors for local middle school and high school students. Although the programs are slowly making progress, students say that they don't go to town much and still yearn for more to do outside of the university.

> For an "easy A," some students recommend "religion courses" and Human Sexuality.

Most Lehigh undergrads come from the tristate region of Pennsylvania, New Jersey, and Delaware, and some students feel that the student body could be more diverse—geographically, racially, and economically. One sophomore said, "I wish it were more diversified. There are very few minorities and very few 'different-looking' people. It is very much of a 'clone campus,' I think." Yet Lehigh students are a very satisfied bunch who enjoy the university's close-knit, self-contained community.

Lehigh is a school with a lot of pride and spirit, and its students enjoy the strong academics and social life. As one student said, "My friends at other schools think I always have about 10 times more work than they ever do, but I also have 20 times more fun than they do!"—*Katherina Payne and Staff*

FYI
The three best things about attending Lehigh are "closeness to Philly, the red and orange hues of the hills in the fall, engineering."
The three worst things about attending Lehigh are "homogeneity, party size limits, and fraternities if you're not in one."
The three things that every student should do before graduating from Lehigh are "take Human Sexuality, party like a madman/madwoman, and take a daytrip to Philadelphia or New York."
One thing I wish I'd known before coming here is "how so many things revolve around alcohol."

Mulhenberg College

Address: 2400 West Chew Street; Allentown, PA 18104-5596
Phone: 610-821-3200
E-mail address: admission @muhlenberg.edu
Web site URL: www.muhlenberg.edu
Founded: 1848
Private or Public: private
Religious affiliation: Lutheran
Location: suburban
Undergraduate enrollment: 2,460
Total enrollment: 2,460
Percent Male/Female: 43%/57%
Percent Minority: 6%

Percent African-American: 1%
Percent Asian: 3%
Percent Hispanic: 2%
Percent Native-American: 0%
Percent in-state/out-of-state: 33%/67%
Percent Pub HS: 70%
Number of Applicants: 3,037
Percent Accepted: 65%
Percent Accepted who enroll: 33%
Entering: 651
Transfers: 8
Application Deadline: 15 Feb
Mean SAT: 580 V, 580 M
Mean ACT: NA

Middle 50% SAT range: 543–615 V, 542–618 M
Middle 50% ACT range: NA
3 Most popular majors: biology, psychology, and business
Retention: 88%
Graduation rate: 71%
On-campus housing: 100%
Fraternities: 35%
Sororities: 36%
Library: 220,000 volumes
Tuition and Fees: $20,085 in; $20,085 out
Room and Board: $5,390
Financial aid, first-year: 60%

Muhlenberg students may complain about their courseload, but most enjoy the challenge. Students are eager to learn. One says, "I like going to class each day. I have interesting courses and like to learn from them." Through many renovations, Muhlenberg is improving resources for its students.

Inside Victorian Academic Buildings

Students must take 34 courses before they graduate. The core requirements are literature, religion, philosophy, 3 semesters of language, 2 sciences, history, 2 courses in behavioral science (psychology, anthropology, sociology etc.), culture, art, and first-year seminar. Many students are pleased with these required courses, adding that they wouldn't have taken such classes if not required. However there are some who find some of the requirements too much. "Religion and philosophy should be electives, regardless that it is a Lutheran campus," believes a student, whereas another says "we have to take two sciences, which is very disturbing to us non-science people." Every major has a set curriculum, which fills up most of the schedules. Students face

some problems with the times of classes while tryingng to form their schedules. Also, they feel that some courses being offered only once a year causes more scheduling problems for them.

Biology, premed, chemistry, and theater arts are considered the toughest and the most competitive majors. Philosophy and especially communications are "very popular" among students and considered less rigorous than other majors. Muhlenberg sponsors many combined undergraduate/graduate programs: a 3-year undergrad–4-year grad dental program with University of Pennsylvania, 3–2 forestry and environmental studies program with Duke University, 3–2 engineering program with Columbia and Washington University as well as a 4–4 medical school admission with MCP/Hahnemann University. Students may also participate in honor programs such as the Dana and the Muhlenberg Scholar's program, create their own majors, or take courses at other schools.

Few classes have over 25 students, except for labs, and students are fond of the "personalization and attention" this brings. However, some complain that the small number of classes also make it harder to get into them, especially in freshman and sophomore years. This problem decreases as students declare their major because then, professors sign the students into classes. Students are pleased with the proficiency of the faculty and believe that they are "accommodating and care a lot about their students." A student says "I run into them [my professors] at the grocery store and it's like running into a friend." Since there are no teaching assistants teaching classes, students have the opportunity to work in classes instructed by professors who are eminent in their fields like Dr. Marjory Hardy, a professor in psychology or like Dr. Daniel Klem, "a world leader on why birds fly into windows. People from all over call him up for help in designing bird-safe buildings," is how one of his students describes Dr. Klem.

Smashmouth Isn't the Only One

Besides well-known professors, students also benefit from and enjoy the guest speakers that come to campus. Chie Abad, who was on a national tour about sweat shops, stopped at Muhlenberg with the help of students organizations such as Amnesty International and PAT. Smashmouth also visited campus and gave a spectacular concert. Besides Smashmouth, Citizen King, Jim Breuer, Wallflowers, George Clinton, Blues Traveler, Bob Cat have come to Muhlenberg.

> "I run into them [my professors] at the grocery store and it's like running into a friend."

Being underage has not prevented students from drinking since fraternity parties offer alcohol to all. But, the administration has become stricter about alcohol, students report, and forces students to sign in when they enter certain parties. Kegs are not allowed on campus, and students say, "frats have been temporarily closed down because of alcohol problems." Many over 21 prefer going to the bars in Allentown.

The non-drinkers also find a lot of things to do. Dances like the West Side Story dance, senior balls, semi-formals, and fraternity or sorority formals have an important role in the social life. The shuttle running to the malls, shopping centers, and to theaters are useful for freshmen since they cannot have cars on campus usually. Besides Activities Council, which provides most of the programs on campus, other popular and respected student organizations are the radio station, Hillel, and APO (community service).

Prevalent Homogenity among Preppy Muhlenbergers

A typical Muhlenberg student is chic, wearing J.Crew, GAP and Abercrombie, and driving a nice car. Students say that there are cliques, and even though groups aren't formed right away, people do tend to stick with those whom them meet during the first months of school through dormlife or organizations. Students find the their peers homogeneous and also classify a typical Muhlenberg student as a "white, preppy student."

Renovations Revive Campus Life

The renovated gym has offers a great weight-lifting room and new equipment. There are also tennis courts and a pool available for students. Football, men and women's soccer, and basketball are among the popular sports. There are some traditions like the Greek Week where sororities and fraternities compete against each other. Another tradition is the annual Scotty Wood Basketball tournament. Intramurals are very popular.

Freshman dorms Prosser and New West have undergone recent renovations. However, the worst dorm, East Hall, remains unchanged and continues to experience bug problems. A few years ago, a turf field and a stadium were built, and the press box and soccer fields were redone. The Union, which includes the cafeteria, mailboxes, and meeting rooms has been renovated to provide a greater space. All dorms except Brown are coed; however, all have single-sex bathrooms. Brown, the all-girls dorm, has higher ceilings and larger rooms compared to others. Quiet hours exist during the week to help those who are studying or sleeping. Off-campus housing is not very popular. After freshman year, a lottery settles rooming, and most upperclassman rooms are quite nice.

There are two meal plans in school, and students prefer the larger one. Banana flambé is a specialty of the dining halls.

Chefs cooking in front of students assure students of the hygiene of the kitchen. There is always a pasta bar and decent vegetarian options. The two dining halls, one for grab and go, the other for sit and talk, offer a variety for students.

Safe and Sound in Allentown

Students enjoy the beauty of their safe campus. Victorian stone buildings make up the majority of the small, green campus. The campus is close to parks and forests. Students have to satisfy themselves with the squirrels running around on campus because pets aren't allowed anywhere on campus, including campus apartments. A couple of call boxes for emergencies and a security staff, with members on foot, bicy-cle, and car, enhance security. Near campus are the Katherine P. Taylor mall, several bars, a couple of coffee shops like Perks, and restaurants: Parma Pizza, Outback, MiChongs Chinese, TGI Fridays, Rudy Tuesday, Arby's, Perkinds, and the more upscale Olive Garden, King George Inn, and Carabas.

Away from Problems

On lazy Sundays, or in spring, whenever the weather is nice, students don't bother about what to do, or where to go. They take a blanket, their radio and their tons of reading, head to a nearby park or to the center of the campus, and enjoy the feeling of learning and being challenged.
—*Yakut Seyhanli*

FYI

The three best things about attending Muhlenberg are "its friendly atmosphere, the small-sized classes, and the attention paid to students."

The three worst things about attending Muhlenberg are "the limited offerings of Allentown, everybody knowing everything about each other because of the small community, and not having anonymity."

The three things that every student should do before graduating from Muhlenberg are "walk through the rose garden of the campus, go to a candlelight carol, and go to a soccer game."

One thing students would like to have known before coming to Mulhenberg is "that the social life's major component is frat parties."

Pennsylvania State University

Address: 201 Shields Building, Box 3000; University Park, PA 16802-3000
Phone: 814-865-5471
E-mail address: admissions@psu.edu
Web site URL: www.psu.edu
Founded: 1855
Private or Public: public
Religious affiliation: none
Location: suburban
Undergraduate enrollment: 34,264
Total enrollment: 40,471
Percent Male/Female: 54%/46%
Percent Minority: 11%

Percent African-American: 3%
Percent Asian: 5%
Percent Hispanic: 3%
Percent Native-American: 0%
Percent in-state/out-of-state: 79%/21%
Percent Pub HS: NA
Number of Applicants: 23,262
Percent Accepted: 47%
Percent Accepted who enroll: 38%
Entering: 4,101
Transfers: NA
Application Deadline: 31 Jan
Mean SAT: 593 V, 617 M
Mean ACT: NA

Middle 50% SAT range: 540–640 V, 561–670 M
Middle 50% ACT range: NA
3 Most popular majors: elementary education, accounting, and marketing
Retention: 93%
Graduation rate: 77%
On-campus housing: 100%
Fraternities: 15%
Sororities: 15%
Library: 2,700,000 volumes
Tuition and Fees: $5,832 in; $12,306 out
Room and Board: $4,338
Financial aid, first-year: 61%

They say to recognize a fellow Penn State alumnus one need only yell out the obligatory "Joe-Pa" and wait for the almost automatic response of "terno." And don't be surprised if you hear this booming football chant along a familiar neighborhood street, considering 1 in 30 college graduates in the United States are graduates of Penn State. Indeed, football rules over this sprawling university nestled at the base of the awe-inspiring Mount Nittany.

"Papa Joe," as Penn State students affectionately call their longtime coach, looks down from atop his perch at Beaver Stadium and sees nothing but beauty, beauty, and football. Perhaps the greatest college ritual of all time has its ultimate expression here at Penn State—pre-game tailgating. From the crusty old alumni, to the gray metallic kegs, to the inebriated college freshman, one truly feels like those Bright College Days will never end when visiting this verdant campus.

But Penn State isn't just about beer pong and sideline BBQs. It is a lively community of 40,000 students bonded together by a love of learning and the implacable pursuit of truth.

Joe Pa Says Study!

A venerable academic tradition lies at the heart of the Penn State philosophy. Although Main Campus is the flagship of the Pennsylvania State University system, there are 22 satellite campuses throughout the state at which rigorous academic requirements such as "reading books" are strictly enforced by a group of crack professors and teaching assistants. Thanks to its gargantuan size and well-known football squad, the Penn State name might be one of the most recognizable university names in the world. And as a result, Penn State has its share of top name professors and academicians. Once home to the likes of Joseph Heller, and now currently housing such top-notch intellectuals as E. Cal Golumbick and Yale alumnus Emily Rolfe Grosholz, who, according to one student, "feeds us learning like candy," the Penn State faculty is certainly not lacking in talent.

In addition to outstanding faculty, Penn State also offers some extraordinarily reputable degree programs—two of which are architecture and engineering. The department of meteorology, also a highlight, is routinely consulted on national weather matters and provides the *New York Times* with the majority of its weather information.

Lest one think Penn State is focused solely on the sciences, the philosophy department is also well thought of and according to one student is the "best philosophy department on the eastern seaboard." Requirements vary depending upon the major. One requirement common to all students is the ESEC requirement, which can be fulfilled by taking such classes as Scuba Diving and Ballroom Dancing.

A bright and shining star in the Penn State academic galaxy remains Schreyer Honors College. Routinely named one of the top honors colleges in the nation, Schreyer boasts an exceedingly competitive admissions process and a student body that rivals those of the Ivy League. Schreyer students get to take specialized classes in intimate settings, and register before other undergrads.

For the rest of the student body, intro classes tend to be relatively large and registration is hectic. Some intro courses such as Biology top out at over 900 kids. In this kind of setting it is easy for the student to feel isolated and occasionally lost, but there are plenty of resources that can help eliminate this academic ennui. There are complaints that science TAs fail to speak even rudimentary English. As one student asked, "How can I learn if I can't understand a damn thing the guy is saying?"

But overall, "the academics at Penn State are as good as you make them. . . . for the slackers we have electrical engineering and for the go-getters we have political science. And by go-getters I mean myself and by slackers I mean my roommate."

Ode to Tracy

This somewhat cryptic title simply refers to Penn State's own incarnation of Greek Divinity—Tracy, the Goddess of Partying. Throughout the weekend, Penn State students look to Tracy, rumored to be the first coed to really get down, for divine guidance in partying, and party they do. Penn State boasts a ubiquitous Greek system, composed of nearly 10% of the student body—4,000 undergrads. The fraternities and sororities, located mere blocks from Old Main, are the central locale for any serious party. Two of the hottest frats on campus are Sigma Pi and Sigma Tau, both of which are rumored to throw some fairly kick-ass soirees.

By far the most popular pastime, socially speaking at least, is drinking. Now while this may come as a surprise to some, Penn State students insist that they are bona fide beer connoisseurs, preferring the smooth taste of Red Dog and Rolling Rock, brewed in Latrobe, PA. While frat parties tend to be exclusive, invitation-only affairs, there are plenty of other locations near campus to guzzle down a few brews. The university itself tries its best to curtail binge drinking and alcoholic consumption among minors, but when one student was asked about underage drinking on campus he replied, "Hold on. My sixteen-year-old girlfriend is back with the keg. Lemme get the door." Asked if he could relay the past weekend's activities, he responded with a mumbled, "I don't really remember my freshman or sophomore years." Suspicious?

> **"I don't really remember my freshman or sophomore years."**

Despite this student's wanton disregard for all laws regulating alcoholic beverages in the state of Pennsylvania, the Penn State president has taken an active role in discouraging binge drinking on campus. And a residential advisor (RA) system is in place to enforce university regulations, although according to one student, "If you don't flaunt the rules you'll be fine."

One may wonder whether non-drinkers would feel comfortable in this "wet" setting. One student stated quite reassuringly that "seventy-five percent of Penn State students feel it's okay not to drink while the other twenty-five percent are complete assholes." President Spanier has implemented a series of "late-night activities" for those students who aren't interested in indulging in spirits. Popular bands such as Reel Big Fish and Goldfinger have also performed on campus.

With abuse of alcohol comes the natural question of frequency of hookups. The question "Are there are a lot of random hookups on campus?" garnered responses ranging from "not with me" to "hell yeah there are!" While random hookups are frequent, dating is certainly not expected but is "somewhat the social norm." With all this charged sexual tension on campus one cannot help but wonder about the physical beauty of the Penn State student body. Many describe their community as a "moving Abercrombie and Fitch catalog."

Although the student body is relatively attractive, it is said by many to be ethnically homogenous. The large majority of the students on campus are of the Caucasian persuasion. But this doesn't prevent minorities on campus from being active in ethnic organizations and outspoken on ethnic issues.

The House That Gram Spa Built

Dorm life and extracurriculars play crucial roles in the lives of most Penn State students. While freshmen are relegated to the relatively unattractive East Halls, far from major academic buildings, upperclassman, when they choose to remain on campus, and honors students take advantage of centrally located housing near the hub of campus activity and an unlimited supply of chicken wings. The dorm rooms for freshman tend to be somewhat small and composed mainly of cinder blocks, but for a state university, this is normal. The best dorm is rumored to be Simmons Hall, while Pennypacker sits at the bottom of the heap. Springfield Hallway, situated in Simmons, has a reputation as being one of the most congenial hallways on campus. The university has almost 40 dormitories, with upperclassmen vying for the spacious Nittany Apartments. Upperclassmen also have the popular option of living off campus or in their respective Greek houses.

Food on campus, unlike that at many other universities, gets relatively high marks from Penn State students. Some have even gone as far as to call it "delicious." State College, rated by *Senior Citizen Magazine* as one of the safest cities in the country, offers a plethora of dining opportunities with fare as exotic as Indian and as hometown as McDonald's.

When they're not chillin' in the dorms or cafeterias, Penn State students are fully engrossed in a host of extracurricular activities. Among the 400 campus organizations are the Shakespeare Club and the *Collegian*, Penn's daily newspaper. Among the more popular organizations on campus is the No Refund Theatre, a troupe of skilled actors who present particularly modernist interpretations of classic plays and pieces.

The Dance Marathon, known as Thon, is also a popular campus activity, during which students jig, twist, and twirl for 48 hours in order to raise money for the Four Diamonds Fund, which provides hospital care for kids with cancer and money for cancer research. It is the first student-run philanthropic organization in the U.S. to make $3 million. Penn State also offers the standard religious and political organizations. Overall, the campus political mood has been described by some as conservative, with a fairly vocal religious minority present in the backdrop.

Penn State can be summed up in one single catch phrase, "food, folks, fun, and learning." These four traits are what makes Penn State what it is today, a public university forever searching for that eternal truth perhaps only Joe Pa is fully aware of.—*Sean McBride*

FYI

The three best things about attending Penn State are "the honors college, the campus, and the active social scene."

The three worst things about attending Penn State are "the lack of diversity, large class sizes, conservative mentality."

The three things every student should do before graduating from Penn State are "do the Night Vision Run—where you buy night vision goggles and run around Old Main naked—smoke with Erin at Simmons Hall, accrue enough credits to graduate."

One thing I'd like to have known before coming here is "that this place was so fun (I would have skipped senior year)."

Susquehanna University

Address: 514 University Avenue; Selinsgrove, PA 17870
Phone: 570-372-4260
E-mail address: suadmiss@susqu.edu
Web site URL: www.susqu.edu
Founded: 1858
Private or Public: private
Religious affiliation: Lutheran
Location: rural
Undergraduate enrollment: 1,765
Total enrollment: 1,765
Percent Male/Female: 42%/58%
Percent Minority: 5%

Percent African-American: 2%
Percent Asian: 1%
Percent Hispanic: 2%
Percent Native-American: 0%
Percent in-state/out-of-state: 64%/36%
Percent Pub HS: 85%
Number of Applicants: 2,003
Percent Accepted: 79%
Percent Accepted who enroll: 30%
Entering: 475
Transfers: NA
Application Deadline: 1 Mar
Mean SAT: NA
Mean ACT: NA

Middle 50% SAT range: 520–620 V, 510–630 M
Middle 50% ACT range: NA
3 Most popular majors: business administration, communication/theater arts, and psychology
Retention: 87%
Graduation rate: 67%
On-campus housing: 100%
Fraternities: 25%
Sororities: 25%
Library: 260,000 volumes
Tuition and Fees: $19,380 in; $19,380 out
Room and Board: $5,500
Financial aid, first-year: 72%

Located in rural Pennsylvania, Susquehanna University can be easy to overlook. Prospective students who find out about it will see, however, that Susquehanna provides a close-knit atmosphere with small classes and quality education.

The school attracts many of its students from the Northeast, especially New Jersey, Pennsylvania, and New York. While the student population once consisted mainly of white middle- and upper-class undergrads, recent outreach efforts and scholarship programs have increased the number of minority students and programs.

A recently initiated merit aid program called Assistantships offers promising incoming freshmen an annual scholarship as well as an opportunity to obtain work experience under the supervision of a faculty or staff member. Another unique program is the Write Option: students in the top one-fifth of their class and enrolled in a college-preparatory program at their high school are allowed to submit two graded writing samples in place of SAT or ACT scores.

Name Games

Although the name of the school implies otherwise, there are no graduate students at Susquehanna. Many undergraduates are attracted to Susquehanna's highly rated biology and music programs. The business department, accredited by the American Assembly of Collegiate Schools of Business, is also popular; acknowledged as outstanding by business and non-business students alike, it is one of only a few schools of its size to be accredited.

The school's curriculum requires students to take courses from three broad categories: perspectives on the world (history, literature, and fine arts), intellectual skills (math, logic, writing seminars, and foreign languages), and contemporary world (social science, hard science, and technology). Few students complain about the requirements; many say that this diverse grounding adds to their educational experiences at Susquehanna. Special programs enhance Susquehanna's standard curriculum. Students can create their own major with the help of a faculty member, or can elect to travel abroad.

Students seem pleased in general with the student-faculty interaction as well as the small class sizes. Classes usually have about 20 to 25 students, and the teaching is done by professors rather than TAs, who are "practically unheard of."

Service

Community service is a popular option at Susquehanna. In recent years, over half the student body has participated in volunteer services, including the Habitat for Humanity program, the Student Association for Cultural Awareness (SACA), the university's Study Buddy program with students from local schools, the Ronald McDonald House for hospitalized children, and the Pennsylvania Service Corps. Other extracurricular activities are popular as well, and the university's Degenstein Center Theater and Lore Degenstein Gallery, both with state-of-the-art equipment, provide major new showcases for student musicians, artists, and actors.

> Classes usually have about 20 to 25 students, and the teaching is done by professors rather than TAs, who are "practically unheard of."

Susquehanna has a lot of school spirit, as many of the athletic teams are nationally ranked in NCAA Division III. Students frequently show support not only for their football team but also for the basketball, volleyball, and soccer teams. Intramural sports are also important at Susquehanna, and many students take advantage of the newly remodeled gymnasium. Because of Susquehanna's location in Selinsgrove, Pennsylvania, where "there's practically no downtown," social life is limited to campus activities sponsored by SAC (Student Activities Committee) and the Greek system. Most upperclassmen also own cars for trips to nearby cities for shopping, clubbing, and other diversions.

Greek Life and Beyond

Some students feel that the Greeks divide the campus, but most Greek activities are open to everyone. The two biggest social events of the year are Greek Week, which consists mostly of fraternity- and sorority-sponsored partying, and Spring Weekend, a festival held before final exams. Students report that, while both events are widely attended, Greek Week is more exclusive to Greeks, and Spring Weekend better involves the entire campus. Another popular campus event is the annual Thanksgiving dinner, where professors serve students special holiday food in the cafeteria, which is decorated with candles.

While everyone at Susquehanna University is guaranteed campus housing, incoming students have complained in the past about the crowded freshman dorms, which consisted of mostly triples. The recent construction of three new residence halls, the renovation of a fourth hall, and new apartment-like dorms and suites, however, has made housing more spacious. Students can also choose to live in the University Scholars House, which includes study areas, a seminar room, a resident assistant's quarters, and a visitor's apartment that allows special university guests to interact informally with students. Some of the most popular dorms include Hassinger Hall, which features newly installed air-conditioning; also known as "Hotel Hassinger," it houses a small theater and several computer labs.

Students report that security is "good and reliable" on the Susquehanna campus, due in part to such security measures as the Walk Safe escort service.

Susquehanna offers intimate classes, a strong sense of community, and great athletics. "You can walk across campus and know everybody's face," one senior said, "but you can also go away from everyone you know and be by yourself for a while."
—*Seung Lee and Staff*

FYI

The three best things about attending Susquehanna are "friendly professors and staff, the opportunity to be a scholar, athlete, musician, and leader at the same time, a beautiful campus."

The three worst things about attending Susquehanna are "the athletic facilities, not enough parking for students, limited choice for electives."

The three things every student should do before graduating from Susquehanna are "swim in the Susquehanna River, go to the Lewisburg Theater, and take Rock Music and Society."

One thing I'd like to have known before coming here is "how hard I would have to work on academics."

Swarthmore College

Address: 500 College Avenue; Swarthmore, PA 19081
Phone: 610-328-8300
E-mail address: admissions @swathmore.edu
Web site URL: www.swarthmore.edu
Founded: 1864
Private or Public: private
Religious affiliation: none
Location: suburban
Undergraduate enrollment: 1,388
Total enrollment: 1,388
Percent Male / Female: 47% / 53%
Percent Minority: 23%

Percent African-American: 1%
Percent Asian: 14%
Percent Hispanic: 8%
Percent Native-American: 0%
Percent in-state / out-of-state: 11% / 89%
Percent Pub HS: 63%
Number of Applicants: 4,585
Percent Accepted: 19%
Percent Accepted who enroll: 41%
Entering: 357
Transfers: 5
Application Deadline: 1 Jan
Mean SAT: 713 V, 705 M
Mean ACT: NA

Middle 50% SAT range: 650–780 V, 660–750 M
Middle 50% ACT range: NA
3 Most popular majors: biology, economics, and English literature
Retention: 95%
Graduation rate: 96%
On-campus housing: 100%
Fraternities: 5%
Sororities: 0%
Library: 1,000,000 volumes
Tuition and Fees: $23,964 in; $23,964 out
Room and Board: $7,500
Financial aid, first-year: 52%

Described as "idyllic and intense," "weird and diverse," Swarthmore College in Pennsylvania is absolutely one of a kind. Consider, for instance, the fact that the campus itself is situated on the 330-acre Scott Arboretum, which one student, waxing poetic, described as "a lush, wooded Arcadia." Or the tradition of the "Primal Scream," when on the evening before finals everyone opens the window and screams for several minutes simultaneously into the dark night, so that "there's this eerie howl all across campus." With a student body of just under 1,400, classes are small and the community tight, which allows for connections in the classroom and the dorm room, on the sports field and the party floor.

Kiss Your Sleep Good-bye

Academically, Swarthmore is unusually rigorous. With a normal course load of four classes a semester, it is common to have over a thousand pages of reading per week, plus a paper or two. (But don't let that intimidate you; one student promises that "you'll find yourself growing to love sleep-deprivation—it's the Swattie way.") Disciplines are grouped into three broad distributions: Humanities, Natural Sciences

& Engineering, and Social Sciences. Three courses are taken in each, two of which must be Primary Distribution Courses (PDCs)—basically writing-intensive intro classes. Those who pass one year of a foreign language at Swarthmore—or three years of a language in high school—are not bound to do more. Few complain about the requirements, attesting that they are "pretty loose" and that "you end up fulfilling them without even knowing it."

During the spring of sophomore year, each student chooses a major from a wide range of traditional disciplines (English and biology are the most popular) and newer interdisciplinary fields, such as Peace & Conflict Studies and Interpretation Theory. Several often opt to design their own major. Many also apply for the selective External Examination/Honors Program for which the college is renowned. Participating students take two double-credit seminars per semester, working closely with professors and engaging in massive amounts of reading, writing, and independent research. At the end of senior year, those in the program take the External Examination—a process of both written and oral exams that are evaluated by a panel of professors and scholars from outside institutions.

In an age of ubiquitous TAs, all classes at Swat are taught by professors, who in general are described as being "cool, competent, approachable" and "willing to talk about class and about life." And because virtually all professors live in the town of Swarthmore, many hold classes in their own homes, providing snacks and tea as well as a good discussion. Not all classes are tiny (the average runs between 15 and 25 people), but anything with over 90 people (Intro Bio and Chem classes are the biggest) is unheard of, and even as a freshman you may find yourself in several classes of 10 people or less.

In a popular policy, freshmen for their first semester take all their classes pass/fail, so that there is less pressure and more adjustment time. Four more pass/fail classes are allowed for the remaining three years also. The Tri-Co setup allows Swatties to take other classes at nearby Bryn Mawr and Haverford for free. For those eager to venture farther from campus, there is an extensive study-abroad/foreign-exchange network (Swat's own programs in Grenoble and Madrid are very popular).

Even a Club for Knitters . . .

The range of extracurricular opportunities is just as broad. Musicians have numerous orchestral, chamber, and choral groups to pick from, as well as a Jazz Ensemble and even a Balinese percussion ensemble. There is a deep commitment to community service among Swatties; Cooperative Involvement and Volunteers in Committees, or CIVIC, is an umbrella organization overseeing projects, and the Swarthmore Foundation endows grants for new proposals from students. Other popular activities include the debate team, the *Phoenix* student newspaper, *Spike*, the humor magazine, Earthlust (an environmental organization), and Swat's own WSRN radio station. For the more eclectic, there are other groups like the Opera Club, Yggdrasill (the Scandinavian Society), the KnitWits (a society of knitters), and even a volunteer fire brigade. Most freshmen are amazed "how easy it is to get involved in stuff and to do fairly significant things fairly fast."

Swatties compete in Division III athletics, and about 30 percent of the student body plays on varsity. (But "it's true that the football team sucks," a student admits rather casually.) Intramurals and club sports teams include water polo, rugby, aikido, ice hockey (the Mother Puckers), and ultimate Frisbee (the Swarming Earthworms). To raise money, teams hold parties and other events—the men's and women's rugby players, for instance, streak and grab donations from spectators in their annual Dash for Cash. Classes in such activities as folk dancing, scuba diving, and fencing are also offered. Despite the enthusiastic participation in many sports, however, attendance at weekend games is low for the most part. "We have a lot of superb athletes, but sports simply aren't prioritized."

There are two frats (the members of which tend to be football and basketball players), but neither has a notable presence on campus except through their weekend parties. Their parties are no different from other non-frat parties—"everyone goes, but the beer is worse." Students say that the administration is fairly lax when it comes to enforcing drinking laws. The Student Affairs Committee often funds the alcohol at some social events. Most people do drink, but "there is no pressure, and drinking is definitely not the focus" of the social scene. "Parties are safe," adds another student, "people look out for one another." Nor have drugs been a significant issue—although weed is quite prevalent.

Despite the close proximity to Philadelphia, relatively few people actually go out into the city, simply because there's always so much to do on campus. Since every event at Swat, Bryn Mawr, and Haverford is free for any Tri-Co student, there are chances to meet people beyond the immediate campus. But when in need of clubs, movie theaters, restaurants, and in general a wider range of options, the city is a mere 20 minutes away by train—there's a stop right on campus.

People have "pretty healthy love/sex lives," and while hookups are constant, most relationships are serious. "It's not really dating as it is just spending lots of time with each other," according to a sophomore. A recent insider's game involves the "Swarthmore Six Degrees of Separation" phenomenon. Theoretically, any Swattie can be linked to any other

Swattie via people who have hooked up with each other. There's not much privacy, and in what's known as the infamous Walk of Shame, Swatties who walk across campus back to their rooms on the morning after often are seen by everyone else from their windows.

Escaping It All

Whether for more privacy or for new diversions, moments definitely come when the Swattie will want to get away. Food and hangout places feel limited after a while, and except for the frequented Bean Bag Cafe, the town of Swarthmore doesn't have much to offer. Students usually take their meals at Sharples Dining Hall—the only cafeteria on campus (continuing a Quaker tradition of sharing meals under the same roof). The Tarble Social Center also contains a snack/coffee hangout, lounge, student activities offices, performance spaces, and the bookstore. As for the dining-hall food, students warn against the meat—or meat-like—products as well as anything fried. But other than those sketchy items, there are plenty of edible options: a huge salad bar, a deli, a grill (where burgers are custom-made), a vegetarian bar, and a self-stir-fry wok; for the truly desperate, waffles and yogurt/ice cream are available at every meal.

> "People will get drunk here and then go play chess or have an intellectual discussion in their dorm after the party ends."

Housing is guaranteed for all four years, and most students—over 90 percent—choose to remain on campus in the dorms, which "vary but are overall pretty acceptable." After freshman year, students select housing by lottery and many upperclassmen get singles. There is no theme housing, but residential halls do occasionally develop their own character. One dorm, for instance, is known for its "spontaneous wrestling matches" in the corridors.

Among the more eccentric Swattie traditions is Genderfuck—supposedly a cross-dressing dance but described more vividly as "a dance/party where guys dress as girls and girls dress as sluts." Another dance, Screw-Your-Roommate, involves roommates setting each other up on blind dates, and then each paired couple dressing up in thematic costumes or performing skits in order to find each other. Members of the Dip-of-the-Month Club meet regularly for skinny-dipping sessions in Crum Creek—a freezing, two-foot-deep stream running through campus. And then there's the McCabe Mile, a "mile-long race around the stacks in the library, started by slamming a scholarly book and rewarded with a roll of toilet paper."

Comfortable, Supportive Atmosphere

Swat is extremely diverse in every way; in general people are open and friendly, and everyone tends to have a wide range of friends—"it's the very opposite of cliquey," remarked a junior. There are a variety of support networks, such as the Black Cultural Center, Swarthmore Asian Organization, Hispanic Organization for Latino/a Awareness, Swarthmore Queer Union, and the Women's Resource Center. But the real diversity extends beyond these formations. As one student said: "Earthytypes hang out with goth-girls who are friends with the basketball player who's going out with the violinist who is the best friend of the kilt-wearer." Nor is there much real division between freshmen and upperclassmen. The stereotypical Swattie is "hardworking, PC, vegetarian, and trendy without trying to be," and the school as a whole is "definitely on the liberal side, but there is no such thing as a typical Swattie."

One thing that does seem intrinsic to every Swattie is a passion for something—or, often, for many things. "People come to Swarthmore because they really care about something, whether it's engineering, art, or literature," a sophomore declared. "I've had wonderful conversations about everything from situation comedy to semiotics, even once with a friend about whose translation of Gabriel Garcia Marquez we each preferred—and all on my own time rather than just in class." Another student agrees: "You can't help but learn here, from classes, extracurricular opportunities, or from your peers—people will get drunk here and then go play chess or have an intellectual discussion in their dorm after the party ends."

Although virtually all tend to acknowledge the uniqueness of their Swat experience, not everyone is completely happy here. The smallness of the college that fosters closeness for some translates into a sometimes stifling lack of anonymity. That "every face is a familiar one" could be both a good and bad thing, as "reputations are easily gotten, rarely forgotten," and "if you get raving drunk you can't hide the next day and have people forget." Some also perceive that students' ambitiousness occasionally leads to a self-involvement that puts work before friends. "Egos are not that huge," however, and "people are relatively modest." And while there is "a kind of playful, joking intellectual elitism here," a freshman observes, "no internal elitism exists in terms of social structures."

The college T-shirt declaring, "Anywhere else it would've been an A—really" does not exaggerate—Swatties probably do work harder than anyone else. But what makes Swat particularly special for most Swatties, as one student said, is how the school "self-selects for a kind of intellectual sensibility—it can be an incredibly total experience; I've found the people that I want to spend my time with, and Swarthmore has been wonderful because of that." —*Chinnie Ding and Staff*

FYI

The three best things about attending Swarthmore are "the individual attention from small classes, all activities and parties are free, and school has a LOT of money (top ten in endowment per student) and they use the money to fund a lot of student-run organizations."

The three worst things about attending Swarthmore are "bad or lack of sports teams, annoying to every tree with a name plate (the school is an arboretum), and sometimes the tiny student body gets to you."

The three things that every student should do before graduating from Swarthmore are "have lunch in the Rose garden, do the 'McCabe Mile,' and go to the 'Screw-Your-Roommate' dance where roommates set up each other with blind dates."

One thing I'd like to have known before coming here is "that the weather in the Mid-Atlantic really does suck."

Temple University

Address: 1801 North Broad Street; Philadelphia, PA 19122-5096	**Percent Asian:** 1%	**Middle 50% ACT range:** NA
Phone: 215-204-7200	**Percent Hispanic:** 4%	**3 Most popular majors:** psychology, business administration, and early childhood / elementary education
E-mail address: tuadm@mail.temple.edu	**Percent Native-American:** 0%	
Web site URL: www.temple.edu	**Percent in-state / out-of-state:** 22% / 78%	
Founded: 1884	**Percent Pub HS:** 77%	**Retention:** 75%
Private or Public: public	**Number of Applicants:** 8,848	**Graduation rate:** 37%
Religious affiliation: none	**Percent Accepted:** 68%	**On-campus housing:** NA
Location: urban	**Percent Accepted who enroll:** 39%	**Fraternities:** 3%
Undergraduate enrollment: 17,620	**Entering:** 2,346	**Sororities:** 3%
Total enrollment: 28,473	**Transfers:** 2,037	**Library:** 2,100,000 volumes
Percent Male / Female: 43% / 57%	**Application Deadline:** 1 Apr	**Tuition and Fees:** $5,830 in; $10,752 out
	Mean SAT: 510 V, 502 M	
Percent Minority: 34%	**Mean ACT:** NA	**Room and Board:** $5,772
Percent African-American: 29%	**Middle 50% SAT range:** 450–570 V, 450–560 M	**Financial aid, first-year:** 72%

If your childhood dreams have ever included becoming the star of one of America's top-rated family situation comedies, perhaps you should consider Temple University. After all, Bill Cosby is an alumnus of this Philadelphia school. But even if making people laugh isn't your primary concern, neither is Temple's. Indeed, Temple University has a very structured academic program with Philadelphia as its playground.

The Core

Although requirements may be different for certain majors, all students are required to fulfill core requirements. These include mathematics, lab sciences, composition, American culture, art, and social sciences. Additionally, all students must become proficient in a foreign language, or take classes in international studies. To round off their course, all students must take a class in race studies and a year known as "intellectual heritage," which covers Western civilization from the ancient world to the modern. While many students are happy that these requirements encourage experimentation in different subjects, some students feel the core is actually quite weak. In regards to the race requirement, one student commented, "Goodness, I'm putting it off 'til senior year. It's a really PC class that professors are not keen on teaching, so it's of very low quality." Within the subject requirements, Temple students must also take a number of writing-intensive classes. According to one junior, "I sometimes think this reduces the quality of classes because people are out to take classes that fall under race and writing-intensive at the same time just to get rid of requirements."

As for actual classes, students agree that the sciences are pretty rigorous, while American Studies offers many manageable classes. Students looking for a more intense atmosphere can take honors classes. Upon successful completion of eight honors courses, students receive an honors certificate at graduation. Getting into classes itself is not a problem provided that the student registers early enough through the school's automated telephone system. "The system is really great and convenient, but it does sometimes leave students unadvised," said one student. Class sizes rarely exceed 30 students and all students agree that there is an extraordinary amount of individual attention from professors.

To Philadelphia and Beyond

Weekends on the Temple campus are pretty low-key. "This is very much a local school," said one student, "so people leave school on the weekends and after 4:30 in the afternoon, the campus is pretty empty." However, the school is in the process of building new dorms to encourage students back on campus and to augment campus life. Being in Philadelphia, though, there is a reasonable excuse for escaping from the campus. Temple students have myriad possibilities within the city. Philadelphia boasts one of the best art museums and a rich theater life, where students attend shows at the Wilma Theater and the Walnut Street Theater. Temple often arranges free or reduced tickets for students to attend special shows. For those with less of a penchant for cultural activities, there are plenty of bars and restaurants on South Street. Students like going to diners, including Oak Lane Diner and the Melrose Diner. For a night at an Irish pub, Temple students often frequent Moriarty's and Sassafrass in the Old City.

Despite the low-key campus social scene, there is a large student center, simply known as the SAC. With a food court, movie theater, and arcade, students are often found lounging or studying. "Since there are a lot of commuters, they need places to hang out." However, the newest hot spot on campus is the Tuttleman Learning Center, which just recently opened and houses 500 brand-new computers complete with ethernet access.

Living in a Hotel

For on-campus students, Temple offers a variety of dorms, and is in the process of erecting new ones. Most rooms are standard doubles with just enough room for a small fridge. Peabody, the oldest dorm on campus, has the smallest rooms. The new buildings, White and New Residence

Hall are cited as the best dorms on campus, composed of suites with shared bathrooms for four people. Also popular are the Temple Towers, university-owned apartments which support a pool. However, one junior mentioned, "they have some problems with roaches and rats." As campus life is beginning to grow, the demand for dorms has gone up, causing the school to have purchased a number of rooms in a local Best Western for roughly 130 kids. Most students, though, choose to live off campus. "In the long run, it was actually cheaper for me to live off anyway," said one student. There is no requirement that freshmen live on campus, so students of all years live in local apartments. "Also, the dorms shut down for every break, even the four-day Thanksgiving holiday, so you're forced to leave if you're not a local. This means a train ticket at best, and quite possibly a plane ticket," said one junior who lives off campus.

On-campus students choose to eat in Johnson-Hardwick Dining Hall, affectionately called "the Caf." The food is described as "above par for a cafeteria, but you can't eat it for too long." The dining hall is a very social setting. As one freshman said, "dinner is a big production." In the evening, the dining hall becomes quite crowded, where one can find a number of people dressed up for a night in the cafeteria. For those on the run, there is a food court in the SAC and a café in the Tuttleman Learning Center—Fresh Bytes. While the dining options on campus are pretty good, students unanimously cite the Lunch Trucks as the "staple and highlight" of dining at Temple. From 11:30 to 12:30, independent food stands line the streets serving everything from Soul Food to all types of Asian foods, and pizza. Of course, each of the lunch trucks also serves Philly Cheesesteaks.

The People

The Lunch Trucks seem to reflect the diversity of the students themselves. Temple is a tremendously diverse school with a very large African-American population. Moreover, there are a number of Indians and Asians and international students. "I've met people from Australia, Ireland, Russia, even Argentina," said one student. "Diversity truly abounds." Temple manages to bring all these students together in various extracurricular activities, such as Student Government, fraternities, and academic fraternities (which act like honor societies). However, as one junior said, "Temple is very much a working class school so almost all of the students work jobs as their major extracurricular activity." Additionally, included among Temple students are returning adult students who may have families, and little time to devote to Temple extracurriculars. Regardless, "there are no idle Temple students."

> **While the dining options on campus are pretty good, students unanimously cite the Lunch Trucks as the "staple and highlight" of dining at Temple.**

When they get a break from their various activities, Temple students really enjoy basketball games. The new Apollo arena provides a world-class venue. Nationally renowned coach and defensive guru, John Chaney, provides a basketball team frequently among the nation's best. Although most students don't really have time to devote to athletics, there is the Independence Blue Cross workout center. There, students profit from a full-service workout club with everything from Nautilus machines to freeweights. Additionally, the Student Pavilion has both indoor and outdoor basketball and tennis courts. Other students sign up in teams to play intramural sports or take part in aerobics.

Temple, set in a lively and historic city, provides a solid education. Some students choose to spend semesters at Temple's campuses in Rome and Japan, adding an international flair to the university. "I like being here a lot and it really was the perfect choice for me," said one student. "I've learned a lot about myself and love living in a city with all sorts of people."—*Shu-Ping Shen*

FYI

The three best things about attending Temple are "being in a city, the honors program, and the Lunch Trucks."

The three worst things about attending Temple are "financial aid, politically correct humanities core, the faulty transcript system."

The three things that every student should do before graduating from Temple are "go to the Rodin museum, see a Temple play, see a Temple basketball game."

One thing I'd like to have known before coming here is "that the language departments were so lacking."

University of Pennsylvania

Address: 1 College Hall; Philadelphia, PA 19104
Phone: 215-898-7507
E-mail address: info@admissions.ugao.upenn.edu
Web site URL: www.upenn.edu
Founded: 1740
Private or Public: private
Religious affiliation: none
Location: urban
Undergraduate enrollment: 9,501
Total enrollment: 22,148
Percent Male / Female: 51% / 49%
Percent Minority: 29%
Percent African-American: 6%

Percent Asian: 19%
Percent Hispanic: 4%
Percent Native-American: 0%
Percent in-state / out-of-state: 10% / 90%
Percent Pub HS: 62%
Number of Applicants: 16,658
Percent Accepted: 29%
Percent Accepted who enroll: 49%
Entering: 2,408
Transfers: 254
Application Deadline: 1 Jan
Mean SAT: 695 V, 715 M
Mean ACT: NA

Middle 50% SAT range: 640–730 V, 660–750 M
Middle 50% ACT range: 28–31
3 Most popular majors: English, history, and psychology
Retention: NA
Graduation rate: 87%
On-campus housing: NA
Fraternities: 30%
Sororities: 30%
Library: 4,200,000 volumes
Tuition and Fees: $24,230 in; $24,230 out
Room and Board: $7,910
Financial aid, first-year: 46%

Founded by one of America's most famous statesmen in 1740, the University of Pennsylvania has grown into a prestigious institution of higher learning. It is also one of the eight schools that form the Ivy League. Although UPenn is best known for its top academic programs, the school provides its students with much more. From its community of tight-knit "college houses" to a dynamic urban setting, UPenn brings together all the best that college has to offer.

Work Before Play

Depending on their choice of major, prospective Quakers apply to one of the university's four undergraduate schools— the College of Arts and Sciences, the School of Engineering and Applied Science, the School of Nursing, and the Wharton School of Business. Unlike many other Ivy League schools, UPenn has undergraduate programs geared toward students considering a specific career. Academics at UPenn are rigorous, and students must fulfill several requirements before they graduate. The requirements are "a fair amount" but "very general stuff and easy to complete," students said. Core requirements also differ among the various undergraduate schools within the university, but most include basic courses in writing, quantitative, and language skills.

Subject areas receiving high marks include anthropology, English, history, and Spanish. "All the Spanish teachers I've had have been cute women in their mid-twenties," one student said. Other high points include abnormal psychology, which is "one of the most popular classes at Penn, even among non–psychology majors." Courses in the famed Wharton School of Business also garnered praise. "Legal Studies 101 was sensational," one student gushed. "The legal studies department is very well liked by all of the students on campus, not just Whartonites." Courses receiving low marks include introductory economics and Operations and Information Management 101, an introductory computer class. A thumbs-down also went to lower-level science courses. UPenn students also dread the "Wharton Curve," utilized in some courses. While this grade distribution guarantees that a certain percentage of the class will get A's and B's, it also means that a part of the class must receive C's. "Theoretically, you can get a ninety on an exam and that will still be a C, because sixty-five percent did better than you," one student cautioned. Students also had negative comments about the advising system and lack of support. "I felt like I was in an academic free fall freshman year," one junior complained.

UPenn's best students can apply to the Benjamin Franklin Scholars program. To graduate from this program, a student needs to have at least a 3.4 GPA and take at least four honors courses. All honors courses at UPenn are open to any student who wishes to take one. The Wharton School offers several joint programs with several of the university's other schools. These include the Huntsman Program in International Studies and Business, the Jerome Fisher Program in Management and Technology, and the Healthcare Management Nursing Program. Admission to these programs is also very selective. Although students select a major in one school, they are able to take courses offered in any of the three other schools.

Eat, Drink, Sleep— Quaker-Style

Quaker life centers around the university's residential college system. Ranging from century-old buildings to modern high-rise towers, each of the 12 "college houses" has its own resident faculty master, dean, graduate student associates, and residential advisors. Other faculty members and their families may live in the college houses as well. Besides providing students a place to sleep and eat, college houses "create a community atmosphere for students who want to have a smaller sphere to interact amidst the larger Penn campus," one student said. "Every Wednesday night, [my master and his wife] invite everyone over to watch *Dawson's Creek* and to have coffee and cookies later on in the evening. I honestly can say that students really think of the college house as a home . . . because of things like this," another student added. Rooms in the college houses are a mixture of singles, doubles, triples, and quads. Some have amenities such as kitchens and private bathrooms as well. Students caution that some of the freshman dorm rooms can be quite small. "If you want to really live large, you need to move off campus," one junior said. Four undergraduate dining halls are scattered all over campus and are usually located near or in the college houses. Food is served buffet-style and "isn't bad." Students give high marks to the food at Irv's Place, the university's kosher dining hall. Other places to eat that students recommend are the food trucks parked in various locations around the campus. "They are clean, cheap, and delicious," one student said. Although the university does not require students to live on campus, almost all freshmen do.

Life in the Big City of Brotherly Love

Although Philadelphia may not be the top reason that most Quakers choose to attend UPenn, but this major urban area provides them a whole new world beyond the campus. The city is in the midst of a revitalization, as crime rates have fallen and run-down areas are being renovated. "Philly doesn't give the greatest first impression, but as many Penn students say, 'It kind of grows on you,'" one sophomore said. When dining hall food gets tiresome, students can venture off campus for an endless array of options. "I like going down to Chinatown for an authentic and inexpensive meal," one student said. For beer and famous Philly cheese steaks, the place to go is Billy Bob's. Other options include the all-night El Diner and the Italian Market, a weekend bazaar offering meats, cheeses, and fish. For a night of entertainment, students head to downtown clubs like Envy, Egypt, Polly Esther's, and Shampoo. Other popular weekend hangouts include Rittenhouse Square, the Gallery, Liberty Place, and South Street. Every student should have a drink at Smokey Joe's before graduating, one junior said. Besides food and drink, the city offers a wide variety of cultural and sporting events. Students can catch Phillies baseball games at Veterans' Stadium, while those more interested in the performing arts can attend performances of the Pennsylvania Ballet Company and the Philadelphia Philharmonic. The city is packed with museums and important historic sites, like Independence Hall, and the Liberty Bell.

Come Out and Play

Although Quakers are serious about their academics, they maintain active social lives as well. "This campus is populated by students who are bright and motivated but also know when to relax and how to have fun," one junior said. Greek life has a strong presence at UPenn, as almost a third of the student population are members of a fraternity or sorority. Weekends usually mean large frat parties, although there is a "smattering of cool, smaller parties" as well. "Greek life is both big but not that big a deal," one student said. Although Sundays are usually reserved for studying, Friday and Saturday nights mean going out and relaxing. "Usually, students plan to go out on Friday or Saturday night, and then stay in the other night and do something low-key, such as watching a movie," a junior said. Diversions include a wide variety of student-produced theater, comedy, and a cappella singing performances. Attending sporting events and having coffee at nearby cafés are also common ways to spend a weekend evening.

UPenn also offers its students plenty of extracurricular activities. The Kite and Key Society is the campus' oldest and largest community service group. A plethora of planning and steering committees allow students to become involved in every facet of college life, from organizing social events for their college houses to advising administrators on academic policies. Many students find part-time jobs working in the university's offices. Students interested in

journalism can join the award-winning *Daily Pennsylvanian*, just one of many publications on the UPenn campus.

Basketball and football are the most popular sports on campus. Basketball games at the Palestra, the university's home court, are well attended, especially during the season's biggest matchup, the UPenn–Princeton game. "Everyone is so pumped up that the air becomes electric during big games," a student said. The football games also attract a large following. When UPenn wins the Ivy League title at home, as it did in 1998, fans rush onto the field, tear down the goalpost, and throw it into the Schuylkill River. After the third quarter of a football game, students sing "Drink a Highball," whose last line is, "Here's a toast to dear old Penn." Although the word *toast* refers to alcoholic drinks here, Quakers throw slices of toasted bread onto the sidelines.

> Said one undergrad, "This campus is populated by students who are bright and motivated but also know when to relax and how to have fun."

Being over 250 years old, UPenn has its share of traditions. One of the oldest is Hey Day, which takes place on the last day of classes during the spring term. Juniors are officially declared seniors by the university's president. Another big event is the yearly Spring Fling, held during the weekend before spring finals begin. The campus "gets drunk four days straight," a student said. Music is a focal point of the festivities, as major acts perform on campus. Recent acts have included the Roots and Ben Folds Five. One popular and very un-Quaker-like myth says students must have sex under the Button, a giant aluminum sculpture in the shape of a button in front of the Van Pelt Library.

When asked for five adjectives to describe UPenn, one junior said, "Fun, active, balanced, diverse, and not-too-big." With its mix of top-notch academics, a vibrant social scene, and driven students, the school seems to package all the best parts of the college experience into a neat bundle.—*Robert Yi*

FYI

The three best things about attending the University of Pennsylvania are "the wide range of opportunities, the lively party scene, and the history classes."

The three worst things about attending the University of Pennsylvania are "the tough curves in some classes, the introductory science courses, and weak academic advising."

The three things that every student should do before graduating from the University of Pennsylvania are "go to a UPenn–Princeton basketball game, take a class at the Wharton School, and eat a crepe at Le Petit Creperie Food Truck next to Gimbel Gymnasium."

One thing I'd like to have known before coming here is "what a Quaker really is."

University of Pittsburgh

Address: Second Floor, Bruce Hall; Pittsburgh, PA 15260
Phone: 412-624-PITT
E-mail address: oafa@pitt.edu
Web site URL: www.pitt.edu
Founded: 1787
Private or Public: public
Religious affiliation: none
Location: urban
Undergraduate enrollment: 16,798
Total enrollment: NA
Percent Male/Female: 47%/53%
Percent Minority: 6%
Percent African-American: 1%

Percent Asian: 4%
Percent Hispanic: 1%
Percent Native-American: 0%
Percent in-state/out-of-state: 85%/15%
Percent Pub HS: NA
Number of Applicants: 13,580
Percent Accepted: 68%
Percent Accepted who enroll: 34%
Entering: 3,140
Transfers: 688
Application Deadline: rolling
Mean SAT: 569 V, 569 M
Mean ACT: 25

Middle 50% SAT range: 500–610 V, 500–610 M
Middle 50% ACT range: 21–27
3 Most popular majors: speech, engineering, and psychology
Retention: 85%
Graduation rate: 36%
On-campus housing: NA
Fraternities: 10%
Sororities: 7%
Library: 3,500,000 volumes
Tuition and Fees: $5,884 in; $12,918 out
Room and Board: $5,598
Financial aid, first-year: 70%

According to one student: "If you can get over trudging up and down the Hill all day, Pitt's a wonderful place." Students at the University of Pittsburgh, situated on a hill just a few miles from downtown Pittsburgh, rave about accessible professors, a bursting social scene, and the inevitable physical fitness gained from hiking to class.

Well-rounded, Rigorous, and Rewarding

"Whether film major or premed," Pitt students are all exposed, or some might say subjected, to a list of requirements that can take up to one-third of their schedules. Graduation requirements include general education classes in such areas as the humanities and social and natural sciences. As well as general education, students must fulfill skills requirements, which consist of composition and quantitative/formal reasoning, a broad category that can be fulfilled through a math, computer science, or philosophy course. Students can elect to test out of these requirements through scores on the SATs or AP tests. Though the framework is the same for everyone, students have a broad selection of courses to choose from to fulfill their requisites. Most agree that the obligations are generally not cumbersome, and many enjoy the well-rounded education they feel the requisites promote. Popular majors are in both the sciences and humanities and include mathematics, English literature, psychology, and communications.

As with any school, there is the usual assortment of "joke classes." Freshman

Studies, an orientation class, is said to be "a waste of time," and business calculus and statistics lighten the workload for some. Beware of a certain science professor, though, who likes to make students in "Rocks for Jocks" earn their course credits. However, even those with rigorous schedules consider their workload to be fair. "It's a lot of work, but I'm managing okay," said one freshman. Another adds that schedules can be "very rigorous but extremely rewarding."

Professors teach all classes, while recitations, smaller sections with more personal interaction and frequent quizzes, are taught by graduate teaching assistants. Pitt students agree that the professors work hard to supplement the course work by giving the material a living face. They often arrange field trips for their students, with history classes visiting the battlefields at Gettysburg and German-language students embarking on a seven-day trip to Germany. The professors are described as "approachable and competent" educators who continually try to make the students feel more comfortable and to offset the serious work with a little play. One biology teacher plays "Bio-jeopardy," while a calculus professor is known to play relaxing classical music before the start of each class.

Living in a Can of Comet
A point of pride for the University of Pittsburgh is the Cathedral of Learning, a 42-story-tall structure in the Gothic style that is "the second-tallest education building in the world." It houses a variety of classrooms and offices, as well as the Nationality Classrooms, themed rooms each scaled to a different culture. However, in contrast to the Cathedral of Learning, students describe the rest of the campus' modern architecture as rather "blah."

> **"Pitt students are intelligent and think that academics are important, but not all-consuming."**

Freshmen usually live in one of three tall, round dorms known as Towers, which look like "big cans of Comet." Two of the towers consist of doubles, and one houses singles. While some students claim that freshman housing is "decent," others declare that it's "horrible." The rooms are air-conditioned and 24-hour-quiet floors are available, though even on the regular floors a tight rein is kept on late-night noise. Housing is coed by floor, and about 30 students live on each floor. Rooms are pie-shaped and are "way too small" in general. The size of the desks is also a big complaint, and one student grumbled that because his desk is so tiny, he has to put his keyboard on his lap to type. Students are assigned resident associates, who help the freshmen make the transition to college and also enforce the bans on candles, halogen lamps, smoking of any variety, and other fire hazards. After freshman year, students usually live in suites or off-campus apartments.

The meal plan is arranged in blocks. Students on the meal plan are allotted six blocks a day, each worth $4.85. While they are free to spend blocks either in the traditional dining halls or at various participating restaurants, unused blocks are deleted at the end of the week and students complain about the inevitable loss of money. Many end up going on a Starbucks spending spree at the end of the week to get their money's worth. Students enjoy the variety of places to eat, but some complain that dining hall hours on Friday and Saturday nights are a problem: "The dining hall operates on the assumption that this is still a commuter campus. They ignore the fact that there has been a recent boom in on-campus living."

You've Gotta Do Something Besides Study!
Students agree that one of Pitt's main attractions is the diversity of entertainment the city offers. One student said, "I honestly can't think of anything this campus can't offer." Another student added, "Pitt students are intelligent and think that academics are important, but not all-consuming. We know how to get out and have a good time." Dance clubs are popular, but students also spend their weekends playing football on the Cathedral lawn, going to parties, or just hanging out with friends. While there's a sizable amount of drinking, students who choose not to drink don't feel left out of the social

scene. Many students also take advantage of a variety of school-sponsored activities, such as weekend trips to Niagara Falls and local productions of such musicals as *The Lion King*. Others choose to attend the abundant parties, usually hosted by students living off campus or the Greeks. According to one student, some frats do charge an admission of about five dollars, but the parties are often free, "especially for good-looking freshman girls."

In addition to entertainment options, there is a huge variety of student clubs and organizations; most students are involved in some type of extracurricular activity. Especially popular is the Outdoors Club, which goes skydiving and rock climbing. Many students also participate in community service projects, such as Habitat for Humanity. Some choose to manage the stress of the academic life by joining the Campus Fools and learning to juggle or ride a unicycle. Another popular option is the Pitt Pathfinders, a student group that is paid to lead tours of the campus. "It's so hard not to find something you can participate in and be passionate about," one student explained.

Sports are an integral part of the Pitt experience. Football gets especially high marks, boosted by Pitt's triumph last year over Penn State. Pitt actively recruits its football players, and the recruiting tent has a presence at most football games. For those who don't join the varsity teams, intramurals are a popular alternative and there is always someone playing sports on the lawn.

Many students come to the University of Pittsburgh expecting to get lost among the thousands of undergraduates, but most are pleasantly surprised. One freshman explained, "It's a lot more personal than I thought it would be." Pitt's large, urban campus can be intimidating, but below the surface is "a very close, tight-knit university."—*Tracy Serge*

FYI

The three best things about attending the University of Pittsburgh are "the professors, the Pitt–Penn State game (but only if we win), and the students."

The three worst things about attending the University of Pittsburgh are "the requirements, Towers, and walking up the Hill."

The three things that every student should do before graduating from the University of Pittsburgh are "go to a football game, have fries at the O, and live for a year in the Towers."

One thing I'd like to have known before coming here is that "college is neither all studying nor all partying; you have to find a balance."

Villanova University

Address: 800 Lancaster
Avenue; Villanova, PA
19085-1672
Phone: 610-519-4000
E-mail address: gotovu
@email.villanova.edu
Web site URL:
www.villanova.edu
Founded: 1842
Private or Public:
private
Religious affiliation:
Catholic
Location: suburban
**Undergraduate
enrollment:** 7,130
Total enrollment: 1,019
Percent Male / Female:
49% / 51%
Percent Minority: 9%

Percent African-American:
3%
Percent Asian: 3%
Percent Hispanic: 3%
Percent Native-American:
0%
**Percent in-state / out-of-
state:** 31% / 69%
Percent Pub HS: 50%
Number of Applicants:
9,278
Percent Accepted: 62%
**Percent Accepted who
enroll:** 28%
Entering: 1,611
Transfers: NA
Application Deadline:
15 Jan
Mean SAT: 600 V, 620 M
Mean ACT: NA

Middle 50% SAT range:
560–640 V,
580–660 M
Middle 50% ACT range:
NA
3 Most popular majors:
finance, biology, and
nursing
Retention: 92%
Graduation rate: 75%
On-campus housing: NA
Fraternities: 29%
Sororities: 40%
Library: 680,000
volumes
Tuition and Fees:
$20,555 in; $20,555 out
Room and Board: $3,040
Financial aid, first-year:
NA

L
ooking for a good combination of
great basketball and the Catholic
tradition? If so, then Villanova University is probably the place to be. Students at Villanova are wildly supportive of
their Wildcats basketball team. During
basketball season, "the games are sold out
all the time. People get painted up. And
everyone is wearing their 'V' shirts, said
one student. But while Villanova offers
basketball thrills, students can gain so
much more.

The Academics

Regardless of academic department, be
it nursing, engineering, or business, all
Villanova students are required to take
core humanities requirements, including
courses in theology and philosophy. Normally taken in the freshman year, these
core classes explore different themes and
time periods, from the ancient and medieval all the way up to the modern. According to one student, "I think our basic
requirements are pretty good, but it really
was a lot of work." Aside from these core
classes, students are allowed to explore
the various options offered within the respective departments. According to most
students, engineering and nursing are

probably the most difficult departments.
One sophomore described how her friend
"has really long days. Sometimes I don't
see her for more than a few minutes." The
departments in the liberal arts are not
deemed quite as difficult and many students, in fact, feel the need to strengthen
those departments.

Still, students have few complaints
about their class experiences. One junior
mentioned that "even for my general lecture courses, I don't think there's ever
been more than 60 people." Furthermore,
the professors are reportedly very accessible. One engineering major commented
that "the professors don't have problems
helping you after class is over or even calling them at their houses. They're really
great." Another student gave a more
mixed review; "I've had a few professors
grossly underprepared," she said, "but,
still, the teachers here are great." Villanova does not have large numbers of
TA's teaching undergraduates, although
they do help to grade and provide help in
certain laboratory courses. While registration may often be difficult for freshmen,
who sit lowest on the priority ladder, Villanova students are extremely happy with
academics. "I really think I'm getting more

than I'm paying for," declared one freshman.

Chugging Along . . .

Alcohol is quite present on the Villanova campus, but the administration is very adamant about restricting alcohol to students of age. Generally, to drink, Wildcats attend fraternity parties. The Greek system is very big, although those who don't rush can still attend the numerous Greek parties. For those interested in calmer activities, movies are shown every weekend in the student center and there are plenty of concerts throughout the semester. Additionally, for those in pursuit of more intellectual activities, "there are lots of forums, colloquiums, and the like— everyday. So you can definitely find one of those if you want." Other on-campus activities can be found at Connelly, the student center. There, students can play pool, foosball, board games, use the internet, and take advantage of a huge lounge. Many juniors and seniors have cars, although freshmen are not allowed to bring cars to campus. "It's okay though," said another student, "freshmen will find plenty to do on campus." While freshman generally stay on campus, upperclassmen do mention that they enjoy going into nearby Philadelphia often. Favorite hangouts include Club Egypt, Fels Planetarium with their Laser Light show, and South Street.

Abercrombie & Fitch Anyone?

One freshman described the general Villanova student to be "a well off, white, Abercrombie and Fitch–wearing, business type." Aside from the somewhat preppy atmosphere, "people here are really friendly," said one junior. Still, students generally agree that the school could use a little more ethnic diversity.

> One freshman described the general Villanova student to be "a well-off, white, Abercrombie and Fitch– wearing, business type."

Villanova "Wildcats" can be found participating in various extracurricular activities. Fraternities are the most popular groups, and they often carry out service projects. Other service organizations include Habitat for Humanity, and Project Sunshine, where students can devote just an hour of their time each week to helping poor children in the inner city. Student government is prevalent on campus and well-respected, as is the *Villanovan*, the school newspaper, which, reportedly, "everyone loves." Additionally, for those who absolutely love Villanova, there is the Blue Key Society, in which students lead outside tours of the campus.

As mentioned earlier, basketball is the most attended sporting event of the year. Football, apparently, "is good, but doesn't attract a lot of people." Students in search of physical activity outside of varsity athletics can participate in intramurals, of which basketball, flag football, soccer, and softball are the most popular. Furthermore, there are two weight rooms which, while in constant use, are never packed. "It's nice because the athletes have their own facilities, so the rest of us can have access to the gyms," said one student. Other sports facilities include indoor and outdoor basketball courts, as well as tennis courts, all easily accessible by foot.

Beautiful Surroundings

Due to its Catholic attachment, one of the most noticeable buildings on the Villanova campus is their Roman Catholic Church. "The building is absolutely lovely, and it's a nice contrast to the new buildings on campus," said one sophomore. One of these more recent buildings is the new Center for Engineering Education and Research, while a new business school is soon to be erected. The campus is quite small; a 15-minute walk is all that's necessary for a walk from corner to corner.

Dorm life is "very nice actually," said one freshman. "The freshmen get treated really well here, and their dorms are all basically new." Aside from comfortable pads, Villanova dorms observe quiet hours and enforce visitation policies. For first-year students, visitation goes up until midnight during the week, while upperclassmen get 24-hour visitation rights. One upperclassman commented on his freshman room, "I was very happy with it—I even had a room with a sink." After freshman year, students are put into a general lottery, although everyone hopes to live in Sheehan, Sullivan, or Good Council, which reportedly have the largest rooms and act as big social hangouts. Since Villanova only guarantees three years of on-campus housing, most seniors move off, although there are some junior apartments, sponsored by the school, which are always in high demand. Unfortunately, many students find residence hall staff rather negligent in fixing things. "I really think they don't like kids," said one student. As for safety issues, one student commented that "it's pretty good. They check the dorms every night and there's a guard sitting at every dorm after 11." While some students sometimes find the guards and dorm policies restricting, they are generally happy with the security system at Villanova.

On this lovely campus are a number of places to eat. All students living on campus must purchase a meal plan, ranging from 19 meals per week, to the "new alternative," which provides a set number of meals during the semester, or an unlimited plan. There are three dining halls, and about eight "à la carte" dining areas. As one upperclassman described, "the dining halls are fun, especially for freshmen, who inevitably spend too many hours just chatting away." Additionally, two of the dining halls remain open until two in the morning. While no food is served at this late hour, "it's a really nice place to go and study." When seeking the excitement of restaurant food, students enjoy going off campus to local favorites such as Bertucci's, Marble's, and Minella's.

Clearly, Villanova is a school with a solid academic tradition where students still find time to be socially and physically active. While set in suburbia, the students also have access to a nearby city, where they can leave any worries of school behind. For the students of Villanova, a Catholic tradition is all part of the academic experience. But as a result, there is a clear sense of family at Villanova, which is something the Wildcats are very happy with.—*Shu-Ping Shen*

FYI

What is the typical weekend schedule? "Friday and Saturday at Villanova are you will see everyone on campus at off-campus parties. But Sundays are for going to mass and refraining from drinking."

Campus Slang? "Going down south?"—You might be if you're going to south campus. "Going on a blind date?"—Maybe you should plan to meet at the "Oreo," a black and white structure that looks nothing like the cookie, before you head to the cafeteria, known fondly as the "Pit Spit."

What do students at your school look forward to the most? "Everyone wants to get *rich* at Villanova."

What three things should every student at your school do before graduating? "Go to the courts, watch Nova basketball game, and drink a Natty Light."

Rhode Island

Brown University

Address: Box 1876; Providence, RI 02912
Phone: 401-863-2378
E-mail address: admission_undergraduate @brown.edu
Web site URL: www.brown.edu
Founded: 1764
Private or Public: private
Religious affiliation: none
Location: small city
Undergraduate enrollment: 6,108
Total enrollment: 7,758
Percent Male / Female: 47% / 53%
Percent Minority: 27%
Percent African-American: 6%

Percent Asian: 14%
Percent Hispanic: 6%
Percent Native-American: 0.5%
Percent in-state / out-of-state: 95% / 5%
Percent Pub HS: 60%
Number of Applicants: 14,756
Percent Accepted: 17%
Percent Accepted who enroll: 56%
Entering: 1,413
Transfers: 57
Application Deadline: 1 Jan
Mean SAT: 690 V, 690 M
Mean ACT: 29

Middle 50% SAT range: 640–750 V, 650–740 M
Middle 50% ACT range: 26–31
3 Most popular majors: biology, history, English literature
Retention: 97%
Graduation rate: 93%
On-campus housing: 100%
Fraternities: NA
Sororities: NA
Library: 3,000,000 volumes
Tuition and Fees: $26,184 in; $26,184 out
Room and Board: $7,346
Financial aid, first-year: 38%

Set atop a quiet hill, overlooking picturesque Providence, Rhode Island, you will find Brown University. Long known for it's liberal atmosphere, Brown students have the option of taking all of their classes pass/fail and have no core requirements. However, do not be deceived. Brownies take their academics seriously, and with a small graduate school, professors are able to devote much of their attention to undergraduate teaching.

Academic Freedom

One feature that sets Brown apart from its Ivy League counterparts is that there is no core curriculum. Students are free to pick and choose from a plethora of course offerings, without worrying about satisfying science, writing, or foreign language requirements. However, each "concentration," Brown-speak for major, has a certain number of course requirements, ranging from 8 (history) to 20 (environmental science). Brown requires 30 credits to graduate, so most students take three or four classes per semester. Students describe the workload as "demanding" but "doable." One student recommended, "Take at least one class pass/fail just out of pure interest while you're at Brown." Most students choose to use this option wisely and are discouraged from taking classes within their concentration Pass/Fail.

Tough concentrations include computer science, engineering, and the natural sciences, and Latin-American studies, English, education, and biology are all popular. Although most students are happy with the class sizes, getting into some courses can be a problem. Many classes and seminars have enrollment caps, and while most agree such courses foster good discussion, some are frustrated nonetheless. Said one student: "Registration's a bitch. You have to be waiting outside the registrar's office at five A.M. to get the classes you want. There needs to be a better system."

The small number of graduate students at Brown make it a decidedly undergraduate-oriented school. While some Brownies raved about the enthusiasm of their professors and the "new ideas they present about tackling problems," others say that you have to follow the good teaching and choose your classes accordingly. Although the focus on undergraduate teaching is generally an asset, some say that there is not as much opportunity for undergraduate research, as there are few graduate students to work for.

Socially Skilled

Although Brownies are proud of their individuality, one thing many students agreed on was how much they loved the people at Brown. "The students here are laid-back, not elitist," one freshman described them. "The people are so intelligent and creative." On the weekends, freshmen can be found exercising their social skills at frat parties or other campus get-togethers. Others take the 15-minute walk into downtown Providence and catch a movie at the new Providence Place mall. The streets surrounding Brown, notably Thayer Street and Wickenden Street, are packed with restaurants, coffee shops, and small stores as well. There are a plethora of campus-wide events, ranging from dances sponsored by student organizations to lectures given by visiting academics. There are several opportunities for Buronians to get out their ball gowns and tuxes each year, with the Presidential Ball being the most formal. Fall Ball, Winter Ball, and Final Fling are less formal.

Most students are involved in some sort of extracurricular activity. The Swearer Center is an umbrella organization for tons of social justice groups, environmental organizations, and community service groups. The *College Hill Independent*, put out by both Brown students and students from the Rhode Island School of Design (RISD), whose campus shares the hilltop with Brown, is a well-respected weekly paper. The *Brown Daily Herald*, student council, and Brown Lesbian, Gay, Bisexual and Transgendered Alliance (LGBTA) are other big organizations on campus.

The Greek system is described as being "very, very small," comprising a handful of fraternities and sororities. Since students must live on campus until their senior year, Greek houses contain standard dorms in the front and meeting space in the back. The university is reportedly "cool about alcohol." "As long as you behave and are not a disturbance, they don't mind." Though there are "plenty of hookups, it's not ragingly disgusting." There is some dating, but "it's hard to date in the traditional sense. It's more long-term." And for all those wondering, assured one student, "There are PLENTY of attractive people here!"

Though students come people from all four corners of the world, and the school maintains a fair amount of ethnic and cultural diversity, students tend to agree that economic diversity is lacking, which some attribute to the lack of need-blind admissions. "The majority of students are upper-middle-class." Or as one student summarized, "It's about as diverse as you can get at a place where you are required to pay thirty thousand dollars a year." Things may change, however, as Brown just recently switched to a need-blind admissions policy.

Bear Dens

Each freshman is assigned to a unit, comprising 20 to 30 students living in the same hallway or section of a dorm. Each unit is under the guidance of three counselors: a residential counselor, a minority peer counselor (MPC), and a women's peer counselor (WPC). Counselors are generally sophomores and are "terrific." "They are there to help you, not to enforce rules." Virtually all freshmen live in one-room doubles, some of which are "good-sized, and some are very small." While students don't rave about campus housing in general, most find it functional. "It's a roof over my head," said one junior. After freshman year, Brownies enter the housing lottery in groups ranging from four to seven students. Many sophomores find themselves with singles, since it is hard for sophomores to get suites. Most floors are coed but with single-sex bathrooms. Martin Gregorian Quad, or "New Dorm," is reportedly the best, and Perkins, which houses only freshmen, is one of the worst. After freshman year, students can also live in program houses such as King House, which is a literary house, West House (environmental awareness), or Machado House (Latino and Hispanic cultural interest). While freshmen, sophomores, and juniors are required to live on campus, most seniors move off into nearby apartments, the majority of which have reasonable rent.

Beautiful Brown

"Very New England," is how one student described her campus. With an eclectic mix of both new and old, traditional brick and some modern architecture thrown in for good measure, set among grassy quads and small, narrow streets, "beautiful" is a word that is used frequently among students when talking about their campus. Getting around the relatively small campus is no problem. Several students say they wish Brown had a student center and a better fitness center. "The athletic facilities are terrible for non-athletes," griped one student. Great hiding spots on campus include the Treehouse on the third floor of the Pembroke Center for Women's Studies. Complete with vaulted ceilings and a fireplace, the Treehouse reportedly got its name from the placards on the windows cautioning students to keep the windows closed, as the Treehouse is a favorite spot for squirrels and birds living in nearby trees. Other good study places include the "Absolute Quiet Room" at the Rockefeller Library, known as "the Rock," and the back porch of Manning Hall, overlooking a green.

> **"There are PLENTY of attractive people here!"**

Surrounded by several bustling retail streets and a quiet residential neighborhood, Brownies report feeling safe on campus. Thayer and Wickenden Streets, downtown Providence, and quiet parks are all easily accessible from campus, and Boston is only 45 minutes and eight dollars away by bus. Several new buildings also add beauty to the campus. Smith-Buoyano is a newly renovated converted gym that now houses history and religion classes. "They even kept the stripes on the floor!" Macmillan is a new high-tech chemistry and environmental studies building, housing both classrooms and labs.

Dining In, Dining Out

Students' opinions regarding the meal plan were varied. "It's good—they have lots to choose from," said one. "It's a rip-off," said another. "Although the vegetarian options are good, the vegan options are terrible." Freshmen are required to purchase a meal plan, and students can choose to have as many as 20 meals per week and as few as 4. Each meal plan comes with a certain number of flex points, which can be used at other campus eateries such as the Blue Room, the Campus Market, or the Ivy Room. If you miss a meal your account is credited $3.50, which can be used toward a snack or late dinner, valid only that day. The food is "edible," and you can always find something to eat at "the Ratty," the main dining hall. If students get tired of dining hall fare, Providence has plenty of good restaurants. Louis, Paragon, and Tortilla Flats are all favorites, while Meeting Street Café is a favorite place to go on a date or just hang out. Spike's Hot Dogs is a campus tradition for late-night dining. Coffee Exchange, Starbucks, and Oceans provide good places to sit and enjoy a cup-o'-joe.

Students looking for hard-core school spirit will probably not find it at Brown. Though many of Brown's teams are quite successful, "there's not much school spirit." Both men's and women's crew have posted winning seasons recently, with the women winning the NCAA Championship in 2000. Football, women's hockey, and men's soccer are some of the more popular teams at Brown. Intramurals are reportedly "huge," with a sport for pretty much anybody.

Although the academic and social freedom found at Brown is not for everyone, students agree that it is the open-minded people and top-rate academics that make the experience worthwhile. "There is an eagerness to learn in a new way and to approach things in a new manner," said one student. The relaxed academic environment creates a community at Brown where students are free to discover their own interests, making for a diverse and stimulating college experience.—*Melissa J. Merritt*

FYI

The three best things about attending Brown are "the student body, the academic attitude, and the general attitude of friendliness and openness."

The three worst things about attending Brown are "the food, the lack of need-blind admissions, and the housing."

The three things that every student should do before graduating from Brown are "go to an Arch sing, camp out on the Main Green or in the SciLi, take a good class just for the hell of it for the love of the subject."

One thing I would have liked to have known before coming here is "the housing sucks."

Rhode Island School of Design

Address: 2 College Street; Providence, RI 02903

Phone: 401-454-6300

E-mail address: admissions@risd.edu

Web site URL: www.risd.edu

Founded: NA

Private or Public: private

Religious affiliation: none

Location: small city

Undergraduate enrollment: 1,847

Total enrollment: NA

Percent Male/Female: 40%/60%

Percent Minority: 18%

Percent African-American: 2%

Percent Asian: 11%

Percent Hispanic: 4%

Percent Native-American: 0.5%

Percent in-state/out-of-state: 9%/91%

Percent Pub HS: NA

Number of Applicants: 2,366

Percent Accepted: 38%

Percent Accepted who enroll: 43%

Entering: 385

Transfers: NA

Application Deadline: 15 Feb

Mean SAT: NA

Mean ACT: NA

Middle 50% SAT range: NA

Middle 50% ACT range: NA

3 Most popular majors: fine arts, graphic design and commercial art, industrial design

Retention: 94%

Graduation rate: 89%

On-campus housing: NA

Fraternities: NA

Sororities: NA

Library: NA

Tuition and Fees: $21,405 in; $21,405 out

Room and Board: $6,490

Financial aid, first-year: 95%

Students at more traditional liberal arts schools often stereotype art school students as strange idlers who don't do any real work. This is far from the truth at the Rhode Island School of Design. With a reputation as one of the premier art schools in the country, RISD (affectionately known as "rizdee") combines a rigorous art curriculum with traditional academic requirements.

Students are required to take three English classes, four art and architectural history classes, three courses in history, politics, or social science, and four liberal arts electives—in addition to the demanding studio courses required for the fine or applied arts majors. Because students can cross-register at Brown University after freshman year, the course selections are practically endless. However, only a handful of students actually take advantage of

the resources at the neighboring university, and the number of cross-registered courses for which a student can receive credit are limited. The largest departments at RISD are industrial design, graphic design, and architecture. The fine arts "suffer a little" because of this, but there is still a waiting list for all the fine arts departments.

Frosh Boot Camp

All RISD freshmen take the same foundation classes. The course load is heaviest during this first year, and as a result many feel that they have "no time to do anything social." One undergrad put it, "All of Freshman Foundation is hell . . . like boot camp, so after freshman year anything is a breeze." A deep sense of community develops as all freshmen collectively slave over their 2-D and 3-D drawing, art history, and English courses. One student said, "Since freshmen take all the same classes and live in the same dorm complex, we are all one, big happy family."

All freshmen must live in one of four halls in the quad. Each hall is coed by floor, and each floor accommodates 15 to 30 freshmen and an RA. Students have drafting tables in their rooms, and each floor also has a well-ventilated work room, TV room, and lounge. Residents say the work rooms are especially valued, since freshmen are not eligible for campus studio space. The South Hall is notable because it is equipped with air-conditioning. East Hall is reserved for people who agree not to smoke and to observe quiet hours; some students call this dorm the "hippie haven." However, designated smoking rooms are more difficult to obtain as a result of their popularity. Overworked freshmen find that their main social activity involves "just hanging out in the dorm."

RISD students are required to declare their major at the beginning of the second semester freshman year, which some feel is "way too soon." One student elaborated, "You have to choose before you have any substantial experience in your potential major."

Life after Freshman Year
Most students agree that RISD gets less intense after the grueling freshman year. Depending on their major, upperclassmen spend two to four afternoons per week in the studio, and divide their mornings and evenings between academic and technical classes. Although a demanding five-year program requires architecture students to "sleep in the studio," most other students work at home. "I always read in the guidebooks that RISD students don't go out, they only work," one student said. "To a certain extent, that is actually very true. But artwork is different from academic work in that you can talk with people while you do it, and you need to. It's essential to get feedback from people while you are working."

Professors serve as harsh critics at RISD. Although students acknowledge that professors must view their work not only as teachers but as professional artists, their criticism can be discouraging. "My photography professor was so harsh during his critiques," one photography major confided, "that I haven't picked up my camera in a week. I am going to start my final project soon and do it for me, not for him." Intensive studio settings in which students aren't fond of their professors can be frustrating, but students say they generally admire their professors and point out that the small classes foster strong relationships with faculty.

Breaks from the Routine
RISD undergrads rave about the six-week-long winter session between semesters, which allows them a greater degree of freedom. "You get to take classes that have nothing to do with your major," one student explained. "Plus, it gives you a little bit of breathing room—you're only in class three times a week, so it's a relief from the usual high pressure of RISD classes." Students also use these six weeks for more independent study, often traveling internationally.

> "Some people like RISD but realize they need more variety. People need to be very dedicated to feel happy here. But if you are interested in getting an education in art, then RISD is an amazing place."

RISD prides itself on exhibiting student work, and the campus art museum has added a wing to display its modern art collection. When it comes to libraries and athletics, however, most students rely upon Brown University's resources. RISD does have its own library, and the modest student center offers occasional student-taught dance and self-defense classes, but Brown's facilities are more extensive. RISD students are proud of their hockey team, however. Known for their losing record each season, the RISD Nads attract fans who love to shout, "Go Nads! Go Nads!"

Providence Provides
Most upperclassmen live off campus. The historic houses on Benefit Street are popular, but can be expensive—students who don't want to spend as much money live

closer to the Brown campus in the Fox Point neighborhood. Although this area is closer to the less affluent sections of Providence, students say they feel very safe. However, students may take advantage of the coordinated Brown and RISD shuttle buses that run until 3 A.M., or the 24-hour Brown escort service.

A student described Providence as "too big to be small-towny, but too small to be exciting." Restaurants in the Thayer Street section of town offer a more palatable alternative to RISD cafeteria fare, which many students call bland and expensive. Freshmen are required to purchase $1,500 worth of meal points a semester, with 40 percent of it refundable. RISD lets students transfer leftover meal points to the Pit, a snack bar that specializes in hamburgers and french fries. Another popular option is the Carrhaus, a student-run coffee shop with an eclectic menu including coffee, bagels, hummus, and ice cream.

Many RISD students report that their main extracurricular activities involve "working and smoking a lot of cigarettes." However, some students find time to participate in a broad range of activities outside of class, from teaching children's art classes in the Providence community to writing for RISD's fiction magazine, *Clerestory*, or for the joint Brown-RISD newspaper, the *College Hill*. More adventurous students join the daredevil Street Luging Club and roll downhill through town lying on skateboards.

Despite the low-key social scene, RISD students insist that there is always something to do. Providence is teeming with college students, and shops and restaurants thrive on student business. Boston and New York are both accessible by train or bus when students need a change of scene.

Not So Strange After All

While geographical backgrounds at RISD are diverse, socioeconomic ones are not. "Everyone comes from rich homes!" one student exclaimed. Another undergrad pointed out, "RISD divides all the money it gets from alumni among all the students and studio costs," so there isn't much left over for scholarships. Many students feel that this leads to a certain homogeneity on campus. "I thought an art school would be more accepting of an out-of-the-ordinary attitude," one undergrad said, "but I was surprised at how conservative the people I met were. People look weird and act liberal, but if you dug deeper, they probably would all be Republicans." However, it is generally agreed that the RISD students are "a neat crowd of people."

Students feel a deep connection to their school, and are proud of how respected a RISD education is in the art community. Quite a few students transfer out each year, however, so students have this advice for prospectives: "Some people like RISD but realize they need more variety. People need to be very dedicated to feel happy here. But if you are interested in getting an education in art, then RISD is an amazing place."—*Siddhartha Shukla and Staff*

FYI

The three best things about attending RISD are "fun people, professors with experience in the real world, and small classes."

The three worst things about attending RISD are "Freshman Foundation, no RISD library, hard work."

The three things that every student should do before graduating are "take a class at Brown, write for the paper, and go to a hockey game."

One thing I'd like to have known before coming here is "most people here have money."

University of Rhode Island

Address: 8 Ranger Road, Suite 1; Kingston, RI 02881-2020
Phone: 401-874-7000
E-mail address: uriadmit@uri.edu
Web site URL: www.uri.edu
Founded: 1892
Private or Public: public
Religious affiliation: none
Location: rural
Undergraduate enrollment: 10,223
Total enrollment: NA
Percent Male/Female: 44%/56%
Percent Minority: 13%

Percent African-American: 4%
Percent Asian: 4%
Percent Hispanic: 4%
Percent Native-American: 0.5%
Percent in-state/out-of-state: 69%/31%
Percent Pub HS: NA
Number of Applicants: 10,034
Percent Accepted: 75%
Percent Accepted who enroll: 29%
Entering: 2,199
Transfers: NA
Application Deadline: 1 Mar

Mean SAT: NA
Mean ACT: NA
Middle 50% SAT range: 490–590 V, 500–600 M
Middle 50% ACT range: NA
3 Most popular majors: NA
Retention: 77%
Graduation rate: 50%
On-campus housing: 42%
Fraternities: 6%
Sororities: 7%
Library: NA
Tuition and Fees: $4,928 in; $13,148 out
Room and Board: $6,378
Financial aid, first-year: NA

D id someone say par-tay? At URI everyone seems to be saying "party." However, the once top ranked party school apparently has started to lose some of its party animal charm. According to one student "URI isn't the party school it used to be." That is welcome news to an administration that has tried, in recent years, to quell the "Animal House" and focus more intently upon academics.

Hard-Core Curriculum

Party animals, don't pack your bags just yet. The University of Rhode Island does require its students to meet graduation requirements by taking courses in the natural sciences, fine arts, mathematics, languages, and social sciences. While this subject load may seem daunting, prospective students should not distress. The requirements, according to one sophomore, are "fairly easy if you pay attention in class and take semi-decent notes."

But be forewarned, introductory classes, especially at large state universities, can be ridiculously large. Some courses at URI enroll as many as 500 students. However, according to students, the average class size is 40 to 50 students. Certain majors also require its participants to take specific classes. Students rave about the Chemical Engineering and German departments in particular, and URI has long been known for its marine biology programs.

Again, a common problem at major universities is the glut of TAs teaching classes. While URI does try to ensure that courses are taught by professors, some students complained about the high number of TA-taught lecture courses. However, when the professors are present, and that is the majority of the time, they are easily approachable when the students make the effort.

For the more academically inclined graduate of the Rhode Island public school system, the University offers a rather impressive and prestigious honors program. The class sizes are generally smaller and the course load more rigorous. Students can apply directly after high school or after their freshman or sophomore years. Like most other universities, URI, extends to its students the possibility of study abroad that, for some Rhode Island–weary scholars, is a great chance to "escape and have a blast." URI also offers a "Centennial Scholarship" for motivated and qualified students that can provide the lucky few with a full ride. You know what that means, freshmen? More disposable income and leeway with the parents!

In terms of academic upgrades, the University of Rhode Island recently committed itself to building a new $9 million environmental studies center on the Kingston campus. The price tag includes a whopping $1 million federal grant.

URI also sponsors numerous academic lectures. Recent talks have centered on such topics as "Genetic Diversity of Life," "Global Youth Cultures," and "Vietnam." Lectures are popular options for academically inclined students.

Home Sweet Home

The campus of URI is a random smattering of gothic, colonial, and modern architecture. The Quad, at the center of campus, is picturesque and, at least according to one student, a great place to "do homework or have sex." The Quad is surrounded by academic buildings, while the Greek houses are relegated to the outskirts of the sprawling campus. Campus dorms, the student center, and the library were recently renovated. "The campus feels like it's brand spankin' new! I absolute love it!"

> "As a sophomore, I'm already dreading having to leave here."

The dorms at Rhode Island get mixed reviews. However, one enthusiastic student stated that her dorm "had a large common room, which we can easily veg out in." All dorms, save one, are coed by floor. There is an all-female dorm for those interested. For the non–substance-using students there is a "Wellness Dorm" that prohibits smoking and drinking. Sorority and frat houses are also popular options for upperclassmen. Many upperclassmen complain about the inadequacy of on-campus housing. However, one of the best options available for upperclassman housing are the apartments along the nearby beach. Surf's up!

After a hard day's night in the library students can chow down at one of URI's three main dining rooms or the oft-praised "Ram's Den." Several meal plans are available to URI students, including a 10-, 15-, or 20-meal plan. At the Ram's Den students use food points purchased at the beginning of the semester to buy the delectable goodies offered at "by far the best food joint on campus." The other dining halls vary, with some serving fast food and others serving actual entrees. The Den offers some well liked grilled entrees. The university has made strides recently in helping to provide for the needs of its vegetarian students. Despite the improvements in dining students still complain about the lack of weekend service.

One student described the town of Kingston, "It's like Disney World without the rides and wonderful Florida climate." Drinking is the only thing that seems to dull the monotony of this one-horse town nestled in the vast wilderness of Rhode Island. Yet, some students relish the small-town setting, describing it as "the ideal little college town!" But where do students crash after a hearty night of hard drinking and wild fun?

Getting Soaked on a Dry Campus

The official administration policy is one of "no alcohol." But according to most students on campus the university is wet to the point of deluge. As with most large state universities, Greek life is the dominant form of social activity on campus. All parties must be registered with the university police but this has not drastically altered the availability of alcohol. One student loudly exclaimed, "Rams party more than study." This, of course, results in the non-drinkers feeling ostracized from the mainstream and has spurred animosity between Greek and non-Greek students. Luckily for those not interested in the frat scene, the University does have an entertainment committee that brings in speakers, theatrical productions, and concerts to campus.

Extracurricular activities are also major parts of student's lives here on campus. Basketball and football games are particularly popular draws especially when URI is playing cross state rival Providence College. Other notable sports teams are the baseball, volleyball, soccer, and sailing team. The sailing team has earned numerous national and international distinctions.

Student senate and the student-run newspaper, *The Five Cent Cigar*, also garner favorable attention on campus. One of the more fascinating clubs at URI is the Experimental Art Society that sponsors such activities as film production and instrument production. The perennial favorite Surf Club also holds September lessons for surfing novices.

The political atmosphere on URI's campus is one of liberal toleration. Racial issues do occasionally surface on campus as a result of several racially self-segregated dorms. Student groups are attempting to combat this problem. A large part of the student body is also comprised of commuters who live nearby and drive to school.

Overall, despite academics playing second fiddle to social life, many students say that URI offers its motivated students a healthy learning experience and for all students a positive college experience. "As a sophomore, I'm already dreading having to leave here. I *LOVE* this place—and it was actually my last choice in high school. Give URI a chance, you won't regret it."—*Sean McBride and Staff*

FYI

The three best things about attending URI are "the friendly and diverse student body, inexpensive cost of living, and the professors who are willing to help with just about anything."

The three worst things about attending URI are "the lack of student involvement, there's nothing to do on weekends (except drink), and the majority of students commute."

The three things everyone should do before graduating from URI are "to take part in Homecoming, to run naked across the Quad, and to change their major at least once."

One thing I'd like to have known before coming here is " that URI ain't as much a party school anymore!"

South Carolina

Address: 105 Sikes Hall; Clemson, SC 29634-5124
Phone: 864-656-2287
E-mail address: NA
Web site URL: www.clemson.edu
Founded: 1889
Private or Public: public
Religious affiliation: none
Location: rural
Undergraduate enrollment: 13,375
Total enrollment: 16,396
Percent Male/Female: 55%/45%
Percent Minority: 10%
Percent African-American: 8%
Percent Asian: 1%

Percent Hispanic: 0.5%
Percent Native-American: 0.5%
Percent in-state/out-of-state: 71%/29%
Percent Pub HS: 90%
Number of Applicants: 9,501
Percent Accepted: 68%
Percent Accepted who enroll: 45%
Entering: 2,893
Transfers: 1,151
Application Deadline: 1 May
Mean SAT: 564 V, 581 M
Mean ACT: NA
Middle 50% SAT range: 520–620 V, 540–640 M

Middle 50% ACT range: 23–27
3 Most popular majors: mechanical engineering, marketing, elementary education
Retention: 84%
Graduation rate: 71%
On-campus housing: 96%
Fraternities: 15%
Sororities: 25%
Library: 1,400,000 volumes
Tuition and Fees: $3,470 in; $9,456 out
Room and Board: $4,122
Financial aid, first-year: 19%

To the casual observer, it might appear that there are many ways in which a student at Clemson would be prevented from graduating. Take, for example, Calhoun Mansion, where, legend has it, any student who takes a tour will never receive his or her degree from the university. Another calls to mind the plaque on the statue of Thomas Green Clemson. It is said that if a student reads this, he or she doesn't stand a chance of graduating. Yet another legend points to the names of previous graduates etched on campus sidewalks, saying that if a student steps on his or her own last name, he or she is destined never to graduate. Despite these terrors, Clemson is attracting a lot of bright young minds and was named *Time* magazine's Public School of the Year in 2000.

From Farms to Foreign Languages

Clemson offers its students a wide variety of academic options, from the popular yet reputedly challenging computer science and engineering majors to Parks, Recreation, and Tourism Management, which is also known by students as Party Right Through May. Students are required to fulfill general education requirements, including a certain amount of class hours in most general subjects, which encompass oral communication, writing, and computer skills. The requirements aren't too limiting and, as one student simply put it,

"Yes, there are academic requirements. They are fair."

Clemson students are placed in one of five colleges according to major. Two of the more popular are the College of Engineering and Science and the College of Architecture, Arts and Humanities. Engineering and computer science are traditionally large majors, while agriculture retains a strong following due to the university's original role as an agricultural school. Other majors, however, are capped each year.

Most Clemson students offer few complaints when it comes to academics. Being a large state university, Clemson offers many options. Some students do say, however, that it is sometimes difficult to get into certain classes. Others note that some "professors can't speak English" and that this precludes any possible relationship, especially when many classes are taught by teaching assistants. Still others praise the ability of their professors, and one commented that "all professors give out their home phone numbers in case you have questions."

Eat, Drink, and . . . Drink

The typical Clemson student, most will tell you, can be described as "a flat-out conservative southerner." The city of Clemson, South Carolina, is definitely a college town, and most students agree that "the town wouldn't be here if it wasn't for the students." Many head into town on Friday and Saturday nights, generally choosing to stay on campus during the week. Bars in downtown Clemson, however, close at midnight due to blue laws. There are two private bars that close at two, and "they are packed after midnight." After the bars close downtown, students generally have parties fondly known as Twelve-Oh-Ones. One student comments that Clemson has an "affinity for ticketing underage drinkers," and most drinking occurs off campus, though there is an on-campus bar. Many Clemson students do have cars, although most complain about the significant lack of parking. According to one student, anyone with a car "more than likely already has one or two parking tickets this year."

While many students choose not to live on campus, there are a variety of on-campus dorms. The average freshman dorm is "single-sex . . . and you can loft the beds," said one student. Another commented, "I lived in the crappiest dorm but had the best time and met the greatest girls." Others agree, saying that dorms are where students often meet their best friends. All dorms have residential advisors, but students report that female dorms tend to have stricter visiting policies and rules. There are also many coed dorms, most of which are divided by floor. In addition, honor students may live in their own dorm, known as Holmes Hall, which comes complete with a kitchen in each four-person suite.

Clemson is currently undergoing a "building period," including a renovation of older buildings, the construction of three new dorms, and a recently completed student union. The campus itself is very large, and as one student commented, "Be prepared to build up your legs—it's a big campus and there are a bunch of hills." Clemson has a variety of food choices for students and a recently improved meal plan. There are two dining halls, a restaurant-type dining hall, a canteen, two cafés, and a food court. Students agree that there are many options, "even for those with a vegetarian bent." One student especially praised the desserts in the cafeterias, saying, "Clemson makes its own ice cream, and it's awesome!"

Orange-Blooded Greeks

Ask average Clemson students what they look forward to most, and you will almost always get the same answer: football. Tiger football is not only huge on campus but also well respected across the country. Besides being "very friendly and willing to help anyone with anything," Clemson students also have something else in common: as one student put it, "My blood runneth orange." During the fall, claimed one student, "it's all about football." Said another: "When there are eighty-six thousand people in Death Valley (the stadium) and the football players come running down the hill, you can't hear the person next to you." As football players enter the stadium, they rub Howard's Rock, originally from Death Valley, California. When players rub the rock, "they are pledging that they will give 110% during the game."

The athletics program at Clemson is such a strong force that it is also heavily supported financially. Most Clemson students are familiar with IPTAY Collegiate Club. Begun in 1934 when Dr. Rupert H. Fike organized the first athletic support group, IPTAY has grown into the largest athletic support group in the nation. It stands for "I Pay Ten [Dollars] A Year," and while the contribution figure has risen significantly, IPTAY has continued to be a powerful force on campus, developing an athletic scholarship endowment and rebuilding athletic facilities.

Although athletes are an important force on campus, most students say that with the large student population, they do not overpower campus life. "You always have classes with athletes and they are treated the same as students," one person commented. There are also a lot of opportunities for non-varsity sports, including intramurals and clubs. In general, most students say there is little division among students. There are cliques, most say, but everyone can find their own niche. One student describes Clemsonites as "aware of image but not slaves to it." One also said that while the school is furthering diversity, there are still "too many white southerners." Others disagree, saying that the most important factor on campus is that students are "Tiger fans and extremely proud to be at Clemson."

"My blood runneth orange."

There is a significantly large Greek life on campus, which, according to campus publications, involves about 25% of the student body. "Rushing is time-consuming, but not really difficult or embarrassing," said one student. The Greek system includes business fraternities, community service sororities, and large social fraternities and sororities. There are Greek houses on each end of campus, although technically sororities cannot have houses thanks to "a really ignorant state law that a house with more than four girls living in it is considered a brothel." As one student put it, "Greek life is hugely integral to Clemson life."

In sum, Clemson provides its students with an accommodating academic program, a nice campus, and lots of school spirit. So much, in fact, that many students would agree that never graduating may not actually be so bad a fate.—*Jessamyn Blau*

FYI

The three best things about attending Clemson are "the parties, the football, and the parties for football."

The three worst things about attending Clemson are "the lack of a big city nearby, some of the dorms aren't so great, and the lack of parking."

The three things that every student should do before graduating from Clemson are "have a night they do not fully remember, attend a Greek life function, and learn how to love independence."

One thing I'd like to have known before coming here is "that home football games are such an event—and that I'd love it so much!"

Furman University

Address: 3300 Poinsett
Highway; Greenville, SC
29613
Phone: 864-294-2034
E-mail address:
admissions@furman.edu
Web site URL:
www.furman.edu
Founded: 1826
Private or Public: private
Religious affiliation: none
Location: small city
**Undergraduate
enrollment:** 2,812
Total enrollment: 2,840
Percent Male / Female:
45%/55%
Percent Minority: 9%
Percent African-American:
5%

Percent Asian: 2%
Percent Hispanic: 1%
Percent Native-American:
0.5%
**Percent in-state / out-of-
state:** 31%/69%
Percent Pub HS: 75%
Number of Applicants:
3,200
Percent Accepted:
66%
**Percent Accepted who
enroll:** 33%
Entering: 684
Transfers: 56
Application Deadline:
1 Feb
Mean SAT: 622 V,
626 M
Mean ACT: NA

Middle 50% SAT range:
570–670 V,
580–670 M
Middle 50% ACT range:
25–30
3 Most popular majors:
political science, business
administration, biology
Retention: 91%
Graduation rate: 79%
On-campus housing:
98%
Fraternities: 30%
Sororities: 35%
Library: 390,000 volumes
Tuition and Fees:
$19,152 in; $19,152 out
Room and Board: $5,144
Financial aid, first-year:
42%

Few universities give their students the opportunity to receive a top-notch education on a campus recognized by the American Society of Landscape Architects as one of the most beautifully landscaped areas in the country. Located on a spacious 750-acre campus nearby Greenville, South Carolina, Furman University offers just this. Furman students will tell you that their campus is truly remarkable, but they will also be quick to note that their challenging course load doesn't leave them too much time to stop and smell the roses.

The Secret of My Success

The campus might be a park, but classes at Furman are no picnic. Academics are a "top priority" here. Paladins take pride in the high quality and challenging nature of their academic program. The stress put on academics has its downside though, as many feel that grading is overly harsh. Students commonly expressed feelings like "I am here to get a better than average education, so the work is something I expect, but I feel like the professors are a little too hard on students at times when it comes to papers and tests." Indeed, Fur-

man professors are notorious for limiting the amount of As given out in their classes, but are otherwise highly praised. Students like the fact that professors teach all classes and TAs only hold tutoring sessions. Just to emphasize this point, one student retorted, "What's a TA look like? I've never even seen one around." Under this system, classes average around 20 students—"nice and small, so everyone can get to know everyone else"—and students can generally get into any class they want to take.

Furman ensures that each of its students receive a well-rounded liberal arts education by requiring a large dose of general-education classes. Ranging from English Composition and Intro to Biblical Literature to Principles of Biology, the wide scope of the General Education Requirement, or GER, lays a solid foundation of learning for each and every Paladin. For the most part, students do not seem to mind this program and take advantage of their required classes to figure out exactly what they want to study. Integrated into the gen-ed curriculum is the Cultural Life Program, which seeks to expose each and every Paladin to a broad range of cultural events throughout the school year. Students can choose to attend events ranging from lectures on the crisis in Kosovo to a performance by the Furman Symphony Orchestra. They must attend 9 CLPs per year, for a total of 36, in order to graduate.

The academic year at Furman is split into an uneven trimester system that students either love or hate. During the three-month-long fall and spring sessions each student takes three 50-minute classes that meet every day. Between the fall and spring, there is a two-month winter session during which students take only two classes, but meet every day for 75 minutes. This "wacko trimester system," as described by one student, "is really a blessing in disguise. Having so few classes at a time really lets me concentrate on the ones I'm taking, and the transition in schedule between the three trimesters keeps things new and fresh." One student exclaimed, "I can't even imagine taking more than three classes at a time!"

However, for every happy comment about the course load, there is a complaint about the way in which this system affects vacation time. "Yeah, spring break is always a blast when you get let out in mid-February," griped one student. Another student grumbled, "Whenever I'm out of class, my non-Furman friends are in, and vice versa. It's really a pain."

A Place in the Sun

Furman students do not have any problem finding activities to keep them busy in their spare time. In fact, the only complaint you might hear around campus is that they have too many things going on at once. Two of the most popular groups on campus are Furman University Student Activities Boards (FUSAB) and Collegiate Educational Service Corp. (CESC). FUSAB acts to coordinate different social, cultural, recreational, and educational activities for students. Events planned by FUSAB include Homecoming, Parent's Day, and the annual music-filled bacchanalia, the Spring Weekend. Also, the body is in charge of attracting local and national performers to the campus. FUSAB has been extremely proud to host Dave Matthews and Tim Reynolds. Prospective FUSAB members must apply to join. Still,

the organization continually keeps its ear to the ground by asking any and all students for suggestions.

CESC is the campus's major community service organization, with an emphasis on the word "major." With more than 1,500 members active in some capacity on the campus, 70 percent of the Furman population has worked for the CESC on one project or another. Under the large CESC umbrella, there are more than 80 agencies that serve the public. These programs range from Child Enrichment and Book Buddies to Big Brother/Big Sister and Church Ministries. The organization also hosts workshops on subjects such as child management and working with the elderly at its yearly High Rocks conference. Plus, the CESC puts on the annual May Day Play when Furman volunteers invite all the kids and adults that participate in CESC programs come to the campus for a day of fun, food, and games.

With more than one third of students involved in a fraternity or sorority, the Greek scene on campus is large, though nonintrusive—"going Greek at Furman is good for those who want it, but not a big deal for those who don't." Furman has no fraternity or sorority houses, and since students must live on campus for at least three years, it's impossible for Greeks to self-segregate. As one female student explained, "my dorm hall has about the same number of sorority and nonsorority girls, and all but one of the sororities are represented, so that shows you just how mixed the population is." This commingling helps make the Greek scene at Furman inclusive, and results in annual parties like Biker Bash and Beach Weekend that are open to all students.

However, because the campus is dry, most parties occur off campus. Students also frequently head to dance clubs in Greenville. Although putting a damper on the social lives of some students, the dry campus rule is not looked at as a major obstacle by most. "For drinkers, where there's a will there's a way" was the claim of one upperclassman, "and we also have a relatively high percentage of nondrinkers who aren't affected anyway." Said another, "Nondrinkers do not feel out of place. If anything, drinkers feel out of place when first introduced to Furman. The great thing is that many people who do not drink party just as hard as those who do!"

What, Me Play Sports?
Football season at Furman does not receive as much attention as at some of the bigger southeastern universities, but the student population at this Division I-AA school is still very involved in athletics. The university's 17 varsity teams attract recruits in most major sports, while club and intramural teams satisfy those with a hunger for sports like rugby, Ultimate Frisbee, and lacrosse. Students rate each other as "very fit and health conscious," and joggers and Rollerbladers can be seen cruising around the scenic campus at all hours of the day.

> "[Furman is] just like that *Cheers* song where 'everybody knows your name.'"

Being health conscious is just one way in which the average Paladin blends in with his or her peers. "There is definitely a lack of diversity in the student body," noted one sophomore, "upper middle-class conservative white kids walking around in North Face jackets are pretty much the norm." Another joked that "Everyone here has a car, although you don't need one since everyone here has a car . . . and fitting in is as simple as these three words: sport utility vehicle." Students also consider one another attractive, yet for some mysterious reason there is little dating on the campus. One student noted that "some people might have significant others, but I never see anyone holding hands or anything like that," while another commented that "it seems like people are only married or totally single, with nothing in between."

Life Is Beautiful
When comments like "this is the most beautiful place you will ever spend four years of your life" are so common, it can only mean that students are happy with their campus. Students love Furman's exquisite park-like environment and the atmosphere it creates. Visitors are greeted by a row of huge oak trees separating the

main road from acres of well-manicured grass lawns. Once through the front gates, two large fountains and groups of students studying or playing Frisbee mark the center of campus between Daniel Chapel and Duke Library. Redbrick colonial–style buildings dot a landscape that's centered on a small lake that is famous for birthday dunkings. Nearby, visitors can take in the beauty of the campus rose garden and quaint Japanese teahouse.

Living Single
For those who do spend four years of their life at Furman, dorming and dining are a top priority. Many seniors take advantage of off-campus apartments, but all other students must live in university-provided housing. With two exceptions, all dorms are single sex. Most men live in the five buildings of South Housing, while the women live in Lakeside Housing. All freshman halls have at least four upperclassman RAs and freshman advisors. Most dorms have community bathrooms, although some buildings are arranged in suites with one bathroom for every two rooms. Juniors and seniors have the option of residing in the highly regarded North Village Apartments, which provide on-campus living with an off-campus feel. Here, roommates share newly built apartments that contain four singles and two baths. All dorms have visitation rules that many students consider harsh. No one is allowed in an opposite-sex building past midnight on weekdays and two in the morning on weekends, and though the rule is enforced, one student confided that "people break it all the time and are never caught."

The word most often used by students to describe their dining hall is "decent." "You know, I've seen much worse, but for some reason the cooks think that everything has to be fried," was how one student depicted the situation at Charles E. Daniel Dining Hall. Overall though, students consider their food selection pretty diverse. Meal plans come with a points system allowing students the alternative of eating at the food court instead of the dining hall, and there are plenty of fast-food options around campus. Additionally, those willing to make the 15-minute drive into Greenville can visit either the mall or the "strip" for a great assortment of local and national restaurants.

The Furman Show
If your college-shopping list includes high academic standards and immaculate scenery, Furman might be just what you're looking for. Small enrollment and intimate classes make for an environment

that's "just like that *Cheers* song where 'everybody knows your name,'" remarked one satisfied sophomore. Those who do choose to spend their college years at Furman try not to let the breathtaking campus keep them from their studies, but in such an outgoing and friendly atmosphere, even these high-achievers have their work cut out for them.—*Robert Berschinski*

FYI

The three best things about attending Furman are that "the people are so nice, the campus is beautiful, and the students are very involved."

The three worst things about attending Furman are "students have to live on campus for three years, getting an A in a class is overly hard, and it is so pretty visitors use it as a park."

The three things that every student should do before graduating from Furman are "get thrown in the lake on their birthday, fountain hop, and work for the CESC."

One thing I'd like to have known before coming here is "there is so much to do that a lot of people overcommit and stress out."

University of South Carolina

Address: Columbia, SC 29208
Phone: 803-777-7700
E-mail address: admissions-ugrad@sc.edu
Web site URL: www.sc.edu
Founded: 1801
Private or Public: public
Religious affiliation: none
Location: small city
Undergraduate enrollment: 14,403
Total enrollment: 23,430
Percent Male/Female: 45%/55%
Percent Minority: 24%
Percent African-American: 19%
Percent Asian: 3%

Percent Hispanic: 1%
Percent Native-American: 0.5%
Percent in-state/out-of-state: 16%/84%
Percent Pub HS: NA
Number of Applicants: 10,162
Percent Accepted: 67%
Percent Accepted who enroll: 39%
Entering: 2,668
Transfers: 983
Application Deadline: NA
Mean SAT: 550 V, 548 M
Mean ACT: 24
Middle 50% SAT range: 490–610 V, 490–610 M

Middle 50% ACT range: 20–27
3 Most popular majors: experimental psychology, engineering, biology
Retention: 81%
Graduation rate: 60%
On-campus housing: 82%
Fraternities: 13%
Sororities: 13%
Library: 3,143,505 volumes
Tuition and Fees: $3,740 in; $9,814 out
Room and Board: $4,167
Financial aid, first-year: 41%

If you were asked to find a cocky student at the University of South Carolina, you would probably be hard-pressed to do so. You would, however, certainly find "Cocky," the big red mascot that leads the South Carolina Gamecocks in spirit at the football games. Football is, without doubt, the most popular sport on campus, with near full attendance at each game. And though Williams Brice Stadium is

packed every weekend in the fall, students at the University of South Carolina are also busily engaged in extremely diverse studies.

Varied Studies
One of South Carolina's greatest assets is the range of course options it offers. While most students lean toward the study of traditional subjects in the College

of Liberal Arts or the College of Science and Mathematics, they can also pursue degrees in more unique fields by attending the School of Applied Professions, which includes hotel, restaurant, and tourism administration, or the School of Library and Information Sciences. Students unanimously agree that the College of Business is probably the strongest program. "International business is especially strong; it was ranked number one in the country," said one freshman. Another student stated that "the journalism school is also pretty good for our region." Regardless of the school chosen, all students at USC have a number of requirements to complete. Each student must have a complete year of basic science and must take English 101 and 102, although these requirements may be waved through AP work. They must also study a year's worth of social sciences and humanities. For many majors, another required class is University 101. This class for freshmen is an introduction to college life, covering such topics as sex and how to study effectively. Although not reported to be a difficult class, one freshman said that many students "have lots of complaints about it. It's a cheesy waste of time and you have to do a lot of mindless work." After these requirements, it is necessary to begin taking classes in the major.

For the most part, students are happy with their professors, although they are not always so pleased with the classes themselves. This disappointment is an outcome of the school's registration system, which sometimes precludes students from getting into the classes they want. One freshman exclaimed that the registration system "is a pain! It's a frustrating time because so many of the classes fill up fast, and if you miss your appointment time, it's a mess." The only redeeming aspect of the registration process, according to another student, is that "you can do it over the computer, so that's kind of helpful." Aside from scheduling difficulties, the major grievance regarding classes is the size. "Sometimes they are just too large," said one junior. Introductory classes generally run about 150 to 200 students at minimum. Past the introductory level, however, many students said that smaller classes are available. Nevertheless, students are enthusiastic about their studies and, according to one freshman, so are the professors. "A lot of my professors are very enthusiastic about what they do. They want to make the class interesting because they know a lot of nonmajors end up taking their class." While there appears to be an overabundance of TAs, one student said, "There may be a lot, but they're good TAs. I haven't really run into any bad ones." Most TAs are older graduate students rather than those just having received their bachelor's degree. TAs rarely teach classes, but lead discussion groups for larger classes or facilitate laboratory work. In general, USC students assert that academics are very strong and any course of study is worthwhile.

So-So Social Options

While the view of academics is rather universal, the view of social life is not. Regarding USC, a junior stated that "academics is fine, but social life stinks," while one freshman said, "There's something for everyone here." Most students find that social options are adequate. One student said that "Columbia is a nice place. You can go see plays, movies, and the like." A popular hangout is Five Points, an area with lots of bars and eating establishments. Some students enjoy going to Tombstone, a local country dance club, but as one student said, "that's very South Carolina." Other students, many of whom live in South Carolina, chose to leave Columbia over the weekend, preferring the social life in their respective hometowns.

On campus, there do not seem to be as many options. Most campus activities are limited to guest lecturers, ranging from Spike Lee to various academics. The University also recently hosted an academic conference on the Civil War. Students looking for less academically geared activities take advantage of a campus cable channel that shows movies every day. Greek life is rather prevalent on campus, but, as one non-Greek freshman said, "I don't feel at all like I'm out of the loop. It's not a school where you have to fit in to have a social life." As for drugs on campus, one student said, "It's such a big campus that I'm sure there's some of it going on, but I've never seen it myself."

Because USC is located in a southern

state, most students joke that the school is full of "a lot of sweet, hospitable southern people." Even so, South Carolina also plays home to many international students and northeners. One freshman commented that USC is "made up of all different kinds of people." However, another student complained that "there always seems to be a black/white kind of thing. It's bothersome that our society hasn't moved on from that. It seems the people always move their own ways." Even so, one student said that "my next-door neighbors are from Philadelphia and South Carolina. Being with them has expanded my horizon by getting to know people I would have never met."

Living Arrangements

Regardless of home state or ethnicity, most South Carolina students make on-campus dormitories their home. One student simply commented that "the dorms aren't bad, depending on the building. Some of them have high ceilings so you can install lofts." Another plus is that all the dorms have air conditioning, so that the muggy South Carolina air is bearable during the spring and summer. Most freshmen live in the Towers, a group of coed dorms, though there is also one all-male dorm. The rooms there were described as "less than stellar" by one freshman, but bearable. Women searching for all-female housing can be placed in McClintock, Simms, or Wade-Hampton dorms. Coed dorms have men living on one side, while the women live on the other. Most dorms have a strict policy restricting visitors of the opposite sex to the hours of from 10 A.M. to 2 A.M. "That's plenty of time to visit, but in the coed dorms, it's usually pretty easy to sneak visitors in," said one upperclassman. The best on-campus housing is reportedly the apartment complex called the South Quad or the Horseshoe apartments, usually reserved for upperclassmen.

While most students are pretty satisfied with their living arrangements, there are still complaints. Some students have also had problems with bugs in their rooms, but as another student aptly pointed out, "Don't come to the South if you don't like roaches!" To avoid hassles like these, many students move off campus, although "you don't feel a need to move off campus. It's not dorky to live on campus at all," said one sophomore. Students living off campus, though, usually invest in a car as many apartment complexes are not within walking distance of the campus. Be forewarned, however, that "parking is the biggest pain in the butt!" as one student put it. A car is also a must for off-campus students because "Columbia has a horrible public transportation system."

Good Food on a Great Campus

Though many students gripe about housing, few complain about campus food. USC has many places to eat, the most frequented being the Grand Market Place. "It's cafeteria-style, but you can get sandwiches and other hot food. It is a little expensive, though," said one student. Students in a rush usually find the food court below the Grand Market Place extremely helpful, where they can dine at Taco Bell, Sub City, and Freshen's Yogurt. Other dining options on campus include the Roost, the Bates, and the Patio, although for some students it is a long hike to get to these facilities. Students do have a few complaints about the dining system hours. "For any-place that's all-you-can-eat, there's only a two-hour window when it's open," said one freshman. Another source of discontent is the meal plan, in which each student purchases a specific number of meals each week, ranging from 10 to 21. But, as one sophomore complained, "If you don't use a meal, it goes to waste." There are decent vegetarian options, but one student said "the dining halls don't really cater to vegetarians." Students do go off campus to eat occasionally, but as one student said, "There's really a variety on campus. Why spend money?"

> "It's a nice mix between a secluded campus, but with the advantages of a city," said one student.

The campus itself is in the middle of downtown Columbia. However, according to one student, "It's really it's own little place. It's very defined, even though it's spread out." The heart of the campus is called the Horseshoe; it is a big open courtyard-like area where "people come and jog, lay out in the sun, and just relax," reported one undergrad. USC will soon boast a new state-of-the-art physical education center as well as a new science building. Recent additions have included a new law center and the South Quad dorm. As for safety, one student said, "it's really safe as far as big schools go." Most students claim to feel safe knowing that there are call stations all over campus in case trouble should arise. One freshman said, "Use common sense and you'll be fine." Most USC students enjoy being on campus and find that while the campus is in the city, it does not exude a big-city feel. "It's a nice mix between a secluded campus, but with the advantages of a city," said one student.

Clubs and Sports

South Carolina is a very active campus. The Greek system is strong, and so are a number of ethnic clubs, including a chapter of the NAACP. Community service is extremely popular, exemplified by such clubs as Carolina for Kids, in which students go into local schools to tutor and play with local children. "Everyone is involved to a point. Many people pick one club to do on campus that they really enjoy," said one student. Other clubs include those concerned with athletics, including aerobics, bodybuilding, and fencing.

As for sports, football is, without question, the most anticipated sport of the year. USC students regularly attend football games, starting with tailgating hours before a game begins. Describing the weekly ritual, one student said, "everyone gets dressed up and then it's like a migration to Williams Brice Stadium. There's a lot of school spirit." After football, students say basketball is probably the most followed sport on campus. The USC basketball team has traditionally performed well in its conference. For non-varsity athletics, students participate in intramurals or go to the Blatt Center, where "you have your choice of treadmills, stair-climber machines, and a pool too."

The University of South Carolina is an extremely large school, which sometimes serves as a point of criticism for many students. However, with a large school also comes numerous educational and extracurricular activities. A freshman, who thought going to a big school would be a problem said, "I haven't found that to be true. You find your own little niche in a group of people. You don't have to belong to a certain group. You find your own way."
—*Shu-Ping Shen and Staff*

FYI
The three best things about attending USC are "the mascot, good cafeteria food, and surprising diversity."
The three worst things about attending USC are "bugs, parking, and registration."
The three things that every student should do before graduating from USC are "paint a letter on your chest for a football game, dance at Tombstone, and tan on the quad."
One thing I'd like to have known before coming here is "how useful a car would be."

Wofford College

Address: 429 North Church Street; Spartanburg, SC 29303-3663
Phone: 864-597-4130
E-mail address: admissions@wofford.edu
Web site URL: www.wofford.edu
Founded: 1854
Private or Public: private
Religious affiliation: United Methodist
Location: small city
Undergraduate enrollment: 1,094
Total enrollment: 1,094
Percent Male/Female: 53%/47%
Percent Minority: 11%

Percent African-American: 9%
Percent Asian: 1%
Percent Hispanic: 0.5%
Percent Native-American: 0.5%
Percent in-state/out-of-state: 63%/37%
Percent Pub HS: 75%
Number of Applicants: 1,279
Percent Accepted: 85%
Percent Accepted who enroll: 28%
Entering: 307
Transfers: 15
Application Deadline: 1 Feb
Mean SAT: 590 V, 600 M
Mean ACT: 24

Middle 50% SAT range: 540–610 V, 540–650 M
Middle 50% ACT range: 22–27
3 Most popular majors: biology, finance, business economics
Retention: 90%
Graduation rate: 82%
On-campus housing: 96%
Fraternities: 56%
Sororities: 59%
Library: 192,776 volumes
Tuition and Fees: $17,730 in; $17,730 out
Room and Board: $5,235
Financial aid, first-year: 55%

When the Rev. Benjamin Wofford of Spartanburg, South Carolina, passed away, he left money to found a college "for literary, classical and scientific education." One hundred and fifty years later, Wofford College still stands as a bastion of solid education in an environment designed to nurture personal growth and experience.

A Select Education
Founded in 1854 and still affiliated with the United Methodist Church, Wofford has remained small by choice. The administration reportedly has no plans to expand enrollment but instead plans to concentrate on providing a select group of students with a strong education in the humanities, arts, and sciences. Professors are accessible and maintain an "open-door policy," according to students. Undergrads are required to take courses in the humanities, English, fine arts, foreign language, science, history, philosophy, math, physical education, and religion. These general education requirements are meant to ensure that by the end of their first two years, students have taken classes they normally would not have considered. Students are also required to complete four interim projects. The month of January is Interim, when students can research, travel, take an internship, or work on an independent

project. Among the most popular majors at Wofford are biology, business, chemistry, English, and history. The science department is reported to be particularly strong, with "most students getting into their first or second choice of medical schools," according to one undergrad. Students also recommend the philosophy and zoology introductory courses.

Wofford's active student body puts their full support behind their impressive athletics program. As part of the deal, Wofford built a brand-new athletic complex, the Richardson Physical Activities Building, which opened in the summer of 1995. Wofford basketball, football, and soccer games already draw crowds, especially when the Terriers play rivals Citadel or Presbyterian College. "Student interest tends to drop off a bit when one of the teams is not performing well," one student said, "but overall, we are very proud of our sports teams."

Using New Technology
The F. W. Olin Building is one of Wofford's most prized possessions. Designed as a model for integrating technology in teaching the liberal arts, this state-of-the-art academic building houses high-tech audiovisual equipment, ultramodern language labs, computer science facilities (including the computer center for the school's network), and classrooms. Plans

for a new science building are also in the works. "The older buildings on campus are always kept in good shape," one student said.

> **"No one here is just a number."**

Students seem content with Wofford's living conditions, and few of them choose to live off campus. A new all-female dorm gets good reviews for its two-room suites, and Dupree is considered one of the best and most social dorms for upperclassmen. Many students consider Marsh dormitory to be Wofford's least popular: it houses first-year male students, and the lack of privacy (especially in the huge bathrooms) is the biggest complaint. "The guys who live there get rowdy a lot and the place usually ends up getting trashed after a while," one student said. The fraternity houses are not residential.

Social Life
The Greek system is strong at Wofford, although kegs are banned from campus. Students say they usually have no problem finding parties off campus if there isn't anything happening on fraternity row. "There is some pressure to join a frat, but that's only because rush period starts three weeks into the fall semester," one student said. Pressure to rush is reportedly heavier among Wofford men than women.

Wofford students tend to describe their classmates as "interesting and colorful." Although the majority of Wofford students are from South Carolina, a large percentage come from other southeastern states. Before the school went coed, its name brought to mind the image of the "Wofford Man," which one student said was a "cultured, well-liked individual—a southern gentleman." Today Wofford students preserve their traditions, but they point out that the school now "prides itself on progressive thinking." Not too progressive, however: Wofford students and administrators alike tend to be politically conservative, although one undergrad said the administration is "liberal enough to let the students do what they want." "Clashes at Wofford don't last very long. There isn't a lot of activism here," one senior reported. Life at Wofford is best described as "mellow"; life moves a bit slower than in big cities, and the atmosphere on campus is relaxed. "Wofford students are not afraid to look a campus visitor in the eye and say hello," one student said. "The school is small enough so that you know almost everyone. No one here is just a number." One student reported that it is not unusual for undergrads to "give the president of the college a high-five as he walks by."

Living in the South
The city of Spartanburg, which students describe as a "blue-collar town," offers a reasonable variety of restaurants and entertainment at low prices. It is a place where you can "find a K-mart very easily, but not a Banana Republic," one student said. The city is no bustling metropolis, but one student predicted that a new BMW manufacturing plant has the potential to "turn Spartanburg into another Raleigh."

According to undergrads, Wofford offers a friendly southern environment and a solid education, particularly for those considering a career in law, medicine, or the ministry. "Wofford transcends the classroom in many ways," one student said. "It does have the potential to be too personal due to its atmosphere and size, but I'd have to say that the positive effects outweigh the negative ones." Another student added, "If you want an outstanding overall college experience, come to Wofford, but if you want to spend four years with your nose buried in a textbook, don't."—*Jeff Kaplow and Staff*

FYI
Three best things about attending Wofford are "small classes, excellent frat parties, and mellow students."
Three worst things about attending Wofford are "no kegs on campus, crappy salad bar, and nothing to do in Spartanburg."
Three things every student should do before graduating from Wofford are "go to a frat party, attend a basketball game against Citadel, and take a road trip to the beach."
One thing I'd like to have known before coming here is "how claustrophobic campus can sometimes get."

South Dakota

University of South Dakota

Address: 414 East Clark Street; Vermillion, SD 57069
Phone: 877-677-5206
E-mail address: admiss@usd.edu
Web site URL: www.usd.edu
Founded: 1862
Private or Public: public
Religious affiliation: none
Location: rural
Undergraduate enrollment: 5,342
Total enrollment: 10,119
Percent Male/Female: 43%/57%
Percent Minority: 5%

Percent African-American: 0.5%
Percent Asian: 0.5%
Percent Hispanic: 0.5%
Percent Native-American: 3%
Percent in-state/out-of-state: 78%/22%
Percent Pub HS: 91%
Number of Applicants: 2,500
Percent Accepted: 88%
Percent Accepted who enroll: 43%
Entering: 962
Transfers: 778
Application Deadline: rolling
Mean SAT: NA

Mean ACT: 21
Middle 50% SAT range: NA
Middle 50% ACT range: 19–25
3 Most popular majors: business, biology, psychology
Retention: NA
Graduation rate: 46%
On-campus housing: NA
Fraternities: 23%
Sororities: 11%
Library: NA
Tuition and Fees: $3,460 in; $7,533 out
Room and Board: $2,946
Financial aid, first-year: 33%

One might say that the University of South Dakota has a split personality: Monday through Friday the college whirls and bustles, while over the weekend it seems like a ghost town that dawdles and yawns. During the week the college offers exotic extracurricular activities, small classes led by attentive professors, and a thriving Greek scene. But on the weekends, you will find that most of the students have either gone home, or to nearby Sioux Falls, South Dakota, and Sioux City, Iowa.

Premeds Study Together

Most students at USD are enrolled in the College of Arts and Sciences, which features traditional majors, including chemistry, mathematics, and English. Core requirements here usually account for about 10 of the courses that the students take. Among the requirements are at least one course in the humanities, one in the social sciences, one in math or computer science, and one in health and wellness. Students identified the biology department of the College of Arts and Sciences as particularly strong. Many of those who major in biology go on to med school at the University of South Dakota. According to several students, the premeds are grade-conscious, but not deathly competitive; in spite of their desire to succeed, said one student, most of "the premeds still study together."

Undergrads at the university may enroll in other colleges, including the School of Business, the School of Education, and the College of Fine Arts. Students cited the nationally accredited School of Business as especially good, and many involved in campus media find advisors in the Mass Communications department of the College of Fine Arts.

USD offers few colossal-sized classes. Even the lectures are tiny by state-school standards. The largest lectures might enroll about 250 students, but lectures average about 100. By junior year, classes range from about 20 to 30 students. Lectures and seminars alike are usually led by professors; TAs are a rare sight at the university. "Just about all my classes have been taught by professors," said one student, "and just about all my professors have known my name." Students work reasonably hard at USD, with many claiming to spend upward of 20 hours a week on their studies, but conceded that it is possible to get by with as little as six. The business, mathematics, and education majors were cited as burdening their students with much work.

Weekday Fun, Weekend Boredom?

Social opportunities abound Mondays through Thursdays. On Tuesdays, a local movie theater (one of two in Vermillion) offers discount movie night. Thursdays, the student association brings in a comedian to perform at Charlie's After Dark, an on-campus club. Famous speakers also appear during the week; recent speakers have included Larry King and Tom Brokaw. Promised one student, "There's a lot going on, if you pay attention to the posters." There are also plays put on through the theater department, which offers cheaper tickets to students, and several art galleries both on-campus and downtown.

Thursday evenings also feature frat parties, widely attended in part because the campus is dry. You cannot miss the Greek presence on campus. According to one independent student, people in frats and sororities are often invited to more parties and make more friends. The benefits of being in one of them are not just social; one independent student lamented that students in Greek organizations seemed to have more leadership opportunities, as they have an identity and a network in campus organizations. However, not every independent student complained about the Greek scene; one student commented that she never felt at all hindered by being independent. While Greeks may have an edge in terms of leadership opportunities and social connections, other networks like residential life, student government, and activities run through the Student Activities Center are equally open to all students.

> "Just about all my professors have known my name."

Vermillion, according to students, has little to offer in way of fun. While there are a few bowling alleys, two movie theaters, and fast-food restaurants, most students see Vermillion as little more than a place to live, shop, and drink. There are a fair number of bars, and during Dakota Days, the annual homecoming game, which is often against South Dakota State, they may open as early as 6:30 A.M. Housing is plentiful, although students must stay on campus for at least two years before they can move into an apartment off campus. There are only a few stores in town, so finding what you want can be difficult. Complained one student, "Vermillion doesn't even have a Wal-Mart nearby," although another claimed that there was one 25 miles away in Yankton, which "to a South Dakotan is 'nearby,'" in part due to South Dakota's higher speed limit of 75 miles per hour on the highway.

And so on the weekends, students leave campus. Many go home to work and earn money for college, even if home is many hours away. "To people here, every city in South Dakota is close," explained one student. But, many also go to Sioux Falls, Sioux City, or even Minneapolis, to find the kind of fun that most college students take for granted: plays, rocks concerts, and exotic restaurants, to name a few. This weekly exodus is not a very widely advertised fact; said one a USDer, "I was really surprised to see how quiet it is here on the weekends." Other students, however, say that despite the number of students who leave campus on the weekends, "if one is creative, it really isn't that hard to find something fun to do" and can find "many activities to fill the weekends."

Getting Involved

Extracurricular opportunities for students abound at USD. Students can work at the *Volante*, the weekly paper founded by *USA Today* creator Al Neuharth, and

KAOR, an alternative radio station that broadcasts 24 hours a day. Those who choose to major in mass communications can also work for the campus television station, KYOT, Monday through Friday. News broadcasts are watched in homes and dorm rooms all around Vermillion. Cherry Street Promotions, a student-run advertising agency, handles marketing for campus and local businesses.

The Coyote (pronounced "Cah-yoat" here) Student Center is a popular hangout for students during the day, and also houses the Program Council, an umbrella organization of student agencies, and a student film society that shows free films on campus once a week. Community service opportunities abound in Vermillion, and many students are very proud of how much their time can be used to aid those in the surrounding areas. In fact, there are so many service options at USD that an umbrella organization called SERVE (Students Enriching the Vermillion Environment) broke away from the Program Council, and now includes programs like Adopt-a-Grandparent, Big Pal/Little Pal, Into the Streets, Vermillion Heroes, and Adopt-a-School.

For the more athletically inclined, USD offers a vibrant intramural program. Students form their own teams; games are played once or twice a week. Among the more popular intramural sports are flag football, softball, and volleyball.

The dorms at USD receive praise from many students. Four of the dorms on the north side of campus, Beede, Mickelson, Olson, and Richardson, are attached to one another, and the complex has its own dining facility. The dorms on the south side, including Julian, are reputed to be more party-oriented. Students can also request to live on a quiet floor, where loud music and socialization are strictly forbidden, or a single-sex, smoke-free, or substance-free floor. Most rooms are one-room doubles, with the occasional quad and triple. Rooms are not spacious, but certainly adequate and are generally in good repair. Still, many students choose to move off campus as soon as they are allowed, in large part due to the dry-campus policy and in order to have kitchens.

Dining hall facilities were recently privatized, and one student swears the food has vastly improved as a result. Another student appreciated the dining halls' attempts to make food healthier and less greasy, but wished for greater variety in the dishes offered. Off-campus options include The Silver Dollar for steak and Chae's for Chinese food.

Leaning Left

Stepping onto the University of South Dakota's three-square-block campus is a bit like dropping down the rabbit hole; the Vermillion university is not your typical state school. The classes are small. The professors get to know you personally. There is no alcohol on campus. And on the weekends, the university is desolate. But if taken full advantage of, the academic and extracurricular opportunities just might be to one's liking.—*William Chen and Staff*

FYI

The three best things about attending the University of South Dakota are: "that Vermillion is a bastion of liberal thought, even in such a conservative state, friendly Midwesterners, and opportunities for academic excellence through an honors program, a Phi Beta Kappa chapter, and study-abroad opportunities."

The three worst things about attending the University of South Dakota are: "the freezing cold winters, the constant threats to cutting funding that come from the state government, and the difficulty of overcoming negative opinions of on-campus weekends to find something fun to do."

The three things that every student should do before graduating from the University of South Dakota are: "visit a reservation and learn about the Native American tribes who live there, find the river and walk the trails, and stay on-campus at least one weekend and discover how many things there are to do, contrary to popular belief."

One thing I'd like to have known before coming here is: "how fast the time would go."

Tennessee

Rhodes College

Address: 2000 North Parkway; Memphis, TN 38112
Phone: 901-843-3700
E-mail address: adminfo@rhodes.edu
Web site URL: www.rhodes.edu
Founded: 1848
Private or Public: private
Religious affiliation: Presbyterian
Location: urban
Undergraduate enrollment: 1,499
Total enrollment: 1,499
Percent Male/Female: 46%/54%
Percent Minority: 9%

Percent African-American: 4%
Percent Asian: 3%
Percent Hispanic: 1%
Percent Native-American: 0.5%
Percent in-state/out-of-state: 29%/71%
Percent Pub HS: 64%
Number of Applicants: 2,283
Percent Accepted: 77%
Percent Accepted who enroll: 25%
Entering: NA
Transfers: 48
Application Deadline: 1 Feb
Mean SAT: NA

Mean ACT: 86
Middle 50% SAT range: 590–700 V, 600–690 M
Middle 50% ACT range: 26–30
3 Most popular majors: biology, business administration, English
Retention: 73%
Graduation rate: NA
On-campus housing: NA
Fraternities: 58%
Sororities: 50%
Library: NA
Tuition and Fees: $18,719 in; $18,719 out
Room and Board: $5,454
Financial aid, first-year: 45%

Many colleges talk about their sense of community, but Rhodes students say their school takes this notion to an entirely new level. Even the iron gates and ivy-draped walls that surround the college seem to emphasize the importance of drawing students into a connected campus. While there are downsides to a close-knit environment, students say they are willing to overlook them for all the advantages that come with being a part of the "Rhodes community."

Bigger Isn't Always Better

Rhodes has all the advantages that one expects from a small liberal arts school—small student body, intimate class size, and personal interaction with faculty. The college is small enough, with 1,499 full-time students, for undergrads to get to know many of their classmates and see familiar faces when walking across campus. Some students feel restricted by this familiarity and regret that they are not always meeting new people. Others complain that the campus can be a "rumor mill, kind of like high school when everyone knew what everyone else did." Despite these grumblings, many students said they enjoy the opportunity to get to know their classmates so well.

Most classes have less than thirty students, and typically class size is about fifteen. The only exceptions are introductory science classes, like freshman year biology. Students stress, though, that large lecture courses are rare, and no class enrolls more than one hundred students. This personal attention requires a higher level of preparation by students. "Coming in to Rhodes, I didn't know I'd be so involved in my classes," explained one undergrad. "Professors expect everyone to participate in discussion and offer theories—and who's to say your ideas aren't better than the professor's?"

Not surprisingly, small classes lead to greater student-faculty interaction. Students rave about the easy access to professors on campus. Many professors give out home telephone numbers and encourage calls at home. "One professor told us to call her at home at any time," said one student. "One catch, though—if we woke her baby, we failed the class. Luckily, that didn't happen!" Professors are willing to meet with students outside of class, to answer questions or to shoot the breeze, and students often see their professors around campus, at the school-wide Rites of Spring festival, or even auditing a class.

Like many liberal arts colleges, Rhodes has a core curriculum, structured so that students are exposed to a wide range of academic fields. Undergrads take classes in each of four divisions: social sciences, natural sciences (including a lab), humanities, and fine arts, as well as required physical education and religion classes. Despite the school's affiliation with the Presbyterian Church (U.S.A.), students do not detect a religious bias. The religion requirement can be filled by taking one of two tracks: Search or Life. Search focuses on the integration of history and its values within religion, and Life looks at particular religious traditions, examining sacred literature and practices. Students say Search is more inclusive of different religious traditions, but Life is considered easier.

Most departments at Rhodes are well regarded, although students say the engineering program is weak. International studies and biology are popular majors. The small size of the school limits the choice of courses and professors in some departments, but students seem willing to sacrifice some variety for close fellowship with the faculty. Rhodes supplements its offerings with exchange programs such as engineering exchanges with Washington University in St. Louis and Maymester foreign study programs. Rhodes also allows students to study abroad through programs sponsored by other schools.

"Walking in Memphis"
Rhodes students find far more to do with their time than just study. The Greek system sets the scene for much of the social activity around campus, with more than half of all students belonging to fraternities and sororities. Rush for fraternities and sororities envelope freshmen as soon as they arrive on campus, and new members are tapped by the end of the first week of classes. Students, even Greeks themselves, are ambivalent about this setup. "It's a great opportunity to meet people, but rush and the Greek system can shut doors and cause divisions on campus," commented one fraternity member. Generally, though, choosing not to rush does not restrict anyone from Greek parties and is not perceived as a barrier to having a thriving social life. Greeks tend to see fraternity and sorority life as one of the few options on campus, while independents downplay the prominence of Greek life. Greek ties are significant but students say they do not overcome one's connections to the college as a whole.

Beyond Greek activities, social opportunities on campus can be lacking. Many students head into Memphis, home to the famed Beale Street, a haven for blues music. The renowned musical atmosphere—noted by Marc Cohn's "Walking in Memphis" and Bob Dylan's "Stuck Inside of Mobile with the Memphis Blues Again"—attracts students to clubs and restaurants. Having a fake ID is usually necessary to get in, although one student claims developing friendships with bouncers is just as effective. With the monopoly that the Greek system can exert over social life on campus, downtown spots are often prime gathering places for Rhodes students—don't be surprised to run into classmates when wandering around the city. Greek or not, drinking is a large part of Rhodes social life. Students say there's no pressure to drink, but alcohol is present at most social events. A new Dean of Student Affairs has shown signs of tightening alcohol use on campus but has not affected drinking practices yet.

Beyond Parties
Community service draws even more participants than the Greek system. Students rave about volunteer opportunities in Memphis, a typical big city with problems. Working at soup kitchens, building with Habitat for Humanity, and mentoring Memphis kids are some of the more popular choices.

Most of these groups are encompassed within the Kinney Volunteer Program, which includes all kinds of options for community service. The small campus is instrumental in getting word out about different causes. "It's hard not to know what's going on," explained one volunteer. The administration places great emphasis on volunteerism, rewarding dedicated students with special housing and scholarships in exchange for commitments to particular projects. The sense of community at Rhodes does not stop at its gates but includes the city of Memphis as well.

Students are involved in bettering Rhodes, too. In addition to traditional student government, which has poor student participation, the Honor Code Council and Students Regulations Council allow for student direction. Upon entering Rhodes, all students commit to following the Honor Code, an agreement to respect others in the Rhodes community. While it is believed that it is not universally followed, most say they like the atmosphere of trust that it creates. The Student Regulations Council is responsible for punishing students who have violated the rules, rather than having the issue brought up before a faculty committee. In essence, students are allowed to uphold the values and rules important to their community.

> "One professor told us to call her at home at any time," said one student. "One catch, though—if we woke her baby, we failed the class. Luckily, that didn't happen!"

Student groups cater to a myriad of interests. The drama department puts on several productions each year, and there are numerous musical groups. Despite the prevailing opinion that the student body is moderate to conservative politically, multicultural groups are active on campus in promoting understanding of various cultures. While religious fellowships, Christian and non-Christian, are common, Rhodes' location in the Bible Belt and its church affiliation do not translate into an aggressive religious atmosphere on campus.

The emphasis on community does not always manifest itself in activity. Students note the lack of school spirit and consider their classmates to be "apathetic" in supporting athletic teams, which compete in the Southern Collegiate Athletic Conference. Students tend to see themselves as homogenous. "There are a lot of preppy Southern white kids around," admitted one undergrad. Minorities exist only in small numbers. While recent classes show growth in representing different backgrounds, students question how a liberal arts school can expose students to a broad range of perspectives with such underrepresentation of many ethnic groups. Still, minorities feel quite comfortable among their peers, and these concerns do not seem dampen the affection that students have for their classmates.

Living in dorms is a further extension of the Rhodes community. Suites are common in freshmen dorms and most dorms have only fifty residents each. A new rule requires freshmen and sophomores to live on campus, and many upperclassmen do as well, causing a housing crunch in recent years. Students living off campus reportedly feel less connected to Rhodes, particularly since many of the neighborhoods surrounding the school are not the safest or most affluent. On-campus meal opportunities are limited to the cafeteria, affectionately titled the Rat, and the Lynx Lair, a fast-food–style alternative, both of which are included in the meal equivalency plan. The Rat does not garner rave reviews for its food, but students do appreciate the study breaks that it sponsors at exam time.

From small classes that facilitate involved class discussions to coaching a basketball team of inner city Memphis teenagers, the focus at Rhodes is on community and getting to know those around you—students, professors, and Memphis residents. Positioned on a beautiful campus replete with Gothic-style buildings made of stone, there is a sense that Rhodes is its own world, set apart from its midtown location. The emphasis on personal interaction is Rhodes' strongest drawing point, and students are not disappointed.—*Alexa Frankenberg*

FYI

The three best things about attending Rhodes are "the size of the school, being in Memphis, and close interaction with the faculty."

The three worst things about attending Rhodes are "everyone knowing what's going on with everyone else, the homogenous student body, and the unsafe neighborhoods surrounding campus."

The three things every student should do before graduating from Rhodes are "ride the Lynx, visit Graceland, and spend an afternoon in Fischer Gardens."

One thing I'd like to have known before coming here is "the participation that teachers demand of the students."

University of Tennessee / Knoxville

Address: 320 Student Services Building; Knoxville, TN 37996-0230

Phone: 865-974-2184

E-mail address: admissions@utk.edu

Web site URL: www.utk.edu

Founded: 1794

Private or Public: public

Religious affiliation: none

Location: urban

Undergraduate enrollment: 19,830

Total enrollment: 26,437

Percent Male / Female: 49%/51%

Percent Minority: 10%

Percent African-American: 6%

Percent Asian: 2%

Percent Hispanic: 1%

Percent Native-American: 0.5%

Percent in-state / out-of-state: 89%/11%

Percent Pub HS: NA

Number of Applicants: 10,605

Percent Accepted: 67%

Percent Accepted who enroll: 58%

Entering: 4,155

Transfers: 1,427

Application Deadline: 15 Jan

Mean SAT: 550 V, 553 M

Mean ACT: 24

Middle 50% SAT range: 500–600 V, 490–610 M

Middle 50% ACT range: 21–26

3 Most popular majors: business / marketing, social sciences / history, engineering

Retention: 79%

Graduation rate: 57%

On-campus housing: 86%

Fraternities: 8%

Sororities: 8%

Library: 1,846,695 volumes

Tuition and Fees: $3,104 in; $9,172 out

Room and Board: $4,430

Financial aid, first-year: 34%

Is there such a thing as too much school spirit? If there is, do not tell any members of the University of Tennessee's Volunteer Nudists society. These fans of Big Orange football are not ashamed to bare their fannies for Smokey (a hound) the mascot to almost 20,000 undergraduates at this stronghold of southern spirit.

"Heh, heh. Yeah, we're pretty good at sports" is how one "Vol" explained another's mantra that "football is life here!" UT's newly expanded Neyland Stadium, the largest collegiate football arena in the nation, seats as many as 107,000 fans. When the big game against either Florida or Alabama hits town, true UT fans gather on Yale Avenue two hours before kickoff to cheer the players on as they walk to the locker room. If the band's performance of "Rocky Top" "doesn't get you excited about UT football," says one student, "nothing will!"

Student spirit, however, is all downhill from Neyland Stadium. At this large state school, there is a small group of involved students, but in general student apathy toward campus issues runs high. As one student government participant complained, "Getting student input on any topic, political or otherwise, is like pulling teeth."

Concrete City

Another student concern is the necessity of having a vehicle, despite the perennial parking problems (a campus permit costs about $175 per year). A few daredevils try biking on campus (one student calls it "bicycle lacrosse"), but most find that they can walk from one end of campus to the other in less than 20 minutes.

In the words of one undergrad, the UT campus is "a pad of concrete set between the river and downtown." Others, however, recommend several spots with a view to kill for: the top of the Hill, where one can see from downtown Knoxville to Ayers Hall, and the view from high in McClung Tower, where the Great Smoky Mountains can be seen in the distance. Some dorm rooms enjoy a view of the Tennessee River, where the Labor Day fireworks festival, Boomsday, is held.

Dorm Dilemmas

And where can you enjoy the fireworks with that special someone? Not in your dorm room. UT's dorms are mostly single-sex, which some students cited as a good reason to move off campus, although some are coed by floor. Beds are "very narrow," and only one dorm has unlimited visitation hours; all of the others having varying rules on opposite-sex visitation that are enforced by RAs (usually upperclassmen), so romance can be quite a feat.

One student described the drinking scene on UT's officially dry campus as "pretty big for some people, but there is a growing majority who don't participate." The dating is considered "a definite plus," although one student said that "there is a large Christian element, so some people are definitely against premarital sex."

> "If you take a course you think should fulfill a requirement, you can petition it by talking to the professor, who has the ultimate say in whether you get in."

With all of these distractions, Vols (as all UT students and Tennesseans in general refer to themselves) still manage to find time not only to register but also to attend classes. Registration is done by phone, with priority given to seniors.

Prerequisites vary by major and by college. UT frosh must choose to enter one of the vocational colleges (education, nursing, agricultural sciences), or can choose to enter the College of Arts and Sciences if they are unsure about their projected major. Depending on the college, prerequisites might include languages and always include some humanities courses, but most students see the prerequisites as beneficial to their education, not a hassle. Through a petitioning system, "if you take a course you think should fulfill a requirement, you can petition it by talking to the professor, who has the ultimate say in whether you get in," one student said.

Class sizes are not in proportion to the large university. Introductory classes of close to 200 students are not uncommon, but between 20 and 30 students is a closer approximation of average class size. Students found professors approachable, although the large size of the university makes the classic "lunch with the prof" meeting of small liberal arts schools a rarity.

Spaces to Study

Undergrads who are serious about studying recommend the John C. Hodges Library (UT's main library with 2 million volumes) over the smaller Hoskins, Taylor Law, and Ag-Vet libraries. Hard-core studying is done in the stacks on the fourth through sixth floors of Hodges. Social studying is popular in the library study rooms, the Golden Roast (a coffee shop within a few minutes' walk), the Daily Grind (another coffee shop), and on the steps of Glocker, a building in the center of campus. Freshmen tend to congregate around the Presidential courtyard while upperclassmen hang out on the Humanities Plaza. The Waffle House and the International House of Pancakes (IHOP) are the 24-hour restaurants of choice for those burning the orange candle at both ends.

With many students commuting from home, extracurriculars do not play the role at UT that they would at a smaller, more close-knit university, but the sheer size of UT guarantees that certain activities will be popular. The Greek scene is large and students feel some pressure to rush, although some non-Greeks are completely happy with their status: "Yuck! [They're] a waste of time and money."

Is UT worth the time and money? Students say yes. Many cite UT's value as the strongest factor in their decision to attend. As one student said: "I could have gone to GA Tech or MIT, where the school was everything I wanted, and graduate in debt. Or I could come to UT, change the school to fit my needs, and graduate with no debt."—*Vladimir Cole and Staff*

FYI

The three best things about attending UT are "awesome football program, awesome basketball program, and the school spirit."

The three worst things about attending UT are "getting used to living in Tennessee, a very homogenous social scene, and it's hard to get a sense of community here, you have to find your little niche fast."

The three things that every student should do before graduating from UT are "attend as many football and basketball games as you can, visit Dolly World, and casually date as often as you can."

One thing I'd like to have known before coming here is "that as a non-Southerner, getting into the country music culture isn't as hard or as bad as I thought."

University of the South (Sewanee)

Address: 735 University Avenue; Sewanee, TN 37383-1000
Phone: 931-598-1238
E-mail address: collegeadmission @sewanee.edu
Web site URL: www.sewanee.edu
Founded: 1857
Private or Public: private
Religious affiliation: Episcopal
Location: rural
Undergraduate enrollment: 1,308
Total enrollment: NA
Percent Male/Female: 46%/54%

Percent Minority: 6%
Percent African-American: 4%
Percent Asian: 0.5%
Percent Hispanic: 0.5%
Percent Native-American: 0.5%
Percent in-state/out-of-state: 82%/18%
Percent Pub HS: 54%
Number of Applicants: 1,642
Percent Accepted: 73%
Percent Accepted who enroll: 33%
Entering: 392
Transfers: NA
Application Deadline: 1 Feb
Mean SAT: NA

Mean ACT: NA
Middle 50% SAT range: 570–660 V, 560–660 M
Middle 50% ACT range: 24–29
3 Most popular majors: English, history, psychology
Retention: 88%
Graduation rate: 82%
On-campus housing: NA
Fraternities: 65%
Sororities: 55%
Library: NA
Tuition and Fees: $19,080 in; $19,080 out
Room and Board: $5,230
Financial aid, first-year: 42%

What do you do when you are on top of a mountain on a 10,000-acre campus and the closest cities, Chattanooga and Nashville, are hours away? Make sure you have a car. Such are the lessons that students learn at the University of the South (called Sewanee nearly universally) along with the more traditional ones inherent to a liberal arts education.

A Work Hard Kind of School

"During the week, I would say that Sewanee students are intense about studying. The library is packed until it closes at 1:00 A.M.," said one sophomore. "If you are accepted into the school in the first place, it should never be impossible to do well in your classes. You can't be lazy here. You have to put forth a true, concentrated effort in able to succeed," commented another student. Sewanee students say that attending classes is important: "People go to class probably 90 to 95 percent of the time. . . . Every test I have ever taken here requires your presence and participation in class as well as preparation by reading the assignments," said one upperclassman. However, if a student is unable to make class, a southern sense of common courtesy and respect prevails and he or she will be sure to tell the professor ahead of time. This same attitude is taken in personal relationships with teachers outside of class. "At Sewanee it is unheard of to pass a professor on the street and not say hello," one student explained. Going to class and making good grades can make a difference.

Students with high GPAs are invited to join the Order of the Gownsmen, an honor that gives students special privileges, like the right to pick their classes before others and to leave a class if the professor doesn't arrive after fifteen minutes.

Picking classes early can sometimes be important. Because classes are so small (the largest being the freshman premed classes, which have only 60–70 students), students say they can sometimes get closed out of a class. However, persistent students can ask special permission from the professor and often get into an otherwise closed class. Students report that a typical class load is four classes a semester. Such a schedule gives them time to complete graduation requirements, which include a choice of classes from a series of subject-divided lists.

A common complaint about classes is the repetition of professors. History is a "big department," consisting of ten professors. According to students, most other departments' faculty can be counted on one hand. Some students enjoy this, though. Having so few professors means that they can get the attention they need. In fact, students say it's common for students to talk of going to their professors' houses for dinner and having department-wide parties.

A Play Hard Kind of School

"It is Sewanee," one student said. "Of course there's a lot of drinking." If students work through Thursday, they party hard through the weekend. Students admit that frats make up a large part of the social scene, but nonmembers are invited to every party, with the exception of some formals. Beer is plentiful and easily attainable, and students say that many drink often and to excess. According to students, there was an effort made by the administration to make alcohol less readily available on campus. However, the measure was defeated for fear that Sewanee students would drive off the mountain to do their drinking, forcing them to drive back while drunk.

A nonchalant attitude toward strict rules marks other parts of campus life. According to the university rule book, "Dormitories (or, with regard to coed dormitories, the individual dormitory rooms) are open to visitors of the opposite sex from 9:00 A.M. until 12:00 P.M. Sundays through Thursdays, and from 9:00 A.M. until 1:00 A.M. Friday and Saturday nights." Violators can face penalties ranging from a reprimand or a fine to eviction from campus. Nonetheless, students report that the rule is seldom, if ever, enforced. "As long as your roommate is not complaining, and you're not making too much noise, nobody looks twice," one sophomore explained.

The fact that Sewanee social life is based around drinking can reportedly create problems for nondrinkers. "Sewanee is a wonderful school if you find your niche right off the bat. If you don't drink and don't have a car, you could have problems if you don't find friends that support you in your decisions and interests," a light-drinking senior complained.

However, one sophomore who described herself as less of a drinker than her schoolmates said that a happy balance is easy to find. "The frats have great bands, and everybody dances like fools. I think that the rest of the campus is pretty liquored up for most of the weekend, though. . . . However, my social life is a testament that you don't have to drink to have a great time at Sewanee."

Students can also take advantage of "drier" activities on the college's location on 10,000 acres of Cumberland plateau. The Domain, as it's called, is "a dream for people who like to hike," so the school attracts "Thoreau people" interested in spending time outdoors. Without even leaving the property of the school, students can hike and go spelunking. Tennessee Williams endowed a theater on campus, and students describe the theater studies department as strong both for education and performances. During the week, students can hang out at "BC," the Bishop's Commons student union.

Leave Them in the Dust!

Sewanee is over 50 percent southern and overwhelmingly white. Said one senior, "You've got your Sewanee student running around in the woods with their hiking boots on, and then you've got your Sewanee student who's suburban and running around in his jeep." Another student pointed out, "the campus is pretty homogeneous. We are mostly upper-class white kids who come from two-parent homes." Others stress the Episcopalian affiliation of Sewanee and note the overwhelmingly Christian nature of the student body but argue that students interpret their Christianity to mean that they should focus on openness. "We have traditions," said one senior, "but we don't cling to the unhelpful ones."

Living in a Hospital

Students generally laud Sewanee housing, and 98 percent of the student body lives on campus. Seniors, who get priority, can nearly always get singles, as do many juniors. The favorite dorm for upperclassmen used to be a hospital, and local students have stories of their parents being patients in the very rooms in which they are now living. There is widespread approval for freshman housing, as well. The newer dorms are divided into suites of two bedrooms, two common rooms, and a bathroom, shared among four people; other freshmen live in more traditional hall-based dorms. Fraternities and sororities do not have their own housing. Each freshman dorm has a group of senior Assistant Proctors living among the underclassmen and one Head Proctor, also a student. While the APs, as they're called, are ostensibly there to enforce rules, "they're students, so they're not going to go out of their way to get someone in trouble," a freshman stressed. "APs are more or less our friends."

Sewanee students say they strike a balance between their Greek partying and Greek studying. A clear line is drawn between the extensive drinking of the weekend and the hard work of the school week. Said one student, "At Sewanee we work hard and play just about as hard. During the week the focus is almost religiously centered on classwork and by the weekend everyone is ready to have a good time at the many open frat parties on campus."— *Jacob Remes and staff*

FYI

The three best things about attending Sewanee are "the hiking opportunities, awesome dorms, faculty are friendly and available."

The three worst things about attending Sewanee are the "the limited number of faculty, Greek-centered social life, and the amount of studying we have to do."

The three things every student should do before graduating from Sewanee go to the Mountain Top Ball, participate in the Sewanee Outing Program, hang out at Stirling's Coffee House."

One thing I wish I'd known before coming to Sewanee is "how small the departments are."

Vanderbilt University

Address: 2305 West End Avenue; Nashville, TN 37203
Phone: 615-322-2561
E-mail address: admissions @vanderbilt.edu
Web site URL: www.vanderbilt.edu
Founded: 1873
Private or Public: private
Religious affiliation: none
Location: urban
Undergraduate enrollment: 5,752
Total enrollment: 10,022
Percent Male / Female: 47%/53%
Percent Minority: 15%

Percent African-American: 5%
Percent Asian: 6%
Percent Hispanic: 3%
Percent Native-American: 0.5%
Percent in-state / out-of-state: 13%/87%
Percent Pub HS: 58%
Number of Applicants: 8,494
Percent Accepted: 61%
Percent Accepted who enroll: 31%
Entering: 1,633
Transfers: 69
Application Deadline: 7 Jan
Mean SAT: NA
Mean ACT: NA

Middle 50% SAT range: 600–690 V, 620–710 M
Middle 50% ACT range: 27–31
3 Most popular majors: social sciences, engineering, psychology
Retention: 92%
Graduation rate: 81%
On-campus housing: 100%
Fraternities: 34%
Sororities: 48%
Library: 2,568,190 volumes
Tuition and Fees: $23,598 in; $23,598 out
Room and Board: $8,032
Financial aid, first-year: 42%

"I t rocks!" This peppy student, like so many of her classmates, is raving about Vanderbilt, one of the top universities in the South, and meriting national attention as a first-rate private university. With the blend of challenging academics and a social life that receives "two very enthusiastic thumbs up," it is easy to see why so many have become so enamored with "Vandy."

Classes at Vandy

A school that prides itself on academic excellence, Vanderbilt has a top-notch undergraduate program that boasts a faculty dedicated to the intellectual pursuits of its students. TAs rarely teach except for the occasional lab or discussion section, and class sizes are small, allowing the professors to have close contact with their students. In fact, one freshman is the only student in her French literature class. It is this individual attention that sets Vandy apart from other universities. Though the students admit that academics are definitely challenging, there is no cutthroat competition for grades. This relaxed atmosphere lends an incredible environment for the undergraduate to explore and grow intellectually. The most popular departments include economics, engineering, English, and education. Students are hard-pressed to name a weak department.

All freshmen choose from among four undergraduate schools: arts and sciences, engineering, George Peabody College for Education and Human Development, or the Blaire School of Music. While a majority of the students are in the school of arts and sciences, the other schools receive good reviews from students as well. One freshman in the music school said that students particularly like it because it allows them the freedom to decide their own level of commitment, and the core curriculum includes courses that music majors would want to take anyway.

Students in the School of Arts and Sciences must complete a core curriculum called Core Program for Liberal Education (CPLE), which includes courses in the humanities, natural and social sciences, and history. Proficiency in a foreign language is also required. This curriculum receives mixed reviews from students. Some praise it for its intellectual variety and depth: "It certainly gives an excellent background in the liberal arts and really helped me decide on my major," said one student. Others don't share this enthusiasm. One freshman described the program as "a necessary evil." Another student complained, "I expected college to be a place where I could explore those subjects that interested me the most, but it [CPLE] doesn't allow me to do that." One upperclassman believes that the program tends to result in classes that students take only to fulfill the requirements, not for learning's sake. This can also affect the professor's attitude toward the class and create an unsatisfying experience.

While academics are an integral part of Vandy life, these students really know how to have a good time. The social scene is dominated by the Greek system, and every weekend at least one fraternity is having a party. Because the sororities and fraternities offer the main weekend entertainment, non-drinkers and those students not interested in pledging complain that there are very few alternatives. One senior said that if you didn't have a car and are not into the Greek scene, your options are pretty limited. Other students, however, say that if you take the initiative, you can find other things to do, although organized, campus-wide activities are limited. In fact, some undergrads complain that the administration does not do enough to organize more social activities, but others say such events would be poorly attended. But do not worry if the concept of the Greek lifestyle doesn't float your boat. Most agree that there isn't any pressure to join and all students can attend the parties whether they are members of the frat or not. Independents say they do sometimes feel isolated in the spring when there are a number of fraternity and sorority formals.

After Class

One of the biggest campus-wide parties of the year is the Rites of Spring, a three-day festival that has featured music from the Dave Matthews Band and the Violent Femmes in recent years. Accolade, a black-tie homecoming dance, is popular with juniors and seniors, and the proceeds go toward scholarships for minority students. Vandy is in the heart of Nashville, and some students use the opportunities that the city has to offer to their advantage. Some students go to area restaurants such as Chili's, Houston's, and the Cooker, while others head to the city to dance and hang out at the many local bars that receive rave reviews from the upperclassmen. Such popular clubs include the Exit Inn, the Underground (for those with alternative music tastes), Mickey Gilley's (not to be missed for all y'all country mu-

sic fans), and the Mix Factory. One upperclassman, however, notes that the "Vanderbubble" keeps most on campus and therefore holds students back from taking advantage of the opportunities in their own backyard.

The most unpopular administration regulation by far is the new policy on alcohol, although many students agree that something had to be done. Three alcohol-related deaths in recent years have led the administration to take every effort to stop underage drinking. The first time an underage student is caught drinking (or even holding an unopened container), he or she will be put on probation, which goes on the student's permanent record; with the second offense, the student is suspended for six months; with the third offense the student is expelled. This policy is on the whole strictly enforced both by the freshman RAs (seniors who live in the freshman halls) and the Inter-fraternity Council, although one RA admitted that the policy is not enforced fairly all the time. Most students agree that the system is working. In fact, one freshman said that a tenth of her hall is already on probation. This year, before going into any frat party, each student must sign in if he/she is underage. Some say this policy has created problems because now many students are going off campus to drink and then have to drive back to campus.

Athletics are a big deal at Vandy. Though in the past few years the football team has "sucked," a new football coach has arrived recently and the Commodores are hoping to turn things around. "Woodyball," as it is affectionately called, has become huge, and the games are packed. Football games are also major social events, where many students get dressed up and go with a date. Men's and women's basketball and soccer teams have had strong seasons lately. Students are also involved in many club and intramural sports. The intramural sports are sponsored by fraternities, dorm floors, and student associations. Soccer, basketball, and softball are especially popular. Don't hold your breath—yes, they do have inner-tube water polo.

Community service keeps many students busy. A popular community-service project is the Alternative Spring Break Program in which students spend their spring breaks building houses in inner cities. Others become Vanderbuddies and tutor local children. Students who participate in a similar program, Culture Shock, once a month adopt an inner-city kid and entertain him or her on campus. The university has several a cappella singing groups, the most popular being the Dodecaphonics, and student publications such as the *Hustler*, the campus newspaper, and *Slightly Amusing*, a humor magazine, are other popular activities that claim the time of many students.

> "The social scene is dominated by the Greek system, and every weekend at least one fraternity is having a party."

As for the comforts of home, housing at Vandy earns high marks from students. In fact, one claims that the dorms are like "hotels" compared with those of other schools. Freshmen live in one of three dorms: Vanderbilt-Barnard Hall, the Kissam Quadrangle, or the Branscomb Quadrangle. These living arrangements seem to be enjoyed by the freshmen as they get a chance to meet and bond with their classmates. The Kissam Quad is known as the quiet dorm, primarily because it contains only single rooms; the best rooms are said to be in Branscomb. The four dorms in Charmichael Towers are considered to be the best place for upperclassmen to live. In those residence halls, students share six-person suites and have a food court on the first floor which includes Alpine Bagel (recently replacing the Dairy Queen and Taco Bell), a pizza parlor, a deli, and a grocery store. Seniors can apply for off-campus housing, but in an attempt to maintain community spirit, the administration reportedly discourages students from living off campus.

Unlike Vanderbilt housing, the cafeteria food is pretty sketchy. In fact, some say the meals in Rand Dining Hall are downright nasty. It may not be a bad idea to have your mother stick around and cook for you. Yes, things move in the food and often you're not really sure whether you are having tapioca pudding or grits, but as one student optimistically puts it, "there is always the salad bar." Freshmen are required to be on a meal plan, but that only covers dinners six days a week. The other meals can be purchased at other places around campus that are worlds more appetizing than Rand Dining Hall. The Over Cup Oak Pub receives amazing reviews from students, and you can even get sweet tea there (it is a Southern thing). You can get all this and much more with the Commodore Card, a unique Vandy invention. In essence, each student has his or her own personal credit card to buy anything on campus, from meals to books to laundry or a midnight snack at the Mini-mart.

The Vanderbilt Student

Students definitely do not go to Vandy for a diverse student body. Recent classes have been the least diverse in a decade, though the administration recently spent more time and money than they ever have before in recruiting a diverse class. Why this lack of diversity? "Imagine lots and lots of people from J. Crew catalogs multiplying," replies one student. Another student agreed: "White, upper class, and conservative, that's Vanderbilt." The homogeneity is one of the things that many Vandy students wish they could change about their school.

Vandy is definitely a southern school, and it is this distinctive Southern feel that attracts many students to Vandy. Combine this with friendly students who like to have fun, a dedicated faculty, challenging academics, a beautiful campus, and a wide selection of extracurricular activities, and you have a top-notch university.
—*Melissa Droller and Staff*

FYI
The three best things about attending Vanderbilt are "the Greek life, the small class size, and the location."
The three worst things about attending Vanderbilt are "the administration's super-strict alcohol policy, the homogeneous student body, and the cafeteria food."
The three things every student should do before graduating from Vanderbilt are "be a Vanderbuddy, watch a campus band at the Rites of Spring, go to the Accolade formal."
One thing I wish I'd known before coming to Vanderbilt is "how strong the Greek influence is here."

Texas

Baylor University

Address: PO Box 97056;
Waco, TX 76798-7056
Phone: 254-710-3435
E-mail address: Admission
_Serv_Office@baylor.edu
Web site URL:
www.baylor.edu
Founded: 1845
Private or Public:
private
Religious affiliation:
Baptist
Location: small city
**Undergraduate
enrollment:** 11,394
Total enrollment:
12,472
Percent Male / Female:
42%/58%
Percent Minority: 20%

Percent African-American:
6%
Percent Asian: 5%
Percent Hispanic: 8%
Percent Native-American:
0.5%
**Percent in-state / out-of-
state:** 80%/20%
Percent Pub HS: NA
Number of Applicants:
7,209
Percent Accepted: 87%
**Percent Accepted who
enroll:** 44%
Entering: 2,772
Transfers: NA
Application Deadline:
rolling
Mean SAT: NA
Mean ACT: NA

Middle 50% SAT range:
520–630 V,
540–650 M
Middle 50% ACT range:
22–27
3 Most popular majors:
teacher education, biology,
business marketing
Retention: 82%
Graduation rate: 69%
On-campus housing: 96%
Fraternities: 20%
Sororities: 25%
Library: 1,500,000
volumes
Tuition and Fees:
$11,988 in; $11,988 out
Room and Board: $5,238
Financial aid, first-year:
41%

In the heart of Waco, Texas, Baylor University shines. More than just another southern, Baptist-affiliated private institution, Baylor is proud of its education and traditions. Whether they're studying biology or volunteering their time to improve the surrounding community, Baylor Bears make the most of their time at school. "The best thing about Baylor is the multitude of things to which you can devote yourself. You can always find something that interests you at this school."

The Cores

Baylor is wonderful for keeping students slightly more well rounded than they might care to be. Students are required to take two semesters of Chapel Forum, a seminar where guest speakers lecture students twice a week. In addition, there are other degree regulations, including minimum number of semester hours and residence requirements. Students believe that the academic requirements are "fair and understandable." Some complain about having to take courses in fields unrelated to their course of study, but most agree that because of today's ever-changing job market, the requirement is "very useful."

Biology is regarded as the hardest major at Baylor, which is well known for its premed program. Professors use the program to weed out those who won't be able to handle the pressure. As far as easier majors go, business and education are known to be less stressful. "A class on how to make a bulletin board? PLEASE!" remarked one student about the education major. However, because of the high-achieving students at the school, the environment is still cutthroat. "I'm not aware of any majors that aren't competitive—this is Baylor!" said one senior.

For those students who are looking for even more of a challenge, there is the Baylor Interdisciplinary Core (BIC), which takes the top professors in each discipline at Baylor to create classes that teach more than one subject at a time. Students enter the highly selective program as freshmen and continue it through their senior year. One participant says that "it is vastly more interesting, memorable, and ultimately more practical than the regular basic courses required for the major of your choice."

Coors Light Anyone?

The social lifc is pretty limited at Baylor. Approximately half the students are in a frat or sorority. Parties revolve around the Greek system and are often the best in frats. Drinking is present at this school even though it is Baptist-affiliated. However, students think "there's not a lot of pressure to drink if you don't want to. Most parties will serve canned sodas as well as alcohol." As far as rushing these frats and sororities, Bears say that some cruel things go on. One student claimed that she's "had to help clean up guys smeared in excrement by frats they rushed and weren't wanted at" and "help girls who had been drawn on in permanent pen on their naked bodies as to what they needed to improve on their figures before getting a bid."

If Greek life isn't your thing, don't worry. A popular and well-respected group on campus is the Baptist Student Union. It's known for not letting non-Baptists lead the various ministries, even if they aren't Christian. Mission Waco is another religious group on campus that is highly respected for its work with the homeless and needy. However, if you're not religious, there are over 250 other organizations at Baylor, from singing groups to ethnic associations. A popular volunteer group is Steppin' Out. Students in this group set aside days to help the Waco community with various service projects. One student said extracurriculars are "the best way to meet and make friends."

Appearance Only Goes So Far

The students are downright beautiful at Baylor. One student commented that there are enough "attractive people, but not beyond the physical aspect." One problem students at this school seem to deal with is appearance. "There's a lot of bulimia and anorexia here," said one girl. "People try to look wealthy, but a majority are from middle-class families." However, one student stated that people are very casual and wear jeans and T-shirts. Dating is a rarity at Baylor. One student said that people "just get laid or engaged." But do not fret, because people are reported to be "really friendly and easy to get to know." Whether it be in class or through activities, you're sure to find some people you click with.

Two If by Land, Green If by Victory

Sports are pretty dry for the Baylor Bears. Although most people go to the football games, it's just to "hang out and pretend to support the team." But there is one team that Bears do "hate with a passion"—the Texas A&M Aggies. Although they have not won any championships lately, Baylor students are still shooting for glory.

> "The best thing about Baylor is the multitude of things to which you can devote yourself. You can always find something that interests you at this school."

As the oldest university in Texas, Baylor definitely has many traditions. Bears know when their athletic teams have won a game or not. It's a tradition to light up the tower of Pat Neff Hall with green floodlights for victories and with white floodlights for losses. Another tradition is the Homecoming bonfire, which was originally set around the campus for protection against Baylor's opponents. And even for non-athletes, the gym facilities are excellent: "We have the best gym in the South." Intramurals are a part of many students' lives, which explains the "athletic look" of most Bears at this beautiful southern school.

Living in the Comfort of Protection

"It's an attractive and typical college campus with brick buildings and nicely manicured lawns and gardens," said one student about Baylor. The campus is spread out, with many great hiding spots. Students enjoy spending time at Cameron Park or Lover's Leap, either reading or sleeping on a blanket. There are also some coffee shops where people hang out or just relax. "There are so many little nooks to run away to when you just want to spend some time alone." Crime is not an issue at Baylor. Students feel safe on campus because of "the Baylor DPS. They're wonderful!" With no recent issues in crime, it's no wonder people feel able to leave their doors unlocked without a threat.

Baylor students aren't very fond of the dining options at the school. The food is "gross, but bearable," said an off-campus student. Another student said that he gets "filled up, so it's good." The food in the SUB is reportedly the only "good stuff," according to most students. The SUB includes chains like Chick-Fil-A, Subway, Dunkin' Donuts, and Starbucks. Many prefer to eat off-campus at restaurants like Crickets, Ninfa's, and Outback Steakhouse.

One thing that might distinguish Baylor from many universities is the visitation hours for its on-campus residents. All dorms at this school are single-sex and have residential advisors to regulate visitation hours for members of the opposite sex. There are only several hours a week when visitation is allowed, a policy many students think is "too restrictive, but understandable." Another downer is that the rooms are a "bit on the small side." Dorms are nevertheless clean and lively, with different personalities for different dorms. The women's halls—there are eight—are a good example. North and South Russell are for non-Betty freshman girls. Alexander Hall is labeled as the dorm with the "smart and beautiful girls." For the men, there are three residence halls, with Penland Hall the largest and most diverse. Many students go off campus after their frosh year for privacy and quiet, but the rent can be expensive and some say the lifestyle is not as exciting as dorm life.

Baylor Bears enjoy the unity they have through the strong Christian presence on campus. Many students take pride in their traditions and beautiful campus. With its southern atmosphere and world-class education, Baylor is a university full of opportunities for people interested in many different things. "As with any college, your experience at Baylor depends on your attitude towards everything around you," said one junior. "It's a matter of whether or not you take advantage of the awesome prospects Baylor has to offer."—*Jane Pak*

FYI

The three best things about attending Baylor are "the student life center, the multitude of things to get involved in, and its closeness to Dallas and Austin."

The three worst things about attending Baylor are "Waco, the fakeness about a lot of people, and rushing."

The three things every student should do before graduating from Baylor are "have a frozen mochaccino at Common Grounds, have a water fight at the fountain in the center of campus, make fun of the newspapers on campus."

One thing I'd like to have known before coming here is "how there's absolutely nothing to do in Waco."

Rice University

Address: MS 17; PO Box 1892; Houston, TX 77251-1892	**Percent African-American:** 6%	**Middle 50% SAT range:** 650–760 V, 670–775 M
Phone: 713-348-4036	**Percent Asian:** 15%	
E-mail address: admission@rice.edu	**Percent Hispanic:** 10%	**Middle 50% ACT range:** 29–33
Web site URL: www.rice.edu	**Percent Native-American:** 0.5%	**3 Most popular majors:** economics, English, electrical engineering
Founded: 1912	**Percent in-state / out-of-state:** 46% / 54%	
Private or Public: private	**Percent Pub HS:** NA	**Retention:** 95%
Religious affiliation: none	**Number of Applicants:** 6,463	**Graduation rate:** 90%
		On-campus housing: 100%
Location: urban	**Percent Accepted:** 24%	**Fraternities:** NA
	Percent Accepted who enroll: 42%	**Sororities:** NA
Undergraduate enrollment: 2,764	**Entering:** 642	**Library:** 1,600,000 volumes
Total enrollment: 4,062	**Transfers:** 54	**Tuition and Fees:** $15,796 in; $15,796 out
Percent Male / Female: 54% / 46%	**Application Deadline:** 2 Jan	**Room and Board:** $6,600
Percent Minority: 32%	**Mean SAT:** NA	**Financial aid, first-year:** 34%
	Mean ACT: NA	

Rice University in Houston, Texas, offers an Ivy League–quality experience, a manageable tuition, a perpetually warm climate, and an upscale urban location. And, students say, the quality of academic and campus resources of Rice matches that of any Ivy.

Academic Excellence

Students claim that academic competition between peers is minimized at Rice. "Students here are driven but not cutthroat," says one senior English major. Instead, Rice students strictly adhere to an honor code, violations of which are punishable by suspension. As one student advises, "Don't $%^& with the Honor Code."

Despite the tame level of competition, students say Rice academics are intense. Especially demanding majors are Biology and Engineering (particularly Chemical Engineering). Though traditionally Rice has excelled in engineering and science, the English and History Departments have made great strides in recent years. The establishment of the Baker Institute for Public Policy, which funds scholars and provides a forum for public policy debate, has strengthened the Political Science department as well. Students say

that Managerial Studies and Sports Medicine are less intense than other majors.

> **Most students develop strong college loyalty and close friendships within their colleges.**

The core curriculum demands that students take courses in three areas: the humanities, the social sciences, and the natural sciences. With the exception of Introductory lectures, classes are generally small. Students select courses during "shopping period," the first two weeks of each semester. One student explains, "You can sit in on as many courses as interest you and leave if you don't like the professor, syllabus, or course." Favorite courses include "Sex with Chad," or "Sexuality and the Social Order" taught by Professor Chad Gordon. Environmental and Energy Economics draws raves, and "students sleep in the hall outside his office the night before registration" to get into Professor Dennis Brown's public speaking class. Students also recommend Professor John Zamito's class on European Intellectual History. For the many Rice students who aspire to careers in medicine, engineering, or science, introductory physics and chemistry are "notoriously difficult." Students must do more than "memorize formulas" and "plug and chug." Rather, they must "think through their work" to attain success in such science courses.

Residential Colleges: Centers of Life
Upon matriculation, all students become residents of one of eight colleges (a new college is under construction, and a tenth college may soon be added as well). Offering such facilities as a TV room, a game room, and weight room, colleges serve as dorms and social centers. Most students develop strong college affiliations and close friendships within their colleges. One student says, "the dorm setup at Jones College is the best." Another claims, "Will Rice College is the college of Gods and Goddesses," while Baker students bond during a naked (except for strategically placed whip cream), drunken run through campus known as the "Baker 13." In addition, each college has its own Master and staff of Associates. The Master, a tenured professor, lives and eats with students, organizes activities, and settles personal and academic problems among students. The Associates, comprised of faculty members, community members, and Rice employees advise students on classes and careers; the great majority of associates live outside of Rice, but each college houses two associates, who reportedly interact frequently with students.

Aesthetic Excellence
Rice boasts a beautiful, architecturally eclectic campus. One student gushes, "Rice's campus is gorgeous. Legend has it that the university charter requires areas with wild strawberries, violets, and rabbits." Another says, "We don't even have sidewalks. The founder insisted on Pebble Paths." The buildings themselves receive mixed comments; Duncan Hall "is like Willy Wonka's magic factory or landing in the Wizard of Oz—people at Rice either love it or hate it." Also, the campus has many large quadrangles which provide room for frequent games of Ultimate Frisbee and touch football. However, students criticize the form of the colleges: "The college buildings are the least attractive. Weiss was originally built as temporary army barracks, and looks like it. Lovett is somehow a cross between a toaster and a prison."

Constant Stimulation
Students say that life at Rice provides constant stimulation; activities abound and fun is usually available. The Cabinet, the University's student government, and the *Thresher*, Rice's newspaper, are extremely popular. The Campus Crusade for Christ (CCC) maintains a large membership but draws criticism for excessive zeal in trying to convert non-Christians. The Residential Colleges offer great extracurricular opportunities in the arts and intramural athletics; Frisbee is especially popular, and because of the warm and sun-drenched setting, students can play any outdoor sport in any season.

Chilling
Students often spend much of their time "chilling" with friends. Students talk about "normal college things—you know, sex, gossip, funny events, football," but people at Rice often extend classroom discussions into their college dining halls or into their suites through the early morning hours. Rice students describe each other as "open with lots of J.Crew Junkies."

Colleges and various campus organizations hold frequent parties. Students say the drinking policy is "extremely lax," and "you just won't get in trouble for underage drinking." Alcohol is "an option for everyone," many claim, but those who do not drink feel little pressure to do so. Esperanza in the fall and Rondolet in the spring are the two major formals. The "Screw-yer-Roommate" dance involves finding one's roommate a blind date for a night and formulating a unique way for the roommate to find his or her date. One junior explains, " I had to gallop around the main academic quad with a stick horse and a cowboy hat and my date had to come bucking out of one of the archways with horns—I had to rope him." Students attend the Night of Decadence (NOD) dressed as minimally as possible; one student says, "It's all about Plastic Wrap—lots of Plastic Wrap." For such reasons, *Playboy* magazine has named NOD one of the top college parties.

Beer Bike, held in the spring, may be the largest social event of the year. Each college picks a theme and marches in a huge parade to the track where a nontraditional bike race is held. After a team member rides around the track twice, another team member chugs either 24 ounces (for males) or 12 ounces (for females and alumni) of beer. Most colleges "start chug practices at the beginning of the year."

One campus hangout is the Coffeehouse, "a student-run organization that donates its profits to charity and provides a forum for student performers. Further, students seem to love the two campus bars: "You gotta love Willy's Pub and Val Halla." On Thursdays, students congregate at Willy's Pub and naked Baker 13 runners receive free beer from Val Halla. For Mexican food aficionados, there are the popular Taco Cabana and Mission Burrito restaurants. House of Pies, "known as 'House of Guys' because of the transvestites who frequent it at 3 A.M.," also attracts many students.

Outside of Rice, Lai-Lai's in Chinatown offers " tantalizing, authentic, and cheap" Chinese food to groups of Rice students. Mai's and Van Loc serve excellent Vietnamese fare.

Venturing beyond the boundaries of Rice, students can visit art gallery openings and festivals in the cosmopolitan city of Houston. The Westheimer Street Festival, which showcases musicians, jewelry, dancing, and crafts, also draws some Rice students. However, most Rice students say they tend to stay within campus bounds: "The hedges that surround Rice are a flimsy physical barrier but are almost impossible to penetrate mentally. There is a zoo, a free theater, and half a dozen museums across the street from Rice, but almost no one leaves campus. Although Rice is completely surrounded by Houston, it is also completely separate from it."

A warm climate, a close-knit community within each residential college, outstanding academics, and pleasant people define Rice University in order to make their college experience satisfying.—*Brian Abaluck*

FYI
The three best things about attending Rice are "the very friendly, comfortable social atmosphere, the spacious, immaculate campus, and O-week, an orientation program to help freshmen adjust to college life."
The three worst things about Rice are "lack of food options on campus—there's nothing except the college cafeterias and Sammy's (which is overpriced), that you have to have a car to get around and live comfortably after freshman year (most sophomores get booted out of campus housing for a year), and the rampant political apathy on campus."
The three things that every student should do before graduating are "Run the Baker 13—it's not just a group of exhibitionists, swim in President Gillis's personal pool (without permission, of course), and go Steamtunneling—again, blatantly illegal, this involves breaking into the underground tunnel system beneath the campus and exploring."
One thing I'd like to have known before coming here is "there is a TON of work—it doesn't matter what you're majoring in—you'll be bustin' your butt."

Southern Methodist University

Address: PO Box 750296; Dallas, TX 75205	**Percent African-American:** 7%	**Middle 50% SAT range:** 520–620 V, 520–630 M
Phone: 214-768-2058	**Percent Asian:** 6%	
E-mail address: ugadmission@smu.edu	**Percent Hispanic:** 9%	**Middle 50% ACT range:** 22–27
Web site URL: www.smu.edu	**Percent Native-American:** 0.5%	**3 Most popular majors:** business administration, finance, psychology
Founded: 1911	**Percent in-state / out-of-state:** 62% / 38%	
Private or Public: private	**Percent Pub HS:** 71%	**Retention:** 85%
Religious affiliation: United Methodist	**Number of Applicants:** 4,280	**Graduation rate:** 71%
Location: suburban	**Percent Accepted:** 89%	**On-campus housing:** 95%
Undergraduate enrollment: 5,426	**Percent Accepted who enroll:** 35%	**Fraternities:** 36%
Total enrollment: 9,464	**Entering:** 1,331	**Sororities:** 37%
Percent Male / Female: 47% / 53%	**Transfers:** 452	**Library:** 2,300,000 volumes
Percent Minority: 23%	**Application Deadline:** 1 Apr	**Tuition and Fees:** $18,510 in; $18,510 out
	Mean SAT: NA	**Room and Board:** $6,901
	Mean ACT: NA	**Financial aid, first-year:** 35%

Outsiders think of Southern Methodist University (SMU), located in the ritzy Highland Park section of Dallas, as a college in country club clothing. Despite the student body's reputation as Beamer-driving, Gap-wearing preprofessional elites, the university is equally known for its academic pressure and commitment to excellence.

The Road to Moola

The course requirements at SMU include rhetoric, two science labs, two PE courses (generally more like health education, not gym class), one math class, and one class dealing with computers or technology. Students must also take at least five "Perspectives" courses, from the following six categories: arts, literature, religious and philosophical thought, history, politics and economics, and behavioral sciences. In addition two "Cultural Formations" courses, or CFs are required, which are "designed to be in-depth interdisciplinary approaches to knowledge within the humanities and the social sciences," and are generally taken in the second year at SMU. Students describe the requirements as "more flexible than they appear. There are quite a few choices."

Popular majors at SMU include business, communications, psychology, and English. Students also cite theater as one of SMU's finest departments. Less popular programs include the engineering, geology, and chemistry departments. Many SMU students have pre-professional aspirations, hoping "to make a lot of money after graduation," according to one undergrad.

Class sizes at SMU vary, but students generally agree that the average course is not "gigantic." Typical introductory classes range in size from 25 to 100 students, but most are fewer than 50, and are generally broken into discussion sections of 15 to 20 students. It is not unusual even for freshmen to have classes with fewer than 30 students, and class size decreases as students move into higher-level courses, with 14 to 20 students about the average size. These relatively small classes allow students and professors to interact daily. Students say that "professors are very eager to help," providing office hours in order to increase their accessibility. Teaching assistants do not play a large role at SMU, and are most commonly found in the math, science, and occasionally business departments, where they lead sections and help out in labs.

Students say that gut or "booster" classes, such as Modern Electrical Technology and Wellness, exist in the hidden nooks of the SMU course book. Recently, the administration improved the registration process by allowing students to register by computer and to add and drop classes online. Students applaud this step, as it enables them to avoid the long registration lines that once marked the beginning of each semester. However, students still must go in person at the end of the semester to confirm their class registration, and lines for that can be very long.

Greek or Geek?

SMU is officially a dry campus, which translates into a harsh crackdown on underage drinking. Students say that unless you are "21 and in your room," drinking can be very risky. The administration has imposed a series of penalties for those caught violating school policy. Upon the first infraction, students are required to go to counseling. Future infractions of the policy involve fines as well as more counseling.

This strict policy reportedly is freely ignored on the sacrosanct grounds of the fraternity and sorority houses, although "you will rarely find anything stronger than cheap beer," one student said. SMU fraternities are getting stricter with drinking, and the Phi Delt fraternity has gone alcohol-free. Approximately half of SMU students are affiliated with the Greek system, and students agree that it plays a large role in campus social life. It is possible to remain independent and still enjoy the Greek party scene, though, since most Greek parties are "easy to get invitations to." However, due to the "cliquishness" of groups, undergrads say there is a "definite pressure to rush" in order to avoid the "Greek-or-geek" syndrome. Besides SMU's campuswide block party, the biggest festivities of the year are overwhelmingly Greek events such as the Shrimp Fest, the Fiji Island Party, Phi Delt's Casino Party, SAE's Guys and Dolls, and Lagnaf weekend.

Students unaffiliated with the Greek system still find plenty to do both on and off campus. Besides frat parties, students enjoy hanging out in Deep Ellum, an eclectic area of Dallas replete with bars and clubs. Although the drinking age is 21, many of the dance clubs—like Eden 2000 and Arcadia—do admit those 18 and older (still 21 to drink, of course). Downtown Dallas's West End, with such upscale hot spots as Planet Hollywood, is another popular rendezvous for students as well as tourists. In order to get around Dallas, though, a car is almost a necessity, since the city is so spread out and public transportation is limited. Students without cars say that an abundant selection of campus eateries and coffeehouses within walking distance of campus keeps them busy. For socializing, the Student Center is the destination of choice.

Campus Facilities

Many of the dorms at SMU have recently undergone renovations, and have been converted to spacious, suite-style rooms. Suites in Virginia-Snider, Morrison-McGinnis, and Cockrell-McIntosh consist of bedrooms connected by their own bathroom with bathtub, counter, and sink, and also connected to a common study room big enough for four desks and shelving units. McElvaney is the most popular dorm for freshmen, which boasts spacious and bright rooms, despite the fact that it is not one of the renovated dorms. Housing is all coed, except in dorms where bathrooms are in the hallways rather than within suites, in which case they are coed by either wing or floor. SMU requires freshmen to live on campus unless they commute from home, but some upperclassmen prefer off-campus housing in apartments.

Eating options include Mac's Place, which is located on the southern end of campus, and Umphrey Lee, which is located on the northern end of campus. Students generally eat at the location closer to them, but since Mac's Place is in one of the more common freshman dorms, more freshmen eat there. Some students claim that Umphrey Lee is "better by far," and thus more upperclassmen opt to eat there. Other options for food on the SMU campus include a Blimpie's, a Burger King, Pangeos Wraps, and a restaurant called the Mane Course which is located in the student center.

Surrounded by the upscale suburban neighborhood of Highland Park, SMU students have few concerns about security. Nevertheless, undergrads describe campus security as tight. Campus police patrol the grounds, and emergency phones are widely accessible. At night, a student escort service will accompany anyone who does not want to walk alone from one campus building to another.

> **SMU is officially a dry campus, which translates into a harsh crackdown on underage drinking.**

SMU students take advantage of the school's numerous extracurricular opportunities. A wide variety of cultural and religious groups sponsor meetings and campus activities. The Student Foundation, a university service organization, and the Program Council, made up of planning committees, are two popular student activities. SMU's wide variety of club and intramural sports, such as lacrosse, flag football, and volleyball, have gained tremendous appeal. Aspiring journalists can write for the *Daily Campus*.

SMU's football team recently won the Western Athletic Conference Championship against Eastern Tennessee under the leadership of Coach Mike Cavin. Although traditionally known to have a weaker football program than many in Texas, SMU is definitely on the rise.

Roughly half of the students at SMU are Texans, born and bred. That does not mean that an equally large number wear cowboy boots and six-shot revolvers. According to students, SMU is "definitely a very wealthy school," but it is also "more down-to-earth than you might think." While some students fit the SMU stereotype—white, upper-class, Texan—they have increasingly reflected more economic diversity, and students report that approximately 70% of the student body receive some financial assistance.

In addition to the warm climate, students especially appreciate how SMU's picturesque, colonial, "Ivy League looking" campus provides the best of two worlds: a tranquil setting within a cosmopolitan academic environment. —*Brian Abaluck and Staff*

FYI

The three best things about attending Southern Methodist University are: small classes, caring and enthusiastic professors, and the opportunities for educational enrichment (lectures, exhibits, performances, seminars, fairs, etc.).

The three worst things about attending Southern Methodist University are "the heavy emphasis on Greek life, the focus of the administration on politics and the appearance of the school, and the food."

The three things every student should do before graduating from Southern Methodist University are "get cheese fries from Snuffer's on Greenville Avenue, get to know your professors on a first-name basis, and go to Deep Ellum for some sort of cultural experience."

One thing I'd like to have known before coming here is: that money and politics could get you further than brains

Texas A&M University

Address: Mail Stop 1265;
College Station, TX
77843-1265
Phone: 409-845-3741
E-mail address:
admissions@tamu.edu
Web site URL:
www.tamu.edu
Founded: 1876
Private or Public: public
Religious affiliation: none
Location: small city
Undergraduate
enrollment: 36,045
Total enrollment: 43,442
Percent Male/Female:
52%/48%
Percent Minority: 16%
Percent African-American:
3%

Percent Asian: 3%
Percent Hispanic: 9%
Percent Native-American:
0.5%
Percent in-state/out-of-
state: 95%/5%
Percent Pub HS: NA
Number of Applicants:
14,453
Percent Accepted:
74%
Percent Accepted who
enroll: 62%
Entering: 6,695
Transfers: 2,174
Application Deadline:
15 Feb
Mean SAT: 577 V,
603 M
Mean ACT: 25

Middle 50% SAT range:
520–630 V,
550–660 M
Middle 50% ACT range:
23–27
3 Most popular majors:
biomedical sciences,
interdisciplinary studies,
marketing
Retention: 88%
Graduation rate: 72%
On-campus housing: 64%
Fraternities: 5%
Sororities: 14%
Library: 1,506,107 volumes
Tuition and Fees:
$3,167 in; $9,647 out
Room and Board: $4,898
Financial aid, first-year:
29%

The first word that should come to mind when thinking about Texas A&M is "tradition." Events such as the Bonfire, Yell Practice, and the Core Cadets are only a few of the numerous traditions that this university was built upon and that are still very much alive today. Founded in 1876 as the Agricultural and Mechanical (hence the A&M) College of Texas, the university was originally an all-male military school. Nowadays, Texas A&M is comprised of roughly 43,000 students divided into 10 academic areas. The one thing that unifies this immense student body, with its students from all 50 states and 113 other nations, is the "Aggie Spirit."

Traditions

The first thing that new Aggies must learn are the many traditions that enhance student life. Each year, for the infamous and spirited football game against the archrival University of Texas Longhorns, Aggies express their "burning desire" for triumph by constructing a massive 55-foot-high bonfire. To replace trees felled for the bonfire, students gather each spring to "replant" seedlings. During the games, students chant, cheer, and sing their fight songs proudly, directed by Yell Leaders, juniors and seniors elected by the student body to foster school spirit. One student noted that "just about everybody" goes to the games, because "if you go once, you want to go back over and over again."

Not all of the Aggie traditions are as festive. Since 1898, students have honored and recognized the Texas A&M students who have died while enrolled by congregating on the first Tuesday of every month. Students gather in front of the Academic Building and solemnly listen to the honor guard from the Corps fire a 21-gun salute. The atmosphere is so hushed and "dead silent" that "the only thing you hear are the pigeons taking off and, once its over, the Core Cadets' boots on the gravel." Students attest to the fact that "it's one of those moments you never forget."

Hitting the Books

The undergraduate education at Texas A&M is divided into colleges that each represent a particular major. Students can enroll in the general studies program for two years, but must eventually choose a college that specializes in their major. Academic requirements, mostly described as "fair" or "not too bad," largely depend on the major. Generally, students must maintain a 2.0–2.5 GPA to stay in the college, change majors, or avoid Scholastic Probation, called "Scho Pro." Some majors such as engineering require "particularly brutal" classes. One student said that chemistry majors are known to take Math 151-Calculus three times: "Everyone's dropped out once, failed once, and gotten a B or C on the third time."

In general, class sizes for introductory or required courses, or "everything in the first two years," range from 300 to 500 students. Most students report that the large class size "doesn't pose much of a problem." Many students are comfortable with these large classes and feel that they are "adequate [and] not too bad because there is a guaranteed curve with so many people." However, as students reach upper-level courses, class sizes tend to slim down to 50 students or less while honors classes commonly enroll less than 20.

While students appreciate that professors teach most of the classes, contentment with the level of instruction varies greatly. One student characterized her professors as "very caring, you can always go to them if you have a problem. They're always very approachable—you feel welcome when you start talking to them." But another student complained that he "hardly interacts with the professors. You can if you want to, but they [have] other things on their minds." Other complaints include "my profs don't cover anything regarding the tests and don't care if you fail," and "my TA fell asleep during physics lab, sprawled across the desk." On the whole, the faculty was deemed "okay, but certainly not the highlight of academics here."

The Students

Though the university is unquestionably large, students often complain that it is "mostly white—there are minorities here, but not a lot." Other students characterize the student body as "mostly cowboys" and "conservative." Regardless of the student mix, Aggies often praise the friendliness of their peers: "If anything happens to you, you can count on anyone here to

help you out." In fact, many students reported that they often receive a "howdy" from friends and strangers alike.

The most prominent student group on campus is the Core Cadets. Each year, over 800 freshmen ("Fish") join the Core Cadets; a program most often compared to ROTC, but without the national military requirement. One Core member said that "you live it, you love it. Everyone else looks up to you, though the physical training and harassment are tough to handle." Cadets not only wear their uniforms daily, but they live and eat together.

Parties and Rodeos

Texas A&M is located in College Station, a small college town that provides Aggies with many opportunities to get off campus once in a while. There are many restaurants, bars, a movie theater, and a mall in the area. The most famous off-campus eatery, the Dixie Chicken, is home to the Aggie tradition of senior "dunking," an event that gives seniors the same number of seconds as the year of their graduation to drink a pitcher of beer.

On-campus, many of the organizations such as the Aggie Angels and the Howdy Ags coordinate social activities. Because of the prominence of the Core Cadets, there is only a small Greek scene. Though alcohol at parties is prevalent, "there are virtually no drugs." Students claim that the party scene is good "most of the time, but every now and then, it can get quite dull."

> **Tradition mandates that guys must kiss their dates after each A&M touchdown, extra point, or field goal.**

Unique to the social scene at Texas A&M is "its quality." One student said that "there are plenty of beautiful girls here; and not only are they beautiful, they have class." There are reportedly some Aggie girls, called Bootchasers, who fawn over the Senior Core Cadets that wear "expensive, big, brown boots with spurs—girls think it's great." Contributing to this "great dating scene" is another Aggie football tradition. Tradition mandates that guys must kiss their dates after each A&M touchdown, extra point, or field goal.

Living Arrangements

Students of Texas A&M complain that campus housing is not the school's strong point. Though students describe dorms as "adequate" overall, the university is "famous for overbooking dorms." One student had to live in temporary housing for a week in a tripled-up dorm room while another reportedly was forced to live in a converted study lounge for an entire semester.

Once accepted, students apply for on-campus housing depending on size, facilities, and cost of particular dorms. All students suggest applying early to have a better chance of getting the dorm that you want. Kreuger Hall, one of the better dorms, was lauded for its locking doors, nice interior and large rooms. Meanwhile, Crocker Hall was described as being "weird: they have their own traditions, and it's in its own little part of campus." Resident advisors are available freshman year for those students who need advice about academics or social issues.

Sports and Activities

For most Aggies, sports shape and enhance the college experience. Texas A&M University plays at the Division I level as a member of the Big 12 Conference. The school has 19 varsity sports: 9 for men and 10 for women. Club and intramural sports are also popular on campus. The university offers intramural competition in events including preseason basketball, outdoor soccer, team bowling, racquetball, and sand volleyball.

Aggies attribute the numerous and diverse extracurricular activities to the school's large student population. Students guarantee that "if there is something you are interested in, there is a club here for you." Student organizations range from academic and preprofessional to cultural and political. Various opportunities for involvement range from the Fade to Black Dance Ensemble to the Students for a Free Tibet or the Aggie Wranglers. Community service is also popular, particularly among students in groups such as Circle K International and Aggie Habitat for Humanity.

Thanks to the variety of activities, many students report that the "sense of belonging is overwhelming." Indeed, it seems that the energy of the A&M student body is manifest in the school's traditions, school spirit, and enthusiasm for their community.—*Kurtland Ma and Staff*

FYI

The three best things about attending Texas A&M are "the Aggie school spirit, the opportunities of a large school, and the athletics."

The three worst things about attending Texas A&M are "the huge student body, the housing, and some of the TAs."

The three things that every student should do before graduating from Texas A&M are "make the bonfire, go to the Dixie Chicken for 'dunking,' and experience the silent remembrance of students who have died while enrolled here."

One thing I'd like to have known before coming here is "that I couldn't keep all the stuff I'd brought in my tiny dorm room!"

Texas Christian University

Address: TCU Box 297013; Fort Worth, TX 76129	**Percent Asian:** 2%	**Middle 50% SAT range:** 520–620 V,
Phone: 817-257-7490	**Percent Hispanic:** 5%	520–640 M
E-mail address: frogmail@tcu.edu	**Percent Native-American:** 0.5%	**Middle 50% ACT range:** 23–28
Web site URL: www.tcu.edu	**Percent in-state / out-of-state:** 73%/27%	**3 Most popular majors:** nursing, finance, marketing
Founded: 1873	**Percent Pub HS:** 91%	**Retention:** 82%
Private or Public: private	**Number of Applicants:** 5,028	**Graduation rate:** 63%
Religious affiliation: Christian	**Percent Accepted:** 75%	**On-campus housing:** 91%
Location: urban	**Percent Accepted who enroll:** 38%	**Fraternities:** 27%
Undergraduate enrollment: 6,267	**Entering:** 1,426	**Sororities:** 33%
Total enrollment: 7,551	**Transfers:** 376	**Library:** 1,885,702 volumes
Percent Male / Female: 41%/59%	**Application Deadline:** 15 Feb	**Tuition and Fees:** $13,125 in; $13,125 out
Percent Minority: 12%	**Mean SAT:** NA	**Room and Board:** $4,240
Percent African-American: 4%	**Mean ACT:** NA	**Financial aid, first-year:** NA

Texas Christian University (TCU) is a college that was *made* for view books. With its lovely campus, beautiful, sunny weather, and good-looking student body, its attractiveness is hard to beat. Just as enticing are TCU's academic offerings and plentiful student organizations. TCU's fine reputation is clearly well founded.

P.E. for Big Kids

Most students agree that TCU's academics have a lot to offer. The required core curriculum makes sure that entering students take classes in a number of disciplines. All students must complete nine hours of Foundation courses (writing and math), six hours of languages and literature, 36 hours of Exploration classes (physical and life sciences, religion, history, philosophy, and fine arts), and, interestingly, two hours of physical education. "P.E. is fun. They have cool classes, like fencing, bowling, scuba diving, and stage combat," said one sophomore. "You also have to take a health class. I took one on prescription drugs, and it was really interesting." TCU is also known for its 3-2 program, which allows students to get a bachelor's degree and MBA in five years.

There are slackers at TCU, as at any college, but for the most part, TCU students take their academics seriously. "It's all what you put into it," said a criminal justice major, "so if you put in the work, you get a lot out of your classes." According to one freshman, opportunities for work are definitely not lacking: "They work you pretty hard. I'm still just in the basic freshman core requirements, and I have massive amounts of reading for every class." Popular majors include nursing, business, communications, and psychology, which is known as one of the easier "athlete" majors. The honors program gets mixed reviews. Honors students do have a lot more work and get to take a few of the smaller honors classes each semester, but some students say there isn't much of an advantage to being in it. "It's a bunch of crap," said one business major. "When you graduate, you're recognized with maybe a stamp, but other than that, there's not much."

Professors at TCU are accessible and earn praise from students. "They work hard, they really know their stuff, and they expect students to also," said a freshman. Many students cite the individual attention from professors as one of TCU's greatest strengths. "They listen to you and keep track of you ... if you're absent a few times, they'll give you a call, stuff like that," explains a sophomore. Barring your standard huge lectures, class size at TCU is small, usually around 40 students at most, and gets no complaints.

Let's Go Eyeball Blood-Spitting Lizards!

With over 160 registered student organizations including the *Daily Skiff* newspaper, the *Image* magazine, dance, music, and theater groups, religious organizations, and a radio station, TCU has an impressive array of extracurriculars that offers students great opportunities for leadership. TCU also has a variety of intramural sports that are popular, as well as student government.

Varsity athletics at TCU are Division I. Football games, featuring not just cheerleaders but also "showgirls" "that are really pretty to look at," said one male student, are especially popular with students and alumni. In addition, the tennis team, which lost to Stanford in the NCAA Championship last year, is always in the top five in the nation, and basketball usually does well. Despite the strong football following, though, "there's not a lot of school spirit, since nobody stays on campus," said one sophomore. The school mascot is the horn frog. "It's actually a lizard, but it's called a horn *frog*," explains a business major. "It's not a good mascot because it's not very intimidating. It spits blood out of its eye or something like that." Ooh, scary.

Animal, Er, Dorm

Some of the most visible organizations at TCU are the fraternities and sororities. With 10 each of national fraternities and sororities, there is no way around the fact that going Greek is big at TCU, for better or for worse. Students in the system get designated dorms instead of houses, which they say has its perks. Besides nicer furnishings in the dorms due to alumni donations and other funds just for Greek groups, they enjoy theme parties, mixers, formals, and an instant niche. They also do volunteer work. "Each group has their own philanthropy. Ours works with Alzheimer's, so we volunteer at a nursing home and do stuff like that," said one junior sorority member.

> **"Everybody is so nice, which really surprised me because we're supposed to be snobby."**

Students who are not involved in the system tend to be either disgusted by it or indifferent to it. Whatever their attitude, there seems to be some separation between Greeks and non-Greeks on campus. "They [fraternities and sororities] are perceived as really snobby by people who aren't in them," admitted one sorority girl. In fact, one non-Greek sophomore said he decided not to rush fraternities because "the frat guys I talked to were rich little pieces of . . . uh, jerks that were stuck-up and conceited. I didn't want to hang out with those kinds of guys." Still, some Greek parties are open to all students, and as one student said, "If you bring girls, you don't have to pay."

Dude, Where's Your Car?

Regardless of the strong Greek presence at TCU, there are plenty of other opportunities to socialize and party. TCU has a dry campus, and residential advisors do rounds in dorms to enforce the rules. Students of the opposite sex are forbidden to be in each other's rooms after a certain time, and a campus police force known as the "Froggy Five-O" also helps keep things under control. One student confirmed, as one might expect, that "a lot of people break the rules."

Not surprisingly, most partying happens off campus. With downtown Fort Worth only one exit away, going downtown to bars and clubs, like Longhorn's, Cowboy Cats, Neon Moon, and City Streets, is also popular. The clubs usually have 18 and over nights with regular dance music on weekends, though most of the bars are strict about carding before serving alcohol. A lot of students leave campus to eat, since food at the Main, the TCU cafeteria, is "really expensive and pretty awful." Popular restaurants include steak houses like Texas De Brazil and Del Frisco's and a "gourmet hole-in-the-wall thing" called "Michael's." Dallas–Fort Worth has a lot of cultural attractions as well, such as art museums and concert centers. With all there is to do downtown, students report that a car is "a must."

Three Cute Girls for Every Boy

The overwhelming majority of students at TCU are from Texas, and the homogeneity doesn't end there. There is very little racial and ethnic diversity, and the stereotype of the Kate-Spade-bag-toting TCU student going to class dressed in Banana Republic is very much a reality. Still, students agree that TCU "is a really friendly campus. Everybody is so nice, which really surprised me because we're supposed to be snobby," said a junior. "Walking around, everybody says hi to each other." The campus, which takes 10 minutes to walk across, is also beautiful. It's comprised of southwestern cream-colored brick buildings with red Spanish-style roofs and "pretty flowers everywhere"—an idyllic scene in the year-round Texas sunshine.

TCU is also a hottie haven—there is no dispute that it's "a very, very pretty school," said one happy freshman boy. "It's what the guys talk about all the time," he laughs. "Our girls are really pretty," agreed one sophomore, "and they dress up a lot. Most people make an effort to look nice." With the nearly 3-to-1 girl-to-guy ratio, it's safe to say that TCU is pretty much crawling with cute chicks. "Because of the ratio, I'm sure we girls do try to look nicer so we can be noticed," said a sorority girl. Not a bad deal, especially for the males of the student body. As one of the lucky guys admits, "We can't complain."
—*Patricia Stringel*

FYI
The three best things about attending TCU are "the friendliness, the beautiful campus, and the good-looking students."
The three worst things about attending TCU are "the Greek system, the lack of school spirit, and the desertion on weekends."
The three things every student should do before graduating from TCU are "jump through the Frog Fountain, get to know Fort Worth, and do the 'Walk of Shame.'"
One thing I'd like to have known before coming here is "the guy-to-girl ratio is great for guys but stinks for girls!"

Texas Technology University

Address: New Students Relations; Box 45005; Lubbock, TX 79409-5005
Phone: 806-742-1482
E-mail address: nsr@ttu.edu
Web site URL: www.texastech.edu
Founded: 1923
Private or Public: public
Religious affiliation: none
Location: small city
Undergraduate enrollment: 20,227
Total enrollment: 24,249
Percent Male / Female: 54%/46%
Percent Minority: 16%
Percent African-American: 3%

Percent Asian: 2%
Percent Hispanic: 10%
Percent Native-American: 0.5%
Percent in-state / out-of-state: 94%/6%
Percent Pub HS: NA
Number of Applicants: 8,100
Percent Accepted: 75%
Percent Accepted who enroll: 58%
Entering: 3,536
Transfers: 1,676
Application Deadline: rolling
Mean SAT: 541 V, 554 M
Mean ACT: 23

Middle 50% SAT range: 480–580 V, 490–600 M
Middle 50% ACT range: 20–26
3 Most popular majors: marketing, management info systems, psychology
Retention: 79%
Graduation rate: 46%
On-campus housing: 82%
Fraternities: 10%
Sororities: 16%
Library: 4,245,818 volumes
Tuition and Fees: $3,107 in; $9,587 out
Room and Board: $4,787
Financial aid, first-year: 47%

Located in the High Plains of West Texas, Texas Tech benefits from the nurturing environment of a medium-sized city without the congestion and stress of a major metropolis. Most buildings on campus, with clay roofs and red and beige brick walls, resemble Spanish-style fortresses. In fact, campus planner William Ward Watkin chose Spanish architecture as the model for Texas Tech's buildings because of the geographic similarity of Western Texas and central Spain. As one student said, "If you can't afford a trip to Spain, bring a banjo, go to the Tech campus, and eat at Taco Cabana. It's the closest you'll get to the real thing."

More Than Agriculture

Texas Tech's academics live up to its impressive campus. Although Texas Tech once functioned primarily as an institute for agriculture and technology, education at Tech no longer revolves around computer chips and corn. The university's core curriculum includes courses in the humanities in an effort to better prepare students to meet the challenges of the future. Most of the academic departments are expanding their curricula to become more liberal arts oriented.

With an undergraduate school, several graduate schools, a law school, and a medical school all on one campus, Texas Tech University is the most comprehensive public university in the state. The undergraduate side of the campus is split up into eight academic colleges: Agricultural Sciences and Natural Resources, Architecture, Arts and Sciences, Business Administration, Education, Engineering, Human Sciences, and the Honors College. Most students consider engineering, education, business, and architecture the strongest and most popular majors. The education program is well known because a good number of Tech students go on to become teachers. Less popular majors include fine arts and theater. For the most part, each college sets its own requirements in addition to the mandated writing courses.

Class sizes range from 300 to 400 students at the introductory level in such fields as astronomy, political science, and other science courses to as few as 20 students in English seminars and higher-level courses. The chief complaint of many students is that the majority of freshman and sophomore classes are taught by TAs instead of professors, though many undergrads report that the student-faculty interactions during junior and senior years make up for this drawback.

Campus Facilities

Tech's vast campus offers a wealth of places where students can study, especially the recently renovated and very quiet main library, which reportedly resembles a stack of books turned on its side, the "B.A. Rotunda" of the business administration building, which is reportedly shaped like a calculator, and various dorm lounges. Texas Tech also has a Student Union and a Student Recreation Center, both about to be renovated, which offer more options for students to get together and study or just hang out.

Opinions of campus housing range from "much better than most state schools" to "mediocre." According to one sophomore RA, "The residence hall staff takes pride in providing students with the best possible environment for living and studying by organizing dorm activities and study breaks." Once a year, the residence hall administration sponsors a campus-wide event featuring country singers like Tim McGraw. The freshman residence hall Chitwood/Weymouth is considered by some students the worst dorm because of its location, although others claim that it is the "place to live when you are a freshman," because it is the only high-rise dorm available for freshman and it is very social. The Strangel/Murdough residence hall is often praised for its convenient location and "chillin'" courtyard. Most Tech dorms consist of two buildings—one for men and one for women—connected by offices, lounges, and a common cafeteria. Each dorm has its own cafeteria offering diverse cuisine including southwestern, Italian, and the "sometimes risky" Chinese entrees. While most dining hall food is considered "boring" or "old," Tech has earned the reputation for having "the best dining halls of any school in Texas." Most dorm rooms are doubles with built-in furniture and are generally considered comfortable. Although the Tech campus is not crime ridden, campus security is tight and there are security guards at dorm entrances and surveillance cameras in various parts of the campus.

Although Tech students are happy with the residence halls, many upperclassmen prefer to move off campus, ond one cited a figure as high a 70% of upperclassmen living off. "Living off campus is more convenient because I can cook my own food and I don't have to deal with the noise," one junior said.

Class. Beer. Bed.

One student said social life at Tech "revolves around fraternity parties and the beer keg," since the town of Lubbock has little to offer beside a few movie theaters and a minor league hockey team, the Cotton Kings, which draws many student fans since their games are played at the Coliseum, a sporting arena right on campus. One student described Lubbock as having "enough to do to keep you occupied, but not enough to get you into trouble." However, recently a new concert venue called the United Spirit Arena was built in town, and several popular bands, including Kiss and Elton John, have played there.

Nonetheless, most students say that the Greek scene is the primary way of socializing, drinking, and meeting people at Tech. And there are numerous opportunities to do so, particularly during weekly parties. One student summarized his typical week as "going to class, then getting wasted, then going to bed." The campus and Lubbock are dry (the largest dry town in the nation), so some students obtain their alcohol from "the Strip," a row of liquor stores just outside the city which are designed to look just like Las Vegas. Some students also hang out at off-campus dance clubs such as the Warehouse, which is the most fun when local bands play there, and Midnight Rodeo. Sports bars such as the Conference Cafe are also popular, as is Liquid 2000 for techno aficionados. Other popular hangouts include Cricket's, which boasts of a full bar, over 100 beers to choose from, pool tables and several TVs, and bars like Tom's Daquaris, Clousseau's Martini bar, Bleacher's Sports Cafe, and Athens. Those looking to satisfy their midnight cravings can do so at Spanky's, IHOP, Taco Cabana, Jazz Louisiana Kitchen, or One Guy's Pizza.

The Mighty Raiders

Athletics are definitely a major part of Tech student life. In 1996, both the men's and women's basketball teams qualified for the "Sweet 16" round of the NCAA tournament. Now in the Big 12 conference, Tech battles athletic powerhouses like UT/Austin, Oklahoma, and its ultimate rival, Texas A&M. The Red Raider football team consistently ranks among the top 25 nationally, and has beaten Texas A&M 4 out of the past 5 years. Football games are usually well attended, and the spirited crowd keeps traditions alive, including "tortilla tossing," in which students toss tortillas every time the team scores. The Saddle Tramps, a group of male students, also decorate the campus with red and black streamers before games. The Lady Raiders basketball team is consistantly ranked in the top 25, and baseball games are also popular, as the team s usually in the running for the conference championship. Tech administrators also show their spirit by ringing the bells in the administration building for 30 minutes each time an athletic team wins a conference championship.

Aside from varsity athletics, Tech offers many opportunities to compete in intramural sports. Students say that IM competition at Tech is more fierce than most varsity sports. Undergrads may form their own teams or compete with different organizations on campus. One sophomore said that over 260 different teams registered to compete in the IM flag football tournament. Tech houses state-of-the-art fitness equipment, tennis courts, and swimming pools for non-varsity athletes, and a local corporation recently donated $10 million for construction of a new basketball arena.

The Heartland Ethos

Although Greek life and athletics are dominant, student life at Tech is not limited to them, since there are over 300 student organizations to choose from. Texas Tech reportedly has the second-largest College Republican Club in the U.S. There are also political groups for more liberal students, the University Democrats and the Campus Libertarians, but students report that these groups "barely" have a presence at Tech due to the more conservative nature of the student body. Other popular organizations include Student Senate, Campus Crusade for Christ, the Marching Band, and the Future Farmers/Ranchers of America. Many students also write for the *University Daily*, Texas Tech's free daily newspaper.

Texas Tech is a conservative school that primarily fits what some students call the "Christian, white, Texan, Republican" stereotype. Although the University is trying to recruit more minority students, there is a definite lack of diversity on campus. Regardless, Tech students are very happy with their school selection, which is evident in their spirit and unity. As one student said, "We have the school spirit and traditions of Texas A&M, but with half the people." Texas Tech is a school where students can learn in a friendly, supportive Texan atmosphere for a not so Texas-sized price.—*Brian Abaluck and Staff*

FYI

The three best things about attending Texas Tech are "the school spirit, the friendliness of West Texans, and the football fever."

The three worst things about attending Texas Tech are "waiting in long lines (3 hours or more) for financial aid checks, the bovine emanations from the cattle farms, and the lesser recognition than UT or A&M."

The three things that every student should do before graduating from Texas Tech are "attend a football game, play IMs, and try to drink all the different beers at Crickets."

One thing I'd like to have known before coming here is "that there is very little diversity."

Trinity University

Address: 715 Stadium Drive; San Antonio, TX 78212-7200
Phone: 210-999-7207
E-mail address: admissions@trinity.edu
Web site URL: www.trinity.edu
Founded: 1869
Private or Public: private
Religious affiliation: Presbyterian
Location: urban
Undergraduate enrollment: 2,264
Total enrollment: NA
Percent Male/Female: 49%/51%
Percent Minority: 21%

Percent African-American: 2%
Percent Asian: 8%
Percent Hispanic: 10%
Percent Native-American: 0.5%
Percent in-state/out-of-state: 72%/28%
Percent Pub HS: NA
Number of Applicants: 2,743
Percent Accepted: 76%
Percent Accepted who enroll: 31%
Entering: 637
Transfers: NA
Application Deadline: 1 Feb
Mean SAT: NA

Mean ACT: NA
Middle 50% SAT range: 580–690 V, 590–680 M
Middle 50% ACT range: 25–30
3 Most popular majors: business administration, biology, English
Retention: 86%
Graduation rate: 76%
On-campus housing: NA
Fraternities: 26%
Sororities: 28%
Library: NA
Tuition and Fees: $15,804 in; $15,804 out
Room and Board: $6,330
Financial aid, first-year: 44%

Amid the rolling lawns and perfectly manicured oak trees in San Antonio sits Trinity University, a country club by any gardener's standards. But don't let this atmosphere fool you. Besides having a "practically 2-to-1 student to gardener ratio" and a special endowment just for landscaping, Trinity offers a solid liberal arts education with motivated students and a top-notch, dedicated faculty.

Common Curriculum

Trinity has consistently ranked high in a variety of publications like the *U.S. News & World Report*, *Money* magazine, and the *Princeton Review* as one of the best small liberal arts universities west of the Mississippi—and it is not hard to see why. Since classes rarely enroll more than 50 and can be as small as 5 and because there are very few teaching assistants, professor–student interaction is said to be "fabulous" and "a cornerstone of a Trinity education." "I don't think there even are TAs here," said one junior. Besides small classes, Trinity offers a first-rate faculty, all of whom have Ph.D.s in their respective fields. "They are really there to help you learn inside and outside of the classroom," with extensive office hours, mentoring programs, and countless opportunities for undergraduates to do research with professors.

Trinity has the Common Curriculum, which emphasizes seven "understandings," including world culture, Judeo-Christian culture, and cognitive thinking. "The requirements do fill up a lot of your schedule the first couple years unless you have AP credits, which can be a pain, but it's still worth taking a wide variety of classes if not to learn about a few topics outside your major, to find a major which really interests you," said one senior who changed his major six times in the course of his first two years. All the majors are reputable, with the sciences, business, and education programs being the strongest. "We have great placement success with education graduates and students bound for medical school," boasted one student.

Facilities of a Country Club

The Trinity campus has been described as nothing less than "beautiful." The buildings are made from 'Trinity Red' brick and sit among a lush landscape. Dorms are considered very decent. "I lived in Prosths last year, which is not considered to be the best dorm on campus, but it's still luxurious by most standards, with big rooms and a great view of the skyline of San Antonio," said one student. Students can choose to live in quiet, dry dorms, or, for the more rowdy, there are more social, wet dorms, where alcohol is allowed. Yet there are some complaints about some dorms, like Herdon, being isolated from the rest of the campus.

Safety is a non-issue for Trinity students. "I always feel safe when I'm walking around campus alone, day or night," a female student said. With campus phones and 24-hour police patrol, most say crime is really rare and students don't often feel the need to use the free escort service that is available to anyone who doesn't feel safe walking around campus alone.

Social Life

The social life at Trinity circles around the Greek system. Approximately 30–35% of the students are members of a fraternity or sorority. "I love my sorority because it gives a great structured social life, but I'm able to have friends outside my sorority, too," one student said. Those who don't wish to be a frat brother or sorority sister are welcome at most Greek events, but many are disappointed with the social life outside the frat parties. There are 10 bars in San Antonio on St. Mary's Strip, including Crazy Horse Saloon and Tycoon Flats, but "good luck getting in as a freshman, because they card practically all the time." In addition, there are some good clubs for blues and other places for country-western dancing. San Antonio also offers a Sea World, the Alamo, Hemisphere Park, Riverwalk, and a mall, for some daytime fun as well. For the dance club–bound, Austin offers some "fun places" that are reportedly much less strict about checking IDs than clubs in San Antonio.

There are two places to go for food on campus: C and Maybee. Since at least one is open until 12, students can always get a snack. C offers food for students on the go, while Maybee offers sit-down meals with several different themes. "The quesadillas from the Mexican food line are the best," said one energetic student. People say Aramark, the food company responsible for the cafeteria cuisine, does a fair job making sure everything is edible and the food is sometimes actually pretty good.

Outside the Classroom

As a Division III school, Trinity does not give athletic scholarships, but "we still hold our own on the fields," said one football player. Saturday football games bring in a good crowd of around 2,500. "We put on our cowboy hats and cheer like crazy," according to one football fan. Other solid teams include men's and women's tennis, soccer, and volleyball. While Trinity's athletics are not quite at the level of UT/Austin, the school has enjoyed a solid showing in the SCAC (Southern Collegiate Athletic Conference) in the last few years in particular.

For those who are not up to the commitment of varsity sports, "intramurals are huge!" exclaimed one student, summing up feelings toward the program. Teams made up of fraternities, sororities, and independents come together to play ferocious games against each other in every sport from inner tube water polo to pole vaulting. Besides intramurals, there are a tremendous number of activities for students to get involved in, like the *Trinitonian*, the student daily newspaper, although it is said that students tend to be apathetic when it comes to active student organizations.

The Students

Although Trinity is Presbyterian-affiliated, one student said, "I don't feel like it's a particularly religious school." However, Christian religious groups have a strong presence on campus. "But there is something here for everyone. Almost everyone can find a niche here," said one student.

That said, students agree that the population is relatively homogeneous. "Everyone here is white, upper-middle-class, and says 'y'all,'" said a student. Yet the school administration has admittedly taken tremendous strides to diversify the student body. An increasing portion of students hail from out of state. However, ethnic diversity still lags and continues to be a high priority of the admissions office. As a consequence, the campus tends to be fairly conservative, although most are tolerant toward all viewpoints.

> **"Everyone here is white, upper-middle-class, and says 'y'all.'"**

With an administration dedicated to consistent improvement on academic and social fronts, there is no doubt that at Trinity undergraduates receive a top-notch education in a community of "tightly knit" students, enthusiastic faculty, and incredible gardeners.—*Jessica Morgan*

FYI

The three best things about attending Trinity are "the small class size, the willingness of the professors and staff to help, and the focus on undergraduate studies."

The three worst things about attending Trinity are "the small size of the student body means you don't get to do some of the things students at bigger universities get to do, lack of student support for athletics, and we have to live on campus for three years."

The three things that every student should do before graduating from Trinity are "go to a football game, play an IM sport, and get thrown in the fountain."

One thing I'd like to have known before coming here is "Texas geography."

University of Dallas

Address: 1845 East Northgate; Irving, TX 75062-4799
Phone: 972-721-5266
E-mail address: undadmis@acad.udallas.edu
Web site URL: www.udallas.edu
Founded: 1956
Private or Public: private
Religious affiliation: Catholic
Location: suburban
Undergraduate enrollment: 1,143
Total enrollment: 2,897
Percent Male / Female: 41%/59%
Percent Minority: 23%

Percent African-American: 2%
Percent Asian: 6%
Percent Hispanic: 14%
Percent Native-American: 0.5%
Percent in-state / out-of-state: 39%/61%
Percent Pub HS: 58%
Number of Applicants: 1,213
Percent Accepted: 76%
Percent Accepted who enroll: 33%
Entering: 310
Transfers: 122
Application Deadline: 15 Feb
Mean SAT: 613 V, 590 M

Mean ACT: NA
Middle 50% SAT range: 575–680 V, 540–650 M
Middle 50% ACT range: 24–28
3 Most popular majors: biology, English, history
Retention: 83%
Graduation rate: 59%
On-campus housing: 95%
Fraternities: NA
Sororities: NA
Library: 300,000 volumes
Tuition and Fees: $14,420 in; $14,420 out
Room and Board: $5,416
Financial aid, first-year: 48%

Students often dream of visiting foreign cities such as Athens and Rome. While others dream, students at the University of Dallas, commonly known as UD, enjoy the opportunity to travel and study in these cities easily for a semester. The emphasis that the university puts on foreign exchange distinguishes this Catholic liberal arts university from many others in its league.

"Baby-sitting" Plus

Located on the outskirts of Dallas in Irving, Texas, the University of Dallas offers a core curriculum reflecting its Catholic religious tradition—all students, for example, must take two theology courses as part of their liberal arts distribution requirements. Undergrads agree that classes at UD are challenging, but not overwhelming, while "'guts' are few and far between"; many students said they would never take a class simply to raise their GPA. English is considered one of UD's strongest departments as well as one of the most popular majors. Philosophy and politics offer strong programs as well, and the sciences, particularly the pre-med track, are considered to be excellent. One student reported that 85% of pre-med students with a 3.3 GPA or

higher get into their top-choice medical school.

While undergrads claim that there are no "bad" departments, some claim that UD's non-pre-med science departments are a bit weaker. Others complain about UD's research facilities; the university has only one small library, forcing many students to use the libraries at nearby Southern Methodist University. Professors teach all classes at UD. Small class sizes allow for frequent interaction between students and faculty, and professors often join students for dinner in the cafeteria.

UD has an attendance policy that allows students to miss no more than three classes during a semester; violators must report to the dean. Students have mixed reactions to the policy: some find it effective in making them learn, but others call it a "bureaucratic baby-sitting mechanism." One student complained, "I can't sleep in and recover from hangovers because of the mandatory attendance."

Exchange Programs

Many undergrads choose the University of Dallas for its foreign-exchange program in Rome. Participants (almost 100 percent of UD students!) spend one semester of their sophomore year on a newly built UD campus 10 minutes outside of Rome. Professors accompany students on trips and teach classes just as they would on the Texas campus. On weekends, the architecture and art classes take tours of the city. Students in the program also get 10 days off to travel "wherever they can make it," one participant said. During this break, many students go to Russia, Spain, Greece, England, or Ireland. Many participants enjoy the trip immensely, and find that it helps them gain a more intimate understanding of the Western Tradition courses they took during the prior year.

UD's main campus is a 20-minute drive from Dallas, making the city a popular weekend destination for students with cars. Undergrads describe the hillside campus as small and fairly isolated. The university has little contact with the surrounding community, although some students tutor children at nearby schools.

> Some feel that coed dorms are in the highest demand, because the single-sex dorms have strict limits on visits by members of the opposite sex.

The university requires students to live on campus unless they live with their families in the Dallas area or are at least 21 years old. Some feel that coed dorms are in the highest demand, because the single-sex dorms have strict limits on visits by members of the opposite sex. However, others point out the fact that the opposite-sex limitations are just as severe in the coed dorms. Students also say the noisiest and rowdiest dorm is the all-female Jerome. After their first year, students can choose their dorms and their roommates. O'Connell Hall, which houses mainly upperclassmen, reportedly is one of the most popular dorms, and is harder to get into, although many recently renovated dorms which offer even more perks are quickly taking its place. Most students share double rooms. About half of UD's upperclassmen move off campus, usually to Tower Village Apartments right across

the street, for cheaper housing and the possibility of keg parties on weekends.

Campus residents must be on the meal plan (either 14 or 19 meals), and students report that the food is less than appetizing. The Rat, a recreation center in the basement of the student center, is an alternative food source that also houses pool tables and a jukebox. Many students prefer the Rat's hamburgers, french fries, and pizza to the cafeteria food, although another student claimed that the food had gotten much better over her four years, and the amount of variety made meals satisfying.

Fun and Games
UD students describe their classmates as mostly white, religiously conservative Texans. There are few minority students, and even fewer openly gay men or lesbians. The general attitude toward drugs and sex is fairly restrained. "It's a pretty moral school," one student said. The social scene consists mainly of small parties in off-campus apartments where beer is reportedly easy to obtain, even though Irving County is dry.

Student government and dorm committees plan other social activities. The biggest unofficial bash of the year is Groundhog Day. On this special day, students take buses into the woods, set up kegs, and party all night, waiting for the groundhogs to come out. In the fall, the big event is Charity Week, a fund-raiser for local charities, involving karaoke contests, dunking booths for professors, and student "jails." University-sponsored trips and social events are attended mostly by freshmen and sophomores; upperclassmen tend to "do their own thing."

Students report that the sense of competition they feel in their academic pursuits is not quite as strong in intercollegiate athletics. UD only recently joined the NCAA Division III, and its rugby team, a club sport, has the longest reputation in the state. The women's soccer team, however, made it to the playoffs last year and is one of the more successful teams on campus. The athletic program launched its first baseball season a few years ago, and it has done very well, too. UD does not offer athletic scholarships, and as for mascots, one student said, "If we have one, you never see it at all."

Undergrads praise UD's small size and its commitment to a liberal arts education. Students have a common desire to learn, and although the school's rigorous academics and stern codes of conduct give parents peace of mind, many students like UD for the sense of spirit and adventure it instills in them.—*Melissa Chan and Staff*

FYI

The three best things about attending the University of Dallas are "small classes, close relationships with professors, and the spiritual and moral awareness of the student body."

The three worst things about attending the University of Dallas are "the isolation of campus if you don't have a car, the lack of privacy in double rooms, the attendance policy."

Three things every student should do before graduating from the University of Dallas are "go abroad, go to the Groundhog Day celebrations (wacky but worth it), and eat a meal with a professor."

One thing I'd like to have known before coming here is "start saving money early for extra travel and recreation expenses if you plan to go abroad."

University of Houston

Address: Houston, TX 77204-2161	**Percent Asian:** 20%	**Middle 50% SAT range:** 450–560 V,
Phone: 713-743-1010	**Percent Hispanic:** 19%	460–580 M
E-mail address: admissions@uh.edu	**Percent Native-American:** 1%	**Middle 50% ACT range:** 18–23
Web site URL: www.uh.edu	**Percent in-state/out-of-state:** 93%/7%	**3 Most popular majors:** psychology, education,
Founded: 1927	**Percent Pub HS:** NA	finance
Private or Public: public	**Number of Applicants:** 8,306	**Retention:** 76%
Religious affiliation: none	**Percent Accepted:** 70%	**Graduation rate:** 37%
Location: urban	**Percent Accepted who**	**On-campus housing:** 40%
Undergraduate enrollment: 25,626	**enroll:** 57%	**Fraternities:** 15%
Total enrollment: 31,602	**Entering:** 3,303	**Sororities:** 15%
Percent Male/Female: 48%/52%	**Transfers:** 4,045	**Library:** 1,900,000 volumes
Percent Minority: 55%	**Application Deadline:** 15 May	**Tuition and Fees:** $2,444 in; $7,604 out
Percent African-American: 15%	**Mean SAT:** 515 V, 533 M	**Room and Board:** $4,513
	Mean ACT: NA	**Financial aid, first-year:** NA

Looking for a big Texas school that still provides a great liberal arts education? The University of Houston, with a new image, a new logo, and a $5 million campaign to encourage you to come, is on its way up.

Diversity in Academics

UH is a gigantic, diverse campus in every way. It houses more than 30,000 students, yet manages to maintain an academic program that seems to satisfy everyone. Fourteen colleges make up the UH system, each one with a specialty, such as the College of Education; of Business Administration; of Natural Sciences and Mathematics; or of Humanities, Fine Arts, and Communications. Students choose from classes in any of these colleges, allowing departmentalized studying over a wide range of topics. One of the most respected colleges is the Conrad N. Hilton School of Hotel and Restaurant Management, which has an on-campus hotel to give students hands-on experience.

Though a large university, UH takes its role as a liberal arts school very seriously. Core requirements make up a large portion of the underclassmen's schedules. The requirements include a total of 42 class hours, consisting of 6 hours in communication (English), 3 hours math, 3 hours of math or logic and reasoning, 3 hours of humanities, 3 hours of visual or performing arts, 6 hours of natural sciences, 6 hours of social sciences, 6 hours of history, and 6 hours of government. While some students feel "bogged down" by these requirements, most are simply "indifferent." The requirements, while often tedious, provide students with a solid background in subjects one would otherwise avoid.

Of the 120 different concentrations undergrads have to choose from, the most difficult are considered to be the math-based ones, including engineering and architecture. While there are no definite "slacker" majors, one student believed that geology would be a safe bet "because when I took that class I skipped the second half of the semester (except the tests) and still got an A." Majors with good reputations are optometry (for which there is an entire college), engineering, and journalism. The sciences wields its own reputation, as well, offering impressive resources such as the Texas Center for Superconductivity Research, now known simply as "Paul's House" in honor of Paul Chu, a UH professor who did early research in superconductivity. The theater department boasts the Pulitzer Prize–winning playwright Edward Albee, who teaches and works to produce entertaining shows for the entire student body.

Every year 300 hard-working students go through a thorough application process in order to join the Honors College. This college—the only interdisciplinary college at UH—gives selected students the opportunity to have a small liberal arts college atmosphere within a huge university setting. Members of this elite group must maintain a high GPA. In exchange for their efforts, honors students enjoy other perks including the chance to live in the best dorms on campus, access to smaller classes, and priority registration.

For the other students at UH, there is not too much about which to complain. They register for classes through a phone system, and are rarely unable to get the classes they want. While some lectures in the core system can have up to 600 students, most upper-level courses enroll no more than 30 students.

A Diverse Crowd

Despite the decent dorms, good food, and quiet atmosphere, UH remains a commuter school. Less than a fifth of the students live on campus and despite all the racial and ethnic diversity, 67% of the student body is from the same county in Texas. Students often live in off-campus apartments, or, more commonly, choose to stay at home and drive to school. The average age of UH students is significantly higher than that of other colleges, and many students are adults taking classes part time, or returning to school after time out in the real world.

But campus residents are fairly happy with the UH culture. Because of the distance between housing complexes, solidarity develops from the four different residence halls: Cougar Place (lots of varsity athletes and a suite setup), Moody Towers ("the dorms that suck the most . . . with cramped rooms and communal showers"), the Quadrangle, and Cambridge Oaks (privately run on-campus apartments). Students living on campus have the opportunity to know one another better, as they are often the only ones around during weekends, without a home to "zip back to and do a load of laundry."

> "Commuters do things that they have to and then go home."

The UH meal plan actually allows students to eat and pay for what they want. Instead of specified meal costs, the card works like a debit card, taking money out of an account set aside for food. This allows students to eat all over campus in places from the Horizon's Café, with a Pizza Hut, Fresh Grill, and Little Kim Son, to the new Millennium 2000 Café, with a Wendy's, a Taco Bell, and a coffee shop. In addition, students can use their "meal money" to shop at any of several convenience stores and make food on their own. In the past, students have protested the food, but the administration is making efforts to improve it, with the addition of fast-food and convenience-store options.

Hanging Out Off Campus

Houston is the fourth largest city in the country and has much to offer UH students. Unfortunately, UH is not in the best area of Houston. Ten minutes from downtown (by car or the Metro, Houston's public transit) and right off the interstate, as one student put it, "UH is in the middle of the ghetto, you have to go over to Rice for things like cool coffee shops." But again, the administration is looking to change all that. With an on-campus police department and a multitude of emergency phones, crime is at a low. Nevertheless, students remind that just as you should not walk around anywhere late at night, "you don't want to walk around alone on the campus perimeter late at night." As long as students use common sense, UH is a safe campus.

Students maintain that having a car is almost essential, as there is little campus night life. Hence, many students, even those who live on campus, own cars. In Houston itself, students hang out in clubs like Numbers, which has live alternative music, and Rockefeller's. Coffee shops are ever popular with the college crowd, and in the city many frequent the new Magic Bus, a combined bar and coffee house. During the daylight hours students can go to the museum district and learn about natural history, science, or art, or shop in the Galleria, a mall complete with an ice skating rink. For a day trip, students may choose to go to the beaches at Galveston or to Freeport for a change of pace.

Staying On Campus

On-campus life is relaxed between classes and schoolwork. A typical UH student wears jeans and T-shirts, and is "way casual." Unless you are one of the few in a Greek organization or in an academic honor society, the chances to get dressed up are few and far between. But diversity, in dress and attitude, is abundant.

The campus itself is fairly compact, yet "very beautiful," with the country's largest sculpture garden, and plenty of grassy areas and trees. One student stated, "you keep on discovering new areas of the campus every day." Statues such as the "person sitting in a box" in front of the science building add to the aesthetic appeal of the campus. The incredible new opera house/music building also makes seeing performances that much more enjoyable.

There are over 250 student organizations at UH, and they range from the Cattle Rustler, to the Young Socialists, to the Shotokan Karate Club, to the National Leadership Honor Society. The Student Program Board oversees all student social activities. In mid-April, the annual Frontier Fiesta and Cook-Off rouses school spirit with a weekend of "Broadway-like" performances, cultural dances, and food—all in a carnival-like atmosphere.

Without any exceptional sports teams, school spirit has waned in the past few years, and is, according to one student, "not so healthy," while another comments that "I have better things to do than go watch the football team lose." Others, however, say support for the sports teams is increasing. With past athletic greats like Carl Lewis and NBA MVP Hakeem Olajuwan as UH alumni, the athletic department definitely has the potential for greatness.

UH is a large, incredibly diverse school with plenty going on to suit anyone's taste. Every option is available both academically and culturally in this growing and changing institution, led by an administration set upon improving in the new millennium.—*Kyla Dahlin*

FYI

The three best things about attending UH are "the honors program, Frontier Fiesta, and downtown Houston."

The three worst things about attending UH are "the parking, the lack of school spirit, and the fact that so many students commute."

The three things that every student should do before graduating from UH are "to study by the Cullen Spring fountain on a nice spring day, to hear a concert in the new opera house, and to join a club!"

One thing I'd like to have known before coming here is that "advisors don't usually know how to help you."

The University of Texas/Austin

Address: Campus Mail Center D0700; Austin, TX 78712-1111
Phone: 512-475-7440
E-mail address: frmn@uts.cc.utexas.edu
Web site URL: www.utexas.edu
Founded: 1883
Private or Public: public
Religious affiliation: none
Location: small city
Undergraduate enrollment: 36,164
Total enrollment: 48,008
Percent Male/Female: 50%/50%
Percent Minority: 33%
Percent African-American: 3%

Percent Asian: 15%
Percent Hispanic: 14%
Percent Native-American: 0.5%
Percent in-state/out-of-state: 94%/6%
Percent Pub HS: NA
Number of Applicants: 18,919
Percent Accepted: 63%
Percent Accepted who enroll: 59%
Entering: 7,040
Transfers: 1,123
Application Deadline: 1 Feb
Mean SAT: 601 V, 620 M
Mean ACT: NA
Middle 50% SAT range: 530–640 V, 550–660 M

Middle 50% ACT range: 22–27
3 Most popular majors: business management, communications, engineering
Retention: 88%
Graduation rate: 65%
On-campus housing: NA
Fraternities: 5%
Sororities: 6%
Library: 1,600,000 volumes
Tuition and Fees: $3,128 in; $9,608 out
Room and Board: $4,854
Financial aid, first-year: 26%

Everything is bigger in the Lone Star State, and the University of Texas/Austin is no exception to this rule. Nestled in the gently rolling hills of central Texas, the flagship state school enrolls nearly 50,000 students. From a vibrant social scene to top-notch academics, UT offers the best of college life to its students. Despite the fact that out-of-state students make up a very small percentage of the student body, UT is an extremely diverse school with students representing a wide range of ideas and interests. "You'll find every type of person imaginable at this school. There is a little of everything. No matter how you dress or what your interests are, you'll find lots of people just like you," one junior said.

Charging into Classes

With such a large student body, trying to get into the classes you want may take a little work, as popular classes and time slots can fill up in the blink of an eye. "Many times you can't get classes you want because things fill up so quickly. Sometimes you have to rearrange your entire schedule to take a required class or just postpone taking it," one student complained. Most Longhorns register for classes through a telephone registration system known as "TEX" or through "ROSE," the on-line equivalent. Although signing up for classes may be one of the bigger hassles facing UT students, "with a little persistence and initiative, you can pretty much get into any class you want," one student said. The university also offers four-day orientation sessions during the summer to ease the transition to life at UT.

Introductory and general science courses can enroll up to 500 students, "with 100–200 being typical." Upper-division classes are usually smaller. Freshman seminars with topics ranging from King Arthur and legends to political philosophy offer first-year students the opportunity to take smaller classes. As at almost every other university, the quality of classes at UT ranges from "awesome to absolutely awful." Subjects receiving raves include literature, biology, and business. While offerings in the government and history departments are generally well received, students gave warnings about the heavy reading load. "Statistics and physics are unfortunately not on UT's priority list in providing the necessary professors to teach the course," one student lamented. UT also has a core curriculum that is "relatively easy to satisfy." Requirements include courses in writing proficiency, Texas government, and a foreign language. Students may place out of some requirements through results from SAT II, Advanced Placement, and International Baccalaureate exams. The university has several large libraries, including the Undergraduate Library and Perry Castnedal Library, better known as "PCL." UT also possesses a large collection of manuscripts and personal documents from some of the world's most famous literary figures.

UT offers a prestigious honors program called "Plan 2." The multidisciplinary liberal arts major offers small classes taught by some of the university's best professors. Students can choose Plan 2 as their only major, although many choose to double-major in Plan 2 and another subject like government or economics. Prospective Plan 2 students apply for the program with a separate application in conjunction with their application to UT. The competition for admission into Plan 2 is tough—SAT scores well above 1400 and top class ranks are the norm for accepted students. "I can't tell you how many Plan 2 people have been accepted to Ivy League schools but turned them down," one Plan 2 junior said. Other well-known UT honors programs include Business Honors, which is modeled after the MBA program of UT's McCombs School of Business and taught in small classes of 30 to 45. Students entering the Business Honors program in 2000 had an average SAT score of 1425, with a class rank in the top 3% of their high school class.

Longhorn Life

Most freshmen live on campus, although the school does not require it. UT allocates about 70% of dormitory rooms to freshmen; the rest are distributed to upperclassmen through a lottery. Competition for on-campus housing can be fierce. Many high school seniors send in a housing application and deposit even before they are accepted to the school. UT's largest dormitory is Jester, a high-rise building that houses almost 3,000 stu-

dents and has its own zip code. Other dormitories include the all-girl Kinsolving and the newly built San Jacinto. Honors students have the option of living in one of the two honors dorms, Carrothers and Andrews. The university also offers the option of coed or single-sex accommodations. Although students in general describe the rooms as being nice (UT provides a small refrigerator, microwave, and air-conditioning in each room), their small size is a common complaint. The majority of Longhorns live off campus. Students report no problems in finding housing convenient to the campus. "You can find apartments anywhere around campus, and prices can be pretty cheap to pretty expensive," one off campus student said. For students who live beyond walking distance to campus, UT operates a shuttle system to transport students between home and school. "Personally, I prefer to have an off-campus apartment because it gives us time away from campus and space," one junior said.

While the food at UT does not garner praise, students say it is pretty decent. The dining halls, especially at Jester, have improved a lot, according to one. Most students who live on campus purchase a meal plan, since the dorms are not equipped with kitchens, and they can eat at any on-campus dining hall with their meal plans. A wide variety of food is offered at meals, including vegetarian selections and a salad bar. Pizza, pasta dishes, and Mexican foods are a few favorites mentioned by students. A variety of fast-food restaurants and eateries are located in and around the campus, giving students even more dining options. Most dining halls do not serve dinner on Sunday nights, giving students the perfect opportunity to sample the fare at some of Austin's restaurants.

Awesome Austin

UT is located in the heart of Austin, the capital of Texas. In fact, the campus sits under the shadow of the tall pink granite state capitol building, which is even taller than the nation's Capitol in Washington, D.C. The city has undergone a boom during the past decade, attracting many high-tech firms to the area. "Hopefully it will keep its classy taste and heart as it turns into the next Silicon Valley," a student said. Austin also has a reputation as a live music city, attracting both established and unknown acts. Sixth Street is a popular area for nightclubs, bars, and trendy restaurants and attracts many UT students looking for a fun night on the town. Numerous coffeehouses give students a relaxing place to study, read poetry, or perform music. "Austin is a great college town. Austin takes pride in its university, and it's a great combination of students and residents," one student said. Many lakes and swimming areas like Hippie Hollow, Lake Travis, Lake Austin, and Canyon Lake surround the city and are popular sites for Longhorns looking for a quick break. Austin weather is quite pleasant and sunny throughout the year. School is out before the summer really heats up, and winter temperatures rarely drop below freezing. Unlike most Texas towns, Austin is easy to navigate without a car. Students walk, bike, or ride the bus to their destinations. Some students bring cars, although the expense and difficulty in finding parking are enough to deter most.

For such a large school, the UT campus is pretty compact. Students can get around quickly and easily just by walking. Many students also use Rollerblades or bicycles to move around campus. Popular spots around campus to rest and study include the Six-Pack—a lawn surrounded by three buildings on each side, the Tower, West Mall, and the Student Union. The beautiful campus is covered with grassy areas and rolling hills.

School Events

Sports and school pride are a big part of life at UT. Every student mentioned football games when asked about big campus events. Fall is the time for the highly anticipated football season, bringing out students and alumni to Saturday games and tailgate parties. The biggest games of the year are those with UT's biggest rivals: Texas A&M and Oklahoma. While football is king at UT, baseball and basketball are also very popular. The UT Tower glows in various combinations of orange and white, depending mostly on sports victories. A complex set of rules determines which lighting scheme will be used to honor a particular event.

> Said one student, "I can't tell you how many Plan 2 people have been accepted to Ivy League schools but turned them down."

Extracurricular activities run the gamut, including the school's newspaper, the *Daily Texan*, student government, and various service and volunteering organizations. Since the school is in the state capital, many students work in government offices. "Many jobs are available on campus and easy to find, thanks to an on-line service of listings," one junior said. Theater and fine arts, especially music, have a strong presence on campus as well. The UT campus has a large Greek system, as sororities and fraternities are also popular among Longhorns. "There is always some big frat party every weekend," one student said.

UT students are very proud of their school and agree that UT is an unforgettable, incredible experience. Although the school's size makes it easy to get lost in the crowd, freshmen should make an effort to become involved in their school. "Join clubs and groups that interest you; don't be afraid to meet new people and to try new classes," one senior said. "My time at UT has been one of the best times of my life, and I want to make sure that I don't miss anything."—*Robert Yi*

FYI

The three best things about attending UT/Austin are "Austin, the very active and vibrant campus, the laid-back and friendly atmosphere."

The three worst things about attending UT/Austin are "lots of distractions from studying; it can take a while to find your way around campus; people tend to hang out in cliques."

The three things that every student should do before graduating from UT/Austin are "go clubbing on Sixth Street, take a tour up to the Tower, go to a UT–Texas A&M football game."

One thing I'd like to have know before coming here is "you have to go through a lot of red tape to get anything done."

Utah

Address: A-153 ASB;
Provo, UT 84602
Phone: 801-378-2507
E-mail address:
admissions@byu.edu
Web site URL: www.byu.edu
Founded: 1875
Private or Public: private
Religious affiliation:
Church of Jesus Christ of
Latter-Day Saints
Location: urban
Undergraduate
enrollment: 33,365
Total enrollment: NA
Percent Male / Female:
49% / 51%
Percent Minority: 7%
Percent African-American:
0.5%

Percent Asian: 3%
Percent Hispanic: 3%
Percent Native-American:
0.5%
Percent in-state / out-of-
state: 34% / 66%
Percent Pub HS: NA
Number of Applicants:
8,078
Percent Accepted:
64%
Percent Accepted who
enroll: 81%
Entering: 4,197
Transfers: NA
Application Deadline:
15 Feb
Mean SAT: NA
Mean ACT: 27
Middle 50% SAT range: NA

Middle 50% ACT range:
25–29
3 Most popular majors:
business management,
elementary education,
zoology
Retention: 87%
Graduation rate: 62%
On-campus housing: NA
Fraternities: NA
Sororities: NA
Library: NA
Tuition and Fees: $2,830
for Latter-Day Church
Members in; $4,250 for
non-members out
Room and Board:
$4,350
Financial aid, first-year:
NA

Nestled among the majestic mountains of Utah, Brigham Young University serves to unite members of the Church of Jesus Christ of Latter-Day Saints from across the country. Students come to BYU seeking a top-rated education as well as a community in which they will be able to find a future mate of the same faith to spend their lives with. The ever-present reminders of the religious nature of the school further this community atmosphere, as the rules of the Book of Mormon are followed without need for much enforcement.

Hittin' the Books

Although the first reason many students choose BYU is religious dedication, the academic side of BYU is certainly not a drawback. The rigors of academics at BYU are apparent from the outset. Before graduation, students must complete a set of general education requirements that in-

clude classes in mathematics, biology, the physical sciences, American Heritage, Wellness (physical education), and the History of Civilization, as well as at least 14 credit hours of religious study. With so many requirements, freshmen find themselves attending most of their classes with other freshmen, which "serves as a means to get to know other freshmen even though classes are usually huge." However, the large class sizes decrease once students choose their areas of concentration.

With a large undergraduate population of nearly 30,000, freshman year can be quite daunting. However, the BYU administration strives to make the transition from high school to college as smooth as possible. One way in which they do this is through the Freshman Academy. Participating freshmen live near one another and take three classes in common (a math class, a writing class, and a foreign language class) for their first semester of school. One student reports that "the Freshman Academy is great because you really feel a sense of community with other freshmen. Especially since you all live together."

"We are at BYU because we want to live as Mormons."

For the most academically and religiously focused students, BYU offers an honors track open to all students upon matriculation to the university. The honors program requires that students take specified honors classes and maintain a GPA above 3.5, but it also goes beyond the classroom. To graduate with honors, students must also complete a study of 16 great works of literature/cinema/performance in a self-directed program, as well as complete courses in advanced languages (either foreign or mathematical), show commitment to the community through service activities, and have faculty sponsors to support their bid for an honors degree.

Beautiful Utah
The only way to describe the atmosphere of Provo, Utah, is "awe-inspiring." Many buildings on campus are made of special glass, and on a bright day, the Utah scenery is reflected throughout campus. The sprawling modern, architecturally innovative campus gets rave reviews from students. As one student puts it, "It is so refreshing to walk to class on a clear day and breathe in everything. I feel very inspired here and know that this place is where I am meant to be."

Living the Book of Mormon
So how, among all this beauty, do students live? Students are not required to live on campus at any time in their years at BYU. This is especially key because the older you get, the more married couples you will find, as well as the number of people returning to school after their mandatory two-year missions. However, the school does follow a strict code of housing that students living both on and off campus must adhere to. This includes restrictions as to when students may have members of the opposite sex in their rooms (always with the doors open and usually not after midnight) as well as modesty of dress (no bikinis allowed by the pool). Although these rules are strict, they do not often have to be rigorously enforced because the student body generally toes the line. As one student notes, "We are at BYU because we want to live as Mormons and follow the Book of Mormon. If we wanted to have random sex and party all the time we would've gone somewhere else."

All These Rules
Because of the religious nature of the school, students at BYU find themselves inundated with religion in all aspects of their lives. However, to BYU students this is not at all a negative. Although Mormonism is one of the fastest-growing religions, it is still relatively uncommon in many parts of the country. Thus for many Mormons BYU is a haven. At the university students are active within their wards (church congregations), and also participate in community service projects and campus extracurriculars. Also, upon matriculation to BYU, students sign an honor code of both an academic and religious nature. Besides agreeing to things like being honest and not cheating, students also agree to avoid mood-altering substances (including caffeine and alcohol). This means not chatting at a coffee shop, no indulging in chocolate bars and the like. However, growing up with Mormon backgrounds makes these restrictions nothing new to students.

Finding "the One"
Due to the strict laws of the Book of Mormon, Mormons must marry within their religion, and where better to find a Mormon spouse than at a Mormon school? Thus upon coming to BYU, finding a future mate is one of the main focuses of most students. This focus on marriage rather than random hookups is further encouraged by the school's policies against couples visiting alone in dorm rooms together. Students are often found going out on group dates, and according to one, "Most kids date around quite a bit" in their quest to find that perfect person they will spend the rest of their lives with. Also, it is not uncommon to see young newly mar-

ried couples on campus. As for partying, there is not much of that. As one student puts it, "There are no problems getting beer if you really want it, but most don't." The parties that students tend to go to are dances sponsored by the school. However, the most popular form of dating tends to be going to dinner in groups of couples. Many students can be found on dates at the Skyroom (an on-campus restaurant on the sixth floor of the Wilkinson Student Center, the Wilk).

Cougar Pride

If you're not up for going on a dinner date, what about attending a football or basketball game? As one student puts it, "The stands are packed for football games, basketball games, and devotionals," which

might tell you something about students' priorities. The BYU Cougars are Division I and belong to the Mountain West Athletic Conference. Their nationally ranked football team often plays in nationally televised games. With such a sense of community at the school, it is no surprise that students rally so fervently behind their mascot, Cosmo the Cougar.

In all aspects of life, BYU is a place of community. "It is so gratifying to be able to practice our faith and to feel the presence of God in our lives as we strive to become spiritually fulfilled adults," notes one student. And nothing could be more of an inspiration toward a fulfilled life than being among members of your own faith in the majestic Utah surroundings.
—Engin Yenidunya

FYI
The three best things about attending BYU are "the great friends, the unity of faith, and beautiful Utah skiing."
The three worst things about attending BYU are "the large size of the school, all the general education requirements, and the curfew rules."
The three things that every student should do before graduating from BYU are "eat at the Skyroom (a restaurant on campus), hike to the Y on the hill, and most important . . . get married."
One thing I'd like to have known before coming here is that "the pressure to find a mate is everywhere."

University of Utah

Address: 201 South 1460 East Room 250S; Salt Lake City, UT 84112-9057	**Percent Hispanic:** 3%	**Middle 50% SAT range:** 430–580 V, 480–650 M
Phone: 801-581-7281	**Percent Native-American:** 0.5%	**Middle 50% ACT range:** 21–27
E-mail address: NA	**Percent in-state / out-of-state:** 10%/90%	
Web site URL: acs.utah.edu	**Percent Pub HS:** NA	**3 Most popular majors:** psychology, sociology, political science
Founded: 1850	**Number of Applicants:** 5,726	
Private or Public: public	**Percent Accepted:** 97%	**Retention:** 62%
Religious affiliation: none	**Percent Accepted who enroll:** 43%	**Graduation rate:** 43%
Location: suburban	**Entering:** 2,399	**On-campus housing:** NA
Undergraduate enrollment: 19,763	**Transfers:** NA	**Fraternities:** 3%
Total enrollment: 25,803	**Application Deadline:** 1 Jun	**Sororities:** 3%
Percent Male / Female: 55%/45%	**Mean SAT:** 487 V, 522 M	**Library:** NA
Percent Minority: 8%	**Mean ACT:** NA	**Tuition and Fees:** $2,790 in; $8,495 out
Percent African-American: 0.5%		**Room and Board:** $4,890
Percent Asian: 4%		**Financial aid, first-year:** 24%

The University of Utah was once just a small university in a sleepy western state. However, Salt Lake City's growing population and its winning bid to host the 2002 Winter Olympic Games have contributed to the growth of student opportunities in recent years. Now, students at U of U can do more than just take a tour of the Mormon Tabernacle when they have time to spare. Instead, they can hit the latest downtown brew pub, take in a Jazz basketball game, or even try their hand at Olympic luge.

Do You Speak English?

Students cite the science departments, especially biology and chemistry, as the strongest departments at U of U. In fact, Pons and Fleischman, the scientists of the controversial cold fusion experiments, did their work at the University of Utah. Undergrads agree that the business, communications, and English departments have excellent professors, although some feel the philosophy department is "too research-oriented." The math department was criticized for its shortage of teachers who "speak English." For more academically gifted students, U of U offers an honors program that gives qualified students easy access to top-notch professors. One student added, however, that this program did not seem to be "too diverse."

Locals Abound

Most undergrads are from in state, and many are Salt Lake City natives (some even go home for lunch). For students in need of housing, campus facilities are described as "pretty spare" and "not too great. Most people live off campus if they can." Thus, only a very small number of undergrads live on campus. Others choose fraternity, sorority, or off-campus housing, which is abundant in the university area. However, a significant amount of dorm space is being built to house future Olympians on the U of U campus, and campus housing is "scheduled to double after the Olympics are over!" one undergrad reported. Since most students commute, parking spaces on and near campus are nearly impossible to find. As one commuter explained, "I often have to arrive on campus an hour before my first class just to find space." U of U is also predomi-

nantly "an all-white school," and one student reported that ethnic minorities are not represented in large numbers.

> However, a significant amount of dorm space is being built to house future Olympians on the U of U campus, and campus housing is "scheduled to double after the Olympics are over!"

Campus activities provide students, especially those new to the city, with opportunities for meeting people. The "most visible social organization on campus" is the university's student association, the ASUU, which sponsors a variety of weekly speakers and monthly concerts, the most popular of which is the two-day reggaefest in May. The weekend social scene is dominated by fraternity and sorority parties, although according to one student, the Greek system "used to be stronger on campus." Students report that because the Greek scene is relatively small, there is little pressure to rush.

Finicky Support

Many undergrads socialize at the Pie, a pizza place decorated with years of graffiti and student signatures. The lobby of the Marriott Library is also considered a prime spot to hang out and meet members of the opposite sex. In spite of U of U's less-than-impressive football record, attendance at the games is strong. Students also take pride in the men's basketball and women's gymnastic teams. However, according to one student, school spirit doesn't extend to much more than "the football and basketball seasons." Less competitive students participate in various intramural sports.

Four More Years

Although Salt Lake City lacks the sophisticated urban attitude of many eastern cities, it has recently experienced a population influx, and is considered one of the best places to live in the United States. The city's cultural attractions include the locally based Ballet West, the Utah Symphony, and the Mormon Tabernacle Choir.

The city attracts major rock, pop, and jazz performers as well. In the past five years, a new arena has been built for the Utah Jazz (the Delta Center) and the local ice arena and convention center were rebuilt in anticipation of the 2002 Olympics. The national ski team trains within 30 minutes of the university, and several popular ski resorts are within driving distance. Other outdoor attractions include camping, rock climbing, hiking, and mountain biking.

The university recently built new facilities for the dance and communications departments (but no new parking lots, one student lamented). The communication facility is equipped with more than 300 computers in five computer labs. A new computer research facility and biology building are both currently under construction. In addition, the recently completed Huntsman Cancer Institute is the largest facility in the United States devoted to cancer research and offers students many unique opportunities to gain exposure to scientific research.

Long a school dominated by Utah Mormons, the university has recently begun to branch out, thanks to the growth of the Salt Lake City area. U of U may not be the place for those seeking great ethnic and religious diversity, but its strong sense of family, local cultural offerings, and proximity to the great outdoors will continue to draw students regardless of religion or origin.—*Brian Abaluck and Staff*

FYI

The three best things about attending the University of Utah are: the opportunity for experience and research in the field of medicine and science, the amazing view of the mountains from campus, and the available outdoor activities including skiing, snowboarding, and waterskiing.

The three worst things about attending the University of Utah are: that campus life suffers from the fact that it is largely a commuter campus, the lack of funding from the state of Utah, and the shortage of parking.

The three things that every student should do before graduating from the University of Utah are: learning how to snowboard, go to Lake Powell, and watch the sun set over the Great Salt Lake.

One thing I'd like to have known before coming here is: that there is so little in the way of on-campus housing.

Vermont

Bennington College

Address: Bennington, VT 05201
Phone: 800-833-6845
E-mail address: admissions @bennington.edu
Web site URL: www.bennington.edu
Founded: 1932
Private or Public: private
Religious affiliation: none
Location: rural
Undergraduate enrollment: 511
Total enrollment: 635
Percent Male/Female: 30%/70%
Percent Minority: 6%

Percent African-American: 2%
Percent Asian: 2%
Percent Hispanic: 2%
Percent Native-American: 0%
Percent in-state/out-of-state: NA
Percent Pub HS: NA
Number of Applicants: 491
Percent Accepted: 35%
Percent Accepted who enroll: 0%
Entering: NA
Transfers: 27
Application Deadline: 782
Mean SAT: 623 V, 543 M

Mean ACT: NA
Middle 50% SAT range: NA
Middle 50% ACT range: NA
3 Most popular majors: visual and performing arts, interdisciplinary studies, literature and languages
Retention: NA
Graduation rate: NA
On-campus housing: 100%
Fraternities: NA
Sororities: NA
Library: 120,000 volumes
Tuition and Fees: $22,500 in; $22,500 out
Room and Board: $5,650
Financial aid, first-year: NA

The town of Bennington may seem to be a tranquil outpost of rural Vermont, but artistic passions seethe beneath its placid surface. "What struck me about coming here is how passionate people are about what they do," one student said. "There's so much energy and raw passion." Not surprisingly, the creative energy of Bennington students often defies and overturns traditions, whether they be societal or artistic. But the college does uphold one important tradition—that of being on the cutting edge of just about everything.

Independent Thinking

No core curriculum confines students to specific courses, and majors as such do not exist; students simply must complete eight courses a year and do senior project to graduate. This unstructured academic environment places the burden of decision making on students. "You really have to be self-motivated and self-inspired," one student said. Another agreed, saying, "If you're not motivated enough, you're either going to leave or not do well at all." Academic flexibility allows students essentially to custom-tailor their own education; reportedly, one student concentrated on costume design and physics. This freedom also leads to a great deal of student/faculty interaction, since each student works very closely with an advisor and a "plan committee" to form his or her own individual program of concentration.

Upholding this flexible non-curriculum is a lack of a structured grading policy. Students do not receive written grades, and GPAs are nonexistent. Rather, teachers issue written evaluations of students' course work. Since students work closely with their teachers in small classes from the start of their freshman year, "the teachers remember you and your projects."

Bennington's faculty is comprised of "teacher-practitioners" who work in their field while teaching. To further encourage students to bridge the gap between theory and practice, a part of the academic year is set aside as a work-study term. During this "Field Work Term" (FWT), students go out and work rather than go to school. The jobs they take vary greatly, and reflect the diversity of interest among the student body. "Not many go out and look for high-paying internships with big firms," one student said. According to her, one student took massage courses in Portugal; another worked at a bookstore; and another did research with a prominent scientist.

While this system helps students connect course work to real life experience, its implementation several years ago met with heated opposition. At the beginning of the 1994 fall term, many academic departments were eliminated, resulting in the firing of tenured faculty members. In place of the departments, the disciplines (music, art, humanities, sciences, and technology) are now taught by teacher-practitioners. The elimination of academic departments caused one student to remark, "We're in a state of total chaos." But since that time, the chaos has subsided. The class of 1997 was the last class to have witnessed the uproar caused by the changes in 1994, and students agree that the situation has improved tremendously.

Living Art

The flexibility of course work at Bennington allows students to pursue their artistic and educational aims independently. Some fulfill one students' description that "they live art, they breathe art, they are art," by essentially locking themselves in their studios. The Visual Arts and Performing Arts Center (VAPA) remains open 24 hours a day, and students work together or individually on projects at all hours of the day or night. This building houses all of the visual and performing arts spaces at Bennington (with the exception of music, for which there is a separate building called Jennings Hall), including dance studios, performing spaces, theater spaces, darkrooms, and studios for all kinds of visual art and design, from painting to architecture to ceramics. One student said, "I think that the biggest way we participate in each others' lives outside of classes would be in supporting each other in our artistic endeavors."

> One student reminisced about his second or third party at Bennington, "I must have kissed about 10 people there."

While the atmosphere at Bennington is eminently accepting and tolerant, it may be difficult for students who are not immersed in art to adjust. "I know that for some people who aren't interested in the arts, it can be very intimidating," one student said.

An "Alternative" Community

Echoing the freedom of the academic atmosphere, Bennington's social atmosphere is open and, according to one student, "liberal to the extreme." In previous years, some students have dressed in drag for graduation. Completely accepting of one another's lives, students report that no tension over homosexuality or bisexuality disturbs campus life. Racial tension is likewise nonexistent on the Bennington campus. Some students, however, expressed dissatisfaction over the low minority representation. "We're pretty much a bunch of whites," one said. Perhaps because of the widespread acceptance of difference at Bennington, no formalized interest groups exist. All groups are, for the most part, unstructured. "Even our literary magazine isn't really a club. People come and put something together. It's that kind of thing," one student said.

The small size of Bennington and its isolated setting have a strong impact on the social life of the college. One student described the campus as "incestuous" due to its small population. "Everybody knows who you're with, what you're doing, and who you're sleeping with," he said. The fact that everybody knows everybody else often results in a feeling of claustrophobia. Cliques develop easily, and one student warned, "I think because it's so small, it's dangerous to get yourself stuck into one group of friends." The dating scene can be dismal, although it does exist. Women comprise the majority of Bennington's population, and this lopsided statistic worsens the problem. "There isn't that much dating going on," one student claimed. "It's just a lot of people sleeping around."

Means of Escape

In order to flee Bennington's occasionally claustrophobic atmosphere, students drive to Albany or Manchester, the nearest cities to Bennington. Cars are not only a mode of transportation, but a means of escape. For those who do not own cars, trips planned by the Student Life Organization offer a good alternative. The organization plans trips to shopping malls, ski slopes, and various places in the area. "They're really good to us," one student said appreciatively.

On-campus options also relieve students from routine. In addition to art exhibitions, concerts, and plays, student bands perform on Friday and Saturday nights in the Cafe, which serves "amazing nachos and smoothies" in addition to providing a meeting place for students. On some weekends, major parties liven up placid Bennington. Among them, the Dress to Get Laid Party (a parody of frat parties at more "mainstream" colleges), the Redneck Party, and '70s and '80s theme parties are popular. One student reminisced about his second or third party at Bennington, "I must have kissed about 10 people there."

While campus social life can be lively, the sports scene is not alive and kicking. There are no hard-core sports at Bennington, although the college has a coed soccer team. Students report that anybody can sign up to play, "even if you've never kicked a ball in your life." Bennington might lack the "school spirit" occasioned by athletics at other schools, but students do not seem to mind. "Bennington probably has 'school spirit' in what it stands for and what it should stand for.... People here have always appreciated that it goes against the tide," one student said.

Food and Housing

Bennington also differs from the mainstream in its food: it actually tastes good. In addition to serving a variety of foods, the cafeteria caters to individual requests. Living is likewise surprisingly good. Nearly all students live one of the 12 houses situated on the Commons lawn. Each New England-style house (white with green shutters) accommodates about 30 people and has its own "personality." While students cannot choose their house, they are assigned according to a housing questionnaire they fill out. Some are designated smoking or nonsmoking houses, while some are unofficially recognized among students as "raise hell houses." Each house contains a little kitchenette and a large living room with a fireplace. After freshman year, all students automatically get singles in the houses. Bennington's long-standing problem of underenrollment guarantees that students have all the space they need. It also means that those who are there really want to be. "It's not for everyone, definitely," one student said. "But I've gotten so much out of this place."—*Susanna Chu and Staff*

FYI

The three best things about attending Bennington College are "getting to live in small, homey houses instead of crowded dorms, the freedom of choosing your own program, interacting with teachers who are actually versed in the ways of how their discipline functions in the real world."

The three worst things about attending Bennington College are "the claustrophobically small community, the chaos from the freedom of choosing your own program, and the difficulty of getting to a city if you don't have a car."

The three things every student should do before graduating from Bennington are "do something absolutely fabulous during FWT, try every smoothie flavor at the Cafe, check out what people are wearing at the Dress to Get Laid party."

The one I'd like to have known before coming here is "what a great community Bennington is."

Marlboro College

Address: Marlboro, VT 05344
Phone: 802-258-9236
E-mail address: admissions@marlboro.edu
Web site URL: www.marlboro.edu
Founded: 1946
Private or Public: private
Religious affiliation: none
Location: rural
Undergraduate enrollment: 290
Total enrollment: 290
Percent Male / Female: 37% / 63%
Percent Minority: 4%
Percent African-American: 1%

Percent Asian: 1%
Percent Hispanic: 2%
Percent Native-American: NA
Percent in-state / out-of-state: 18% / 82%
Percent Pub HS: NA
Number of Applicants: 308
Percent Accepted: 80%
Percent Accepted who enroll: 40%
Entering: 99
Transfers: 29
Application Deadline: 1 Mar
Mean SAT: 610 V, 580 M
Mean ACT: NA

Middle 50% SAT range: 560–700 V, 470–620 M
Middle 50% ACT range: NA
3 Most popular majors: writing, environmental studies, theater
Retention: 78%
Graduation rate: 40%
On-campus housing: NA
Fraternities: NA
Sororities: NA
Library: 52,000 volumes
Tuition and Fees: $19,585 in; $19,585 out
Room and Board: $6,750
Financial aid, first-year: 85%

The intimate quality of the college experience at Marlboro College extends beyond its rustic surroundings into the social lives of students both inside and outside the realm of academics. According to students, the tightness of the community is one of Marlboro's most attractive qualities, but also one of the "most challenging" aspects of being a student.

Rigorous Academics

Students call Marlboro academics "rigorous," often featuring one-on-one tutorials with professors. These tutorials are very popular with undergrads. Most introductory classes enroll 15 to 20 people, while the higher-level seminars are even smaller. Literature and the social science departments are reportedly strong at Marlboro, with the former ranking as one of the more popular majors. Religion, Literature, and Philosophy is considered the most difficult and rewarding course. As one student said, "It's the history of Western thought in one year: the *Iliad* in one week, *The Divine Comedy* the next."

Marlboro has few academic requirements. Regardless of their major (or "field of concentration" in Marlborian terms), students must fulfill a writing requirement before their sophomore year and submit a 20-page portfolio of their writing at the end of the semester, which is judged by the faculty. If the instructors view a submission unacceptable, the student has two more opportunities to pass the requirement. If a student fails to pass within three tries, he or she is asked to leave the college, regardless of previous academic achievements. The requirement can sound intimidating to incoming freshmen, but students describe it as a "good thing" that pressures them into writing clearly and concisely. One of Marlboro's most interesting opportunities is its World Studies Program where students focus on International Relations as an academic discipline and often study and work abroad during the first semester of their junior year. Students are required to write about their experiences upon their return.

Marlboro undergrads consider themselves "extremely lucky" to have strong relationships with the faculty. Teaching assistants are relatively nonexistent, although some students often choose to co-teach a course with another student as their final "Plan of Concentration," a cumulative interdisciplinary effort of their last two years of study. Otherwise described as a "senior thesis times ten," this final work is relatively flexible—some opt for writing a 120-page paper while others produce a play. The intimacy students and their professors enjoy is a highlight of Marlboro, and it is not uncommon for students to enjoy dinner at any one of their professors' homes. Marlboro has one centrally located cafeteria, which encourages both students and faculty to enjoy one another's company at mealtimes.

Although upperclassmen receive priority during class registration, one student said that he "never heard of anyone not being able to take a class because it was full." The average class size is seven or eight students, and class sizes of three or four are not uncommon, which "makes it awfully hard to hide if you haven't done your work," remarked one student. The professors, for the benefit of the students, provide 20-minute introductory lectures during the first two days of each term. Although courses are described as "demanding," faculty advisors make sure their advisees keep up with the course load. The lack of organized athletics at Marlboro encourages students to focus on their schoolwork, "so what you do here is study," one student explained.

Beside dorm rooms, places for students to hang out on campus are limited, and those not interested in going to the Campus Center find themselves seeking a ride into Brattleboro, a small town popular for its "cultural and liberal" atmosphere, about 15 minutes from campus. The Campus Center functions as a campus coffeehouse, alternate cafeteria (with limited hours), game room, post office, and general location for all campus-wide events. For those who want a more sociable study place, the center is the place to meet.

Marlboro Living

All Marlboro undergrads are required to live on campus freshman year (although exceptions are made for married students and those with dependents), though most students live on campus all four years. Students praise the dorm rooms, some of which have balconies. The rooms are favorably-sized, and usually only frosh live in triples. The priority for housing selection is based on how many credits a student has earned. All the Way is one of the more popular dorms because of its large kitchen, while Howland is generally the

least favorite due to "dumpy" conditions and higher noise levels. The thin walls in Howland "really affect your love life," one student moaned. However, dorm favorites change annually depending on who lives there. Resident advisors (RAs) live in each dorm and organize meetings to vote on "quiet hours" and other inter-dorm issues. One student remarked, "Unlike other colleges, the RAs at Marlboro are more like advisors and less like police." Dorm halls are coed, and only one dorm, Half Way, is reserved for women. Each year, one building is designated "substance-free" and one is "smoke-free." Security reportedly is not an issue at Marlboro, and some students do not worry if they forget to lock their doors.

> Marlboro's emphasis on "self-reliance" academics makes it a particularly attractive school to those who seek a rigorous curriculum balanced with a lot of attention from faculty.

Marlboro's isolated location limits the availability of off-campus housing. College-owned cottages are designed for students who desire a close-to-campus location and independence from typical dorm living. Each cottage, usually occupied by juniors or seniors, consists of four bedrooms. Renting houses in the woods from townspeople is another option, and Brattleboro, despite the commute, attracts many looking for alternatives to dorm housing.

The Grub

Dining hall food at Marlboro is reportedly decent. Many students complain about the lack of variety, although vegetarian and vegan options are available at every meal. There is freshly baked bread every day, which one student described as "fantastic." Student workers do the cooking, and accept suggestions by their peers. Dining hours are limited, but those who miss a meal can find snacks at the Campus Center. According to one undergrad on the meal plan, "You can eat as much as you want, and you don't have to pay per item." Every Sunday is Ben & Jerry's Night and both on- and off-campus students are welcome to partake of delicious, free ice cream.

What's Happening in Vermont?

The popular Outdoor Program allows Marlborians to take advantage of the pristine Vermont countryside. Students often suggest new activities, such as hang gliding, and as long as there are enough people (at least five) and money, the activity is organized and implemented. One student described campus athletics as "do-it-yourself sports," since no official varsity program exists. There is a soccer team, but apart from that formal competition is limited.

The party scene is reportedly diverse. In addition to going to parties organized by the Social Activities Council, most people spend time with friends either at private parties or in the Campus Center. The Cabaret, the main social event of the year, involves an exhibition of student entertainment. Social drinking is common on campus, and some students smoke marijuana, but as one undergrad said, "Neither drugs nor alcohol are in your face. They're not a requirement for attending parties."

The small size of the college "makes it hard to have casual sex relationships," one student said, "as you invariably see your fellow classmates quite often." Another student indicated that there are only "six couples" on campus. A lack of privacy is supposedly responsible for hindering random hookups.

Politically, Marlboro is predominantly liberal. Students say the gay community is quite vocal and is "very accepted" on campus. Participation in student groups, whatever the cause, is popular, and although the student body is not ethnically diverse, its geographical diversity lends itself to many different ideas and experiences from those willing to contribute. Environmental concerns are a hot topic among students. Recently, mass mailings and their impact on deforestation has been a subject of debate.

School spirit at Marlboro is surprisingly high for a school that lacks a formal athletics department. Most undergrads have a "fierce loyalty and love" for Marlboro, and many alumni remain active in college affairs. *The Citizen* is a biweekly student newspaper, and another popular group is the Live Action Role-Playing Group, a band of students who perform for the entertainment of the campus community.

Marlboro's emphasis on "self-reliance" academics makes it a particularly attractive school to those who seek a rigorous curriculum balanced with a lot of attention from faculty. The isolation of the college is great for those who want "to get away from it all," but most students warn that you really should know what you want in a school before coming to Marlboro: "Make sure you want someplace really independent," and do not forget to pack "some good sturdy shoes" for those wintertime hikes to class.—*Susannah Chu and Staff*

FYI

The three best things about attending Marlboro are "the quiet, the personal attention, and the alumni dedication to the place."

The three worst things about attending Marlboro are "the quiet, no varsity athletics, and Brattleboro."

The three things that every student should do before graduating from Marlboro are "join an environmental rally, hang at the Campus Center, and chow some yummy Ben & Jerry's."

One thing I'd like to have known before coming here is "know how to write because it makes the portfolio requirement a thousand times less stressful."

Middlebury College

Address: The Emma Willard House; Middlebury, VT 05753-6002

Phone: 802-443-3000

E-mail address: admissions @middlebury.edu

Web site URL: www.middlebury.edu

Founded: 1800

Private or Public: private

Religious affiliation: none

Location: small town

Undergraduate enrollment: 2,265

Total enrollment: 2,265

Percent Male/Female: 49%/51%

Percent Minority: 12%

Percent African-American: 2%

Percent Asian: 4%

Percent Hispanic: 5%

Percent Native-American: 0.5%

Percent in-state/out-of-state: 5%/95%

Percent Pub HS: 54%

Number of Applicants: 4,869

Percent Accepted: 26%

Percent Accepted who enroll: 42%

Entering: 524

Transfers: 5

Application Deadline: 15 Dec

Mean SAT: NA

Mean ACT: NA

Middle 50% SAT range: 670–730 V, 650–720 M

Middle 50% ACT range: 28–31

3 Most popular majors: English, economics, political science

Retention: 95%

Graduation rate: 89%

On-campus housing: 100%

Fraternities: NA

Sororities: NA

Library: 1,200,000 volumes

Tuition and Fees: $32,600 total annual expenses

Room and Board: NA

Financial aid, first-year: 36%

How many people get to say that they graduated from college on skis, or that while doing the stationary bike every day they looked out through a picture window onto Vermont's Green Mountains? Many Middlebury grads have done these things and more. Middlebury students are not only known for their academic prowess, but also for their active enjoyment of the natural setting that surrounds them.

Academics: A Course on Star Trek

Middlebury students must fulfill two sets of requirements: Cultural Civilization and General Academic. For the Cultural Civilization requirements, students must take one class in each of three groups: European, American, and other cultures. To fulfill the General Academic requirements, students must take classes in seven out of the following eight groups: the arts, deductive reasoning, history, sociology, philosophy, science, language, and literature. Students in general say the requirements are "easy to fulfill." One student said she had "never heard anyone complain about them."

Students report that both the foreign language and English departments are exceptional. Middlebury offers many intensive foreign-language classes, as well as a special intensive-language school in the summer. Middlebury also stresses good writing skills, and has a two-class requirement: one freshman writing seminar and a "writing-intensive" course. Popular departments include psychology, economics, history, biology, environmental studies, and political science. Students say there are no "gut" classes at Middlebury, but some of the easier options are nicknames "Physics for Poets" and "Chemistry for Citizens." Undergrads study in the main library, the Crest Room (a late-night dining hall), common rooms in the dorms, the science library, or the very comfortable and quiet music library.

All classes are taught by professors, and average class size is small, generally around 15 students, with the largest lectures, like Intro Biology, enrolling 105 students at the most. Students say they have no problems getting into all the classes they want. If a class fills up, students report that professors will often open up an extra section. Professors are known for their availability and friendliness. Undergrads go to professors' office hours, call their professors at home, see them around campus, or even baby-sit for their children.

Two distinctive aspects of a Middlebury education are the February entering class and the January Term (J-Term). Because Middlebury is so focused on foreign languages, and because the school is small, many students go abroad in the spring term. To fill their places, the administration admits an extra 100 students to Middlebury in February. Although some people have the misconception that these students are the leftovers who "didn't really get in," this is not the case. Middlebury chooses extremely active, leadership-oriented students for February admission so they will be up to the challenge of adjusting so quickly. "I know everyone in my class, and everyone at Middlebury knows not to mess with one of us, because we have 99 other people behind us," one February-class student said. January term is a chance for students to study a subject, such as a language, intensely. Many professors also offer January classes on the subjects of their independent research. Students also can opt for a more laid-back, fun January course, like a class on Star Trek, and spend extra time on outdoor winter activities.

Skinny-Dipping . . . In Winter?

Middlebury students are interested in outdoor activities no matter what the weather. In the spring and fall students swim and canoe on Lake Champlain, and hike and rock-climb on local trails. The Mountain Club organizes weekly outings, although students are welcome to go on their own as well. In the winter, Middlebury is an outdoor sports utopia with its own alpine ski slope, the Middlebury College Snowbowl, only 12 miles away. The college also owns a cross-country ski area called Breadloaf. The cross-country running trail turns into a cross-country skiing trail in the winter. And for those who are brave, the Polar Bear Club goes skinny-dipping every Wednesday throughout the year.

What makes Middlebury students different from other college students? According to one student, it's "how well-rounded they are; they do a little of everything, academics and extracurriculars." Many par-

ticipate in the student government, write for the weekly student paper, the Campus, attend lectures, join ISO (the International Students Organization), or start their own group. Many students also participate in community service in the town of Middlebury, where town-gown relations are not considered strained at all; "the college does a lot for the community," one student said. Many students participate in local Big Sib/Little Sib and Habitat for Humanity programs.

Middlebury students characterize their fellow classmates as generally "athletic," with everyone doing something active. Students are also required to fill a two-class PE requirement (less athletic students can choose classes like canoeing and ballroom dancing). Students call the gym facilities "spectacular," with a new hockey rink on the way, a new swimming pool that one student claimed is the "nicest in New England," a climbing wall, a private golf course, a football stadium with a view of the mountains, and a new eight-lane track. Men's ice hockey is the most popular sport, perhaps because it has won its division title for a few years in a row; fans show their school spirit by waiting all night for tickets.

While students find that the dating scene at Middlebury is "pretty nonexistent," random hookups and partying with friends are common. Many students start a weekend evening by going to a movie or concert on campus, and the Fun Club sponsors other nonalcoholic events. Upperclassmen 21 and over go to the few bars in Middlebury, such as Mr. Upps and Angelo's. Vermont alcohol policy is strict: in order to drink, you must show a Vermont State ID or a passport, so underage drinking in town is not much of an option. On the other hand, some students say they can drink in their rooms as long as the door is shut and they are not being noisy.

Social Houses: A Free Trip to Hawaii

Social houses are Middlebury's alternative to the Greek system, which was disbanded in 1990. Students rush social houses in their sophomore year, and everyone who rushes gets into at least one of them. According to one student, "A bulk of the student population, but not the majority" joins the social houses, and their parties are open to anyone. The administration gives the social houses money for events throughout the year, so IDs are checked at the door. At least one of the social houses throws a party almost every weekend, and some get wild. One social house throws an annual "tropical island" theme party and raffles off a ticket to Hawaii. Some guests bring packed suitcases.

Groups of dorms called commons organize parties and other social events, mainly for people who do not want to join a social house, although all students are welcome. Once the keg is kicked at a social house or commons party, at around 1 A.M., students, often very drunk, head over to McCollough Student Center, where a DJ dance party sponsored by the social houses, commons, or MCAB (Middlebury College Activities Board) rages until everyone gets tired and goes home.

> **"You've probably seen the J. Crew jokes on e-mail."**

Home for about 90 percent of the students is campus dorms. The other 10 percent live either in their social houses, in college-owned senior housing on the fringe of campus, or in one of the many cultural and specialty houses, such as the Italian House, the Chinese House, the International Student House, or the Weybridge Environmental House.

Dorms and Dining

Residents consider the dorms "fair," although some say Battelle, Coffren ("Coffin"), and the New Dorms, which are "very sterile," rank at the bottom of the pack, while Voter, Hepburn, and the top floors of most dorms (reserved for seniors) are considered the best rooms. Students report that "rooms are pretty bad, but if you like the people, it doesn't matter." After freshman year, undergrads choose their own dorms with a group of their friends. Some students choose substance-free and quiet halls. Junior counselors live in freshman dorms to answer academic questions, social questions, or anything else.

Freshmen find their JCs more as friends than authority figures, and upperclassmen feel the same about RAs and Residence Life directors (recent grads in charge of the administration and maintenance of the dorms), who live in all dorms.

All full-time students are enrolled in the meal program and can choose from four different dining halls, all run by the same catering service. Students say the dining service staff seems to care about them and makes special meals once a month. For example, on Halloween, all the dining hall staff dresses in costume and prepares Halloween theme food. Proctor is the main dining hall; Lower Proctor (with pink walls) caters to the "ultimate Frisbee and artsy crowd." Freeman serves regular dining hall food and Hamlin serves fast food, but also has a good salad bar. The Chateau dining hall has language tables at lunch. The Crest Room, located in the student center, is a snack bar where students eat, study, or hang out until it closes at two or three o'clock in the morning. Students cannot transfer their meals there, but can charge them on their ID card. The student center also offers billiards, a bar, a stage for performances, and a cybercafe. The school has also recently built the Bicentennial Hall.

If students want to eat off campus, they often walk into town. Middlebury has several restaurants, many of which are family-run. Most students have cars, so if they want to go a little farther for food, go shopping, or go out at night, they take the one-hour drive to Burlington or drive two hours to Montreal.

Middlebury students tend to classify themselves as the "preppy, L. L. Bean, Eddie Bauer type. You need warm, comfortable clothes in the winter; it isn't a surprise that everyone orders from L. L. Bean," one student said. Another student remarked, "You've probably seen the J. Crew jokes on e-mail." Many students come from the New England area, although there is a large international student population. One non-East Coast student joked that nearly everyone comes from "a little town outside Boston." Students report that there is not much diversity and that this can be "frustrating" sometimes. Nor is there much political activism, although students consider themselves relatively liberal and environmentally conscious. Minority groups are well accepted, and the MOQA (Middlebury Open Queer Alliance) has a strong presence on campus.

Annual Events

Middlebury hosts many annual events, such as Winter Carnival, which centers on ski races, followed by snowman-carving contests and other winter games, and a formal ball. More recent traditions include Winter Olympics and a Charity Ball sponsored by the social houses. All social houses throw parties for Robin Hood days in the spring. Some students report that this event is an excuse for everyone on campus to get very drunk, although Middle-

bury also sponsors a concert that draws big-name bands. In the past, Middlebury has been host to the Dave Matthews Band and the Samples.

Never described as anything less than spectacular, Middlebury was built in such a way that you will have a view. Middlebury's "marble buildings tucked in the background of the Champlain Valley" are breathtaking, while its academics are highly lauded, and "the openness and friendliness of the student body and professors" is unanimously praised. As one student said, "It definitely becomes home." All this plus graduating on skis— what else could the nature-loving academic want?—*Marion Ringel and Staff*

FYI
The three best things about attending Middlebury are "beautiful campus, hot ultimate players during the spring, and DJ dance parties every weekend."
The three worst things about attending Middlebury are "everyone looks like they're from J.Crew, winter is 9 months long, and Middlebury's in the middle of nowhere."
The three things that every student should do before graduating from Middlebury are "sled down the hill in front of Mead Chapel, hook up after getting drunk, and ski up the Snow Bowl."
One thing I'd like to have known before coming here is "the closest McDonald's is an hour's walk away."

University of Vermont

Address: 194 S. Prospect Street; Burlington, VT 05401-3596
Phone: 802-656-3370
E-mail address: admissions@vuvm.edu
Web site URL: www.uvm.edu
Founded: 1791
Private or Public: public
Religious affiliation: none
Location: small town
Undergraduate enrollment: 7,470
Total enrollment: 10,246
Percent Male/Female: 45%/55%
Percent Minority: 4%
Percent African-American: 0.5%

Percent Asian: 2%
Percent Hispanic: 1%
Percent Native-American: 0.5%
Percent in-state/out-of-state: 42%/58%
Percent Pub HS: 66%
Number of Applicants: 7,564
Percent Accepted: 80%
Percent Accepted who enroll: 30%
Entering: 1,818
Transfers: 320
Application Deadline: 15 Jan
Mean SAT: 562 V, 566 M
Mean ACT: 24

Middle 50% SAT range: 510–610 V, 520–620 M
Middle 50% ACT range: 21–26
3 Most popular majors: psychology, English, business administration
Retention: 81%
Graduation rate: 67%
On-campus housing: 95%
Fraternities: NA
Sororities: NA
Library: NA
Tuition and Fees: $8,044 in; $19,252 out
Room and Board: $5,620
Financial aid, first-year: 50%

Life in Vermont has its upsides and its downsides. The University of Vermont campus looks idyllic in the winter, with its snow-covered hills and icicle-tipped buildings. Two renowned ski resorts, Sugarbush and Stowe, are less than a half-hour drive from the university grounds, and school-organized transportation brings students to and from the slopes. Burlington's Waterfront Park is just blocks from campus and offers outdoor ice-skating. However, with the average low in January an icy eight degrees, one student said the winter can "put a damper on a lot of activity. When it's two degrees out, no one is too motivated to go walk and find a party." During their four-year stay in the Green Mountain State, University of Vermont students learn to both love and loathe the wintry climate.

Academic Options

There is no set of academic requirements common to all UVM students. Mandatory classes vary depending on school, program, and major. However, most students say "requirements are fair, and easy to fulfill in four years if you know what you want to study." One freshman raved that "a lot of the classes that take care of re-

quirements are also fun" and can be practical. Classes like Applications of Finite Math fulfill requirements while giving students vital skills for the future.

All undergraduates are required to take a Race and Culture class and fulfill two credits of physical education. PE offerings range from traditional sports, like tennis and volleyball, to more creative offerings, like figure skating and rappelling. One undergrad marveled at the fact that students receive course credit for everything from Walking for Fitness to Stress Reduction.

Class size at UVM varies depending on the level of the course. According to one junior, "Intro classes are about as bad as they get . . . five-hundred-person lecture halls, dry professors, and two exams to evaluate you." However, things improve dramatically once students get past the basics: "Upper-level classes are 20 people or less, discussion-based, and much more interesting." Popular offerings include the sociology class Sex, Marriage and Family, which examines issues like how the view of sex has changed over time and how childhood experiences affect parents' behavior.

Students' primary complaint is that many get shut out of classes. Athletes get first pick, then seniors, juniors, sophomores, and finally freshmen. One undergraduate complained, "Classes fill up too early and you sometimes have to wait two or three semesters to get a class you want, which screws up your class requirements for your major." All students must complete a major, and the most popular programs include business administration, biology, and elementary education. UVM offers a variety of pre-professional programs, including pre-law, pre-med, and pre-vet.

> "At any time during the week, day or night, you can and will find people ready to party."

All students tackle five classes a semester, leading some to groan about the "ton of work." However, others assure you that the academic load is manageable. "I think it is useful to do all the work teachers give you, but for some classes it isn't really necessary," said one student. PE classes, which usually don't have homework, also lighten the load.

Home, Sweet Home
UVM students call Burlington, the largest city in Vermont, their home. Downtown features a mall, nice stores, and a pedestrian shopping area that is off-limits to cars. Students consider their city "quaint" and a "very spiritual place" and frequently venture into Burlington for meals, shopping, and relaxation. They also take advantage of the wilderness around Burlington, enjoying the splendid scenery and wild terrain that lie just outside the city. "The best part of Vermont is often the unexplored parts," said one student. Undergraduates often spend their free time hiking, swimming, and biking around Burlington.

Students also get involved in the local community, through the university's multitude of volunteer programs. UVM Volunteers-in-action is the "student-run umbrella organization for 12 different volunteer programs." Through this group, students devote their time in Burlington's soup kitchens and battered women's homes, among others. Every year about 40 volunteers go to Burlington elementary

schools to teach creative writing and produce the *Vermont Children's Magazine.* One junior described the volunteer program as "one of the most rewarding things I have done at UVM."

Hockey is *the* sport for UVM students. According to one undergrad, "The games are always filled," as everyone flocks to see the NCAA Division III Catamounts face off against rival ECAC teams. Club and intramural athletics thrive as well, and "lots of people" use the campus fitness center regularly. Students also stay in shape by hitting the slopes at one of the many local ski resorts.

Room and Board
UVM underclassmen usually live on one of three mini-campuses: Main Campus, East Campus, or Redstone. Most freshmen live in Harris-Millis, which primarily holds doubles, with a few triples mixed in. Main Campus houses an additional group of freshmen, in the infamous "shoeboxes," known for their tiny size. Freshman dorms are "fun, social places . . . but you won't get any work done there at all," and floors are single-sex. Most sophomores live on Redstone Campus, which is farther from classes but "really nice and with newer furniture." One of the best parts of the UVM housing system is that it is flexible and "you have the option to move around a lot," with no deadlines for changing rooms. Juniors and seniors are allowed to move off campus and many do. They often live in Burlington apartments and houses, but due to high demand, off-campus housing can be "really expensive." Undergrads can also reside in the Living and Learning complex, in which students who share a common interest live with one another.

The on-campus food is provided by Marriott and is "pretty good" according to most students. Students pay for meals using either points or blocks. Points work like cash and can be used to pay for meals at the cafeteria, food at Alice's (think "Mobil Mart"), or pizza. Blocks can only be used at the all-you-can-eat cafeteria that has nightly pasta, pizza, and grill options in addition to hot entrées. All students choose from a variety of meal plans, which can be comprised entirely of points, blocks, or some combination of the two.

Party Hardy

By all accounts, UVM lives up to its reputation as a party school: "At any time during the week, day or night, you can and will find people ready to party." Since the campus is officially dry, students party at off-campus fraternity houses and independent bashes. Fraternities usually charge five dollars for admission and sometimes host theme parties. One student recalls a "disease" party, where students were handed cards with the name of an illness. If partiers found the student with the matching card, they were rewarded with shots of alcohol. In addition to drinking, "all frats have music and dancing and most house parties do, too."

Most students agree that non-drinkers do not feel out of place on campus. "If you are sober, you can have a great time, too," remarked one freshman. Staying in to chill with friends is a pretty common alternative to partying. However, the party scene dominates UVM social life, and despite the occasional a cappella concert or dance, alternative social gatherings are "not always an option." The administration is attempting to crack down on on-campus and underage drinking. Burlington city cops, as well as residential advisors, patrol the dorms, and according to the disgruntled student, "They are not looking out for your best interests. Ever." Drug use is also widespread on campus. "The pot scene is unbelievable at UVM—practically unavoidable," said one upperclassman. Another student contends that while drugs are around, "it really depends on the people who you hang out with."

In addition to on-campus entertainment, UVM students enjoy Burlington's "hoppin' nightlife," letting loose at one of the city's two dance clubs or the numerous bars, which require ID. The area around UVM boasts an active concert scene. "Burlington is a young, hip city, and everything comes through: reggae, hip-hop, bluegrass, you name it," as well as the jam-oriented music for which the area is particularly known. One of the most popular venues is Higher Ground, in nearby Winooski, Vermont, which brings in a continual stream of talented musicians.

Hippies—Too Many or Too Few?

Most undergrads say that their schoolmates have a great variety of attitudes, styles, and interests. One student complained that there are "too many hippies," but another said there are not as many as she expected. One junior warned that "if you like Phish, you'll get to know a lot more about them. And if you don't, well, you better learn to tolerate them." More than half of the student body are Vermont natives, and cultural and racial diversity are not the school's strongest points.

On the whole, students at the University of Vermont celebrated the fact that their peers possess "a liberal attitude and an open mind." Whether it is in the classroom or the frat houses or on Church Street in downtown Burlington, their classmates are "genuinely nice people" and receptive to different ideas, pastimes, and fellow students.—*Pamela Boykoff*

FYI

The three best things about attending UVM are "Burlington is a really nice-sized town, UVM has a number of outstanding professors, and we have a good library staff and interlibrary loan considering the small size of the school."

The three worst things about attending UVM are "northeasterners are fairly rude to strangers, good classes but poor class offerings, not much of a feel for community."

The three things every student should do before graduating from UVM are "ski/snowboard at Stowe Mt., learn how to balance academics and fun, get involved in the Burlington community."

One thing I'd like to have known before coming here is "how late the winters last. It seems like they don't bother to start until January but don't end until almost May."

Virginia

College of William and Mary

Address: PO Box 8795, Williamsburg, VA 23187-8795
Phone: 757-221-4223
E-mail address: admiss@facstaff.wm.edu
Web site URL: www.wm.edu
Founded: 1693
Private or Public: NA
Religious affiliation: none
Location: small city
Undergraduate enrollment: 5,552
Total enrollment: 7,553
Percent Male/Female: 42%/58%
Percent Minority: 14%
Percent African-American: 4%

Percent Asian: 7%
Percent Hispanic: 3%
Percent Native-American: 7%
Percent in-state/out-of-state: 64%/36%
Percent Pub HS: 78%
Number of Applicants: 6,878
Percent Accepted: 45%
Percent Accepted who enroll: 42%
Entering: 1,301
Transfers: 137
Application Deadline: 5 Jan
Mean SAT: 662 V, 651 M
Mean ACT: NA

Middle 50% SAT range: 620–710 V, 610–700 M
Middle 50% ACT range: 29–32
3 Most popular majors: psychology, biology, economics
Retention: 95%
Graduation rate: 88%
On-campus housing: 99%
Fraternities: 32%
Sororities: 29%
Library: 1,418,932 volumes
Tuition and Fees: $4,610 in; $16,434 out
Room and Board: $4,897
Financial aid, first-year: 30%

Students at William and Mary quickly become accustomed to giving directions. When the weather is nice, it is not uncommon for a student to be stopped en route to class by a bewildered tourist looking for a historic landmark. After all, this is the second-oldest school in the nation, and it's located in Colonial Williamsburg, a popular vacation spot. While the hordes of wandering "tourons" can sometimes be irritating, students agree that the attention is flattering, and they are proud to show off their school. "Besides," explained a senior, "it's a constant reminder that we get to go to everything in Colonial Williamsburg for free . . . so we might as well help out!"

A Tight-knit Community

William and Mary's small size is relatively unusual among its public school counterparts, but students insist that is not *too* small. Says one upperclassman, "I can walk across the Sunken Gardens and run into people I know, but I could also meet someone new every day." The small size fosters a close community, which is made even tighter by a number of William and Mary traditions. Everybody looks forward to the annual Yule Log Ceremony, where representatives of different cultures explain their traditions for the holiday season and the president of the university, dressed as Santa Claus, reads to the whole student body. Worries are burned away on a Yule log, and the evening ends with hot cider, cookies, and a bonfire. Ghost tours of Colonial Williamsburg are popular around Halloween, and spring brings the formal King and Queen's Ball. Although these "traditional" William and Mary events are beloved and well attended, students complain that university sporting events do not enjoy the same support. "This is not a spirited campus," sighed one senior. "We are an academic school, not an athletic one." Another student blamed the lack of spirit on William and Mary students' tendency to be overcommitted to their own extracurriculars: "People are faithful to their own activities, but it takes a lot to make them participate in others'."

The extracurriculars that command the attention of William and Mary students are many and varied. The a cappella and theater communities are "very tight," and intramural sports are extremely popular. Community service is also a big deal here, and the majority of William and Mary students participate in some form of it. Religious organizations are another strong presence; said one senior, "This is one of the most religious public schools I've seen." Although the campus is not very culturally or ethnically diverse, students here appreciate diversity and say that there is a definite emphasis on multiculturalism. Cultural events such as the Taste of Asia celebration are well attended by the entire student body. "There is an interest in diversity here, but it is not exemplified," said one student. On the other hand, students also say that the size of the student body means that the campus does not self-segregate. As one student said, "Groups here *have* to integrate because it is such a small community."

Students at William and Mary tend to dress relatively conservatively, but one can find styles here ranging from "hippie" to "label-conscious" and "preppy." The off-center male–female ratio can be a source of woe, prompting one female student to ask, "Where are the guys?" Students say that formal dating is not too common on campus; most relationships seem to be either "serious" or "hookups." Socializing at William and Mary is done in groups rather than couples, but those who do date will certainly have many a "relationship talk" on the benches scattered around Colonial Williamsburg. According to one senior, "Pretty much every relationship here starts or ends in Colonial Williamsburg."

Getting Down to Business

A student from Virginia claims that the instate reputation of William and Mary students is that "all we do is study." While this is certainly an exaggeration, students at William and Mary *do* take their studies very

seriously, and they say that they are continually impressed by the intellectualism of their peers. "We're not afraid to challenge ourselves," one junior asserted. Class sizes are generally small, although introductory courses are often large lectures. Students rave about their professors, describing them as "friendly," "knowledgeable," and "approachable." As one student put it, "All my professors know my name, and I can go up to them and talk about anything, whenever." Stories that illustrate professors' commitment to students abound; Professor Scholnik, for example, is known for inviting his entire American Renaissance Literature class over to his house for a winter holiday dinner.

Students who want a rewarding—if extremely challenging—academic experience often opt to take a class with Prof. Hans Tiefel of the religion department, the best-known of which is his "Death" course. Tiefel's students should prepare for a heavy workload; as one senior joked, "If you get into the class, it *means* death!" Courses in economics, chemistry, and introductory philosophy are popular with students for fulfilling general requirements, although one student warns that "organic chemistry kicks everyone's butt!" Courses known for having lighter workloads include "Rocks for Jocks" and "Physics for Non-Majors." The government and biology departments draw rave reviews from students, while the sociology department is said to offer many easy courses. A portion of the incoming freshman class are chosen to be Monroe Scholars. These students have the option of living in Monroe Hall, and they are given funds to pursue an independent study project over the summer.

While there is no specific core curriculum, students must fulfill general education requirements (GERs) in seven areas. They are also required to demonstrate proficiency in a foreign language, writing, and physical activity. The academic requirements are praised for being "very reasonable" and for exposing students to different subjects. As one upperclassman explained, "You fulfill a lot of [the GERs] just by moving through the school." Freshmen are required to take a writing seminar each semester. These professor-led seminars of 15 students or less are offered in a variety of focused subjects, which change from year to year. "Everyone loves his or her freshman seminar," one student declared. Those with advanced academic standing—either by being upperclassmen or by matriculating with AP credits—can choose their classes (and rooms) before others, and most are eventually able to take the classes they want. However, there are so many course offerings that "even if you do not get into the class you want, you can always find something else."

Taking It All In

Despite its charm to visitors, Colonial Williamsburg—or "CW," as it is referred to by the students—is not the cultural mecca many would like. The school is working with the city to provide more social options, but social life is "very campus-centered," and most students seem to like it that way. Although 65% of the student body hail from Virginia, the campus does not empty out on the weekends. Said one junior, "We live by the weekends here." The Greek scene is a "staple," since one-third of the campus belong to a fraternity or sorority. However, non-Greeks can easily take advantage of the parties as well, and students are quick to point out that Greek life is only part of the social scene. Underage drinking typically occurs in private or Greek parties, as the off-campus delis and other venues require ID. William and Mary students agree that while drinking is present, it is not a huge problem and there is hardly any peer pressure. "It's a healthy environment," said one student.

> "Pretty much every relationship here starts or ends in Colonial Williamsburg."

The university and the surrounding area offer plenty of cultural events, school-organized activities, movies, and restaurants as alternatives or additions to the party scene. There are several "delis" just off campus that function as bars for those with proper ID and serve as hangouts for the student body in general. Undergrads also frequent Lodge One, the student center, which brings in comedians and local bands for entertainment, or sip cups of java at the Daily Grind, a 24-hour on-campus coffee shop built recently at the request of the student body. For those who desire more nightlife, Virginia Beach, Norfolk, and Richmond are always just a short trip away.

The Campus Experience

William and Mary students describe their campus as "beautiful, colonial, and green." Everyone seems to have a favorite spot to study. "This place has so many nooks and crannies," said one freshman. There are two parts to the campus: Old Campus is distinguished by old colonial buildings, while New Campus is a mix of colonial and modern architecture. People relax in the Sunken Gardens and enjoy the beauty of the Crim Dell, a shaded pond. *Playboy* magazine listed the bridge over the Crim Dell as one of the most romantic spots on an American campus, and the legend at William and Mary is that you will marry the person you kiss on the bridge. The Crim Dell and Sunken Gardens are also part of another William and Mary tradition, the "triathlon." Before graduating, every student is supposed to streak across the Sunken Gardens, jump in the Crim Dell, and jump the wall of the Governor's Palace in Colonial Williamsburg.

The food on campus is described as "pretty good," although some students complain about recent changes in the meal plans. Most eat on campus, but when they tire of college food there are plenty of off-campus options. The Trellis is famous for its desserts, and the Cheese Shop is known for its "house dressing," made from a recipe so secret that employees have to sign an agreement not to reveal it.

Most students live on campus at William and Mary, and rooms are chosen by a lottery system. Those who move off tend to be seniors, students who want more independence, or students with very low lottery numbers, and many of them discover that a car helps get them around. Freshmen are housed together, and most people agree that their closest friends are their hallmates from freshman year. Housing quality varies from DuPont, known as the "hotel" for freshmen, to dorms that are not renovated and lack air-conditioning. Upperclassmen with good lottery numbers can opt to live in one of the coveted lodges, which are centrally located "houses" for six or seven people. Theme and single-sex housing is also available.

Students at William and Mary truly love their historic and tight-knit school, and they thoroughly enjoy their experience here. The beautiful campus and dedicated professors are continually cited as big draws, but students insist that their peers are the most wonderful part of William and Mary. Said one freshman: "People here are just so friendly . . . they like you for who you are. That's why I chose this place." —*Alison Schary*

FYI

The three best things about attending William and Mary are "great professors, access to Colonial Williamsburg, and a really diverse group of people you can learn a lot from."

The three worst things about attending William and Mary are "parking (or the complete lack thereof), sometimes it rains too much, and I wish there were a shopping center closer by."

The three things that every student should do before graduating from William and Mary are "take a class in the Wren Building (oldest building on campus), eat at the Cheese Shop, and compete in the triathlon."

One thing I'd like to have known before coming here is "how accessible the professors are. I wish I would have gotten to know my professors right from the start."

George Mason University

Address: 4400 University Drive, MSN 3A4; Fairfax, VA 22030-4444
Phone: 703-993-2400
E-mail address: admissions@gmu.edu
Web site URL: www.gmu.edu
Founded: 1957
Private or Public: public
Religious affiliation: none
Location: suburban
Undergraduate enrollment: NA
Total enrollment: NA
Percent Male/Female: NA
Percent Minority: 0%

Percent African-American: NA
Percent Asian: NA
Percent Hispanic: NA
Percent Native-American: NA
Percent in-state/out-of-state: 92%/8%
Percent Pub HS: NA
Number of Applicants: 6,035
Percent Accepted: 63%
Percent Accepted who enroll: 55%
Entering: 2,110
Transfers: 2,034
Application Deadline: 1 Feb
Mean SAT: NA
Mean ACT: NA

Middle 50% SAT range: 460–570 V, 470–580 M
Middle 50% ACT range: 17–23
3 Most popular majors: psychology, administrative services, speech and rhetoric
Retention: 74%
Graduation rate: 51%
On-campus housing: NA
Fraternities: 8%
Sororities: 8%
Library: NA
Tuition and Fees: $3,756 in; $12,516 out
Room and Board: $5,080
Financial aid, first-year: 38%

Just 30 minutes outside of Washington, D.C., George Mason University was founded in 1957 as a two-year branch of the University of Virginia. After gaining university status in 1972, it has come into its own and earned national recognition, although a large majority of its students are commuters from northern Virginia (parking lots are an integral part of the campus). The architecture is modern and new buildings are always under construction. The sprawling tree-lined campus seems barely able to contain GMU's academic and physical growth. "It used to be thought of as a backup school, but now people who come here really want to come here," one student reported.

An Academic Mall

Recent additions to the academic curriculum have propelled GMU from a regional university into national prominence. It offers over 100 undergraduate and graduate programs along with over 100 more certificate, interdisciplinary, and minor programs. One student said that the overall academic atmosphere is "not overly competitive," but she felt she was "receiving a great education at a reasonable cost."

Business, biology, and psychology are reportedly among the most popular majors. Business majors report that the recently built Enterprise Hall, with its new facilities and updated equipment, will revolutionize the department, whereas some students listed communications and theater as weaker departments. Almost all upper-level courses are taught by professors (as opposed to TAs, who do some teaching at lower levels) and are relatively small, with 20 to 30 students. GMU offers University 101 courses that allow freshmen to orient themselves to the university and the surrounding area. Registration for classes is done over the phone. Students with high GPAs can enroll in the Robinson Courses, which are taught by visiting professors. This prominent group has included journalist Roger Wilkins (Pulitzer Prize winner for coverage of Watergate scandal), anthropologist Mary Catherine Bateson, and African anthropologist John Paden, among others.

GMU has four innovative programs that are popular with students. The Plan for Alternatives to General Education (PAGE) provides an option that differs from general education courses. Faculty members from various disciplines team-teach the two-year program in small seminar-like classes. In the New Century College program, a student may design his or her own major with the help of a faculty advisor. The Linked Courses program allows freshmen to join the required composition class, English 101, with an introductory course in communication, government, philosophy, sociology, anthropology, psychology, or history. The fourth program is the Bachelor of Arts in Interdisciplinary Studies (BAIS), which allows students to major in a combination of disciplines.

Commuting to School

Undergrads report that George Mason is not the "typical college experience," because the student body includes a large number of commuters. Only about 15 per-

cent of all students live in campus dorms. The on-campus social scene is limited to the small number of students who live there, but because they are a small group, they tend to be "very close and very active." People tend to hang out in definite cliques and "it is hard to make friends here if you don't live on campus," one student said. "You have to either be Greek or very social."

Freshmen who live on campus are required to live in President's Park, dorms that some consider "the worst on campus." Residents of Commons and student apartments consider their accommodations spacious and comfortable. The first-year dorms are officially alcohol-free, but residents reportedly interpret the rule liberally. On-campus living can provide a family-like experience. "The on-campus students bond together and have a lot of school spirit," said one undergrad. Popular hangouts include Taco Bell and Pizza Hut, as well as "the Rat," the only place on campus where students of legal age can buy alcohol. On the other hand, "most people go off campus to do stuff."

> **George Mason is relatively young and current undergrads have the opportunity to have a formative influence on shaping campus life.**

For those who live on campus, Greek life is very popular. The most active frats include Sigma Chi and AON. Alpha Xi Delta is a popular sorority. Frat parties tend to be exclusive, and while students say it is not hard for girls to get in (life is not fair), guys have a tough time. Most parties tend to be in private homes or in D.C. clubs. Alcohol figures heavily into the social scene. Despite the strict control of alcohol sales (hard liquor is sold in VA only through state-owned Alcohol Beverage Control, or ABC, centers), some students say underage drinking is easy if you "have connections."

Being in DC

Washington, D.C., is a great source of academic, social, and internship experiences. Many students choose to come to Mason because of its proximity to D.C. "It's close enough to D.C., but you get to enjoy the peaceful and convenient living of the suburbs." Clubbing and frequenting the bars in the Georgetown and Adams Morgan neighborhoods of D.C. are very popular for students with cars (which is just about everybody).

Other popular extracurricular activities at GMU include student government and the university's weekly newspaper, the *Broadside*. Those with rebellious blood can write for the underground independent newspaper, the *Expulsion*, which makes fun of the university's official paper. Students use these publications to get their ideas across to the administration, and many feel their ideas actually make an impact that might not be possible at an older, more tradition-bound school. Students report that there is almost always "something going on in the quad," from speakers to poets to comedians. Mason Day, an annual celebration, recently featured a concert by the Violent Femmes. Recent famous speakers have included mayor of D.C. Marion Barry, G. Gordon Liddy, Oliver North, news anchorman Ed Bradley, Candace Bergen, and Richard Dreyfus.

Diversity Abounds

Despite the high in-state population at GMU, students are impressed by their classmates' diverse ethnic and geographical origins. One student went so far as to say that "GMU is the most ethnically diverse campus in Virginia." There is also a large, active gay and lesbian population on campus, and reportedly there is also much interracial dating. Many older students and part-time students take classes at GMU although they have little contact with traditional-age undergrads.

In keeping with the "newness" of George Mason, the campus has modern architecture, and construction is under way as the college continues to expand. There are already two student centers, and the new University Center will house retail stores, a theater, a library center, lounge, eateries, and classrooms for the New Century College. The arts center has hosted such performers as Itzhak Perlman. Student tickets are free and all performances are open to the public.

Students report that contact between George Mason and the town of Fairfax is minimal. "Fairfax is not a college town like Charlottesville," complained one student, who said there is little to do in Fairfax. Students rely on D.C. for entertainment instead.

The biggest complaint students have about George Mason is the lack of traditions. But, many students see a positive side to this too because George Mason is relatively young and current undergrads have the opportunity to have a formative influence on shaping campus life. It may not have the rich, historical atmosphere of an older university, but GMU offers a college experience devoid of the stereotypes and prejudices that often accompany tradition.—*Seung Lee and Staff*

FYI
The three best things about attending GMU are "the incredible speakers who visit, the proximity to DC, and 'the Rat.'"
The three worst things about attending GMU are "the lack of traditions that define a school, a lackluster Fairfax, and living in President's Park."
The three things that every student should do before graduating from GMU are "go clubbing in D.C., keep your eyes posted for awesome speakers, and get invited to a frat party."
One thing I'd like to have known before coming here is "that you will need a car to take advantage of D.C."

Hampden-Sydney College

Address: PO Box 667;
Hampden-Sydney, VA
23943
Phone: 804-223-6120
E-mail address:
hsapp@tiger.hsc.edu
Web site URL: www.hsc.edu
Founded: 1776
Private or Public: private
Religious affiliation:
Presbyterian
Location: rural
**Undergraduate
enrollment:** NA
Total enrollment: 996
Percent Male/Female: NA
Percent Minority: 0%
Percent African-American:
NA

Percent Asian: NA
Percent Hispanic: NA
Percent Native-American:
NA
**Percent in-state/out-of-
state:** 60%/40%
Percent Pub HS: 65%
Number of Applicants:
991
Percent Accepted:
74%
**Percent Accepted who
enroll:** 42%
Entering: 307
Transfers: 9
Application Deadline:
1 Mar
Mean SAT: 551 V, 557 M
Mean ACT: 22

Middle 50% SAT range:
500–600 V,
510–610 M
Middle 50% ACT range:
19–25
3 Most popular majors:
economics, history,
political science
Retention: 80%
Graduation rate: 64%
On-campus housing: 100%
Fraternities: 30%
Sororities: NA
Library: 220,172 volumes
Tuition and Fees:
$16,531 in; $16,531 out
Room and Board: $5,898
Financial aid, first-year:
80%

Tradition, excellence, and honor: at all-male Hampden-Sydney, these are not just words. They are a way of life.

Academic Excellence

Excellence in academics comes in the form of the Rhetoric Program, a set of first- and second-year core requirements. Although many of their classes are predetermined by the Rhetoric Program, freshmen get a taste of the individual attention they will receive at Hampden-Sydney through faculty advisors who help plan their schedules.

The Rhetoric Program consists of challenging classes in English, writing, and speech, ten papers a semester, stringent grammar testing, and a final proficiency exam. A follow-up exam is given after the program to ensure that students have actually retained what they've learned. As one student put it, "The Rhetoric Program totally killed me my freshman year." However, students seem to appreciate the program and say that it helps later on with courses in their majors.

The economics, political science, and history departments are quite strong and popular. Languages and sciences are reportedly not as strong, yet students agree that most of the departments are quite challenging. As one sophomore put it, "If you get an A here, you really had to earn it."

The largest classes at Hampden-Sydney enroll about 35 people. Upper-level classes usually contain no more than 10 students. Students know all their professors well, and some professors invite students to dinner and other social events. The accessibility of professors also comes in handy when extensions on assignments are needed. As one student reported, "Since professors know all their students so well, they're usually willing to accept a late paper or reschedule an exam if need be. It's really easy to talk to the teachers." The college also runs a Writing Center, whose staff will read and critique any written assignments. Students agree that all of these personal services help them excel.

Living Quarters

Although only freshmen are required to live on campus, almost all upperclassmen remain in campus housing. Students choose their preferred dorm before attending Hampden-Sydney. One student explained that students almost always pick the dorms they stayed in during their visits as prospective students.

Cushing, the oldest and one of the most popular dorms, houses half the freshman class. "All the freshmen want to live there," one student remarked, because of its "Animal House, party-dorm" reputation and large rooms. Other popular dorms are Carpenter, which has carpeting in all the rooms, and the Hampden House apartments, which are complete with private bathrooms. The dorms are divided into four "passages," hallways where neighboring students form strong and lasting friendships.

Typical College Food

Pannill Commons, the main dining hall on campus, serves "typical college food—not great," one student said. Most undergrads prefer the Tiger Inn restaurant, a campus hangout equivalent to a student center, with pool tables and a big-screen television. Although it's not part of the meal plan, the Tiger Inn attracts many students and even hosts bands and comedians.

> "It does get a little old only having 900 guys around."

Students also venture off campus to the town of Farmville for food. Some like Charlie's and Macado's for sandwiches or steak dinners. The Hitchin' Post, right off campus, draws quite a crowd for sandwiches as well. Although Farmville has about "half a dozen good restaurants," one student said, it does not have much else for the college crowd. The nearest mall is 45 minutes away, in Lynchburg, and Richmond, the largest city nearby, is an hour's drive away. Students admit that "you really need a car here, or at least have a friend with a car." Freshmen are allowed to have cars on campus, reportedly a tremendous asset for visiting the women's schools about an hour away from Hampden-Sydney.

Where the Women Are

There are four women's colleges close to Hampden-Sydney: Mary Baldwin, Sweet Briar, Randolph-Macon, and Hollins. Longwood, a coed state school, is also nearby. Hampden-Sydney social functions have a "definitely noticeable" female presence. The College Activities Committee occasionally hosts frequent mixers with the women's schools, and the fraternities, which include half of the student body, throw parties with the sororities from the Universities of Richmond and Virginia. As one student remarked, "It's initially really easy to meet girls. It seems like almost everyone here has a girlfriend."

Going Out

Most parties and weekend activities occur at the Circle, Hampden-Sydney's fraternity row. Despite the administration's recent enforcement of the alcohol policy by making Cushing a dry dorm, the attitude toward alcohol among students is pretty laid-back. Fraternity parties, open to all students, provide a steady supply of alcohol.

Although Greek life is a large part of the campus scene, it is not divisive. According to one non-Greek, "People consider themselves Hampden-Sydney men first, Greeks second." The Greeks are responsible for all the big parties and social events on campus. The biggest is Greek Week, an annual spring weekend of partying and dancing. Greek Week hosts popular bands, which have included Hootie and the Blowfish, Big Head Todd and the Monsters, the Dave Matthews Band, Blues Traveler, and the Spin Doctors. Road trips to the women's colleges are also popular weekend activities.

Extracurriculars

The favorite extracurricular activity for Greeks and non-Greeks alike is intramural sports. Students organize their own teams and compete in a variety of sports, including football, basketball, and soccer. Varsity sports also receive enthusiastic student support, especially the football team, whose homecoming performance kicks off a weekend of parties with students from the competing school. The Young Republicans is one of the many popular extracurricular groups. Political sentiment on campus is conservative, and students say they are politically active. Other popular activities include the debate society, the literary organization, the Key Club, and the Outsider's Club, which sponsors white-water rafting and adventure trips.

Honorable Men

One of the most prestigious campus organizations is the student government, which is responsible for enforcing the honor code. Hampden-Sydney has a strictly enforced honor code; students can be expelled for cheating, stealing, or dishonesty. Any infraction of the honor code is addressed by the student-run honor court, which assigns the accused undergrad a student lawyer and decides his punishment. Although very few cases come in front of the court, students take their judicial process seriously. They say the honor code allows them freedom to feel safe and govern themselves.

As a result of the honor code, students report, Hampden-Sydney has almost no crime. As one student said, "I leave my books everywhere. You can walk into your friend's room and start watching TV and no one will mind. Even the dorms are always open."

With a deeply entrenched honor code and strong sense of tradition, Hampden-Sydney students enjoy a special camaraderie on campus. Although one student remarked, "It does get a little old only having 900 guys around," most students agree that the all-male environment creates a sense of true fellowship, and that the college would lose much of its special character if women were admitted. Other students point out that relationships with the faculty, strong academics, and accessibility to the many surrounding women's colleges outweigh any disadvantages.
—*Susanna Chu and Staff*

FYI

The three best things about attending Hampden-Sydney are "student pride, the honor code, and the sense of security around campus."

The three worst things about attending Hampden-Sydney are "the lack of cute girls down the hall, the core requirements, and the need for a car."

The three things that every student should do before graduating from Hampden-Sydney are "walk around the dorms in boxers, spend a night at a sorority house, have a humiliating experience during Greek Week."

One thing I'd like to have known before coming here is "your really can have fun at an all-guys college."

Hollins University

Address: PO Box 9707; Roanoke, VA 24020-1707	**Percent Asian:** NA	**Middle 50% SAT range:** 530–650 V, 500–580 M
Phone: 540-362-6401	**Percent Hispanic:** NA	
E-mail address: huadm@hollins.edu	**Percent Native-American:** NA	**Middle 50% ACT range:** 23–27
Web site URL: www.hollins.edu	**Percent in-state / out-of-state:** 34%/66%	**3 Most popular majors:** psychology, English, biology
Founded: 1842	**Percent Pub HS:** 76%	
Private or Public: private	**Number of Applicants:** 722	**Retention:** 79%
Religious affiliation: none	**Percent Accepted:** 86%	**Graduation rate:** 68%
Location: suburban		**On-campus housing:** NA
Undergraduate enrollment: NA	**Percent Accepted who enroll:** 38%	**Fraternities:** NA
Total enrollment: 1,102	**Entering:** 238	**Sororities:** NA
Percent Male / Female: NA	**Transfers:** 35	**Library:** NA
	Application Deadline: 15 Feb	**Tuition and Fees:** $16,710 in; $16,710 out
Percent Minority: 0%		**Room and Board:** $6,125
Percent African-American: NA	**Mean SAT:** NA	**Financial aid, first-year:** 64%
	Mean ACT: NA	

When the first frost falls on the beautiful campus of Hollins University, the entire community celebrates Tinker Day. Dorm halls are filled with the sound of seniors banging pots and pans, noise known as the Tinker Day Scares. Upon hearing the great clamor, students rise and do what classes before them have been doing for years; they go to the dining hall to eat breakfast in their pajamas. Classes are canceled for the entire day and everyone dons a crazy outfit and prepares to climb nearby Tinker Mountain, one of the many hills that surround the Hollins campus. At the top, students enjoy a huge picnic buffet and spend the rest of the day celebrating with songs and skits. Tinker Day is just one example of the many traditions observed at Hollins University. Students enjoy themselves at Hollins; they also recognize that Hollins is a place dedicated to providing a great education.

Broad-Based Academics

Hollins, a four-year women's university, divides its academic coursework into four divisions: humanities, social sciences, fine arts, and natural sciences. Each student must take eight credits from each division as part of a "broad based academic curriculum." Freshmen have to fulfill an additional writing requirement. Students praise the English department as exceptionally strong. As one undergrad said, "The department has like quadruple the number of professors of any other department." Aside from English, other popular majors include history and psychology. The political science department "is pretty good, but the professors are incomparably harder than in any other department." Although many undergraduates tend to major in the humanities, the natural sciences reportedly are "still pretty good and the facilities are up-to-date." Some students said that "easy" majors include communications and religion. Regardless of particular department credentials, most undergrads praise their professors for innovative assignments. For example, students in a sociology class were required to go into a store and write a paper on how they would steal money from that establishment. Not only do professors often "devise cool projects for class," but many live on the Hollins campus and are "always open" to student interaction, one undergrad said.

Class registration at the beginning of each term is "straightforward and fast," according to students. Few students have trouble getting into the classes they want, although some introductory classes in psychology, computer science, and art do fill up, due to caps put on course enrollment. To help students choose classes, course and faculty evaluations from previous semesters are readily accessible. Hollins students are also positive about the small class sizes. One freshman said that most of her classes "only had 15 people and the largest class I have had here has been only 45 students."

Short Term

Hollins divides the year into two semesters plus a short, four-week term that occurs in January. "Short Term is the reason I came to Hollins," said one freshman. Many upperclassmen use this time to do internships made possible through an extensive alumni network run by the career development office. Other students stay on campus for intensive seminar courses. The school also sponsors many off-campus opportunities during Short Term, such as travel to Greece, Spain, or Germany to improve language proficiency. By graduation, each student must have accumulated four Short Term credits, although as one senior noted, "Who would want to miss Short Term anyway?"

Car—A Must-Have

As for social life, Hollins students often find their options limited. Many go off-campus on the weekends to meet male undergrads at either Washington and Lee University or Hampden-Sydney College, both within an hour's drive. In fact, many students say having a car is a "major necessity" at Hollins. According to one senior, "There's just no bus system provided or sponsored by the administration. I have to say that it's really inconvenient not to have a car when a walk to the supermarket is half a mile." The student government does fund a taxi service on the weekends. "It's great," said one undergrad. "You can get $3 vouchers that take you to the mall or downtown." The area around Hollins is "a small district—a bit too provincial for my taste," one student said. Popular eating establishments in town include Macado's and the Mill Mountain Coffee House. One student complained, however, that "Roanoke just isn't really geared to students." Campus parties, particularly ones thrown by upperclassmen who are of age, reportedly are "uncool if you are under 21 because they won't let you near a keg."

Tradition, Tradition, Tradition

Many campus activities revolve around tradition at Hollins. Aside from Tinker Day, another popular event is Ring Night, which often "snowballs into a weeklong event." Juniors are put into groups and together do the seniors' bidding. After performing "idiotic gags and making morons of ourselves," the juniors are finally awarded their class rings. Another event is called Founder's Day, during which the seniors walk in their graduation gowns to the statue of the founder and place a wreath at its base. On certain occasions, members of a religious group called Freya don black robes and walk around campus in the middle of the night, advocating higher standards of morality.

> "Women who are going places start at Hollins."

Hollins students often criticize themselves for not "providing enough diversity." One student said that most people tend to think of Hollins students as "preppy, almost arrogant, and aloof," as many students come from higher socioeconomic backgrounds. One freshman said, "In my first few days, I did not see one person of color." One senior said that Hollins is particularly lacking in African-American students, and another said, "The diversity here tends to come from international students rather than from actual minority students from the U.S." Hollins is trying to change this image, however, in part by making substantive changes to the scholarship program for minority students.

Luxurious Housing, Crummy Food

At Hollins, all freshman live in one dorm comprised of singles and doubles. All of these rooms have built-in desks, dressers, closets, and mirrors, and air-conditioning and heating controls. One freshman living in a single said, "It's not huge, but I'm comfortable. The doubles, though, are huge." The most popular dorm on campus is Main Dorm (it "has two closets in each room as opposed to one"). Apartments across the street from the main campus house seniors and are considered "quite luxurious for on-campus housing." One of the less popular dorms is Randolph, which was built in the 1970s and reportedly "doesn't have the charm that all the other dorms do." As a result, some call it "the projects." After freshman year, housing is assigned through a lottery system, with preference given to upperclasswomen. Regardless of which dorm they live in, though, the women at Hollins are on the whole pleased with their accommodations.

The food, however, does not get such rave reviews. Though many students find campus food tolerable, others complain that it is "extremely distasteful." One student said, "I didn't expect the food to be so crummy or for there to be such a limited choice of food." Hollins only has one dining hall, with specific hours assigned for every meal. Some students find the hours inconvenient; dinner, for example, goes from 4:30 until 6:30. "I'm just not used to eating so early," one sophomore said. Despite these complaints, students praise the dining hall for its cleanliness and for "providing ice-cream sundaes every Friday at lunch as well as special theme nights every now and then." The Hollins meal plan is included in the cost of tuition. One freshman claimed, "Once you've paid, you can eat twice a week or 50 times a week." Also, as one student reported, "Probably any girl could come here and have a meal because they never check your ID." For other dining alternatives, students often go to the Rat, a place that serves as the Hollins student center and has food "like a McDonald's," or head over to the local, off-campus deli, Boomer's.

Campus Views

Hollins students are very enthusiastic about their surroundings. Many call the campus "absolutely gorgeous." The architecture is an elegant southern/Georgian style with wide porches and grand white columns. As one student noted, "We're situated in a valley, and the surrounding mountains are just beautiful." Students praise the administration for constantly revamping and updating its buildings and facilities. Recently, renovations have been undertaken on Moddey, the student services building, and the old library. The new library, which opened in the spring of 1999, is "great; it's the first literary landmark in Virginia." One student did complain that the weight room in the gym could use a little work. Another student added, "We also could use a few more male bathrooms. We do get visitors now and then." Campus security issues are also important to the administration. As one student pointed out, "Hollins is isolated and it's all girls, so security concerns are pretty high." Students are encouraged to go to officials if they feel security is lacking, and "panic boxes" are posted all over campus to connect students with campus security officers.

Active Student Body

Aside from basking in the beauty of their school, Hollins students are also extremely involved in campus life. Student Government Association is a popular activity and has multiple committees that are open to any interested students. The volunteer group SHARE is also extremely well respected by Hollins women, and coordinates the large amount of community service done by students. Many students also go into the mountains to work with various ecological programs. In addition to these groups, students participate actively in sports. The riding team consistently performs well, as do the fencing and swimming teams. Hollins recruits athletes, but any student interested in a sport can find a team to join. Even students who are not active in organized sports make good use of the gym. As one student said, "Though there's a lack of treadmills, we have a climbing wall and a really great pool."

One recent area of concern on campus is that in July of 1998, Hollins changed from a college to a university. This change reportedly came as a result of the need for more money, but brought with it an increased selection of classes and majors, and many building upgrades. However, many upperclasswomen are not pleased about the shift in status. Although Hollins already offers coed graduate programs, many fear that the undergraduate program will become coed. As one senior commented, "They've changed our bumper sticker from reading 'Women are going places' to 'People are going places.'" One freshman reported, however, "The president says that there is absolutely no way that the school is going coed, and I believe her." A sophomore explained, "Hollins is still very much a small liberal arts college dedicated to personal attention and women's education."

The students of Hollins University clearly love their campus, community, academic program, and learning from each other. Though one senior said, "I wish it weren't as hard finding guy friends and developing male relationships, but I'd definitely come here again—in a flash."—*Jeff Kaplow and Staff*

FYI
The three best things about attending Hollins are "the many traditions, the women's atmosphere (it provides a big comfort level), and the fact that all the professors know you."
The three worst things about attending Hollins are "the small course selection, the lack of diversity, and the scarce resources in the library."
The three things that every student should do before graduating from Hollins are "walk on the front quad, have a rope passed down to you, and go to the Spring Cotillion."
One thing I'd like to have known before coming here is "how limited classes at a small school are."

J a m e s   M a d i s o n   U n i v e r s i t y

Address: Sonner Hall MSC 0101; Harrisonburg, VA 22807
Phone: 540-568-6211
E-mail address: gotojmu@jmu.edu
Web site URL: www.jmu.edu
Founded: 1908
Private or Public: public
Religious affiliation: none
Location: small city
Undergraduate enrollment: NA
Total enrollment: NA
Percent Male / Female: NA
Percent Minority: 0%
Percent African-American: NA

Percent Asian: NA
Percent Hispanic: NA
Percent Native-American: NA
Percent in-state / out-of-state: 70% / 30%
Percent Pub HS: 95%
Number of Applicants: 12,980
Percent Accepted: 65%
Percent Accepted who enroll: 36%
Entering: 3,039
Transfers: 587
Application Deadline: 15 Jan
Mean SAT: NA
Mean ACT: NA

Middle 50% SAT range: 540–620 V, 540–640 M
Middle 50% ACT range: NA
3 Most popular majors: psychology, English, community health liaison
Retention: 91%
Graduation rate: 87%
On-campus housing: NA
Fraternities: 14%
Sororities: 18%
Library: NA
Tuition and Fees: $3,926 in; $9,532 out
Room and Board: $5,182
Financial aid, first-year: NA

Students new to James Madison University are usually struck first by the school's great academics and great people. Having grown from an obscure state-funded teachers' college, Madison College has become one of the foremost academic institutions in the South, impressing its students not only with its academics but also with its relaxed and friendly atmosphere.

Abercrombie and Fitch Meets Main Street, USA

One of the "Ten Reasons You Know You're at JMU," according to a T-shirt seen on campus, is "you introduce yourself to someone new every day." Friendly, courteous, and down-to-earth people are many students' number-one reason for choosing JMU. One student enthused, "I get a feeling around campus that everyone wants you to be there. You can always exchange a friendly hello with a passerby and get help when you need it." The campus atmosphere is "friendly and upbeat," conducive to meeting people and making friends. Students described the student body as "preppy" and "homogeneous." The stereotypical JMU Duke is an upper-

middle-class Abercrombie and Fitch–wearing suburban white kid from the East Coast. Minority students tend to self-segregate and sometimes have a hard time, but all are upbeat about the "nice, friendly" student body.

Party Hearty

Most Dukes follow a "work hard, play hard" philosophy, while the social scene, according to most students, revolves around "drink hard." Some students said that non-drinkers can feel out of place; one student commented that most non-drinkers tend to be more involved in extracurricular activities or have part-time jobs. Students described the dating scene as "average" and mentioned that "because of alcohol, there are more random hook-ups than usual." The administration provides a number of popular non-alcoholic social alternatives like Thursday and Saturday two-dollar movie screenings of recent releases and concerts featuring big-name bands. Recent performers include Vertical Horizon and Nine Days. Students can also choose from an incredibly wide range of extracurricular activities and club sports. Although the Greek scene is big, with about 30% of students involved, no students reported feeling pressure to rush.

Frat parties are a popular weekend destination, but the most popular parties—especially for non-Greeks—are those held in off-campus student apartments. One student described them as "very cool"; another said, "Most anybody can get in if you are dressed nice, but it helps if you have girls with you." The university has a "three strikes" alcohol policy, and campus police and residential advisors are described as "average" in their enforcement of rules ("so long as you aren't loud and destructive, you won't get caught"). The city police department, however, is "very ruthless" in its alcohol enforcement and routinely breaks up off-campus parties. One of these breakups, involving a back-to-school block party, degenerated into a riot last year. Most students felt the police department was responsible for the incident, which marked an all-time low in student–police relations. The poor relationship between students and Harrisonburg police doesn't affect campus safety, though; the campus police are "well respected and do their jobs." The university police and student cadets patrol the campus around-the-clock, and blue-light security phones were recently installed. Though there was an incident involving the rape of a student some time ago, students agreed that they "wouldn't think twice" if they had to walk across campus alone at night.

Major Mecca

JMU academics received rave reviews from students, who lauded the huge choice of major programs and academic flexibility the school offers. The School of Media Arts and Design (SMAD) was praised as a "hidden jewel"; popular (and difficult) majors include business, computer science, and the prestigious College of Integrated Science and Technology (CISAT) programs.

Classes range in difficulty from the "credit-getter" introductory ROTC classes (a "guaranteed A" often taken by non-ROTC students) to "weed-out" classes like Computer Science 139 and 239, which Comp Sci majors must pass with a B. Classes are usually small and almost never taught by teaching assistants. The professors are generally accessible and

enthusiastic—especially in upper-level classes—though students report the occasional oddball who "couldn't teach a bull to charge." Most of those in the latter category teach large mandatory (and often unpopular) general education classes. The caliber of the faculty is high; singled out for praise by their students were writing teacher and punk singer Jennifer Holl, known to leap to windowsills during lectures; history professor Raymond Hyser; and World War II fighter ace *cum* English professor Geoffrey Morley-Mower. TAs are few and of widely varying quality: many students praised their TAs as "great and helpful"; a few told horror stories. One student noted that JMU's rigid academic honor code (subject, according to some students, to widespread abuse) prevents TAs from offering much assistance on assignments.

"JMU is an amazing school."

Of the 120 credits JMU students need to graduate, about 40 are general education requirements. Though they do have some latitude in choosing these courses, most students view the requirement as an academic chore. Most majors require about 60 credits for graduation, and many students elect minors as well. Students typically take 15 to 18 credits per semester. Grading was universally described as "fair," and most said the academic programs were challenging and competitive but not impossible for students who keep up with their work.

Food and Shelter

JMU students enjoy a choice of 11 on-campus dining options, ranging from conventional dining halls such as Gibbons Hall ("D-Hall") and Festival to commercial chains like Sbarro and Chick-Fil-A. Students preferring to eat off campus can find a wide variety of restaurants nearby, including chains like Applebee's and Chili's and ethnic restaurants like El Charro and La Italia. Most students praised the quality of the food, and all were positive about the range of options. There is an enormous variety of on-campus housing, and dormitories come in all forms—old and new, air-conditioned and cooled by Mother Nature, towers and conventional dorms, coed and all-women, substance-free, smoke-free, and international. Housing can be a trade-off, though: newer dorms are generally nicer but are located farther away from the main campus. Freshmen, who are required to live on campus, are assigned rooms based on their answers to a five-part questionnaire. Upperclassmen who want to live on campus must enter a housing lottery, but most students move off campus in their sophomore or junior year. Off-campus housing is "reasonably priced" (about $300 per month, according to one student) and readily accessible via a free bus service. RAs got high marks, and most students agreed that they "strike a good balance between enforcing the rules and being your friend."

Freight Trains and Superhighways

The JMU campus is vast, hilly, and beautiful. Interstate 81 and a railroad line run directly through the campus and divide it into "old" and "new" halves. The new half is almost completely new, built to house the College of Integrated Science and Technology. Though "prison-like" in appearance, the buildings are "high-quality and conducive to student life." The old half is home of the university's original gorgeous bluestone buildings and the famous "Kissing Rock," a campus landmark and romantic hangout; it is also the location of the Quad, a collection of old bluestone academic buildings. Crisscrossing under the Quad are a set of tunnels that, according to campus legend, were closed off long ago, after a student died there. Her ghost is said to appear on foggy nights in the bell tower of Wilson Hall, and though the tunnels are still *verboten* to students, the adventurous will occasionally sneak in to have a look around.

Campus facilities are mostly new, popular, and of high quality, especially the five-year-old UREC recreation center, which features weight rooms, racquetball and basketball courts, a pool, a suspended track, and a climbing wall. Also popular is Taylor Down Under, a student center featuring a coffee shop, pool hall, performance space, and various information and student life offices. The only major facility that students singled out for criticism was the Carrier Library, described as "not what you'd expect at a university like ours." The city of Harrisonburg, students agree, "doesn't have anything besides JMU," and many students look forward to getting out of town.

Go, Dukes!

JMU runs a popular and successful athletic program, and students often turn out for football, soccer, basketball, and track-and-field events, especially against perennial rival Virginia Tech. Most teams are NCAA Division I, and the school puts a lot of money and effort into sports. Club sports are also very popular and often successful. But is the Dukes' school spirit any surprise when they attend a rising star that is rapidly becoming one of the top universities in the nation? As one freshman put it simply, "JMU is an amazing school—COME HERE!"—*Jeff Howard*

FYI
The three best things about attending JMU are "the faculty is always willing to help you out, very friendly people, beautiful campus."
The three worst things about attending JMU are "parking is not the best, registering for classes can be difficult, weather varies throughout the day."
The three things every student should do before graduating from JMU are "go skiing and snow tubing at Massanutten, go to a 'dive-in' movie at the pool, and go to Melrose (an off-campus cabin that hosts parties)."
One thing I'd like to have known before coming here is "the people are very friendly, so you need to like friendly people."

Randolph-Macon Woman's College

Address: 2500 Rivermont Avenue; Lynchburg, VA 24503
Phone: 804-947-8100
E-mail address: admissions@rmwc.edu
Web site URL: www.rmwc.edu
Founded: 1891
Private or Public: private
Religious affiliation: United Methodist
Location: small city
Undergraduate enrollment: NA
Total enrollment: NA
Percent Male/Female: NA
Percent Minority: 0%
Percent African-American: NA

Percent Asian: NA
Percent Hispanic: NA
Percent Native-American: NA
Percent in-state/out-of-state: 40%/60%
Percent Pub HS: 74%
Number of Applicants: 719
Percent Accepted: 84%
Percent Accepted who enroll: 33%
Entering: 201
Transfers: NA
Application Deadline: rolling
Mean SAT: 607 V, 568 M
Mean ACT: 25

Middle 50% SAT range: 543–670 V, 500–610 M
Middle 50% ACT range: 24–29
3 Most popular majors: psychology, politics, biology
Retention: 78%
Graduation rate: 63%
On-campus housing: 100%
Fraternities: NA
Sororities: NA
Library: NA
Tuition and Fees: $17,080 in; $17,080 out
Room and Board: $7,010
Financial aid, first-year: 61%

L ynchburg, Virginia, is the home of Randolph Macon Woman's College, a small, private, single-sex institution. The campus, which has seen few changes since its construction, consists of majestic redbrick buildings surrounded by a redbrick wall. Inside this wall, lives a close-knit community of women who are as serious about their commitment to their school as they are about their studies.

Noses to the Grindstone

Academics at Randolph Macon are anything but easy. Students are required to take one course each in compositional English, literature, history, European culture, women's studies, Asian or African civilization, a physical science (including a lab), math, physical education, fine arts, and a foreign language. Students say the requirements are a strong selling point of the college, as they expose students to "courses that you wouldn't think of taking." Registration is done alphabetically by last name on a rotating basis per semester. Students claim that it is very rare to get shut out of a class, even for first-years.

They also stress the benefits of their

small school on student-faculty relations. Students consider the fact that there are no teaching assistants anywhere in the school to be a bonus as professors do all the grading and teaching themselves. Professors are described as "fantastic," and often become friends and mentors as well as instructors to their students. Although all departments are considered to be "academically strong," biology, math, and psychology are thought to be the most popular, primarily because these subjects encompass a wide variety of courses students find useful. Be warned, however— classes are not simple. Many science courses could be described as "death wish" classes by those who do not have a lot of time to spend on their work.

> "Randolph Macon Woman's College is not for everyone: it is single-sex, small, and highly challenging."

Thanks to such a demanding course load, students find themselves hitting the books more often than not. Lipscomb

Library, a six-story building set in the middle of one of Macon's hills, is described as "adequate" for both studying and research. Although Lipscomb is not very large, the school offers its students a free interlibrary loan system, allowing them to obtain books from nearby schools. For those with some serious work to do, the Ethyl Center, with on-site tutors, computers, comfortable chairs, and solo study rooms, provides an ideal spot. For group work, the student center is a popular choice due to its central location.

Beautiful Rooms

Of course, students can also study in their spacious dorm rooms. While off-campus living is prohibited to those under 25, unmarried, or not living at home in Lynchburg, there are no complaints about the rooming alternatives. Room options comprise everything from singles to suites, and the rooms generally are large, carpeted, with ample windows and closet space. One student remarked, "Believe it or not, it's humungous, and bigger than my room at home!" Male visitors are allowed in the dorms until midnight Mondays through Thursdays, and allowed to stay overnight on weekends. The dorms also have TV lounges and old-fashioned "date parlors" that are used mostly for studying. The worst thing anyone reported about dorms were that they did not have elevators.

They Have Fun, Too . . .

When they are not busy studying or going to meetings for their extracurricular activities, Randolph Macon women go to coffeehouses and cafes in town, rent movies, or go to school-sponsored activities such as lectures. On the weekends, students make time for low-key partying, go to local bars, or visit nearby campuses such as Hampden-Sydney. There is no need for a car at Randolph Macon, and although the town is described as "boring" by some, there are plenty of on-campus activities to choose from. Favorite events include Tacky Party, where everyone "dresses up real tacky and plays seventies music," in November, and the Senior Dinner, a formal weekend that includes a cocktail and casino night.

Students are very active in extracurricular activities, which range from sports to writing for the school newspaper the *Sundial*, or the literary magazine *Hail! Muse*, to community service projects such as BIONIC, which stands for Believe It or Not I Care. MAC, Macon Activities Counsel, arranges the school's social activities. A recently added rugby team has proved popular among students. The Black Women's Alliance both provides support for African-American students as well as sponsors dances and other social events. The organization, Bridges, provides support for gay students on campus. Randolph Macon women are also fairly politically active, and the campus chapters of the Young Democrats and Republicans enjoy a large degree of student participation. The new weight-training center, an Olympic-size pool, refurbished playing fields, and tennis and basketball courts provide ample space for the Randolph Macon Wildcats to play, and those not involved in organized sports to keep in shape.

Spoiled Rotten

As the meal plan is included in the tuition, there are no real options, but students have few complaints about the food. "The food is really good," said one student. "We get spoiled rotten." The one main dining hall has both a hot food line and "stations" where the staff cooks food to students' specifications. Vegetarians can order meals without meat. The Skellar, a student-run snack bar, provides an on-campus alternative to the dining hall. On the weekends, many students go out to eat at a variety of restaurants ranging from fast-food to Meriwhethers-Godsy, a restaurant for special occasions, run by a Macon alum.

Evens v. Odds and Other Traditions

Tradition holds a very important place at Randolph Macon. The campus is filled with gardens and gazebos, and on beautiful days, students enjoy hanging out on front campus or in the Dell, an open-air amphitheater. There are no sororities, but some students join secret societies. There is a traditional class rivalry between "evens and odds," those whose classes end in even or odd years, which involves practical jokes and spray-painting slogans around campus. Randolph Macon women are intensely proud of their school, and report feeling "overwhelmed by school spirit." One student reported that those who do not like it transfer out, leaving a cohesive group. Another student bragged about her dorm: "It's a great community—we all get along really well. It's like having 65 sisters!" The school's small size also fosters interaction between the faculty and students. As classes are rarely bigger than 20 or 30 students, and can be as small as one, professors get to know their pupils well, even too well, for the less studious: "Many professors eat at the dining hall, so you don't want to skip class and see them there," reported one undergrad.

For some, however, the small size and relative isolation of the campus can be a drawback. There is not much to do in Lynchburg in terms of entertainment, especially for those used to big cities. While the school attracts students from all over the globe, Randolph Macon is still not as diverse as some might like it. One student complained the student body as a whole was "lacking certain aspects of American background. We are mostly white Christians from well-to-do families—Land's End, Eddie Bauer, and J. Crew kids."

A Warm Community

Randolph Macon Woman's College is not for everyone: it is single-sex, small, and highly challenging. Yet, for those who choose to attend, there is a lot to be gained from its selective atmosphere. Students have the opportunity to study abroad, as many do, during their junior year. The college also provides its students with a variety of popular internship programs. Undergrads even have the option to design their own major, for a more personalized program of study. They also cannot say enough about the pride and love they have for their school. Traditionally, RMWC has been like a second home for many students, and as with all Macon traditions, they want to keep it that way.—*Ann Zeidner and Staff*

FYI

The three best things about attending RMWC are "the personal attention, the camaraderie, and the even v. odd pranks."

The three worst things about attending RMWC are "the academic rigor, the absence of a male presence in the classroom, and the lack of diversity."

The three things that every student should do before graduating from RMWC are "go to Tacky Party, order from the J.Crew catalog, and make friends with a professor."

One thing I'd like to have known before coming here is "how much I like having men around."

Sweet Briar College

Address: PO Box B; Sweet Briar, VA 24595
Phone: 804-381-6142
E-mail address: admissions@sbc.edu
Web site URL: www.sbc.edu
Founded: 1901
Private or Public: private
Religious affiliation: none
Location: rural
Undergraduate enrollment: NA
Total enrollment: 582
Percent Male/Female: NA
Percent Minority: 0%
Percent African-American: NA
Percent Asian: NA

Percent Hispanic: NA
Percent Native-American: NA
Percent in-state/out-of-state: 37%/63%
Percent Pub HS: 67%
Number of Applicants: 499
Percent Accepted: 89%
Percent Accepted who enroll: 42%
Entering: 186
Transfers: 18
Application Deadline: 15 Feb
Mean SAT: 580 V, 530 M
Mean ACT: 24

Middle 50% SAT range: 520–620 V, 470–580 M
Middle 50% ACT range: NA
3 Most popular majors: psychology, government, English
Retention: 80%
Graduation rate: 67%
On-campus housing: 100%
Fraternities: NA
Sororities: NA
Library: 474,818 volumes
Tuition and Fees: $17,324 in; $17,324 out
Room and Board: $7,016
Financial aid, first-year: 93%

Sitting tranquil at the foothills of the South Ridge Mountains in Virginia, Sweet Briar College feels quaint with its old-Georgian style buildings and small town, rural setting. Rich with traditions established since its inception in 1901, Sweet Briar is also a place where "things are happening," as one student said, bringing to light the dynamic student body, the involved faculty, and the energetic environment. "You can do what you want here." Most Sweet Briar students agree that the intimate environment, the professors, and the highly motivated women make the school a tremendous learning experience and four remarkable years.

Strong Academics
As a liberal arts school, SWC emphasizes learning in a variety of disciplines with basic distribution requirements in addition to those requirements of your major. There is a core of courses in a variety of departments one must take to graduate. A student must take one course in art and literature, non-Western study, social science, history, English, physical education, an oral- and writing-intensive course, as well as quantitative reasoning. Other requirements include foreign language and community service. "I didn't find the required classes to be a problem at all," said one student. "There are not too many requirements and they are pretty flexible." For a small college, (the entering freshman class is around 160 students) Sweet Briar offers a variety of very strong departments. A student can choose from thirty-four majors or you can construct your own major, which "is really easy to do." Being the most popular major, Biology has a tremendous faculty and boasts a new wing of Guion, the science building, which houses equipment capable of chromatographic and electrophoretic analyses among other things. Another popular major is government. "After taking the prerequisites I am now doing independent work on governmental urban development with a professor," said one government major. Psychology and teaching certification are also well-liked.

Another aspect of Sweet Briar academics is the honors program. It offers a variety of honors seminars of all disciplines, which are team-taught by the top scholars in the field. In the spring of your junior year you have the opportunity to work closely with a faculty member and write an honors thesis over the course of three semesters, on a topic of your choice. Sweet Briar also offers cross-enrollment programs with the Seven-College Exchange program, a Dual-Degree Engineering Program with Columbia and Washington University in St. Louis, and strong junior-year-abroad programs.

Amazing Professors
"Professors really care about teaching you something. And after the semester is over they still remember you and are genuinely interested in what you are doing. I'm still friends with many of my professors from freshman year," said one senior. Living near or on campus, the faculty at Sweet Briar makes the academic environment what it is, since there are no teaching assistants. With introductory classes averaging around 25, close interaction with professors begins freshman year. "They learn your name and are always accessible. They really care about what they are teaching," said one English major. The administration is also well-liked by students and is very involved in enhancing the Sweet Briar experience. "Our president even teaches a class." By interacting with professors in class, through research in the lab, or in a game of basketball, "you really learn to look to them as mentors and friends, not just people you see a few days a week for an hour. That really distinguishes Sweet Briar from other schools."

Room and Board
Virtually everyone lives on campus. There is a wide variety of housing available. Most freshwomen live in dorms with some quads or triples, which have bedrooms and a common room attached. Residential advisors, or upperclasswomen, live among freshwomen, as do professional resident coordinators. Besides having assistance with living conditions, freshwomen also have key leaders, upperclasswomen with expertise in a certain academic department or health issues, which can help with any academic or social problems students may have. "We are basically there if freshmen have problems adjusting to college life, have questions about academic stuff

at Sweet Briar, or just want to hang out with some upperclasswomen," said one RA. Upperclasswomen can choose to live in corridor-style housing or there are also houses near or on campus that are very popular for seniors. The dorm rooms and houses are the most common hangout place for students. There are parlors and recreation rooms, complete with pool tables, Ping-Pong, TVs, and stereo systems. A new student center is also in the middle of being designed. The state-of-the art facility will include student study, meeting, and lounge areas; large multipurpose rooms for student events; student services offices; college postal, mailing, and shipping facilities; a full-service copy center; Book Shop; a grill restaurant; and outdoor recreational areas.

> "With a low minority presence and limited socioeconomic backgrounds, the term "Suzy Sweet Briar," the nickname given to the typical student, "who drives a nice car, dresses nicely, and wears pearls," holds some truth still.

"Food here is great!" says one freshwoman. Prothro Commons, the cafeteria, offers a great variety of food that "tends to be non-greasy." SWC students have no complaints. "And when you don't like the hot meal, that's ok because there is a full salad and sandwich bar and side dishes to choose from."

Who Goes to Sweet Briar?

"We are really motivated here," said one student. "I think most of us are pretty serious about academics." At the same time, students are "genuinely friendly and good-natured." With a low minority presence and limited socioeconomic backgrounds, the term "Suzy Sweet Briar," the nickname given to the typical student, "who drives a nice car, dresses nicely, and wears pearls," holds some truth still. However, the administration is working to change that. The diversity of the activities makes up for the homogeneity of the student population. Activites range from SWEBOP (Sweet Briar Outdoor Program to the "Learning

on the Land" archeological-wildlife orientation program for freshwomen. Sweet Briar also has a unique collection of groups called tap-clubs, which vary in selectivity, themes, and seriousness. Some include "Aints-N-Asses (a loud, comic group), Taps-N-Toes (for dancers and those that help with dance concerts), Ear Phones (for loud people who can't sing), Sweet Tones (our a cappella group), Chung Mungs and Tau Phi (two community service based groups)."

There are a lot of things to do on Sweet Briar's "beautiful" campus. With "bike trails out the wazoo" and horseback riding at the on-campus Equestrian Center, "one of the best in the country," in addition to the varsity sports SBC offers, like field hockey, lacrosse, riding, soccer, swimming, tennis, and volleyball. Students often hangout at the Bistro, a restaurant in town that often hosts bands and DJs. Another popular joint is the Briar Patch, another restaurant near campus. A coffeehouse in the Meta Glass ("Glass") Dorm is a great place for students to get a little caffeine and socialize with friends. Parties on campus tend to be small, and underage drinking is prevented, so "when you turn twenty-one it's a big deal." The Administration has been trying to work with the Campus Events Organization to increase the number of events on campus. Certain events like the four dell parties, outdoor band events, and two formals through the year draw a big crowd of men and women. SWC has been able to attract many groups to campus like Richmond Ballet, Urban Bush Women, and others for SB's Babcock season. In addition, there are a variety of traditional social events throughout the year. One is the Junior Banquet, "one of the biggest nights of the year," where Juniors receive their class rings. There is also a step-singing tradition in the fall and spring. "Founders' Day and Lantern Bearing are our most beautiful traditions. For Founders' Day the seniors wear their robes and ask a sophomore to walk with them to the monument. A bagpiper leads the community on the walk to the monument where we place daisies on our founders' graves. Lantern Bearing is at the end of the year. Again, the seniors wear their robes. We ask an underclassman to bear our lantern—a basket of flowers they get for us—as we walk around the quad at night. Then lantern bearers sing sad songs to us. This tradition definitely produces the most tears," a senior said.

But often Sweet Briar students must go off campus to find a social life, since the campus is "kind of dead" socially. A car is "definitely a must," as many students go to nearby colleges and universities. Some students go to Lynchburg, a twenty-minute drive away, "which has a little to be desired," or another option is the all-male Hampden-Sydney College. Nearby Washington and Lee and Virginia Military Institute are other popular destinations. "Guys are a big deal on the weekends," admits one student, "since we don't see many of them during the week."

Sweet Briar College offers tremendous academic experience in a tight-knit community of inspiring women. "This place does something to you," one student said. "When we leave here, we love Sweet Briar."

FYI

The three best things about Sweet Briar College are "the food, the professors, and the academics."

The three worst things about Sweet Briar are "being far from a city, lack of diversity, no social life on campus."

The three things that every student should do before leaving campus are "get to know a professor, find a boyfriend nearby so you don't have to scramble for stuff to do on the weekends, and bear a lantern."

One thing I'd like to have known before coming here is "how homogenous this place is."

University of Richmond

Address: 28 Westhampton Way; University of Richmond, VA 23173	**Percent Asian:** NA	**Middle 50% SAT range:** 600–680 V, 620–690 M
Phone: 804-289-8640	**Percent Hispanic:** NA	
	Percent Native-American: NA	**Middle 50% ACT range:** 27–30
E-mail address: admissions @richmond.edu	**Percent in-state / out-of-state:** 17%/83%	**3 Most popular majors:** business, biology, political science
Web site URL: www.richmond.edu	**Percent Pub HS:** 70%	
Founded: 1830	**Number of Applicants:** 6,234	**Retention:** 92%
Private or Public: private	**Percent Accepted:** 45%	**Graduation rate:** 83%
Religious affiliation: none		**On-campus housing:** 99%
Location: suburban	**Percent Accepted who enroll:** 32%	**Fraternities:** 39%
Undergraduate enrollment: NA	**Entering:** 886	**Sororities:** 50%
Total enrollment: 3,777	**Transfers:** 30	**Library:** 1,068,000 volumes
Percent Male / Female: NA	**Application Deadline:** 15 Jan	**Tuition and Fees:** $20,430 in; $20,430 out
Percent Minority: 0%	**Mean SAT:** NA	**Room and Board:** $4,240
Percent African-American: NA	**Mean ACT:** NA	**Financial aid, first-year:** 34%

"Country club" is how one student described the University of Richmond. According to a freshman, Richmond is "a very trendy school where most people are generically prep." In the Richmond fashion world, J. Crew, Gap, and Abercrombie & Fitch all reign supreme. Nevertheless, the well-dressed Spiders of the University of Richmond follow rigorous academic schedules and profit from a rich social life.

Strong Academics

Academically, students are encouraged to receive a broad-based education through required classes in various disciplines.

Students must take classes in science, English, symbolic reasoning (which can be satisfied by calculus), fine arts, and must demonstrate proficiency in a foreign language. In addition, CORE, a class that entails a lot of different readings from all over the world, is required, as is Wellness, a course in health. These classes can usually be completed by second semester of sophomore year, after which students devote their schedules to their majors. One sophomore said that some of the courses "are ridiculous because I already did the work in AP classes." The general opinion, though, as another student described, is that "they're pretty beneficial. By forcing you to take a broad spectrum, you find out what you're interested in." While most students choose traditional concentrations in the arts and sciences, Richmond also boasts a strong business school, as well as the only program in the nation offering a degree in leadership studies. Although there are differing opinions regarding easy majors, all students said that science classes are the toughest. The typical response to biology majors is, as one student said, "I'm so sorry."

Whether the classes are easy or tough, though, class size is extremely small. Most classes enroll 20 to 25 people, giving students close contact with their professors. One junior said, "I think the professors are very open and ready to give you all the help you need. It differs from just being a number." Another junior said, "The professors really care about their students." Undergrads rarely have contact with TAs except in lab settings or for drill sessions in the introductory languages. Students have few negative comments about their classes, although one student did not like the attendance policies. "You can only miss three, otherwise they start taking a letter grade off." Another student simply said the worst thing about Richmond academics was "the 8:15 classes." As for the workload, one student said, "It's hard!" Academics at Richmond are strong and as one junior put it, "You get out of it what you put into it."

Social Options

When the Spiders aren't working on the weekend, they can be found engaging in the lively social atmosphere of the school. Washington, D.C., and the beach are both a little more than an hour away from campus, although most students choose to stay nearby for entertainment purposes. For those determined to leave campus, Richmond "has a lot for the arts, restaurants all around, bars, and the James River," said one student. Social life on campus, however, is by far the most popular option. Greek life is very strong at Richmond; students estimate that at least half of the student body rushes. However, non-Greeks are always welcome at parties on the weekend, so it is definitely not a necessity to join. Other than Greek parties, Richmond students have the option to go to movies shown every Thursday through Sunday, to hear guest lecturers, or to concerts, all organized by the Campus Activities Board (CAB). Alcohol has a definite presence and while the administration "doesn't want anything to get out of hand, if no one is getting hurt, then they look the other way," reported one undergrad.

Country Club Kids, Country Club Campus

With regards to the student body, the general consensus is that the typical student "is really rich, has more money than common sense; the kid that Mommy and Daddy gave a credit card to before coming to Richmond." As mentioned previously, style plays an important role at Richmond, where "girls always wear black pants and no one wears sweats." Richmond students universally complain about the lack of diversity. A freshman said that Richmond "breeds naiveté. Some students that come here have never seen a person of color and they think 10 percent minority is big. I would like to see more awareness of other races." With regards to diversity, one junior did say that "it's one of the things the university is trying to change."

The University of Richmond's campus is unanimously described as "gorgeous." As one junior described it, "there are flowers everywhere, it's very well kept by the physical plant workers, and the architecture is amazing." Another student went so far as to describe the campus as the main reason why students come to Richmond. In the middle of campus is a large lake that separates the two halves of the campus.

Over the lake sits Commons, a student union building that ranges in function from housing campus organizations to hosting karaoke nights in its restaurant. A gazebo also sits on the lake; legend has it that whomever you kiss in the gazebo will be your future spouse. The only way to avoid this fate is "to be thrown over the bridge into the water," said one junior. Aside from being happy with the physical appearance of the campus, Richmond students are also pleased with the security system. One junior said that "you always see plenty of policemen and there is a shuttle for students after 7 o'clock until 2 or 3 in the morning." In addition, dorms have card-only access, meaning only people affiliated with the university can come and go freely. According to one student, "The school is set off in suburban Richmond and is very secure. Everyone feels safe walking around."

The Coordinate System

The physical formation of the campus lends itself well to the living situation at Richmond, which is rather unique, with each half of the campus playing host to one of two residential colleges. The Coordinate system, as it is called, separates the campus so that men belong to Richmond College, while women make up Westhampton College. This separation provides for two separate student governments and judicial boards, allowing students of both genders to participate actively in the life of the university. Generally, students like the system and find that it is perhaps the most defining characteristic of their school. A freshman in Richmond College said, "I am a fan of it. An all-guy dorm means I can walk around in my boxers if I want. Plus, I would be too easily distracted if girls were in my dorm or on this side of campus." Another junior said, "I'm not an advocate for or against it, but it creates an atmosphere where a lot more studying gets done." For students who do not enjoy the system as much, there is little chance that there will be any changes. According to one sophomore, "Alums give us a lot money to keep the system in place, so we're stuck with it no matter what."

Almost all students decide to live on campus as part of the coordinate system. Very few students live off campus, even though it is slightly cheaper to do so. Freshmen can expect their rooms to be "the size of what's in it. You could get anything from a palace to something just adequate." For the most part, all dorms have air-conditioning, although one sophomore said that "AC is kind of a trade-off, because the bigger rooms don't have it, while the smaller ones do." After freshman year, rooms are chosen through lottery, with priority given to upperclassmen. Upperclassmen have the option of hall bathrooms or suite-style living quarters. In addition, there are two international houses, as well as substance-free dorms for both men and women. Furthermore, the university just instituted this year a smoke-free housing option. Students say that the best dorms for men are Thomas and Freeman, while for the women they are North Court and Lora Robins. At the other end of the spectrum are Marsh for men, which "smells bad and doesn't have air-conditioning," and South Court for women. Each dorm also has an RA on each floor. Though most students find them friendly and helpful, one sophomore said "they are really too strict for their own good with the girls." Despite these minor grievances, one junior said housing "is just really nice."

> "An all-guy dorm means I can walk around in my boxers if I want. Plus, I would be too easily distracted if girls were in my dorm or on this side of campus."

Students are generally pleased with the dining hall fare. One sophomore said "we're supposed to have one of the best dining halls in the country." While the food "gets repetitive, it's a lot better than some places I've been to," said another student. On campus, Richmond students can either go to the main dining hall or an alternative fast-food facility. One part of the dining hall named Harvest Place serves only vegetarian food, but students find the vegetarian options only "decent." Even though the food may be great, students are unhappy that all eating establishments on campus are closed by 8 P.M.

Students can, however, use their meal card to order pizza, and the school is negotiating a deal with a local grocery store. Freshmen and sophomores must stick to the 19-meals-per-week plan, with no other options. One sophomore said, "I eat a lot in my room or off campus, so I really don't need that many meals." Students enjoy going to off-campus restaurants, the most frequented being Pasta Luna, the Strawberry Street Cafe, and Ukrops. Those more interested in a casual coffeehouse setting can go to the World Cup Cafe or the Fourth Street Cafe.

Service-Minded Students

As an outgrowth of Greek life, community service is extremely popular at Richmond. Community service is often a requirement for fraternities and sororities, although the Volunteer Action Council and Habitat for Humanity also provide such outlets for non-Greeks. Students who don't get involved with these groups might partake in a singing group, debate, or an academically related club, including computer science and physics. A number of students work on-campus jobs, which are "relatively easy to find and mostly minimum wage." Other students look for off-campus employment, although for them, a car is a necessity.

Basketball is Richmond's most followed sport. The team has consistently ranked high in its conference, which leads to a fair degree of team spirit, although one student said team spirit is "pretty low overall." Football games are also popular in the fall, but one junior said it was really "the tailgates that are a big deal." Another junior commented that "most people end up going to get drunk rather than to actually watch the game." Students interested in athletics, but not at the varsity level can participate an intramurals or club sports, popular ones including crew, soccer, ultimate Frisbee, and equestrian. Students can also take advantage of Robins Center, the university gym, which is reportedly "really nice."

Regardless of its faults, Richmond Spiders are extremely proud and happy with their school. The small size allows for close interaction both in academics and social life. One sophomore pointed out that "it's a very close environment. I didn't expect to get to know so many people so closely." With the quaint charm of a small campus, but also the lures of nearby big cities, Richmond students prosper from a milieu that supplies all. A junior, very enthusiastic about her Richmond experience said, "I don't think I could be happier anywhere else."—*Shu-Ping Shen and Staff*

FYI

The three best things about attending University of Richmond are "the location, the beautiful campus, and the friendly people."

The three worst things about attending University of Richmond are "the lack of communication between students and administration, the coordinate system, and the lack of diversity."

The three things that every student should do before graduating from University of Richmond are "go to the Pig Roast, the Ring Dance, and the Potter's Pub (but not before you're 21)."

One thing I'd like to have known before coming here is "there is no health/sport medicine department."

University of Virginia

Address: PO Box 400160; Charlottesville, VA 22904-4160
Phone: 804-982-3200
E-mail address: undergrad-admission@virginia.edu
Web site URL: www.virginia.edu
Founded: 1819
Private or Public: public
Religious affiliation: none
Location: small city
Undergraduate enrollment: NA
Total enrollment: 22,433
Percent Male/Female: NA
Percent Minority: 0%
Percent African-American: NA

Percent Asian: NA
Percent Hispanic: NA
Percent Native-American: NA
Percent in-state/out-of-state: 68%/32%
Percent Pub HS: 76%
Number of Applicants: 16,461
Percent Accepted: 34%
Percent Accepted who enroll: 52%
Entering: 2,924
Transfers: 540
Application Deadline: 2 Jan
Mean SAT: 648 V, 659 M
Mean ACT: 28

Middle 50% SAT range: 600–700 V, 610–710 M
Middle 50% ACT range: 26–31
3 Most popular majors: commerce, psychology, economics
Retention: 96%
Graduation rate: 91%
On-campus housing: 100%
Fraternities: 30%
Sororities: 30%
Library: 4,588,606 volumes
Tuition and Fees: $4,130 in; $16,603 out
Room and Board: $4,589
Financial aid, first-year: NA

Tradition and pride abound at the University of Virginia (UVA). Thomas Jefferson founded the school; Edgar Allan Poe went here, as did Woodrow Wilson. There are no "freshmen" and "sophomores" at UVA; instead, there are first-years and second-years and so on. Why, one may wonder? Because Mr. Jefferson believed that learning never ends; thus a "freshman" is just in the first year of a lifelong education.

The "A," The "E," The "Comm"
Undergraduates at UVA are enrolled in one of six schools: the Engineering School, the Architecture School, the College of Arts and Sciences, the McIntire School of Commerce, the Nursing School, and the Curry School of Education. Academic requirements differ based on the school and the major. The core curriculum in the liberal arts college is "basic: 12 credits of math and science, 8 of humanities, 3 of history, 6 of social science, and 3 in non-Western perspectives." In addition, there is a foreign language requirement and a writing proficiency requirement. These requirements do not seem to bother too many students "since they are really flexible, and you can space out anything that you detest so that you aren't stuck with a ton of courses that you hate in any given semester." Another student added, "Requirements give one a chance to look into unexpected and interesting academic fields." Many students think that majors in the Engineering School ("E-School") and the commerce school ("Comm-School") are the hardest as well as the most competitive. In the E-School, "you don't have much choice on what classes you can take; the workload is unbearable." A lot of the teaching assistants in the E-School reportedly "barely speak English. But usually, there is a teacher somewhere nearby (or head TA) who speaks English fluently, so there isn't any major problem with that." A second-year in the college said, "My favorite part is the review sessions which some TAs give that cover the outside reading material."

Class size "depends greatly on which classes you take." Lectures can go up to 500, whereas 2 people can form a small class. "Any class I felt that I wanted to be small because of its content has been small, and big lectures for the intro stuff are nice because you can find big study groups." Some classes, such as Public Speaking, are hard to get into, but "a lot of times you can course-action into them." UVA has its share of guts such as Physics

105 ("How Things Work"), Mental Health, lower-level astronomy classes, and any physical education class.

Most students are happy with their professors. Said one student, "They are interesting and they seem generally excited to be teaching, instead of being jaded." A third-year added, "The professors here want you to learn, so they try and be available as much as possible." Professor Elzinga in the economics department and Professor Sabato in government and foreign affairs are among UVA's most famous professors. Grading is "usually tough but fair." "In some departments there is grade inflation, but generally it is not excessive and I still have to work hard to get good marks," said one student. About her overall academic experience at UVA, a third-year said, "I love it here. . . . [it's] challenging but you always learn something."

Sex, Drugs, and the Honor Code

UVA students are known as "Wahoos" and Charlottesville is nicknamed "'Hooville" after a fish named "Wahoo," which doesn't know when to stop drinking and explodes as a result. It would be right to say that UVA students truly live up to their nicknames: "Alcohol is everywhere on campus!" However, most students say that "non-drinkers do not feel left out of it. They go to parties, too; they just don't drink." The administration has very strict alcohol policies. Kegs are not allowed "on the grounds itself." Not too many people do hard drugs at UVA, but there is a "good deal of weed use." A second-year added, "Quite a lot smoke pot, but mostly casually and not too openly, and never confrontationally."

> "The odd thing here is running . . . people are always running . . . it's excessive; it is just really big . . . everyone runs."

Fraternities that are lined up on Rugby Road take the center stage in the party scene. "Sometimes it's hard to get in, but not if you bring girls with you," said one male student. Being underage is a problem at bars but not at fraternities. The fraternity parties are "okay, but get a little monotonous." There is usually no charge. Mid-Winters and the Foxfield Races are the biggest parties. In addition to fraternity bashes, upperclassmen go to bars, house parties, other colleges, and Washington, D.C.

While "some people have a lot of random hookups," most upperclassmen reportedly have significant others, "some of them very long-term." Dating is also said to be "very common." Most students agree that "there are enough attractive people." There is also a "good deal of sex, but most people tend to be discreet."

There are lots of occasions to get dressed up. Besides the formal events of fraternities and sororities, one tradition here is to get dressed up for the football games. According to one student, there are "tons of things to do on the weekends besides going to football games—you can go to the Downtown Mall or the Corner; both have good food and stores." Also, there are "always local bands playing all over the place." The UVA theater shows two-dollar movies every weekend: one old movie and one new one. Said one student, "We have great speakers that come, so that is something to look forward to." The Virginia Film Festival held once a year brings big Hollywood names like Anthony Hopkins and Sigourney Weaver. The Dalai Lama and Ralph Nader were among the speakers on campus in the last three years. Campus-wide organized activities are "wonderful, frequent, and fun." "Good movies and amazing lectures" are easy to come across. One student summarized the experience: "I am very happy with the social scene at UVA—the frat people keep to themselves, and so those who are not interested in that still have plenty to do."

"Honor" at UVA is far more than a word. The Honor System provides students with substantial benefits enjoyed every day, like taking unproctored exams in your own room or in a pavilion garden. A third-year noted that "the Honor System helps develop and improve this community."

Who Are the Wahoos?

The stereotypical UVa student is "white, preppy, and well groomed; wears khakis and polo shirts or skirts with nice tank tops; probably upper/middle-class." Opinions on the student body differ from "very diverse" to "too homogeneous (predominantly white)." Several students mentioned "the need to have more minority students," as the "admissions for minorities has decreased due to lack of applicants." An aspect of the student body that most agree on is that "there is a lot of self-segregation," which is "a big issue here." Another student added, "I don't know who the typical UVA student is, but sometimes walking to class you can sort of pick out the guy who applied early admission because his father went here and his grandfather went here and so on."

Most people exercise and are "in good shape." "The odd thing here is running . . . people are always running, but it's excessive; if you walk around at any point in the day, you will see people running alone or in big groups, but it is just really big . . . everyone runs," said one student.

Living and Dining

First-years live on campus, in either the New Dorms or the Old Dorms. Rooms in the Old Dorms are "small," but these dorms are "more social." Those living in the New Dorms "get really big rooms with a suite area for every five rooms, and some rooms have air-conditioning." There is a residential advisor for every 20 first-years. "Some are strict; some couldn't care less. Most are strict when they need to be," said one student. After the first year, "there are tons of people who move to live 'off Grounds,' many who relocate to fraternity and sorority houses as well as the two residential colleges on Grounds." The residential colleges, Brown and Hereford, "have personality, but other than that, the housing areas are pretty standard." There are also special houses such as the French, Spanish, and Russian Houses, where students with common interests live together. On-campus floors and bathrooms are not coed. Living off campus is "very popular," though rents and proximity to campus can vary greatly.

The dining hall food reportedly "is not terrible, but not good, either, and the wait is often bad." The dining halls are "fairly clean," but some students complain about dinner ending too early. Students also have "plus points" that come with the meal plans that they can use at different stores, bakeries, or the Pav, the Castle, and the Treehouse—food courts that house chain restaurants like Pizza Hut and Chick-Fil-A. Also, students "love delivery here, and the Castle delivers." There is also a large food selection for vegetarians, and "the restaurants in Charlottesville are great, basically one from each cost category that is about five minutes away."

The Good Ole' Song

At UVA, "almost everyone belongs to some society or another, and many belong to more than one." As one third-year said, people are "very devoted" to extracurricular activities. Some of the most well respected organizations are the Madison House (community service), the Jefferson Society (debate), the *Cavalier Daily*, and the University Guides. Community service is very popular among students. A good number of students also have paying jobs, and UVA offers a lot of employment opportunities for students.

The most popular sport by far is football, but soccer and basketball are also big. Everyone, students and alumni, goes to the football games. "If you walk around campus on game days, all you see is beer everywhere and everyone dressed up," said one student. There are many traditions surrounding the football games. A student described one: "Everyone puts their arms around each other and sways while singing 'The Good Ole' Song' after the team scores." There is also the "Fourth-year fifth," which is the challenge of fourth-year students drinking a fifth of bourbon at the last football game of the season. The Cavalier fans possess and express a great amount of team spirit. Besides varsity sports, the Aquatic and Fitness Center has great facilities for swimming, weight lifting, and the like. Many people do intramurals, and there are always pickup games to be found.

History and Modernity Come Together

The campus is "beautiful . . . hilly, open, historical architecture yet with a modern vibe." "Wonderful buildings" and "lots of trees" contribute to the attractiveness of campus. The university is centered on the Lawn, which is adjacent to the Rotunda and hosts a statue of Homer and Frisbee games on sunny afternoons. It is also a popular hangout on lazy Sundays.

Scott Stadium has recently been renovated, "making it one of the nicest stadiums in the nation," holding about 60,000 people. There are also plans to expand the basketball court, the University Hall. One student added, "They are generally just revamping the older buildings and adding to the science library."

UVA is a "really friendly place." The people are "generally enthusiastic and happy, and they don't stress out like at other schools." The "great thing about UVA is for a public university, you get an Ivy League education for about half-price, and the campus is great . . . plus, it's also a huge party school if you dig that sort of thing . . . there is something for everyone." —*Engin Yenidunya*

FYI

The three best things about attending UVA are "Charlottesville, the Honor Code, and the burgers at Riverside."

The three worst things about attending UVA are "Charlottesville, people's obsession with running, and it's hard to get into classes."

The three things that every student should do before graduating from UVA are "go to Foxfield horse races, streak the Lawn, go to the Rocket Party at Serp."

One thing I would like to have known before coming here is "the dominance of fraternities and sororities in social life."

Virginia Polytechnic Institute and State University

Address: 201 Burruss Hall; Blacksburg, VA 24061
Phone: 540-231-6267
E-mail address: vtadmiss@vt.edu
Web site URL: www.vt.edu
Founded: 1872
Private or Public: public
Religious affiliation: none
Location: rural
Undergraduate enrollment: NA
Total enrollment: 25,783
Percent Male/Female: NA
Percent Minority: 0%
Percent African-American: NA
Percent Asian: NA
Percent Hispanic: NA

Percent Native-American: NA
Percent in-state/out-of-state: 76%/24%
Percent Pub HS: NA
Number of Applicants: 16,109
Percent Accepted: 74%
Percent Accepted who enroll: 39%
Entering: 4,655
Transfers: 854
Application Deadline: 1 Feb
Mean SAT: 573 V, 594 M
Mean ACT: NA
Middle 50% SAT range: 520–620 V, 540–640 M

Middle 50% ACT range: NA
3 Most popular majors: biology, communication studies, management science
Retention: NA
Graduation rate: NA
On-campus housing: NA
Fraternities: 20%
Sororities: 10%
Library: 2,000,000 volumes
Tuition and Fees: $3,620 in; $11,844 out
Room and Board: $3,865
Financial aid, first-year: 65%

When the name of the school says Virginia Polytechnic, they aren't kidding about the "poly." It is not often that you find a school at which students agree that the best programs are as dissimilar as architecture and engineering. The eight colleges that make up Virginia Tech attract a wide variety of preprofessional students with diverse interests.

Eight Plus One

By the time they graduate, Hokies (as students at Virginia Tech call themselves, in reference to their giant, purple turkey mascot) must enroll in one of the eight colleges: Agriculture and Life Sciences; Architecture and Urban Studies; Arts and Sciences; Business; Engineering; Forestry and Wildlife Resources; Human Resources and Education; and Veterinary Medicine. While many students apply to the college of their choice from the beginning, many others start out in a program called University Studies, which provides students with an administrative division without forcing them to chose a college until the after sophomore year. Students say that it is also not difficult to change colleges, as long as your grades are good. Nonetheless, students caution that it's a good idea to know what you want to study because between distribution requirements (which vary within each college) and the requirements of each major, there isn't a whole lot of room for experimentation or electives. "You may have a few extra credits now and then," said one student. The business school has fewer requirements and is therefore considered easier by many undergrads.

Students report that preprofessionals make up a majority of the honors program. Based on high school grades and test scores, prefrosh are invited to apply for the program, which gives them access to small, honors-only colloquia and priority for other classes. Once they are in the program, Hokies must maintain a 3.5 GPA. Even if an applicant's high school grades aren't strong enough to get into the program at the time of matriculation to the university, anyone in the school who achieves a 3.5 is invited to apply, regardless of year.

Although most of the student body is technical-minded, students say there is room at the school for nontechnical majors. Each of the schools' requirements includes humanities classes, such as freshman English. "I've known quite a few psychology and humanities majors. The curriculum is quite diverse; it's not just technical," said one sophomore computer science major. The difficulty of classes also varies. "Some [majors] have bigger workloads than others," one student said, citing psychology and health and food services as particularly easy majors. Among the more popular gut classes is Introduction to Film. "You just go twice a week and watch movies. It's pretty slick," said one undergrad.

Students report that some elective classes can be difficult to get into, although they are quick to qualify that if a class is required for your major, you're guaranteed a spot. Advanced classes tend to have about 30 students, although some Hokies complain that many intro classes are too large, sometimes running up to 600 students. "You can usually expect them to be at least 300 people," complained one junior.

Intramurals, Graffiti Parties, and Greeks

When Hokies stop working, alcohol often comes into play, students say. "There's not much to do here if you don't drink, to be honest," said one student, who estimated that about 50 percent of campus is involved with the Greek scene. Others disputed his description of booze-soaked weekends. "Nobody forces anyone to drink," one sophomore said, explaining that even at big parties not everyone drinks. Another sophomore explained: "I expected a lot worse in terms of drinking. Once you get past your freshman year, [the dominance of frat parties] . . . turns into apartment parties for the most part."

> **"The curriculum is quite diverse; it's not just technical."**

For those who do not drink, the school is trying to increase the number of alternatives. At the beginning of the 1998–99 school year, an announcement was made by the Virginia attorney general that there would be a crackdown on campus underage drinking. In response, the administration created the Alcohol Free Programming Fund at the beginning of the 1999–2000 school year to help student groups plan dry activities. The fund has yet to see widespread use; the few student groups that know about the program have generally taken advantage of it. Students point out that "even without the new fund, every day of the week there's something going on. You can always find a concert or an organization or a movie."

For those who come from urban or suburban areas, living in tiny Blacksburg can require a bit of an adjustment. "It's definitely a change from home," said a junior from the Washington, D.C., area. Hokies occasionally travel to Roanoke to go shopping or to D.C., about three hours away, to go clubbing or see concerts. Most students at Virginia Tech have cars, although they agree that it isn't a necessity.

On the weekends, Hokies can often be found supporting their sports teams. Home football games are major occasions, particularly against rival University of Virginia. Even those not involved in "regular, full-fledged varsity sports" are often active athletes, participating in the popular intramural leagues. There are volleyball courts next to all the dorms and "there's always someone throwing a Frisbee, baseball, football, or something," said one student. In addition, students report that you can usually find a pick-up game somewhere on the Drill Field, a large courtyard around which all the residential and academic building are centered.

The First-Year Experience

All freshman Hokies must live on campus, in one of several coed-by-floor dorms; after the first year, students have the option of moving off campus. Typically, students say the number of students living on campus drops by half for sophomores, and nearly all juniors and seniors choose to live off campus. Student reviews of freshman housing are mixed, but are overwhelmingly positive about a new dorm called "The First-Year Experience," an all-freshman dorm. Other dorms include a large all-male dormitory, an athlete-only building full of suites, and a handful of upperclassman suite dorms, which have air conditioning. All the buildings are wired with an ethernet network for Internet access.

Students have a variety of options in choosing a meal plan. Many freshmen are on a meal plan that gives them 19 meals a week at a variety of dining halls around campus. Others are on "flex," a system in which students buy points that they can use at any dining hall, including franchise restaurants in the student center, vending machines, or even the laundromat. Aside from a few horror stories about fried chicken, Hokies are pretty happy about their food. "Virginia Tech has one of the best meal plans and dining facilities," boasted one junior.

Virginia Tech, the largest college in Virginia and a member of the state university system, is clearly a technical university. But unlike other such schools, the arts and sciences school is large enough so that there are plenty of opportunities for all types of students.—*Jacob Remes and staff*

FYI

The three best things about attending Virginia Tech are "the laid back atmosphere, great sports teams, and a wide range of majors."

The three worst things about attending Virginia Tech are "the boring town of Blacksburg, isolation from civilization, and having to pay to get in to a lot of parties."

The three things that every student should do before graduating from Virginia Tech are "go to the football game against UVA, go tubing on the New River, and do something outdoorsy."

One thing I'd like to have known before coming here is "how cold and windy it gets during the winters."

Washington and Lee University

Address: Letcher Avenue; Lexington, VA 24450-0303	**Percent Asian:** NA	**Middle 50% SAT range:** 630–710 V, 640–720 M
Phone: 540-463-8710	**Percent Hispanic:** NA	
E-mail address: admissions@wlu.edu	**Percent Native-American:** NA	**Middle 50% ACT range:** 27–30
Web site URL: www.wlu.edu	**Percent in-state/out-of-state:** 12%/88%	**3 Most popular majors:** economics, journalism, history
Founded: 1749	**Percent Pub HS:** 60%	**Retention:** 94%
Private or Public: private	**Number of Applicants:** 3,082	**Graduation rate:** 86%
Religious affiliation: none	**Percent Accepted:** 36%	**On-campus housing:** 60%
Location: rural	**Percent Accepted who enroll:** 42%	**Fraternities:** 82%
Undergraduate enrollment: NA	**Entering:** 467	**Sororities:** 70%
Total enrollment: 2,096	**Transfers:** 7	**Library:** 503,931 volumes
Percent Male/Female: NA	**Application Deadline:** 15 Jan	**Tuition and Fees:** $17,105 in; $17,105 out
Percent Minority: 0%	**Mean SAT:** NA	**Room and Board:** $5,547
Percent African-American: NA	**Mean ACT:** NA	**Financial aid, first-year:** NA

Are you a closet Republican? Are you an out-of-the-closet Republican? When you wake up in the morning and put on something other than a coat and tie, do you feel underdressed? If you answered yes to any of these questions, Washington and Lee could be your dream school.

Just Say Hello

Situated in the lush foothills of the Blue Ridge Mountains, Washington and Lee University is not your typical school. Students say the campus makes them feel transported back to a time when America was a kinder and friendlier place. Above all else, students praise W&L's honor system, under which they promise not to lie, cheat, or steal. Some students say they can leave their doors open when they are not in their rooms without worrying; all campus buildings are left unlocked; exams are unproctored. "The last time that I felt this secure must have been in my mother's womb," one undergrad said. When they are not busy in class, Washington and Lee students spend a lot of time saying hi to one another. The university's "speaking tradition" requires all students to say hello to any person that they make eye contact with while walking around campus. In the words of one student, "This isn't anyplace for a recluse."

There is an undeniable old-boy, bourbon-drinking, cigar-smoking Republican tradition on the Washington and Lee campus. Many students do not mind this image; in fact, many embrace it. "It is not uncommon to see students attend classes in coats and ties, or dresses," said one undergrad. The social scene reportedly is dominated by fraternities, but as one member said, "Students at other schools drink cheap beer at frat parties. Here, everyone drinks bourbon and Coke." Well over half of all W&L students go Greek, which led one student to say, "You have to be Greek to have any kind of a social life at all."

Working Damn Hard

Despite their fondness for sipping bourbon or talking about what color Jaguar they plan to buy someday, Washington and Lee students have a demanding course load. Undergrads agree that there are no "easy-A" courses to be found. "Student here work damn hard. Every A we get, we work our butts off for," said one. Many consider the politics and history departments excellent, and students in a variety of majors have nothing but praise for their professors. "Profs here are the best. They teach all classes. They read all papers. They care, like you're one of their children," said one student. Among some of the more famous faculty members are Professors Mudd, a former anchor for CBS news, and Yoder, a Pulitzer Prize-winning journalist.

> **It is easy to surmise that General Lee would look upon this university with as much pride as current undergrads do.**

In line with the strong sense of tradition at Washington and Lee, students follow a core curriculum, which ensures that they take courses in a foreign language, English, science, and history. Students do not seem to mind studying at Washington and Lee, as they have top-notch facilities in which to learn. Leyburn Library is open 24 hours a day, and a new science center opened recently. Students also call the gym "super." The university recently spent millions of dollars refurbishing the tennis courts.

Greek Spirit
Spirit at W&L reportedly centers on the Greek system. Frats and sororities regularly compete against one another in a wide range of intramural sports. As one student said, "We have everything from shooting to water polo." In addition to intramurals, students take advantage of university-sponsored dances, especially Christmas Weekend and Mock Convention. Christmas Weekend is a week long party with formals and a concert featuring a major performer (including such big names as Hootie and the Blowfish). The Mock Convention, in addition to being a major time for parties, is also a popular extracurricular activity. Every four years Washington and Lee holds a mock convention for the political party not in power. Students do extensive research on likely state voting trends and try to predict the candidate most likely to win each state's endorsement for the presidency. According to one student, "It's a mess of work, but all the fun we have during the convention week amply makes up for it."

Great Food
Washington and Lee undergrads love the dining hall food, which draws such comments as "great," "healthy," and "an utter joy." All freshmen eat at Evans dining hall. Upperclassmen can also eat at Evans, or at General Head Quarters (GHQ) or the Co-op snack bar. Most, however, elect to eat at their fraternity or sorority house. Each house has its own team of chefs, and the food, in the words of one student, "is better than anything my mother could even hope to make." Those in search of off-campus culinary adventures often head to Palms, Spanky's, Harb's, or Lee-Hi, a 24-hour truck stop.

Not Just Resume-Padding
Washington and Lee students say they participate in as many extracurriculars as possible, not for "resume padding," but instead "to bring honor upon the university." Among the most popular activities are Mock Convention, the College Republicans (surprise, surprise), many musical groups (both vocal and instrumental), and the college's two weekly newspapers, *Ring Tum-Phi* and the *Trident*.

The on-campus crypt of Robert E. Lee is a year-round tourist attraction. One can only imagine what this revered general would think of his namesake institution after all these years. With its tradition-laden campus, a student body tremendously respectful of these traditions, and a deep sense of honesty, it is easy to surmise that General Lee would look upon this university with as much pride as current undergrads do.—*Jeff Kaplow and Staff*

FYI
The three best things about attending Washington and Lee are "the conservative spirit, the speaking tradition, and Christmas weekend."
The three worst things about attending Washington and Lee are "you have to go Greek, drinking bourbon, and the lack of alternative, liberal viewpoints."
The three things that every student should do before graduating from Washington and Lee are "join Mock Convention, visit the crypt, and rush a frat."
One thing I'd like to have known before coming here is "how stodgy we can sometimes be."

Washington

Evergreen State College

Address: 2700 Evergreen Parkway NW; Olympia, WA 98505
Phone: 360-866-6000
E-mail address: admissions @evergreen.edu
Web site URL: www.evergreen.edu
Founded: 1967
Private or Public: public
Religious affiliation: none
Location: small city
Undergraduate enrollment: NA
Total enrollment: 4,486
Percent Male/Female: NA
Percent Minority: 0%
Percent African-American: NA

Percent Asian: NA
Percent Hispanic: NA
Percent Native-American: NA
Percent in-state/out-of-state: 73%/27%
Percent Pub HS: NA
Number of Applicants: 1,526
Percent Accepted: 86%
Percent Accepted who enroll: 35%
Entering: 462
Transfers: 835
Application Deadline: 1 Mar
Mean SAT: 588 V, 590 M
Mean ACT: 65

Middle 50% SAT range: 530–660 V, 490–610 M
Middle 50% ACT range: 21–26
3 Most popular majors: B.A. and B.S. awarded/ no majors
Retention: 55%
Graduation rate: NA
On-campus housing: 75%
Fraternities: NA
Sororities: NA
Library: NA
Tuition and Fees: $2,792 in; $9,794 out
Room and Board: $5,136
Financial aid, first-year: 44%

Open-mindedness, liberal ideas, social consciousness, and culture of the 1960s touch every aspect of life at Evergreen State College. Evergreen was founded in 1967 on the unconventional idea that "Greeners" would have no mandatory areas of study and nearly absolute academic freedom. Evergreen students choose an "area of interest" and create their own course of study from a wide variety of academic options. This is a freedom these students take seriously.

Challenge Us

The academic atmosphere at Evergreen "challenges students to challenge themselves," one undergraduate explained. There is no grading at Evergreen; instead, professors write evaluations of student performance. By pinpointing areas of strength and weakness, these evaluations help students improve their academic standing and learn through the process. Some students warn that "if you're not self-motivated, Evergreen is not the best place for you to be." Small classes encourage student-teacher interaction, which is evidenced by the fact that most students call their professors by their first names. The only requirement is a freshman core course that teaches research, planning, and writing by focusing on one specific topic such as wildlife in the streams and "modeling nature." "I really like my core course because instead of taking a generic chemistry course, I'm learning all the chemistry that applies to a specific problem. For once I feel as if I'm really applying my knowledge," said one freshman.

Evergreen divides its school year into quarters. After the freshman core, students select programs, or areas of study that include multiple courses running through multiple quarters concentrating on a particular theme. For instance, the program "Molecule to Organism" includes a course in organic chemistry, a course in cell biology, and a course in organismal biology; "In the Enchanted Kingdom" incorporates, among other classes, a class in Russian and Slavic folk culture and a class in the psychology of myth and legend. One junior explained, "I really feel like I come away from each program with a thorough understanding of something, not just a bunch of memorized facts that I'll forget in a few years."

The Greener Crew

Although most Greeners are Washington State residents, a considerable number come from out of state. The majority of students are Caucasian. A sizable gay and lesbian population on campus is open and supported by the rest of the student body. According to one student, "We have a whole lot of hippies here" who tend to dress in hemp and tie-dye, listen to Bob Dylan, eat organic food, and talk about Buddhism. Many discuss intellectual ideas outside of the classroom.

On weekends, "just hanging out" is popular. Students often dine out at the Corner, a student-run vegetarian cooperative that prepares food grown on Evergreen's own organic farm. Most Evergreen parties are small, private affairs, held in student rooms. There is no Greek system on campus. Super Saturday, the biggest social event of the year, showcases live music, arts and crafts, and game booths in the spring. The annual "All Freakfest Night," a 12-hour "cheesy horror film" marathon held at a local independent film theater, also attracts many students. Students say it's fairly easy to catch a ride to Olympia, Seattle, and Portland which are only an hour's drive from campus.

> "Evergreen offers a non-traditional education that attracts a group of freethinking students."

Students at Evergreen involve themselves heavily in extracurricular activities, even though they have a relaxed attitude about them. Free Tibet and the Washington Public Interest Research group are two of "the many groups committed to social action." Many Greeners write for the *Cooper Point Journal* or the *Evergreen Times* newspapers. Another option is to work as a disc jockey for CHAOS, the Evergreen radio station, which plays everything from punk and industrial music to folk and contemporary jazz. Students play intramural rugby, basketball, and ultimate Frisbee, and a new varsity basketball team has drawn large crowds. However, many students argue that "sports are just here for fun."

Rainy Days

Washington's temperate rain forests engulf the Evergreen campus. "There are just so many trees here. It's gorgeous," gushed one student. Indeed, the cement buildings, which comprise most of the campus, seem to blend with the wooded surroundings. One student described moss and algae growing on the cement buildings "taking the landscape back to nature in a really beautiful way." The rural setting provides rock-climbing, hiking, and beach-strolling opportunities for the "very outdoor-oriented" students. This willingness to enjoy the outdoors is also attributed to the fact that most Greeners feel safe on campus.

Evergreen offers students several housing alternatives: four- to six-person apartments, two-person studios, and traditional single rooms. No matter where they live, Evergreen students tend to cook for themselves and avoid the dining halls. The dorms, small apartments with living rooms and kitchens, are popular for their social atmosphere, but "it's hard to find someplace in the dorms that's quiet" to study. The "mods," or modular housing units, are set on the outskirts of campus and surrounded by thick woods. Each mod has two double bedrooms, a kitchen, a living room, a front porch, a bathroom with a bathtub, and a yard. Many living in the mods can point out the unit where Nirvana gave its first performance.

Because the buildings, including the dorms, are all located on one side of campus, students can get to all classes within five minutes. One notable feature of campus is the recreational center, open to all students, which offers activities ranging from ceramics to martial arts to yoga. The center also sports Nautilus equipment, a rock-climbing wall, a camping-gear center, saunas, racquetball courts, and an 11-lane Olympic-size pool.

Evergreen offers a nontraditional education that attracts a group of freethinking students. To get the most out of academics, students must be motivated, because "it's easy to slack off and get by.

But it's ultimately up to you to learn if you want to." The independence and tolerance provided at Evergreen allow students to chart their own academic and social paths.—*Brian Abaluck and Staff*

FYI

The three best things about attending Evergreen State are "being challenged to think on your feet, emphasis on experiential learning, and abilty to craft your own course of study through individual and group contracts."

The three worst things about attending Evergreen State are "limited number and variety of courses, Washington's pop sterotype of a 'hippie school with no grades and lots of drugs,' and having emphases instead of majors and minors."

The three things that every student should do before graduating from Evergreen State are "experiment with all the media equipment, take only what you want to learn, and make your way into the wilderness."

One thing I'd like to have known before coming here is "that the classes offered change from year to year."

University of Puget Sound

Address: 1500 North Warner Street; Tacoma, WA 98416-0062
Phone: 253-879-3211
E-mail address: admission@ups.edu
Web site URL: www.ups.edu
Founded: 1888
Private or Public: private
Religious affiliation: none
Location: suburban
Undergraduate enrollment: NA
Total enrollment: 2,973
Percent Male / Female: NA
Percent Minority: 0%
Percent African-American: NA

Percent Asian: NA
Percent Hispanic: NA
Percent Native-American: NA
Percent in-state / out-of-state: 32%/68%
Percent Pub HS: 78%
Number of Applicants: 4,138
Percent Accepted: 74%
Percent Accepted who enroll: 22%
Entering: 684
Transfers: 109
Application Deadline: 1 Feb
Mean SAT: 621 V, 620 M
Mean ACT: 27

Middle 50% SAT range: 570–670 V, 580–660 M
Middle 50% ACT range: 25–29
3 Most popular majors: business administration, English, psychology
Retention: 83%
Graduation rate: 73%
On-campus housing: 95%
Fraternities: 25%
Sororities: 24%
Library: 463,233 volumes
Tuition and Fees: $20,605 in; $20,605 out
Room and Board: $5,270
Financial aid, first-year: 72%

Looking for a liberal arts college with the demanding curriculum of a major university? Amid the torrential rains (and therefore beautiful, lush greenery) lies the University of Puget Sound. As a mid-sized liberal arts school, UPS allows for a diverse curriculum and challenging courses in a more personalized setting. Though they often take five years to get there, graduates are prepared well for handling the challenges of the real world.

"The Work Load Is Exceptional"

UPS expects quite a lot from its students, and they tend to deliver. The school requires a basic core of classes for a bachelor of the arts degree. Students must take English, a natural science, math, communications, and physical education in order to graduate, and while this basic curriculum is regarded as necessary, "many of the core classes are lectures and if they're not in your field of interest they can become extremely dull," as one student said.

However, as a smaller school, even the lectures seem personal. UPS only enrolls about 80 people in its largest classes, regardless of their popularity. Not that this means that you will have a hard time getting the classes you want—one student pointed out that "even the classes that are already closed aren't impossible to get into. If you speak to the professor, 9 times out of 10 you'll be admitted." TAs have actually been deemed "unconstitutional" at UPS, at least for teaching classes, so you can really build a relationship with your professors, even in the first year.

For the ambitious, UPS has a highly selective honors program available for freshmen whose SAT scores and/or high school records prove them eligible. This program has the same requirements as the regular core system, but the classes are taught at a faster pace and at a more in-depth level. Honors students, however, also must live in separate housing and write a senior thesis.

> "TAs have actually been deemed 'unconstitutional' at UPS, at least for teaching classes, so you can really build a relationship with your professors, even in the first year."

For those looking for a more diverse college experience, UPS offers an extremely liberal independent study program. Students can apply to do anything from traveling abroad for a year to working in nearby Rainier National Park as a ranger. On a more practical note, for those who find the courses at UPS too challenging or expensive (as a smaller college UPS cannot offer as much financial aid as it would like), Washington has a statewide program in which you can attend any community college in the state for a year and have your credits transfer without any hassle. As one student stated, "This way you get the same credits for the classes you don't care about, but at half the difficulty and one-fifth the cost."

As students become deeper entrenched in their major, the heavier the workload becomes—but it's all worth it. Small classes (typically 14 students) allow for a very personal educational experience. "Stay in touch with your professors. The relationship with them becomes extremely intense due to small class sizes, and they can be of great value years after graduating," advised one senior.

Proximity to Seattle, Vancouver, Portland

"The beauty of Tacoma is its centralized geographic location to all the happenings in the northwest." Seattle is 40 minutes north, Portland is a two-hour drive, Vancouver is three and a half, the coast is three hours away, and Mt. Rainier National Park is a mere hour and a half away. Seattle offers everything a student could want in terms of urban life, sports, and cultural events, and if it can't be found there, any of the other cities will do.

This is not to say that everyone leaves Tacoma to have a good time. The small city offers several independent theaters, Narrows Alley—the local bowling center, and fantastic coffee shops like Grounds for Coffee and Shakabra. Of course, the college population has spawned many downtown bars and nightclubs, not to mention an underground party scene. According to one student, "some of the best DJs in the northwest reside here in Tacoma."

While the campus is dry, drinking "can still be fairly popular around the school." Students frequent several local bars, namely Magoo's, Engine House 9, Roselli's, and the Ram Brewery. But chemical consumption is neither expected nor pressured, and there is even a substance-free freshman dorm. Other drugs that have recently become extremely prevalent in the northwest, such as speed and heroin, are not a problem on the UPS campus. The only substance in abundance seems to be marijuana, and "students are able to locate some of the finest bud in the world within a week of first arriving to campus." Despite this, students reiterate that UPS is a low-pressure environment, and the rumors that "mushrooms which grow on campus can be brewed into a tea for hallucinatory madness" are unfounded.

Greek Life

Fraternities and sororities play a vital role in the social life at UPS. They throw some of the coolest parties throughout the year. However, unlike many colleges, the UPS frats are not exclusive, nor does a majority of the student body participate. This means pretty much anyone can go to a frat party and be welcomed. Each frat throws its own formals throughout the year, but as one student stated, "the hottest party of the year is a seven-house block party called The Rail thrown every Halloween weekend." This party is open to anyone and everyone.

To counteract the frat scene, the student government throws many dances and events. One of the highlights of the year is the Xmas Mistletoast and homecoming (which includes a singing contest and a pre-football game parade). Homecoming weekend also features musical acts, and in the past this has included the Stone Temple Pilots, Sky Cries Mary, and Chuck Mangione.

The Great Outdoors

If the urban scene is not your thing, the Pacific Northwest has much, much more to offer. Students often bike, hike, and walk around UPS. The Residents of the Outhouse organize backpacking trips almost every weekend. Further, the Sailing Club is extremely popular. Along with all this are ski areas, a national park, and even hunting. The weather does not hinder UPS students. As one student joked, "many students come out of March wondering what the hell that bright ball of light coming out of the sky is since we haven't seen the sun for a while."

UPS students also participate in choir, band, the radio station, and theater. While the sports teams are not necessarily respected as they are at major universities, the women's volleyball team has a good record, and intramurals are a popular extracurricular. Popular IMs are volleyball and crew. If organized sports seem like too much effort, the Pamplin Fitness Center, built in 1994, is considered a "fantastic place to burn calories, socialize, and de-stress."

But, Where Do I Live?

During the first year at UPS students live in campus dorms, which are considered cramped. Most of the dorms are coed; however, a women's floor is available. After freshman year, the upperclassmen decide whether to stay in dorms or to move into a university-owned residence (these house between 5 and 6 people, whom you choose). Theme houses are popular, and range from the foreign language house to the sailing house, and even the "Outhouse" for nature enthusiasts. If you cannot find a theme house that suites your needs, it is possible to petition the school and start a new one.

While students tend to be open-minded and liberal, the student body does not necessarily reflect that. As one student put it, "A lack of diversity has been a problem for some time at this school and has been addressed, but not really solved." The student body tends to be Caucasian and middle class, although the administration claims to be making efforts to recruit minority students from more diverse backgrounds.

Due to the lack of diversity, "interracial dating is rare," but not frowned upon. Dating does occur, or as one student put it, "Not too many are celibate here, so yeah, they date." And according to some, the campus is getting better looking with each new crop of freshmen. Homosexuality is accepted, and couples of all types are seen around campus, and as one student commented, "lots of sex on all fronts."

UPS is a challenging liberal arts school where students work to their potential, but do not forget to unwind. Students consider UPS a strong foundation for the world beyond.—*Kyla Dahlin*

FYI
The three best things about attending UPS are "the personal relationships with your professors, the ability for any individual to make a difference on campus, and the beauty of the campus itself."
The three worst things about attending UPS are "the weather, the cost, and the small size."
The three things that every student should do before graduating from UPS are "to work, to work some more, and then relax!"
One thing I'd like to have known before coming here is "that they expect a lot from you academically, and they don't like to keep around loafers."

University of Washington

Address: 1410 NE Campus Parkway, 320 Schmitz Hall Box 355840; Seattle, WA 9819-5840
Phone: 206-543-9686
E-mail address: askuwadm @u.washington.edu
Web site URL: u.washington.edu
Founded: 1861
Private or Public: public
Religious affiliation: none
Location: urban
Undergraduate enrollment: NA
Total enrollment: 35,367
Percent Male / Female: NA
Percent Minority: 0%

Percent African-American: NA
Percent Asian: NA
Percent Hispanic: NA
Percent Native-American: NA
Percent in-state / out-of-state: 77% / 23%
Percent Pub HS: NA
Number of Applicants: 12,785
Percent Accepted: 77%
Percent Accepted who enroll: 0%
Entering: NA
Transfers: 2,900
Application Deadline: 15 Jan
Mean SAT: NA
Mean ACT: NA

Middle 50% SAT range: 510–630 V, 610–650 M
Middle 50% ACT range: 22–27
3 Most popular majors: business, biology, political science
Retention: 91%
Graduation rate: 69%
On-campus housing: NA
Fraternities: 13%
Sororities: 12%
Library: 5,100,000 volumes
Tuition and Fees: $3,638 in; $12,029 out
Room and Board: $5,844
Financial aid, first-year: 36%

Founded in 1861, the University of Washington claimed only a single building on a ten-acre hill where the faculty—one professor—taught Latin, Greek, English, history, algebra, and physiology. Such humble beginnings would hardly be expected from today's dynamic university, affectionately nicknamed "U-Dub," where its strong athletics and academics have given it a national reputation.

Science Bias?

As one of the largest research institutions in the country, U-Dub's specialization lies in the sciences. Students claim that the hardest but best majors are computer science, engineering sciences, biochemistry, and the natural sciences—chemistry, cell and molecular biology, and physics. Thanks to its state-of-the-art facilities, cutting-edge faculty, and great internship opportunities, degrees in the sciences "are totally worth all the hard work." One student lamented the work that his biochemistry major required, observing that the school's average GPA for humanities was 3.1 while the average GPA for sciences was 2.8. The difference, he claimed, "speaks for itself." While students unanimously agreed that sciences are the toughest and most demanding majors, there was disagreement about the school's slacker majors. Some students contended that "psychology is a joke," and others labeled English, art, and political science as "wimp classes."

Despite this obvious division between the liberal arts and the sciences, U-Dub requires that students in the School of Arts and Sciences take courses in three areas: social sciences, humanities, and natural sciences. Easy classes include Psychology 101 and Music 185. These popular classes enroll nearly 800 students, while most introductory-level classes enroll 300. Some students admit that they were fooled into thinking "intro equals easy." Instead, some of the classes are taught by professors who "assign homework as if you're taking only that class." But because "professors are really interested in students' learning," the workload is not overwhelmingly difficult. "After all, I've survived so far," explained one senior.

Tri-Campus System

The university operates on a three-campus system, with the main campus in Seattle and two others in Bothell and Tacoma, which have mainly evening and weekend programs. Students praise their campus as being "beautiful!" U-Dub's lakeside location provides students not only with a great view, but also with many opportunities to sail, canoe, kayak, or windsurf. The Cascade and Olympic mountains draw many students, from skiers to backpackers and other nature lovers. The campus is full of joggers and cyclists at all hours of the day, thanks to the "exceptionally safe" environment. The only complaint about the Seattle campus was the city's "nine-month gray spell" and the rainy winters.

The great campus has attracted an increasing number of out-of-staters, causing many undergrads to opt for campus housing. Students can opt for the "study dorm," the "party dorm," the "single-room dorm," or even the "all-nighter dorm." Most of these dorms are coed, and all are modern and comfortable: common rooms have couches and grand pianos, and computer and weight room facilities are state-of-the-art. Stylistically, the dorms are "small and concrete," claimed one student. Some students, while grateful that the rooms are furnished, wished that "there was just a little more space." The campus, however is unquestionably spacious. The size of the campus makes a bicycle a treasure, but students warn that sidewalk tag with pedestrians is frustrating. For those with a car, parking is expensive, and spaces in the lots are at a premium.

> **"I had the freshman 15 . . . except it was negative."**

The most popular off-campus housing is in the nearby "U District," where rents are low and food is cheap on "the Ave" (First Avenue). Students with purple hair "flip-flopping about," make the U District, also nicknamed the "student ghetto," what one sophomore termed "the hangout for the most diverse people in the world." Many students frequent the U District to get relatively edible food, as the school cafeterias provide only "limited choices, unpleasant service, stale ingredients, and

small portions." One student conveyed the quality of the food by explaining, "I had the freshman 15 . . . except it was negative." Another student complained about his dining experience at U-Dub: "One time my pizza crust was uncooked, and the other time there was only one slice of pepperoni on my entire slice of pizza. Friends who work at the food service told me they save all the leftovers and dump it into every Friday's special 'soup of the day.'"

Students throw parties each week at the HUB (the Husky Union Building), but students generally agree that the best parties are on the Greek Row or the "big, upperclassmen apartments off-campus." The Greek system at U-Dub is "less influential than WSU [Washington State University]," for frats and sororities are "only popular among themselves." For alternatives to the frats and the heavy drinking that tends to characterize such parties, the burgeoning city of Seattle offers a wealth of shops, restaurants, dance clubs, and coffee shops to entertain. The student government also offers free movies weekly, along with occasional dances and activities. One senior said, "I have never had trouble finding something to do."

Sport Shorts

That "the wave" supposedly was first introduced in the U-Dub stadium is an indication of the popularity of the school's sporting events. The Huskies' football team commands great loyalty from the student body, thanks to this Pac-10 team's recent Rose Bowl appearance and perennial strength. Huge crowds come to cheer on the Huskies against their biggest rivals, the Washington State Cougars, in the annual Apple Cup showdown. To get tickets to any football or basketball game, students must endure a "minimum three-hour wait" in line, but the wait is worth it, "something every student should do."

Most students commit to some level of sports: from club sports to intramural sports (which are "hugely popular") to a relaxing afternoon of Frisbee tossing. Undergraduates enjoy the campus' "incredibly large" recreational gym, the Intramural Activities Building, or IMA, which houses the headquarters for hundreds of competing intramural teams. Such sports as aikido, fly fishing, skiing, and snowboarding are also popular with students.

In addition to sports, U-Dub offers "every club imaginable." Students encourage the freshmen to get involved in student activities, as they often facilitate great friendships and sometimes, claimed one junior, "a date!" Among the many extracurricular options are the Swing Club, the Pagan Students Association, the Asian Dance club (which has 1,000 members), the Sci-Fi club, political groups, and Christian fellowships.

Undergrads, especially the science majors, dedicate a lot of time to their intense studying. Many find the Suzallo Graduate Study Reading Room the best place to go for "studying where it's dead quiet." On the opposite extreme is the Odegaard Undergraduate Library, which one student called the "loudest place I've ever tried to study." Despite their access to a dozen libraries, most students opt to hit the books in their own rooms.

The University of Washington, with its attractive Seattle location, its great athletic tradition, its solid academic programs, and its variety of activities, welcomes students from around the world. No longer is this school the little building on a ten-acre hill; it has evolved into a "fabulous university endowed with countless opportunities."
—*Marti Page and Staff*

FYI

The three best things about attending University of Washington are "the awesome view of Mt. Rainier, the relaxed no dress-code atmosphere, and the strong computer science and medicine programs."

The three worst things about attending University of Washington are "rain—it's worst when the weather gets colder, professors never remember you because classes are too big, and professors are hard to contact."

The three things every student should do before graduating from the University of Washington are "work out at the intramural activities center, walk up 'The Ave,' and go to Canada."

One thing I'd like to have known before coming here is "this is a fun school, but definitely not a party school."

Washington State University

Address: Pullman, WA 99164-1067
Phone: 509-335-5586
E-mail address: admiss@wsu.edu
Web site URL: www.wsu.edu
Founded: 1890
Private or Public: public
Religious affiliation: none
Location: rural
Undergraduate enrollment: NA
Total enrollment: 20,799
Percent Male / Female: NA
Percent Minority: 0%
Percent African-American: NA
Percent Asian: NA

Percent Hispanic: NA
Percent Native-American: NA
Percent in-state / out-of-state: 91%/9%
Percent Pub HS: NA
Number of Applicants: 7,132
Percent Accepted: 84%
Percent Accepted who enroll: 50%
Entering: 2,978
Transfers: 1,923
Application Deadline: 1 May
Mean SAT: 526 V, 527 M
Mean ACT: NA

Middle 50% SAT range: 470–590 V, 470–580 M
Middle 50% ACT range: NA
3 Most popular majors: business administration, communications, social sciences
Retention: 83%
Graduation rate: 59%
On-campus housing: 97%
Fraternities: 17%
Sororities: 16%
Library: NA
Tuition and Fees: $3,662 in; $10,696 out
Room and Board: $4,618
Financial aid, first-year: 40%

Students at Washington State University have a number of reasons for being there, but location isn't usually on top of the list. Washington State University is located in what one student called "the middle of nowhere." Despite the isolated environment, however, many students find their experiences at WSU to be better than they expected.

Farmer School? Not Really

Like many other land-grant universities throughout the United States, WSU emphasizes agriculture and engineering. The university is divided into nine colleges: the most popular include agriculture, arts and sciences, business, communications, and veterinary science. Students report that communications is the strongest department, ranking among the top programs in the region. No matter which college they choose, however, all undergraduates must fulfill a complicated system of core requirements that vary depending upon a student's major and entrance date to the school. Students with superior high school grades and standardized test scores can qualify for a selective honors program, but students in the regular program say they do not find the core requirements overwhelming.

Big Classes

Classes at WSU are relatively large. Introductory classes, especially those that meet the core requirements, can enroll as many as 500 students, and the norm in the other introductory courses is 100 to 200. Even advanced courses in popular colleges such as business or communications enroll 30 or 40 people. Students often want to sign up for the same classes and must wait to enroll in the ones they want, or even the ones they need. As a result, many undergrads need to take a fifth year to graduate.

The Town of Pullman

What on earth can a student do in Pullman for five years? "Drink, and drink, and drink" is a popular response. Despite its small size, Pullman has many bars and clubs—including Chaser's, Rico's, Doc's, and the Cavern—that attract students every weekend. The Washington–Idaho border is five miles away, and three miles beyond that is Moscow, Idaho, home of the University of Idaho. For the truly adventurous (and those with cars), Spokane is about 70 miles away, offering an even wider variety of nightlife.

Cracking the Whip

On campus, students report with some dismay that the administration's traditionally lenient attitude toward drinking has changed in recent years. The administration has banned kegs, limited fraternity and sorority parties, and prohibited alcoholic beverages at Greek functions. According to one junior, however, the rules are "broken all the time." Waterburst, a weekend party that used to take place before the beginning of school in the fall, was recently eliminated, and some students believe the traditional Greenstock Bash, WSU's version of Woodstock, will also be discontinued in future years. Many undergrads fear this could mark the demise of the active social life at Washington State, leaving little else to do on campus except drink.

Greeks? Gone

About one-fifth of WSU's undergraduate population belongs to a fraternity or a sorority, but with recent restrictions on alcohol, the Greeks no longer dominate the social scene. "If the Trojans had had this administration on their side," one student said, "they wouldn't have had any trouble with the Greeks." Nonetheless, the presence of more than 30 fraternities and sororities creates some pressure to rush.

> **"Many undergrads take a fifth year to graduate."**

For students who do not want to participate in Greek life, Washington State offers excellent dorms, which residents say are comfortable and foster a sense of unity. Of particular interest is the International House, which houses a culturally diverse group of undergrads. Some students complain, however, that food quality is a major drawback to dorm life—the food in the fraternity and sorority houses reportedly is much better.

The dorms are not the only facilities students praise at WSU. The CUB (Compton Union Building) is a favorite undergrad hangout, complete with a bowling alley, a game room, and a full-size movie theater. The three gyms are also popular, and the main one has a large new weight room. The university's recent renovation of the Ernest Holland Library makes it one of the largest in the Pacific Northwest.

Extra! Extra! Read All About It!

While drinking and partying are the favorite pastimes, many WSU students get involved in extracurricular activities. The "fantastic" intramural sports program allows students to participate in anything from badminton to water polo. For those interested in writing, the school has such outlets as the *Daily Evergreen* newspaper. Cultural groups are also gaining popularity, and their activities are coordinated by a central governing body known as the Council of Minority Student Presidents.

The popular Pac-10 football and basketball teams usually attract large crowds of undergrads to their games. While the basketball team has not performed well in recent years, many students feel it will fare better in the future, and might even make the NCAA tournament someday. The Cougars football team at WSU has had a winning record in recent years. Cougars especially enjoy annual sport battles against their state and Pac-10 rivals, the University of Washington Huskies, in the Apple Cup. Although WSU victories are rare in this showdown, the occasional victory "makes them all the more sweet," one sophomore said.

Though a geographically diverse student body is not one of WSU's strong points, since most students come from Washington, especially from the Spokane and Seattle areas, many undergraduates report that the university has a great deal to offer, both socially and academically, in a relatively relaxed and tranquil environment. The town of Pullman is not the most interesting college town, but students are confident that the years they spend at Washington State University will be the best four (or five or six) years of their lives.
—*Melissa Chan and Staff*

FYI

The three best things about attending WSU are "everything's in walking distance, people are friendly, and the Greek system is large but not exclusive."

The three worst things about attending WSU are "that it's in the middle of nowhere, the campus is too hilly, and the area is too windy."

The three things that every student should do before graduating from WSU are "visit Cougar Country, go to Moscow, Idaho, and have one humiliating drunk experience."

One thing I'd like to have known before coming here is "how to pace yourself through everything."

Whitman College

Address: 345 Boyer Avenue; Walla Walla, WA 99362-2083
Phone: 509-527-5176
E-mail address: admission@whitman.edu
Web site URL: www.whitman.edu
Founded: 1859
Private or Public: private
Religious affiliation: none
Location: small city
Undergraduate enrollment: NA
Total enrollment: 1,380
Percent Male / Female: NA
Percent Minority: 0%
Percent African-American: NA

Percent Asian: NA
Percent Hispanic: NA
Percent Native-American: NA
Percent in-state / out-of-state: 47% / 53%
Percent Pub HS: NA
Number of Applicants: 2,151
Percent Accepted: 50%
Percent Accepted who enroll: 34%
Entering: 368
Transfers: 21
Application Deadline: 1 Feb
Mean SAT: 656 V, 644 M
Mean ACT: NA

Middle 50% SAT range: 610–720 V, 600–700 M
Middle 50% ACT range: 27–30
3 Most popular majors: biology, English, politics
Retention: 91%
Graduation rate: 80%
On-campus housing: 99%
Fraternities: 41%
Sororities: 33%
Library: 282,540 volumes
Tuition and Fees: $21,742 in; $21,742 out
Room and Board: $6,090
Financial aid, first-year: 86%

Ever feel like exploring your natural side? If so, Whitman is the place for you. Whitties are known for their love of hiking, biking, skiing, backpacking, and camping. With the tranquil eastern Washington landscape, who could resist! However, all is not lost if you don't value your hiking boots over your life; there are plenty of on-campus organizations and, due to the laid-back nature of Whitman students, you can join or form any club you can dream up.

The Core of Academics

Besides their love of outdoors, Whitties also take their academics seriously. Currently there are seven distributional groups, including fine arts, history, language and rhetoric, physical sciences, descriptive sciences, philosophy and religion, and social sciences. However, beginning with the class of 2006, there will only be four distributional groups. Currently students must complete study in six of the seven groups by the end of junior year, but these policies will be changing over the next two years. Amid all this change there is *one* constant, and that is the dreaded "Core." The Core is a yearlong class taken by all incoming freshmen and is officially titled "Antiquity and Modernity." This is

quite possibly "the worst part of Whitman." Almost all students would agree that the "Core SUCKS!" However, one student did comment that "you take it, and hopefully you're smarter for it, and all freshmen take it, so it's a bonding experience, because you all get to complain together."

Once they get the Core out of the way and need to pick a major, students are much happier. Most of the major areas of study have similar levels of difficulty. Because class size is small, students are always accountable to their professor and cannot get away with doing none of the reading. However, for those desiring to push themselves to the academic limit, astrophysics is said to be the hardest major possible. Ultimately, students pick what they like so they have fun studying. And of course they leave time for other things, such as lounging around Ankeny Field.

Home, Sweet Home

Whitman is a small school situated around Ankeny Field. In fall and spring, many students can be seen playing intramural sports such as soccer, touch football, or rugby on the field. Ankeny is also a good place to meet friends or study in the sun. Surrounding Ankeny are all the main buildings on campus. Most of the campus architecture has an eclectic flavor to it. While some of the older administration buildings and residences have a colonial feel to them, most of the academic buildings are much more modern in style.

> **"The frats are way more chill than at state schools."**

As for living on campus, there is a never-ending list of possibilities. All freshmen and sophomores live on campus and have required meal plans. Most freshmen live in Lyman and Jewitt Halls, which are the two biggest dorms, in the center of campus next to Ankeny Field. Sophomores move into much smaller residence halls that hold fewer than 80 students and no more than 9 students in the case of language houses. There is one dorm, Prentiss Hall, that is all-female and houses the school's five sororities. All the other housing is coed. Most people live in suites; however, some upperclassmen live in apartment-style housing at the edge of campus if they do not want to move off campus. A large number of students move off after two years. Besides dorms, there are many special-interest houses: anything from the Global Awareness House, to the Writing House, to the Asian Studies House, and many more. According to students, the food they get is good but repetitive. One perk about living in the language houses is that they are reputed to have the best food on campus. Also, there are four fraternities associated with Whitman—known to the students as the Tkes, Phis, Betas, and Sigs—that serve as the center of campus social life. They host most of the campus parties, both with and without alcohol.

Chillin' Out

Partying at Whitman is what you make of it. Most students drink, but for those who do not, there is "not too much pressure because there are people at parties all the time who don't drink and there are things where drinking isn't a big part of it." There are many campus-wide school-sponsored parties that are alcohol-free, but many people "pre-funk" (drink before they go to the party) with their friends. On most weekends, the place to go is the frats. According to one student, "The frats are way more chill than at state schools and there's always something going on. It's never hard to find out what parties are going on." Also, one of the most widely talked-about annual events is the Beer Mile. The school sponsors this event, in which students drink lots of beer and run around the town of Walla Walla. As for getting busted by the cops, one student reports, "We can do whatever we want; they just don't look." Outside of partying, the social world is much more limited. Students report dating to be "non-existent" because "if you have a bad breakup, it makes it difficult not to see the person, because the student body is so small."

Whitties

Because Whitties are small in number, with fewer than 1,500 undergraduates, Whitman is not known for its diversity. Sometimes referred to by its students as "Whiteman," Whitman is almost entirely an "Abercrombie and Fitch–wearing bunch of outdoorsy kids." However, that is changing slowly as Whitman seeks to admit a diverse class and emphasize multiculturalism through special-interest housing. One such house is MECCA House (a multiethnic house), which seeks to create a community for minority and international students at Whitman. Also, as one student points out, "There is a lot of diversity within the white." People at Whitman come from all different parts of the country and the world at large and have had many unique experiences that make them all unique, interesting people.

Athletics for All

Although it is a small school and has no football team or cheerleaders and school spirit does not revolve around going out to "the Big Game," Whitman boasts a highly competitive ski team and a huge array of intramural athletic programs. The most popular intramurals are basketball and touch football. Unlike large state schools where all athletes are recruited and the jocks are set apart from the rest of the school, there is a place for everyone in Whitman athletics. According to one student, the "ulty" team (Ultimate Frisbee team) "is a bunch of hippies." Also, there is always the option of going hiking or backpacking in the surrounding Washington forests.

Get On Your Hiking Boots

Extracurriculars at Whitman fit all its stereotypes. There are a plethora of outdoor activities clubs that focus on hiking, skiing, biking, and camping. Also, with such a laid-back student body, Whitman students are always up for trying something weird and new that sounds even re-motely enticing. There is a club for everything on campus! There is even "the SPAM Alliance." As you might have guessed, if there isn't already a club for what you want, you are encouraged to start your own. Cheeze Whiz club, anyone?

Overall, even with the dreaded freshman Core, Whitman is a place that those who attend love. As one student so eloquently put it, "If Whitman is for you, it's the best place in the world. If it's not for you, you probably wouldn't have applied in the first place!"—*Sophie Jones*

FYI

The three best things about attending Whitman are "the relaxed campus atmosphere, the awesome people, and the professors that know you on a first-name basis."

The three worst things about attending Whitman are "the distance from a city, the small number of students, the Core SUCKS!"

The three things that every student should do before graduating from Whitman are "streak Ankeny Field (at the center of campus), run the Beer Mile (clothed or naked), and watch a sunset in the wheat fields."

One thing I'd like to have known before coming here is that "Whitman is basically a White-man's campus."

West Virginia

Marshall University

Address: 400 Hall Greer Boulevard; Huntington, WV 25755
Phone: 800-642-3499
E-mail address: admissions@marshall.edu
Web site URL: www.marshall.edu
Founded: 1837
Private or Public: public
Religious affiliation: none
Location: suburban
Undergraduate enrollment: NA
Total enrollment: NA
Percent Male/Female: NA
Percent Minority: 0%
Percent African-American: NA

Percent Asian: NA
Percent Hispanic: NA
Percent Native-American: NA
Percent in-state/out-of-state: 85%/15%
Percent Pub HS: NA
Number of Applicants: 2,278
Percent Accepted: 98%
Percent Accepted who enroll: 82%
Entering: 1,847
Transfers: NA
Application Deadline: NA
Mean SAT: NA
Mean ACT: 21
Middle 50% SAT range: NA

Middle 50% ACT range: 18–24
3 Most popular majors: elementary education, biological science, secondary education
Retention: 72%
Graduation rate: NA
On-campus housing: NA
Fraternities: 6%
Sororities: 3%
Library: NA
Tuition and Fees: $2,886 in; $6,958 out
Room and Board: $4,652
Financial aid, first-year: 42%

Green and white or blue and gold? Almost a century and a half after West Virginia split off from its eastern neighbor to fight with the north, an affiliation with either of WV's large state universities can still pit brother against brother. For over 12,000 undergraduates, the choice is clear. Marshall University, located in the heart of downtown Huntington, West Virginia, is sometimes eclipsed by the more renowned WVU, West Virginia's other large state school. Yet, Marshall's rich traditions in service, academic excellence, and student involvement, easily allows it to stand proudly as a solid university with a wealth of offerings.

Seen and Herd
In recent years, Marshall has gained increased national exposure due to the overwhelming success of its football team, *The Thundering Herd*. This addi-

tional attention garnered by Marshall through the success of its athletic alums (recent NFL Rookie of the Year Randy Moss), has upped the influx of out of state applicants, an area in which the university is noticeably lacking. School spirit runs markedly high in Huntington, and students take pride in supporting their team, which boasts several consecutive undefeated seasons and multiple victories in the Mid-Atlantic Conference title game. However, as one undergrad jokingly notes, "the football games stop being fun after a while. We always win." Game-day is always eventful in Huntington, and fans from around the state crowd through "Tent City" on their way to the big game. Yet, despite the success of Marshall athletic teams, the university is likely better known for the tragedy that formerly surrounded its program. The away game plane crash in which all of the football players and coaches on board were killed is still associated with the school's name and reminders linger on campus in the form of the Memorial Student Center and an outdoor fountain commemorating the tragedy.

Academics

Coincidentally, many of those doing the reporting on Marshall are grads themselves. Marshall's journalism program is reportedly one of its most difficult and well respected. While majors give high praise to the faculty and curriculum, many of them complain of the higher grading scale that is used in many of the journalism classes. Communications and business programs typically enroll large numbers of students and health sciences are rapidly gaining popularity. In general, Marshall academics get high marks and while, as one student notes, "there are plenty of ways to slide by," most students agree that those who are looking for a challenging program should have no trouble finding their niche at Marshall.

The prestigious Yeager Scholars Program, requiring a separate application, awards full room and board for four years, a personal computer, a stipend for textbooks, and a travel-aboard allowance for especially academically qualified students. Yeager Scholars also receive priority scheduling, special high-level seminar courses, and a special mentor to guide them through their academic career and senior projects. Marshall has been recognized nationally for both this and other full- and partial-tuition scholarships, and is consistently ranked as one of America's "Best College Buys."

For such a large university, students point out Marshall's unusually small class sizes and the genuine enthusiasm of their professors. "It's great," one student gushes. "All my professors know my name!" "My math teacher is all about his office hours," another freshman remarked. "He comes to class angry if students didn't come and visit him the afternoon before." Students also report that its not unusual for one their fellow classmates to actually be *older* than the professor. Marshall's heavy emphasis on community education often brings in

adults looking to complete a degree or earn additional credit. Marshall provides students with multiple scheduling options, allowing them to register for courses in person, over the telephone, or on the internet, although, regardless of the method, students still find registration "a giant pain in the rear."

Centralized Campus

Even if students happen to get stuck in an early morning section, however, getting to class is rarely a problem. Marshall's centralized, flat campus allows one student to "roll out of bed at 7:55 and still make it to my 8:00 class." Marshall's notorious housing shortage has made headlines in recent years when the university was forced to put up students at a local Holiday Inn while they sorted out rooming troubles. Students continue to marvel at the absurdity of a rule that requires students to live on campus for their first two years when dorms are already overcrowded. Yet, on the whole, undergrads are very satisfied with their living arrangements. Most students live in the university's massive air-conditioned Towers dorms, but its smaller rooms cause others to opt for the more spacious Buskirk and Hodges dorms. With the exception of Holderby Hall, all Marshall dorms are single sex, and each reportedly has its tradeoffs (the Hodges males notoriously complain about their group showers). All dorms are required to observe "quiet hours" beginning at 9 P.M. on weeknights and midnight on weekends and students must sign-in all guests. While students complain about rules that restrict opposite-sex visitors to 11 P.M., Marshall's dorms are lauded as being very safe and are a social center for many of its students. Indeed, the campus as a whole is thought to be very secure, and many undergrads note the heavy presence of both the University Police and city officers on bike patrol.

Social Scene

When students want to get out of the dorm the surrounding area provides a lively nightlife, with Huntington's many bars pulling in the largest following, most of which line central 4th Street. Student favorites such as The Drink, The Union, and The Wild Dog attract large crowds nightly and are reportedly fairly lax about carding. However, students note that, even with the wide variety of options, most bars take on distinct personalities and students tend to frequent their one specific venue. Fraternities and sororities also play a large role in the Marshall social scene, although students feel there is a much higher pressure for males to rush than females. For non-drinkers, the Memorial Student Center holds popular evening events and their Thursday open-mike nights typically draw several undergrads. While students don't see having a car to be a necessity, many recommend some sort of transportation to get to a "real" restaurant or to the Huntington Mall and movie theaters, which are actually in nearby Barboursville. Many of Marshall's students tend to be from nearby in-state locations, causing the campus to "almost completely clear out" on the weekends, often an annoyance for many out-of-state undergrads.

> "Everyone here is so friendly. I have my home family, and then I have my Marshall family."

Indeed, while most of Marshall's students tend to hail from West Virginia, out-of-state students typically don't report having trouble adjusting. However, several students do see the Marshall community as racially lopsided, with Marshall having a relatively low minority population. Students note that the undergraduate population tends to self-segregate, and the university is currently attempting to implement programs which add to campus diversity and cultural awareness. Yet, students find Marshall easy to adapt to, and praise the overall friendliness of the student body. "Everyone here is so friendly," one sophomore remarks. "I have my home family, and then I have my Marshall family."

The lively undergraduate dating scene also keeps undergrads social. While students admit that "random hook-ups abound," casual and serious relationships are generally easy to come by. Whether it's an evening at a concert at the Huntington Civic Arena, only blocks from campus, or a quick lunch date at the Calamity Café, Marshall students have plenty of options for their get-togethers.

Marshall's students tend to be very involved in a wide range of extra-curriculars, with intramural sports, The Christian Center, and *The Parthenon*, the daily student newspaper, drawing several participants. Most undergrads also hold some type of part-time employment and several students participate in community outreach programs. Students remark on the usually high level of town/gown cooperation, and see the city of Huntington as taking an active interest in the life of the university and vice-versa.

Futuristic Facilities

With a new science building and classrooms that are frequently renovated, Marshall's facilities have received lots of positive attention. One student favorite is Drinko Library, a four-floor state-of-the-art facility which provides students with several meeting rooms and quiet study clusters which can be accessed with an ID Keycard. Drinko is also home to several classrooms with "a laptop for every student," and its 1st floor is open to the Marshall community 24 hours a day.

Students can eat in one of Marshall's three large dining halls, and most rate the food as at least "average." However, those who would rather dine elsewhere can head to the Student center where a Chick-Fill-A, a Pizza Hut, and a student snack shop provides additional offerings to the typical student meal plan.

As Marshall continues to pick up national momentum, its role in the collegiate world will undoubtedly increase. Students, community leaders, and the administration are cooperatively working on their "Vision 2020" plan, a course of action for the university that continues to broaden its scope and includes the construction of several new state-of-the-art facilities. For now, however, Marshall manages to remain one of the nation's best kept secrets as a low-cost, challenging, enthusiastic university.—*Conor Knighton*

FYI

The three best things about attending Marshall are "the safe and well laid out campus, caring professors, and the 4th Street Bars."

The three worst things about attending Marshall are "overly strict dorm regulations, a self-segregating student body, and the mass exodus that occurs on the weekends."

The three things that every student should do before graduating from Marshall are "get involved, party the whole weekend of the MAC Championship, and go to at least one football and basketball game."

One thing I'd like to have known before coming here is "do all the things that sound cheesy—'Welcome Weekend' might sound dumb at first, but you'll wish you'd gone when you see how many friends your roommate made."

West Virginia University

Address: PO Box 6009; Morgantown, WV 26506-6009

Phone: 304-293-2121

E-mail address: WVUAdmissions @arc.wvu.edu

Web site URL: www.wvu.edu

Founded: 1867

Private or Public: public

Religious affiliation: none

Location: suburban

Undergraduate enrollment: NA

Total enrollment: 23,000

Percent Male/Female: NA

Percent Minority: 0%

Percent African-American: NA

Percent Asian: NA

Percent Hispanic: NA

Percent Native-American: NA

Percent in-state/out-of-state: 60%/40%

Percent Pub HS: NA

Number of Applicants: 8,124

Percent Accepted: 94%

Percent Accepted who enroll: 47%

Entering: 3,567

Transfers: 1,000

Application Deadline: 1 Mar

Mean SAT: 516 V, 515 M

Mean ACT: 22

Middle 50% SAT range: 460–560 V, 460–560 M

Middle 50% ACT range: 19–25

3 Most popular majors: business administration and management, journalism, psychology

Retention: 68%

Graduation rate: 56%

On-campus housing: 95%

Fraternities: 16%

Sororities: 19%

Library: 1,500,000 volumes

Tuition and Fees: $2,748 in; $8,100 out

Room and Board: $4,990

Financial aid, first-year: 51%

"Almost heaven, West Virginia . . ." For over 22,000 proud Mountaineers, the words of John Denver's 1971 song still ring loudly today. Situated in the picturesque hills of Morgantown, West Virginia University boasts one of the most enthusiastic student bodies in the nation. As one student put it, "you'll never find a group of people with more school spirit than you will at WVU."

Two-Pronged Pride

Much of WVU's school spirit centers on its athletic teams. In fact, many students cite seasonal trips to Mountaineer Field as a key aspect of their college life. When not cheering on one of WVU's 20 Division I squads, students participate in a wide variety of intramural sports. As one partici-

pant explained, "you don't have to be athletic at all—everyone just comes out to have a good time. Intramurals are a great way to meet fellow Mounties."

WVU's football team draws national attention each year and often vies for one of the top slots in the Big East athletic conference. One student described the opening kick-off of the first game of the season as "the best ten seconds of the semester." The state legislature has recently mandated that the Mounties play Marshall University, WVU's state rival to the south. While football carries the largest fan base by far, sports like basketball, baseball, and gymnastics receive a smaller but equally devout following.

West Virginians take pride in their academics as well. Mountaineers are quick to point to their unusually high numbers of Rhodes scholars (sixth among public universities) and to the long-term success of graduates. The much-touted University Honors Program helps high achievers get the most out of their college experience. In addition to receiving priority housing and scheduling, honors students may take exclusive "honors only" seminars taught in small groups by the university's top faculty. To be accepted into the program, students must meet specific grade and test score requirements, although those who demonstrate success once in college can also earn their way into the program.

> One student noted that Mountaineers are "far less likely to gain the infamous freshman fifteen" than their counterparts across the nation.

WVU professors are described as "very clear and precise about what they want." When confusion does arise, "professors seem to go out of their way to be helpful," noted one student. However, some undergrads complain about foreign teachers being difficult to understand. "If you're going to take a math class, be sure to bring a translator," warned one undergrad. Introductory courses have been known to enroll over 500 people, but students say that the average class size is less than 30, allowing for individual interaction between student and professor.

Unfortunately, getting into classes isn't always easy. Students gripe about the university's STAR system, a telephone course registration service and the source of endless busy signals and headaches. Often, students will sacrifice precious sleeping time in order to break through before peak calling hours and schedule the classes they want. "It's much better to wake up at 6 A.M. on the first day of scheduling than to be stuck waking up at 8:30 A.M. every day of the semester," explained one student.

In 1997, WVU entered into a partnership with the F.B.I. to create the world's first biometrics program, training students in the digital verification of identity by observation of biological patterns such as fingerprint swirls or eye blood vessel webs. Students in this highly competitive major work with state-of-the-art technology and regularly hone their skills by sorting through mock crime scenes. Many others turn to the popular business, economics, and health sciences programs that are said to attract thousands of Mountaineers each year. With over 130 possible majors, students praise the wide course variety at WVU.

Campus Living

All freshmen are required to live on campus, with the majority living in one of two mammoth, air-conditioned dorms known as the Towers. Many freshmen apply to live in Boreman South, hoping to take advantage of the dorm's unique "suite-style" living areas. Honors students are assigned to Dadisman Hall, and females can elect to live in Boreman North, WVU's only single-sex dorm.

Unique among state universities is WVU's new Operation Jump Start program. The program matches an incoming freshman with one of WVU's nine residential "houses" ("a fancy way of saying 'dorm,'" explained one student), each functioning as a small community within the larger university. Students are placed near others with similar academic and extracurricular interests, and they frequently interact with faculty member advisors who live in on-campus houses near the dorms. Operation Jump Start also helps to coordinate Fall Fest, a giant celebration at the beginning of the first semester, featuring top musical acts as Busta Ryhmes, Puff Daddy, the Verve Pipe, and the Goo Goo Dolls.

After freshman year, some students choose to live off-campus in a fraternity or sorority house, or one of Morgantown's many student apartment complexes. Of those who remain, most choose to live in Stalnaker Hall, widely regarded as the best dorm on campus.

Dining halls are generally given low marks, but Morgantown provides a wide variety of local restaurants within walking distance. Student favorites include the Boston Beanery, Pargo's, and the Mountainlair—a centrally located student union home to several fast-food chain restaurants as well as a bowling alley, a movie theater, and a game room.

One student noted that Mountaineers are "far less likely to gain the infamous freshman fifteen" than their counterparts across the nation. A general source of complaints, WVU's mountainous terrain can make for a tiring hike to class. Divided into two separate campuses—the main campus is downtown and the other is in nearby Evansdale—getting to class can often be a problem. Recently ranked as one of the best "people movers" in the nation, the PRT is an above-ground train that connects the two locations, running regular shuttles to several campus locations. Each fall during Mountaineer Week, various student organizations participate in a competition to cram as many people as possible into one of the small cars (the current record is 98). While students complain of the PRT's occasional breakdowns, one student joked that "it gives us a great excuse to miss class."

WVU's extensive campus is currently under heavy renovation, and while some complain of the rampant construction, one freshman noted that "good things come to those who wait." When all is said and done, WVU will be home to a state-of-the-art 200,000-square-foot Student Recreation Center, a brand-new biology building, and an addition to the central library facility.

Social Center

With a large Greek system exerting a heavy influence over social life, weekends at WVU generally revolves around fraternity and sorority parties. Pre-game football tailgates also attract thousands of students in the fall. Unable to shake its party school reputation, Morgantown is well known for its many bars and dance clubs. Student favorites include Phantoms, Shooters, Dr. Longshot's, and the Brass Alley. For non-drinkers, one student

quipped that "all three of us" still feel accepted and rarely have a problem finding alternate activities. WVU's new *Up All Night* program provides students with school-sponsored, alcohol-free activities every weekend night and generally receives high marks from the student body. Games such as Virtual Reality Soccer, Astro Bowling, and Make Your Own Music Video—coupled with "an insane amount of free food"—make *Up All Night* a popular stop on a typical weekend night.

Students are quick to point out that the best part of WVU is "its people" which are described as "incredibly friendly, outgoing, and always willing to lend a helping hand." WVU students participate in a wide range of extra-curriculars, with popular activities such as the Residence Hall Association, the drama club, and the student-written Daily Athenian enlisting several Mountaineers. However, many complain that the student body is too homogeneous; one student remembers being initially surprised by how few minority students there were at such a large university.

Getting Your Money's Worth

For the last several years, WVU has consistently remained a bargain in a field of increasingly expensive state schools. Many students remarked that while they could have gone to a more costly university, the money that they save now can be applied to the hefty price tag of graduate school down the line. Most importantly, Mountaineers seem happy about their choice. "I love it here," gushed one student. "I immediately felt like I was part of a family." A family that is proud to claim top-notch athletes, dedicated scholars and equally dedicated socialites among its members, WVU offers a well-rounded college experience for those who are willing to bleed blue and gold.—*Conor Knighton*

FYI

The three best things about attending WVU are "the atmosphere in general (especially on football game days), the desire of the faculty to help the students succeed, and the friendly student body."

The three worst things about attending WVU are "the hills, the lack of diversity, overly large intro classes."

The three things that every student should do before graduating from WVU are "live in the dorm at least once; Attend Fall/Spring Fest; take a "fun" course, e.g., photography, tennis, or fishing."

One thing I'd like to have known before coming here is "don't restrict yourself to a major your freshman year."

Wisconsin

Beloit College

Address: 700 College Avenue; Beloit, WI 53511
Phone: 608-363-2500
E-mail address: admiss@beloit.edu
Web site URL: www.beloit.edu
Founded: 1846
Private or Public: private
Religious affiliation: none
Location: urban
Undergraduate enrollment: NA
Total enrollment: NA
Percent Male/Female: NA
Percent Minority: 0%
Percent African-American: NA
Percent Asian: NA

Percent Hispanic: NA
Percent Native-American: NA
Percent in-state/out-of-state: 21%/79%
Percent Pub HS: NA
Number of Applicants: 1,472
Percent Accepted: 70%
Percent Accepted who enroll: 30%
Entering: 308
Transfers: 60
Application Deadline: 15 Jan
Mean SAT: 640 V, 600 M
Mean ACT: 27

Middle 50% SAT range: 590–690 V, 550–650 M
Middle 50% ACT range: 24–29
3 Most popular majors: anthropology, biology, English
Retention: 93%
Graduation rate: 69%
On-campus housing: NA
Fraternities: 15%
Sororities: 5%
Library: NA
Tuition and Fees: $21,550 in; $21,550 out
Room and Board: $4,882
Financial aid, first-year: 63%

Upon entering Beloit College, most students "realize that they have the opportunity to be treated as adults, and that their opinions really do matter," one undergrad explained. This understanding creates a "productive" atmosphere filled with a "go get 'em" attitude, as well as fostering a strong sense of responsibility. As a result, many Beloit students get involved with all sorts of school activities while keeping up with their academic work.

Challenging You to Think

Students describe the Beloit curriculum as "challenging." The strongest and most popular departments are anthropology and geology, although, as one student said, "no departments are bad here, some are just understaffed." General academic requirements include two courses in each of three divisions (natural sciences, social sciences, and humanities), which students must complete within their first two years. Upperclassmen currently take classes toward either a double major or a major and a minor, although an overhaul of the curriculum has been discussed and the requirements may change in the coming years. Class size is small: introductory classes reportedly enroll 20 to 30 students, and upper-level classes are often even smaller.

Student-faculty interaction is said to be strong and personal; one student said most professors are on a first-name basis with undergrads. Another said the faculty is "really open and willing to help with problems both during class and outside of class." Many opportunities are available for one-on-one research projects with professors, and student contact with the Beloit faculty does not end when class ends: professors often support their students by attending various school activities. One student exclaimed, "Beloit is the only place you can play poker with your professors and borrow their cars!" TAs do not teach classes, but some lead lab sessions in the natural sciences courses.

Beloit has a local chapter of the Phi Beta Kappa honor society, and students can participate in off-campus study in the U.S. and abroad. They also can choose from an urban studies program in Chicago, a political science program in Washington, D.C., or study-abroad destinations such as Indonesia, Zimbabwe, Brazil, Ecuador, Germany, France, and Japan.

Campus Architecture and Life
When they are on campus, Beloit students enjoy the architecture of their surroundings, which ranges from late-nineteenth to various twentieth-century styles. (The newest building at Beloit was constructed in 1964.) Many facilities, including the Logan Museum of Anthropology and five dorms, have undergone recent renovations. The Morse Library was modernized recently, but one student reported that it is still "not so hot." The library's resources are limited. "They are just becoming outdated and there are many periodicals which are absent and should be there," one undergrad complained. Beloit is a member of the Wisconsin Interlibrary Loan System, however, which allows students to obtain resources from any library in the state. Many undergrads do their research at the nearby University of Wisconsin at Madison.

All students must live on campus for six semesters, and most stay through their senior year. One reason for this is the scarcity of off-campus housing, and, as one student put it, "The townies don't like us." Dorms at Beloit house students from all classes together. The best dorms are reportedly the "'64 halls," which include Peet, Bushnell, Blaisdell, Whitney, and Porter. All of these dorms were recently renovated and feature carpeting and air-conditioning; they also have many singles. Most students agree that if you want a single as a frosh, these are the dorms in which to find them. Haven and Wood are among the most coveted dorms, while Aldrich is supposedly the worst place to end up because, as one student reported, "it is noisy and there are too many frosh." Maurer is the only all-female dorm at Beloit; all others are either coed by room (such as Peet, Bushnell, and Blaisdell) or

by floor (such as Haven and Wood). Other housing options include three fraternity houses and two sorority houses, language houses for French, Spanish, Russian, and German speakers, the art co-op, the Outdoor Environmental house (OEC), and the Black Students United house (BSU).

> **"Beloit is the only place you can play poker with your professors and borrow their cars!"**

Students praise Beloit's athletic facility, the Flood Arena. One basketball player described it as the "best facility in our conference." The football and basketball teams have had good records in recent years and draw the most student support. Most athletes agree that even if the entire student body does not show up at the games, "athletes in general support their athletic friends." Intramural sports are not as popular as they once were, but two new coaches were recently hired for the women's basketball and track teams.

What's Cooking?
All first-year students must purchase a plan of 20 meals per week. After freshman year, undergrads can choose either 14 or 10 meals per week. Most eat their evening meals at the Commons, a central cafeteria on the north side of campus, where almost all of the residential buildings are located. On the south side of campus, which consists mainly of academic buildings, a snack bar in the student union called D.K.'s serves fast food; students can also use their meal cards there. Popular off-campus restaurants include Domenico's (an Italian restaurant), State Street Cafe, and the local International House of Pancakes.

Town-Gown Troubles
Relations between students and residents of Beloit are reportedly poor, and most undergrads stay on campus. As one student put it, "We live in a two-block-by-two-block bubble." The Java Joint cafe is a popular spot for social study and for pure socializing. The Coughy Haus, known as C Haus to regulars, is a popular campus bar. Organizations such as BSU

and the Alliance for Gay and Bisexual Students and Straight Supporters often rent the C Haus for a night to host large dance parties. Fraternities and sororities throw parties almost every weekend, and students also hang out on the quad, known as the Wall. Those looking for a mellow night out can catch a movie sponsored by the film club every Wednesday, Friday, and Sunday night. Students for a Better Education (SABE) funds other social activities. Annual Beloit parties include the Art Co-op's Deb Ball, a funky dance where women dress as men and vice versa; Folk and Blues, a two-day festival in September where bands play until midnight; and Spring Day, a Greek-sponsored festival of food and music to raise money for local charities. When students do venture off campus, they often go to Goodies, a bar (and Beloit College tradition) that recently changed locations, or Phazes, a new bar downtown. To promote responsibility, the administration encourages students to avoid dangerous situations connected to alcohol, drugs, and sex. Sex education material is readily available, especially from the resident advisors, who sell condoms and talk about sexually transmitted diseases.

Extracurricular activities play a big part in campus life. *The Roundtable*, a weekly newspaper, is the main publication on campus. Many students are djs on the campus radio station, WBCR. Syzygy is a popular Beloit poetry-reading group. Other campus groups include: the Cult Movie Club; ECHO, which promotes the legalization of marijuana; the International Club; the Rock Climbing Club; and the SCUBA Club.

Unfortunately, the surrounding community has its share of crime. Beloit has responded to this problem by maintaining an extensive and effective security system. Students report that the campus is always well lit, and security officers are on duty 24 hours a day. Students agree that the officers are very friendly. As one student said, "They want to get to know students better, so they try to reach out because it makes their job much easier." Just as professors and students are on a first-name basis, so are the security officers and students. "It's not just, 'There goes a security officer,' it's, 'Oh, there goes Bob.'" This close relationship makes students feel safe on campus.

Most Beloit students are from Wisconsin or Illinois, but several are international students. Undergrads insist that there is no real student stereotype at Beloit; everyone is an individual. Liberalism is the main political view, though one student noted that "there are a lot of closet conservatives." Students come from a variety of backgrounds, and find many opportunities to learn from each other.

Beloit makes students work for everything, and as one senior said, "They have not taught me to think for myself—they have *pushed* me to think for myself." When students take the initiative to do something, the administration is extremely supportive. According to one student, "They say, 'You can do it!'" Another student added, "The school opens your eyes to things that you never dreamt of—different people, different ideas, and different ways of life."—*Lisa Smith and Staff*

FYI

The three best things about attending Beloit are "the push to think for yourself, the tight Beloit community, and the swingin' social scene."

The three worst things about attending Beloit are "town-gown relations, largely Wisconsin/Illinois-based student body, and crappy library resources."

The three things that every student should do before graduating from Beloit are "join the SCUBA club, hang out at Folk and Blues, and buy a round of drinks at Coughy Haus."

One thing I'd like to have known before coming here is "how crummy our relations are with the town."

Lawrence University

Address: PO Box 599;
Appleton, WI 54912
Phone: 920-832-6500
E-mail address:
excel@lawrence.edu
Web site URL:
www.lawrence.edu
Founded: 1847
Private or Public: private
Religious affiliation:
none
Location: small city
**Undergraduate
enrollment:** NA
Total enrollment: NA
Percent Male / Female: NA
Percent Minority: 0%
Percent African-American:
NA

Percent Asian: NA
Percent Hispanic: NA
Percent Native-American:
NA
**Percent in-state / out-of-
state:** 45%/55%
Percent Pub HS: NA
Number of Applicants:
1,307
Percent Accepted:
84%
**Percent Accepted who
enroll:** 30%
Entering: 327
Transfers: 51
Application Deadline:
15 Jan
Mean SAT: NA
Mean ACT: NA

Middle 50% SAT range:
590–690 V,
580–690 M
Middle 50% ACT range:
25–30
3 Most popular majors:
biology, psychology, art
and music
Retention: 81%
Graduation rate: 65%
On-campus housing: 100%
Fraternities: 35%
Sororities: 25%
Library: 370,000 volumes
Tuition and Fees:
$21,849 in; $21,849 out
Room and Board: $4,791
Financial aid, first-year:
68%

L awrence University, located in Appleton, Wisconsin, has been coeducational since its founding in 1847, making it the second-oldest coed university in the nation. While other schools have followed Lawrence's lead, Lawrence remains one of the leaders in coeducation. It has evolved to offer students diverse academic possibilities within the confines of a close-knit social environment.

Small Classes

The small student body strongly affects Lawrence academics. Introductory science lectures, for example, usually enroll no more than 60 students, and students cite close relationships with professors as one of the best parts of the Lawrence experience. "You spend a lot of time with your professors here," said one sophomore. "They expect a lot of you." The close student-faculty relations also provide the opportunity for students to do independent work with faculty members. Despite the small classes, few students experience any major problems enrolling in the classes that they want.

Lawrence operates on a quarter system, with students normally enrolling in three classes per term. Among the 36 courses re-

quired for graduation, students must take both introductory and upper-level classes in four distribution groups and fulfill a language requirement. All freshmen must take a two-quarter Freshman Studies, or "Great Books," course, typically containing 14 to 19 students. Undergrads consider the course "the core of [their] common experience at Lawrence." A wide range of departments receive praise from undergrads. One said the sciences are "really incredible" at Lawrence, due to the excellent instructors. "For a school of this size, the science professors are really quite good," one chemistry major said, adding, "we have really state-of-the-art science equipment." Other students praise the English, art, and philosophy departments. Lawrence undergrads refuse to describe their school as intense or stress-filled despite the rigorous academic offerings. "Students work hard, and professors expect a lot of their students, but it's definitely not cutthroat," said one senior. Another student described the academic atmosphere as "really cooperative."

In addition to a strong liberal arts and sciences program, the university has one of the top music conservatories in the country. Although the "connie" students only take about one-third of their classes in the college, they participate in Lawrence life in most other ways. Each year about 15 to 20 students take part in a five-year double degree program, which grants both a bachelor of music and a bachelor of arts degree. Lawrence also offers a BA in music, which allows students in the regular liberal arts college to take advantage of the conservatory programs. Students see the conservatory as a "very central and defining part of the university," and even non-musicians feel its presence.

When the atmosphere of Lawrence begins to feel too confining, students often choose to enroll in one of the "excellent" off-campus study programs. Although the university sponsors 25 programs, students can travel nearly anywhere in the world through the Associated Colleges of the Midwest program. Popular Lawrence programs include the London Study Center and the Wilderness Field Program in northern Minnesota. For those who opt to stay on campus, the library, with a small but adequate collection, is a popular place to study, and the Media Center has an excellent collection of music and movies.

Centralized Social Life

Students describe the surrounding community of Appleton, a middle-sized town in Wisconsin, as very safe. The self-contained nature of the campus led one student to remark, "I've never been afraid to walk on campus, at any time of night." However, the praise for Appleton only goes so far; one sophomore said, "The town is culturally dead, as far as I'm concerned." Another undergrad agreed that "downtown doesn't really cater to college students." On the other hand, some restaurants, bookstores, and coffeehouses have opened over the past few years on the main street, giving students an alternative to campus hangouts. Many students, for example, travel to Peggy's Coffeeshop or Zacateca's, a popular Mexican restaurant, for good food and company.

Because of the conservatory, "there're nearly always recitals and guest artists" on campus, one student said, and internationally famous classical and jazz artists often perform at the school. Many people hang out at the union, which includes the Grill, a coffeehouse, and the Viking Room bar. The Grill attracts students in search

of late-night greasy food, and the new student-run coffeehouse sponsors live music nearly every weekend. Only students 21 and older can visit the Viking Room.

Although some students warn that those in search of a big party school "should not come to Lawrence," the five fraternity houses on campus often organize big parties. The Lawrence drinking policy prohibits "all kegs and keg substitutes." Even so, interested students can still reportedly find "a lot of beer" at an average weekend party. One freshman said, "If you don't want to go to frat parties, you have to create your own fun," but a senior felt that the sense of community at Lawrence makes finding a good time easy: "Sometimes it doesn't even matter what you're doing, it's just that you're doing it with friends."

> **Students see the conservatory as a "very central and defining part of the university," and even non-musicians feel its presence.**

All undergrads are required to live on campus, which contributes to a "centralization" of social life. One student called the housing situation merely "tolerable." Ormsby Hall, with hardwood floors and a central location, and the substance-free Kohler both rank high with students. Upperclassmen often choose Sage Hall, which has suites, quads, and singles. Despite a slight housing crunch in recent years—some study lounges have been converted into student rooms—Lawrence still guarantees housing for all. Other popular living options include the co-op house (where students prepare their own food), the five frat houses, and the five theme houses. Each year, upper-class students organize and create proposals for the theme houses, whose residents must participate in service to Lawrence or the surrounding community. Theme houses in recent years have included a feminist house, a vegetarian house, an outdoor recreation house, and a house devoted to youth outreach through the arts.

Students describe the campus food as

"very predictable." "There's a lot of variety, but it can get old kind of fast," said one freshman. Regulations require that freshmen purchase a 19-meal plan, but all students (except those living in fraternity houses) must choose some form of meal plan. The main dining hall is Downer Commons, and according to Lawrence students, "the name says it all." Although the more popular facility in Colman Hall only opens for breakfast and lunch on weekdays and serves a limited menu, students appreciate the better food and table service.

Limited Diversity

About 40 percent of Lawrence students come from Wisconsin, which often creates a feeling of insularity on campus, according to several students. Although the admissions office actively recruits a large percentage of international students to campus, few describe the school as ethnically or racially diverse. "This is a very white campus," one student said. Another said that much of the student body consists of "upper-middle-class white kids." One sophomore felt, however, that the administration was making an effort to change things: "They really try to bring in a variety of people."

Because of the music conservatory, "Lawrence is very unusual in the amount of music opportunities for majors and non-majors." Music comprises a major portion of extracurricular activities on campus, with students participating in the symphony, concert band, and several student-organized recital groups. Lawrence International, the international students' organization, sponsors many activities, as does the Outdoor Recreation Club. Publications on campus include the biweekly *Lawrentian* and the conservative *Lawrence Review*, as well as *Tropos*, a yearly art and literary magazine. Aspiring actors often participate in one of three major productions put on at Lawrence each year. "If there isn't something here that you really want, you can start it," one sophomore said. However, some students criticize the sense of apathy on campus. "A lot of the time things don't get off the ground because students either aren't interested or don't have the time to be interested," one junior said.

Although Lawrence has a strong Division III athletic program, students agree that "the sports at this school are for the athletes and it's not a school-spirit thing." The Division III status means that "virtually anyone can participate in a sport if they're interested." Varsity teams practice at Alexander Gym, leaving the modern Buchanen-Kiewit Recreation Center open for intramural sports and general student use. "I wouldn't say the facilities are state-of-the-art, but they're better than average, especially for a school this size," said one student. Both the men's and women's swim teams have been highly ranked in their conferences recently, and the volleyball and hockey teams are also described as standout varsity sports.

In general, students describe Lawrence as a very good place to spend four years. "People say 'hi' all the time," one student said. "It's a very comfortable place." The academics offer students a challenging and stimulating undergraduate experience in a small-size setting. As one undergrad said, "A lot of the time, they expect the students to provide structure and focus for themselves." Students with enough initiative often find that at Lawrence they can do just that.—*Kathryn Eigen and Staff*

FYI

The three best things about attending Lawrence are "the music, the music, and the music."

The three worst things about attending Lawrence are "Appleton, the all-white faces, and the frat system."

The three things that every student should do before graduating from Lawrence are "hang out at Peggy's, pick an extracurricular you love, and sign up for an off-campus study program."

One thing I'd like to have known before coming here is "that you better like music because you will get an ear full."

Marquette University

Address: PO Box 1881; Milwaukee, WI 53201-1881

Phone: 414-288-7302

E-mail address: admissions@marquette.edu

Web site URL: www.marquette.edu

Founded: 1881

Private or Public: private

Religious affiliation: Roman Catholic

Location: urban

Undergraduate enrollment: NA

Total enrollment: 10,780

Percent Male/Female: NA

Percent Minority: 0%

Percent African-American: NA

Percent Asian: NA

Percent Hispanic: NA

Percent Native-American: NA

Percent in-state/out-of-state: 47%/53%

Percent Pub HS: 58%

Number of Applicants: 6,925

Percent Accepted: 84%

Percent Accepted who enroll: 30%

Entering: 1,723

Transfers: 168

Application Deadline: 1 Feb

Mean SAT: 576 V, 584 M

Mean ACT: 26

Middle 50% SAT range: 520–620 V, 520–640 M

Middle 50% ACT range: 23–28

3 Most popular majors: business, engineering, health sciences

Retention: 88%

Graduation rate: 72%

On-campus housing: 90%

Fraternities: 7%

Sororities: 7%

Library: 719,906 volumes

Tuition and Fees: $17,336 in; $17,336 out

Room and Board: $6,086

Financial aid, first-year: 84%

W hether you are interested in a traditional college atmosphere or an urban lifestyle, Marquette University offers both options. Marquette's strong religious foundation may seem incongruous with its urban setting and spirit, but students enjoy the opportunities it offers for both intellectual and social growth.

Marquette University was founded in 1881 as a Jesuit institution for a city with a large Roman Catholic population. It was named for a figure out of Wisconsin's history, Père Jacques Marquette, a 17th-century Jesuit explorer who charted much of what is now the Midwest. The school's status as a church-related institution reportedly does not dominate its character, but students say it has a presence in campus life. The administration and faculty consider an understanding of Christian thought an integral part of a Marquette education, and this is one of the only absolute requirements in an otherwise flexible core curriculum. Few students find this an infringement of their freedom, either academic or religious. One undergrad said she regarded her theology class as "more oriented toward the philosophy of religion than specifically Catholic thought." Courses in theology are required of all students in the nine undergraduate schools and two professional schools, with the exception of Dental Hygiene. Other distribution requirements vary among the colleges.

The Curriculum

Marquette's undergraduate colleges include nursing, engineering, arts and sciences, business administration, communication, journalism, the performing arts, medical technology, and a school of education. Though business is one of the most popular majors, students say engineering is the most competitive. One junior said that the international business program is "wonderful" and that it encourages students to go abroad during their junior year to supplement their study. Other departments generally earn praise from students, although one education student complained of "a weak teaching program" that did not offer a lot of class variety. Marquette has the only dental school in Wisconsin and the only four-year curriculum available in dental hygiene. In addition, Marquette is one of the few schools in the country to offer a six-year combined bachelor's and master's program in physical therapy.

According to students, Marquette matches solid academics with accessible professors. This has recently been reflected in a sizable increase in the admissions pool, with the class of 2003 being the first to have an admissions cap imposed. Class size, however, can be an obstacle in the introductory-level courses, which often enroll 200 or more. Students must take a number of these large introductory courses to fulfill their requirements. Students report that upper-level classes have an average enrollment of about 20 to 30.

Life Outside of Class

Volunteer activity is widespread on campus, although some students think that it is "not that a lot of people are involved, just that those who are involved are very serious about their work." With a large number of religious organizations acting as a campus social-service network, there is no lack of opportunity for the service-oriented. Campus groups with church affiliation include Knights of Columbus, Campus Ministry, Marquette University Community, and Campus Crusade for Christ. Popular volunteer projects include Midnight Run, which began at Marquette to distribute food to the homeless, and construction work for Habitat for Humanity. As one junior said, "There are a lot of social problems around us, like homelessness, poverty, etc.," due to Milwaukee's urban environment, so opportunities for community service abound.

Another strong campus network is the Greek system, which is an influential part of Marquette student life. The Christian educational ethic is not daunted by the escapades of the average college student at Marquette, and many students say they "party hard." Fraternities sponsor most of the popular campus parties, which can be, as one student put it, "exclusive." Weekly house parties also are common, but according to one student, are "attended only by freshmen and people from other area colleges." Fraternities also engage in such activities as the Booze Cruise, for which members take their kegs out to the lakefront and go boating, and the Pub Crawl, in which participants go from one bar to the next along a scheduled route and do a shot at each. Although many Marquette students say they do not drink despite Milwaukee's reputation as Beer City, one senior reported that some fraternity parties "take at least two weeks to clean up."

Fraternity parties owe some of their popularity to the strict regulations against drinking in the dorms, where freshmen are required to live. Security officers stationed at entrances of dorm parties can ask dorm residents and guests to submit to a bag search for alcohol. Beer often finds its way into the dorms anyway, however, and one student said it is not uncommon "to see a keg hidden away in a garbage can." Marquette students describe their campus as "friendly." "I met my best friends here my first day at Marquette, and I continually meet new ones, " said one undergrad.

A Compact Campus

Students describe Marquette's campus as "compact." The main part of the campus measures about eight blocks long and two blocks wide. Marquette has five residence halls. Tower and East halls are popular for their spaciousness, while McCormick draws less enthusiasm from undergrads, partly because it has a reputation for wild parties. Some say it also suffers from an excess of "architectural vision"—it is a modern, circular building with small rooms in the shape of pie slices. However, one student said that McCormick is a "cool place to live because it is the only coed freshman residence hall." Priests live in the dorms to serve as advisors and friends, and also to conduct weekly masses. Most of the dorms for upperclassmen are coed, but students say that "intervisitation," or going to the rooms of those of the opposite sex, is strictly regulated. On weekends, the administration allows 24-hour visitation, but on weeknights members of the opposite sex must be out of the room by 1 A.M.

> With a large number of religious organizations acting as a campus social-service network, there is no lack of opportunity for the service-oriented.

After the second year, the majority of undergrads move off campus. In past years, good off-campus housing has been expensive and difficult to find. Marquette addressed the problem by buying property near the campus and converting it into student apartment complexes, making the off-campus living experience much more pleasant. Humphrey Hall and Renee Row are popular housing options, and the new Campus Town on Wall Street has many upperclassmen excited about its coffee shops, laundry, and bowling alley.

In the city of Milwaukee, as one undergrad said, "there is never a dearth of activity." Local attractions include shopping malls like Grand Avenue, which features blocks of boutiques, department stores, and restaurants; the Bradley Center, home to Marquette basketball and the NBA's Milwaukee Bucks, and Mecca Arena, which brings in big-name concerts; great restaurants, including many that represent Milwaukee's German-American population; and the nearby shore of Lake Michigan, site of many festivals and boating events. The Milwaukee Brewers also play near the campus. Those interested in the arts will not be disappointed; Milwaukee offers the Rep Theater and the Performing Arts Center, among other resources. Students with cars have easy access to Kettle Moraine, a region known for its hiking and skiing, and Chicago, which is only a two-hour drive away.

On campus, students generally hang out in the Memorial Union student center to enjoy its pub, fast food, and grand ballroom. Wells Street is home to popular restaurants and pubs like Whales on Wells, Giuliano's Pizza, and the Avalanche. Although students who live on campus must purchase a meal plan, many call the food at the cafeteria "not very good" and "unhealthy." One student mentioned a long-running campaign for low-calorie salad dressings.

The Marquette campus is constantly changing, a result of a university-led urban renewal project. One student reported that new buildings have been going up "throughout the year" in a program meant to benefit both the city and the student body. Recent additions include a theater, art museum, and a math/computer science building as well as a recreation center that one student said has "prime workout facilities" and space for Marquette's intramural games. All varsity teams enjoy strong student support. "Marquette is a basketball campus," one student said, but the men's soccer and track teams and women's tennis team also attract a following. In 1995, the basketball team made it to the NIT finals and the student body marched through the streets of the city to celebrate the team's success. Marquette does not have a football team; while some students find this to be a disadvantage, they say the situation will probably not change, as the possibility of a football team has been discussed and rejected "many times before."

A Final Look

The spiritual heart of the Marquette campus is the St. Joan of Arc Chapel, built in 1400 and brought to Wisconsin from France. Students agree that the chapel serves as an emblem of Marquette's Jesuit tradition, which characterizes the school to this day. According to students, Marquette's great basketball team, awesome gym, and city life enrich, but do not define the Marquette experience. Marquette is largely about tradition, from its predominantly religious and politically conservative faculty and student body to its close-knit, "family feel."—*Jay Munir and Staff*

FYI

The three best things about attending Marquette are "the Catholic tradition, a city rich in activities, and the energy of the campus."

The three worst things about attending Marquette are "having priests living in dorms, the visitation regulations on weekdays, and the lack of a football team."

The three things every student should do before graduating from Marquette are "take advantage of what Milwaukee has to offer, participate in the Midnight Run, get involved in a service project you believe in."

One thing I'd like to have known before coming here is "how terrific Milwaukee is."

University of Wisconsin/Madison

Address: 3rd Floor, Red Gym, 716 Langdon Street; Madison, WI 53706-1400
Phone: 608-262-3961
E-mail address: on.wisconsin @mail.admin.wisc.edu
Web site URL: www.wisc.edu
Founded: 1836
Private or Public: public
Religious affiliation: none
Location: urban
Undergraduate enrollment: NA
Total enrollment: 40,109
Percent Male/Female: NA
Percent Minority: 0%

Percent African-American: NA
Percent Asian: NA
Percent Hispanic: NA
Percent Native-American: NA
Percent in-state/out-of-state: 70%/30%
Percent Pub HS: NA
Number of Applicants: 17,241
Percent Accepted: 73%
Percent Accepted who enroll: 44%
Entering: 5,604
Transfers: 1,717
Application Deadline: 1 Feb
Mean SAT: NA
Mean ACT: NA

Middle 50% SAT range: 520–640 V, 550–680 M
Middle 50% ACT range: 23–28
3 Most popular majors: engineering, NA
Retention: NA
Graduation rate: NA
On-campus housing: 82%
Fraternities: 10%
Sororities: 8%
Library: 4,800,000 volumes
Tuition and Fees: $3,650 in; $12,400 out
Room and Board: $5,250
Financial aid, first-year: 28%

With an undergraduate population of nearly 30,000, the University of Wisconsin/Madison offers its students a diversity generally not associated with the Midwest. For many students from Wisconsin and around the country, Madison is an obvious choice for its challenging academics, large sports program, and overall general appeal. As one of the highest-rated state schools in the country, Madison offers a booming college life and a solid academic program.

School Days

Academics at Madison are very stimulating, students say, although one was quick to pronounce that many people maintain the mantra: "Don't let school get in the way of your education." Students explain that a typical undergrad is appreciative of the "great education at a reasonable price" but wants to be "able to enjoy life to the fullest." English, communication arts, and political science are popular majors and generally deemed to be fairly easy, while computer science and engineering are two of the harder programs. While many people from the Midwest who want

to stay close to their families and friends choose Madison, students explain that the school is different because "it attracts the same type of student who could make it in notable East or West Coast schools."

Students must fulfill general education requirements in natural science, communications, humanities, and quantitative reasoning. While one student asserted that the academic requirements at Madison are "fair or too lax," most others seem to agree that they can be an obstacle. Students complained specifically about "unnecessary classes that don't have anything to do with your major." Registration can also be a problem, as many students don't get into the classes that they signed up for. There are many large lectures—as can be expected on such a large campus—although one student noted that "in small classes, I had good rapport with my professors." Most say that this is particularly the case "once you get to classes within your major." Students say that as professors get to know them well, they are "always more than willing to help with anything, even if it isn't school-related." Some students complain about foreign teaching assistants, who are sometimes "hard to understand."

Madison has an honors program that eligible students enter during the initial application process. That program, as well as the Medical Scholars program, allows students to distinguish themselves from the greater population. In the honors program, students are required to take specific honors courses and maintain a high grade point average.

Football and Other Fun

While academics are a high priority, students admit that "football comes first at certain times of the year." Madison, already a "college town," is overrun during game days, when "you can't bike or drive through the downtown area." During football season, a large percentage of the student population spend their time at "'Camp Randall,' where hopefully the Badgers are winning." If the football game is at home, students will often get up around eight to "start pre-game parties or tailgates." The football team is a frequent Rose Bowl contender, and the basketball team is a perennial Big Ten powerhouse. Students say that you can't get enough of the team spirit at Madison—as one student explained, "Here, we are all Badgers!" Most students will say that even if the team is not number one, "we're absolutely the greatest." Another was quick to add that when there is a Badger game "we drink before, during, and after the game."

Madison is definitely known as a party school, but most students say that "things are kept under control and people stay safe." Students, many say, simply like to "maximize the social opportunities in life while attending a good school." There are a lot of parties, usually with a significant amount of drinking, but non-drinkers do not feel isolated, because Madison "is such a large school that you can always be yourself and find people who share the same interests as you." Or, as another student explained, abstaining is sometimes better "because you will definitely remember everything that happens during the night." A lot of students frequent the bars on State Street, one of the main streets in Madison located near the dorms. Others, however, say that Madison "can be pretty boring" and that to find something to do "you have

to go out and look for it." If there is no football game, "you don't always see a lot of students out of bed before noon on weekends." While some students "spend their weekends being productive," most do go to some parties. Freshmen tend to party from Thursday night through the weekend, and others claim that "there's a fair amount of students who think [the weekend] starts on Wednesday."

> **"You can always be yourself and find people who share the same interests as you."**

One student explained that Madison undergrads tend to spend about one-fourth of their time studying. People are "pretty devoted" to extracurricular activities, which span the active fraternity scene to the Go Club, dedicated to the Asian board game. Tau Beta Pi is a well-respected fraternity at the school, and students are also very actively involved in social movements. The school is well known for its protests of the Vietnam War, during which Sterling Hall, the physics building, was bombed. This tradition of protest continues today; as one student explained, these go year-round. There are many religious and political organizations, and sports are also important extracurricular activities for many people. Madison is a Division I school and does a fair amount of recruiting. However its top-notch athletic facilities, including "three gyms, outdoor and indoor tennis courts, volleyball and basketball courts, swimming pools, and a running track," are available to all students.

Madison, the City

Madison, the university's host city and the Wisconsin state capital, is definitely a great place to be, according to most students. The city is surrounded by lakes and hills, giving the whole campus a very natural aura. As one noted, "Madison is a city where everyone smiles when they see you." Students also say, though, that because of the college town atmosphere, "you need to go out of here just to get a taste of reality." Contrary to the situation on most college campuses, many students have off-campus jobs in the city.

Madison is generally a very liberal campus with a fairly large gay community, though "there aren't any gay pride activities here." Interracial couples are also visible on campus. Students are very laid-back and can often be seen walking around in "sweatpants or pajama bottoms." While some students say that dating at Madison consists of random hookups, others do have serious relationships.

Students also praise Madison's diverse student population. Although one student identified a typical Madisonian as "reading *Badger Herald* while having lunch, wearing an Abercrombie jacket, studying and partying through the weekend," the environment of the school is changing, as diversity, particularly international, increases. One international student explained that "there are so many places and activities through which you can connect with both Americans and other international students." Students also mentioned the number of ethnic festivals and other opportunities to learn about different cultures. There are no real cliques, although people are often identified by what major they are in. The school is "full of interesting people," from MTV celebrities like Noah from Road Rules and the famous spring breakers from 1999 to alums like John Lange, the U.S. ambassador to Botswana, and Jack St. Clair Kilby, a Nobel Prize winner.

Overall, Madison provides students an amazing environment for "four great years." While some are unimpressed by the gargantuan size of the school, others will assert that this provides for an amazing wealth of opportunities. From academics, to football, to the abundance of parties, students at Madison claim their school to be "one of, if not the, best universities in America!"—*Jessamyn Blau*

FYI

The three best things about attending the University of Wisconsin/Madison are "the thousands of people you can meet, Badger football, and Halloween time for parties."

The three worst things about attending the University of Wisconsin/Madison are "the sheer number of people, the long, cold winter, and sometimes registration is a pain."

The three things that every student should do before graduating from the University of Wisconsin/Madison are "go to a Badger game, go to Memorial Union, and just stare at Lake Mendota—it's beautiful—and eat Babcock's ice cream; it's the best!."

One thing I'd like to have known before coming here is "that people in southeastern Wisconsin call a water fountain a 'bubbler.'"

Wyoming

University of Wyoming

Address: PO Box 3434; Laramine, WY 82071
Phone: 307-766-5160
E-mail address: undergraduate.admissions @wuwyo.edu
Web site URL: www.uwyo.edu
Founded: 1886
Private or Public: public
Religious affiliation: none
Location: rural
Undergraduate enrollment: NA
Total enrollment: 11,126
Percent Male/Female: NA
Percent Minority: 0%

Percent African-American: NA
Percent Asian: NA
Percent Hispanic: NA
Percent Native-American: NA
Percent in-state/out-of-state: 79%/21%
Percent Pub HS: NA
Number of Applicants: 2,466
Percent Accepted: 97%
Percent Accepted who enroll: 51%
Entering: 1,225
Transfers: 1,107
Application Deadline: 10 Aug
Mean SAT: NA

Mean ACT: 24
Middle 50% SAT range: NA
Middle 50% ACT range: 21–26
3 Most popular majors: elementary education, psychology, accounting
Retention: 76%
Graduation rate: 48%
On-campus housing: 54%
Fraternities: 6%
Sororities: 4%
Library: 1,393,055 volumes
Tuition and Fees: $2,575 in; $7,693 out
Room and Board: $4,568
Financial aid, first-year: 42%

D oes the majesty of the mountains call your name, or perhaps the serenity of the open plain whistle in your ear? If so, head west—way out west, to the University of Wyoming. Whether it's the outdoor scenery of Vedauwoo State Park, or the night life of nearby Denver, students at UW appreciate their slice of western bliss.

Studies With a Smile

"The difference between UW and my old school," remarked one transfer student, "is that even though it's a state school, the professors really care about my studies here." Although class sizes admittedly run into the hundreds, many students rave over the quality of professors at UW. Long office hours and teachers interested in getting to know their pupils are the norm, although this trend seems to lose steam when students discuss TA attention.

The engineering department is regarded among the university's strongest. Students also consider UW extremely well-rounded in terms of fields of study which includes UW's esteemed nursing school, tough science departments, and Latin classes. On the softer side, students consider social work to be a slack major, and any of the classes within the University Studies program to be "completely lame." University Studies is a program that is mandatory for graduation and is supposed to promote good study habits and help to make the adjustment to college life easier. Unfortunately, many students find this to be a "big joke."

For those wishing to enhance their studies, UW offers a well-regarded honors program. Available to students with a 3.7 high school GPA, or an ACT of 28 or SAT of 1240, the University Honors Program challenges its students to improve upon their thinking and writing skills. The program consists of five courses, of which two are taken in the freshman year, and one course for the remaining three years. Specific honors classes change yearly, but follow consistent themes such as "Non-Western Perspectives" and "Modes of Understanding."

Dorming and Dining

When students say UW is situated in a small-town environment, they really mean it. Town-gown relations take on a new meaning when the local town of Laramie is made up primarily of students from the UW. When asked whether most students live on or off campus, one student jokingly replied "Around here, even if you live off campus, you're still pretty much on campus!" Although no one is required to live in university-provided housing, a majority of UW's freshmen and substantial percentage of upperclassmen elect to live in one of the UW's six dorms. Centrally located between most classroom buildings on West Campus and the sports buildings of East Campus, dorm living situates students in the middle of UW life. Hill and Crane house most of the UW's graduate students, while Downey, McIntyre, White and Orr are primarily home to undergrads. Dorms are coed by wing or floor, and students can choose to live in halls with restricted opposite-sex visiting hours and substance free floors. Overall, students give high marks to their dorms for both size and convenience features such as in-room sinks.

> "Imagine Mayberry with many well-dressed people and no parking spots and you've got UW!"

Those choosing to live on campus eat most of their meals in the Washakie dining hall. Located centrally to the undergraduate residence halls, Washakie contains a computer lab, game room, workout room, and a convenience store known as the Pokeskellar. More than just a store, the Pokeskellar often acts as a social center for "dormies." While Washakie is not known for its quality of food, students have many other options both on and off campus. "Laramie has your standard set of both fast food and more sit-down oriented restaurants," reported one student, "selection really isn't a problem." Additionally, students rave over their UW Campus Expre$$ ID cards, which act as credit cards at many on campus eateries. Whether it's a mid-day burrito craving at the Taco Bell or a late night cup of Joe at the local coffee spot, satisfaction is only a card swipe away.

The Rowdy Life of a Cowboy

Although most of UW's students are from Wyoming, not many return home on the weekends. More popular destinations include Denver, Ft. Collins, and the ski slopes of the Colorado Rockies. Closer to school is Vedauwoo State Park, which offers scenic trails, intense rock climbing and gorgeous views. On any given weekend though, most students stick around campus and party, especially during football season.

During the fall the UW Cowboys take center stage as they make their annual run at the Mountain West conference championship. This season is no different, with the entire school celebrating the football victory over rival Air Force Academy, snapping an eleven game losing streak that was the longest in division 1-A. Football is not the only game in this town though. Sports enthusiasm runs strongly through the veins of many Cowboys and Cowgirls, and basketball and volleyball also draw large crowds. In addition to these more common intercollegiate sports, Wyoming plays host to rock climbing, skiing and ultimate frisbee teams, and its western nature shines through both the men's and women's top-ranked Rodeo Club teams.

While roping calves might not be your idea of the perfect way to spend an afternoon, UW supplies a myriad of clubs and activities to satisfy even the most discerning of students. Aspiring writers work can work for the campus daily paper the *Branding Iron*, or for *Frontiers* magazine. Religious organizations, including Campus Ventures and the Intervarsity Christian Fellowship, abound on the primarily conservative campus, although liberal groups such as "Students Together in Opposition of Prohibition (of Hemp)" also make their mark. Students consider UW's relatively homogeneous population a mixed blessing. "If you fit the Abercrombie and North Face look here, you'll do fine," remarked one student, "but diversity isn't most people's first concern."

Centered along the aptly named "Fraternity Mall," the Greek system at UW is a substantial, yet non-dominating, aspect of campus social life. Greeks engage themselves in various charity events and hold parties throughout the school year, but non-Greeks do not report feeling left out. As one undergrad observed, "If you want to party, you don't need to be a Greek, but it doesn't hurt, either. Parties can be found pretty consistently around town."

Anyone Wanna Make a Snowman?

Students consider the UW campus an extremely safe place to live and work. Emergency phones are scattered throughout, and there is a nighttime campus escort service for students walking at night, although many female students say they feel safe even without this precaution. Many also report leaving their cars with the doors unlocked and the windows rolled down—if they are lucky enough to find a parking space. "Most people do have cars, and there is NO parking anywhere," noted one student, while another reported "imagine Mayberry with many well-dressed people and no parking spots and you've got UW!"

Students consider the UW campus attractive and scenic, with a distinct western architectural flair. Most notably among campus buildings is the Centennial Complex, which houses the University Art Museum and the American Heritage Center. Designed by internationally recognized architect Antoine Predock, the Centennial Complex reminded one student of "a big fortune cookie . . . either that or an oversized teepee." More importantly, the Centennial Complex has gathered an impressive accumulation of cultural artifacts. With collections ranging from 18th-century Persian paintings to 20th-century photography and sculpture, the Art Museum holds something for art lovers of all kinds, and also stages forums and lectures by invited notables. Other remarkable buildings on campus include War Memorial Stadium, home of the Cowboys, and "Old Main," the building that contained the university in its entirety in 1886 and now serves as the President's office.

There is one additional item worth mentioning about the UW campus—most of the year it will be covered in snow. The first thing every new UW student learns is that if you do not like the cold white stuff, it is going to be a long year. With sub-freezing lows by the end of September, summer exits to fall pretty quickly in Cowboy country. Snowy days have even become the subject of legend around Laramie, where every good UW student knows that the first snowfall of the year can be expected on Halloween, and a blizzard will try and trap students on the last day before winter break.

With a friendly smile and easy-going nature, life out in out-of-the-way Laramie offers its students energetic professors, a safe environment and a full social schedule, all for a bargain price. Nearby skiing, hiking, and rock climbing cater to those with an interest in the outdoors, while intellectual stimulation can likewise be found at the Art Museum and American Heritage Center. So who wants to spend four years fighting off blizzards as a Cowboy? At the University of Wyoming, everyone does.

—Robert Berschinski

FYI

The three best things about attending the University of Wyoming are "the amazing scenery, the friendly people, and most importantly, those great apple bagels at the Union."

The three worst things about attending the University of Wyoming are "the cold, the wind, and the cold wind."

The three things that every student should do before graduating from the University of Wyoming are "learn to ski, rock climb in Vedauwoo, and go to the hot springs in Saratoga."

One thing I'd like to have known before coming here is "that everyone rides something to school. I definitely would have brought my bike if I knew I was going to able to use it all the time."

Canada

For the American student seeking the adventure of a foreign university but reluctant to travel halfway around the world, Canada may be the ideal location. A different culture, fine programs, and low tuition are just across the border. But there's more to Canada than mountain ranges, friendly people, and cold beer; before you pack your skis and buy a plane ticket, you should know what awaits you.

Don't Say We Didn't Warn You

First, let us offer these words of warning: If generalizations about all the students in a particular university are risky, then generalizations about all the universities in a particular country are even more so. As always, there will be exceptions and differences of degree with respect to everything that follows. Research everything carefully. Individual universities, as well as different programs within the universities, can vary from the exceptional to the inadequate, and it is crucial to find out as much as possible about the school that interests you before you commit.

The greatest difference between Canadian and American universities is that in Canada there are no private colleges; all Canadian schools are government-funded. This has many implications, from overt funding problems to students' attitudes about the purpose of a university and a university education. As any administrator of a state school in the United States will tell you, legislators never seem to allocate as much funding as a school thinks it needs, and Canadian schools have suffered from budget cutbacks in recent years just as American schools have. Many Canadian institutions have problems with their buildings and the quality of specialized equipment for science classes. Of course, this is not universally true, so it's impor-

tant to find out which schools are strong in the subjects that interest you.

To get a general overview of all Canadian colleges, it is helpful to know if the school is situated in a French-speaking province. That can make a big difference. Ontario and British Columbia have the most colleges of the provinces, so you may want to start there in a general search.

One thing to look for in government-funded Canadian schools is a phenomenon known as "warm-body admissions." Since Canadian schools are funded based on the number of students enrolled, some schools lower their admissions standards to fill seats and raise funding. This often leads to inflated numbers of first year students and high first-year dropout rates. This generally does not occur at the better Canadian schools, such as those included in this guide. Admissions standards tend to be based more on the students' cumulative high-school grades than on other qualities, but standards vary from school to school and from program to program. It is wise to check the standards for a particular program before you apply.

Although there are now more and more exceptions, Canadian universities often lack that elusive entity known as "school spirit" or "school unity." This can be explained in part by the size of most schools and the number of students who live at home or off campus. Unlike many Americans, most Canadians don't seem to be looking for the ideal "college experience." Instead, they are looking primarily for the right education for their future careers, and convenience is an important concern. By and large, Canadian students are unabashedly preprofessional. Students view a degree as a prerequisite for a job and attend university as a means to that end.

If you decide that a unversity in Canada is right for you, there are certain procedures to follow and documents to obtain. Start early! Some schools may not be prepared to handle foreign students. For information, write or call the school and ask to be put in contact with their foreign students' office. Once accepted, you will need a visa and a student authorization. These must be obtained at a Canadian embassy or consulate in the United States, not in Canada. To get the documents, you will need proof of U.S. citizenship (usually a passport a birth certificate), a letter of acceptance to a Canadian institution, and proof of adequate funds to support yourself while in Canada. If you decide that it's for you, strap on a sense of adventure and get ready for a unique experience, but remember that it's a four-year-long trek.—*Seung Lee*

Carleton University

Address: 1125 Colonel By Drive; Ottawa, Ontario K1S 5B6
Phone: 613-520-7400
E-mail address: NA
Web site URL: www.carleton.ca
Founded: 1942
Private or Public: public
Religious affiliation: none
Location: urban
Undergraduate enrollment: 14,721
Total enrollment: 17,137
Percent Male/Female: 49%/51%
Percent Minority: NA

Percent African-American: NA
Percent Asian: NA
Percent Hispanic: NA
Percent Native-American: NA
Percent in-state/out-of-state: 90%/10%
Percent Pub HS: NA
Number of Applicants: NA
Percent Accepted: NA
Percent Accepted who enroll: NA
Entering: NA
Transfers: NA
Application Deadline: 10 Apr
Mean SAT: NA

Mean ACT: NA
Middle 50% SAT range: NA
Middle 50% ACT range: NA
3 Most popular majors: biology, English, political science
Retention: NA
Graduation rate: NA
On-campus housing: NA
Fraternities: 0%
Sororities: 0%
Library: 2,000,000 volumes
Tuition and Fees: $2,500 in; $10,000 out
Room and Board: $4,164
Financial aid, first-year: 39%

Located on the south side of Ottawa, Carleton is ideally situated for students to take advantage of the capital's offerings. The campus offers easy access to national institutions and governmental operations. Carleton offers several specialized programs such as journalism, mass communications, and aerospace engineering that greatly benefit from the university's location.

Winter Wonderland

Carleton is bounded by the Rideau River and Rideau Canal, which in winter is transformed into the world's longest outdoor skating rink. The original college was founded after World War II to educate veterans, so the university is relatively young. Although Carleton is not in the heart of the city, a 15-minute bus ride takes students downtown. Ottawa is a big city with many offerings, and undergraduates often take advantage of the opportunities for political internships in the Houses of Parliament and other government institutions. Ottawa has its own professional football team, as well as a new Triple-A baseball team, the Lynx, and an NHL team, the Senators. Ottawa also benefits from the traditional perks of capital cities, including several national museums and galleries, as well as the National Arts Centre and its orchestra. Students frequently look to the city for entertainment, and report that city-university relations are good.

Hearty snowfalls turn Carleton into a winter wonderland, especially during the ten days of Winterlude, a city-organized festival celebrating winter with the Rideau Canal as its focal point. In the spring and summer, Ottawa is a beautiful place to enjoy the many bicycle and jogging paths. As one student reported, "Walking to class can become nightmarish, as Ottawa is said to have the highest amount of bicycle traffic in North America."

Journalism and More
Journalism is among the most prestigious programs Carleton offers, attracting students from around the country and abroad; it is surely this great program that puts Carleton on the map. Students say they love it, and cite the accessibility of the faculty as one main reason. Mass communications, public administration, and political science are other strengths at Carleton. Students majoring in the aerospace and environmental studies programs can earn either a B.A. or a B.S. degree. The university also offers an aboriginal studies major as part of the Centre for Aboriginal Education and Research and Culture (CAERC), an interdisciplinary program for academic research and cultural studies of Canada's indigenous people. Carleton recently established a unique four-year Bachelor of International Business with Honours degree program that involves studies in international business as well as a foreign language. Students in this program take courses in the social sciences and spend a year at a foreign university.

Social Life
Social life often centers on the residences and on the campus pubs (the drinking age in Ontario is 19). The Unicentre, a hub of student life, includes a pub called Rooster's and Porter Hall, where various college bands perform. The residences get involved in student life by sponsoring popular intramural games and other activities. "Intramurals are fairly popular, and probably better attended than most varsity matches," said one student. A lottery system determines who will get housing (either a single or a double) in the residences, and the only on-campus housing guarantees are given to students with at least an A-minus average. Few undergrads have trouble finding accommodation off campus, and many use the housing referral

service, an innovative service provided by the university. The surrounding neighborhoods reportedly are dominated by students.

Carleton students can join more than 100 campus clubs and societies. Like most Canadian schools, Carleton forbids fraternities and sororities because of their exclusive nature. But, students find other ways to fill their time, participating in organizations such as the undergraduate student paper, the *Charlatan*, the radio station, CKCU, and varsity athletics, which tend to attract spectators only when the seasons come to their respective finales. The big football game of the season is the Panda Game (named after the victory prize, originally a stuffed panda bear, but now a bronze bear trophy) against rival University of Ottawa.

> **Ottawa is a big city with many offerings, and undergraduates often take advantage of the opportunities for political internships in the Houses of Parliament and other government institutions.**

As most students will admit, Carleton tries to keep its doors open to anyone who wants to learn. Most students approve of this policy—especially those who would not be in school if that were not the case—although some complain that it leads to overcrowding. Although it is relatively easy to get accepted at Carleton, students report that staying in a select program is more challenging. Spaces available in second-year classes are often limited, especially in journalism and other popular programs.

Strong fund-raising campaigns have enabled Carleton to maintain, modernize, and expand its facilities. The MacOdrum Library houses more than a million volumes as well as microfilms, archival material, maps, documents, and prints; the Carleton University Art Gallery opened in 1992 to an enthusiastic response from the community.

A telephone registration system has eliminated long lines at the beginning of each semester, although students report that "you'd better get some snacks and a blanket and prepare yourself to camp out on the phone for a good chunk of time." Another much-appreciated feature is the underground tunnel system that connects several points on campus. The tunnels provide easy access for students with disabilities and an alternative to cold cross-campus treks during those harsh Canadian winters.

Combining the advantages of the nation's capital with a variety of educational opportunities, Carleton attracts students from throughout Canada and abroad. Students can pursue their interests with diverse academic programs and extracurricular activities, all in a relaxed and friendly environment.—*Alison Pulaski and Staff*

FYI
The three best things about attending Carleton are "the Unicentre, the journalism program, and spending time at the Art Gallery."
The three worst things about attending Carleton are "cold winters, the lack of a Greek scene, and having the Panda Game—come on, it's a panda!"
The three things that every student should do before graduating from Carleton are "use the tunnels when it gets unbearably cold, get an internship in Ottawa, and go to Winterlude."
One thing I'd like to have known before coming here is "how cold it gets."

McGill University

Address: 845 Sherbrooke St. West; Montreal, Quebec H3A 2T5	**Percent African-American:** NA	**Mean ACT:** NA
	Percent Asian: NA	**Middle 50% SAT range:** NA
Phone: 514-398-4455	**Percent Hispanic:** NA	**Middle 50% ACT range:** NA
E-mail address: admissions @aro.lan.mcgill.ca	**Percent Native-American:** NA	**3 Most popular majors:** psychology, political science, commerce
Web site URL: www.mcgill.ca	**Percent in-state / out-of-state:** NA	**Retention:** NA
Founded: 1821	**Percent Pub HS:** NA	**Graduation rate:** NA
Private or Public: public	**Number of Applicants:** 14,783	**On-campus housing:** 28%
Religious affiliation: none	**Percent Accepted:** NA	**Fraternities:** 0%
Location: urban	**Percent Accepted who enroll:** NA	**Sororities:** 0%
Undergraduate enrollment: 15,889	**Entering:** NA	**Library:** 2,900,000 volumes
Total enrollment: 20,348	**Transfers:** NA	**Tuition and Fees:** $3,168 in; $12,000 out
Percent Male / Female: 42%/58%	**Application Deadline:** 15 Jan	**Room and Board:** $6,412
Percent Minority: NA	**Mean SAT:** NA	**Financial aid, first-year:** NA

L ocated in the heart of Montreal, McGill University offers its students the best of two worlds: a college experience in a safe urban setting. Come rain or subzero weather, McGill students can always be found gracing the streets of Montreal, taking advantage of its numerous resources. About McGill's location, one student said, "Where in the States can you find an amazing university in a safe urban setting—the key word being 'safe'?" But despite its urban location, the McGill campus is no less collegiate than a suburban or rural one. Indeed, looking at McGill's luxurious lawns and plethora of trees, a student may forget that just footsteps away from campus lies one of the world's most happening cities. All things considered, it's no wonder McGill students keep coming and never want to leave!

Learning the Canadian Way

When applying to McGill, students are asked to indicate the academic field they intend to enter. At McGill, the different academic disciplines are called "faculties." The faculties cover a wide range of interests including everything from the arts to agricultural science, with each faculty having its own department and specific requirements. Most of the faculties are housed on the main campus; only agricultural studies is on MacDonald campus.

Few students complain about the requirements. Said one student, "The requirements are extremely reasonable. They truly allow one to explore what fields one is interested in without having to be loaded down." A typical four-year B.A.-degree candidate needs about 120 credits to graduate. First-year students in the arts are required to take one class in three out of the four following disciplines—humanities, social sciences, languages, and math and science. These requirements are intended to give students a wide view of available options. After this initial year of experimentation, students declare a major and are assigned an advisor in their specific department.

But the choices given to each student do not end there. Within each department, a student can choose to complete a single or double major and an honors or joint-honors degree. Honors students typically take more specialized classes and work more closely with individual professors. In addition, an honors degree might require a senior thesis, depending on the individual department.

In terms of the classes themselves, many departments require introductory lectures that, like those at other universities, tend to be quite massive. TAs help lead discussion sections, which somewhat compensates for the immense lectures. But whereas at other universities class size shrinks as courses become more advanced, at McGill classes remain large, a cause of many student complaints. At McGill, classes are taught in English, but students can elect to take tests and write papers in French.

Canadian Cutbacks

When asked about the living environment at McGill, one student replied, "All the problems with living at McGill are due to three problems, "Cutbacks, cutbacks, cutbacks." For instance, even though McGill's libraries house over 2.9 million volumes, the libraries themselves are described as pretty pitiful; few students actually study there.

What distinguishes McGill from many American universities is that few of its students actually live on campus. Most live off campus or commute from home. First priority in on-campus housing is given to international students, primarily first-years.

McGill dorms are formally called residences, but students refer to them as "rez." Four of the main residences are found on the hill, a location first-year students never stop complaining about. Said one student, "The rezes are not that near anything and you have to climb this huge hill."

> "Where in the States can you find an amazing university in a safe urban setting—the key word being 'safe'?"

Each "rez" has a unique reputation. Gardener is known as the place for quiet studious students, although current first-year students say that reputation is beginning to change; Molson, the typically rowdy dorm, has become tamer in the past two years. McConnell remains the party dorm, as well as the rez with single-sex bathrooms. All three are coed. But if coed living is not your thing, Royal Victoria College is an all-female dorm with a more central campus location.

Students from the three dorms eat in the same cafeteria; students in Douglas, situated slightly lower down the hill, have a separate facility. Known for its aesthetic beauty, Douglas is the favorite among many. However, due to seemingly never-ending construction, Douglas has begun to lost its charm to some.

Solin Hall, the newest "rez," is also located away from the hill. Students often complain about its location, explaining it is too far from everything. With its apartment-like rooms, Solin offers more independent living for some; for others, it may be the cause of constant problems and hassles since Solin students have to cook their own meals.

But judging from the overall negative view of McGill food, cooking for yourself in Solin may not be such a bad thing after all; all other students are required to purchase a meal plan. McGill food was described as completely inedible and the meal plans as stingy because McGill limits what students can take at meals. In response to the sometimes-ludicrous dining guidelines, one student griped, "Since when is orange juice a desert?" For vegetarians, food options are even worse or nonexistent.

After the first year, students escape the meal plan as they move out of residences and, more often than not, into the "McGill ghetto." But don't be fooled by the name. In reality, the "ghetto" is a neighborhood of nice yet affordable apartment houses located just steps away from campus. Other popular places for upperclassmen include "The Plateau" or "The Main," which is situated near St. Laurent Street, a center of activity with its numerous bars and restaurants.

Extracurriculars Exist?

A McGill freshman asked to name organizations he belonged to could not list a single one. With the exception of sports, extracurricular activities do not enjoy high student participation, largely due to the high percentage of students living off campus. Greek life, too, has minimal campus presence. When asked to list a few clubs, most students would name The Stonecutters, a popular group whose sole activity is to gather and watch *The Simpsons* together every Sunday.

Students involved in sports compete at the club, intramural, and varsity levels. An interesting fact most people don't know is that Harvard is McGill's historical rival. Indeed, the first North American football game was reportedly a McGill-versus-Harvard rugby game that took a bizarre turn, and football was "invented." Nowadays, McGill's more commonly rec-

ognized rival is Queen's University in Kingston, Ontario. And even though football is not very popular at McGill, students still get a chance to show their school spirit at the annual Homecoming game, a.k.a. the "I-didn't-know-we-had-a-football-team game." Another instance of school spirit displayed occurred when the men's soccer team won the national championship back in 1997.

For more literary minds, McGill offers numerous student publications. Published three times a week, the *McGill Daily* comes out twice a week in English and once in French. In addition, literary alternatives include the weekly *McGill Tribune* and the *Red Herring*, a humor magazine. But at McGill, out-of-class life typically revolves around off-campus venues.

Bars on Campus

For American natives, McGill's on-campus bar may be a strange sight. Unlike American schools where the majority of the students are underage, McGill social life truly capitalizes on the local drinking age, which is only eighteen. So whereas most freshman orientations at other schools center on talks and maybe pizza dinners, according to one student, the goal of freshman orientation at McGill is "to get the freshman drunk." Almost all activities revolve around drinking; even the breakfast menu features bagels and beer. Drinking is truly a central part of McGill social life.

Besides bars, other popular social spots include Peels Pub with 14-cent wings and shots for under a dollar. Angel's is known for great dancing. Gert's is the convenient and popular on-campus bar. Overall, clubbing and barhopping are the main events of a McGill student's weekend nights.

So with such a bustling social life, why would McGill students ever choose to stay in? As most McGill students would answer: the cold. Without a doubt, the freezing temperatures were one of McGill students' main complaints. But for those prospectives able to foresee themselves wearing woolen clothes for the next four years, McGill is the place to be.—*Alyssa Blair Greenwald*

McMaster University

Address: 1280 Main Street West, Suite 20; Hamilton, Ontario L8S 4L8
Phone: 905-525-9140
E-mail address: macadmit@mcmaster.edu
Web site URL: www.mcmaster.ca
Founded: 1887
Private or Public: public
Religious affiliation: none
Location: suburban
Undergraduate enrollment: 14,130
Total enrollment: 18,806
Percent Male/Female: 43%/57%
Percent Minority: NA

Percent African-American: NA
Percent Asian: NA
Percent Hispanic: NA
Percent Native-American: NA
Percent in-state/out-of-state: NA
Percent Pub HS: NA
Number of Applicants: 19,652
Percent Accepted: 66%
Percent Accepted who enroll: 29%
Entering: NA
Transfers: NA
Application Deadline: 1 May
Mean SAT: NA

Mean ACT: NA
Middle 50% SAT range: NA
Middle 50% ACT range: NA
3 Most popular majors: kinesiology, commerce, sociology
Retention: 92%
Graduation rate: 86%
On-campus housing: 70%
Fraternities: 0%
Sororities: 0%
Library: 1,700,000 volumes
Tuition and Fees: $3,907 in; $12,000 out
Room and Board: $5,450
Financial aid, first-year: 50%

McMaster University, located in Hamilton, a city at the heart of the Golden Horseshoe area of southern Ontario, is known for its dedication to innovative education and ground-breaking research. Many report that McMaster, home to about 18,000 students, is second-to-none in diversity of programs offered, ethnic makeup of student body, and vibrant social scene. Named after a senator, McMaster University was founded in 1887 in Toronto but moved to its current location in 1930. The beautiful ivy-clad buildings that intersperse the campus testify to the institution's distinguished history.

Choices Galore

If there is one thing about McMaster's academics that differentiates it from other post-secondary schools, it is the broad range of programs of study. Undergrads can choose from a whopping 141 degree programs from six faculties. Specific academic requirements vary by program, but students must take 30% of their courses outside of their program. Students report that the hardest programs can be found in engineering, the health sciences, and science and that the easiest ones are bunched in the social sciences, business, and humanities. "I don't know how these people can say they're struggling with only twelve hours of class each week," commented a science student up to his neck with calculus problem sets and lab reports.

Students unanimously gave thumbs-up to the "elite" arts and science program, designed to provide students with a broad-based liberal education. "I love the program, mainly because the classes are very small," praised one student. Said another: "The profs are as excited about teaching us as we are about learning from them. Class discussions are intelligent, and even intimidating in the first years of the program." One student reported, "After a biology teacher mentioned how asparagus makes your urine smell funny, a group of 'ArtScis' cooked some up, and the professor ate it in front of the class's 300-plus students." Professors genuinely seem to care about their quality of teaching. Said one fourth-year student: "One of my profs took our class to his cottage in Algonquin for a weekend. A technology and society professor brought in a chain saw to class to cut a pound of butter and later in the year took a hammer to an old VCR in order to demonstrate a Neo-Luddite approach to technology."

The undergraduate M.D. program and the undergraduate nursing program are two fields of study that are often extolled. Both are well known for their problem-based learning approach to medical education, a method that has been adopted by medical programs around the world. The interdisciplinary engineering and management program is also worth a mention, as it remains Canada's only "discipline-specific joint engineering and business degree program."

> **The campus is "a funny mix of beautiful ivy-clad buildings and modern concrete monoliths."**

Also highly praised is the kinesiology program, which is one of the top three kinesiology programs in the country. It's a very holistic program—it takes a scientific, psychological, and sociological approach in a variety of disciplines within the realm of kinesiology. Class sizes differ from program to program, but one student remarked that "compared to similar schools like the University of Toronto, Mac classes are quite small." Small classes translate into a "close-knit" academic environment, in which there is ample interaction between students and teaching staff. Students also laud the professors and teaching assistants, describing them as "approachable," "interested in seeing you succeed," and "down-to-earth."

Not all comments concerning academics are positive, however. First-year students,

in particular, are often surprised at the difficulty of the courses. "It is really hard to get good grades. You have to work hard even in intro classes," claimed one student.

Getting Rid of Stress

To relieve pent-up stress, McMaster students play hard and party hard. From huge parties to theme dances, this school has it all. Students can choose from on-campus bars such as the Rat, the Downstairs John, and the Phoenix and off-campus bars with outlandish names like "Snooty Fox," "The Funky Monkey," "Billy Bob's," and the "Texas Border." For frosh, the school year kicks off with Welcome Week, formerly known as Frosh Week, during which time students get their first taste of the freedom and fun of university life by partying, gathering in bars, and attending concerts. Mac freshmen tend to travel in packs, so dating is not common during the first few months. However, according to one second-year student, by January things calm down and people begin to fall into their niches. One of the biggest dances of the year is the McMaster Student Union's (MSU's) Charity Ball, which reportedly draws as many as 800 students. "Besides being a great occasion to get dressed up, it also unites the school to some extent," said one student. Other big events include Frost Week—the first week back after Christmas break—Homecoming, faculty formals throughout the year, public speakers, and concerts. "There's a good selection of musical groups that come to campus each year," said one undergrad.

The consensus regarding drug use is that "people definitely do them, but they aren't blatantly obvious about it." In other words, drugs are accessible to students looking to get high but not perceived by the administration or the student body as being a threat to the school's reputation. After alcohol and nicotine, "marijuana is the drug of choice, with mushrooms and Ecstasy following," reported one insider to the drug scene. Despite the widespread drinking on and off campus, non-drinkers don't feel left out. "You can hang out with your friends at the bars, keep your hands away from the booze, and still have a great time," reported one student.

For those who would prefer to stay away from alcohol, there are always plenty of alternatives. "Why do you need to go out, get drunk, put a dent in your wallet, and suffer a hangover in the morning when you could just sit back in the lounge, play pool, and watch a good movie with friends?" asked one student.

Not Just for a Good-Looking Resumé

While it is true that some McMaster students join tons of extracurricular activities hoping to make themselves look good to potential employers and grad schools, most students get involved to gain new skills, for the rewarding experiences, and, of course, to have fun. One student said it well: "There's always going to be a few pre-med types who have ulterior motives behind their getting involved in volunteering, athletics, cultural organizations, special interest groups, and student government. But for the most part, people get into it just for the hell of it." There are many extracurricular options open to undergraduates, from campus newspapers to intramural sports, the Conservative Party to the Queer Club. Some students say, however, that participation is lacking in many of them. Said one junior, "There are a million and one things to get into, but nobody does." Part of the reason for this is that a vast number of students live off campus, making it difficult for them to get involved. The major student-run organization is the MSU, which basically runs all student activities, including the weekly newspaper, the *Silhouette*. The Student Union also runs two bars frequented by Mac students, a day-care center, a grocery store, and a radio station, all of which are staffed entirely by students.

On the upside, athletics at the varsity and intramural levels seem to be popular. One student on the rugby team commented, "Being a varsity athlete, most of the people I know are really into athletics at Mac. The football and basketball teams are really big here, often going to the nationals." The Pulse, the on-campus fitness center, is highly popular among students who want to stay fit but do not have the time to be on a team.

Mixed Feelings About the City

One concern often raised by prospective students is the city of Hamilton. "I spent four years at Mac and all I got was black

lung," one graduate jokingly complained. In reality, McMaster is located in suburban West Hamilton, far from the city's smog-producing steel mills. Pollution is not a problem, nor is transportation into the city. A bus pass is included in tuition fees, and the HSR, the bus network, is reportedly excellent. The city itself, however, is not so great. Apart from a strong local music scene, Hamilton offers few cultural events and loses most touring artists to nearby Toronto, located 45 minutes away. McMaster students report that they rarely venture outside of the Westdale area around the school. The city is "rough and industrial," but there are some gems: the Hudson, "a small club that's good for beats [and] DJs"; the Raven, a new bar that features indie rock groups and local acts; and Hess Street, a street lined with outdoor patios that are packed during the summer. Most people brush off the negative aspects of the city by simply saying, "I came here for the school, not the city."

Awesome Campus, Dorms

McMaster students consistently give high ratings to the campus and residences. As one student described the campus, "It's a funny mix of beautiful ivy-clad buildings (such as the old student building Hamilton Hall) and modern concrete monoliths (such as the massive hospital and engineering building), mostly built around a large central green space. Come nice weather, students and Frisbees use the space well, but the campus can get eerily quiet when students go home on weekends." The most popular hangout seems to be the Togo Salmon Hall cafeteria, but students agree that this will change once the McMaster University Student Center is built. Places to study abound, but students reportedly stick to their own turf: arts students go to Mills Library, engineering and science students hit the books at the Thode Science and Engineering Libraries, and health science and biology students crowd the Health Science Library.

Students report that they met most of their friends through their residences. Most are evenly divided in their opinion when asked whether their new friends tend to be similar to high school friends. "They're definitely different from the type of people I hung out with in high school," said one student, while another commented, "If you were in a clique during high school, you're most likely to join the same kind of clique at Mac." Nevertheless, the consensus is that friends are an integral part of the university experience: "They're linked to my enjoyment of life. Most of the fun comes from the things (sports, parties, classes) I do with my friends." First-years usually occupy doubles and thus have the opportunity to find out what it is like to live with a roommate. After first year, however, students may choose to live on or off campus. Theme housing is abundant at Mac—among them are La Maison Française, International House, and Quiet House.

On campus, there are four cafeterias that are good for school grub. Students can also eat at one of the six fast-food kiosks around campus. There is no general meal plan; instead, students can buy each meal, often in the main cafeteria, which has a fast-food court and is open 24/7, ideal for midnight snacking. The food is very expensive, however, so many undergraduates eat off campus. La Luna, a restaurant serving Lebanese food, is fairly popular thanks to an inexpensive menu.

An exceptional reputation and vast breadth of programs naturally leads many students toward McMaster University. And with such a vibrant community of scholastic and social stimulation, it is easy to understand why.—*Tak Nishikawa*

FYI

The three best things about attending McMaster are "the huge range of possible programs to study, the meal plan, and the size of the student body."

The three worst things about attending McMaster are "the lack of attention paid to non–science and business students, the tough grading system, and the cliquey atmosphere."

The three things that every student should do before graduating from McMaster are "take a road trip to Toronto or beyond, make the dean's list, and explore Hamilton for yourself."

One thing I'd like to have known before coming here is "that I'd make more friends than I ever could imagine."

Queen's University

Address: 99 University Avenue, Room 206; Kingston, Ontario K7L 3N6	**Percent African-American:** NA	**Mean SAT:** 558 V, 606 M
		Mean ACT: NA
	Percent Asian: NA	**Middle 50% SAT range:** NA
Phone: 613-533-2000	**Percent Hispanic:** NA	**Middle 50% ACT range:** NA
E-mail address: admissn @post.queensu.ca	**Percent Native-American:** NA	**3 Most popular majors:** commerce, NA
Web site URL: www.queensu.ca	**Percent in-state / out-of-state:** NA	**Retention:** NA
Founded: 1841	**Percent Pub HS:** 89%	**Graduation rate:** 90%
Private or Public: public	**Number of Applicants:** 17,085	**On-campus housing:** 85%
Religious affiliation: none		**Fraternities:** 0%
Location: small city	**Percent Accepted:** 47%	**Sororities:** 0%
Undergraduate enrollment: 10,998	**Percent Accepted who enroll:** 32%	**Library:** 1,900,000 volumes
Total enrollment: 15,973	**Entering:** 2,600	**Tuition and Fees:** $4,540 in; $11,000 out
Percent Male / Female: 45% / 55%	**Transfers:** 75	**Room and Board:** $5,600
Percent Minority: NA	**Application Deadline:** 15 May	**Financial aid, first-year:** 55%

D o not be fooled by Queen's University's reputation as the "Harvard of the North." Although both universities boast a tradition of academic excellence, Queen's is a uniquely Canadian university, not a mere replica of its Cambridge ally. Located on the north shore of Lake Ontario in Kingston, Ontario, Queen's University is one of Canada's premier schools. Rivaling McGill University for first ranking, Queen's University demands excellence and dedication from its students which begins at admission and persists until graduation. Fortunately, Queen's students tend to be a driven bunch and, overall, survive and even flourish in the school's often competitive environment.

Survival of the Fittest

"Queen's academics are hard. There is no other way to describe them. But I'm not complaining," one student reported. Although requirements and course loads vary from major to major, all students should expect to be challenged academically while at Queen's.

The commerce and concurrent education programs are known to be two of the best majors at Queen's. The engineering and sciences are also known to be top-notch, but are no picnic for first-year students, who often face course loads of 30-plus hours per week.

First-year courses tend to fairly large, but numbers dwindle down to about 20 people in upper-level courses. Introductory lectures usually are not overcrowded with students who simply want to meet requirements since many departments do not require students to take courses outside of their major. In general, Queen's students report that they are generally pleased with the courses they are taking.

A universal comment was praise for the dedication of the professors at Queen's. Only a handful of courses are taught by TAs, and even those TAs tend to be highly qualified. Many distinguished professors, including key political thinkers, grace the halls of Queen's University, which has produced some of the most influential men and women in Canadian government.

Life Outside the Classroom

First-year students typically live on campus although a few choose to remain at home. Dorms vary from single-sex to co-ed. One popular coed freshman hall is Vic Hall. Some dorms have special international or "quiet" floors. Although students can request where and with how many roommates they wish to live, they are not always guaranteed that their requests will be met.

Residence halls were given good marks overall with few student complaints about strict regulations. Although all residential students are required to purchase a meal plan, each dorm has its own kitchen. Food is reportedly edible, but one student warned against eating the school meat. Other options for on-campus dining include Taco Bell, Pizza Hut, Subway, and Tim Horton's.

After first year, most students move off campus, though do not tend to move far. Most students remain within one mile of campus in what is dubbed the "student ghetto apartments" for their cheap rents and less-than-stellar conditions. Off-campus housing in Kingston, Ontario, is not hard to come by, and most students would concur that Kingston is great a place to live. A small city with only 120,000 residents, it often caters to the student population with its abundance of bars and restaurants. At times, however, the city's small size "can be stifling."

> **"Although Queen's students may work hard during the week, we sure know how to party on the weekends."**

The campus itself has a great location right in the heart of Kingston. Bordering a lake, the campus boasts beauty in the form of wide open spaces, old limestone buildings, and a plethora of trees. Although Queen's students often get teased by their counterparts at rival McGill because of all the provincial jails located in Kingston, crime at Queen's is not a significant problem. Perhaps this is the result of the administration's tight security and strict regulations. "The regulations can be a pain, but at least you feel safe," one student said.

Unlike students at most American universities, most students at Queen's are of legal drinking age, and the social life clearly reflects this fact. Frosh Week is packed with beer-drinking and partying. During the day, frosh bond at administration-organized events, but at night festivities, beer is the thing as students kick back and meet one another. "I met some of my closest friends during Frosh week," stated one upperclassman.

The drinking does not stop with the end of Frosh Week. Social life tends to center around three campus pubs: Clark Hall, Alphie's, and QP (the Quiet Pub). At Clark Hall, engineering students carry on the Friday noon ritual of "pounding beers till you can't get up." For those who prefer off-campus partying, the Shot received rave reviews as did A.J.'s and Stages.

Overall, the social scene at Queen's is described as excellent. "Although Queen's students may work hard during the week, we sure know how to party on the weekends," one student boasted. Such partying usually starts Thursday night and continues throughout the weekend.

Extracurricular Haven

Despite their busy academic schedules, Queen's students still participate in a wide array of extracurricular activities. Popular clubs include Queen's Model Parliament, Alma Mater Big Brothers (AMS), a student environmental coalition, and intramurals. Students can also elect to participate in one of two weekly publications: the *Queen's Journal* newspaper or the satirical *Golden Words*. Other more zany activities include the juggling club, and although small and few in number, the Jewish organizations on campus tend to be quite visible.

With the Golden Gale as their school mascot, Queen's students are a spirited bunch when it comes to sports. Although the school actively recruits for athletes, prospective athletes must still adhere to high academic entrance standards. Per-

haps as a consequence, Queen's does not always have the strongest sports teams.

Some of the most popular teams at Queen's are the football, rugby, and hockey teams. The annual "kill McGill" game draws huge crowds, and many students come dressed in tams and overalls to show their Golden Gale pride. Engineers are known for their unusual tradition of dying themselves purple to show their Queen's spirit. Some students complain about the tight security at the games, but most students agree the games are "fun social events."

Even at the intramural level, sports tend to be very popular. Students say the intramurals are very well-organized and are well-divided so that students can pick and choose the intensity and level they wish to compete at. The only complaint is with regard to the condition of athletic facilities. Many of the stadiums are old and need to be renovated. As one student said, "We need a better sports arena in a big way."

Although many of the Queen's students are from either Toronto or Ottawa, the student body is still described as "diverse." Nevertheless, students cite the predominant Queen's student as "preppy" and from a high socioeconomic background. Minorities can feel at home with the school's plethora of minority groups, but according to some students, most people tend to interact within their own ethnic group. Overall however, Queen's is not described as a cliquish school, and most students report that they are satisfied with the shape of their student body.

In fact, some students would agree that the student body is one of the best things about Queen's. "I feel I have met some of the most amazing people here, people whose friendships will last a lifetime," said one undergrad. "I love that students here are smart, but still know how to have fun. I couldn't be happier."—*Alyssa Blair Greenwald*

University of British Columbia

Address: 2075 Westbrook Mall; Vancouver, British Columbia V6T 1Z1
Phone: 604-822-2211
E-mail address: registrar. admissions@ubc.ca
Web site URL: www.ubc.ca
Founded: 1915
Private or Public: public
Religious affiliation: none
Location: urban
Undergraduate enrollment: 25,743
Total enrollment: 31,971
Percent Male/Female: 44%/56%
Percent Minority: NA

Percent African-American: NA
Percent Asian: NA
Percent Hispanic: NA
Percent Native-American: NA
Percent in-state/out-of-state: NA
Percent Pub HS: NA
Number of Applicants: 22,849
Percent Accepted: 48%
Percent Accepted who enroll: 29%
Entering: 3,181
Transfers: NA

Application Deadline: NA
Mean SAT: NA
Mean ACT: NA
Middle 50% SAT range: NA
Middle 50% ACT range: NA
3 Most popular majors: NA
Retention: NA
Graduation rate: NA
On-campus housing: 5%
Fraternities: NA
Sororities: NA
Library: NA
Tuition and Fees: $2,550 in; $14,048 out
Room and Board: $4,516
Financial aid, first-year: 16%

Located just outside of Vancouver and the sandy beaches of the Pacific Ocean and some of the greatest skiing mountains in North America, the University of British Columbia offers students the chance to experience their college years in a million different ways.

Not only does the University of British Columbia have the reputation for being one of Canada's premiere academic institutions, but it is also one of the largest, with over 40,000 students. Accordingly, the extensive course offerings support a wide range of academic interests. The diverse social atmosphere and relaxed attitude toward underage drinking (the legal drinking at in Canada is 19, so most students can legally drink) provide numerous opportunities for students to kick back and relax at campus bars like The Pit, at popular beer garden parties, and in the fraternity houses. According to one student, the typical life of the residential dorms revolves around "party, sleep, procrastinate, party, sleep, procrastinate, intramural sport, and last-minute homework."

So Many Engineers, So Little Time

Despite the emphasis on social life within the campus dorms, course requirements at the University of British Columbia are demanding. English is required for all first year students, although freshmen claim that "it's really, really boring." Students feel the number of credits required for graduation is reasonable, even though some complained about a distribution requirement that makes students concentrating in the arts take courses in a science department (and vice versa). Sciences are particularly strong at UBC, and the majority of students major in either commerce or engineering. "There are so many engineering students here," said one undergrad. "They walk around in their stupid red jackets and play lots of pranks. And even more than engineering students, there are masses and masses of commerce students." The university also offers competitive programs in forestry and nursing. But if you are looking for an easy major, sociology, music appreciation, and French are rumored to be the slackers' favorites.

In a school as big as UBC, class size tends to be large. Lecture classes with 200 to 300 students are the norm, but classes offered in the evening can be smaller. Still, most students report being generally satisfied with the level of teaching at UBC. An undergrad noted, "All of my teachers make themselves as accessible to the students as they can in a school with 40,000 students."

Large lecture classes often break up into small discussion sections run by graduate students. In one freshman English class, a TA opened a class on Margaret Atwood's *The Edible Woman* by bringing soda and cookies for the entire class.

Undergrads report that Science One (a three-course program that concurrently studies physics, chemistry, and biology), which accepts only a limited number of students, is among the most difficult classes, although some freshmen reported that Science One does not require serious work. According to one student, "The thing that thrills me the most about my classes is that there are only three, and they are easy!" Registering for classes is done by telephone and gives priority to students who make the best grades. The registration process is jokingly described as the one most difficult aspect of academic life for some UBC students.

Parties, Nude Beaches, and Drinking

Because of UBC's diversity and size, student social life varies widely. University-sponsored movies and guest lectures at the "SUB" (student union building) are reportedly well attended. Past speakers have even included a professional hypnotist. Frat parties and beer garden parties remain a favorite for most students, who generally feel that alcohol plays a significant role in most social activities at the school. The frats also host a number of theme parties throughout the year, usually featuring such events as a toga night, a "boxers" bash, and several formal affairs. Among the more unusual student hangouts is a nude beach right off campus called the Wreck. It is reported to be a "place with no laws."

Much social life at UBC is divided between students who live on campus and those who commute. Because housing is limited, many students are unable to get campus housing and a large percentage of the student body lives off campus. Vancouver's high rental rates make off-campus living fairly expensive, and many students choose to commute from home. Since a fair amount of freshman social life centers on dorm parties, many students living off campus report feeling isolated from campus life. One off-campus student observed, "It kind of takes away from the university atmosphere, that most people live far away from the school; it's also really hard to make friends here."

Thirteen Women Make a Whorehouse

Students who live on campus say the rooms are definitely livable and even nice, depending on how much you expect in a residential dorm. One major complaint, however, is that there is not enough female housing for a school some dub "the University of a Billion Chicks." Housing options include two coed complexes primarily for freshmen and a variety of apartments and family units for upperclassmen and graduate students. Single-sex and coed housing are available, and students can also choose to live in special theme housing. Fraternity houses provide additional housing for students involved in UBC's active Greek life. An old Canadian law defining houses of prostitution as those with more than 12 females under one roof prevents sororities from living together on campus.

A nighttime walking service and an on-campus bus make students feel secure on campus. Vancouver has a low crime rate for a large city, and students report they feel perfectly safe walking around campus or through the city after dark. Still, some students report that use of date-rape drugs and prowlers in the residential colleges are increasing threats to security. Unfortunately according to one student, UBC has a reputation for having "one of the highest rape rates in Canadian universities."

> Education subsidies from the Canadian government make UBC a relatively affordable institution, comparable with in-state tuition at most public colleges in the U.S.

Dining options at the university are pretty extensive. There are cafeterias in almost every building. Students report that the food served in the dining halls is definitely edible and the veggie wraps are particularly tasty. One student even warned,

"Beware of the cinnamon buns—they are highly addictive!" For those who refuse to ingest cafeteria food, the Village, an international food fair, serves everything from sushi to Subway sandwiches. All campus facilities serve only Coca-Cola products, so do not expect to find Pepsi or Snapple beverages. For those students who crave culinary diversity, Vancouver also provides a wide range of restaurants.

Pros and Cons of Diversity

Education subsidies from the Canadian government make UBC a relatively affordable institution, comparable with in-state tuition at most public colleges in the U.S. Still, many students are surprised to find a high concentration of students from upper- and upper-middle-class families. As one student noted, "The UBC student stereotype is a well-dressed commerce student. A lot of the people at this school seem to be pretty rich and quite snobby." But students from less privileged backgrounds also make up a large, if not quite as conspicuous, percentage of the student body. The UBC student body also is one of the most multicultural in Canada. Asian students form a large portion of the university's minority population, but students report that other minorities are also well represented. International students at UBC bring still more diversity to the campus, and interracial and homosexual couples are definitely accepted.

However, great diversity takes its toll on school spirit. One student remarked that school spirit is only present "among engineers, forestry [students], and at sport-

ing events." Athletic competitions are reportedly poorly advertised and rarely attended. While some students promote their Thunderbirds with pride, others do not even know that the Thunderbird is their mascot. While varsity sports are not so popular, many students do participate in the intramural sports. Undergrads describe athletic facilities for both varsity athletes and the student body at large as good, and UBC offers roughly comparable facilities to both groups. Students agree that other campus facilities are also maintained in fair condition. Although some students find the large buildings "grotesque," many others find the UBC campus aesthetically pleasing. The combination of Gothic buildings and modern glass complexes contribute to the campus's eclectic atmosphere. To nature lovers' delight, study breaks at UBC can mean taking a stroll through the botanical, rose, and Japanese gardens scattered throughout campus.

Student opinion about UBC varies as widely as its diverse population. Some students absolutely recommend the university; others complain, "it's big, it's ugly, and it's really, really lonely." While each student's perspective depends on his or her experiences, UBC has a lot to offer all its students. With a reputation for academic excellence, a unique location, and an immensely diverse student body, it's not hard to see why the University of British Columbia holds its own as one of Canada's most popular colleges.—*Letitia Stein and Staff*

FYI
The three best things about attending UBC are "how affordable it is, how safe I feel, and how strong the academics are here."
The three worst things about attending UBC are "the lack of school spirit, the commuter school mentality, and the lack of diversity."
The three things that every student should do before graduating from UBC are "tan nude at the Wreck, have a beer at the Pit, and drink lots of Coca-Cola."
One thing I'd like to have known before coming here is "how huge this place really is."

University of Toronto

Address: 27 King's College Circle; Toronto, Ontario M5S 1J4
Phone: 416-978-2011
E-mail address: adk@adm.utoronto.edu
Web site URL: www.utoronto.ca
Founded: 1827
Private or Public: public
Religious affiliation: none
Location: urban
Undergraduate enrollment: 41,873
Total enrollment: 52,796
Percent Male/Female: 44%/56%
Percent Minority: NA

Percent African-American: NA
Percent Asian: NA
Percent Hispanic: NA
Percent Native-American: NA
Percent in-state/out-of-state: NA
Percent Pub HS: NA
Number of Applicants: 34,089
Percent Accepted: 61%
Percent Accepted who enroll: 65%
Entering: 13,477
Transfers: NA
Application Deadline: 1 Mar

Mean SAT: NA
Mean ACT: NA
Middle 50% SAT range: NA
Middle 50% ACT range: NA
3 Most popular majors: NA
Retention: NA
Graduation rate: NA
On-campus housing: 7%
Fraternities: 0%
Sororities: 0%
Library: 10,000,000 volumes
Tuition and Fees: $3,322 in; $9,500 out
Room and Board: $6,000
Financial aid, first-year: NA

Looking for great classes, a great nightlife, and 50,000 other people to share it with? At U of T, students know how to work and play hard, all in Canada's largest city.

Personalized Attention Despite the Size

Coming to the University of Toronto for the first time can be intimidating for freshmen—the enormous size of the school makes it difficult to see the same face twice. Most students, though, are able to find their own niches and are enthusiastic about their experience.

At U of T, as the university is affectionately called, everyone agrees that the education is top-notch. There are four main programs, or faculties, as they are known: engineering, arts and science, music, and physical education and health. The Arts and Science Faculty is by far the most popular program. Each has its own specific requirements, and students apply directly to the faculty of their choice. Classes at U of T are strong, and there is a wide selection available. Although intro classes can be huge—"I've heard of classes with 1,500 people that had to be held in Convocation Hall to accommodate everybody" commented one student—most find class sizes become smaller and more personalized as they go up in years. One senior in engineering noted that: "by 4th year you get to know the people in your program really well, since you all take the same classes year after year." The workload is demanding, but students at U of T know how to work hard. With all the choices available there is a class for everyone, and it is relatively easy for most to find a schedule that fits their needs.

The staff is also greatly admired—many professors are leaders in their field. Students agree that the faculty is highly intelligent; although some say that this doesn't necessarily make for great teaching skills. Often the number of foreign professors in the science-based departments can especially be frustrating when it comes to understanding lectures. Still, most observe that professors are generally accessible even in the biggest classes. Grading is fair, and depending on the professor, can even be somewhat stringent. One student recalled classes where only a few people passed, and a significant number failed. "There was more grade inflation in my high school," added another senior. TAs are also a helpful option, although many students grumbled about the disruption caused by a recent strike by TAs. On the whole though, most agree on the strength of teaching at U of T, and consequently on the depth of its programs.

Like at other Canadian institutions, there is a co-op program whereby students alternate between attending classes and working. Formally known as the "Professional Experience Year," or PY, the program is relatively young and is geared toward the engineering and computer sciences. Compared to other co-op programs where work terms last about four months, PY runs anywhere from 12 to 16 months at a time, which students say allows for more depth on the job. "When employers know you're going to be staying longer, they're willing to give you more responsibility, which really helps build good relationships for possible future employment," explained one student.

Life on Campus

At U of T the nine colleges make up the center of campus life. Usually it's the students in arts and science who live in the colleges, but anybody can apply. Seven of the nine are located on the university's central Toronto campus, while the other two, Erindale and Scarborough, are both about a half hour's drive away respectively. While they have their own specific religious backgrounds (St. Michael's, for example, is predominantly Roman Catholic), they are open to everyone. Also, the colleges function as somewhat autonomous units with U of T, each with its own administrative powers (registration, etc.), dining services, housing, and traditions. They serve as smaller communities within the larger one at the school, and most are enthusiastic about the sense of belonging the colleges provide that may otherwise be lacking in such a huge place. Students tend to live on campus their first and sometimes second years (housing is guaranteed for the first year), but after that many choose to live off campus. With the help of the housing office at U of T, finding a place to live outside is relatively easy and prices are affordable, if people share. Moreover, with the extensive subway system available, students don't necessarily find it inconvenient to live a distance away from campus. Since a great proportion of the student body comes from the metro Toronto area, some also choose to live at home and commute.

> "If you know what you want in an education, there's no better place than U of T for the number of opportunities it offers."

The food in the colleges is of typical cafeteria-style fare, and the meal plan offers flex dollars that can be transferred to local restaurants, which students praise. In any case, finding good dining in Toronto is not a problem at all—the amazing selection will satisfy anyone's palate. Furthermore, students strongly recommend checking out Chinatown, which borders the campus, for great food. There are some cooking facilities available in the colleges too for those who long for home-cooked meals.

After Hours

When classes are over for the day, there's a still lot to do. With such a wide variety of extracurricular activities available, "if you want it, chances are there's already a club for it," as one student commented. In a school of such mammoth size, being part of a club can be a good way to meet people. Most activities run out of Hart House, a building that boasts athletic and meeting facilities convenient for student groups to use. Still, a broad mix of students exists: while some are very involved in extracurriculars, others don't care as much about participating in campus affairs. With so many students living off campus, people find themselves separating their school lives from their outside lives. Often the sheer size of U of T, coupled with its location in a bustling city makes for a disconnected atmosphere. Students can be very businesslike at U of T, as one mentioned: "A lot of people are just here to go to class—otherwise their lives are pretty separate from the university."

There isn't a great deal of unity or support for the varsity sports teams; school spirit is mainly to be found within individual colleges or programs (such as engineering, etc.). Since each group runs its own activities and events and has its own pubs, most socializing occurs within. The divisions among colleges surprised some students—there are a number of inter-college competitions and friendly rivalries as opposed to friendships, so it can be hard to meet people from other colleges. On the upside, students of a college are often especially close and develop strong bonds with one another.

Only Toronto

If there's one-thing students at U of T all agree upon, it's the umpteen number of opportunities that going to school in a city like Toronto provides. "Toronto is great," one sophomore raved; "I couldn't imagine being anywhere else." Many die-hard fans attend Maple Leafs hockey games at the new Air Canada Center, and NBA basketball at the Skydome is becoming popular. There is also a well-developed entertainment scene. From the Art Gallery of Ontario to the music of the famous Roy Thomson Hall, theater, the arts hold their own in Toronto. There is a myriad of recreational activities available—Canada's Wonderland, the country's best amusement park, is less than an hour away. Students are enthusiastic about the nightlife too—clubbing is the thing to do, with places like the "Whiskey Saigon" and "The Brunswick House" among some of the favorite U of T haunts. No matter what one's interests are, there is literally something for everybody in Toronto. Drinking is a popular activity but according to students, alcoholism isn't a big problem. The dating scene is, as one individual put it, "what you make of it . . . it's not like we lack of people at U of T if you're looking for someone."

Leader for the Future

At the University of Toronto, great academics plus a great location make the school a good choice for anyone. While the size can be intimidating at first, most students are able to take initiative and carve a place for themselves somewhere. Above all students here are passionate about what they do, which helps explain U of T's high job placement rate after graduation. Many of Canada's future leaders emerge here, and with the university's recent acceptance of an $80 million (CAN) grant from the provincial government this year, U of T is even more firmly on the path to leading the way in Canada, if not North America, in higher education. Students on the whole give their experience two thumbs up—"if you know what you want in an education, there's no better place than U of T for the number of opportunities it offers."—*Florence Han*

FYI
The three best things about attending U of T are "being in the middle of Toronto, the extensive resources available, and all the activities you can join."
The three worst things about attending U of T are "the lack of good parking, the automated registration, and the long distance between buildings that makes getting to class on time a hassle!"
The three things every student should do before graduating from U of T are "get involved in the many activities, participate in all of frosh week, and go to a Leafs game."
One thing I'd like to have known before coming here is "that the colleges would be so segregated from each other socially."

University of Waterloo

Address: 200 University Avenue West; Waterloo, Ontario N2L 3G1
Phone: 519-885-1211
E-mail address: visitus@uwaterloo.ca
Web site URL: www.uwaterloo.ca
Founded: 1959
Private or Public: public
Religious affiliation: none
Location: urban
Undergraduate enrollment: 16,200
Total enrollment: 18,000
Percent Male / Female: 55% / 45%
Percent Minority: NA

Percent African-American: NA
Percent Asian: NA
Percent Hispanic: NA
Percent Native-American: NA
Percent in-state / out-of-state: 97% / 3%
Percent Pub HS: NA
Number of Applicants: 18,857
Percent Accepted: 46%
Percent Accepted who enroll: 40%
Entering: 361
Transfers: 354
Application Deadline: 1 May

Mean SAT: NA
Mean ACT: NA
Middle 50% SAT range: NA
Middle 50% ACT range: NA
3 Most popular majors: NA
Retention: NA
Graduation rate: NA
On-campus housing: 64%
Fraternities: NA
Sororities: NA
Library: 2,500,000 volumes
Tuition and Fees: $3,400 in; $14,000 out
Room and Board: $5,400
Financial aid, first-year: NA

Where else can you get great academics, great work experience, and great bratwurst, all at Canadian prices? According to students at the University of Waterloo, you can get everything you want all in one place.

A Taste of the Real World

Although it is smaller than most major Canadian universities, the University of Waterloo is well known among its peers for its rigorous and demanding academic programs. With a total of forty classes required for graduation (ten per year), there is always a lot to do particularly for students who double-major and are struggling to fit in those extra courses. Academic programs are structured around Waterloo's six faculties: applied health sciences, arts, engineering, mathematics, environmental studies, and science; each has its own requirements. In addition, there is also an Independent Studies Program for those looking for something more specialized. While math and engineering have an especially strong reputation as Waterloo has more students enrolled in math than any other school in the world), the other departments are not slouches. There is little reported grade inflation, and professors are fairly accessible. Overall, undergrads

find that the programs cater to them well. One arts student, noting the close attention students receive, commented that he could not remember taking any English classes with more than forty students per class, even freshman year.

One of Waterloo's biggest highlights is its well-developed Co-op program, where students divide the school year by alternating terms of school and employment. The Co-op program is the largest of its kind in North America with over half of the student body participating. As a result, Waterloo operates on a trimester system, with classes in session all-year long to allow students in the Co-op program to graduate within five years. Current undergrads highly recommend the program, saying, "not only can you get some much-needed cash, but you also get work experience, which is great for future employment." Being a part of the Co-op system means having the opportunity to travel—not just to nearby Toronto, but to places outside of Canada as well. Students also report that coming back to school from the "real world" after working for a term provides a better perspective on classes and university life in general. One adds that "sometimes it's nice just to get away for a change of scenery and to refocus my energies."

Building Friendships

There are two main residences for students at Waterloo, called Village One and Ron Eydt Village. There are no on-campus housing requirements, but most students spend their first and second years in the dorms. Each dorm has a resident advisor, nicknamed a "don," who is an upperclassman. Many students are very enthusiastic about living within a residential church college system. The colleges include St Jerome's, St. Paul's, Conrad Grebel, and Renison. They are small colleges, religiously affiliated with the university. Offering both separate classes and housing spaces, the church colleges reportedly offer a "homier" atmosphere. Although each have their own religious background, students of any affiliation may apply for residence. Some say the church colleges have the most "spirit," and according to some, also have better food—try Conrad Grebel for Mennonite cooking, for one. On the whole, dorm rooms are small, but are the place where "we start to build lasting friendships so it isn't so bad—in a sense, we are all in it together."

Upperclassmen tend to live off campus—there is a lot of available housing conveniently near the school, and the cost of living is more affordable. By living off campus, students are able to avoid the meal plan which is reportedly "a total rip-off." Many find tastier food off campus as popular places to eat include East Side Mario's, Subway, Gino's, and the "plaza," which is open 24 hours a day. Gino's is particularly well known for allegedly holding the Guinness World Record for creating the longest pizza.

Friendly, Outdoorsy Atmosphere

Students find the town of Waterloo, Ontario, a quiet kind of university town, and are quick to differentiate it from nearby "gross, industrial, abandoned factory-like" Kitchener. For the outdoorsy types, the area around Laurel Lake provides the perfect opportunity to jog, swim, and bike. For those eager to explore the social scene, there is the Student Life Center, which organizes free movies and other recreational activities. The town of Waterloo is also famous for its great Oktoberfest celebration every year: people come from all over to sample the bratwurst, take in the dancing, and just to see what the festival is all about. Many students enthusiastically recommend the event, even if it means just taking a tour of the local breweries.

> Students also report that coming back to school from the "real world" after working for a term provides a better perspective on classes and university life in general.

As for the nightlife, there is Fed Hall, Canada's largest campus dance hall, where students go to party. Thursday nights are especially popular as people line up literally hours in advance to get in. Other than that, there are the usual weekend parties with plenty of alcohol available. Waterloo may have the reputation for being a studious school, but as one student commented, "even the engineering students know how to relax once in awhile." A fair number of people leave town for the weekend and head for Toronto, which is about an hour away. However, other students were quick to point out that their peers do not go to Toronto for the weekend often, preferring to hang out with friends on campus.

Intramurals and More

Extracurricular involvement at Waterloo varies as most students do not participate in many. Due to the Co-op system, many students do not have a lot of time to pursue other activities such as various employment opportunities. Extracurricular activities include an active student government and *Imprint*, the main student newspaper. Intramurals are also especially strong given a number of fine facilities available. Any student with interest can play, and the lack of pressure on the field makes the experience enjoyable. Varsity sports are very much in the background at Waterloo.

Quest for the Pink Tie

Waterloo, like all other schools, has its own unique traditions. Among them is the quest for the pink tie, which occurs during freshman week at the start of the school year. Math students, or "mathies" as they are called, go through a mild form of initiation to get the coveted pink tie. Later, a huge pink tie is hung over the side of the math building, and this often adds to the touch of rivalry between the math and engineering departments. During frosh week, engineering students try to steal the giant pink tie, while mathies try to sneak out the "tool," the engineering faculty's prized possession. As one student said, "we love to scheme and plot, but it is really just fun and games."

A Place to Grow

At Waterloo, academics are taken very seriously. "There are lots of smart people, especially in the sciences and engineering," says one undergrad. Students head to the Dana Porter Library to study, and computer clusters are readily available on campus. While the academic atmosphere may not be cutthroat, some complain that there are people who study compulsively. One student remarked that there exists a clear separation between students where "half the students study like crazy, and half have a life." Students at Waterloo can be cliquish, so school unity leaves room for improvement. However, the University of Waterloo still remains one of Canada's foremost educational institutions for the engineering, math and arts, and those who attend do take note of the good job placement rate after graduation. Above all, Waterloo students in general agree about the number of academic and social opportunities available. If there is one thing to remember about the people at Waterloo, it is that "we really know how to go after what we want." It is just that passion that keeps Waterloo growing and its students succeeding.—*Florence Han*

FYI

The three best things about attending Waterloo are "its academic reputation, extensive intramurals, and going to Fed Hall on Thursday nights."

The three worst things about attending Waterloo are "the ugly buildings, food service, and cliques among students."

The three things that every student should do before graduating from Waterloo are "go tubing in Laurel Creek, go out for a team (competitive or intramurals), and check out Oktoberfest."

One thing I'd like to have known before coming here is "that there is more to explore at Waterloo than just the academics."

University of Western Ontario

Address: 1151 Richmond Street; London, Ontario N6A 3K7
Phone: 519-679-2111
E-mail address: reg-admissions@julian.uwo.ca
Web site URL: www.uwo.ca
Founded: 1878
Private or Public: public
Religious affiliation: none
Location: small city
Undergraduate enrollment: 1,916
Total enrollment: 27,722
Percent Male/Female: 46%/54%
Percent Minority: NA

Percent African-American: NA
Percent Asian: NA
Percent Hispanic: NA
Percent Native-American: NA
Percent in-state/out-of-state: 92%/8%
Percent Pub HS: NA
Number of Applicants: 23,525
Percent Accepted: 34%
Percent Accepted who enroll: 92%
Entering: 4,959
Transfers: NA
Application Deadline: 1 Mar

Mean SAT: NA
Mean ACT: NA
Middle 50% SAT range: NA
Middle 50% ACT range: NA
3 Most popular majors: sociology, psychology, biology
Retention: NA
Graduation rate: NA
On-campus housing: 50%
Fraternities: NA
Sororities: NA
Library: NA
Tuition and Fees: $3,129 in; $10,458 out
Room and Board: $5,491
Financial aid, first-year: NA

Located in the west end of the province in London, Ontario, the University of Western Ontario is aptly named. With more than 25,000 full-time students, this university is Canada's fourth-largest post-secondary institution. Established in 1878, Western has since grown to include 12 faculties collectively offering over 200 undergraduate programs, more than enough to support an extensive range of academic interests. Diversity of ethnic backgrounds as well as academic and extracurricular interests allows virtually any student to feel comfortable at Western. Even when it comes to having fun, Western offers a vibrant social scene that caters to all types of students.

Boning Up

Students report that Western has top-notch academics across-the-board, but its program in business administration is in a league of its own. The prestigious and highly popular honors business administration program takes the best and brightest and prepares them to become successful leaders in the business world. So outstanding is this curriculum that it is ranked nineteenth in North America by the *Financial Times*, and many graduates of the Richard Ivey School of Business at Western go on to become CEOs, presi-

dents, and senior executives of companies in Canada and around the world.

"Major in Yourself" is UWO's celebrated catchphrase. Here students can immerse themselves in academic pursuits that range from the traditional to the cutting edge. For instance, in the commercial aviation management program, students graduate with a commercial airline pilot's license and a university degree. Unlike most Canadian schools, where students delve into specialized study from day one, Western encourages most students to explore a wide variety of disciplines in their first year. For students who want even more freedom and flexibility in their course selection, there is Western's Scholar's Elective program, which combines a liberal education with the chance to work with a faculty mentor.

Students report large variations in class size. Said one, "First-year biology has more than fifteen hundred students in one section, and close to three thousand students taking the course." Another mentioned that his largest class was Super-Psych, an introductory psychology class that typically crams 2,000 students into Alumni Hall, an enormous lecture hall. Although "almost all first-year classes have more than 80 students per class," class size significantly declines for upperclassmen. Students are generally very satisfied with their professors and teaching assistants and generously throw around words like "amazing," "approachable," and "quirky, but in a totally likable way" when describing them. "My calculus professor had an overhead which had 'Happy New Year' written in Chinese and showed it to the class on Lunar New Year," remarked one satisfied student enrolled in Western's chemistry and economics program. Another professor "set off firecrackers and pyro" to kick off a psychology class.

Academic requirements differ depending on the faculty, and students' opinions of them vary. While many find the requirements "fair" and "reasonable," others beg to differ: "There are too many. It's too complicated, especially as a first-year student." The consensus among students seems to be that the engineering program is the most demanding, while easier majors tend to be clustered in the arts and social sciences. The workload is described as being "manageable," but students report working much more than they did in high school. One remarked that, for better or worse, "Western seems to be immune to the grade inflation that has plagued other schools."

Play Hard; Party Hard

Students who enroll at Western will find that the school offers a vibrant array of social scenes. The majority of students enter Western as 19-year-olds, owing to Ontario's five-year high school system. This seemingly trivial fact takes on a whole new significance when you learn that Canada's legal drinking age is also 19. "Too bad for college students south of the border," one student gleefully remarked. It is no surprise that Western has something of a party-school reputation. "We party like crazy," said one student succinctly. Popular pubs in London like the Rid Out Club and the Ceeps bar, as well as the on-campus nightclub the Wave, are typically jam-packed on weekends. There are oft-heard incidents of binge drinking on campus, but not many students seem to be into hard drugs. Non-drinkers do not feel left out, as there are plenty of other opportunities for fun and entertainment, ranging from formal and semiformal dances to rock concerts. The University Commu-

nity Centre features a food court, bookstore, convenience store, travel agency, pharmacy, ATM, gym, movie theater, and swimming pool and acts as a popular meeting place. It also houses CHRW FM, Western's radio station, TV Western, and the *Gazette*, the school newspaper. "That place is like a mini–shopping mall," one student remarked. "It sort of eliminates the need to go into town."

The Greek system is popular at Western; students report that there are "at least 21 frats and six sororities." Undergrads note that, by and large, groups of friends form quickly on campus and tend to avoid change. Pranks and wild tomfoolery are reportedly other means of simultaneously having fun and entertaining others: the eight-foot-tall "snow penis" recently erected by fun-loving students aroused the interest of many a passerby.

Getting Involved

At Western, students report that they are "rarely bored." There is literally something for everyone, with more than 125 clubs and associations actively making their presence felt on campus. With organizations like Western Anime Video Explosion, Women in Engineering, Young Liberals, and Medieval Society, Western's extracurricular opportunities encompass interests from ethnic heritage and politics to future careers and martial arts. Students can even join off-the-wall clubs like the Water Buffalo chapter, whose members congregate in large furry blue hats with yellow horns (just like the ones Fred and Barney wore) to "drink beer and watch reruns of *The Flintstones*." In addition, there are ample community service opportunities, and the university hospital seems to be one of the hot spots for volunteerism. For the more athletically inclined student, it is good to know that Western is recognized as having an "awesome" athletic program. Many of the 36 varsity teams are among Canada's very best—in 1999–2000, the men's soccer team won the national championship and 12 other Mustang teams finished in the top 10 in the country. Almost one-third of Western students compete at different levels of intramural play, and "many students work out, so it's safe to say students are quite fit." If students "aren't actively participating in varsity sports or intramurals, then they are at least out supporting the Mustangs," said one student. Indeed, with the newly unveiled 8,000-seat TD Waterhouse Stadium, which will host the 2001 Canada Summer Games, Western students are more enthusiastic about athletics than ever before.

The Lowdown on Campus Dorms

Students have a choice of six residences on campus, including the infamous Saugeen-Maitland Hall, which houses 1,250-odd students. (David Letterman once named Saugeen-Maitland Hall one of the top 10 "party" spots in North America.) Elgin Hall, Alumni House, and Essex Hall are suite-style, meaning there are four bedrooms, a kitchen, and a bathroom in each suite. Thus many students can enjoy "late-night instant noodles while crunching numbers, typing up a report, or just chillin'." The other three residences are traditional-style: students in a wing share bathrooms, and food is served in dining halls. Although living in residence is not mandatory, students who opt to do so report enjoying fast computer network hookups, 24-hour front-desk staff, AC, and parking facilities nearby. As one student explained, "Most of my friends here live on my floor. Residences are also very safe and well maintained." Many prefer faculty-based floors, which house students in the same area of study together. However, some have expressed a few complaints: "There's the rule that only two guests are allowed per person on weekends in your dorm room. Also, in some places, the ladybugs get annoying in late fall, but that's because people take the screens off the windows and it's breeding season for them." Moreover, students lament that the residences are great socially, but that "academically it's impossible to get any work done." A remedy for this situation lies in the numerous libraries on campus, where students can escape from the hustle and bustle of life in their dorm and hit the books. The most popular study place is the D. B. Weldon Library; the truly hardcore academics consider its facilities and study carrels first-rate.

All on-campus students, with the exception of those in Alumni House, must be on a meal plan. Cafeteria food gets a "fair" rating from students, who claim that "in terms of cafeteria food it's not too bad." The university food services pay attention to student feedback; the standard cafeteria fare reportedly is getting better every year because of the recent implementation of student-suggested changes. Students on the meal plan say they like being able to use their meal cards at several fast-food kiosks on campus but warn that "if you lose your card, then you're kind of in big trouble, because the person who finds it can use it." For those who tire of dining hall food, there are several great restaurants, including T. J. Baxter's, close to campus.

> "Western seems to be immune to the grade inflation that has plagued other schools."

To not mention the breathtaking beauty of Western's campus would be a great disservice to the school itself. In addition to the main campus, there are three affiliates: King's College, a Catholic college; Huron College, which is Anglican; and Brescia, a women's college, all located a short distance from the main campus. Well-lit footpaths, the school's own police force, and the volunteer student Foot Patrol all contribute to making Western an extremely safe campus day and night.

Students feel that London, Canada's tenth largest city, is much too homogeneous in ethnic makeup. Although the student body "reflects diverse ethnic backgrounds," this is not the case in the city, which is predominantly white. Others call the city "very rich and very white-collar." Furthermore, diversity of ethnic backgrounds and of interests on campus do not necessarily translate into demographic diversity—although there is a sizable international student population, most students hail from within the province of Ontario.

Ontario's Country Club?

Western has been described by more than one cynical student as a "country club," and if having a good time is what you are interested in, you can find your own little party central in London, Ontario. You will also find self-described "well-rounded students" who combine the good life with a solid academic program. "This place is amazing," one student said. "It's the only school I know of where students can party as hard as they do and still succeed in athletics and academics."—*Takamitsu Nishikawa*

FYI

The three best things about attending Western are "homecoming weekend in September, when alumni return and we have one of the biggest parties of the year, the business administration program, and the scenic views from campus."

The three worst things about attending Western are "grading can be tough, studying in your dorm room is impossible, and the lack of student diversity is sometimes annoying."

The three things that every student should do before graduating from Western are "eat at every food outlet at least once, study at each of the libraries at least once, and get hammered at least once."

One thing I'd like to have known before coming here is "that I would live in a dorm known as 'the zoo.'"

Index